Fodor's

ESSENTIAL COSTA RICA

Welcome to Costa Rica

Miles of pristine beaches, fabulous national parks with plentiful wildlife, world-renowned eco-lodges, and the mellow *pura vida* lifestyle of Costa Rica's welcoming people have made this one of the hottest destinations around. Where else can you gaze upon a volcano while soaking in a hot spring one day, hike deep into a rain forest the next, and end your trip learning to surf at a luxurious seaside resort? As you plan your upcoming travels to Costa Rica, please confirm that places are still open and let us know when we need to make updates by writing to us at this address: editors@fodors.com.

TOP REASONS TO GO

★ **Active Volcanoes:** Five imposing behemoths exude, fume, seethe, and smolder.

★ **Beaches:** From pristine secluded hideaways to palm-fringed resort strands.

★ **Coffee:** A plantation tour shows you what makes the country tick.

★ **Eco-friendly Hotels:** Wilderness lodges set the standard for green tourism with style.

★ **Outdoor Adventure:** Ziplining, canopy tours, hiking, and surfing are all top-notch.

★ **Wildlife Galore:** Monkeys, sloths, and turtles abound, and the birding is superb.

Contents

Fodor's Features

MAPS

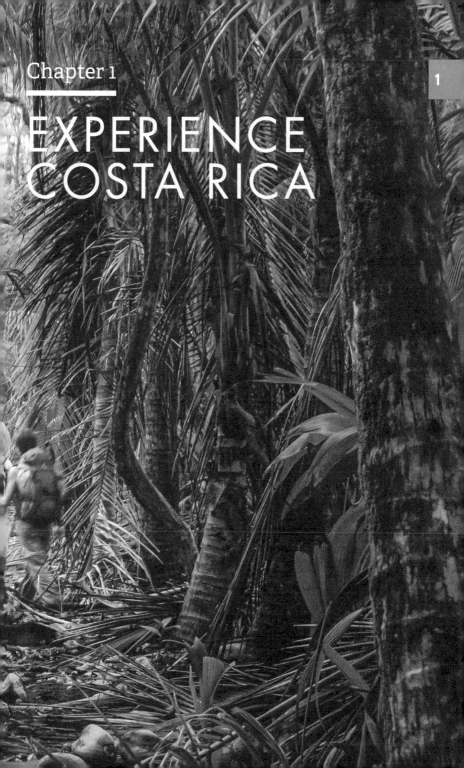

Chapter 1

EXPERIENCE COSTA RICA

18 ULTIMATE EXPERIENCES

Costa Rica offers terrific experiences that should be on every traveler's list. Here are Fodor's top picks for a memorable trip.

1 Discover Tropical Paradise at Manuel Antonio National Park

Costa Rica's most famous national park is also its smallest, logging in at a scant 5 square km (3 square miles) on the Central Pacific coast. You'll find some of the country's best beaches here, as well as lodging of all shapes and sizes and terrific dining. *(Ch. 9)*

2 Catch a Glimpse of Rare Birds

Costa Rica is one of the world's premier birding destinations, with hundreds of resident and migratory species like hummingbirds, toucans, and macaws. *(Ch. 10)*

3 Strike a Yoga Pose

Costa Rica is the land of pura vida (literally, "pure life"), and yoga retreats around the country offer a nirvana-like experience. *(Ch. 7, 8)*

4 Stand in Awe of Volcán Arenal

Local seismologists refer to Arenal as "resting," but it remains one of the country's five active volcanoes. Its last major eruption took place in 2010. *(Ch. 6)*

5 Go White-Water Rafting

From family-friendly floats to wild multiday adventures, Costa Rica's long, May–November rainy season creates great white-water experiences for rafters and kayakers. *(Ch. 5)*

6 Float with Butterflies

Costa Rica counts 1,500 butterfly species—the most famous is the blue morpho, with its neon wings. Several enclosed, netted gardens around the country showcase these insects. *(Ch. 5)*

7 Gobble Gallo Pinto

Take yesterday's leftover rice, add some black beans, onion, and chopped red pepper. Top with a dollop of sour cream or Salsa Lizano, and you have gallo pinto, or "spotted rooster." *(Ch. 4)*

8 Scuba and Snorkel Coral Reefs

Two oceans and 1,465 km (910 miles) of coastline make Costa Rica a popular diving and snorkeling destination. Try the North Pacific's Gulf of Papagayo. *(Ch. 7)*

9 Get Wild in Corcovado National Park

Costa Rica's largest national park is also its most biologically diverse, with tapirs, sloths, jaguars, peccaries, and all four of the country's monkey species. *(Ch. 10)*

10 Soak in a Hot Spring

Ranging from luxurious resorts to roadside rivers, Costa Rica has a collection of hot-springs complexes dotting the area around La Fortuna, thanks to the presence of the Arenal Volcano. *(Ch. 6)*

11 Look into a Smoldering Volcano

The Poás Volcano, about an hour outside San José, lets visitors gaze into a seething cauldron and sulfurous lake. Visit early in the morning for the best views. *(Ch. 5)*

12 Go Surfing on the Nicoya Peninsula

Costa Rica has no shortage of beaches, but nothing tops the Nicoya Peninsula on the north Pacific coast. From hippie beach towns to all-inclusive resorts, there's a place for every skill level. *(Ch. 8)*

13 Witness a Sea Turtle Hatching

Remote Tortuguero, on the north Caribbean coast, is Costa Rica's most famous spot to take in the amazing spectacle of turtle nesting. *(Ch. 11)*

14 Learn About the Origins of Coffee

A handful of coffee estates—Britt, Doka, Don Juan, and Monteverde—offer informative half-day tours and let you see it all, from picking to brewing. *(Ch. 5)*

15 Get Cultured at the Teatro Nacional

San José's Teatro Nacional was built in 1897 as a venue for international operas. Today, the ornate theater offers tours, concerts, plays, and performances. *(Ch. 4)*

16 Get a Bird's-Eye View of the Rain Forest

Costa Rica has hundreds of ziplines, hanging bridges, and even gondolas that take you on a thrilling ride through the forest canopy. *(Ch. 6)*

17 Stay at an Ecolodge

Costa Rica's premier ecolodges offer secluded comfort surrounded by nature. Cabo Matapalo's Lapa Ríos is one of the best. *(Ch. 10)*

18 Celebrate Carnaval on the Caribbean Coast

For a week in October, the Afro-Caribbean port city of Limón is awash in colorful parades and dances. *(Ch. 11)*

WHAT'S WHERE

1 **San José.** The capital city is increasingly trendy, with great restaurants and nightlife, in addition to fascinating museums dedicated to gold and jade. Almost everyone passes through on their way to the beach or the mountains.

2 **The Central Valley.** You likely won't linger long in the Central Valley, as it lacks big-name attractions. But there are day-trip possibilities from San José, including exploring mountain villages, rafting through whitewater rapids, and seeing volcanoes.

3 **Arenal, Monteverde, and the Northern Lowlands.** After zipping along cables through Monteverde Cloud Forest, windsurfing on Lake Arenal, or taking in the Arenal Volcano, reward yourself with a dip in Tabacón Hot Springs.

4 **Guanacaste.** If you came for beaches, this area is for you. Each has a unique personality: Tamarindo's nightlife is legendary; Avellanas's swells challenge surfers; and the Papagayo Peninsula's all-inclusive resorts provide every creature comfort.

Elevation	
4,019	1,225
2,952	900
2,624	800
2,296	700
1,968	600
1,640	500
1,312	400
984	300
656	200
328	100
feet	meters

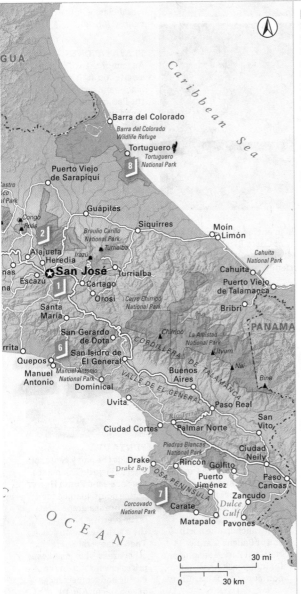

5 The Nicoya Peninsula. Still beachy, the southern peninsula gets rave reviews for its lodgings, smaller and more intimate than those farther north up the coast. Nature lovers flock to Nosara, and the twin towns of Malpaís and Santa Teresa have both surfers' digs and luxury villas.

6 Manuel Antonio and the Central Pacific Coast. The area's not just for spring breakers, although it does include funky surf towns like Jacó. The national park, on a peninsula jutting into the ocean, has the easiest wildlife viewing on the planet.

7 The Osa Peninsula and the South Pacific. Rustic lodges in the Osa Peninsula sit on the edge of the country's wildest region, consisting almost entirely of Corcovado National Park. Hikes reveal toucans and scarlet macaws.

8 Tortuguero and the Caribbean Coast. Come here for the spirited music, the tasty Afro-Caribbean-style food, and the turtle-watching at Tortuguero National Park.

Best Beaches in Costa Rica

PLAYA SÁMARA

A horseshoe-shape cove with an entrance protected by a coral reef keeps Sámara one of Costa Rica's rare, easily swimmable beaches. A friendly town, not too developed but still with many family-friendly activities, anchors the area. *(Ch. 8)*

PLAYA DOMINICAL

Friendly Dominical, a fun surfers' town with a palm-lined beach, is the picture of "laid back." It's one of the few beaches staffed by lifeguards, and there are world-class wildlife refuges nearby. *(Ch. 10)*

PLAYA PAVONES

An end-of-the-world vibe awaits you at this rocky, black-sand beach near the Panamanian border. It's a favorite for surfers, but nonsurfers can enjoy its isolation and lush rain forest. *(Ch. 10)*

PLAYA TORTUGUERO

Nobody comes to rainy Tortuguero to sunbathe. Four sea turtle species nest here, providing a different type of nightlife than Costa Rica's hipper beaches: watching hatchlings scurry toward the sea. *(Ch. 11)*

PLAYA MONTEZUMA

Known for its bohemian town and gray-sand beaches, Costa Rica's onetime "hippie" capital today offers plenty of grown-up offerings among the backpackers' digs and quirky New Age-y shops and restaurants. *(Ch. 8)*

PLAYA UVITA

Some snazzy new dining and lodging options and a growing number of resident expats make Playa Uvita one of Costa Rica's up-and-coming beaches. Uvita anchors the north end of Ballena Marine National Park, a sanctuary for humpback whales and bottlenose dolphins. *(Ch. 10)*

PUNTA UVA

Outside the party center of Puerto Viejo de Talamanca, the dark-sand Punta Uva, or "grape point" (named for its signature sea-grape trees) is the prettiest beach on the south Caribbean coast. There's more rain here than other areas—but that keeps prices lower than on the Pacific and tempers mega-development. *(Ch. 11)*

Manuel Antonio

MANUEL ANTONIO
Costa Rica's powerhouse beach is actually a string of palm-lined strands that go by the collective name Manuel Antonio. A lively tourist scene and a national park of the same name, home to an array of monkeys, birds, and sloths, make this Costa Rica's top tourist attraction. *(Ch. 9)*

PLAYA JUNQUILLAL
Junquillal (pronounced *hoon-key-YAHL*) on the Nicoya Peninsula is a bit more difficult to access than beaches north and south, but the locals and expats who call it home are happy to keep things that way. Though primarily the province of surfers, everyone can love the scenic beach. *(Ch. 7)*

PLAYA HERMOSA
The name of this north Pacific coast playa translates to "beautiful beach"—and it really is. Terrific sunsets and great lodging and dining make it a top choice. What's more, Hermosa's calm waters are an exception to most other Costa Rica beaches: you can actually swim here. *(Ch. 7)*

Best Ecolodges in Costa Rica

THE HARMONY HOTEL, NOSARA
Green goes chic at this holistic retreat on the north Pacific coast. The majority of guests come to Harmony for the yoga—one complimentary class is included in your stay—and the spa treatments. *(Ch. 8)*

PLAYA NICUESA RAINFOREST LODGE, GOLFITO
One of the country's top green lodgings, Playa Nicuesa's commitment to sustainability shines, from the use of fallen wood and recycled materials in construction to the bounty of land and sea served up family-style at dinner. *(Ch. 10)*

DANTICA LODGE & GALLERY, SAN GERARDO DE DOTA
Small, luxurious, white-stucco houses decorated in tropical colors are scattered around Dantica's forested grounds, where you have ample opportunity for hiking and a very good chance of spotting a resplendent quetzal. *(Ch. 10)*

ARENAL OBSERVATORY LODGE, ARENAL
You cannot stay closer than this to a volcano summit—you're less than 3.2 km (2 miles) away—although, admittedly, northern Costa Rica's Volcán Arenal has settled into a less-active phase these days. With the best views of the volcano around, Arenal Observatory Lodge sits amid an 870-acre private reserve perfect for nature walks. Plus, the folks here take active steps to protect the environment and participate in local community projects. *(Ch. 6)*

FINCA ROSA BLANCA COFFEE PLANTATION RESORT, HEREDIA
One of the Central Valley's most sumptuous lodgings is on a hilltop amid a working organic coffee plantation. Although you are in the San José metro area, the capital seems far away; the only reminder is the restaurant's spectacular view of the city lights below. The Gaudí-esque main building and neighboring structures have spacious rooms decorated with local art. *(Ch. 5)*

HOTEL SÍ COMO NO, MANUEL ANTONIO
"Sustainability" is the watchword at Sí Como No, a hip and trendy green hotel with environmentally friendly practices at its core. In addition to its nine buildings on the forested hillside grounds, Sí Como No operates its own Greentique Nature Reserve, a great opportunity to observe wildlife. *(Ch. 9)*

Arenal Observatory Lodge

LA CAROLINA LODGE, VOLCÁN TENORIO

Costa Rica's remote lodges do amazing things with no electricity or Wi-Fi. You can help with chores at this proudly off-the-grid working farm—if the spirit so moves you—or pamper yourself after a forest walk or horse ride with a massage or yoga session.

Swap travel stories over a sumptuous family-style dinner, and wind up your evening with a soak in the fire-heated hot tub. *(Ch. 6)*

RANCHO NATURALISTA, TURRIALBA

A perfect perch for accessing Costa Rica's premier bird-watching location on the fringes of the Central Valley southeast of Turrialba, Rancho Naturalista has upscale rustic rooms and resident birding guides available during the high season. Hiking and horseback riding will also keep you occupied. *(Ch. 5)*

TORTUGA LODGE, TORTUGUERO

A riverside lodge known for its nature packages, Tortuga sets itself apart in location and service. Packages include charter flights to Tortuguero, where guides take you on nocturnal turtle-watching excursions. *(Ch. 11)*

LAPA RÍOS, CORCOVADO NATIONAL PARK

Costa Rica's original green lodging pioneered the concept of the sustainability tour. You'll leave feeling educated about ways you can help conserve nature. The screened, open-air bungalows sit amid a private 1,000-acre reserve. *(Ch. 10)*

What to Eat and Drink in Costa Rica

Arroz con pollo

GALLO PINTO

Costa Rica's signature dish translates to "spotted rooster." It's so typical of the country there's a saying: "Más tico que el gallo pinto" (More Costa Rican than gallo pinto). You'll find this mix of rice, black beans, chopped bell peppers, and cilantro all over the country—even at McDonald's.

TRES LECHES

This sweet, decadent sponge cake gets soaked in a sauce made with three different types of milk: condensed, evaporated, and sweet cream. Though it sounds like the cake would be soggy, successful takes are actually quite light. Some variations substitute whole milk for the cream to cut the sweetness.

ARROZ CON POLLO

Comfort food at its finest, this chicken-and-rice dish is a staple in any Tico home, although you'll see Latin America–wide variations. Even finicky eaters enjoy the shredded chicken, with sautéed and chopped veggies like celery, corn, bell peppers, cilantro, and carrots over rice.

Gallo pinto

CASADO
Fortify yourself with a midday *casado* at a small mom-and-pop restaurant. "Casado" means "married," and the plate "marries" meat, vegetables, rice, and plantains.

IMPERIAL
Far and away, the most popular locally brewed beer is this pale lager. The same brewery—jointly Costa Rican and Dutch owned—also makes Pilsen and Bavaria.

SALSA LIZANO
It's the quintessential Costa Rican condiment, and no self-respecting home or restaurant does without it. It started as a response to Lea & Perrins' 1920 introduction of Worcestershire sauce to Costa Rica. "I can do better," insisted a local man, and Salsa Lizano was born.

FRUTAS
Sure, you know bananas and pineapples, two of Costa Rica's top agricultural exports. But you'll also encounter the egg-shape *maracuyá* (similar to passion fruit) and *guanábana* (soursop).

CAFÉ
Café is coffee, the country's signature product. Here's the kicker: Quality coffee goes for export, leaving an inferior bean behind. Your best bet for a good cup is an upscale restaurant.

ENSALADA DE PALMITO
The cylindrical, ivory-color vegetable comes from the inner stem of coconut and peach palms; you'll equate its flavor with artichokes. A particularly Costa Rican treat, especially popular around Easter, is palmito salad.

SOPA NEGRA
This filling black-bean soup with a poached egg is thick enough to spoon onto a tortilla. Most cooks garnish it to add some visual pizzazz to an otherwise unattractive-looking dish—though there's nothing ho-hum about the flavor.

RONDÓN
Afro-Caribbean immigrants brought this hearty soup to the Caribbean coast. They called it "run down"—made with whatever ingredients the cook could run down. Expect fresh fish, lobster, or crab, with plantains, cassava, and yams.

RICE AND BEANS
This is not gallo pinto. It's a Caribbean dish (its name always in English) with rice and beans steeped in fresh coconut milk.

Costa Rica Today

GOVERNMENT

Costa Rica is a democratic republic whose structure will be familiar to any citizen of the United States—a government with independent executive, legislative, and judicial branches. Citizens are guaranteed equality before the law, the right to own property, and the freedom of speech and religion. The country is justifiably proud of its long-established tradition of democracy, with free elections and peaceful transitions of power.

The country is famous for lacking an army, which was abolished when the constitution was ratified in 1949. The country's stable government and economy have made this possible, even as its neighbors were embroiled in civil wars in the 1970s and 1980s. Costa Rica does maintain a small national guard.

ECONOMY

Costa Rica has diversified its economy beyond traditional agriculture, and tourism brings in more money than its three major cash crops: coffee, bananas, and pineapples. High-tech companies such as Intel, Hewlett-Packard, and Motorola; Internet purveyor Amazon; and pharmaceutical companies like Procter & Gamble and GlaxoSmithKline operate plants and service centers in Costa Rica, providing well-paid jobs for educated professionals. The U.S. chains and big-box stores have arrived, too—most notably Walmart, which operates 13 supercenters here.

Costa Rica has staked hopes on international free-trade agreements in recent years, most notably with Mexico (1995), Canada (2002), the United States (2008), the European Union (2010), and China (2011). Opponents of the treaties are wary of how much benefit they provide for the country, however.

The economy historically bedevils Costa Rica and never more so than in the wake of the worldwide COVID-19 pandemic. Costa Rica received high marks for keeping numbers of cases and deaths far lower than jurisdictions with comparable populations. Like every other country, though, it wonders what the long-term economic impact will be.

TOURISM

In good times, some 3.1 million international visitors inject a much-needed $3.9 billion into Costa Rica's economy. The COVID-19 pandemic meant a several-month shutdown of all ports of entry and abruptly threw those numbers into reverse. As the tourism industry slowly recovers from the crisis, it hopes to reestablish Costa Rica as one of the hemisphere's great travel destinations. When things return to "normal," the industry will return to its classic, spirited debates on how to reconcile ecotourism and sustainable development with resort construction, adventure tourism, and extreme sports. Tourism's various subsectors here do not always see eye to eye.

RELIGION

Because it was a Spanish colony, Costa Rica continues to have a close relationship with the Catholic Church. Catholicism was made the country's official religion in the constitution. Because of this, priests are the only type of clergy authorized to perform civil marriages. (Others require the assistance of a legal official.)

The number of Costa Ricans identifying as Catholic has dropped to 54%. Even among this group, many people do not have a strong identification with the church or with its teachings. The live-and-let-live attitude of most Costa Ricans does not mesh well with religious doctrine. Evangelical churches are gaining ground, but not yet to the same extent as elsewhere in Central America.

Every village has a church on its main square—always hopping once a year, when the town's patron saint is honored. These are times for food, music, and dancing in the streets. If the celebrations lack much religious fervor—well, that's Costa Rica for you.

SPORTS

Like everyone else on this soccer-mad isthmus, Costa Ricans take their game seriously, and passions bubble over when it comes to their beloved national team.

On the national level, the big local rivalry is between LD Alajuelense (*La Liga,* or "the League") and Deportivo Saprissa (*El Monstruo Morado,* or "the Purple Monster"). They have won the Costa Rican championship 30 and 36 times, respectively, which makes the rivalry particularly intense. You can tell how important the sport is when you fly into the country. As your plane flies across the Central Valley, you'll notice that every village, no matter how small, has a soccer field.

CASH CROPS

If nearby Honduras was the original Banana Republic, 19th-century Costa Rica was a Coffee Republic. Coffee remains inexorably entwined with the country, with economists paying close attention to world prices and kids in rural areas still taking class time off to help with the harvest.

The irony is that it's hard to get a decent cup of the stuff here. True to economic realities of developing countries, the high-quality product gets exported, with the inferior coffee staying behind for the local market. (The same is true of bananas, Costa Rica's other signature agricultural product.) The best places to get a cup of high-quality Costa Rican coffee are upscale restaurants and hotels. Owners understand foreign tastes and have export-quality coffee on hand. Gift shops sell the superior product as well.

The Central Valley is where you'll find many of the coffee plantations. You'll recognize them immediately by the rows of brilliant green plants covered in red berries. Because many of these plants are sensitive to light, they are often shaded by tall trees or even by canopies of fabric. Tours of the plantations are a great way to get to know the local cash crop.

In recent years, the producers of coffee have focused on quality rather than quantity. That's why bananas are now the top agricultural export, followed by pineapples. Both grow in sunny lowland areas, which are abundant on both the Atlantic and Pacific coasts. These crops are treated with just as much care as coffee. You're likely to see bunches of bananas wrapped in plastic bags—while still on the tree. This prevents blemishes that make them less appealing to foreign consumers.

Ecotourism in Costa Rica

DEFINING ECOTOURISM

Ecotourism has become the buzzword of Costa Rica's travel industry. From the original concept revolving around travel to enjoy nature, it has morphed into everything from hiking through the rain forest to rumbling over hillsides in all-terrain vehicles. We'll go with the oft-stated definition that ecotourism is "environmentally responsible travel." Costa Rica does itself proud in the domain of adventure tourism and extreme sports, but those activities sometimes conflict with that lofty ecotourism goal. That is not to say that adventure sports can't be part of a green vacation. It all depends what impact they have on the environment and the local community.

GOING GREEN

Over the past decade, the concept of ecotourism has made a strong impression on the average traveler. Many people now realize that mass tourism can be damaging to environmentally sensitive places like Costa Rica but that much can be done to alleviate the negative effects. At the same time, "ecotourism" has become a marketing term used to attract customers who have the best intentions.

In addition to giving travelers the chance to observe and learn about wildlife, ecotourism should accomplish three things: refrain from damaging the environment, strengthen conservation efforts, and improve the lives of local people.

The last part might seem a bit beside the point, but environmentalists point out that much of the deforestation in Costa Rica and other countries is by poor people trying to eke out a living through subsistence farming. Providing them with other ways to make a living is the best way to prevent this.

WHAT CAN YOU DO?

Make sure the hotel you choose is eco-friendly. A great place to start is the Costa Rican Tourism Board (⊕ *visitcostarica.com*). It has a rating system for hotels and lodges called the Certification for Sustainable Tourism. The New York–based Rainforest Alliance (⊕ *rainforest-alliance.org*) has a convenient searchable database of sustainable lodges. The International Ecotourism Society (⊕ *ecotourism.org*) also has a database of tour companies, hotels, and other travel services that are committed to sustainable practices.

Use locally owned lodges, car-rental agencies, or tour companies. Eat in local restaurants, shop in local markets, and attend local events. Enrich your experience and support the community by hiring local guides.

Make sure your tour company follows sustainable policies, including contributing to conservation efforts, hiring and training locals for most jobs, educating visitors about the local ecology and culture, and taking steps to mitigate negative impacts on the environment.

Don't be overly aggressive if you bargain for souvenirs, and don't shortchange local people on payments or tips for services.

Stray from the beaten path—by visiting areas where few tourists go, you can avoid adding to the stress on hot spots.

Support conservation by paying entrance fees to parks and protected sites. You can go a few steps further by making donations to local or international conservation groups such as Conservation International, the Rainforest Alliance, and the World Wide Fund for Nature.

Costa Rica Outdoor Adventures

Ziplining and Canopy Tours

Costa Rica gave the world the so-called canopy tour, a series of ziplines that let you glide through the treetops, attached to a secure harness. Although billed as a way to get up close and personal with nature, your focus and attention will likely be on the ride rather than spotting that elusive resplendent quetzal. No matter. Ziplining has become one of Costa Rica's signature activities for visitors. The term "canopy tour" has expanded to include hanging bridges and elevated trams where you walk or ride through the forest canopy. The latter two really are more effective ways to view all the nature the treetops have to offer.

Ziplines are a fast-paced, thrilling experience. You're attached to a zipline with a safety harness, and then you "fly" at about 15–40 mph from one tree platform to the next. (You may be anywhere from 60 to 300 feet above the forest floor.) Tree-to-tree ziplines date from the 19th century and have been a bona fide activity for visitors to Costa Rica since the mid-1990s when the first tour opened in Monteverde. These tours are tremendous fun, but you won't see any animals. An average fitness level—and above-average level of intrepidness—are all you need. Be brutally frank in assessing your desire and ability to do this, and remember that once you start, there's no turning back.

Bridges and trams are canopy tours in a literal sense, where you walk along suspension bridges, ride along in a tram, or are hoisted up to a platform to get a closer look at birds, monkeys, and sloths. They're also called hanging-bridges tours, sky walks, or platform tours. If seeing nature at a more leisurely pace is your goal, opt for these, especially the bridge excursions. Early mornings are the best time for animal sightings—at 50–250 feet above ground, the views are stupendous.

BEST CANOPY TOURS

El Santuario Canopy Adventure Tour, Manuel Antonio National Park. The mile-plus cable system here is Costa Rica's longest single zipline.

Hacienda Guachipelín, Rincón de la Vieja National Park. Combine ziplines with horseback riding and sulfur springs on the summit of northern Costa Rica's best-known volcano.

Original Canopy Tour, Limón. A branch of Costa Rica's first zipline tour is the highlight of a nature-themed park near the Caribbean coast.

Osa Canopy Tour, Uvita. One of the South Pacific's few such operations combines ziplines with rappelling stations and a Tarzan swing.

Rainforest Adventures, Braulio Carrillo National Park. These folks pioneered the concept of guided gondola rides through the canopy.

Selvatura, Monteverde Cloud Forest. Some of the longest ziplines in the country are here. There is also an extensive bridge system that lets you walk through the canopy at your own pace.

Sportfishing

Adventurous anglers flock to Costa Rica to test their will—and patience—against an assortment of feisty fresh- and saltwater fish. Just remember: catch-and-release is usually expected, so the pleasure's all in the pursuit. With so many options, the hardest decision is where to go. Inshore fishing in the country's rivers and lakes yields roosterfish, snapper, barracuda, jacks, and snook. Fly-fishing aficionados love the extra-large tarpon and snook because of their sheer size and fight. The country's coasts swarm with a multitude of bigger game, including the majestic billfish—the marlin and the sailfish. There are many top-notch fishing outfitters up and down both coasts and around rivers and lakes, so planning a fishing trip is easy. Charter boats range from 22 feet to 60 feet in length. With a good captain, a boat in the 22- to 26-foot range for up to three anglers can cost from $500 to $900 a day. A 28- to 32-foot boat fits four and costs from $800 to $1,500 per day. A boat for six people costs $1,400 to $2,000 and measures between 36 and 47 feet. A 60-foot boat for up to 10 anglers costs about $3,000 a day. A good charter boat company employs experienced captains and offers good equipment, bait, and food and beverages.

You're guaranteed a few good catches no matter what the season, as demonstrated by the cadre of sportsmen who circle the coasts year-round chasing that perfect catch. If your heart is set on an area or a type of fish, do your research ahead of time and plan accordingly. Costa Rica teems with a constant supply of fish, some of which might seem unique to North Americans.

Northern Lowlands: Lake Arenal and Caño Negro are great freshwater spots to snag extra-large tarpon, snook, and the ugly-but-fascinating guapote bass. Start your fishing journey in nearby La Fortuna.

Guanacaste: Tamarindo is the main departure point for anglers looking to find big game, including tuna, roosterfish, and marlin. Boats also leave from Playas del Coco, Ocotal, Tambor, and Flamingo Beach, which are best fished May through August. All are close to the well-stocked northern Papagayo Gulf.

Central Pacific coast: If you're hunting sailfish and marlin between December and April, head to the Central Pacific coast around Los Sueños and Quepos, where up to 10 sailfish are caught per boat.

South Pacific: Puerto Jiménez, Golfito, and Zancudo are less developed than the other Pacific regions and are famous for their excellent inshore fishing for snapper and roosterfish, though offshore big game is also good in the area, especially November through January.

Caribbean coast: Barra del Colorado is a popular sportfishing hub and a great departure point for freshwater fishing on the Caribbean side of the country. Fly-fishers looking for the ultimate challenge head to the San Juan River for its legendary tarpon. The Colorado River lures anglers with jack, tuna, snook, tarpon, and dorado. Transportation and tours can be arranged by the hotels listed in Tortuguero or Puerto Viejo de Sarapiquí.

Scuba Diving and Snorkeling

For snorkelers and scuba divers, Costa Rica is synonymous with swarms of fish and stretches of coral that hug the country's 1,291 km (802 miles) of coastline. Submerge yourself in crystalline waters and enter another world, with bull sharks, brain coral, and toothy green eels. The variety and abundance of marine life are awe-inspiring.

Beach towns on both coasts are riddled with diving schools and equipment-rental shops. Look for outfitters that are PADI (Professional Association of Diving Instructors) trained or give PADI certifications. If you're a first-timer and plan to go diving just once, taking a basic half-day class isn't difficult, and it will allow you to dive up to 40 feet with an instructor. A three- or four-day certification course gets you a lifetime license and allows you to dive up to 130 feet and without a guide.

The Pacific tends to be clearer than the Caribbean, and the fish are bigger and more abundant. Northern waters are generally best May through July, after winds die down and the water turns bluer and warmer. The southern Osa Peninsula is popular during the dry season, from January to April. The Caribbean, known for its diverse coral and small fish, is good for beginners because it has less surge. The best months are September and October, when the ocean is as calm and flat as a swimming pool. April and May also offer decent conditions, but steer clear during the rest of the year, when rain and strong waves cloud the water.

Cahuita. Mounds of coral and a barrier reef (dubbed Long Shoal) run from Cahuita to Punta Mona, along 25 km (15 miles) of Caribbean coastline. Arches, tunnels, and canyons in the reef form a playground for small fish, crabs, and lobsters. Even though sediment and wastewater have damaged much of the coral, the healthy sections are dense, colorful, and delightfully shaped. Gentle pools right off the beach allow for some of the country's best snorkeling.

Golfo de Papagayo (Papagayo Gulf). This northern gulf has Costa Rica's highest concentration of snorkel and dive shops. Calm, protected waters make it the best place for beginner divers on the Pacific.

Isla de Caño (Caño Island). With visibility of 20 to 80 feet, strong currents, and very changeable conditions, Caño is best suited for advanced divers. The huge schools of large fish and potential shark sightings are the attractions here. Novice snorkelers can frolic in the Coral Garden, a shallow area on the north side of this biological reserve.

Isla del Coco (Cocos Island). One of the world's premier sites for advanced divers lies 295 nautical miles and a 36-hour sail from Puntarenas. Visibility is good all year, and hammerhead and white-tipped reef sharks are the main attractions.

Isla Murciélago (Bat Island). Located inside Santa Rosa National Park, this cluster of rocks is good for advanced divers and famous for its fearsome bull sharks.

Isla Santa Catalina (Santa Catalina Island). Known for sightings of golden cownose rays and giant mantas, these big rocks near Playa Flamingo have spots for beginner and advanced divers. Snorkelers should head to shallower waters, near the beach.

Bird-Watching

Even if you've never seen yourself as a bird-watcher, Costa Rica will get you hooked. Waking you before dawn, calling to you throughout the day, and serenading you through tropical nights, birds are impossible to ignore here. Luckily, Costa Rica has a wealth of world-class ornithologists and local bird guides who can answer all your questions. Every licensed naturalist guide also has some birding expertise, so many tours you take in the country will include some bird-watching.

The sheer variety and abundance of birds here make bird-watching a daily pastime—with less than 0.03% of the planet's surface, Costa Rica counts some 900 bird species, more than the United States and Canada combined. Armed with a pair of binoculars and a birding guide, the sky is literally the limit for the number of birds you can see; catching sight of a brilliantly colored bird is exciting, but being able to identify it after a couple of encounters is even more thrilling. For kids, spotting birds makes a great game. With their sharp young eyes, they're usually very good at it—plus it's wildly educational. About 10% of Costa Rica's birds are endemic, so this is a mecca for bird-watchers intent on compiling an impressive life list.

The best time to bird is November to May, when local species are joined by winter migrants. Breeding season, which varies by species throughout the year, is the easiest time to spot birds, as males put on displays for females, followed by frequent flights to gather nesting material and then food for the chicks. Also keep your eye on fruit-bearing trees that attract hungry birds.

The most sought-after bird is the aptly named resplendent quetzal, sporting brilliant blue, green, and red plumage and long tail feathers. The best places to spot it are **Los Quetzales National Park** in the **Cerro de la Muerte** highlands, the **San Gerardo de Dota** valley, and the **Monteverde Cloud Forest Reserve.** Another bird high on many bird-watchers' lists is the scarlet macaw, the largest of the parrot family here. You'll see pairs performing aerial ballets and munching in beach almond trees in **Corcovado National Park,** along the Osa Peninsula's coastline, and around **Carara National Park** in the Central Pacific region. The **Tempisque River** delta's salty waters, at the north end of the Gulf of Nicoya, are famous for a wealth of water birds, notably wood storks, glossy ibis, and roseate spoonbills. Farther north, in **Palo Verde** and **Caño Negro National Parks,** look for the rarest and largest of wading birds, the jabiru. The network of jungle-edged natural canals in **Tortuguero National Park,** in the northern Caribbean, is home to a host of herons, including the spectacular rufescent tiger heron

and the multihued agami heron. More than 50 species of hummingbirds hover around every part of the country. Look for them around feeders at lodges in the **Cerro de la Muerte** area, Monteverde, and the Turrialba region.

Sea Turtle-Watching

Five species of sea turtle visit Costa Rican shores: olive ridley, green sea turtle, loggerhead, hawksbill, and leatherback. The gentle giants, which can weigh up to 1,000 pounds, spend most of their time at sea but come ashore by the thousands for two or three nights to lay their eggs. There are just seven places in the world where these mass nesting events, called arribadas, happen. This includes both of Costa Rica's coasts, with the most turtles coming to the Nicoya Peninsula on the Pacific coast and Tortuguero on the Caribbean coast.

Head to the Nicoya Peninsula on the Pacific coast during the rainy season. In September, October, and November, at least once a month and sometimes twice, more than 100,000 olive ridley sea turtles come to Ostional National Wildlife Refuge north of Nosara, filling the beach over the course of three or four days with more than 100 million eggs in one of the largest arribadas in the world. Around 60 days later, in a flurry of flying sand, the tiny hatchlings emerge from their shells, dig their way to the surface, and make their cumbersome and perilous journey to the sea. After many years and thousands of miles at sea, olive ridleys will return to the exact beach where they were born when it is their time to nest.

On the east coast in Tortuguero, you are likely to see different types of turtles' mass nesting events. There is a good chance of seeing leatherbacks nesting on the shore from March to July, green sea turtles from June to October, and hawksbills from July to October. While the numbers aren't quite as grandiose as in Ostional—leatherback sea turtle numbers continue to decline, and scientists estimate that there may be as few as 32,000 nesting females left in the world—they're still a sight to behold.

■ TIP→ **Book a turtle-watching tour ahead of your trip, noting that a responsible guide never allows animal interactions. Below is a handy guide of where to spot turtles around the country and where to stay.**

Ostional. See turtles at Ostional National Wildlife Refuge (☎ 506/682–0400) and stay at Luna Azul (☎ 506/4500–1400 ⊕ hotellunaazul.com). (Ch. 8)

Tortuguero. See turtles with the Sea Turtle Conservancy (☎ 506/2767–1576) and stay at Tortuga Lodge (☎ 800/963–1195 ⊕ tortugalodge.com). (Ch. 11)

Montezuma. See turtles with ASVO (☎ 506/2222–3612) and stay at Ylang Ylang Beach Resort (☎ 888/795–8494 ⊕ ylangylangbeachresort.com). (Ch. 8)

Sámara. See turtles at the Camaronal National Wildlife Refuge (☎ 506/2659–8190) and stay at Villas Kalimba (☎ 506/2656–0929 ⊕ villaskalimba.com). (Ch. 8)

Playa Hermosa. See turtles at Playa Hermosa/Punta Mala National Wildlife Refuge (inquire at hotel about tour) and stay at DoceLunas (☎ 506/2643–2211 ⊕ docelunas.com). (Ch. 9)

Cabo Matapalo. See turtles with Osa Conservation (☎ 506/8719–8582) and stay at Bosque del Cabo (☎ 506/2735–5206 ⊕ bosquedelcabo.com). (Ch. 10)

Puerto Viejo de Talamanca. See turtles at Gandoca Manzanillo National Wildlife Refuge with ATEC Eco-Tours

(☎ 506/2750–0398) and stay at Cariblue Beach & Jungle Resort (☎ 506/2750–0035 ⊕ cariblue.com). (Ch. 11)

Surfing

Costa Rica's big surfing community, consistent waves, and not-too-crowded beaches make surfing accessible to anyone who is curious enough to paddle into the lineup; surf schools and board rentals are plentiful.

At many of Costa Rica's top surf spots, a wide range of ages and skills can be found bobbing together in the water. With the right board—ideally a foam longboard for first timers—and good instruction, just about anybody can stand up and ride. Trained instructors can adapt lessons to different levels, ages, and body types. If you want to get a head start before your vacation, practice pop-ups at home (YouTube has dozens of tutorials) or swim laps at your local pool to get in shape before your first wipeout.

With warm water, offshore winds, and friendly locals, you really can't find a better place to learn the sport. Costa Ricans are known for their pura vida attitude, and this usually translates into a welcoming vibe in the water. Just steer clear of the hotshots until you know local protocol.

On the Pacific, waves are consistent from December through April. As you move southward, the breaks are best from May to November. On the Caribbean side, conditions are best January through April.

Dominical, Pacific Coast. A long set of fast, powerful breaks that are great for advanced levels. When waves get too big, head south to Dominicalito.

Esteríllos, Pacific Coast. Divided into three beaches, this wide stretch of coast is uncrowded to the point of desolation. The surf and currents can be tough for beginners, and Este and Centro have waves much like Hermosa. Oeste has softer waves.

Jacó, Pacific Coast. Unless the surf gets too big, the consistent beach breaks produce forgiving waves that are good for beginner to intermediate surfers.

Malpaís, Pacific Coast. A variety of beach breaks plus a point break that's good when waves are pumping.

Manuel Antonio, Pacific Coast. Playitas, at the national park's north end, is perhaps the most consistent spot here. It's only good at high tide, about three hours per day, and usually flat September through December.

Pavones, Pacific Coast. This advanced and fickle spot is said to be one of the world's longest lefts, lasting nearly three minutes.

Playa Cocles, Caribbean Coast. Plenty of beach breaks and good for all levels, but beware of riptides.

Playa Guiones, Pacific Coast. If not the best surf in the vicinity of Nosara, it's the best beach break for beginners and longboarders, with plenty of long rights and lefts.

Playa Hermosa, Pacific Coast. A steep beach break just south of Jacó with some of the country's best barrels and surfers. Waves can get big, mean, hollow, and thunderously heavy.

Salsa Brava, Caribbean Coast. When it's on, this is arguably Costa Rica's best and most powerful wave, breaking right over a shallow coral reef.

Sámara, Pacific Coast. Protected, mellow beach breaks great for beginners, yet close to advanced spots like Playa Camaronal.

Tamarindo, Pacific Coast. Surfer's paradise for all levels, with famous breaks like Ollie's Point, Playa Avellanas, and Playa Negra (south), and Witch's Rock (north). Solid waves are formed at a point break called Pico Pequeño and at the river mouth called El Estero at the beach's north end.

Weddings and Honeymoons

Ever dreamed of getting married on a sandy beach shaded by palm trees? Many people who envision such a scene immediately think of the Caribbean. But Costa Rica is fast becoming a favored destination for tropical nuptials.

Compared with the complicated procedures in many other destinations, getting married in Costa Rica is easy. There are no residency restrictions or blood-test requirements. At least a month in advance, couples who are over 18 should provide their local wedding planner with a copy of their birth certificates and passports so they can be submitted to the local authorities. With Costa Rica legalizing same-sex marriage in 2020, all couples, gay and straight, may tie the knot here.

Any previous marriage complicates things a bit. The couple needs to provide documentation that the marriage was terminated. Divorce papers or death certificate of a previous spouse must be translated into Spanish and notarized.

THE BIG DAY

Judges, attorneys, and Catholic priests have legal authority to certify a marriage in Costa Rica. (Most foreign couples avoid the latter because a Catholic wedding requires months of preparation.) The official ceremony is simple, but couples are free to add their own vows or anything else they would like. The officiant will register the marriage with the civil registry and the couple's embassy.

At the wedding, the couple needs to have at least two witnesses who are not family members. Many couples choose their best man and maid of honor. If necessary, the wedding planner can provide witnesses.

The license itself takes three months to issue and is sent to the couple's home address. For an extra fee, couples can ask for the process to be expedited. Virtually all Western countries recognize the legality of a Costa Rican marriage.

BEAUTIFUL BACKDROPS

Although Costa Rica offers no shortage of impressive backdrops for a ceremony, the Central Pacific coast sees the most tourist weddings and honeymoons. May and June are the most popular months for foreigners, but many people choose January or February because you are virtually guaranteed sunny skies. (Costa Ricans favor December weddings.) Manuel Antonio's Makanda by the Sea, La Mariposa, Sí Como No, and Punta Leona's Villa Caletas are among the many lodgings here with events staff well versed in planning ceremonies and tending to the legalities.

There are many details to attend to: flowers, music, and photography. Most large hotels have on-staff wedding planners to walk you through the process. Couples can also hire their own wedding planner, which is often less expensive. Either way, wedding planners have a wide range of services available, and couples can pick and choose.

HONEYMOONS

As far as honeymoons go, no place in Costa Rica is inappropriate. Although honeymoons on the beach, especially along the Northern Pacific and Central Pacific coasts, are popular, many couples opt for treks to the mountains or the rain forests. Dozens of newlyweds choose offbeat adventures, such as spotting sea turtles along the Caribbean coast or swimming with pilot whales off the Osa Peninsula.

The People of Costa Rica

Unlike many of its neighbors, Costa Rica never had a dominant indigenous population. When Christopher Columbus arrived in 1504, he didn't encounter empires like those in present-day Mexico and Peru. Instead, a small contingent of indigenous Caribs rowed out in canoes to meet his ship. The heavy gold bands the indigenous peoples wore led to Columbus mistakenly calling the land Costa Rica, or "Rich Coast."

On the mainland, the Spanish encountered disparate peoples like the Chorotega, Bribri, Cabécar, and Boruca peoples. Archaeological evidence shows that they had lived in the region for thousands of years. But that would change with breathtaking speed. European diseases felled many of their members, and the brutality of slavery imposed by the colonial power drove most of those remaining into the mountains.

Some of these peoples still exist, although in relatively small communities. Several thousand Bribri, Kekoldi, and other peoples live in villages scattered around Talamanca, a mountainous region close to the border of Panama. Although many traditions have been lost over the years, some have managed to retain their own languages and religions. If you're interested in seeing the local culture, tour companies in the coastal communities of Limón and Puerto Viejo de Talamanca can arrange visits to these villages.

That isn't to say that there's no local culture. More than 90% of the country's residents are descendants of the Spanish. But few people express any pride in their Spanish heritage. Perhaps that is because Spain had little interest in Costa Rica, the smallest and poorest of its Central American colonies. Instead, the people here created a unique culture that mixes parts of Europe, Latin America, and the Caribbean. There's a strong emphasis on education, and the 97% literacy rate is by far the highest in the region. There's a laid-back attitude toward life, typified by the common greeting of *pura vida,* which translates literally as "pure life" but means something between "no worries" and "don't sweat the small stuff."

It sounds like a cliché, but Costa Ricans are an incredibly welcoming people. Anyone who has visited other Central American countries will be surprised at how Ticos seem genuinely happy to greet newcomers. If you ever find yourself lost in a town or village, you may find locals willing to not only point you in the right direction but walk you all the way to your destination. A trip to Costa Rica will supply you with memories of beaches, nature, and adventure, but we wager you'll also remember the friendly people here.

Kids and Families

With so much to keep them interested and occupied, Costa Rica is a blast with kids. The activities here are things the whole family can do together: discovering a waterfall in a rain forest, snorkeling with sea turtles, or white-water rafting down a roaring river. There are also activities for kids that will allow parents time to stroll hand in hand down a deserted beach.

CHOOSING A DESTINATION

Basing yourself in one place for several days is a great idea. Climbing into the car every day or two not only makes the kids miserable but means that the best part of the day is spent traveling. (Kids who are prone to carsickness won't do well on the winding, twisting roads, like the road to Monteverde Cloud Forest.) The good news is that there are many destinations where you could stay for a week and still not do and see everything.

Headed to the beach? Remember that for families, not all beaches are created equal. Choose a destination with a range of activities. Manuel Antonio, on the Central Pacific coast, is your best bet. The proximity to the national park is the main selling point, but you're also close to other nature preserves. As for activities, there's everything from snorkeling and surfing lessons to kayaking excursions to zipline adventures. And the range of kid-friendly restaurants is unmatched anywhere in the country. On the Nicoya Peninsula, Playas del Coco and Playa Tamarindo have a decent amount of activities for the small fry.

Santa Elena, the closest town to Monteverde Cloud Forest Biological Reserve, is another great base. There are several nature preserves in the area, and they offer both day and night hikes. If skies are cloudy—as they often are—there are indoor attractions like the display of slithering snakes. The town is compact and walkable, and has many eateries with children's menus. La Fortuna, the gateway to the Lake Arenal area, has activities from waterfall hikes to canopy tours. The town itself isn't attractive, so you'll want to choose a place nearby.

Believe it or not, the San José area is not a bad base. Activities like white-water rafting are nearby, and on rainy days you can visit the city's excellent museums dedicated to gold and jade. The hotels in the surrounding countryside are often a long drive from good restaurants. We prefer the hotels in the city, as dozens of restaurants line the pedestrian-only streets.

KID-FRIENDLY ACTIVITIES

You can't beat the beach in Costa Rica. Unfortunately, few have lifeguards; take warning signs about rip currents very seriously. Snorkeling and surfing lessons are great for older kids, but stick with a licensed company rather than that enthusiastic young person who approaches you on the beach.

Canopy tours are good for kids of all ages. Ask the staff about how long a tour will take, because once you set out on a hike over a series of hanging bridges, you have no choice but to continue on to the end. Ziplines are appropriate for older teens, who should always be accompanied by an adult.

For the smallest of the small fry, the butterfly enclosures and hummingbird gardens that you find near many resort areas are wonderful diversions. Indoor activities, like the display of frogs at Santa Elena, fascinate youngsters. And don't avoid the easier hikes in the national parks. Seeing animals in the wild is likely to start a lifelong love of animals.

What to Watch and Read

AFTER EARTH

In a postapocalyptic world, Will and Jaden Smith are a dad and son whose spaceship crash-lands on 31st-century Earth—with humanity long since departed for another planet. As they struggle to return home, the steaming, gurgling, bubbling landscape around Arenal Volcano is the backdrop.

THE BLUE BUTTERFLY

Entomologist William Hurt accompanies a terminally ill 10-year-old boy from Montreal to Costa Rica in this 2004 film. His goal? Fulfill the boy's final wish to see the country's wondrous blue morpho butterfly. See if you can spot the lush scenery of Puerto Viejo de Talamanca on the south Caribbean coast.

CARNIVAL IN COSTA RICA

In this 1947 movie, a young man and woman return to Costa Rica after time abroad to discover their families have arranged for them to marry. The problem is that they're in love with other people. Technicolor filming was done in Hollywood; on-location footage of San José's carnival celebration and coffee harvest was patched in.

THE ENDLESS SUMMER II

Credit this documentary by Bruce Brown for putting Costa Rica on the map in surfing circles. His original Endless Summer (1966) did not visit here, but three decades later, this sequel coincided with the launch of Costa Rica's tourism boom. The film follows two surfers around the world. First stop? Costa Rica.

DOWN TO EARTH WITH ZAC EFRON

One episode of this 2020 Netflix series brings Efron and wellness expert Darin Olien to Costa Rica. Ziplines, beaches, animal-rescue centers, and community-based tourism lead them to conclude the country holds a key to sustainable living—and is a lot of fun to boot.

JURASSIC PARK

Contrary to popular belief, movies in the Jurassic Park franchise were not filmed in Costa Rica. Yes, author Michael Crichton based his fictional Isla Nublar on the real-life Isla del Coco, some 350 miles southwest of Costa Rica, but director Steven Spielberg found Hawaii simpler to reach for the films.

MONKEYS ARE MADE OF CHOCOLATE: EXOTIC AND UNSEEN COSTA RICA BY JACK EWING

Onetime cattle rancher Jack Ewing let nature reclaim his deforested land near Dominical in the 1980s, resulting in Hacienda Barú, one of Costa Rica's best nature reserves. In 32 essays—arguably the quintessential modern nature guide to the country—Ewing paints a picture of Costa Rica's flora and fauna, with humans as guests who inhabit the land.

PURA VIDA (LOVE HAS NO BOUNDARIES) BY SARA ALVA

You'll hear the expression ¡Pura vida! a lot during your Costa Rica trip. Literally translated as "pure life," it serves as a greeting, a farewell, and an all-around expression of approval. Most important, it describes a uniquely Costa Rican enjoyment of life. Tourist Simon, on vacation with his family, finds a holiday romance with Costa Rican Juan in this breezy 100-page novella by Sara Alva.

RADICAL SABBATICAL BY GLEN TIBALDEO AND LAURA BERGER

A husband and wife duo write about taking the expat plunge with wit and style. You can dive into and out of the book's 42 fun short- to medium-length chapters at will, in any sequence. If you find yourself saying "Let's move here!" during your vacation, give this book a read first.

Chapter 2

TRAVEL SMART

Updated by
Jeffrey Van Fleet

★ **CAPITAL**
San José

👥 **POPULATION**
5.2 million

💬 **LANGUAGE**
Spanish

$ **CURRENCY**
Costa Rican colón

☎ **AREA CODE**
506

⚠ **EMERGENCIES**
911; U.S. Embassy in San José: 506/2519–2000

🚗 **DRIVING**
On the right side

⚡ **ELECTRICITY**
120 volts/60 cycles; plugs are U.S. standard two- and three-prong

🕙 **TIME**
Two hours behind New York during U.S. daylight saving; one hour behind otherwise

🌐 **WEB RESOURCES**
www.visitcostarica.com,
www.ticotimes.net,
www.therealcostarica.com

Know Before You Go

When should I go to Costa Rica? What should I pack? Do I need a visa? Is there Uber? Is it safe? What if I get hurt? We've got the answers and a few tips to help you make the most of your visit.

YOU CAN'T SEE THE WHOLE COUNTRY IN ONE TRIP

No matter how small Costa Rica looks on a map—it's the size of Vermont and New Hampshire combined—your best-laid plans to see the entire country will never materialize. Choose two or three destinations to see in two weeks.

THE RAINY SEASON IS A GREAT TIME TO VISIT

Don't let the May-through-November wet season stop you from visiting. Dubbed the "green season" by the tourist industry, crowds are smaller, prices are lower, and the countryside is lush and verdant. There are showers for a couple of hours in the afternoon, but you plan around that. (Rains do become heavier and more prolonged in September and October.) Most nature activities go on rain or shine, though, and many outfitters provide ponchos and boots.

THE CLOUD FOREST CAN GET CHILLY

Much of your time spent in Costa Rica won't require warm clothing, but make sure to pack layers; if you're visiting the Cloud Forest, include a sweater. The forest is aptly named and full of mist. It can get quite chilly, and not just in the morning and late at night.

EXPECT TO STAY AT SMALL LODGINGS

All-inclusives exist, but they've never been the focus of tourism here. Although you will see Hilton, Hampton, Marriott, Radisson, Four Seasons, and Best Western here, Costa Rica remains the province of smaller, independently owned lodgings with local touches, where the owners will give you nearby dining and sightseeing recommendations, or where you can exchange such information with your fellow travelers over breakfast.

COSTA RICA DOES NOT USE ADDRESSES AS WE KNOW THEM

If street names exist, nobody here knows or uses them. Costa Rica relies instead on a charming, exasperating system of expressing locations in reference to a landmark. Think in units of 100 meters, which denote how far it is to the next cross street. Historically, the reference point was the church, always in the center of town ("200 meters north and 50 meters west of the church," for example); these days, that landmark could be anything: a bakery, a gas station, a Taco Bell. Just keep asking.

RESEARCH SPORTS OUTFITTERS

Costa Rica lets you raft, hike, zipline, swim, surf, kayak, rappel, bike, climb, sail, spelunk, hang glide, bungee jump, snorkel, balloon, dive, fish, trek, and skydive. Be brutally frank with yourself about your capabilities, and evaluate the outfitter carefully. No government body here sets standards. Remember that you're not at a giant outdoor amusement park. This is real nature with all its accompanying forces.

NO HAGGLING

Bargaining is not the sport here that it is in other countries. Souvenir prices are fixed and fair, certainly at brick-and-mortar establishments, and attempts to haggle down the amount might come across as rude. Merchants pay high credit-card fees, so you might get a small discount (*descuento*) if you pay in cash and with local currency (the *colón*). Do feel free to bargain, say, for produce at an outdoor farmers' market or if you want to negotiate hiring a taxi for a day.

YOU HAVE TO GET CAR RENTAL INSURANCE

Insurance in Costa Rica is a government monopoly. At a minimum, you must take the third-party insurance the rental agency offers. Your back-home car insurance does not exempt you, and neither does any coverage your credit card provides. Don't be fooled by online offers for car rental that will cost you "Only $10 a day!" as such rates are impossible. Ask what is included when you get a price quote. Some agencies tell you everything up front while others advertise only the base rate.

KEEP CALM AND DOWNLOAD WAZE
Speaking of driving, when you get out on the road, be extremely cautious. A mountainous spine bisects the country, and even on the beaten tourist track you can encounter some of Costa Rica's legendarily rough roads. Consider downloading a navigation app like Waze, which seems to work best here, and slow down. If you're really worried, you can cut down on driving by taking domestic flights.

STAY CONNECTED WITH WHATSAPP
To avoid massive roaming charges, consider a prepaid local SIM card for your unlocked phone, from one of Costa Rica's three cell companies—Kölbi, Claro, or Movistar. (Kölbi has counters in the arrivals area of both international airports, in San José and Liberia.) Better yet, download the free messaging app, WhatsApp, and hunt down a Wi-Fi hotspot to make phone calls and send messages.

DON'T FORGET THE DEPARTURE TAX
Costa Rica levies a $29 airport departure tax, payable in dollars or the equivalent in colones. Nearly all airlines bundle the tax into ticket prices; charter flights often do not. If not already included, you pay the tax at the airport upon departure. Paying with a MasterCard or Visa credit card means the transaction will be processed as a cash advance and incur additional fees. A few hotels will collect the tax for you as well.

EVERYONE CAN GET MARRIED HERE
Costa Rica's 2020 legalization of same-sex marriage means both gay and straight couples can say a tropical "I do." You need to be at least 18 and supply your wedding planner—as a foreigner, you should use one to navigate logistics—with copies of your and your witnesses' passports and birth certificates. (Witnesses cannot be related to you.) Some big resort lodgings have a planner on staff.

THE HEALTH CARE IS GOOD
We hope you don't require medical attention during your trip, but if you do, you can expect some of the best care in Central America, despite the overburdened public health system. Medications generally cost a fraction of what you'd pay in the United States.

LEARN THE PHRASE "PURA VIDA"
You can't go wrong by saying an amiable *pura vida*, which serves as "hello," "good-bye," "thanks," "cool," and so on. The phrase has become synonymous with the country and its way of life.

SOME NATIONAL PARKS CLOSE ONCE A WEEK
Make sure to plan your trips to the national parks around weekly closures. Manuel Antonio, one of the most popular national parks in Costa Rica, is closed on Tuesday.

COSTA RICANS PREFER FORMAL SPANISH
If you're going to speak Spanish in Costa Rica, err on the side of formality. For example, use *con mucho gusto* (with much pleasure) instead of the typical *de nada* for "you're welcome." And note that it's considered impolite to ask about marital status and family.

NO VISA NEEDED
A valid passport is all you'll need for a tourist stay of up to 90 days. To be on the safe side, be sure your passport is valid for at least 90 days from your date of entry.

UBER OPERATES, ALBEIT WITH ISSUES
You can hail Uber rides here, but the company operates without proper government permits and is always under threat of being shut down. Until Uber and the government work out their differences, we recommend not using the service.

Getting Here

Air

If you are visiting several regions of the country, flying into San José, in the center of Costa Rica, is your best option. Flying into Liberia, in northwest Costa Rica, makes more sense if you are planning to spend your vacation entirely in the North Pacific. Fares are usually lower to San José than to Liberia. San José also has many more flights each day, making it easier if you miss a flight or have some other unexpected mishap.

Rarely does an international flight arrive in San José early enough to make a domestic connection, particularly in the rainy season, as the weather is typically difficult for flying small planes in the afternoon. You'll likely end up spending your first night in or near San José, leaving for your domestic destination the next morning.

It's very rare, but afternoon and evening storms during the May-to-November rainy season occasionally cause flights coming into San José to be rerouted to Liberia or, sometimes, to Panama City, where you may be forced to spend the night. October, with its frequent evening fog, tends to be the worst month for reroutes.

■ TIP➜ In the rainy season, try to book a flight with the earliest arrival time available.

Once you're in Costa Rica, a few airlines recommend that you call them about three days before your return flight to reconfirm. Most explicitly say it's not necessary. It's always a good idea to check the day before you are scheduled to depart to make sure your flight time hasn't changed.

If you arrive in Costa Rica and your baggage doesn't, the first thing you should do is go to the baggage claims counter and file an official report. Then contact your airline to let them know where you will be staying. Bags are usually located within two days and can be sent to you just about anywhere in the country. Don't expect too much from local agents; try to get updates directly from your airline.

If your bag has been searched and contents are missing or damaged, file a claim with the Transportation Security Administration's Consumer Response Center as soon as possible. If your bags arrive damaged or fail to arrive at all, file a written report with the airline before leaving the airport.

Costa Rica levies a $29 airport departure tax, payable in dollars or the equivalent in colones. Nearly all airlines bundle the tax into ticket prices; charter flights often do not. You'll need to check with your airline. If not already included, you pay the tax at the airport upon departure. Paying with a MasterCard or Visa credit card means the transaction will be processed as a cash advance and incur additional fees. A few resort hotels will collect the tax for you as well.

AIRPORTS

Costa Rica has two international airports. Aeropuerto Internacional Juan Santamaría (SJO) is the country's main airport, about 17 km (10 miles) northwest of downtown San José, just outside the city of Alajuela. The drive takes about 30 minutes. Domestic airline SANSA operates from here in its own terminal. The country's other international airport is Aeropuerto Internacional Guanacaste (LIR), a small airport near the city of Liberia in the North Pacific. It's about 13 km (8 miles) west of the city.

The small Aeropuerto Tobías Bolaños, in the Pavas district on San José's west side, serves a few local charter airlines.

Other places where planes land in Costa Rica aren't exactly airports. They're more like carports with landing strips, and airline representatives arrive a few minutes before a plane is due to land or take off. (A few of these actually do have a tiny terminal building.)

Most international flights arrive in the evening and depart early in the morning. Prepare yourself for long waits at immigration and customs. When you're departing the country, prepare for security checkpoints at both airports. Liquids and gels of more than 3 ounces are not permitted. Carry-on bags are sometimes searched again at the gates for flights to the United States. Get to the airport three hours before your flight.

GROUND TRANSPORTATION

At Aeropuerto Internacional Juan Santamaría, you exit the terminal into a fume-filled parking area flanked by hordes of taxis and tour vans. If you're with a tour, you need only look for a tour company representative with a sign that bears your name. If you need a taxi, a uniformed agent will escort you to one of the orange Taxi Aeropuerto cabs (no other taxis are allowed in the arrivals area). The metered fare to most areas of San José is $25 to $40.

Transportation at Aeropuerto Internacional Guanacaste is also a mix of taxis and tour vans. The big Pacific-coast resorts provide transportation, but always check with your lodging for recommendations on the best way to arrive.

FLIGHTS

From North America to San José: American flies from Miami, Dallas, Charlotte, and Chicago O'Hare; United flies from Houston (IAH) and Newark, and, from December to April, from Chicago O'Hare, Denver, Los Angeles, and Washington Dulles (IAD); Delta flies from Atlanta and Los Angeles; Alaska flies from Los Angeles; Spirit flies from Fort Lauderdale, Orlando, and Miami; Frontier flies from Orlando; JetBlue flies from Orlando, Fort Lauderdale, New York (JFK), and Los Angeles; Southwest flies from Houston Hobby (HOU); Air Canada flies from Toronto and, from December through April, from Montreal; WestJet flies from Toronto; Avianca offers connections from several U.S. airports through its hubs in San Salvador, El Salvador, or Bogotá, Colombia. Mexico's AeroMéxico and Volaris do the same via their hubs in Mexico City, and Panama's Copa also offers connections through its hub in Panama City.

From New York or Los Angeles, nonstop flights to San José are 5½ hours. San José is 2½ hours from Miami, 3½ hours from Houston, and 4 hours from Charlotte and Dallas. In general, nonstop flights aren't that much more expensive. Ticket prices from hubs such as New York, Los Angeles, and Miami hover between $500 and $600, although the range varies widely.

From North America to Liberia: American flies from Dallas, Charlotte, Miami, Chicago O'Hare, and Austin; Delta flies from Atlanta and Los Angeles, and, from December through April, from Minneapolis; United flies from Houston, and, from December through April, from Newark, Chicago O'Hare, Denver, Los Angeles, and San Francisco; JetBlue flies from New York (JFK), and, from December through April, from Boston; Alaska flies

Getting Here

from Los Angeles; Southwest flies from Baltimore and Houston Hobby (HOU), and from December through April, from Baltimore (BWI); Frontier flies from Orlando; Air Canada Rouge, the low-cost division of Air Canada, flies from Toronto, and, from December through April, from Montreal; and WestJet flies from Toronto, and, from December through April, from Calgary. Copa connects its U.S. gateways to Liberia via its hub in Panama City.

Avianca and Copa connect San José with other Central American cities.

Given Costa Rica's often-difficult driving conditions, domestic flights are a desirable and practical option. The informality of domestic air service—"airports" other than Liberia and San José usually consist of only an airstrip with no central building at which to buy tickets—means you should purchase your domestic airplane tickets in advance. You can also buy them at travel agencies once you're in the country. We recommend grabbing a seat as soon as you know your itinerary, especially during the December–April high season.

SANSA is the largest domestic commercial airline, and it flies to 13 destinations around the country from San José. You can buy tickets online, over the phone, and at most travel agencies in Costa Rica. The tiny, domestic passenger planes in Costa Rica require that you pack light. SANSA imposes a luggage weight limit of 30 pounds. Extra luggage is sometimes allowed, but costs $1 to $3 per pound and will go standby. Skyway flies from San José to eight destinations in Costa Rica, as well as Bocas del Toro, Panama. Costa Rica Green Airways connects San José with Quepos and Tambor. The three domestic airlines cannot store extra baggage, but hotels and lodges *may* be able to store your luggage—ask ahead and bring a smaller bag for your

domestic travels. None has interline ticketing or baggage transfers with the international airlines serving Costa Rica.

Charter flights within Costa Rica are not as expensive as you might think, and can be a good deal if you are traveling in a group. The price per person will be only slightly more than taking a regularly scheduled domestic flight, and you can set your own departure time. The country has dozens of airstrips that are accessible only by charter plane. Charter planes are most often booked through tour operators, travel agents, or remote lodges. Most charter planes are smaller than domestic commercial planes.

■TIP➜ **Don't book a domestic flight for the day you arrive in or leave Costa Rica; connections are extremely tight, and you'll be at the mercy of the weather.**

 ## Bus

Tica Bus has daily service to Panama and Nicaragua, with connections to Honduras, El Salvador, Guatemala, and far southern Mexico. Transnica serves Nicaragua and Honduras. Central Line offers service to Nicaragua. We recommend Tica Bus—it's more established and serves more destinations—but Transnica and Central Line are acceptable, too. All three companies have comfortable, air-conditioned coaches with videos and onboard toilets, and help with border procedures.

All Costa Rican towns are connected by regular bus service that's reliable, comprehensive, and inexpensive. Buses between major cities are modern, but in rural areas you may get a converted U.S. school bus without air-conditioning. On longer routes, buses stop midway at modest restaurants. Near their destinations many buses turn into large taxis, dropping passengers off one by one along the way. To save time, take a *directo* (express) bus, which still might make a few stops. Be prepared for bus-company employees and bus drivers to speak only Spanish.

The main inconvenience of long-distance buses is the time spent getting there. For example, a bus from San José to the Osa Peninsula is nine hours or more, whereas the flight is one hour. Shorter distances reduce the difference—the bus to Quepos is 3½ hours, while the flight is 30 minutes. There is no central bus station in San José; buses leave from a variety of departure points, depending on the region they serve. You frequently have to return to San José to travel between outlying regions.

■ TIP→ **Avoid putting your belongings in the overhead bin. If you must, keep your eye on them.**

If anyone—even someone who looks like a bus employee—offers to put your things in the luggage compartment, politely decline. If you have to put your luggage underneath the bus, get off quickly when you arrive to retrieve it.

Most bus companies don't have printed schedules, although departure times may be posted on a sign at the ticket window. Phones are usually busy or go unanswered.

■ TIP→ **For the most reliable schedules, go to the bus station a day before your departure.**

The official tourism board, the Instituto Costarricense de Turismo (ICT), provides bus schedules on its website, but the information is updated infrequently. Hotel employees can usually give you the information you need.

Buses usually depart and arrive on time; they may even leave a few minutes early if they are full. Tickets are sold at bus stations and on the buses themselves; reservations aren't accepted, and you must pay in person with cash. Be sure to have loose change and small bills handy; employees won't have change for a 10,000-colón bill. Buses to popular beach and mountain destinations often sell out on weekends and holidays. It's difficult to get tickets to San José on Sunday afternoon. Some companies won't sell you a round-trip ticket from the departure point; if that's the case, make sure the first thing you do on arrival at your destination is to buy a return ticket. Sometimes tickets include seat numbers, which are usually printed on the tops of the seats or above the windows. Smoking is not permitted.

Interbus, a private bus company, travels to the most popular tourist destinations in modern, air-conditioned vans. Vehicles seat 10 to 20 people. (Interbus can also supply coaches for large groups.) Costs from San José range from $45 to $105 one way, but can take hours off your trip. Reservations must always be made at least 24 hours in advance. Be sure to double-check information on the website—published prices do change and routes may be discontinued. Costa Rica Shuttle offers minivan service that's great if you're traveling in a group. Rates range from $65 to $465 for up to five people.

 # Car

Renting a car with a driver makes the most sense for sightseeing in and around San José. You can also usually hire a taxi driver to ferry you around; most will stick to the meter, which will tick at a rate of about $25 for each hour the driver

Getting Here

spends waiting for you. At around $150 per day plus the driver's food, hiring a driver for areas outside the San José area costs almost the same as renting a four-wheel-drive vehicle, but is more expensive for multiday trips because you also have to pay for the driver's lodging. Some drivers are also knowledgeable guides; others just drive. Unless they're driving large passenger vans for established companies, it's doubtful that drivers have any special training or licensing.

Hotels can usually direct you to trusted drivers. Alamo provides professional car-and-driver services for a minimum of three days. On top of the rental fee, you pay $90 for the driver, plus food and lodging.

GASOLINE
You'll usually find 24-hour stations (*gasolineras*) only in San José or along the Pan-American Highway. Most other stations are open 7 to 7, although some are open until midnight. Regular unleaded gasoline is called *regular,* and high-octane unleaded, required in most modern vehicles, is called *súper.* Gas is sold by the liter.

Try to fill your tank in cities—gas is more expensive (and more likely to be dirtier) at informal fill-up places in rural areas, where gas stations can be few and far between. Major credit cards are widely accepted. There are no self-service gas stations in Costa Rica. It is not customary to tip attendants. If you want a *factura* (receipt), ask for it.

PARKING
On-street parking is scarce in downtown San José. Where you find a free spot, you'll also find *guachimanes* ("watchmen," informal, usually self-appointed guards). They won't actually get involved if someone tries something with your car, but it's best to give them a couple of

dollars (1,000-1,500 colones) anyway. It's illegal to park in zones marked by yellow curb paint, or in front of garage doors or driveways, usually marked *no estacionar* (no parking). Downtown parking laws are strictly enforced; the fine for illegal parking may be as high as $90. In places like Alajuela and Heredia, you'll find signs with a large E in a red circle, and the words *con boleto* (with a ticket). These tickets can be bought for ½-hour (250 colones), one-hour (500 colones), or two-hour (1,000 colones) increments. San José has abandoned this ticket system in favor of an online app.

Safer and ubiquitous are the public lots (*parqueos*), which average about $3 per hour. Most are open late, especially near hopping nightspots or theaters, but check beforehand. Never leave anything inside the car.

Outside San José and the surrounding communities, parking rules are far more lax. Guarded hotel or restaurant parking lots are the rule, with few public lots.

RENTAL CARS
When you reserve a car, ask about cancellation penalties, taxes, drop-off charges (if you're planning to pick up the car in one city and leave it in another), insurance, and surcharges (for being under or over a certain age, for additional drivers, or for driving beyond a specific distance). Most firms will not rent to drivers under 25; a few will levy a daily surcharge for drivers 21–25 years old. All these things can add substantially to your costs. Request such extras as car seats and GPS devices when you book. You will not be provided with a transponder for paying tolls on the highways in the San José metro area. You'll pay manually yourself in colones or U.S. dollars (nothing larger than a $20 bill).

■TIP→ **If you're visiting only one or two major areas, taking a shuttle van or a domestic flight is cheaper and more convenient than driving.**

Renting is a good choice if you're destination hopping, staying at a hotel outside town, or going well off the beaten path. Car trips to northern Guanacaste from San José can take an entire day, so flying is a better option if you don't have a lot of time. Flying is definitely better than driving for visiting the South Pacific.

A standard vehicle is fine for most destinations, but a *doble-tracción* (four-wheel-drive vehicle) is often essential to reach the remote parts of the country, especially during the rainy season. Even in the dry season, a 4WD vehicle is necessary to reach Monteverde and some off-the-beaten-path destinations on the North and South Pacific coasts. The biggest 4WD vehicles can cost twice as much as an economy car, but compact 4WDs are more reasonable. Any damage caused by fording a body of water voids your rental contract entirely, as a few shocked foreign visitors have found out as they were presented a bill for the entire cost of the vehicle.

Japanese and Korean cars are all the rage in Costa Rica, and that's what your rental vehicle will be too. Most cars in Costa Rica have manual transmission.

■TIP→ **Specify when making a reservation if you want automatic transmission; it usually costs around $10 more per day.**

Costa Rica has around 30 car-rental firms. Most local firms are affiliated with international chains and offer the same guarantees and services. Tricolor, a local company, gets high marks from visitors. Renting in or near San José is by far the easiest way to go. Around a dozen rental offices line San José's Paseo Colón. It's getting easier to rent outside San José,

particularly on the Pacific coast. Several rental companies have branches in Liberia, Quepos, Manuel Antonio, Jacó, Tamarindo, and La Fortuna. In most other places across the country, it's either impossible or very difficult and expensive to rent a car.

Rental cars may not be driven across borders to Nicaragua and Panama. For a $50 fee, Alamo will let you drop off a Costa Rican rental car at the Nicaraguan border at Peñas Blancas and provide you with a Nicaraguan rental on the other side. Another $50 fee applies when returning to Costa Rica. Transfers must be scheduled in advance.

High-season rates in San José begin at $65 per day and $400 per week for an economy car with air-conditioning, manual transmission, and unlimited mileage, along with obligatory insurance. Rates fluctuate considerably according to demand, season, and company. (Although July and August are technically "low season" here, most rental agencies levy high-season rates during those months.) Rates for a 4WD vehicle during high season start at $100 per day and $600 to $900 per week. Companies often require a $1,500 deposit, payable by credit card. Some levy a larger amount. Debit cards and cash are not accepted for deposits.

A very few firms levy a 13% surcharge for cars picked up at or returned to San José's Aeropuerto Internacional Juan Santamaría or Liberia's Aeropuerto Internacional Guanacaste. Check cars thoroughly for damage before you sign the contract. Even tough-looking 4WD vehicles should be coddled.

■TIP→ **Repair charges levied by rental companies for damage—no matter how minor—are outrageous even by U.S. or European standards.**

Getting Here

One-way service surcharges are $50 to $150, depending on the drop-off point. To avoid a hefty refueling fee, fill the tank just before you return the car. Routine dirt and grime on the outside of the vehicle will be overlooked upon return; cleaning on the inside, other than normal vacuuming, will incur a cleaning fee. Smoking is not permitted inside rental vehicles.

It's wise to opt for full insurance coverage. Auto insurance in Costa Rica is a government monopoly. At a minimum, you are required to purchase a collision-damage waiver as well as third-party liability insurance through the rental agency to cover damages to other persons and vehicles. Your own credit-card coverage does not exempt you from this charge. Some rental agencies include such costs in your quoted rates. Many do not, however, and we hear numerous tales of clients shocked at the final tally when they pick up the car. Always ask what is included when you reserve. A few websites trumpet rental vehicles here for as little as $10 per day. Such rates are impossible all-in; you'll always end up paying much, much more.

International driving permits (IDPs), which translate your license into 10 languages, are not necessary in Costa Rica. Your own driver's license is good for a maximum of 90 days. You must carry your passport, or a copy of it with the entry stamp, to prove when you entered the country.

ROAD CONDITIONS

Many travelers shy away from renting a car in Costa Rica. Indeed, this is not an ideal place to drive. In San José, traffic is bad and car theft is rampant (look for guarded lots or hotels with parking). Roads in rural areas are often unpaved or potholed—and tires usually aren't covered by the basic insurance. Ticos have a reputation as reckless drivers—with one of the highest accident rates in the world. Although driving can be a challenge, it's a great way to explore certain regions, especially the North Pacific, the Northern Lowlands, and the Caribbean coast (apart from roadless Tortuguero). Keep in mind that winding roads and poor conditions make most trips longer than you'd normally expect.

The winding Pan-American Highway south of the capital is notorious for long snakes of traffic stuck behind slow-moving trucks. Look out for potholes, even in the smoothest sections of the best roads. Also watch for unmarked speed bumps where you'd least expect them, particularly on main thoroughfares in rural areas. During the rainy season, roads are in much worse shape. Check with your destination before setting out. Roads are prone to washouts and landslides, especially the highway through Braulio Carrillo National Park, north of San José, the route to the Caribbean coast.

San José and the metro area are terribly congested during weekday rush hours (7 to 9 am and 4 to 6 pm). Try to avoid returning to the city on Sunday evening, when traffic from the beaches can be backed up for miles. Frequent fender benders tie up traffic. Keep your windows rolled up in the center of the city, because thieves may reach into your car at stoplights and snatch purses, jewelry, and valuables.

Signposting off main highways is notoriously bad but improving. Distances are given in kilometers (1 km = 0.6 miles). Watch carefully for *No Hay Paso* (Do Not Enter) signs; one-way streets are common, and it's not unusual for a two-way street to suddenly become one way. Single-lane bridges are common in rural areas. A *Ceda el Paso* (Yield) sign facing you means just that: let oncoming traffic proceed before you enter the bridge.

Highways are numbered on signs and maps, but few people use or even know the numbering system. Asking for directions to "Highway 27" will probably be met with a blank stare. Everyone calls it the "Carretera a Caldera" (highway to Caldera, on the Pacific coast) instead. Your best bet is to download the Waze app to navigate. Outside San José you may run into long stretches of unpaved road. Look out for potholes, landslides during the rainy season, and cattle on the roads. Driving at night outside cities and towns is not recommended, because roads are poorly lighted and many don't have painted lines. The sun sets here around 5:30 pm all year long with little variation. Make a point to arrive at your destination before then.

ROADSIDE EMERGENCIES

Costa Rica has no highway emergency service organization. In Costa Rica, 911 is the nationwide number for accidents and all emergencies. Traffic Police (*tránsitos*) are scattered around the country, but Costa Ricans are very good about stopping for people with car trouble. Whatever happens, don't move the car after an accident, even if a monstrous traffic jam ensues. Call 911 first if the accident is serious (nearly everyone has a mobile phone), then call the emergency number of your car-rental agency.

RULES OF THE ROAD

■ TIP→ **Obey traffic laws religiously, even if Costa Ricans don't.**

Fines are frightfully high—a speeding ticket could set you back over $500—and evidence exists that transit police target foreigners. Don't plan on skipping the country with an unpaid traffic fine. Your rental agency will get the ticket and bill it to your credit card after your return home.

Driving is on the right side of the road in Costa Rica. The highway speed limit is usually 90 kph (54 mph), which drops to 60 kph (36 mph) in residential areas. In towns, limits range from 30 to 50 kph (18 to 31 mph). Speed limits are enforced in all regions of the country. *Alto* means "stop" and again, *Ceda el Paso* means "yield." Right turns on red are permitted except where signs indicate otherwise, but in San José this is usually not possible because of one-way streets and pedestrian crossings.

Local drunk driving laws are strict. You'll get nailed with a $510 fine if you're caught driving in a "predrunk" state (blood alcohol levels of 0.05% to 0.075%). If your level is higher than that, the car will be confiscated, your license will be taken away, and you risk jail time. Police officers who stop drivers for speeding and drunk driving are sometimes looking for payment on the spot—essentially a bribe. Asking for a ticket instead of paying the bribe discourages corruption and does not compromise your safety. You can generally pay the ticket at your car-rental company, which will pay it on your behalf.

Seat-belt use is mandatory ($175 fine). Car seats are required for children ages four and under; older children must use a booster seat until age 12 ($250 fine). Children over 12 are allowed in the front seat. Drivers are prohibited from texting or using handheld cell phones ($175 fine). Although drivers here appear to park anywhere, parking tickets can set you back up to $90.

Getting Here

Taxi

Taxis are cheap and your best bet for getting around San José. Just about every driver is friendly and eager to use a few English words to tell you about a cousin or sister in New Jersey; however, cabbies truly conversant in English are scarce. Tipping is not expected, but it's a good idea when you've had some extra help, especially with your bags. Taxis are not shared with strangers here; the ride is for you and your party only.

Cabs are red, usually with a yellow light on top. To hail one, extend your hand and wave it at about hip height. If it's available, the driver will often flick his headlights before pulling over. The city is dotted with *paradas de taxi,* taxi queues where you stand the best chance of grabbing one. Taxis generally congregate around the central park in most other cities and towns. Your hotel can usually call you a reputable taxi or private car service, and when you're out to dinner or on the town, ask the manager to call you a cab—it's much easier than hailing one on the street, and safer, too.

■ TIP→ **Taxi drivers are notorious for "not having change." If it's just a few hundred colones, you may as well round up. If it's a lot, ask to go to a store or gas station where you can make change.**

To avoid this situation, never use a 10,000-colón bill in a taxi, and avoid paying with 5,000-colón bills unless you've run up almost that much in fares. Drivers will round the fare up to the nearest 100 colones.

Outside the capital area, drivers often use their odometers to creatively calculate fares. Manuel Antonio drivers are notorious for overcharging. It's illegal, but taxis charge up to double for hotel pickups or fares that take them out of the province (such as San José to Alajuela). Ask the manager at your hotel about the going rate. Try to avoid taking an unofficial taxi (*pirata*), although it's sometimes the only option. It's better to ask your hotel for recommendations.

It's always a good idea to make a note of the cab number (painted in a yellow triangle on the door), and sit in the back seat for safety.

The ride service Uber operates in Costa Rica with service primarily in San José and the metro area. The legality of its status here is unsettled. Until Uber and the authorities work out their differences, you use its services at some risk.

Essentials

⊕ Customs and Duties

When shopping in Costa Rica, keep receipts for all purchases. Be ready to show customs (*aduanas*) officials what you've bought. Pack purchases together in an easily accessible place. The only orchids you can take home are packaged in a tube and come with an export permit.

Visitors entering Costa Rica may bring in 500 grams of tobacco, 5 liters of wine or spirits, 2 kilograms of sweets and chocolates, and the equivalent of $500 worth of merchandise. You can also bring one camera and one video camera, six rolls of film, binoculars, and electrical items for personal use only, including laptops and other electronics. Make sure you have personalized prescriptions for any medication you are taking. Customs officials at San José's international airport rarely examine tourists' luggage by hand, although all incoming bags are x-rayed. If you enter by land, they'll probably look through your bags. Officers at the airport generally speak English and are generally your best (only, really) option for resolving any problem. It usually takes about 30 minutes to clear immigration and customs when arriving in Costa Rica.

⊕ Dining

Dining options around Costa Rica run the spectrum from elegant and formal to beachy and casual. San José and popular tourist centers, especially Manuel Antonio, offer a wide variety of cuisine types. Farther off the beaten track, expect hearty, filling local cuisine. Increasingly common as you move away from San José are the conical thatch roofs of the round, open *rancho* restaurants that serve a combination of traditional staples with simple international fare.

By law, smoking is prohibited in all restaurants and bars.

Every town has at least one *soda*—that's Costa Rican Spanish for a small, family-run restaurant frequented by locals. Don't expect anything as fancy as a menu. A board usually lists specials of the day. The lunchtime *casado* (literally, "married")—a "marriage" of chicken, pork, or beef with rice, beans, cabbage salad, and natural fruit drink—sets you back about $3. No one will bring you a bill; just pay the cashier when you're finished. Having a meal at the local soda always provides a good opportunity to practice your Spanish.

MEALS AND MEALTIMES

In San José and surrounding cities, most sodas are open daily 7 am to early evening, though some close Sunday. Other restaurants are usually open 11 am to 9 pm, and in resort areas some restaurants may stay open later. Normal dining hours in Costa Rica are noon to 3 and 6 to 9. *Desayuno* (breakfast) is served at most sodas and hotels. The traditional breakfast is *gallo pinto,* which includes eggs, plantains, and fried cheese; hotel breakfasts vary widely and generally offer lighter international options in addition to the local stick-to-your-ribs plate. *Almuerzo* (lunch) is the biggest meal of the day for Costa Ricans, and savvy travelers know that lunch specials are often a great bargain. *Cena* (dinner or supper) runs the gamut.

Except for those in hotels, many restaurants close between Christmas and New Year's Day and during Holy Week (Palm Sunday to Easter Sunday). Unless otherwise noted, the restaurants listed in this guide are open daily for lunch and dinner. Credit cards are not accepted at many rural restaurants. Always ask before you order to find out if your credit card will be accepted. Visa and MasterCard are

Essentials

the most commonly accepted cards; American Express and Diners Club are less widely accepted. Discover card is increasingly accepted.

■ **TIP→ Remember that 23% is added to all menu prices: 13% for tax and 10% for tip.**

Legally, menus are required to show after-tax, after-tip prices in colones; in practice, many tourist-oriented places do not. Because a gratuity (*propina*) is included, there's no need to tip, but if your service is good, it's nice to add a little money to the obligatory 10%.

RESERVATIONS AND DRESS

Costa Ricans generally dress more formally than North Americans. For dinner at an upscale restaurant, long pants and closed-toe shoes are standard for men except in beach locations, and women tend to wear high heels and dressy clothes that show off their figures. Shorts, flip-flops, and tank tops are not acceptable, except at inexpensive restaurants in beach towns.

VEGETARIAN OPTIONS

Vegetarians sticking to lower-budget establishments won't go hungry, but may develop a love-hate relationship with rice, beans, and fried cheese. A simple *sin carne* (no meat) request is often interpreted as "no beef," so specify *solo vegetales* (only vegetables), and for good measure, *nada de cerdo, pollo, o pescado* (no pork, chicken, or fish). More cosmopolitan restaurants are more conscious of vegetarians—upscale Asian restaurants often offer vegetarian options.

WINES, BEER, AND SPIRITS

The ubiquitous sodas generally don't have liquor licenses, but getting a drink in any other eatery isn't usually a problem. This is not a wine-drinking culture; the fruit of the vine you do find likely will come from Chile or Argentina. Don't let

Holy Thursday and Good Friday catch you off guard; both are legally dry days. In general, restaurant prices for imported alcohol—which includes just about everything except local beer, rum, and *guaro*, the local sugarcane firewater—may be more than what you'd like to pay.

News reports have surfaced in recent years of methanol-tainted alcohol.

⚠ **Drink distilled spirits only in reputable hotels and upscale establishments.**

Health

COVID-19

COVID 19 has disrupted travel since March 2020, and travelers should expect sporadic ongoing issues. Always travel with a mask in case it's required, and keep up to date on the most recent testing and vaccination guidelines for Costa Rica.

SPECIFIC ISSUES IN COSTA RICA

Costa Rica is one of several Latin American countries where transmission of the mosquito-borne Zika virus has been identified. Because risks to fetal development during any trimester of pregnancy have been reported, the CDC recommends that pregnant women avoid travel to Costa Rica. If travel is necessary, take strict steps to avoid mosquito bites.

The CDC marked Costa Rica as an area infested by the *Aedes aegypti* (dengue-carrier) mosquito, but not as an epidemic region. The highest-risk area is the Caribbean, especially in the rainy season. The mosquito-borne chikungunya virus began appearing in Costa Rica in 2015. In areas with Zika, chikungunya, and dengue, use mosquito nets, wear clothing that covers your whole body, and use *repelente* (insect repellent) and *espirales* (mosquito coils), sold in supermarkets, pharmacies, and, sometimes, small country stores.

■ TIP→ **Repellents made with DEET or picaridin are most effective.**

Perfume and aftershave can actually attract mosquitoes.

It's unlikely that you will contract chikungunya or dengue, but if you start suffering from high fever, the shakes, or joint pain, make sure you ask to be tested for these diseases at a local clinic. Your embassy can provide you with a list of recommended doctors and dentists. Such symptoms in the weeks following your return should also spark concern.

Poisonous snakes, scorpions, and other pests pose a small threat in Costa Rica.

Water is generally safe to drink, especially around San José, but the quality can vary; to be safe, drink bottled water. In rural areas you run a mild risk of encountering drinking water, fresh fruit, and vegetables contaminated by fecal matter, which in most cases causes a bit of traveler's diarrhea but can cause leptospirosis (which can be treated by antibiotics if detected early). Stay on the safe side by avoiding uncooked food, unpasteurized milk, and ice—ask for drinks *sin hielo* (without ice). Ceviche, raw fish cured in lemon juice—a favorite appetizer, especially at seaside resorts— is generally safe to eat.

Mild cases of diarrhea may respond to Imodium (known generically as loper-amide) or Pepto-Bismol, both of which can be purchased over the counter. Drink plenty of purified water or tea; chamo-mile (*manzanilla* in Spanish) is a good folk remedy. In severe cases, rehydrate yourself with a salt-sugar solution (½ teaspoon salt and 4 tablespoons sugar per quart of water).

Heatstroke and dehydration are real dangers, especially for hikers, so drink lots of water. Take at least 1 liter per person for every hour you plan to be on the trail. Sunburn is the most common traveler's health problem. Use sunscreen with SPF 30 or higher. Most pharmacies and super-markets carry sunscreen in a wide range of SPFs, though it is relatively pricey.

The greatest danger to your person actually lies off Costa Rica's popular beaches: riptides are common wherever there are waves, and tourists run into serious difficulties in them every year. If you see waves, ask the locals where it's safe to swim; and if you're uncertain, don't go in deeper than your waist. If you get caught in a rip current, swim parallel to the beach until you're free of it, and then swim back to shore.

■ TIP→ **Avoid swimming where a town's main river opens up to the sea. Septic tanks aren't common.**

Do not fly within 24 hours of scuba diving.

OVER-THE-COUNTER REMEDIES

Farmacia is Spanish for pharmacy, and the names for common drugs like *aspiri-na, ibúprofen,* and *acetaminofina* (Tylenol or Panadol) are basically the same as they are in English. Some drugs for which you need a prescription back home are sold over the counter in Costa Rica. Pharmacies throughout the country are generally open from 8 to 8. Some phar-macies in San José stay open 24 hours.

Government facilities—the so-called Caja hospitals (short for Caja Costarri-cense de Seguro Social, or Costa Rican Social Security System)—and clinics are of acceptable quality, but notoriously overburdened. Private hospitals are more accustomed to serving foreigners.

Essentials

🖊 Immunizations

No specific immunizations or vaccinations are required for visits to Costa Rica from the United States, however, all visitors must have valid proof of COVID-19 vaccination and/or a booster; while the need and frequency of boosters is still being discussed in the medical community, it's important to verify the most recent requirements with your physician before you travel.

The U.S. Centers for Disease Control and Prevention recommends that all travelers to Costa Rica be up to date on routine immunizations, namely seasonal influenza, tetanus, diphtheria, and pertussis (whooping cough). (Measles reappeared in Costa Rica in 2019, imported by an unvaccinated visitor. The country had been measles-free for many years.) The CDC also suggests being immunized against typhoid and hepatitis A, especially if you're headed off the beaten path or staying a few weeks. The agency no longer recommends malaria prophylaxis for travel to Costa Rica for most visitors, except for a couple of small pockets near the Nicaraguan border. The CDC does suggest taking precautions to avoid mosquito bites. You must have the yellow fever vaccination if arriving directly from certain countries in South America and Africa.

🛏 Lodging

Costa Rica excels in its selection of boutique hotels, tasteful bungalows, and bed-and-breakfasts, which offer a high degree of personalized service. Because they're generally small, you may have to book one or two months ahead, and up to six months in the high season, especially around Christmas or Easter. Reserving through an association or agency can significantly reduce the time you spend scanning the Internet, but you can often get a better deal and negotiate longer-stay or low-season discounts directly with the hotel.

High-end accommodations range from luxury tents to exquisite hotels to villa rentals. You'll find all the amenities you expect at such areas, with one notable exception: the roads and routes to even five-star villas can be atrocious. Resorts are generally one of two kinds: luxurious privileged gateways to the best of the country (such as Punta Islita) or generic medium-budget all-inclusives (such as the Spanish hotel chain Barceló). Several chain hotels have franchises in Costa Rica, and they are rarely booked solid.

Nature lodges in the South Pacific may be less expensive than they initially appear, as the nightly rate usually includes three hearty meals and sometimes even guided hikes. Internet access isn't a given, even if a place has a website. Many have an eco-friendly approach (even to luxury), so air-conditioning might not be included. Consider how isolated you want to be; some lodges are miles from neighbors and have few rainy-day diversions. The voluntary "green leaf" rating system evaluates eco-friendly lodgings. A listing can be found at ⊕ www.turismo-sostenible.co.cr.

Be sure to reserve well in advance for the dry season (mid-December to April everywhere except the Caribbean coast, which has a short September to October "dry" season).

■ TIP➜ If you're having trouble finding accommodations, consider contacting a tour operator. Because they reserve blocks of rooms, you might have better luck.

During the rainy season (May to mid-November except on the Caribbean coast, where it's almost always rainy) most hotels drop their rates considerably, which sometimes sends them into a lower price category than the one we indicate.

Most hotels and other lodgings require you to give your credit-card details before confirming your reservation. Get confirmation in writing and have a copy of it handy when you check in.

Be sure you understand the hotel's cancellation policy. Some places allow you to cancel without any kind of penalty—even if you prepaid to secure a discounted rate—if you cancel at least 24 hours in advance. Others require you to cancel a week in advance or penalize you the cost of one night. Small inns and bed-and-breakfasts are most likely to require you to cancel far in advance. Most hotels allow children under a certain age to stay in their parents' room at no extra charge, but others charge for them as extra adults; find out the cutoff age for discounts.

The lodgings we list are Costa Rica's cream of the crop in each price category. When pricing accommodations, always ask what's included and what costs extra. Keep in mind that prices don't include 16.4% service and tax. Smoking is prohibited in all hotels, both in rooms and public areas.

Our local writers vet every hotel to recommend the best overnights in each price category, from budget to expensive. Unless otherwise specified, you can expect private bath, phone, and TV in your room. Hotel reviews have been shortened. For full information, visit Fodors.com.

APARTMENT AND HOUSE RENTALS

Rental houses are common all over Costa Rica, particularly in the Pacific coast destinations of Manuel Antonio, Tamarindo, and Jacó. Homes can accommodate whole families, often for less money and at a higher comfort level than a hotel. Properties are often owned by foreigners, most of them based in the United States, with property managers in Costa Rica.

Resort communities with villa-style lodgings are also growing. Escape Villas Costa Rica lists rentals in Manuel Antonio, Dominical, Uvita, Ojochal, Jacó, Playa Flamingo, Tamarindo, Tambor, Montezuma, Santa Teresa, and Arenal. Villas & Apartments Abroad has a good selection of rentals on the North and Central Pacific coasts. For the southern Nicoya Peninsula and Playa Hermosa on the North Pacific coast, check Costa Rica Beach Rentals.

BED-AND-BREAKFASTS

A number of quintessential bed-and-breakfasts—small and homey—are clustered in the Central Valley, generally offering hearty breakfasts and friendly inside information for $60 to $120 per night. You'll also find them scattered through the rest of the country, mixed in with other self-titled bed-and-breakfasts that range from small cabins in the mountains to luxurious boutique-hotel-style digs in the North Pacific region. The service Airbnb brokers many lodgings and homestay experiences in Costa Rica.

HOME EXCHANGES

With a direct home exchange, you stay in someone else's home while they stay in yours. Some outfits also deal with vacation homes, so you're not actually staying in someone's full-time residence, just their vacant weekend place.

Home exchanges are an excellent way to immerse yourself in the true Costa Rica, particularly if you've been here before. Drawbacks include restricted options and dates. Many companies list home exchanges, but we've found Home Exchange, which lists a handful of jazzy houses around Costa Rica, to be the most reliable.

Essentials

Money

In general, Costa Rica is cheaper than North America or Europe, but travelers looking for dirt-cheap developing-nation deals may find it's more expensive than they bargained for—and prices are rising as more foreigners visit.

The tourism industry quotes prices in dollars. You may certainly pay for hotels and tours in local currency, but they will be priced at that day's equivalent colón exchange rate.

Food in modest restaurants and public transportation are inexpensive. A 2-km (1-mile) taxi ride costs about $2. Although they are springing up at a healthy rate, don't count on using an ATM outside San José.

CURRENCY AND EXCHANGE

Costa Rica's currency is the *colón* (pronounced *koh-LOHN*; the plural is *colones*). Prices are shown with a "¢" sign in front of the number. At this writing, the colón is about 640 to the U.S. dollar and 725 to the euro. Coins come in denominations of 5, 10, 25, 50, 100, and 500 colones. Be careful not to mix up the very similar 100- and 500-colón coins. Bills come in denominations of 1,000 (red), 2,000 (blue), 5,000 (yellow), 10,000 (green), and 20,000 (orange) colones. As you'd expect, prices have a lot of zeroes. If you want to approximate a colón price in dollars, lop off the last two digits and divide by 6. You'll be pretty close (3,000 colones = a little less than $5). Avoid using larger-denomination bills in taxis, on buses, or in small stores. Many tourist-oriented businesses accept U.S. dollars, although the exchange rate might not be favorable to you. Make sure your dollars are in good condition—no tears or writing—and don't use or accept anything larger than a $20. Many counterfeit $50 and $100 bills circulate here and almost no one will accept them for payment.

Assuming you can find them at all, Costa Rican colones are sold abroad at terrible rates, so wait until you arrive in Costa Rica to get local currency. U.S. dollars are still the easiest to exchange, but euros can be exchanged for colones at just about any Banco Nacional office and at the San José and Escazú branches of other banks. The four state banks—Banco Nacional, Banco de Costa Rica, Bancrédito, and Banco Popular—come complete with horrendous lines. Private banks—Scotiabank and BAC Credomatic—are the best places to change U.S. dollars and traveler's checks. The arrivals area of the international airports in San José and Liberia both have ATMs and are your best bet for getting cash after you land. There is a branch of the BAC Credomatic upstairs in the check-in area of Juan Santamaría airport where you can exchange money when you arrive or depart—it's a much better deal than the Global Exchange counter in the baggage-claim area or at the departure gates. Airport taxi and van drivers accept U.S. dollars. Outdoor money changers are rarely seen on the street, but avoid them if they approach; you will most certainly get a bad deal, and you risk robbery by pulling out wads of cash.

■ TIP→ Even if a currency-exchange booth has a sign promising no commission, rest assured that there's some kind of huge, hidden fee. (Oh ... that's right. The sign didn't say no fee). And as for rates, you're almost always better off getting foreign currency at an ATM or exchanging money at a bank.

🌐 Passport

U.S. citizens need only a passport to enter Costa Rica and a return plane ticket home or to another country for stays of up to 90 days. Make sure it's up to date. We've received much conflicting information, even within officialdom, about how long your passport must be valid—the official answer is "for the duration of your trip," but government officials, passport officers, and airline check-in agents frequently interpret the rules differently.

⚠ **To be on the safe side, make sure your passport is valid for at least six months after date of arrival.**

➕ Safety

Violent crime is not a serious problem in Costa Rica, but thieves can easily prey on tourists, so be alert. The government has created a Tourism Police unit whose more than 250 officers can be seen on bikes or motorcycles patrolling areas in Guanacaste, San José, and the Arenal area.

For many English-speaking tourists, standing out like a sore thumb can't be avoided. But there are some precautions you can take:

■ Don't bring anything you can't stand to lose.

■ Don't flash expensive jewelry or watches.

■ In cities, don't carry expensive cameras or lots of cash.

■ Wear backpacks on your front; thieves can slit your backpack and run away with its contents before you notice.

■ Don't wear a waist pack, because thieves can cut the strap.

■ Distribute your cash and any valuables (including credit cards and passport) between a deep front pocket, an inside jacket or vest pocket, and a hidden money belt. (If you use a money belt, have some small bills handy so you don't have to reach for it in public.)

■ Keep your hand on your wallet if you are in a crowd or on a bus.

■ Don't let your purse dangle from your shoulder; always hold on to it with your hand for added security.

■ Keep car windows rolled up and car doors locked at all times in cities.

■ Park in designated lots—car theft is common—or if that's not possible, accept the offer of the guachimán (a term adopted from English, pronounced "watchie man")—men or boys who watch your car while you're gone. Give them the equivalent of a dollar an hour when you return.

■ Never leave valuables in a car, even in an attended parking lot.

■ Padlock your luggage.

■ Talk with locals or your hotel staff about any areas you should avoid. Never leave a drink unattended in a club or bar: scams involving date-rape drugs have been reported, targeting both men and women.

■ Never leave your belongings unattended, including at the beach or in a tent.

■ Use your hotel room's safe, even if there's an extra charge. If your room doesn't have one, ask the manager to put your valuables in the hotel safe and ask him or her to sign a list of what you are storing.

Essentials

■ **If someone does try to rob you, immediately surrender your possessions and don't try to be a hero.**

Scams do occur in San José. A distraction artist might squirt you with something, or spill something on you, then try to clean you off while his partner steals your backpack. Pickpockets and bag slashers work buses and crowds. Beware of anyone who seems overly friendly, aggressively helpful, or disrespectful of your personal space. Be particularly vigilant around San José's Coca-Cola bus terminal, one of the dicier areas but a central transportation hub.

A few tourists have been hit with the slashed-tire scam: someone punctures the tires of your rental car (often right at the airport, when you arrive) and then comes to your "aid" when you pull off to the side of the road and robs you. Forget about the rims: always drive to the nearest open gas station or service center if you get a flat.

Costa Rica remains a *mostly* safe destination for solo travelers, but a few high-profile cases of violence against visitors in recent years have rattled everyone here. Striking a proper balance—being guarded without refusing all contact with people—can be done, but also can be difficult. Ask at your hotel which neighborhoods to avoid at night. If you want to fend off persistent admirers, you can politely say, *Por favor, necesito un tiempo a solas* (I'd like some time on my own, please). Stronger is *Por favor, no me moleste* (Please, stop bothering me).

Ⓢ Taxes

The airport departure tax for tourists is $29. Most airlines include the tax in the ticket price. A few do not, which will require you to pay the tax upon departure in cash (dollars or colones) or with a Visa or MasterCard. All Costa Rican businesses charge a 13% sales tax, called the IVA. It is included in the shelf price you see. There is no additional hotel tax. You'll pay only the IVA, usually on top of the posted rates. Restaurants add the 13% IVA tax and 10% service fee to meals. By law, menu prices are supposed to reflect the final price you pay in local currency; many tourist-oriented dining spots ignore the requirement. Tourists are not refunded for taxes paid in Costa Rica.

Ⓢ Tipping

Costa Rica doesn't have a tipping culture, but positive reinforcement goes a long way to fostering a culture of good service; good intentions are usually there, but execution can be hit or miss. Tip only for good service.

■ **TIP→ Tipping in colones is best. Never tip with U.S. coins, because there's no way for locals to exchange them.**

Ⓥ Visa

A visa is not required for U.S. citizens for stays less than 90 days, but you must have a return ticket.

⦿ Visitor Information

The official tourism board, the Instituto Costarricense de Turismo (ICT), has an office on Avenida Central in San José and a small desk in the baggage claim area at Juan Santamaría airport. The airport counter contains a few brochures but is staffed only sporadically. Visitor information is provided by the Costa Rica Tourism Board in the United States.

Tipping

Bellhop	$1–$5 or 500 colones per bag, depending on the level of the hotel
Hotel Concierge	$5 or more, if he or she performs a service for you
Hotel Doorman	$1–$2 if he or she helps you get a cab
Hotel Maid	$1–$3 or 500–1,500 colones per day (either daily or at the end of your stay, in cash)
Hotel Room-Service Waiter	$1–$2 or 500–1,000 colones per delivery, even if a service charge has been added
Tour Guide	$10 or 5,000 colones per group member per day
Hired Driver	10% of the rental
Waiter	10%–15%, with 15% being the norm at high-end restaurants; nothing additional if a service charge is added to the bill
Bartender	$1 per drink
Restroom Attendant	$1
Coat-check	$1–$2 per item checked unless there is a fee, then nothing
Taxi Driver	200–300 colones if they've helped you navigate a complicated set of directions, or 500 colones if they've helped you with luggage; otherwise nothing

ONLINE TRAVEL TOOLS

The REAL Costa Rica slips in a bit of attitude with its information, and is a bit lax on updating, but scores high marks for overall accuracy. Scope out detailed maps, driving distances, and pictorial guides to the locations of hotels and businesses in some communities at ⊕ CostaRicaMap.com. The Association of Residents of Costa Rica online forums are some of the region's most active and informed, with topics ranging from business and pleasure trips to the real-estate market, with loads of information if you're interested in moving to the country. *The Tico Times* publishes news about Costa Rica, much of it of interest to visitors.

🗓 When to Go

HIGH SEASON

The sunniest, driest season in most of the country occurs from mid-December through April, with Christmas and Easter bracketing the busiest tourist season. March and April are sweltering in lowland areas, with temperatures in the arid North Pacific frequently exceeding 90°F.

LOW SEASON

Afternoon showers kick in by May and last through November, with a brief drier season in June and July. Rain or not, North American and European summer vacations do increase the influx of visitors from June through August. Rains become heavy in September and October.

VALUE SEASON

The transition periods between rainy and dry seasons and back again make a marvelous time to visit Costa Rica. Visitor numbers are smaller and the threat of rain is minimal.

Helpful Phrases in Spanish

BASICS

Hello	Hola	oh-lah
Yes/no	Sí/no	see/no
Please	Por favor	pore fah-**vore**
May I?	¿Me permite?	may pair-**mee**-tay
Thank you	Gracias	**Grah**-see-as
You're welcome	De nada	day **nah**-dah
I'm sorry	Lo siento	lo see-**en**-toh
Good morning!	¡Buenos días!	**bway**-nohs **dee**-ahs
Good evening!	¡Buenas noches!	**bway**-nahs **no**-chess
Good-bye!	¡Adiós!/¡Hasta luego!	ah-dee-**ohss/ah**-stah **lwe**-go
Mr./Mrs.	Señor/Señora	sen-**yor**/sen-**yohr**-ah
Miss	Señorita	sen-yo-**ree**-tah
Pleased to meet you	Mucho gusto	**moo**-cho **goose**-toh
How are you?	¿Cómo está usted?	**ko**-mo es-**tah** oo-**sted**

NUMBERS

one	un, uno	oon, **oo**-no
two	dos	dos
three	tres	tress
four	cuatro	**kwah**-tro
five	cinco	**sink**-oh
six	seis	saice
seven	siete	see-**et**-eh
eight	ocho	**o**-cho
nine	nueve	new-**eh**-vey
ten	diez	dee-**es**
eleven	once	**ohn**-seh
twelve	doce	**doh**-seh
thirteen	trece	**treh**-seh
fourteen	catorce	ka-**tohr**-seh
fifteen	quince	**keen**-seh
sixteen	dieciséis	dee-**es**-ee-**saice**
seventeen	diecisiete	dee-**es**-ee-see-**et**-eh
eighteen	dieciocho	dee-**es**-ee-o-cho
nineteen	diecinueve	dee-**es**-ee-new-ev-eh
twenty	veinte	**vain**-teh
twenty-one	veinte y uno/veintiuno	**vain**-te-oo-noh
thirty	treinta	**train**-tah
forty	cuarenta	kwah-**ren**-tah
fifty	cincuenta	seen-**kwen**-tah
sixty	sesenta	sess-**en**-tah
seventy	setenta	set-**en**-tah
eighty	ochenta	oh-**chen**-tah
ninety	noventa	no-**ven**-tah
one hundred	cien	see-**en**
one thousand	mil	meel
one million	un millón	oon meel-**yohn**

COLORS

black	negro	**neh**-groh
blue	azul	ah-**sool**
brown	café	kah-**feh**
green	verde	**ver**-deh
orange	naranja	na-**rahn**-hah
red	rojo	**roh**-hoh
white	blanco	**blahn**-koh
yellow	amarillo	ah-mah-**ree**-yoh

DAYS OF THE WEEK

Sunday	domingo	doe-**meen**-goh
Monday	lunes	**loo**-ness
Tuesday	martes	**mahr**-tess
Wednesday	miércoles	me-**air**-koh-less
Thursday	jueves	hoo-**ev**-ess
Friday	viernes	vee-**air**-ness
Saturday	sábado	**sah**-bah-doh

MONTHS

January	enero	eh-**neh**-roh
February	febrero	feh-**breh**-roh
March	marzo	**mahr**-soh
April	abril	ah-**breel**
May	mayo	**my**-oh
June	junio	**hoo**-nee-oh
July	julio	**hoo**-lee-yoh
August	agosto	ah-**ghost**-toh
September	septiembre	sep-tee-**em**-breh
October	octubre	oak-**too**-breh
November	noviembre	no-vee-**em**-breh
December	diciembre	dee-see-**em**-breh

USEFUL WORDS AND PHRASES

Do you speak English?	¿Habla usted inglés?	ah-blah oos-**ted** in-**glehs**
I don't speak Spanish.	No hablo español	no **ah**-bloh es-pahn-**yol**
I don't understand.	No entiendo	no en-tee-**en**-doh
I understand.	Entiendo	en-tee-**en**-doh
I don't know.	No sé	no **seh**
I'm American.	Soy americano (americana)	soy ah-meh-ree-**kah**-no (ah-meh-ree-**kah**-nah)
What's your name?	¿Cómo se llama usted?	koh-mo seh **yah**-mah oos-**ted**
My name is . . .	Me llamo . . .	may **yah**-moh
What time is it?	¿Qué hora es?	keh o-rah es
How?	¿Cómo?	**koh**-mo
When?	¿Cuándo?	**kwahn**-doh
Yesterday	Ayer	ah-**yehr**
Today	hoy	oy
Tomorrow	mañana	mahn-**yah**-nah

Tonight	Esta noche	**es**-tah **no**-cheh
What?	¿Qué?	keh
What is it?	¿Qué es esto?	keh es **es**-toh
Why?	¿Por qué?	pore **keh**
Who?	¿Quién?	kee-**yen**
Where is ...	¿Dónde está ...	**dohn**-deh es-**tah**
... the train station?	la estación del tren?	la es-tah-see-**on** del trehn
... the subway station?	la estación del tren subterráneo?	la es-ta-see-**on** del trehn la es-ta-see-**on** soob-teh-**rrahn**-eh-oh
... the bus stop?	la parada del autobus?	la pah-**rah**-dah del ow-toh-**boos**
... the terminal? (airport)	el aeropuerto	el air-oh-**pwar**-toh
... the post office?	la oficina de correos?	la oh-fee-**see**- nah deh koh-**rreh**-os
... the bank?	el banco?	el **bahn**-koh
... the hotel?	el hotel?	el oh-**tel**
... the museum?	el museo?	el moo-**seh**-oh
... the hospital?	el hospital?	el ohss-pee-**tal**
... the elevator?	el ascensor?	el ah-sen-**sohr**
Where are the restrooms?	el baño?	el **bahn**-yoh
Here/there	Aquí/allá	ah-**key**/ah-**yah**
Open/closed	Abierto/cerrado	ah-bee-**er**-toh/ ser-**ah**-doh
Left/right	Izquierda/derecha	iss-key-**eh**-dah/ dare-**eh**-chah
Is it near?	¿Está cerca?	es-**tah sehr**-kah
Is it far?	¿Está lejos?	es-**tah leh**-hoss
I'd like ...	Quisiera ...	kee-see-**ehr**-ah
... a room	un cuarto/una habitación	oon **kwahr**-toh/**oo**-nah ah-bee-tah-see-**on**
... the key	la llave	lah **yah**-veh
... a newspaper	un periódico	oon pehr-ee-**oh**-dee-koh
... a stamp	un sello de correo	oon **seh**-yo deh korr-**eh**-oh
I'd like to buy ...	Quisiera comprar ...	kee-see-**ehr**-ah kohm-**prahr**
... soap	jabón	hah-**bohn**
... suntan lotion	Loción bronceadora	loh-see-**ohn** brohn-seh-ah-**do**-rah
... envelopes	sobres	**so**-brehs
... writing paper	papel	pah-**pel**
... a postcard	una tarjeta postal	**oon**-ah tar-**het**-ah post-**ahl**
... a ticket		
How much is it?	¿Cuánto cuesta?	**kwahn**-toh **kwes**-tah
It's expensive/cheap	Está caro/barato	es-**tah kah**-roh/ bah-**rah**-toh
A little/a lot	Un poquito/mucho	oon poh-**kee**-toh/ **moo**-choh
More/less	Más/menos	mahss/**men**-ohss
Enough/too (much)	Suficiente/	soo-fee-see-**en**-teh/

I am ill/sick	Estoy enfermo(a)	es-**toy** en-**fehr**-moh(mah)
Call a doctor	Llame a un medico	**ya**-meh ah oon **med**-ee-koh
Help!	Socorro	soh-**koh**-roh
Stop!	Pare	**pah**-reh

DINING OUT

I'd like to reserve a table ...	Quisiera reservar una mesa ...	kee-**syeh**-rah rreh-sehr-**bahr** oo-nah **meh**-sah ...
... for two people.	para dos personas.	**pah**-rah dohs pehr-**soh**-nahs
... for this evening.	para esta noche.	**pah**-rah **ehs**-tah **noh**-cheh
... for 8 PM	para las ocho de la noche.	**pah**-rah lahs **oh**-choh deh lah **noh**-cheh
A bottle of ...	Una botella de ...	oo-nah bo-**teh**-yah deh
A cup of ...	Una taza de ...	oo-nah **tah**-sah deh
A glass of ...	Un vaso de ...	oon **vah**-so deh
Bill/check	La cuenta	lah **kwen**-tah
Bread	El pan	el pahn
Breakfast	El desayuno	el deh-sah-**yoon**-oh
Butter	La mantequilla	lah man-teh-**kee**-yah
Coffee	Café	kah-**feh**
Dinner	La cena	lah **seh**-nah
Fork	El tenedor	el ten-eh-**dor**
I don't eat meat	No como carne	noh koh-moh **kahr**-neh
I cannot eat ...	No puedo comer ...	noh **pweh**-doh koh-**mehr**
I'd like to order ...	Quiero ordenar ...	**kee**-yehr-oh **ohr**-deh-nahr
I'd like ...	Me gustaría ...	Meh goo-stah-**ee**-ah
I'm hungry/thirsty	Tengo hambre.	**Tehn**-goh **hahm**-breh
Is service/the tip included?	¿Está incluida la propina?	es-**tah** in-cloo-**ee**-dah lah pro-**pee**-nah
Knife	El cuchillo	el koo-**chee**-yo
Lunch	La comida	lah koh-**mee**-dah
Menu	La carta, el menú	lah **cart**-ah, el meh-**noo**
Napkin	La servilleta	lah sehr-vee-**yet**-ah
Pepper	La pimienta	lah pee-mee-**en**-tah
Plate	plato	
Please give me ...	Por favor déme ...	pore fah-**vor deh**-meh
Salt	La sal	lah sahl
Spoon	Una cuchara	**oo**-nah koo-**chah**-rah
Sugar	El ázucar	el ah-**su**-kar
Tea	té	teh
Water	agua	**ah**-gwah
Wine	vino	**vee**-noh

What to Pack for Costa Rica

FRAMELESS BACKPACK OR DUFFEL BAG

Even if you're planning to stay only in luxury resorts, odds are that at least once you'll have to haul your stuff a distance from the shuttle drop-off or the airport. Consider, too, that domestic airlines have tight weight restrictions—at this writing 11 to 13 kilograms, or 25 to 30 pounds—and not all buses have luggage compartments. Frameless backpacks and duffel bags can be squeezed into tight spaces and are less conspicuous than fancier luggage.

COMFORTABLE, HAND-WASHABLE CLOTHING

T-shirts and shorts are acceptable near the beach and in tourist areas; long-sleeve shirts and pants protect your skin from ferocious sun and, in coastal regions, mosquitoes. Leave your jeans behind—they take forever to dry.

WATERPROOF, LIGHTWEIGHT JACKET

A lightweight jacket and sweater will be welcome on cool nights, early mornings, and trips up volcanoes; you'll need even warmer clothes for trips to Chirripó National Park or Cerro de la Muerte and overnight stays in San Gerardo de Dota or on the slopes of Poás Volcano.

ONE WRINKLE-FREE NICE OUTFIT

While daytime activities require your active gear, you'll still want to go to a nice dinner or a bar when you're in Costa Rica, too. You likely won't need anything too fancy. By "nice," we mean a casual wrinkle-free dress or pants.

YOUR OWN TOILETRIES

It's sometimes tough to find tampons, so bring your own and, since septic systems here generally cannot handle them, refrain from flushing them down the toilet. For almost all toiletries, including contact lens supplies, a pharmacy is your best bet once you arrive. Don't forget sunblock, and expect to sweat it off and reapply regularly in the high humidity.

PACKING CHECKLIST FOR COSTA RICA

- Quick-drying synthetic-fiber shirts and socks

- Hiking boots or shoes that can get muddy and wet

- Waterproof sport sandals (especially for the Osa Peninsula)

- Knee-high socks for rubber boots that are supplied at many lodges

- A pair of lightweight pants

- Waterproof, lightweight jacket, windbreaker, or poncho

- Day pack for hikes

- Sweater for cool nights and early mornings

- Swimsuit

- Insect repellent with DEET

- Flashlight with spare batteries

- Sunscreen with a minimum SPF 30

- Large, portable water bottle

- Hat and/or bandannas

- Binoculars (with carrying strap)

- Imodium and Pepto-Bismol

- Swiss Army knife

- Zip-style plastic bags

- Toilet paper (rarely provided in public bathrooms) and toiletries

- One wrinkle-free, nice outfit

- Frameless backpack or duffel bag

Tours

Bicycle

Costa Rica is mountainous and rough around the edges. It's a rare bird who attempts a road-biking tour here. But the payoff for the ungroomed, tire-munching terrain is uncrowded, wildly beautiful off-road routes. Most bike-tour operators want to make sure you're in moderately good shape and do some biking at home. Operators generally provide top-notch equipment, including bikes and helmets, but welcome serious mountain bikers who bring their own ride. Operators usually meet you at the airport and take care of all logistics.

Useful topographical maps (not biking maps per se) are generally provided as part of the tour, and include unpaved roads. If you're striking out on your own, these maps can usually be found at downtown San José's Lehmann bookstore for about $7. Some basic Spanish is highly recommended if you're going to do it yourself.

■ TIP➔ **Check with individual airlines about bike-packing requirements.**

Cardboard bike boxes can be found at bike shops for about $15; more secure options start at $40. International travelers often can substitute a bike for a piece of checked luggage at no charge (if the box conforms to regular baggage dimensions), but U.S. airlines will sometimes charge a $100 to $200 handling fee each way.

🚶 Bird-Watching

You will get more out of your time in Costa Rica by taking a tour rather than trying to find birds on your own. Bring your own binoculars, but don't worry about a spotting scope; if you go with a company that specializes in birding tours, your guide will have one. Expect to see about 300 species during a weeklong tour. Many U.S. travel companies subcontract with Costa Rican tour operators. By arranging your tour directly with local companies, you save money.

Birdwatching Costa Rica
SPECIAL-INTEREST TOURS | Comprehensive multiday birding tours are offered by this company, with eight options in various regions of Costa Rica as well as tours customized to your own requirements. You can opt for a single-day excursion as well. ☎ *2771–4582 in Costa Rica* ⊕ *www. birdwatchingcostarica.com* ✉ *From $294 per person for 1-day tour.*

🚶 Diving

Costa Rica's remote Cocos Island—one of the world's best dive spots—can be visited only on multiday scuba safaris, but Guanacaste, the South Pacific, and, to a lesser extent, the Caribbean offer some respectable underwater adventures. Also in the south lies Caño Island, a good alternative to Cocos Island, particularly in the rainy season, when dive sites closer to shore are clouded by river runoff.

Bill Beard's Costa Rica
ADVENTURE TOURS | This Gulf of Papagayo outfitter pioneered Costa Rican diving tours and offers several Pacific-coast options. ☎ *877/853–0538 in North America, 2479–7089 in Costa Rica* ⊕ *www. billbeardcostarica.com* ✉ *From $85 for ½-day dive.*

Sirenas Diving Costa Rica
ADVENTURE TOURS | Based in Playa Hermosa, Sirenas Diving has trips to all the dive sites in Guanacaste and the North Pacific coast, as well as the complete range of PADI courses. ☎ *8481–0663 in Costa Rica* ⊕ *www.sirenasdivingcostarica.com* ✉ *From $150.*

Tours

Undersea Hunter
ADVENTURE TOURS | The *Argo* and *Sea Hunter* make eight-day, seven-night excursions, or longer, several times a year to Cocos Island. ☎ *2228–6613, 800/203–2120 in North America* ⊕ *www. underseahunter.com* ✉ *From $4,695.*

⚐ Fishing

If fishing is your primary objective in Costa Rica, you are best off booking a package. During peak season you may not even be able to find a hotel room in the hot fishing spots, let alone one of the top boats and skippers. The major fish populations move along the Pacific coast through the year, and tarpon and snook fishing on the Caribbean is subject to the vagaries of seasonal wind and weather but viable year-round.

Costa Rica Outdoors

SPECIAL-INTEREST TOURS | San José–based Costa Rica Outdoors is one of the best bets for full service and honest advice about where to go and works with the widest range of operators around the country. ☎ *800/308–3394 in North America* ⊕ *www.costaricaoutdoors.com* ✉ *4-night packages from $990.*

J. P. Sportfishing Tours
SPECIAL-INTEREST TOURS | This longtime operator is the place to get hooked up for fishing in Quepos and the Central Pacific coast. Experienced skippers are fluent in English and, depending on the season, offer the chance to catch marlin, dorado, Pacific sailfish, snapper, yellowfin, or roosterfish. You'll need to obtain your own fishing license. ☎ *2777–1613, 866/620–4188 in North America* ⊕ *www. jpsportfishing.com* ✉ *From $900 for 1–4 anglers for ½ day.*

The Zancudo Lodge
SPECIAL-INTEREST TOURS | Near Golfito on the South Pacific coast, this lodge mixes sportfishing with upscale accommodations and a variety of other activities. ☎ *2776–0008, 800/854–8791 in North America* ⊕ *www.zancudolodge.com* ✉ *From $2,995 for 3 days' fishing, accommodations, and meals.*

◉ Spanish-Language Programs

Thousands of people travel to Costa Rica every year to study Spanish. Dozens of schools in and around San José offer professional instruction and homestays, and there are several smaller schools outside the capital. Bundling a homestay with a local family into the course is always a way to increase your proficiency.

CPI Spanish Immersion School
SPECIAL-INTEREST TOURS | You can sign up for four or five hours per day of study at CPI's schools in Heredia, Monteverde, and Playa Flamingo. ☎ *8681–6552, 877/373–3116* ⊕ *www.cpi-edu.com* ✉ *From $460 (1 wk).*

Escuela d'Amore
SPECIAL-INTEREST TOURS | In beautiful Manuel Antonio, this is one of Costa Rica's prime places to combine language study and beach time. ☎ *2777–1143, 800/261–3203 in North America* ⊕ *www. edcostarica.com* ✉ *From $845 (2 wks).*

ILISA
SPECIAL-INTEREST TOURS | Cultural-immersion classes are based in San Pedro, San José's preeminent east-side suburb. ☎ *2280–0700, 727/230–0563 in North America* ⊕ *www.ilisa.com* ✉ *From $450 (1 wk).*

Institute for Central American Development Studies (*ICADS*)

SPECIAL-INTEREST TOURS | Language programs here include optional academic seminars in English about Central America's political, social, and economic conditions. ☎ 2225–0508 ⊕ *www.icads. org* ✉ *From $1,990 (4 wks).*

🏄 Surfing

Most Costa Rican travel agencies have packages that ferry both veterans and newcomers between the country's famed bicoastal breaks.

Del Mar Adventures

SPECIAL-INTEREST TOURS | Based in Nosara and with a branch at Playa Hermosa on the Central Pacific coast, this company offers a variety of surf lessons, including women-only classes. ☎ 8385–8535 in *Costa Rica* ⊕ *www.delmaradventures. com* ✉ *Lessons from $85.*

📍 Volunteer Programs

In recent years more and more Costa Ricans have realized the need to preserve their country's precious biodiversity. Both Ticos and far-flung environmentalists have founded volunteer and educational concerns to this end.

Volunteer opportunities span a range of diverse interests. You can tag sea turtles as part of a research project, build trails in a national park, or volunteer at an orphanage. Many of the organizations require at least rudimentary Spanish. Beach cleanups, recycling, and some wildlife projects don't require proficiency in Spanish.

Costa Rican Humanitarian Foundation (*Fundación Humanitaria*)

SPECIAL-INTEREST TOURS | Volunteer opportunities include working with indigenous communities, women, children, community-based clinics, and education centers. ☎ 8390–4192 in Costa Rica, 310/402–2377 in North America ⊕ *www.crhf.org* ✉ *$50–$100/day donation to foundation, plus $40/day for homestay.*

Institute for Central American Development Studies (*ICADS*)

SPECIAL-INTEREST TOURS | The Institute delves into development and social justice in a variety of 13-week volunteer programs that let you work with schools and disadvantaged communities. ☎ 2225–0508 in Costa Rica ⊕ *www. icads.org* ✉ *From $13,450 (13 wks).*

Talamancan Association of Eco-Tourism and Conservation (*ATEC*)

SPECIAL-INTEREST TOURS | As well as designing short group and individual outings centered on Costa Rican wildlife and indigenous culture, ATEC keeps an updated list of up to 30 Caribbean-based organizations that welcome volunteers. A two-month commitment is required. ☎ 2750–0398 in Costa Rica ⊕ *www. ateccr.org.*

Great Itineraries

Great Itineraries in Costa Rica

Costa Rica looks disarmingly small on the map. This country the size of Vermont and New Hampshire combined *should* be easy to take in, right? Arrive here and you'll see that a mountainous spine transects the country and dirt roads make driving downright abysmal. Ambitious plans to see the entire country never materialize. Rather than rushing around—and rushing is something you can't easily do here—pick and choose a couple of destinations and get to know them well.

LAY OF THE LAND

San José and the Central Valley. Costa Rica's congested capital sits smack-dab in the center of the country. Because it's the country's transportation hub, you'll likely pass through, even if only on your first and last days here. Coming to Costa Rica on business? You'll probably get to know the city well. San José gives way to bustling suburbs, then smaller towns, then pastoral countryside ringing the capital in a mountain valley (elevation 3,000–5,000 feet). Take in the valley as day trips from the city or base yourself out here. San José's Aeropuerto Internacional Juan Santamaría sits in the Central Valley, too.

The North. Transportation is straightforward in the vast, mostly flat northern one-third of the country that makes up the Northern Lowlands. This area has two of Costa Rica's biggest attractions, Arenal Volcano and Monteverde Cloud Forest. Main roads are decent here. You'd think a highway, north to south, would line the northern Pacific coast, making it easy to bop among this region's famed beaches and down through the Nicoya Peninsula. However, you frequently have to head back inland to get to the next strand of sand down the coast. If this area is your sole destination, book your flights to Liberia's Aeropuerto Internacional Guanacaste, rather than down to San José.

Manuel Antonio and the Central Pacific Coast. A spiffy highway puts San José 90 minutes to two hours from the beaches along this section of the coast. That's great for the tourism industry here, but you should book space for holidays and high-season weekends in advance: Costa Ricans love to take minibreaks to this region, too.

The Osa Peninsula and the South Pacific. The south is rarely first-timer's territory—even most Costa Ricans have never ventured to the southern third of their country, a land of remote beaches, mountains, and wilderness ecolodges. Transportation is improving to and within this splendid region, but can still be a chore. Sample it, though, and you might count yourself among the growing number of fans.

Tortuguero and the Caribbean Coast. Once you get over the hump of the mountains north of San José, a good road puts you directly en route to the sultry, tropical southern Caribbean coast, still largely the province of European visitors and less known in American circles. The northern Caribbean coast near Tortuguero National Park is a different story entirely: no roads exist up here, making boat or plane your only travel options.

NICARAGUA
CARIBBEAN SEA
The North
Tortuguero and the Caribbean Coast
San José
San José and the Central Valley
Manuel Antonio and the Central Pacific Coast
Osa Peninsula and the South Pacific
PANAMA
PACIFIC OCEAN

TIMING

Costa Rican Tourist Board surveys show that U.S. visitors spend an average of nine days on a trip here. That's ample occasion to take in destinations in a couple of regions, and it accounts for time to get from one place to the other. (Depending on the places you choose, that last part can be more of a chore than you may realize.) Rather than packing too much in, keep repeating that most Costa Rican of expressions, *si Dios lo quiere*: "If God is willing," you'll get back here to partake of what you didn't see the first time around.

ITINERARIES

We proffer five possible itineraries, each taking in a small slice of the country and showcasing some of the crowd-pleasing destinations for which Costa Rica is known. The San José, Central Valley, and Tortuguero itinerary leans toward the "leave the driving to them" end of the spectrum; the Osa Peninsula itinerary incorporates domestic air travel. If you have time, these itineraries can be combined or broken apart and reassembled to suit your needs. If you are doing the driving, remember the sun sets here around 5:30 pm all year long, give or take about 15 minutes. Always plan to arrive at your destination before dark.

PEAK SEASON: DECEMBER TO APRIL

The Christmas-to-Easter period essentially defines Costa Rica's high season. With little rain and temperatures in the 80s and higher, the country makes an ideal escape for North Americans and Europeans fleeing those frigid winters.

Great Itineraries

Best of Costa Rica: 7-Day Itinerary

Volcanoes and beaches are two of the things Costa Rica does best, so the classic first-timer's itinerary to Costa Rica takes in two of its most popular destinations: the impressive Arenal Volcano and the beaches of the Central Pacific coast's lovely Manuel Antonio.

DAY 1: SAN JOSÉ

Arrive in **San José's Aeropuerto Internacional Juan Santamaría** (most arrivals are in the evening) and head straight to one of the small hotels north of the city in the **Central Valley.** The airport lies northwest of the capital, so staying in San José requires a bit of backtracking. The **Hampton Inn** just across from the airport lets you ease into your Costa Rican experience in familiar surroundings; the **Xandari Resort & Spa** offers a far more local, and pricier, first night here. Brace yourself for lines at immigration if you arrive in the evening along with several other large flights from North America. Try to get a seat near the front of the plane, and don't dawdle when disembarking.

DAY 2: POÁS VOLCANO AND ARENAL

(45 minutes by paved road from airport to Poás Volcano; 2½ hours by paved road from airport to La Fortuna)

If you have the time, set out early for **Poás Volcano,** where you can peer over the edge of the crater. It makes an interesting start to your first full day in Costa Rica. Fortify yourself with the fruits, jellies, and chocolates sold by vendors on the road up to the summit. Otherwise, get going to the Arenal area right away. Set out on the scenic drive—turn north at San Ramón—to **La Fortuna,** which sits at the foot of **Arenal Volcano**

and is its hub. Bear in mind that portions of the route twist and turn and fog over by noon. Drop your luggage at one of many fantastic hotels, and partake of the myriad activities here. Take a zipline or hanging-bridges tour through the forest canopy north of the volcano with amazing views of the mountain itself. Follow up with a visit to one of many hot-springs complexes in the area as the sun sets behind Volcán Arenal. They all line the road that runs west from La Fortuna around the north side of the volcano.

Shuttle vans have hotel-to-hotel service, usually from the Hampton Inn to many Arenal-area hotels. We like **Nayara Gardens** with its terrific views of the volcano.

DAY 3: CAÑO NEGRO WILDLIFE REFUGE

(90 minutes by paved road from La Fortuna)

Spend the day in the **Caño Negro Wildlife Refuge,** a lowland forest reserve replete with waterfowl near the Nicaraguan border. Book your trip the night before; tour operators in La Fortuna keep evening hours for exactly that reason. All transport is included, and it's far easier than trying to visit the refuge on your own.

DAY 4: SCENIC DRIVE TO THE CENTRAL PACIFIC

(4–4½ hours by paved road from La Fortuna)

Today's a traveling day—a chance to really see the country's famous landscape. Four hours' drive from Arenal takes you to fabled **Manuel Antonio** on the Central Pacific coast. Beyond-beautiful hotels are the norm here, and you have your choice of seaside luxury—we like the **Arenas del Mar Beachfront and Nature Resort**—or tree-shrouded lodges like **Villas Nicolás.**

Hotel-to-hotel shuttle-van services can get you from Arenal to Manuel Antonio.

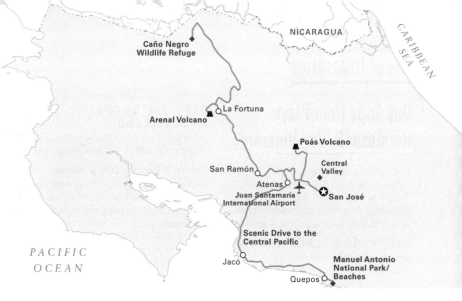

If you drive instead, start out as early as possible. You'll pass again through the mountainous stretch between La Fortuna and San Ramón—that's the way you came—to get back to the main highway heading east. Exit at **Atenas,** a pleasant town that makes a good lunch stop. South of Atenas, hook up with the Pacific Highway—follow the signs directing you to Caldera. The Jacó exit takes you on the fairly good road to Manuel Antonio.

DAY 5: MANUEL ANTONIO NATIONAL PARK
(10–20 minutes from most area lodgings)

Manuel Antonio is Costa Rica's most famous national park for a reason: it has beaches, lush rain forest, mangrove swamps, and rocky coves with abundant marine life. You can—and should—spend an entire day exploring the park, home to capuchin monkeys, sloths, agoutis, and 200 species of birds. It's also one of two locales in the country where you'll see squirrel monkeys. Almost all Manuel Antonio hotels have transport to the park. If yours doesn't, taxis are plentiful and cheap. Don't forget: the park is closed on Tuesday.

DAY 6: BEACHES
(10–20 minutes from most area lodgings)

Days 1 through 5 were on-the-go days. Reward yourself today with lots of relaxation. One of Costa Rica's most popular strands of sand, **Playa Espadilla** hums with activity on weekends and holidays. Alas, riptides can make swimming risky here. Within the national park, **Playa Manuel Antonio** and **Playa Espadilla Sur** offer more seclusion, but no real facilities. Manuel Antonio and its neighboring town, **Quepos,** have the best selection of restaurants of any beach community in the country.

DAY 7: SAN JOSÉ
(2–2½ hours by paved road from Manuel Antonio)

An easy morning drive back to San José gives you time to spend the afternoon in the city. Visit the **Teatro Nacional** and the **Museo de Oro Precolombino,** and save time for late-afternoon shopping. An evening meal caps off your trip before you turn in early to get ready for tomorrow morning's departure. We recommend that you check in three hours before your flight.

Great Itineraries

Day Trips from Playa Hermosa: 6-Day Itinerary

The province of Guanacaste and the Nicoya Peninsula are known as Costa Rica's "fun in the sun" destination. Kids and adults alike enjoy the region's huge variety of land- and water-based activities.

DAYS 1 AND 2: PLAYA HERMOSA
(30 minutes by paved road from Liberia airport)

Most arrivals to **Liberia's Aeropuerto Internacional Guanacaste,** Costa Rica's second international airport, are in the early afternoon. You can't go wrong with any North Pacific beach, but we like **Playa Hermosa** for its location about 30 minutes from the airport—it's convenient as a base for visiting area attractions. The smaller lodgings here make the perfect antidote to the megaresorts that are not too far away. They can arrange to have transport waiting at the airport, with advance notice. The **Hotel Playa Hermosa Bosque del Mar** hugs the beach itself. The big all-inclusives up here have their own minivans to whisk you in air-conditioned comfort from airport to resort. Otherwise, the airport contains the full selection of car-rental counters.

Start Day 2 off lazing on the beach. Morning is a great time of day to hit the beach in this part of Costa Rica—the breezes are refreshingly cool and the sun hasn't started to beat down yet. After lunch, explore Playa Hermosa's "metropolis," the small town of **Playas del Coco.** Quite frankly, Coco is our least favorite beach up here. But we like the town for its little souvenir shops, restaurants, and culture.

Taxis are the easiest way to travel between Playa Hermosa and Coco, about 10 minutes away. Have your hotel call one, and flag one down on the street in town when it's time to return.

DAY 3: RINCÓN DE LA VIEJA VOLCANO
(1½-hour drive from Playa Hermosa, the last 45 minutes by dirt and stone road)

The top of **Rincón de la Vieja Volcano,** with its steaming, bubbling, oozing fumaroles, lies about 90 minutes from Hermosa. Lather on the sunscreen and head for the **Hacienda Guachipelín**—tours are open to nonhotel guests, too—and its volcano-viewing hikes, canopy tours, rappelling, horseback riding, mountain biking, and river tubing. Cap off the day with a spa treatment, complete with thermal mud bath.

If you don't have a rental car, book a private driver for the day, which can usually be arranged through your hotel. The region has seen an increase in tour operators who can take you to area attractions, too, which your hotel can arrange.

If you are driving yourself, you may wish to spend the night up here and not trek back down to the coast the same day. Hacienda Guachipelín itself is a solid lodging value.

DAY 4: GOLF OR DIVING
(30 minutes by paved road from Playa Hermosa to Papagayo Golf & Country Club; 10 minutes by paved road from Playa Hermosa to Playas del Coco)

Golf is big up here. The 18-hole **Vista Ridge Golf & Country Club** is just southeast of Playas del Coco. The other popular, slightly pricey, sport here is scuba diving. Dive operators are based in nearby Playas del Coco—we like **Rich Coast Diving**—or Playa Panamá. A daylong diving course won't certify you, but gives you a taste of the deep. A taxi can transport you to and from the golf course, and dive operators will pick you up from and return you to your hotel.

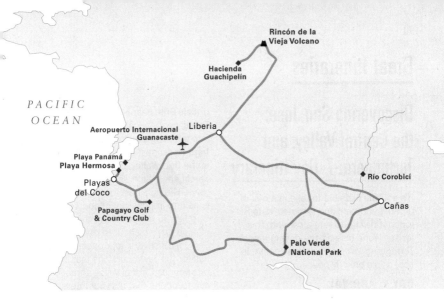

A map showing the Pacific Ocean region with locations including Rincón de la Vieja Volcano, Hacienda Guachipelín, Aeropuerto Internacional Guanacaste, Liberia, Playa Panamá, Playa Hermosa, Playas del Coco, Papagayo Golf & Country Club, Río Corobicí, Cañas, and Palo Verde National Park.

DAY 5: PALO VERDE NATIONAL PARK

(1½ hours by paved road from Playa Hermosa to Palo Verde, the last 45 minutes by dirt road)

Start with a morning guided tour at **Palo Verde National Park,** one of the last remaining dry tropical forests in Central America. The **Organization for Tropical Studies,** which operates the biological station here, has terrific guides. Spend the afternoon observing nature in a more relaxed fashion with a float (easy Class I and II rapids) down the nearby Río Corobicí. The aptly named **Safaris Corobicí,** near Cañas on the Pan-American Highway, specializes in the floating trips. This excursion is a bit roundabout, so this is the day your own vehicle would come in handiest. But you can also hire a private driver or get a tour operator to fix you up (arranged through your hotel). Bring water to drink: it gets hot here.

DAY 6: DEPARTURE

(30 minutes by paved road from Playa Hermosa)

Grab a last dip in the ocean this morning, because your flight departs from Liberia in the early afternoon. The airport terminal is modern and spacious, but you should still allow yourself plenty of time for check-in.

Tips

■ A car is ideal for this itinerary, yet many area attractions and tour operators provide transport to and from area lodging if you aren't too far afield.

■ All-inclusive resorts do a good job of organizing local excursions with local operators, so if you're staying at one, take advantage of them.

■ Getting from beach to beach often requires travel back inland. There is no real (i.e., navigable) coastal road.

■ If ever there were a case for an off-season vacation, this is it. This driest, hottest part of the country gets very dry and hot from January through April. We prefer the region during the low season after April.

Great Itineraries

Discovering San José, the Central Valley, and Tortuguero: 7-Day Itinerary

It's entirely possible to take in a mix of urban, suburban, and remote Costa Rica without having to rent a car with this let-someone-else-do-the-driving itinerary. Tortuguero, on the Caribbean coast, is accessible only by boat.

DAY 1: ARRIVAL

Following your evening arrival in **San José,** head to one of the many in-town lodgings. **Hotel Grano de Oro,** west of downtown, or the **Gran Hotel Costa Rica,** downtown, are good options. Your hotel can arrange for transport with advance notice. The big players have their own hotel shuttle vans, but smaller lodgings can arrange for a taxi. Otherwise, grab one of the official orange airport cabs at the customs exit. Plan on spending $30 for a taxi ride into the city.

DAY 2: SAN JOSÉ

A full day in the city gives you time to spend the morning visiting the **Teatro Nacional** and the **Museo de Oro Precolombino**—they're on the same block. Duck into the **Museo del Jade** in the afternoon, especially if it's raining, or partake of some late-afternoon crafts shopping. An evening meal at one of San José's fine restaurants caps off the day. Asian restaurant **Tin Jo** is one of the country's top dining experiences.

DAY 3: DAY TOURS TO THE CENTRAL VALLEY

San José's location makes it the perfect place from which to fan out to the Central Valley's many sights. The list of things to see and do in the valley is impressive: learn all about coffee at the installations of **Café Britt,** near Heredia, or the **Doka Estate,** near Alajuela; peer over the rim into bubbling cauldrons of the **Poás** or **Irazú** volcanoes; step back into history in the **Orosi Valley**; or shop for crafts in **Sarchí,** the country's signature artisan town. Hitting all the attractions in one day is next to impossible, of course—Café Britt lies 30 minutes from the capital, but plan on up to an hour to reach the others. San José's several tour operators offer half- or full-day excursions that incorporate various Central Valley attractions, or can tailor one that fits your interests. Plan to be picked up from your hotel between 7 and 8 in the morning and return after midday for a half-day tour, or around 5 for a daylong excursion.

DAYS 4 AND 5: TORTUGUERO

(2 hours by paved road plus 2–2½ hours by boat from San José)

An early-morning pickup at your San José hotel and you are off to one of Costa Rica's most remote destinations. Once you traverse **Braulio Carrillo National Park** north of the capital, you switch from van to boat at a put-in point in the Caribbean lowlands. The final stretch to **Tortuguero** takes place by boat; this is a roadless part of Costa Rica. Arrive at your lodge by midafternoon. Rest and get cleaned up for a sumptuous dinner.

Although you can do Tortuguero on your own, most visitors opt for an all-inclusive tour. **Pachira Lodge,** along the main canal, or the more secluded **Evergreen Lodge** are good options.

The knock at the door comes early in the morning of Day 5 as you are roused out of bed to go on a prebreakfast bird-watching excursion in **Tortuguero National Park.** (Remember: there are no roads, so transport is by boat.) The day entails a guided hike in the national park

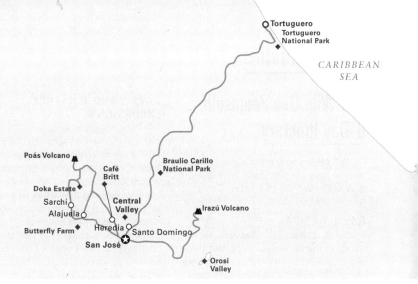

and a stroll through the tiny village of the same name. Evenings give way to turtle-watching during the nesting season (July through October).

Tortuguero is the rainiest spot in Costa Rica, and the rains spread evenly throughout the year. Plan to get wet (it's half the fun). Most of the lodges here provide ponchos and rain boots.

DAY 6: BACK TO SAN JOSÉ
(60–90 minutes by boat plus 2 hours by paved road from Tortuguero)

Day 6 is your fourth day in reverse. After a hearty breakfast at your lodge, you board the launches back to civilization. The boat travels faster than it did on the way up here. You transfer to a waiting van at the put-in point and head back to your city hotel, arriving in the afternoon. Tortuguero lodges do offer two-day/one-night excursions, but go for the extra day if your schedule permits.

DAY 7: DEPARTURE
(30–45 minutes from San José)

Most international flights depart Aeropuerto Internacional Juan Santamaría in the morning. Recommended check-in time is always three hours in advance of departure.

Tips

■ Forget the car. Tortuguero has no roads. Someone else has to take care of your transportation needs.

■ A few San José hotels might allow you to leave your things while you're touring outside the city, a particular boon when you're headed to Tortuguero. Space inside the small boats is limited.

■ July through October is prime turtle-nesting season in Tortuguero.

■ If you have more money than time, the Tortuguero lodges can arrange for you to fly to and from San José on domestic airline SANSA.

Great Itineraries

The Wild Osa Peninsula: 8-Day Itinerary

Most travelers who make it this far south already have a trip to Costa Rica under their belts, but feel free to break that rule. All you need is a spirit of adventure.

DAY 1: ARRIVAL

Following your arrival in **San José,** head to one of the several lodgings near the airport. We recommend staying out here rather than heading into San José itself, about 30 minutes away; you need to be back at the airport the next morning for your flight to the Osa Peninsula, and you'll appreciate the extra time. You cannot get closer to the airport than the **Hampton Inn,** just across the highway. Wherever you stay, your hotel can arrange for transport with advance notice, whether its own shuttle vans or sending a taxi for you. Otherwise, grab one of the official orange airport cabs as you exit customs.

DAY 2: SAN JOSÉ TO PUERTO JIMÉNEZ TO CABO MATAPALO

(1 hour by air to Puerto Jiménez and 1 hour by gravel road)

You're back at the airport for your hourlong flight to Puerto Jiménez on domestic airlines SANSA or Skyway. Check-in is a leisurely affair, but you should arrive at the airport at least 45 minutes before departure. Arrival at the airstrip in Puerto Jiménez, Osa's "metropolis," is even more low-key. Our recommended lodgings in Cabo Matapalo, 21 km (14 miles) south, can arrange for transfers. Each has its own style: **Lapa Ríos** rates as one of the world's premier ecolodges; **El Remanso** is quiet and intimate; **Bosque del Cabo** draws an engaging, sociable clientele.

DAYS 3 AND 4: NATURE EXCURSIONS

The Cabo Matapalo lodges offer their own nature-themed activities. They range from quiet hikes to snorkeling to horseback riding to more strenuous rappelling and climbing. Highly regarded local tour operator **Everyday Adventures** takes you on excursions that skew toward the adrenaline-rush end of the spectrum. The end of the day puts you back at your lodge, chatting with other guests well into the evening about what you saw that day.

DAY 5: CABO MATAPALO TO CARATE

(1 hour by road)

Carate is literally Osa's end of the road. The lodges here can arrange for an overland transfer from Cabo Matapalo or all the way from Puerto Jiménez if you're skipping Matapalo entirely. Accommodations here have their own personalities, too: **Finca Exótica** caters to nature lovers, **Luna Lodge** is for the yoga or wellness devotee. A trip to the beach rounds out your day. Alas, as is the case elsewhere in Costa Rica, riptides are dangerous here.

DAY 6: CORCOVADO NATIONAL PARK

(45-minute hike to La Leona park entrance from Carate; half day or full day of hiking in park)

If you've come this far, Costa Rica's famed **Corcovado National Park** should be on your agenda. The lodges here can arrange for guided walks to the park—it's the only way to approach Corcovado from this direction. You must enter Corcovado accompanied by a guide, and you must pay your entry fee in advance. Accommodation inside the park—advance reservations are mandatory—is rustic. Any overnights would necessitate

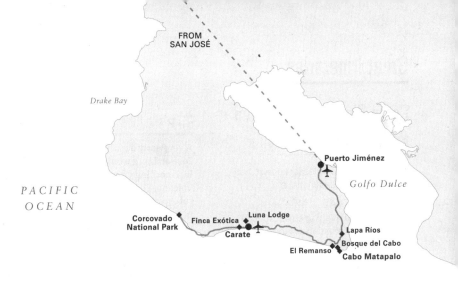

FROM SAN JOSÉ

Drake Bay

Puerto Jiménez

Golfo Dulce

PACIFIC
OCEAN

Corcovado
National Park   Finca Exótica   Luna Lodge
                        Carate

Lapa Ríos
Bosque del Cabo
El Remanso   Cabo Matapalo

adding extra days onto this itinerary. No one ever tires of repeating the platitudes about Corcovado, most often citing *National Geographic*'s description of the park as "the most biologically intense place on earth in terms of biodiversity."

DAYS 7 AND 8: CARATE TO PUERTO JIMÉNEZ TO SAN JOSÉ
(2 hours by road and 1 hour by air to San José)

The lodges here can arrange for an overland transfer back to Puerto Jiménez, or you can take the *colectivo,* the public transport here. Carate does have its own tiny airstrip with charter planes making the quick jaunt back to Puerto Jiménez. If timing does not coincide with SANSA or Skyway's schedules, a night in Puerto Jiménez gives you a dose of civilization again in the style of a tropical frontier town. You can catch a flight back to San José the next morning, from where you can depart for other destinations in Costa Rica.

Tips

■ Opt for morning flights during the rainy season.

■ Same-day international-to-domestic and domestic-to-international air connections are risky; both SANSA and Skyway advise against them.

■ Domestic airlines limit your luggage to anywhere from 15 to 30 pounds, depending on your fare. Pack lightly, or make advance arrangements with your hotel.

■ September and October are the wettest months of the rainy season and Osa roads occasionally become impassable.

■ Lodges and tour operators here can take care of your advance fee payment to enter Corcovado National Park. Visitor numbers are limited; make arrangements far in advance.

Great Itineraries

Costa Rica Off the Beaten Path: 9-Day Itinerary

Avoid the crowds in lesser-known, but up-and-coming, destinations.

DAY 1: ARRIVAL

Following your evening arrival at Juan Santamaría International Airport, head into San José. The airport lies northwest of the capital, and because you'll be heading east out of the city the next morning, this gets you well on your way there. The west-side **Hotel Grano de Oro** or the downtown **Gran Hotel Costa Rica** are tried-and-true favorites and make for wonderful ways to ease into your Costa Rican experience.

DAY 2: SAN JOSÉ TO CARTAGO TO THE OROSI VALLEY
(1 hour by road)

Allow yourself a leisurely breakfast at your hotel and avoid San José's morning rush hour. Get going by 10 and you'll be fine. A half-hour drive takes you to Cartago and its only real sight. Tradition holds that the **Basílica de Nuestra Señora de los Ángeles** was the site of a 17th-century apparition of the Virgin Mary. A leisurely drive east takes you to Paraíso. Just before Paraíso lies the **Jardín Botánico Lankester,** a must for orchid lovers. Turn south at the center of town and descend steeply into the Orosi Valley. Spend the night at the rustic, but smart, **Hotel Quelitales** or the sumptuous **La Casona del Cafetal.**

Tips

A very early departure from San José on Day 2 would let you squeeze in a morning visit to the Irazú Volcano. The early bird always catches the best volcano views in Costa Rica, of course, and the volcano is only a short detour from Cartago. A stop at Dominical, one of the country's quintessential beach towns, could add an extra day or two onto this itinerary. While the Costanera is a modern highway by Costa Rican standards, do be careful navigating its ever-growing truck traffic.

DAY 3: OROSI VALLEY

A loop road lets you easily navigate the entire valley. **Ujarrás** houses the ruins of Costa Rica's first church. The town of Orosi itself contains the **Church of San José de Orosi,** the country's oldest house of worship still in use. Whether you stay there or not, **La Casona del Cafetal** is one of Costa Rica's most famous lunch stops. Expect a long wait on weekends.

DAY 4: OROSI VALLEY TO SAN GERARDO DE DOTA
(2 hours by road)

For optimal driving conditions, get an early start today. Head back toward Paraíso and Cartago, then south on the Pan-American Highway. You'll pass over the ominously named Cerro de la Muerte (Hill of Death). You'll be fine, but the high-elevation stretch of highway fogs over by noon. At Km 80, turn off to San

Gerardo de Dota and navigate the steep descent carefully. You'll welcome the sight of the **Savegre Hotel** or **Dantica Cloud Forest Lodge,** both wonderful places to spend a couple of nights.

DAY 5: SAN GERARDO DE DOTA

San Gerardo means bird-watching. The activity generally requires some hiking here. The two lodges we suggest both have top-notch on-site guides. If you're not a birder, don't forget that this is one of Costa Rica's premier trout-fishing and horseback-riding destinations.

DAY 6: SAN GERARDO DE DOTA TO COSTA BALLENA

(2 hours by road)

Another early start today and it's back up the road and back down the Pan-American Highway. The highway descends to the hub city of San Isidro de El General, a good refueling stop. An hour-long descent to the coast takes you to the beach town of Dominical. Your reward for the rugged highway conditions you've endured so far is the so-called Costanera, a modern highway that hugs the Pacific Ocean. Head south along the coast.

DAYS 7 AND 8: COSTA BALLENA AND BALLENA MARINE NATIONAL PARK

A couple of days of exploring this stretch of coast between Dominical and Ojochal allow you to experience up-and-coming Costa Rica. **El Castillo Boutique Luxury Hotel** and **Kura Boutique Hotel** offer some amazing luxury down here, but **Río Tico Safari Lodge** provides comfort at affordable prices. Ballena Marine National Park, the region's original sine qua non, provides whale- and dolphin-watching tours, along with terrific sunsets and sections with swimming—a treat hard to come by at many of the country's beaches.

DAY 9: COSTA BALLENA TO SAN JOSÉ

(3–4 hours by road)

You need not return to San José the same way you came. At Dominical, the Costanera continues northwest to Quepos and Jacó, from where you can catch the tolled Carretera a Caldera (Highway 27) back to the capital with much better road conditions.

Contacts

Air

AIRPORT INFORMATION
Aeropuerto Internacional Guanacaste. (*LIR*). ✉ Liberia ☎ 2666–9600 ⊕ *www. guanacasteairport.com.*
Aeropuerto Internacional Juan Santamaría. (*SJO*). ✉ Alajuela ☎ 2437–2400 ⊕ sjoairport.com.

DOMESTIC AND CHARTER AIRLINES Aerobell Air Charter. ☎ 4000–2030 in Costa Rica ⊕ *www.aerobell.com.* **Costa Rica Green Airways.** ☎ 4070–0771, 888/828–8471 ⊕ *www. costaricagreenair.com.* **SANSA.** ☎ 2290–4100 in Costa Rica, 877/767–2672 in North America ⊕ *www. flysansa.com.* **Skyway.** ☎ 4010–0244, 877/841– 8330 ⊕ *www.skywaycr. com.*

Bus

Central Line. ✉ Avda. 9, C. 12, Barrio La Merced ☎ 2221–9115 ⊕ *www. transportescentralline. com.* **Tica Bus.** ✉ Avda. 3, C. 26, 200 meters (656 feet) north and 100 meters (328 feet) west of Torre Mercedes, Paseo Colón ☎ 2296–9788 ⊕ *www.ticabus.com.* **TransNica.** ✉ C. 22, Avdas. 3–5, San José ☎ 8408– 0000 ⊕ *www.transnica. com.*

SHUTTLE-VAN SERVICES
Costa Rica Shuttle. ☎ 4000– 1040, 800/849–9403 in North America ⊕ *www. costaricashuttle.com.*
Interbus. ☎ 4100–0888 ⊕ *www.interbusonline. com.*

🚗 Car

LOCAL AGENCIES
Economy. ☎ 877/326–7368 in North America, 2299–2000 in Costa Rica ⊕ *www.economyrentacar. com.* **Tricolor.** ☎ 800/949– 0234 in North America, 2440–3333 in Costa Rica ⊕ *www.tricolorcarrental. com.* **Vamos.** ☎ 4000–0557 in Costa Rica, 800/601– 8806 in North America ⊕ *www.vamosrentacar. com.*

🇺🇸 Embassy

United States Embassy. (*Embajada de los Estados Unidos*). ✉ C. 120 and Avda. 0, Pavas ☎ 2519– 2000 ⊕ cr.usembassy.gov.

🛏 Lodging

Airbnb. ⊕ www.airbnb. com. **Costa Rica Beach Rentals.** ☎ 8340–3842, 973/917–8046 in North America ⊕ *www.costarica-beachrentals.com.* **Escape Villas Costa Rica.** ☎ 8932–4731, 888/672– 3673 in North America ⊕ *www.villascostarica. com.* **Home Exchange.** ☎ No phone ⊕ www.home-exchange.com. **Villas & Apartments Abroad.** ✉ 385 Fifth Ave., Suite 1008, New York ☎ 212/213–6435 in North America ⊕ *www. vaanyc.com.*

📍 Visitor Information

Association of Residents of Costa Rica. (*ARCR*). ☎ 2220–0055 ⊕ *www. arcr.net.* **CostaRicaMap. com.** ⊕ *www.costaricam-ap.com.* **Instituto Costarricense de Turismo.** (*ICT, Costa Rica Tourism Board*). ☎ 2299–5800 ⊕ *www. visitcostarica.com.* **The REAL Costa Rica.** ⊕ *www. therealcostarica.com.* **The Tico Times.** ⊕ *www. ticotimes.net.*

Chapter 3

BIODIVERSITY

Updated by
Jeffrey Van Fleet

Costa Rica's forests hold an array of flora and fauna so vast and diverse that scientists haven't even named thousands of the species found here. The country covers less than 0.03% of Earth's surface, yet it contains nearly 5% of the planet's plant and animal species. Costa Rica has at least 9,000 plant species, including more than 1,200 types of orchids, some 2,000 kinds of butterflies, and 876 bird species.

Costa Rica acts as a natural land bridge between North and South America, so there is a lot of intercontinental exchange. But the country's flora and fauna add up to more than what has passed between the continents. Costa Rica's biological diversity is the result of its tropical location, its varied topography, and the many microclimates resulting from the combination of mountains, valleys, and lowlands. The isthmus also acts as a hospitable haven to many species that couldn't complete the journey from one hemisphere to the other. The rain forests of Costa Rica's Caribbean and southwestern lowlands are the northernmost home of such southern species as the crab-eating raccoon. The tropical dry forests of the northern Pacific slope are the southern limit for such North American species as the Virginia opossum. And then there are the dozens of northern bird species that spend their winter holidays here.

Research and planning go a long way toward making your travel to Costa Rica a success. A short trip around the country can put you in one landscape after another, each with its own array of plants and animals, from the false bird of paradise and guanacaste tree to the three-toed sloth and the holy grail of birds, the resplendent quetzal. The country's renowned national park system holds examples of all of its major ecosystems, including cloud forests, mangroves and wetlands, rain forests, and tropical dry forests, and some of its most impressive sights. In terms of activities, there's more interesting stuff to do here than could possibly ever fit into one vacation. But keep in mind that somewhere around three-fourths of the country has been urbanized or converted to agriculture, so if you want to see the spectacular nature that we describe in this book, you need to know where to go.

In addition to this section on biodiversity, you'll find regional planning information and a list of our favorite ecolodges at the front of the book.

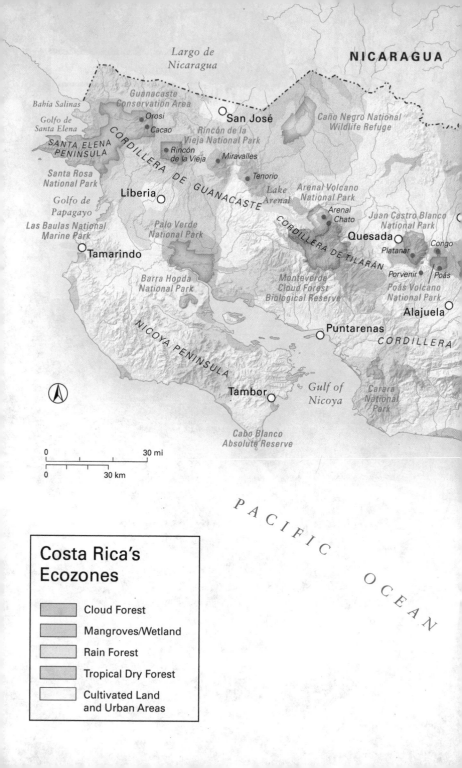

Largo de
Nicaragua

NICARAGUA

Bahía Salinas

*Golfo de
Santa Elena*

Guanacaste
Conservation Area

● Orosi

● Cacao

○ San José

SANTA ELENA
PENINSULA

Rincón de la
Vieja National Park

Caño Negro National
Wildlife Refuge

● Rincón
de la Vieja

● Miravalles

*Santa Rosa
National Park*

CORDILLERA DE GUANACASTE

● Tenorio

Arenal Volcano
National Park

Liberia ○

Lake
Arenal

● Arenal
Chato

Juan Castro Blanco
National Park

*Golfo de
Papagayo*

Palo Verde
National Park

CORDILLERA DE TILARÁN

Quesada ○

Platanar ●

Congo ●

*Las Baulas National
Marine Park*

Porvenir ● | Poás

Tamarindo ○

Barra Honda
National Park

Monteverde
Cloud Forest
Biological Reserve

Poás Volcano
National Park

Alajuela ○

NICOYA PENINSULA

Puntarenas ○

CORDILLERA

Tambor ○

*Gulf of
Nicoya*

Carara
National
Park

*Cabo Blanco
Absolute Reserve*

0 ——— 30 mi

0 ——— 30 km

P A C I F I C

O C E A N

Costa Rica's
Ecozones

Cloud Forest

Mangroves/Wetland

Rain Forest

Tropical Dry Forest

Cultivated Land
and Urban Areas

Costa Rica's Ecozones

Barra del Colorado Wildlife Refuge

Caribbean Sea

La Selva
La Virgen
Braulio Carrillo National Park

Cacho Negro
Barva

Tortuguero National Park

Limón

Turrialba Volcano National Park

Heredia
Turrialba
Irazú

SAN JOSÉ ★
Cartago
Irazú Volcano National Park

A CENTRAL

Cahuita National Park

Chirripó National Park

La Amistad International Biosphere

Chirripó (Highest point in Costa Rica 3,810 m) ▲

San Gerardo de Dota

Quepos

CORDILLERA DE TALAMANCA

Eli ▲
Ena ▲
Utyum ▲

PANAMA

San Isidro de El General

Nai ▲

Manuel Antonio National Park

VALLE DE EL GENERAL

Buenos Aires

Bine ▲

Ballena National Marine Park

Río Terraba

Drake
Drake Bay

Golfito

Piedras Blancas National Park

OSA PENINSULA

Golfo Dulce

Corcovado National Park

KEY	
▲	Mountain
●	Volcano
▢	National Parks, Wildlife Refuges and Biological Reserves

RAIN FOREST

Warm and wet, Costa Rica's rain forest is the quintessential dripping, squawking, chirping, buzzing jungle. In this sultry landscape of green on green, birds flap and screech overhead and twigs snap under the steps of unseen creatures. All the ingredients for life—water, sunlight, and more water—drench these areas.

The amount of rain in a rain forest is stunning. The enormous swath of forest in the Caribbean lowlands averages more than 13 feet of rain a year. Corcovado National Park, on the Osa Peninsula, can get 18 feet. September and October, Costa Rica's rainiest months, can mean difficult travel to these areas. The rest of the year, you should still count on getting rained on, but not washed out.

The soaring canopy soaks up the lion's share of sunlight, seriously depriving the plants below. Underneath the highest trees are several distinct layers of growth. The understory is made up of smaller and younger trees,

shaded but also protected from harsh winds and rainfall. Shrubby species and even younger trees stand farther below, and small plants, fungus, dead trees, and fallen leaves cover the constantly decomposing forest floor.

Light rarely passes through these layers and layers of growth. At the forest floor, plants lie poised, in a stasis of sorts, waiting for one of the giants above to fall and open a patch of sky. When this does happen, an incredible spectacle occurs as the waiting plants unveil an arsenal of evolutionary tricks. Vines twist out, looking for other trees to pull themselves up along, shoots explode from hidden bulbs, and ferns and lianas battle for height and access to the sun.

But as competitive as the jungle sounds, it is essentially a series of ecosystems based on interdependence and cooperation. Trees depend on the animals that eat their fruit to disperse their seeds. Fungi feed off the nutrients produced by the decomposing forest floor. From death comes life—an abundance of life.

Costa Rica's rain forests have suffered from incursions by agriculture, logging, and cattle farming, but they're still home to the majority of the nation's biodiversity, with more species per square mile than anywhere else.

TOP DESTINATIONS

Most of Costa Rica's rain forest can be found across the Caribbean lowlands and on the South Pacific coast.

CORCOVADO NATIONAL PARK

This park is the remote, untamed jewel of Costa Rica's biodiversity crown. Covering one-third of the Osa Peninsula, Corcovado National Park holds about one-quarter of all tree species in Costa Rica and at least 140 identified species of mammals. Covering 445 square km (172 square miles), the park includes Central America's largest tract of lowland Pacific rain forest, including some old-growth areas. Corcovado is home to the largest concentration of jaguars left in the country, and the biggest population of scarlet macaws. There are at least 116 species of amphibians and reptiles, and about 370 bird species. Ranger stations and campsites are available for the more adventurous, and luxurious ecolodges surround the park for those who don't like to rough it. *(See Chapter 10.)*

LA SELVA

If anybody knows anything about the rain forest, it is the researchers at La Selva biological station, situated in the midst of 3,900 acres of protected forest in northern Costa Rica. The station, run by the Organization for Tropical Studies,

Squirrel monkey

was founded by famed biologist Leslie Holdridge in 1954 and is one of the most important sites worldwide for research on tropical rain forests. The research station can sleep up to 80 people in dormitory-style rooms and two-room family cabins, and feed as many as 130 in the dining hall. More than 60 km (36 miles) of trails provide access to a variety of ecosystems. *(See Chapter 11.)*

MANUEL ANTONIO NATIONAL PARK

For a tame, up-close glimpse of the rain forest and some of its more photogenic inhabitants, Manuel Antonio National Park is a favorite. Located on the Central Pacific coast, Manuel Antonio is one of Costa Rica's most visited—and smallest—national parks. Capuchin monkeys are used to humans to the point of practically ignoring them, unless a snack is poking out from an unattended backpack. The highly endangered squirrel monkeys are less bold, but can be seen at the park or from nearby hotels. Sloths are a common sight along the trail, as are a host of exotic birds and other creatures. *(See Chapter 9.)*

A green and black poison dart frog

EXPERIENCING A RAIN FOREST

Kayaking in Drake Bay

There are a variety of ways to explore and experience the rain forest, which is only fitting given the diversity of the rain-forest ecosystem.

CANOPY TOURS

Canopy tours are a wonderful way to get a bird's-eye—or sloth's—view of the rain forest. Suspension bridges and ziplines, originally used for canopy research, offer a fantastic glimpse into the upper reaches of the forest. (The famed zipline tours are really more thrill ride than a way to get up close and personal with nature.) If you're not very mobile or don't feel like walking, go on a rain-forest tram; it's a small, slow-moving gondola that carries passengers gently through the jungle canopy.

HIKING

Hiking or walking through any one of Costa Rica's numerous national parks is an easy way to fully experience the vibrancy of the life found there. And we can't say this too many times: guided hikes are the way to go for anyone who hopes to catch a glimpse of the more exotic and hard-to-find species or better understand the complexity of the surrounding ecosystems.

MOUNTAIN BIKING

During the dry season, some parks open up trails for mountain bikers. But once the rains begin, a bike trip can turn into a long slog through the mud. Before you rent a bike, ask about the conditions of the trails.

RAFTING

Gentle, slow-moving rivers beg to be explored by canoe or kayak. It's a wonderful way to experience the deep calm of the jungle, and stealthy enough to increase your chances of seeing wildlife. If you're more of a thrill seeker, choose from any of the white-water rafting tours that pass through rain forests.

FLORA

To enter into a Costa Rican rain forest is to be overwhelmed by the diversity and intensity of life. Just 2½ acres contain almost 100 species of trees, and many of the more than 1,000 species of orchids are nested in their branches.

False bird of paradise

FALSE BIRD OF PARADISE

No avid photographer will return from Costa Rica without snapping a few shots of a heliconia, one of the most vibrant families of plants in the rain forest. This genus of flowering plant, containing between 100 and 200 species, includes the false bird of paradise (*Heliconia rostrata*), a dangling, impossibly colorful flower of alternating bulbous protrusions, colored red and tipped with green and yellow. Its vibrant colors and nectar make it a favorite for hummingbirds.

GUARIA MORADA

Almost every tree here plays host to lichens, woody vines called lianas, and rootless epiphytes, including the national flower, *guaria morada* (*Guarianthe skinneri*). Because this is an orchid species, you'll find it in several different shapes and colors: the flowers can be from pure white to deep magenta, and the base of its lip can range from yellow to white. There can be anywhere from 4 to 14 flowers per stem.

Guaria morada

SILK COTTON TREE

The silk cotton tree (*Ceiba pentandra*), known locally as *ceiba*, is one of the most easily recognizable of the rain-forest giants. Growing nearly 200 feet tall, it can be identified close to the ground by its tall, winding, and narrow roots, which act as buttresses to support the enormous trunk.

The silk cotton tree

STRANGLER FIG

Aptly called *matapalo* in Spanish, meaning "tree killer," the strangler fig begins its life as an epiphyte, living high in the branches of another tree. Over several years, it grows dangling roots to the forest floor that capture nutrients from the soil, thicken, and slowly meld onto the host tree. Eventually—it might take as long as 100 years—the strangler completely engulfs its host. In time the "strangled" tree decomposes and disintegrates, leaving the strangler fig—replete with branches, leaves, flowers, and fruit—standing hollow but victorious.

Strangler fig

FAUNA

Keep an eye out for three-wattled bellbirds, chestnut-mandibled toucans, or the secretive Baird's tapir. A host of wildcats include the ocelot, jaguarundi, puma, margay, and rarely seen jaguar.

HARPY EAGLE

The endangered harpy eagle, nearly extinct from Costa Rica, is the country's largest and most powerful raptor. It's named for the Greek spirits that carried the dead to the underworld of Hades and who are said to have the faces of humans but the bodies of eagles. Harpy eagles are huge—females are more than 2 feet in length and have a 6-foot wingspan. They hunt above the canopy, searching for large mammals or, occasionally, for large birds like the macaw.

Harpy eagle

MORPHO BUTTERFLY

The bright blue morpho butterfly bounces through the jungle like a small piece of sky on a string. The entire life cycle, from egg to death, is approximately 137 days, and adult butterflies live for only about a month. Once they emerge from the cocoon, morphos have few predators, thanks to the poisonous compounds that they retain from feeding habits back in their caterpillar days. In fact, the hairy brown tufts on the morpho caterpillar have been known to irritate human skin.

Blue morpho

SCARLET MACAWS

Every bit the pirate's crimson parrot, these large and noisy birds mate for life, travel in pairs or large groups, and can often be found gathered in almond trees in low-elevation forests of the central and southern Pacific coast. Their cousin, the critically endangered great green macaw, travels across the Caribbean lowlands, following the ripening of the mountain almond.

Scarlet macaw

THREE-TOED OR TWO-TOED SLOTH

Though difficult for us to spot, the barely moving three-toed sloth and two-toed sloth are principal meals for the harpy eagle. This animal's fur is a small self-sustaining ecosystem unto itself: because the forest is so wet and the sloth so inert, two species of blue-green algae thrive on its fur and provide it with needed camouflage. Nonparasitic insects also live here, feeding off the algae and keeping the growth under control.

■TIP→ The vibrantly colored red-eyed tree frog, like the white tent bat, sometimes rests on the underside of large jungle leaves. If you're lucky, your guide may be able to coax one out for you to see.

Three-toed sloth

VOLCANOES

As part of the Pacific Ring of Fire, the country has three volcanic mountain ranges: Guanacaste, Central, and Tilarán. There are around 300 volcanic points in Costa Rica, but only five have formed volcanoes that have erupted in recent memory: Turrialba, Irazú, Poás, Rincón de la Vieja, and Arenal.

Arenal, the crown jewel of volcanoes here, has settled into a less active phase these days. The others have, conversely, experienced more activity, necessitating occasional safety closures of their namesake national parks. Always check with locals before setting out.

Costa Rica's volcanoes are the result of friction between two enormous tectonic plates—the Cocos plate and the Caribbean plate. As these plates rub against each other, the friction partially melts rock. Although everyone uses the term "lava," pyroclastic flow, or hot gas and rock, more accurately describes the product spewed from the volcanoes here. The flow is forced toward the surface,

leaking through cracks or weak spots in the crust along with volcanic gas. In Rincón de la Vieja, gas escapes through craters high on the volcano, as well as seeping up through the surrounding ground, creating bubbling mud pits, hot springs, and fumaroles.

The volcanic mountain ranges divide the country's Pacific and Caribbean slopes and are responsible for the differences in climate between each side. Rain-laden trade winds blowing westward can't pass over these ranges without shedding their precipitation and rising. This creates Guanacaste's rain shadow: the dry plains and tropical dry forest that lie leeward, or west of the mountains. The mountains block the rain-producing weather system and cast a "shadow" of dryness.

Costa Rica's volcanic lakes occur when there is no natural drainage from a crater. The chemicals, minerals, and gases from below the earth's crust infuse the water and vibrantly color it. Irazú's lake is neon green; the baby-blue lagoon in Poás is extremely acidic and gives off toxic sulfur clouds and massive amounts of carbon dioxide.

ADVENTURE HIGHLIGHTS

■ A hike through lush cloud forest will take you to the five magnificent waterfalls at La Paz Waterfall Gardens near Poás Volcano National Park.

■ Anglers love the guapote, tilapia, and machaca pulled from Lake Arenal.

■ The Arenal area is the jumping-off point for Class II–IV white-water rafting trips on the Blancas, Arenal, Toro, and San Carlos rivers.

■ Take the tough hike to La Fortuna Waterfall, near Arenal. Swimming under the waterfall is a slice of paradise.

TOP DESTINATIONS

Costa Rica's volcanoes are often the centerpieces of large national parks.

ARENAL VOLCANO

At 5,512 feet, Arenal Volcano, rising on the northwestern plains of San Carlos, is every bit an awesome sight. Tall and perfectly conical, its sides are scarred by a history of violent eruptions and textured by decades of pyroclastic flow. Located at the northern end of the Tilarán Mountain Range, northwest of the capital, it is Costa Rica's best-known volcano. Arenal exhibits less activity these days, but that's likely temporary. Research suggests that Arenal has a 400-year cycle of major eruptions, and the activity since the 1968 explosion is small in comparison with what it's capable of. *(See Chapter 6.)*

POÁS VOLCANO

Poás Volcano is Costa Rica's most visited national park, in part because it's the closest active volcano to the capital of San José and the Aeropuerto Internacional Juan Santamaría. Located in the Cordillera Volcánica Central Mountain Range, Poás is topped by three craters, the tallest reaching 8,885 feet above sea level. Only the main cone has shown any volcanic eruptions in the last 200 years, but when they happen, they happen. Normally, you can get a

Gaudy leaf frog; Marco13, Fodors.com member

good look at the crater from the viewing deck, but authorities close the park at the slightest hint of unusual activity. *(See Chapter 5.)*

Note: Costa Rica's hot spot (literally) these days is the Turrialba Volcano, which occasionally spews ash over the metro area and periodically closes the international airport. Park entry is allowed at this writing after being prohibited for many years, but periodic closures do take place.

RINCÓN DE LA VIEJA

A mass of slopes, craters, and biodiversity that bridges the Continental Divide, Rincón de la Vieja is in Costa Rica's arid northwest. It's not the classic conical volcano, but rather a ridge made of a series of craters that include bare, rocky bowls with brilliantly colored lakes, and velvety cones covered in rain forest. Scientists believe Rincón de la Vieja was born of simultaneous volcanic activity at nine different eruption points. Rincón de la Vieja National Park covers nearly 35,000 acres and is a wonderland of volcanic activity that includes bubbling mud pits, hot springs, and geysers, as well as refreshing lagoons and spectacular waterfalls. Occasional abnormal activity necessitates the park's closure. *(See Chapter 7.)*

On the Road to Arenal; piper35w, Fodors.com member

EXPERIENCING THE VOLCANOES

Hiking in Arenal

The Guatuso people believed that the fire god lived inside the Arenal Volcano—and in 1968, the gods were not happy. After 500 years of dormancy, Arenal erupted savagely, burying three small villages and killing 87 people. Today, thousands live at its base in the thriving town of La Fortuna, which is literally in Arenal's shadow.

HIKING

Volcano tourism is a major draw for international visitors, but given the dangers at the active sites, activities at the top are limited. The parks have hiking trails. For your safety, we recommend hiking with a guide, especially at Arenal. The volcano has settled into a less active phase these days, but it's still one of those you-never-know situations, and a knowledgeable guide knows where not to tread. At Poás and Irazú, you can go right up to the summit and peer inside.

HORSEBACK RIDING

All of Costa Rica's active volcanoes are the centerpieces of national parks. Arenal and Poás have good horseback-riding trails and many outfitters, especially in Arenal. For safety's sake and the well-being of the animals, stick with the operators we recommend.

GEOTHERMAL WONDERS

Volcanic activity is not limited to a volcano's peak. The underground heat that fuels these giants also results in hot springs, bubbling mud pits, and geysers, among other geological wonders. Minerals from the dormant Tenorio Volcano create a fascinating effect in one of the rivers running down its side, the Río Celeste, giving it a baby-blue tint. Arenal fuels area hot springs, perfect for a well-deserved soak of your tired muscles after a day of hiking.

FLORA

The habitat and ecology of these geologic giants is influenced mostly by their surrounding ecological zones and elevation. Conditions around the crater of an active volcano are intensely harsh, but some tougher species do manage to survive.

FERN

Contrary to popular stereotypes, ferns don't necessarily grow in shady, moist environments. The tongue fern (*Elaphoglossum lingua*) extends long, rubbery tongue-shape leaves and has evolved to grow around volcanic rock and hardened ash. You'll find it around the top of the Poás Volcano. Farther down, you'll find other types of ferns adapted to friendlier conditions.

Ferns

MYRTLE

Myrtle (*Myrtaceae*) and other low-lying shrubs survive this environment thanks to their slow growth rate. Myrtle, poor man's umbrella (*Gunnera insignis*), *papelillo* (*Senecio oerstedianus*), and other shrubs and ferns cover the higher bluffs around Irazú's crater. Mistletoe (*Psittacanthus*) can be found near the major volcanoes in the Central Valley. These flowering plants are interesting because they attach to trees by haustoria, special structures that penetrate the host plant and absorb its water and nutrients. When the mistletoe dies, it leaves a mark on the tree, a woodrose or *rosa de palo*.

Myrtle

OAK

Forests in Costa Rica's higher mountain areas share some plant species with cloud forests. However, the plants here have adapted to live in cold temperatures and, if the volcano is active, in compacted ash. Surrounding the Botos Lagoon, on the south side of the principal Poás crater, is high-elevation cloud forest of oak (*Quercus costaricensis* and *Q. copeyensis*), small cedar (*Brunellia costaricensis*), and flowering cypress (*Escallonia poasana*)—trees that are typically crowded with epiphytes, bromeliads, and mosses.

epiphytes growing on an oak

WILD BALSAM

Wild balsam, oak, and poor man's umbrella carpet the inactive cones around Rincón de la Vieja. Tropical dry-forest species grow farther down. Look for the guanacaste tree (*Enterolobium cyclocarpum*), Spanish cedar (*Cedrela odorata*), oak (*Quercus oocarpa*), and the country's largest wild population of the guaria morada orchid, Costa Rica's national flower.

guaria morada orchid

FAUNA

Like the flora around a volcano, the wildlife diversity of this region is dictated by the ecology around the mountain. Also, the more humans there are, the fewer animals you'll see.

FIERY-THROATED HUMMINGBIRD

Birds are one of the most populous types of creatures to live on the flanks of Poás and many more of Costa Rica's volcanoes. The fiery-throated hummingbird, the summer tanager, the sooty robin, and the emerald toucanet are among the 79 bird species that have been recorded at Poás. The fiery-throated hummingbird is recognizable by its forecrown, throat, and breast colors, as well as its bluish hump and blue-black tail.

Fiery-throated hummingbird

NINE-BANDED ARMADILLO

Irazú is home to smaller creatures such as the nine-banded armadillo, the eastern cottontail, and the little spotted cat. The nine-banded armadillo has a long snout and fantastic sense of smell. It can hold its breath for up to six minutes. This helps it keep dirt out of its nostrils while digging. Under stressful conditions, a female armadillo can prolong her pregnancy for up to three years by delaying the implantation of the fertilized egg into the uterus wall.

Nine-banded armadillo

NORTH AMERICAN PORCUPINE

The much drier region of Rincón de la Vieja has a distinctly different—and broader—set of animal inhabitants, including the North American porcupine and the agouti (a large, short-legged relative of the guinea pig). Pumas, ocelots, raccoons, and three species of monkeys (the howler, the white-faced capuchin, and the Central American spider monkey) are among the larger mammals. More than 300 bird species have been recorded there, including the collared aracari, the bare-necked umbrella bird, and the three-wattled bellbird.

North American porcupine

PUMA

In the Barva region, pumas (also called mountain lions and cougars) and even jaguars still stalk the more remote forests, searching for the tapir or an unlucky spider monkey. The puma is an excellent climber and can jump to branches 16 feet off the ground, essentially giving monkeys nowhere to hide. Pumas have never been hunted for their pelts, but are suffering from habitat destruction. In Costa Rica, they are rarely found outside protected areas.

Puma

CLOUD FOREST

The four mountain ranges that make up Costa Rica's own piece of the Continental Divide split the country into its Caribbean and Pacific regions. At these higher altitudes, temperatures cool, clouds settle, and rainfall increases. The forests found here are shrouded in mist and rich in biodiversity. Welcome to Costa Rica's famed cloud forests.

Like their lowland rain-forest cousins, cloud forests are packed with plant and animal species, thanks largely to their water-drenched conditions. There's an average of 16 feet of rainfall a year, but that number doubles when you factor in the amount of moisture gleaned from the clouds and fog that drift through every day. As in rain forests, giant hardwoods reaching as high as almost 200 feet set the ceiling for this ecology zone, while a variety of smaller trees, ferns, shrubs, and other plants fill the understories. Epiphytes flourish here, as do mosses, lichens, and liverwort. These plants cling to passing moisture and

capture it like sponges. As a result, cloud forests are constantly soaking wet, even when there is no rain.

Because conditions in a cloud forest can be harsh, many of the tougher and more adaptable rain-forest species make their home here. The relentless, heavy cloud cover can block sunlight even from the highest reaches of the forest, and deeper inside, light is rare. Photosynthesis and growth are slower, so the plants tend to be smaller with thicker trunks and stems. These unique conditions also produce an unusually high number of endemic and rare species.

The Monteverde Cloud Forest Biological Reserve, one of the world's most famous protected cloud forests, shelters innumerable life-forms. There are more than 100 mammal species; 400 bird species, including at least 30 species of hummingbird; 500-plus species of butterfly; and more than 2,500 plant species, including 420 types of orchid. Monteverde, in particular, lets you groove to a different style of Costa Rican nightlife: the big reserve and several smaller adjoining ones offer guided nocturnal walks. There are only a handful of protected cloud forests here and worldwide, and this type of ecozone is increasingly threatened by human encroachment.

ADVENTURE HIGHLIGHTS

■ Leave the car at home and travel on horseback to or from the Arenal Volcano area and Monteverde Cloud Forest. Contact Desafío Adventures, the only guides we recommend for this journey.

■ The good folks at the Savegre Hotel will give you an education on one of their daylong natural-history hikes around San Gerardo de Dota cloud forest.

■ Selvatura, right next to Monteverde, is the only canopy tour in the area with a zipline built entirely inside the cloud forest.

TOP DESTINATIONS

Regardless of which cloud forest you visit, bring a raincoat—many outfitters do supply ponchos—and go with a guide if you want to see wildlife. You'll marvel at their ability to spot a sloth at a hundred paces.

BRAULIO CARRILLO NATIONAL PARK

Descending from the Cordillera Volcánica Central Mountain Range, Braulio Carrillo National Park is an awesome, intimidating, and rugged landscape of dense cloud forest that stretches toward the rain forests of the Caribbean lowlands. The enormous park encompasses 117,580 acres of untamed jungle and is less than an hour's drive from San José. The country's principal eastbound highway cuts a path straight through it. Elusive (and endangered) jaguars and pumas are among the many animal species here, and scenic viewpoints are plentiful along the highway. A handful of trails, including the easy-to-access loop trails at the Quebrada González station, can be taken a short distance into the park's interior. *(See Chapter 11.)*

MONTEVERDE CLOUD FOREST BIOLOGICAL RESERVE

Costa Rica's most famous cloud forest reserve is packed with an astonishing

Braulio Carrillo National Park

variety of life: 2,500 plant species, 400 species of bird, 500 types of butterfly, and more than 100 different mammals—many of them bats—have been cataloged so far. The reserve reaches 5,032 feet above sea level, spans the Tilarán Mountain Range, and encompasses 9,885 acres of cloud forest and rain forest. There are 13 km (8 miles) of well-marked trails, zipline tours, and suspended bridges for canopy viewing, as well as bird tours, guided night walks, and a field research station with an amphibian aquarium. Allow a generous slice of time for leisurely hiking; longer hikes are made possible by some strategically placed overnight refuges along the way. *(See Chapter 6.)*

SAN GERARDO DE DOTA

One of Costa Rica's premier nature destinations, San Gerardo de Dota is a damp, epiphyte-laden forest of giant oak trees and an astonishing number of resplendent quetzals. Outdoors enthusiasts may never want to leave these parts—some of the country's best hiking is in this valley, and it's popular with bird-watchers. It's also great for horseback riding and trout fly-fishing. *(See Chapter 10.)*

anteater

EXPERIENCING A CLOUD FOREST

Gearing up for the Tarzan swing at the end of the zipline tour at Selvatura

You may need to get down and dirty—well, more like wet and muddy—to experience a cloud forest's natural wonders, but then, that's half the fun.

BIRD-WATCHING

Bird-watching is rewarding in the cloud forest, where some of the most vibrant and peculiar of nature's winged creatures can be found. Rise early, enjoy some locally grown coffee, and check the aguacatillo trees for quetzals. If you opt to go without a guide, bring along waterproof binoculars and a good guidebook (we recommend *The Birds of Costa Rica,* by Richard Garrigues and Robert Dean) for spotting and identifying birds.

CANOPY TOURS

Canopy tours and suspended bridges run right through the upper reaches of the cloud forest—an ecosystem in its own right. Spot birds, monkeys, and exotic orchids from a viewpoint that was once nearly impossible to reach. Get even closer to butterflies,

amphibians, snakes, and insects at various exhibits in the parks' research centers.

FISHING

If freshwater fishing in spectacular surroundings is right up your alley, check out the Savegre River, in the San Gerardo de Dota Valley. It's been stocked with rainbow trout since the 1950s.

HIKING

Well-guided hikes through this eerie landscape, draped with moss and vines, make it easier to spot the less obvious features of this complex ecosystem. Compared with the barren tropical dry forest and colorful rain forest, cloud forests don't easily offer up their secrets. Binoculars and a good guide will go a long way toward making your hike and wildlife spotting richer experiences.

FLORA

A typical 2½ acres of cloud forest might be home to nearly 100 species of trees. Contrast that with a mere 30 in the richest forests of North America.

EPIPHYTES
Epiphytes thrive in cloud and rain forests, thanks to all the moisture and nutrients in the air. The *stanhopea* orchid is interesting because of its clever pollination tricks. The blossoms' sweet smell attracts bees, but the flower's waxy surface is slippery so they slide down inside. As they slowly work their way out, they brush up against the flower's column and collect pollen. This pollen is then transferred to the sticky stigma of other flowers.

Epiphyte stanhopea

Bromeliads, another family of flowering plants, compete with epiphytes for space on the branches and trunks of the forest's trees. The spiraling leaves form caches for water, falling plant material, and insect excretions. These are mineral-rich little ponds for insects and amphibians, and drinking and bathing water for birds and other animals.

POOR MAN'S UMBRELLA
If you're caught in the rain, take cover under a poor man's umbrella (*Gunnera insignis* and *G. talamancana*), whose broad and sturdy leaves sometimes grow large enough to shelter an entire family. These shrubby plants love the dark, moist interior of the cloud forest.

Poor man's umbrella

ROBLE TREE
Majestic roble, or oak—principally the white oak (*Quercus copeyensis*) and black oak (*Q. costaricensis*)—is the dominant tree of Costa Rica's cloud forests and grows to 200 feet. The deciduous hardwood *cedro dulce*, or Spanish cedar (*Cedrela odorata*), is also a giant at 147 feet. These two are joined by evergreens like the *jaúl*, or alder, and the *aguacatillo,* a name meaning "little avocado" that's given to a variety of trees from the *lauracea* family.

White oak tree

STAR ORCHID
The star orchid (*Epidendrum radicans*) is one of the few orchids that is not an epiphyte. It grows on land and mimics in color and shape other nectar-filled flowers in order to attract butterflies who unwittingly become pollinators.

Star orchid

FAUNA

The resplendent quetzal, the blue-crowned motmot, the orange-bellied trogon, and the emerald toucanet are just some of the hundreds of species that can be logged in a cloud forest.

COLLARED TROGON

The collared trogon and the orange-bellied trogon are in the same family as the quetzal. They all share square black-and-white tail plumage and bright orange or yellow chest feathers. The collared trogon perches very quietly and is easy to miss. Luckily, it doesn't fly far, so its flight is easy to follow.

GLASS FROGS

One of the more bizarre amphibians is the tiny, transparent glass frog of the *Centrolenellu* genus, whose internal organs can be seen through its skin. It lives in trees and bushes and can often be heard at night near the rivers and streams. Cloud forests have fewer amphibian species than rain forests, but amphibian populations worldwide have plummeted in recent decades. No one knows the cause yet. Some blame acid rain and pesticides; others believe it is yet another sign of coming ecological disaster.

HOWLER MONKEYS

One of the largest New World monkeys, howlers are named for their loud, barking roar that can be heard for miles. If you want to spot a howler, be sure to scan the treetops; their diet consists mainly of canopy leaves, and they rarely leave the protection of the trees. Other cloud-forest mammals include the white-faced capuchin monkey, white-nosed coatis, porcupines, red brocket deer, and Alston's singing mouse.

RESPLENDENT QUETZAL

Perhaps the most famed resident of Costa Rica's cloud forests is the illustrious resplendent quetzal. Every year, bird-watchers come to Costa Rica hoping to spot the green, red, and turquoise plumage of this elusive trogon. Considered a sacred creature by the Maya and the namesake of Guatemala's currency, the quetzal spends much of its time perched in its favorite tree, the aguacatillo.

Collared trogon

Glass frogs

Howler monkey

Resplendent quetzal

TROPICAL DRY FOREST

The most endangered biome in the world, these seasonal forests swing between two climate extremes—from drenching wet to bone-dry. To survive, plants undergo a drastic physical transformation: forests burst into life during the rainy months, and are brown, leafless, and seemingly dead during the dry season.

DID YOU KNOW?

On a hike through the tropical dry forest surrounding Rincón de la Vieja Lodge, you can watch howler and white-faced monkey troops cavorting through the trees, swimming underneath the waterfalls, and soaking in the hot springs.

For about half the year, northwestern Costa Rica is almost as wet as the rest of the country. The weather blows in from the Pacific, and you can expect rain most days. During the dry season, from January to April, weather patterns change, winds shift, and the land becomes parched.

Tall deciduous hardwoods are the giants in this ecology zone, with spindly branches creating a seasonal canopy as high as 100 feet. A thorny and rambling understory of smaller trees and bushes thrives thanks to the plentiful light permitted once the canopy leaves fall to the forest floor. The challenges of the dry months have forced

plants to specialize. The hardwoods are solitary and diffuse, their seeds spread far and wide by animals and insects. Some even flower progressively through the dry season, depending on the plant species and the particular bees and birds that have evolved to pollinate them.

If you can take the heat, the dry season is perfect for bird- and animal-watching since the lack of foliage makes wildlife spotting easy. (Water, sunscreen, and wide-brimmed hats are musts.) Keep your eyes peeled for monkeys, parrots, lizards, coyotes, rabbits, snakes, and perhaps even jaguars.

There was once one great, uninterrupted swath of dry forest that began in southern Mexico, rolled across Mesoamerica, and ended in northwest Costa Rica. Today, less than 2% of the Central American tropical dry forest remains, the majority of it in Costa Rica. But even here, the forest is fractured into biologically isolated islands, thanks to decades of logging and agriculture. The Guanacaste Conservation Area has managed to corral off large chunks of land for preservation, and private and government efforts are under way to create biological corridors between isolated dry forests so that animals and plants can roam farther and deepen their gene pools, which is critical to their survival.

ADVENTURE HIGHLIGHTS

■ Adrenaline-spiked tours with Hacienda Guachipelín (bordering Rincón de la Vieja National Park) include river tubing, rappelling, ziplines, and a Tarzan swing.

■ Let the knowledgeable folks from the Organization for Tropical Studies take you on a guided bird-watching tour through Palo Verde National Park. Boat rides float you past hundreds of waterfowl.

■ Take the kids on a bird- and monkey-watching journey down the Río Corobicí, in Palo Verde National Park.

TOP DESTINATIONS

Most of Costa Rica's remaining tropical dry forests are located in the northwest of the country, not too far from the Nicaragua border.

GUANACASTE CONSERVATION AREA

Santa Rosa National Park is part of the larger Guanacaste Conservation Area, which is composed of some tropical dry forest and former farmland that's being regenerated to its natural state. The park is intended to serve as a much-needed biological corridor from Santa Rosa up to the cloud forests of the Orosi and Cacao volcanoes, to the east. Park infrastructure is generally lacking, though three biological stations offer some accommodations to student groups and researchers. *(See Chapter 7.)*

PALO VERDE NATIONAL PARK

Farther south, Palo Verde National Park skirts the northeastern side of the Río Tempisque, straddling some of the country's most spectacular wetlands and tropical dry forest. Thanks to these two very different ecology zones, Palo Verde is packed with very diverse bird, plant, and animal species—bird-watchers love this park. The Organization for Tropical Studies has a biological station at Palo Verde and offers tours

White-nosed coati in Palo Verde National Park

Canopy tour at Rincón de la Vieja National Park

and accommodations. Park guards also maintain a ranger station with rustic overnight accommodations. *(See Chapter 8.)*

RINCÓN DE LA VIEJA NATIONAL PARK

More tropical dry forest can be found inside the Rincón de la Vieja National Park, ringing the base of the two volcanoes of this protected area—the dormant Santa María and the active Rincón de la Vieja. The park hosts some 300 bird species as well as cougars, kinkajous, and the shy, elusive jaguar. A handful of lodges inside the park and the proximity to the city of Liberia make Rincón an easy destination to visit. *(See Chapter 7.)*

SANTA ROSA NATIONAL PARK

The largest piece of tropical dry forest under government protection in Central America spreads out over Santa Rosa National Park, about 35 km (22 miles) north of Guanacaste's capital, Liberia. The park, which covers 380 square km (146 square miles), also includes two beaches and coastal mangrove forest. Thanks to trails and equipped campsites, you can venture deep into the park. During the dry season, visibility is excellent and chances are good that you'll spot wildlife. *(See Chapter 7.)*

EXPERIENCING A TROPICAL DRY FOREST

Las Chorreras Waterfalls near Rincón de la Vieja National Park

Many of Costa Rica's roads are rough at best, and tropical forests are often remote. We recommend renting a four-wheel-drive vehicle for getting around.

BIKING

Some parks allow biking, but again, this is certainly something you don't want to do during the rains. Contact the park that you'll be visiting ahead of time for trail and rental information.

BIRD- AND WILDLIFE-WATCHING

Most people come to these areas for bird-watching and wildlife spotting, but it's best done during the dry season, when all the foliage drops from the trees. Bring a good bird or wildlife guide, binoculars, lots of water (we can't stress this enough), and plenty of patience. It's a good idea to find a watering hole and just hunker down and let the animals come to you. If you don't want to explore the forest alone, tours can be arranged through hotels, ranger stations, and private research centers inside the parks. In terms of bird and wildlife guides, we recommend *The Birds of Costa Rica* by Richard Garrigues and Robert Dean and *The Mammals of Costa Rica* by Mark Wainwright. If you'd like to know more about plants, pick up *Tropical Plants of Costa Rica* by Willow Zuchowski.

HIKING

The best way to experience these endangered woods is to strap on your hiking boots, grab a hat and lots of water, and get out and walk. Most of the dry forests are protected lands and found in Guanacaste's national parks. Some have road access, making it possible to drive through the park, but most are accessible only by hiking trails. During the rainy season, roads become mud pits and hiking trails are almost impassable.

FLORA

Among other types of flora, tropical dry forests are filled with deciduous hardwoods, such as mahogany (*Swietenia macrophylla*), black laurel (*Cordia gerascanthus*), ronrón (*Astronium graveolens*), and cocobolo (*Dalbergia retusa*). Much of the wood is highly prized for furniture and houses, so many of these trees are facing extinction outside national parks and protected areas.

CORNIZUELO

The spiky *cornizuelo* (*Acacia collinsii*) is an intriguing resident of the lower levels because of its symbiotic relationship with ants. This small evergreen tree puts out large thorns that serve as a home for a certain ant species. In exchange for food and shelter, the ants provide the tree protection from other leaf-munching insects or vines. Sometimes the ants will even cut down encroaching vegetation on the forest floor, allowing the tree to thrive.

Cornizuelo

FRANGIPANI TREE

The frangipani tree (*Plumeria rubra*) can grow up to 26 feet and has meaty pink, white, or yellow blossoms. The flowers are most fragrant at night to lure sphinx moths. Unfortunately for the moth, the blooms don't produce nectar. The plant simply dupes their pollinators into hopping from bloom to bloom and tree to tree in a fruitless search for food.

Frangipani

GUANACASTE

Perhaps the most striking and easy-to-spot resident of Costa Rica's tropical dry forest is the *Guanacaste* (*Enterolobium cyclocarpum*), an imposing tree with an enormous, spherical canopy that seems straight out of the African savanna. The guanacaste is the northwest province's namesake and Costa Rica's national tree. It is most easily identified standing alone in pastures: Without the competition of the forest, it sends massive branches out low from its trunk, creating an arching crown of foliage close to the ground. The ear-shape seedpods are also a distinct marker; the hard seeds inside are popular with local artisan jewelers.

Guanacaste

GUMBO-LIMBO

Costa Ricans call the gumbo-limbo tree (*Bursera simaruba*) *indio desnudo* (naked Indian) because of its red, peeling bark. This tree is also found in Florida, and the wood has historically been used for making carousel horses in the United States.

Gumbo-limbo

FAUNA

Tropical dry forests are literally crawling with life. Bark scorpions, giant cockroaches, and tarantulas scuttle along the forest floor, and the buzz from wasps and cicadas gives the air an almost electric feel. A careful eye may be able to pick out walking sticks frozen still among the twigs. The jaguar, and one of its favorite prey, the endangered tapir, also stalk these forests.

BLACK-HEADED TROGON

With an open canopy for much of the year, and plentiful ground rodents and reptiles, these forests are great hunting grounds for birds of prey like the roadside hawk and the spectacled owl. The white-throated magpie jay travels in noisy mobs, while the scissor-tailed flycatcher migrates from as far north as the southern United States. The rufous-naped wren builds its nest in the spiky acacia trees. The black-headed trogon, with its bright yellow breast, and the elegant trogon both nest exclusively in Costa Rica's tropical dry forest.

COYOTE

Nearly unique to the dry tropical forest is the coyote, which feeds on rodents, lizards, and an assortment of small mammals, as well as sea turtle eggs (when near the beach) and other improvised meals. Like the Virginia opossum and the white-tailed deer, the coyote is believed to have traveled south from North America through the once-interconnected tropical dry forest of Mesoamerica.

NEOTROPICAL RATTLESNAKE

The venomous neotropical rattlesnake and the exquisite painted wood turtle are among the reptiles that exclusively call this region home. Salvin's spiny pocket mouse, the eastern cottontail rabbit, and both spotted and hooded skunks are unique to Costa Rica's dry forests.

WHITE-FACED CAPUCHIN

Monkeys are common all over Costa Rica, and the dry forests are home to three species: the howler monkeys, with their leathery black faces and deep barking call, are the loudest of the forest's mammals; the white-faced capuchin travel in playful packs; and the endangered spider monkey requires large, undisturbed tracts of forest for a healthy population to survive. This last group is in steep decline—another indicator of the overall health of this ecoregion.

Black-headed trogon

Coyote

Neotropical rattlesnake

White-faced capuchin

WETLANDS AND MANGROVES

Wetlands are any low-lying areas that are perpetually saturated with water. Their complex ecosystems support a variety of living things—both endemic species unique to the area and visitors who travel halfway around the hemisphere to get here. Here, land species have evolved to live much of their lives in water.

One common type of wetland in Costa Rica is a floodplain, created when a river or stream regularly overflows its banks, either because of heavy rains or ocean tides. Thanks to huge deposits of sediment that are left as the floodwaters recede, the ground is extremely fertile and plants thrive, as do the animals that feed here.

Mangroves are a unique type of wetland that cover a scant 1% of the country. They are found at the edges of tidal areas along both coasts, such as ocean inlets, estuaries, and canals where saltwater mixes with fresh. Mangrove forests are made up of a small variety of plants—principally mangrove trees—but attract a variety of animals.

Costa Rica's seven species of mangrove trees are able to survive in this stressful habitat because they have developed the ability to cope with constant flooding, tolerate a lack of oxygen, and thrive in a mix of salt and fresh water thanks to uniquely adapted roots and leaves. The nutrient-rich sediment and mud that build up around these trees and between their prop roots create habitat for plankton, algae, crabs, oysters, and shrimp. These, in turn, attract larger and larger animals that come to feed, giving mangrove forests a remarkable level of biodiversity.

What they lack in number, mangroves make up for in biological impact. These thick coastal forests are protective barriers for inland ecosystems; they dissipate the force of storm winds and sudden surges in tides or floods triggered by coastal storms or tsunamis. Working in the opposite direction, a fully functioning mangrove prevents erosion of the coastline.

Sadly, coastal development is a big threat to mangroves. It is illegal to clear mangrove forests, but enforcement is weak.

ADVENTURE HIGHLIGHTS

■ Witness the spectacle of nesting turtles at Tortuguero National Park. Turtle-watching excursions require a certified guide and take place only between February and November.

■ Anglers can hook mackerel, tarpon, snook, calba, and snapper in the canals and along the coast of Tortuguero and Barra Colorado.

■ Take a kayaking tour through the mangrove estuary of Isla Damas, near Manuel Antonio. You'll see monkeys, crocodiles, and numerous birds.

TOP DESTINATIONS

The Ramsar Convention on Wetlands is an intergovernmental treaty to provide a framework for the conservation of the world's wetlands. There are 12 Ramsar wetlands in Costa Rica: all are impressive, but we've listed only our top three.

CAÑO NEGRO NATIONAL WILDLIFE REFUGE

Ramsar wetland Caño Negro National Wildlife Refuge lies in the remote northern plains close to the border with Nicaragua. Caño Negro has a seasonal lake that can cover as many as 1,975 acres and grow as deep as 10 feet. The lake is actually a pool created by the Frio River that dries up to nearly nothing between February and May. The park also has marshes, semipermanently flooded old-growth forest, and other wetland habitats. *(See Chapter 6.)*

PALO VERDE NATIONAL PARK

Within Palo Verde National Park is perhaps Costa Rica's best-known wetland—a system that includes permanent shallow freshwater lagoons, marshes, mangroves, and woodlands that are seasonally flooded by the Tempisque River. A good portion of this 45,511-acre park is covered by tropical dry forest. In fact, this park has 12 different habitats, creating one of the most diverse collections of life in the country.

Alpha howler monkey

Turtles sunbathing in Tortuguero

At least 55 aquatic plants and 150 tree species have been identified here, and the largest number of aquatic and wading birds in Mesoamerica can be found in Palo Verde wetlands. (A total of 279 bird species has been recorded here.) The Organization for Tropical Studies maintains a research station at the park with limited accommodations but great views of the marshes, as well as extremely knowledgeable guides. *(See Chapter 8.)*

TORTUGUERO NATIONAL PARK

Ninety-nine percent of mangrove forests are found on Costa Rica's Pacific coast. But the best place to see some of the remaining 1% on the Caribbean side is Tortuguero National Park. Like Palo Verde, Tortuguero is home to a wide variety of life—11 distinct habitats in total, including extensive wetlands and mangrove forests. Beach-nesting turtles (*tortugas*) are the main attraction, but the park is included in the Ramsar list of internationally important wetlands. Many species can be spotted along Tortuguero's famous canals. *(See Chapter 11.)*

EXPERIENCING THE WETLANDS AND MANGROVES

Paddling through Tortuguero at dawn; Thornton Cohen, Fodors.com member

Wildlife viewing in general can be very rewarding in these areas because a wide variety of creatures come together and share the habitat.

BIRD-WATCHING

The most populous and diverse of the creatures that live in and depend on wetlands and mangroves are birds, so bring some binoculars and your field guide, and prepare to check off some species. For good photos, take a long lens and tripod, and get an early start; midday sun reflecting off the ubiquitous water can make your photos washed out or create some challenging reflections.

BOATING

The best way to see Costa Rica's remaining mangrove forests is by boat; we recommend using a kayak or canoe. These vessels allow you to slip along canals and protected coastlines in near silence, increasing your chance of creeping up on many of the more impressive creatures that call this habitat home. A guided boat tour is also recommended—a good naturalist or biologist, or even a knowledgeable local, will know where creatures habitually hang out and will be able to distinguish between thick branches and a knotted boa at the top of a shoreside tree.

FISHING

Canals that are not part of protected areas can be ripe for fishing—another, tastier way to get a close-up look at some of the local fauna. Make sure to ask about what's biting, as well as local fishing regulations.

VIEWING PLATFORMS

Hiking can be more difficult in these areas because wetlands are by definition largely underwater. But some areas have elevated platforms that make for great up-close viewing of the interior parts of marshes and shallow lagoons.

FLORA

Wetland and mangrove plants share an ability to live in soggy conditions. However, not all wetland plants are able to survive brackish water in the way coastal mangrove flora can.

BLACK MANGROVE

The black mangrove can grow as tall as 40 feet and has adapted to survive in its habitat by excreting salt through special glands in its leaves. It grows on the banks above the high-tide line and has evolved to breathe through small roots it sends up vertically in case of flooding.

Black mangrove

RED MANGROVE

Costa Rica has seven species of mangrove trees, including red mangrove (*Rhizophora mangle*), black mangrove (*Avicennia germinans*), white mangrove (*Laguncularia racemosa*), and the rarer tea mangrove (*Pelliciera rhizophorae*). Red mangrove is easily identified by its tall arching prop roots that give it a firm foothold against wind and waves. The tidal land is also unstable, so all mangroves need a lot of root just to keep upright. As a result, many have more living matter underwater than aboveground. They also depend on their prop roots for extra nutrients and oxygen; the red mangrove filters salt at its roots.

Red mangrove

THORNY SENSITIVE PLANT

Aquatic grasses and herbs grow along the shallower edges of swamps and marshlands where they can take root underwater and still reach the air above. The curious *dormilona,* or thorny sensitive plant (*Mimosa pigra*), is another invasive wetland shrub and can be identified by the way its fernlike leaves wilt shyly to the touch, only to straighten out a little later.

Thorny sensitive plant

WATER HYACINTH

The succulent floating water hyacinth (*Eichornia crassipes*) is recognizable by its lavender-pink flowers that are sometimes bundled at 8–15 per single stalk. The stems rise from a bed of thick floating green leaves, whereas the plant's feathery roots hang free in the still fresh water. The water hyacinth is prolific and invasive; they've even been known to clog the canals of Tortuguero.

Water hyacinth

FAUNA

Though the diversity of plant life in mangrove swamps and wetlands is small compared with other ecozones, this habitat attracts an extremely wide variety of fauna.

BLACK-BELLIED WHISTLING DUCK

Bird-watchers love the wide-open wetlands and marshes, with flocks of thousands of migrating and resident species. In these tropical floodplains pink-tinged roseate spoonbills will be found stalking the shallow water alongside the majestic great egret and the bizarre and endangered jabiru stork. Keep an eye out for the black-bellied whistling duck, which actually perches and nests in trees. These migrant ducks can also be found in some southern U.S. states.

Black-bellied whistling duck

BLACK-CROWNED NIGHT HERON

Mangroves are critical nesting habitats for a number of birds, including the endangered mangrove hummingbird, the yellow-billed continga, the Amazon kingfisher, and the black-crowned night heron. Interestingly, black-crowned night herons don't distinguish between their own young and those from other nests, so they willingly brood strange chicks.

Black-crowned night heron

CRAB-EATING RACCOON

Bigger creatures are attracted to these mangroves precisely because of the veritable buffet of sea snacks. The crab-eating raccoon will prowl the canopy of the mangrove forests as well as the floor, feeding on crabs and mollusks. The endangered American crocodile and the spectacled caiman can also be found lurking in still waters or sunning themselves on the banks of mangrove habitats.

Crab-eating raccoon

RAINBOW PARROTFISH

Rainbow parrotfish, in addition to many other fish species, spend time as juveniles in mangrove areas, feeding in the relative safety of the roots until they're big enough to venture out into more open water. Parrotfish have a few unusual abilities: they are hermaphroditic and can change sex in response to population density; at night they wrap themselves in a protective mucus cocoon; and they eat algae off the coral and excrete a fine white sand. One parrotfish can create up to 200 pounds of sand per year, which ultimately washes ashore. Think about it the next time you're lying on the beach.

Rainbow parrotfish

SHORELINE

Costa Rica has a whopping 1,290-km-long (799-mile-long) coastline that varies from expansive beaches to tranquil bays, muddy estuaries, and rocky outcroppings. They're backed by mangrove, transitional, and tropical rain and dry forests.

Few visitors who come to the Costa Rican shore think of it as an ecosystem in its own right. But venture beyond the tanned bodies and the accompanying party scene and you'll be rewarded with a panorama of life that rivals that of any rain forest. Each of Costa Rica's coastal environments, as well as the currents and the wind, has its own distinct impact on the ecology of the beach.

By law, all of Costa Rica's beaches are public, but beaches near population centers get strewn with trash quite quickly. It's one of the great ironies of Costa Rica that a country renowned for its environmental achievements litters with such laissez-faire. Limited access tends to make for more scenic beaches. If you're worried about pollution, keep an eye out for

Blue Flag beaches (marked on our maps with blue flags), an ecological rating system that evaluates water quality—both ocean and drinking water—trash cleanup, waste management, security, signposting, and environmental education. Blue Flags are awarded to communities rather than to individual hotels, which feeds a sense of cooperation. Flags are also awarded to inland communities.

Costa Rica's sand beaches come in different shades and textures: pulverized black volcanic rock (the Caribbean's Playa Negra), and on the Pacific, crushed white shells (Playa Conchal) or finely ground white coral and quartz (Playa Carrillo), and gray rock sediment (many stretches along both coasts). These strips of sand may seem devoid of life, but they're actually ecological hotbeds, where mammals, birds, and amphibians live, feed, or reproduce. The hardiest of creatures can be found in the tidal pools that form on rockier beaches; keep an eye out for colorful fish, starfish, and sea urchins, all of which endure pounding waves, powerful tides, broiling sun, and predator attacks from the air, land, or sea.

ADVENTURE HIGHLIGHTS

■ From October 15 to February 15, Playa Grande sees lumbering, huge leatherback turtles come ashore to nest. Sixty days later, the hatchlings will scramble toward the water.

■ Gentle, consistent waves and a couple of good surfing schools make Sámara, on the north Pacific coast, a good choice for first-timers hoping to catch a wave.

■ Snorkeling is phenomenal near Cahuita's coral reef and at Punta Uva on the Caribbean coast. Look for colorful blue parrotfish, angelfish, sponges, and seaweeds.

TOP DESTINATIONS

Costa Rica's beach scenes are wildly diverse, so a little planning can go a long way.

BALLENA MARINE NATIONAL PARK

This unique park is along one of the more remote stretches of coastline, on the southern end of the Central Pacific region, and encompasses several beaches. Parque Nacional Marino Ballena (*ballena* is Spanish for "whale") gets its name from the humpback whales who feed here, and for a peculiar sandbar formation at Playa Uvita that goes straight out toward the ocean before splitting and curving in two directions, much like a whale's tail. *(See Chapter 10.)*

THE CARIBBEAN

This rainier side of the country has an entirely different feel from the Pacific. North of Limón, there are miles of undeveloped, protected beaches where green sea turtles come from July to October to lay eggs. There have also been sightings of the loggerhead, hawksbill, and leatherback turtles. The currents here are strong, so don't plan on swimming.

To the south of Limón, beaches are bordered by dense green vegetation all year long, and the quality of the

Playa Uvita

Black Iguana in Marino Ballena National Park

sand can change dramatically as you wander from cove to cove. Some of the country's healthiest living coral reefs are offshore, so snorkeling is worthwhile. Beaches of note are Cahuita's Playa Negra and Playa Blanca, and Puerto Viejo de Talamanca's Punta Uva. *(See Chapter 11.)*

MANUEL ANTONIO NATIONAL PARK

On the Central Pacific coast, Manuel Antonio National Park shelters some of the country's most gorgeous beaches. A series of half-moon bays with sparkling sands are fronted by transitional forest—a combination of flora and fauna from the tropical dry forests farther north and the tropical rain forests that stretch south. Wildlife is abundant at Manuel Antonio, and the towering jungle at the beach's edge can give the area a wild and paradisiacal feel. *(See Chapter 9.)*

THE NICOYA PENINSULA

A succession of incredible beaches are scattered along this region of the Pacific coast, from Playa Panamá in the north all the way south to Montezuma. Playas Grande and Ostional offer something none of the others can: the turtle *arribada* (mass nesting). *(See Chapter 8.)*

EXPERIENCING THE SHORELINE

Nesting olive ridley turtles at Ostional Wildlife Refuge

Costa Rica's beaches have tons of activities. If you like getting wet, the ocean is bathwater-warm and there are watersports outfitters just about everywhere. There are also plenty of hammocks and cafés.

HORSEBACK RIDING

Horseback riding on the beach is great fun, but you can't do it everywhere. Many of the most popular beaches have outlawed it for health reasons, especially if it's where a lot of people swim.

SURFING

Costa Rica is a world-class surfing destination, and the Pacific coast in particular has enough surf spots to satisfy both pros and novices. You can arrange lessons in most beach towns. Surfing is an activity that involves a lot of floating, so it allows for plenty of wildlife-watching: keep a weather eye for jumping fish, stingrays, dolphins, and squads of brown pelicans.

TURTLE TOURS

Witnessing the nesting ritual of Costa Rica's visiting sea turtles is a truly unforgettable experience. Various organizations oversee the nesting beaches and arrange tours. A licensed guide is required. The onslaught of mother sea turtles is most intense throughout the night, so be ready to go when your guide tells you.

■ TIP → **Take great care at beaches that drop off steeply as you enter the water. This is an indicator not only of large waves that crash straight onto the shore but also of strong currents. Few Costa Rican beaches have lifeguards.**

FLORA

The plants along the coast play an important role in maintaining the dunes and preventing erosion in the face of heavy winds and other forces.

COCONUT PALMS

Coconut palm trees are the most distinctive plants in any tropical setting. No postcard photo of a white-sand beach would be complete without at least one palm tilting precariously over the shore. Palm trees (from the *Arecaceae* family) require a lot of sunlight and, thanks to their strong root system, will often grow at nearly horizontal angles to escape the shade of beachside forests. The coconut palm is also the proud parent of the world's largest seed—the delicious coconut—which can float long distances across the ocean, washing up on a foreign shore and sprouting a new tree from the sand.

MANGROVE

Mangrove swamps are rich, murky forests that thrive in brackish waters up and down Costa Rica's coasts. They grow in what's known as the intertidal zone, the part of the coast that's above sea level at low tide and submerged at high tide. Mangrove trees (*rhizophora*) are just one of the species that live in these coastal swamps—you can recognize them by their stilt roots, the long tendril-like roots that allow the tree to breathe even when it's partially submerged. These forests are vibrant and complex ecosystems in their own right.

MANZANILLO DE PLAYA

Steer clear of the poisonous manchineel, or *manzanillo de playa* (*Hippomane mancinella*), the most toxic tree in Costa Rica. Its fruit and bark secrete a white latex that's highly irritating to the touch and poisonous—even fatal—if ingested. Don't burn it either, because the smoke can also cause allergic reactions. The tree can be identified by its small yellowish apples and bright green leaves. It's found along the north Pacific coast, stretches of the Nicoya Peninsula, the Central Pacific's Manuel Antonio National Park, and on the Osa Peninsula.

SEA GRAPE

Sea grape (*Coccoloba uvifera*) and similar types of shrubby, ground-hugging vegetation grow close to the water, around the edges of the beach. These plants play a part in keeping the beach stable and preventing erosion.

Coconut palms

Mangrove tree

Manzanillo de playa

Sea grape

FAUNA

Beaches are tough environments where few animals actually make their home. But as we all know, you don't have to live on the beach to enjoy it.

BROWN PELICAN

Brown pelicans fly in tight formation, dropping low over the sea and running parallel with the swells in search of shoals of fish. Browns are unique in that they're the only pelican species that plunge from the air to catch their food. After a successful dive, they have to guard against gulls, who will actually try to pluck the freshly caught fish from their pouch.

IGUANAS

A common sight on Costa Rica's sandy shores are iguanas. The green iguana (*Iguana iguana*) and the black spiny-tailed iguana, or black iguana (*Ctenosaura similis*), are often found sunning themselves on rocks or a few feet from the shade (and protection) of trees. Interestingly, the green iguana has been known to lay eggs and share nests with American crocodiles and spectacled caimans.

OLIVE RIDLEY TURTLE

At 75 to 100 pounds, the olive ridley (*Lepidochelys olivacea*) is the smallest of the five marine turtles that nest in Costa Rica. During mass nesting times (arribada), anywhere from tens to hundreds of thousands of females drag themselves ashore, gasping audibly, to lay their eggs. Between dusk and dawn, the prehistoric creatures crawl over the beach, sometimes even over one another, on their way between the ocean and their nests. People who are lucky enough to witness the event never forget it. Costa Rica's shores are also visited by the green turtle, the hawksbill, the loggerhead, and the leatherback turtle.

PAINTED GHOST CRAB

These intriguingly named crabs are called "ghosts" because they move so quickly that they seem to disappear. They're also one of the few creatures that actually live full-time on the beach. Sun beats down, wind is strong, danger lurks everywhere, but there's little to no cover, but painted ghost crabs (*Ocypode gaudichaudii*) survive all this by burrowing deep under the sand where the temperature and humidity are more constant and there's protection from surface threats like the black iguana.

Brown pelican

Iguanas

Olive ridley turtle

Painted ghost crab

Did You Know?

You can spot green iguanas and black iguanas sunning themselves along Costa Rica's coastline.

Chapter 4

SAN JOSÉ

Updated by
Jeffrey Van Fleet

◉ Sights   🍴 Restaurants   🛏 Hotels   🛍 Shopping   🍸 Nightlife

★★★☆☆   ★★★★★   ★★★★★   ★★★★☆   ★★★★★

WELCOME TO SAN JOSÉ

TOP REASONS TO GO

★ **Eating out:** Instead of relying on mostly rice and beans and chicken like the rest of Costa Rica, San José's diverse restaurants offer a welcome change of pace.

★ **Gold and jade museums:** For a sense of indigenous Costa Rica, frequently forgotten during the nation's march to modernity, the country's two best museums are must-sees.

★ **Historic Barrios Amón and Otoya:** These northern neighborhoods abutting and sometimes overlapping downtown have tree-lined streets and century-old houses turned into trendy hotels and restaurants.

★ **Location, location, location:** From the capital's pivotal position, you can be riding river rapids or taking a coffee tour atop a giant volcano in an hour or less.

★ **Shopping:** San José is the best place to stock up on both essentials and souvenirs. Look for leather-and-wood rocking chairs, ceramics, textiles, and, of course, wonderful coffee.

The metropolitan area holds around 2.2 million residents, but the city proper is small, with some 340,000 people living in its 44 square km (17 square miles). Most sights are concentrated in three downtown neighborhoods—La Soledad, La Merced, and El Carmen—named for their anchor churches. Borders are fuzzy: one *barrio* (neighborhood) flows into the next, districts overlap, and the city itself melts into its suburbs with nary a sign to denote where one community ends and another begins.

1 **Downtown.** This area holds San José's historic and commercial districts and many top attractions: the Museo del Jade (Jade Museum), Museo del Oro Precolombino (Pre-Columbian Gold Museum), Mercado Central (Central Market), and Teatro Nacional (National Theater).

2 **West of Downtown.** The mostly residential neighborhoods here are anchored by large Parque Metropolitano La Sabana (La Sabana Park) and the Museo de Arte Costarricense (Museum of Costa Rican Art).

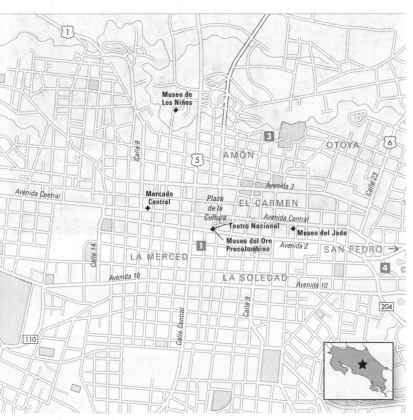

3 North of Downtown.
Historic barrios Amón and Otoya and the Museo de los Niños (Children's Museum) are a few of the attractions to the north.

4 East of Downtown.
Several good restaurants and hotels and the Universidad de Costa Rica (University of Costa Rica) are ensconced in and on the way to the San Pedro suburb.

SOUVENIR SHOPPING IN SAN JOSÉ

Handwoven baskets

San José's shops and markets can be crowded, but they're great fun for the savvy shopper and a great way to explore. The city's bustling downtown is compact enough to make it easy to visit a few markets in a day, or even an afternoon.

Coffee. The most authentic modern-day Costa Rica souvenir, and the most appreciated back home. Load up on whole bean (*grano entero*), or if you prefer ground (*molido*), buy the *puro* (otherwise it might have added sugar). Café Britt is the most famous brand ($5/lb).

Coffee brewers. The original Costa Rican coffeemaker is called a *chorreador*. It's a simple wooden stand that's fitted with cloth socklike filters. Finely ground coffee is dumped in the sock, and hot water is filtered into the mug beneath. Unadorned ones in sleek cherrywood cost around $15. Don't forget extra filters ($1).

Local libations. If you don't have room for a six-pack, be sure to take home the Imperial beer label on a stein or T-shirt (both $5). Or snag a bottle of Costa Rica's signature sugarcane liquor, *guaro*.

Mayan ocarinas. Calling the ocarina two-faced would be an insult, but only because you wouldn't be giving it nearly enough credit. The Mayan resonant vessel flutes ($10–$20) depict more than a half-dozen animal faces when flipped around and were often given as gifts to travelers by the Chorotega indigenous group in northwestern Guanacaste.

Hammocks. Swinging in one of these is the official *pura vida* posture. Structured hammocks with wooden dowels on the ends ($50 and up) are optimal, but dowel-less, cocoonlike hammocks ($35 and up) are infinitely more packable. Get a chair hammock ($25) if you have limited space back home.

Oxcarts. From the Sarchí region, the oxcart has become Costa Rica's most iconic craftsman artifact. Full-size ones can run several hundred dollars, and dealers can arrange to have them shipped. There's also a coffee table–size version ($35) or, better yet, an oxcart napkin holder ($5).

Boruca ceremonial masks. The Boruca people, one of the country's last active indigenous groups, don these masks in their annual end-of-the-year festival, Dansa de los Diablitos (Dance of the Devils). Cheaper imitations abound, but Chietón Morén has the best—and most authentic—selection ($120–$150).

Machetes. Knives and machetes are commonly used in the country's rural jungle areas and happily sold in leather slings to travelers ($15). Also, knives ($5–$10) and other items, like frogs and butterflies made out of colored resin, might not be considered traditional but represent the Rastafarian side of the country.

A coffee vendor bags Costa Rica's top souvenir.

Boruca ceremonial mask

Jewelry. Go for oversize wooden hoop earrings ($10), wire-wrought gold and silver baubles ($10), or plaster-molded earrings adorned with toucans, frogs, and pineapples ($5). Jewelry made from carved-out coco shells is popular, too.

Tropical woods and papers. Sleek mango-wood vases ($15), inlaid rosewood cutting boards ($15), and hand-painted rum-wood mugs ($10) are among the many elegant woodworks here. There are also scratch-and-sniff writing materials that would make Willy Wonka proud, with banana, mango, lemon, and coffee-scented stationery sets ($7).

Folkloric dresses and shirts. While they're often only pulled out on national holidays like Independence Day, a flounced dress ($15 and up) or pinafore ($10) might be just the gift you're looking for. Ranchero-style shirts ($15) and straw hats ($8) are also options.

San José is the center of all that is Costa Rica, and to Ticos in the countryside at least, it glitters every bit as much as New York City. True to developing-country patterns, everything—politics, business, art, cuisine, nightlife, and culture—converges here in the capital. It may not be the center of your trip to Costa Rica—those rain forests and volcanoes have your name written on them. But the city is worth a day or two of exploring, as a way to ease into Costa Rica at the start of a visit or to wrap things up with a well-deserved dose of civilization following your adventures to more remote parts of the country.

San José is—dare we say it—hip these days. Hands down, it has Costa Rica's best dining and nightlife scene, with the east-side neighborhoods of Barrios Escalante and La California leading the way as the new places to be. Amid the noise and traffic—and make no mistake: San José still serves up those annoyances in abundance—shady parks, well-maintained museums, lively plazas, great hotels, cool shops, and fun tours do exist. Further, the city makes a great base for day trips: from downtown it's a mere 30- to 40-minute drive to the tranquil countryside and myriad outdoor activities of the surrounding Central Valley.

You'd never know San José is as old as it is—given the complete absence of colonial architecture—but settlers founded the city in 1737. After independence in 1821, San José cemented its position as the new nation's capital. Revenues from the coffee and banana industries financed the construction of stately homes, theaters, and a trolley system (later abandoned and now visible only in old sepia photographs). As recently as the mid-1900s, San José was no larger than the present-day downtown area; old-timers remember the vast coffee and cane plantations that extended beyond its borders. The city began to mushroom only after World War II, when old buildings were razed to make room for concrete monstrosities. The sprawl eventually connected the capital with nearby cities. Today, the city spells out its new slogan, ¡SJO VIVE! ("San José lives!"), in colorful 8-foot letters in Central Park, near the National Theater, and in front of the post office. Caught up in that new spirit, Costa Ricans visiting the capital like to have their pictures taken in front of those signs. You might enjoy that, too.

San José has attracted people from all over Costa Rica, yet it remains, in many ways, a collection of distinct neighborhoods where residents maintain friendly small-town ways. For you, this might mean the driver you're following will decide to abruptly stop his vehicle to buy a lottery ticket or chat with a friend on the street. Or it might mean you have to navigate a maze of fruit-vendor stands on a crowded sidewalk. But this is part of what keeps San José a big small town.

Planning

When to Go

HIGH SEASON: MID-DECEMBER TO APRIL

San José's 3,800-foot altitude keeps temperatures pleasant and springlike year-round. The capital's status as a business-travel destination means lodging rates rarely vary throughout the year. The dry season literally blows in with a change in wind patterns that makes December and January brisk but sunny. February warms up; by March and April, the heat and dust pick up considerably.

LOW SEASON: MAY TO MID-NOVEMBER

The wet season moves in gradually, with manageable brief afternoon showers from May through July. August becomes wetter. September and October might mean constant rain for days at a time, and navigating a traffic-clogged city in a torrential rush-hour downpour is not fun.

SHOULDER SEASON: MID-NOVEMBER TO MID-DECEMBER

Rains wind down by mid-November and you'll even experience a bit of a nip in the air—it's still the tropics, though—as the city decks itself out for the holidays. The big influx of tourists won't arrive until just before the end of the year, so this is the time to enjoy the capital at its best.

Planning Your Time

SAN JOSÉ IN A DAY

If you have only a day to spend in San José, the must-see stops are the Teatro Nacional (National Theater) and the Museo del Oro Precolombino (Pre-Columbian Gold Museum). It's easy to accomplish this because they sit on the same block.

With more time, take in the Museo del Jade (Jade Museum) and Museo Nacional (National Museum). The Museo de los Niños (Children's Museum) is a kid pleaser. It's in a dicey part of the barrio El Carmen, more north of downtown than actually in downtown; take a taxi.

DAY TRIPS FROM THE CAPITAL

The capital sits smack-dab in the middle of the country in the fertile Central Valley. Although a day trip to either coast would be grueling—despite Costa Rica's small size, it takes longer than you think to get from place to place—you can easily pop out to the Central Valley's major sights and be back in the city in time for dinner. A couple of these attractions provide pickup service in San José, some for a nominal additional cost. Alternatively,

Destination	From San José (By Car)
Basílica de Nuestra Señora de los Ángeles	30 mins southeast
Café Britt	30 mins north
Carara National Park	2 hrs southwest
Doka Coffee Estate	1 hr west
Guayabo National Monument	2 hrs southeast, 4WD necessary
Irazú Volcano	1 hr east
Jardín Botánico Lankester	45 mins southeast
La Paz Waterfall Gardens	2 hrs north
Orosi Valley	1 hr southeast
Poás Volcano	1 hr northwest
Rainforest Adventures	1 hr north
River Rafting	2–2½ hrs southeast or north
Sarchí	1 hr northwest
Tortuga Island	3 hrs west
Zoo Ave	45 mins west

tour operators include many of these attractions on their itineraries.

BYPASS SAN JOSÉ?

San José isn't necessarily the Costa Rica you came to see. Those beaches and rain forests beckon, after all. If that is, indeed, the case, you can avoid the city altogether.

The international airport actually lies just outside the city of Alajuela, about 30 minutes northwest of the capital. Look for lodgings in Alajuela, San Antonio de Belén, Escazú, or Santa Ana—all within striking distance of the airport. Or head west. *For information about lodgings near Aeropuerto Internacional Juan Santamaría, see Chapter 5.*

Few international flights arrive in the morning, but they do exist, especially via

Miami. Get here early and you can head out of town immediately.

If your vacation takes you only to northwest Costa Rica (including the North Pacific beaches), don't fly into San José at all. Use Aeropuerto Internacional Guanacaste outside the northwestern hub city of Liberia. Search for airport code *LIR* instead of *SJO*.

Getting Here and Around

AIR

Aeropuerto Internacional Juan Santamaría, 16 km (10 miles) northwest of downtown, receives international flights and those of domestic airlines SANSA, Skyway, and Costa Rica Green Airways.

BUS

San José has no central bus terminal. The city's public bus stations are all in sketchy neighborhoods. Always take a taxi to and from them. Bag-snatching is common inside the so-called Coca-Cola terminal, a onetime Coke bottling plant converted into a bus station. Watch your things carefully. Even better: use air-conditioned minivan shuttles operated by Interbus instead of public buses to travel between the capital and key tourist destinations.

City buses are cheap (¢100–¢150) and easy to use. For Paseo Colón and La Sabana, take buses marked "Sabana–Cementerio" from stops at Avenida 2 between Calles 5 and 7 or Avenida 3 next to the post office. For Los Yoses and San Pedro, take the various "San Pedro" buses from Avenida Central between Calles 9 and 11.

BUS TERMINALS Gran Terminal del Caribe. ✉ *C. Ctl., Avda. 13, Barrio Tournón* ☎ *2222–0610.* **Terminal Coca-Cola.** ✉ *Avda. 1, C. 16, Barrio La Merced.* **Terminal Empresarios Unidos.** ✉ *C. 16, Avda. 12, Barrio La Merced* ☎ *2221–6600* ⊕ *www. eupsacr.com.* **Terminal MEPE.** ✉ *C. 12, Avda. 9, Barrio La Merced* ☎ *2257–8129* ⊕ *www.mepecr.com.* **Terminal 7-10.** ✉ *C.*

10, Avda. 7, across from former Cine Líbano, Barrio La Merced ☎ *2519–9743* ⊕ *www.terminal7-10.com.* **Terminal Tracopa.** ⊠ *C. 5, Avda. 20, Barrio El Pacífico* ☎ *2221–4214* ⊕ *www.tracopacr.com.*

SHUTTLE COMPANIES Interbus. ☎ *4100–0888* ⊕ *www.facebook.com/interbus/.*

CAR

Paved roads fan out from Paseo Colón west to Escazú and northwest to the airport, Alajuela, and Heredia. For the North Pacific coast, Guanacaste, and on to Nicaragua, take the Pan-American Highway north (CA1). The Carretera a Caldera (Highway 27) takes you to Escazú, Santa Ana, and beyond to the Central Pacific coast. Calle 3 runs north into the highway to Guápiles, Limón, and the Atlantic coast through Braulio Carrillo National Park, with a turnoff to Sarapiquí. Follow Avenida Central or 2 east through San Pedro to enter the Pan-American Highway south (CA2), which has a turnoff for Cartago, Volcán Irazú, and Turrialba before it heads toward the South Pacific coast and Panama.

Avoid driving in the city if you can help it. Streets are narrow, rush hour (7 to 9 am and 5 to 7 pm) traffic is horrible, and drivers can be reckless. What's more, San José and neighboring San Pedro enforce rigid weekday driving restrictions (6 am to 7 pm) for all private vehicles, including your rental car. The last digit of your license plate determines your no-driving day: Monday (1 and 2), Tuesday (3 and 4), Wednesday (5 and 6), Thursday (7 and 8), and Friday (9 and 0).

Street parking is difficult to find and requires payment by a locally available app. Park your vehicle instead in a guarded lot and plan to pay $2 per hour. Leave nothing of value inside the car.

Driving is forbidden on 48 blocks in the center city—sections of Avenidas Central and 4, and Calles 2, 3, 8, 9, and 17—which have been turned into pleasant pedestrian-only thoroughfares. More

of these *bulevares* are on the drawing board. Thank China and the European Union for much of the funding.

TAXI

You can hail cabs on the street or call for one. Licensed cabs are red with a gold triangle on the front doors. A 3-km (2-mile) ride costs around $3; tipping isn't customary. By law cabbies must use *marías* (meters) within the metropolitan area; the meter starts at about $1.15. Any taxi can take you to the airport. Taxi Aeropuerto—whose vehicles are orange—is the only authorized taxi service from the airport into San José. Expect to pay $25 to $40 depending on your destination in the city. Cab drivers hate it if you slam the door; close the door gently.

The ride service Uber operates in San José and surrounding suburbs, albeit without proper government permits. Until Uber and the authorities work out their differences, you use the service at some risk.

TAXIS Alfaro. ☎ *2221–8466.* **Coopetaxi.** ☎ *2235–9966.* **San Jorge.** ☎ *2221–3434.* **Taxi Aeropuerto.** ☎ *2221–6865* ⊕ *www.taxiaeropuerto.com.*

Health and Safety

San José is safer than other Latin American capitals. Violent crime is rare; the greatest threat you're likely to face is petty theft. Standard big-city precautions apply.

Use only licensed red taxis with yellow triangles on the front doors. The license plate of an official taxi begins with TSJ (Taxi San José).

Park in guarded, well-lighted lots ($2 an hour). If you must park on the street, make sure informal *guachimen* (watchmen) are present. Usually this is someone with a big stick who will expect payment of about $2 per hour. Never leave anything valuable in your parked vehicle.

MEDICAL ASSISTANCE Clínica Bíblica.
⊠ *Avda. 14, Cs. Ctl.–1, Barrio El Pacífico*
☎ *2522–1000* ⊕ *www.clinicabiblica.com.*
Hospital La Católica. ⊠ *C. Esquivel Bonilla, Guadalupe* ☎ *2246–3000* ⊕ *www.hospitallacatolica.com.*

Money Matters

San José state banks—Banco Nacional, Banco de Costa Rica, Bancrédito, Banco Popular—come complete with horrendous lines. The private BAC Credomatic and Scotiabank are better bets. Bypass that process entirely and get cash with your ATM card instead. Cash machines inside a bank, during the day while a guard keeps watch, are your safest bet. For security reasons, many ATMs shut down overnight, frequently from 10 pm to 6 am.

BANKS/ATMS BAC Credomatic. ⊠ *Avda. 2, Cs. Ctl.–1, Barrio El Carmen* ☎ *2295–9797* ⊕ *www.baccredomatic.com.* **Banco Nacional.** ⊠ *Avda. 1, Cs. 2–4, Barrio La Merced* ☎ *2212–2000* ⊕ *www.bncr.fi.cr.* **Scotiabank.** ⊠ *C. 5, Avdas. Ctl.–2, behind Teatro Nacional, Barrio La Soledad* ☎ *2521–5680* ⊕ *www.scotiabankcr.com.*

Sights

In San José some streets have names, but no one seems to know or use them. Streets in the center of the capital are laid out in a grid, with *avenidas* (avenues) running east and west, and *calles* (streets) north and south. Odd-number avenues increase in number north of Avenida Central; even-number avenues to the south. Streets east of Calle Central have odd numbers; those to the west are even. Locals rarely use the numbers, however.

Costa Ricans rely instead on a charming and exasperating system of designating addresses by the distance from landmarks, as in "100 meters north and 50 meters west of the school." Another quirk: "100 meters" always refers to one city block, regardless of how long it actually is. Likewise, "200 meters" is two blocks, and so on.

Historically, the reference point was the church, but these days it might be a bar, a Taco Bell, or even a quirky landmark: the eastern suburb of San Pedro uses the *higuerón*, a prominent fig tree. The city has embarked on an ambitious project to name all its streets once and for all. Even after it's completed, it's improbable that anybody will know or use the names. Your best bet is to follow the time-honored practice of *ir y preguntar* (keep walking and keep asking).

Tours

★ Art City Tour
SPECIAL-INTEREST TOURS | The city sponsors a monthly evening showcase of its cultural venues from February through November. (The date varies each month.) Several museums and galleries around town participate. You won't be able to hit them all in the 4:30–8 pm timeframe, but grab one of the free shuttles and check out a few of them. ⊠ *San José* ⊕ *www.gamcultural.com.*

Barrio Bird Walking Tours
GUIDED TOURS | Despite the name, the specialty of this company is not birding but rather two-hour walking tours of the city, with a focus on sights, art, and food. Maximum group size is eight. ☎ *6280–6169* ⊕ *www.toursanjosecostarica.com* ▭ *From $32.*

Carpe Chepe
WALKING TOURS | Among a variety of city tours, these enthusiastic folks operate a popular Friday- and Saturday-evening Pub Crawl excursion ($30) and a Central Market tour ($48) weekday afternoons. Local hotel pickup and dropoff can be arranged for an added fee. ☎ *8347–6198* ⊕ *www.carpechepe.com* ▭ *From $30.*

San José Free Walking Tour

WALKING TOURS | As the name promises, the 2½-hour walk is free and covers downtown sights. The 9 am walk departs from in front of the Aurola Holiday Inn on the north side of Parque Morazán, but advance reservations are required. The cheery guides do a good job. They rely on tips: be generous. ☎ *8721–9443* ⊕ *sanjosewalking.com.*

★ San José Urban Adventures

GUIDED TOURS | Partake in a selection of fun half-day or evening walking tours with these knowledgeable folks. Bites & Sites and San José by Night are especially popular. ☎ *4000–5730, 888/927–2128 in North America* ⊕ *www.sanjoseurbanadventures.com* ✉ *From $38.*

VIP City Bus

GUIDED TOURS | You'll see the city between downtown and La Sabana Park from the vantage point of a double-decker bus on VIP's four-hour tours that include snacks and commentary from bilingual guides. Morning tours include lunch; afternoon, dinner; and evening, dinner and drinks. ☎ *2282–0240* ⊕ *www.vipcitybus.com* ✉ *From $75.*

Restaurants

Costa Rica's capital beckons with the country's most varied and cosmopolitan restaurant scene. Italian, Spanish, Asian, French, Middle Eastern, Peruvian— they're all here, along with upscale Costa Rican cuisine.

Wherever you eat in San José, be it a small *soda* (mom-and-pop eatery) or a sophisticated restaurant, dress is casual. Meals tend to be taken earlier than in other Latin American countries; few restaurants serve past 9 or 10 pm. Local cafés usually open for breakfast at 7 and remain open until 7 or 8 in the evening. Restaurants serving international cuisine are usually open from 11 am to 9 pm. Some downtown eateries that serve mainly San José office workers limit evening hours and close entirely on Sunday. Restaurants that do open on Sunday do a brisk business: it's the traditional family day out (and the maid's day off). Remember: all dining places are no-smoking.

Folks here are serious about *tomando café* (taking a coffee break) in this land that coffee built. But many places they partake in the city feel bland and institutional. We do know of a few gems that serve export-quality coffee to the tune of a trendy café vibe; we list them under Coffee and Quick Bites. The generic term in Spanish for a coffee shop is a *cafetería*, which bears no resemblance to a cafeteria as we know it.

⚠ **Watch your things, no matter where you dine. Even at the best restaurants, thieves occasionally target purses slung over chair arms or placed under chairs.**

Prices in the reviews are the average cost of a main course at dinner or, if dinner is not served, at lunch. Restaurant reviews have been shortened. For full information, visit Fodors.com.

What it Costs in U.S. Dollars			
$	$$	$$$	$$$$
RESTAURANTS			
under $10	$10–$15	$16–$25	over $25

Hotels

San José may be a big city, but it truly shines in its selection of small to medium-size inns. They're all locally owned, and their friendly, attentive staff will make you feel as if you're staying in an oasis in the middle of Costa Rica's noisy, congested capital.

San José has plenty of chains, including Best Western, Holiday Inn, Radisson, Quality Inn, Meliá, and Barceló (the last two are Spanish). But it also has historic houses with traditional architecture that have been converted into small lodgings.

The historic houses are usually without a concierge or pool and are found mainly in Barrios Amón and Otoya, and in the eastern suburb of San Pedro. The city also has a lower tier of lodgings with the simplicity (and prices) beloved of backpackers. Most smaller hotels don't have air-conditioning, but it rarely gets hot enough at this altitude to warrant it. Beware of any place that calls itself a *motel*; it likely rents by the hour.

Many lodgings operate at near-full occupancy in high season (December–April), but the capital's status as a business-travel destination means lodging rates remain constant year-round. Reconfirm all reservations 24 hours in advance. If you're flying out early in the morning and prefer to stay near the airport, consider booking a hotel near Alajuela or San Antonio de Belén in the Central Valley. *(See Chapter 5.)*

Hotel prices are the lowest cost of a standard double room in high season. Hotel reviews have been shortened. For full information, visit Fodors.com.

What it Costs in U.S. Dollars			
$	$$	$$$	$$$$
HOTELS			
under $75	$75–$150	$151–$250	over $250

Nightlife

No one can accuse San José of having too few watering holes; finding one welcoming to visitors is a bit more of a challenge. Downtown, hotels and the couple of places we recommend are good bets for a quiet drink. The rest of the center city can get boozy and brawly at night. Be careful. Barrios Amón and Otoya,

north of downtown, have little in the way of nightlife; even hotel bars are rare.

East of downtown, Barrios Escalante and La California house the places to see and be seen these days. Some of the city's trendiest nightspots have sprung up here in these two neighborhoods that connect central San José with the eastern suburb of San Pedro. The young and the restless hang out in the student-oriented places around the University of Costa Rica in San Pedro. Most rock loudly each night. Finding the few quiet university bars and cafés where you can carry on a real conversation takes some hunting.

Other nightlife has migrated to the Central Valley suburbs of Escazú and Heredia. *(See Chapter 5.)* Both are about 20- to 30-minute taxi rides southwest and north, respectively, from downtown San José.

Take taxis to and from when you're out at night; it's always the safest option after dark. Most places will be happy to call you a cab—or, if there's a guard, they can hail you one—when it's time to call it a night. Remember that all venues are no-smoking.

Performing Arts

The best source for theater, dance, film, and arts information is the "Viva" entertainment section of the Spanish-language daily *La Nación.* The paper also publishes the "Tiempo Libre" section each Friday, highlighting what's going on over the weekend. *GAM Cultural,* a free monthly flyer found in many upscale hotels and restaurants, publishes features about what's going on around town. Listings in both publications are in Spanish but are easy to decipher. The website of the English-language *The Tico Times* (⊕ www.ticotimes.net) lists many events of interest to visitors and the expat community.

Unfortunately, arts offerings in the city are nearly nonexistent during the high-season weeks from mid-December through early February. That's holiday and school vacation time.

Dubbing of movies is rare; films are screened in their original language, usually English, and subtitled in Spanish. Children's movies, however, *are* dubbed (*doblada*), although a multiplex cinema may offer some *hablada en inglés,* or screenings in English. Plan to pay $6 for a ticket. Don't expect anything too avant-garde in most theaters; month-old Hollywood releases are the norm. Following trends seen elsewhere, theaters have fled downtown for the suburban malls.

More than a dozen theater groups (many of which perform slapstick comedies) hold forth in smaller theaters around town. If your Spanish is up to it, call for a reservation. The curtain rises at 8 pm, Friday through Sunday, with some companies staging performances on Thursday night, too. If your Spanish isn't quite theater-ready, there are plenty of dance and music performances.

Shopping

Although it might seem more "authentic" to buy your souvenirs at their source, you can find everything in the city—a real bonus if you're pressed for time. If the capital has any real tourist shopping district, it's found loosely in the cluster of streets around Parque Morazán, just north of downtown, an area bounded roughly by Avenidas 1 and 7 and Calles 5 and 9. Stroll and search, because many other businesses congregate in the area as well.

The northeastern suburb of Moravia has a cluster of high-quality crafts and artisan shops—for good reason very popular with tour groups—in the three blocks heading north from the Colegio María Inmaculada high school. The street is two blocks behind the city's church.

Prices in shops are fixed and fair. You might be able to bargain at the Mercado Municipal de Artesanías, but bargaining isn't the sport it is in other countries. Haggling, even if not ill-intended, will come off as rude. Your best bet for getting a deal is to simply suggest you'll come back later and walk away. If the vendors really want to lower the price, they will.

Visitor Information

No official tourist office holds court downtown. The ubiquitous "Tourist Information" signs you see around town are really private travel agencies looking to sell you tours rather than provide unbiased information.

Downtown

It's a trend seen the world over: businesses and residents flee city centers for the space, blissful quiet, and lower-priced real estate of the 'burbs. Although Costa Rica's capital is experiencing this phenomenon, downtown still remains the city's historic and vibrant (if noisy and congested) heart. Government offices have largely stayed put here, as have most attractions. It's impossible to sightsee without finding yourself downtown.

Boundaries are fuzzy. For example, the subneighborhoods of El Carmen, La Merced, and La Soledad are anchored in downtown but sprawl outward from the center city. And, in an effort to seem trendier, several establishments in downtown's northern fringes prefer to say that they're in the more fashionable barrios of Amón or Otoya.

The city has only three must-see sights—the Teatro Nacional, the Museo del Oro Precolombino (Pre-Columbian Gold Museum), and the Museo del Jade (Jade Museum)—and they are simply fabulous. All sit within a three-block walk of each

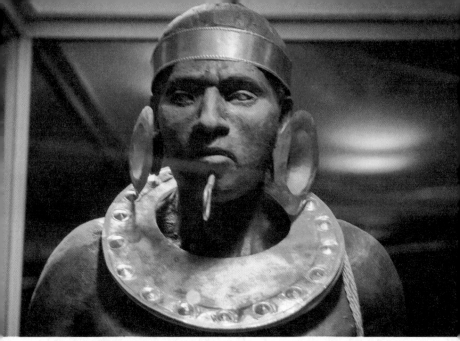

The Museo del Oro Precolombino has the largest collection of pre-Columbian gold jewelry in Central America.

other and could fill a day if that's all the time you have in the capital.

Sights

Catedral Metropolitana (*Metropolitan Cathedral*)

CHURCH | Built in 1871 and completely refurbished in the late 1990s to repair earthquake damage, the neoclassical cathedral, topped by a corrugated tin dome, isn't terribly interesting outside. But inside are patterned floor tiles, stained-glass windows depicting various saints and apostles, and framed polychrome bas-reliefs illustrating the Stations of the Cross. A magnificent 1891 Belgian pipe organ fills the church with music.

The interior of the small Capilla del Santísimo (Chapel of the Host) on the cathedral's north side evokes ornate old Catholicism, much more so than the main sanctuary itself. A marble statue of Pope John Paul II stands guard over the garden on the building's north side.

Masses are held throughout the day on Sunday starting at 7 am, with one in English each Saturday at 4 pm. Although not part of the cathedral complex, a small statue of Holocaust victim Anne Frank graces the pedestrian mall on the building's south side. It was donated by the Embassy of the Netherlands. ⊠ *C. Ctl., Avdas. 2–4, San José* ☎ *2221–3820.*

Centro Nacional de la Cultura (*National Cultural Center*)

FACTORY | Rather than tear it down, the Ministry of Culture converted the sloped-surface, double-block 1853 Fábrica Nacional de Licores (National Liquor Factory) into a 150,000-square-foot cultural center, with government offices, two theaters, and a museum. The Teatro FANAL and Teatro 1887 are two of the capital's foremost performing-arts venues. Both spaces were used for storage and testing in the original factory complex. ⊠ *C. 13, Avdas. 3–5, San José* ☎ *2257–5524* ⊕ *www.mcj.go.cr* ✉ *Tours free.*

Correos de Costa Rica
(Central Post Office)

GOVERNMENT BUILDING | The handsome carved exterior of the post office, dating from 1917, is hard to miss among the bland buildings surrounding it. The lobby is not as interesting as the exterior, but it and the small pedestrian plaza in front are a perpetual hive of activity. ⊠ *C. 2, Avdas. 1–3, San José* ☎ *2202–2900* ⊕ *correos.go.cr* ⊗ *Closed Sun.*

Estatua de John Lennon
(Statue of John Lennon)

PLAZA/SQUARE | A whimsical statue of John Lennon sits on a small, slightly out-of-the-way plaza across from La Soledad church. Sculptor José Ramón Villa's work marks the spot where, in 1966, Costa Ricans smashed Beatles records in protest of Lennon's statement that the iconic pop group was "more popular than Jesus." The official name of the statue is *Imagine All the People Living Life in Peace*, evoking the lyrics of Lennon's song "Imagine." After more than a half century, bygones are apparently bygones: residents and tourists alike enjoy having their photos taken sitting with the casually seated figure. ⊠ *C. 9, Avda. 4, Barrio La Soledad.*

Mercado Central *(Central Market)*

MARKET | This one-block-square melting pot is a warren of dark, narrow passages flanked by stalls packed with spices (some purported to have medicinal value), fish, fruit, flowers, pets, and wood and leather crafts. The 1880 structure is a kinder, gentler introduction to a Central American market; there are no pigs or chickens or their accompanying smells to be found here. A few stands selling tourist souvenirs congregate near the entrances, but this is primarily a place where the average Costa Rican comes to shop. There are dozens of cheap restaurants and snack stalls, including the country's first ice-cream vendor. Be warned: the concentration of shoppers makes this a hot spot for pickpockets, purse snatchers, and backpack slitters. Enter and exit at the southeast corner of the building (Avenida Central at Calle 6). The green-and-white *salida* signs direct you to other exits, but they spill onto slightly less-safe streets. Use the image of the Sacred Heart of Jesus, the market's patron and protector, near the center of the building, as your guide; it faces that safer corner by which you should exit. (We doubt it was planned that way.) ⊠ *Bordered by Avdas. Ctl.–1 and Cs. 6–8, San José* ⊗ *Closed Sun.*

Museo de Arte y Diseño Contemporáneo
(Museum of Contemporary Art and Design)

ART MUSEUM | This wonderfully minimalist space is perfect as the country's premier modern-art venue. The MADC, as it's known around town, hosts changing exhibits by artists and designers from all over Latin America. While the museum holds a permanent collection, space constraints mean that even that must rotate. You will probably not recognize the artists here, but names such as Miguel Hernández and Florencia Urbina tower over the field of contemporary art in Costa Rica. You can arrange for a guided visit with a couple of days' notice. The museum occupies part of a government-office complex in the Centro Nacional de la Cultura (CENAC). ⊠ *Centro Nacional de la Cultura, C. 15, Avdas. 3–5, San José* ☎ *2257–9370* ⊕ *www.madc.cr* ⊠ *$4* ⊗ *Closed Sun. and Mon.*

Need a Break?

A slew of unnamed *sodas*—that's the Costa Rican term for a mom-and-pop eatery—populate the heart of the Mercado Central. Grab a quick bite while you explore. It's all very informal.

4

San José DOWNTOWN

Downtown San José

TO AIRPORT

Avenida 13
Avenida 11
MÉXICO
Avenida 3
Avenida 5
Calle 24
Calle 22
Calle 20
COCA-COLA
Avda. 9
Calle 14
Calle 12
Calle 10
Calle 8
Calle 6
LA MERCED
Avenida 1
Avenida Central
Avenida 7
Avenida 5
Avenida 3
Parque México
Río Torres
TOURNÓN
AMÓN
Calle Central Alfredo Volio
Avenida 11
Avenida 9
EL CARMEN
Morazán Park
Plaza de la Cultura
Calle 4
Paseo Colón
Parque de la Merced
Avenida 2
Avenida 4
Avenida 6
Central Park
SANTA LUCÍA
Avenida 4
Avenida 6
Avenida 8
Avenida 10
Calle 20
Calle 16
Calle 14
Calle 2
Calle Central
LA SOLEDAD
Avenida 12
BOLÍVAR
A. Pochet e Odio
Avda. 20
Calle 18
Calle 16
DOLOROSA
Avenida 14
Avenida 16
Avenida 18
Avenida 20
Calle 3
Calle 5
Calle 7
PACIFICO
Avda. 22

0 ____ 300 yards
0 ____ 300 m

Sights ▼

1 Catedral Metropolitana **D4**
2 Centro Nacional de la Cultura **F3**
3 Correos de Costa Rica **D4**
4 Estatua de John Lennon **E5**
5 Mercado Central **C4**
6 Museo de Arte y Diseño Contemporáneo ... **G3**
7 Museo del Jade **F4**
8 Museo del Oro Precolombino **E4**
9 Museo Nacional **G4**
10 Parque Central **D4**
11 Parque España **F3**
12 Parque Nacional **G4**
13 Plaza de la Democracia **F4**
14 Teatro Nacional **E4**

Restaurants ▼

1 Alma de Café **E4**
2 La Criollita **F3**
3 Nuestra Tierra **F5**
4 Shakti **F6**
5 Tin Jo **F5**

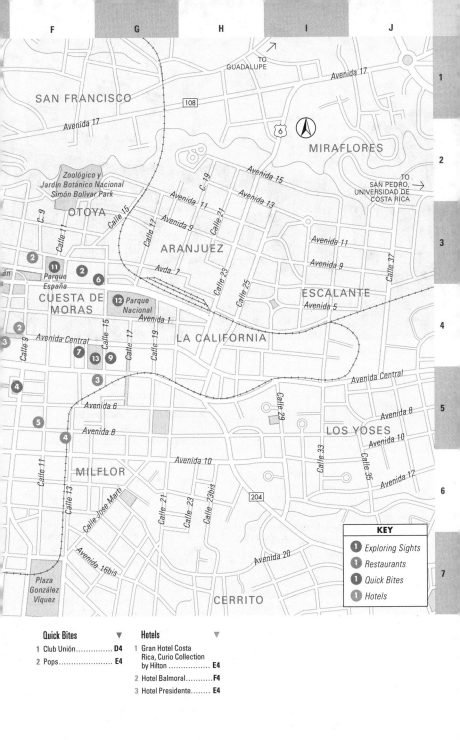

F G H I J

1

TO
GUADALUPE

Avenida 17

SAN FRANCISCO

108

Avenida 17

MIRAFLORES

2

Zoológico y
Jardín Botánico Nacional
Simón Bolívar Park

Avenida 15

TO
SAN PEDRO,
UNIVERSIDAD DE
COSTA RICA

C.-9

OTOYA

Calle 15

C.-19

Avenida 11

Avenida 13

Calle 1

Avenida 9

Calle 17

Avenida 11

Calle 21

ARANJUEZ

Avenida 11

3

Parque
España

Calle 23

Calle 25

Avenida 9

Calle 37

Avda. 7

CUESTA DE
MORAS

Parque
Nacional

Avenida 1

ESCALANTE

Avenida 5

4

Calle 9

Avenida Central

Calle 15

Calle 17

Calle 19

LA CALIFORNIA

Avenida Central

Avenida 6

Calle 29

5

Avenida 8

LOS YOSES

Avenida 8

Calle 33

Avenida 10

Calle 35

Avenida 10

MILFLOR

Avenida 12

Calle 11

Calle 13

Avenida 10

6

Calle José Martí

Calle 21

Calle 23

Calle 23bis

204

Avenida 16bis

Avenida 20

7

Plaza
González
Víquez

CERRITO

KEY

1 Exploring Sights

1 Restaurants

1 Quick Bites

1 Hotels

Quick Bites ▼
1 Club Unión **D4**
2 Pops **E4**

Hotels ▼
1 Gran Hotel Costa
  Rica, Curio Collection
  by Hilton **E4**
2 Hotel Balmoral **F4**
3 Hotel Presidente **E4**

San José's ornate Correos de Costa Rica building houses a stamp museum on the second floor.

★ **Museo del Jade** (*Jade Museum*)
HISTORY MUSEUM | San José's starkly modern Jade Museum displays the world's largest collection of the green gemstone. The holdings log in at 5,000-plus pieces, and are, in a word, amazing. Nearly all the items on display were produced in pre-Columbian times, and most of the jade (pronounced *HAH-day* in Spanish) dates from 300 BC to AD 700. A series of drawings explains how this extremely hard stone was cut using string saws with quartz-and-sand abrasive. Jade was sometimes used in jewelry designs, but it was most often carved into oblong pendants. The museum also has other pre-Columbian artifacts, such as polychrome vases and three-legged *metates* (small stone tables for grinding corn), as well as a gallery of modern art. Also included on display is a startling exhibition of ceramic fertility symbols. While the collection is undeniably fabulous, the pieces may begin to look the same after a time. Let your own tastes and interests guide you in how much time you spend here.

✉ *Avda. Ctl., C. 13, San José* ☎ *2521–6610* ⊕ *museodeljade.ins-cr.com* ✆ *$16.*

★ **Museo del Oro Precolombino**
(*Pre-Columbian Gold Museum*)
OTHER MUSEUM | This dazzling modern museum in a three-story underground structure beneath the stark plaza north of the Teatro Nacional contains Central America's largest collection of pre-Columbian gold jewelry—20,000 troy ounces in more than 1,600 individual pieces—all owned by the Banco Central (the country's central bank) and displayed attractively in bilingual exhibits. Many pieces are in the form of frogs and eagles, two animals perceived by the region's early cultures to have great spiritual significance. A spiffy illumination system makes the pieces sparkle. All that glitters here is not gold: most spectacular are the various shaman figurines, which represent the human connection to animal deities. One of the halls houses the Museo Numismática (Coin Museum), a repository of historic coins and bills and other objects used as legal tender

throughout the country's history. Rotating art exhibitions happen on another level. ✉ *C. 5, Avdas. Ctl.–2, San José* ⚓ *Eastern end of Plaza de la Cultura* ☎ *2243–4202* 🌐 *www.museosdelbancocentral.org* 🎫 *$15, includes Museo Numismática.*

Museo Nacional (*National Museum*)
MILITARY SIGHT | In the mango-color Bellavista Fortress, which dates from 1870, the museum gives you a quick and insightful lesson (in English and Spanish) on Costa Rican culture from pre-Columbian times to the present. Cases display pre-Columbian artifacts, period dress, colonial furniture, religious art, and photographs. Some of the country's foremost ethnographers and anthropologists are on the museum's staff. Nearly 1,000 pre-Columbian Costa Rican stone and ceramic objects dating from about AD 1000 are on display here. The artifacts were taken from the country in the late 19th century by businessman Minor Keith during the construction of the Atlantic Railroad and were repatriated from the Brooklyn Museum in 2012. Outside are a veranda and a pleasant, manicured courtyard garden. A former army headquarters, this now-tranquil building saw fierce fighting during a 1931 army mutiny and the 1948 revolution, as the bullet holes pocking its turrets attest. But it was also here that three-time president José Figueres abolished the country's military in 1949. ✉ *Bellavista Fortress, C. 15, Avdas. Ctl.–2, San José* ⚓ *Eastern end of Plaza de la Democracia* ☎ *2211–5700* 🌐 *www.museocostarica. go.cr* 🎫 *$11* 🕐 *Closed Mon.*

Parque Central (*Central Park*)
PLAZA/SQUARE | At the city's nucleus, the tree-shaded Central Park is more plaza than park. A life-size bronze statue of a street sweeper (*El Barrendero*) cleans up some bronze litter; look also for *Armonía* (*Harmony*), a sculpture of three street musicians. In the center of the one-square-block park is a spiderlike gazebo donated by onetime Nicaraguan dictator

Did You Know?

What's an old theater without its resident ghost? Patrons have claimed to see figures moving in the Teatro Nacional's second-floor paintings. Sightings were common during the theater's early days, although none have been reported in years.

Anastasio Somoza. ✉ *Bordered by Avdas. 2–4 and Cs. 2–Ctl., San José.*

Parque España
CITY PARK | This shady little park is a favorite spot for locals and visitors alike. A bronze statue of Costa Rica's Spanish founder, Juan Vázquez de Coronado, overlooks an elevated fountain on its southwest corner; the opposite corner has a lovely tiled guardhouse. A bust of Queen Isabella of Castile stares at the yellow compound to the east of the park, the Centro Nacional de la Cultura. The bright yellow colonial-style building to the east of the modern INS building is the 1912 Casa Amarilla, home of Costa Rica's Foreign Ministry. The massive ceiba tree in front, planted by John F. Kennedy and the presidents of all the Central American nations in 1963, gives you an idea of how quickly things grow in the tropics. A garden around the corner on Calle 13 contains a 6-foot-wide section of the Berlin Wall donated by Germany's Foreign Ministry after reunification. Ask the guard to let you into the garden if you want a closer look. As with all San José parks, safety declines markedly after dark. Be on your way out before 5 pm. ✉ *Bordered by Avdas. 7–3 and Cs. 11–17, San José.*

Parque Nacional (*National Park*)
CITY PARK | A bronze monument commemorating Central America's battles against North American invader William Walker in 1856 forms the centerpiece of the large, leafy park. Five Amazons,

Did You Know?

In addition to the world's
largest collection of
American jade, the Museo
del Jade in San José
has a risqué display of
pre-Columbian ceramic
fertility symbols—indica-
tive of humankind's
eternal preoccupation
with sex.

representing the five nations of the isthmus, attack Walker, who shields his face from the onslaught. Costa Rica maintains the lead and shelters a veiled Nicaragua, the country most devastated by the war. Guatemala, Honduras, and El Salvador might dispute this version of events, but this is how Costa Rica chose to commission the work by French sculptor Louis Carrier Belleuse, a student of Rodin, in 1895. Bas-relief murals on the monument's pedestal depict key battles in the war against the Americans. As with all San José parks, you should avoid the space after dark. ⊠ *Bordered by Avdas. 1–3 and Cs. 15–19, San José.*

Plaza de la Democracia

PLAZA/SQUARE | President Óscar Arias built this terraced space west of the Museo Nacional to mark 100 years of Costa Rican democracy and to receive dignitaries during a 1989 hemispheric summit. The view west toward the dark green Cerros de Escazú is nice in the morning and fabulous at sunset. The Jade Museum lines the plaza's western edge. ⊠ *Bordered by Avdas. Ctl.–2 and Cs. 13–15, San José.*

★ Teatro Nacional

NOTABLE BUILDING | The National Theater is Costa Rica at its most enchanting. Chagrined that touring prima donna Adelina Patti bypassed San José in 1890 for lack of a suitable venue, wealthy coffee merchants raised import taxes and hired Belgian architects to design this building, lavish with cast iron and Italian marble. Soft, illuminated coppers, golds, and whites highlight the theater's exterior nightly from 6 pm to 5 am.

The sumptuous neo-baroque interior is of interest, too. Given the provenance of the building funds, it's not surprising that frescoes on the stairway inside depict coffee and banana production. Note Italian painter Aleardo Villa's famous ceiling mural *Alegoría del Café y Banano* (*Allegory of Coffee and Bananas*), a joyful harvest scene that appeared on Costa

Rica's old 5-colón note. You can see the theater's interior by attending one of the performances that take place several nights a week; intermission gives you a chance to nose around. Stop at the *boletería* (box office), just off the lobby, and see what strikes your fancy. Ticket prices are a fraction of what you'd pay at a similar stateside venue. Don't worry if you left your tuxedo or evening gown back home; as long as you don't show up for a performance wearing shorts, jeans, or a T-shirt, no one will care.

For a fee you can also move beyond the lobby for a guided tour in Spanish and English; offered hourly on the hour from 9 until 4 daily, except at noon. If you're downtown on a Tuesday from March through November, take in one of the Teatro al Mediodía (Theater at Midday) performances that begin at 12:10 pm. It might be a chamber-music recital or a one-act play in Spanish. ⊠ *Plaza de la Cultura, C. 3, Avda. 2, San José* ☎ *2010–1100* ⊕ *www.teatronacional.go.cr* ▱ *$7 tour.*

🍴 Restaurants

Alma de Café

$ | **COSTA RICAN** | Duck into the Teatro Nacional's sumptuous café, off the theater lobby, to sit at a marble table and sip a hazelnut mocha beneath frescoed ceilings. The frescoes are part of an allegory celebrating the 1897 opening of the theater. **Known for:** cake and sandwiches; artistic surroundings; coffee (with option to add ice cream and alcohol). **$** *Average main: $8* ⊠ *Teatro Nacional, C.3, Avda. 2, San José* ☎ *2010–1110* ⊕ *www.teatronacional.go.cr/Cafeteria* ⊗ *Closed Sun. May–Nov.*

La Criollita

$ | **COSTA RICAN** | Kick off your day with a breakfast platter here: the *americano* (U.S.-style) or the *tico* (Costa Rican), with eggs, fried plantains, and *natilla* (sour cream). Snag one of the precious tables in the back garden, an unexpected refuge from noise and traffic, in the morning or late afternoon. **Known for:** bargain prices; coffee and dessert; crowded lunch spot. [$] *Average main: $9* ⊠ *Avda. 7, Cs. 7–9, San José* ☎ *2256–6511* ⊕ *www.face-book.com/restlacriollita* ⊘ *Closed Sun. No dinner Sat.*

Nuestra Tierra

$ | **COSTA RICAN** | The generous home-made meals at this ranch-style restaurant are delicious, and the incredibly friendly waitstaff, who epitomize Costa Rican hospitality and dress in folkloric clothing, prepare your coffee filtered through the traditional cloth chorreador. The place keeps late hours, just in case those late-night *gallo pinto* (Costa Rican–style rice and beans) pangs hit. **Known for:** lots of tourists; generous portions; típico setting. [$] *Average main: $9* ⊠ *Avdas. 2–4, C. 13, San José* ☎ *2258–6500* ⊕ *www. nuestratierra.co.cr.*

Shakti

$$ | **VEGETARIAN** | The baskets of fruit and vegetables at the entrance and the wall of herbal teas, health-food books, and fresh herbs for sale by the register signal that you're in a vegetarian-friendly joint. The bright and airy macrobiotic restaurant serves homemade bread, soy burgers, pita sandwiches (veggie or chicken), fruit shakes, and a hearty *plato del día* that comes with soup, green salad, and a beverage. **Known for:** local ingredients; monster salads; vegetarian oasis. [$] *Average main: $10* ⊠ *Avda. 8, Cs. 11–13, San José* ☎ *2222–4475* ⊘ *Closed Sun. No dinner.*

★ Tin Jo

$$$ | **ASIAN** | The colorful dining rooms of this converted house evoke Japan, India, China, Indonesia, and Thailand. Start with a powerful Singapore sling (brandy and fruit juices) before trying such treats as Thai shrimp and pineapple curry in coconut milk, Chinese mu shu stir-fry with crepes, Indian samosas, and sushi rolls. **Known for:** impeccable service; vegetarian options; one of Costa Rica's best restaurants. [$] *Average main: $19* ⊠ *C.*

11, Avdas. 6–8, San José ☎ *2221–7605* ⊕ *www.tinjo.com.*

 Coffee and Quick Bites

Club Unión

$ | **CAFÉ** | This elevated, glassed-in café lets you survey the ongoing hive of activity on the small, shaded plaza in front of the post office. While Club Unión is a membership organization comprised of the movers and shakers in Costa Rican society, everyone is welcome in its informal café to enjoy coffee and pastries. **Known for:** great view of the world passing by; windows frame view of the post office across the way; sleek, modern structure contrasts with early-1900s architecture on block. [$] *Average main: $6* ⊠ *Between Avdas. 1 and 3, on C. 2, Downtown* ⊹ *Across from post office* ☎ *506/2257–1555* ⊕ *www.clubunion.com* ⊘ *Closed Sun.*

Pops

$ | **COSTA RICAN** | To sample the crème de la crème of locally made ice cream, head to Pops. After a long walk on crowded sidewalks, it may be just what the doctor ordered. **Known for:** good spot for a quick break; a Costa Rica institution; mango ice cream. [$] *Average main: $2* ⊠ *C. 3, Avda. Ctl., San José* ☎ *2222–2336* ⊕ *www. pops.co.cr* ⊟ *No credit cards.*

Hotels

Staying in the downtown area allows you to travel around the city as most Ticos do: on foot. Stroll the parks, museums, and shops, and then retire to one of the many character-filled small or historic hotels.

★ Gran Hotel Costa Rica, Curio Collection by Hilton

$$$ | **HOTEL** | You cannot get more centrally located than this grande dame of San José lodgings, the first choice among travelers who want to be where the action is. **Pros:** central location;

impeccable service; modern amenities. **Cons:** sometimes congested traffic to get here; some rooms look into interior skylight rather than outdoors; modern rooms don't reflect building's history. $ *Rooms from: $158* ☒ *Avda. 2, C. 3, San José* ☎ *2103–9000, 844/442–8746 in North America* ⊕ *www.hilton.com* ⇨ *79 rooms* ⍥ *Free Breakfast.*

Hotel Balmoral

$$ | HOTEL | You'll find all the standard amenities of a medium-price business-class hotel here, but leisure travelers also enjoy using the Balmoral as their San José base. **Pros:** central location; good restaurant; close to downtown sights. **Cons:** some street noise; many rooms do not face the outside; restaurant service can be slow at times. $ *Rooms from: $109* ☒ *C. 7, Avdas. Ctl.–1, San José* ☎ *2222–5022* ⊕ *www.balmoral. co.cr* ⇨ *112 rooms* ⍥ *Free Breakfast.*

Hotel Presidente

$$ | HOTEL | A largely American clientele looking for all the downtown hubbub enjoys the medium-price business-class accommodations here. **Pros:** close to downtown sights; eco-friendly; rooftop patio. **Cons:** some rooms have thin walls; a few dated furnishings in some rooms; some street noise. $ *Rooms from: $140* ☒ *Avda. Ctl., C. 7, San José* ☎ *2010–0000, 800/707–8604 in North America* ⊕ *www.hotel-presidente.com* ⇨ *92 rooms* ⍥ *Free Breakfast.*

 Nightlife

Azotea Calle 7

COCKTAIL LOUNGES | Downtown's most elegant nightspot perches in a garden on the rooftop of the Hotel Presidente and offers terrific views and inventive cocktails. ☒ *Hotel Presidente, Avda. Ctl., C. 7, Barrio La Soledad* ☎ *2010–0000* ⊕ *www. hotel-presidente.com.*

Be Aware

A few gems really do populate the downtown area, but several bars there double as prostitute pickup joints or are just boozy places where patrons go to pick fights. If you're downtown at night, drink at your hotel or one of the places we recommend, and never wander directly south or west of Parque Central on foot.

Club Teatro

CABARET | RuPaul has nothing on the performers at San José's largest LGBTQ+ venue. The drag shows here aren't just any drag shows; they include gymnastics and trapeze, too. The venue is safe, but the neighborhood is dicey. Take a taxi to and from here. ☒ *Avda. 16, C. 2, Barrio El Pacífico* ☎ *2256–1003* ⊕ *www.facebook. com/el.teatro.cr.*

La Avispa

DANCE CLUBS | An LGBTQ+ crowd frequents La Avispa, which has two dance floors with videos and karaoke, as well as a quieter upstairs bar with pool tables. The last Friday of each month is ladies' night. The neighborhood between downtown and the bar is sketchy; take a taxi. ☒ *C. 1, Avda. 8, San José* ☎ *2223–5343* ⊕ *www.laavispa.com.*

🎭 Performing Arts

Centro Nacional de la Cultura

MUSIC | There are frequent dance performances and concerts in the Teatro FANAL and Teatro 1887, both in the Centro Nacional de la Cultura. ☒ *C. 13, Avdas. 3–5, Barrio Otoya* ☎ *2257–5524* ⊕ *www.mcj.go.cr.*

Teatro Nacional (*National Theater*)

CONCERTS | This 1897 neo-baroque theater is the home of the excellent National Symphony Orchestra, which performs on several Friday evenings and Sunday mornings between March and November. The theater also hosts visiting musical groups and dance companies. Tickets are $10–$50—far less than you'd pay for a comparable production back home. ⊠ *Plaza de la Cultura, Barrio La Soledad* ☎ *2010–1100* ⊕ *www.teatronacional.go.cr.*

Teatro Popular Melico Salazar

MUSIC | San José's second-most-popular theater has a full calendar of music and dance shows, as well as a few offbeat productions. There is something on a couple of nights a week; tickets are $5–$25. ⊠ *Avda. 2, Cs. Ctl.–2, Barrio La Merced* ☎ *2295–6000* ⊕ *www.teatromelico.go.cr.*

Shopping

CRAFTS

★ Chietón Morén

CRAFTS | A nonprofit association assembles the works of 220 artisans from Costa Rica's eight original indigenous communities in this attractively arranged setting on the pedestrian mall south of the Museo Nacional. While the place bills itself as "part museum," all works are for sale at prices fair to the creators and fair to you. (The name translates as "fair deal" in Costa Rica's indigenous Boruca language.) You'll find a good selection of ceramics, jewelry, weavings, and paintings here. ⊠ *C. 17, Avdas. 2–4, San José* ☎ *2221–0145* ⊕ *www.chietonmoren.org.*

Mercado Municipal de Artesanías (*Municipal Crafts Market*)

CRAFTS | Several dozen souvenir vendors congregate in this one-square-block building on the south side of a small downtown plaza. It's a real mix here. Some of the sellers do offer bargains on

hammocks, wood carvings, and clothing; others sell trinkets probably made in China. Look carefully. ⊠ *Avda. 6, Cs. 5–7, Downtown* ☎ *7174–5371* ⊕ *www.facebook.com/mercadoartesanias.sj.*

MUSIC

Universal

MUSIC | In addition to selling everything else imaginable, downtown department store Universal stocks a good selection of Latin CDs in its first-floor music department. ⊠ *Avda. Ctl., Cs. Ctl.–1, San José* ☎ *2222–2222* ⊕ *www.tiendauniversal.com.*

SOUVENIRS

La Traviata

SOUVENIRS | The small shop off the lobby of the National Theater has a terrific selection of thespian-themed postcards, tote bags, and glassware. You can access the shop without an admission ticket to a theater production. In addition to being open Monday through Saturday during the day, the shop is also open before evening performances and during intermission. ⊠ *Teatro Nacional, Plaza de la Cultura, San José* ☎ *2010–1100* ⊕ *www.teatronacional.go.cr.*

Mercado Central

SOUVENIRS | This maze of passageways is where the average Costa Rican comes to stock up on day-to-day necessities, but a few stalls of interest to tourists congregate near the southeast entrance. Pickpockets frequent the crowded market; exercise care. ⊠ *Bordered by Avdas. Ctl.–1 and Cs. 6–8, San José.*

Museo del Jade (*Jade Museum*)

SOUVENIRS | The small shop in the Jade Museum sells replicas of many of the pieces in the museum collection. The shop is accessible only if you've paid the $16 museum admission. ⊠ *Avda. Ctl., C. 13, San José* ☎ *2287–6034* ⊕ *museodeljade.grupoins.com.*

Museo del Oro Precolombino

(*Pre-Columbian Gold Museum*)
SOUVENIRS | The shop at the entrance
of the Museo del Oro Precolombino
(Gold Museum) offers a great selection
of pre-Columbian-themed jewelry, art,
exclusively designed T-shirts, coin key
chains, notebooks, and mouse pads.
You can access the shop without paying
the museum admission. ⊠ *C. 5, Avdas.
Ctl.–2, San José* ☎ *2243–4202* ⊕ *www.
museosdelbancocentral.org.*

★ Tienda Eñe

SOUVENIRS | The big red *Ñ* on the window
marks this cute little boutique with goods
all made by Costa Rican artists and
designers. Look for prints, bags, jewelry,
and a big selection of mugs. ⊠ *Avda. 7, C.
11a, Barrio Amón* ☎ *2222–7681* ⊕ *www.
facebook.com/esquina13y7.*

West of Downtown

Paseo Colón, one of San José's major
boulevards, heads due west from downtown and leads to vast La Sabana Park,
the city's largest parcel of green space.
La Sabana anchors the even vaster west
side of the city. A block or two off its
exhaust-ridden avenues are quiet residential streets, and you'll find the U.S.,
Canadian, and British embassies here.

◉ Sights

Museo de Arte Costarricense

ART MUSEUM | Located in La Sabana Park,
which was once Costa Rica's international airport, this—the country's foremost
art museum—was once its terminal and
control tower. A splendid collection of
19th- and 20th-century Costa Rican art,
labeled in Spanish and English, is housed
in 12 exhibition halls. Be sure to visit the
top-floor Salón Dorado to see the stucco,
bronze-plate bas-relief mural depicting
Costa Rican history, created by French
sculptor Louis Feron. Guided tours are
offered Tuesday through Friday from 10

to 3. Wander into the sculpture garden in
back and take in Jorge Jiménez's 22-foot-
tall *Imagen Cósmica,* which depicts
pre-Columbian traditions. ⊠ *Parque La
Sabana, C. 42, Paseo Colón* ☎ *4060–
2300* ⊕ *www.facebook.com/mac.mcj.cr*
🖙 *Free* ⊗ *Closed Mon.*

Parque La Sabana

CITY PARK | FAMILY | Though it isn't cen-
trally located, the 180-acre La Sabana
("the savannah") comes the closest of
San José's green spaces to achieving
the same function and spirit as New
York's Central Park. La Sabana was once
San José's airport, and the whitewashed
Museo de Arte Costarricense, just south
of the Cortes statue, served as its terminal and control tower.

The round Gimnasio Nacional (National
Gymnasium) sits at the park's southeast
corner and hosts sporting events and the
occasional concert. The Estadio Nacional,
a sleek, futuristic-looking 40,000-seat
stadium—a controversial gift from the
government of China, which decided to
use its own construction workers rather
than employ locals—looms over the
park's northwest corner. It hosts soccer
matches primarily, but Paul McCartney,
Elton John, Shakira, and Lady Gaga have
all performed in the stadium. In between
are acres of space for soccer, basketball,
tennis, swimming, jogging, picnicking,
and kite flying. The park hums with activity on weekends. The stadium grounds
are fine, but avoid walking through the
rest of the park after the sun goes down.
⊠ *Bordered by Cs. 42–68, Avda. de las
Américas, and Carretera a Caldera, Paseo
Colón.*

🍴 Restaurants

★ Grano de Oro Restaurant

$$$ | ECLECTIC | The Hotel Grano de Oro
houses one of San José's premier dining
destinations: a splendid restaurant
wrapped around a lovely indoor patio and
bromeliad-filled garden. The garden area

Did You Know?

The auditorium floor in the Teatro Nacional was designed to be hoisted up to stage level by a manual winch so that it could also be used as a ballroom.

is a perfect spot for lunch on a warm day—choose from among a variety of light sandwiches and salads, or opt for dinner in the elegant indoor dining area for dishes like breaded sea bass with orange sauce and macadamia nuts or *cerdo en salsa tamarindo* (roasted pork in tamarind sauce). **Known for:** yummy desserts; impressive wine selection; elegant hotel setting. [$] *Average main: $23* ✉ *C. 30, Avdas. 2–4, Paseo Colón* ☎ *2255–3322* 🌐 *www.hotelgranodeoro.com.*

L'Olivo

$$$ | **ITALIAN** | The vaulted ceilings and a vineyard mural on one wall evoke old Italy at this restaurant serving homemade pastas—spinach cannelloni and linguine with clam sauce are popular dishes. An extensive wine list rounds out the offerings, and service is attentive—the chef makes the rounds to ensure that you're satisfied. **Known for:** lively atmosphere; reservations recommended; small dining area. [$] *Average main: $16* ✉ *Paseo Colón* ✣ *300 meters (984 feet) north and 50 meters (164 feet) east of ICE Bldg.* ☎ *2220–0453* 🌐 *www.suitescristina.com* 💳 *No credit cards* 🕓 *Closed Sun.*

Lubnan

$$ | **MIDDLE EASTERN** | The Lebanese owners at one of San José's few Middle Eastern restaurants serve a wide variety of dishes from their native region, but if you can't decide, the meze platter serves two people and gives you a little bit of everything. Try the juicy shish kebab *de cordero* (of lamb) or, if you're feeling especially adventurous, the raw ground-meat *kebbe naye* (with wheat meal) and *kafta naye* (without wheat meal). **Known for:** hip bar in back; belly-dancing show on Thursday night; yummy kebabs. [$] *Average main: $12* ✉ *Cs. 22–24, Paseo Colón* ☎ *2257–6071* 🌐 *www.facebook.com/lubnancr* 🕓 *Closed Mon. No dinner Sun.*

Machu Picchu

$$ | **PERUVIAN** | A few travel posters are the only props that evoke Peru, but no matter: the Peruvian food is anything but plain, and the seafood is excellent. The *especial de mariscos* (special seafood platter), big enough for two, presents you with shrimp, conch, and squid cooked four ways. **Known for:** authentic Peruvian-style ceviche; smooth pisco sours; extra-spicy Peruvian hot sauce. [$] *Average main: $12* ✉ *C. 32, Paseo Colón* ✣ *130 meters (426 feet) north of KFC* ☎ *2222–7384* 🌐 *www.facebook.com/restaurante.machu.picchu* 🕓 *No dinner Sun.*

Soda Tapia

$ | **COSTA RICAN** | Don't expect anything fancy at this extremely popular restaurant, but food here is cheap and filling. The ubiquitous gallo pinto for breakfast and *casados* (meat, fish, or poultry, accompanied by rice, cabbage salad, and dessert) for lunch are on the menu, along with a variety of sandwiches and burgers. **Known for:** cheap eats; filling lunch specials; early-morning breakfast hangout. [$] *Average main: $9* ✉ *C. 42, Avdas. 2–4, Sabana Este* ☎ *2222–8401* 🌐 *www.facebook.com/sodatapia* 💳 *No credit cards.*

☕ Coffee and Quick Bites

Juan Valdez Café

$ | **CAFÉ** | This sleek, modern west-side coffee shop and store is an island of all-Colombian products, both beverage and souvenirs, in Costa Rica. They serve cakes, pastries, and delicious coffee milkshakes. **Known for:** tasty coffee milkshakes; lots of coffee and souvenirs—Colombian, of course—for purchase; an island of Colombian coffee in Costa Rica. [$] *Average main: $6* ✉ *Hilton Garden Inn San Jose La Sabana, Blvd. Rohrmoser, Sabana Norte* ✣ *Northwest corner of La Sabana park* ☎ *4700–2361* 🌐 *www.juanvaldezcafe.com.*

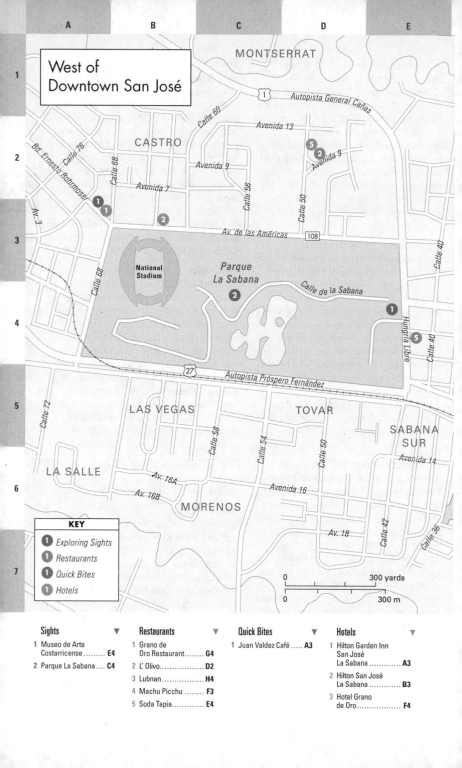

West of
Downtown San José

MONTSERRAT

CASTRO

National
Stadium

Parque
La Sabana

Calle de la Sabana

Av. de las Américas

LAS VEGAS

TOVAR

SABANA
SUR

LA SALLE

MORENOS

KEY

- ① Exploring Sights
- ① Restaurants
- ① Quick Bites
- ① Hotels

| 0 | | 300 yards |
| 0 | | 300 m |

Sights ▼	Restaurants ▼	Quick Bites ▼	Hotels ▼
1 Museo de Arte Costarricense **E4**	1 Grano de Oro Restaurant........ **G4**	1 Juan Valdez Café **A3**	1 Hilton Garden Inn San José La Sabana **A3**
2 Parque La Sabana.... **C4**	2 L' Olivo................. **D2**		2 Hilton San José La Sabana **B3**
	3 Lubnan **H4**		3 Hotel Grano de Oro................. **F4**
	4 Machu Picchu **F3**		
	5 Soda Tapia............. **E4**		

Hotels

San José's vast west side contains only a smattering of lodgings, but among them are two of the city's best, Hotel Grano de Oro and the Park Inn by Radisson.

Hilton Garden Inn San José La Sabana
$$$ | **HOTEL** | This U.S. chain manages to provide all the modern amenities of its well-known brand while incorporating local touches. **Pros:** mountain views; friendly service; comfortable rooms. **Cons:** somewhat generic chain hotel rooms; rooftop pool, but unsheltered; located in an office building. [$] *Rooms from: $159* ✉ *Blvd. Rohrmoser, northwest corner of Parque La Sabana, Sabana Norte* ☎ *2520–6000, 800/445–8667 in North America* 🌐 *www.hilton.com* 🛏 *115 rooms* 🍴 *Free Breakfast.*

★ **Hilton San José La Sabana**
$$$ | **HOTEL** | In a country of low-slung buildings, this 31-story skyscraper hotel—it's Costa Rica's tallest building—stands out as a veritable Manhattan on La Sabana park. **Pros:** stupendous views; first-class amenities; excellent restaurant. **Cons:** far from downtown sights; sameness of a chain hotel; lacks local flavor. [$] *Rooms from: $181* ✉ *Sabana Norte* ✥ *North side of Parque La Sabana, across from National Stadium* ☎ *800/445–8667 in North America, 2220–9000* 🌐 *www.hilton.com* 🛏 *131 rooms* 🍴 *Free Breakfast.*

★ **Hotel Grano de Oro**
$$$ | **HOTEL** | Two wooden houses have been converted into one of the city's most charming inns, decorated throughout with old photos of the capital and paintings by local artists; head up to your room for the old coffee-plantation feel for which the hotel is known. **Pros:** sundeck with beautiful views; sumptuous, old-world decor; superb, elegant restaurant. **Cons:** need taxi to get here; nothing else worth seeing in the neighborhood; far from downtown sights. [$] *Rooms from: $210* ✉ *C. 30, Avdas. 2–4, Paseo Colón* ☎ *2255–3322* 🌐 *www.hotelgranodeoro.com* 🛏 *39 rooms* 🍴 *No Meals.*

★ **Park Inn by Radisson**
$$ | **HOTEL** | This chain lodging incorporates local flair—bright, fresh primary colors and a rotating selection of Costa Rican art throughout—while providing business amenities in a clean, modern hotel. **Pros:** impeccable service; friendly staff; local style despite being a chain hotel. **Cons:** nothing else interesting in the neighborhood; lacks history of other San José hotels; far from downtown sights. [$] *Rooms from: $125* ✉ *Avda. 6, Cs. 28–30, Paseo Colón* ☎ *4110–1100, 800/333–3333 in North America* 🌐 *www.radissonhotelsamericas.com* 🛏 *117 rooms* 🍴 *Free Breakfast.*

Suites Cristina
$$ | **HOTEL** | Our favorite of the capital's many *apartotels* (part apartment house, part hotel) sits on a quiet, out-of-the-way street north of La Sabana Park. **Pros:** friendly staff; quiet street; terrific rates for what is offered. **Cons:** some rooms have no TV; some noise on rare nights when there's an event at the nearby stadium; far from downtown sights and center of town. [$] *Rooms from: $79* ✉ *Sabana Norte* ✥ *300 meters (984 feet) north of ICE Bldg.* ☎ *2220–0453* 🌐 *www.suitescristina.com* 🛏 *50 suites* 🍴 *Free Breakfast.*

Shopping

Hotel Grano de Oro
CRAFTS | The small gift shop at the Hotel Grano de Oro has an impressive selection of carvings and jewelry on hand. ✉ *C. 30, Avdas. 2–4, Paseo Colón* ☎ *2255–3322* 🌐 *www.hotelgranodeoro.com.*

North and East of Downtown

Immediately northeast of downtown lie Barrio Amón and Barrio Otoya. Both neighborhoods are repositories of historic houses that have escaped the wrecking ball; many now serve as hotels, restaurants, galleries, and offices—a few are even private residences. Where these barrios begin and end depends on who's doing the talking. Locales on the fringes of the city center prefer to be associated with these "good neighborhoods" rather than with downtown. Barrio Escalante, to the east, has quickly become San José's hippest neighborhood, with an ever-increasing number of restaurants and bars.

The sprawling suburb of San Pedro begins several blocks east of downtown San José. It's home to the University of Costa Rica and all the intellect and cheap eats and nightlife that a student could desire. But away from the heart of the university, San Pedro is awash with malls, fast-food restaurants, and car dealerships—although it manages to mix in such stately districts as Los Yoses for good measure. To get to San Pedro, take a $3 taxi ride from downtown and get off in front of Banco Nacional, just beyond the rotunda with the fountain at its center.

◎ Sights

Jardín de Mariposas Spyrogyra
(*Spyrogyra Butterfly Garden*)
GARDEN | FAMILY | Spending an hour at this magical butterfly garden is entertaining and educational for nature lovers of all ages. Self-guided tours enlighten you on butterfly ecology and let you see the winged creatures close up. After an 18-minute video introduction, you're free to wander screened-in gardens along a numbered trail. Some 30 species of colorful butterflies flutter about,

Have Some Sauce

Any self-respecting tico home or restaurant keeps a bottle of Salsa Lizano, one of the country's signature food products, on hand. Its tang brightens up meat, vegetable, and rice dishes. Bottles of the stuff make great souvenirs, and you can buy them at **Palí** and **Más x Menos** (pronounced Más *por* Menos) supermarkets throughout the country. The main San José branch of Palí is at Avenida Central, between Calles 11 and 13.

accompanied by six types of hummingbirds. Try to come when it's sunny, as butterflies are most active then. A small, moderately priced café borders the garden and serves sandwiches and tico fare. The place is difficult to find if you're driving, so keep your eyes peeled. ⊠ *Barrio Tournón* ✛ *50 meters (164 feet) east and 150 meters (492 feet) south of main entrance to El Pueblo shopping center* ☎ *2222–2937* ⊕ *www.butterflygarden-costarica.com* ☞ *$7.*

Museo de los Niños (*Children's Museum*)
CHILDREN'S MUSEUM | FAMILY | Three halls of this museum are filled with eye-catching seasonal exhibits for kids, ranging in subject from local ecology to outer space. The exhibits are labeled in Spanish only, but most are interactive, so language shouldn't be much of a problem. The museum's most popular resident is the Egyptian exhibit's sarcophagus; the mummy draws oohs and aahs. Located in a former prison, big kids may want to check it out just to marvel at the castle-like architecture and the old cells that have been preserved in an admittedly gruesome exhibit about life behind bars. The complex that houses the museum is called the Centro Costarricense de Ciencia y Cultura (Costa Rican Center

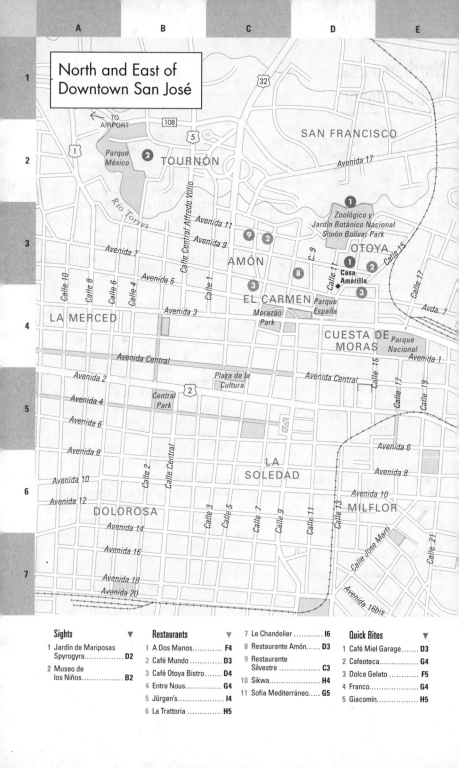

North and East of Downtown San José

SAN FRANCISCO

TOURNÓN

Parque México

Río Torres

AMÓN

EL CARMEN

LA MERCED

Zoológico y Jardín Botánico Nacional Simón Bolívar Park

OTOYA

Casa Amarilla

Morazán Park

Parque España

CUESTA DE MORAS

Parque Nacional

Plaza de la Cultura

Central Park

LA SOLEDAD

DOLOROSA

MILFLOR

Avenida 17
Avenida 11
Avenida 9
Avenida 7
Avenida 5
Avenida 3
Avenida Central
Avenida 2
Avenida 4
Avenida 6
Avenida 8
Avenida 10
Avenida 12
Avenida 14
Avenida 16
Avenida 18
Avenida 20
Avenida 1
Avenida 6
Avenida 8
Avenida 10
Avenida 16bis

Calle Central Alfredo Volio
Calle 10
Calle 8
Calle 6
Calle 4
Calle 1
Calle 2
Calle Central
Calle 3
Calle 5
Calle 7
Calle 9
Calle 11
Calle 13
Calle José Martí
Calle 15
Calle 17
Calle 19
Calle 21

TO AIRPORT
108
32
5
1
2

Hotels ▼

Missing History

Blame it on the earthquakes. Costa Ricans are quick to attribute the scarcity of historic architecture in San José and around the country to a history of earth tremors. Indeed, major earthquakes have struck various locales around Costa Rica 12 times since the mid-18th century (six times in the 20th century, and twice in the present one), felling untold numbers of historical structures.

But blame it on the wrecking ball, too, say historians. The tear-it-down approach really began to take its toll in the 1970s, an era when boxy, concrete buildings were in vogue around the world. Costa Rica didn't establish its first school of architecture until 1972, staffed by faculty from Mexico, England, and Brazil, and a real Costa Rican tradition did not take hold. Mix that with a lack of government regulation and what one historian calls a typical Tico do-your-own-thing penchant, and the result is a city full of squat buildings.

The tide began to turn in 1995 with the passage of the Law of Historic and Architectural Patrimony. More than 300 historic structures in the country are currently protected under the legislation, and new buildings are added to the registry each year. But legal protection is no guarantee of funding necessary to actually restore a historic landmark.

You need to look hard, but San José really does have several diamonds in the rough. The National Theater and Central Post Office remain the two most visited examples of historic architecture in the capital. But the National Museum, the National Center of Culture, and several small hostelries and restaurants around town—especially in Barrios Amón and Otoya—are all modern transformations and restorations of structures with histories.

of Science and Culture), and that will be the sign that greets you on the front of the building. Though just a short distance from downtown, a walk here takes you through a dodgy neighborhood; always take a taxi to and from. ✉ *Centro Costarricense de Ciencia y Cultura, north end of C. 4, Barrio Tournón* ☎ *2105–0500* 🌐 *www.museocr.org* 🎟 *$4* 🕑 *Closed Mon.*

🍴 Restaurants

A Dos Manos

$$ | **BURGER** | The name translates as "with two hands," and that's what it takes to handle the monster burgers here. The capital's best burgers are made from grass-fed beef (except for the veggie and chicken burgers), with inventive toppings such as Caesar salad, mac and cheese, or hash browns. **Known for:** low-carb, vegan, and kosher options available; support for the LGBTQ community; inventive burger toppings. [$] *Average main: $14* ✉ *Avda. 3, between Cs. 25–29, Barrio Escalante* ☎ *8868–2287* 🌐 *www.facebook.com/adosmanoscr.*

Café Mundo

$$ | **CAFÉ** | The upstairs café at this corner restaurant serves meals on a porch, on a garden patio, or in two dining rooms. Try the soup of the day and fresh-baked bread to start; main courses include shrimp in a vegetable cream sauce or *lomito en salsa de vino tinto* (tenderloin in a red-wine sauce). **Known for:** delicious chocolate cake; place to see and be seen; popular LGBTQ hangout. $ *Average main: $14* ⊠ *C. 15, Avdas. 9–11, Barrio Otoya* ☎ *2222–6190* ⊙ *Closed Sun. No lunch Sat.*

Café Otoya Bistro
$$ | ECLECTIC | The warm and welcoming vibe that exudes from this very cool Barrio Otoya café is only enhanced by the friendly, attentive staff. Diners are a real mix: some chow down on a sumptuous tenderloin, while others stop in for baked goods and coffee, but almost everyone partakes in the all-day brunch, especially on weekends. **Known for:** all-day brunch; $24 Work Combo package (breakfast, lunch, a table, and Wi-Fi access); rotating art exhibits and live music performances. $ *Average main: $12* ⊠ *Avda. 7, Cs. 11A-15, Barrio Otoya* ☎ *7118–2762* ⊕ *www. cafeotoya.com.*

Entre Nous
$ | ECLECTIC | It's the crepes—salty or sweet—that draw the crowds here. It's a bright, cheery place with a covered terrace to stop for dessert after an evening out in Barrio Escalante. **Known for:** sampler platters, great for a group; attentive service; to-die-for Grand Marnier crepes. $ *Average main: $8* ⊠ *Avda. 7, Cs. 29–31, Barrio Escalante* ☎ *4034–8030* ⊕ *www. entrenouscreperie.com.*

★ Jürgen's
$$$ | ECLECTIC | A common haunt for *políticos*, Jürgen's attracts San José's elites, and you'll feel pretty elite too when you dine at this contemporary restaurant with leather and wood accents. The inventive menu, with delicacies such as medallions of roasted duck and tuna fillet encrusted with sesame seeds, sets this place apart from the city's more traditional venues. **Known for:** impeccable service; sleek, modern furnishings; haunt for "who's who" of San José society. $ *Average main: $24* ⊠ *Blvd. Dent, Barrio Dent* ⚓ *250 meters (820 feet) north of Grupo Q* ☎ *2224–2455* ⊕ *www.facebook.com/ RestauranteJurgens* ⊙ *Closed Sun. No lunch Sat.*

La Trattoria
$$ | ITALIAN | The excellent, reasonably priced homemade pastas make this popular lunch spot worth the stop. Begin your meal with fresh bread and excellent antipasti, and make sure to save room for tiramisu. **Known for:** hard-to-find location behind a supermarket; friendly service; homemade Italian dishes. $ *Average main: $10* ⊠ *Calle 37, Barrio Dent* ⚓ *Behind Automercado* ☎ *2224–7065* ⊕ *www. facebook.com/trattoriayoses* ⊙ *No dinner Sun.*

★ Le Chandelier
$$$$ | FRENCH | Formal service and traditional sauce-heavy French dishes are part of the experience at this elegant dining room with wicker chairs, tile floors, and original paintings. Start off with saffron ravioli stuffed with ricotta cheese and walnuts, and opt for a unique main course like corvina in a *pejibaye* (peach palm) sauce or hearts of palm and veal chops glazed in a sweet port-wine sauce. **Known for:** impeccable, formal service; San José's most elegant restaurant; duck à l'orange. $ *Average main: $32* ⊠ *C. 49, San Pedro* ⚓ *50 meters (164 feet) west and 100 meters (328 feet) south of the ICE Bldg.* ☎ *2225–3980* ⊕ *www. facebook.com/lechandeliercr* ⊙ *Closed Sun. No lunch Sat.*

Restaurante Amón
$ | COSTA RICAN | Reasonable prices and a hearty breakfast of gallo pinto (beans and rice), scrambled eggs, bread, and coffee at this artsy restaurant will fortify you for a morning of sightseeing. The bargain $7 lunch special consists of the standard casado—choose from fish, chicken, beef, or pork—accompanied by rice, beans, vegetable, salad, and dessert. **Known for:** minimalist setting; rotating art exhibits; typical Costa Rican flavors. $ *Average main: $6* ⊠ *C. 7, Avdas. 7–9, Barrio Amón* ☎ *2221–2960* ⊙ *Closed weekends. No dinner.*

Are You Ready for Some Fútbol?

Sports mean one thing in San José: soccer. Very young boys (and a slowly increasing number of girls) kick around a ball—or some other object if no ball is available—in street pickup games, and they grow into fans passionate about their local team. But everyone puts aside regional differences when the reputation of Costa Rica's national team is on the line, as it is during the World Cup.

Consult the Spanish-language daily *La Nación* or ask at your hotel for details on upcoming games—you simply show up at the stadium box office. Prices range from $6 to $15. *Sombra numerado* (shaded seats) are the most expensive.

Professional soccer matches are usually played on Sunday morning or Wednesday night in either of two San José stadiums. The Estadio Ricardo Saprissa (next to the Clínica Integrada de Tibás) is home to Saprissa, the capital's beloved hometown team, in the northern suburb of Tibás; the Chinese-built Estadio Nacional sits at the northwest corner of La Sabana Park and hosts visiting national teams who come to take on La Sele, Costa Rica's own national squad.

★ **Restaurante Silvestre**

$$$$ | **COSTA RICAN** | Chef Santiago Fernandez is at the helm of this ambitious and wildly successful exploration of upscale contemporary Costa Rican cuisine. The regularly changing menus use local and organic ingredients (along with fish and meat procured through responsible means) to take diners on a journey into some of the most creative (and delicious) food Costa Rica has to offer. **Known for:** prix-fixe menus of sustainable fine dining, including wine pairings; hip downstairs bar; gorgeous setting in a renovated mansion with a plant-filled indoor terrace. [$] *Average main: $28* ✉ *Avda. 11, C. 3A, #955, Barrio Amón* ☎ *2221–2465* 🌐 *www.restaurantesilvestre.com* 🕓 *Closed Sun. No lunch Sat.*

Sikwa

$$ | **COSTA RICAN** | The indigenous cultures of Costa Rica don't get too much attention from tourists, but this small, intimate restaurant in Barrio Escalante is trying to change that by incorporating recipes derived from the history and culture of the eight surviving indigenous ethnic groups. Sikwa has deliciously (and respectfully) bridged the gap between the country's past and present as each meal tells a different story, which the chef and servers will happily share with diners. **Known for:** traditional indigenous dishes like peach palm soup and escarole tomato sauce with white corn and pork; small space best for smaller groups; unique dining experience blending history and storytelling. [$] *Average main: $13* ✉ *Casa Batsú, Avda. 1, C. 33, Barrio Escalante* ✣ *125 meters (410 feet) east of Fresh Market* ☎ *7093–1662* 🌐 *www.facebook.com/sikwarestaurante.cr* 🕓 *Closed Mon. and Tues. No dinner Sun.*

Sofia Mediterráneo

$$ | **MEDITERRANEAN** | Natives of Istanbul, the chef and owner rely on authentic recipes for excellent red peppers stuffed with spicy beef and rice, eggplant-tomato salad, and other Mediterranean treats. You'll find a good selection of vegetarian salads, too. **Known for:** potent Turkish coffee; sceney atmosphere; to-die-for baklava. [$] *Average main: $14* ✉ *C. 33, Avda. 3, Barrio Escalante* ☎ *2224–5050* 🌐 *www.facebook.com/sofiamediterraneo* 🕓 *No lunch Mon.*

☕ Coffee and Quick Bites

Café Miel Garage

$ | **CAFÉ** | A scant two tables and a small counter are the only seating in this tiny converted garage. But the coffee, harvested from its own plantation in Tarrazú in the Los Santos region, is robust and flavorful, as are the cakes and ice creams. **Known for:** fruit smoothies served in a jar; good selection of cakes and pastries; located in a converted garage, hence the name. ⓈAverage main: $6 ⊠ Avda. 9, C. 13, Barrio Otoya ☎ 2221–0897 ⊕ cafemielgarage.com 🗖 No credit cards.

Cafeoteca

$ | **CAFÉ** | This café blends and roasts its own coffee on-site which pairs well with the cakes and pies on offer. All coffees served here are also for sale in the shop, including samplers of eight different varieties from around the country in individual single-cup sachets. **Known for:** knowledgeable baristas; good selection of specialty coffees from around the country; only works with small coffee suppliers. Ⓢ Average main: $8 ⊠ C. 31, Avda. 5, Barrio Escalante ☎ 2253–8426.

Dolce Gelato

$$ | **ICE CREAM** | **FAMILY** | The homemade gelato served at Dolce Gelato gives Costa Rica's ubiquitous Pop's ice cream chain a run for its money. These folks get adventurous with their flavors: maracuyá (passion fruit) and mango are two popular ones. **Known for:** delicious pies and crepes that incorporate gelato, of course; menu options for lactose-intolerant diners; wide variety of whimsical flavors. Ⓢ Average main: $10 ⊠ Avda. 3, C. 25–29, Barrio Escalante ☎ 6462–4320 ⊕ www.facebook.com/dolcegelatocr.

Franco

$ | **CAFÉ** | Fashionable Franco serves gourmet beverages made from the country's premium coffees. Your inner amateur barista may want to check into the slate of coffee workshops offered here. **Known for:** cool, tree-shaded patio is an oasis in the busy city; farm-fresh ingredients from small suppliers; informative coffee workshops. Ⓢ Average main: $8 ⊠ Avda. 7, Cs. 31–33, Barrio Escalante ☎ 4082–7006 ⊕ www.franco.cr.

Giacomín

$ | **BAKERY** | We have to admit that Costa Rican baked goods tend toward the dry-as-dust end of the spectrum, but Italian-style bakery Giacomín, near the University of Costa Rica, is an exception—a touch of liqueur added to the batter makes all the difference. Stand European-style at the downstairs espresso bar or take your goodies to the tables and chairs on the upstairs balcony. **Known for:** espresso bar; upstairs balcony; Italian-style pastries. Ⓢ Average main: $5 ⊠ Los Yoses ⊹ Next to Automercado supermarket ☎ 4001–7478 ⊕ www.giacomincr.com 🗖 No credit cards.

🛏 Hotels

Just north of downtown, old homes converted into small lodgings populate Barrios Amón and Otoya, two of the capital's most historic neighborhoods. The small properties 10 minutes by cab east of downtown, toward the university, offer personalized service and lots of peace and quiet. Plenty of restaurants and bars are within easy reach.

Hotel Aranjuez

$ | **HOTEL** | Several 1940s-era houses with extensive gardens and lively common areas—visitors swap travel advice here—make up this family-run lodging. **Pros:** good budget value; great place to meet other budget travelers; excellent complimentary breakfast. **Cons:** far from sights; can be hard to find space in high season; a few rooms share bath. Ⓢ Rooms from: $57 ⊠ C. 19, Avdas. 11–13, Barrio Aranjuez ☎ 2256–1825 ⊕ www.hotelaranjuez.com ⤴ 35 rooms ⭑❍⭑ Free Breakfast.

In markets, you'll find friendly artists and artisans.

Hotel Dunn Inn

$$ | **B&B/INN** | Adjoining 1926 and 1933 houses fuse to create the cozy Barrio Amón experience at bargain prices. **Pros:** good value; friendly staff; many online specials. **Cons:** interior rooms catch noise from lobby and bar; sits at bottom of steep street; difficult to get reservations. [$] *Rooms from: $119* ✉ *Avda. 11, C. 5, Barrio Amón* ☎ *2222–3232, 800/545–4801 in North America* 🌐 *www.hoteldunninn.com* 🛏 *28 rooms* 🍴 *Free Breakfast.*

Hotel Santo Tomás

$ | **B&B/INN** | The front of this century-old former coffee-plantation house is along a busy street, but close the front door behind you and you'll find an oasis of quiet in the center of the city. **Pros:** pool; friendly staff; central location. **Cons:** safe, but borders a sketchy neighborhood; small rooms; difficult parking. [$] *Rooms from: $72* ✉ *Avda. 7, Cs. 3–5, Barrio Amón* ☎ *2255–0448* 🌐 *www.hotelsantotomas.com* 🛏 *30 rooms* 🍴 *Free Breakfast.*

Nightlife

Café Mundo

CAFÉS | The highly recommended restaurant Café Mundo is a quiet spot for a drink or bite to eat and is frequented by LGBTQ and bohemian crowds. ✉ *C. 15, Avda. 9, Barrio Otoya* ☎ *2222–6190.*

Costa Rica Beer Factory

BREWPUBS | One of Costa Rica's budding brewpubs serves up four of its own craft beers and one seasonally rotating one, as well as possibly the country's best selection of international brews, plus burgers and appetizers. Weekend nights get crowded. The folks here can also arrange guided tours ($9–$29) of their brewery near Heredia in the Central Valley. ✉ *C. 33, Avda. 7, Barrio Escalante* ☎ *8447–9732* 🌐 *www.costaricabeerfactory.com.*

El Observatorio

GATHERING PLACES | El Observatorio strikes an unusual balance between casual and formal: it's the kind of place where an over-30 crowd in ties goes to watch a soccer game. Something is on here every night except Sunday: usually a selection of stand-up comedy, live music, or karaoke. Some evenings present some more highbrow cultural offerings too. ⊠ *C. 23, Barrio La California* ✛ *Across from Cine Magaly* ☎ *2223–0725* ⊕ *www.elobservatorio.tv.*

Mercado La California

GATHERING PLACES | You find food stands (tacos, pizzas, and sandwiches) and a bar kiosk (beer, wine, or mixed drinks) all to your liking at this sprawling place—part bar, part food court, part night market. Order and grab a seat. That's the system at this always-hopping spot. ⊠ *C. 21, Avda. 1, Barrio La California* ⊕ *www.facebook.com/mercadolacalifornia.*

Merecumbé

DANCE CLUBS | Many Costa Ricans learn to merengue, rumba, mambo, cha-cha, and swing (called *cumbia* elsewhere) at a young age. Play catch-up at dance school Merecumbé, which has 16 branches around Costa Rica. With a few days' notice you can arrange a private lesson with an English-speaking instructor. An hour or two is all you need to grasp the fundamentals of merengue and *bolero* (what Costa Ricans call the rumba), both of which are easy to master and work with the pop music you're likely to hear back home. ⊠ *100 meters (328 feet) south and 25 meters (82 feet) west of Banco Popular, San Pedro* ☎ *2224–3531* ⊕ *www.facebook.com/merecumbe. sanpedro.*

Ram Luna

LIVE MUSIC | In the far, far southern suburbs, 14 km (9 miles) south of downtown San José, Ram Luna is most famous for the views—the lights of the Central Valley sparkle at your feet—and the music. Make reservations if you plan to be here for Wednesday or Thursday evening's folklore show—a bilingual emcee fills you in on the cultural background of what you're enjoying—or Friday evening's dancing to live music. ⊠ *Aserrí* ✛ *15 km (9 miles) south of San José between Aserrí and Tabarca* ☎ *2230–3022* ⊕ *www.restauranteramluna.com.*

Stiefel Pub

BREWPUBS | Craft beer is taking hold in Costa Rica, and Stiefel has 10 microbrews on tap to the accompaniment of a lively pub atmosphere. ⊠ *Avda. 7, Barrio Amón* ✛ *50 meters (164 feet) east of INS building* ☎ *6222–8681* ⊕ *www.facebook.com/StiefelPubEscazu.*

 Performing Arts

Eugene O'Neill Theater (*Teatro Eugene O'Neill*)

MUSIC | This theater has chamber concerts and plays many weekend evenings. The cultural center is a great place to meet North American expatriates. ⊠ *Centro Cultural Costarricense–Norteamericano, Avda. 1, C. 37, Barrio Dent* ☎ *2207–7549* ⊕ *www.centrocultural.cr.*

Teatro La Aduana

THEATER | You'll find frequent dance and stage performances at this theater, and it is home to the Compañía Nacional de Teatro (National Theater Company). ⊠ *C. 25, Avda. 3, Barrio La California* ☎ *2257–8305* ⊕ *www.mcj.go.cr.*

🛍 Shopping

BOOKS AND MAGAZINES

Librería Internacional

BOOKS | The city's largest bookstore evokes that Barnes & Noble ambience, though on a much smaller scale. It stocks English translations of Latin American literature, as well as myriad coffee-table books on Costa Rica. There are 21 other smaller branches around San José and the Central Valley. ⊠ *Plaza Antares, Rotonda La Bandera, Barrio Dent* ☎ *2253–9553* ⊕ *www.libreriainternacional.com.*

CRAFTS
Mi Pueblo Verde
CRAFTS | This is a standout among the Moravia shops for its fine carvings made from native cocobolo and guapinol wood. Check out the unusual salad bowls. ⊠ *San Vicente de Moravia* ⊹ *50 meters (164 feet) north of Colegio María Inmaculada* ☎ *2235–5742.*

FARMERS' MARKET
Feria Verde
MARKET | It's a tad out of the way, but just up the street from the Hotel Aranjuez is the city's best Saturday morning farmers' market. Stock up on organic fruits and veggies and take in the local scene. For something tropical, try some coconut water—you'll get a coconut whacked in half by a machete, and you can sip the water through a straw. Things get underway at 7 am and wind down at 12:30. ⊠ *North end of C. 19, Barrio Aranjuez* ⊹ *150 meters (492 feet) north of Hotel Aranjuez, then downhill to left.*

MALLS
Several huge enclosed shopping centers anchor the metro area. These are complemented by dozens of smaller strip malls. Expect all the comforts of home—food courts and movie theaters included. The large Mall San Pedro in the eastern suburb of San Pedro has had some issues with security; we recommend avoiding it.

Terramall
MALL | The mammoth trilevel 160-store Terramall is the far eastern suburbs' prime shopping destination. ⊠ *Autopista Florencio del Castillo, Tres Ríos* ☎ *2278–6970* ⊕ *www.terramall.co.cr.*

SOUVENIRS
Artesanía Zurquí
SOUVENIRS | You'll find a well-rounded selection of ceramics, wood, and leather at Artesanía Zurquí. ⊠ *San Vicente de Moravia* ⊹ *50 meters (164 feet) north of Colegio María Inmaculada* ☎ *2240–5302.*

THE CENTRAL VALLEY

Updated by
Jeffrey Van Fleet

⊙ Sights   🍴 Restaurants   🛏 Hotels   🛍 Shopping   🍸 Nightlife

★★★★★   ★★★★☆   ★★★★★   ★★★☆☆   ★★★★☆

WELCOME TO THE CENTRAL VALLEY

TOP REASONS TO GO

★ **Avian adventures:** Flock to Tapantí National Park to see emerald toucanets, resplendent quetzals (if you're lucky), and nearly every species of Costa Rican hummingbird. Rancho Naturalista is the bird lover's hotel of choice.

★ **Coffee:** Get up close and personal with harvesting and processing on coffee tours at two of the valley's many plantations: Café Britt and Doka Estate.

★ **Poás Volcano:** Peer right down into the witches' cauldron that is the Poás Volcano.

★ **The Orosi Valley:** Spectacular views and quiet, bucolic towns make this area a great day trip or overnight from San José.

★ **Rafting the Pacuare River:** Brave the rapids as you descend through tropical forest on one of the best white-water rivers in Central America.

The Central Valley is something of a misnomer, and its Spanish name, the *meseta central* (central plateau) isn't entirely accurate either. The two contiguous mountain ranges that run the length of the country—the Cordillera Central range (which includes Poás, Barva, Irazú, and Turrialba volcanoes) to the north and the Cordillera de Talamanca to the south—don't quite line up in the middle, leaving a trough between them. The "valley" floor is about 3,000 to 5,000 feet above sea level. In the valley, your view toward the coasts is obstructed by the two mountain ranges. But from a hillside hotel, your view of San José and the valley can be spectacular.

1 **Escazú.** Posh town with a growing number of shops and restaurants.

2 **Santa Ana.** Explore the wildlife refuge and traditional church in quaint Santa Ana.

3 **Grecia.** Home to the area's best farmers' market and a unique metal church.

4 **Sarchí.** This relaxing town is known for its crafts and oxcarts.

5 **Carara National Park.** Spot monkeys and toucans in the biologically diverse park.

6 **San Antonio de Belén.** Convenient departure town for trips to the western Central Valley and more.

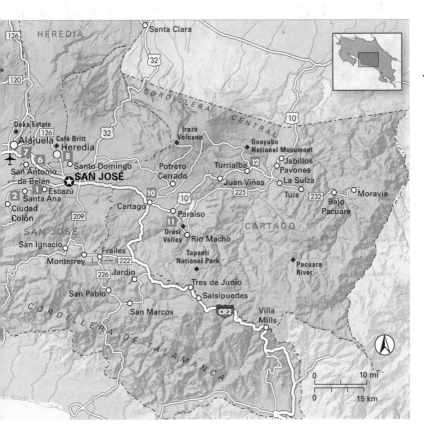

7 Alajuela. Costa Rica's second most populated city is a 30-minute ride from San José.

8 Heredia. An important coffee center and buzzing city with university life and old colonial structures.

9 Poás Volcano National Park. Peer into the crater of Costa Rica's most famous volcano.

10 Cartago. Costa Rica's oldest city and colonial capital is home to the country's national shrine.

11 The Orosi Valley. This pastoral land is the cradle of Costa Rican history.

12 Turrialba. Near the bustling market town are its namesake volcano and the archaeological ruins of Guayabo.

CARARA NATIONAL PARK

Carara National Park

One of the last remnants of an ecological transition zone between Costa Rica's drier northwest and more humid southwest, Carara National Park holds a tremendous collection of plants and animals.

Squeezed into its 47 square km (18 square miles) is a mixed habitat of evergreen and deciduous forest, river, lagoon, and marshland. Much of the park's terrain is blanketed with dramatic primary forest, massive trees laden with vines and epiphytes. This is a birder's and plant lover's haven. The sparse undergrowth makes terrestrial wildlife and ground birds easier to see. The most famous denizens—aside from the crocodiles in the adjoining Río Tárcoles—are the park's colorful and noisy scarlet macaws, which always travel in pairs. An oxbow lake (a U-shaped body of water that was once part of a river) adds an extra wildlife dimension, attracting turtles and waterfowl—and the crocodiles that dine on them. Bring lots of drinking water; this park can get very hot and humid.

(For more information, see the review in this chapter.)

BEST TIME TO GO

Dry season, January to April, is the best time to visit. The trails get muddy during the rainy season and usually close in the wettest months. This small park can feel crowded at the trailheads, so arrive early and walk far.

FUN FACT

The crowning glory of Carara is the successful conservation program that has doubled its scarlet macaw population. You can't miss these long-tailed, noisy parrots—look for streaks of blue and red in the sky.

BEST WAYS TO EXPLORE

BIRD-WATCHING

With more than 400 species recorded here, Carara is on every bird-watcher's must-visit list. It's an especially good place to see elusive ground birds, such as antpittas (a small ground-dwelling bird that eats ants), early in the morning and late in the afternoon. Around the lake and in the marshy areas, you may also spot roseate spoonbills, northern jacanas, and stately boat-billed herons. The park's most famous fliers are the scarlet macaws. Once almost absent from the area, a decades-long conservation program has revitalized the local population.

HIKING

The best and really only way to explore this park is on foot. Trails are well marked and maintained but the ground is often muddy—this is rain forest, after all. The shortest—and most popular—loop trail can be done in only 15 minutes. But if you venture farther afield, you'll quickly be on your own. The longer trail that connects with the Quebrada Bonita loop takes about 90 minutes to hike. There is also a short wheelchair-accessible route that starts at the main entrance. It goes deep enough into the forest to give visitors a sense of its drama and diversity.

WILDLIFE-WATCHING

Carara is famous for an amazing variety of wildlife, given its relatively small area. Keep alert (and quiet) while walking and you'll have a good chance of spotting lizards, coatimundis (a member of the raccoon family), and sloths. You're almost guaranteed to see white-faced monkeys and, with luck, howler and spider monkeys, too. You may even see a nine-banded armadillo.

Visitors spot wildlife in Carara National Park.

TOP REASONS TO GO

BIRDS

With a varied habitat that attracts both forest and water birds, Carara is a treasure trove for birders. Even if you're not a birder, you'll get a thrill hearing the raucous crowing of beautiful scarlet macaws as they soar over the forest canopy.

THE JUNGLE

The forest here is simply magnificent. Even if you don't spot a single bird or animal, you will experience the true meaning of jungle. Carara has one of the most diverse collections of trees in the country. Breathe deeply, be alert to the symphony of forest sounds, and bask in a totally natural world.

WILDLIFE

For most visitors, wildlife is the park's main attraction. You can count on seeing monkeys and lots of lizards as you walk the trails. Although they are a little harder to spot, look for anteaters, sloths, and armadillos.

POÁS VOLCANO

Poás Volcano

Towering north of Alajuela, the verdant Poás Volcano is covered with a quilt of farms and topped by a dark green shawl of cloud forest.

That pastoral scene disappears once you get to the 8,885-foot summit, and you gaze into the steaming, bubbling crater with smoking fumaroles and a gurgling, gray-turquoise sulfurous lake. You'll swear you're peering over the edge of a giant witches' cauldron. That basin, 2 km (1 mile) in diameter and nearly 1,000 feet deep, is thought to be the largest active volcanic crater in the world.

Poás is one of Costa Rica's five active volcanoes—it has erupted more than 40 times since the early 1800s—and is one of those rare places that permits you to see volcanic energy this close with minimal risk. Authorities closely monitor Poás's activity following several eruptions in March 2006, the first significant increase in activity since 1994. The most recent activity took place in late 2019 and produced clouds of smoke. Access is normally open, but park officials close the route up here when there is evidence of any activity they deem "irregular."

BEST TIME TO GO

The peak is frequently shrouded in mist, and you might see little beyond the lip of the crater. Be patient and wait awhile, especially if some wind is blowing—the clouds can disappear quickly. Aim to get here before 10 am. The earlier you arrive, the better the visibility.

FUN FACT

Forgot your umbrella? Duck under a *sombrilla de pobre* (poor man's umbrella) plant. These giant leaves can grow to diameters of 3 to 5 feet.

BEST WAYS TO EXPLORE

BIRD-WATCHING

Although birding can be a little frustrating here because of cloud and mist, more than 330 bird species call Poás home. One of the most comical birds you'll see in Costa Rica is usually spotted foraging in plain sight on the ground: the big-footed finch, whose oversize feet give it a clownish walk. Its cousin, the yellow-thighed finch, is easy to recognize by its bright yellow, er ... thighs. Arrive early and bird around the gate before the park opens, and stop along the road to the visitor center wherever you see a likely birding area. In the underbrush you may find spotted wood quail or the elusive buffy-crowned wood partridge. The trees along the road are a favorite haunt of both black-and-yellow and long-tailed silky flycatchers.

NO HIKING FOR NOW

The park's two hiking trails are closed at this writing. Although visiting Poás is considered safe these days, in the event of an evacuation, officials here want to be able to round up everybody quickly and get them out.

VOLCANIC TIPS

A paved road leads all the way from Alajuela to Poás's summit. No one is allowed to venture into the crater or walk along its edge.

■ TIP→ **Take periodic breaks from viewing: step back at least every 10 minutes, so that the sulfur fumes don't overcome you. Be sure to bring a sweater or a jacket—it can be surprisingly chilly and wet up here.**

TOP REASONS TO GO

A+ FACILITIES

You're on your own in many national parks, most of which are lacking in facilities, but this wheelchair-accessible park is a pleasant exception, with a visitor center containing exhibits, a cafeteria, gift shop, and restrooms.

BUBBLES AND ASH

"Up close and personal with nature" takes on a whole new meaning here. Costa Rica forms part of the Pacific Rim's so-called Ring of Fire, and a visit to the volcano's summit gives you a close-up view of a region of the earth that is still in formation.

LOCATION, LOCATION, LOCATION

Poás's proximity to San José and the western Central Valley makes it an easy half-day trip.

SAFETY FIRST!

Advance reservations (made at ⊕ *www.sinac. go.cr*) are required as numbers are limited. Upon arrival, you'll see a mandatory safety presentation and will be required to wear a helmet during your visit.

Peer into Poás Volcano from the park's overlook.

IRAZÚ VOLCANO

Irazú Volcano

The word *Irazú* is likely a corruption of Iztaru, a long-ago indigenous community whose name translated as "hill of thunder." The name is apt.

Volcán Irazú, as it's known in Spanish, is considered active, but the gases and steam that billow from fumaroles on the northwestern slope are rarely visible from the peak above the crater lookouts. The mountain's first recorded eruption took place in 1723; the most recent was a series of eruptions that lasted from 1963 to 1965. Boulders and mud rained down on the countryside, damming rivers and causing serious floods, and the volcano dumped up to 20 inches of ash on sections of the Central Valley.

When conditions are clear, you can see the chartreuse lake inside the Cráter Principal. The stark moonscape of the summit contrasts markedly with the lush vegetation of Irazú's lower slopes, home to porcupines, armadillos, coyotes, and mountain hares. Listen for the low-pitched, throaty song of the *yigüirro,* or clay-color thrush, Costa Rica's national bird. Its call is most pronounced just before the start of the rainy season. *(For more information, see the review in this chapter.)*

BEST TIME TO GO

Early morning, especially January–April, affords the best views of the craters. Clouds appear by late morning. Wear warm, waterproof clothing if you come early.

FUN FACT

Irazú has dumped a lot of ash over the centuries. The most recent began on the day John F. Kennedy arrived in Costa Rica in 1963. Old photos show him giving an outdoor speech in San José; everyone listening is holding umbrellas. The "ash storm" that ensued lasted on and off for two years.

BEST WAYS TO EXPLORE

BIRD-WATCHING

The road to Irazú provides some of the best roadside birding opportunities in the country, especially on a weekday when there isn't a constant parade of cars and buses heading up to the crater. Some of the most fruitful areas are on either side of the bridges you'll pass over. Reliable bird species that inhabit these roadsides are acorn and hairy woodpeckers; the brilliant flame-throated warbler; buzzing around blossoms, the fiery-throated green violetear; and (aptly named) volcano hummingbirds. Once past the main entrance, there are also plenty of opportunities to stop and bird-watch roadside. Look for volcano juncos on the ground and slaty flowerpiercers visiting flowering shrubs.

HIKING

Even before you get to the main entrance, check out the park's Prusia Sector, which has hiking trails that pass through majestic oak and pine forests and picnic areas. They're popular with Tico families on weekends, so if you want the woods to yourself, come on a weekday. Trails in the park are well marked; avoid heading down any paths marked with *"paso restringido"* (passage restricted) signs.

VOLCANIC TIPS

A paved road leads all the way to the summit, where a small coffee shop sells hot beverages, and a persistent pair of coatis cruise the picnic tables for handouts. (Please resist the urge to feed them!) The road to the top climbs past vegetable fields, pastures, and native oak forests. You pass through the villages of Potrero Cerrado and San Juan de Chicuá before reaching the summit's bleak but beautiful main crater.

TOP REASONS TO GO

EASY TO GET TO

Irazú's proximity to San José and the entire eastern Central Valley makes it an easy half-day or day trip. Public transportation from the capital, frequently a cumbersome option to most of the country's national parks, is straightforward.

THE VIEW

How many places in the world let you peer directly into the crater of an active volcano? Costa Rica offers you two: here at Irazú and at Poás Volcano. Poás's steaming cauldron is spookier, but Irazú's crater lake with colors that change according to the light is nonetheless impressive.

MORE VIEWS

"On a clear day, you can see forever," goes the old song from the musical of the same name. Irazú is one of the few places in Costa Rica that lets you glimpse both the Pacific and Atlantic (Caribbean) oceans at once. "Clear" is the key term here: clouds frequently obscure the view. Early morning gives you your best shot.

Irazú's crater lake changes color with the light.

San José sits in an almost-mile-high mountain valley ringed by volcanoes whose ash has fertilized the soil and turned the region into Costa Rica's historic breadbasket. This will always be the land that coffee built, and the small cities of the Central Valley exhibit a tidiness and prosperity you don't see in the rest of the country. The valley is chock-full of activities and is Costa Rica at its most *típico*, giving you the best sense of what makes the country tick.

You can't find a more ideal climate than out here in the valley. When people refer to Costa Rica's proverbial "eternal spring," they're talking about this part of the country, which lacks the oppressive seasonal heat and rain of other regions. It's no wonder the Central Valley has drawn a growing number of North American and European retirees.

There's no shortage of terrific lodgings out here—everything from family-run boutique hotels to the big international chains are yours for the night. It used to be that everyone stayed in San José and took in the various attractions in the Central Valley on day trips. With the good selection of quality accommodations out here, why not base yourself in the Central Valley, and make San José your day trip instead?

MAJOR REGIONS

The communities immediately **west of San José** are the capital's booming, upscale suburbs. Things turn more pastoral the farther west you go, and you'll find one of the country's best craft communities, Sarchí, and pleasant countryside lodges near Atenas, a thriving agricultural center and quintessential Costa Rican town. Heading farther west toward the Central Pacific coast, Carara National Park is home to an impressive collection of plants and animals.

Coffee farms and small valley towns dominate the area **north of San José.** Their beautiful hotels attract visitors on their first and last nights in the country. Coffee plantations Café Britt and Doka Estate are both here, as is the international airport, near Alajuela. North of Alajuela, Poás Volcano's turquoise crater lake and steaming main crater make it many visitors' favorite volcano stop.

The less visited eastern Central Valley (**east of San José**) holds Cartago, older than San José, with a couple of historic attractions. Irazú is Costa Rica's tallest volcano. On a clear day you can see both the Atlantic and Pacific oceans from its peak. The nearby Orosi Valley is an often overlooked beauty. The drive into the valley is simply gorgeous, and a tranquil way to spend a day. Birding destination Tapantí National Park is at the southern edge of the valley. Rafting trips on the Pacuare and Reventazón are based in bustling, growing Turrialba. The nearby Guayabo National Monument, ruins of a city deserted in AD 1400, is Costa Rica's only significant archaeological site.

Planning

When to Go

HIGH SEASON: MID-DECEMBER TO APRIL

The Central Valley's elevation keeps temperatures pleasant and springlike year-round, slightly warmer to the west and slightly cooler to the east. Turrialba and the Orosi Valley represent a transition zone between the valley and the Caribbean slope; expect warmer temperatures there. December and January kick off the dry season with sunny days and brisk nights. February, March, and April warm up considerably. Most hotels here keep rates constant throughout the year; a few follow high-season/low-season fluctuations.

LOW SEASON: MAY TO MID-NOVEMBER

The rainy season moves in gradually with afternoon showers from May through July. August becomes wetter, and September and October can mean prolonged downpours. The valley's western sector—Alajuela, San Antonio de Belén, Escazú, and Santa Ana—always catches a tad less rain than its eastern counterpart.

SHOULDER SEASON: MID-NOVEMBER TO MID-DECEMBER

Rains start to wind down by mid-November, and the month before December holidays is a terrific time to enjoy the Central Valley at its most lush and green, and before the big influx of tourists arrives. As an added bonus, the coffee harvest is underway in earnest in this part of the country, too—always a bustling, fascinating spectacle.

Planning Your Time

You could spend an entire week here without getting bored, but if you have only a week or two in Costa Rica, we recommend a maximum of two days before heading to rain forests and beaches in other parts of the country. Spending a day after you arrive, then another day or two before you fly out, gives you a taste of the region, breaks up the travel time, and makes your last day interesting, rather than spent in transit back to San José. The drive between just about any two points in the Central Valley is two hours or usually less, so it's ideal for short trips. Tour operators in and around San José offer daylong excursions that mix and match the valley's sights—perhaps a volcano visit in the morning and a coffee tour in the afternoon.

Getting Here and Around

AIR

Although Aeropuerto Internacional Juan Santamaría (SJO) is billed as San José's airport, it sits just outside the city of Alajuela in the near northwestern part of the valley. You can get taxis from the airport to any point in the Central Valley for $10–$120. Some hotels arrange pickup.

BUS

Many visitors never consider taking a local bus to get around, but doing so puts you in close contact with locals—an experience you miss out on if you travel by taxi or tour bus. It's also cheap. Always opt for a taxi at night or when you're in a hurry.

CAR

All points in the western Central Valley can be reached by car. For San Antonio de Belén, Heredia, Alajuela, and points north of San José, turn right at the west end of Paseo Colón onto the Pan-American Highway (Autopista General Cañas or Highway CA1). A left at the west end of Paseo Colón and then a right is the start of the Highway to Caldera (Highway 27). It takes you to Escazú and Santa Ana and beyond to the Pacific coast. The eastern Central Valley is accessible from San José by driving east on Avenida 2, then Central, through San Pedro, then following signs from the intersection to Cartago on Highway CA2. To get to the Orosi Valley, head straight through Cartago, turn right at the Basílica de Nuestra Señora de los Angeles, and follow the signs to Paraíso. The road through Cartago and Paraíso continues east to Turrialba. Driving from one side of the valley to the other means you need to get across San José. There's no efficient way to bypass the capital.

You'll encounter toll plazas just before Juan Santamaría International Airport on the way to Alajuela; across from the mammoth Terramall shopping center on the way to Cartago; just beyond the first Escazú exit on the way to Santa Ana; and north of San José near the entrance to Braulio Carrillo National Park on the way to the Caribbean coast.

The best way to get around the Central Valley is by car. Most of the car-rental agencies in San José have offices at or near the airport in Alajuela. They will deliver vehicles to many area hotels, but not those in Turrialba and the Orosi Valley.

TAXI

All Central Valley towns have taxis, which usually wait for fares along their central parks. The rideshare service Uber operates, albeit without proper permits, in a few of the larger suburbs—Escazú, Santa Ana, Alajuela, Heredia, and Cartago—in the Central Valley. Until Uber and the government reconcile their differences, you use the service at some risk.

Restaurants

Growing Escazú has become as metropolitan as San José and has the restaurant selection to prove it. Elsewhere, as befits this cradle of the country's tradition, typical Costa Rican cuisine still reigns.

Hotels

Most international flights come into Costa Rica in the evening and head out early in the morning, meaning you likely have to stay your first and last nights in or near San José, and the Central Valley can be considered "near." For getting away from it all and still being close to the country's main airport, the lodgings around San José make splendid alternatives to staying in the city itself. It may pain you to tear yourself away from that beach villa or rain-forest lodge, but you can still come back to something distinctive here on your last night in Costa Rica. Small mom-and-pop places, sprawling coffee plantations, nature lodges, and hilltop villas with expansive views are some of your options. The large chains are here as well, but the real gems are the boutique hotels, many of which are family-run places and have unique designs that take advantage of exceptional countryside locations. Subtropical gardens are the norm, rather than the exception. The Central Valley's climate is often a great surprise to first-time visitors—it's usually cool enough at night to go without air-conditioning, so don't be surprised if many hotels don't have it.

HOTEL AND RESTAURANT PRICES

Restaurant prices are the average cost of a main course at dinner or, if dinner is not served, at lunch. Hotel prices are the lowest cost of a standard double room in high season. Restaurant and hotel reviews have been shortened. For full information, visit Fodors.com.

What it Costs in U.S. Dollars

$	$$	$$$	$$$$
RESTAURANTS			
under $10	$10–$15	$16–$25	over $25
HOTELS			
under $75	$75–$150	$151–$250	over $250

Escazú

5 km (3 miles) southwest of San José.

Costa Rica's wealthiest community and the Central Valley's most prestigious address, Escazú (pronounced *es-cah-SOO*) nevertheless mixes glamour with tradition, BMWs with oxcarts, trendy malls with farmers' markets, Louis Vuitton with burlap produce sacks. As you exit the highway and crest the first gentle hill, you might think you made a wrong turn and ended up in Southern California, but farther up you return to small-town Central America. Narrow roads wind their way up the steep slopes, past postage-stamp coffee fields and lengths of shoulder-to-shoulder, modest houses with tidy gardens and the occasional oxcart parked in the yard. Unfortunately, the area's stream of new developments and high-rises has steadily chipped away at the rural landscape—each year you have to climb higher to find the kind of scene that captured the attention of many a Costa Rican painter in the early 20th century. In their place are plenty of fancy homes and condos, especially in the San Rafael neighborhood. Escazú's

historic church faces a small plaza, surrounded in part by weathered adobe buildings. The town center is several blocks north of the busy road to Santa Ana, which is lined with a growing selection of restaurants, bars, and shops.

During colonial days, Escazú was dubbed the "City of Witches" because many native healers lived in the area. Locals say that Escazú is still Costa Rica's most haunted community, home to witches who will tell your fortune or concoct a love potion for a small fee, but you'd be hard-pressed to spot them in the town's busy commercial district. Try a soccer field instead: the city's soccer team is christened Las Brujas (the Witches). You'll see a huge number of witch-on-a-broomstick decals affixed to vehicles here, too; it's the city's official symbol.

GETTING HERE AND AROUND

To drive to Escazú from San José, turn left at the western end of Paseo Colón, which ends at the Parque La Sabana. Take the first right onto the Caldera Highway, and get off the highway at the second exit. The off-ramp curves right, then sharply left; follow it about 1 km (½ mile), sticking to the main road, to El Cruce at the bottom of the hill (marked by the large Physiomed orthopedic clinic). Continue through the traffic light for San Rafael addresses; turn right for the old road to Santa Ana. The trip takes about 20 minutes, much longer during rush hour. A steady stream of buses for Escazú runs from several stops near, but not inside, the Terminal Coca-Cola in San José (Avenidas 1–3, Calles 14–16), with service from 5 am to 11 pm.

⚠ **Be careful: the Coca-Cola neighborhood is a dicey part of downtown San José.**

TAXIS Coopetico. ☎ 2224–7979.

ESSENTIALS

BANKS/ATMS BAC Credomatic. ✉ 200 meters (656 feet) south of El Cruce, San Rafael, Escazú ☎ 309/2295–9797 ⊕ www.bac.net. **Banco de Costa Rica**

ATM. ✉ *125 meters (410 feet) west of Municipalidad, Escazú.* **Banco Nacional.** ✉ *Southwest side of Parque Central, Escazú* ☎ *2228–0009* 🌐 *www.bncr.fi.cr.*

MEDICAL ASSISTANCE Hospital CIMA. ✉ *12 km (7½ miles) west of downtown San José, next to PriceSmart, just off hwy. to Santa Ana, Escazú* ☎ *2208–1000, 855/782–6253 in North America* 🌐 *www.hospitalcima.com.*

PHARMACY Farmacia San Miguel. ✉ *North side of Parque Central, Escazú* ☎ *2228–2339.*

POST OFFICE Correos. ✉ *100 meters (328 feet) north of church, Escazú* 🌐 *correos.go.cr.*

Sights

Butterfly Kingdom

FARM/RANCH | FAMILY | Butterflies are the "livestock" at this working farm in the heart of Escazú, where caterpillars are raised and then exported in chrysalis form. A two-hour tour of the operation takes you through the stages of a butterfly's life. The highlight is the garden where fluttering butterflies surround you. Sunny days fuel the most activity among them; they are quieter if the day is overcast. (The latter conditions make for easier photos.) Bilingual tours in English and Spanish are included in the admission price. The place can be difficult to find. Call for directions or take a taxi. Drivers know the facility as the *mariposario.* ✉ *Bello Horizonte, 1 km (½ mile) south and 100 meters (328 feet) west of Distribuidora Santa Bárbara, Escazú* ☎ *2288–6667* 🌐 *www.butterflykingdom.net* 🎫 *$5.*

Iglesia San Miguel Arcángel

(*Church of St. Michael the Archangel*) **CHURCH** | According to tradition, ghosts and witches work their spells, good and bad, over Escazú. The founders of this haunted town fittingly chose the archangel Michael, reputed to have driven Satan from heaven, as their patron saint. The original church on this site dates from 1796, but earthquakes took their toll, as they have on so many historic sites throughout Costa Rica. A complete reconstruction was done in 1962, remaining as true as possible to the original design, but up to current earthquake building codes. The results are still impressive six decades later. A statue of St. Michael watches from the left side of the main altar. ✉ *Parque Central, Escazú* ☎ *2228–0635.*

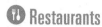

Restaurants

Barbecue Los Anonos

$$ | BARBECUE | FAMILY | Costa Ricans flock here to enjoy Los Anonos' family-friendly grill fest. Your best bet is the grilled meat, and there is plenty to choose from, including imported U.S. beef and less expensive Costa Rican cuts. **Known for:** family-friendly service; reasonably priced weekday lunch specials; hearty grilled steaks. [$] *Average main: $14* ✉ *400 meters (1,312 feet) west of Los Anonos Bridge, Escazú* ☎ *2228–0180* 🌐 *www.restaurantelosanonos.com* 🕒 *Closed Mon.*

Búlali

$$ | CAFÉ | The name means "honey" in Costa Rica's indigenous Bribri language, and that—rather than refined sugar—provides the added sweetness to the baked goods here. Croissants, quinoa pancakes, and omelets make for filling breakfasts while light beef, chicken, and veggie fare with salads round out the lunch offerings. **Known for:** fruit and honey smoothies; mouthwatering baked goods; plenty of gluten-free offerings, a rarity in Costa Rica. [$] *Average main: $14* ✉ *Avda. Escazú, Autopista Próspero Fernández, Escazú* ☎ *2519–9090* 🌐 *www.bulaliartesanal.com.*

Gallo Rojo

$$ | ASIAN | An upscale tour of the street food of East and Southeast Asia focuses primarily on the owner's mother's native

Taiwan, with flavors from Japan, Korea, Vietnam, Thailand, and Singapore mixed in for good measure. The wealth of riches includes *gua bao* (a Taiwanese steamed meat or chicken sandwich), *gyoza* (Japanese-style pork and ginger rolls), pad Thai, and Singapore noodles. **Known for:** friendly staff; several gluten-free options; gastronomic tour of Asia. $ *Average main: $12* ⊠ *Escazú* ✛ *100 meters (328 feet) east, 300 meters (984 feet) north of Centro Comercial El Paco* ☎ *2289–5254* ⊕ *www.gallorojocr.com* ☽ *No dinner Sun.*

★ La Divina Comida

$$$$ | **PERUVIAN** | The country's top Peruvian restaurant uses fresh local ingredients to re-create Peru's greatest hits, served with style. A variety of ceviches accompany favorites such as aji chicken risotto, grilled octopus in balsamic vinaigrette, or *lomito saltado* (beef tenderloin in tomato sauce). **Known for:** impeccable service; sceney vibe; attention to detail. $ *Average main: $26* ⊠ *Avda. Escazú, Autopista Próspero Fernández, Escazú* ☎ *2208–8899* ⊕ *www.ladivinacomidacr.com.*

Plaza España

$$$ | **SPANISH** | Generous portions of Spanish tapas and entrées draw diners to this whitewashed adobe house up the hill near San Antonio de Escazú. Presentation isn't the strong suit here: straight-up good food is, as are reasonable prices. **Known for:** friendly, informal setting; mouthwatering sangrias; reasonably priced Spanish menu. $ *Average main: $16* ⊠ *Del Cruce del Barrio El Carmen, San Antonio de Escazú, Escazú* ☎ *2228–1850* ☽ *Closed Mon. and Tues. No dinner Sun.*

★ Taj Mahal

$$$ | **INDIAN** | This burst of northern Indian flavor is a surprising treat. Richly swathed in warm fuchsias, red ochers, and golds, the mansion's dining area sprawls through a handful of small, intimate rooms and out to a gazebo in the tree-covered backyard. **Known for:** impressive vegetarian offerings in a

mostly meat-devouring country; pleasant, helpful waitstaff; great tandoori menu. $ *Average main: $20* ⊠ *1 km (½ mile) west of Paco mall on old road to Santa Ana, Escazú* ☎ *2228–0980* ⊕ *www.thetajmahalrestaurant.com.*

 ## Hotels

Casa de las Tías

$$ | **B&B/INN** | The full range of city services is at your doorstep here, but you're blissfully apart from them at this tranquil bed-and-breakfast at the quiet end of a short road. **Pros:** tranquil, without sacrificing convenience; service goes the extra mile; excellent breakfast. **Cons:** slightly dated feel; no kids under 10; walls could be a little thicker. $ *Rooms from: $84* ⊠ *100 meters (328 feet) south and 150 meters (492 feet) east of El Cruce; turn east just south of Restaurante Carpe Diem, Escazú* ☎ *2289–5517* ⊕ *www.casadelastias.com* ⊐ *5 units* ⦵ *Free Breakfast.*

Costa Verde Inn

$ | **B&B/INN** | When they need to make a city run, many beach-living expats head straight for this quiet B&B on the outskirts of Escazú, and it's a good example to follow. **Pros:** inviting public areas; excellent value; friendly staff. **Cons:** can be difficult to find; pool is for plungers, not swimmers; large student groups in summer. $ *Rooms from: $72* ⊠ *Escazú* ✛ *300 meters (984 feet) south of southeast corner of second cemetery (the farthest west)* ☎ *2228–4080, 800/773–5013* ⊕ *www.costaverdeinn.com* ⊐ *19 rooms* ⦵ *Free Breakfast.*

Posada El Quijote

$$ | **B&B/INN** | Perched on a hill in Escazú's Bello Horizonte neighborhood, with a great view of the city, this B&B strikes the right balance between a small inn and a tasteful private residence. **Pros:** peaceful, friendly place to spend first or last night; excellent staff; stupendous views. **Cons:** can be difficult to find;

Costa Rica's oxcarts are folkloric symbols and a common canvas for local artisans.

standard rooms not quite as nice; need a car to get around. $ Rooms from: $85 ✉ 1st street west of Anonos Bridge, 1 km (½ mile) up hill, Bello Horizonte, Escazú ☎ 2289–8401 ⊕ www.quijote.cr ➥ 8 units ❙◎❙ Free Breakfast.

Nightlife

Escazú is the Central Valley's hot spot for nightlife—many San José residents head here for the restaurants, bars, and dance clubs that cater to a young, smartphone-toting crowd. You can't miss the bright lights as you swing into town off the toll highway.

Henry's Beach Cafe

CAFÉS | A popular watering hole with the under-30 set, this spot has televised sports by day, varied music by night, and an island theme of beach paintings and surfboards. Costa Ricans refer to this style of bar as an "American bar," which is fairly accurate. ✉ Plaza San Rafael, 200 meters (656 feet) north of Centro Comercial Paco, Escazú ☎ 2289–6239 ⊕ www.henrysbeachcafe.com.

Jazz Café Escazú

LIVE MUSIC | Music fans chill out here. The boxy club hosts an eclectic live-music lineup. ✉ First exit after tollbooths, next to Confort Suizo, across hwy. from Hospital Cima, Escazú ☎ 2288–4740 ⊕ www.jazzcafecostarica.com.

Pocket

BARS | A great cocktail selection with very smooth gin-tonics is yours at this unassuming place in downtown Escazú. Occasional live music is on the schedule, too. ✉ Escazú ✛ 175 meters (574 feet) south of Musmanni bakery ☎ 2289–3432 ⊕ www.pocketcr.com.

Tintos y Blancos

WINE BARS | Although part of the enormous Multiplaza mall, sophisticated wine bar Tintos y Blancos ("reds and whites," as in wine colors) has its own entrance in back. It offers a quality selection of libations, primarily Chilean and Argentine wines, with several French and Italian to round out the choices. ✉ *Multiplaza mall, C. Multiplaza, Escazú* ☎ *2201–5937* ⊕ *www.tintosyblancos.com.*

🛍 Shopping

Escazú's Saturday-morning farmers' market makes a terrific place to stock up on fresh fruit and vegetables if you're preparing a do-it-yourself lunch or just want to snack. Vendors start lining the street on the south side of the church around dawn, and things begin to wind down by late morning. If you get the shopping bug and absolutely must visit a mall while on vacation, Escazú is the place to do it. Multiplaza, on the south side of the toll highway, approximately 5 km (3 miles) west of San José, is Costa Rica's most luxurious mall.

★ Biesanz Woodworks

CRAFTS | Expat artist Barry Biesanz creates unique, world-class items from Costa Rican hardwoods, which are turned (a form of woodworking) on-site. Local artisans also ply their trade here. It's difficult to find, so take a taxi or call for directions from your hotel. ✉ *Bello Horizonte, 800 meters (2,624 feet) south of Escuela Bello Horizonte, Escazú* ☎ *2289–4337* ⊕ *www.biesanz.com.*

Congo

CRAFTS | Congo offers a good selection of wood carvings and ceramic bowls and vases made by local artisans. It's a small four-store chain. ✉ *Avda. Escazú, Autopista Próspero Fernández, Escazú* ☎ *2201–8017* ⊕ *www.costaricacongo.com.*

Multiplaza

MALL | Costa Rica's most upscale mall—think Kenneth Cole, Giorgio Armani, Oscar de la Renta, and many of their Costa Rican counterparts—looms over the highway with its 194 stores between Escazú and Santa Ana. ✉ *Caldera Hwy., between Escazú and Santa Ana, Escazú* ☎ *4001–7999* ⊕ *www.multiplaza.com.*

🏃 Activities

HIKING

High in the hills above Escazú is the tiny community of **San Antonio de Escazú,** famous for its annual oxcart festival held the second Sunday of March. The view from here—of nearby San José and distant volcanoes—is impressive by both day and night. If you head higher than San Antonio de Escazú, brace yourself for steep roads that wind up into the mountains toward **Pico Blanco,** the highest point in the Escazú Cordillera, which is a half-day hike to ascend. You can also hike **San Miguel,** one peak east. We recommend you go with an outfitter—far safer than hiking on your own.

Aventuras Picotours

HIKING & WALKING | The owner of Aventuras Picotours was the first Costa Rican to reach the summit of Everest; he can lead you on a variety of far less daunting daylong hikes in the hills above town. ✉ *Escazú* ☎ *8880–2676* ⊕ *www.facebook.com/aventuraspicotours* ✉ *Tours from $59.*

Santa Ana

17 km (10 miles) southwest of San José.

Santa Ana's tranquil town center, with its rugged stone church, has changed little through the years, even though condos and shopping malls now spread out in all directions. The church, which was built between 1870 and 1880, has a Spanish-tile roof, carved wooden doors, and two pre-Columbian stone spheres flanking its entrance. Its rustic interior—bare wooden pillars and beams and black iron lamps—seems appropriate for an area with a tradition of ranching. Because it's warmer and drier than the towns to the east, Santa Ana is one of the few Central Valley towns that doesn't have a good climate for coffee. (It is Costa Rica's onion capital, however.) Though development encroaches every year—Santa Ana is well on its way to becoming another Escazú—you can still find pastures and patches of forest around the area; it isn't unusual to see men on horseback here.

GETTING HERE AND AROUND

From San José, turn left at the western end of Paseo Colón, which ends at the Parque La Sabana. Take the first right, and get on the highway. Get off at the sixth exit; bear left at the flashing red lights, winding past roadside stands selling ceramics and vegetables before hitting the town center, about 2 km (1 mile) from the highway. The trip takes about 25 minutes if there's little traffic. Blue buses to Santa Ana leave from inside San José's Terminal Coca-Cola every 8 to 10 minutes during the day.

⚠ **Be careful: the Coca-Cola area is a dodgy part of downtown San José.**

To get to places along the toll highway or Piedades, take buses marked "Pista" or "Multiplaza." Those marked "Calle Vieja" leave every 15 minutes and pass through Escazú on the old road to Santa Ana. Buses run from 5 am to 11 pm.

ESSENTIALS

BANKS/ATMS Banco de Costa Rica. ✉ *Northwest corner of central park, Santa Ana* ☎ *2203–4281* 🌐 *www.bancobcr.com.* **Banco Nacional.** ✉ *100 meters (328 feet) south of church, Santa Ana* ☎ *2282–2479* 🌐 *www.bncr.fi.cr.*

MEDICAL ASSISTANCE Clínica Bíblica. ✉ *Autopista Próspero Fernández, Santa Ana* ☎ *2522–1000* 🌐 *www.clinicabiblica.com.* **Farmacia Sucre.** ✉ *25 meters (82 feet) south of church, Santa Ana* ☎ *2282–1296.*

POST OFFICE Correos. ✉ *Next to Municipalidad, Santa Ana* 🌐 *correos.go.cr.*

👁 Sights

Refugio Animal

WILDLIFE REFUGE | FAMILY | This former "herpetology refuge" between Santa Ana and Escazú has opened its doors to more than just snakes: macaws, monkeys, and crocodiles reside here, too. As with all such facilities around Costa Rica, the ultimate goal is to release animals back into the wild. But for many, their fragile condition means they will live out their days here. ✉ *Santa Ana* ✥ *2 km (1 mile) east of Santa Ana on old road to Escazú* ☎ *2282–4614* 🌐 *www.refugioanimalcr.com* 🎟 *$20* ⏲ *Closed Mon.*

🍴 Restaurants

★ Andiamo Là

$$$ | ITALIAN | One of the Central Valley's trendiest restaurants stands out with its daily fish and meat specials, including starter carpaccios of salmon, octopus, and beef. The sea bass and jumbo shrimp combination plate comes with a sauce of chopped fresh tomatoes, white wine, and garlic. **Known for:** terrific-value lunch specials; polished, friendly service; delicious homemade pastas. [$] *Average main: $21* ✉ *Next to Más X Menos supermarket, Santa Ana* ☎ *2282–7879* 🌐 *www.andiamola.com* ⏲ *No dinner Sun.*

Bacchus

$$$ | ECLECTIC | Take a Peruvian chef who trained in France and an Italian owner, and the result is this solid member of the local dining scene. Duck breast in a port sauce, baked mushroom-and-polenta ragout, and a variety of pizzas are among the delights to be found on the menu. **Known for:** extensive wine list; elegant setting with modern art and garden terrace; impressive French and Italian menu. [$] *Average main: $19* ✉ *200 meters east and 100 meters north of church, Santa Ana* ☎ *2282–5441* 🌐 *www.facebook.com/bacchusrestaurante* ⏲ *Closed Mon.*

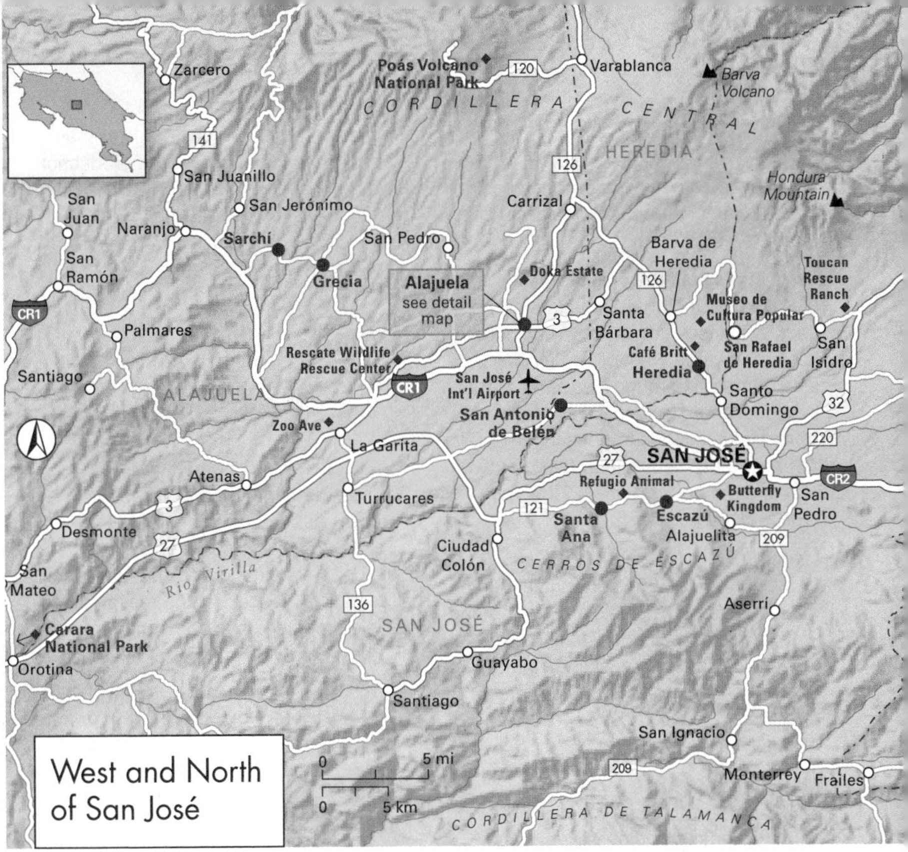
West and North of San José
Zarcero
Poás Volcano National Park
120
Varablanca
Barva Volcano
CORDILLERA CENTRAL
141
126
HEREDIA
San Juanillo
Hondura Mountain
San Juan
San Jerónimo
Carrizal
Naranjo
Sarchí
San Pedro
San Ramón
Grecia
Alajuela see detail map
Doka Estate
Barva de Heredia
Toucan Rescue Ranch
CR1
Museo de Cultura Popular
Santa Bárbara
3
Palmares
San Rafael de Heredia
San Isidro
Rescate Wildlife Rescue Center
Café Britt
Heredia
Santiago
ALAJUELA
San José Int'l Airport
Santo Domingo
32
San Antonio de Belén
Zoo Ave
La Garita
220
27
SAN JOSÉ
CR2
Atenas
Refugio Animal
Butterfly Kingdom
San Pedro
Turrucares
121
Santa Ana
Escazú
Alajuelita
Desmonte
209
Ciudad Colón
CERROS DE ESCAZÚ
San Mateo
Río Virilla
136
Aserrí
SAN JOSÉ
Carara National Park
Orotina
Guayabo
Santiago
San Ignacio
Monterrey
Frailes
0 5 mi
0 5 km
CORDILLERA DE TALAMANCA

Hotels

Hotel Alta Las Palomas
$$$ | **HOTEL** | The view from this hotel perched on a hillside above Santa Ana is impressive, but so is the building itself with its blend of colonial and modern style—think archways, hardwoods, and leather. **Pros:** classy service; panoramic views; excellent value for the price. **Cons:** little to do within walking distance; best to have a car to stay here; lower-floor rooms lose out on the view. [$] *Rooms from: $180* ✉ *2½ km (1½ miles) west of Paco shopping center, on old road between Santa Ana and Escazú, Alto de las Palomas, Santa Ana* ☎ *2282–8882, 800/242–0500 in North America* 🌐 *www.thealtahotel.com* 🛏 *23 rooms* 🍴 *Free Breakfast.*

★ **Hotel Villa Los Candiles**
$$ | **HOTEL** | You'd never expect to find such a quiet, homey oasis smack-dab in the middle of a suburban business neighborhood, but here it is. **Pros:** attentive staff; suites have kitchenettes; pet-friendly. **Cons:** hot water sometimes takes time to heat up; middle of busy commercial area; can be difficult to find. [$] *Rooms from: $113* ✉ *350 meters (1,148 feet) east, 25 meters (82 feet) south of Más X Menos supermarket, Santa Ana* ☎ *2282–8280* 🌐 *www.hotelvillaloscandiles.com* 💳 *No credit cards* 🛏 *28 rooms* 🍴 *Free Breakfast.*

Nightlife

As metro-area development marches west, a few nightspots have set up shop out here, too.

Costa Rica's Craft Brewing Company
BREWPUBS | One of the pioneers of the country's nascent microbrewery industry has set up shop west of Santa Ana, serving two year-round ales and several seasonal ones. They make a nice change from the ubiquitous Imperial beer. ⊠ *Santa Ana ✛ 200 meters (656 feet) south of Parques del Sol* ☎ *2249–4277* ⊕ *www. facebook.com/lacraftcr.*

Latitud 9
GATHERING PLACES | This stylish bar serves good cocktails in a sleek, modern setting with indoor and outdoor seating. DJs take over after 9 on weekend nights. ⊠ *City Pl., Santa Ana ✛ 200 meters (656 feet) north of Red Cross* ☎ *4035–3111* ⊕ *latitud-9o.negocio.site.*

MAD Burger & Beer
BARS | These folks make some of the country's best burgers, served to the accompaniment of a good selection of beer and other drinks. ⊠ *Santa Ana Town Center, Santa Ana ✛ 100 meters (328 feet) east of Red Cross* ☎ *4700–1888* ⊕ *www.facebook.com/madbarcr.*

Tap House
BREWPUBS | This low-key, mostly local place serves up 30 types of beer— domestic and imported—with the requisite selection of chicken wings, nachos, and other appetizers. ⊠ *City Pl., Santa Ana ✛ 200 meters (656 feet) north of Red Cross* ☎ *2100–8447* ⊕ *www. facebook.com/TapHouseCR.*

Shopping

Cerámica Las Palomas
CERAMICS | Large glazed pots with ornate decorations that range from traditional patterns to modern motifs are the specialties here. Flowerpots and lamps are also common works here, and the staff will happily show you the production process, from raw clay to art. ⊠ *Old road to Santa Ana, opposite Hotel Alta, Santa Ana* ☎ *2282–7001* ⊕ *www.ceramica-laspalomas.webs.com.*

Grecia

26 km (16 miles) northwest of Alajuela, 46 km (29 miles) northwest of San José.

The quiet farming community of Grecia—the name means "Greece" in Spanish—is reputed to be Costa Rica's cleanest town, and some enthusiastic civic boosters extend that superlative to all of Latin America, but the reason most people stop here is to admire its unusual church. A growing number of expats now call the town home.

GETTING HERE AND AROUND
From San José continue west on the highway past the airport—the turnoff is on the right—or head into Alajuela and turn left just before the Alajuela cemetery. Buses leave Calle 20 in San José for Grecia every 30 minutes from 5:30 am to 10 pm. From Alajuela, buses to Grecia/Ciudad Quesada pick up on the southern edge of town (Calle 4 and Avenida 10).

ESSENTIALS
BANKS/ATMS BAC Credomatic. ⊠ *100 meters (328 feet) north of central park, Grecia* ☎ *2295–9696* ⊕ *www.bac.net.* **Banco Nacional.** ⊠ *Northwest corner of central park, Grecia* ☎ *2444–0690* ⊕ *www.bncr.fi.cr.*

Sights

Church of Our Lady of Mercy (*Iglesia de Nuestra Señora de las Mercedes*)
CHURCH | This brick-red Gothic-style church is made of prefabricated iron. It's one of two buildings in the country made from steel frames and iron sheets imported from Belgium in the late 19th century (the other is the metal

schoolhouse next to San José's Parque Morazán), when some prominent Costa Ricans decided that metal structures would better withstand the periodic earthquakes that had taken their toll on so much of the country's architecture. The frames were shipped from Antwerp to Limón, then transported by train to Alajuela—from which the metal walls of the church were carried by oxcarts. Locals refer to the building as simply the "Iglesia Metálica" (Metal Church). The splendid 1886 German pipe organ, regarded as Costa Rica's finest, is worth a look inside. ⊠ *Avda. 1, Cs. 1–3, Grecia* ☎ *2494–1616.*

Shopping

★ Feria del Agricultor

MARKET | Grecia's covered weekend farmers' market is one of Costa Rica's liveliest and best. It runs Friday afternoon and evening until 9—fairy lights sparkle during the evening hours—and starts up again at 5 the next morning, winding down around noon. Fresh produce is yours for the buying and, if you time it right, homemade tortillas and cinnamon rolls too. While either day is fun to attend, there's a better selection of produce on Friday. ⊠ *Grecia ✛ 200 meters (656 feet) west of Tribunales de Justicia* ☎ *2494–7360.*

Sarchí

8 km (5 miles) west of Grecia, 53 km (33 miles, 1½ hrs) northwest of San José.

Tranquil Sarchí is Costa Rica's premier center for crafts and carpentry. People drive here from all over the country to shop for furniture, and tour buses regularly descend upon the souvenir shops outside town. The area's most famous products are its brightly painted oxcarts—replicas of those traditionally used to transport coffee. Sarchí, as Costa Rica's consummate day-trip destination,

has developed little acceptable lodging of its own. There are plenty of places to stay, however, in the nearby communities (San Ramón, Atenas, and Alajuela).

GETTING HERE AND AROUND

To get to Sarchí from San José, take the highway well past the airport to the turnoff for Naranjo; then veer right just as you enter Naranjo. Direct buses to Sarchí depart from Alajuela (Calle 8, Avenidas 1–3) every 30 minutes from 6 am to 9 pm; the ride takes 90 minutes.

ESSENTIALS

BANK/ATM Banco Nacional. ⊠ *South side of soccer field, Sarchí* ☎ *2454–3044* ⊕ *www.bncr.fi.cr.*

POST OFFICE Correos. ⊠ *South side of soccer field, Sarchí* ⊕ *correos.go.cr.*

Sights

Else Kientzler Botanical Garden

(*Jardín Botánico Else Kientzler*)
GARDEN | FAMILY | Some 2,000 plant species, tropical and subtropical, flourish on 17 acres here, and all are well labeled. The German owner named the facility, affiliated with an ornamental-plant exporter, after his late plant-loving mother. About half of the garden's pathways are wheelchair accessible. When the tropical fruit trees are in season, visitors are permitted to pick and eat the fruit. Kids enjoy the maze and playground. ⊠ *400 meters north of soccer field, Sarchí* ☎ *2454–2070* ⊕ *www.elsegarden.com* 🗺 *$6.*

★ La Carreta

OTHER ATTRACTION | The world's largest oxcart, constructed and brightly painted by longtime local factory Souvenirs Costa Rica and enshrined in the *Guinness Book of World Records,* can be found in Sarchí's central park. The work—locals refer to it as simply La Carreta (the Oxcart)—logs in at 45 feet and weighs 2 tons. Since no other country is attached to oxcarts quite like Costa Rica, we doubt that record will be broken anytime soon. Oxcarts were used by 19th-century coffee farmers to transport the all-important cash crop to the port of Puntarenas on the Pacific coast. Artisans began painting the carts in the early 1900s. Debate continues as to why: the kaleidoscopic designs may have symbolized the points of the compass, or may have echoed the landscape's tropical colors. In any case, the oxcart has become the national symbol. ✉ *Center of Sarchí, central park, Sarchí.*

Souvenirs Costa Rica
(*Taller Eloy Alfaro e Hijos*)
FACTORY | Costa Rica's only real remaining oxcart factory was founded in 1920, and its carpentry methods have changed little since then. The guiding spirit of founder Eloy Alfaro lives on here, but the business and tradition have passed onto subsequent generations of his family. The two-story wooden building housing the wood shop is surrounded by trees and flowers—mostly orchids—and all the machinery on the ground floor is powered by a waterwheel at the back of the shop. Carts are painted in the back, and although the factory's main products are genuine oxcarts—which sell for up to $2,500—there are also some smaller mementos that can easily be shipped home. A cavernous restaurant serves food, buffet-style. ✉ *Sarchí* ✥ *200 meters (656 feet) north of soccer field* ☎ *2454–4131.*

🍴 Restaurants

Restaurante La Finca
$ | COSTA RICAN | This is a good place to stop for lunch when you need a break from shopping, with a variety of steaks, spicy chorizos, *arroz con pollo* (rice and chicken), and soups—we recommend the maize soup—on the menu. You might not expect it in this mix, but the pizza is pretty good, too. **Known for:** nice variety of pizza; popular with tour groups; hearty tico food. [$] *Average main: $9* ✉ *Down road at turnoff next to Plaza de Artesanía, Sarchí* ☎ *2454–1602* 🌐 *www.restaurantelafincasarchi.com* 🕒 *No dinner.*

🛍 Shopping

Sarchí is the best place in Costa Rica to buy miniature oxcarts, the larger of which are designed to serve as patio bars or end tables and can be broken down for easy transportation or shipped to your home. Another popular item is a locally produced rocking chair with a leather seat and back.

Plaza de la Artesanía
SHOPPING CENTER | Sarchí's answer to a shopping mall gathers a dozen artisan and souvenir shops under one roof. Expect to find oxcarts, the town's signature symbol, and everything else imaginable. If you can't find it here, it probably doesn't exist in Costa Rica. ✉ *Sarchí Sur* ✥ *2 km (1 mile) south of Sarchí.*

Carara National Park

43 km (27 miles) southwest of Atenas, 85 km (53 miles) southwest of San José.

In the wilderness of Carara National Park and surroundings, you might encounter white-faced capuchin monkeys in the trees or crocodiles lounging on a riverbank. The region is extremely biologically diverse, making it an excellent destination for bird-watchers and other wildlife enthusiasts.

GETTING HERE AND AROUND

Take Highway 27 west of San José beyond Orotina and follow the signs to Jacó and Quepos. The reserve is on the left after you cross Río Tárcoles. From San José, you can hop on a bus to Jacó, Quepos, or Manuel Antonio, and ask to be dropped off near the park entrance, about a two-hour drive. An organized tour is far easier. Jacó is the nearest town and the most logical base for trips into the park. Local travel agencies and tour

En Route

Zarcero. The central park of this small, tidy town 15 km (9 miles) north of Sarchí on the road to Ciudad Quesada looks as if it were designed by Dr. Seuss. Evangelista Blanco, a local landscape artist, modeled cypress topiaries in fanciful animal shapes—motorcycle-riding monkeys, a lightbulb-eyed elephant—that enliven the park in front of the town church. (An NPR feature on Zarcero once dubbed Blanco "Señor Scissorhands.") Soft lighting illuminates the park in the evening. The church interior is covered with elaborate pastel stencil work and detailed religious paintings by the late Misael Solís, a well-known local artist. Sample some cheese if you're in town, too; Zarcero-made cheese is one of Costa Rica's favorites, and it's available in a few shops on the west side of the central park. The town is frequently included as a short stop on many organized tours heading to the northern region of the country. ⊠ *Zarcero.*

operators arrange transportation to and guides through the park.

⚠ **Cars parked at the trailhead have been broken into. If you don't see a ranger on duty at the Sendero Laguna Meandrica trailhead, avoid leaving anything of value in your vehicle. You may be able to leave your belongings at the main ranger station (several miles south of the trailhead), where you can also buy drinks and souvenirs and use the restroom. Otherwise, visit the park as a day trip from a nearby hotel.**

TOURS

Horizontes

ECOTOURISM | The country's premier nature-tour operator can arrange visits to Carara National Park as a day trip from San José or as part of a longer tour. ☎ *4052–5850, 888/786–8748 in North America* ⊕ *www.horizontes.com* ⊠ *From $45.*

Jaguar Riders

SPECIAL-INTEREST TOURS | This Jacó-based tour operator can arrange guided ATV tours through the forests of Carara National Park. ⊠ *Avda. Pastor Díaz, next to Pancho Villa restaurant, Jacó* ☎ *2643–0180* ⊕ *www.jaguariders.com* ⊠ *From $69.*

Sights

Carara National Park

(*Parque Nacional Carara*)

NATIONAL PARK | Sparse undergrowth here makes wildlife easier to see than in most other parks, although proximity to major population centers means that tour buses arrive regularly in high season, prompting some animals to head deeper into the forest. Come very early or late in the day to avoid the crowds. Bird-watchers can call the day before to arrange admission before the park opens. If you're lucky, you may glimpse armadillos, basilisk lizards, coatis, and any of several monkey species, as well as birds such as blue-crowned motmots, chestnut-mandibled toucans, and trogons. A network of trails takes 15 minutes to four hours to navigate. (Many of the trails are wheelchair accessible.) The park has guides, but you must arrange their services in advance. Camping is not permitted. ⊠ *Orotina ✛ East of Costanera, just south of bridge over Río Tárcoles* ☎ *2637–1080, 1192 national park hotline* ⊕ *www.sinac.go.cr* ⊠ *$10.*

San Antonio de Belén

17 km (10 miles) northwest of San José.

San Antonio de Belén has little to offer visitors but its rural charm and proximity to the international airport. The latter led developers to build several of the San José area's biggest hotels here. The country's sole Church of Jesus Christ of Latter-day Saints temple is also found here, open only to visitors of the Mormon faith. The town is a convenient departure point for trips to the western Central Valley, Pacific coast, and northern region. If you stay at any of the big hotel chains here, you likely won't even see the town, just the busy highway between San José and Alajuela.

GETTING HERE AND AROUND

From San José, turn right at the west end of Paseo Colón onto the Pan-American Highway (Carretera General Cañas). The San Antonio de Belén exit is at an overpass 6 km (4 miles) west of the Heredia exit, by the Real Cariari Mall. Turn left at the first intersection, cross over the highway, and continue 1 km (½ mile) to the forced right turn, driving 1½ km (1 mile) to the center of town. San Antonio is only 10 minutes from the airport.

ESSENTIALS

BANK/ATM Banco de Costa Rica. ✉ *50 meters (164 feet) north of rear of church, San Antonio* ☎ *2239–1149* 🌐 *www.bancobcr.com.*

MEDICAL ASSISTANCE Farmacia Sucre. ✉ *North side of church, San Antonio* ☎ *2293–9160.*

POST OFFICE Correos. ✉ *3 blocks west and 25 meters (82 feet) north of church, San Antonio* 🌐 *correos.go.cr.*

TAXIS Taxi Belén. ✉ *San Antonio de Belén, San Antonio* ☎ *2293–3300.*

Hotels

Costa Rica Marriott Hacienda Belén
$$$$ | HOTEL | FAMILY | The stately Marriott offers comprehensive luxury close to the airport, and, despite being a U.S. chain, has many distinctively Costa Rican touches. **Pros:** excellent service; lavish grounds; close to airport. **Cons:** tricky car access from highway; far from all sights; tendency to nickel-and-dime guests. [$] *Rooms from: $298* ✉ *1 km (½ mile) west of Bridgestone/Firestone, off Autopista General Cañas, San Antonio* ☎ *2298–0000, 800/535–4028 in North America* 🌐 *www.marriott.com* 🛏 *300 rooms* 🍴 *No Meals.*

El Rodeo Estancia
$$ | HOTEL | This quiet hotel bills itself as a "country hotel," though this is more in image than fact—El Rodeo's proximity to the airport and major business parks is the real draw. **Pros:** proximity to airport; spacious rooms; popular steak house restaurant. **Cons:** generic feel; best to have a car to stay here; cat on premises, so not a place to go if you dislike felines. [$] *Rooms from: $85* ✉ *Road to Santa Ana, 2 km (1 mile) east of Parque Central, San Antonio* ☎ *2293–3909* 🌐 *www.elrodeohotel.com* 🛏 *29 rooms* 🍴 *Free Breakfast.*

Alajuela

20 km (13 miles) northwest of San José.

Because of its proximity to the international airport (5–10 minutes away), many travelers spend their first or last night in or near Alajuela (pronounced *ah-lah-WHAY-lah*), but the beauty of the surrounding countryside persuades some to stay longer. Alajuela is Costa Rica's second-most-populated city, and a mere 30-minute bus ride from the capital, but it has a decidedly provincial air compared with San José. Architecturally, it differs little from the bulk of Costa Rican towns:

Alajuela Cathedral's painted domed cupola was rebuilt after the 1991 earthquake.

it's a grid of low-rise structures painted in dull pastel colors. A slightly lower elevation keeps Alajuela a couple of degrees warmer than the capital.

GETTING HERE AND AROUND

To reach Alajuela, head west on the highway past the San Antonio de Belén turnoff and turn right at the airport (watch for the overhead signs). Buses travel between San José (Avenida 2, Calles 12–14, opposite north side of Parque La Merced), the airport, and Alajuela, and run every five minutes from 4:40 am to 10:30 pm. The bus stop in Alajuela is 400 meters (1,312 feet) west, 25 meters (82 feet) north of the central park (Calle 3 and Avenida 1). Buses leave San José for the Rescate Wildlife Rescue Center (formerly Zoo Ave) from La Merced church (Calle 14 and Avenida 4) daily on the hour from 8 am to noon, returning on the hour from 10 am to 3 pm.

TAXIS Cootaxa. ☎ 2443–3030.

ESSENTIALS

BANKS/ATMS BAC Credomatic. ✉ *100 meters north of cathedral, Alajuela* ☎ *2295–9797* ⊕ *www.bac.net.* **Banco de Costa Rica.** ✉ *50 meters west of southwest corner of central park, Alajuela* ☎ *2440–9039* ⊕ *www.bancobcr.com.* **Banco Nacional.** ✉ *West side of central park, Alajuela* ☎ *2441–0373* ⊕ *www.bncr. fi.cr.*

HOSPITAL Hospital San Rafael. ✉ *1 km (½ mile) northeast of airport, on main road to Alajuela, Alajuela* ☎ *2436–1001.*

MEDICAL ASSISTANCE Farmacia Chavarría. ✉ *C. 4, Avdas. 1–Ctl., Alajuela* ☎ *2441–1231* ⊕ *www.facebook.com/ farmaciachavarriaexpress.*

POST OFFICE Correos. ✉ *Avda. 5, C. 1, Alajuela* ⊕ *correos.go.cr.*

◉ Sights

Alajuela Cathedral (*Catedral de Alajuela*)
CHURCH | The large neoclassical Alajuela Cathedral has columns topped by interesting capitals decorated with local agricultural motifs, and a striking red metal dome. Construction was completed in 1863. The interior is spacious but rather plain, except for the ornate cupola above the altar. ⊠ *C. Ctl., Avdas. 1–Ctl., Alajuela* ☎ *2443–2928*.

★ Doka Estate
FARM/RANCH | The Central Valley is coffee country. Consider devoting an hour of your vacation to learning about the crop's production. Doka Estate, a working coffee plantation for more than 70 years, offers a comprehensive tour that takes you through the fields, shows you how the fruit is processed and the beans are dried, and lets you sample the local brew. The best time to take this tour is during the October-to-February picking season. Transportation can be arranged from San José, Alajuela, Heredia, Escazú, or San Antonio de Belén. Various add-on packages include breakfast and/or lunch. Doka features on many organized area tours in combination with various other Central Valley attractions. ⊠ *10 km (6 miles) north of Alajuela's Tribunales de Justicia, Sabanilla* ✛ *Turn left at San Isidro and continue 6 km (4 miles), follow signs* ☎ *2449–5152, 888/946–3652 in North America* ⊕ *www.dokaestate.com* 🎫 *$25*.

Museo Juan Santamaría (*Juan Santamaría Museum*)
JAIL/PRISON | The heroic deeds of Juan Santamaría are celebrated in this museum housed in the old jail, on the north side of Parque Central. It's worth a quick look if you have the time; Santamaría's story is an interesting one. A pleasant café inside is a great place to stop for a coffee. ⊠ *Avda. 3, Cs. Ctl.–2, Alajuela* ☎ *2441–4775* ⊕ *www.museojuansantamaria.go.cr* 🎫 *Free* ⊗ *Closed Mon.*

Parque Central
CITY PARK | Royal palms and massive mango trees fill Alajuela's central park—residents frequently refer to the park as the Parque de los Mangos—which also has a lovely fountain imported from Glasgow and concrete benches where locals gather to chat. Everyone agrees the futuristic gazebo at the center of the park is a bit of an eyesore. Surrounding the plaza is an odd mix of charming old buildings and sterile concrete boxes. ⊠ *C. Ctl., Avdas. 1–Ctl., Alajuela*.

Rescate Wildlife Rescue Center
WILDLIFE REFUGE | FAMILY | Spread over lush grounds, the zoo has a collection of large cages holding toucans, hawks, parrots, and free-ranging macaws as part of a breeding project for rare and endangered birds, all of which are destined for eventual release. It has 115 bird species, including such rare ones as the quetzal, fiery-billed aracari, several types of eagles, and even ostriches. An impressive mural at the back of the facility shows Costa Rica's 850 bird species painted to scale. Wingless animals include crocodiles, caimans, a boa constrictor, turtles, monkeys, wildcats, and other interesting critters. A botanical garden rounds out the offerings here. The facility was formerly known as Zoo Ave, and many locals still refer to it that way. ⊠ *La Garita de Alajuela, Alajuela* ✛ *Head west from Alajuela center past cemetery, turn left after stone church in Barrio San José, continue for 2 km (1 mile); or head west on Pan-American Hwy. to Atenas exit, then turn right* ☎ *2433–8989* ⊕ *www.rescatewildlife.org* 🎫 *$30*.

🍴 Restaurants

Bar y Restaurante El Mirador
$$ | ECLECTIC | Perched on a ridge several miles north of town, El Mirador has a sweeping view of the Central Valley that is impressive by day but more beautiful at dusk and after dark. Get a window table in the dining room, or one on

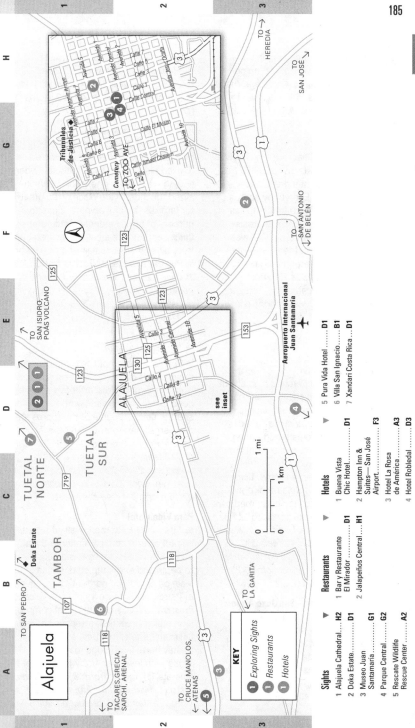

Alajuela

TUETAL NORTE

TUETAL SUR

TAMBOR

Doka Estate

ALAJUELA

Aeropuerto Internacional
Juan Santamaría

TO SAN PEDRO
TO TACARES, GRECIA, SARCHÍ, ARENAL
TO CRUCE MANOLOS, ATENAS
TO LA GARITA
TO SAN ISIDRO, POÁS VOLCANO
TO SAN ANTONIO DE BELÉN
TO HEREDIA
TO SAN JOSÉ

Tribunales de Justicia
Cemetery
TO ZOO AVE

1 mi
1 km
0

KEY

1 Exploring Sights
1 Restaurants
1 Hotels

Sights ▶

1 Alajuela Cathedral.... **H2**
2 Doka Estate............. **D1**
3 Museo Juan
 Santamaría............. **G1**
4 Parque Central......... **G2**
5 Rescate Wildlife
 Rescue Center......... **A2**

Restaurants ▶

1 Bar y Restaurante
 El Mirador **D1**
2 Jalapeños Central.... **H1**

Hotels ▶

1 Buena Vista
 Chic Hotel.............. **D1**
2 Hampton Inn &
 Suites— San José
 Airport.................. **F3**
3 Hotel La Rosa
 de América **A3**
4 Hotel Robledal **D3**

5 Pura Vida Hotel **D1**
6 Villa San Ignacio..... **B1**
7 Xandari Costa Rica ... **D1**

the adjacent porch if it isn't too cool.
Known for: lomito (tenderloin) in variety of sauces; friendly service; stunning views of Central Valley. $ *Average main: $12* ✉ *Road to Poás, 5 km (3 miles) north of Tribunales de Justicia, Alajuela* 🕿 *2441–9347.*

Jalapeños Central

$$ | **MEXICAN** | Tasty, hearty, filling Tex-Mex food and a gregarious owner make this basic downtown joint a great place for lunch or dinner. Everybody seems to know everybody else here—this is a favorite hangout among the area's expat community—and you'll be welcome, too. **Known for:** friendly service; fun dining atmosphere; great fajitas. $ *Average main: $13* ✉ *150 meters (492 feet) north of cathedral, Alajuela* 🕿 *2430–4027* ⊕ *www.facebook.com/jalapenoscentralIG.*

 ## Hotels

Buena Vista Chic Hotel

$$$ | **HOTEL** | **FAMILY** | Perched high above Alajuela, this hotel's superb staff make up for the somewhat dated, uninspired interior, and it does have the "good view" it is named for, although most rooms overlook the lawns or pool area. **Pros:** excellent service; family-friendly; great views from some rooms. **Cons:** farther from the airport than other options; best to have a car to stay here; mediocre restaurant. $ *Rooms from: $155* ✉ *Road to Poás, 6 km (4 miles) north of Alajuela's Tribunales de Justicia, Alajuela* 🕿 *2442–8605, 855/877–3732 in North America* ⊕ *www.hotelbuenavistacr.com* 🛌 *22 rooms* ⦿⦿ *Free Breakfast.*

Hampton Inn & Suites – San José Airport

$$$ | **HOTEL** | A longtime favorite for first-and last-night stays, this chain hotel lets you ease into and out of Costa Rica in familiar surroundings. **Pros:** airport proximity; U.S. amenities; friendly staff. **Cons:** sameness of a chain hotel; as with all airport hotels, your stay here may be very short; some noise from planes in the evening. $ *Rooms from: $155* ✉ *Blvd. del Aeropuerto, Alajuela* 🕿 *2436–0000, 877/461–1402 in North America* ⊕ *www.hamptoninn.hilton.com* 🛌 *100 rooms* ⦿⦿ *Free Breakfast.*

Hotel La Rosa de América

$$ | **HOTEL** | **FAMILY** | This small hotel tucked off the road to La Garita is a simple and relaxed place to unwind, with its owners adding welcoming energy and personalized touches to the place. **Pros:** great for families; helpful owners; close to a number of family-friendly restaurants. **Cons:** best to have a car to stay here; far from all sights; lacks flair of other options in this price range. $ *Rooms from: $113* ✉ *Calle La Rosa, Alajuela* ⊹ *1 km (½ mile) east of Zoo Ave.* 🕿 *2433–2741* ⊕ *www.larosadeamerica.com* 🛌 *16 rooms* ⦿⦿ *Free Breakfast.*

Hotel Robledal

$$ | **HOTEL** | A *robledal* is an oak grove in Spanish, and ample oak trees shade the grounds of this quiet oasis not far from the airport. **Pros:** attentive service; good Costa Rican restaurant; free airport shuttle. **Cons:** a couple of the rooms are dark; small bathrooms; can be difficult to find. $ *Rooms from: $104* ✉ *400 meters (1,312 feet) west of Iglesia El Roble, Alajuela* 🕿 *2438–3937, 812/962–4386 in North America* ⊕ *www.hotelrobledal.com* 🛌 *15 rooms* ⦿⦿ *Free Breakfast.*

Pura Vida Hotel

$$ | **B&B/INN** | Extremely well-informed, helpful owners and proximity to the airport (15 minutes) make this a good place to begin and end a trip, and thanks to its location on a ridge north of town, several of its rooms have views of Poás Volcano. **Pros:** owners active in the local community; stellar breakfast; attentive service. **Cons:** stairs to climb; best to have a car to stay here; large dogs may turn off those with less-than-fuzzy feelings for animals. $ *Rooms from: $100* ✉ *Tuetal, 2 km (1 mile) north of Tribunales de Justicia; veer left at Y intersection, Alajuela*

The verdant Central Valley is Costa Rica's breadbasket.

☎ 2430–2929 ⊕ www.puravidahotel.com ↝ 6 units ¶○¶ Free Breakfast.

Villa San Ignacio

$$ | **B&B/INN | FAMILY** | The friendly Villa San Ignacio, with its classy Spanish-style architecture, proves that affordable does not have to equal generic. **Pros:** spirited environment; great for first or last night; excellent service. **Cons:** pet friendly; can be difficult to find; roadside rooms can be noisy, opt for garden rooms. $ *Rooms from: $140* ⊠ *2½ km (1½ miles) north-west of the Princesa Marina, Alajuela* ☎ *2433–6316* ⊕ *www.villasanignacio. com* ↝ *16 rooms* ¶○¶ *Free Breakfast.*

★ Xandari Costa Rica

$$$$ | **HOTEL** | The tranquil and colorful Xandari is a strikingly original inn and spa, tailor-made for honeymooners and romantic getaways. **Pros:** ideal setting for romance; guilt-free gourmet delights; eco-friendly, including on-site nature reserve. **Cons:** should have car to stay here; far from any sights; some noise from other rooms. $ *Rooms from: $265* ⊠ *5 km (3 miles) north of Tribunales de*

Justicia, Alajuela ✛ *Turn left after small bridge, follow signs* ☎ *2443–2020, 866/363–3212 in North America* ⊕ *www. xandari.com* ↝ *24 villas* ¶○¶ *Free Breakfast.*

Shopping

City Mall

MALL | Central America's largest shopping mall weighs in at 330 stores and is most notable for its indoor snow-themed amusement park. ⊠ *Radial Francisco J. Orlich, Alajuela* ☎ *4200–5100* ⊕ *www. citymall.net.*

Goodlight Books

BOOKS | One of Costa Rica's largest used-book stores stocks around 9,000 volumes, and a huge number of those are in English. It's also a great place to hang out for coffee and baked goods. ⊠ *Alajuela* ✛ *100 meters (328 feet) north and 300 meters (984 feet) west of La Agonía church* ☎ *2430–4083.*

Heredia

4 km (3 miles) north of Santo Domingo, 11 km (6 miles) northwest of San José.

The lively city of Heredia, capital of the important coffee province of the same name, contains a couple of the country's best-preserved colonial structures, along with a contrasting, youthful buzz provided by the National University (UNA) and century-old *colegios* (high schools) scattered around the town. Heredia is nicknamed the City of Flowers (La Ciudad de Flores, in Spanish), which refers less to the flowers that decorate the city than to a leading founding family named Flores. Flores also refers to beautiful women, for which Heredia is known. (On the topic of names, remember that "h" is always silent in Spanish; pronounce the small city's name *air-AY-dee-ah*.) Founded in 1706, the city bears witness to how difficult preservation can be in an earthquake-prone country; most of its colonial structures have been destroyed by tremors and the tropical climate, not to mention modernization. Still, the city and neighboring towns retain a certain historic flavor, with old adobe buildings scattered amid the concrete structures. Nearby Barva is also notable for its colonial central square and venerable adobe structures. From Heredia, scenic mountain roads climb northeast, passing through the pleasant, high-altitude coffee towns of San Rafael and San Isidro, each anchored by a notable, tico-style Gothic church and a pleasant central park.

GETTING HERE AND AROUND

The narrow routes from San José to Heredia are notoriously clogged at almost all times; avoid them during rush hours if possible—and realize that you may encounter traffic jams at other times of the day, too. Turn right at the west end of Paseo Colón. Follow the Pan-American Highway 2 km (1 mile); take the second exit, just before the highway heads onto an overpass and just after the Hotel Irazú (on the right). To get to the center of Heredia, follow that road for 5½ km (3½ miles), being careful to note which direction traffic in the alternative middle lane is traveling, then turn left at the Universidad Nacional.

Buses run between San José (300 meters [984 feet] east of Hospital San Juan de Dios) and Heredia every 5 to 10 minutes daily, between 5 am and 10 pm. The steady stream of buses leaving from Calle 1, Avenidas 7–9 every three to five minutes, passing through Santo Domingo, is sometimes a better bet during rush hour—particularly the *directo* buses that start after 3:30 pm (these buses also run from midnight to 3:30 am on the hour). Better still, hop aboard the new, modern train, departing San José from the vintage Atlantic Station, on the north side of the Parque Nacional, and arriving in downtown Heredia 30 minutes later. Trains run every half hour on weekdays from 5:30 to 8 am, then 3:30 to 7:30 pm—geared more toward the needs of workaday commuters than tourists—and the fare is about $0.95. If you're without a car, a taxi is the best way to get to Café Britt or Barva.

ESSENTIALS

BANKS/ATMS BAC Credomatic. ⊠ *Paseo de las Flores, Heredia* ☎ *2295–9797* ⊕ *www.bac.net.* **Banco Nacional.** ⊠ *25 meters south of southwest corner of Parque Central, Heredia* ☎ *2277–6900* ⊕ *www.bncr.fi.cr.*

PHARMACY Farmacia Chavarría. ⊠ *South side of Parque Central, Heredia* ☎ *2263–4668* ⊕ *www.facebook.com/farmaciachavarriaexpress.*

POST OFFICE Correos. ⊠ *Avda. Ctl., Cs. Ctl.–2, northwest corner of Parque Central, Heredia* ⊕ *correos.go.cr.*

Continued on page 194

Picking coffee beans from plant

COFFEE, THE GOLDEN BEAN

Tour a working coffee plantation and learn about the product that catapulted Costa Rica onto the world's economic stage, built the country's infrastructure, and created a middle class unlike any other in Central America.

Costa Rica B.C. (before coffee) was a poor, forgotten little colony with scant infrastructure and no real means of making money. Coffee production changed all of that and transformed the country into one of the wealthier and most stable in Central America. Coffee remains Costa Rica's bread and butter—the industry employs one-fourth of Costa Rica's population full- or part-time—and coffee plantations are sprinkled throughout the Central Valley and Northern Lowlands. All cultivate fine Arabica beans (by government decree, the inferior Robusta variety is not grown here). Visit one and learn what makes the country tick.

By Jeffrey Van Fleet

HISTORY IN A CUP

Coffee plantations near Poás Volcano, Central Valley

DRINKING THE GOOD STUFF

Here's the kicker for you, dear coffee-loving visitor: it's tough to find a decent cup in Costa Rica. True to the realities of developing-country economics, the good stuff goes for export, leaving a poorer quality bean behind for the local market. Add to that that the typical household here makes coffee with heaps of sugar. Your best bet for a good cup is an upscale hotel or restaurant, which is attuned to foreign tastes and does use export-quality product. The decorative foil bags you see in souvenir shops and supermarkets are also export-quality and make terrific souvenirs.

The country's first leaders saw this new crop as a tool with which to engineer a better life for their people. After gaining independence, new laws were created to allow average Costa Ricans to become coffee-growing landowners. These farmers formed the foundation of a middle-class majority that has long distinguished the country from the rest of Latin America. Costa Rica's infrastructure, institutional organizations, and means of production quickly blossomed—young entrepreneurs established small import-export houses, growers banded together to promote a better infrastructure, and everyone plowed their profits into improving the country's primitive road system.

SOCIAL TRANSFORMATION
As the coffee business became more profitable, prominent families were sending their children abroad to study, and doctors, lawyers and other skilled professionals in search of jobs began arriving by the boat-

COFFEE TIMELINE

Local workers harvesting coffee beans in 1800s

1720	Coffee arrives in New World.
1791	Coffee plants introduced to Costa Rica.
1820	First coffee exports go to Panama.
1830	Legislation paves way for coffee profits to finance government projects.
1860	Costa Rican coffee first exported to United States.
1890	Atlantic Railroad opens, allowing for easier port access.

Traditional coffee brewing

load. Returning students and well-educated immigrants brought a new world view that contributed to the formation of Costa Rica's liberal ideology.

MODERN TIMES

Development gobbled up land in the Central Valley by the last half of the 20th century, and coffee production began to spread to other areas of the country. A worldwide slump in coffee prices in the 1990s forced many producers out of the business. Prices have risen since 2002, and the government looks to smooth out any fluctuations with added-value eco-certification standards and innovative marketing.

Today, some 70% of the country's *número uno* agricultural crop comes from small family properties of under 25 acres owned by 250,000 farmers. They seasonally employ more than four times that number of people, and kids in rural areas still take class time off to help with the harvest.

CAFÉ CHEAT SHEET

café solo: black
con azúcar: with sugar
con crema: with cream
con leche: with milk
descafeinado: decaffeinated (not easy to find here)

■

grano entero: whole beans
grano molido: ground
tostado claro or tueste claro: light roast
tostado oscuro or tueste oscuro: dark roast

Oxcarts built in the early 1900s to transport coffee

1897	Coffee barons construct San José's ornate Teatro Nacional.
1992	Costa Rica adopts new environmental laws for coffee industry.
1997	Tourism displaces coffee as Costa Rica's top industry.
Today	Costa Rica turns to eco-certification and fair-trade marketing of coffee.

COSTA RICA'S BEAN COUNTRY

Coffee plantations from Cervantes to Orosi Central Valley

Monteverde

Tilarán
Monteverde Coffee Tour
La Virgen
Puerto Viejo de Sarapiquí
Cariari

Bagaces
Don Juan Coffee Tour
La Fortuna
San Miguel

Santa Elena
Ciudad Quesada
Cinchona
Guápiles

CORDILLERA DE TILARÁN

8 GUANACASTE
San Ramón
Doka Coffee Estate

Santa Cruz
Nicoya
Isla Chira
VALLE OCCIDENTAL
Atenas
Café Britt
TRES RIOS

Tamarindo
Puntarenas
4
Alajuela
2
Turrialba

Nosara
Carmona
Orotina
SAN JOSÉ
Cartago
OROS
5

Nicoya Peninsula
Jicaral
Caldera
3
TARRAZÚ
Orosi

Sámara
Punta Islita
Paquera
Tárcoles
VALLE CENTRAL
1

Carrillo
Tambor
San Marcos

Cobano
Jacó
San Gerardo de Dota

30 miles
Mal País
Montezuma
Parrita

45 km
Cabo Blanco
Quepos

Dominical

Costa Rica possesses all the factors necessary—moderately high altitude, mineral-rich volcanic soil, adequate rainfall but distinct rainy and dry seasons—to be a major coffee player. Costa Rican growers cultivate only Arabica coffee beans. The industry eliminated the inferior Robusta variety in 1989 and hasn't looked back. The Costa Rican Coffee Institute certifies eight regional coffee varieties.

The coffee-growing cycle begins in April or May, when rains make the dark-green bushes explode in a flurry of white blossoms. By November, the fruit starts to ripen, turning from green to red. The busy harvest begins as farmers race to get picked "cherries" to beneficios (processing mills), where beans are removed, washed, machine-dried, and packed in burlap sacks either for export or to be roasted for local consumption.

Coffee plantations, Central Valley

1 Aficionados wax poetic about the beans that come from **Tarrazú**, the high-altitude Los Santos Region in the Southern Pacific. It has good body, high acidity, and a chocolaty flavor.

2 Coffee grown in **Tres Ríos**, east of San José, has high acidity, good body, and a nice aroma.

3 Altitude of the **Valle Central** (around San José, Heredia and Alajuela) affects the size and hardness of the coffee bean and can influence certain components, particularly the acidity. This is an important characteristic of Arabica coffee.

4 **Valle Occidental**, in the prosperous western Central Valley, gives you hints of apricots and peaches.

Arabica coffee beans

Coffee beans | Coffee bean pickers | Hand picking Coffee beans

Coffee plant

Siquirres
Moín
6 TURRIALBA
Puerto Viejo de Talamanca
Cahuita
Bribri
Sixaola
PANAMA
CORDILLERA DE TALAMANCA
San Isidro
Buenos Aires
Salitre
7 BRUNCA
Palmar Norte
Paso Real
Ciudad Cortés
San Vito
Palmar Sur
Pan-American Hwy
Ciudad Neily
Drake
Rincón
Golfito
Río Claro
Osa Peninsula
Puerto Jiménez
Paso Canoas
Zancudo
Carate
Pavones
Matapalo

❺ Tasters describe **Orosi** coffee, from the southeastern Central Valley, as "floral."

❻ The lower altitudes of nearby **Turrialba** give its product a medium body.

❼ The high-altitude **Brunca** region, near San Vito in southern Costa Rica, produces coffee with excellent aroma, good body, and moderate acidity.

❽ Guanacaste is a diverse region that includes Monteverde and the central Nicoya Peninsula. Here they produce a medium-body coffee.

PLANTATIONS WITH TOURS

Wonder where your cup of morning coffee originates? The following purveyors give informative tours of their facilities and acquaint you with the life and times of the country's favorite beverage.

Tours guide you through the plant-to-crop process in English or Spanish, taking you from picking to drying to roasting to packing to brewing.

Reservations are essential. Plan on spending a half-day for any of these outings. The whole package will set you back about $30–$40 per person.

CAFÉ BRITT Barva, Heredia Café Britt incorporates a small theater production into its informative tour, presenting the history of Costa Rican coffee in song and dance.

CAFÉ MONTEVERDE Monteverde Monteverde Coffee offers you some hands-on experience. Depending on the time of year, you can help with picking, drying, roasting, or packing.

COOPEDOTA SANTA MARIA Santa Maria de Dota A tour here acquaints you with the standard bean-to-bag experience, as well as the cooperative's pioneering environmental practices.

DOKA COFFEE ESTATE San Luis de Sabanilla, Alajuela Doka Coffee Estate offers a comprehensive tour through the entire growing and drying process and lets you sample the local brew.

DON JUAN COFFEE TOUR Monteverde A personalized excursion with a small group is the hallmark of this tour to a coffee plantation a few miles outside the town of Santa Elena.

Sights

★ Café Britt

FACTORY | The producer of Costa Rica's most popular export-quality coffee gives a lively Classic Coffee Tour highlighting the history of Costa Rica's coffee cultivation through a theatrical presentation that is admittedly a bit hokey. Your "tour guides" are professional actors, and pretty good ones at that, so if you don't mind the song and dance, it's fun. (You might even be called upon to participate.) During the 1½-hour tour, you'll take a short walk through the coffee farm and processing plant, and learn how professional coffee tasters distinguish a fine cup of java. A two-hour Coffee Lovers tour delves into the process at a more expert level. You'll leave the new all-day Coffee Origins tour feeling like even more of an expert, delving into the environmental issues surrounding coffee. You can also stop in at Britt's Coffee Bar and Factory Store. Although all three tours are devoted entirely to the production and history of Costa Rica's most famous agricultural product, Britt is also a purveyor of fine chocolates, cocoas, cookies, macadamia nuts, and coffee liqueurs; you'll see its products for sale in souvenir shops around the country and at the airport as you leave. The standard coffee tour is often a half-day inclusion on many Central Valley tours operated by San José tour companies, combined with the Poás volcano, the La Paz waterfall gardens, or Rainforest Adventures. ✉ *Heredia* ✛ *From Heredia, take road to Barva, follow signs* ☎ *2277–1600, 800/462–7488 in North America* ⊕ *www.coffeetour.com* 🎫 *From $27.*

Costa Rica Meadery

WINERY | Costa Rica's climate sadly doesn't allow for wine grapes to flourish, but crafty brewers have discovered perhaps the next best thing: mead, which is created by fermenting honey with water. This farm is the first and currently only meadery in the country, with the mead's honey coming directly from the farm's nearby beehives and other local beekeepers. The meads are flavored with a variety of tropical fruits and flowers, including passion fruit and hibiscus. Book ahead to enjoy one- or two-hour tours of the farm, hives, and production facility, all ending with a tasting. You can also just visit the tasting room for a half-hour tasting, accompanied by honey and cheeses (advance reservations are still required). They occasionally host dinners too. The meadery proudly practices environmentally sound, socially equitable, and economically viable sustainability. ✉ *The Ark Herb Farm, Calle La Sabaneta, Santa Bárbara de Heredia* ✛ *800 meters (2,624 feet) north of Escuela Rosales* ☎ *8718–4094* ⊕ *www.costaricameadery. com* 🎫 *Tour $25.*

Fortín (*Little Fort*)

MILITARY SIGHT | On the north side of the Parque Central in its own little park stands a strange tower, built as a military post in the 1870s. It never did see action and now serves as the symbol of the city, one of the few military monuments in this country without an army. The tower is closed to the public. The old brick building next to the Fortín is the Palacio Municipal (Town Hall). ✉ *C. Ctl., Avda. Ctl., Heredia.*

Iglesia de la Inmaculada Concepción (*Church of the Immaculate Conception*)

CHURCH | On the east side of the park stands this impressive neoclassical church that locals refer to as simply "La Inmaculada." It was built between 1797 and 1804 to replace an adobe temple dating from the early 1700s and is one of the few structures in Costa Rica remaining from the colonial era. The flat-fronted, whitewashed church has thick stone walls, small windows, and squat buttresses, which have kept it intact through two centuries of earthquakes and tremors. The serene, white interior has two rows of stately, gold-trimmed Ionic columns marching down a long aisle, past 20 lovely stained-glass windows constructed in France. The church is flanked by tidy side gardens, where you can stroll among sculpted trees along concrete paths incised with a floral pattern. The church's soft exterior illumination brightens up the park nightly from 6 pm until midnight. ⊠ *Eastern side of Parque Central, Heredia* ☎ *2237–0779.*

Mercado Nuevo (*New Market*)
MARKET | Three blocks southeast of the Parque Central is Heredia's covered New Market—that's how everybody refers to it here—officially the Mercado Central, which holds dozens of *sodas* (simple restaurants) along with the usual food stands and vendors supplying the day-to-day needs of the average Costa Rican. While generally safe, the crowded conditions here do invite the occasional pickpocket. Watch your possessions. ⊠ *C. Ctl., Avda. 6, Heredia.*

Museo de Cultura Popular (*Museum of Popular Culture*)
OTHER MUSEUM | At the edge of a middle-class neighborhood between Heredia and Barva, this museum is housed in a farmhouse with a large veranda built in 1885 using an adobe-like technique called *bahareque.* Run by the National University, the museum is furnished with antiques and surrounded by a garden and a small coffee farm. Just walking around the museum is instructive, but calling ahead to reserve a hands-on cultural tour (such as one on tortilla making) really makes it worth the trip. An open-air restaurant serves bread baked in a clay oven, and fresh tortillas and tamales. ⊠ *Heredia* ✛ *From Musmanni bakery in Santa Lucía de Barva, go 100 meters (328 feet) north, then turn right for 1 km (½ mile); follow signs* ☎ *2260–1619* ⊕ *www.museo.una.ac.cr* 🏷 *$2* 🕘 *Closed Sat.*

★ Parque Central
CITY PARK | Heredia is centered on tree-studded Parque Central, which gets our vote for the country's loveliest and liveliest central park, surrounded by some notable buildings spanning more than 250 years of history. The park has a large, round, cast-iron fountain imported from England in 1879 and a Victorian bandstand where the municipal band plays on Sunday morning and Thursday night. Families, couples, and old-timers sit on park benches, shaded by fig and towering palm trees, often inhabited by noisy and colorful flocks of crimson-fronted parakeets. Drop into Pops, a national ice-cream chain, at the south side of the park and pick up a cone, then take a seat on a park bench and watch the passing parade. ⊠ *C. Ctl., Avda. Ctl., Heredia.*

San Rafael de Heredia
TOWN | This quiet, tidy coffee town 2 km (1 mile) northeast of Heredia has a large church notable for its stained-glass windows and bright interior. The road north from the church winds its way up Barva Volcano, ending atop the Monte de la Cruz lookout point with a commanding vista of San José and the Central Valley. ⊠ *San Rafael de Heredia.*

★ Toucan Rescue Ranch
WILDLIFE REFUGE | One of Costa Rica's many animal-rescue facilities, Toucan Rescue Ranch is a great place to see wildlife. There are more than just toucans—the good-hearted folks here care for many sloths and owls, too. The ultimate goal is to return the animals to the wild; the frail condition of some means that this will be their permanent home. The general 2½-hour walk focuses on observing the facility's work with toucans and sloths. Tickets must be purchased in advance on the facility's website. ⊠ *San Josecito, Heredia* ☎ *2268–4041* ⊕ *www. toucanrescueranch.org* 🏷 *From $62* 🕘 *Closed Mon.* ♿ *Reservations required.*

Restaurants

Bromelias del Río

$$ | COSTA RICAN | This simple garden dining spot in the far northern Central Valley makes a great breakfast stop if you're on your way to the Caribbean. Fortify yourself with the *tradicional* (gallo pinto, eggs, bread, and coffee) or *americano* (ham, eggs, bacon, toast, and juice) breakfasts. **Known for:** good value; coffee drinks; hearty, filling breakfasts. $ *Average main: $11* ⊠ *San Isidro de Heredia, Heredia* ✛ *North side of Parque Central* ☎ *2268–8445* ⊕ *www.facebook. com/cafeteriayrestaurantebromeliasdelrio* ☽ *No dinner.*

Hotels

★ Finca Rosa Blanca Coffee Farm & Inn

$$$$ | B&B/INN | Set amid fields of green coffee, this exclusive, hilltop B&B hideaway has a much-deserved reputation as one of the country's sumptuous splurges. **Pros:** eco-consciousness; indulgence with style; service par excellence. **Cons:** expensive restaurant; hard to find if you are driving your own car; some units short on closet and drawer space. $ *Rooms from: $290* ⊠ *800 meters (2,624 feet) north of Café Britt Distribution Center, Santa Bárbara de Heredia, Heredia* ☎ *2269–9392, 305/395–3042 in North America* ⊕ *www.fincarosablanca. com* ⤵ *14 suites* ۩ *Free Breakfast.*

Hotel Hojarrascas

$ | HOTEL | The entrance here resembles any other storefront downtown, and you could pass right by without noticing this quiet, family-run gem. **Pros:** good value for what is offered; attentive owner; great service. **Cons:** access can be difficult in your own vehicle because of street congestion; difficult parking; can hear a bit of noise from the hallway. $ *Rooms from: $74* ⊠ *Avda. 8, Cs. 4–6, Heredia* ☎ *2261–3649* ⊕ *www.hotelhojarascas.com* ▭ *No credit cards* ⤵ *15 units* ۩ *Free Breakfast.*

Hotel Valladolid

$$ | HOTEL | The classiest hotel in downtown Heredia, this four-story narrow building attracts business travelers and visiting professors at the nearby National University, although guests are just as likely to be vacationers. **Pros:** central location; friendly staff; extensive buffet breakfast with homemade tortillas. **Cons:** a few rooms show their age; on slightly steep hill if walking; limited parking. $ *Rooms from: $87* ⊠ *C. 7, Avda. 7, Heredia* ☎ *2260–2905* ⊕ *www.hotelvalladolid. net* ⤵ *12 rooms* ۩ *Free Breakfast.*

Shopping

Feria

MARKET | On Saturday morning starting at 5, Heredia's open-air *feria*, a lively farmers' market, stretches for almost a kilometer (½ mile) along Avenida 14. Things start to wind down around noon. ⊠ *Avda. 14, Heredia.*

Paseo de Las Flores

MALL | This airy, pleasant, and huge shopping mall with 320 stores is on the main road south of town. It has a branch of almost every international fashion boutique, as well as a multiplex cinema and a wide choice of cafés and restaurants. ⊠ *2 km (1 mile) south of town on hwy. to San José, Heredia* ☎ *2261–9898* ⊕ *www. paseodelasflores.com.*

Sibö Chocolate

CHOCOLATE | Get to know a bean of another kind during a private tasting at the workshop of the country's best artisanal chocolate makers. It starts with an informative talk about the historical and cultural significance of the cacao bean, includes a demonstration of tempering chocolate by hand, and ends, of course, with a sampling of exquisite chocolates made from 100% organic cacao. Tasters can also stay for an elegant lunch on Sibö's pretty terrace. Reserve 48 hours in advance. ⊠ *Heredia* ✛ *Turnoff for San Isidro de Heredia, 1½ km (1 mile) off hwy.*

En Route

Barva de Heredia. About 3 km (2 miles) due north of Heredia, this colonial town is famous for mask making and for its Parque Central, still with the original adobe buildings with Spanish-tile roofs on three sides, and a white-stucco church to the east. The park is filled with whimsical sculptures, including a park bench shaped like an entire seated family, and bizarre masks and clown's heads decorating garbage receptacles. An amphitheater and stage stand ready for the annual mask festival held every August. (A less pleasant part of the August festival is the tradition of smacking one's fellow townspeople with cow or pig bladders—perhaps *not* a good time to visit.) The stout, handsome church with terra-cotta bas-relief flourishes dates from the late 18th century and has a lovely grotto shrine to the Virgin Mary in the church garden. On a clear day you can see verdant Volcán Barva towering to the north. ⊠ *3 km (2 miles) north of Heredia, Barva.*

to Braulio Carrillo National Park ☎ 2268–1335 ⊕ *www.sibuchocolate.com.*

Poás Volcano National Park

37 km (23 miles, 45 mins) north of Alajuela, 57 km (35 miles, 1 hr) north of San José.

Arenal may be Costa Rica's most famous volcano, but you can peer right into the crater here at Poás—from the vantage point of an observation platform. That gives it an edge in the "cool volcano visit" department.

GETTING HERE AND AROUND

From the Pan-American Highway north of Alajuela, follow the signs for Poás. The road is in relatively good condition. One public bus departs daily at 8 am from San José (Avenida 2, Calles 12–14) and returns at 2 pm. Taxis from San José are around $100 (and around $50 from Alajuela). A slew of tours from San José take in the volcano and combine the morning excursion with an afternoon at La Paz Waterfall Gardens, or with tours of Café Britt near Heredia or the Doka Estate near Alajuela.

Sights

La Paz Waterfall Gardens

GARDEN | FAMILY | Five magnificent waterfalls are the main attractions at these gardens on the eastern edge of Volcán Poás National Park, but they are complemented by the beauty of the surrounding cloud forest, an abundance of hummingbirds and other avian species, and the country's biggest butterfly garden. A concrete trail leads down from the visitor center to the multilevel, screened butterfly observatory and continues to gardens where hummingbird feeders attract swarms of these multicolor creatures. Other exhibits are devoted to frogs and snakes. The trail then enters the cloud forest, where it leads to a series of metal stairways that let you descend into a steep gorge to viewing platforms near each of the waterfalls. A free shuttle will transport you from the trail exit back to the main building if you prefer to avoid the hike uphill. Several alternative paths lead from the main trail through the cloud forest and along the river's quieter upper stretch, providing options for hours of exploration—it takes about two hours to hike the entire complex. (Enter before 3 pm to give yourself adequate time.) The

La Paz Waterfall Gardens attracts 24 different species of hummingbirds and has a huge butterfly garden.

complex's Jungle Cat exhibit serves as a rescue center for felines (jaguars, ocelots, and pumas). The visitor center has a gift shop and open-air cafeteria with a great view. The gardens are a stop on many daylong tours from San José that take in the Poás Volcano or area coffee tours. The complex is especially busy on weekends. ⊠ *6 km (4 miles) north of Vara Blanca, Poás Volcán National Park* ☎ *2482–2720, 954/727–3997 in North America* ⊕ *www.waterfallgardens.com* ✉ *From $48.*

★ **Poás Volcano National Park** (*Parque Nacional Volcán Poás*)

VOLCANO | This is widely regarded as Costa Rica's coolest volcano experience. An observation platform lets you peer right inside what is thought to be the largest active volcanic crater in the world. The ride up here is disarming: pleasant farms and lush green cloud forest line the volcano's slopes; friendly fruit and jam vendors along the road beckon you to stop and sample their wares. Only when you get to the bubbling, gurgling, smoking summit do you leave those pastoral scenes behind and stare into the crater. Arrive here as early as possible in the morning for the best views. Clouds occasionally move in as early as midmorning.

It's wise to step away from the crater and its fumes for fresh air at least once every 10 minutes, and a good place to take that break is the park's bustling visitor center—the country's best—with complete park information, a cafeteria, and a gift shop. The volcano features prominently on many itineraries of area tour operators. Increased volcanic activity in recent years forces periodic closure of the park. Check conditions before heading up here on your own.

Entries are timed and must be reserved and paid for in advance at the national parks website. You'll undergo a mandatory safety presentation on arrival and must wear a helmet during your visit. The park's famed hiking trails are closed at this writing.

For more information, see the color feature at the beginning of this chapter. ✉ *Poás Volcán National Park* ✥ *From Alajuela, drive north through town and follow signs* ☎ *2482–2424, 1192 national park hotline* 🌐 *www.sinac.go.cr for required advance ticketed entry time* 🎟 *$15.*

🍴 Restaurants

Freddo Fresas

$$ | **COSTA RICAN** | *Fresas* means "strawberries," and they're the star at this rustic wooden place on the way to the volcano. They end up on your corn pancakes, in juices, as desserts, or as sides to the variety of típico dishes here. **Known for:** piping hot coffee; strawberry everything; tortillas aliñadas (huge corn tortillas with cheese and cream). [$] *Average main: $11* ✉ *Poás Volcán National Park* ✥ *200 meters (656 feet) north of Fraijanes cemetery* ☎ *2482–2800* 🌐 *www.facebook.com/freddofresas* ⏲ *No dinner.*

Restaurante Chubascos

$$ | **COSTA RICAN** | Dine amid tall pines and colorful flowers on the upper slopes of Poás Volcano. There's a small menu of traditional Tico dishes that includes platters of *gallos* (homemade tortillas with meat, cheese, or potato filling) as well as delicious daily specials. **Known for:** refreshing fruit drinks; pleasant countryside setting; terrific Tico cooking. [$] *Average main: $11* ✉ *1 km (½ mile) north of Laguna de Fraijanes, Poás Volcán National Park* ☎ *2482–2280* 🌐 *www.facebook.com/chubascos.co.cr* ⏲ *Closed Tues. No dinner.*

🛏 Hotels

Peace Lodge

$$$$ | **HOTEL** | These rooms overlooking the misty forests of La Paz Waterfall Gardens seem like something out of the *Lord of the Rings,* with their curved, clay-stucco walls, hardwood floors, stone fireplaces, four-poster beds made of varnished logs, and grottolike bathrooms with private waterfalls. **Pros:** many activities, plus admission to the Waterfall Gardens, included in rates; whimsical furnishings; excellent river trail. **Cons:** popular with tour groups; all but the top floors can be a bit noisy because of creaky stairs; pricey. [$] *Rooms from: $400* ✉ *6 km (4 miles) north of Vara Blanca, Poás Volcán National Park* ☎ *2482–2100, 954/727–3997 in North America* 🌐 *www.waterfallgardens.com* 🛏 *18 units* 🍽 *No Meals.*

★ Poás Volcano Lodge

$$$ | **B&B/INN** | Stylish luxury prevails here: king-size beds, outdoor whirlpool tubs, and luxurious fabrics grace the rooms, and many have balconies overlooking the volcano. **Pros:** close to volcano; coffeemakers and electric teakettles in rooms; great breakfasts. **Cons:** a bit pricey; best to have a car to say here; hotel is often fully booked. [$] *Rooms from: $240* ✉ *500 meters (1,640 feet) west of gas station, Vara Blanca, Poás Volcán National Park* ☎ *2482–2194* 🌐 *www.poasvolcanolodge.com* 🛏 *12 rooms* 🍽 *Free Breakfast.*

🛍 Shopping

Volcán Poás National Park Visitor Center

SOUVENIRS | The park's visitor center has a well-stocked shop that sells nature-themed T-shirts, cards, and posters. A portion of the profits goes to support conservation projects. ✉ *Poás Volcán National Park* ☎ *2482–2424.*

Cartago

22 km (14 miles) southeast of San José.

Although most of its structures from the colonial era are gone, Cartago still has some attractive restored buildings, most of them erected after the devastating 1910 earthquake. The city served as the country's first capital until 1823, when the seat of government was moved to

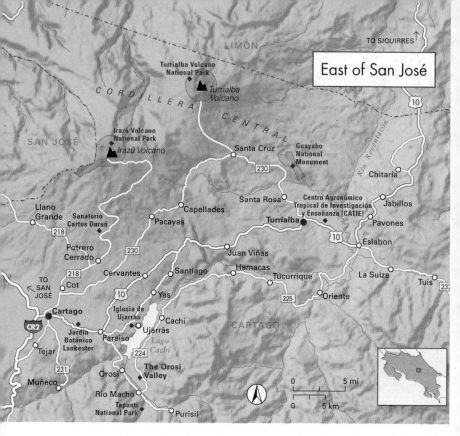

East of San José

the emerging economic center of San José. Today, Cartago is a bustling market town, 900 feet higher in elevation and a few degrees cooler than San José. Most visitors see Cartago on their way to or from the Orosi Valley or Turrialba, and there is little reason (or place) to stay the night. The Orosi Valley, a short drive away, has better lodging choices. A couple of interesting sights warrant a half day if you're out this way, however.

GETTING HERE AND AROUND

For the 25-minute drive from San José, drive east on Avenida 2 through San Pedro and Curridabat to the toll highway entrance, where you have three road options—take the middle one marked Cartago. Shortly before Cartago, a Y intersection marks the beginning of the route up Irazú, with traffic to Cartago veering right.

Buses between San José and Cartago leave every 10 minutes daily (Avenida 10 and Calle 5, 400 meters [1,312 feet] south of the Teatro Nacional) from 5 am to 6 pm; after 6 the buses leave from Avenida 2 between Calles 1–3, in front of the National Theater. Cartago buses to San José pick up 300 meters (984 feet) west of the Municipal Museum of Cartago (formerly called the Comandancia), from 4:35 am to 11 pm. Buses to Orosi leave Cartago every 15 minutes from 5:15 to 7:30 am, then every 30 minutes until 7 pm, with a bus at 8 and 9 pm, 100 meters (328 feet) east, 25 meters (82 feet) south of the southeast corner of Las Ruinas.

TAXIS Taxis El Carmen. ✉ *Cartago*
☎ *2551–4646.*

Bulls dressed in their finest for an oxcart parade in Cartago

ESSENTIALS

BANKS/ATMS BAC Credomatic. ✉ *100 meters (328 feet) south of Ruinas, Cartago* ☎ *2295–9797* ⊕ *www.bac.net.* **Banco Nacional.** ✉ *Southeast corner of Las Ruinas, Cartago* ☎ *2550–1400* ⊕ *www. bncr.fi.cr.*

HOSPITAL Hospital Dr. Max Peralta. ✉ *200 meters (656 feet) south, 150 meters (492 feet) west of Las Ruinas, Cartago* ☎ *2550–1999.* **Hospital Universal.** ✉ *400 meters (1,312 feet) south of Las Ruinas, Cartago* ☎ *4052–5700* ⊕ *www.hospital-universal.com.*

PHARMACY Farmacia Fischel. ✉ *300 meters (984 feet) west of Basílica de Nuestra Señora de los Angeles, Cartago* ☎ *2552–2430.*

POST OFFICE Correos. ✉ *Avda. 2, Cs. 15–17, Cartago* ⊕ *correos.go.cr.*

Sights

Basílica de Nuestra Señora de los Angeles (*Our Lady of the Angels Basilica*)
CHURCH | Cartago's major tourist sight is a hodgepodge of architectural styles from Byzantine to baroque, with a dash of Gothic thrown in. The interior of this 1926 basilica is striking, with a colorful tile floor, intricately painted, faux-finish wood columns, and lots of stained glass. Tradition holds that an apparition of the Virgin Mary in the form of a dark stone occurred here in 1635. This "Black Virgin" (La Negrita) is Costa Rica's patron saint, and she sits high above the main altar. To the left as you face the altar is a room decorated with amulets given in dedication to the Virgin for her intercession in everything from triumphs over disease to triumphs on the soccer field. ✉ *C. 16, Avdas. 2–4, 7 blocks east of central square, Cartago* ☎ *2551–0465* ⊕ *www. santuarionacional.org.*

Cartago's Basilica de Nuestra Señora de los Angeles is the focus of the annual pilgrimage to celebrate the appearance of La Negrita, the Black Virgin.

Irazú Volcano National Park (*Parque Nacional Volcán Irazú*)

VOLCANO | Costa Rica's highest volcano, at 11,260 feet, is one of the most popular with visitors, since you can walk right down into the crater. Its presence is a mixed blessing: the ash fertilizes the Central Valley soil, but the volcano has caused considerable destruction through the centuries. ⚠ **Do not leave anything of value in your car while you visit the volcano. There have been a lot of thefts in the parking lot here, even though it is supposed to be guarded.**

Most San José and area tour operators include the volcano among their excursions, and this is the easiest way to visit. With the Poás Volcano National Park near Alajuela limiting visitors these days, numbers have risen dramatically at Irazú, where no such restrictions exist. Weekends here get *very* busy. Things are a lot more manageable during the week. *For more information, see the highlighted listing in this chapter.* ✉ *Irazú Volcano National Park* ☎ *2200–5025, 1192 national-al park hotline* 🔊 *$15.*

Las Ruinas

RUINS | Churches in one form or another stood at the site of the present-day central park from 1575 to 1841; they kept being knocked down by earthquakes and reconstructed again and again. After a major earthquake in 1841, the citizens of Cartago began work on a new, Romanesque cathedral. But a devastating earthquake in 1910 ended that project, too. Is there a connection between building churches on this spot and the occurrence of earthquakes? No one knows, but townspeople have decided not to tempt fate any longer. Among the many legends attributed to the ruins is the gruesome story of the priest who, after falling in love with his sister-in-law, was murdered by his brother. Folks here say his headless ghost still haunts the grounds at night. ✉ *Avda. 2, Cs. 1–2, Cartago* 🔊 *Free.*

Sanatorio Carlos Durán (*Carlos Durán Sanatorium*)

HOSPITAL | These ruins of a former sanatorium were featured on the Syfy TV series *Ghost Hunters International* and have acquired cult status among visitors interested in paranormal phenomena. The complex sits just off the highway on the way to the Irazú Volcano and functioned as Costa Rica's hospital for tuberculosis patients from 1918 to 1973. The institution bears the name of its physician-founder, who also served as the country's president in the late 19th century. The attendant who takes your admission can provide some information, but you're essentially on a self-guided visit here. Most of the alleged spectral sightings are of the nuns who cared for the patients, with a few visitors claiming to see images in their photos they didn't notice when they were snapping pictures. Other visitors don't see anything but claim to hear what they assume are the nuns' voices. We can't promise you'll spot any ghosts, but don't let that spoil the intrigue. Your greatest risk here is likely natural, rather than supernatural: the outdoor walkways get slippery on rainy days. Tread carefully. ⊠ *Cartago* ✛ *Prusia de Cartago, 18 km (11 miles) southeast of Irazú volcano, 8 km (5 miles) north of Cartago* ☎ *2240–3016 in San José* 🌐 *$3.*

🍴 Restaurants

Although you can find decent pasta and pizza, haute cuisine just doesn't exist here. Cartago does give you a fine opportunity to eat some *comida típica* (typical food). On just about any street downtown you'll find a soda, and the women in the kitchen will serve you the same style of food they cook at home for their own families. One rule of thumb: the busier, the better—the locals know where to eat well.

La Puerta del Sol

$$ | **COSTA RICAN** | A cut above the usual soda, this large, long-established restaurant across from the basilica has been feeding pilgrims for seven decades. Along with hearty portions of seafood, grilled meats, and typical casados, the restaurant has a popular bar and terrace. **Known for:** decent dining in a town that generally lacks it; good view of the basilica; ample servings. 💲 *Average main: $11* ⊠ *North side of basilica plaza, Cartago* ☎ *2551–0615* 🌐 *www.facebook.com/ restaurantlapuertadelsol.*

Restaurant 1910

$$ | **COSTA RICAN** | The menu here at this upscale countryside spot is predominantly Costa Rican, with such traditional specialties as *trucha* (trout) and rice with chicken, along with some more sophisticated dishes, like corvina (sea bass) fillet with a coconut-liqueur sauce. The Sunday típico buffet is a great introduction to Costa Rican cooking. **Known for:** pleasant rural setting; vintage photo exhibit; variety of trout dishes. 💲 *Average main: $11* ⊠ *Road to Parque Nacional Volcán Irazú, 300 meters (984 feet) north of Cot–Pacayas turnoff, Irazú Volcano National Park* ☎ *2536–6063* 🚫 *No credit cards* 🌣 *No dinner Sun.*

🏃 Activities

CYCLING

San José Urban Adventures

BICYCLE TOURS | A six-hour tour, beginning and ending in San José, takes you by train to Cartago, followed by a cycling jaunt around town. ☎ *2208–3838* 🌐 *www. urbanadventures.com/en/san-jose.*

The Orosi Valley

45 km (28 miles) southeast of San José.

If you have a day to spend near San José, this idyllic valley makes a classic day trip, passing through coffee plantations shaded by poró trees—their flame-color flowers make a stunning sight during the dry season—oceans of chayote-squash vines, and small towns backed by verdant landscapes, with countless breathtaking views. It's a popular weekend drive for Costa Ricans, but still relatively off the beaten tourist path. The region is one of the few areas in Costa Rica that has remnants (ruins and churches) of the 17th-century Spanish colonial era. Paraíso, the valley's not-so-interesting metropolis, is your first point of access. Heading counterclockwise around the loop road are the area's real gems: Orosi, Tapantí National Park, Cachí, and Ujarrás.

GETTING HERE AND AROUND

A good road makes a loop around the valley, and it's easy to take in all the sights along the circle if you have your own vehicle, or if you go on a guided tour—it's a staple of most San José tour operators' offerings. Buses to the town of Orosi leave Cartago every 15 minutes from 5:15 to 7:30 am, then every 30 minutes until 7 pm, with a bus at 8 and 9 pm, 100 meters (328 feet) east and 25 meters (82 feet) south of the southeast corner of Las Ruinas. Public transportation around the valley is tricky: buses travel clockwise and counterclockwise, but neither route completes the circle.

ESSENTIALS

BANKS/ATMS Banco Nacional. ⊠ *Orosi* ⊹ *200 meters (656 feet) south of soccer field* ☎ *2533–1390* ⊕ *www.bncr.fi.cr.*

PHARMACIES Farmacia Candelaria. ⊠ *Orosi* ⊹ *North side of Restaurante Coto, across from soccer field* ☎ *2533–1919.*

POST OFFICE Correos. ⊠ *100 meters (328 feet) north of Municipalidad, Paraíso* ⊕ *correos.go.cr.*

 Sights

Iglesia de San José de Orosi (*Church of San José de Orosi*)
CHURCH | The town of Orosi, in the heart of the valley, has but one major sight: this beautifully restored 1743 church, the country's oldest house of worship still

in use, and one of the few structures in Costa Rica remaining from the colonial era. Set in a garden, against a green mountainside, it has a classic Spanish colonial whitewashed facade and bell tower, with a roof made of cane overlaid with terra-cotta barrel tiles. Inside are an antique wooden altar and ancient paintings of the Stations of the Cross and the Virgin of Guadalupe, all brought to Costa Rica from Guatemala. The religious-art museum next door has a small but exquisite collection of furniture and artifacts from the original Franciscan monastery here. A huge modern parish church sits beside the historic one, but happily, it's just far enough away not to spoil photos of the picturesque original structure. ⊠ *West side of soccer field, Orosi* ☎ *2533–3051* ⊠ *Museum $1* ⊘ *Closed Mon.*

Iglesia de Ujarrás (*Church of Ujarrás*)
CHURCH | The ruins of Costa Rica's first church lie past the Cachí dam near the small hamlet of Ujarrás (*oo-hah-RRASS*). An unlikely Spanish victory over a superior force of invading British pirates was attributed to a stop here to ask for the protection of the Virgin Mary, and a church was constructed in thanksgiving to honor the Virgin of Ujarrás. The entire village was abandoned in 1833 after a series of earthquakes and floods wreaked havoc in this lowest point of the Orosi Valley, and the inhabitants resettled at the site that would become the present-day town of Paraíso. Today the impressive, often-photographed limestone ruins sit in a beautifully maintained park with lawns, flower gardens, and a pretty picnic area. A final, scenic 6-km (4-mile) winding drive to Paraíso from Ujarrás completes the road that loops the valley. Visitors fill the site on weekends, but on weekdays you'll likely have the place to yourself. ⊠ *In a small park, 1 km (½ mile) from Restaurante Típico Ujarrás, Orosi* ☎ *2574–8366* ⊠ *Free.*

Iglesia de San José de Orosi is the county's oldest church that is still in use.

Jardín Botánico Lankester

GARDEN | The lush gardens of Lankester Botanical Garden, operated by the University of Costa Rica, house one of the world's foremost orchid collections, with more than 1,100 native and introduced species. Bromeliads, heliconias, and aroids also abound in the 7-acre garden, along with 80 species of trees, including rare palms. A Japanese garden has a graceful bridge and a teahouse. ⊠ *4 km (2½ miles) east of Cartago at west entrance to Paraíso, Cartago* ☎ *2511–7939* ⊕ *www.jbl.ucr.ac.cr* ⌨ *$10.*

Tapantí National Park

(*Parque Nacional Tapantí*)
NATIONAL PARK | Stretching all the way to the Talamanca Mountains, this reserve encompasses 47 square km (18 square miles) of largely pristine, remote cloud forest, a refuge for more than 400 bird species, including the emerald toucanet, violaceous trogon, and many of the country's hummingbirds. The rangers' office and visitor center are on the right just after the park entrance. You can leave your vehicle at a parking area 1½ km (1 mile) up the road. From here loop trails head off into the woods on both sides. Get an early start—you can enter on foot before 8 am, as long as you pay as you leave. The park clouds over markedly by afternoon and, with between 250 and 300 inches of rain annually, it's renowned as the country's wettest national park. (Fittingly, Tapantí means "torrent from heaven.") Be prepared with a poncho or sturdy umbrella. ⊠ *14 km (8 miles) south of Orosi, Orosi* ☎ *2206–5615* ⌨ *$10.*

🍽 Restaurants

Bar y Restaurante Coto

$$ | COSTA RICAN | A local institution since 1952, this large rancho restaurant and bar is famous for its huge meat platters—we're talking 1 to 1½ kilos (2¼ to 3½ pounds) of meat—with all the típico side dishes. Or you can dine more daintily on sautéed trout. **Known for:** good seafood dishes; pleasant view of Orosi church; enormous meat platters. Ⓢ *Average main: $14* ⊠ *Northeast corner of soccer*

field, Orosi ☎ *2533–3032* 💳 *No credit cards.*

La Casona del Cafetal

$$ | **COSTA RICAN** | The valley's most scenic and famous lunch stop sits on a coffee plantation overlooking the Cachí Reservoir. It's firmly on the beaten path, which means frequent visits from tour groups. **Known for:** yummy coffee desserts; solid menu of típico food; immensely popular weekend lunch buffet. [$] *Average main: $13* ✉ *2 km (1 mile) south of Cachí Dam, Orosi* ☎ *2577–1414* 🌐 *www.lacasonadelcafetal.com* 🕒 *No dinner.*

Hotels

★ **Hotel Quelitales**

$$ | **B&B/INN** | For quiet, get-away-from-it-all seclusion, this eco-friendly lodging can't be beat. **Pros:** quiet seclusion; great views; careful attention to sustainability and environment. **Cons:** best to have a car; steep walk to a couple of bungalows; rough final road to get here. [$] *Rooms from: $145* ✉ *3 km (2 miles) east of Cachí, Orosi* ☎ *2577–2222* 🌐 *www.hotelquelitales.com* 🔑 *9 bungalows* 🍴 *Free Breakfast.*

La Casona del Cafetal

$$ | **B&B/INN** | This sophisticated lodging offers dark-wood queen or king rooms in units scattered around a coffee plantation. **Pros:** amenities such as flat-screen TVs and Wi-Fi, which are uncommon in these parts; attentive service; quiet seclusion. **Cons:** best to have a car to stay here; restaurant gets extremely busy on weekends; all units, especially standard rooms, are a bit dark. [$] *Rooms from: $120* ✉ *2 km (1 mile) south of Cachí Dam, Orosi* ☎ *2577–1414* 🌐 *www.lacasonadelcafetal.com* 🔑 *7 rooms* 🍴 *Free Breakfast.*

Orosi Lodge

$ | **B&B/INN** | Run by a young German couple who have built a warm rapport with the community, the little lodge blends in with Orosi's pretty, old-town architecture: whitewashed walls are trimmed in blue, ceilings are high, and natural wood is used throughout. **Pros:** charming decor; affordable and pleasant; views from second-floor rooms. **Cons:** reception sometimes closes early; no restaurant, just a café. [$] *Rooms from: $66* ✉ *350 meters (1,148 feet) south, 100 meters (328 feet) west of soccer field, Orosi* ☎ *2533–3578* 🌐 *www.orosilodge.com* 🔑 *8 units* 🍴 *No Meals.*

Shopping

★ **Casa del Soñador** (*House of the Dreamer*)

CRAFTS | Stop in at this unique artisan shop, a picturesque wood cottage embellished with monumental carvings by local wood sculptor Macedonio Quesada, the creator of the House of the Dreamer. Though Macedonio died years ago, his sons Miguel and Hermes continue the tradition, carving interesting, often comical little statues out of coffee roots, which they sell for only $10 to $25. ✉ *2 km (1 mile) south of Cachí Dam, Orosi* ☎ *2577–1812.*

Turrialba

58 km (36 miles) east of San José.

The well-to-do agricultural center of Turrialba is a bustling town, with a youthful vibe from the nearby university, a colorful open-air market, and a tree-shaded central park filled with an intriguing collection of large-scale animal sculptures. The region's moist cheese, made in nearby Santa Cruz, is famous all over Costa Rica. As you begin the descent to Turrialba town, the temperature rises markedly and sugarcane alternates with fields of neat rows of coffee bushes. Turrialba also makes a product you might have heard of: Rawlings makes all the baseballs used in the major leagues. (The plant does not offer tours.) Thanks to some spectacular scenery, patches of rain forest in the surrounding countryside, and a handful of upscale nature lodges, ecotourism is increasingly the focus of the town's efforts. Significant numbers of kayakers and rafters also flock here to run the Pacuare and Reventazón rivers. And looming above the town is Volcán Turrialba. Recent eruptions of ash, along with a heavily damaged road, prevent visitors from going to the top or even getting near the base. Although volcanic activity keeps you away from the behemoth for safety reasons, don't let that scare you off from visiting other area attractions.

GETTING HERE AND AROUND

There are two ways to reach this area from San José, both of which pass through spectacular landscapes. The more direct route, accessible by heading east through Cartago, continues east through Paraíso, where you turn left at the northeast corner of the central park to pick up the road to Turrialba. Marked by signs, this road leads north to Guayabo National Monument. For the second route, turn off the road between Cartago and the summit of Irazú near the town of Cot, heading toward Pacayas. That narrow route twists along the slopes of Irazú and Turrialba volcanoes, with some stunning scenery—stately pollarded trees lining the road, riotous patches of tropical flowers, and metal-girder bridges across crashing streams.

Direct buses between San José and Turrialba leave hourly from 8 to 8 (slower buses run as early as 5:15 am and as late as 10 pm) from Calle 13, Avenida 6, just west of the downtown court buildings. Direct buses depart from the Turrialba terminal (at the entrance to Turrialba) for San José on the hour from 5 to 5, on the half hour to Cartago, and every two hours to Siquirres.

TAXIS Asocut. ⊠ *Turrialba* ☎ *2556–7070.*

ESSENTIALS

BANKS/ATMS Banco de Costa Rica. ⊠ *Avda. 0, C. 1, Turrialba* ☎ *2556–0472.* **Banco Nacional.** ⊠ *C. 1, Avda. Ctl., Turrialba* ☎ *2556–1211* ⊕ *www.bncr.fi.cr.*

HOSPITAL Hospital Dr. William Allen. ⊠ *Avda. 2, 100 meters (328 feet) west of C. 4, Turrialba* ☎ *2558–1300.*

PHARMACY Farmacia San Buenaventura. ⊠ *50 meters (164 feet) south of east side of central park, Turrialba* ☎ *2556–0379.*

 Sights

Guayabo National Monument (*Monumento Nacional Guayabo*)

RUINS | On the slopes of Turrialba Volcano lies Costa Rica's only true archaeological site. The city, once home to possibly 10,000 people, was abandoned in AD 1400, probably because of disease or war. Starting from the round, thatch-roof reception center, guided tours will take you through the rain forest to a lookout from which you can see the layout of the excavated circular buildings. Only the raised foundations survive, since the conical houses themselves were built of wood. As you descend into the ruins, notice the well-engineered surface and covered aqueducts leading to a trough of drinking water, which still functions today.

Guayabo has been recognized by the American Society of Civil Engineers as a feat of Latin American civil engineering second only to Machu Picchu. The hillside jungle is captivating, and the trip is further enhanced by bird-watching possibilities: 200 species have been recorded. ⊠ *Turrialba* ✢ *Drive through center of Turrialba to girdered bridge; take road signed Guayabo National Monument northeast for total of 16 km (10 miles), about 25–30 mins driving; watch for signed left turnoff, which will take you final 3 km (2 miles) to monument. If you've taken scenic Irazú foothills route to Turrialba, the Santa Cruz route—11 km (7 miles) (about 35 mins*

Try rafting the Pacuare River in October or November when the water is high.

driving)—is an option. Turn left on rough road from Santa Cruz; climb 5 km (3 miles), past the Escuela de Guayabo; turn right at the sign for the monument; the road descends 6 km (4 miles) to the site ☎ 2559–1220, 8534–1063 to reserve a guide, 1192 national park hotline ✉ From $5.

Turrialba Volcano National Park (*Parque Nacional Volcán Turrialba*)
VOLCANO | Although you've never been able to drive up to its summit as you can at Poás and Irazú, Volcán Turrialba is an impressive sight from a distance. The park reopened in 2022 after being closed for 10 years, a combination of increased volcanic activity and COVID precautions. The volcano became increasingly active in 2010. A series of explosions from 2015 well into 2020 spewed out steam and ash to far reaches of the country and periodically closed Juan Santamaría International Airport. (Volcanic ash can corrode airplane engines.) Sulfur dioxide fumes emanate from the volcano, a

phenomenon that has taken its toll on plant and animal life in the immediate vicinity.

While the park is open again, entry comes with major restrictions. Advance reservations and the services of a park guide are required. Tours depart hourly from 6 am to 10 am and take you on a trail 4 km (2½ miles) in length, billed as a "moderate to difficult" hike. Although you can still not go directly to the crater, observation platforms allow for viewing from a safe distance. Park authorities constantly monitor Turrialba's rumblings and close the park at the slightest hint of abnormal activity.

⚠ **If you suffer from a heart or respiratory condition or are pregnant, stay away.**
✉ 20 km (12 miles) east of Cot, Turrialba ☎ 1192 national parks hotline, 8534–1063 to reserve tour and mandatory guide ✉ $12, plus $10 per group for guide.

Off the Beaten Path

Centro Agronómico Tropical de Investigación y Enseñanza. A good place for bird-watchers and garden enthusiasts, the Tropical Agricultural Research and Higher Education Center—better known by its Spanish acronym, CATIE—is one of the leading tropical research centers in Latin America, with headquarters here and affiliates in nine other countries. You might catch sight of the yellow-winged northern jacana or the purple gallinule in the lagoon near the main building. The 10-square-km (4-square-mile) property includes landscaped grounds, seed-conservation chambers, greenhouses, orchards, experimental agricultural projects, a large swath of rain forest, labs and offices, and lodging for students and teachers. The most popular attraction is the **Botanical Garden Tour,** a two-hour guided walk to taste, smell, and touch tropical fruits, along with cacao, coffee, and other medicinal and stimulant plants. A favorite stop is the "miracle fruit" tree, whose berries magically make anything sour taste sweet. Reservations are required for guided tours. ✉ *3 km (2 miles) outside Turrialba, on road to Siquirres, Turrialba* ☎ *2558–2000* 🌐 *www.catie.ac.cr* 🎟 *From $15.*

Restaurants

La Garza Bar y Restaurante
$ | **COSTA RICAN** | With weathered, blond-wood tables and chairs, and big windows with a view out onto the central park, La Garza is a popular meeting spot with a little more atmosphere than most of the eateries in town in spite of its extremely plain interior. The menu runs the gamut from hamburgers to chicken and has a good seafood selection. **Known for:** nice outdoor view, even if plain interior; late-night eats; decent burgers. [$] *Average main: $9* ✉ *Northwest corner of central park, Turrialba* ☎ *2556–1073.*

Hotels

★ **Casa Turire**
$$$ | **B&B/INN** | Lush gardens and manicured lawns surround this gorgeous, hacienda-style luxury hotel overlooking a scenic lake. **Pros:** beautiful grounds; attention to sustainable tourism; luxurious suites. **Cons:** standard-room bathrooms could use a little upgrading; can be difficult to find; small, one-room spa. [$] *Rooms from: $190* ✉ *8 km (5 miles) south on Carretera a la Suiza from Turrialba, Turrialba* ☎ *2531–1309* 🌐 *www.hotelcasaturire.com* 🛏 *16 rooms* 🍴 *Free Breakfast.*

Guayabo Lodge
$$ | **B&B/INN** | If fresh mountain air appeals to you, this upscale mountain retreat has comfortable rooms, a first-class restaurant, and spacious, glassed-in sitting areas to enjoy unbeatable volcano and valley views by day and blazing fireplaces by night. **Pros:** cozy and comfortable; high sustainability consciousness; great views. **Cons:** clouds can obscure the view; can be difficult to get through by phone; weather can be wet and cool. [$] *Rooms from: $105* ✉ *2 km (1 mile) west of Santa Cruz de Turrialba, Turrialba* ☎ *2538–8400* 🌐 *www.guayabolodge.co.cr* 🛏 *26 rooms* 🍴 *Free Breakfast.*

Hotel Villa Florencia
$$ | **HOTEL** | **FAMILY** | This country inn a few miles outside of Turrialba offers peace and quiet, a rural feel, and friendly owners and staff. **Pros:** warm, helpful staff; family-friendly; quiet surroundings. **Cons:** best to have car to stay here; can be difficult to find; some rooms have

dated furnishings. $ *Rooms from: $145*
⊠ *La Susanita de Turrialba, 800 meters
(2,624 feet) west, Turrialba* ☏ *2557–3536*
⊕ *www.villaflorencia.com* ⇌ *20 rooms*
❖ *Free Breakfast.*

★ Rancho Naturalista

$$$$ | B&B/INN | Unparalleled bird-watching within a 160-acre private nature
reserve with more than 450 recorded
species, plus first-class food and comfortable lodging are the reasons nature
lovers from all over the world stay here.
Pros: birder's paradise; warm atmosphere; gourmet meals included. **Cons:** not
a convenient base for day trips; rough
final stretch of road to get here; some
rooms are a little dated. $ *Rooms from:
$380* ⊠ *20 km (12 miles) southeast of
Turrialba, 1½ km (1 mile) south of Tuís,
then up rough road, Turrialba* ☏ *8704–
3217, 2100–1855 for reservations*
⊕ *www.ranchonaturalista.net* ▭ *No credit
cards* ⇌ *13 rooms* ❖ *Free Breakfast.*

Turrialtico Lodge

$$ | B&B/INN | Dramatically positioned on a
hill overlooking the valley east of Turrialba,
this Costa Rican–owned rustic wood
lodge is a good budget option. **Pros:** rich
views at budget prices; coffeemakers in
rooms; good opportunity to mingle with
Ticos. **Cons:** less service-oriented than
other area options; need a car to stay
here; thin walls in main lodge. $ *Rooms
from: $77* ⊠ *8 km (5 miles) east of
Turrialba on road to Siquirres, Turrialba*
☏ *2538–1111* ⊕ *www.turrialtico.com*
⇌ *19 units* ❖ *Free Breakfast.*

Activities

Costa Rica Ríos

WHITE-WATER RAFTING | Specializing in
weeklong rafting, kayaking, and canoeing
excursions on the Pacuare and Pejibaye
rivers, this outfitter has rafter-to-guide
ratios of no more than 5:1. ⊠ *50 meters
(164 feet) north of central park, Turrialba*

☏ *2556–8664, 888/829–8246 in North
America* ⊕ *www.costaricarios.com* ⊠ *Ex-
cursions from $1,899/week.*

Ecoaventuras

LOCAL SPORTS | All the best activities—
horseback riding, mountain biking,
kayaking, and rafting—are covered with
this adventure company's one- to three-
day excursions with pickup from San
José area hotels. ⊠ *750 meters (2,461
feet) south of bus terminal, Turrialba*
☏ *2556–7171* ⊕ *www.ecoaventuras.co.cr*
⊠ *From $90.*

Explornatura

LOCAL SPORTS | This downtown company
organizes kayaking, horseback riding,
mountain biking, and rafting tours,
including a family-friendly Class II rafting
trip with lots of thrills but fewer chances
of spills. ⊠ *40 meters (131 feet) west of
Hotel Wagelia, Turrialba* ☏ *6357–5071*
⊕ *www.explornatura.com* ⊠ *From $89.*

Ríos Adventure

LOCAL SPORTS | The knowledgeable folks
here offer one- to four-day white-water
excursions on the nearby Río Pacuare,
with pickups in San José and Puerto Viejo
de Talamanca on the south Caribbean
coast. ⊠ *Turrialba* ☏ *6077–5209* ⊕ *www.
riosadventure.com* ⊠ *From $89.*

Volcán Turrialba Lodge

HIKING & WALKING | The lodge here can
arrange for guided walks and horseback
tours of the area, all at a safe distance
from the volcano. You'll find only very
rustic accommodation here. ⊠ *Turrialba
⊹ 20 km (12 miles) east of Cot, turn right
at Pacayas on road to Volcán Turrialba,
4 km (2½ miles) on dirt road; or from
Turrialba side, follow signs in La Pastora
for national park, 14 km (8½ miles)
along patchy paved road; 4WD advised
because last 3 km (2 miles) is on rough
road* ☏ *2273–4335* ⊕ *www.facebook.
com/turrialbalodge* ⊠ *From $55.*

Chapter 6

ARENAL, MONTEVERDE, AND THE NORTHERN LOWLANDS

Updated by
Rachel White

◉ Sights	🍴 Restaurants	🛏 Hotels	🛍 Shopping	🍸 Nightlife
★★★★★	★★★☆☆	★★★★☆	★★☆☆☆	★☆☆☆☆

WELCOME TO ARENAL, MONTEVERDE, AND THE NORTHERN LOWLANDS

TOP REASONS TO GO

★ **Soak in a volcano-heated hot spring:** For four decades Arenal was one of the world's most active volcanoes, but it has been in a state of slumber since 2010. It still provides a majestic backdrop for the steamy thermal waters nearby.

★ **Hike to a waterfall:** The reward for a tough hike down to La Fortuna Waterfall is a magnificent waterfall, plummeting nearly 76 meters (250 feet) into a freshwater pool.

★ **Float on a cloud:** Explore Monteverde's misty world on treetop walkways or on exhilarating ziplines up to 1 meter (3.28 feet) off the ground.

★ **Watch wildlife:** Birds, monkeys, turtles, caiman, and sloths abound in the 25,000-acre Caño Negro National Wildlife Refuge.

★ **Set sail:** Lake Arenal is one of the top windsurfing and kitesurfing spots in the world; winds can reach 50 to 60 mph mid-November through April.

The rich, lush terrain of the Zona Norte (Northern Zone), as it is known locally, runs from the base of the Cordillera Central in the south to the Río San Juan, on the border with Nicaragua in the north. Most visitors begin their visit to Costa Rica in San José, and then head north to La Fortuna. This adventure hub is a base for exploring the Arenal Volcano, La Fortuna Waterfall, and Caño Negro National Wildlife Refuge, and for sportfishing, windsurfing, and kitesurfing at Lake Arenal and rafting on the Sarapiquí River.

1 Arenal and La Fortuna. A three-hour drive northwest of San José brings you to Arenal Volcano, one of the top 10 most visited attractions in Costa Rica. Book the right hotel, such as Arenal Kioro, and you can wake up to views of the 5,300-foot-tall dome from your window. Although the volcano is in a passive stage, you might see a few plumes of smoke during your visit. La Fortuna is the closest town to the volcano; nearby diversions include hot springs, hanging bridges, white-water rafting, ziplines, waterfalls, and rain forest tours.

2 Nuevo Arenal. About an hour away from Arenal Volcano, the "nuevo" or "new" town of Arenal is popular for windsurfers who come to visit Lake Arenal. It also makes a good base for exploring the area, offering a few truly memorable restaurants and hotels.

3 Monteverde Cloud Forest and Santa Elena. Home to the rainiest of cloud forests, the Monteverde Cloud Forest area is also the canopy-tour capital of Costa Rica. Hanging bridges, treetop tram tours, and ziplines abound. As if that's not enough, horseback riding, coffee tours, and nature hikes are also available. Santa Elena, the closest town to Monteverde Cloud Forest, is the best base for a trip here.

4 Tenorio Volcano and the Río Celeste. Located about an hour north of Arenal in a verdant national park, the lesser known but magnificent Tenorio Volcano is surrounded by great hiking trails, a waterfall, hot springs, and Costa Rica's most striking blue river, the Río Celeste.

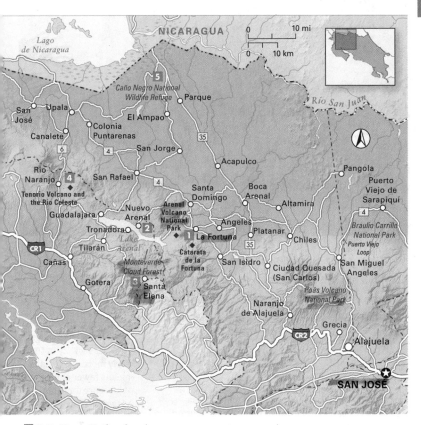

5 Caño Negro National Wildlife Refuge. In the far northern lowlands, this rain forest reserve and wetland, reminiscent of a small Florida Everglades, is a great place for fishing, bird-watching, and communing with nature. Boat tours are a popular way to take in all the flora and fauna of the area. It's about 90 minutes driving from La Fortuna.

ARENAL VOLCANO

Arenal Volcano

Rising to a height of roughly 5,000 feet, Arenal Volcano, Costa Rica's youngest volcano, dominates the region's landscape.

Volcanologists estimate Arenal's age at around 7,000 years, and it was dormant for nearly 500 years until 1968. On July 29, 1968, an earthquake shook the area, and 12 hours later Arenal blew.

Until October 2010, Arenal was in a constant state of activity—thunderous, rumbling eruptions occurred sometimes as frequently as once per hour. Tourists flocked here for the nightly show of rocks spewing skyward. Experts believe the volcano could now remain in a "resting" state for up to 800 years. After heavy rainfall, puffs of steam occasionally rise from the crater, making for an impressive photo of plumes over its cone. Sleeping or not, the lack of lava hasn't dissuaded travelers from seeing the magnificent mound or even hiking its flanks, which offer views of Lake Arenal in the distance. It still remains among the most visited attractions in the country.

For more information, see the review in this chapter.

BEST TIME TO GO

Despite its size, viewing Arenal Volcano can be hit or miss any time of year. January through April, especially in the early morning, usually means fewer clouds to obscure daytime views.

FUN FACT

It's no wonder Arenal Volcano is so photogenic—the conical supermodel has the third-most-picture-perfect crater in the world. Take aim quickly if you want to get a good shot, as cloud cover makes this natural attraction camera shy.

BEST WAYS TO EXPLORE

BIRD-WATCHING

If you decide to hike Los Tucanes trail, chances are you'll see at least one of the five species of toucan that have been recorded here: chestnut-billed and keel-billed toucans, the yellow-eared and emerald toucanet, and the collared aracari. You'll never look at a box of Froot Loops the same way after seeing the real thing. Hummingbirds also abound on the volcano's slopes. Look for anything tiny and purple.

HIKING

For intrepid hikers, Las Heliconias trail ($15), which starts at the national park's reception center, wends through secondary forest and passes by the cooled lava flow from the 1968 eruption. Outside the park, Los Tucanes trail ($10) also leads to the lava fields, but it's more of an uphill hike, beginning near the entrance to the Arenal Observatory Lodge. There's also a steep and arduous four-hour hike up to Cerro Chatto ($10), a dormant volcano with a lopsided, extinct crater partially filled with water, creating a pretty lake. The Los Miradores trail is completely paved and handicap accessible. It leads you through 1.3 km (0.8 miles) of forest to views of Lake Arenal, then takes you right to its shores. Arenal Observatory Lodge has a day pass ($32) including 11 km (7 miles) of trails, lunch, and use of swimming pools.

VOLCANIC TIPS

Two words: "from afar." Under no circumstances should you hike the volcano's trails on your own. In rainy season, some trails like Cerro Chatto are extremely muddy and treacherous. Pre-2010, lava rocks and volcanic gas occasionally killed trekkers who got too close to the action. The tour operators we recommend know where the danger lies and take appropriate precautions.

Waterfalls, streams, and lush rain forest surround Arenal.

TOP REASONS TO GO

ALL BUDGETS WELCOME

Travelers on tight budgets are being priced out of the market in some regions of Costa Rica. Not so here. You'll find everything from backpackers' digs to luxury hotels in the area around Arenal.

A PERFECT VOLCANO

Arenal's perfect cone, hiking trails, and thermal activity that heats neighboring hot springs keep the volcano at the top of the "must see" list despite the fact that its dormant phase may last another 800 years.

SPORTS AND ADVENTURE

It might have been the volcano that put Arenal on the map, but it's the area's recreational activities that keep travelers coming back. From ziplines and hanging bridges to waterfalls and raging rivers, Arenal has more attractions than any other destination in the country.

6

Arenal, Monteverde, and the Northern Lowlands

ARENAL VOLCANO

CAÑO NEGRO NATIONAL WILDLIFE REFUGE

Caño Negro National Wildlife Refuge

Think of a smaller version of Florida's Everglades and you'll have a good picture of the Refugio Nacional de Vida Silvestre Caño Negro.

This lowland rain-forest reserve in the far northern reaches of Costa Rica near the Nicaraguan border covers 98 square km (38 square miles). It looks remote on the map but is easily visited on an organized day tour, especially from La Fortuna. Caño Negro is the core of a UNESCO biosphere called Agua y Paz (Water and Peace), which encompasses more than 2 million acres of wildlife habitat in Costa Rica and Nicaragua.

Caño Negro has suffered severe deforestation over the years, but most of the length of the Río Frío, its principal river, is still lined with trees. The park's vast lake, which floods after seasonal rains, is an excellent place to watch waterfowl. The reserve is home to more than 350 migratory and resident bird species and 310 types of plants. On land, pumas, tapirs, ocelots, cougars, and the always-elusive jaguar are among the more than 160 mammal species that thrive here—consider yourself fortunate if you spot a jaguar.

BEST TIME TO GO

It gets *hot* here, with March and April brutally so, but the January–March dry season is the best time to spot the reserve's migratory bird population. Opportunities abound the rest of the year, too, though. No matter what season, bring sunscreen, a hat, and bug spray.

FUN FACT

In addition to other bird species, the reserve is the best place to spot the Nicaraguan grackle. This New World blackbird is found only in Nicaragua and northern Costa Rica.

BEST WAYS TO EXPLORE

BIRD-WATCHING

This is the best place in the country to see waterbirds. Just sit back in your tour boat and survey the passing parade. You're sure to see anhingas spreading their wings to dry; both glossy and white ibis recognizable by their long curved beaks; roseate spoonbills, often mistaken for flamingos; and the jabiru, king of the storks. Herons and kingfishers lurk on the banks, ready to spear fish, while jacanas, with their huge feet, forage in the water lettuce, looking as though they are actually walking on water. Above the water, watch for gray-color snail kites, which, true to their name, are hunting for snails.

BOAT TOURS

In the dry season you can ride horses, but a visit here chiefly entails a wildlife-spotting boat tour. You could drive up here on your own—roads to the area are in good shape until you approach Los Chiles; then it's 19 km (12 miles) on a gravel road to the park entrance in Caño Negro Town. Once here, you'd need to arrange for boat transportation. You can book the most reputable guides directly through Natural Lodge Caño Negro. Visiting with a tour company out of La Fortuna—it's a two-hour ride each way—is the most common way to see the park, but keep in mind that most Fortuna-based companies tour the perimeter of the reserve rather than the park interior in order to avoid the $5 entrance fee.

CAIMAN TOURS

Famous for its caimans, Caño Negro boasts a sizable population. They're smaller than crocodiles, though—at most, 8 feet long—and relatively unthreatening, because they're too small to eat large mammals (such as humans). It's a thrill to see them sunning on a bank.

TOP REASONS TO GO

BIRD-WATCHING

The reserve is one of Costa Rica's lesser-sung bird-watching and wildlife-viewing destinations. Caño Negro is growing in popularity, but, for now, a visit here still feels special.

FISHING

It's not all about wildlife viewing here: Caño Negro is also one of Costa Rica's prime freshwater fishing destinations, with tarpon, snook, and garfish yours for catch-and-release bragging rights during the September–March season (fishing is prohibited April–July, and the garfish ban is March–August). The two lodges inside the reserve can hook you up.

GREAT TOURS

It's easy to get here from the Arenal area, with tour operators organizing day tours from La Fortuna. If time allows, stay overnight in Caño Negro and reserve a tour through one of the lodges. When selecting a company, make sure the tour actually enters the reserve.

Jungle River Cruise Boat tour is a great way to see Caño Negro.

The vast expanse that locals call the Zona Norte (Northern Zone) packs in a larger variety of activities than any other part of the country. You'll find almost everything in this region that Costa Rica has to offer, from volcanoes to rain forests to waterfalls. Everything except beaches, of course.

Spend any amount of time here and you can partake of—take a deep breath—horseback riding, canoeing, kayaking, rafting, rappelling, windsurfing, kite-surfing, wildlife viewing, bird-watching, bungee jumping, shopping, cloud- and rain-forest hiking, swimming, hot-springs soaking, and volcano (albeit now dormant) viewing. The zipline canopy tour deserves special mention. The activity was invented in Costa Rica and has spread to all corners of the planet, while zipping along cables from platform to platform high in the trees has become Costa Rica's signature adventure activity.

The myriad activities make this, and especially Monteverde, Costa Rica's most kid-friendly region. Young children will "oooooh" (and "eeewwww") at various area animal exhibits devoted to bats, frogs, butterflies, hummingbirds, and snakes. Guided nature hikes abound; shorter treks can be entertaining and cater to younger ones' shorter attention spans. Most sure-footed and confi-dent teenagers can participate in adult activities such as white-water rafting and canopy tours.

A few operators around here will tell you that kids older than eight can participate in canopy tours. Even if their brochures show children happily zipping from platform to platform, the gondola-like trams and hanging bridges are far safer ways for preteens to see the rain-forest canopy.

Most nature- and adventure-themed excursions go on rain or shine, so don't feel you have to avoid a rainy-season visit here. (While rare, thunder and lightning *do* cancel such activities.) During the wet months, it's almost a given that you'll get a bit damp on your canopy tour, hike, or horseback ride, and most tour operators provide ponchos. But to avoid a thorough soaking, plan activities for the morning. Rains usually begin around 2 pm, like clockwork, from July through December, although they can be more prolonged in September and October. The clearest time of day is normally before 8 am.

MAJOR REGIONS

About 3½ hours from San José, the **Arenal Volcano** area is one of Costa Rica's biggest attractions. Whether you come here from San José or Liberia, prepare yourself for some spectacular scenery and curvy roads. Although the roads are well paved, they are quite narrow in places with steep drops and sharp turns. Any discomfort passengers might occasionally experience is more than made up for by the swaths of misty rain forest and dramatic expanses of the Cordillera Central.

Monteverde Cloud Forest is 167 km (104 miles, 3½ hrs) northwest of San José and 110 km (67 miles, 4 hrs) southwest of La Fortuna, and **Santa Elena** is 6 km (4 miles, 30 mins) north of Monteverde and 35 km (22 miles, 2 hrs) southeast of Tilarán.

Northwest of Monteverde is **Tenorio Volcano National Park and the Río Celeste,** home to an azure river and a dazzling waterfall that proves to be the most underrated attraction in Costa Rica. Also largely undiscovered, but with great bird-watching and wildlife, is **Caño Negro National Wildlife Refuge** in the far north reaches of the area.

Planning

When to Go

HIGH SEASON: MID-DECEMBER TO APRIL

Climate is difficult to pinpoint in this vast region. The Northern Lowlands link the rainier Caribbean in the east to drier Guanacaste in the west. Precipitation generally decreases from east to west. Monteverde is cool, damp, and breezy much of the time, with high winds in January and February. Elsewhere, rain can occur outside the official wet season since the area's low elevation frequently hosts battles between competing weather fronts. Visibility changes daily (and hourly), so your chances of seeing the Arenal volcano crater are more or less the same year-round, though you may have more luck from February to April, the hottest and driest time of the year.

LOW SEASON: JUNE TO MID-NOVEMBER

Throughout the entire region, the warm and humid rainy season normally lasts from June to December. Many places in Arenal and Monteverde are beginning

to impose high-season rates in July and August to correspond with prime North American and European vacation times.

We frequently overhear comments such as "I didn't know it would be so rainy in the rain forest." You heard it here first: that's why they call it the rain forest! During the rainy season it's not unusual for it to rain for several days straight, and even during the dry season, brief showers will come up without notice. Be sure to bring a poncho or rain jacket and waterproof footwear.

SHOULDER SEASON: MAY TO JUNE

The wet season just starts to kick in by May, but rarely to a degree that will interfere with your travels. A little precipitation provides a welcome clearing and freshening of the air in the countryside.

Planning Your Time

Although not centrally located, the Northern Lowlands can be easily tacked onto stays in other regions of Costa Rica. Fairly decent—decent for Costa Rica, that is—transportation links the region to San José, the Central Valley, and the North Pacific.

A week is more than enough time to experience a great deal of this area—especially if you're longing to get out and get moving. Give yourself four days in La Fortuna and the surrounding Arenal area, a great base for exploring the region. Devote the rest of your week to the Monteverde Cloud Forest. If your stay here is limited to two or three days, make La Fortuna–Arenal your base. Don't miss the inactive volcano, a day at the hot springs, or a trip to Caño Negro National Wildlife Refuge.

Most tour operators who have hikes end the day at one of the various thermal springs in the area. The most popular are Baldi, Ecotermales, Springs Resort, and Tabacón, all with cascading pools at varying temperatures and day packages that include lunch or dinner. With waterslides, buffet lines, and busloads of tourists, the larger hot springs can feel a bit like the Disneyland of relaxation. If you plan on spending a good amount of time soaking in the hot springs, opt for staying at a hotel with on-site thermal pools.

■ TIP→ **There are free public hot springs past the yellow gate next to Tabacón.**

"Half-day" tours to Caño Negro actually take most of the day, from around 7:30 am to 4 pm, and you'll spend about two hours each way in a bus or van.

Getting Here and Around

AIR

SANSA has daily flights from their own airport in San José to La Fortuna (FTN). It's located directly next to the international airport, with a fleet of puddle jumpers and a fast and easy check-in of only 30 minutes before boarding. Most travelers to this region fly into San José's Aeropuerto Internacional Juan Santamaría or Liberia's Daniel Oduber Airport and rent a car. Monteverde and Arenal are equidistant from both. Base your choice of airport on which other areas in Costa Rica you plan to visit in addition to this one—if you're headed to Guanacaste, Liberia may be your best bet. If you plan to hit the Caribbean coast or the Southern Pacific, it may be wise to fly into San José.

BUS

Buses in this region are typically large, clean, and fairly comfortable, but often crowded Friday through Sunday. Don't expect air-conditioning. Service tends toward the agonizingly slow: even supposedly express buses marked *directo* often make numerous stops. Terminal 7-10 (⊕ *terminal7-10.com/en*) in San José serves most of the major towns in this chapter.

CAR

Road access to the northwest is by way of the paved two-lane Pan-American Highway, which starts from the west end of Paseo Colón in San José and runs northwest to Peñas Blancas at the Nicaraguan border. Turn north at Naranjo for La Fortuna; at Lagarto for Monteverde; and at Cañas for Tilarán. This region manages to mix some of the country's smoothest highways with some of its most horrendous roads. The various roads to Monteverde are legendary in the latter regard—but the final destination makes it worth the trip. Four-wheel-drive vehicles are best on the frequently potholed roads. If you don't want to pay for 4WD, at least rent a car with high clearance (many rental agencies insist you take a 4WD vehicle if you mention Monteverde as part of your itinerary). You'll encounter frequent one-lane bridges; if the triangular *Ceda el Paso* sign faces you, yield to oncoming traffic. Driving in this region can be slow going if you get behind a large truck transporting sugarcane. As the north is prime sugar country, that's quite likely.

It is possible to rent a car in La Fortuna, but for a far better selection, most visitors pick up their rental vehicles in San José or Liberia. Consider downloading the Waze app to help guide you with directions.

Health and Safety

This region is Costa Rica's capital of adventure tourism—it gave birth to the zipline canopy tour—so any risks up here are far more likely to be natural than criminal. Before you set out rafting, ziplining, rappelling, or bungee jumping, be brutally frank with yourself about your abilities, your physical condition, and your fear levels: it's almost impossible to turn back on many excursions once you've started. Even an activity as innocuous as hiking or horseback riding poses a certain amount of risk, and you should never go alone. Nature here is not an amusement park.

Remember also that there is little government oversight of adventure tourism here. Pay close attention during any safety briefings and orientation. Don't be afraid to ask questions, and don't be afraid to walk away if something seems off to you. Look for zipline tours with built-in brake systems, double cables, and chest harnesses in addition to the normal waist harness. Many companies include GoPro helmet mounts so you can document your canopy adventure hands-free. If you have travel insurance, make sure it covers action sports or adrenaline activities—most standard packages do not cover injuries related to kayaking, horseback riding, ziplining, kitesurfing, or other such sports.

Money Matters

Outside the centers of Monteverde, La Fortuna, Nuevo Arenal, San Carlos, and Tilarán, ATMs are still few and far between. Stock up on cash when you get a chance.

Restaurants

The north is the country's breadbasket, and the hotels and restaurants out here make use of the bounty to whip up the best in *típico* Costa Rican cuisine. Don't be afraid to ask for tap water; it is safe to drink in all but the most rural areas. Service is generally slow but well worth the wait at most restaurants. Your final bill will include a 13% sales tax and a 10–12% service charge, though we suggest you tip a little extra.

Hotels

A few sumptuous resorts hold court in northern Costa Rica, but this region is largely the province of smaller, nature-themed lodgings that invite you to partake of all their eco-activities, and offer good value. Due to the comfortable inland temperatures, most hotels do not have air-conditioning. Also, it's not uncommon for some hotels to request that toilet paper be disposed of in a bin rather than flushed down the toilet, due to local plumbing challenges. Hotel rooms are taxed at the national rate of 13%.

HOTEL AND RESTAURANT PRICES

Restaurant prices are the average cost of a main course at dinner or, if dinner is not served, at lunch. Hotel prices are the lowest cost of a standard double room in high season. Restaurant and hotel reviews have been shortened. For full information, visit Fodors.com.

What It Costs in U.S. Dollars			
$	$$	$$$	$$$$
RESTAURANTS			
under $10	$10–$15	$16–$25	over $25
HOTELS			
under $75	$75–$150	$151–$250	over $250

Arenal and La Fortuna

50 km (30 miles, 45 mins) northwest of Ciudad Quesada, 17 km (11 miles) east of Arenal Volcano, 190 km (118 miles, 3½ hrs by car, 25 mins by plane) northwest of San José.

As they say, "Location, location, location." Who would think that a small town sitting at the foot of massive Arenal Volcano would attract visitors from around the world? Nobody comes to La Fortuna—an ever-expanding mass of hotels, tour operators, souvenir shops, and *sodas* (small, family-run restaurants)—to see the town alone. Instead, thousands of tourists flock here each year to use it as a hub for visiting the natural wonders that surround it. The volcano, as well as waterfalls, vast nature preserves, hot

Canyoneering and waterfall rappelling near the currently inactive Arenal Volcano

springs (*termales*), great rafting rivers, and an astonishing array of birds are to be found within an hour or less of your hotel. La Fortuna is also the best place to arrange trips to the Caño Negro National Wildlife Refuge.

Many people who settled the Northern Lowlands came to the then-isolated region in the 1940s and '50s from other parts of the country to take part in government-sponsored homesteading programs. Thanks to its rich volcanic soil, the agricultural region became one of the most productive in Central America. After the 1968 eruption of Arenal Volcano, La Fortuna was transformed from a tiny, dusty farm town to one of Costa Rica's tourism powerhouses, where visitors converged to see the volcano in action.

As of 2010, the volcano went into a rest-ing phase, which means it is still "active" below the surface, but it's doubtful you'll see more than a puff of steam. Viewing the volcano's peak can be hit or miss, especially during the rainy season (May through November). One minute Arenal

Volcano looms menacingly over the village; the next minute clouds shroud its cone. Early morning (and sometimes late afternoon), especially in the dry season, is the best time to catch a longer glimpse.

GETTING HERE AND AROUND

Choose from two routes from San José: for a slightly longer but better road, leave the Pan-American Highway at Naranjo, continuing north to Zarcero and Ciudad Quesada. Head northwest at Ciudad Quesada to La Fortuna; or for a curvier but shorter route, continue beyond Naranjo on the Pan-American Highway, turning north at San Ramón, arriving at La Fortuna about 90 minutes after the turnoff. (Opt for the first route if you are prone to motion sickness.) Either route passes through a mountainous section that begins to fog over by afternoon. Get as early a start as possible. SANSA flies daily to La Fortuna (FTN); flights land at an airstrip at the hamlet of El Tanque, 7 km (4 miles) east of town. Van transport ($10 one way) meets each flight to take you into La Fortuna.

Tropical Tours has a daily shared shuttle bus service between San José, La Fortuna, and Arenal ($54), and Monteverde ($54). Interbus has connections from here to a few of the North Pacific beaches. Public buses depart five times daily from San José's Terminal Atlántico Norte. Travel time is four hours. Although billed as an express route, the bus makes many stops.

Desafío Adventures provides a fast, popular, three-hour transfer between Monteverde and La Fortuna via taxi, boat, then another taxi, for $32 each way. If you're up for an adventure, there's a pedal and paddle option that takes you from Arenal to Monteverde on bicycles and stand-up paddleboards ($150). It also offers private transfers from San José to La Fortuna for $167 one way.

Taxis in and around La Fortuna are relatively affordable and will take you anywhere; a taxi to the Tabacón resort should run about $20. Get a cab at the stand on the east side of Parque Central.

The string of properties on the highway between La Fortuna and the Tabacón resort has led to a noticeable increase in traffic. It is hardly the proverbial urban jungle, and it is one of the country's prettiest stretches of road, but you should drive with caution. Cars dart in and out of driveways. Visitors congregate along the side of the road (likely sloth-spotting), and drivers gaze up at the volcano that looms over the highway. Keep your eyes on the road.

RENTAL CARS Alamo. ⊠ *100 meters (328 feet) west of church, La Fortuna* ☎ *2479–9090* ⊕ *www.alamocostarica. com.* **Mapache.** ⊠ *800 meters (2,624 feet) west of church, La Fortuna* ☎ *2586–6300* ⊕ *www.mapache.com.*

SHUTTLES Tropical Tours Shuttles.
☎ *2640–0811, 2640–1900* ⊕ *tropicaltour-shuttles.com.*

ESSENTIALS

BANKS/ATMS BAC San José. ⊠ *75 meters (246 feet) north of gas station, La Fortuna.* **Banco de Costa Rica.** ⊠ *East of Parque Central, in front of the school, La Fortuna* ☎ *2479–9113.* **Banco Nacional.** ⊠ *Central Plaza, 100 meters (328 feet) east of Catholic church, La Fortuna* ☎ *2479–9355.*

MEDICAL CLINIC Clínica La Fortuna CCSS. ⊠ *300 meters (984 feet) east of Parque Central, La Fortuna* ☎ *2479–8565.*

PHARMACY Farmacia Fishel. ⊠ *On main road, 25 meters (82 feet) east of public park, La Fortuna* ☎ *2479–9778.*

POST OFFICE Correos. ⊠ *Across from north side of church, La Fortuna* ☎ *2479–8070.*

◉ Sights

Arenal Volcano National Park

(*Parque Nacional Volcán Arenal*)
VOLCANO | Although the volcano is in a resting phase, you might see an occasional plume of smoke. It is still worth visiting the network of three easy trails leading to old lava flows, secondary rain forest, and a lookout point. (You are still limited in how close you can get, since no one can predict when Arenal will roar to life again.) The park is home to more than 200 species of birds, as well as monkeys, sloths, coatis, deer, and anteaters. A top trail within the park is Heliconias (0.61 km [0.38 mile]), which has a lookout point and connects to Las Coladas Trail (2 km [1 mile]). You'll see hardened lava streams from 1992 and a 200-year-old ceiba tree on El Ceibo loop (2.3 km [1.43 miles]) toward the edge of the park. Los Miradores Trail (1.29 km [0.8 mile]) takes you on a paved trail to Lake Arenal. Old lava flows are also visible on the popular Los Tucanes Trail that begins near the Arenal Observatory Lodge. Guides are available for hire at the neighboring tour office, Arenal 1968. Bring plenty of water, but remember that

single-use plastics are prohibited in all of Costa Rica's national parks (a reusable water bottle will make a nice souvenir).

Outside the national park is the noteworthy Cerro Chatto, an inactive volcano which you can hike from a trailhead near La Fortuna Waterfall at the Green Lagoon Lodge. Expect to pay an entrance fee of up to $10. The challenging, steep, and often muddy Cerro Chatto Trail is for experienced hikers in good physical condition. It takes about three to four hours to reach the stunning, emerald green crater lake. ⊠ *1½ km (1 mile) from police station, on road to Arenal Observatory Lodge, La Fortuna* ☎ *2460–0620 regional office, 2200–4192 park administration* ⌨ *$15 cash only.*

Church of San Juan Bosco
CHURCH | The town's squat, pale, concrete church, unremarkable on its own, just might win Costa Rica's most-photographed-house-of-worship award. The view of the church from across the central park, with the volcano in the background, makes a great photo of the sacred and the menacing. ⊠ *West side of Parque Central, La Fortuna.*

Eco Termales
HOT SPRING | Open hours at these family-owned hot springs are divided into two intervals per day (9 to 4 and 5 to 10), with only 80 guests permitted entry per segment. This means the six pools and restaurant never get too crowded. Temperatures range from 37° to 41°C (98.6° to 105.8°F), and there is one chilly waterfall to cool you off. Admission includes towel and locker. This is a great alternative to the overcrowded Baldi Hot Springs across the road or the mammoth Tabacón Hot Springs. ⊠ *3½ km (2 miles) east of Catholic church, across from Baldi, diagonal from Volcán Look Disco Club, La Fortuna* ☎ *2479–8787* ⊕ *www.ecotermalesfortuna.cr* ⌨ *From $44.*

Ecocentro Danaus (*Danaus Ecocenter*)
NATURE SIGHT | FAMILY | A small ecotourism project outside town exhibits 60 species of medicinal plants, abundant animal life—including sloths and caimans—and butterfly and orchid gardens. This is a great place to see Costa Rica's famed red poison dart frogs up close. You can also learn about the indigenous Maleku culture and see their art displayed. Seven guided tours are offered daily from 8 am to 3:30 pm. A two-hour guided evening tour begins at 5:45 and should be reserved in advance. The center can arrange your transportation, too. ⊠ *2 km (1 mile) south of La Fortuna, 600 meters (1,969 feet) above road to Agua Azul, La Fortuna* ☎ *2479–7019, 506/8588–9314 WhatsApp* ⌨ *From $30.*

★ La Fortuna Waterfall
(*Cataratas de la Fortuna*)
WATERFALL | A strenuous walk down 500 steps (allow 25 to 40 minutes) is worth the effort to swim in the pool under the waterfall. Wear sturdy shoes or water sandals with traction, and bring snacks and water. You can get to the trailhead from La Fortuna by walking, by horseback, or by taking a taxi (approximately $10). Arranging a tour with an agency in La Fortuna is the easiest option. There are restrooms, free parking, a restaurant, and gift shop. ⊠ *Yellow entrance sign off main road toward volcano, 7 km (4 miles) south of La Fortuna, La Fortuna* ☎ *2479–9515* ⊕ *www.cataratalafortuna.com* ⌨ *$18.*

Lake Arenal
BODY OF WATER | Costa Rica's largest inland body of water, shimmering Lake Arenal, all 85 square km (33 square miles) of it, lies between rolling green hills and a picture-perfect volcano. Many visitors are surprised to learn it's a man-made lake, created in 1973 when a giant dam was built to provide hydroelectric power for the country. A natural depression was flooded, and a lake was born. Depending on the season,

Off the Beaten Path

Venado Caves. In 1945 a farmer in the mountain hamlet of Venado fell into a hole, and thus discovered Cavernas de Venado, subterranean limestone chambers extending about 2½ km (1½ miles). If you're not claustrophobic, willing to get wet, and don't mind bats or spiders (think carefully) this could be the ticket for you. Rubber boots, flashlights, and helmets are provided. Bring insect repellent and knee pads but leave your phone at the hotel—it will get wet. If you want to capture the adventure, consider hiring their on-site photographer to follow you through the 10 caves. Lunch is an option here; it must be reserved in advance. Most La Fortuna–based tour companies run trips to Venado Caves for about $90 or you can book directly with the caves for $28. ⊠ *45 mins north of La Fortuna and 20 mins southeast of San Rafael, La Fortuna* ☎ *2478–8008, 8653–2086* ⊕ *www.cavernasdelvenadocr.com* 🍽 *From $28.*

the depth varies between 100 and 200 feet, with rainbow bass and machaca fish lurking below the surface. When water levels drop, you can see ruins of a cemetery and church jutting from the lake. The almost constant winds from the Caribbean make this area a windsurfing and kiteboarding mecca. Outfitters in La Fortuna, Nuevo Arenal, and Tilarán run fishing, windsurfing, and kiteboarding trips on the lake. Desafío, an operator based in La Fortuna and Monteverde, has a half-day horseback trip between the two towns, with great views of the lake. For the best lake views, reserve a hotel in Nuevo Arenal. ⊠ *15 km (9 miles) southwest of La Fortuna, La Fortuna.*

Místico Arenal Hanging Bridges

TRAIL | A series of trails and bridges form a loop through the primary rain forest of a 250-acre private reserve, providing great bird-watching and volcano viewing. Sixteen fixed and hanging bridges allow you to see the forest at different levels. There are self-guided tours, but if you want to spot animals in addition to the breathtaking views, we recommend a guide. Trails are open rain or shine, and there are things to do in both types of weather, including horseback-riding tours that start at 9 am and 1 pm. Shuttle service from La Fortuna and area lodgings can be arranged. ⊠ *2½ km (1½ miles) east of Lake Arenal dam on paved road, La Fortuna* ☎ *2479–8282* ⊕ *www.misticopark.com* 🍽 *From $26.*

The Spa at Tabacón

HOT SPRING | Grab a robe and settle into the jungle Jacuzzi while spa valets serve you healthy smoothies. Treatments like the volcanic mud wrap and the couples' two-hour massage in private jungle bungalows utilize locally made products and end with champagne and fresh fruit. For a full day of pampering, request the spa package, which includes access to the thermal baths, lunch or dinner, and spa services. ⊠ *13 km (8 miles) northwest of La Fortuna on hwy. toward Nuevo Arenal, across from Tabacón Resort, La Fortuna* ☎ *2479–2027* ⊕ *www.tabacon.com* 🍽 *From $60.*

🍴 Restaurants

Chipotle's

$$ | **MEXICAN** | Fresh bold flavors, local products, first-class service, and marvelous murals elevate this basic roadside restaurant to a delightful dining experience. The chef and owner trained in Mexico, so you can taste the authenticity in the tacos and the mezcal in the

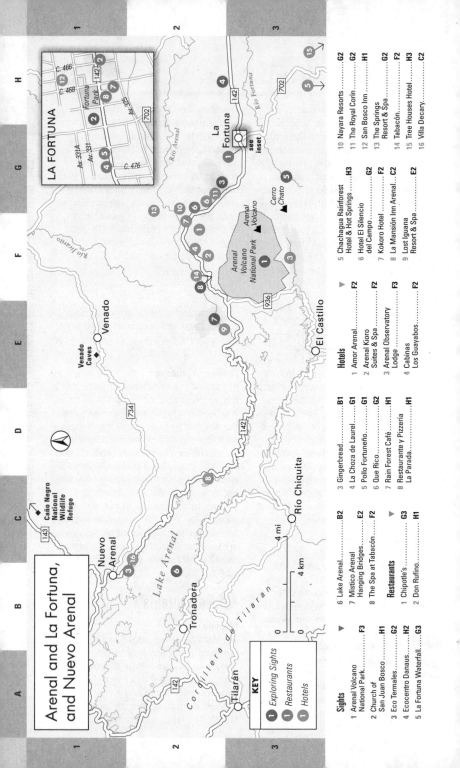

Arenal and La Fortuna, and Nuevo Arenal

LA FORTUNA

C. 466
C. 468
Fortuna Park
Av. 331A
Av. 331
Av. 325
C. 476
702

Caño Negro National Wildlife Refuge
Cordillera de Tilarán
Lake Arenal
Río Jilanito
Río Arenal
Río Fortuna

Venado Caves
Venado
Nuevo Arenal
Tronadora
Tilarán
Río Chiquita
El Castillo
La Fortuna
see inset

Arenal Volcano National Park
Arenal Volcano
Cerro Chato

143
734
142
142
702
936

0   4 km
0   4 mi

KEY

▶ 1 Exploring Sights
1 Restaurants
1 Hotels

Sights   ▶

1 Arenal Volcano National Park F3
2 Church of San Juan Bosco H1
3 Eco Termales G2
4 Ecocentro Danaus H2
5 La Fortuna Waterfall G3
6 Lake Arenal B2
7 Místico Arenal Hanging Bridges E2
8 The Spa at Tabacón F2

Restaurants   ▶

1 Chipotle's G3
2 Don Rufino H1
3 Gingerbread B1
4 La Choza de Laurel G1
5 Pollo Fortuneño G1
6 Que Rico G2
7 Rain Forest Café H1
8 Restaurante y Pizzería La Parada H1

Hotels   ▶

1 Amor Arenal F2
2 Arenal Kioro Suites & Spa F2
3 Arenal Observatory Lodge F3
4 Cabinas Los Guayabos E2
5 Chachagua Rainforest Hotel & Hot Springs H3
6 Hotel El Silencio del Campo G2
7 Kokoro Hotel F2
8 La Mansión Inn Arenal C2
9 Lost Iguana Resort & Spa E2
10 Nayara Resorts G2
11 The Royal Corin G2
12 San Bosco Inn H1
13 The Springs Resort & Spa G2
14 Tabacón F2
15 Tree Houses Hotel H3
16 Villa Decary C2

margaritas. **Known for:** tacos every which way; churros; fresh guacamole and homemade chips. $ *Average main: $10* ✉ *Plaza Arenal, La Fortuna* ✛ *500 meters (1,640 feet) west of parque de la Fortuna de San Carlos* ☎ *2479–9700.*

Don Rufino

$$$ | ECLECTIC | The L-shape bar fronting the main street is a popular expat and tourist hangout. The user-friendly menu is marked with symbols of chili peppers for spicy dishes, a tomato for vegetarian dishes, and a check mark for those that are highly recommended, like the chicken seasoned with chocolate, coffee, and tarragon or forest lasagna made with wild mushrooms, caramelized onions, and ricotta cheese. **Known for:** friendly service and clientele; occasional live music; organic, local meats. $ *Average main: $17* ✉ *Across from gas station, La Fortuna* ☎ *2479–9997* ⊕ *donrufino.com.*

La Choza de Laurel

$$ | COSTA RICAN | The aroma of rotisserie chicken, porterhouse steak, and fresh fish bathed in garlic attracts passersby to this open-air restaurant a short walk from the center of town. Wooden picnic tables and a cigar shop storefront replicate an old Costa Rican village, adding a cultural touch to your meal. **Known for:** Choza plate with chicken; black bean soup with homemade tortillas; banana splits served in a pineapple. $ *Average main: $12* ✉ *400 meters (1,312 feet) northwest of church, La Fortuna* ☎ *2479–7063* ⊕ *lachozadelaurel.com/en.*

Pollo Fortuneño

$ | COSTA RICAN | FAMILY | This bustling open-air eatery has an extensive menu, but they specialize in wood-fired chicken and ribs. It's worth a stop to grab a rotisserie chicken if your room has a mini-refrigerator or a barbecue picnic lunch for your hike. **Known for:** delicious patacones (fried plantains) and dips; pollo; fall-off-the-bone ribs. $ *Average main: $9* ✉ *Rte. 142, La Fortuna* ✛ *100 meters*

En Route

Viento Fresco Waterfalls. On the road from Monteverde, just south of Tilarán, this private farm boasts five cascading waterfalls and swimming holes. The largest plunges 1 meter (3.28 feet) into a freshwater pool. Note that it's not great for anyone with mobility issues or for children. The site also offers hiking trails, a dairy farm, several caves, changing facilities, and a restaurant serving Costa Rican fare. Horseback riding is also available. ✉ *Tilarán* ✛ *11 km (6 miles) south of Tilarán near San Miguel* ☎ *2695–3434* ✑ *$15 waterfalls; $55 horseback riding.*

(328 feet) west of the Catholic church ☎ *2479–7475.*

★ Que Rico

$$$ | ITALIAN | This lovely Italian-inspired restaurant adds touches of romance with wooden tables draped with red-and-white linens and soft music and candles. The menu is long, with options ranging from local ceviche to tamarind chicken, but the Italian specialties are best: the brick-oven Volcán pizza with ham, mushrooms, bacon, and pepperoni is a local favorite. **Known for:** Baci Peruguna pastries stuffed with Nutella and caramelized onions; wine-pairing recommendations; above and beyond service. $ *Average main: $20* ✉ *6½ km (4 miles) west of church, La Fortuna* ☎ *2479–1020* ⊕ *www.quericoarenal.com.*

Rain Forest Café

$ | COSTA RICAN | Reasonable prices and excellent quality have made this café a traveler's favorite, with meals ranging from *churrasco* (grilled meat) and empanadas to salads and sandwiches. There's typical Costa Rican *casado* (chicken, beef, or fish served with rice, beans, plantains, and salad) along with tempting desserts like chocolate pie, carrot cake, flan, and a variety of pastries. **Known for:** local coffee; Crazy Monkey smoothie made with banana, milk, cinnamon, and coffee; scrumptious macadamia cakes. [$] *Average main: $8* ✉ *In front of Hotel Las Colinas, 125 meters (410 feet) south of park, La Fortuna* ☎ *2479–7239.*

Restaurante y Pizzería La Parada

$$ | **COSTA RICAN** | This locals' favorite late-night eatery (open until midnight) does a brisk business serving pizza, pasta, nachos, burgers, and grilled fish. There's a buffet, if you'd rather just point and choose. **Known for:** surprisingly impressive wine selection; busy atmosphere; quick, cheap food. [$] *Average main: $11* ✉ *Across from Parque Central and regional bus stop, La Fortuna* ☎ *2479–9098* 🌐 *www.restaurantelaparada.com.*

Hotels

★ Amor Arenal

$$$$ | **RESORT** | Perched canyonside with views of the forest and the volcano beyond, these spacious, modern cabins of stone and wood below soaring ceilings and massive windows are cozy and comfortable. **Pros:** many amenities as well as on-site trails; delectable farm-to-table buffet breakfast; close to town but it feels like you're in the middle of the forest. **Cons:** no kids allowed; bathrooms lack privacy; long walks to casitas (resort provides golf-cart rides 24 hours). [$] *Rooms from: $575* ✉ *West of Centro de La Fortuna 7 km (4½ miles) on Ruta 142, La Fortuna* ☎ *2479–7070* 🌐 *amorarenal.com* 🛏 *31 casitas* 🍴 *Free Breakfast.*

Arenal Kioro Suites & Spa

$$$$ | **RESORT** | This is one of the closest properties to the volcano, with rooms boasting hydromassage Jacuzzis, sitting areas, jaw-dropping views, Juliet balconies, and nearly 700 square feet of space. **Pros:** plentiful breakfast; all rooms face the volcano; enormous rooms. **Cons:** no bottled water or ceiling fans in rooms; steep walkways; dim rooms. [$] *Rooms from: $368* ✉ *10 km (6 miles) northeast of La Fortuna, before Tabacón, Arenal Volcano National Park* ☎ *2479–1700* 🌐 *www.hotelarenalkioro.com* 🛏 *53 rooms* 🍴 *Free Breakfast.*

★ Arenal Observatory Lodge

$$$ | **HOTEL** | These cozy, comfortable, and simple rooms allow you to sleep as close as anyone should to a volcano—it's a mere 2¾ km (1¾ miles) away, and stellar views and outdoor activities are what the place is all about. **Pros:** best volcano views; secluded location; rate includes breakfast, taxes, and guided hike. **Cons:** isolated location; patchy Wi-Fi; rough road to get here. [$] *Rooms from: $178* ✉ *5 km (3 miles) from national park entrance, La Fortuna* ☎ *2479–1070 lodge, 2290–7011 in San José, 877/804–7732 in U.S. and Canada* 🌐 *www.arenalobservatorylodge.com* 🛏 *48 rooms* 🍴 *Free Breakfast.*

Cabinas Los Guayabos

$ | **HOTEL** | As one of the low-priced options with a volcano view, these orange adobe cabins are basic but clean with big windows and private patios, which are great for viewing wildlife and, on clear days, Arenal. **Pros:** good budget value; friendly owners; great volcano views. **Cons:** breakfast not included; inconvenient if you don't have a car; rustic rooms. [$] *Rooms from: $72* ✉ *9 km (5½ miles) west of La Fortuna, La Fortuna* ☎ *2479–1444* 🌐 *www.facebook.com/cabinaslosguayabosoficial* 💳 *No credit cards* 🛏 *9 cabins* 🍴 *No Meals.*

Chachagua Rainforest Hotel & Hot Springs

$$$ | **HOTEL** | If you fancy toucan spotting from your room or the deck of your bungalow, Chachagua will be right up your alley. **Pros:** feels private and secluded; nice hot springs and restaurant-bar area; nature walk on-site. **Cons:** rooms a bit dark; rough road to hotel; 30 minutes from La Fortuna. [$] *Rooms from: $248* ✉ *12 km (7 miles) south of La Fortuna, La Fortuna* ☎ *833/216–2355 from U.S.,*

4000–2026 🌐 www.chachaguarainforest-hotel.com 🛏 19 units 🍴 Free Breakfast.

Hotel El Silencio del Campo
$$$ | **HOTEL** | **FAMILY** | From the villas to the farm to the on-site hot springs, kids and adults alike are enthralled by this peaceful property. **Pros:** cute little farm; warm and friendly Costa Rican–family owned; clean and comfortable villas. **Cons:** rooms lack a lot of natural light; service at restaurant can be slow; can be loud at times. *[$] Rooms from: $216 ✉ Rte. 142, La Fortuna ✥ 5 km (3 miles) west of La Fortuna Central Park ☎ 2479–7055 🌐 www.hotelsilenciodelcampo.com 🛏 12 villas 🍴 Free Breakfast.*

Kokoro Hotel
$$ | **HOTEL** | **FAMILY** | Spacious and clean rooms at this hot-springs hotel are like mini log cabins with hardwood floors and sugarcane ceilings—Nos. 16, 17, and 18 even offer views of the volcano. **Pros:** lovely pool; private hot springs; tour desk with good rates. **Cons:** cleanliness of pools could be improved; hot springs open at 4 pm; dim lighting in rooms. *[$] Rooms from: $110 ✉ 500 meters (1,640 feet) west of Quebrada la Palma, La Fortuna ☎ 2479–1222 🌐 kokoroarenal.net 🛏 29 rooms 🍴 Free Breakfast.*

Lost Iguana Resort & Spa
$$$$ | **HOTEL** | Despite the relative isolation, travelers flock to this rain-forest resort largely because each hillside room has a huge picture window and door opening to an individual balcony with volcano views. **Pros:** good breakfast; great volcano views in rain-forest setting; plenty of wildlife; nice spa and gym. **Cons:** small pool; removed from sights; poor lighting in rooms. *[$] Rooms from: $325 ✉ Off Hwy. 142, 20 km (12 miles) west of La Fortuna, La Fortuna ☎ 2479–1557 🌐 www.lostiguanacr.com 🛏 42 rooms 🍴 Free Breakfast.*

★ **Nayara Resorts**
$$$$ | **RESORT** | Scattered over expansive grounds are freestanding casitas, villas, and "tents," all tastefully decorated with dark-wood furnishings and equipped with luxurious touches like indoor-outdoor showers, four-post canopy beds, plasma TVs, and whirlpool tubs. **Pros:** attentive staff, luxe accommodations; early check-in can be arranged; excellent breakfast. **Cons:** villas lack volcano views; need to use golf carts to get around sprawling grounds; hotel books up early. *[$] Rooms from: $700 ✉ 7 km (4½ miles) west of La Fortuna, Arenal Volcano National Park ☎ 2479–1600, 888/332–2961 in North America 🌐 www.arenalnayara.com 🛏 66 units 🍴 Free Breakfast.*

The Royal Corín
$$$$ | **HOTEL** | This hotel has a volcano view along with luxury perks like a swim-up bar, five-star cuisine, a swanky lobby, and an impressive spa. **Pros:** on-site hot springs; pleasant hotel-style surroundings; excellent showers. **Cons:** poor lighting in the rooms; not a lot of local flavor; some street noise. *[$] Rooms from: $304 ✉ 4 km (2½ miles) west of La Fortuna, La Fortuna ☎ 2479–2201, 800/742–1399 in North America 🌐 www.royalcorin.com 🛏 54 rooms 🍴 Free Breakfast.*

San Bosco Inn
$$ | **HOTEL** | In downtown La Fortuna, this inn has clean, bright rooms linked by a long veranda lined with benches and potted plants, and added perks like a large pool and in-room Wi-Fi. **Pros:** gated property; good value; close to center of town; use of spa at sister property Volcano Lodge. **Cons:** boxy design; small rooms; some rooms get street noise. *[$] Rooms from: $88 ✉ La Fortuna ✥ 220 meters (722 feet) north of gas station ☎ 2479–9050, 800/393–0902 in North America 🌐 www.hotelsanbosco.com 🛏 33 rooms 🍴 Free Breakfast.*

The perfect way to end the day: a nice soak in the hot springs in Arenal Volcano National Park

The Springs Resort & Spa

$$$$ | RESORT | FAMILY | With its own adventure park, hot-springs complex, and activities for all ages, this resort caters to both hotel guests and the outside public with day passes to its massive grounds. **Pros:** stupendous volcano views; hot springs rich in minerals; excellent sushi bar. **Cons:** rooms are pricey; Wi-Fi signal weak in some areas; property has a theme-park feel. $ *Rooms from: $875* ✉ *9 km (5½ miles) west of La Fortuna, then 4 km (2½ miles) north, La Fortuna* ☎ *2401–3313, 954/727–8333 in North America* ⊕ *www.thespringscostarica. com* ⌁ *47 units* ❍❑ *No Meals.*

Tabacón

$$$$ | RESORT | At one of Central America's most relaxing and romantic resorts, it's the hot springs and lovely spa, coupled with attractive rooms (the suites are some of the country's finest) that customarily draw happy guests inland from the ocean. **Pros:** luxurious hot springs; great volcano views; good restaurant; elegant hotel. **Cons:** hot springs can get crowded; two-night minimum stay. $ *Rooms from: $430* ✉ *13 km (8 miles) northwest of La Fortuna on Hwy. 142, La Fortuna* ☎ *2479–2000, 2519–1999 in San José, 855/822–2266 in North America* ⊕ *www.tabacon.com* ⌁ *102 rooms* ❍❑ *Free Breakfast.*

Tree Houses Hotel

$$$ | B&B/INN | Whether whiling away the mornings on the porch amid the toucans, trekking to the river, or spotting nocturnal creatures on night hikes, nature lovers will be enthralled with the stilted cabins of this 10-acre property in the trees. **Pros:** lots of wildlife including sloths, monkeys, birds; unique perspective from the treetops without sacrificing A/C; complimentary perks like morning coffee delivery to your porch and guided hikes. **Cons:** remote location 25 minutes from major attractions; limited Wi-Fi and cell signal; some road noise. $ *Rooms from: $246* ✉ *Ciudad Quesada* ✛ *300 meters (984 feet) north of the cemetery* ☎ *2475–6507* ⊕ *www.treehouseshotelcostarica.com* ⌁ *7 tree houses* ❍❑ *Free Breakfast.*

Nightlife

People in La Fortuna tend to turn in early, though there are a couple of spots for night owls.

Lava Lounge

LIVE MUSIC | This La Fortuna hot spot has local and imported beers plus plenty of cocktails to get you in the mood for live music every Wednesday and Saturday from 7 to 10. An unorthodox happy hour is from 9 to 11 am, and you're likely to have desperate-looking dogs underfoot, telepathically begging you to take them home. Lava Lounge owner Scott Alan runs a dog rescue at this pooch-friendly establishment. Donations to the cause are always appreciated. ⊠ *25 meters (82 feet) west of Catholic church, La Fortuna* ☎ *2479–7365.*

Shopping

Cianikal

SOUVENIRS | Stop into this atelier for a unique, elevated gift or keepsake that you will not see in the big souvenir shops: jewelry, art, T-shirts, chocolate, honey, spices, and soaps, all handmade in Costa Rica by local artisans. You can even watch the jewelry being made, and a portion of the proceeds goes to reforestation efforts. ⊠ *La Fortuna ⊹ 100 meters (328 feet) west of La Fortuna Church* ☎ *2479–7421.*

🏃 Activities

CANOPY TOURS

Ecoglide Arenal Park

ZIP LINING | Unlike most zipline companies, Ecoglide adds an element of safety with their double cables and allows guests to request starting times outside of their regular tour schedule. There are 12 standard ziplines and a Tarzan swing at platform No. 8. For those who want to film while they fly, Ecoglide rents helmets with front camera mounting systems. As with all zipline tours in Costa

Rica, reservations should be made in advance. Set tours start at 8, 10, noon, and 3. ⊠ *3 km (2 miles) west of La Fortuna, La Fortuna* ☎ *2479–7472* ⊕ *www. arenalecoglide.com* 🌐 *$78.*

★ Sky Adventures Arenal Park

LOCAL SPORTS | This adventure park on the outskirts of Arenal Volcano operates another park in Monteverde. Alpine-style gondolas transport you to the site, from which you can descend via 3 km (2 miles) of ziplines, hike through the cloud forest along a series of suspended bridges, or go back the way you came, on the tram. You'll pass from rain forest into cloud forest, and can fly above the treetops with gorgeous views of the lake and volcano. Adrenaline seekers might opt for biking, canyoning, or tubing back to base camp. You can mix and match tours for a full-day adventure, too. The company is Safe Travel certified by the World Travel & Tourism Council. ⊠ *26 km (16 miles) west of La Fortuna, El Castillo* ☎ *2479–4100, 844/486–6759 in North America* ⊕ *www. skyadventures.travel* 🌐 *From $41.*

RAFTING AND KAYAKING

Canoa Aventura

CANOEING & ROWING | Canoeing trips with ample wildlife viewing on the Río Peñas Blancas are a specialty, as are daylong canoe tours of the Caño Blanco Wildlife Refuge. The three-hour Caño Negro tour takes place on the Río Frío near the Nicaraguan border, where you're sure to see birds, monkeys, caimans, iguanas, and bats. Tours are appropriate for beginners, with a selection of easy floats if you're not feeling too adventurous, and instruction is provided, but the folks here can tailor excursions if you're more experienced. ⊠ *1 km (½ mile) west of the church, La Fortuna* ☎ *2479–8200* ⊕ *www. canoa-aventura.com* 🌐 *From $63.*

Flow Trips

KAYAKING | Local guides lead rafting excursions on the Sarapiquí River (Classes II, III, and IV), as well as biking trips, kayaking trips on Lake Arenal, and wildlife

Did You Know?

Many rain forests have hanging bridges and elevated platforms to give you a bird's-eye view of the canopy.

safaris by raft on the Peñas Blancas River. ⊠ *1 km (½ mile) west of La Fortuna, La Fortuna* ☎ *2479–0075* ⊕ *www. flowtrips.com* ⊠ *From $72.*

RAPPELLING
Pure Trek Canyoning
ROCK CLIMBING | Rappel down three waterfalls and one rock wall ranging in height from 39 to 164 feet. Two guides lead small groups—10 is the maximum size—on a four-hour tour ($101) that departs at 7 am or noon to a private farm near La Fortuna, with plenty of wildlife-watching opportunities along the way. There is a bit of hiking between waterfalls and long periods of waiting for others in your group, so patience and proper shoes are a must. The excursion includes transportation, all rappelling gear, and a light lunch. ⊠ *7 km (4½ miles) west of town center, La Fortuna* ☎ *2479–1313, 866/569–5723 in North America* ⊕ *www. puretrekcanyoning.com* ⊠ *$109.*

TOUR OPERATORS
★ Desafío Adventure Company
HIKING & WALKING | Expert Desafío guides can take you rafting, horseback riding, hiking, rappelling—you name the adventure. Desafío pioneered rafting trips in this region, and has day trips on the Sarapiquí River (Class III–IV) for experienced rafters ($95) and half-day rafting on the Balsa River (Class II–III) for less experienced paddlers ($75). Kayaking outings on Lake Arenal ($65) are ideal for beginners. If you're in the mood for something different, Desafío has half-day stand-up-paddling excursions on the lake ($75), and the popular Mambo Combo tour that combines waterfall rappelling and white-water rafting ($155).

If you're interested in getting up to Monteverde from the Arenal–La Fortuna area without taking the grinding four-hour drive, there's an alternative: Desafío Adventures has a six-hour guided mountain bike trip along trails and country back roads ($136). ⊠ *Behind church, La Fortuna* ☎ *2479–0020, 855/818–0020 in*

Caution

Four-wheel-ATV adventures are popular in Monteverde and Arenal, but not recommended. They can disturb vegetation and the ecosystem, not to mention that the noise often frightens wildlife.

North America ⊕ *www.desafiocostarica. com* ⊠ *From $65.*

Jacamar Naturalist Tours
SPECIAL-INTEREST TOURS | The variety of tours here ranges from bird walks and sunset lake cruises to white-water rafting and safari float trips. There are boat trips on Lake Arenal and Caño Negro Lagoon in the morning. ⊠ *Across from Parque Central, south side of Catholic church, La Fortuna* ☎ *2479–9767, 800/719–6377 in North America* ⊕ *www.arenaltours.com* ⊠ *From $63.*

Sunset Tours
GUIDED TOURS | One of the country's best tour operators pioneered excursions to the Caño Negro National Wildlife Refuge and Venado Caverns. (Note, though, that like most La Fortuna tour operators, its tours do not actually enter Caño Negro itself.) They also offer tours to La Fortuna Waterfall, the volcano, Lake Arenal, and nearby rivers. ⊠ *Across from south side of church, La Fortuna* ☎ *2479–9585, 2479–9800, 6169–7648* ⊠ *From $45.*

Nuevo Arenal

40 km (25 miles, 1 hr) west of La Fortuna.

Much of the original town of Arenal, at one of the lowest points near Lake Arenal, was destroyed by the volcano's 1968 eruption, and the rest was destroyed in 1973, when Lake Arenal flooded the region. This new (*nuevo*) town was created about 30 km (19 miles) away from the site of the old. It is about halfway between La Fortuna and Tilarán, making it a good stop for a break, and an even better base, with a few truly lovely lodgings and restaurants nearby.

GETTING HERE AND AROUND

The route from La Fortuna to Nuevo Arenal around the north shore of Lake Arenal has been greatly improved over the years. Watch out for the raccoonlike coatimundis (*pizotes* in Spanish) that scurry along the road. Longtime human feeding has diminished their ability to search for food on their own, and the cookies and potato chips they're frequently fed make matters worse. Don't contribute to the problem. Public buses run twice daily from La Fortuna to Nuevo Arenal and five times daily from Tilarán. You can catch a taxi from La Fortuna for around $45. On the main road, at the entrance of town, there's a small shopping area with a pharmacy, post office, and a gas station across the street. The small town has three grocery stores including Super Compro on the main road.

🍴 Restaurants

Gingerbread

$$$ | **ECLECTIC** | Choose from the ever-changing menu or let the chef guide you through what might just be the best meal you'll have in Costa Rica. You'll discover fresh dishes like filet mignon, shrimp risotto, organic Greek chicken, and blackened tuna. **Known for:** wine cellar; macadamia cheesecake; lamb curry. [$] *Average main: $20* ✉ *Next to Villa Decary, Nuevo Arenal* ☎ *2694–0039* 🌐 *www.gingerbreadarenal.com* 🕒 *Closed Sun. and Mon. No lunch.*

🛏 Hotels

La Mansión Inn Arenal

$$ | **HOTEL** | Nicely decorated cottages are scattered around 25 acres on Arenal's northeast shore at the point where the volcano begins to disappear from sight, but the lake views (and the sunsets) remain as spectacular as ever. **Pros:** luxurious furnishings; stupendous lake views from private terraces; great pool area. **Cons:** far from sights; need a car to stay here; very slippery path after rain. [$] *Rooms from: $150* ✉ *Hwy. 142, 34 km (21 miles) west of La Fortuna, Nuevo Arenal* ☎ *2692–8018* 🌐 *www.lamansionarenal.com* 🛏 *18 units* 🍽 *Free Breakfast.*

★ **Villa Decary**

$$ | **B&B/INN** | There's much to recommend at this hillside property, including the large picture windows and balconies overlooking Lake Arenal and the attentive service from the owners. **Pros:** attentive owners; great breakfasts; yoga classes offered. **Cons:** minimal road noise; Wi-Fi reaches only lower-level rooms and common areas; need a car to stay here. [$] *Rooms from: $109* ✉ *2 km (1 mile) east of Nuevo Arenal, Nuevo Arenal* ☎ *2694–4330, 800/556–0505 in North America* 🌐 *www.villadecary.com* 🛏 *8 units* 🍽 *Free Breakfast.*

Monteverde Cloud Forest and Santa Elena

Monteverde is 167 km (104 miles, 3½ hrs) northwest of San José and 110 km (67 miles, 4 hrs) southwest of La Fortuna, Santa Elena is 6 km (4 miles, 30 mins) north of Monteverde and 35 km (22 miles, 2 hrs) southeast of Tilarán.

Monteverde is a rain forest, but you won't be in the tropics—rather in the cool, gray, misty world of the cloud forest. Almost 900 species of epiphytes,

Continued on page 240

Zip lining is an exhilarating experience.

CANOPY TOURS

Costa Rica invented the concept of the canopy tour, and the idea has spread across the globe. Zip lining through the treetops is a once-in-a-lifetime experience, and exploring the jungle canopy is the best way to see the most eye-catching animals.

A canopy tour is an umbrella term describing excursions that take you to the jungle's ceiling. The experience is distinctly Costa Rican and is one of the country's signature activities for visitors. There are two types of tours: one gives you a chance to see animals (from bridges and platforms), and the other lets you swing through the trees on zip lines. We know of around 80 tours nationwide but recommend only about a third of that number. *You'll find tour information in most chapters of this book.*

By Jeffrey Van Fleet

WHAT EXACTLY IS A CANOPY TOUR?

Canopy zip line tour at Rain Forest Adventures

WHAT TO EXPECT

Plan on a half-day for your canopy tour, including transportation to and from your hotel and a safety briefing for zip line excursions. Most zip line tours begin at fixed times and reservations are always required, or at least advised. A tour over hanging-bridges is far more leisurely and can be done at your own pace. The latest craze on zip line tours is an optional Tarzan swing, a freefall drop similar to bungee jumping but with swinging instead of bouncing. Several outfitters also offer rappelling as part of the package. The occasional mega-complex, such as Monteverde's Selvatura, offers both types of tours. For most, it's one or the other.

BRIDGES AND TRAMS

These are canopy tours in a literal sense, where you walk along suspension bridges, ride along in a tram, or are hoisted up to a platform to get a closer look at birds, monkeys, and sloths. They're also called hanging-bridges tours, sky walks, or platform tours. If seeing nature at a more leisurely pace is your goal, opt for these, especially the bridge excursions. Early mornings are the best time for animal sightings—at 50–250 feet above ground, the views are stupendous.

ZIP LINES

This type of tour is a fast-paced, thrilling experience. You're attached to a zip line with a safety harness, and then you "fly" at about 15–40 miles per hour from one tree platform to the next. (You may be anywhere from 60–300 feet above the forest floor.) Tree-to-tree zip lines date from the 19th century and have been a bona fide activity for visitors to Costa Rica since the mid-1990s when the first tour opened in Monteverde. These tours are tremendous fun, but you won't see any animals. An average fitness level—and above-average level of intrepidness—are all you need.

TOP CANOPY TOURS BY REGION

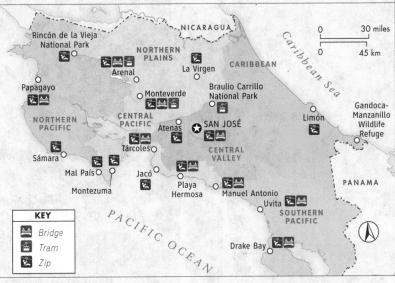

TOUR OPERATER	LOCATION	TYPE		
Místico Arenal Park	Arenal		Bridge	
Sky Adventures	Arenal	Zip	Bridge	Tram
Canopy Safari	Manuel Antonio	Zip	Bridge	
Canopy Mal Pais	Malpaís	Zip		
Montezuma Waterfall Canopy Tour	Montezuma	Zip		
Ecoglide Arenal Park	Arenal	Zip		
Hotel Villa Lapas	Tárcoles	Zip	Bridge	
Hacienda Guachipelín	Rincón de La Vieja National Park	Zip	Bridge	
Original Canopy Tour	Monteverde	Zip		
Original Canopy Tour	Drake Bay	Zip	Bridge	
Original Canopy tour	Veragua, Limón	Zip		
Rain Forest Adventures	Braulio Carrillo National Park	Zip	Bridge	Tram
Rain Forest Adventures	Jacó	Zip	Bridge	Tram
Las Pavas Zip Line	Rincón de la Vieja National Park	Zip		
Selvatura	Monteverde	Zip	Bridge	
Tití Canopy Tour	Manuel Antonio	Zip		
Sky Adventures	Monteverde	Zip	Bridge	Tram
Wing Nuts Canopy Tour	Sámara	Zip		
Witch's Rock Canopy Tour	Papagayo	Zip	Bridge	
Osa Canopy Tour	Uvita	Zip	Bridge	
El Santuario Canopy Adventure Tour	Manuel Antonio	Zip	Bridge	

SAFETY FIRST

(top left) Kids enjoy zip lining. (bottom left) Brown-Throated Three-Toed Sloth. (right) Sky Tram, Rainforest Canopy Tour, Arenal

PLAYING IT SAFE

Flying through the air, while undeniably cool, is also inherently dangerous. Before you strap into a harness, be certain that the safety standards are first rate. There's virtually no government oversight of the activity in Costa Rica. Here is a list of questions you should ask before you book:

1. How long has the company been in business?

2. Are they insured?

3. Are cables, harnesses, and other equipment manufacturer-certified?

4. Is there a second safety line that connects you to the zip line in case the main pulley gives way?

5. What's the price? Plan on paying $50 to $80— a low price could indicate a second-rate operation.

6. Are participants clipped to the zip line while on the platform? (They should be.)

KEEP IN MIND

■ Listen closely to the guides' pre-tour safety briefing and obey their instructions.

■ Never argue with the guide when s/he is making a decision to preserve your safety.

■ Don't attempt to take photos in flight.

■ Gauge your abilities frankly. Remember, once you start, there's no turning back.

■ If anything seems "off" or makes you uncomfortable, walk away.

including 450 orchids, thrive here; most tree trunks are covered with mosses, bromeliads, ferns, and other plants. Monteverde spans the Continental Divide, extending from about 4,920 feet on the Pacific slope and 4,430 feet on the Atlantic slope up to the highest peaks of the Tilarán Mountains at around 6,070 feet. Make Santa Elena your base of operations when visiting this area.

The area's first residents were a handful of Costa Rican families fleeing the rough-and-tumble life of nearby gold-mining fields during the 1940s. They were joined in the early 1950s by Quakers, conscientious objectors from Alabama fleeing conscription into the Korean War. A number of things drew them to Costa Rica: just a few years earlier it had abolished its military, and the Monteverde area offered good grazing. The cloud forest that lay above the dairy farms soon attracted the attention of ecologists. Educators and artisans followed, giving Monteverde and its "metropolis," the village of Santa Elena, a certain mystique. These days, Monteverde looks quite a bit different than it did when the first wave of Quakers arrived. New hotels have sprouted up everywhere, traffic grips the center of town, and there's a small shopping center outside of town on the way to the mountain. A glut of rented all-terrain vehicles (ATVs) contributes to the increasing din that disrupts Monteverde's legendary peace and quiet, and the paving of one access route will no doubt increase visitor numbers. Some define these moves as progress while others lament the gradual chipping away at what makes one of Costa Rica's most special areas so special. Reminiscent of a ski town in summer, Monteverde still lets you get away from it all, but you'll have to work harder at it than you used to. In any case, you'll not lack for things to do if seeing nature is a primary reason for your visit. The only way to see the area's reserves, including the Monteverde Cloud Forest, is to hike them.

Did You Know?

Monteverde's Quakers, or more officially, the Society of Friends, no longer constitute the majority here these days, but their imprint on the community remains strong. Their meetinghouse at Escuela de los Amigos, just south of the Cheese Factory on the road to the reserve, welcomes visitors at meetings of worship, 10:30 am Sunday and 9 am Wednesday. Most of the time is spent in quiet reflection.

Note that a casual reference to "Monteverde" generally indicates this entire area, but officially the term applies only to the original Quaker settlement, which is by the dairy-processing plant just down the mountain from the reserve entrance. If you follow road signs exclusively, you'll end up outside the town of Santa Elena, halfway to the reserve.

It takes a little effort to get here, and it can get crowded during high season, but this exceptionally well-protected reserve affords visitors one of the country's best opportunities to view abundant—and stunning—wildlife and colorful high-elevation flora.

GETTING HERE AND AROUND

Monteverde's isolation is coming to an end with the paving of one access route. The completion of "Highway" 606—remember that Costa Ricans rarely use or know highway numbers—via Sardinal has made the area more accessible than ever. Whether that's good or bad depends on your point of view. (Other roads in and out still mean negotiating some of the country's legendarily rough roads.) Your own vehicle gives you the greatest flexibility, but a burgeoning number of shuttle-van services connect Monteverde with San José and other tourist destinations throughout the country.

Buses from San José leave twice daily from the Terminal 7-10 (at Calle 10 and Avenida 7), at 6:30 am and 2:30 pm. It's around a five-hour trip, stopping in the center of Santa Elena and at various locations on the way up the mountain as far as the Cheese Factory. Buses from Santa Elena leave for San José at 6:30 am and 2:30 pm daily. Taxis from Santa Elena are $10 to $13. Buses from Tilarán to Santa Elena leave once a day, at 12:30 pm. Desafío Adventure Company offers shared transportation from San José to Monteverde for $52 one way. The San José–Monteverde public bus route is notorious for theft; watch your bags, and never let your passport and money out of your sight—or off your person. Never take advice from the "guides" who meet incoming buses in Monteverde and La Fortuna. They claim to want to help you find accommodations and tours, when in reality they receive kickbacks for sending tourists to less-than-desirable hotels or to unqualified "tour guides."

If you can handle the curvy roads, a windy track leads from Tilarán via Cabeceras to Santa Elena, near the Monteverde Cloud Forest Biological Reserve, doing away with the need to cut across to the Pan-American Highway. You need a 4WD vehicle, and you should inquire locally about the current condition of the road. The views of Nicoya Peninsula, Lake Arenal, and Arenal Volcano reward those willing to bump around a bit. Note, too, that you don't really save much time—on a good day it takes about 2½ hours as opposed to the 3 hours required via Cañas and Río Lagarto on the highway.

By car from the Fortuna area, it's at least three hours by bumpy road around Lake Arenal; some tour companies provide the trip via minibus and boat (called "Taxi-Boat-Taxi" or "Jeep-Boat-Jeep") for about $30 one way. Gray Line has daily shuttle bus service between San José, La Fortuna, Arenal ($50), and Monteverde ($49). Interbus also connects San José with La Fortuna and Monteverde (each $49) daily, with connections from here to a few of the North Pacific beaches. There will be times you wish you had your own vehicle, but it's surprisingly easy to get around the Monteverde area without a car. Given the state of the roads off the main track, you'll be happy to let someone else do the driving. Taxis are plentiful; it's easy to call one from your hotel, and restaurants are happy to summon a cab to take you back to your hotel after dinner. Taxis also congregate in front of the church on the main street in Santa Elena. If you're taking a tour, many companies will pick you up from your hotel and bring you back at the end of the day, either free or for a small fee.

ESSENTIALS

BANK/ATM Banco Nacional. ✉ *50 meters (164 feet) north of Catholic church, and 50 meters (164 feet) east of first corner, next to Orchid Garden, Santa Elena* ☎ *2645–5610.*

MEDICAL CLINIC Clínica Monteverde. ✉ *150 meters (492 feet) south of soccer field, Santa Elena* ☎ *2645–5076.*

PHARMACY Farmacia Vitosi. ✉ *Across from Chamber of Tourism, Santa Elena* ☎ *2645–5004.*

POST OFFICE Correos. ✉ *Rte. 620, Santa Elena* ✛ *North side of the Centro Comercial Plaza* ☎ *2202–2900.*

TOURIST INFORMATION Chamber of Tourism Monteverde. ✉ *Across from Súper Compro supermarket, Santa Elena* ☎ *2645–6565* ⊕ *www.exploremonteverde.com.*

Sights

The Bat Jungle

NATURE PRESERVE | FAMILY | Butterflies, frogs, and snakes have their own Monteverde-area exhibits, and bats get equal time with guided tours that provide insight into the life of one of the planet's most misunderstood mammals. If you've

had an aversion to bats in the past, be prepared to start loving them. Admission includes a 45-minute guided tour through a small exhibit and glass enclosure housing nearly 100 live bats. You can watch them fly, eat, and even give birth. Reservations are recommended. ⊠ *Across from Tramonti restaurant, Monteverde* ☎ *2645–9999* ⊕ *www.batjungle.com* ✉ *$15 for guided tour, $7 self-guided.*

Butterfly Garden (*Jardín de Mariposas*)
NATURE PRESERVE | FAMILY | Thirty species of butterflies flit about in four enclosed botanical gardens, and you'll learn about a variety of other insects and arachnids. Morning visits are best, since the butterflies are most active early in the day. Your entrance ticket includes an hour-long guided tour under tin roofs, meaning you won't get wet on rainy days. Be sure to visit the nonprofit gift shop benefiting the local community. ⊠ *Near Monteverde Inn, Monteverde* ✤ *Take right-hand turnoff 4 km (2½ miles) past Santa Elena on road to Monteverde, continue for 2 km (1 mile)* ☎ *2645–5512* ⊕ *www.monteverdebutterflygardens.com* ✉ *$17.*

Cafe Monteverde Coffee Tour
FACTORY | Bite your tongue before requesting Costa Rica's ubiquitous Café Britt up here. Export-quality Café Monteverde is the local, sustainably grown product, and the tour lets you see the process up close from start to finish from the area's Turín plantation, 3 km (2 miles) north of Santa Elena, where the plants are grown in the shade; transported to the *beneficio,* the processing mill where the beans are washed and dried; and finally to the roaster. Reservations are required, and pickup from area hotels is available. They also operate the Monteverde Coffee Center (coffee shop) in town next to CASEM and the Café Monteverde in Santa Elena. ⊠ *Monteverde* ☎ *2645–7550* ⊕ *www.cafedemonteverde.com* ✉ *$35.*

Children's Eternal Rain Forest
(*Bosque Eterno de los Niños*)
FOREST | FAMILY | The 54,000-acre rain forest dwarfs the Monteverde and Santa Elena reserves. It began life as a school project in Sweden among children interested in saving a piece of the rain forest, and blossomed into a fund-raising effort among students from 44 countries. The reserve's Bajo del Tigre trail makes for a gentle self-guided 3½-km (2-mile) hike through secondary forest. Along the trail are 27 stations at which to stop and learn about the reserve, many with lessons geared toward kids. A separate guided twilight walk with a knowledgable guide ($25) begins at 5:30 pm and lasts two hours, affording the chance to see the nocturnal side of the cloud forest; reservations are required. Much of the rest of the reserve is not open to the public, but the Monteverde Conservation League offers stays at San Gerardo and Poco Sol, two remote field stations within the forest. The $79 packages include dormitory accommodation and meals. ⊠ *100 meters (328 feet) south of CASEM, Monteverde* ☎ *2645–5200* ⊕ *acmcr.org* ✉ *From $16.*

Curi Cancha Reserve
NATURE PRESERVE | FAMILY | There's no shortage of nature walks in Monteverde, but this newer, less crowded reserve—with more than 6½ km (4 miles) of trails progressing through different types of forests, fields, and gardens filled with hummingbird feeders—is one of the best. You'll get the chance to see fauna like the elusive quetzal, motmots, owls and other birds, plus sloths and snakes, as well as flora like mammoth trees, bromeliads, epiphytes, and orchids. Trails are wide and in great shape; there are bathroom facilities and benches for taking a rest, and the reserve is totally handicap accessible, with carts for folks who need them. We recommend a guide—you'll see much, much more that way. ⊠ *300 meters (984 feet) west of the cheese factory, Monteverde* ☎ *2645–6915* ⊕ *reservacuricancha.com* ✉ *$20.*

A leisurely stroll across a suspension bridge in the Monteverde Cloud Forest.

Don Juan Coffee Tour

FACTORY | Small groups are the hallmark of these tours that last about two hours and let you see the coffee process from start to finish at the plantation of Don Juan Cruz, one of the original settlers in the area. You can also learn about chocolate and sugarcane. Transportation can be arranged from all Monteverde-area lodgings. To get a taste without the tour, you can visit their café and gift store next to the post office in Santa Elena. ⊠ *2 km (1 mile) northwest of soccer field, Monteverde* ☎ *2645–7100* ⊕ *www.donjuancoffeetour.com* ⊠ *$45.*

★ El Trapiche

FACTORY | Two-hour tours departing at 10 am and 3 pm guide you from the bean to the cup at this coffee plantation and old-fashioned *trapiche* (sugarcane mill) where you can sample liquor, java, and other locally made products. The hands-on tour includes a ride on an oxcart and some sweet treats made from homegrown coffee beans, sugarcane, and cacao. ⊠ *Hwy. 606, 2 km (1 mile) northwest of Santa Elena, Santa Elena* ☎ *2645–7650* ⊕ *www.eltrapichetour.com* ⊠ *$35.*

★ Monteverde Cloud Forest Biological Reserve (*Reserva Biológica Bosque Nuboso de Monteverde*)

NATURE PRESERVE | One of Costa Rica's best-kept reserves has 13 km (8 miles) of well-marked trails, lush vegetation, and a cool, damp climate. The collision of moist winds with the Continental Divide here creates a constant mist whose particles provide nutrients for plants growing at the upper layers of the forest. Giant trees are enshrouded in a cascade of orchids, bromeliads, mosses, and ferns, and in those patches where sunlight penetrates, brilliantly colored flowers flourish. The sheer size of everything, especially the leaves of the trees, is striking. No less astounding is the variety: more than 3,000 plant species, 500 species of birds, 500 types of butterflies, and 130 different mammals have so far been cataloged at Monteverde. A damp and exotic mixture of shades, smells, and sounds, the cloud forest is also famous for its population of resplendent quetzals, which can be spotted feeding on the *aguacatillo* (similar to avocado) trees; best viewing times are early mornings from January until September, and especially during the mating season of April and May. Other forest-dwelling inhabitants include hummingbirds and multicolor frogs.

For those who don't have a lucky eye, a short-stay aquarium is in the field station; captive amphibians stay here just a week before being released back into the wild. Although the reserve limits visitors to 250 people at a time, Monteverde is one of the country's most popular destinations. We do hear complaints (and agree with them) that the reserve gets too crowded with visitors at times. Early visitors have the best chance at spotting wildlife in the protected reserve.

Allow a generous slice of time for leisurely hiking to see the forest's flora and fauna; longer hikes are made possible by some strategically placed overnight refuges along the way. At the gift shop you can buy self-guide pamphlets and books; a map is provided when you pay the entrance fee. You can navigate the reserve on your own, but the 2½-hour guided Natural History Walk (7:30 am, 11:30 am, and 1:30 pm) is invaluable for getting the most out of your visit. You may also take advantage of two-hour guided night tours starting each evening at 5:45 (reservations required). The reserve provides transport from area hotels for an extra $5. Guided walking bird-watching tours up to the reserve leave from the park entrance daily at 6 am for groups of four to six people. Advance reservations are required.

If you'd like to stay in the reserve itself, you'll find six rooms of lodging at the site's La Casona. Rates of $90 per person include three meals and entrance to all park trails. ⊠ *10 km (6 miles) south of Santa Elena, Monteverde* ☎ *2645–5122* ⊕ *cloudforestmonteverde.com* ⌑ *From $25.*

Monteverde Ecological Sanctuary

WILDLIFE REFUGE | This family-run, 52-acre wildlife refuge is laced with four trails and houses birds, sloths, agoutis, and coatimundis. They focus on small group tours, including a coffee tour, cooking classes, and day hikes, where you'll come upon two waterfalls and a coffee plantation. If you can't make it all the way up to the Monteverde Reserve for the day hike, there's a two-hour guided twilight walk that begins each evening at 5:30 and 7:30. Reservations are required. ⊠ *Turnoff to Jardín de Mariposas, off main road just south of Santa Elena, Monteverde* ☎ *2645–5869* ⊕ *www.santuarioecologico.com* ⌑ *From $18.*

Orchid Garden (*Jardín de Orquídeas*)

GARDEN | More than 460 species of orchids, one of which is the world's smallest, are on display. The workers' passion for orchids is contagious and you might find yourself inspired to create a garden of your own. Admission includes a 30-minute tour. ⊠ *150 meters (492 feet) south of Banco Nacional, Santa Elena* ☎ *2645–5308* ⊕ *www.monteverdeorchidgarden.com* ⌑ *$14.*

Santa Elena Cloud Forest Reserve (*Reserva Bosque Nuboso Santa Elena*)

NATURE PRESERVE | Several conservation areas near Monteverde are attractive day-trip destinations, especially when the Monteverde Reserve is too busy. The 765-acre Santa Elena Reserve just west of Monteverde is a project of the Santa Elena high school, and has a series of trails of varying length and difficulty that can be walked alone or with a guide on tours that depart daily at 7:30, 9:15, and 11:30 am, and 1 pm. The 1½-km (1-mile) Youth Challenge trail takes about 45 minutes to negotiate and includes an observation platform with views that extend as far as the Arenal Volcano—that is, if the clouds clear. If you're feeling hardy, try the 5-km (3-mile) Caño Negro trail. There's a shuttle service to the reserve with fixed departures and returns; reservations are required, and the cost is $3 each way. ✉ *6 km (4 miles) north of Santa Elena, Monteverde* ☎ *2645–5390* ⊕ *www.monteverdeinfo.com/tours/santa-elena-cloud-forest-reserve* 💲 *From $16.*

★ Selvatura

NATURE SIGHT | FAMILY | If your time in Monteverde is limited, consider spending it at Selvatura, a kind of nature-themed adventure park—complete with a canopy tour and hanging bridges—just outside the Santa Elena Reserve. A 100-bird hummingbird garden, an enclosed 20-species *mariposario* (butterfly garden), a sloth sanctuary, a *herpetario* (frog and reptile house), and insect exhibition sit near the visitor center. The only zipline tour built entirely inside the Monteverde Cloud Forest has 12 lines and 18 platforms, with an optional Tarzan swing at the end to round out the excursion. The Tree Top Walkway takes you to heights ranging from 36 feet up to 180 feet on a 3-km (2-mile) walk. These are some of the longest and strongest bridges in the country and run through the same canopy terrain as the zipline tour, which sometimes makes for a not-so-quiet walk.

You can choose from numerous mix-and-match packages, depending on which activities interest you, or take it all in, with lunch included, for $169. Most visitors get by for much less, given that one day isn't enough for all there is to do here. ✉ *Office across from church in town; Selvatura park 7 km (4 miles) northwest of Banco Nacional, Santa Elena* ⟴ *Next to San Gerardo Cloud Forest Reserve* ☎ *4001–7899, 800/771–1803 in North America* ⊕ *www.selvatura.com* 💲 *From $50.*

 Restaurants

Café Caburé

$$ | MODERN ARGENTINE | This restaurant/bakery/chocolateria is one of only a few in Costa Rica that grinds its own cocoa beans. Start with a meal in the open-air restaurant serving savory empanadas, mole dishes, and chipotle wraps with a creamy secret sauce before getting to the sweet stuff, like ganache with blackberry sauce, chocolate-passion-fruit mousse, and exquisite chocolate truffles. **Known for:** curried chicken and mango salad; tours of adjoining chocolate factory; vegetarian options. 💲 *Average main: $13* ✉ *Paseo de Stella Tourist Center in Old Monteverde, near the Bat Jungle, Monteverde* ☎ *2645–5020* ⊕ *www.cabure.net* 🕙 *Closed Tues.*

★ Celajes

$$$ | COSTA RICAN | In the wood-polished dining room of Hotel Belmar, this elegant restaurant, whose name means "sunset clouds," is indeed the best place to admire the stunning views, with soft jazz and artisanal cocktails that set the tone for the farm-to-table menu. Start with the gorgeous cheese platter or the refreshing grilled-watermelon salad before moving on to the divine chicken stuffed with goat cheese, prosciutto, and spinach, and bathed in a white-wine-and-passion-fruit sauce. **Known for:** filet mignon with coffee glaze; homemade pastas; local organic ingredients from the Belmar family ranch. 💲 *Average main: $22* ✉ *Hotel Belmar, 4 km (2½ miles) north of town, adjacent to Monteverde Cloud Forest, Monteverde* ☎ *2645–5201, 866/978–6424 from U.S. and Canada* ⊕ *www.hotelbelmar.net.*

Morpho's

$$ | COSTA RICAN | With its rain-forest murals, glass patios, and tree-stump tables, you're never far from nature in this pleasant restaurant. Parsley potatoes, and creative sauces like pineapple curry, blue cheese, or bay-leaf-and-garlic sauce (a take on chimichurri) infuse the menu of flavorful chicken, pork, beef, or fish dishes. **Known for:** fresh salads; peanut butter pie; friendly service. 💲 *Average main: $15* ✉ *Santa Elena* ⟴ *50 meters (164 feet) east of Banco Nacional* ☎ *2645–7373.*

★ **Orchid Coffee Shop** (*Cafe Las Orquideas*)
$$ | **BAKERY** | An astonishing level of culinary perfection comes out of this A-frame shack serving breakfast, lunch, and early dinner. The menu is enormous, with crepes, pancakes, granola, and French toast alongside tomato soup, veggie panini, 25 types of coffee, and fresh smoothies made with homemade yogurt and local ingredients like pineapple, cucumber, carrot, and basil. **Known for:** neighboring Orchid Garden; careful attention to detail in preparation; espresso mocha made with hot chocolate, whiskey, and mint. $ *Average main: $10* ✉ *Santa Elena* ✥ *Next to Orchid Garden, 150 meters (492 feet) south of Banco Nacional* ☎ *2645–6850* 🌐 *www.orchidcoffeecr.com.*

Stella's Bakery
$ | **CAFÉ** | This local institution is a good place to get an early-morning fix before heading to the Monteverde Cloud Forest. Pastries, rolls, muffins, natural juices, and coffee are standard breakfast fare, and light sandwiches, soups, and quiches are on offer at lunch. **Known for:** homemade lasagna; local art; terrific pastries. $ *Average main: $8* ✉ *Across from CASEM, Monteverde* ☎ *2645–5560* 🌐 *stellasmonteverde.com.*

Taco Taco
$ | **MEXICAN FUSION** | This always-busy casual eatery is a great place to stop for tacos, burritos, and other Tex-Mex fare, which you can eat in the dining room or outside on the patio. The meat is slow-cooked and flavorful, but fish and veggie options abound as well. **Known for:** pork carnitas; extensive beer list; Baja tacos with tempura-battered fresh avocado. $ *Average main: $6* ✉ *Southeast of Banco Nacional in El Corazon de Santa Elena, Santa Elena* ☎ *2645–7900* 🌐 *tacotaco.net.*

Tramonti
$$ | **ITALIAN** | This glass-walled restaurant is warm and inviting, with dangling fairy lights, hardwood floors, candles dripping onto old wine bottles, and chefs tossing dough high overhead beside a wood-fired oven. The *pulpo* (octopus) and beef carpaccio are ultrathin, a perfect accompaniment for the pizzas that come piled high with toppings like asparagus, mushrooms, ricotta, and Gorgonzola. **Known for:** eggplant ravioli; romantic atmosphere; homemade rolls. $ *Average main: $14* ✉ *3 km (2 miles) from Monteverde Cloud Forest, across from Bat Jungle, Monteverde* ☎ *2645–6120* 🌐 *www.tramonticr.com.*

🛏 Hotels

Most hotels in Monteverde don't have air-conditioning or heaters in the rooms, so you might have to crack a window or grab an extra blanket. It also helps to pack accordingly. Since Monteverde caters to wildlife enthusiasts and bird-watchers, most hotels serve breakfast from 6 to 9, with checkout at 10 am. If you're not an early riser, be sure to request a wake-up call so that you don't miss breakfast.

Arco Iris Lodge
$$ | **HOTEL** | You're almost in the center of town, but you'd never know it at this tranquil spot set on 4 acres of birding trails, where cozy cabins range from rustic to plush and come with porches. **Pros:** attentive owner and staff; terrific breakfast; centrally located. **Cons:** Wi-Fi can be spotty at times; front rooms get a bit of street noise; mattresses may not be to everyone's liking. $ *Rooms from: $111* ✉ *50 meters south of Banco Nacional, Santa Elena* ☎ *2645–5067* 🌐 *www.arcoirislodge.com* 🛏 *21 units* 🍴 *Free Breakfast.*

Casa Batsú
$$ | **B&B/INN** | This charming B&B is owned and operated by a lovely Costa Rican family that takes pride in every detail, from the homemade breakfasts and manicured gardens to the spotless

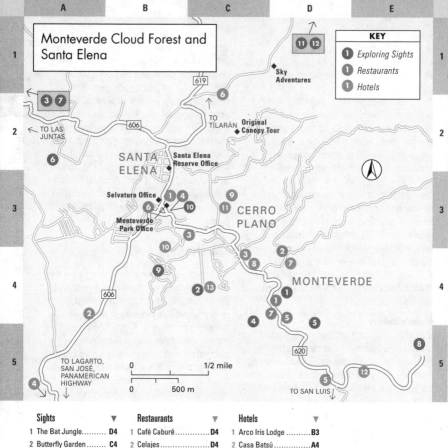

Monteverde Cloud Forest and Santa Elena

KEY

- 1 Exploring Sights
- 1 Restaurants
- 1 Hotels

Sky Adventures

619

TO TILARÁN

Original Canopy Tour

606

TO LAS JUNTAS

SANTA ELENA

Santa Elena Reserve Office

Selvatura Office

Monteverde Park Office

CERRO PLANO

MONTEVERDE

606

620

TO SAN LUIS

TO LAGARTO, SAN JOSÉ, PANAMERICAN HIGHWAY

0 ——— 1/2 mile
0 ——— 500 m

rooms and warm hospitality. **Pros:** excellent value; outstanding breakfasts; gracious hosts. **Cons:** thin walls; often books up well in advance. $ *Rooms from: $129* ✉ *Hwy. 606, 1½ km (1 mile) south of Santa Elena, 100 meters (328 feet) northeast from El Tubu gas station, Monteverde* ☎ *2645–7004* ⊕ *www.casa-batsu.org* ⊷ *5 rooms* ¶◎¶ *Free Breakfast.*

El Establo Mountain Hotel
$$$ | HOTEL | The area's largest hotel gets high marks for its huge suites, plush decor, a long list of amenities, and many activities. **Pros:** spacious rooms; many activities; great views. **Cons:** large size means no personalized service; Wi-Fi doesn't reach all rooms; massive grounds require shuttle van to navigate. $ *Rooms from: $180* ✉ *3½ km (2 miles) northwest of Monteverde, Monteverde* ☎ *2645–5110* ⊕ *www.elestablo.com* ⊷ *155 rooms* ¶◎¶ *No Meals.*

El Sol
$$ | HOTEL | A charming family tends to guests at this peaceful, bohemian Shangri-la just 10 minutes down the mountain from—and a noticeable few degrees warmer than—Santa Elena. **Pros:** great views; whimsically decorated cabins; same rates year-round. **Cons:** cash only; Wi-Fi in common areas only; need a car to get here. $ *Rooms from: $145* ✉ *5 km (3 miles) southwest of Santa Elena in La Lindora, Monteverde* ☎ *2645–5838* ▭ *No credit cards* ⊷ *4 cabins* ¶◎¶ *No Meals.*

Fonda Vela
$$$ | HOTEL | Steep-roofed chalets have large bedrooms with wood floors and huge windows; some have views of the wooded grounds, and others, of the far-off Gulf of Nicoya. **Pros:** secluded location close to reserve; large rooms; indoor pool. **Cons:** rough road to get here; restaurant closed in low season; far from town. $ *Rooms from: $153* ✉ *1½ km (1 mile) northwest of Monteverde Reserve entrance, Monteverde* ☎ *2645–5125* ⊕ *www.fondavela.com* ⊷ *38 rooms* ¶◎¶ *No Meals.*

★ Hidden Canopy Treehouses
$$$$ | B&B/INN | Nestled among 13½ acres of rolling hills nearly 3 km (2 miles) from town, luxury tree houses have wraparound decks, driftwood headboards, tree-stump nightstands, waterfall showers, and skylight ceilings, ultimately fading the line between nature and decor. **Pros:** great happy hour at sunset; huge film library and board games for guests; exceptional breakfast; rooms have dehumidifiers. **Cons:** no kids under 14; checkout at 10 am; two- or three-night minimum stay depending on season; patchy Wi-Fi in rooms. $ *Rooms from: $299* ✉ *Santa Elena* ✛ *300 meters (984 feet) east of crossroad to Los Nubes, before Sky Adventures Park* ☎ *2645–5447* ⊕ *www.hiddencanopy.com* ⊗ *Closed Sept. 15–Dec. 1* ⊷ *7 units* ¶◎¶ *Free Breakfast.*

★ Hotel Belmar
$$$ | HOTEL | Inspired by the owners' years in Austria, two spacious chalets built into a hillside command expansive views of the Gulf of Nicoya and the hilly peninsula, and contain elegant, airy, and downright regal rooms—all with balconies, minibars, polished woods, and plush white duvets. **Pros:** excellent restaurant; free in-room coffee delivery; beautifully maintained; eco-friendly. **Cons:** steep walk if on foot; breakfast not included in rate; far from town. $ *Rooms from: $239* ✉ *4 km (2½ miles) north of Monteverde, Monteverde* ☎ *2645–5201* ⊕ *www.hotelbelmar.net* ⊷ *25 rooms* ¶◎¶ *No Meals.*

★ Koora Hotel
$$$$ | HOTEL | FAMILY | Tucked into the mountainside, the main lodge with the restaurant and bar has a decidedly sophisticated feel, with spectacular views of the Pacific in the distance. **Pros:** super-spacious bungalows for families; attentive service; great restaurant and bar on-site. **Cons:** rooms get warm during the day; bungalows seem far from main lodge at night; capuchin monkeys can get cheeky. $ *Rooms*

from: $280 ✉ *Monteverde* ✣ *300 meters (984 feet) northeast of Banco de Costa Rica* ☎ *4000–3385* 🌐 *www.koorahotel.com* 🛏 *4 suites, 4 bungalows* 🍴 *Free Breakfast.*

Los Pinos

$$ | **HOTEL** | **FAMILY** | This 18-acre private reserve contains 16 cozy cabins with fully equipped kitchens in which you can prepare meals with produce from the hotel's hydroponic vegetable garden. **Pros:** free vegetables from on-site garden; excellent value; spacious cabins that are good for families or groups. **Cons:** no restaurant or meals; steep hike to some cabins; some cabins are slightly dated. [$] *Rooms from: $80* ✉ *Monteverde, Santa Elena* ✣ *200 meters (656 feet) east of Cerro Plano School* ☎ *2645–5252* 🌐 *www.lospinos.net* 🛏 *16 cabins* 🍴 *No Meals.*

Monteverde Lodge and Gardens

$$$$ | **HOTEL** | Reminiscent of a ski lodge, this longtime favorite has extremely comfortable rooms with vaulted ceilings and great views with rates often packaged with a long list of nature activities. **Pros:** rustic luxury; attentive service; private dinners in the butterfly garden; great hiking trails. **Cons:** rooms have poor lighting; breakfast ends at 8:30; ground-floor rooms can be noisy. [$] *Rooms from: $300* ✉ *After Hotel Poco a Poco, 500 meters to lodge entrance on right, Santa Elena* ☎ *2645–5057* 🌐 *www.monteverdelodge.com* 🛏 *28 rooms* 🍴 *Free Breakfast.*

Senda Monteverde Hotel

$$$$ | **B&B/INN** | Situated on 3 acres with private nature trails, these completely updated casita duplexes with large windows, separate bedrooms, porches, and luxe linens are lovely, but it's the top-notch service that sets Senda apart. **Pros:** spacious, bright, newly renovated casitas; exemplary service and welcome; impressive grounds. **Cons:** mix of styles lacks aesthetic harmony; furniture less luxurious than price would reflect; chilly in the evenings. [$] *Rooms from: $380* ✉ *North of the BCR in Cerro Plano, Monteverde* ☎ *4001–6349, 866/380–4032 from U.S.* 🌐 *www.sendamonteverde.com* 🛏 *24 casitas* 🍴 *Free Breakfast.*

Trapp Family Hotel

$$ | **HOTEL** | The closest lodge to the Monteverde reserve (but 6 km [4 miles] from the town center) has enormous rooms, with wood-paneled walls and ceilings, marvelously crafted wood furniture, balconies, and lovely views from most. **Pros:** spacious rooms; same rates year-round; closest lodging to reserve entrance. **Cons:** no A/C, fans, or screens on windows; spotty Wi-Fi in rooms; rough road to get here; 6½ km (4 miles) from town. [$] *Rooms from: $130* ✉ *Main road from Monteverde Cloud Forest, Monteverde* ☎ *2645–5858* 🌐 *www.trapphotelmonteverde.com* 🛏 *26 rooms* 🍴 *Free Breakfast.*

Valle Escondido Nature Reserve Hotel

$$ | **HOTEL** | The basic rooms here have stunning views of the Gulf of Nicoya as well as hardwood floors, firm beds, and powerful, hot showers—and are a great budget option. **Pros:** good rock-bottom budget value; good views; hearty breakfasts. **Cons:** cash only; rough road to hotel; spartan rooms. [$] *Rooms from: $91* ✉ *100 meters south of Butterfly Garden, Monteverde* ☎ *2645–5156* 🌐 *valleescondidocr.com* 💳 *No credit cards* 🛏 *14 rooms* 🍴 *No Meals.*

🍸 Nightlife

"Wild nightlife" takes on its own peculiar meaning here. You can still get up close with nature after the sun has gone down. Several of the reserves have guided evening walks—advance reservations and separate admission are required—and the Frog Pond of Monteverde, the Herpetarium, and the Bat Jungle keep evening hours. Beyond that, you'll probably while away the evening in a restaurant or your hotel dining room chatting with fellow travelers. Monteverde is an early-to-bed, early-to-rise kind of place—some hotels end breakfast as early as 8:30, so it's best not to oversleep.

Shopping

Cooperativa de Artesanía de Santa Elena y Monteverde (CASEM)

CRAFTS | This artisans' cooperative is made up of 45 people, mostly women, who sell locally made crafts. The prices are higher than they are at most other places, but the high quality and the knowledge that you are contributing to the livelihood of the community justifies paying a bit more. The attached restaurant serves typical Costa Rican dishes. ✉ Next to El Bosque Lodge, Monteverde ☎ 2645-5190 ⊕ casemcoop.blogspot.com.

Dicoma

SOUVENIRS | Although the strip mall doesn't provide the most picturesque setting, inside you'll find lovely souvenirs and other Costa Rican–made items that you won't see at the typical tourist traps. The store features handmade leather purses, beautiful and affordable jewelry, totes, art, scarves, and home goods. ✉ Centro Comercial, Monteverde ☎ 2645-6832 ⊕ www.tiendadicoma.com.

Hummingbird Gallery

ART GALLERIES | Standouts among the books, jewelry, T-shirts, and Costa Rican coffee on display here are photographs by local nature specialists Michael and Patricia Fogden. This is a great place to emulate their efforts: you can capture an image of a hummingbird in action as hundreds flutter around the feeders. No flash photography is allowed. ✉ Outside entrance to Monteverde Cloud Forest, Monteverde ☎ 2645-5030 ⊕ www.facebook.com/monteverdehummingbirdgallery.

Monteverde Art House

ART GALLERIES | This lovely art gallery offers local paintings, sculptures, photography, pottery, and jewelry. The wooden artwork is amazing, and some of it is displayed inside a unique gazebo. ✉ 100 meters (328 feet) north of Cerro Plano School, Monteverde ☎ 2645-5275 ⊕ www.monteverdearthouse.com.

Monteverde Wholefoods (Coopesanta Elena)

CRAFTS | This small local store carries organic goods and is the distributor for the area's gourmet Monteverde coffee and accoutrements. ✉ Next to CASEM, Monteverde ☎ 2645-5927.

Activities

Hiking through the cloud forest is beautiful, but if you'd like to see birds and animals and learn about the history and the flora and fauna of Monteverde, your best bet is to get a naturalist guide. Enthusiastic and passionate about where they call home and highly educated about the environment, these guides will show you so much more than you would ever see on your own.

ADVENTURE TOURS

Original Canopy Tour

ZIP LINING | FAMILY | The first company to offer zipline tours in Costa Rica has set up 12 platforms in the canopy. Included is an optional Tarzan swing and tree rappel. Tours last about 2½ hours and begin at 7:30, 10:30, and 2:30. They offer free pickup from most Monteverde hotels. ✉ Monteverde ☎ 2291-4465 in San José for reservations, 305/433-2241 in U.S. ⊕ www.canopytour.com ☞ $52.

Rafael Elizondo Nature Tours

GUIDED TOURS | You'll feel the enthusiasm of these passionate and knowledgeable English-speaking guides with years of experience. Share in the wonder of the biodiversity and beauty of the birds, mammals, and plants on a nature tour. ✉ Monteverde ☎ 8838-8145 ⊕ rafaelelizondo.com ☞ 23.

Sky Adventures

ZIP LINING | FAMILY | Here's a tram/zipline/hanging-bridges entertainment complex all in one. A tram takes you on a 1½-km-long (1-mile-long) gondola ride through the rain-forest canopy. You can descend via the tram, or along a series of six hanging bridges, at heights of up to 138 feet, connected from tree to tree. Your third descent option is 3 km (2 miles) of ziplines through the cloud-forest canopy. Imposing towers, used as support, mar the landscape somewhat. The site's Arboreal Tree Climbing Park takes you on an eight-tree climbing circuit (33 to 60 feet) courtesy of hand-hold straps that do no damage. ✉ *4 km (2½ miles) northeast of town on road toward Santa Elena Reserve, Santa Elena* ☎ *2645–6384 office, 844/468–6759 in North America* ⊕ *www.skyadventures.travel* ✆ *From $41.*

HORSEBACK RIDING

Horseback riding can be one of the most peaceful ways to see the cloud forest. A ride to a waterfall is a magical way to spend a morning. Just make sure the horses look well cared for and healthy, and if something feels off, cancel and reschedule with someone else.

■ **TIP→ During rainy season (July–December), book horseback trips in the morning, since rains usually begin around 2 pm.**

Caballeriza El Rodeo

HORSEBACK RIDING | Escorted 1½-hour horseback-riding tours ($45) with Caballeriza El Rodeo are on a private farm. Excursions are for everyone from beginner to experienced riders. A two-hour sunset tour ($45) begins at 3:30 pm. ✉ *Santa Elena* ✛ *West entrance of town of Santa Elena* ☎ *2645–6306* ✆ *$45.*

Smiling Horses

HORSEBACK RIDING | Owner Sabine—who speaks English, French, German, and Spanish—offers two-hour treks starting at $60. In addition to the regular waterfall and canyon tours, excursions at full moon are also offered once a month. Experienced riders can make reservations to go on longer, faster rides. ✉ *1 km (½ mile) west of the cemetery, Santa Elena* ☎ *8385–2424* ⊕ *www.horseback-riding-tour.com* ✆ *From $60.*

Ants on Parade

Tread carefully when you see a tiny green parade on the ground before you. It's a troop of leaf-cutter ants carrying compost material to an underground nest.

Tenorio Volcano and the Río Celeste

109 km (68 miles, 3½ hrs) northwest of Monteverde Cloud Forest Biological Reserve and 92 km (57 miles, 2 hrs) northeast of Palo Verde National Park.

Tenorio Volcano National Park is one of the newest and most underrated parks in Costa Rica. It has easy hiking trails through primary and secondary rain forests to one of the most beautiful rivers in Costa Rica, not to mention an exquisite waterfall.

Legend says that when God was painting the sky he dipped the paintbrush into the Río Celeste, giving it its otherworldly cerulean hue. Recently, University of Costa Rica scientists discovered that it's actually an optical illusion caused by the sunlight scattering off the suspended aluminosilicate then reflecting off of the riverbed turning the water turquoise. Nevertheless, the wow factor remains.

■ **TIP→ Because it's just over an hour from the Liberia airport, Tenorio Volcano National Park makes a great stop for beachgoers who are spending time on the Pacific but**

would also like to get some rain forest and volcano viewing in on their vacation.

GETTING HERE AND AROUND

The best way to get to the river and park is to drive your own rental, as no buses run directly to the national park. That may change since this "local secret" has been discovered and is becoming more popular by the day, but for now, you have to take a bus to Upala, then catch a taxi to the national park. You could also hire a private shuttle. From Arenal, the 30 miles (47 km) is a pleasant 1½-hour drive to the Río Celeste. Leaving La Fortuna, head east on Route 142 for a short distance, then turn left on Route 4. Follow signs to Upala, where you'll begin to see signs for the Parque Nacional Volcan Tenorio and Río Celeste.

Driving from San José will be a roundabout no matter which route you drive, and will take a little under four hours. It's easiest to take the Pan-American Highway (Route 1 on a map) to Cañas, where you'll see a turnoff onto Route 6 toward Bijagua.

At the entrance to the park you'll see a secure parking lot with a guard. Parking costs $3.50 (2,000 colones). Never leave valuables in the car.

Sights

★ Tenorio Volcano National Park
NATIONAL PARK | Better known for its aquamarine river and waterfall than its namesake volcano, this park is one of the lesser known but most stunning parks in Costa Rica. The hike is not terribly arduous, but there are a lot of steps. The first part of the hike, about 1½ km (1 mile), features a trail with well-maintained steps down to a breathtaking waterfall. At this point, you may choose to head back up the same way you came, especially if you have young children or have reached your limit. More adventurous hikers can go back up the steps and continue to a lookout point, the Laguna Azul (Blue Lagoon), and bubbling hot springs. The trail has some hanging bridges, and at the end, you can see the two rivers converging, as if by magic, creating an azure color. Head back the same way you came; the round-trip is 6 km (3½ miles). Plan for around four hours of hiking. Swimming is prohibited inside the national park, but there are public entrances outside the park. One is about 1 km (½ mile) past the entrance near the bridge, or you can pay $4 for access at Cabinas Piuri. Make sure you arrive before 2 pm, when the park stops allowing visitors. The trail can get very muddy, so don't go in flip-flops. If you don't have hiking shoes, there are rubber boots to rent ($5) at the park entrance. Remember that national parks in Costa Rica no longer allow single-use plastic, and they check bags, so bring along your reusable water bottle, bug spray, and your credit card; they don't accept cash. ✉ *Bijagua* ☎ *2206–5369* 🎟 *$12.*

Hotels

Celeste Mountain Lodge
$$ | **B&B/INN** | This funky little mountain ecolodge has fabulous views of the neighboring Tenorio and Miravalles volcanoes and is a great base for viewing nearby Rio Celeste. **Pros:** private rain-forest trail; innovative gourmet food; eco-friendly, sustainable tourism. **Cons:** very firm beds not for everyone; sparse decor; some noise from neighboring rooms. [$] *Rooms from: $142* ✉ *Bijagua* ✥ *4 km (2½ miles) on access road to Tenorio Volcano National Park* ☎ *2278–6628* 🌐 *celestemountainlodge.com* 🛏 *20 rooms* 🍴 *Free Breakfast.*

★ La Carolina Lodge
$$$ | **ALL-INCLUSIVE** | **FAMILY** | Hark back to a simpler time as you relax in a rocking chair next to a stone fireplace, sip ever-available coffee, and listen to the river flow past at this rustic lodge, but don't think the lack of electricity and Wi-Fi means you will be deprived; it's quite the opposite. **Pros:** beautiful setting on a farm next to the river; chance to unplug and

Did You Know?

Like a small Florida Everglades, Costa Rica's Caño Negro Wildlife Refuge is home to lowlands, swamps, and floodplains filled with wildlife like the great egret.

get away from it all; family-style meals. **Cons:** rustic cabins; staff has very limited English; limited electricity and Wi-Fi only in office. [$] *Rooms from: $221* ✉ *San Miguel, Bijagua de Upala, Caño Negro National Wildlife Refuge* ☎ *2466–6393, 843/343–4201 from U.S.* 🌐 *lacarolinalodge.com* 🛏 *12 units* 🍴 *All-Inclusive.*

Río Celeste Hideway

$$$$ | **B&B/INN** | Set in the rain forest, these marvelous, secluded casitas have elegant furnishings, sizable bathrooms with private garden showers, and terraces that entice you to spend time in nature. **Pros:** spacious, well-appointed casitas in the rain forest; terrific pool and hot tubs; close to Tenorio Volcano National Park and hike to Río Celeste. **Cons:** far from other restaurants; pool can get chilly; restaurant is expensive with limited menu. [$] *Rooms from: $375* ✉ *1 km (½ mile) southeast of Tenorio Volcano, Alajuela* ☎ *2206–4000, 954/234–2372 from U.S.* 🌐 *www.riocelestehideaway.com* 🛏 *26 casitas* 🍴 *Free Breakfast.*

Caño Negro National Wildlife Refuge

100 km (60 miles, 2 hrs) north of La Fortuna.

If you're seeking a national park experience without the crowds, Caño Negro should be on your list; its excellent birding and wildlife viewing still have an "undiscovered" feel. Long a favorite among fishing enthusiasts and bird-watchers, this remote area is off the beaten track and may be difficult to get to if your time in Costa Rica is short. You can cross into Nicaragua, via Los Chiles, but there are almost no roads in this part of southern Nicaragua, making access to the rest of the country nearly impossible. The border crossing at Peñas Blancas, near the North Pacific coast, is far more user-friendly.

GETTING HERE AND AROUND

The highway from La Fortuna to Los Chiles, the gateway to the Caño Negro National Wildlife Refuge, is one of the best maintained in the northern lowlands. You can catch public buses in San José at Terminal 7–10 twice a day for a trip of about five hours to Los Chiles, with many stops. Public buses also operate between La Fortuna and Los Chiles. If they have room, many tour companies will allow you to ride along on their shuttles for around $30. If you're not staying way up here, an organized tour of the reserve from La Fortuna is the way most visitors get to and from.

Sights

★ **Caño Negro National Wildlife Refuge**
(*Refugio Nacional de Vida Silvestre Caño Negro*)

WILDLIFE REFUGE | It's a shame that Caño Negro doesn't grab the same amount of attention in wildlife-viewing circles as other destinations in Costa Rica. Due to the recent saturation of visitors at Tortuguero National Park to the east, however, Caño Negro is starting to gain recognition among bird-watchers and nature lovers for its isolation, diversity, and abundant wildlife. As a feeding ground for both resident and migratory birds, the refuge is home to more than 350 bird species, 310 plants, and at least 160 species of mammals. The reserve is a splendid place to watch waterfowl and resident exotic animals, including cougars, jaguars, and several species of monkeys. It's also one of the best places to see a basilisk, more commonly known as the "Jesus Christ Lizard" because of its ability to run on water. Comprising the vast wetland sanctuary is a web of channels and lagoons ideal for exploring by boat, and even more so by canoe to reach remote lowlands, swamps, and seasonal floodplains. If you're not staying at one of the two lodges up here, the refuge is easily visited as a day trip from La Fortuna. Note that most

Arenal-area tour operators do not actually enter the refuge (to avoid paying the $5 per person entrance fee). Tour companies often claim that the areas surrounding the park are equally spectacular, but this is not the case. Although you're likely to see wildlife on the outskirts of the refuge, you won't see a fraction of what you encounter inside the park, which lacks the parade of tour boats disturbing the habitat. For the best tour of the refuge, book through resident guide Jimmy Gutierrez at Natural Lodge Caño Negro. There are no public facilities in the park, which consists mostly of wetlands fed by the Frio River and best explored only by boat. Bring a camera, binoculars, and plenty of bug spray.

For more information, see highlighted listing in this chapter. ✉ *Off Hwy. 35, 180 km (112 miles) north of La Fortuna, Caño Negro National Wildlife Refuge* ☎ *2471–1580* 🌐 *www.sinac.go.cr* 🎫 *$5; fishing license $30.*

Hotels

Hotel de Campo

$$ | HOTEL | Under the shade of tropical fruit trees, white bungalows of high-quality wood each contain two bright, sparkling rooms with terra-cotta tile floors and front patios that open onto a central swimming pool. **Pros:** secluded location; close to reserve; tons of wildlife. **Cons:** food slightly overpriced; small pool; need a car to get here and road is very rough. [$] *Rooms from: $98* ✉ *Caño Negro National Wildlife Refuge* ✣ *Caño Negro village, 100 meters (328 feet) past grocery* ☎ *2471–1012* 🌐 *www.hoteldecampo.com* 💳 *No credit cards* 🛏 *14 rooms, 7 bungalows* 🍴 *Free Breakfast.*

Natural Lodge Caño Negro

$$ | HOTEL | It might come as a surprise to find such attractive and comfortable rooms, with nice appointments and high ceilings, in so remote a place, but the lack of pretense and laid-back atmosphere fit right into the surroundings on the east side of the reserve. **Pros:** secluded location; close to reserve; excellent boat tour; great for bird-watching. **Cons:** no Wi-Fi in the rooms; rough and bumpy road; need a car to get here. [$] *Rooms from: $140* ✉ *Caño Negro village, Caño Negro National Wildlife Refuge* ✣ *250 meters (820 feet) west of the school* ☎ *2471–1426, 8352–6555* 🌐 *www.canonegrolodge.com* 🛏 *42 rooms* 🍴 *Free Breakfast.*

Activities

Natural Lodge Caño Negro

GUIDED TOURS | Unlike the La Fortuna–based tour operators visiting the area, Natural Lodge Caño Negro offers excursions that actually take place inside the reserve rather than along its outskirts. Their resident guides are experts on local wildlife and can arrange motorized boat tours or excursions by canoe to reach remote areas not accessible by motorboat. A two-hour wetlands tour departs at 8 am and 2 pm and costs $48. Sportfishing, day hikes, and night tours are also available. Rates do not include the $5 park entrance fee. ✉ *Caño Negro National Wildlife Refuge* ✣ *250 meters (820 feet) west of the school* ☎ *2471–1426, 8352–6555* 🌐 *www.canonegrolodge.com* 🎫 *From $48.*

Chapter 7

GUANACASTE

7

Updated by
Rachel White

⊙ Sights	🍴 Restaurants	🛏 Hotels	🛍 Shopping	🍸 Nightlife
★★★☆☆	★★★★★	★★★★☆	★★★☆☆	★★★★★

WELCOME TO GUANACASTE

TOP REASONS TO GO

★ **Beaches:** White sand, black sand, palm-fringed strands, beaches for swimming, partying, surfing, and sunbathing—the sheer variety of Guanacaste's beaches can't be beat.

★ **Big wind:** From November to May, the trade winds whip across Northern Guanacaste with a velocity and consistency that make the Bahía Salinas a world-class windsurfing and kitesurfing destination.

★ **Endangered nature:** Guanacaste's varied national parks protect some of Central America's last remaining patches of tropical dry forest, a distinctive ecosystem where you might spot magpie jays or howler monkeys in the branches of a gumbo-limbo tree.

★ **Scuba diving:** Forget the pretty tropical fish. Sharks, rays, sea turtles, and moray eels are the large-scale attractions for divers here.

★ **Surfing:** Offshore winds, warm water, and hollow barrels make for epic waves at more than a dozen Guanacaste beaches.

1 **Bahía Salinas.** Haven for kitesurfers with mostly pristine, undeveloped beaches.

2 **Playa Bahía Junquillal.** Bordered by Bahía Junquillal National Wildlife Refuge.

3 **Santa Rosa National Park.** Forests and beaches combine for untouched beauty.

4 **Guanacaste National Park.** A biological corridor and migratory passage with hiking trails.

5 **Rincón de la Vieja National Park.** Wildlife, rivers, waterfalls, and mudbaths are the tip of the volcano.

6 **Liberia.** The capital of Guanacaste has an international airport and many shopping centers.

7 **Papagayo Peninsula.** Remote paradise with a bevy of all-inclusive luxury hotels.

8 **Playa Hermosa.** Wide, curved beach with warm waters.

9 **Playas del Coco.** Messy, noisy, and colorful, with lots of dive shops and lively nightlife.

10 **Playa Ocotal.** Quiet and serene; a welcome respite from its noisy neighbor.

11 **Las Catalinas.** Car-free village with utopian beaches and mountain biking trails.

12 **Playa Pan de Azúcar.** An almost deserted strand of tropical beach.

13 **Playa Potrero.** Community with a church, school, and supermarket.

14 **Playa Flamingo.** Boating and swimming wonderland.

15 **Brasilito and Playa Conchal.** Brasilito is cluttered and noisy, a lively contrast to the gated Playa Conchal to the south.

16 **Playa Grande.** Wide, beautiful, pristine, and one of the best surfing beaches. Its Las Baulas National Marine Park protects sea turtles.

17 **Tamarindo.** Funky beach town full of surfers and the best restaurants on the coast.

18 **Playa Langosta.** Tranquil, elegant community with an unsullied beach.

19 **Playa Avellanas.** Lovely spot for anyone who likes sea, sand, and surfing.

20 **Playa Negra.** A laid-back surfer community.

21 **Playa Junquillal.** Serene, uncrowded beaches and hardly a building in sight.

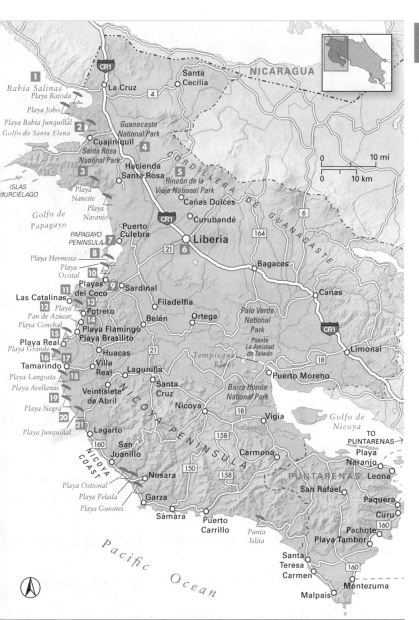

RINCÓN DE LA VIEJA NATIONAL PARK

Rincón de la Vieja National Park

Rincón de la Vieja National Park is Costa Rica's mini-Yellowstone, with volcanic hot springs and bubbling mud pools, refreshing waterfalls, and cool forest trails. Often shrouded in clouds, the currently active volcano dominates the landscape northwest of Liberia, rising above the sunbaked plains.

It has two windswept peaks, Santa María, at 6,323 feet high on the east slope, and Rincón de la Vieja at 6,254 feet on the west. The latter slope has an active crater that hardy hikers can climb to when the trail is open. It's usually closed in the wet season, and when the crater is too active. Fumaroles on its lower slope constantly let off steam. Las Pailas entrance has the most accessible trails, including an easy loop trail that wends past all the interesting volcanic features and a waterfall that flows from August to November. When the volcano is very active, the entire park is closed to visitors, so check with lodges or tour operators before you go.

(For more information, see the review in this chapter.)

BEST TIME TO GO

Good times to visit are January through May, during the dry season. December and January can be very windy, but that means temperatures stay cooler for hiking. May to November—the green season—is when the fumaroles and boiling mud pots are most active, but the crater is often covered in clouds, so it's not the best time to hike to the top. During the wet season, trails are slippery and muddy, and can get crowded during school break (from mid-December through February).

BEST WAYS TO EXPLORE

BIRD-WATCHING

Birding is excellent most of the year, except for December and January when the weather is dry and often too windy. You're bound to hear the three-note song of the long-tailed manakin wherever you walk—it sounds something like "Toledo," which is what the locals call this bird. Along with their lavish, long tail feathers, the males are famous for their cooperative courting dance: two pals leap back and forth over each other, but only the senior male gets any girl who falls for this act. The hard-to-spot rock wren lives closer to the top of the volcano.

HIKING

The only way to explore the park trails is on foot, along well-marked paths that range from easy loops to more demanding climbs. The ranger station at Las Pailas entrance provides maps of the park trails and restrooms before you set off. Las Pailas loop (3 km [2 miles]), which starts just past the ranger station, is the easiest hike; it takes about two hours. Remember to bring sunscreen and reusable water bottles; plastic bottles are not allowed in the park. If you want to venture farther afield, follow the signs for La Cangreja trail. After passing through dense, cool forest, you'll emerge through an avenue of giant agave plants into an open, windy meadow. Your reward is the cool waterfall and swimming hole at the end of the trail.

ON HORSEBACK

Local ranches and lodges organize daylong trail rides to waterfalls and sulfur springs on the lower slopes of the volcano, just outside the park borders. The distinctive rotten-egg smell of sulfur will tell you when you're near the springs

Mud-bathing in Rincón de la Vieja National Park

TOP REASONS TO GO

WILDLIFE

Here you can find more than 300 species of birds, plus mammals such as white-tailed deer, coyotes, howler and capuchin monkeys, armadillos, and the occasional harlequin snake (not venomous).

CLIMBING TO THE CRATER

Due to volcanic activity, the hike to the crater has been closed and looks to stay closed for the foreseeable future.

GEOLOGICAL WONDERS

Three-kilometer (2-mile) Las Pailas loop trail showcases the park's famous geothermal features. Along the trail you'll see fumaroles with steam hissing out of ground vents, a *volcancito* (baby volcano), and boiling mud fields.

SANTA ROSA NATIONAL PARK

Sunset sky in Santa Rosa National Park

Renowned for its wildlife, Santa Rosa National Park, part of the larger Guanacaste Conservation Area, protects the largest swath of extant lowland dry forest in Central America, about 91,000 acres. *Dry* is the operative word here, with less than 59 inches of rainfall a year in some parts of the park.

If you station yourself near watering holes in the dry season (January to April) you may spot deer, coyotes, coatis, and armadillos. The park also has the world's only fully protected nesting beach for olive ridley sea turtles. Treetop inhabitants include spider, capuchin, and howler monkeys, as well as hundreds of bird species. The deciduous forest here includes giant kapok, guanacaste, and mahogany, as well as calabash, acacia, and gumbo-limbo trees with their distinctive peeling bark. The park is also of historical significance to Costa Rica because it was here, in 1856, that an army of Costa Rican volunteers decisively defeated an invading force of mercenaries.

BEST TIME TO GO

Dry season is the best time to visit if you want to see wildlife. The vegetation is sparse, making for easy observation. It's also the best time to drive to the park's beaches. In the rainy season, trails can become mud baths, excluding the Indio Desnudo Trail, which is fine year-round.

FUN FACT

Moving from sparse, sunlit secondary forest into the park's shady primary forest areas, you can experience an instant temperature drop of as much as 5°C (9°F).

BEST WAYS TO EXPLORE

GETTING AROUND

Only the first 12 km (7 miles) of the park's roads are accessible by vehicles. The rest of the park's 20 km (12 miles) of hiking trails have been significantly improved. It's easy to drive to La Casona headquarters along a paved road and pick up a short loop hiking trail, but beyond that point, you need a 4WD vehicle. We do not recommend going past La Casona during rainy season.

A HISTORICAL TOUR

Costa Rica doesn't have many historical sites—relics of its past have mostly been destroyed by earthquakes and volcanic eruptions. So La Casona, the symbolic birthplace of Costa Rica's nationhood, is a particularly revered site. Most Costa Ricans come to Santa Rosa on a historical pilgrimage. The place was burned to the ground in a fire purposely set in 2001 by disgruntled poachers who had been fined by park rangers. The government, schoolchildren, and private businesses came to the rescue, raising the money to restore the historic hacienda and replace the exhibits.

TURTLE-WATCHING

Thousands of olive ridley sea turtles emerge from the sea every year, from July to December, to dig nests and deposit eggs on the park's protected beaches at Playa Nancite and Playa Naranjo. Pacific green sea turtles and the huge leatherbacks also appear, but in much smaller numbers. You can hike the 12 km (8 miles) to Playa Naranjo and pitch your tent near the beach; this is a natural spectacle you'll get to witness far from any crowds. Playa Nancite is a 22-km (13-mile) hike; you'll need prior written permission from a park ranger to visit this protected beach as only 30 people can visit a day.

TOP REASONS TO GO

EXPLORE THE FOREST

The short (about 1-km [½-mile]) Casona nature-trail loop, which starts from the park headquarters, is a great way to get a sampling of dry tropical forest and to spot wildlife. Look for signs leading to the Indio Desnudo (Naked Indian) path, named after the local word for gumbo-limbo trees.

SERIOUS SURFING

Off Playa Naranjo lies the famous Witch's Rock, a towering rock formation famous for its surfing breaks. If you're interested in checking it out, take a boat from Playas del Coco, Playa Hermosa, or Playa Tamarindo.

WILDLIFE-WATCHING

Wildlife is easy to spot here thanks to the low-density foliage of this tropical dry forest. Scan the treetops and keep an eye out for spider, white-faced capuchin, and howler monkeys. If you're lucky, you might even spot an ocelot.

The wild coastline near Santa Rosa National Park

Reliably sunny, dry weather brings planeloads of sun-starved Northerners to the North Pacific area of Costa Rica every winter, and a windswept coastline makes Guanacaste popular with surfers eager to relive the legendary "Endless Summer" of the sport's early years.

Ever since the 1966 cult-classic film put Costa Rica on the map, surfers and travelers alike have flocked to the beaches where waves peel, hammocks sway, and monkeys and iguanas clamber in treetops. It's easy to understand why many who come to visit return year after year or even devise a plan to stay; Guanacaste casts its spell the moment you hit the coast. From the luxury resorts and cattle ranches to the fishing villages and surf towns, the region serves up everything from high-rise resorts to utter isolation with a side of sustainable living. An abundance of marine life and stellar diving spots also lure fishers and underwater aficionados. Add in some stunningly scenic national parks and a range of thrilling outdoor adventures, and you have all the ingredients that make this region an all-around top spot to experience Costa Rica's charms. Although most tourists head here for the dry "high" season, it's even more beautiful—and cheaper, cooler, and less crowded—in the "green" or low season, April to December.

MAJOR REGIONS

Guanacaste Province—a vast swath of land in northwestern Costa Rica—is bordered by the Pacific Ocean to the west and the looming Cordillera de Guanacaste volcanic mountain range to the east.

Far Northern Guanacaste. Dry, hot Far Northern Guanacaste is traditionally ranching country, but it does include the impressive wildernesses of Santa Rosa and Rincón de la Vieja national parks, the latter of which holds one of Costa Rica's most active volcanoes. Liberia, the capital of Guanacaste Province, is the closest town to Costa Rica's second-largest airport. Farther to the north is Bahía Salinas, second only to Lake Arenal for wind- and kitesurfing.

Guanacaste Pacific Coast. The number and variety of beaches along the northern border of the Nicoya Peninsula, from the Papagayo Peninsula to Tamarindo and down to Playa Junquillal, make it a top tourist destination. Each beach has its specialty, be it surfing, fishing, diving, or just plain relaxing. Hotels and restaurants are in generous supply.

Planning

When to Go

HIGH SEASON: MID-DECEMBER TO APRIL

This is the driest region of the country, with only 65 inches of average annual rainfall. It's also the hottest region, with average temperatures around 30°C to

35°C (86°F to 95°F) in high season. It's no wonder that winter-weary Northerners come here for guaranteed sunshine and heat. The beaches and trails can get packed during these drier months, especially mid-December to February, when school is out in Costa Rica. January can be quite breezy, especially along the coast, thanks to the annual Papagayo winds. February through April are the driest months: skies are clear, but the heat is intense and the landscape is brown and parched. Fishing and scuba diving are at their best during this period, though.

LOW SEASON: MAY THROUGH OCTOBER

Major downpours are frequent in the afternoon during the rainy season, which brings lower prices, fewer crowds, and a lush green landscape. But mornings are usually fresh and clear. Unpaved beach roads can become quite muddy, making travel difficult and some roads impassable.

SHOULDER SEASON: NOVEMBER TO MID-DECEMBER

This is the best time to visit, when the rains have abated, the landscape is lush, and the evening air is cool. Hotels and restaurants are prepped for the impending tourist influx, and staff are fresh and eager to please. Except for the popular U.S. Thanksgiving week, you can usually get a deal. High-season rates begin mid-December.

PLANNING YOUR TIME

Visiting this region for 10 days to two weeks will introduce you to its wonders and give you a real taste of the North Pacific. Schedule plenty of beach time for lounging, sunbathing, surfing, diving, and snorkeling. Logistically, you also need to take into consideration slow travel over bumpy roads. A beach like Tamarindo with lots of restaurants and nightlife can keep you entertained for a week or more, whereas a more solitary beach might merit only a couple of days. Also

plan to visit some protected areas to enjoy canopy tours, wildlife viewing, and hiking. Outdoorsy types should consider spending a few days around Rincón de la Vieja National Park for its amazing hiking, bird-watching, and horseback riding. Other parks to consider are Palo Verde National Park, Santa Rosa National Park, and Barra Honda National Park. Many North Pacific beaches are just a few hours' drive from the Arenal Volcano area, so the region can be combined with the Northern Lowlands.

Getting Here and Around

AIR

Aeropuerto Internacional Daniel Oduber Quirós (LIR) in Liberia is an international gateway to the coast, with a large, air-conditioned terminal. Tamarindo also has a small airstrip. Flying from San José is the best way to get here if you are already in the country. If your primary destination lies in Guanacaste, make sure you investigate the possibility of flying directly into Liberia instead of San José, which saves some serious hours on the road.

Many airlines have direct service between major U.S. hubs and Costa Rica's two international airports in San José and Liberia. SANSA has a scheduled flight between San José, Liberia, and Tamarindo, but you'll need to go directly to the airline's website to schedule flights. Don't forget to factor in the exit tax, $29 by air and $7 by land, payable in U.S. dollars, colones, or credit card. Some airlines include this fee in the ticket price.

AIR CONTACTS SANSA. ☎ *877/767–2672* ⊕ *flysansa.com.*

BUS

Interbus has door-to-door minivan shuttle service from San José to all the major beach hotels (in Papagayo, Flamingo, Tamarindo, and Coco). Fares range from

$42 to $57 per person. Reserve 48 hours in advance to guarantee a seat.

BUS CONTACTS Interbus. ☏ *4100–0888* ⊕ *www.interbusonline.com.*

CAR

Most unpaved roads here alternate between being extremely muddy and treacherous during the rainy season and extremely dusty during the dry season. That said, it can be a real adventure exploring the coastline if you have a 4WD or a hired driver with a good, sturdy car. The major artery in this region is the Pan-American Highway (CA 1), which heads northwest from San José to Liberia, then due north to the Nicaraguan border. It's fairly well maintained, but the convoys of trucks and buses often create heavy traffic and there are few passing opportunities. To skip the hours of frustrating driving, consider flying into Liberia, whose airport provides easy access to the region. Local hotels and tour companies can help you arrange for ground transportation in many cases. In Guanacaste, it's usually safe to take *pirata* (pirate, or unofficial) taxis, but always negotiate the price before getting into the cab, or ask your hotel to call a reputable driver.

The northwest is accessed via the paved two-lane Pan-American Highway (CA 1), which begins at the top of Paseo Colón in San José. Take the Friendship Bridge (aka Río Tempisque Bridge) across the Tempisque River to get to the Pacific beaches south of Liberia. Once you get off the main highway, dust, mud, potholes, and other factors come into play, depending on which beach you visit. The roads to Playa Flamingo, Playa Conchal, Playa Brasilito, Tamarindo, Playa Grande, Playas del Coco, Hermosa, and Ocotal are paved all the way; every other destination may require some dirt-road maneuvering.

Restaurants

Seafood and fresh fish are tops here, followed by fast food—pizza, tacos, barbecue—to satisfy the hordes of hungry surfers and beachgoers. But there are many sophisticated restaurants, too, offering Asian-fusion, Italian, French, and international cuisine, especially in the tourist-heavy beach towns of Hermosa, Flamingo, and Tamarindo.

■ **TIP →** **Many restaurants, especially tourist-oriented ones with dollar-denominated menus, do not include the 13% national sales tax plus mandatory 10%–12% service. By law, menus are required to show the total price including tax, but many owners flout this law. Be sure to ask if taxes are included; otherwise you may be surprised by a bill that's 25% higher than you expected.**

Hotels

A wide range of lodging options awaits you here, so choose wisely. If your goal is to take leisurely swims and lounge quietly on the beach with a cocktail in hand, then avoid the beaches that are renowned for surfing waves. Expensive resorts like the Four Seasons are generally well balanced with budget hotels that charge less than $75 per night. Wherever you stay, be sure to factor in the 13% sales tax. As in all of Costa Rica, the places we recommend most highly are the small owner-operated hotels and bed-and-breakfasts that blend in with unspoiled nature and offer one-on-one attention from the staff and owners. Costa Rica's most precious resource is its people, and most hotels will be able to connect you with local tour operators and knowledgeable staff members who can help show you the best aspects of each destination, whether it's a local park with howler monkeys, a great family-run restaurant on the beach, or a thrilling canopy tour.

HOTEL AND RESTAURANT PRICES

Restaurant prices are the average cost of a main course at dinner or, if dinner is not served, at lunch. Hotel prices are the lowest cost of a standard double room in high season. Restaurant and hotel reviews have been shortened. For full information, visit Fodors.com.

What it Costs in U.S. Dollars			
$	$$	$$$	$$$$
RESTAURANTS			
under $10	$10–$15	$16–$25	over $25
HOTELS			
under $75	$75–$150	$151–$250	over $250

Tours

Horizontes Nature Tours

ADVENTURE TOURS | With a focus on nature and adventure, Horizontes has independent, private tours with your own guide and driver as well as small-group tours. Customized tours are available for bird-watchers, families, couples, yogis, and beachgoers. Average tours are six nights. ☎ 4052–5850, 888/786–8748 toll-free in U.S. ⊕ www.horizontes.com ⊠ From $1,440 per person.

Bahía Salinas

15 km (9 miles) west of La Cruz.

The large windswept bay at the very top of Costa Rica's Pacific coast is the second-windiest area in the country, after Lake Arenal, making it great for windsurfers and kitesurfers, as well as beachgoers looking for breezy, uncrowded, pristine beaches. It also happens to be the sunniest and driest side of Costa Rica. Strong onshore breezes blow from November to May, when only experienced riders are out on the waves and the water grows

steadily cooler. The south (bay) side has the strongest winds, and choppy, colder water from January to May.

In July and August the wind is more appropriate for beginner kitesurfers and windsurfers, whereas any time of year you can enjoy the area's diving and beaches. On the sheltered Golfo de Santa Elena, to the west, are two beaches that rank among the most beautiful in all of Costa Rica: Playa Rajada and Playa Jobo, although Dreams Las Mareas Resort has claimed ground at Jobo Bay. Other beaches lining the bay are Playa Copal, Playa Papaturro, and Playa Pochotes. Still, it's a far cry from the overdeveloped beaches of Guanacaste's gold coast farther to the south.

GETTING HERE AND AROUND

From Liberia, drive 45 minutes toward La Cruz, the last town before the Peñas Blancas border crossing. From a high point in La Cruz, the road to Salinas descends both in altitude and condition. Turn left toward Bahía Salinas, the only road leading to the beaches. Signs direct you to Puerto Soley where the road splits shortly thereafter and heads right to El Jobo. Playa Copal is about 13 km (8 miles) along the same road from La Cruz. The first few kilometers of the beach road are paved, but expect a bumpy ride most of the way.

 Beaches

Playa Copal

BEACH | Playa Copal is a narrow, dark-beige rocky beach that is one of the main venues for kitesurfing. Winds are often gusty but consistent November to May, which is why several kite schools have set up shop nearby. A couple of kilometers to the east is Playa Papaturro, another windy beach where you'll find simple accommodations and a kitesurfing school at Blue Dream Hotel. **Amenities:** food and drink. **Best for:** solitude. ⊠ *About 2 km (1 mile) east of branch road that leads to Ecoplaya, Bahía Salinas.*

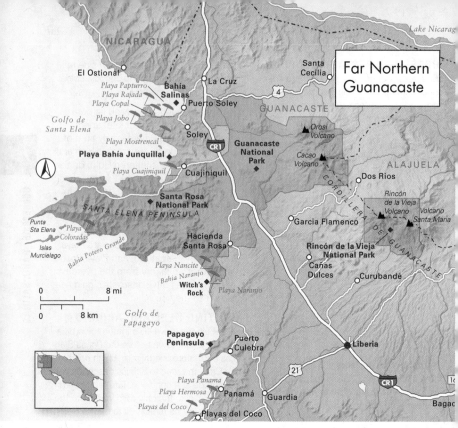

Playa Jobo

BEACH | Dominated by the massive Dreams Las Mareas Resort, Playa Jobo is still one of the most beautiful beaches in the area. Cradled within the sheltered cove is fine brown sand and calm water, making this beach safe for swimming. Motorized water sports are not allowed, so despite the resort's size, the bay remains relatively quiet. A few sailboats are anchored offshore. Playa Jobo is fringed with acacia trees that have sharp thorns, and there are rocks jetting on either side of the cove where many people begin a snorkel adventure (beware of sea urchins and jellyfish). This beach is a refuge to turtles and manta rays, which you might see in the shallow, clear waters. Windy days are frequent, so watch for blowing sand. At high tide, the beach is narrow. This, combined with the slight slope to the shore, has most people sunbathing by the pool or lounging in the grassy area between the sand and the resort. Although all beaches in Costa Rica are public, this strand is difficult to reach unless you're staying at Dreams Resort. Your other options are to approach by boat or access from around the cove at low tide. **Amenities:** food and drink. **Best for:** snorkeling; sunset; swimming. ⊠ *Dreams Las Mareas Resort, 3-km (2-mile) walk or drive west from Ecoplaya Beach Resort, Bahía Salinas.*

Playa Rajada

BEACH | Gorgeous, horseshoe-shaped Playa Rajada is a wide sweep of almost-white fine-grain sand that, so far, has evaded tourists. Shallow, warm waters make it perfect for swimming, and an interesting rock formation at the north end invites snorkelers, plus there's plenty of shade. It's also a favorite beach for watching sunsets. **Amenities:** none. **Best for:** snorkeling; sunset; swimming. ✉ *5 km (3 miles) west of Ecoplaya Beach Resort or 3 km (2 miles) north of town of El Jobo, Bahía Salinas.*

Hotels

Blue Dream Hotel

$ | HOTEL | FAMILY | Catering predominantly to kitesurfers, this breezy property on a steep hillside is one of the more affordable lodging options in Bahía Salinas, with suites, bungalows, rooms, and dorms just minutes from the water. **Pros:** very affordable; kitesurfing lessons; water views. **Cons:** not much to do outside of kitesurfing; stray animals and neglected grounds; steep climb to top rooms. [$] *Rooms from: $51* ✉ *60 meters west of Playa Papaturro entrance, Bahía Salinas* ☎ *8826–5221, 2676–1042* 🌐 *www.bluedreamhotel.com* 🛏 *16 units* 🍴 *No Meals.*

★ **Cañas Castilla**

$ | B&B/INN | Swiss expats Guido and Agi spent their first years in Costa Rica living off the land without running water or electricity, but today their little paradise is a full-fledged farm with cows, horses, chickens, and rustic cabins for overnight guests. **Pros:** friendly owners; nature abounds; all rooms are wheelchair-accessible; delicious food. **Cons:** no phones; patchy Wi-Fi in common areas only; muddy in rainy season. [$] *Rooms from: $70* ✉ *5 km (3 miles) north from La Cruz, La Cruz* ✣ *Turn off the hwy. to right into Sonzapote after school. Follow signs 2 km (1 mile) east to Finca Cañas Castilla* ☎ *8381–4030 mobile* 🌐 *www.canas-castilla.com* 🛏 *6 rooms* 🍴 *No Meals.*

★ **Dreams Las Mareas Costa Rica**

$$$$ | RESORT | FAMILY | As the first all-inclusive luxury resort in the Bahía Salinas area and the first hotel in Guanacaste to feature swim-up rooms, Dreams Las Mareas stands out from the AI pack with no hidden charges, no restaurant reservations, no towel cards, and no plastic wrist bands. **Pros:** lovely swim-up rooms; calm beach; designated kids' pool. **Cons:** steep, vast grounds require a lot of walking; patios and bathrooms lack privacy; isolated on a bumpy road. [$] *Rooms from: $560* ✉ *Playa Jobo, west of Bahia Salinas, Bahía Salinas* ☎ *2690–2400, 866/237–3267 in U.S.* 🌐 *www.dreamsresorts.com/las-mareas* 🛏 *447 rooms* 🍴 *All-Inclusive.*

The First Guanacastecos

The Chorotega tribe first settled the Guanacaste area and grew corn and fished. Chief Nicoya was the Chorotegan leader who greeted the conquistadores in 1523 and bequeathed his name to the town and peninsula.

Activities

Inshore fishing is quite good in the bay during windy months, when snapper, roosterfish, wahoo, and other fighters abound. Scuba divers might also encounter big fish from December to May, though visibility can be poor then. From May to December the snorkeling is good around the rocky points and Isla Bolaños.

KITESURFING AND WINDSURFING

Blue Dream Kitesurfing School

WINDSURFING | Ideally situated near windy Playa Papaturro (11 km [7 miles] west of La Cruz, turn left at sign for Papaturro), this kitesurfing school is run by Nicola Bertoldi, a multilingual instructor with lots of experience; private lessons cost $45 per hour. Nine hours of beginner's kitesurfing private lessons cost $360, including equipment. But the best deals are all-inclusive packages starting at $499 that include five days of lessons, lodging, and meals at the school's Blue Dream

Hotel, on a ridge with ocean views. Check their website for wind conditions and closure dates, as the school often shuts down once the breezes stop. ✉ *Bahía Salinas* ✣ *60 meters (197 feet) east Playa Papaturro entrance* ☎ *8826–5221, 2676–1042* 🌐 *www.bluedreamhotel.com* 🎟 *Private lessons $45 per hr.*

TOUR OPERATORS

Costa Kite

WINDSURFING | All levels are welcome here, from first-timers who want to get their feet wet or advanced kitesurfers who are ready to jump. All instructors are certified, and they use new gear. ✉ *Bahía Salinas* ✣ *100 meters (328 feet) south of Hotel Bolaños* ☎ *8907–9889* 🌐 *costakite.com* 🎟 *Three-hour group lesson $90; rentals $60 per day.*

Playa Bahía Junquillal

26 km (16 miles) northwest of Santa Rosa National Park entrance.

This 2½-km (1½-mile), tree-fringed beach is as close as you can get to a white-sand beach in this part of Guanacaste. Not to be confused with the Playa Junquillal farther south, this beach is part of the Guanacaste Conservation Area, and is a wildlife refuge to the north of Santa Rosa.

GETTING HERE AND AROUND

From the Pan-American Highway, take the road signed for Cuajiniquil, 43 km (26 miles) northwest of Liberia and 8 km (5 miles) north of Santa Rosa National Park. Follow the paved road 14 km (8 miles) to the beach turnoff, along a dirt road for another 4 km (2½ miles). From the Bahía Salinas area, take the scenic dirt road (4WD recommended); then follow the road near Puerto Soley (signed for Cuajiniquil) 7 km (4½ miles) to the beach entrance. It's about 30 minutes from the Pan-American turnoff and one hour from Bahía Salinas.

Beaches

Bahía Junquillal

(*Junquillal Bay Wildlife Refuge*)

BEACH | The warm, calm water and relative isolation makes this one of the best swimming beaches on the Golfo de Santa Elena. Stay for the day or camp out right on the beach in the well-kept, shaded camping area with cold-water showers, bathrooms, firepits, grills, and picnic tables ($15 per person onetime park entrance for foreigners, plus $19 per person per night to camp). Compared with other camping areas in Costa Rica, prices are steep since this is part of the Junquillal Bay Wildlife Refuge. You can snorkel if you bring your own gear. **Amenities:** showers; toilets. **Best for:** fishing; solitude; swimming. ✉ *18 km (11 miles) west of Pan-American Hwy., Cuajiniquil turnoff* 🌐 *www.acguanacaste.ac.cr/turismo/sector-junquillal* 🎟 *$15.*

Hotels

Santa Elena Lodge

$$ | **B&B/INN** | This simple family-run lodge with cozy rooms on the outskirts of Cuajiniquil provides the closest accommodations to both Playa Bahía Junquillal and Santa Rosa National Park, making it a good option for nature lovers and anyone who wants to stray from the vacationing crowds. **Pros:** friendly owners; near beach and park; clean and comfortable rooms. **Cons:** little English spoken; sounds can carry; basic accommodations. [$] *Rooms from: $80* ✉ *10 km (6 miles) west of Pan-American Hwy., 4 km (2½ miles) east of Junquillal, Cuajiniquil* ☎ *2679–1038* 🌐 *www.facebook.com/santaelenalodge* 🛏 *8 rooms* 🍴 *Free Breakfast.*

Santa Rosa National Park

35 km (22 miles) northwest of Liberia.

Santa Rosa National Park blends forest and pristine beaches overlooking the famed surf spot Witch's Rock. North of Liberia, the park is less frequented than other national parks in Costa Rica due to the difficult terrain (especially in rainy season) and the remote location far off the beaten path. The country's first national park, it still has an untouched beauty that is evident from the chirping birds among the treetops to the white-tailed deer drinking from watering holes. There are several campsites where travelers can soak in the sounds of Santa Rosa's symphony, comprised of howler monkeys, coyotes, bats, and (if you're lucky) the occasional jaguar. The best time to experience the typical dry-forest vegetation and wildlife is during dry season when leaves are sparse and roads are accessible.

GETTING HERE AND AROUND

The turnoff for Santa Rosa National Park from the Pan-American Highway is well marked, about 30 minutes outside of Liberia. From Liberia you can hop on a bus heading north to La Cruz and get off at the park entrance, but you'll have to hike 7 km (4½ miles) in the hot sun to the Casona park headquarters from there.

 ## Sights

Santa Rosa National Park

(*Parque Nacional Santa Rosa*)
NATIONAL PARK | Thanks to sparse foliage, it's not difficult to spot wildlife within Santa Rosa's tropical dry forest, especially if you're with an experienced guide. There are impressive flora and fauna, and even on a half-day visit you might see monkeys, birds, deer, and coatis hiding in the dry-forest vegetation. Santa Rosa's wealth of natural beauty is due in part

to its remoteness—it isn't as busy as some of Costa Rica's other parks. Most trails are easily accessible and relatively flat. To get deep into the park, you must have a 4WD vehicle, and many roads are impassable in rainy season. The park headquarters, a historic ranch house and museum called La Casona, and a nearby camping area are 7 km (4½ miles) from the Pan-American Highway via a paved road.

From park headquarters it's 11 km (7 miles) to **Playa Naranjo,** where the famed Witch's Rock surf break is located (surfers get there by boat). The road here is rough (4WD only). **Playa Nancite**—the site of one of the world's few completely protected olive ridley turtle *arribada,* or mass nesting (permit required)—is an additional 3 miles (5 km) by footpath north of Playa Naranjo. The arribadas occur during rainy season (July to November). A permit can be obtained from the Ecotourism Office in the administrative center. The most impressive coastal views are from the Mirador Valle Naranjo and Mirador Tierras Emergidas. For bird-watching, follow the Los Platos trail about 5 km (3 miles) past the administrative center on the way to the coast. It's best to visit the park with a guide. ✉ *Km 269, Pan-American Hwy. 35 km (22 miles) north of Liberia, Santa Rosa National Park* ☎ *2666–0623* ⊕ *www.acguanacaste. ac.cr* ➋ *$15 park entrance; $19 camping* ☉ *Closed Tues.*

 ## Hotels

Tierra Madre

$$ | B&B/INN | FAMILY | Located 25 km (15½ miles) northeast of La Cruz, this remote eco-estate is made up of four hillside bungalows with stunning volcano views and a backdrop of Lake Nicaragua. **Pros:** gourmet farm-to-table meals; way off the beaten path; unique activities led by friendly and passionate owners. **Cons:** long muddy road; lots of insects in the area; Wi-Fi in common areas only.

$ *Rooms from: $120* ✉ *La Cruz* ✛ *25 km (15½ miles) northeast of La Cruz, 5 km (3 miles) from nearest village of Los Andes* ☎ *8705–4249* ⊕ *www.tierramadre. co.cr* ⤴ *4 bungalows* ⎤⎞ *Free Breakfast* ☞ *Two-night minimum stay.*

🏃 Activities

HIKING

Several trails to the beaches lead off the road before it becomes impassable to vehicles. The hike to Playa Naranjo (11 km [7 miles] west of La Casona) requires good physical condition and lots of water. You can get a map of the trails at the park entrance. Call ahead for seasonal closures.

Casona Nature-Trail Loop (*Sendero Indio Desnudo*)

HIKING & WALKING | The short (about 1-km [½-mile]) Casona nature-trail loop from the park headquarters is worth taking to get a brief sampling of the woods. Look for the handicap-accessible Indio Desnudo (Naked Indian) path, named after the local word for gumbo-limbo trees. This is one of the few trails that doesn't get overly muddy, even after a heavy rain in wet season. Carry plenty of water and insect repellent. ✉ *Santa Rosa National Park.*

SURFING

Witch's Rock (*Pena Bruja*)

SURFING | Witch's Rock towers offshore over a near-perfect beach break off Playa Naranjo in Santa Rosa National Park. The massive boulder once howled and whistled, causing passersby to believe the rock was haunted by a witch. In reality, it was only the offshore winds billowing between the water and stone that made the eerie sound. Years of erosion have silenced the howling, but the boulder, and the name, remain. If you are interested in surfing Witch's Rock, take a boat tour from Playas del Coco, Playa Hermosa, or Playa Tamarindo, to the south. Tropic Surf offers surf trips to

Witch's Rock from its shop at Four Seasons Resort Peninsula Papagayo. ✉ *Santa Rosa National Park.*

Guanacaste National Park

30 km (18 miles) north of Liberia.

The 325-square-km (125-square-mile) park was created to preserve rain forests around Cacao Volcano and Orosi Volcano.

👁 Sights

Guanacaste National Park

NATIONAL PARK | The 325-square-km (125-square-mile) Parque Nacional Guanacaste, bordering the east side of the Pan-American Highway 30 km (18 miles) north of Liberia, was created to preserve rain forests around Cacao Volcano (5,443 feet) and Orosi Volcano (4,879 feet), which are seasonally inhabited by migrant wildlife from Santa Rosa National Park. The connecting border of these two national parks serves as a biological corridor for birds resettling between cloud, rain, and dry forests. Popular with researchers, the park is just beginning to cater to tourists. There are a few trails for a leisurely stroll and a bird observation deck; if you want a serious hike, it's best to hire a professional guide. In rainy season, roads are impassable; a 4WD vehicle is required year-round. Established under Dr. Daniel Janzen, the park is part of the Guanacaste Conservation Area, a mosaic of interdependent protected areas, parks, and refuges; the goal is to accommodate the migratory patterns of animals, from jaguars to tapirs. Much of the park's territory is cattle pasture, which is regenerating into new forest faster than predicted. Today the park has howler and capuchin monkeys, collared peccaries, white-tailed deer, pumas, sloths, coatis, bats, and more than 5,000 species of butterflies and moths. Among the 300 different birds are parakeets, hawks, cuckoos, and magpie-jays. ✉ *35 km (22 miles) north of Liberia* ⬦ *Adjacent to Santa Rosa National Park* 🎟 *$15.*

Rincón de la Vieja National Park

25 km (15 miles) northeast of Liberia.

Wildlife, rivers, waterfalls, and mud baths are just the tip of the volcano when it comes to the natural wonders of Rincón de la Vieja National Park. Dominating the scenery east of the Pan-American Highway just north of bustling Liberia, the national park's 34,800 acres are home to two peaks, the most impressive being Rincón de la Vieja at 6,254 feet, which is often enveloped in clouds. Expect to see monkeys, sloths, and birds in a single day's exploration.

■ TIP→ **If your vacation plans only include the Pacific Coast but you really want to visit a volcano, this is your chance. Rincón de la Vieja is a great alternative and much shorter trip than the more popular Arenal.**

For lodging, take your pick from working ranches, river lodges, rustic B&Bs, and garden villas; just be sure to rent a 4WD vehicle to reach the more remote properties, especially in rainy season. To get a taste of the area, there are plenty of activities that blend nature and adventure, like horseback riding, river rafting, ziplining, and hiking on a network of trails that set off from the Santa María ranger station and wind past hot springs, mud baths, and waterfalls. Lathering up with the volcanic mud softens the skin and detoxifies the body, and it makes for a fun photo op.

GETTING HERE AND AROUND

There are two park entrances on the volcano's southern slope: the less traveled one at Hacienda Santa María on the road leading northeast from Liberia (one hour),

where there is camping available; and the one at Las Pailas, past Curubandé off the Pan-American Highway. To get to Las Pailas entrance from Liberia, take the first entrance road 5 km (3 miles) northwest of Liberia off the Pan-American Highway. The turnoff is easy to miss—follow signs for Hacienda Guachipelín or the town of Curubandé. It's a 17-km (10½-mile) road, paved until the final stretch beyond Hacienda Guachipelín. Non–hotel guests must pay a small toll (about $1.50) to access the private road to the park entrance. The Santa María entrance is 25 km (15 miles) northeast of Liberia along the Colonia Blanca route, which follows the course of the Río Liberia. The turnoff from the Pan-American Highway to the hotels on the western slope of the volcano is 12 km (7 miles) northwest of Liberia, turning right at the road signed for Cañas Dulces. A 4WD vehicle is recommended for all these slow and bone-rattling rides.

◉ Sights

★ **Rincón de la Vieja National Park** (*Parque Nacional Volcán Rincón de la Vieja*)
NATIONAL PARK | It might be a trek to get here, but Rincón de la Vieja National Park doesn't disappoint with its multitude of natural wonders from hot springs and mud baths to refreshing waterfalls and a smoldering volcano. Dominating 140 square km (54 square miles) of the volcano's upper slopes, this tropical rain forest is usually blanketed in clouds, with a short dry transition between January and April. The park has two peaks: Santa María and the barren Rincón de la Vieja. The latter has an active crater, leading park authorities to close some trails, especially during wet season (check the status before you visit).

The wildlife here is diverse, with birds, deer, coyotes, monkeys, and armadillos. There are two main entrances: Santa María and Las Pailas; the latter is the most common place to enter the park and is closest to the trails (there's a $1.50 charge for private road use). The park does not have guides; we recommend the nature guides at Eco Explorer and Tours Your Way. Many of the attractions people visit in Rincón de la Vieja are accessible without actually entering the park, since the ranches that border it also hold significant forest and geothermal sites. (⇨ *For more information, see the highlighted listing in this chapter.*) ✉ *Rincón de la Vieja National Park* ☎ *2666–5051* 🎟 *$15.*

Hotels

★ Blue River Resort
$$ | **RESORT** | **FAMILY** | Named for the blue river that flows nearby, this property on the volcano's northern slope is worth the trek to experience the resort's hot springs, mud baths, butterfly gardens, adventure tours, and spacious rustic cabins with terrace-hammocks. **Pros:** family-friendly; great activities; nearby waterfalls. **Cons:** limited, somewhat pricey menu; Wi-Fi in common areas only; rough, unpaved road. [$] *Rooms from: $140* ✉ *Rincón de la Vieja National Park* ✣ *600 meters (1,968 feet) west of Río Celeste Bridge* ☎ *2206–5000, 2206–5506, 954/688–3646 in U.S.* 🌐 *www.blueriverresort.com* 🛏 *25 rooms* 🍴 *Free Breakfast.*

Borinquen Mountain Resort & Spa
$$$ | **RESORT** | The spacious villas and bungalows on this 570-acre ranch are lovely, and the room rate includes access to their hot springs, mud baths, and a Costa Rican breakfast. **Pros:** attractive, well-equipped bungalows; peaceful environment; lots of outdoor activities. **Cons:** Wi-Fi only in restaurant and reception areas; occasional sound of ATVs, golf carts, and leaf blowers; 12-km (7½-mile) unpaved road; far from park entrance. [$] *Rooms from: $180* ✉ *13 km (8 miles) northwest of Liberia on Pan-American Hwy., then 19 km (12 miles) north on dirt road toward Cañas Dulces, Rincón de la Vieja National Park* ☎ *2690–1900* 🌐 *www.borinquenresort.com* 🛏 *39 units* 🍴 *Free Breakfast.*

Buena Vista Del Rincón
$$ | **B&B/INN** | Beautiful views abound at this truly Costa Rican ecolodge, with rustic hacienda-style rooms and plenty of cultural activities. **Pros:** many activities; breathtaking views; Costa Rican culture. **Cons:** patchy Wi-Fi; mediocre food; rooms may be too basic for some. [$] *Rooms from: $121* ✉ *Buena Vista Del Rincón, Rincón de la Vieja National Park* ☎ *506/2690–1414* 🌐 *www.buenavistadelrincon.com* 🛏 *76 rooms* 🍴 *Free Breakfast.*

Hacienda Guachipelín
$$ | **HOTEL** | **FAMILY** | One of the best values in the Rincón area for hair-raising adventure and nature tours, this hotel also gets top billing for its comfortable rooms, excellent restaurant, and friendly service. **Pros:** near park entrance; lots of activities; excellent value; home-cooked Costa Rican cuisine. **Cons:** some rooms are near horse stables; $50 fee for check-out after noon; caters to large groups and day visitors. [$] *Rooms from: $119* ✉ *Rincón de la Vieja National Park* ✣ *17 km (10 miles) northeast of Pan-American Hwy., on road to Las Pailas park entrance* ☎ *2666–8075, 888/730–3840 toll-free in U.S.* 🌐 *www.guachipelin.com* 🛏 *66 rooms* 🍴 *Free Breakfast.*

Activities

TOUR OPERATORS

★ Buena Vista Del Rincón Eco Adventure Park
HORSEBACK RIDING | An hour's drive west of the national park, this lodge lies on a large ranch where visitors enjoy horseback riding, waterfall hikes, a canopy tour, hanging bridges, and hot springs. Tours are $20 to $50 per person; a combination tour that lasts six to seven hours costs $85, including lunch. ✉ *Rincón de la Vieja National Park* ✣ *Western slope of*

volcano, 10 km (6 miles) north of Cañas Dulces, near Borinquen Mountain Resort ☎ *2690–1414 in Liberia* ⊕ *buenavistadelrincon.com* 🖅 *From $20.*

★ Hacienda Guachipelín Adventure Tours
HORSEBACK RIDING | This experienced outfitter has the most exciting tours in the area, including horseback riding, river tubing, hot springs and mud baths, guided waterfall hikes, and hikes on the slopes of the national park volcano (from $27 to $65). The popular canopy tour includes rock climbing, rappelling, ziplines, suspension bridges, and a Tarzan swing. The one-day, all-you-can-do adventure pass, including lunch, is a great deal for $105. ⊠ *Road to Rincón de la Vieja National Park, Rincón de la Vieja National Park* ☎ *2690–2900, 888/730–3840 toll-free in U.S.* ⊕ *www.guachipelin.com* 🖅 *From $27.*

Sensoria
ECOTOURISM | If you want to experience the area's natural attractions without all the adrenaline-pumping activities, Sensoria has peaceful jungle trails, waterfalls, pools, and an observation tower. The entrance fee includes lunch and a guided three-hour hike during which you'll visit vibrant blue waterfalls, hot springs, and natural pools. Bring a change of clothes, bug spray, and water shoes. The hiking tour begins daily at 9:30 am. Tours are by reservation only, and no children under six are allowed. ⊠ *Rincón de la Vieja National Park* ✛ *From Pan-American Hwy., turn right toward Quebrada Grande. Turn left toward Dos Ríos. Left at high school and continue toward Buenos Aires de Upala. Turn right at sign for "AyA." Follow signs for Sensoria and continue 3.7 km (2.3 miles) to entrance* ☎ *506/8955-4971* ⊕ *www.sensoria.cr* 🖅 *$125* ☞ *Reservation only.*

Tours Your Way
GUIDED TOURS | Playas del Coco–based Mainor Lara Bustos guides tours to Rincón de la Vieja or Palo Verde for $120, including transportation, entrance fees, lunch, and snacks. Ask about family discounts. ⊠ *Rincón de la Vieja National Park* ☎ *8820–1829* ⊕ *www.tours-your-way.com.*

HIKING
Nearly all the lodges and outfitters in the area offer guided hikes through the park to the fumaroles, hot springs, waterfalls, and (when possible) to the summit or the edge of the active crater.

If you're doing a self-guided hike, stop for trail maps and hiking information at the park stations at both entrance gates. To give yourself enough time to complete the longer hikes, make sure you start out between 7 and 9 am.

La Cangreja Waterfall Loop
HIKING & WALKING | A popular hike out of Las Pailas is the four-hour 10-km (6-mile) Cangreja Waterfall loop, passing through beautiful primary forests and windswept savannas. The *catarata* (waterfall) has a cool swimming hole below; the surrounding rocks have pockets of hot springs. Check with park rangers to make sure this trail is open. Entry closes at noon; the trail is closed Saturday, Sunday, and Monday. ⊠ *Rincón de la Vieja National Park* ⊕ *www.acguanacaste.ac.cr* 🖅 *$17.*

Loop Through the Park (Las Pailas)
HIKING & WALKING | A less strenuous option than the trail to the summit is the fascinating 3-km (2-mile) loop through the park, which takes about two hours to complete, starting at Las Pailas entrance. Along the well-marked trail you'll see fumaroles exuding steam, a *volcancito* (little volcano), and Las Pailas, the boiling mud fields named after pots used for boiling down sugarcane. From the mud pots, a spur trail leads 5 km (3 miles) to a

series of hot springs. If you tread softly in the nearby forest, you may spot animals such as howler, capuchin, and spider monkeys, as well as raccoonlike coatis looking for handouts. Remember the cardinal rule of wildlife encounters: don't feed the animals. ⊠ *Rincón de la Vieja National Park* ⊕ *www.acguanacaste. ac.cr/turismo/sector-pailas* 🎫 *$17.*

HORSEBACK RIDING

Borinquen Mountain Resort & Spa

HORSEBACK RIDING | A day package here begins with a horseback ride and a 90-minute canopy tour, followed by lunch and free time to soak in the hotel's hot springs and relax in the natural steam bath. ⊠ *12 km (7½ miles) northwest of Liberia on the Pan-American Hwy., then 23 km (14 miles) north on the dirt road that passes Cañas Dulces, Rincón de la Vieja National Park* ☎ *8418–0101* ⊕ *www. borinquenresort.com* 🎫 *From $65.*

Buena Vista Del Rincón

HORSEBACK RIDING | This lodge and tour operator has horseback trips to hot springs and waterfalls. If not everyone in your party is a horse lover, tractor transport ($35) is available to the hot springs as well. ⊠ *Western slope of volcano, 10 km (6 miles) north of Cañas Dulces, near Borinquen Mountain Resort, Rincón de la Vieja National Park* ⊕ *buenavistadelrincon.com* 🎫 *From $60.*

Hacienda Guachipelín

HORSEBACK RIDING | This is the premier working ranch in the area, with more than 100 well-bred and well-trained horses, and miles of trails to three waterfalls, tropical dry forest, and hot springs. In addition to horseback tours, the Hacienda also offers a cowboy-for-a-day tour that includes harnessing your horse, rounding up cattle, and milking a cow. ⊠ *Hacienda Guachipelín, Rincón de la Vieja National Park* ☎ *2690–2900, 888/730–3840 toll-free in U.S. or Canada* ⊕ *www.guachipelin.com* 🎫 *Horseback tours from $35; cowboy-for-a-day tour $70.*

Liberia

214 km (133 miles, 4–5 hrs) northwest of San José.

Once a dusty cattle-market town, Liberia has galloped toward modernization, becoming the commercial, as well as the administrative, capital of Guanacaste. There are still a few vestiges of its colonial past on quieter side streets. But Liberia has virtually become one big shopping mall, complete with fast-food restaurants, familiar superstores, and a multiplex theater. Walk a couple of blocks south of the main street along Calle Real, though, and you can still find some of the whitewashed adobe houses for which Liberia was nicknamed the "White City," as well as some grand town houses that recall the city's glory days. A few have been restored and are now hotels and cafés. Liberia today is essentially a good place to have a meal and make a bank stop at any one of a dozen banks, including Scotiabank, Citibank, and HSBC. Liberia can also serve as a base for day trips to Santa Rosa and Rincón de la Vieja national parks. Keep in mind that Liberia is the hottest city in Costa Rica, getting up to 115°F (46°C) in April. The drive from San José takes between four and five hours, so it makes sense to fly directly into Liberia if you're going only to the North Pacific. It's easy to rent a car near the airport.

GETTING HERE AND AROUND

From San José, follow the Pan-American Highway west past the Puntarenas exit, then north past Cañas to Liberia. The road is paved and in decent condition... for Costa Rica. It's a heavily traveled truck and bus route, and there are miles and miles where it is impossible to pass, but many drivers try, making this a dangerous road. Hourly direct buses leave San José for Liberia each day, and there are half a dozen daily flights, so it might be worth busing or flying to Liberia and

Did You Know?

In the geothermal areas around Rincón de la Vieja, you'll find mud pots (pools of bubbling mud), fumaroles (holes that emit steam and gases), and hot springs.

renting a car from here. There are many international flights directly into Liberia.

The *avenidas* (avenues) officially run east–west, whereas the *calles* (streets) run north–south. Liberia is not too big to walk easily, but there are always taxis lined up around the pleasant central park.

RENTAL CARS Alamo. ✉ *Liberia* ✣ *2 km (1 mile) northeast of Liberia airport* ☎ *2668–1111, 800/522–9696 in U.S..* **Budget.** ✉ *1 km (½ mile) east of Liberia airport, Liberia* ☎ *2436–2061.* **Enterprise.** ✉ *Liberia* ✣ *2 km (1 mile) northeast of Liberia airport* ☎ *2242–7818* 🌐 *www.enterprise.com.* **Hertz.** ✉ *Hwy. 21, 3 km (2 miles) east of airport, Liberia* ☎ *4002–0712* 🌐 *hertz.com.* **Vamos Rent-A-Car.** ✉ *5 km (3 miles) east of Liberia Airport on Hwy. 21, Liberia* ☎ *4000–0557, 800/601–8806 from U.S., 213/261–8586 text from the U.S.* 🌐 *www.vamosrentacar.com.*

ESSENTIALS

BANK/ATM Banco de Costa Rica. ✉ *C. Ctl., Avda. 1, diagonally across from central park, Liberia* ☎ *2666–9002.*

HOSPITAL Liberia Hospital. (*San Rafael Arcangel Medical Center*) ✉ *North end of town, Liberia* ✣ *Near Ascención Esquivel School* ☎ *2666–1717.*

PHARMACY Farmacia Lux. ✉ *Avda. 25 de Julio, Liberia* ✣ *In front of Super Compro, 100 meters (328 feet) west of the park* ☎ *2665–1002.*

POST OFFICE Correo. ✉ *Near Banco Nacional, Liberia* ✣ *300 meters (984 feet) west of hwy., 200 meters (656 feet) north of Avda. Ctl.* ☎ *2666–1649.*

🍴 Restaurants

Restaurante Café Europa (*Panaderia Alemana*)

$$$ | GERMAN | FAMILY | The aroma of baking bread is irresistible as you pass this German bakery, just south of the Liberia airport, whose baked goods are delivered all over the peninsula. The display case is filled with tempting strudels, Bundt cakes, and flaky fruit pastries. **Known for:** savory scallops; beer garden with a playground for the kids; apple strudel and other tempting bakery desserts. [$] *Average main: $16* ✉ *Liberia* ✣ *5 km (3 miles) west of Liberia airport* ☎ *8361–2777, 2668–1081* 🌐 *www.panaleman.com.*

🛏 Hotels

Hilton Garden Inn Liberia Airport

$$$ | HOTEL | Comfortable and convenient, especially if you're catching an early-morning flight or you need a break from driving before heading south to the beach, this five-story contemporary Hilton has all the mod cons, including Wi-Fi, HDTVs, microwaves, and refrigerators. **Pros:** kids under 12 stay free; excellent amenities; free shuttle to and from airport. **Cons:** service is inconsistent; some airplane noise; no shaded parking area. [$] *Rooms from: $174* ✉ *Across from Liberia International Airport on main hwy., Liberia* ☎ *2690–8888* 🌐 *www.liberiaairport.hgi.com* 🛏 *169 rooms* 🍽 *No Meals.*

Papagayo Peninsula

47 km (29 miles) west of Liberia.

The Papagayo Peninsula, a crooked finger of land cradling the west side of Bahía Culebra (Snake Bay), enjoys guaranteed sun from January to April, making it a prime site for all-inclusive hotels catering to snowbirds escaping North American winters. Probably one of the most luxurious parts of Costa Rica, five large hotels are already situated around Papagayo Bay, and others are slated to be built here, all part of a government-sponsored development program modeled after Cancún. Just before the entrance to Andaz Resort is the impressive Marina Papagayo, where luxury yachts and sailboats dock. Although the hotels are reminiscent of their Caribbean counterparts, the beaches are distinctly Costa Rican, with brown sand and aquamarine water that grows cool from January to April. Isolation is the name of the game here, which means that getting out of the man-made "paradise" to explore anything off-property often entails a pricey tour.

High season here coincides with dry season, when the heat is intense and the landscape becomes brown and brittle. In the rainy season (August to December), the landscape is greener and lusher, and the prices a bit lower. The sparkling water and spectacular sunsets are beautiful year-round.

GETTING HERE AND AROUND

All hotels here have airport pickup. To get to the Four Seasons from the Liberia airport (the hotel refuses to put up directional signs in order to protect its privacy), drive 10 km (6 miles) south of Guardia, over the Río Tempisque Bridge, then take the turn on the right signed for Andaz Peninsula Papagayo Resort. Follow this road about 20 km (12 miles) to its end at the entrance to the resort. For Casa Conde Hotel, El Mangroove, and Secrets Papagayo, take the road toward Playa Panama.

Beaches

Playa Panama

BEACH | **FAMILY** | On the southern end of Culebra Bay, this calm beach with black sand stretches 2 km (1 mile), and is frequented by guests staying at nearby El Mangroove resort and Casa Conde Beachfront Hotel. It's a great beach to visit with kids if you're staying in nearby Play Del Coco as well. Devoid of rocks and waves, the water is virtually flat, making this a popular spot for stand-up paddleboarding, kayaking, and swimming. There's a wooden shack next to El Mangroove offering overpriced water activities and equipment. Local vendors stand beachside, selling everything from sarongs to snow cones. With a minimum of six people, you can organize a snorkeling tour on a boat to the outer bay. There isn't much shade on the sand, but a grassy area between the resorts and the beach is lined with swaying palms and mesquite trees. A path meanders from one end of the bay to the other, meaning you can stroll without getting too much sun. There's guarded parking ($1 tip) between the two hotels. **Amenities:** food and drink; water sports. **Best for:** kayaking; swimming; walking. ✉ *Playa Panama, at Culebra Bay, in front of El Mangroove.*

Restaurants

Makoko

$$$ | **INTERNATIONAL** | At El Mangroove's trendy poolside restaurant, guests can dine with a glimpse of the ocean or head indoors to the more formal dining room enclosed in glass. Most ingredients are locally grown, and nearly every item on the menu is organic, including the grass-fed beef. **Known for:** Worcestershire-glazed short ribs slow-cooked for 24 hours; extensive wine list; seared scallops. [$] *Average main: $22* ✉ *At intersection near Hilton Resort, Playa Arenilla* ☎ *4701–0000* 🌐 *www.elmangroove.net* 🕒 *No lunch.*

Hotels

Andaz Costa Rica Resort at Peninsula Papagayo

$$$$ | **RESORT** | Earth tones and natural details prevail in this Hyatt property created by architect Ronald Zürcher, who utilized indigenous woods, sugarcane, and bamboo in the design of the rooms, each contemporary and bright with ocean views. **Pros:** friendly staff; free Kids' Club; design reflects natural surroundings. **Cons:** rooms have dim lighting; small and rocky beach; pricey meals. [$] *Rooms from: $927* ✉ *Peninsula Papagayo, next to Four Seasons Resort, Papagayo Peninsula* ☎ *2690–1234* 🌐 *www.andazpapagayo.com* 🛏 *153 rooms* 🍴 *No Meals.*

Casa Conde Beachfront Hotel

$$$$ | **HOTEL** | **FAMILY** | Spread over verdant grounds just behind relatively pristine Playa Panama, this all-inclusive property has an excellent location with bay views, balmy breezes, and a huge swimming pool. **Pros:** spacious rooms; immaculate grounds; close to beach. **Cons:** rooms near pool can be noisy; no activities; early check-ins cost $25 per person. [$] *Rooms from: $400* ✉ *Playa Panama, 3 km (2 miles) north of Playa Hermosa* ☎ *2586–7300 San José office, 2672–1008* 🌐 *www.ccbeachfront.com* 🛏 *50 rooms* 🍴 *All-Inclusive.*

El Mangroove

$$$$ | **HOTEL** | Barefoot luxury abounds at this hip boutique hotel where an airy courtyard leads to a 45-meter pool lined with beach bungalows and modern rooms. **Pros:** 24-hour room service; nice gym and spa; gorgeous rain showers; all-inclusive plan available. **Cons:** mosquitoes in common areas; staff lack attention to detail; poolside cabana costs $150 per day; only two rooms have ocean views. [$] *Rooms from: $395* ✉ *Bahia Papagayo, at Playa Panama, at intersection before Hilton Resort, Playa Arenilla* ☎ *4701–0000, 855/219–9371* 🌐 *www.elmangroove.net* 🛏 *85 rooms* 🍴 *No Meals.*

★ **Four Seasons Resort Costa Rica**

$$$$ | **RESORT** | With an indulgent spa, restaurants, and retail boutiques, Four Seasons is one of the most luxurious hotels in Costa Rica, but it's the unparalleled service and secluded location between two golden-sand beaches that make this resort one of a kind. **Pros:** impeccable service; lovely beach; surf trips to Witch's Rock. **Cons:** 30 minutes from main road; expensive; breakfast not included. [$] *Rooms from: $1,630* ✉ *25 km (15 miles) west of Guardia* ✥ *Follow signs to Andaz Resort and continue to end of road* ☎ *2696–0000, 800/781–5700 in U.S and Canada* 🌐 *www.fourseasons.com/costarica* 🛏 *159 units* 🍴 *No Meals.*

Activities

CANOPY TOUR

Witch's Rock Canopy Tour

ZIP LINING | Taking advantage of one of the few remaining patches of dry tropical forest on the Papagayo Peninsula, Witch's Rock Canopy Tour gives you your money's worth: 24 platforms, with a thrilling 1,485-foot cable zip between two of them; three hanging bridges; a waterfall in rainy season; and hiking trails. The 1½-hour tour is $95 per person; includes transportation from area hotels. ✥ *On road to Four Seasons Resort, 17 km (10 miles) west of DYI Center on main hwy. from Liberia* ☎ *6060–1631, 2696–7103* 🌐 *www.witchsrockcanopy.com* 🎟 *From $95.*

GOLF

Four Seasons Golf Course at Peninsula Papagayo

GOLF | Teeing off from one of the highest points on the peninsula, this 18-hole, par-72 championship course was designed by Arnold Palmer and has breathtaking views on every play. Surrounded by ocean and forest, you're likely to encounter howler and white-faced monkeys during your game. Several holes are perched on cliffs backed by ocean, like hole 17 with spectacular views from both the tee and the green. Increasing the challenge are tough drops from the tees and small greens. Signature hole 6 demands skill; it's a long 446-yard par 4 with a tee shot that plays 200 feet downhill to a valley. In addition to the award-winning course, there's a driving range, a sand-bunker practice area, putting and chipping greens, and a pro shop. Tee times are offered from 7 am to 4 pm. You can rent clubs for $85, and if you're staying at the hotel you can enjoy an all-you-can-play during your stay for $750. ✉ *Four Seasons Resort Costa Rica* ✥ *26 km (16 miles) north of Liberia, follow signs to Andaz Resort* ☎ *2696–0000* 🌐 *www.fourseasons.com/costarica* 🎟 *$240 morning for outside guests, $175 afternoon* ⛳ *18 holes, 6800 yards, par 72.*

SURFING
Tropic Surf

SURFING | No one mixes surfing and luxury better than this highly professional outfitter, offering lessons ($110) and half-day excursions ($350) to Witch's Rock and Ollies Point aboard their fleet of boats. Their quiver is top-notch, ranging from shortboards to stand-up paddleboards. Trained instructors are on hand for all levels, delivering water and sunscreen while you surf. In addition to their location at Four Seasons Resort Peninsula Papagayo, they have more than 20 destinations worldwide. ⊠ *Four Seasons Peninsula Papagayo* ⊕ *www. tropicsurf.net* ✆ *From $110.*

Playa Hermosa

27 km (17 miles) southwest of Liberia airport.

Beautiful Playa Hermosa, once a laid-back fishing community, has grown exponentially with condominiums and villas covering the scrubby hills overlooking the wide, curved beach. Warm, swimmable water, prime dive sites, choice fishing grounds, and sunset views of the Papagayo Peninsula are all reasons why Canadian and American expatriates are buying condos here. In the early morning, though, Playa Hermosa is still the kind of place where the beach is the town's main thoroughfare, filled with joggers, people walking their dogs, and families out for a stroll. Not to be confused with the mainland surfers' beach of the same name south of Jacó, this Playa Hermosa has long been occupied by small hotels, restaurants, and homes along the length of the beach, so the newer hotel behemoths and other developments are forced to set up shop off the beach or up on the surrounding hillsides.

GETTING HERE AND AROUND

Heading south from Liberia along Highway 21, take the turnoff in Comunidad signed for Playa Hermosa and Playas del Coco. Playa Hermosa is about 15 km (9 miles) northwest. The paved road forks after the small town of Sardinal, the right fork heading into Hermosa and the left leading to Playas del Coco. Local directions usually refer to the first and second entrance roads to the beach, the first entrance being the southern one. There is no through-beachfront road, so you have to approach the beach from either of these two roads. Transportes La Pampa buses leave from Liberia for Playa Hermosa daily starting at 4:40 am (to get workers to their hotel jobs), then at 7:30 and 11:30 am and 3:30 pm. The trip takes around an hour. A taxi from Playa Hermosa to Playas del Coco costs about $15 and takes about 15 minutes.

ESSENTIALS

Playa Hermosa has a large supermarket, Luperón, on the main road, between the first and second beach entrances, open 8 am to 9 pm most days, where you can stock up on just about everything you need—food, wine, liquor, toiletries, and fresh-baked bread. There's even a pharmacy.

 Beaches

Playa Hermosa

BEACH | Not to be confused with the surfers' beach near Jacó by the same name, Playa Hermosa's 2-km-long (1-mile-long) crescent of dark-gray volcanic sand attracts heat, making the early morning or late afternoon the best time to visit (with the latter providing spectacular sunsets). The beach fronts a line of shade trees, so there's a welcome respite from the heat of the sun. The crystal clear water—it's a Blue Flag beach—is usually calm, with no strong currents and with comfortable temperatures of 23°C to 27°C (74°F to 80°F). For offshore diving, there's an average visibility of 20 feet, and rock reefs that attract large schools of fish, sea turtles, sharks, manta rays, and moray eels. Sea views are as picturesque as they get, with bobbing fishing boats, jagged profiles of coastline, rocky outcroppings, and at night the twinkling lights of the Four Seasons Resort across the bay. At the beach's north end, low tide creates wide, rock-lined tidal pools. Food and drinks are available at Hotel El Velero. Amenities: food and drink; water sports. Best for: swimming; walking. ⊠ *Playa Hermosa*.

Restaurants

Aqua Sport

$$ | PERUVIAN | There's not much "aqua sport" going on at this Peruvian beachfront restaurant, unless drinking margaritas in a hammock somehow qualifies. It's the kind of place you drop by on day one, and find yourself coming back to for the remainder of your vacation—blame the setting of Adirondack chairs lining the beach combined with fresh fish like grilled snapper served with shoestring fries. **Known for:** cheerful location on the beach with a tree swing for the littles; Tato burger—juicy beef patty with bacon, cream cheese, and whiskey; delectable fish tacos. $ *Average main: $14* ⊠ *Playa Hermosa* ⊹ *2nd entrance to Playa Hermosa, at beach* ☎ *2672–0151*.

Ginger Restaurant Bar

$$$ | TAPAS | This tapas restaurant, featuring Asian and Mediterranean flavors, is in a modern glass-and-steel tree house that's cantilevered on the side of a hill and includes a spacious deck. Delectable appetizer-size offerings include seared pepper-crusted tuna atop pickled ginger slaw, or panfried sea bass fillets with a divine ginger-and-mandarin-orange butter sauce. **Known for:** pavlova; small plates, tapas-size dishes to share; spring rolls. $ *Average main: $18* ⊠ *Main hwy., south of Hotel Condovac, Playa Hermosa* ☎ *2672–0041* ⊕ *www.gingercostarica. com* ⊙ *Closed Mon. No lunch*.

Hotels

Hotel & Villas Huetares

$ | HOTEL | FAMILY | The best bargain in town, this long-established family hotel offers two-bedroom garden villas surrounding a central pool, as well as a two-story annex with 16 spacious rooms. **Pros:** close to beach; good kitchens; beautiful grounds and pool. **Cons:** basic rooms; weak Wi-Fi signal; lots of noise from kids, especially on weekends. $ *Rooms from: $72* ⊠ *Playa Hermosa* ⊹ *2nd entrance road to Playa Hermosa, 100 meters (328 feet) in from the main hwy.* ☎ *2672–0052, 4000–1274* ⊕ *huetarescr.com* ⊷ *40 rooms* ⊙ *Free Breakfast*.

★ Hotel Bosque del Mar Playa Hermosa

$$$ | HOTEL | This beachfront hotel on the southern end of Playa Hermosa features luxurious rooms and suites on a beautiful, spacious property shaded by century-old vine-draped trees. **Pros:** superb garden and beachfront location; beautiful restaurant; all rooms have terraces. **Cons:** mosquitoes; expensive for the area; some rooms near the pool are dark. $ *Rooms from: $226* ⊠ *Playa Hermosa* ⊹ *End of 1st entrance to Playa Hermosa* ☎ *2672–0046* ⊕ *www.hotelplayahermosa.com* ⊷ *33 units* ⊙ *No Meals*.

Villa del Sueño

$$ | HOTEL | Although the handsome garden restaurant is the main attraction at this elegant hotel, the spacious rooms and well-equipped villas are quite comfortable, too, and the hotel is about a block from the beach. **Pros:** excellent restaurant; good value; updated rooms. **Cons:** can be noisy when there's live music; mosquitoes; not on the beach. $ *Rooms from: $110* ⊠ *Playa Hermosa* ⊹ *1st entrance to Playa Hermosa, 500 meters (1,640 feet) west of main hwy.* ☎ *2672–0026, 800/378–8599* ⊕ *www. villadelsueno.com* ⊷ *44 units* ⊙ *Free Breakfast*.

▼ Nightlife

Hotel El Velero

THEMED ENTERTAINMENT | This lively beach-front hotel has live music select nights, and Taco Tuesday (half-off tacos). The crowd is thirtyish and up. ⊠ *Playa Hermosa ⊕ 2nd entrance to Playa Hermosa, then 100 meters (328 feet) north of Aqua Sport on beach road ☎ 2672–1017 ⊕ costaricahotel.net.*

Villa del Sueño

LIVE MUSIC | In high season, Villa del Sueño hosts live music on Friday and Sunday nights, as well as occasional concerts featuring top national bands and performers. ⊠ *1st entrance to Playa Hermosa, 500 meters (1,640 feet) west of main hwy., Playa Hermosa ☎ 2672–0026 ⊕ www.villadelsueno.com.*

Activities

BOATING AND FISHING

The fishing at Playa Hermosa is mostly close to the shores, and yields edible fish like dorado (mahimahi), snapper, amberjack, tuna, and wahoo. Roosterfish, marlin, and sailfish are all catch-and-release. Some local restaurants are happy to cook your catch for you. You can rent a boat or snorkel with **North Pacific Tours.** Most Hermosa-based snorkeling companies head to nearby spots where you may see turtles, eagle rays, eels, parrotfish, snapper, puffer fish, and angelfish. Start out early when waters are calm.

Charlie's Adventure

BOATING | This tour company organizes snorkeling and beach barbecue trips in the morning and at sunset. ⊠ *Panama Beach, Playa Hermosa ☎ 8842–9219, 2697–0594 (24 hrs) ⊕ www.facebook.com/CharliesAdventureTravel ⊠ From $85.*

Papagayo Gulf Sport Fishing–North Pacific Tours

BOATING | Based in Playa Hermosa, this reliable outfitter has private and customized charters for fishing, surfing, and snorkeling tours aboard a 28-foot center-console panga. They run various fishing tours in the area. ⊠ *Playa Hermosa ☎ 8398–8129 ⊕ www.northpacifictours.com ⊠ Tours from $60; half-day fishing excursion $400.*

Playas del Coco

25 km (16 miles) southwest of Liberia airport, 10 km (6 miles) south of Playa Hermosa.

Noisy, colorful, and interesting, Playas del Coco has the best souvenir shopping, the most dive shops, and the liveliest nightlife and barhopping on this part of the coast. It's still a working fishing port, with a port captain's office, a fish market, and an ice factory for keeping the catch of the day fresh—not for cooling margaritas, although many are enjoyed here. The beach has a beautiful boardwalk with palm trees, benches, and cold showers. Coco has had an explosion of condominium and villa projects, along with new commercial development, including the upscale Pacifico Village shopping center at the entrance to town. This center boasts a flagship AutoMercado, the country's top grocery chain, as well as a bank, pharmacy, restaurants, fast-food chains, a UPS office, and a few clothing boutiques. Fresh seafood, myriad souvenir shops, and plenty of bars have always drawn tourists here, but Playas del Coco also has a high concentration of tour operators offering diving, fishing, and surfing excursions at remote breaks such as Ollie's Point and Witch's Rock. Because Coco is mere minutes from Playa Hermosa, however, you can just as easily enjoy those sports while staying at that more pleasant beach. If

7

Guanacaste **PLAYAS DEL COCO**

Continued on page 289

Choosing a Beach

From pulverized volcanic rock and steady waves to soft white sand and idyllic settings, all of the beaches along the Nicoya Peninsula's coast have their own distinct merits. Playa Tamarindo has a restaurant so close to the ocean the surf spray salts your food; playas Hermosa and Sámara are family-friendly spots with swimmable waters; and playas Langosta and Pelada are made for contemplative walks.

GUANACASTE PACIFIC COAST

Playa Tamarindo

1 Popular luxury resorts line the beaches of the **Papagayo Peninsula**.

2 **Playa Hermosa** is one of the few Costa Rican beaches with calm, crystal-clear waters.

3 Diving and fishing are the name of the game at **Playas del Coco** and its lively beach town.

4 **Playa Ocotal** is a quiet black-sand beach with great views, diving, and good snorkeling.

5 **Playa Pan de Azúcar** is practically deserted once you get there.

6 **Playa Potrero** is the jumping-off point for diving trips to the Catalina Islands.

7 Busy white-sand **Playa Flamingo** is ideal for swimming and sunning.

8 Shells sprinkle the sand at chilled-out **Playa Conchal**, where you'll find the area's best snorkeling.

9 Lively **Tamarindo** is a hyped-up surfing and water-sports beach with wild nightlife. Tamarindo and Grande are great places to take surf lessons.

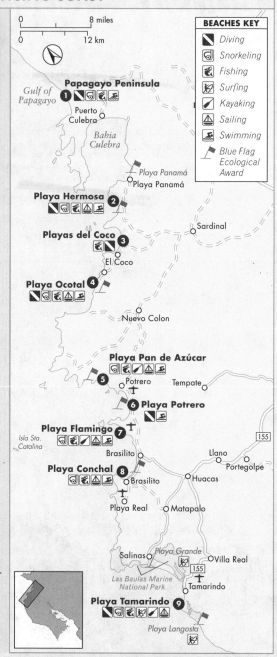

BEACHES KEY

Diving
Snorkeling
Fishing
Surfing
Kayaking
Sailing
Swimming
Blue Flag Ecological Award

Gulf of Papagayo

Papagayo Peninsula 1

Puerto Culebra

Bahía Culebra

Playa Panamá
Playa Panamá

Playa Hermosa 2

Sardinal

Playas del Coco 3

El Coco

Playa Ocotal 4

Nuevo Colon

Playa Pan de Azúcar 5

Potrero
Tempate

Playa Potrero 6

Playa Flamingo 7

Isla Sta. Catalina

Brasilito

Llano
Portegolpe

Playa Conchal 8

Brasilito
Huacas

Playa Real
Matapalo

Salinas
Playa Grande
Villa Real

Las Baulas Marine National Park
155
Tamarindo

Playa Tamarindo 9

Playa Langosta

0   8 miles
0   12 km

GUANACASTE AND NORTHERN NICOYA PENINSULA

(top) Playa Avellanas (bottom) Sunset at Sámara

❶ **Playa Langosta** is great for walks up its estuary and watching dramatic sunsets.

❷ **Playa Avellanas** is a perfect spot to relax with a cold drink between surf sessions.

❸ **Playa Negra** has some of Costa Rica's best surfing waves.

❹ Peaceful and difficult to reach, **Playa Junquillal** is all about relaxation.

❺ Hemmed in by rocks, **Playa Pelada** is staked out by territorial Tico surfers.

❻ Long, clean **Playa Guiones** is backed by dense jungle.

❼ **Sámara's** gentle waters make it perfect for kayakers, swimmers, and novice surfers.

❽ Perhaps the most beautiful beach in the country, **Playa Carrillo** fronts an idyllic half-moon bay.

❾ Rocky **Punta Islita** has interesting tidal pools to explore.

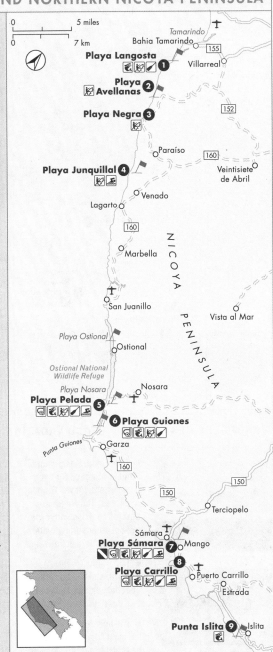

SOUTHERN NICOYA PENINSULA

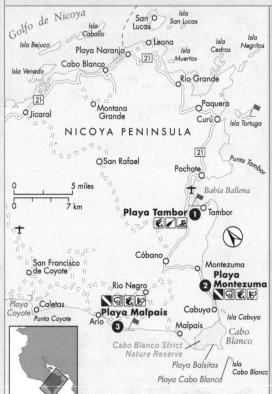

(top) Montezuma (bottom) Surfing at Malpaís

❶ Crescent-shaped, shallow **Playa Tambor** is flanked by an all-inclusive resort and a fishing village.

❷ **Montezuma's** off-beat town is as much a draw as its bayside beach.

❸ Some of the largest surfing waves in Costa Rica are at **Malpaís**.

MAKING THE BEST OF YOUR BEACH VACATION

■ Tamarindo, Nosara, and Sámara are good for beginning surfers. Playas Grande, Avellanas, and Negra are best left to those with experience; other surfing waters are somewhere in between.

■ Tamarindo, Nosara, Sámara, and Tambor are beaches with air service to San José.

■ The beach road connecting most Nicoya Peninsula beaches is hard to stomach any time of year, and virtually impassable during the August through December rains. Take easier inland routes instead.

■ Riptides are seriously dangerous and hardly any Costa Rican beaches have lifeguards; get information from your hotel about where to swim safely.

you like to shop and party, Coco's slightly raucous ambience is appealing.

GETTING HERE AND AROUND

The easy drive from the Liberia airport to Playas del Coco takes about 30 minutes. The paved highway turns into a grand, divided boulevard as you enter town; it ends at the beach. If you don't have a car, the best way to get here from Playa Hermosa is in a taxi, for about $20 one way. A taxi from the Liberia airport will run you around $30.

ESSENTIALS

BANKS/ATMS BAC San José. ✉ *At Pacific Village, next to AutoMercado, Playas del Coco.* **Banco Nacional.** ✉ *At entrance to town on main road, across street from Hard Rock Cafe, Playas del Coco.*

PHARMACY Farmacia Azul. ✉ *7 Plaza Colonial, Playas del Coco* ☎ *2670–0339* 🌐 *www.farmaciaazul.com.*

POST OFFICE Correo. ✉ *At entrance to town on main road, Playas del Coco* ✣ *100 meters (328 feet) south of Hotel Flor de Itabo.*

🍴 Restaurants

La Dolce Vita

$$ | ITALIAN | Two Italian brothers offer well-prepared Italian classics and thin-crust pizza, as well as some interesting seafood dishes like tuna tartare and tagliolini with crab in a cream sauce. For dessert there's an intriguing panna cotta or classic tiramisu. **Known for:** catch of the day; beautiful courtyard setting; homemade pasta. [$] *Average main: $14* ✉ *Playas del Coco* ✣ *In El Pueblito shopping center, 350 meters (1,148 feet) north along road running parallel to beach* ☎ *2670–1384.*

★ The Lookout

$$$ | SEAFOOD | As if the breathtaking view high in the hills above Playas del Coco weren't enough (you may recognize it from its feature on the television series *Restaurants on the Edge*), the innovative menu at one of the few oyster bars in Costa Rica takes it a step further. Try the oysters raw or grilled or order the tuna nachos alongside a spicy ginger margarita or watermelon mojito. **Known for:** tuna poke bowl; 17 Monkey Head Brewing company beers on tap; fresh raw oysters, delivered Wednesday. [$] *Average main: $20* ✉ *Rooftop of Chantel Suites, up hill in Vista Marina, Playas del Coco* ☎ *4033–7588* 🌐 *www.thelookoutcoco.com* ⏲ *Closed Mon.*

Santorini

$$ | GREEK | If you're in the mood for something more Mediterranean head to this open-air Greek restaurant for some moussaka or the fresh catch of the day prepared Greek-style—fried whole and served with potatoes and Mykonos salad. There are gluten-free and vegan options, just ask your server. **Known for:** authentic Greek food; baklava and homemade ice cream; freshly caught seafood in scrumptious preparations. [$] *Average main: $15* ✉ *Main St., next to Papagayos Seafood, Playas del Coco* ☎ *4703–6633.*

☕ Coffee and Quick Bites

Guayoyo Coffee House

$ | AMERICAN | An exuberant mix of American and Venezuelan favorites makes this breakfast spot a favorite of locals and tourists alike who come for the coffee and stay for the pillow-soft cinnamon rolls and other tasty baked goods. Make sure you try the chicken avo *chachapa* (a Venezuelan sweet corn pancake with shredded chicken in hogada sauce, cheese, avocado, and egg) or the eponymous *guayoyo* (a Venezuelan pour-over coffee), or a dirty chai latte. **Known for:** delicious coffee selection; baked goods; arepas and other Venezuelan delights. [$] *Average main: $8* ✉ *La Chorrera Shopping Center, Plaza Costa Mar, Playas del Coco* ☎ *2101–1398* 🌐 *guayoyo-coffee-house.business.site* ⏲ *No dinner.*

Hotels

La Puerta del Sol

$$ | HOTEL | Facing a formal garden with sculpted shrubs and a lovely pool, this tranquil enclosure just two blocks from the beach has airy, Mediterranean-style guest rooms splashed with tropical colors. **Pros:** intimate; comfortable; new bar and restaurant. **Cons:** hard beds; rooms lack charm; a few cats prowling the garden. $ *Rooms from: $115* ✉ *Playas del Coco* ✥ *180 meters (590 feet) to right (north) off main road to town* ☎ *2670–0195* 🌐 *lapuertadelsolhotel.com* 🛏 *9 rooms* 🍴 *Free Breakfast.*

Nightlife

Coconutz

BARS | Local expats meet up at this popular sports bar and grill, which has an all-day happy hour from 9 to 7, TVs for *Monday Night Football,* a full range of bar food, craft beer, and live music most nights. Tuesday features karaoke at 7:30. There's also free Wi-Fi, but don't expect to be able to focus on work over the noise. ✉ *Main road, across from El Coco Casino, Playas del Coco* ☎ *2670–1982* 🌐 *coconutzbar.com.*

Shopping

Souvenir stalls and shops line the main drag near the entrance to the beach.

Activities

BOATING

Marlin Del Rey

BOATING | FAMILY | With operations in Tamarindo and Playas del Coco, Marlin Del Rey offers sailing tours on their 65-foot catamaran. Trips will take you to quiet white-sand beaches and include snorkeling, lunch, and an open bar. Sunset tours depart at 1:30 pm. ✉ *Main St., Playas del Coco* ☎ *2653–1212, 877/827–8275 in U.S.* 🌐 *www.marlindelrey.com* 🎟 *$95 per person.*

DIVING AND SNORKELING

Half a dozen dive shops populate this small town. The standard price for a two-tank dive is $95; Catalina Island dives are $115. This coast doesn't have the coral reefs or the clear visibility of the Caribbean coast, but it does have a lot of plankton (hence the lower visibility) that feeds legions of fish, some of them really, really big. Manta rays and sharks (white-tipped, nurse, and bull varieties) are among the stars of the undersea show. It takes about 20 to 45 minutes to reach most dive sites.

Deep Blue Diving Adventures

SCUBA DIVING | This organization has daily scuba-diving trips to the top dive spots in the Papagayo Gulf and Catalina Islands. They also do open-water certification. ✉ *Corner of Chorrera and Cangrejo, Playas del Coco* ☎ *2670–1004* 🌐 *www.deepblue-diving.com* 🎟 *From $85.*

★ Rich Coast Diving

SCUBA DIVING | This longtime operator has enthusiastic guides and is the only PADI five-star CDC facility with the Green Star Award in Costa Rica. It offers daily fun dives, PADI courses, and local snorkeling trips. New divers can book a discovery session—a pool session with two dives for $175. ✉ *Main street, near intersection with road to Playa Ocotal, near Medical Center, Playas del Coco* ☎ *2670–0176* 🌐 *www.richcoastdiving.com* 🎟 *From $85 without equipment.*

Sirenas Diving Costa Rica

SCUBA DIVING | With more than 20 years of experience, this dive operation has a full range of scuba activities, from beginner training to open-water PADI certification. Multitank dives are organized at more than 20 sites. Guides and trainers are very good, and their safety standards have the DAN (Divers Alert Network) seal of approval. Diving trips are personalized and private, with no more than six people. Prices range from $150 for two-tank morning dives to $975 for the PADI open-water certification course, with discounts for more than one person. Courses are offered from their PADI dive boat in Playas del Coco, and there's no physical office, so reservations are essential. They also offer combo tours with any combination of fishing, surfing, diving, and snorkeling. ⊠ *Playas del Coco* ☎ *8481–0663, 8387–4710* ⊕ *www.sirenasdivingcostarica.com* ✉ *From $150.*

Summer Salt Dive Center

SCUBA DIVING | This longstanding small dive center is especially good for beginners, but great for every level. They focus on safety and fun in diving and snorkeling. ⊠ *Main St., Playas del Coco* ✛ *100 meters (328 feet) south of the park* ☎ *2670–0308* ⊕ *www.summer-salt.com* ✉ *From $80, plus $25 for equipment.*

FISHING

Fishing charter boats go out 24 to 64 km (15 to 40 miles) seeking yellowfin tuna, mahimahi, grouper, and red snapper close in, and sailfish, marlin, and roosterfish offshore (beyond 64 km [40 miles]).

Blue Marlin Sportfishing

FISHING | This downtown fishing-charter office has eight boats to choose from, ranging from a 30-foot boat for close-in fishing ($430 for a half day) to larger boats that go out to sea for a full day offshore all-inclusive ($1,650). Prices are for four to five fishers. ⊠ *Main street, south of police station, Playas del Coco* ☎ *6002–0720* ✉ *From $430.*

GOLF

Papagayo Golf & Country Club – Vista Ridge

GOLF | This 18-hole, par-72 course is affordable and just 10 minutes from Playas del Coco. You can play the whole course for $50, including a golf cart and a cooler with ice and water (and clubs if you need them), but don't expect the Four Seasons. The greens are small and slow once the afternoon winds kick in, with some challenging holes toward the back tees. Long drives through the rain forest mean you'll encounter plenty of wildlife while you play. Signature hole 18

(par 3) drives 171 yards directly through the towering trees. The first tee time is at 7:30, and the last is at noon. There's a driving range and putting green. ✛ *10 km (6 miles) southeast of Playas del Coco* ☎ *2697–0169, 8843–9598* ⊕ *www. facebook.com/papagayogolf* ✉ *$65 for 18 holes* ⚑. *18 holes, 6028 yards, par 72.*

SURFING

Witch's Rock and Ollie's Point

SURFING | These legendary surfing spots are no more than an hour's boat ride away from Playas del Coco off the coast of Santa Rosa National Park, you just need to pay the $15 park entrance fee. You can sign up for a surfing trip with any beach-town tour operator, but local authorities allow excursions to Witch's Rock and Ollie's Point to originate only from the main dock at Playas del Coco, in boats owned by local boat owners, in order to curb overcrowding and undue environmental stress. This is not a trip for a beginner. The 40-minute boat trip to Witch's Rock costs about $250, or $350 to surf both Witch's Rock and Ollie's Point, which is located an additional 20 minutes north. For those prices, your boat captain will spend the day waiting aboard while you surf. Luxury surf excursions to both breaks are also available through Tropic Surf, based at the Four Seasons Resort on Peninsula Papagayo. ⊠ *Playas del Coco.*

Playa Ocotal

3 km (2 miles) south of Playas del Coco.

Just a few minutes south of Playas del Coco, this beach couldn't be more different than its rapidly developing neighbor. Quiet and serene, there is little commercial development, aside from a couple of beachfront restaurants. A large resort hotel dominates the beach, and private condominium complexes and luxurious villas pile up on the steep hills overlooking the ocean. Bring your mask and flippers—the tranquil water here is perfect for snorkeling.

GETTING HERE AND AROUND

The drive is 10 minutes from Playas del Coco on a paved road to the gated entrance of Playa Ocotal. The road winds through a heavily populated Tico residential area, so be on the lookout, especially at night, for bicyclists without lights, children playing, or dogs, cows, and horses on the road. There are no buses from Playas del Coco to Ocotal, but it's about $6 by taxi.

Sights

The Monkey Farm

FARM/RANCH | Despite the name, you're likely to see more goats, ducks, chickens, pigs, and other farm animals than you are monkeys. During interactive tours, you can feed a baby goat, harvest and brew tea, and pet baby peacocks. Advanced reservations required. At this volunteer-run operation, animals are rescued, rehabilitated, and released back into the wild. At any given time, you might see reptiles, raccoons, and (usually) a monkey or two that are being treated for injuries. Keep in mind this is not a zoo, nor is it a tourist trap, meaning that animals roam free and the sanctuary survives on a donation basis. The sustainable farm has an impressive aquaponics setup and offers horseback-riding tours for all levels—$55 per hour in the jungle or $70 for two hours on the beach. ⊠ *Ocotal* ⊹ *On road from Playas del Coco to Ocotal, 1 km (½ mile) from Playa Ocotal* ☎ *8853–0165* ⊕ *www.themonkeyfarm.org* 🎫 *$10* ☯ *Closed Tues. and Thurs.*

Beaches

Playa Ocotal

BEACH | One of the most dramatic beaches in the country, this serene crescent of black-sand beach ringed by rocky cliffs contrasts nicely with the sparkling, clean turquoise water. It's only ½ km (¼ mile) long, but the views stretch for miles and include

nearby offshore islands and the jagged profile of the Santa Elena Peninsula 34 km (21 miles) away. This is prime fishing, diving, and relaxing territory. Right at the entrance to the Gulf of Papagayo, it's a good place for sportfishing enthusiasts to hole up between excursions. There's good diving at Las Corridas, just 1 km (½ mile) away, and excellent snorkeling in nearby coves and islands, as well as around the rocks at the east end of the beach. **Amenities:** food and drink. **Best for:** snorkeling. ⊠ *10-min drive south of Playas del Coco, Ocotal.*

Nightlife

Father Rooster

BARS | The best place to enjoy a quiet sunset margarita—or make that a "rooster-rita"—is at this laid-back bar and restaurant on the beach. You can relax on the wooden deck, or at the tables right on the sand, and enjoy a romantic dinner featuring fresh fish and Tex-Mex favorites. Portions here are huge, and there's free Wi-Fi, a pool table, a big-screen TV, and occasional live music to keep you entertained. It's open 11 to 10, though it does close for private parties so you may want to call ahead. Guests from the Four Seasons often anchor here for a drink before sailing back to Peninsula Papagayo. ⊠ *Ocotal* ⊹ *100 meters (328 feet) west of El Ocotal Beach Resort, 3 km (2 miles) south of Playas del Coco* ☎ *2670–1246* ⊕ *www.fatherrooster.com.*

Activities

DIVING AND SNORKELING

The rocky outcrop at the north end of the beach near Los Almendros is good for close-to-shore snorkeling.

Rocket Frog Divers

SCUBA DIVING | Rocket Frog promises a faster boat out to the dive site, leaving more time for diving. They offer local trips around Papagayo ($85), trips to Catalina Island ($135), and, depending on the season, they go to the Bat Islands, where

Did You Know?

Magnificent beaches and a dramatically sculpted shoreline are southern Guanacaste's trademarks. Here you'll find no shortage of wildlife-watching opportunities. Be sure to check out the tide pools that form on the rocky headlands at each end of Playa Ocotal.

you may see bull sharks ($165). You dive with knowledgeable guides—some with backgrounds in marine biology—for a unique perspective, and are likely to see rays, eels, tropical fish, and turtles. There are scuba courses for novices through instructors. ⊠ *Hotel Colono Beach, Playas del Coco* ✛ *50 meters (164 feet) west of Supercompro* ☎ *2670–1589, 315/222–8801 from U.S.* ⊕ *www.scuba-dive-costa-rica.com* ⊠ *From $85.*

Las Catalinas

16 km (10 miles) southwest of Playa Ocotal via Cam. del Cielo.

Take a stroll through the car-free pedestrian village of Las Catalinas, and though it may feel contradictory to walk through the new streets and feel like you've gone back in time—perhaps to a European village—that's where the magic begins. Let the kids play on the Tarzan rope swings while you lounge under the trees and take in views of Paya Danta, lounge in a hammock, or mosey to the surf shop for gelato, shave ice, or some of that famous Costa Rican coffee. Feeling ambitious? Bike on some of the 22 km (13 miles) of trails through the forest.

GETTING HERE AND AROUND

From the Liberia airport, take a right out of the airport and, after 10 km (6 miles), head right toward Huacas. After passing through Brasilito, you will reach Potrero. Go around the soccer field and turn right. Follow the "Las Catalinas" signs. Ecotrans offers shared rides and transfers to Las Catalinas. It's best to stock up on groceries and cash in Potrero—there's not much here in the way of markets.

 Beaches

Playa Danta

BEACH | Surfers will need to go elsewhere to find their waves; this natural beach, dotted with shade trees and with the Limonada restaurant a stone's throw away, has a low swell, which makes it great for kids, swimming, stand-up paddleboarding, and snorkeling. For those seeking something more remote, a quick hike north through the forest gets you to secluded Playa Dantita, your own private oasis. **Amenities:** food and drink. **Best for:** swimming. ⊠ *Playa Danta, Las Catalinas.*

Playa Pan de Azúcar

BEACH | A seemingly endless stretch of soft, light-color sand, this Blue Flag beach is the idyllic paradise people picture in their tropical dreams. There is only one property on the entire beach, the Hotel Sugar Beach, offering parking, restrooms, and a restaurant open to the public except during private events. The north end of the beach has some good snorkeling when the sea is calm—usually around low tide—and swimming out from the middle of the beach is relatively safe. Watch out for a few rocks on both sides of the cove, and if the swell is big, children and weak swimmers shouldn't go in past their waist. This beach is frequented by Ticos on weekends, but it is still relatively peaceful compared with neighboring beaches. Playa Penca, a short walk south along the beach, can be a good swimming beach as well. A large part of the attraction here is the forest that hems the beach, where you may see howler monkeys, black iguanas, magpie jays, trogons, and dozens of other bird species. **Amenities:** food and drink; parking (no fee); toilets. **Best for:** solitude; swimming. ⊠ *Playa Pan de Azúcar, Potrero.*

Restaurants

★ Limonada
$$ | LATIN AMERICAN | Friendly staff are at your service while you kick back on cushioned sectional seating or long wooden tables with your toes in the sand. The menu offers a fresh, casual, and creative take on Costa Rican food—don't miss the homemade guacamole, served with homemade tortilla chips, fresh veggies, and tostones. **Known for:** ceviche; jalapeño margaritas; unhurried, mellow atmosphere where kids can play while adults relax. [$] *Average main: $12* ✉ *Sugar Beach Rd., Playa Danta* ☎ *2654–4600* ⏲ *No breakfast.*

Sentido Norte
$$$ | COSTA RICAN | Come for the ocean views, stay for the bounty of Costa Rican cuisine. The chef here uses local favorites like chayote and hearts of palm, as well as the usual mahimahi and tuna, in innovative and delicious ways. **Known for:** sea-to-table ingredients; infinity pool; spectacular views. [$] *Average main: $19* ✉ *Las Catalinas* ☎ *2103–1200* 🌐 *www.sentidonorterestaurant.com.*

Hotels

★ Casa Chameleon
$$$$ | HOTEL | Tucked into the hillside with jaw-dropping panoramic views of the beach and the forest, this luxury hotel with a modern Balinese feel offers private and secluded villas for couples who want to unwind and take it easy. **Pros:** private saltwater plunge pool in every room; excellent restaurant; true barefoot elegance. **Cons:** adults only; no TVs; not directly on the beach. [$] *Rooms from: $845* ✉ *Playa Danta, just before you drive into Las Catalinas, Las Catalinas* ☎ *860/333–6199 from U.S., 2103–1200* 🌐 *www.casachameleonhotels.com/las-catalinas* 🛏 *16 rooms* 🍴 *Free Breakfast.*

Activities

Pura Vida Ride
BIKING | When it comes to bicycling in Costa Rica, many people ride the roads and take their lives into their own hands. Las Catalinas aims to change that with 22 km (13 miles) of mountain-biking trails and a large selection of mountain bikes to rent (prices start at $45 per hour). They also offer stand-up paddleboards and kayaks for the relatively calm bay. The multisport pass offers all of their toys for a full day for $100. ✉ *Las Catalinas at Playa Danta, Las Catalinas* ☎ *2654–6137* 🌐 *www.puravidaride.com* 🎫 *$45 per hr.*

Playa Potrero

4 km (2½ miles) north of Flamingo.

A typical small town with a school, church, and supermarket arranged around a soccer field, Potrero's main attraction is the long beach on the curve of Flamingo Bay. there are a smattering of small hotels and restaurants lining the road to town.

GETTING HERE AND AROUND

Just before crossing the bridge at the entrance to Flamingo, take the right fork signed for Playa Potrero. The road follows the shoreline. Local buses run from Flamingo to Potrero, but it's so close that you're better off taking a taxi.

ESSENTIALS

An ATM is available at the Flor de Pacifico center on the east side of Potrero. For groceries, there's Super Wendy across from Hotel Isolina and a small convenience store called Super Potrero next to Bar Las Brisas.

Beaches

Playa Potrero

BEACH | Stretching 4 km (2½ miles), this relatively undeveloped wide, brown-sand beach, across Potrero Bay from built-up Flamingo, catches ocean breezes and spectacular sunsets, which you can watch while bobbing in the warm, swimmable water. The pelican-patrolled beach is anchored at one end by the small Tico community of Potrero and at the other end by the Flamingo skyline. Although large houses and condominium developments have sprung up on any hill with a view, at beach level there is only one unimposing hotel and some low-lying private houses set well back from the beach; beachgoers never feel hemmed in or crowded, thanks to the local folks who keep the beach clean and deserving of Blue Flag status. The best area for swimming is midway between Flamingo and Potrero town, near the Bahía del Sol Hotel. About 10 km (6 miles) offshore lie the Catalina Islands, a barrier-island draw for divers and snorkelers; dive boats based in Flamingo can get there in 10 minutes. **Amenities:** food and drink. **Best for:** sunset; swimming; walking. ✉ *Playa Potrero, Potrero.*

Restaurants

The Beach House

$$ | **AMERICAN** | On the road connecting Potrero and Flamingo, this beachfront restaurant welcomes travelers with cheerful decor and witty signs like "Trespassers will be *offered a* shot." Water laps just a few feet from your table, and there's a pier out back, making this a popular lunch spot for American classics like hamburgers, chicken sandwiches, BLTs, and fried shrimp. The tasty sangrias and margaritas are sure to keep you dazed during sunset. **Known for:** breathtaking sunsets; volcano dessert to share; onion ring tower. [$] *Average main: $15* ✉ *800 meters (2,624 feet) north of Banco Nacional, Potrero* ✥ *North end of Playa Flamingo on way to Potrero* ☎ *2654–6203* 🌐 *www.beachhousecr.com.*

Café Del Sol

$$$ | **AMERICAN** | There's something for everyone any time of day at this three-story bakery/bistro/lounge/cocktail bar. In the morning, there are savory quiches and homemade granola as well as tartlets, pies, and every other type of sweets and bread (including gluten-free), while lunch has a more upscale menu with delectable soups (bouillabaisse), salads (poached lobster), sandwiches, and artisanal pizza. Dinner standouts are linguine *del mare* with lobster, shrimp, octopus, and clams, or tender grilled guava barbecue short ribs. **Known for:** rooftop cocktails; tapas like fresh-from-the-sea tuna tiradito and sea-bass ceviche; European-style patisserie breakfast noshes. [$] *Average main: $20* ✉ *Corner Of Hwy. 911, Potrero* 🌐 *cafedelsolcr.com* 🕓 *Closed Mon. and Tues.*

★ Costa Rica Sailing Center

$$ | **COSTA RICAN** | **FAMILY** | Relax beachside at the most laid-back yacht club you'll ever visit. There are bonfires after dark, live music, and sometimes an event like a chili cookoff or beer fest; plus, the kids can play in the pool while you enjoy a craft beer and good food. **Known for:** sunset views; sailing lessons and boat rentals; cold drinks. [$] *Average main: $14* ✉ *South of Hotel Bahía del Sol Surfside, Potrero* ☎ *2654–6056* 🌐 *www.facebook.com/costaricasailingcenter.*

The Shack

$$ | **AMERICAN** | A popular spot with expats who come for the cold beers, burritos, burgers, and *pura vida* vibe, The Shack successfully blends a Tico menu with American and British favorites. Grab a seat under the tin roof and try the fresh fish-and-chips, heaping nachos, cheeseburgers, or coconut shrimp. **Known for:** nachos to share; friendly owner and welcoming atmosphere; tantalizing breakfast choices. [$] *Average main: $10*

✉ *Potrero ✥ 200 meters (656 feet) west of El Castillo ☎ 2654–6038 🌐 theshackcr.com ⏲ Closed Sat.*

Hotels

★ Bahía del Sol

$$$ | RESORT | FAMILY | Snagging the best spot on the beach, Bahía del Sol has a gorgeous beachfront pool and comfortable rooms built around a garden of tropical shrubs and towering trees. **Pros:** on the beach; lovely grounds; excellent restaurant; friendly, first-rate service. **Cons:** hotel closed during October; some rooms need updates; front terraces are not very private. [$] *Rooms from: $180* ✉ *South end of Potrero Beach, Potrero* ☎ *2654–4671* 🌐 *www.bahiadelsolhotel.com* ⏲ *Closed Oct.* 🛏 *28 rooms* 🍴 *Free Breakfast.*

Hotel Isolina

$$ | HOTEL | This small hotel complex, a little island (*isolina*) of palm trees shading two pools, has basic and clean rooms with some of the best rates in the area. **Pros:** all rooms face the pool; affordable; secure parking; clean rooms. **Cons:** dated rooms need upgrades; Wi-Fi near reception only; loud A/C; breakfast not included for rooms with kitchenettes. [$] *Rooms from: $80* ✉ *Potrero* ✥ *100 meters (328 feet) north of Restaurant La Perla, on beach road* ☎ *8554–7483, 2654–4333* 🌐 *www.isolinabeach.com* 🛏 *34 units* 🍴 *Free Breakfast.*

Nightlife

Café del Sol Lounge and Rooftop Bar

COCKTAIL LOUNGES | Open sunset to midnight for tapas and cocktails, wine, and beer, this open-air lounge on the third floor has tasty drinks, fun music, dancing, guest DJs from New York, and a clubby feel you may not be expecting to find in the middle of the jungle. ✉ *Corner of Hwy. 911, Potrero* ☎ *7221–9855* 🌐 *www.cafedelsolcr.com/lounge.html.*

Perlas

BARS | Expats come for the microbrews, the satellite TV tuned to football, a game of Ping-Pong or pool, and the live music. Although the bar brings the people in, it's the food that keeps them there—braised oxtail, pork ribs, tuna poke, and burgers seem to justify another round. If you stay long enough, you'll find that the sweet homemade cheesecake goes surprising well with a bitter IPA. ✉ *C. Principal, Avda. 3, near the Shack, Potrero* ☎ *2654–4500* 🌐 *perlas.pub.*

Potrero Brewing Co.

BARS | In a land of Imperial, it's nice to find good beer. The friendly staff at this independent brewery serve up a tasty variety of stouts, IPAs, sours, lagers, and even root beer. They're conveniently located next to a beer garden of sorts, an outdoor food court with lots of options from burgers to pizza. Take a load off and sip a cold flight. ✉ *Ruta 911, Potrero* ✥ *200 meters (656 feet) east of Costa Rica Sailing Center, next to Panache Sailing* ☎ *506/4080–3783.*

Activities

DIVING

Catalina Islands

SCUBA DIVING | The Catalina Islands are a major destination for dive operations based all along the coast. These barrier islands are remarkable for their diversity and appeal to different levels of divers. On one side, the islands have 20- to 30-foot drops, great for beginners. The other side has deeper drops of 60 to 80 feet, better suited to more experienced divers. Among the 25 dive sites, the top are **Dirty Rock, Elephant Rock, Big Catalina,** and **Cupcake**. From January to March, when the water is colder, you are almost guaranteed manta ray sightings at these spots. Cownose and devil rays are also spotted here in large schools, as well as bull and white-tipped sharks, several types of eels, and an array of reef fish. Dive operators from Playa Hermosa south to Tamarindo offer trips to these islands. Reserve through your hotel, or directly through a dive shop. The islands are a 30-minute boat trip from Potrero Bay. ⊠ *Potrero.*

Playa Flamingo

80 km (50 miles) southwest of Liberia.

One of the first northern beaches to experience overdevelopment—a fact immortalized in the concrete towers that straggle up the hill above the bay—Flamingo still has some hidden charms. Perhaps most famous for its large sportfishing fleet, Flamingo's marina with over 200 docking spots for yachts gives the beach energy.

GETTING HERE AND AROUND

To get to Playa Flamingo from Liberia, drive 45 km (28 miles) south to Belén and then 35 km (22 miles) west on a good, paved road. The trip takes just over an hour. If you're coming from the Playas del Coco and Ocotal area, you can take a 16-km (10-mile) shortcut, called the "Monkey Trail," starting near Sardinal and emerging at Potrero. It's then 4 km (2½ miles) south to Flamingo. Attempt this only in dry season in a 4WD vehicle with GPS, because there are a few river crossings. The drive from San José takes 4½ hours, and costs about $230 per five-passenger van. You can also take a van from Liberia, a 50-minute scenic drive for around $90 per van. Ecotrans has transportation between Liberia airport and Playa Flamingo for $25 per person. *(See Bus in Travel Smart Costa Rica.)*

CONTACTS Ecotrans. ⊠ *Flamingo* ☎ *2654–5151, 954/353–6737 in U.S.* ⊕ *www. ecotranscostarica.com.*

ESSENTIALS

BANK/ATM Banco de Costa Rica. ⊠ *On the main road to Playa Flamingo, at intersection of road to Playa Potrero, across from Hotel Flamingo Marina Resort, Flamingo* ☎ *2654–4984.*

PHARMACY Farmacia La Plaza Flamingo. ⊠ *La Plaza Flamingo, Central Plaza next to the marina, Flamingo* ☎ *2654–5524.*

 Beaches

Playa Flamingo

BEACH | Hidden away to the southwest of the town, Flamingo Beach is picture-perfect, with almost-white sand sloping into a relatively calm sea, and buttonwood trees separating it from the road. This beach is great for swimming, with a fine-sand bottom and no strong currents, though there are a few submerged rocks in front of the Margaritaville Beach Resort, so you should swim a bit farther south. There's sometimes a bit of surf—if the waves are big, keep your eye on little paddlers. There is minimal shade along the beach's 1-km-long (½-mile-long) stretch, but Margaritaville's 5 O'Clock Somewhere Bar will deliver cocktails and serve food on the beach, or there is the Coco Loco restaurant on the south end. To find the beach, go straight as you enter town, and instead of going up the hill, turn left after the Margaritaville Beach Resort. **Amenities:** food and drink. **Best for:** swimming; walking. ⊠ *Southwest of town, in front of Flamingo Beach Resort, Flamingo.*

🍴 Restaurants

Angelina's

$$$ | **ITALIAN** | Guanacaste-inspired and locally sourced, the cuisine here pays tribute to the owner's Italian roots with dishes like lobster tail served with homemade black pasta. This restaurant is one of the area's more upscale places to dine, with marble tables, parchment lamps, and driftwood-integrated decor under an open-air patio. **Known for:** wide-ranging wine list; juicy steaks aged in custom Himalayan salt chamber; homemade thin-crust pizza. $ *Average main: $18* ⊠ *Plaza Commercial, 2nd fl.,*

Flamingo ☎ *2654–4839* 🌐 *www.angelinasplayaflamingo.com* 🕒 *No lunch.*

Coco Loco

$$ | **SEAFOOD** | The "crazy coconut" is one of the few places where you can dine with your toes in the sand while watching the sunset without anything separating you from the water. Start with the fried calamari or mixed ceviche, and move on to mains like the blackened swordfish wrap, the sesame-crusted yellowfin tuna taco, or the slow-cooked ribs with pineapple barbecue sauce. **Known for:** exquisite sunsets; signature drink served in a fresh coconut; tuna tacos. [$] *Average main: $10* ✉ *Flamingo* ✣ *On Playa Flamingo, 650 meters (2,132 feet) south of Flamingo Beach Resort* ☎ *2654–6242* 🌐 *cocolococostarica.com.*

Marie's Restaurant

$$ | **SEAFOOD** | A Flamingo institution serving beachgoers and locals for more than three decades, this popular restaurant has an array of sandwiches and salads, as well as reliably fresh seafood in large portions at reasonable prices. Settle in at one of the wooden tables beneath the ceiling fans and massive thatch roof for a traditional Costa Rican ceviche, avocado stuffed with shrimp, or heart of palm and *pejivalle* (palm fruit). **Known for:** kebabs featuring fish, chicken, and shrimp; whole red snapper; big breakfast menu. [$] *Average main: $15* ✉ *Plaza commercial center, near north end of beach, Flamingo* ☎ *2654–4136* 🌐 *www.mariesrestaurantcostarica.com.*

★ **The Surf Box**

$ | **AMERICAN** | Pop into this charming spot with "California cool" and cozy up in the corner booth, where the clean white walls set a backdrop for rainbow-hued books and surf-themed wall decor. Outside, be prepared to share the pura vida vibe and maybe a table—it's communal seating, and it gets busy during brunch with treats like homemade bagels with egg and avocado and rich ricotta pancakes. **Known for:** innovative smoothies with eco-friendly metal straws; Miami-inspired Cuban sandwich; acai bowls bursting with healthy goodness like fruit, chia, and homemade granola. [$] *Average main: $9* ✉ *Flamingo* ✣ *25 meters (82 feet) south of Banco Nacional* ☎ *8437–7128* ✉ *surfboxcr@gmail.com* 🕒 *No dinner Sun.*

Hotels

Hotel Guanacaste Lodge

$ | **HOTEL** | On the outskirts of Flamingo, a short drive from the beach, this Tico-run lodge offers basic accommodations for a fraction of what the town's big hotels charge. **Pros:** affordable; nice pool; large rooms. **Cons:** no in-room phones or safes; simple furnishings with few amenities; unattractive from the outside. [$] *Rooms from: $72* ✉ *Flamingo* ✣ *200 meters (656 feet) south of Potrero-Flamingo crossroads* ☎ *2654–4494* 🌐 *www.guanacastelodge.com* 🛏 *10 rooms* 🍴 *Free Breakfast.*

Margaritaville Beach Resort

$$$$ | **RESORT** | **FAMILY** | With a prime spot on the beach and a mammoth pool with swim-up bar to lounge around, this Jimmy Buffet–themed hotel is eager to please. **Pros:** updated rooms and suites; plenty of activities to keep kids busy; friendly staff. **Cons:** nice but not luxurious; some rooms have view of parking lot; food is just okay. [$] *Rooms from: $298* ✉ *Playa Flamingo Santa Cruz, Flamingo* ☎ *2654–4444* 🌐 *www.margaritavillebeachresortcostarica.com* 🛏 *120 rooms* 🍴 *All-Inclusive.*

Activities

BOATING

Lazy Lizard Catamaran Sailing Adventures

BOATING | Laze away a morning or afternoon sailing or sunbathing on either a 34- or 38-foot catamaran. You can swim or snorkel during the four-hour tour, starting at 8:30 am (minimum of eight people) and 2 pm. Included in the price is transportation from your hotel, snorkeling equipment, kayaks, drinks, and food. ⊠ *Flamingo Marina, Flamingo* ☎ *2654–5900* ⊕ *www.lazylizardsailing. com* ⊠ *From $85.*

DIVING AND SNORKELING

Flamingo offers the quickest access to the Catalina Islands, visible from its beach, where big schools of fish, manta rays, and other sea creatures gather. Coastal reefs to the north are visited on day trips that combine snorkeling with time on undeveloped beaches. Most diving excursions to Catalina Islands depart from Potrero Bay.

FISHING

There are plenty of sportfishing boats bobbing in Flamingo Bay from which to choose. Larger boats have moved to moorings in the Papagayo Marina near the Andaz Resort. In December the wind picks up, and many of the smaller, 31-foot-and-under boats head to calmer water farther south. But the wind brings cold water and abundant baitfish, which attract marlin (blue, black, and striped), Pacific sailfish, yellowfin tuna, wahoo, mahimahi, grouper, and red snapper. January to April is consequently prime catch-and-release season for billfish.

Brasilito and Playa Conchal

8 km (5 miles) south of Flamingo.

With a 15-minute stroll along the water's edge separating them, Brasilito and Conchal are worlds apart. Brasilito is a small, scruffy fishing village while Conchal is a lovely shell-sand beach dominated by the gated residential community and Westin Hotel. Brasilito has a jumble of houses huddled around its main square, which doubles as the soccer field. It's cluttered, noisy, and totally tico—a lively contrast to the controlled sophistication of Playa Conchal less than a mile south. Fishing boats moor just off a wide beach, and

The Guanacaste Tree
👁

Massive and wide spreading, with tiny leaflets and dark brown, earlike seedpods, the guanacaste tree is common through this region and is Costa Rica's national tree.

there's a range of seafood restaurants, from inexpensive *marisquerías* to a few notable establishments taking pride in organic and locally sourced ingredients.

GETTING HERE AND AROUND

The drive south to Brasilito from Flamingo is 10 minutes on a paved highway, or a 20-minute drive north from Tamarindo. Brasilito is just 1 km (½ mile) north of the entrance to the massive Westin Golf Resort & Spa and private Reserva Conchal housing development, which blocks the main road access to Playa Conchal. To reach Playa Conchal without driving through the guard-posted resort, turn left at the end of the town square in Brasilito and follow the dirt road across a stretch of beach and over a steep hill; the beach stretch is impassable at high tide. You can also park in Brasilito and take a 15-minute stroll along the beach to Playa Conchal. Buses run from Flamingo to Brasilito three times daily, at 7:30 and 11:30 am and 2:30 pm. A taxi from Flamingo is about $10.

ESSENTIALS

The closest bank and ATM are in Flamingo.

PHARMACY Farmacia El Cruce. ⊠ *Crossroads at Huacas, Playa Conchal* ☎ *2653–8787.*

The reclusive zebra moray eel likes to hide its entire body in rock or coral holes.

Beaches

Playa Brasilito

BEACH | Fishing boats moor just off this wide beach, about 3 km (2 miles) long with golden sand flecked with pebbles and a few rocks. The surf is a little stronger here than at Flamingo Beach, but the shallow, sandy bottom keeps it swimmable. There is one hotel almost on the beach, the quirky Hotel Brasilito. The sea is cleaner off nearby Playa Conchal, which is also more attractive. **Amenities:** food and drink. **Best for:** snorkeling; walking. ✉ *Playa Brasilito, Playa Conchal.*

Playa Conchal

BEACH | Named for the bits of broken shells that cover its base of fine white sand (the Spanish word for shell is *concha*), lovely Playa Conchal is an idyllic strand sloping steeply into aquamarine water and lined with trees. As its Blue Flag attests, it's clean and invites safe swimming. Although it's dominated by the sprawling Westin Playa Conchal, you don't need to stay at that all-inclusive resort to enjoy Conchal, since it's a short beach walk (or drive at low tide in a four-wheel-drive vehicle) south from Brasilito. The point that defines Conchal's northern end is hemmed by a lava-rock reef that is a popular snorkeling area—locals rent equipment on the beach. Waves can be powerful at times, so keep an eye on little ones. Despite the availability of shell jewelry, remember that shell collecting is not officially permitted on Costa Rican beaches. **Amenities:** food and drink. **Best for:** snorkeling; swimming; walking. ✉ *Playa Conchal, Playa Conchal.*

🍴 Restaurants

Gracia Mar Vista

$$$ | MODERN AMERICAN | FAMILY | Tucked into the hills of the gated Mar Vista community, this open-air restaurant comes complete with dazzling ocean views, infinity pools for guests to enjoy, and a made-from-scratch farm- and sea-to-table menu. Chef and owner Frankie Becker cooks up fresh seafood, but vegetarians are in luck too, because the crispy cauliflower and hummus platter are mouthwatering. **Known for:** Cajun barbecue shrimp; amazing views; lobster bisque. [$] *Average main: $17* ✉ *Off Route 180, Mar Vista, Flamingo* ☎ *6110–1687* 🌐 *graciacostarica.com.*

Papaya

$$ | **ECLECTIC** | Grab a table at the second-floor lounge overlooking the pool while the kitchen cooks up fresh seafood delivered daily by local fishermen. Dinner reservations are recommended, so call ahead to try the coconut shrimp, sesame-crusted tuna, or Thai curry. **Known for:** wide array of vegetarian meals; fresh fruit juices (also used in cocktails); guacamole and homemade chips. [$] *Average main: $15* ✉ *Conchal Hotel, Brasilito* ✣ *200 meters (656 feet) south of bridge* ☎ *2654–9125* 🌐 *www.conchalcr.com* ⏲ *Closed Wed.*

★ **Patagonia Del Mar**

$$$ | **ASIAN FUSION** | This open-air Argentinian grill has a lovely ambience, great views of the beach across the street, and even better steak and seafood. Lounge poolside with a cocktail and sushi or sample their good wine selection with some shrimp tempura while the kids play on the swings. **Known for:** fresh seafood poke bowls; beautiful pool; melt-in-your-mouth beef tenderloin with jalapeño sauce. [$] *Average main: $21* ✉ *Brasilito* ✣ *100 meters (323 feet) north of Puente Brasilito* ☎ *8800–0005* 🌐 *patagoniadel-mar.business.site.*

Hotels

★ **Conchal Hotel**

$$ | **HOTEL** | It may not be on the beach, but this quaint boutique hotel is certainly a diamond in the rough in rustic Brasilito, with breezy rooms framing an attractive pool-centered courtyard and a second-story restaurant with wholesome cuisine. **Pros:** B&B feel; outstanding restaurant; friendly owners. **Cons:** 15-minute walk to the beach; hotel often full; some street noise. [$] *Rooms from: $99* ✉ *Brasilito* ✣ *200 meters (656 feet) south of bridge* ☎ *2654–9125* 🌐 *www.conchalcr.com* ➪ *13 rooms* 🍴 *Free Breakfast.*

Hotel Brasilito

$$ | **HOTEL** | Budget travelers who don't need amenities will love this rustic two-story wooden hotel's affordable price and seafront location, if not its no-frills but adequate A-frame rooms. **Pros:** inexpensive; beachfront; family owned and operated. **Cons:** can be noisy; rooms need upgrading; boxy rooms, some without TVs, A/C, or phones. [$] *Rooms from: $89* ✉ *Brasilito* ✣ *Between soccer field and beach* ☎ *2654–4237* 🌐 *www.brasilito.com* ➪ *18 rooms* 🍴 *No Meals.*

W Costa Rica–Reserva Conchal

$$$$ | **RESORT** | Incorporating Costa Rican culture at every turn, this convivial, unique member of the W chain leaves no detail overlooked, from the "forest" of guanacaste trees at the pool and restaurant, to the "pineapple" elevator tower. **Pros:** fun and lively atmosphere; Costa Rica–inspired architecture and decor; beautiful white sand beach. **Cons:** long walk to get anywhere; somewhat pricey; no breakfast included. [$] *Rooms from: $619* ✉ *Reserva Conchal Cabo Villas, Playa Conchal* ☎ *2654–3600* 🌐 *www.marriott.com* ➪ *150 rooms* 🍴 *No Meals.*

The Westin Golf Resort & Spa, Playa Conchal

$$$$ | **RESORT** | **FAMILY** | So vast that guests ride around in biodiesel shuttles, this all-inclusive Starwood property is set on 2,400 acres with nearly every vacation wish granted, from lagoon-style pools and a picture-perfect beach to eight restaurants and a championship golf course. **Pros:** saltwater pools; abundant activities; beach access. **Cons:** only three rooms have ocean views; easy to get lost; no food and drink service on the beach. [$] *Rooms from: $669* ✉ *Entrance less than 1 km (½ mile) south of Brasilito, Playa Conchal* ☎ *2654–3500* 🌐 *www.starwoodhotels.com/westin* ➪ *404 units* 🍴 *All-Inclusive.*

⚡ Activities

GOLF

Reserva Conchal Golf Course

GOLF | One of the best golf courses in a country not known for golf, this 18-hole, par-71 course designed by Robert Trent Jones Jr. is perfectly maintained and reserved for guests of the Westin Golf Resort & Spa, who can try out their swing for $160, cart included; renting clubs costs an extra $60. The well-laid-out course has wide fairways and beautiful views including a couple of holes over-looking the water. Holes 16, 17, and 18 pose a challenge, with downhill tee shots and a drive that lands close to the water. Allow extra time to observe the wildlife, including howler monkeys, lizards, coatis, and birds. ⊠ *The Westin Resort & Spa, Playa Conchal, entrance, less than 1 km (½ mile) south of Brasilito, Playa Conchal* ☎ *2654–3100* ⊕ *www.reservaconchal. com* ⊠ *$160 for 18 holes* ⅄ *18 holes, 6956 yards, par 71.*

Playa Grande

21 km (13 miles) north of Tamarindo.

Down the (long, paved) road from Tamarindo, but only five minutes by boat across a tidal estuary, lies beautiful, pristine Playa Grande. By day, it's one of the best surfing beaches in the country, and by night it's a nesting beach for the increasingly rare giant leatherback sea turtle. The beach has thus far escaped the overdevelopment of nearby Tamarindo, and is consequently lined with thick vegetation instead of hotels and strip malls. But Playa Grande isn't immune to development; developers have sold hundreds of lots. The ongoing battle to protect the beach continues. The good thing is that the homes are 200 meters (656 feet) from the beach, thanks to a legislated buffer zone and a decree that no lights can be visible from the beach, to avoid disturbing the turtles. A few hotels and restaurants make this a pleasant, tranquil alternative to Tamarindo. And if you want to go shopping or barhopping, Tamarindo is only a two-minute boat ride away.

GETTING HERE AND AROUND

The road from Tamarindo is paved for the duration of the 30-minute drive. Alternatively, you can take a small boat across the Tamarindo Estuary for about $3 per person and walk 30 minutes along the beach to the main surf break. A lesser-known break is just a 10-minute walk; boats travel (8–4:30) between the guide kiosk at the north end of Tamarindo and Hotel Bula Bula in Playa Grande. Otherwise, a taxi from Tamarindo to Playa Grande will cost about $30 one way.

◉ Sights

★ **Las Baulas National Marine Park** (*Parque Nacional Marino Las Baulas*)
WILDLIFE REFUGE | Encompassing more than 1,000 acres of beach, mangrove swamps, and estuary, and more than 54,000 acres of ocean, this wide expanse of sand and sea will make you feel small, in the best way possible. *Baula* is the Spanish word for leatherback sea turtles, who have been nesting here for thousands of years. While their numbers continue to decline, guides still lead night hikes here between October and May to see leatherback and olive ridley sea turtles lay their eggs. You can also spot scores of native birds like brown-footed boobies and pelicans, kayak through the mangroves and estuary, or learn to surf on some of the best waves in the country. There are no hotels or restaurants on the beach thanks to government regulation preventing development, but there is a taco stand and a ranger station open from 8 am to 4 pm at the entrance to the beach. Be sure to bring water and sunscreen, and your own shade. The park closes to the public at 6 pm and 5 pm during turtle nesting season. ⊠ *Playa Grande* ⊹ *500 meters (1,640 feet)*

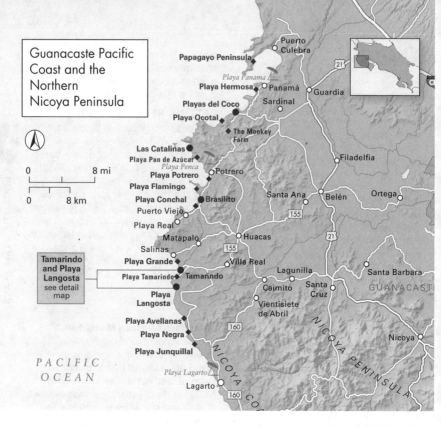

Puerto Culebra

Papagayo Peninsula

Playa Panamá

Playa Hermosa

Panamá

Guardia

Sardinal

Playas del Coco

Playa Ocotal

The Monkey Farm

Filadelfia

Las Catalinas

Playa Pan de Azúcar

Playa Penca

Potrero

Playa Potrero

Playa Flamingo

Santa Ana

Belén

Ortega

Playa Conchal

Brasilito

Puerto Viejo

Playa Real

Matapalo

Huacas

Salinas

Villa Real

Playa Grande

Tamarindo and Playa Langosta see detail map

Playa Tamarindo

Tamarindo

Lagunilla

Santa Barbara

GUANACASTE

Caimito

Santa Cruz

Playa Langosta

Vientisiete de Abril

Playa Avellanas

Playa Negra

Nicoya

Playa Junquillal

PACIFIC OCEAN

Playa Lagarto

Lagarto

NICOYA PENINSULA

0   8 mi

0   8 km

*south of Escuela de Playa Grande 933
☎ 2653–0470 ⊕ www.sinac.go.cr.*

Nesting Giant Leatherback Turtles

WILDLIFE REFUGE | Playa Grande used to host the world's largest visitation of nesting giant leatherback turtles, but the number of turtles has fallen drastically in the past 20 years, from a high of 1,504 in 1989 to less than 40 currently. This loss is due to long-line commercial fishing boats that trap turtles in their nets, causing the turtles to drown, along with poaching of turtle eggs and loss of habitat. The beach is still strictly off-limits 6 pm to 6 am from October 20 to February 15, during the peak nesting season. You can visit only as part of a guided tour with a park ranger, from the headquarters for Las Baulas National Marine Park, 100 meters (328 feet) east of Hotel Las Tortugas. If you are lucky, spotters will find a nesting turtle.

At their signal, you'll walk down the beach as silently as you can, where in the darkness you'll witness the remarkable sight of a 500-pound creature digging a hole in the sand large enough to deposit up to 100 golf-ball-size eggs. About 60 days later, the sight of hundreds of hatchlings scrambling toward open water in the early morning is equally impressive. Turtle-watching takes place around high tide, which can be shortly after sunset, or in the early morning. Plan on spending one to six hours at the ranger station waiting for a turtle to come up, during which you can watch a video on the turtles in English (the guides speak mostly Spanish). You are charged only if a turtle sighting is confirmed. Visitation is limited to 60 people per night (in groups of 15 max) and unregistered visitors are not allowed. Reservations should be made one week in advance either by phone or at Las Baulas National Park headquarters at Playa Grande. ✉ *Playa Grande* ✥ *100 meters (328 feet) east of main beach entrance* ☎ *2653–0470* 🎟 *$25, only if turtle is spotted, includes guided tour.*

Beaches

Playa Grande

BEACH | In addition to being a paradise for surfers and sunbathers, the narrow woodsy patch that lines this wide, pristine Blue Flag beach holds howler monkeys and an array of birds, and the mangrove estuary on the north end of the beach has crocodiles. Because it's a protected area, the beach is unspoiled by buildings and natural beauty abounds. There is not a lot of shade. Be aware that the surf is a little heavy for safe swimming, and there's an abundance of mosquitoes during the rainy months, especially near the estuary, so bring plenty of repellent. The beach's shores and waters are part of Parque Nacional Marino Las Baulas. Admission is free during daylight hours but off-limits at night during the turtle-nesting season (October 20 to February 15), when tourists come on guided turtle tours, hoping to catch the increasingly rare sight of a leatherback turtle building a nest and depositing eggs. The beach gained protected status in part because a surfer who arrived here more than 30 years ago was so upset by the widespread turtle-egg poaching that he adopted a conservationist's agenda. Louis Wilson, owner of Las Tortugas Hotel, spearheaded a campaign to protect the nesting baulas (leatherback turtles) that eventually resulted in the creation of the national park. When walking on the beach, be sure to avoid the dry sand above the high tide line where turtles lay their eggs. **Amenities:** food and drink. **Best for:** surfing; walking. ✉ *Playa Grande.*

Restaurants

Bistro Cantarana

$$ | **INTERNATIONAL** | You can usually count on good food at this second-story restaurant in the trees. You can get wild with crocodile fingers, or try something more familiar, like the handmade pizzas. **Known for:** unfussy breakfast fare; homemade tortillas and sauces; fresh seafood like tuna poke bowl and fish tacos. [$] *Average main: $13* ✉ *Hotel Cantarana, Palm Beach Estates, Playa Grande* ✥ *2 km (1 mile) east of park headquarters* ☎ *2653–0486* 🌐 *www.hotel-cantarana.com* 🕒 *Closed Wed.*

★ Casa Inti

$$$ | **PERUVIAN** | This friendly lunchtime Peruvian café has a revolving menu of flavorful delights made from fresh ingredients that are almost as beautiful as they are tasty. Try the ceviche (a slight change from the usual Costa Rican) in the breezy palapa or the *lomo saltado* or the eggplant—we promise you'll want to return every day for lunch. **Known for:** fresh salads; tasty homemade desserts; authentic Peruvian food. [$] *Average main: $16* ✉ *Playa Grande* ✥ *150 meters (492 feet) west of the Asada on Rte. 933, next to Amigo Realty* ☎ *8520–5411* 🕒 *Closed Sat.–Mon. No dinner.*

Pots and Bowls

$$ | **COSTA RICAN** | Surrounded by a plethora of delightful potted plants you'll indulge in bowls of delicious, nutritious food at this eponymous eatery. The menu is divided into sweet (acai bowls, waffles with homemade caramel-fruit syrup, chia pudding) and salty (teriyaki chicken bowls, orzo miso with mushrooms, spinach, coconut milk, and goat cheese), so there's something for whatever you're craving. **Known for:** breakfast; perfectly brewed coffee, cold-pressed juice, and smoothies; vegan, vegetarian, and allergy-friendly options. [$] *Average main: $11* ✉ *Hwy. 933, Playa Grande* ☎ *4701–2394* 🌐 *potsandbowlscr.com.*

Costa Rica's shores are visited by the green turtle, the olive ridley (above), the hawksbill, the loggerhead, and the leatherback turtle.

Upstairs at the RipJack Inn

$$$ | **SEAFOOD** | Chow down at this casual place a block from the beach, or party at the extensive bar, which occupies about a third of the restaurant. Portions are large, so pace yourself—especially if you order the popular barbecue ribs with mashed potatoes. **Known for:** friendly atmosphere where everyone knows you; yummy breakfast sandwiches; hot garlic shrimp. *Average main: $18 ✉ RipJack Inn, Playa Grande ↔ 100 meters (328 feet) south of park headquarters ☎ 6474–5425, 2653–1636 🌐 www.ripjackinn.com.*

Hotels

The Grateful Hotel

$$ | **HOTEL** | At the eastern edge of the estuary in the gated Palm Beach Estates community, this pleasant hotel (an homage to the band The Grateful Dead) has its own landing for ferrying guests and restaurant patrons to and from Tamarindo (it's a 1 km [½ mile] trip). **Pros:** great food at the restaurant; right across from Tamarindo; friendly staff. **Cons:** music can be loud; poor lighting; Grateful Dead experience may not be for everyone. *Rooms from: $100 ✉ Palm Beach Estates, Playa Grande ☎ 8707–9939 🌐 thegratefulhotel.com ⇆ 10 rooms 🍽 Free Breakfast.*

Hotel Las Tortugas

$$$ | **B&B/INN** | With a prime location on the beach, this place is perfect for surfers, nature lovers, and sun worshippers with a range of budgets. **Pros:** on the beach; friendly owners; good value. **Cons:** spotty service at times; rooms lack amenities; busy location. *Rooms from: $175 ✉ Entrance to Leatherback Marine National Park, 33 km (20 miles) north of Tamarindo, Playa Grande ☎ 2653–0423 🌐 www.lastortugashotel.com ⇆ 37 units 🍽 No Meals.*

ONDA Playa Grande

$$ | **HOTEL** | Less than a five-minute saunter to the sea, this Spanish colonial adults-only hotel has clean, modern rooms that surround a pool. **Pros:** great place to make friends; nice work-while-traveling setup; steps from the beach. **Cons:** lacks in-room amenities;

may skew toward younger crowd; loud music. $ Rooms from: $130 ⌧ Main road, Playa Grande ✛ 250 meters (820 feet) northeast of MINAE ☎ 4002–2779 ⊕ stayonda.com ⤵ 8 rooms, 2 dorms ⍾ No Meals.

 ## Activities

■ TIP→ **Unless you are a strong swimmer attached to a surfboard, don't go in any deeper than your waist here.**

There is calmer water for snorkeling about a 30-minute walk north of Las Tortugas, at a black-sand beach called Playa Carbón. There is a large gathering on the beach every night at sunset. All Playa Grande and Tamarindo hotels can arrange guided boat tours of the estuary for around $25 per person. You may see crocodiles, monkeys, herons, kingfishers, and an array of other birdlife; go either early in the morning or late in the afternoon, and bring insect repellent.

TOUR OPERATORS

All the area hotels can arrange guided boat tours of the estuary for around $25 per person. You may see crocodiles, monkeys, herons, kingfishers, and an array of other birdlife; go either early in the morning or late in the afternoon, and bring insect repellent.

SURFING

Playa Grande is renowned for having one of the most consistent surf breaks in the country. Only experienced surfers should attempt riding this beach break, which often features big barrels and offshore winds. The waves are best at high tide, especially around a full moon.

Hotel Las Tortugas

SURFING | The hotel rents boards for $15 to $20 a day and offers surfing lessons at their beachfront Caribbean-style snack bar. ⌧ Playa Grande ☎ 2653–0423 ⊕ www.lastortugashotel.com.

YOGA

Yoga at RipJack Inn

YOGA | RipJack Inn has its own yoga shala where classes are held daily. Check the website for times. The cost is $15 and yoga mats are provided. ⌧ RipJack Inn, Playa Grande ✛ 100 meters (328 feet) south of Hotel Las Tortugas ☎ 2653–1636 ⊕ www.ripjackinn.com ⤳ $15.

Tamarindo

82 km (51 miles) southwest of Liberia.

Once a funky beach town full of surfers and local fishermen, Tamarindo is now a pricey, hyped-up hive of commercial development and real estate speculation, happily accompanied by a dizzying variety of shops, bars, and hotels, and probably the best selection of restaurants of any beach town on the Pacific coast. There's a shopping center at the entrance to town with an upscale AutoMercado supermarket and ATM. On the downside, the congested two-lane beach road through Tamarindo comes to a halt at times throughout the day, especially when delivery trucks stop in front of shops and restaurants, while drivers inch past the flashing hazards and distracted pedestrians. Strip malls, billboards, and high-rise condominiums clutter the rest of the main street and obscure views of the still-magnificent beach. Beyond the chaos of Diria Grand Boulevard (the commercial center), the main road bends toward Playa Langosta and gains some composure and tranquillity (other than the potholes).

Tamarindo serves as a popular base for surfing at the nearby Playas Grande, Langosta, Avellanas, and Negra. There are plenty of outdoor options in addition to surfing, among them diving, sportfishing, wildlife-watching, and canopy tours. You can also play 18 rounds at the nearby Hacienda Pinilla or Reserva Conchal golf courses, or simply stroll the beach and sunbathe. There have been reports of car break-ins that occur minutes after you leave your vehicle. Most upscale hotels and inns have their own security and gated parking. Once you're on the beach, almost all the negatives disappear (just keep an eye on your belongings).

GETTING HERE AND AROUND

SANSA flies to Tamarindo's tiny airstrip direct from San José. By car from Liberia, travel south on the highway to the turnoff for Belén, then head west and turn left at the Huacas crossroads to Tamarindo, passing through the small village of Villareal. The drive from Liberia to Tamarindo takes just over one hour.

The Tamarindo Shuttle ferries passengers between the various beaches in a comfortable van and will also pick you up at the Liberia airport ($20 per person, minimum of two; evening flights require a minimum of three passengers). Shared shuttles from San José cost $60 per person. Once you're in Tamarindo everything is within walkable distance, or you can rent golf carts to get around. If you want to have a car, reserve early, they often run out.

There are no direct bus connections between Playa Grande or Playa Avellanas and Tamarindo. A taxi or a shuttle van (or a five-minute boat trip over the estuary from Playa Grande) is your best bet to get to and from nearby towns if you don't have a car.

TAXIS Juan Carlos Taxi. ⊠ *Tamarindo* ☎ *8636–6358.*

SHUTTLES Tamarindo Shuttle. ⊠ *Tamarindo* ☎ *2653–4444, 2653–2626* ⊕ *www. tamarindoshuttle.com.*

RENTAL CARS Alamo. ⊠ *On main road, diagonal from Tamarindo Diria hotel, Tamarindo* ☎ *2653–0727.* **Economy.** ⊠ *Main road entering Tamarindo, across from Witch's Rock Surf Camp, Tamarindo* ☎ *2653–0728.* **Hertz.** ⊠ *100 m east of Hotel Pasatiempo, Tamarindo* ☎ *2653–1358.*

ESSENTIALS

BANK/ATM Banco Nacional. ⊠ *Across from Arco Iris Hotel, Tamarindo* ☎ *2653–0366.*

HOSPITALS Beachside Clinic. ⊠ *Brasilito* ✢ *200 meters (656 feet) west of Huacas cruce, about 20 mins out of town on road to Brasilito* ☎ *2653–9911* ⊕ *beachsideclin-iccr.com.*

PHARMACY Farmacia Tamarindo. ⊠ *Main road into town, diagonally across from Best Western Tamarindo Villas, Tamarindo* ☎ *2653–0210.*

POST OFFICE Correo. ⊠ *Across from airport on main road between Villareal and Tamarindo, Tamarindo* ☎ *2653–0676.*

 Beaches

Playa Tamarindo

BEACH | Wide and flat, the sand here is packed hard enough for easy walking and jogging, but swimming and surfing have become questionable since the town's Blue Flag status was taken away (because of overdevelopment and the total absence of water treatment). The water quality is especially poor during the rainy months, when you'll want to do your swimming and surfing at nearby Playa Langosta or Playa Grande. Despite this, surfing is still the main attraction here, and there's a young crowd that parties hard after a day riding the waves. Witch's Rock Surf Shop has showers, toilets, surfboard rental, a swimming pool, and a restaurant where you can watch the surfers over a cold beer. Strong currents at the north end of the beach get a lot of swimmers into trouble, especially when they try to cross the estuary without a surfboard. Steer clear of the estuary, where there have been crocodile sightings. There's street parking and a public dirt lot in front of El Vaquero Brewpub. **Amenities:** food and drink; parking; showers; toilets. **Best for:** partiers; surfing; walking. ⊠ *Tamarindo.*

🍴 Restaurants

Bamboo Sushi Club

$$ | **SUSHI** | As soon as you cross the bamboo bridge, you'll be instantly transported from a strip mall to an ocean-side Zen garden where the fish is bought fresh from the boats. Try a frozen mojito and start with a seaweed salad and steamed dumplings, then dive into the sashimi and sushi. **Known for:** frozen passion-fruit mojitos; spicy edamame; fresh-off-the-boat sushi. [$] *Average main: $10* ✉ *Tamarindo* ✣ *20 meters (65 feet) after Diria Hotel on Main St.* ☎ *2653–4519.*

Dragonfly Bar & Grill

$$$ | **ECLECTIC** | Paper lanterns suspended over wooden tables and polished concrete floors bring rustic elegance to this A-frame restaurant supported by tree-trunk columns. The place has been a favorite for years and remains trendy with international fusion dishes like Buddha bowls or seared yellowfin tuna with wasabi aioli. **Known for:** wood-fired grill; laid-back charm; tender beef. [$] *Average main: $17* ✉ *Behind Hotel Pasatiempo, past Pizzeria La Baula, Tamarindo* ✣ *100 meters (328 feet) past turnoff for Langosta Beach road, then left 50 meters (164 feet)* ☎ *2653–1506* 🌐 *www.dragonflybarandgrill.com* 🕒 *No lunch.*

Green Papaya

$ | **MEXICAN FUSION** | **FAMILY** | Sit back and relax in the outside swinging seats at this taco and burrito haven. The polished wood and laid-back atmosphere are perfect for sipping a cocktail and snacking on chips with a trio of dips before indulging in made-from-scratch tortillas and mama's secret beef stew. **Known for:** fresh and innovative tacos and burritos; friendly staff; amazing homemade hot sauce. [$] *Average main: $9* ✉ *Behind Oveja Negra Hostel, Tamarindo* ☎ *2653–0863* 🌐 *www.facebook.com/Gr33nPapaya* 💳 *No credit cards* 🕒 *Closed Mon.*

★ **La Bodega**

$ | **CAFÉ** | Linger as long as you'd like for breakfast or lunch on the open-air deck, where you'll be served fresh, local, and organic food. Daily specials include heaping salads or sandwiches on homemade bread, and specialty coffees like cappuccino and from-scratch baked goods round out the menu. **Known for:** breakfast sandwiches; hibiscus lemonade; food-allergy friendly. [$] *Average main: $9* ✉ *Hotel Nahua, Tamarindo* ✣ *Diagonal from Banco Nacional* ☎ *8395–6184* 🌐 *www.facebook.com/LaBodegaCR* 🕒 *No dinner.*

Little Lucha

$ | **MEXICAN** | Decorated with figurines and images of Mexican wrestlers, with a VW bus for the bar, this restaurant serves authentic Mexico City street tacos. Feel the taco love with a platter: the *cochinita pibil,* which features pork shoulder slow-cooked in banana leaves and seasoned to citrus perfection, the veggie (not just for vegetarians) with mushrooms, onions, roasted peppers, and garlic, and the classic beer-battered fish taco topped with white sauce and a few drops of hot sauce. **Known for:** tequila cocktails and Mexican beers; colorful punk-rock atmosphere; Taco Tuesday (all tacos $2). [$] *Average main: $6* ✉ *Tamarindo* ✣ *20 meters (65 feet) north of Super Compro, diagonal from skate park* ☎ *8723–4297* 🕒 *Closed Sun.*

Nogui's

$$$ | **SEAFOOD** | Pleasing a loyal legion of local fans since 1974, Nogui's offers a hearty menu of seafood and meat dishes that pair perfectly with a tamarind margarita. With feet-in-the-sand dining and ocean views, it's a great place to let the kids play on the beach while you enjoy one of Tamarindo's best places to watch the sunset. **Known for:** colorful Adirondack chairs on the beach; breakfast; legendary selection of pies like pineapple, chocolate, and coconut cream. [$] *Average*

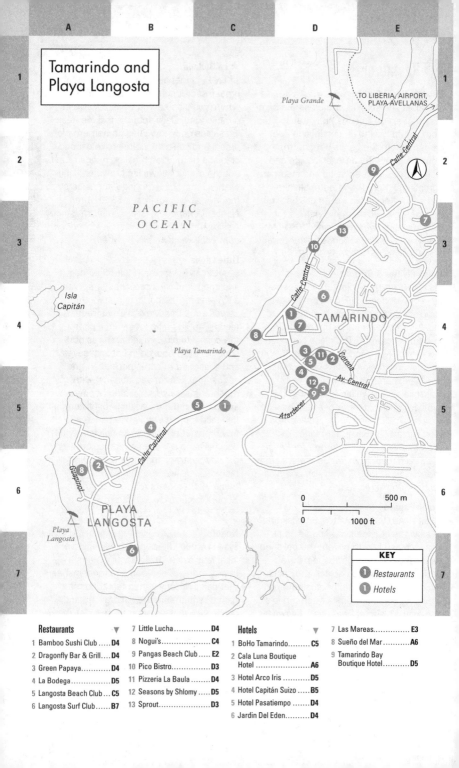

Tamarindo and Playa Langosta

PACIFIC OCEAN

Playa Grande

TO LIBERIA, AIRPORT,
PLAYA AVELLANAS

Isla Capitán

TAMARINDO

Playa Tamarindo

Calle Central

Corona

Av. Central

Atardecer

Calle Cardinal

Guapinol

PLAYA LANGOSTA

Playa Langosta

| 0 | | 500 m |
| 0 | | 1000 ft |

KEY

🔵 *Restaurants*

🔵 *Hotels*

Restaurants ▼

1 Bamboo Sushi Club **D4**
2 Dragonfly Bar & Grill.... **D4**
3 Green Papaya.............**D4**
4 La Bodega **D5**
5 Langosta Beach Club ... **C5**
6 Langosta Surf Club **B7**
7 Little Lucha...............**D4**
8 Nogui's..................**C4**
9 Pangas Beach Club **E2**
10 Pico Bistro..............**D3**
11 Pizzeria La Baula **D4**
12 Seasons by Shlomy **D5**
13 Sprout...................**D3**

Hotels ▼

1 BoHo Tamarindo.........**C5**
2 Cala Luna Boutique
  Hotel **A6**
3 Hotel Arco Iris **D5**
4 Hotel Capitán Suizo **B5**
5 Hotel Pasatiempo **D4**
6 Jardin Del Eden..........**D4**
7 Las Mareas...............**E3**
8 Sueño del Mar **A6**
9 Tamarindo Bay
  Boutique Hotel..........**D5**

main: $16 ⊠ Tamarindo ✛ South side of Tamarindo Circle, on beach ☎ 2653–0029 ⊕ www.noguistamarindo.com ⊙ Closed Wed.

★ Pangas Beach Club

$$$ | FRENCH FUSION | You can't get any closer to the water than at this outdoor beach garden, where rustic tables are shaded by enormous ficus trees draped with wicker lamps. Classic French cuisine with Costa Rican flavors include dishes like fresh seafood with fruit reductions and organic meats seared on hot lava stones. **Known for:** lovely setting on the beach; lamb seared on hot lava stones; sunset dinners. $ Average main: $25 ⊠ Tamarindo ✛ 500 meters (1,640 feet) southwest of Automercado ☎ 2653–0024 ⊕ pangasbeachclubcr.com.

Pico Bistro

$ | AMERICAN | Cool off inside or relax outside on the deck at this little gem on the beach, the perfect spot to replenish the reserves with some healthy food or a good cup of coffee while you watch surfers ride the waves. Pico has the best Wi-Fi in town, so if you must look at your computer on your vacation, do it from here. **Known for:** brunch; unimpeded beach views; fresh salads and Buddha bowls. $ Average main: $9 ⊠ Calle Central, Tamarindo ☎ 8841–5338 ⊕ pico-bistro-tamarindo.business.site.

Pizzeria La Baula

$$ | PIZZA | FAMILY | Wildly popular, this casually chic, alfresco pizzeria on a quiet side street has plenty of cars parked outside most nights, with patrons inside feasting on the consistently delicious thin-crust pizzas. Families are especially fond of La Baula (the Costa Rican name for the leatherback turtle) because of its reasonable prices, noisy buzz, and adjacent playground and picniclike dining area. **Known for:** great place for large groups; open-air dining in a lighthearted

atmosphere; prosciutto, arugula, and Parmesan pizza. $ Average main: $15 ⊠ Next door to Dragonfly Bar & Grill, Tamarindo ✛ 100 meters (328 feet) north of Hotel Pasatiempo, behind Banco Nacional ☎ 2653–1450 ⊕ www.facebook.com/PizzeriaLaBaula ⊙ No lunch.

★ Seasons by Shlomy

$$$ | MEDITERRANEAN | At his intimate, poolside restaurant in the casually chic Hotel Arco Iris, innovative Israeli-born and Cordon Bleu–trained chef Shlomy Koren transforms fresh local ingredients into sophisticated Mediterranean-fusion dishes you would pay a small fortune for on the Riviera. The alluring smell of sautéed garlic teases the senses for what's ahead: salty soft focaccia with chicken liver pâté, perhaps a rare fillet or red snapper with sun-dried tomatoes, finished with white-chocolate mousse with strawberries. **Known for:** seafood pasta; consistently delicious meals; seared tuna. $ Average main: $19 ⊠ Hotel Arco Iris, uphill from turnoff to Playa Langosta road, Tamarindo ☎ 8368–6983 ⊕ www.seasonstamarindo.com ▭ No credit cards ⊙ Closed Sun. No lunch.

Sprout

$$ | CAFÉ | The simple but spot-on menu, especially good for those with food sensitivities, features fresh, local, and organic ingredients in sandwiches, salads, and smoothies blended with fruits and vegetables so delightful that you'll forget they're good for you. Sink your teeth into top picks like the blackened mahimahi sandwich with mango-habanero mayo on toasted ciabatta or the piled-high hamburger on homemade brioche. **Known for:** pork sliders; fish tacos; scrumptious salads and sandwiches. $ Average main: $10 ⊠ Entrance to Tamarindo, across from Witch's Rock Surf Camp, Tamarindo ☎ 8937–2506 ⊙ Closed Sun.

Hotels

BoHo Tamarindo

$$ | B&B/INN | This chic and charming breezy boutique hotel is a welcome hideaway from the dusty bustle of Tamarindo, but still walking distance to everything. **Pros:** good value; clean, comfortable, stylish rooms; excellent hospitality from owners. **Cons:** doesn't feel very Costa Rican; not on the beach; no coffeemaker in room. [$] *Rooms from: $150* ✉ *Calle Cardinal, Tamarindo* ☎ *8709–5674* ⊕ *www.boho-tamarindo.com* ⇌ *8 rooms* ⦿| *Free Breakfast.*

Hotel Arco Iris

$$ | HOTEL | With eight ultraspacious, deluxe rooms with two queen beds, and five beautiful bungalows boasting high, sloping cane ceilings, handsome contemporary furniture, and sleek marble bathrooms, there's something for everyone on this chic compound, half a block off one of Tamarindo's main drags. **Pros:** transportation service and concierge; boutique feel; great restaurant. **Cons:** no water views; small pool; not a lot of privacy in bungalows. [$] *Rooms from: $142* ✉ *Follow signs past turnoff to Playa Langosta and go up hill to right, Tamarindo* ☎ *2653–0330* ⊕ *www.hotelarcoiris. com* ⇌ *13 units* ⦿| *Free Breakfast.*

Hotel Pasatiempo

$$$ | HOTEL | FAMILY | Built around a tropical garden, this pretty collection of bungalows is clean and comfortable, making this laid-back spot a great option for families. **Pros:** fun and friendly bar area; gorgeous pool and garden; 10% discount when booking directly through hotel. **Cons:** rooms close to the bar can be noisy; some mosquitoes; seven-minute walk to beach. [$] *Rooms from: $160* ✉ *Tamarindo* ⊹ *100 meters (328 feet) southeast of high-rise Pacific Park condo at turnoff for Playa Langosta Rd.* ☎ *2653–0096, 2653–4701* ⊕ *www.hotelpasatiempo.com* ⇌ *22 rooms* ⦿| *Free Breakfast.*

Jardin Del Eden

$$$$ | HOTEL | An oasis with luxurious rooms, this adults-only boutique hotel just off the main street feels a million miles away from the busy 9-to-5. **Pros:** exquisite gardens; poolside organic restaurant; beachside garden across the street. **Cons:** a lot of steps to some rooms; not all rooms are the same high quality; hotel isn't directly on the beach. [$] *Rooms from: $324* ✉ *Tamarindo Beach, Tamarindo* ☎ *2653–0137, 4070–0303* ⊕ *www.jardindeleden.com* ⇌ *46 rooms* ⦿| *All-Inclusive* ☞ *Breakfast and dinner included, no lunch.*

Las Mareas

$$$ | HOUSE | If space, privacy, luxury, and location are your priorities, then these 2,800-square-foot vacation rentals are your best option, with Balinese decor and all the comforts of home. **Pros:** ideal for large groups; five-minute walk to central Tamarindo; high-end amenities. **Cons:** one-week minimum stay during holidays; maid service every other day; no meals. [$] *Rooms from: $200* ✉ *Across from Las Pangas Beach Club, at entrance to Tamarindo, Tamarindo* ☎ *2653–1561, 8832–5773* ⇌ *6 villas* ⦿| *No Meals.*

★ Tamarindo Bay Boutique Hotel

$$ | HOTEL | This boutique hotel built from recycled materials is inspired by the owners' travels to Southeast Asia and has nine contemporary rooms overlooking a pool-centered courtyard. **Pros:** outstanding breakfasts; huge rooms; immaculate and peaceful property; UV-treated pool. **Cons:** ground-floor rooms get some noise from above; no kids under 18; no ocean views. [$] *Rooms from: $145* ✉ *Tamarindo* ⊹ *100 meters (328 feet) south of Banco Nacional, next to Hotel Arco Iris* ☎ *2653–2692, 8706–9470* ⊕ *www.tamarindobayhotel.com* ⇌ *9 rooms* ⦿| *Free Breakfast.*

Nightlife

Tamarindo is one of the few places out-side San José and Jacó where the night-life really jumps. Although party-hearty hot spots come and go with the tides, Tamarindo does have some perennially popular nightspots, along with a couple of low-key options.

Crazy Monkey Bar

DANCE CLUBS | Popular with the surfing crowd, Crazy Monkey Bar features live salsa music, a fire show, and DJs that attract locals who really know how to move—and a crowd of appreciative onlookers. Friday night is ladies' night. ✉ *Best Western Tamarindo Vista Villas, main road entering Tamarindo, across from Witch's Rock Surf Camp, Tamarindo* ☎ *2653–0114.*

El Vaquero Bar

BARS | After a sunset surf session, pull up a bar stool in the sand and enjoy a craft beer made at the neighboring Volcano Brewing Company. Happy hour is from 5 to 7, and there's live music on week-ends. If you've worked up an appetite, try the chicken wings, jalapeño poppers, hamburgers, and nachos. This is the best place to watch the surfers over a cold one. ✉ *In front of Economy Rental Car, next to Witch's Rock Surf Camp, Tamarindo* ☎ *2653–1238* ⊕ *www.witchsrocksurf-camp.com/el-vaquero-brewpub.*

Sharky's

BARS | This is the biggest, most popular sports bar in town, with huge TV screens showing up to six games at once. After the game, both floors play extremely loud music for dancing. There's live music on Monday, karaoke on Tuesday, and ladies' night Saturday. If sports aren't your thing, the bar food is amazingly good. The action starts at 11:30 am and goes to 2:30 am. ✉ *Avda. Ctl., across from Plaza Tamarindo, Tamarindo* ☎ *2653–4705* ⊕ *www.sharkysbars.com.*

Shopping

Most stores lining the main road along Diria Grand Boulevard sell the same souvenirs. It's hard to leave town without at least one sarong or T-shirt in your suit-case. There are a few upscale clothing and jewelry shops as well, and some worthy farmers' markets.

Azul Profundo Boutique

SWIMWEAR | The theme of this Tamarindo boutique is "Don't worry, be hippy," with a collection of upscale beachwear and jewelry ranging from tie-dyed sundresses and OM pendants to pura vida earrings and wool belts. They also have beach bags, hats, and bikinis. Here you can find nicer clothes for men and women; head next door to Azul Profundo Kids for the little ones. ✉ *Local #1 Centro Comercial Plaza, Tamarindo* ☎ *2653–0395* ⊕ *www. azulprofundoboutique.com.*

Buena Nena

SOUVENIRS | If you've bought too many souvenirs on your trip, stop in this funky boutique to pick up one of their handmade bags—they have a glorious selection of cool patterns and sizes. If you haven't bought enough souvenirs, stop in to pick something out from their selection of well-made dresses, hats, and jewelry. ✉ *Store #1 Hotel Zullymar, on road to rotunda, Tamarindo* ☎ *2653–1991.*

Tama Market

MARKET | On Saturday from 8 am to 4 pm, the farmers' market in Oneida Park is bustling. Stop by for some fresh organic fruits and veggies, homemade kombucha, or baked goods. ✉ *Next to Green Papaya restaurant and behind Oneida Park, Playa Tamarindo, Tamarindo* ☎ *8779–8800* ⊕ *www.facebook.com/ Market.Tamarindo.*

Tamarindo Night Market

MARKET | On Thursday evening from 5:30 to 9:30 pm, join in the buzzing crowd to sample food and cocktails from around the world, buy jewelry, and listen to live music. ⊠ *In the parking lot up the road from Hotel Pasatiempo, Tamarindo* ☎ *6051–6634.*

Activities

BOATING

Rocky Isla El Capitán, just offshore, is a close-in kayaking destination, full of sand-dollar shells. Exploring the tidal estuaries north and south of town is best done in a kayak at high tide, when you can travel farther up the temporary rivers. Arrange kayaking trips through your hotel. A number of boats offer sunset trips that allow you to snorkel, and provide food and beverages.

Blue Dolphin Sailing

BOATING | FAMILY | Set sail on a 40-foot catamaran for an afternoon of sunning, snorkeling, and kayaking aboard the *Blue Dolphin.* The boat departs at 1 pm from the beach next to El Chiringuito Restaurant and returns around sunset. It's $95 per person, including a light meal and open bar. During high season there's also a morning tour, from 8 am to noon, for $80 (including snorkel gear and fishing poles). The boat is also available for private tours. ⊠ *Meet on beach outside Chriniguito restaurant, Tamarindo* ☎ *8842–3204, 855/842–3204 toll-free* ⊕ *www.bluedolphinsailing.com* ⌑ *From $80.*

Iguana Surf

BOATING | This longtime surf shop, with an office across from the beach, organizes jungle boat tours of the Tamarindo Estuary and offers a full roster of local tours, including snorkeling. ⊠ *Tamarindo* ✛ *Across from beach, 100 meters (328 feet) north of El Diriá Hotel* ☎ *2653–0613* ⊕ *www.iguanasurf.net* ⌑ *From $50.*

Marlin del Rey Sailing Tours

BOATING | This custom-built, 66-foot cat-amaran, with a large, comfortable main saloon, takes you on a day tour ($75, minimum 15 people) that includes snorkeling, an open bar, lunch, and snacks. It

leaves at 8 am. The sunset tour departs at 1:30 pm ($85, no minimum), with time to snorkel, walk along a deserted beach, and enjoy the open bar and a gourmet feast, complete with homemade choc-olate-chip cookies. You can also rent the whole boat for private parties. ⊠ *Plaza Esmeralda, next to Subway, Tamarindo* ☎ *2653–1212, 877/827–8275 in U.S.* ⊕ *www.marlindelrey.com* ⌑ *From $75.*

FISHING

Go Fish Costa Rica

FISHING | Steve and Liisa specialize in custom-made fishing trips for everyone from serious sportfishermen to families out for fun, matching you with the best boat and captain for your experience level. On inshore fishing trips, you'll likely catch roosterfish, snapper, and grouper. On deepwater trips you'll go for tuna, mahimahi, and wahoo; marlin and sailfish will get live released. ⊠ *Langosta Beach, Tamarindo* ✛ *Boats usually depart from beach near Chiringuito Restaurant* ☎ *2653–0709* ⊕ *gofishcr.com* ⌑ *Half day from $425.*

Rhino Charger Sportfishing

FISHING | With more than 30 years of sportfishing experience, this U.S.-owned and-operated company has a well-main-tained 31-foot *Island Hopper,* the only boat in the Tamarindo fleet equipped with a flybridge. There are always two English-speaking crew members onboard, with enough room for up to seven anglers per trip. Charters cost $750 for a half day and $1,100 for a full day. Rates include fishing gear, snacks, and beverages. ⊠ *Tamarindo Bay, Tamarindo* ☎ *506/8835–8263 cell, 772/905–2941 in U.S.* ⊕ *www.rhinocharger.com* ⌑ *From $750.*

SURFING

Costa Rica Surf Club

SURFING | Owners Diego and Sabrina go out of their way to share their love of surfing with everyone that walks through the doors. From the novice to the advanced surfer, everyone will enjoy the waves with individual ($55) or group lessons ($35). They also have a large collection of surfboards if you'd like to rent. ⊠ *Main street across from beach in Sunrise Commercial Center, Tamarindo* ☎ *2653–0130* ⊕ *www.facebook.com/crscsurfshop* ⊠ *From $35.*

Iguana Surf

SURFING | FAMILY | Right across from the beach, this popular surf shop rents surfboards ($20 per day) and boogie boards and offers group lessons four times a day ($45, for ages three and up), as well as private lessons ($80). It's open 8 to 6 daily. ⊠ *Tamarindo* ⊹ *Across from beach, 100 meters (328 feet) north of Tamarindo Diria hotel* ☎ *2653–0091* ⊕ *www.iguana-surf.net* ⊠ *From $20.*

Witch's Rock Surf Camp

SURFING | This hip, popular hotel, restaurant, and surf school is surfer central in Tamarindo, with a large surf shop and all the latest gear and board rentals. Surf lessons ($85) include all-day board rental, in-water training, and a surf seminar, such as a shaping tutorial with Robert August of *Endless Summer* fame. Courses for intermediate and advanced surfers are also on offer. If you're just looking to rent a board, this is the place—they have the most solid quiver in town. The shop is right on the beach, just steps from the best surf breaks. ⊠ *North end of beach, main road in Tamarindo, across from Economy Rent a Car, Tamarindo* ☎ *2653–1238, 888/318–7873 toll-free in U.S. and Canada* ⊕ *www.witchsrocksurf-camp.com* ⊠ *From $85.*

TOURS

Black Stallion Surf Saloon

SPECIAL-INTEREST TOURS | FAMILY | This "Costa Rican cowboy saloon with a surfer twist" is a full-day experience that starts with ziplining, horseback riding, and ATV tours, and ends with a barbecue feast of smoked meats like ribs, pork, chorizo, ranch chicken, and grilled vegetables. Homegrown bananas, mangoes,

and citrus are used to infuse cocktails and make dressings and sauces for the farm-to-table dishes. Even vegetarians rave about the endless options of all-you-can-eat grilled fruits, vegetables, and salads. The rustic ranch dining room is intimate and memorable, and the remote location just outside of Tamarindo means you're likely to get a spectacular star show. ⊠ *The Black Stallion Hills Ranch, Tamarindo* ⊹ *10-min drive from Tamarindo* ☎ *8869–9765* ⊕ *www.blackstallion-hills.com* ⊠ *Dinner at 7 pm from $45.*

TURTLE-WATCHING TOURS
ACOTAM

WILDLIFE-WATCHING | FAMILY | ACOTAM, a local conservation association, conducts turtle-viewing tours in Las Baulas National Marine Park in Playa Grande with local guides for $35, including park entrance fee. The group picks you up at your hotel and briefs you at their headquarters on the estuary that separates Tamarindo and Playa Grande. An open boat then takes you across the estuary, where you wait at the park station until a turtle has been spotted. With so few leatherback turtles nesting, you are more likely to see green sea turtles instead. The leatherback nesting season is from mid-October to mid-February. You can see the green sea turtles through April. They also offer covered-boat mangrove tours along the Tamarindo River year-round for $25 per person (minimum two people). ⊠ *Tamarindo* ☎ *2653–1687* ✎ *guiaslocalesta-ma@gmail.com* ⊠ *From $25.*

Playa Langosta

2 km (1 mile) south of Tamarindo.

A chic bedroom community of Tamarindo, just five minutes away by car, Playa Langosta is tranquil and elegant. It has not totally escaped development, but most of the low-rise buildings on the northern half are tucked behind the mangrove trees,

Continued on page 322

SURFING
COSTA RICA

Costa Rica's big surfing community, consistent waves, and not-too-crowded beaches make surfing accessible to anyone who is curious enough to give it a whirl; surf schools, board rentals, and beachside lessons are plentiful. At the most popular beaches, surf tourism is a regular part of the scene. Many instructors are able to bridge generational divides, giving lessons tailored for anyone from tots to retirees. First-timers would be wise to start

by Leland Baxter-Neal

Costa Ricans are known for their laid-back attitude, and this usually translates into a welcoming vibe in the water. Of course, as the waves get more intense, and the surfers more serious, the unspoken rules get stricter, so beginners are advised to stay close to the shore. A good instructor should help keep you out of the way anywhere you go, and if you're on your own, just steer clear of the hot shots until you know the local protocol.

COSTA RICA'S SURF FINDER

THE PACIFIC COAST

For those new to surfing, destinations on the Pacific coast are more welcoming in a number of ways. There are more beaches, hotels, bars, and surf schools than in the Caribbean, and the waves are friendlier. Access to the Northern and Central Pacific coast is also made easy by (sometimes) paved and well-marked roads. As you head southward down the coast, the route becomes untamed. The remoteness of the Osa Peninsula has guarded a couple of world-class breaks surrounded by some of the country's most untouched jungle.

WHEN TO GO: Waves are most consistent from December through April. As you move southward down the coast, the breaks are best from May to November.

THE CARIBBEAN

Costa Rica's truncated Caribbean has comparatively few beaches and they draw only the most dedicated surf seekers. The laid-back culture of that coast seems a perfect match for the surfer vibe. Among the Caribbean waves is perhaps Costa Rica's most famous: Puerto Viejo's Salsa Brava.

WHEN TO GO: Best conditions January through April.

TYPES OF BREAKS

BEACH BREAK: The best type for beginners. Waves break over sandbars and the seafloor. Jacó, Hermosa, and Sámara are all beach breaks.

POINT BREAK: Created as waves hit a point jutting into the ocean. With the right conditions, this can create very consistent waves. Pavones is a point break.

REEF BREAK: Waves break as they hit a reef. It can create great (but dangerous) surf. There's a good chance of getting smashed and scraped over extremely sharp coral or rocks. Salsa Brava, in Puerto Viejo, is a reef break.

PACIFIC

❶ Tamarindo: Very popular with all levels of surfers. It is most famous for its reef breaks like Ollie's Point, Playa Negra (south), and Witch's Rock (north), made famous by the film *Endless Summer*. Nice waves are formed at a point break called Pico Pequeño and at the river mouth called El Estero at the beach's north end.

❷ Playa Guiones: If not the best surf in the vicinity of Nosara, it's the best beach break for beginners and longboarders, second only to Sámara. Lots of long, fun rights and lefts.

❸ Sámara: Protected, mellow beach breaks where the greatest danger is that the waves are too small. Great for beginners and close to lots of breaks like Playa Camaronal for more advanced surfers.

❹ Malpaís: A variety of beach breaks plus a point break that's good when waves get big. Good for beginners and advanced surfers, but hard to reach.

❺ Jacó: Unless the surf gets too big, the consistent beach breaks produce forgiving waves that are good to begin and advance on. The south end is best for beginners.

Tamarindo

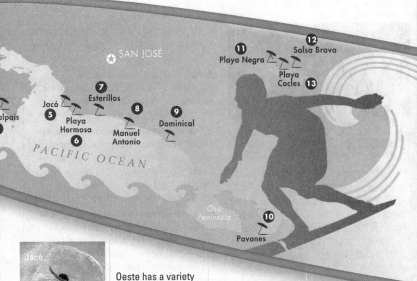

SAN JOSÉ

Playa Negra
Salsa Brava
Playa Cocles

Esterillos
Jacó
Palpaís
Playa Hermosa
Manuel Antonio
Dominical

PACIFIC OCEAN

Osa Peninsula

Pavones

Jacó

Oeste has a variety of beach breaks with softer, friendlier waves.

6 Playa Hermosa:
A steep beach break just south of Jacó with some of the country's best waves and surfers. Waves can get big, mean, and thunderously heavy.

7 Esteríllos:
Divided into three beaches, going north to south: Oeste, Centro, and Este. A beautiful stretch of coast, uncrowded to the point of desolation. The surf and currents can be tough for beginners, and Este and Centro have waves much like Hermosa.

8 Manuel Antonio:
Just outside the national park you'll find a variety of beach breaks. Playitas, at the park's north end, is perhaps the most consistent. This spot only gets good at hightide, about three hours per day. September through December it's ususally flat.

9 Dominical: At the foot of beautiful, forested coastal mountains. A long set of beach breaks that are fun and great for advanced levels. When waves get too big, head south to Dominicalito. This

wave is fast, hollow, and powerful.

10 Pavones: Legendary, remote, and surrounded by rain forest, Pavones is said to be one of the world's longest, left-breaking waves, with a perfect ride lasting nearly three minutes. But with fickle conditions and a tough drive to get here, it's best for the very experienced.

CARIBBEAN

11 Playa Negra:
A largely undiscovered but quality reef break for all skill levels. Be careful at low tide when rocks are exposed.

12 Salsa Brava:
When the conditions are right, this is arguably Costa Rica's best and most powerful wave; it's placed right over a shallow coral reef. For advanced surfers only.

13 Playa Cocles:
Plenty of beach breaks to pick from, good for all levels. But beware the currents or you'll drift out to sea.

SURF SCHOOL TIPS

Surf lesson

Surfing is for the young and the young at heart. At many of Costa Rica's top surf beaches, a wide range of ages and skill sets can be found bobbing together in the water. With the right board and some good instructions, just about anybody can stand up and have some fun in the waves. We strongly recommend taking a lesson or two, but be sure to take them from an actual surf school (there's one on just about every beach) rather than from the eager kid who approaches you with a board. Trained instructors will be much better at adapting their lesson plans to different skill levels, ages, and body types.

If you're a first-timer, there are a few things you need to know before getting in the water.

■ **Pick your beach carefully.** Sámara is a good choice, as is Jacó or Tamarindo. You want beach breaks and small, gentle waves. Make sure to ask about rip tides.

■ **Expect introductory lessons to cover the basics.** You'll learn how to lie on the board, paddle out, pass the incoming waves, and how to pop up on your board. If you're a natural, you'll be able to hop up and stay standing in the white wash of the wave after it breaks.

■ **Have realistic expectations.** Even if you have experience in other board sports, like snowboarding or skateboarding, don't expect to be surfing on the face of the wave or tucking into barrels on your first day. It literally takes years before you can reach that level.

■ **Choose the right gear.** If you're a beginner, start on a longboard, preferably made of foam (aka, "soft top surfboard"). Be sure to wear a rashguard or a wet suit to help protect your chest and stomach from getting scraped or stung by jellyfish. Hydrate, and apply sunscreen.

SURF SLANG (or, how not to sound like a kook)

Barrel: The area created when a wave breaks onto itself in a curl, creating a surfable tube that's the surfer's nirvana. Also called the "green room."

Drop in: To stand up and drop down the face of a wave. Also used when one surfer cuts another off: "Hey, don't drop in on that guy!"

Duck dive: A maneuver where the surfer first pushes his or her board underwater and then dives with it, ducking under waves that have already broken or are about to break. It's difficult with a longboard (⇨ see Turtle roll).

Goofy foot: Having a right-foot-forward stance on the surfboard. The opposite is known as "regular."

Close out: When a wave or a section of a wave breaks all at once, rather than breaking steadily in one direction. A frustrating situation for surfers, giving them nowhere to go as the wave comes crashing down.

Ding: A hole, dent, crack, or other damage to a board.

Grom: A young surfer, usually under 15, who "rips" (is amazing).

Kook: Someone (usually a beginner) trying to pass as a surfer.

Outside: The area farther out from where waves are most regularly breaking. Surfers line up here to catch waves.

Stick: A surfboard.

Turtle roll: A maneuver where the surfer rolls over on the surfboard, going underwater and holding the board upside down. Used by longboarders and beginners to keep from being swept back toward shore by breaking waves.

BOARD SHAPES

Longboard: Lengthier (about 2.5–3 m/ 9–10.5 feet), wider, thicker, and more buoyant than the often-miniscule shortboards. Offers more flotation and speedier paddling, which makes it easier to get into waves. Great for beginners and those with relaxed surf styles. Skill level: Beginner to Intermediate.

Funboard: A little shorter than the longboard with a slightly more acute nose and blunt tail, the funboard combines the best attributes of the longboards with some similar characteristics of the shorter boards. Good for beginners or surfers looking for a board more maneuverable and faster than a longboard. Skill level: Beginner to Intermediate.

Fishboard: A stumpy, blunt-nosed, twin-finned board that features a "V" tail (giving it a "fish" like look, hence the name) and is fast and maneuverable. Good for catching small, steep slow waves and pulling tricks. At one point this was the world's best-selling surfboard. Skill level: Intermediate to Expert.

Shortboard: Shortboards came on the scene in 1967–70 when the average board length dropped from 9'6" to 6'6" (2.9 m to 2 m) and changed the wave riding styles in the surf world forever. This board is a short, light, high-performance stick that is designed for carving the wave with a high amount of maneuverability. These boards generally need a fast steep wave, completely different than a longboard break, which tends to be slower with shallower wave faces. Skill level: Expert.

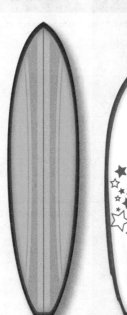

Beginner   Expert

Funboards

Fish

Longboards   Shortboards

Shallow wave faces, easiest surfing   Steeper wave faces, difficult surfing

From family-friendly spots to walkable stretches of sand, Guanacaste has a beach for everyone.

so you can enjoy an unsullied dramatic beachscape, with surf crashing against rocky outcroppings. A few high-rise condominiums have invaded the area, but they are mostly set back. Past Playa Langosta Beach Club are a handful of hotels and B&Bs that outshine properties in neighboring Tamarindo.

GETTING HERE AND AROUND

The municipality is still working on paving the dirt road from Tamarindo to Langosta, so there are some smooth sections and some filled with potholes. A few side roads are still dirt, so to keep down the dust, the road is periodically spread with an industrial molasses mixture, which accounts for the stickiness and the lovely smell of cookies in the air. You can walk along the beach, at low tide, all the way from Tamarindo Beach, but be careful not to get caught on the headland rocks as the tide comes in. Most hotels offer pickup in Tamarindo for car-free visitors. As an alternative you can take a taxi or rent a bicycle for the short trip.

 Beaches

Playa Langosta

BEACH | This Blue Flag beach is actually two beaches: To the north is an upscale residential area where every foot of beachfront has been built up; the beach here is rather narrow, since the coast is lined with rocks, and the light-gray sand is coarse. To the south, the beach is a pristine, protected annex of Las Baulas National Marine Park, where the occasional leatherback turtle nests at night and beachcombers and surfers roam by day. The dividing point is the San Francisco Estuary, the mouth of which is a knee-high wade at low tide, and a deep river with dangerous currents around high tide. The beach here is wider and less rocky, and it's where surfers find the best surf breaks. If you walk up the river at low tide, you may see snowy egrets, baby blue herons, tail-bobbing spotted sandpipers, and, if your eyes are sharp, tiny white-lored gnatcatchers, endemic to these parts. The rockier parts of the beach are excellent for spotting seabirds, including American oystercatchers, and playing in the tide pools. Amenities are available at Playa Langosta Beach Club. **Amenities:** food and drink; toilets. **Best for:** sunset; surfing; walking. ✉ *Playa Langosta.*

🍴 Restaurants

Langosta Beach Club

$$$ | **FRENCH** | This beach club–restaurant–lounge–jazz club is the most romantic and sophisticated dining spot on the beach. By day, you can lounge by the pool or surf between bites of ceviche, panini, burgers, or mussels with fries; by night, you'll find tables set with white linens and candles arranged under swaying palms around two glowing pools. **Known for:** ahi tuna almost too beautiful to eat, topped with arugula and caviar on a tower of thin and crispy potatoes; good wine list and light, refreshing Argentine wines by the glass; beach club atmosphere—stay for the day. $ *Average main: $25* ✉ *Langosta Beach road, Playa Langosta* ✛ *200 meters (656 feet) north of Capitán Suizo* 🕾 *2653–1127* ⊕ *www. langostabeachclub.com* ☞ *Beach club day pass $25.*

★ Langosta Surf Club

$ | **SANDWICHES** | If you want to feel at home on vacation, head to this family-friendly neighborhood sports bar featuring in-house roasted deli meats, local artisanal products, and delectable salads. Choose dine-in or take out lunches like big turkey sandwiches with a side of pineapple slaw or the delightful pear Gorgonzola salad. **Known for:** huge deli sandwiches; healthy, fresh ingredients; fun atmosphere with lots to do. $ *Average main: $8* ✉ *Langosta Beach, Playa Langosta* 🕾 *8332–9339* 🕔 *Closed Sun.*

🛏 Hotels

★ Cala Luna Boutique Hotel

$$$ | **RESORT** | **FAMILY** | For your own "cove of the moon" with casual luxury, Cala Luna is the place in Langosta. **Pros:** yoga classes; gorgeous gardens; complimentary sunset cocktails. **Cons:** rocky beach; mediocre restaurant; five-minute walk to the beach. $ *Rooms from: $249* ✉ *Cala Luna Boutique Hotel and Villas, Playa Langosta* 🕾 *2653–0214* ⊕ *calaluna.com* ⬏ *49 units* ⏺ *Free Breakfast.*

★ Hotel Capitán Suizo

$$$$ | **HOTEL** | Nature, tranquility, luxury, and an unbeatably beautiful beach setting make this environmentally conscious boutique hotel the most elegant choice in town. **Pros:** secluded beachfront hotel; excellent restaurant; lovely gardens and pool. **Cons:** pricey; no TVs; not all rooms are beachfront. $ *Rooms from: $274* ✉ *Playa Langosta* ✛ *Right side of Playa Langosta road, halfway between Tamarindo and Langosta* 🕾 *2653–0075* ⊕ *www. hotelcapitansuizo.com* 🕔 *Usually closed for maintenance between Sept. and Oct.* ⬏ *35 units* ⏺ *Free Breakfast.*

Sueño del Mar

$$$ | **B&B/INN** | The name of this beachfront bed-and-breakfast means "Dream of the Sea," and the front gate opens into a dreamy world of intimate gardens, patios, and hand-painted tiles. **Pros:** intimate; well-appointed; amazing breakfast; great beachfront. **Cons:** lack of privacy in small rooms; pricey; tiny pool. $ *Rooms from: $250* ✉ *Playa Langosta* ✛ *130 meters (426 feet) south of Capitán Suizo, veer right for 45 meters (147 feet), then right again for about 90 meters (295 feet) to entrance gate, across from back of Cala Luna Hotel* 🕾 *2653–0284* ⊕ *www.suenodel-mar.com* ⬏ *6 units* ⏺ *Free Breakfast.*

Nightlife

Playa Langosta Beach Club

PIANO BARS | Sink into a comfortable chair at this chic poolside lounge on Playa Langosta to watch the sunset over the Pacific and listen to jazz under the stars (Tuesday 7 to 9 pm), or treat your ears to some Brazilian music on Friday. ✉ *Tamarindo–Playa Langosta Rd., Playa Langosta* ✛ *200 meters (656 feet) north of Hotel Capitán Suizo* ⊕ *langostabeachclub.com.*

 Activities

Tour operators in Tamarindo, just a few miles north, offer activities in the Playa Langosta area.

Playa Avellanas

17 km (11 miles) south of Tamarindo.

Traditionally a far cry from its northern neighbor's boom of real estate development, Avellanas has seen Tamarindo escapees slowly encroaching on it for years, building private houses and a smattering of small hotels. If they ever pave the road, it may get busy at this beach, but for now, as you bump along the dusty, rough beach road, most of the cars you pass have surfboards on top. But nonsurfers are welcome, as Avellanas (pronounced *ah-vey-YA-nas*) is a lovely spot for anyone who just likes sea and sand.

GETTING HERE AND AROUND

You have to drive inland from Tamarindo to Villareal, where you turn right for the 13-km (8-mile) trip down a bumpy road to reach Playa Avellanas. It takes about 20 minutes. All of the roads in the gated community of Hacienda Pinilla are paved.

If you're without a car, take the Tamarindo Shuttle van. They have private transport to Playa Avellanas for $50 or to the JW Marriott at Hacienda Pinilla for $35.

SHUTTLES Tamarindo Shuttle. ☎ *2653–4444* ⊕ *www.tamarindoshuttle.com.*

 Beaches

Playa Avellanas

BEACH | This beach's main claims to fame are surfing and hanging around at Lola's, a sexy beach restaurant-bar. Wide and sandy at the main access point, the beach itself is beautiful, with a line of palms and beach almonds for shade. Rocky outcroppings and a small river mouth mark its southern end, and a mangrove swamp lies behind its northern half. Its Blue Flag designation means the water is clean, but you shouldn't go in deeper than your waist when the waves are big, because of rip currents. That's when the surfers take over. Jellyfish can be a problem, so you might want to wear a rash guard. Unfortunately, security is an issue here, as at most Costa Rican beaches; posted signs warn visitors not to leave anything of value in parked cars or unattended on the beach. There is guarded parking at the beach entrance near Lola's; be sure to have small bills to tip the attendant when you leave. If you are staying in the gated resort community of Hacienda Pinilla, it's better to park in the private lot and enter from its beach club. **Amenities:** food and drink; parking (no fee). **Best for:** surfing; walking. ✉ *Playa Avellanas.*

 Restaurants

★ **Cactus**

$ | **COSTA RICAN** | It's easy to miss this unassuming eatery surrounded by cactus on the road to the beach, but you would be missing out on some of the area's best Costa Rican food. Starting with the humble dishes of his childhood, the chef elevates the menu with made-from-scratch corn tortillas made into *tayuyás*: sandwiches brimming with sweet and savory fillings like an omelet with cheese curd, ripe banana, honey, and custard, or shredded chicken spiced to perfection with avocado, tomato, and lettuce. **Known for:** breakfast with ice cream; great value; mouthwatering casado. $ *Average main: $8 ✉ Carretera Playa Avellanas, Playa Avellanas ☎ 2215–3899 ⊘ Closed daily 3–6.*

La Purruja

$$ | **AMERICAN** | **FAMILY** | While the day away listening to reggae, sipping on cold drinks, watching the surfers, and snacking on beach food. You can't beat the views or the service, and it's a great family spot owing to the large portions, good prices, and on-site ice cream parlor. **Known for:** fish tacos; wonderful hospitality; beautiful vistas. $ *Average main: $10 ✉ Main entrance to Playa Avellanas, Playa Avellanas ☎ 8703–7231.*

★ Lola's

$$ | **VEGETARIAN** | This hip beach café has exactly the kind of ambience one comes to Costa Rica for, with tables scattered along the beach amid palm and almond trees, hammocks swinging in the wind, palm fronds rustling, and surfers riding the glistening waves in front. Seating, or more precisely, lolling, is on reclining, African-style hardwood chairs, or at shaded tables. **Known for:** great spot to camp out for the day; flatbread pizza, fresh-fruit smoothies, and organic meats; Ave and Ana the pigs, their mascots. $ *Average main: $14 ✉ At main entrance to Playa Avellanas, Playa Avellanas ☎ 2652–9097 ⊕ www.lolascostarica.info.*

🛏 Hotels

Cabinas Las Olas

$$ | **B&B/INN** | **FAMILY** | Frequented mainly by surfers, this is a good option for anyone seeking easy beach access, relative solitude, and comfortable, if not fancy, lodging. **Pros:** near beach; surf shop with board rental and lessons; secluded. **Cons:** simple rooms; patchy Wi-Fi; mosquitoes a problem in rainy season. $ *Rooms from: $100 ✉ 1 km (½ mile) before*

Avellanas, on right, Playa Avellanas ☎ 2652–9315 ⊕ www.cabinaslasolas. com ⊘ Closed Oct. ⇦ 10 rooms ⦿ Free Breakfast.

JW Marriott Guanacaste Resort & Spa

$$$$ | **RESORT** | In the gated community of Hacienda Pinilla, this luxury resort is centered around a 25,000-square-foot infinity pool that merges with a short stretch of beach in the west, making every sunset a major event. **Pros:** largest infinity pool in Central America; luxurious; equestrian center. **Cons:** beach is rocky; ground-level rooms facing walkways get outside noise; very pricey. $ *Rooms from: $538 ✉ In Hacienda Pinilla Beach resort and residential community, Playa Avellanas ☎ 2681–2000 ⊕ www.marriott.com/sjojw ⇦ 310 rooms ⦿ No Meals.*

★ Los Altos de Eros Luxury Inn & Spa

$$$$ | **HOTEL** | This intimate adults-only inn is the place to be for honeymooning couples with enough money left over after the wedding to pamper themselves, or for stressed-out high achievers in need of some serious relaxation therapy. **Pros:** secluded location; excellent service, including the outstanding spa; complimentary transportation for hotel guests to Tamarindo and Avellanas 6:30–8:30. **Cons:** no kids under 18; difficult to find; scheduled mealtimes. $ *Rooms from: $330 ✉ Cañafistula ✛ 14 km (8½ miles) southeast of Tamarindo ☎ 8850–4203, 800/391–1944 ⊕ www.losaltosdeeros. com ⇦ 6 rooms ⦿ Free Breakfast.*

🏃 Activities

GOLF

Hacienda Pinilla Golf Course

GOLF | Mike Young, who has designed some of the best golf courses in the southern United States, designed the par-72 championship course at Hacienda Pinilla. It has ocean views and breezes, and plenty of birds populate the surrounding trees. Not as busy as some of the other courses in Guanacaste, the fairways are wide with long par 4s, and Holes 15 and 9 are challenging. The latter, a par 4, shoots over a few bunkers to an elevated green. Non–hotel guests pay $150 for 18 holes in high season, including carts and range balls; club rental is $50 more. ✉ *In Hacienda Pinilla gated community, next to JW Marriott, 10 km (6 miles) south of Tamarindo via Villa Real, Tamarindo* ☎ *2681–4500* 🌐 *www.haciendapinilla.com* 🎫 *$150 for 18 holes* 🏌 *18 holes, 7200 yards, par 72.*

SURFING

Locals claim there are eight breaks here when the swell is big, which means Avellanas doesn't suffer the kind of overcrowding as the breaks at Playas Negra and Langosta. Tamarindo-based surf schools can arrange day trips here.

Cabinas Las Olas

SURFING | You can rent boards at Cabinas Las Olas for $20 a day and they offer private lessons for $80. ✉ *Main road, on right, Playa Avellanas* ☎ *2652–9315* 🌐 *cabinaslasolas.com* 🎫 *from $20.*

Playa Negra

3 km (2 miles) south of Playa Avellanas.

Surfer culture is apparent here in the wave of beach-shack surfer camps along the road that leads to the rocky strand of beach. But Playa Negra is growing up fast, with some interesting cafés and restaurants popping up to cater to beachgoers and residents of an upscale residential development called Rancho Playa Negra.

A Surf Classic

Americans—surfer Americans, at least—got their first look at Playa Negra in 1994's *The Endless Summer II*, a film by legendary surf documentarian Bruce Brown.

GETTING HERE AND AROUND

From Playa Avellanas, continue south 10 minutes on the rough beach road to Playa Negra. If it's rainy season and the road is too rough, you can approach along a slightly more civilized route from Santa Cruz. Drive 27 km (16½ miles) west, via Veintisiete de Abril, to Paraíso, then follow signs for Playa Negra for 4 km (2½ miles). Taxis are the easiest way to get around if you don't have a car; they cost about $40 from Tamarindo.

Beaches

Playa Negra

BEACH | Contrary to the name, the beach is not black, but rather beige with dark streaks. This is primarily a surfer's beach, so it's not great for swimming because it tends to have fast hollow waves and is lined with rocks. There is one calm, short stretch of clear sand to the south of the Playa Negra Hotel, and at low tide a large tidal pool forms there. The spindly buttonwood trees that edge the beach provide sparse shade. The dirt road to Playa Negra is always bumpy and muddy during rainy season, so drive with caution. Food and drink are served at Playa Negra Hotel's *palapa* restaurant on the beach. **Amenities:** food and drink; parking (no fee). **Best for:** surfing; walking. ✉ *Playa Negra.*

Restaurants

Café Playa Negra

$$ | **PERUVIAN** | This surf café features such Peruvian specialties as ceviche and *causa* (cold mashed potatoes studded with shrimp and tuna chunks). The menu also includes a few familiar favorites like hamburgers and BLTs. **Known for:** pisco sour cocktails; beautiful presentation; ceviche and sushi. [$] *Average main: $12* ✉ *Main street, Playa Negra* ☎ *2652–9351* 🌐 *www.cafeplayanegra.com* 🕒 *Closed Tues. and Oct.*

Kon-Tiki

$$ | ITALIAN | A favorite local hangout, this rustic pizzeria has an outdoor clay oven and an open kitchen. There are 14 types of pizza, like the house special with goat cheese, pesto, and caramelized onions. **Known for:** busy atmosphere; sangria; amazing crispy crust. $ *Average main: $14 ✉ Playa Negra ✛ 700 meters (2,296 feet) after soccer field at Los Pargos ☎ 2652–9117 ⊕ www.facebook.com/kon-tikiplayanegra ⊙ Closed Mon. No lunch.*

★ Restaurant Deevena

$$$ | FRENCH FUSION | An unexpected outpost of divine French cuisine, this oasis of elegance overlooks a sparkling blue pool edged by lush palms, while lounge chairs shaded by orange umbrellas tempt diners to stay overnight (six stylish rooms are available). Lunch and dinner feature lots of local seafood, produce, and goat cheese from the chef's nearby farm. **Known for:** volcano dessert with chocolate lava; fresh catch of the day; tantalizing pasta, steak, and seafood prepared in a French style. $ *Average main: $24 ✉ Playa Negra ✛ 25 meters (82 feet) off main road that runs through Playa Negra; watch for Villa Deevena sign ☎ 2653–2328 ⊕ www.villadeevena.com ⊙ Closed Mon. and Sept.–Oct.*

Hotels

Cafe Playa Negra Hotel

$$ | HOTEL | This "boho chic" boutique hotel is charming, close to the beach, and a good value. **Pros:** great restaurant; short walk to the beach; good value. **Cons:** no TVs; small pool; rough road to get here. $ *Rooms from: $100 ✉ Calle Principal De Los Pargos, Playa Negra ☎ 6084–5053 ⊕ cafeplayanegra.com ⇄ 8 rooms ⦿| Free Breakfast.*

Hotel Playa Negra

$$ | HOTEL | Pastel-color, round cabinas are sprinkled across sunny lawns strewn with tropical plants at this gorgeous oceanfront place with a huge round pool. **Pros:** in front of reef break; comfortable accommodation; family suites available. **Cons:** rocky road to hotel; some rooms lack a/c and Wi-Fi; not a great swimming beach. $ *Rooms from: $96 ✉ 4 km (2½ miles) northwest of Paraíso on dirt road (watch signs for Playa Negra), then follow signs carefully at forks in road; or 10 mins south of Playa Avellanas on beach road, Playa Negra ☎ 2652–9134 ⊕ playanegra.com ⊙ Restaurant closed Sept. and Oct. ⇄ 17 units ⦿| No Meals.*

Villa Deevena

$$ | HOTEL | Although most travelers visit this out-of-the-way spot for its famed French restaurant by the same name, Deevena is equally gaining renown for its hospitable staff and elegant rooms that surround a pool. **Pros:** excellent restaurant; saltwater pool; family-run business. **Cons:** not on the beach; breakfast not included; outdoor showers attract bugs. $ *Rooms from: $145 ✉ Playa Negra ✛ 25 meters (82 feet) off main road that runs through Playa Negra; watch for Villa Deevena sign ☎ 2653–2328 ⊕ www.villadeevena.com ⊙ Closed Sept. and Oct. ⇄ 6 rooms ⦿| No Meals.*

Activities

SURFING

Surfers dig the waves here, which are almost all rights, with beautifully shaped barrels. It's a spectacular, but treacherous, rock-reef break for experienced surfers only. There's also a small beach break to the south of the rocks where neophytes can cut their teeth. Both breaks can be ridden from mid- to high tide.

Hotel Playa Negra

SURFING | The point break is right in front of the only beachfront hotel, which can arrange surfing classes ($40 per hour for a private lesson) and rent boards ($20 per day). ✉ *Playa Negra ✛ 4 km (2½ miles) northwest of Paraíso on dirt road, then follow signs carefully at forks in road; or 10 mins south of Playa Avellanas on rough* *beach road* ☎ *2652–9298* 🌐 *playanegra.com* 🛏 *From $40.*

Playa Junquillal

4 km (2½ miles) south of Paraíso, 34 km (22 miles) southwest of Santa Cruz.

Seekers of oceanfront tranquility need look no further than Junquillal (pronounced *hoon-key-YALL*), a beach town as far away from the crowd as you can get on a decent road. A surprisingly cosmopolitan mélange of expats has settled in this out-of-the-way area. There's a supermarket at the entrance to an upscale housing development, but Junquillal is still barely on the tourist map; consequently its few hotels offer some of the best deals on the North Pacific coast. Avoid visiting between September and November, when hotels close, beaches are empty, and Junquillal virtually turns into a ghost town.

GETTING HERE AND AROUND

In rainy season, the 4-km-long (2½-mile-long) beach road from Playa Negra to Playa Junquillal is sometimes not passable. The alternative is driving down from Santa Cruz one hour on a road that's paved most of the way. There is a bus to Junquillal from the central market in Santa Cruz; the trip takes about 40 minutes. A taxi from Santa Cruz or Tamarindo costs about $50; from the Liberia airport, $95 to $100.

ESSENTIALS

The closest town for most services is Santa Cruz, 34 km (22 miles) northeast.

Beaches

Playa Junquillal

BEACH | **FAMILY** | This wide swath of light-brown sand stretches over 3 km (2 miles), with coconut palms lining much of it and hardly a building in sight. Two species of sea turtle nest here, and a group of young people collect and protect their eggs, releasing the baby turtles after sunset. The surf is a little strong, so watch children carefully. There's a kids' playground right at the beach, and a funky little restaurant with concrete tables amid the palms. At low tide, it's a perfect beach for taking long, romantic strolls or for exploring active tide pools. Surfers head here to ride the beach break near Junquillal's northern end because it rarely gets crowded. **Amenities:** food and drink. **Best for:** surfing; walking. ✉ *Playa Junquillal.*

Hotels

★ **Guacamaya Lodge**

$$ | **HOTEL** | **FAMILY** | Spread across a breezy hill with expansive views above the treetops of the surrounding forest and the sea, the Guacamaya is a real find, with affordable, spacious cabinas surrounding a generous-size pool, lawn, and tropical plants. **Pros:** excellent value; clean; friendly. **Cons:** meals and taxes not included in rate; some rooms may need updating; hilly five-minute walk to the beach. [$] *Rooms from: $105* ✉ *Playa Junquillal* ✥ *275 meters (902 feet) east of Playa Junquillal* ☎ *2658–8431* 🌐 *www.guacamayalodge.com* ⏲ *Closed Sept. and Oct.* 🛏 *12 units* 🍴 *No Meals.*

Mundo Milo Eco Lodge

$$ | **B&B/INN** | This hidden ecolodge with a kidney-shape pool is made up of five bungalows themed after Africa, Persia, and Mexico. **Pros:** 300 meters (984 feet) from the beach; great value; delicious food at restaurant. **Cons:** closed September and October; bumpy road; ecolodge equals natural, so there may be some bugs. [$] *Rooms from: $77* ✉ *C. Mundo Milo, Playa Junquillal* ✥ *300 meters (984 feet) from beach* ☎ *2658–7010* 🌐 *www.mundomilo.com* 💳 *No credit cards* ⏲ *Closed Sept. and Oct.* 🛏 *6 units* 🍴 *Free Breakfast.*

Chapter 8

THE NICOYA PENINSULA

8

Updated by
Marlise Kast-Myers

 ◉ Sights
★★★★☆

 🍴 Restaurants
★★★☆☆

 🛏 Hotels
★★★★☆

 💼 Shopping
★★★☆☆

 🍸 Nightlife
★★★★☆

WELCOME TO THE NICOYA PENINSULA

TOP REASONS TO GO

★ **Beaches:** Whether you enjoy hidden coves or popular spots to share a sunset with new friends, there is a beach for you here.

★ **Flora and fauna:** From sea turtles and howler monkeys to caves and deciduous forest, nature abounds.

★ **Laid-back vibes:** Life moves a little slower here, so expect to linger over dinners and endless beach days. It's the *pura vida* everyone keeps talking about.

★ **Yoga:** Now a major wellness destination, the Nicoya Peninsula has yoga on seemingly every corner (and monkeys leaning in to watch your vinyasa).

★ **Surfing:** There are gentle beach breaks and overhead swells and barrels; the consistent waves of the Nicoya Peninsula are ideal for experts and newbies alike.

Lively beach towns dot the coast of the Nicoya Peninsula from Nosara down to Playa Tambor, at the southern tip. In the south, communities are small and quiet, with a funky, European vibe. National parks Palo Verde and Barra Honda are the main attractions in the interior of the peninsula. The former is a prime bird-watching park; the latter has caves and waterfalls to explore.

1 Nosara. Despite its growth, this surf and yoga haven retains its sleepy, offbeat feel.

2 Sámara. Popular beach bars and an array of restaurants make this a lovely little international beach community.

3 Playa Carrillo. Long, reef-protected crescent beach backed by swaying coconut palms and sheltering cliffs.

4 Punta Islita. One of the few places aside from the capital with art, Punta Islita also has a beautiful rocky beach and a tiny tuft of land that becomes an island at high tide.

5 Palo Verde National Park. A hot, dry deciduous forest that is decidedly not lush, but is home to deer, monkeys, peccaries, lizards, and thousands of waterfowl.

6 Barra Honda National Park. A massive peak with hiking trails leading to dazzling vistas and a labyrinth of caves to be explored.

7 Curú National Wildlife Refuge. This private refuge has some of the best wildlife-viewing opportunities on the Nicoya Peninsula, a pristine beach, and cool bioluminescent kayaking tours.

8 Playa Tambor Area. One of the lesser developed group of beaches and towns on the peninsula, perfect for solitary relaxing and soaking up the sun.

9 Isla Tortuga. A lavish and impressive, if somewhat crowded, island oasis; a quick boat ride away from Playa Tambor or Montezuma.

10 Montezuma. An artsy, eccentric beach community beautifully positioned on a sandy bay that has avoided overdevelopment.

11 Malpaís and Santa Teresa. Small-town surfers' paradise with a stretch of hotels, restaurants, and shopping centers lining a sometimes sandy and sometimes rocky beach filled with wave seekers.

PALO VERDE NATIONAL PARK

Aerial view of the Tempisque River.

One of the best wildlife- and bird-watching parks in the country, Palo Verde extends over 198 square km (76 square miles) of dry deciduous forest, bordered on the west by the wide Tempisque River.

With fairly flat terrain and less density than a rain forest, wildlife is often easier to spot here. Frequent sightings include monkeys, coatis, peccaries, lizards, and snakes. Keep an eye out for the harlequin snake. It's nonpoisonous but its coloring mimics the deadly coral snake.

The park contains seasonal wetlands at the end of the rainy season that provide a temporary home for migratory and resident aquatic birds, including herons, wood storks, jabirus, and flamingo-like roseate spoonbills. Crocodiles can be spotted in the waters of the Tempisque River year-round, and storks nest on islands at the mouth of the river where it empties into the Gulf of Nicoya. Trails are well marked, but the weather here can be very hot and windy. Mosquitoes, especially in the marshy areas, are rampant during the wet season (May–December).

(For more information, see the review in this chapter.)

BEST TIME TO GO

The best time of year to visit is at the beginning of the dry season, especially in January and February, when the seasonal wetlands are shrinking and birds and wildlife are concentrated around smaller ponds. During the month of April, the wetlands are completely dry.

FUN FACT

The park is named after the light-green palo verde bush, also known as the Jerusalem thorn. Even when it loses its leaves, this tree can still photosynthesize through its trunk.

BEST WAYS TO EXPLORE

BIRD-WATCHING

The greatest number of wildlife species you're likely to see here are birds, close to 300 recorded species. Many of them are aquatic birds drawn to the park's vast marshes and seasonal wetlands. The most sought-after aquatic bird is the jabiru stork, a huge white bird with a red neck and long black bill. You may well spot it soaring overhead—it's hard to miss. Palo Verde and surrounding areas are the most important breeding sites for this species.

PARK STRATEGIES

Unlike many of the other national parks, you can drive 7 km (4½ miles) of fairly rough road from the park entrance to the Organization for Tropical Studies (OTS) research station, where most of the trailheads begin. From that point, the best way to see the park is on foot. Plan to spend a couple of nights in the dormitory-style park lodge so that you can get an early-morning start. You'll want to get out early because this is a very, very hot area. Hike open areas in the cooler mornings and then choose shaded forest trails for hikes later in the day. Make sure you have a good sun hat, too.

RIVER CRUISE

A river does run through the park, so a delightful and less strenuous wildlife-viewing option is to cruise down the Tempisque River on a chartered boat with a guide who'll do the spotting for you. Without a boat, you are limited to observing the marshy areas and riverbanks from a long distance. Be sure the boat you choose has a bilingual naturalist on board who knows the English names of birds and animals. River cruises are by reservation only, which can be arranged through the OTS research station.

Wildlife, like spectacled caiman, abounds in Palo Verde.

TOP REASONS TO GO

BIRDS, BIRDS, BIRDS

Even if you're not used to looking at birds, you'll be impressed by the waves of migratory waterbirds that use this park as a way station on their routes. Think of the 2001 documentary *Winged Migration* and you'll have an idea of the number of birds that flock here.

LOTS OF WILD ANIMALS

Hiking the forest trails is hot work, especially in the dry season. But the wildlife viewing here makes it worthwhile. Watch for monkeys, peccaries, spiny tailed iguanas, and coatis. Take plenty of water, and use insect repellent or wear long sleeves and pants.

OUTDOOR ADVENTURES

The Organization for Tropical Studies has a number of activities to choose from, including guided nature walks, mountain biking, boat tours, and even an occasional nighttime tour. The park service offers bunk-bed lodging without air-conditioning.

The Nicoya Peninsula PALO VERDE NATIONAL PARK 8

On this quirky peninsula south of Tamarindo, you'll find the interesting anomaly of a trendy restaurant or upscale hotel plunked at the end of a tortuous dirt road. The key to enjoying the Nicoya Peninsula is to pick your spot—happening beach town or off-the-beaten-path seclusion.

The parks and wildlife refuges in and around the Río Tempisque are prime places to hike, explore caves, and spot birds and other wildlife. And there's a smattering of culture, too, in the town of Nicoya, with its colonial-era church, and in Guaitil, with pottery made in the pre-Columbian Chorotega tradition. The town of Nicoya is the commercial and political hub of the northern Nicoya Peninsula. By road, Nicoya provides the best access to Sámara, Nosara, and points south and north, and is linked by a smooth, well-paved road to the northern Nicoya beach towns.

The southern tip of the Nicoya Peninsula is one of Costa Rica's less developed regions, where some of the country's most gorgeous beaches, rain forests, waterfalls, and tidal pools lie at the end of some of its worst roads. Within the region are quiet, well-preserved parks where you can explore pristine forests or travel by boat or sea kayak to idyllic islands for bird-watching or snorkeling. Other outdoor options include horseback riding, gliding through the treetops on a canopy tour, or surfing on some of the country's most consistent waves. In the laid-back beach towns of Montezuma, Santa Teresa, and Malpaís, an international cast of surfers, nature lovers, yoga enthusiasts, holistic new-agers, and expatriate massage therapists live out their dreams in paradise.

Planning

When to Go

HIGH SEASON: MID-DECEMBER TO APRIL

The driest and hottest time of the year, with average temperatures hovering between 86°F and 95°F, this is the time to come if you're looking to soak up some sun with nary a raindrop in sight. The beaches and parks are the busiest this time of year, especially when school is out for Costa Ricans, mid-December to February. With the new year in January come the Papagayo winds, bringing lots of gusts, especially along the coast. These breezes usually die down by mid-February. This is the best period for snorkeling, whale-watching, and fishing. The landscape isn't at its most resplendent during this time—much of the green gives way to brown.

LOW SEASON: MAY THROUGH OCTOBER

Although the mornings are usually clear, pretty much every afternoon during low (rainy) season brings showers. These rains are accompanied by smaller crowds, lush green landscapes, and more affordable accommodations. Some roads become impassable during this time, making alternate (longer) routes neccessary.

SHOULDER SEASON: NOVEMBER TO MID-DECEMBER

Shoulder season, verdant and lush, is the best time to visit the Nicoya Peninsula. Smaller crowds and reasonable temperatures make getting around more pleasant, while hotels and restaurants are ready for guests.

PLANNING YOUR TIME

Each little beach town on the peninsula has its own flavor, so it's nice to be able to stay in more than one place. With that said, the roads here are tough going, so schedule driving time into your plans. "As the crow flies" is rare here, so expect bumpy, winding dirt roads. Plan to spend at least a week on the peninsula. Split your time between beach activities like surf lessons, snorkeling, and turtle and whale-watching, in addition to land explorations of the caves and other parks. Whatever you do, don't forget to lounge.

Getting Here and Around

AIR

Aeropuerto Internacional Daniel Oduber Quirós (LIR) in Liberia is an international gateway to the coast, with a large, air-conditioned terminal. Tamarindo, Nosara, Playa Sámara, and Punta Islita also have small airstrips. Flying from San José to these airports is the best way to get here if you are already in the country. If your primary destination lies in Nicoya, make sure you investigate the possibility of flying directly into Liberia instead of

San José, which saves some serious hours on the road.

Many airlines have direct service from major hubs to Costa Rica's two international airports in San José and Liberia. SANSA and Aerobell have scheduled flights between San José and Liberia, as well as destinations on the Nicoya Peninsula. Don't forget to factor in the exit tax, $29 by air and $8 by land, payable in U.S. dollars, colones, or by credit card. Most airlines include this fee in the ticket price.

CAR

You will want to rent a four-wheel-drive vehicle to drive around the peninsula. Waze is the best driving app in Costa Rica—download it before you come for updated road conditions and accurate driving directions. The roads get muddy and full of potholes during rainy season, and they can be dusty and bumpy in the dry season. Depending on whether you look at this as an adventure or an agony, you will either love the trip or wish you had flown the national airlines. Highway 150, which runs from Nicoya to Sámara, is smooth sailing all the way. The same applies to Route 21 from Liberia to the southern Nicoya Peninsula. Route 160 to reach Montezuma and Malpaís takes you a bit off the beaten path, with some gravel, dirt, and river crossings, where it's easy to get stuck in the mud when conditions are wet. The road from Tamarindo south to Nosara has some major river crossings and is not advised during rainy season.

FERRY

If you're headed to the southern Nicoya Peninsula (Curú, Tambor, Montezuma, Malpaís, or Santa Teresa), the ferry ride from Puntarenas to Paquera across the Gulf of Nicoya is not only the fastest route, it's also the most scenic, with great views of the mountainous coast and islands.

Restaurants

The varied and wonderful restaurants of the peninsula, many with tables in the sand, ocean waves in the background, and twinkling lights strung overhead, rival any in Costa Rica. In many of the areas where more Europeans have settled, like Sámara and Malpaís, you will find French and Italian restaurants with homemade pasta and from-scratch sauces. Don't rule out the healthy fare at wellness destinations—dishes are often innovative and enticing.

■ TIP→ **Many restaurants, especially tourist-oriented ones with dollar-denominated menus, do not include the 13% national sales tax plus mandatory 10%–12% service. By law, menus are required to show the total price including tax, but many owners flout this law. Be sure to ask if taxes are included; otherwise you may be surprised by a bill that's 25% higher than you expected.**

Hotels

The hotels on the Nicoya Peninsula range from boutiques perched on mountainsides to cabinas in the jungle where you can wake up to howler monkeys to all-inclusive beach resorts. No matter your choice, you will always get the best hospitality from the eager-to-please independently owned lodging. Hotel owners are generally folks who have come here and fallen in love with the place, so they can usually give you the best tips on hidden waterfalls, good-natured guides, and where to spot the monkeys.

RESTAURANT AND HOTEL PRICES

Restaurant prices are the average cost of a main course at dinner or, if dinner is not served, at lunch. Hotel prices are the lowest cost of a standard double room in high season. Restaurant and hotel reviews have been shortened. For full information, visit Fodors.com.

What it Costs in U.S. Dollars			
$	$$	$$$	$$$$
RESTAURANTS			
under $10	$10–$15	$16–$25	over $25
HOTELS			
under $75	$75–$150	$151–$250	over $250

Tours

Horizontes Nature Tours

GUIDED TOURS | With a focus on nature and adventure, Horizontes has independent, private tours with your own guide and driver as well as small-group tours. Customized tours are available for bird-watchers, families, couples, yogis, and beachgoers. Average tours are six nights. ✉ *Nicoya* ⊕ *www.horizontes.com.*

Nosara

28 km (17 miles) southwest of Nicoya.

One of the last beach communities for people who want to get away from it all, Nosara's attractions are the wild stretches of side-by-side beaches called Pelada and Guiones, with surfing waves and miles of sand on which to stroll, and the tropical dry forest that covers much of the hinterland. While it is becoming one of the most popular destinations in Costa Rica, it somehow manages to feel as if you've discovered your own tropical paradise (nice, after you finally arrive from the bumpy, dusty dirt road). Regulations here limit development to low-rise buildings 600 feet from the beach, where they are thankfully screened by trees. Americans and Europeans, with a large Swiss contingent, are building at an increasingly rapid pace. There still appears to be an aesthetic sense here that is totally lacking in Guanacaste's Tamarindo, despite a plethora of trendy juice bars, fast-food taco stands, and souvenir stalls cropping up at the beach entrances. Offsetting the fast-food wave are the two organic farmers' markets in town, Sunday 9 to 2 and Tuesday starting at 8 am, in the Esquinas Skate Park next to the police station. Hotel owners and community members are participating in a reforestation project along the beachfront to create a lusher biological corridor and the results are beautifully evident already. The town of Nosara itself is inland and not very attractive, but it does have essential services, as well as the airplane landing strip. Almost all the tourist action is at the beaches.

For years, most travelers headed here for the surf. The wide range of surf schools and waves varying from beginner to expert levels make Nosara one of the best places to learn to surf. Along with surfing, the Nosara Yoga Institute, which offers instructor training and daily classes for all levels, is a major draw for health-conscious visitors. Healthy food options, spas, and exercise classes abound. You'll see lots of yoga practitioners on the beaches around sunrise and sunset.

Bird-watchers and other nature enthusiasts can explore the tropical dry forest on hiking trails, on horseback, or by floating up the tree-lined Nosara River in a kayak, guide boat, or paddleboard. The last leg of the access road to Nosara, from either direction, is still abysmal, and the labyrinth of woodsy roads around the beaches and hard-to-read signs make it easy to get lost, which is why most hotels here provide local maps for their guests. Don't get in your car without one—especially at night. For local news and tourist information, pick up a free copy of the excellent monthly bilingual newspaper *The Voice of Guanacaste* (⊕ www.vozdeguanacaste. com).

GETTING HERE AND AROUND

From Liberia, it's about a three-hour drive to Playa Guiones, the beach in Nosara. Take Route 21 south all the way to Nicoya. While on a map the beach drive may look more desirable, in practice, it is infinitely longer and dustier. From Nicoya drive south, almost to Sámara, but take the very first road sign for Nosara, 1 km (½ mile) south of the big gas station before Sámara. This high road is rough for about 8 km (5 miles), but there are bridges over all the river crossings. When you join up with the beach road near Garza, you still have a very bumpy 10 km (6 miles) to go. The roads into Nosara are in poor shape, so a 4WD vehicle is definitely recommended. Budget about one hour for the trip from Nicoya. On the bright side, the main road above the beaches has finally been paved, cutting down on the choking dust in dry season. But all the dirt side roads to the beaches are still either dust bowls or mired in mud. The more remote the area, the more likely that someone will stop to help you change a tire or tow you out of a river. Usually, Good Samaritans won't accept any payment and are more trustworthy than those who offer to "help" in the States.

Coming from San José, you can fly directly to the town of Nosara on daily scheduled SANSA flights, or take an air-conditioned shuttle van from San José. To book flights you need to go directly to the airline's website. Major rent-a-car companies have offices in Playa Guiones.

RENTAL CARS Alamo/National. ⊠ *Playa Guiones road next to Café de Paris, Nosara* ☎ *2682–0894.* **Economy.** ⊠ *Below Marlin Bill's Restaurant, at intersection of main road and Playa Guiones road, Nosara* ☎ *2682–1146.*

AIRLINES SANSA Airlines. ⊠ *Nosara Airport, Nosara* ☎ *2290–4100* ⊕ *www. flysansa.com.*

ESSENTIALS

BANKS/ATMS Banco de Costa Rica.
✉ *Next to Servicentro Nosara gas station, main road, Nosara* ☎ *2682–5232.* **Banco Popular.** ✉ *Main St., next door to Café de Paris, Playa Guiones* ☎ *2682–0011.*

HOSPITAL Centro Médico Nosara. ✉ *Nosara ✛ Next door to Mandala shop, 100 meters (328 feet) west of Café de Paris, on road to Playa Guiones* ☎ *2682–1212.*

PHARMACY Farmacia Elimar Nosara. ✉ *In town, on right side of airstrip, Nosara ✛ 600 meters (1,968 feet) past the airport* ☎ *2682–5149.* **Farmacia Guiones.** ✉ *Nosara ✛ 150 meters (492 feet) east of Café de Paris, next to Medical Center* ☎ *2101–7528.*

POST OFFICE Correo. ✉ *Next to soccer field in town, Nosara* ☎ *2682–0100* ⊕ *correos.go.cr.*

Sights

★ **Ostional National Wildlife Refuge** (*Refugio Nacional de Fauna Silvestre Ostional*)
WILDLIFE REFUGE | FAMILY | This wildlife refuge protects one of Costa Rica's major nesting beaches for olive ridley turtles. If you get to go when the turtles are hatching, it is a magical experience. Locals have formed an association to run the reserve on a cooperative basis, and during the first 36 hours of the *arribadas* (mass nesting) they are allowed to harvest the eggs, on the premise that eggs laid during this time would likely be destroyed by subsequent waves of mother turtles. Though turtles nest here year-round, the largest arribadas, with thousands of turtles nesting over the course of several nights, occur from July to December; smaller arribadas take place between January and May. They usually occur around high tide, the week of a new moon. It's best to go very early in the morning, at sunrise. People in Nosara can tell you when an arribada has begun, or check the Facebook page *Asociacion de Guias Locales de*

Ostional (AGLO) Costa Rica. To avoid overcrowding on the beach, visitors must join a guide-led tour of the nesting and hatching areas for $20 per person. Stop at the kiosk at the entrance to the beach to arrange a tour, or at the Association of Guides office, 25 meters (82 feet) south of the beach entrance on the main road, next to Cabinas Ostional. A new bridge over the Río Montaña has made access easier from Nosara, but it's sometimes difficult to get to from the north during rainy season (May to mid-December). ✉ *7 km (4½ miles) north of Nosara, Nosara* ☎ *2682–0428* 🖘 *$20.*

Beaches

★ **Playa Guiones**
BEACH | This beach is one of the natural wonders of Costa Rica: a wide expanse of light-brown sand, sandwiched between rolling surf and green sea-grape vines starting at the high-tide mark and backed by rejuvenating secondary forest. With some of the most consistent surf on the Pacific coast, Playa Guiones attracts a lot of surfboard-toting visitors, but the always-breezy beach is also a haven for sun lovers, beachcombers, and anyone who wants to connect with nature. The only building in sight is the bizarre Hotel Nosara, which was originally the only choice for lodging in town but is now one of many. Otherwise, this glorious Blue Flag beach has 7 km (4½ miles) of hard-packed sand, great for jogging, riding bikes, and saluting the sun. Because there's a 10-foot tide, the beach is expansive at low tide but rather narrow at high tide, when waves usually create strong currents that can make the sea dangerous for nonsurfers. Most hotels post tide charts. Keep in mind there are no umbrellas for rent on this shadeless beach. Guiones is at the south end of the Nosara agglomeration, with three public accesses. The easiest one to find is about 300 meters (984 feet) past the Harmony Hotel, beyond the parked ATVs and

souvenir stalls. **Amenities:** none. **Best for:** surfing; walking. ✉ *Playa Guiones, Nosara.*

Playa Pelada

BEACH | North along the shore, Playa Guiones segues seamlessly into crescent-shape Playa Pelada, where the water is a little calmer and just as clean, also designated a Blue Flag beach. There are tide pools to explore and a blowhole that sends water shooting up when the surf is big. Lots of trees provide shade. The northern end has a decent surf break, but novice surfers should beware of riptides and rocks. This is the locals' favorite vantage point for watching sunsets—great photo ops, with beached fishing boats adding color and interest to the foreground. Olga's Beach Club bar is nothing fancy, but it's a good place for a cool beer and fried red snapper. More upscale and romantic are the cushioned settees in front of La Luna Bar, on a slight rise overlooking the beach. **Amenities:** food and drink. **Best for:** sunset; surfing; swimming. ✉ *Playa Pelada, Nosara.*

🍴 Restaurants

Il Peperoni

$$ | ITALIAN | FAMILY | Head to this spot for the biggest pizzas in town in a large, roofed-over garden near Playa Pelada. The house pizza is thin crust with carrots, broccoli, olives, red peppers, onions, mushrooms, ham, and pepperoni. **Known for:** spicy dipping oil; family-friendly setting; wood-fired brick-oven pizzas. [$] *Average main: $15* ✉ *Across from Condominios Las Flores, road to Playa Pelada, Nosara* ☎ *8334–9999* 🕓 *Closed Sun.*

★ **La Luna**

$$$ | MEDITERRANEAN | FAMILY | Dawn to dusk, this casually chic restaurant overlooking Playa Pelada is the most scenic place to have breakfast, lunch, cocktails, or dinner, with tables spilling out of the interior onto a wide, covered terrace and onto the sand. The menu is mostly Mediterranean, ranging from Moroccan-spiced or limoncello-marinated fish of the day, to beef or fish carpaccio and brick oven–fired pizzas. **Known for:** Mediterranean platter with hummus and tzatziki; spectacular sunsets; crispy-crust pizza. [$] *Average main: $16* ✉ *Playa Pelada, overlooking beach, Nosara* ☎ *2682–0122.*

Marlin Bill's

$$ | AMERICAN | FAMILY | Carnivores can sink their teeth into a 22-ounce bone-in, rib-eye steak or 16-ounce pork chops in American-size portions at this open-air restaurant with a great sunset view. Lighter choices include grilled fish and salads, eggplant Parmesan, homemade spinach-and-ricotta ravioli in marinara sauce, and delicious "dorado fingers" (battered fish-fillet strips served with tartar sauce). **Known for:** daily specials; margaritas and rum-based drinks; live music on weekends. [$] *Average main: $14* ✉ *Hilltop above main road, near Coconut Harry's Surf Shop, Nosara* ☎ *2682–0458* 🕓 *Closed Sun.*

☕ Coffee and Quick Bites

Café de Paris

$$ | ECLECTIC | FAMILY | Vestiges of the original Swiss-French owners linger on at this bakery and alfresco eatery, open for breakfast and lunch. In addition to hearty sandwiches, the café serves burritos, bowls, and salads. **Known for:** bakery goodies like baguettes, tarts, and pastries; coffee and espresso; lunch with a dip in the pool. [$] *Average main: $12* ✉ *Main road, on corner of Playa Guiones entrance, Nosara* ☎ *2682–0087* 🕓 *Café closed Sun. No dinner.*

Destiny Café & Restaurant

$$ | AMERICAN | A feast for the senses, this plant-filled haven has coffee, smoothies, and food that look lovely and taste delicious. Whether you order the impeccably presented "Eggs Nest" (sous vide eggs in a nest of crispy, fried sweet potatoes) or the art-topped green matcha latte, having an enjoyable meal here is practically kismet. **Known for:** outdoor garden setting; thirst quenchers like the blue majik (spirulina) smoothie; fresh salads, poke bowls, and brunch food like truffle avo toast. $ *Average main: $12 ✉ La Negra Surf Hotel, Playa Guiones Norte, Nosara ☎ 8708–0129 ⊕ www. facebook.com/Destinynosara.cr ⊗ No dinner. Closed Mon.*

Hotels

★ Bodhi Tree Yoga Resort

$$$$ | RESORT | With three pools, a spa, and luxurious rooms, there's more to this resort than just yoga. **Pros:** lush grounds and beautiful rooms; first-rate yoga classes; range of accommodations for every budget. **Cons:** not right on beach; dormitory-style rooms lack privacy; lots of stairs. $ *Rooms from: $280 ✉ Bodhi St., Nosara ☎ 2682–0256 ⊕ www.bodhi-treeyogaresort.com ↘ 42 rooms ⊙ Free Breakfast.*

Casa Romántica

$$ | B&B/INN | Calm, tranquil, and close to the beach, this hotel's name (Romantic House) says it all: the Spanish coloni-al–style house has an upstairs veranda and a graceful arcade with views of a crystal-blue kidney-shape pool surround-ed by a glorious tropical garden. **Pros:** very close to beach; yoga sessions; good value. **Cons:** usually quiet but children can make the pool area noisy at times; often full; rooms comfortable but not spec-tacular. $ *Rooms from: $135 ✉ Nosara ✛ 200 meters (656 feet) southwest of Gilded Iguana ☎ 2682–0272 ⊕ www. casa-romantica.net ↘ 13 units ⊙ Free Breakfast.*

The Gilded Iguana Surf Hotel

$$$$ | HOTEL | FAMILY | This lively hotel-bar-restaurant has been a Nosara fixture for more than 35 years and has a chic, modern aesthetic. **Pros:** upscale and modern; fitness center with classes;

directly across from surf breaks, with surf club. **Cons:** outdoor showers lack pri-vacy; can feel crowded; slow service at restaurant. $ *Rooms from: $279 ✉ Playa Guiones, Nosara ☎ 2682–0259 ⊕ www. thegildediguana.com ↘ 29 rooms ⊙ Free Breakfast.*

★ The Harmony Hotel

$$$$ | B&B/INN | This ultracool, holistic retreat gets top marks for both comfort and sustainability, thanks to American owners who are surfers that believe comfort, quiet, and thinking ecologically are more appealing than partying. **Pros:** on beach; sustainable menu; complimen-tary use of boards and bikes; one free yoga class per guest per stay. **Cons:** not overly kid-friendly but babies welcome; standard rooms are smallish; pricey. $ *Rooms from: $520 ✉ From Café de Paris, take road almost all the way to Playa Guiones, look for sign leading to tree-shaded parking lot on right, Nosara ☎ 2682–4114, 2682–1073 ⊕ www. harmonynosara.com ↘ 24 rooms ⊙ Free Breakfast.*

★ Hotel Lagarta Lodge

$$$$ | B&B/INN | A birders' and nature-lov-ers' Valhalla, this magnificent nature lodge on a promontory has amazing views of the forest, river, and coast north of Nosara. **Pros:** amazing views and grounds; two pool areas; family rooms sleep six. **Cons:** some steps to rooms; steep, rough road to get here; not on the beach. $ *Rooms from: $386 ✉ Top of hill at north end of Nosara, Nosara ☎ 8596–1919 ⊕ www.lagartalodge.com ↘ 36 suites ⊙ Free Breakfast.*

Luna Azul

$$$ | B&B/INN | Sequestered in the green hills above Playa Ostional, 8 km (5 miles) north of Nosara, tranquil, tasteful Luna Azul is full of clever design and health-ful attributes, surrounded by a private nature reserve abounding with birds and wildlife. **Pros:** luxurious rooms; excellent breakfast; ; good restaurant; isolated in a picturesque environment. **Cons:**

getting here involves some rough roads; restaurant prices do not include tax and service; not near the beach or Nosara town. [$] *Rooms from: $170* ✉ *1 km (½ mile) north of Ostional, 8 km (5 miles) north of Nosara, Nosara* ☎ *2682–1400* 🌐 *www.hotellunaazul.com* 🛏 *7 bungalows* 🍴 *Free Breakfast.*

Olas Verdes Hotel

$$$$ | **HOTEL** | **FAMILY** | A private path through native jungle gets you to the beach at this welcoming hotel, which has a surf school and organic restaurant on-site. **Pros:** exemplary service; spacious rooms; highly rated surf school on-site and close to beach. **Cons:** rooms facing pool lack privacy; not in the center of the "action" in town (but a complimentary bike ride away); small pool. [$] *Rooms from: $265* ✉ *Playa Guiones, Nosara* ✥ *500 meters (1,640 feet) west and 300 meters (984 feet) south of Café de Paris* ☎ *2682–0608* 🌐 *www.olasverdeshotel.com* 🛏 *17 suites* 🍴 *Free Breakfast.*

★ Tierra Magnifica

$$$$ | **B&B/INN** | Perched on the mountainside with breathtaking ocean views, Tierra Magnifica has all the attentiveness and personalization of a boutique hotel and all the amenities of a resort. **Pros:** panoramic views; great restaurant that caters to personal needs; chic, clean minimalist aesthetic. **Cons:** yoga costs $67 with four-person minimum; not ideal for families, since no children under 15 allowed; not all rooms are same quality. [$] *Rooms from: $365* ✉ *Proyecto Americano Las Huacas, Lote EE90, Nosara* ☎ *2682–0270, 800/409–4760 from U.S.* 🌐 *www.tierramagnifica.com* 🛏 *14 rooms* 🍴 *Free Breakfast.*

Nightlife

The Gilded Iguana

LIVE MUSIC | Live acoustic music on Saturday night draws a big crowd. ✉ *Playa Guiones, Nosara* ☎ *2682–0259.*

La Luna

CAFÉS | Sip an exotic tropical cocktail or munch on hummus and pita bread while watching the sun set at this lovely Mediterranean restaurant and bar, which has settees and rattan chairs set out on the sand, as well as seats in the chic new indoor lounge. You'll most likely need a reservation for sunset. ✉ *Beachfront, Playa Pelada, Nosara* ☎ *2682–0122.*

Olga's

BARS | Sunsets, with occasional live music, are the main events in the evening on Playa Pelada, and both locals and tourists gather to watch it here at this beach shack and bar with the best view. Olga's also serves an excellent fried whole red snapper. ✉ *End of the road to Playa Pelada, Nosara.*

Shopping

Arte Guay

CRAFTS | This is the place to find the largest selection of local crafts and every imaginable souvenir, plus beachwear and sun hats. ✉ *Just past Café de Paris on road to Playa Guiones, right-hand side, Nosara.*

Love Nosara Store

SOUVENIRS | The owner and designer of this trendy open-air boutique invites you to take a piece of Nosara with you. All the high-quality items they sell are designed in house and consciously crafted in Costa Rica from fair-trade materials. Centering the gallerylike store is a massive tree surrounded by beachwear, hats, bags, jewelry, and more. ✉ *West of Café de Paris, Nosara* ☎ *8468–7716.*

Mandala

OTHER SPECIALTY STORE | Yoga fans will swoon over the pretty yoga tops here, made of feather-light Peruvian pima cotton. There are also yoga pants and cool beachwear of the shop's own design. There's a selection of Birkenstock sandals, too. An array of aromatherapy potions makes the shop a pleasant place to be, along with the air-conditioning. Look for the large Buddha posed in front of the shop; open 9 to 5 daily. ⊠ *Playa Guiones road, beside the medical center* ☎ *2682–1431.*

The Silver Tree

JEWELRY & WATCHES | Follow the smell of incense into this elegant jewelry store, with beautiful handmade pieces from local artists as well as sophisticated resort wear. There are also unusual, high-quality handcrafted gifts, art, and one-of-a-kind curios, locally made and from around the world. ⊠ *2nd fl. in mini-mall beside Café de Paris, on Playa Guiones road, Nosara* ☎ *2682–1422.*

Activities

TOUR OPERATORS

Experience Nosara

LOCAL SPORTS | For in-depth insights into the natural world, join a bilingual naturalist on a three-hour kayak or stand-up paddleboard tour along the Río Nosara ($65 per person), or on a leisurely hike to a hidden waterfall with swimming holes ($65 per person). Out on the ocean, the company offers surfing, and on the calmer side, two-hour stand-up paddleboard lessons and 2½- to 3-hour tours ($100); plus a three-hour snorkeling tour at Playa Juanillo, including coconut water and fruit ($75, minimum four people). ⊠ *Nosara* ☎ *8705–2010* ⊕ *www.experience-nosara. com.*

BIRD-WATCHING

Experience Nosara

BIRD WATCHING | Bilingual naturalist and ornithologist Allan Azofeifa leads serious birders on bird-watching tours, with an early-morning expedition on foot in the Nosara Biological Reserve or a kayak paddle upriver to catch sight of some of the 270 species recorded here. ⊠ *Nosara* ☎ *8705–2010* ⊕ *www.experience-nosara. com* ✉ *$65, minimum 2 people.*

FISHING

Fishing Nosara

FISHING | This outfit can hook you up with local English-speaking captains who can take you fishing for 2½ hours, a half day, or full day, on boats ranging from 20 to 31 feet. The shop sells rods, lures, fishing shirts, hats, and souvenir T-shirts. ⊠ *In Paradise Rentals office on main road to Playa Guiones, Playa Guiones* ☎ *2682–0606* ⊕ *www.fishingnosara.com* ✉ *From $250 for 2½ hours to $950 for a full day on the largest, best-equipped boat.*

SPAS

Tica Massage

SPAS | Relaxing massages, facials, and salt glows in a jungle setting ($95 per hour) are available by appointment at Tica Massage. ⊠ *Across from Harmony Hotel, Playa Guiones* ☎ *2682–0096, 8627–0444* ⊕ *www.ticamassage.com.*

SURFING

Nosara has been called the best place in the world to learn how to surf, so if you've always wanted to try it, this is the place. Surf shops and surf schools are proliferating to satisfy the growing demand. Guiones is the perfect beginners' beach, with no rocks to worry about. Local surf instructors say that the waves here are so consistent that there's no week throughout the year when you won't be able to surf. Every year, the Costa Rica National Surfing Circuit comes here for surf trials.

Coconut Harry's Surf Shop

SURFING | This Nosara surfing institution on the main road has a store full of surfing gear, along with a new taco bar. Most of the surfing action has shifted to a convenient beach location 100 meters (328 feet) from the main Playa Guiones beach entrance. You'll find board rentals ($20 per day), gear, lessons ($55 for 1½ hours, board included, for a group of four; a private lesson is $75), and board storage. ⊠ *Main road, next to Beach Dog Cafe, Nosara* ☎ *2682–1852 main* *road shop, 8602–1852 beach location* ⊕ *www.coconutharrys.com.*

The Gilded Iguana Surf Club

SURFING | **FAMILY** | For the pampered surfer, this surf club offers surf lessons, lockers, showers, dressing rooms, a game room, photography of your session, and a quiver with over 150 surfboards. Simply pick your "stick" and your board caddy will wax your board before you hit the waves, located just a trail-walk away. Post-session, you can power up at the juice bar or relax in the surf lounge. ⊠ *Playa Guiones ⊹ 200 meters (656 feet) from Guones Beach* ☎ *2106–5308* ⊕ *www.thegildediguana.com* ✉ *Club access $15 per day; surfboard rental $20 per day; group lessons $50; private lessons $80.*

Nosara Surf Shop

SURFING | This large surf shop offers group lessons ($65 for 1½ hours), rents boards by the day ($15 to $20), and has lots of gear for sale, too. It also rents ATVs ($55 for the day). ⊠ *Nosara ⊹ 500 meters (1,640 feet) west of Café de Paris, on road to Playa Guiones* ☎ *2682–0186* ⊕ *www.nosarasurfshop.com.*

Safari Surf School

SURFING | This popular beachfront school, owned by a veteran surfer from Hawaii, is certified by the International Surfing Association. There are special packages for women, as well as a kids' surf camp. Most students come on package deals that include transportation and lodging at the school's Olas Verdes surfer lodge, with 17 spacious suites, an alfresco restaurant, and a swimming pool. A short trail through the woods leads straight to the beach and surfing breaks. You can also pay as you learn, $55 for a 1½-hour group lesson or $85 for a private lesson, surfboard included. ⊠ *Olas Verdes, Guiones beach road, 300 meters (984 feet) south of Harbor Reef Hotel, Playa Guiones* ☎ *8611–7954* ⊕ *www.safarisurfschool.com.*

YOGA

★ Bodhi Tree Yoga Resort

YOGA | Up to seven yoga classes are offered daily here, as well as spinning and Pilates. Stop into one of the juice bars after your class for a healthy treat. A free shuttle zips around town hourly, so you can hop on from your hotel and they will give you a ride back as well. ⊠ *Bodhi St., Nosara* ☎ *2682–0256* ⊕ *bodhitreeyogaresort.com* ✉ *From $15 for most classes, $25 for aerial yoga.*

Harmony Healing Center

YOGA | Close to Playa Guiones, the Harmony Hotel holds yoga classes daily. It also has a wide selection of New Age therapeutic massages and a full range of herbal spa services. ⊠ *Playa Guiones road, near beach entrance, Nosara* ☎ *2682–4114* ⊕ *www.healingcentrenosara.com* ✉ *$20 per session.*

Sámara

36 km (23 miles) southwest of Nicoya, 26 km (16 miles) south of Nosara.

Sámara has miles of palm-shaded beach, safe swimming water, and an abundance of budget accommodations and seafront restaurants, making it especially popular with budget travelers, both Tico and foreign. This can be a lively place on weekends, with beach bars and handicraft vendors setting up on the main drag. A sandy roadway with the occasional car runs alongside the coconut palms and Indian almond trees that line the beach, so be sure to look both ways when you move between the surf and the town. Like nearby Nosara, Sámara is becoming more nature- and health-conscious.

GETTING HERE AND AROUND

The drive from Nicoya to Sámara is one of the most scenic in Costa Rica, passing through rolling hills and green vistas before descending to the wide, south-facing bay hemmed by palm-lined sand. The road is paved all the way and takes about an hour.

■ TIP→ **Potholes are spreading, so drivers need to keep their eyes on the road instead of the beautiful views.**

A rough beach road from Nosara is passable in dry season (it's more direct, but takes just as long); do not attempt this road when it rains. To get from Nosara to Sámara via the paved road, drive south 5 km (3 miles) past Garza. At the T in the road, ignore the road toward Sámara (the beach road) and take the road to the left, toward Nicoya. This will take you uphill to merge with the main Nicoya–Sámara highway. There are daily bus routes to Samara from San José ($8) and Nicoya ($2.50). For the latest bus schedule, look online at *samarabeach.com*.

RENTAL CARS Alamo. ✉ *Main road into town, beside Hotel Samara Beach, Sámara* ☎ *2656–0958.*

ESSENTIALS

BANKS/ATMS Banco de Costa Rica. ✉ *North side of soccer field, Downtown, Sámara* ☎ *2656–2112.* **Banco Nacional.** ✉ *Sámara* ✣ *50 meters (164 feet) west of Catholic church* ☎ *2656–0089.*

HOSPITAL Medical Center. (*Dr Freddy Soto*) ✉ *Sámara* ✣ *160 meters (524 feet) east of Supermarket Palí Sámara* ☎ *2656–0992.*

PHARMACY Farmacia Sámara. ✉ *Main road at entrance to Sámara, next door to Miniplaza Patio Colonial, Sámara* ☎ *2215–6093.*

POST OFFICE Correo. ✉ *Beside church, across from soccer field, Sámara* 🌐 *correos.go.cr.*

Beaches

Playa Sámara

BEACH | This is the perfect hangout beach, with plenty of shade, bars, and seafront restaurants to take refuge in from the sun. Devoid of rip currents or big waves, it's also perfect for families with children. Its wide sweep of light-gray sand is framed by two forest-covered hills jutting out at either end. The waves break out on a reef that lines the entrance of the cove several hundred yards offshore, which keeps the water calm enough for safe swimming and leaves enough surf to have fun in. The reef holds plenty of marine attractions for diving and snorkeling excursions. Isla Chora, at the south end of the bay, provides a sheltered area that is especially popular with kayakers and snorkelers—it even has a tiny beach at lower tides. After years of hard work to clean up the beach, Sámara Beach now sports a Blue Flag. Those seeking solitude should head to the beach's western or eastern ends. **Amenities:** food and drink; water sports. **Best for:** snorkeling; surfing; swimming.

Restaurants

Bohemia Café

$ | **CAFÉ** | **FAMILY** | Take a beach break and stop at this funky open-air café for a smoothie or espresso, and stay for a panini or avocado toast—just make sure to get here before the freshly baked bread runs out. The seats may be unconventional (think swings and couches) but the food is pure delight. **Known for:** "Bohemian" smoothie; strong coffee; spicy panini. [$] *Average main: $8* ✉ *In front of Sámara Natural Center, Sámara* ☎ *6346–3590* ⏲ *Closed Mon.*

★ **Gusto Beach Creativo**

$$$ | **ITALIAN** | A romantic setting, ocean breezes, and a creative Italian menu make this the one of the most popular restaurants in Sámara. By day, rustic wooden tables are shaded by white sails strung between palms; by night, diners bask in the glow of white globe lamps and light-festooned trees. **Known for:** prosecco; toes-in-the-sand dining; tuna tartare. [$] *Average main: $16* ✉ *Sámara* ✣ *Beach road, center of town* ☎ *2656–0252.*

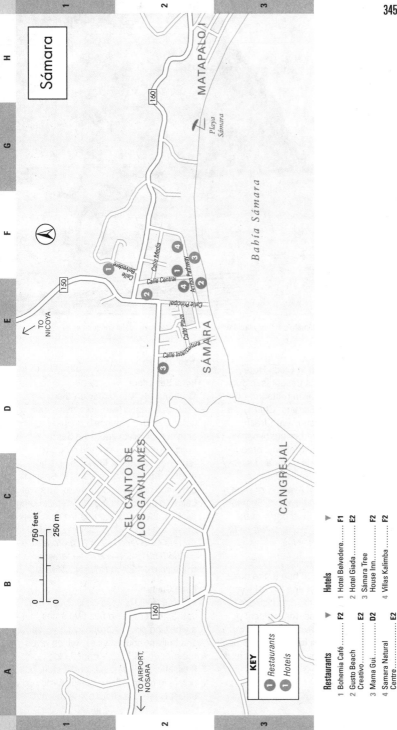

Sámara

TO NICOYA

150

160

MATAPALO

Playa Sámara

Bahía Sámara

Calle Belvedere

Calle María

Calle Central

Arriba Pathway

Calle Principal

Calle Plaza

Calle Intercultura

SÁMARA

EL CANTO DE LOS GAVILANES

CANGREJAL

TO AIRPORT, NOSARA

160

KEY

1 *Restaurants*

1 *Hotels*

0   750 feet
0   250 m

Restaurants ▶

1 Bohemia Café **F2**
2 Gusto Beach Creativo **E2**
3 Mama Gui **D2**
4 Samara Natural Centre **E2**

Hotels ▶

1 Hotel Belvedere **F1**
2 Hotel Giada **E2**
3 Sámara Tree House Inn **F2**
4 Villas Kalimba **F2**

Beginning surfers love Sámara's almost placid water and its undeveloped palm-fringed beach.

★ Mama Gui

$$ | **ITALIAN** | Located at Giada Hotel, poolside tables and ultrasophisticated cuisine make this Italian restaurant the best dining spot in Samara. Chef Gigio Palazzo prepares dishes with fresh local seafood, meat from sustainable farms, and organic-hydroponic produce. **Known for:** homemade pasta and savory sauces; gluten-free pasta; imported Italian ingredients. [$] *Average main: $14* ✉ *Giada Hotel, Calle Principal, Sámara* ✣ *200 meters (656 feet) north of the beach* ☎ *2656–2347* ▭ *No credit cards* ⏲ *Closed Wed. Sept.–Nov.*

Samara Natural Centre

$ | **BAKERY** | This health hub in the heart of Samara has everything to make your vacation green and full of goodness. A juice bar, falafel stand, fitness center, and health-food store are just a few of the offerings. **Known for:** local and organic foods; healthy treats; homemade crafts. [$] *Average main: $5* ✉ *Sámara* ✣ *In front of Gusto Beach.*

Hotels

Hotel Belvedere

$$ | **B&B/INN** | After a day on the beach, it's refreshing to retreat to this small hotel buried in a dense, cool garden on a breezy hill overlooking Sámara. **Pros:** affordable; clean and quiet; rooms renovated annually. **Cons:** Wi-Fi is not reliable and TV shows are all in Spanish; breakfast not included; five-minute walk down to beach and a bit longer climbing back up the hill. [$] *Rooms from: $85* ✉ *Sámara* ✣ *Entering Sámara, go 100 meters (328 feet) left at first cross street* ☎ *2656–0213* 🌐 *www.hotelbelvederesamara.com* 🛏 *22 units* 🍴 *No Meals.*

Hotel Giada

$$ | **B&B/INN** | This eco-conscious hotel in the heart of town has two small swimming pools surrounded by greenery and brilliant bougainvillea, which gives the property a Mediterranean look. **Pros:** affordable rates; friendly staff; hair dryers in rooms. **Cons:** smallish rooms; street noise can affect some rooms;

not right on the beach. $ *Rooms from: $90 ⊠ Main strip, Sámara ⊹ 250 meters (820 feet) north of beach ☎ 2656–0132 ⊕ www.hotelgiada.net ⇆ 24 rooms* ⊙⏐ *Free Breakfast.*

Sámara Tree House Inn

$$$ | **B&B/INN** | One of the few hotels right on the beach, this small inn has lofty, breezy bungalows with air-conditioned bedrooms perfect for folks who love the open air and looking down on the beach action. **Pros:** right on the beach; small and cozy; short walk to restaurants and shops. **Cons:** very small pool; beach bungalows with no screens can get buggy; neighboring bars and restaurants can be noisy. $ *Rooms from: $192 ⊠ Beach road, across from supermarket, Sámara ☎ 2656–0733 ⊕ www.samaratreehouse. com ⇆ 6 units* ⊙⏐ *Free Breakfast.*

★ Villas Kalimba

$$$ | **RESORT** | You may never want to leave this tranquil oasis of luxury villas hidden behind scrolled white-and-orange walls, where the architecture is Mexican but the style is all Italian. **Pros:** spacious villas; all the comforts of home; lovely garden. **Cons:** not right on beach; some noise from beach road; sauna use costs $10 per hour. $ *Rooms from: $175 ⊠ Sámara ⊹ 200 meters (656 feet) east of Sámara police station, along beach road ☎ 2656–0929 ⊕ www.villaskalimba.com ⇆ 9 villas* ⊙⏐ *No Meals.*

Nightlife

Lo Que Hay Bar & Taquería

LIVE MUSIC | Live music plays some nights at this friendly bar right on the beach with free Wi-Fi. If you stayed up all night, this place also serves breakfast starting at 7 am. ⊠ *Beach road, across from Sámara Organics Market Café, Sámara ☎ 8738–0990.*

Micro Bar

BARS | This tiny boîte of a bar is the coolest place in town, with an Escher-inspired tile floor and hip lighting. Bellying up to the bar is a pleasure; in fact, practically the entire space is given over to a handsome bar with an old-fashioned bar rail to lean on. A cool soundtrack accompanies your beer tasting. You can try a sample of any of the 16 Costa Rican craft microbrews on tap. Once you find your favorite, a 12-ounce cold brew costs around $5. A few high tables spill out onto the street, surrounded by groups of happy beer drinkers. Happy Hour runs 2–6, boasting two drinks for $9. ⊠ *Beach road, across from Sámara Tree House Inn, Sámara ☎ 8539–1805.*

Shopping

Souvenir stands are set up along the main street and the entrance to the beach, along with the inevitable handmade-jewelry stalls. Most shops here have pretty much the same beachwear and souvenirs for sale.

Sámara Organics Market

OTHER SPECIALTY STORE | More than a market for a wide range of gluten-free, dairy-alternative, vegetarian options, and organic foods, this spacious, pleasant shop sells imported olive oils and other gastronomic treats—rare in these parts. There's also a selection of artisan-made objets d'art. You can sit in one of the lounge chairs here and sip an espresso, a just-pressed exotic fruit drink, or a healthy, organic potion. Vegetable dips and spreads are packaged to go, along with organic brownies, cookies, and cakes. ⊠ *Sámara ⊹ In the Natural Center, on beach road, across from Gusto Beach ⊕ www.samaraorganics.com.*

Activities

TOUR OPERATORS

Sámara is known more for gentle water sports such as snorkeling, kayaking, and paddleboarding than for surfing, although the calmer waters provide a good place for beginners, so surf schools have multiplied fast. There are also two high-flying adventures here: a zipline tour and ultralight flights and flying lessons. ATV tours, tearing along dirt roads, are popular with travelers who are particularly fond of dust (or mud, according to the season). For a quieter, closer contact with nature, there's a guided hike in a private forest reserve. For information on area activities, visit the informative website ⊕ *www.samaraadventures.com,* or drop into their office 200 meters (656 feet) north of the police station, next to Coco's Mexican Restaurant.

Carrillo Tours Eco Adventures

LOCAL SPORTS | Horseback riding, river and sea kayaking, dolphin-watching, fishing, snorkeling, and trips to Palo Verde, Arenal, and Monteverde national parks can all be booked here. This long-established local tour company also provides daily shuttle service to the Liberia airport at 8:30 am ($57 per person, minimum two people). ✉ *Sámara* ⚓ *200 meters (656 feet) west of Banco Nacional* ☎ *2656–0606* ⊕ *www.carrilloadventures.com* ✉ *From $35.*

Octopus Tour

BOAT TOURS | **FAMILY** | This Costa Rican–owned boat tour company puts an emphasis on respecting animals and the ocean. Half-day dolphin tours begin with pickup at your hotel and are hosted by an experienced, passionate guide. You'll snorkel around the reefs of Playa Carrillo to end your trip. They almost always see dolphins, and you may spot whales, sea turtles, and manta rays as well. Prices include snorkel equipment, water, juice, beer, and pineapple. ✉ *Playa Carrillo, Sámara* ☎ *8638–2320* ⊕ *www.octopustourcr.com* ✉ *From $55.*

Samara Adventures

LOCAL SPORTS | This tour operator offers an array of local tours, including kayaking, dolphin-watching, and mountain-bike tours, as well as paddleboarding and tours in Monteverde and Arenal national parks. It also arranges transportation by private shuttle to other parts of the country. ✉ *Next to Cocos, 200 meters (656 feet) north of the police station, Sámara* ☎ *2656–0920* ⊕ *www.samaraadventures.com* ✉ *From $50.*

Sámara Trails

HIKING & WALKING | Take a 2½-hour hike with a bilingual naturalist guide through a mango plantation and into a private reserve to experience the tropical dry forest and its denizens—howler monkeys, trogons, and motmots, among them. There's a daily morning tour at 6:30 am, or earlier if you want to see more birds, and another at 2:30 pm. Park entrance, a bilingual naturalist guide, snacks, water, and transportation from Sámara are included; book at Sámara Adventure Tours in town. ✉ *Werner Sauter Biological Reserve, 3 km (2 miles) northeast of Sámara, Sámara* ☎ *2656–0920, 800/726–8120 toll-free in U.S.* ⊕ *www.samaratrails.com* ✉ *$40 for 2½-hour hike.*

CANOPY TOURS

Wing Nuts Canopy Tour

ZIP LINING | **FAMILY** | Named after a famous surfer, this three-hour, 10-platform zipline tour flies through a patch of tropical forest just south of town, with ocean views from some of the platforms. It's small but just right for younger or timid children, and they have special tot-size harnesses for kids as young as three years old. Canopy tours take off from 7 am to 2:30 pm; reserve by phone. ✉ *In hills above Sámara, Office 1 km (½ mile) east of downtown Sámara, Sámara* ☎ *2656–0153* ⊕ *www.wingnutscanopy.com* ✉ *$75.*

DIVING AND SNORKELING

The reef offshore is the best place to snorkel. Kayakers also paddle out to Isla Chora to snorkel on the leeward side of the island.

KAYAKING

Samara Adventure Company and Carrillo Adventures organize kayaking tours, on both ocean and river, in plastic sit-on-top kayaks.

C&C Surf School

KAYAKING | You can rent boards or take lessons at this established surf school, which also runs three-hour guided kayak snorkeling tours on the Río Ora and out to Isla Chora and the nearby reef ($45, including gear and a fruit snack). ⊠ *On beach next to Tree House Inn, Sámara* ☎ *6275–6235.*

Ticos Surf School

KAYAKING | This beachfront surf school also has stand-up paddleboards and kayaks to rent. Kayaking tours through the mangroves or on the ocean are $60 per person; 1½-hour paddleboard lessons (also $60) include an extra hour of practice time. Bike rental is $15 per day and surfboards $5 per hour. ⊠ *On beach, Sámara* ☎ *8457–0132.*

SURFING

The surf is relatively gentle at Sámara, so it's a good place for beginners to learn to get up on a board. The challenging waves for more experienced surfers are farther south, at Playa Camaronal, which has both left and right breaks.

C&C Surf School

SURFING | The most experienced beachfront surf school offers lessons from beginner up ($70 per 90-minute private lesson, including five-day board rental; $50 for two or more beginners) with certified instructors, and a huge selection of boards for rent ($5 per hour; $15 per day or $20 for 24 hours). ⊠ *On beach next to Gusto Beach Creativo, Sámara* ☎ *6275–6235.*

ULTRALIGHT FLIGHTS
Fly With Us–Ultralight Tours

SKYDIVING | Take off for a thrilling ride over Sámara on an ultralight flight in an open gyrocopter ($130 cash for 20-minute tour, $170 for 30 minutes.) Pilot Jöerg also gives flying lessons. ⊠ *Playa Buena Vista, 6 km (4 miles) northwest of Sámara, Sámara* ☎ *8828–1000* ⊕ *flywithus.aero.*

Playa Carrillo

7 km (4½ miles) southeast of Sámara.

With its long, reef-protected crescent beach backed by an elegant line of swaying coconut palms and sheltering cliffs, Playa Carrillo (interchangeably called Puerto Carrillo) is a candidate for the most picturesque beach in Costa Rica. A smooth, paved boulevard runs along the beach, with sparkling turquoise waters on the sea side and a hedge of scarlet bougainvillea on the land side. The main landmark here is the Hotel Guanamar, high above the south end of the beach. Unfortunately, the former private fishing club and previously grand hotel has been bought and sold so often that its charm has faded. But its bar still has the best view. Hotel Nammbú, with dozens of villas, is your best bet for lodging on the hill overlooking the beach.

GETTING HERE AND AROUND

It's an easy 15-minute drive south on the smooth, paved road from Sámara. If you're not staying at a hotel in Carrillo, you'll have to park your car either in a sunbaked concrete lot halfway along the beach or on the grassy median at the south end of the beach. You can also take a taxi from Sámara or hop on the local bus.

ESSENTIALS

Sámara is the closest town for banks and other services.

Beaches

★ **Playa Carrillo**

BEACH | Unmarred by a single building at beach level, this picture-perfect pristine white strand is ideal for swimming, snorkeling, strolling, and lounging—just remember not to sit under a loaded coconut palm. Signs posted by the municipality announce that the only entry "fee" is: make no fires, and take your garbage away with you. There are some

Idyllic Playa Carrillo is perfect for swimming, snorkeling, or just sunning.

concrete tables and benches, but they get snapped up quickly. This is a popular beach with locals, and it gets quite busy on weekends. The only commercial activity is a hand-wheeled cart selling fruit ices. **Amenities:** none. **Best for:** snorkeling; swimming; walking.

⚠ **Sometimes crocodiles hang out at the river mouths at both ends of the beach, so keep a lookout and wade or swim only in the middle of the beach.** ✉ *Carrillo.*

🍴 Restaurants

El Colibrí Steakhouse

$$$ | **ARGENTINE** | **FAMILY** | Sink your chops into steak (rib eye, New York, or T-bone) grilled on an open fire and served Argentine-style with garlicky chimichurri sauce at this family-run, pleasant rancho restaurant. Other specialties include grilled chorizo sausages or Milanesa, the classic Argentine breaded steak, served with french fries. **Known for:** mussels with white wine sauce; Argentine wines; mouthwatering steaks cooked to perfection. [$] *Average main: $18* ✉ *Carrillo* ✣ *From main beach road, turn left at soccer field, then left again; 50 meters (164 feet) east of the church* ☎ *2656–0656* 🌐 *www.cabinaselcolibri.com* 🕒 *No lunch.*

🛏 Hotels

Nammbú Beachfront Bungalows

$$$ | **HOTEL** | **FAMILY** | As the most luxurious property near Playa Carrillo, this modern hotel is also one of the newest, with three categories of rooms, some as large as 807 square feet; despite the name, there are no bungalows nor is the property beachfront. **Pros:** modern, clean, spacious rooms; spectacular sunsets at dreamy beach; infinity pool with ocean view. **Cons:** overpriced menu; no closets in rooms; service could use some work. [$] *Rooms from: $250* ✉ *Main road, Carrillo* ✣ *Above Playa Carrillo* ☎ *2696–8080* 🌐 *www.nammbu.com* 🛏 *63 rooms* 🍽 *Free Breakfast.*

Activities

FISHING

From January to April, the boats moored off the beach take anglers on fishing expeditions for catch-and-release marlin and sailfishing, as well as good-eating dorado, yellowfin tuna, and wahoo.

Kingfisher Sportfishing

FISHING | Captain Rick Ruhlow, a U.S. Coast Guard–licensed skipper with years of experience fishing Costa Rican waters, takes up to five anglers out on *Kingfisher*, a fully equipped 31-foot Palm Beach fishing boat; it's the only boat that stays full-time in Carrillo from November to September. A full day's fishing offshore costs $1,250; inshore $900. ⊠ *Carrillo* ☎ *8859–9561, 2656–0091* ⊕ *www.costaricabillfishing.com.*

Punta Islita

16 km (11 miles) south of Playa Carrillo in dry season, 30 km (21 miles) south of Carrillo by alternative mountain route in rainy season.

Punta Islita is named for a tiny tuft of land that becomes an island at high tide. It's synonymous in Costa Rica with Hotel Punta Islita, one of the country's most exclusive, luxurious, and gorgeous resorts, popular with honeymooners and romantics of any age. Just about everything in Punta Islita—from outdoor activities to food—revolves around, and is available through, this resort. Just uphill from the beach, the small village of Punta Islita is an artistic work in progress, thanks to a community art project led by a few renowned Costa Rican artists who have turned almost all the buildings into galleries, workshops, or works of art themselves.

GETTING HERE AND AROUND

Thanks to the bridge over the Río Oro, it's a quick, 25-minute trip south of Playa Carrillo. A 4WD vehicle is recommended since the dirt road on the other side of the bridge is

hilly and rough. Some well-heeled guests fly into the hotel's private airstrip.

Sights

Museo Islita (*Casa Museo*)

MUSEUM VILLAGE | This open-air contemporary art museum—the only one in the country—is a treasure trove of art displayed in a gallery and throughout the entire village. Supported by Hotel Punta Islita, visiting resident artists have inspired local villagers to create colorful murals and mosaics ornamenting public spaces and buildings, even beautifying the recycling center and trees in the village plaza. The museum building showcases one-of-a-kind textile prints, folk-art paintings on wood, jewelry, and objets d'art made from recycled materials, all for sale. ⊠ *Punta Islita, Punta Islita* ☎ *2656–2039* ⊘ *Closed Sun.*

Beaches

★ Punta Islita

BEACH | The curved beach here is rocky but good for walking, especially at low tide when tidal pools form in the volcanic rock. Sunsets are gorgeous, but despite its Blue Flag designation, this is not a great swimming beach. Be sure to take a stroll through the small village up from the beach, which is a memorable experience. Food and drinks are all available through the Aura Beach Club. **Amenities:** food and drink; showers; toilets. **Best for:** sunset; walking. ⊠ *Punta Islita.*

Restaurants

Aura Beach Club

$$$$ | LATIN AMERICAN | The hammocks, palapas, pool, and beach here are open to the public, so take a dip, grab some beach food, and take in a sunset, all the while trying to spot some red macaws. Showers, toilets, tables, chairs, towels, and more are available for use with a $70 minimum food and beverage purchase.

Known for: patacones; brick-oven pizza; ubiquitous seafood, particularly whole red snapper. 🟨 *Average main: $70* ⊠ *Islita Beach, Punta Islita* 🕾 *2656–3500.*

 Hotels

★ Hotel Punta Islita

$$$$ | RESORT | Overlooking the ocean from a forested ridge, this secluded and sublime hotel is luxury incarnate, with villas, casitas, suites, and spacious rooms sprinkled around the bougainvillea-bedecked hillside. **Pros:** gorgeous views; ultraluxurious rooms; top-notch service. **Cons:** left side of the beach is rocky; very pricey; isolated location. 🟨 *Rooms from: $420* ⊠ *16 km (11 miles) south of Playa Carrillo, Punta Islita* 🕾 *2565–3500, 2549–6466 in San Jose* ⊕ *www.hotelpuntaislita.com* 💤 *56 units* ¶◯¶ *Free Breakfast.*

Palo Verde National Park

52 km (32 miles) south of Liberia.

Definitely not most people's idea of a lush, tropical jungle, Palo Verde National Park's deciduous forest is hot, but also very dry and an ideal habitat for easy-to-spot monkeys, deer, peccaries, and lizards. Seasonal wetlands the size of lakes attract waterfowl by the thousands, as well as the photographers who come to shoot the grand avian spectacle.

GETTING HERE AND AROUND

To get to Palo Verde from Liberia, drive south along the Pan-American Highway to Bagaces, then turn right at the small, easy-to-miss sign for Palo Verde, along a rough dirt road for 28 km (17 miles). Count on an hour to drive the distance from the main highway to the park entrance; it's a very bumpy road. You'll have to pay the $12 park entrance fee to get to the Organization for Tropical Studies station. The OTS station is about 7 km (4½ miles) beyond the park entrance; the park headquarters is less than 1 km (½ mile) farther. The gatekeeper takes lunch from noon to 1 pm. The drive from Liberia should take a total of about 1½ hours.

 Sights

Las Pumas Rescue Shelter (*Centro de Rescate Las Pumas*)

WILDLIFE REFUGE | Sad but true, one of the few places left in the country where you are guaranteed to see large wild cats, including a jaguar, is this animal rescue center. The small enclosures also hold jaguarundis, pumas, margays, and ocelots. The shelter houses other species, including otters, grissons, white-faced and spider monkeys, and scarlet macaws, all native to the area. Some animals and birds are rehabilitated and released into the wild. The larger cats are probably here for life, as it's dangerous for them to be released. Donations to the nonprofit foundation, founded in 2003 by a Swiss conservationist, are welcomed. ⊠ *4½ km (3 miles) north of Cañas on main hwy., Palo Verde National Park* 🕾 *2669–6044, 2669–6019 for reservations* ⊕ *www.centrorescatelaspumas.org* 💤 *$12.*

Llanos de Cortés

WATERFALL | Just 3 km (2 miles) north of the Palo Verde road at Bagaces, take the dirt road signed for Llanos de Cortés to get to this hidden waterfall less than 2 km (1 mile) off the highway. About ½ km (¼ mile) along the dirt road you'll see on your right a large rock with "Cataratas" scrawled on it. Follow this bumpy road about 1.3 km (0.8 mile) to its end and then clamber down a steep path to the pool at the bottom of a spectacular, wide 50-foot waterfall. This is a great place for a picnic, especially since there are restrooms; avoid weekends if you can when it's often crowded and noisy. Don't leave anything of value in your car. ⊠ *Off Pan-American Hwy., Bagaces* 💤 *$7.*

★ Palo Verde National Park
(*Parque Nacional Palo Verde*)
NATIONAL PARK | Because this dry deciduous forest is less dense than a rain forest, it's much easier to spot the fauna along the hiking trails, including white-tailed deer, coatis, collared peccaries, and monkeys. This park's 198 square km (76 square miles) of terrain is fairly flat—the maximum elevation is 879 feet. The west boundary of the park is bordered by the Río Tempisque, where crocodiles ply the waters year-round. The park also holds Costa Rica's highest concentration of waterfowl, the most common the black-bellied whistling duck and the blue-winged teal, with close to 30,000 during dry season. Although not as common, other waterfowl spotted here are the fulvous whistling duck, the glossy ibis, the pinnated bittern, the least bittern, the snail kite, and the very rare masked duck. Other birds endemic to the northwest, which you may find in the park's dry-forest habitat, are streaked-back orioles, banded wrens, and black-headed trogons. In the wet season, the river and the park's vast seasonal wetlands host huge numbers of migratory and resident aquatic birds, including herons, wood storks, jabirus (giant storks), and elegant flamingo-like roseate spoonbills. There is a raised platform near the OTS research station, about 8 km (5 miles) past the park entrance, with a panoramic view over a marsh filled with ducks and jacanas. A narrow metal ladder leads to the top of the old tower, big enough for just two people at the top. For a good look at hundreds of waterfowl, there's also a long boardwalk jutting out over the wetlands. It's almost always hot and humid in these lowlands—March is the hottest month—so be prepared with water, a hat, and insect repellent. Hostel-type lodging in rustic dormitory facilities with bunk beds and shared bathrooms ($13), and family-style meals for overnight guests only ($7 breakfast; $9 for lunch or dinner) can be arranged through the park headquarters. ⇨ *For more information, see the highlighted listing in this chapter.* ✉ *Palo Verde National Park* ✥ *29 km (18 miles) southwest of Bagaces* ☎ *2206–5965* 🎟 *$12.*

Hotels

La Ensenada Lodge
$ | **B&B/INN** | Part of a national wildlife refuge, this is the most comfortable and affordable base for bird-watching, crocodile spotting, and nature appreciation on this side of the Río Tempisque. **Pros:** wildlife; interesting setting; good value. **Cons:** large tour groups at times; no air-conditioning; very simple rooms. [$] *Rooms from: $50* ✉ *Take signed turnoff at Km 155 of Pan-America Hwy. and drive along gravel road, about 13 km (8 miles) southwest to lodge, Palo Verde National Park* ☎ *2289–6655 office in San José, 2661–4090 lodge* 🌐 *www.laensenada.net* 🛏 *25 cabin rooms* 🍴 *No Meals.*

Rancho Humo Estancia (*Villa Los Salom*)
$$ | **B&B/INN** | The most comfortable way to experience the birds and wildlife of the Tempisque wetlands is to roost at this eco-boutique hotel, a luxurious version of a traditional hacienda, set in a private reserve directly across from Palo Verde National Park. **Pros:** wetlands setting; incredible bird-watching; most luxurious hotel in the area. **Cons:** thin walls mean noise from neighbors; dusty gravel road for 26 km (16 miles); meager portions at meals. [$] *Rooms from: $121* ✉ *Pozo de Agua, 26 km (16 miles) north of Quebrada Honda, on east side of Puente de la Amistad, Nicoya* ☎ *2105–5400* 🌐 *www.ranchohumo.com* 🛏 *10 rooms* 🍴 *Free Breakfast.*

Activities

BIRD-WATCHING

The best bird-watching in Palo Verde is on the wetlands in front of the Organization for Tropical Studies (OTS) biological station. The OTS has expert guides who can help you see and identify the varied birds in the area ($90 private tour; $54 per person for two or more), but if you have good binoculars and a bird book, you can identify plenty of species on your own. A boat excursion to Isla Pájaros south of the Río Tempisque is particularly interesting for birders. Toward the end of rainy season this 6-acre island near Puerto Moreno is an exciting place to see hundreds of nesting wood storks, cormorants, and anhingas. You can get close enough to see chicks being fed in nests.

■ TIP→ **The best time to go is very early in the morning, to avoid heat and to guarantee the most bird sightings.**

Aventuras Arenal

BIRD WATCHING | This adventure-tour company specializes in ecological tours and has guides with good eyes who usually know the English names for birds. The river safari and Llanos de Cortés waterfall combo is $135 per person. The river safari chugs slowly up the Río Tempisque ($55, including juice and lunch). ⊠ *Palo Verde National Park* ☎ *2479–9133* ⊕ *www.aventurasarenal.com.*

RIVER RAFTING

Safaris Corobici

WILDLIFE-WATCHING | **FAMILY** | This small, local company specializes in three-hour float trips down the Río Corobici ($45) to see birds, bats, crocs, iguanas, and more. They put in (and end) near its office location, near Km 192 on the Pan-American Highway. It also offers an early-morning bird-watching float tour ($60 with lunch) and a half-day float, with lunch in its Cocobolo restaurant afterward ($65). Boats are launched from 7 to 3:30 daily. There are also gentle float trips that connect with the Tenorio River ($60 including lunch). The office is right at the entrance to Las Pumas Rescue Shelter. ⊠ *Km 192 on main hwy. to Liberia, 4½ km (3 miles) north of Cañas, Cañas* ☎ *2669–6191* ⊕ *nicoya.com* 🖃 *From $45.*

TOUR OPERATORS

Organization for Tropical Studies

BIRD WATCHING | This nonprofit scientific consortium of universities offers overnight packages with a guided walk, excellent family-style meals, and lodging in very basic, no-frills rooms, overhead fans, and private bathrooms ($93 per person). Although the accommodations are spartan, staying here is the only way to set off on a 6 am birding tour (the park gates don't open till 8). The biological research station overlooks the Palo Verde wetlands, and expert naturalist guides can arrange a boat tour ($64 plus guide fee) along wetlands lining both sides of the Río Tempisque, as well as long hikes on the park trails. Call at least a day ahead to arrange the boat tour. Bring binoculars and cameras. Guides can direct you to a perennial nest where jabirus are in residence with their chicks, January through February. Guests still have to pay the $12 entrance fee per person to the national park. ⊠ *7 km (4½ miles) past park entrance, Palo Verde National Park* ☎ *2524–0607* ⊕ *tropicalstudies.org.*

Barra Honda National Park

100 km (62 miles) south of Liberia, 13 km (8 miles) west of Río Tempisque Bridge.

You can't miss this park's massive peak, once thought to be a volcano. Within that mountain, however, is an intricate network of caves to be explored, and hiking trails on its slopes lead to scenic cascades and views over the Gulf of Nicoya.

GETTING HERE AND AROUND

From the Río Tempisque Bridge, drive west along a paved highway. Then follow a dirt road (signed off the highway) for 10 km (6 miles) to the park entrance. If you don't have a car, there is a bus that departs from the town of Nicoya at 7:30 am, Monday through Saturday. You can also take a taxi from Nicoya to the park entrance or go with one of many tour companies in beach towns on the Nicoya Peninsula.

Sights

Barra Honda National Park

(*Parque Nacional Barra Honda*)

NATIONAL PARK | FAMILY | A mecca for speleologists, the caves beneath the 1,184-foot Barra Honda Peak were created millions of years ago by erosion after the ridge emerged from the sea. You can explore the resulting calcium carbonate formations on a guided tour, and perhaps catch sight of some of the abundant underground animal life, including bats, birds, blindfish, salamanders, and snails. The caves are spread around almost 23 square km (9 square miles), but many of them remain unexplored.

Every day starting at 8 am, local guides take groups 58 feet down ladders into Terciopelo Cave, which shelters unusual formations shaped (they say) like fried eggs, popcorn, and shark's teeth. You must wear a harness with a rope attached for safety. The tour costs $30 per person (minimum of two) including equipment rental, guide, and entrance fee. Kids under 12 are not allowed into this cave, but they can visit the kid-size La Cuevita cavern ($5), which also has interesting stalagmites. Both cave visits include interpretive nature hikes. The caves are not open during the wet season for fear of flooding.

Those with a fear of heights, or claustrophobia, may want to skip the cave tour, but Barra Honda still has plenty to offer, thanks to its extensive forests and abundant wildlife. You can climb the 3-km (2-mile) Los Laureles trail (the same trail that leads to Terciopelo Cave) to Barra Honda's summit, where you'll have sweeping views over the surrounding countryside and islet-filled Gulf of Nicoya. Wildlife you may spot on Barra Honda's trails include howler and white-faced monkeys, skunks, coatis, deer, parakeets, hawks, dozens of other bird species, and iguanas. It's a good idea to hire a local guide from the Asociación de Guías Ecologistas. The park has camping facilities ($2 per night), and the ranger station, open 8 am to dusk, has potable water and restrooms. There are also a couple of basic cabins to rent ($30). ✉ *13 km (8 miles) west of Río Tempisque Bridge, Barra Honda National Park* ☎ *2659–1551* 🖳 *$12 (cash only); cave tour $30.*

Curú National Wildlife Refuge

7 km (4½ miles) south of Paquera, 1½ to 2 hrs southwest of Puntarenas by ferry.

With miles of trails through forest and mangrove swamp, this uncrowded private refuge is most famous for its pristine beach, perfectly sited for swimming, snorkeling, and easy kayaking to nearby Tortuga Island. The land was once owned by the Pacific Lumber Company, which logged the area's rosewood, cedar, and mahogany trees. Thanks to its protected status, the area is now home to more than 230 species of birds, 78 species of mammals, and 500 species of plants. The entrance fee is $15.

GETTING HERE AND AROUND

From the town of Paquera it's a short drive to Curú National Wildlife Refuge. You can also take a bus bound for Cóbano; just ask the driver to drop you off at the entrance to the refugio.

Activities

TOUR OPERATORS

Seascape Kayak Tours

KAYAKING | From October to May, experienced Canadian guide Bruce Smith leads half- and full-day kayak excursions in Ballena Bay, leaving from Curú and Playa Tambor ($85 to $165, minimum two people). Smith also leads three- and five-day kayaking tours and goes to Tortuguero National Park and Golfo Dulce. ✉ *Curú National Wildlife Refuge, Paquera* ☎ *8314–8605, 866/747–1884 toll-free* 🌐 *www.seascapekayaktours.com* 🎟 *From $85.*

Turismo Curú

LOCAL SPORTS | Guided 90-minute nature walks of the Curú Wildlife Refuge are a specialty of this tour operator ($15, plus $15 admission to refuge). The company also offers inexpensive kayaking trips to nearby Isla Tortuga, including snorkeling; a half-day tour is $67, full day $127, and the refuge admission fee. A bioluminescence tour ($55) allows you to kayak to Quesera Beach and view the otherworldly underwater phenomena after enjoying sunset. You can rent kayaks by the hour ($10 single, $15 double). All tours require a minimum of two people. For large groups, there is boat transportation from Puntarenas directly to Curú. The tour operator has an office in Paquera and a dive shop on-site at the refuge, with tanks, tours, and diving lessons. A two-tank dive, including boat to Isla Tortuga, gear, and cool drinks, is $105 for certified divers; a Discovery tour for non-certified divers is also $115, including 30 minutes of instruction and one tank. You can do a 2½-hour bioluminescence tour at night by boat, snorkeling with the glowing sea creatures for $50. ✉ *Main road, across from Esso station, Paquera* ☎ *2641–0004, 2641–0688* 🌐 *www.turismocuru.com* 🎟 *$15.*

Playa Tambor Area

27 km (17 miles) south of Paquera.

Much of the vast Bahía Ballena shoreline is taken up by a massive all-inclusive hotel and an adjoining private residential development and golf course. But to the south, near the actual village of Tambor, visitors can explore the barely developed Playa Tambor, a beautiful flat beach with nothing more than a volleyball net, a few concrete tables set under shade trees, and one beach shack serving pizza. This beach was never developed as much as Montezuma or Malpaís, making it a better destination for those who want to get away from the crowds. It can serve as a convenient base for fishing excursions, bird-watching, horseback-riding trips, and day trips to Curú National Wildlife Refuge and Isla Tortuga.

GETTING HERE AND AROUND

You can fly directly to Tambor (TMU) from San José on SANSA. Taxis meet every flight and can take you to a nearby hotel ($15), to Montezuma ($50), or to Malpaís ($60).

Hotels

Tambor Tropical

$$$ | **B&B/INN** | Centered on the scenic sweep of placid Bahía Tambor with its warm, shallow water, intimate Tambor Tropical offers "beds with a view" in spacious suites, along with sportfishing, a turtle hatchery, horseback riding, bird-watching, and just lolling in a hammock by the pretty, blue-tile pool. **Pros:** kind and helpful staff; spacious suites; tranquil, beautiful setting. **Cons:** continental, not full, breakfast included; no kids under 16. [$] *Rooms from: $232* ✉ *Tambor* ✥ *From Tambor main street, turn left at beach* ☎ *2683–0011, 866/890–2537 in*

Isla Tortuga, just off the coast near Curú National Wildlife Refuge

U.S. 🌐 *www.tamabortropical.com* 🛏 *12 suites* 🍴 *Free Breakfast.*

★ **Tango Mar Resort**

$$$ | **RESORT** | **FAMILY** | Set on stunning, palm-fringed Playa Quizales and backed by 15 acres of exuberant gardens and a 9-hole executive golf course, this comfortable, contemporary resort has a wide range of luxurious lodging options that appeal to families and couples of every age, including honeymooners. **Pros:** gorgeous setting; friendly service and attention to detail; lots of activity options. **Cons:** large groups on occasion; stairs to climb to villas and some rooms; quiet evenings. [$] *Rooms from: $230* ✉ *Playa Quizales, 3 km (2 miles) south of Tambor, Tambor* ☎ *2683–0001, 800/297–4420 in North America* 🌐 *www.tangomar.com* 🛏 *43 rooms* 🍴 *Free Breakfast.*

Activities

Unlike other beach towns, tiny Tambor doesn't have tour operators on every corner or rental shops of any kind—not even for a basic bike. The receptionist at your hotel can set up tours of the area's diverse natural attractions.

FISHING

In the open sea off the Gulf of Nicoya, sailfish, marlin, tuna, mahimahi, and wahoo are in abundance from November to March. Local fishermen in small boats are your best guides to finding fish in the gulf, including snapper, sea bass, and jacks, almost year-round. Prices for fishing cost $396 for half-day trips.

HIKING

An easy and quick excursion from Tambor is the 1-km (½-mile) hike south of town to the secluded beach of Palo de Jesús. From the town's dock, follow the road south until it becomes a shady trail that winds its way over rocks and sand around Punta Piedra Amarilla. The trees along the way resound with squawks of parakeets and the throaty utterings of male howler monkeys.

HORSEBACK RIDING

The Tango Mar Resort has its own stables and offers horseback tours that can take you down trails through the rain forest or down to the beach to see an array of wildlife. Set off early in the morning or late in the afternoon, when it's cooler and you're more likely to see birds and animals. Tours range from $45 for a two-hour ride on hotel property to $68 for a longer ride to Montezuma, along the beach.

Isla Tortuga

90 mins by boat from Puntarenas.

Soft white sand and casually leaning palms fringe this island of tropical dry forest off the southern coast of the Nicoya Peninsula. Sound heavenly? It would be if there weren't quite so many people. Tours from Jacó, Herradura, San José, Puntarenas, and Montezuma take boatfuls of visitors to drink from coconuts and snorkel around a large rock. On the boat ride from Playa Tambor or Montezuma you might spot passing dolphins. Though state owned, the island is leased and inhabited by a Costa Rican family. It makes for an easy day trip out to sea, costing $20 to $109, depending on the duration and departure point.

GETTING HERE AND AROUND

Every tour operator in Playa Tambor and Montezuma offers trips to Isla Tortuga, one of the area's biggest attractions, or you can kayak from the nearby Curú National Wildlife Refuge. Admission to the island is $7 (included in tour prices).

 Beaches

Isla Tortuga

ISLAND | FAMILY | This idyllic, unpopulated island has a white-sand beach fronting clear turquoise water, where you'll see a good number of colorful fish, though in the company of many tourists, arriving in many boats of all sizes; try to avoid the weekends if you can. A 40-minute hiking trail (small fee) wanders past monkey ladders, strangler figs, bromeliads, orchids, and the fruit-bearing *guanábana* (soursop) and *marañón* (cashew) trees up to a lookout point with amazing vistas. **Amenities:** food and drink; toilets; water sports. **Best for:** snorkeling; swimming. ✉ *Isla Tortuga* 🖾 *$7*.

 Activities

KAYAKING
Turismo Curú

KAYAKING | FAMILY | This tour operator arranges motorboat tours to the island, leaving from Curú Wildlife Refuge at 9 am and spending one hour on a less-frequented beach on one of the Morteros Islands, and two hours on the beach at Tortuga, plus snorkeling ($60 per person, including snorkeling gear, lunch, and entrance fee to Curú). Tortuga Island is only 3 km (2 miles) off the beach of Curú, so experienced kayakers can paddle there ($80 per person). You can also take a boat tour to Tortuga and spend an hour kayaking around the island ($55). ✉ *Main road, across from Esso station, Paquera* 🕾 *2641–0004* ⊕ *www.turismocuru.com* 🖾 *From $55*.

Montezuma

7 km (4½ miles) southeast of Cóbano, 45 km (28 miles) south of Paquera, 18 km (11 miles) south of Tambor.

Beautifully positioned on a sandy bay, Montezuma is hemmed in by a precipitous wooded shoreline that has prevented the overdevelopment that has affected so many other beach towns. Its small, funky town center is a pastel cluster of New Age health-food cafés, trendy beachwear shops, jaunty tour kiosks, lively open-air bars and restaurants and, at last count, three ice-cream shops, two selling Italian gelato. Most hotels are clustered in or around the town's center,

Lovely beaches, yoga, and New Age cafés are the main attractions in Montezuma.

but the best ones are on the coast to the north and south, where the loudest revelers are the howler monkeys in the nearby forest. The beaches north of town, especially Playa Grande, are lovely.

Montezuma has been on the international vagabond circuit for years, attracting backpackers and alternative-lifestyle types. Yoga is a main attraction, with a wide range of classes, and the town is becoming more of a cultural draw, with a low-key film festival of shorts and documentaries, and an occasional poetry festival. At night, the center of town often fills up with tattooed travelers and artisans who entertain each other and passersby. When college students are on break, the place can be a zoo. People used to jokingly refer to the town as "Monte-fuma" (*fuma* means "smoke" in Spanish—get it?) but, for better or for worse, Montezuma is being tamed and becoming more civilized and attractive, with plenty of grown-up lodging and dining options to choose from.

North and south of the town center have always been quiet, and the attractions here include swaths of tropical dry forest, waterfalls, and beautiful virgin beaches that stretch across one national park and two nature preserves. One especially good walk (about two hours) or horseback ride leads to a small waterfall called El Chorro that pours into the sea, where there is a small tidal pool at lower tides.

GETTING HERE AND AROUND
Most people get here via the ferry from Puntarenas to Paquera, which is an hour's drive from Montezuma, with a bumpy dirt-road stretch from Cóbano to Montezuma. The quickest way to get here, however, is to fly to nearby Tambor. One of the taxis waiting at the airstrip will take you to Montezuma for $50, about a 1½-hour drive. There are also one-hour water taxis ($50) that travel every morning between Jacó and Montezuma, departing from Montezuma at 8:30 am and Jacó at 10 am. There are no banks in town; the closest bank is in Cóbano. There is an ATM on the beach road in Montezuma, but it's

not the most secure or reliable place to withdraw money.

ESSENTIALS

BANK/ATM Banco Nacional. ✉ *Main road, Cóbano, Montezuma* ☎ *2212–2000.*

🍴 Restaurants

Cocolores

$$$ | **ECLECTIC** | Follow the glow of multicolor lanterns to this dinner-only, open-air eatery within sight and sound of the ocean. The simple wooden tables are on a patio bordered with gardens or, during the drier months, practically on the beach. **Known for:** mouthwatering coconut curry; unique oceanfront atmosphere; ceviche. [$] *Average main: $16* ✉ *Behind Hotel Pargo Feliz, on beach road, Montezuma* ☎ *2642–0348* 🕓 *Closed Mon. and last 3 wks of Oct. No lunch.*

El Sano Banano Restaurant

$$ | **VEGETARIAN** | Montezuma's first natural-food restaurant is named after the chewy dried bananas made by the owners, who also own the upscale Ylang Ylang resort on the beach. This popular eatery serves the best vegetarian fare in town, including scrambled tofu for breakfast and excellent wraps, salads, fajitas, and spring rolls, with plenty of vegan and gluten-free options. **Known for:** great people-watching; super breakfasts; sandwich with chicken and patacones (smashed and fried plantains). [$] *Average main: $12* ✉ *Main road, Montezuma* ☎ *2642–0638* 🌐 *elsanobanano.com.*

Ice Dream

$ | **ITALIAN** | Literally, the coolest place in town is this blissfully air-conditioned ice-cream parlor with an array of refreshing Italian gelato flavors, cool fruit smoothies, and milk shakes. It's airy and bright, with large windows looking onto the main street and an outdoor terrace. **Known for:** good selection of panini; Lavazza coffee; a variety of gelatos to cool you off. [$] *Average main: $6* ✉ *Southeast corner of main street and beach road, Montezuma* ☎ *2642–0160.*

★ Playa de los Artistas

$$$ | **ITALIAN** | Arty driftwood tables and sculpted chairs scattered along the rocky beach and an inventive Mediterranean menu have made this one of the most scenic, as well as one of the best, restaurants in the country for almost 30 years. The eclectic menu changes daily and features local seafood, lamb, beef, and even duck. **Known for:** homemade ravioli; funky found-art decor; spectacular beach setting. [$] *Average main: $20* ✉ *Montezuma* ✣ *275 meters (902 feet) south of town, near Los Mangos Hotel* ☎ *2642–0920, 2642–0316* 🕓 *Closed Mon.–Wed.*

★ Ylang Ylang Restaurant

$$$ | **VEGETARIAN** | One of Montezuma's most scenic and sophisticated restaurants, Ylang Ylang is nestled between the beach and the jungle, offering views of waves crashing against the rocks. The lunch menu lists a selection of sushi, salads, wraps, and sandwiches with various vegan, gluten-free, and raw dishes. **Known for:** fresh flavorful sushi; blackened tuna; remote location. [$] *Average main: $18* ✉ *On beach, ½ km (¼ mile) north of town, at Ylang Ylang Beach Resort, Montezuma* ☎ *2642–0523* 🌐 *www.ylangylangbeachresort.com.*

🛏 Hotels

Hotel El Jardín

$$ | **HOTEL** | Spread across a hill a few blocks from the beach, this hotel has refreshed rooms and villas with ocean, pool, and garden views. **Pros:** central location; good value; spacious rooms. **Cons:** steep paths to climb; no breakfast; a few rooms catch a bit of noise from bars in town. [$] *Rooms from: $85* ✉ *West end of main road, Montezuma* ☎ *2642–0074* 🌐 *www.hoteleljardin.com* 🛎 *16 rooms* 🍴 *No Meals.*

Sano Banano Beachside Hotel

$$ | **B&B/INN** | If quiet and cool is what you are seeking, these comfortable, tastefully decorated rooms above the popular restaurant of the same name are

air-conditioned and soundproofed—and they are a bargain. **Pros:** budget-friendly; Ylang Ylang Beach Resort privileges; excellent restaurant. **Cons:** can feel a little claustrophobic; lacks some things like hair dryer and TV; most guest rooms lack windows. [$] *Rooms from: $75* ✉ *Main road, Montezuma* ☎ *2642–0638* 🌐 *elsanobanano.com* 🛏 *12 rooms* 🍴 *Free Breakfast.*

★ Ylang Ylang Beach Resort

$$$ | **RESORT** | Secluded and serene, this gorgeous tropical resort with a holistic slant sits in an exuberant garden, nestled between the sea and a lush forest. **Pros:** gorgeous, natural setting; great restaurant; excellent service. **Cons:** 15-minute walk to town along beach; spotty Wi-Fi; ocean-view tent cabins offer limited privacy. [$] *Rooms from: $198* ✉ *Montezuma* ✥ *700 meters (2,296 feet) north of school in Montezuma* ☎ *2642–0523, 888/795–8494 in North America* 🌐 *www.ylangylangbeachresort.com* 🛏 *23 units* 🍴 *Free Breakfast.*

Nightlife

Montezuma's nightlife is focused on a handful of bars where locals and out-of-towners mix, a refreshing change from larger beach towns. A few venues boasting live music have recently appeared on the scene, including El Sano Banano and Ylang Ylang Beach Resort, where guest musicians and bands perform. Street-side artisans selling their creations often animate the area with drumming and dancing that draw passersby to stop and dance, too.

Cafe Restaurant Organico

CAFÉS | There's live music almost every night and open-mic night on Monday at this Italian-owned hot spot. The fun gets started around 7:30 and goes late into the night if enough performers show up. Cool down with a bowl of excellent, chili-spiced, chocolate Italian gelato while you watch the show. ✉ *Across from Cocolores, on beach road, Montezuma* ☎ *2642–1322.*

Restaurante Moctezuma

BARS | You can't get any closer to the beach than at this breezy, casual bar, which serves the cheapest beers in town. At night, candles and moonlight illuminate the tables in the sand. ✉ *Hotel Moctezuma, 1st fl., Montezuma* ☎ *2642–0058.*

Shopping

Beachwear, banana paper, wooden crafts, and indigenous pottery are some of what you find in colorful shops in the town's center. During the dry season, traveling artisans from around the world unfold their streetside tables just before the sun begins to set; candles light up the handmade leather-and-seed jewelry, dream catchers, and knit tops.

Galeria La Floresta

CRAFTS | Visit this outdoor gallery to see a display of fantastical, stunning lamps and sconces made from driftwood, bamboo, and shells. Swiss artist Claudia Bassaeur makes unique and beautiful lamp shades with marbled, handmade paper imported from Santa Fe, New Mexico. She also makes extraordinary jewelry, using found "treasure." Call ahead to make an appointment. The gallery is on the main road in Cabuya, on the way to Cabo Blanco Absolute Nature Reserve. ✉ *7 km (4½ miles) south of Montezuma on road to Cabuya, 200 meters (656 feet) past Hotel Celaje, Montezuma* ☎ *8836–6876.*

Activities

In Montezuma it seems that every other storefront is occupied by a tour operator. In spite of the multitude of signs advertising "Tourist Information," none are officially sanctioned by the Costa Rican tourist office.

HIKING

Hiking is one of the best ways to explore Montezuma's natural treasures, including beaches, lush coastline, jungles, and waterfalls. There are plenty of options around town or in nearby parks and reserves. Just over a bridge, 10 minutes south of town, a slippery path patrolled by howler monkeys leads upstream to two waterfalls and a fun swimming hole. If you value your life, don't jump or dive from the waterfalls. Guides from any tour operator in town can escort you, but save your money. This one you can do on your own. The path is very crowded on weekends, especially in January and around Easter.

El Chorro

HIKING & WALKING | To reach the beach-front waterfall called El Chorro, head left from the main beach access and hike about two hours to the north of town along the sand and through the woods behind the rocky points. The trip takes you across seven adjacent beaches, on one of which there is a small store where you can buy soft drinks. Leave as early in the morning as possible to beat the heat, and bring water and good sunblock. El Chorro can also be reached on a horse-back tour organized by any of the local tour operators. ⊠ *Montezuma*.

J. C.'s Journeys

BIRD WATCHING | On Tuesday, Thursday, Friday, and Saturday, bilingual certified guide Juan Carlos Aguirre leads three-hour bird-watching tours starting at 5:30 am ($60 per person, minimum two people) including breakfast; a local cultural tour where you'll visit with a rural farmer and learn about sustainable farming; and two-hour nocturnal tours, complete with a night-vision scope to help you spot creatures along a forest stream ($30 per person, minimum of two). You can also hire Juan Carlos for a private birding tour. ⊠ *Montezuma* ☎ *8975–8832* ⊕ *www.jcsjourneys.com*.

TOUR OPERATORS

Zuma Tours

SNORKELING | If you want to get out on the water, this reliable agency organizes snorkeling tours to Tortuga Island ($70), and sportfishing trips from five to eight hours.

Chorotegan Pottery

In the country village of Guaitil, 24 km (15 miles) north of Nicoya, artists—most of them women—have revived a vanishing tradition by producing clay pottery handmade in the manner of indigenous Chorotegans. The town square is a soccer field, and almost every house facing it has a pottery shop out front and a round, wood-fired kiln in back. Pottery designs range from traditional Costa Rican to inspired Cubist abstractions. Prices range from $12 to $300; most are around $30.

There are tours of Curú Wildlife Refuge and the Montezuma Waterfall Canopy. They also offer transport by shuttle van, and taxi boats ($50) between Jacó and Montezuma (a much faster trip than by land). ⊠ *Main street, south of El Sano Banano Hotel, Montezuma* ☎ *2642–0024* ⊕ *www.zumatours.net* 🛥 *From $50.*

Malpaís and Santa Teresa

12 km (7½ miles) southwest of Cóbano, 52 km (33 miles) south of Paquera.

Once frequented mostly by die-hard surfers in search of some of the country's largest waves and by naturalists en route to the nearby Cabo Blanco Absolute Nature Preserve, this area is now a 10-km (6-mile) stretch of hotels, restaurants, and shopping centers strung along a mostly dirt road that is choked with dust in the dry season and awash in mud the rest of the year. Despite the congestion, the string of beaches and consistent surf still draw a multitude of surfers.

Health-oriented spas, organic restaurants, and yoga classes are also attracting a very international, young crowd, from Europe, Australia, and North America.

Coming from Cóbano, the road alternates between paved and dirt sections until it reaches an intersection, known locally as El Cruce, marked by a cluster of shopping centers, banks, restaurants, and hotel signs. To the left is the partially paved route to relatively tranquil Malpaís, and to the right is the road to Santa Teresa, which has a few paved sections but is mostly a rutted, narrow dirt road clogged with trucks, ATVs, bicycles, and pedestrians. Playa Carmen, straight ahead, is the area's best place for surfing, though swimmers will want to be careful of rip currents. Malpaís and Santa Teresa are so close that locals disagree on where one begins and the other ends. You could travel up the road parallel to the ocean that connects them and not realize you've moved from one town to the other.

GETTING HERE AND AROUND

From Paquera it's an hour's drive to Malpaís via Cóbano. After Cóbano, the road is partially paved. There are some bumpy dirt sections, which can become quite muddy in the rainy season, so a 4WD vehicle is your best bet. There is a direct bus from San José, leaving at 6 am and 2 pm to Santa Teresa, crossing with the ferry from Puntarenas. The trip takes about six hours and costs about $15, including ferry fare. SANSA has 30-minute flights between San Jose and Tambor for about $150. Taxis waiting at Tambor's airstrip will take up to four people to Malpaís for $50.

SHUTTLES Tropical Tours Shuttles. ⊠ Malpais ⊹ 50 meters (164 feet) north of El Cruce ☎ 2640–1900, 2640–0811 ⊕ www.tropicaltourshuttles.com.

TAXI Taxi. ⊠ Malpaís ☎ 8360–8166.

ESSENTIALS

BANK/ATM Banco Nacional. ⊠ Centro Comercial Playa Carmen, at crossroads, Malpaís ☎ 2640–0640.

MEDICAL CENTER Lifeguard Urgent Medical Centre. ⊠ At crossroads, around corner from BCR bank, Malpais ☎ 4001–9867 ext 12 ⊕ lifeguardcostarica.com.

PHARMACY Farmacia Amiga. ⊠ Centro Comercial Playa Carmen, at crossroads, Malpais ☎ 2640–0830.

Sights

★ Cabo Blanco Absolute Nature Preserve
(Reserva Natural Absoluta Cabo Blanco)
NATURE PRESERVE | Conquistadores named this area Cabo Blanco on account of its white earth and cliffs, but it was a more benevolent pair of foreigners—Swede Nicolas Wessberg and his Danish wife, Karen Mogensen, arriving here in the 1950s—who made it a preserve. Appalled by the first clear-cut in the Cabo Blanco area in 1960, the pioneering couple launched an international appeal to save the forest. In time their efforts led not only to the creation of the 12-square-km (4½-square-mile) reserve but also to the founding of Costa Rica's national park service, the National Conservation Areas System (SINAC). Wessberg was murdered on the Osa Peninsula in 1975 while researching the area's potential as a national park. A reserve just outside Montezuma was named in his honor. A reserve has also been created to honor his wife, who dedicated her life to conservation after her husband's death.

Informative natural-history captions dot the trails in the Cabo Blanco forest. Look for the sapodilla trees, which produce a white latex used to make gum; you can often see V-shape scars where the trees have been cut to allow the latex to run into containers placed at the base. Wessberg cataloged a full array of animals here: porcupine, hog-nosed skunk, spotted skunk, gray fox, anteater, cougar, and jaguar. Resident birds include brown pelicans, white-throated magpies, toucans, cattle egrets, green herons, parrots, and blue-crowned motmots. A fairly strenuous 10-km (6-mile) round-trip hike, which takes about two hours in each direction, follows a trail from the reserve entrance to **Playa Cabo Blanco.** The beach is magnificent, with hundreds of pelicans flying in formation and paddling in the calm waters offshore—you can wade right in and join them. Off the tip of the cape is the 7,511-square-foot **Isla Cabo Blanco,** with pelicans, frigate birds, brown boobies, and an abandoned lighthouse. As a strict reserve, Cabo Blanco is open only five days a week. It has restrooms, picnic tables at the entrance, and a visitor center with information panels on park history and biological diversity, but no other tourist facilities, and overnight camping is not permitted. Most visitors come with their own guide. This is one of the hottest parks in the country, so be sure to bring lots of water with you.

⚠ **An official sign at the entrance warns people with cardiovascular problems NOT to walk the strenuous trail to Cabo Blanco beach.** ⊠ *Cabo Blanco Absolute Nature Preserve, Montezuma* ✛ *10 km (6 miles) southwest of Montezuma via Cabuya* ☎ *2642–0093, 2642–0312* ⊕ *www. costarica-nationalparks.com/caboblanco-absolutenaturalreserve.html* 🎟 *$12.*

 Beaches

Playa Carmen

BEACH | This Blue Flag beach, sometimes referred to as El Carmen, is just a stone's throw from the commercial development along the beach road, so it tends to attract more people. There's a parking lot and palm trees for shade. The waves offer excellent surfing for all levels, with dozens of beach breaks scattered along the wide, sandy strand. The sea grows rough and dirty during the May to December rainy season, with frequent swells that sometimes make it impossible to get out on a surfboard. Swimmers need to be careful of rip currents. Lifeguards are on duty year-round on weekends, from 9 am to sunset; more days during holiday periods. **Amenities:** food and drink. **Best for:** surfing. ⊠ *Playa Carmen, Santa Teresa.*

Playa Malpaís

BEACH | South of the bustle of Playas Carmen and Santa Teresa, this Blue Flag beach is quieter and rockier, with interesting volcanic formations. The tougher surfing here was the original attraction that drew surfers from around the world, with a challenging break over a rock platform. Swimming is not advised, but the dramatic scenery is unbeatable. **Amenities:** food and drink. **Best for:** surfing; sunset. ⊠ *Malpais.*

Playa Santa Teresa

BEACH | Playa Carmen seamlessly segues into Playa Santa Teresa, about 1 km (½ mile) to the north. This flat, sandy Blue Flag beach is edged by forest and punctuated with rocky sections and tide pools at low tide. It's usually a calmer option for surfers, but swimmers need to take care, especially since there are no lifeguards here. The farther north you go, the less crowded the beach is. Beachfront hotels include Trópico Latino, Latitude 10, Florblanca, and Pranamar; Rancho Itauna provides food and entertainment facing the beach. **Amenities:** none. **Best for:** surfing; walking. ⊠ *Santa Teresa.*

 Restaurants

Koji's Restaurant

$$$ | **SUSHI** | North of Santa Teresa, this trendy sushi place off a dusty dirt road is one of the most popular restaurants in the area. Fabulous sushi, sashimi, and tempura are carefully crafted, and there's a daily blackboard menu featuring hand rolls and wraps. **Known for:** locally sourced seafood, fruits, and vegetables; spicy sesame tuna; Koji roll made with shrimp tempura, avocado, cucumber, spicy tuna, and special sauce. $ *Average main: $18* ⊠ *Buenos Aires Rd., below Hotel Horizon, Santa Teresa* ☎ *2640–0815* ⊙ *Closed Sun. and Mon. No lunch.*

Playa Santa Teresa, on the southern tip of the Nicoya Peninsula

★ Nectar

$$$ | **SEAFOOD** | Fresh seafood is the specialty at this poolside alfresco restaurant, with inventive daily specials that focus on the day's catch prepared with Asian and Mediterranean flavors. After 3:30, the dedicated sushi chef produces such treats as panko-crusted prawn roll with ahi tuna, mango, and avocado. **Known for:** Latin, Mediterranean, and Asian influences; organic and local produce; fresh sushi. ⓈAverage main: $25 ⊠ Resort Florblanca, 2 km (1 mile) north of soccer field, Malpais ☎ 2640–0232 ⊕ www. florblanca.com/nectar.

Restaurante Al Chile Viola

$$ | **MODERN ITALIAN** | Chefs Emiliano and Luz from Florence will challenge your taste buds with imaginative dishes using authentic Italian ingredients like traditional homemade pastas including beef lasagna, eggplant Parmesan, and osso buco *alla Romana*. For dessert, Emiliano makes a killer dark-chocolate mousse sprinkled with sea-salt crystals, or try the signature frozen coffee made with local

Cafe Tica liqueur. During high season (December–May), there's live music three times a week. **Known for:** sea bass with grilled vegetables; bull testicle ravioli; creative homemade pastas. ⓈAverage main: $14 ⊠ Santa Teresa ✛ 200 meters (656 feet) north of Super La Hacienda, on main road ☎ 2640–0433 ⓍClosed Sun., and Sept. and Oct. No lunch.

Hotels

★ Casa MarBella

$$ | **HOTEL** | **FAMILY** | It is indeed a picture-perfect view of the "beautiful sea" that you find at this lovely casa, nestled into the side of a hill. **Pros:** significant discounts for cash payment; infinity pool; large three-bedroom option perfect for families. **Cons:** suites are on the smaller side; some rooms lack privacy; steep, bumpy climb up the road. ⓈRooms from: $88 ⊠ Santa Teresa ✛ 125 meters (410 feet) east and 25 meters (82 feet) north of Super Ronny's ☎ 2640–0749 ⊕ www.casamarbel.la ⇆ 12 rooms ⓘ⊙No Meals.

★ Florblanca
$$$$ | **RESORT** | Named for the white flowers of the frangipani trees growing between the restaurant and the beach, this ultraluxurious resort is dedicated to relaxation and rejuvenation. **Pros:** gorgeous villas and grounds; friendly; great yoga classes; no kids under age six. **Cons:** on rocky stretch of beach; insects sometimes a problem; very expensive. [$] *Rooms from: $600* ✉ *2 km (1 mile) north of soccer field, Santa Teresa* ☎ *2640–0232, 800/685–1031 toll-free in North America* 🌐 *www.florblanca.com* 🛏 *11 rooms* 🍴 *No Meals.*

Hotel Tropico Latino
$$$ | **HOTEL** | **FAMILY** | This beachfront hotel has everything: a spectacular beach with a major surf break; a trendy restaurant with ocean views; a round, palm-fringed pool; bungalows and rooms sprinkled throughout a mature garden; twice-daily yoga sessions on the beach; and a full-service spa. **Pros:** lush gardens; great location on beach; large pool. **Cons:** not quiet—more of a buzz with lots of people coming and going; cheaper rooms are dark and close to dusty, noisy road. [$] *Rooms from: $160* ✉ *Santa Teresa* ✣ *700 meters (2,296 feet) north of crossroads* ☎ *2640–0062* 🌐 *www.hoteltropicolatino.com* 🛏 *22 units* 🍴 *No Meals.*

Nightlife

Ranchos Itauna
LIVE MUSIC | This beachfront restaurant-lounge in Santa Teresa is a fixture on the nightlife scene, with "SoundLab" Tuesday and Saturday, featuring international live and DJ music, from 4 to 11 pm. Salsa lessons, bonfires, and torch-fire shows add to the excitement. The crowd is a mix of locals and tourists. ✉ *100 meters (328 feet) north of Super Costa, Santa Teresa* ☎ *2640–0095, 8760–7785* 🌐 *www.ranchos-itauna.com.*

Activities

CANOPY TOURS

Canopy Malpaís
ZIP LINING | The only canopy tour in the area has an 11-platform adventure with ocean views that takes about an hour ($55). Transportation to the zipline, near the entrance of Cabo Blanco Absolute Nature Reserve, is $10 round-trip. ✉ *Near entrance to Cabo Blanco Absolute Nature Reserve, Malpais* ☎ *2640–0360* 🌐 *www.canopymalpais.com* 🎫 *From $55.*

SURFING

From November to May, the Malpaís area has some of Costa Rica's most consistent surf, as well as clear skies and winds that create idyllic conditions.

Kina Surf Shop
SURFING | This shop stands out among the dozens of surf shops scattered along the beach road for its surfing expertise and wide range of boards and accessories. If you're a first-time surfer, they can fit you with the correct board from their stock of more than 60 different shapes and sizes. Surf lessons for all levels cost $70 (minimum two people) for about two hours, including board for the rest of the day and a rash guard. ✉ *Plaza Solar, in front of Brunelas, main street, Santa Teresa* ☎ *2640–0627* 🌐 *www.kinasurfcr.com* 🎫 *From $70* ☞ *Cash only.*

MANUEL ANTONIO AND THE CENTRAL PACIFIC COAST

Updated by
Marlise Kast-Myers

 Sights
★★★★★

 Restaurants
★★★★☆

 Hotels
★★★★★

 Shopping
★★★☆☆

 Nightlife
★★★★☆

WELCOME TO MANUEL ANTONIO AND THE CENTRAL PACIFIC COAST

TOP REASONS TO GO

★ **Adventure sports:** Snorkel among colorful fish, get muddy on mountain adventures, and zip through treetops near Jacó and Manuel Antonio.

★ **Fishing:** Deep-sea fishing at Quepos, Jacó, or Herradura gives a chance to hook a sailfish, marlin, wahoo, or yellowfin tuna.

★ **Nature and wildlife:** Explore the seaside forest and see sloths, iguanas, agoutis, monkeys, and 450 species of birds at Manuel Antonio National Park.

★ **Sunsets:** Whether you view it from the beach or while sipping hilltop cocktails in Manuel Antonio, this region has some of the country's best venues for watching the sunset.

★ **Surfing:** This is Costa Rica's surf central. Jacó, Playa Hermosa, Esterillos, and Manuel Antonio beckon surfers, from beginners to pros.

Most of the Central Pacific is mountainous, and beach towns are backed by forested peaks. Humid evergreen forests, oil-palm plantations, and cattle pastures blanket the land. The coastal highway connects all towns from Tárcoles to the southern Pacific. The hub town of Jacó makes a good base for visiting surrounding beaches and wildlife areas. Farther south are neighboring Quepos and Manuel Antonio, Costa Rica's most popular destination, followed by smaller towns barely touched by tourism.

1 Tárcoles. This small town is famous for its crocodiles. You can get a peek at the huge reptiles as they lounge on the riverbanks or take a river tour.

2 Punta Leona. Past Tárcoles on the Central Pacific Coast, Punta Leona is worth a trip if your ideal stay is an upscale villa in the lush rain forest with killer views and access to a private beach.

3 Playa Herradura. Just north of Jacó, this beautiful coastal town named for its horseshoe-shaped beach is known for its marina, golf course, and sportfishing.

4 Jacó. Famous for nightlife and surfing, this lively, popular destination is the most developed beach town in Costa Rica and offers something for both beach lovers and adventure seekers.

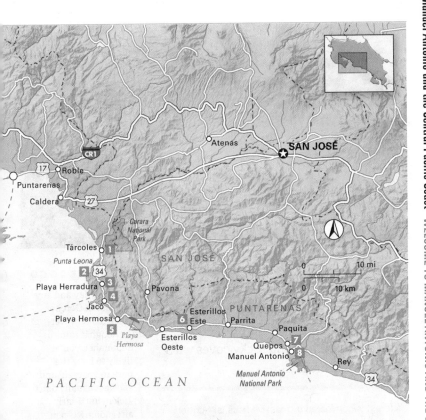

5 Playa Hermosa. Not to be confused with the beach of the same name in Guanacaste, this surf town south of Jacó has ample outdoor activities, including turtle tours and surfing lessons.

6 Esterillos Este. Midway between the busy towns of Jacó and Quepos, this under-the-radar community has some great beachfront boutique hotels.

7 Quepos. The gateway town to Manuel Antonio is good for stocking up on supplies, visiting the area's nature reserve, and booking canopy tours.

8 Manuel Antonio. One of the most popular spots in Costa Rica is home to the wildlife-rich, beachlined Manuel Antonio National Park and a nice selection of restaurants and hotels.

MANUEL ANTONIO NATIONAL PARK

Manuel Antonio National Park

At only 7 square km (3 square miles), Manuel Antonio National Park—Costa Rica's smallest park—has impressive natural attractions: wildlife, rain forest, white-sand beaches, and rocky coves with abundant marine life.

The forest is dominated by massive ficus, silk-cotton trees, black-and-white Guapinols, and Panama trees as well as guacimo colorado, bully tree, cedar, and ceniza-ro. It's home to both two- and three-toed sloths, green and black iguanas, agoutis (similar to the guinea pig, but with longer legs), raccoons, coatis, three species of monkey, and more than 450 species of birds.

The well-maintained trails are short, mostly paved—and heavily traveled. Make no mistake about it: this is no undiscovered wilderness. In fact, Manuel Antonio is Costa Rica's most visited attraction. There are 5 km (3 miles) of coastline, and it's one of the few parks where you can combine nature walks with swimming off idyllic beaches. There's no commercial beach development, so the beaches are picture-perfect.

(For more information see the review in this chapter.)

BEST TIME TO GO

Visit any day and any month but October, when it's very wet. Although it rains in September, you're likely to have the park to yourself, and showers usually don't kick in until early afternoon. Keep in mind that the park is closed on Monday.

FUN FACT

The park's territory is too small to support all of its monkeys, so forested corridors and suspended bridges have been built to allow them to come and go.

BEST WAYS TO EXPLORE

HIKING

Don your hiking shoes and set off on Sloth Trail, the main route that leads to Manuel Antonio beach. The coral reef here makes it a good spot for snorkeling. A second trail leads to Playa Espadilla Sur. These two stunning beaches lie on either side of a tombolo, a sandy strip that connects the mainland to rocky Punta Catedral, which used to be an island thousands of years ago. Farther east, where fewer visitors venture, Playa Escondido is rocky and secluded. Trails from the entrance to Punta Catedral and Playa Escondido are in excellent shape. Trails farther east are progressively rougher due to the steep terrain. Sturdy walking sandals are good enough for most of the trails, but light hiking boots or closed shoes will help you avoid nasty encounters with biting ants.

WILDLIFE-WATCHING

Manuel Antonio is famous for its monkeys, especially the noisy white-faced monkeys that pester tourists at the beach. A troop of rare squirrel monkeys also lives here, one of the few places in the country where you can still find them. These tiny monkeys—*mono titi* in Spanish—are endangered. Catching sight of them is a real wildlife coup. The smallest of Costa Rica's four monkey species, these little guys have squirrel-like bushy tails, but they use them only for balance—they can't swing from them.

Watch, too, for less active creatures, such as the more-or-less stationary sloth, especially along the park's Sloth Trail. They sleep much of the day, curled up high in the trees. Look for clumps of green and brown and watch carefully to see if they move. You'll see many more animals and birds with a guide than without one. Hire an official guide at the park entrance.

TOP REASONS TO GO

BEACHES

There are gorgeous beaches with no commercial clutter or noise, but you need to bring your own snorkeling gear, snacks, and drinks. Only sandwiches, fruit, and nonalcoholic beverages are allowed in the park. There are toilet facilities and cold-water, open-air showers.

MONKEYS

Along with the ubiquitous capuchin monkeys performing for visitors on the beaches, you'll also find howler monkeys (*congos*) draped over tree branches in the forest, and more rarely, the endangered squirrel monkey.

PELICANS

Just off Playa Espadilla, you can swim out to some rocks and tread water while pelicans dive for fish.

VIEWS

For a fabulous coastal view, take the path that leads up to Punta Catedral's rocky hill, draped with thick jungle. You'll pass a lookout point with a view out at the Pacific and the park's islets.

An iguana sunbathes in Manuel Antonio.

The Central Pacific region of Costa Rica is a long swath of gorgeous land, encompassing sublime coastline dotted with national parks and palm-lined beaches, and inland stretches of ranches, coffee plantations, small villages, and forested mountains. There's a reason this is a popular place to visit: the region has a lot of *pura vida* to offer.

If you're a first-timer to Costa Rica, this region is all about Manuel Antonio and the acclaimed national park of the same name. (Manuel Antonio and the Arenal Volcano in the Northern Lowlands make the classic "get your feet wet" visit to Costa Rica.) For Costa Ricans, the Central Pacific often means Jacó, the closest beach town to San José, and an odd mix of burgeoning condo developments, nightclubs, hotels, and surf shops. But you need not limit yourself to these two anchors: Herradura, Playas Hermosa, Esterillos, and Bejuco along this stretch of coast offer a little more solitude, although development is slowly creeping up here, too.

The region is easily accessible by way of the San José–Caldera Highway CR27, which connects to the Southern Coastal Highway CR34.

MAJOR REGIONS

From Tárcoles to Quepos along Costa Rica's **Central Pacific Coast,** you'll find patches of undeveloped jungle, small surf towns, and some of the country's most accessible beaches. The proximity of these strands to San José leads Costa Ricans and foreigners alike to pop down for quick weekend beach vacations. Surfers have good reason to head for the consistent waves of Playas Jacó and Hermosa, and anglers and golfers should consider Playa Herradura for its golf courses and ocean access. You might find Herradura and Jacó overrated and overdeveloped, but the latter is a good option if you're looking for shopping, surfing, and nightlife.

South of the beach communities and surf stops along the Central Pacific coast are the towns of Quepos and **Manuel Antonio,** as well as the popular Manuel Antonio National Park. Unless you're stocking up on supplies or making a bank run, it's better to bypass Quepos, a former banana port and now a somewhat run-down fishing town. Most travelers head straight to Manuel Antonio, where boutique hotels and luxury resorts are perched on beachside cliffs or frame the national park. Between surf lessons, canopy tours, exploring the national park, and relaxing on the beach, it's easy to fall in love with this quaint town where the jungle meets the shore. Equally impressive is the town's reputation for sustainability practices, from green hotels to organic cuisine. Although some consider Manuel Antonio overdeveloped, nobody can deny its spectacular natural beauty.

Planning

When to Go

HIGH SEASON: DECEMBER TO APRIL

Dry season means high season here. Your payback for braving the crowds is nearly ideal weather. Expect warm, sunny days and pleasant evenings. If, however, you're not big on heat, March and April may feel stiflingly hot. Lots of visitors push hotel prices up and crowd the beaches, especially on dry-season weekends. Weekdays offer a slight respite from the crowds. During Holy Week and the last week of December, rooms are even harder to come by. If you're in the area during high season and want to visit one of the parks, especially Manuel Antonio, get an early start and arrive by 7 am.

LOW SEASON: SEPTEMBER TO NOVEMBER

This is the wettest of the rainy season, when showers become frequent and prolonged. The landmass and wind patterns that cause hurricane activity off the Caribbean coast create significant rain in the Central Pacific. Nature-themed activities usually go on rain or shine, but beach-lazing plans may well go awry. Keep in mind that some smaller hotels and restaurants actually close for several weeks during low season.

SHOULDER SEASON: MAY TO AUGUST

The rains begin in mid-May, but the first half of the wet season sees warm, mostly sunny days with lighter afternoon showers. It's easy to plan around them, and the precipitation keeps everything lush and green. Midyear school vacations fall in early July, with Costa Rican families flocking to the beach, especially Jacó and Manuel Antonio.

Planning Your Time

A week gives you enough time to visit several beaches on the central coast and still explore the wildlife of Manuel Antonio National Park. Adventure seekers might want to set aside a day for a surf lesson, forest hike, or canopy tour. The perfect balance is three days in scenic Manuel Antonio, two days at a secluded beach near Tárcoles or Playa Bejuco, and a couple of days for surfing and action close to bustling Jacó.

Getting Here and Around

AIR

The 20-minute flight between San José and Quepos on SANSA can save you the three-hour drive and costs between $85 and $100 one way. From San José, all airlines have daily flights to Quepos departing between 8 and 3.

AIRLINES SANSA Airlines. ⊠ *Juan Santamaría International Airport (SJO), Alajuela* ☏ *877/767–2672 from U.S., 2290–4100* ⊕ *www.flysansa.com.*

BUS

Public buses to and within this entire region are punctual and economical, and local shuttles from San José can drop you off at your hotel's doorstep. Public buses leave San José almost hourly between 6 am and 7:30 pm and take four hours to reach Quepos. From here you have to take local transportation to your hotel in Manuel Antonio. Interbus is more direct, with hotel pickup in San José and Quepos or Manuel Antonio. The company offers a morning and afternoon trip for around $62 one way.

BUS CONTACTS Interbus. ☏ *4100–0888* ⊕ *www.interbusonline.com.*

CAR

Highway 27 connects San José to the Pacific port of Caldera, near Puntarenas. This 77-km (46-mile) toll road eliminates a winding drive through the mountains and puts the coast just one hour from the capital. Costa Ricans call the modern road the Carretera a Caldera (Caldera Highway). Before the coast, an exit to the two-lane paved coastal highway, or Costanera, leads southeast to Tárcoles, Herradura, Jacó, Hermosa, Esterillos, Bejuco, and Quepos. An asphalt road winds its way over the hill between Quepos and Manuel Antonio National Park—plan on about 1½ hours to drive to Jacó and 2½ hours to Quepos.

Tours

King Tours

ADVENTURE TOURS | A roster of tours includes trips to renowned attractions like Manuel Antonio National Park, as well as crocodile boat adventures, whale-watching, deep-sea and coastal fishing trips, horseback rides to waterfalls, and canopy tours. The company can also book tours to destinations elsewhere in the country, such as Poás and Arenal volcanoes, Monteverde Cloud Forest, and Isla Tortuga. ✉ *Main road into Playa Herradura, in front of Los Sueños, Herradura* ☎ *8819–1920, 800/213–7091 in North America* ⊕ *www.kingtours.com* ✉ *From $85.*

Restaurants

You'll find the liveliest dining mix in the country outside San José here, especially in Manuel Antonio. The crowd of international visitors has brought international restaurants ranging from Japanese to Italian, but as you'd expect in a coastal region, seafood still reigns here.

For traditional Costa Rican cuisine, your best bet is a roadside *soda* where locals gather for their daily *casado* (rice, beans, plantains, and an entrée of chicken, beef, or fish). Your final bill will include a 13% sales tax and a 10%–12% service charge.

Hotels

The Central Pacific has a good mix of high-quality resorts, ecolodges, rental villas, boutique hotels, and *cabinas* (usually low-cost, freestanding cabins with more amenities than a standard room). You'll also find some of the country's priciest lodgings. As a rule, prices drop 20% to 30% during the rainy season. Hotel rooms are taxed at the national rate of 13%. Reserve as far in advance as possible during the busy dry season, especially on weekends. Near Manuel Antonio National Park, the cliff-side hotels with ocean views are the more activity-rich, attractive, and expensive places to stay.

HOTEL AND RESTAURANT PRICES
Restaurant prices are the average cost of a main course at dinner or, if dinner is not served, at lunch. Hotel prices are the lowest cost of a standard double room in high season. Restaurant and hotel reviews have been shortened. For full information, visit Fodors.com.

What it Costs in U.S. Dollars			
$	$$	$$$	$$$$
RESTAURANTS			
under $10	$10–$15	$16–$25	over $25
HOTELS			
under $75	$75–$150	$151–$250	over $250

Tárcoles

90 km (54 miles) southwest of San José.

Crocodile boat tours on the Río Tárcoles are this small town's claim to fame. You don't actually have to drive to Tárcoles to do the tour; operators can pick you up in Herradura or Jacó. Budget (or time-conscious) travelers may want to simply stop near Río Tárcoles bridge where dozens of crocodiles gather on the banks. It's easy to snap a few photos from the top of the bridge, but be sure to lock your car and watch for oncoming traffic and Tourist Police, who make this a regular ticketing location for speedy drivers. The muddy river has gained a reputation as the country's dirtiest, due to San José's inadequate sewage system, but it amazingly remains an impressive refuge for wildlife. A huge diversity of birds results from a combination of transitional forest and the river, which houses crocodiles, herons, storks, spoonbills, and other waterbirds. This is also one of the few areas in the country where you can see scarlet macaws, which you may spot on a boat tour or while hiking in a private reserve nearby. If you have the time, drive 12 km (8 miles) south of the Río Tárcoles bridge and take a dip in the pools of Catarata Manantial de Agua Viva. As the highest waterfall in Costa Rica, these freshwater cascades are located 4 km (2½ miles) past Hotel Villa Lapas.

GETTING HERE AND AROUND

By car, head west from San José on Highway 27 to Orotina and follow the signs to Herradura, Jacó, and Quepos. After crossing the bridge over the Río Tárcoles, look for the entrance to the town of Tárcoles on the right. On the left is the dirt road that leads to the Hotel Villa Lapas and the waterfall reserve. Any bus traveling to Jacó can drop you off at the entrance to Tárcoles. Let the driver know in advance.

🍽 Restaurants

Steven Lisa's

$$ | ECLECTIC | A convenient location, free Wi-Fi, and good food make this roadside restaurant, just south of the entrance to Tárcoles, a popular pit stop for those traveling between San José and the Central Pacific beaches. The menu includes breakfast, lunch, and dinner with entrées that range from hamburgers and pasta to fried shrimp and a pricey surf and turf. **Known for:** shrimp with fries; local casado; great breakfast. Ⓢ *Average main: $10* ⊠ *On Costanera Sur, north of gas station near Río La Pita, Tárcoles* ☎ *2637–0665.*

🛏 Hotels

Hotel Villa Lapas Jungle Village

$$ | RESORT | FAMILY | Within a tranquil rain-forest preserve, the stucco rooms here are nothing special, but are a great escape for nature lovers who want lodging, tours, and wildlife all in one location. **Pros:** surrounded by forest; lots of activities; birds. **Cons:** property is a bit tired looking; often busy with tour groups; rooms sometimes musty. Ⓢ *Rooms from: $79* ⊠ *Off Costanera, 3 km (2 miles) after bridge over Río Tárcoles, turn left on dirt road for 600 meters (1,968 feet), Tárcoles* ☎ *4080–8900* ⊕ *www.villalapas.com* ➹ *76 rooms* ◉ *Free Breakfast.*

🏃 Activities

BOAT TOURS

On the two-hour riverboat tours through the mangrove forest and Tárcoles River, you might see massive crocodiles, Jesus lizards, iguanas, and some of roughly 50 colorful bird species, including the roseate spoonbill and boat-billed heron. Tours reach the river's mouth, providing nice sea views, especially at sunset.

■ **TIP→ Around noon is the best time to spot crocs sunbathing; bird enthusiasts prefer afternoon rides to catch scarlet macaws. During the rainy season (May to November),** the river may grow too rough for boats in the afternoon.

Crocodile Man Tour

ADVENTURE TOURS | Small scars on the hands of the two brothers who run the company are the result of the tour's most original (and optional) attraction: feeding fish to the crocs. The boats are small enough to slide up alongside the mangroves for a closer look. Transportation is provided from nearby beaches (at an added cost), but not from San José. Daily tours take place every two hours from 8 to 4. They also offer a bird-watching tour at 6 am. ⊠ *Main road into Tárcoles, Tárcoles* ☎ *2637–0771* ⊕ *www.crocodilemantour.com* ⊠ *$35.*

DIVING
Okeanos Aggressor

SCUBA DIVING | Ten-day dive safaris to Cocos Island operate year-round. ⊠ *Tárcoles* ☎ *800/348–2628 in U.S.* ⊕ *www.aggressor.com* ⊠ *From $6,599.*

Undersea Hunter

DIVING & SNORKELING | The boat operates 10-day dive trips to Cocos Island year-round and is part of a fleet that also includes *Argo* and *Sea Hunter*. Park fee of $490 not included in rate. ⊠ *Tárcoles* ☎ *2228–6613 in San José, 800/203–2120 in North America* ⊕ *www.underseahunter.com* ⊠ *From $5,950.*

HIKING
Catarata Manantial de Agua Viva

TRAIL | This is Costa Rica's tallest waterfall, cascading 600 feet into freshwater pools where you can cool off after a strenuous 3-km (2-mile) hike to the river basin. You're not likely to see other tourists here—it's not one of the more well-known waterfalls. This trek is not suitable for children, the elderly, or those with health conditions. Bring drinking water and wear proper shoes as rocks can be sharp and slippery. ⊠ *On dirt road 4 km (2½ miles) past Hotel Villa Lapas, Tárcoles* ✛ *Look for a sign reading "cascada"* ☎ *8831–2980* ⊠ *$20.*

Sky Way

HIKING & WALKING | Hotel Villa Lapas manages this suspension-bridge nature walk, consisting of five bridges spread out over a 2½-km (1½-mile) old-growth-forest nature trail. You can do the trail with a guide ($40), and will most likely see scarlet macaws, yellow-billed cotinga, and the black-hooded antshrike. A shuttle picks you up at the hotel. ⊠ *Hotel Villa Lapas, off Costanera, after bridge over Río Tárcoles, Tárcoles* ☎ *2637–0232* ⊕ *www.villalapas.com* ⊠ *Sky Way $20; guided tours $40.*

Punta Leona

13 km (8 miles) south of Tárcoles.

Past Tárcoles, the first sizable beach town of the Central Pacific coast is Playa Herradura. In between, the road passes tiny Playa La Pita, then heads inland where it crosses the entrance to Punta Leona, a vast hotel and residential complex. The road then winds its way up a steep hill, atop which is the entrance to the luxury hotel Villa Caletas. On the other side of that ridge is the bay and beach of Herradura.

Beaches

Playa La Pita

BEACH | About a kilometer (½ mile) south after the entrance to Tárcoles, the Costanera passes this small beach that provides your first glimpse of the Pacific if you're coming down from San José or the Central Valley. The beach is rocky, and its proximity to the crocodile-infested Río Tárcoles makes the water murky and dangerous for swimming, but it's a nice spot to stop and admire the ocean and birds. **Amenities:** food and drink. **Best for:** sunset; walking. ⊠ *Tárcoles.*

Diving the Deep at Cocos Island

Rated one of the top diving destinations in the world, Isla del Coco is uninhabited and remote (32 hours by boat), and its waters are teeming with marine life. It's no place for beginners, but serious divers enjoy 100-foot visibility and the underwater equivalent of a big-game park. Scalloped hammerheads, white-tipped reef sharks, Galápagos sharks, bottlenose dolphins, billfish, and manta rays mix with huge schools of brilliantly colored fish.

Encompassing about 22½ square km (9 square miles), Isla del Coco is one of the largest uninhabited islands on Earth. Its isolation has led to the evolution of dozens of endemic plant and animal species. The rocky topography is draped in rain forest and cloud forest and includes more than 200 waterfalls. Because of Isla del Coco's distance from shore (484 km [300 miles]) and its craggy topography, few visitors to Costa Rica—and even fewer Costa Ricans—have set foot on the island.

Costa Rica annexed Coco in 1869, and it became a national park in 1978. Today only extremely high-priced specialty cruise ships, park rangers, volunteers, and scientists visit this place. The dry season (December to April) brings calmer seas and is the best time to see silky sharks. During the rainy season large schools of hammerheads can be seen, but the ocean is rougher.

Two boats, *Okeanos Aggressor* and *Undersea Hunter*, offer regular 10-day dive cruises from Puntarenas that include three days of travel time on the open ocean and cost roughly $6,000 to $7,000, depending on the boat and dates.

 Restaurants

Mirador Restaurant

$$$$ | **ECLECTIC** | White tablecloths, glass walls, and yellow-and-blue-checkered curtains contribute to the sophisticated but not overly stuffy atmosphere of this hotel dining room on the top terrace at Hotel Villa Caletas. Appetizers range from the traditional escargots to a shrimp-and-lobster bisque, and entrées include beef tenderloin with chimichurri, jumbo shrimp sautéed with white wine and passion fruit, and roasted duck with truffle oil. **Known for:** creamy risotto; stunning sunset views; extensive wine list. $ *Average main: $50* ⊠ *Villa Caletas hotel, off coastal hwy., 3 km (2 miles) south of Punta Leona, Tárcoles* ☎ *2630–3000* ⊕ *www.hotel-villacaletas.com* ⊗ *No lunch* ⌔ *During low season, open weekends only.*

Hotels

★ Villa Caletas

$$$ | **RESORT** | Perched 1,200 feet above the sea on a promontory south of Punta Leona, the elegant rooms sequestered in the jungle have jaw-dropping views of the surrounding foliage and sea below. **Pros:** gorgeous views; all rooms have king bed, Jacuzzi, and ocean view; luxury at a reasonable price. **Cons:** lots of stairs; 15-minute drive to rocky beach; challenging for wheelchairs and elderly. $ *Rooms from: $230* ⊠ *Off coastal hwy., 3 km (2 miles) south of Punta Leona, on right, Tárcoles* ☎ *2630–3000, 2257–3653 in San José* ⊕ *hotelvillacaletas.com* ⌔ *53 units* ⦿ *Free Breakfast.*

Playa Herradura

20 km (12 miles) south of Tárcoles.

Just north of bustling Jacó, this small beach town, named for its horse-shoe-shape bay, is made up of hotels, a golf course, and a marina. Once a sleepy fishing village, it has transformed into one of the country's fastest-developing areas. The entrance to town is marked by a shopping complex complete with fast-food chains and a surf shop. A paved road connecting the coastal highway to the beach dead-ends at the sand where three seafood shacks line the shores; the best is the more upscale El Pelicano. Golfers and sportfishing fans alike are drawn to the pristine beauty of Playa Herradura, and the placid waters tend to keep surfers farther down the coast, where waves are abundant. It's an attractive alternative to Jacó if you'd like to be driving distance to the hustle and bustle but in a more tranquil spot.

GETTING HERE AND AROUND

By car, head 20 minutes straight down the Pacific Highway. The town's entrance is on the right-hand side, where a long paved road leads to the beach. Follow the signs to the Marriott.

Beaches

Playa Herradura

BEACH | If sportfishing, boating, and golfing are your priorities, this is a good option. If you're looking for seclusion, a beautiful beach, or a bargain, keep driving. Rocky Playa Herradura is a poor representative of Costa Rica's breathtaking beaches, although its tranquil waters make it considerably safer for swimming and stand-up paddleboarding than most central and southern Pacific beaches. It gets its name from the Spanish word for "horseshoe," referring to the shape of the deep bay in which it lies. Playa Herradura's safety factor, coupled with the fact that it's the closest beach to San José, has turned it into a popular weekend getaway for Josefinos, who compete for shade beneath the sparse palms and Indian almond trees that line the beach. On the north end is Los Sueños, which includes a large marina, shopping center, hundreds of condos, a golf course, and a massive Marriott hotel. This is the sportfishing capital of Costa Rica, so expect plenty of boats anchored offshore. The rough black sand makes the water look somewhat dark and dirty at times. The best spot to grab a bite is Restaurante El Pelicano across from the beach. **Amenities:** food and drink; toilets; water sports. **Best for:** swimming. ✉ *Near Los Suenos Marriott, 4 km (2½ miles) north of Jacó, Herradura.*

Restaurants

Restaurante El Pelícano

$$$ | **SEAFOOD** | It may not look like much at first glance, but this open-air restaurant across the street from the beach serves some dishes you'd be hard-pressed to find in other casual beach-town places. Request one of the outdoor tables under the bamboo dome and dine on dishes like fish croquettes in a lemon sauce, grilled tuna in mango sauce, and clams au gratin. **Known for:** deep-fried whole red snapper; tagliata: lobster, octopus, jumbo shrimp, and mahimahi complete with tableside fire show; "formal" beachfront dining. [$] *Average main: $20* ✉ *Herradura* ✥ *Turn left at end of main road into Playa Herradura* ☎ *2637–8910* 🌐 *www.elpelicanorestaurante.com.*

Hotels

Los Sueños Marriott Ocean and Golf Resort

$$$$ | **RESORT** | **FAMILY** | This mammoth multimillion-dollar resort in a palatial colonial-style building has a gorgeous view of Herradura Bay and combines modern amenities with traditional Central American decorative motifs, such as barrel-tile roofing and hand-painted tiles. **Pros:**

good base for excursions; kids' club with activities throughout the day; swimming pool the size of a soccer field. **Cons:** so-so rooms; beach can be dirty; expensive. [$] *Rooms from: $269* ✉ *Herradura* ✣ *1 km (½ mile) west of road to Jacó from San José, follow signs at entrance of road to Playa Herradura* ☎ *2630–9000, 888/236–2427 in North America, 2298–0000 in San José* 🌐 *www.marriott.com* 🛏 *201 rooms* 🍴 *No Meals.*

Activities

Few activities are available directly in Playa Herradura, but most of the area's diverse outfitters can pick you up at your hotel for activities near Jacó and Playa Hermosa. Your hotel's reception desk is often a good source of information.

FISHING

Maverick Sportfishing

FISHING | One of the area's oldest and most reputable sportfishing outfitters offers trips to fishing grounds just an hour offshore in calm waters. As the only authorized charter operator in Los Sueños, tours leave the marina at 7 am and return at 4 pm. Also available are sunset cruises and boat trips to Tortuga Island. ✉ *Los Sueños Marina, at charter dock at Playa Herradura, Herradura* ☎ *4001–6366, 205/579–1612 in North America* 🌐 *www.mavericksportfish.com* 🎟 *From $1,900 for up to 4 people.*

GOLF

La Iguana Golf Club

GOLF | Designed by Ted Robinson, this course at Los Sueños Marriott is cradled between rain forest and ocean, allowing you to play alongside local wildlife like macaws, iguanas, and monkeys (known to steal the ball when you're not looking). The championship course is long, narrow, and well manicured, and there's a putting green, driving range, and PGA-qualified golf instructors. Overlooking the 18th hole is a restaurant where you can take a break and admire the scenery. Marriott members get a discount on the greens fees; otherwise expect a pricey game of golf and expensive restaurant and pro shop. ✉ *Los Sueños Marriott, Herradura* ✣ *1 km (½ mile) west of Herradura entrance* ☎ *2630–9151* 🌐 *www.golflaiguana.com* 🎟 *18 holes from $195* ⛳ *18 holes, 6698 yards, par 72.*

Jacó

7 km (4 miles) south of Playa Herradura, 114 km (70 miles) southwest of San José.

Its proximity to San José has made Jacó the most developed beach town in Costa Rica. Nature lovers and solitude seekers may want to skip this rather seedy but bustling town. While in the past, Jacó has been known mostly for its nightlife, surf scene, and prostitution, recent efforts to make it a more family-friendly destination include parks, playgrounds, an open-air mall, and kid-friendly restaurants. More than 80 hotels and cabinas back its long, gray-sand beach, and the mix of restaurants, shops, and bars lining Avenida Pastor Díaz (the town's main drag) give it a cluttered appearance devoid of any greenery. Any real Costa Rican–ness evaporated years ago, but if you need creature comforts, you can pretty much find anything you need— from law offices and dental clinics to tattoo parlors and appliance stores. In recent years, several expats have opened a handful of cheerful cafés, restaurants, and hotels on side streets, offering a splash of color to the grungy town. Jacó does provide everything in terms of tours and outdoor activities, and makes a convenient hub for exploring neighboring beaches and attractions. Theft can be a problem here.

GETTING HERE AND AROUND

The drive from San José takes less than two hours; take Highway 27 west of San José beyond Orotina, and then take the exit to Jacó and Quepos. The exit, on

the right after Herradura, is well marked. There's a gas station at the second entrance to town close to Club del Mar. Buses leave from San José's Terminal 7-10 station seven times daily, with an extra run on weekends.

RENTAL CARS Alamo. ✉ *Avda. Pastor Díaz, 50 m south of Subway, Jacó* ☎ *2643–1752* 🌐 *www.alamocostarica.com.* **Economy.** ✉ *Avda. Pastor Díaz, 100 m south of Best Western, Jacó* ☎ *2299–2000* 🌐 *www.economyrentacar.com.* **Hertz.** ✉ *Plaza Coral 20, Jacó* ✣ *Next to MegaSuper* ☎ *2221–1818* 🌐 *www.hertzcostarica.com.*

TAXIS Taxi services. ✉ *Jacó* ☎ *2643–2020, 2643–2121, 2643–3030.*

ESSENTIALS

BANKS/ATMS BAC San José. ✉ *Centro Comercial Il Galeone, Jacó* ☎ *2295–9797.* **Banco Nacional.** ✉ *Avda. Pastor Díaz, Jacó* ☎ *2212–7555* 🌐 *www.bncr.fi.cr.*

HOSPITAL Clínica De Jacó. ✉ *In front of Plaza de Deportes, Jacó* ☎ *2643–1767.*

PHARMACIES Farmacia Jacó. ✉ *Plaza El Jardín, Avda. Pastor Díaz, across from Mas X Menos supermarket, Jacó* ☎ *2643–3205.* **Farmacia La Económica.** ✉ *Avda. Pastor Díaz, across from Banco Nacional, Jacó* ☎ *2643–6544.*

POST OFFICE Correos. ✉ *Avda. Pastor Díaz, Jacó* ✣ *Across from the municipality and Transit Police* ☎ *2643–2175.*

Beaches

Playa Jacó

BEACH | This long, palm-lined beach west of town is a pleasant enough spot in the morning but can burn the soles of your feet on a sunny afternoon. Though the gray sand and beachside construction make this spot less attractive than most other Costa Rican beaches, it's a good place to soak up the sun or enjoy a sunset. The beach is popular with surfers for the consistency of its waves, but when the surf is up, swimmers should beware of dangerous rip currents. Smaller waves make this beach ideal for surf lessons or longboarders. Bigger waves are found 5 km (3 miles) south at Playa Hermosa (a blue flag beach). During the rainy months, the ocean here is not very clean. The stretch near Jacó Laguna Resort is less crowded and their tiki bar is a great spot to grab a cocktail at sunset. **Amenities:** food and drink; toilets (at local restaurants and hotels). **Best for:** sunsets; surfing. ✉ *Jacó.*

Restaurants

★ Amancio's Pizza Pasta and Drinks

$$ | **ITALIAN** | Taste the passion that the chef and owner has for the simple things in life: fresh ingredients, made-from-scratch bread and pasta, and sauces that simmer all day. Grab some calzones to take to the beach, or dine in on the Italian plate, an overflowing platter of house-cured salami and other meats, along with olives and cheeses straight from Italy. **Known for:** chicken parmigiana; lobster fettuccine; pizza. [$] *Average main: $15* ✉ *Centro Comercial El Jardín, Jacó* ☎ *2643–2373* 🕒 *Closed Wed.*

El Hicaco

$$$ | **SEAFOOD** | It's the setting that will lure you, but the food that will keep you on repeat at this seafood restaurant just steps from the sand. Bamboo, wood, and rattan decor will make you want to throw on a Tommy Bahama shirt and order a mai tai. **Known for:** tuna with crunchy plantain; sunset views; lobster dishes. [$] *Average main: $20* ✉ *Calle Hicaco, Jacó* ✣ *In front of the beach* ☎ *2643–3226* 🌐 *www.elhicaco.com.*

Graffiti Restro Cafe and Wine Bar

$$ | **ECLECTIC** | The gritty-gourmet concept of this upscale Jacó hot spot plays with the senses with a menu that features fresh, locally grown ingredients. Check the blackboard for specials—whatever has inspired the chef that day—and wash

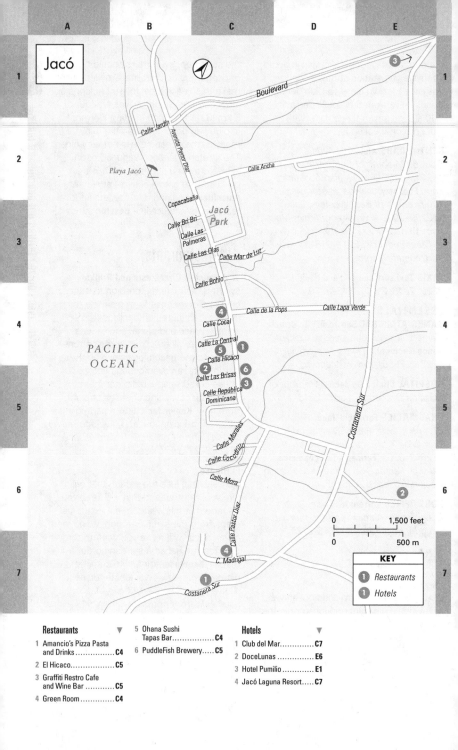

Jacó

PACIFIC OCEAN

Playa Jacó

Jacó Park

Boulevard

Calle Jardin
Avenida Pastor Diaz
Calle Ancha
Copacabaña
Calle Bri Bri
Calle Las Palmeras
Calle Las Olas
Calle Mar de Luz
Calle Bohío
Calle de la Pops
Calle Lapa Verde
Calle Cocal
Calle La Central
Calle Hicaco
Calle Las Brisas
Calle República Dominicana
Calle Morales
Calle Cocodrilo
Calle Mora
Calle Pastor Diaz
Costanera Sur
C. Madrigal
Costanera Sur

4
5
1
2
6
3
3
2
4
1

0   1,500 feet
0   500 m

KEY

1 *Restaurants*

1 *Hotels*

it down with a signature lemongrass martini. **Known for:** tuna tower; happy hour 4–5 with $4 drinks and tapas; cacao-and-coffee-rubbed beef tenderloin. $ *Average main: $15* ⊠ *Jacó Walk Open Air Shopping Plaza, Avda. Pastor Diaz, Jacó* ☎ *2643–1708* ⊕ *www.graffitirestro. com* ⊘ *No lunch.*

Green Room
$$ | **CAFÉ** | Bordered by a white picket fence, this charming art café serves meals prepared with organic ingredients delivered daily by local farmers. The ever-changing chalkboard menu usually features home-ground burgers with fresh-baked buns or seared ahi on buckwheat noodles with roasted vegetables. **Known for:** live entertainment every night; chipotle basil margarita; barbecue ribs. $ *Average main: $10* ⊠ *Corner of Avda. Pastor Díaz and C. Cocal, Jacó* ☎ *2643–4425* ⊕ *greenroomjaco.com.*

Ohana Sushi Tapas Bar
$$ | **ASIAN FUSION** | Don't worry about getting dressed up for this unfussy sushi fusion restaurant, built from a colorful shipping container, found driftwood, and recycled pallets. The food is made with as much innovation, creativity, and care, blending flavors perfectly in popular sushi, salads, and Asian-fusion meat dishes. **Known for:** yaki sticks (grilled skewers with tenderloin, fish, seafood, or chicken); vegan and gluten-free options; consistently fresh, delicious sushi. $ *Average main: $15* ⊠ *Calle El Hicaco, Jacó* ⊹ *50 meters (164 feet) before beach* ☎ *2643–2226* ⊕ *ohana-sushi-tapas-y-bar. business.site* ⊘ *Closed Thurs.*

PuddleFish Brewery
$$ | **MODERN AMERICAN** | **FAMILY** | This brewery tasting room serves tasty American-style pub grub. Sit in the modern outdoor area under the shade, or belly up to the bar inside and try a beer flight to go along with your burger or sandwich. **Known for:** tuna steak sandwich; Sunday brunch with bottomless mimosas; flavorful craft beers. $ *Average main:*

$12 ⊠ *South end of Playa Jacó at the entrance of Calle Madrigal, Jacó* ⊹ *100 meters (328 feet) southwest of the Delta gas station* ☎ *4703–6301* ⊕ *www.puddlefishbrewery.com.*

Hotels

Club del Mar
$$$ | **RESORT** | **FAMILY** | At the second entrance to Jacó on the beach's southern end, one of the town's better lodgings includes green-and-cream-hue rooms with private teak balconies and spacious one- and two-bedroom condos. **Pros:** beautiful beachfront location; washer and dryer; friendly, helpful staff. **Cons:** hard mattresses; no bathtubs in standard rooms; some highway noise reaches back to condos. $ *Rooms from: $160* ⊠ *Costanera, Jacó* ⊹ *300 meters (984 feet) south of Delta gas station* ☎ *2643–3194, 866/978–5669 in North America* ⊕ *www.clubdelmarcr.com* ⤴ *31 units* ⦿ *Free Breakfast.*

DoceLunas
$$$ | **HOTEL** | The spacious, teak-furnished rooms at "Twelve Moons" are a couple of miles from the sea and sand, and noise, set amid 5 acres of lawns shaded by tropical trees and luxuriant gardens with a mountainous green backdrop. **Pros:** more secluded than other Jacó lodgings; terrific restaurant; beautiful grounds. **Cons:** the restaurant closes at 3 pm most days; resident dogs and cats are friendly but not ideal if you aren't into pets; 20-minute walk to beach. $ *Rooms from: $170* ⊠ *Jacó* ⊹ *On coastal hwy. from San José, pass 1st entrance to Jacó; take dirt road on left with signs for DoceLunas at main entrance to Quebrada Seca* ☎ *2643–2211* ⊕ *www.docelunas. com* ⤴ *20 rooms* ⦿ *Free Breakfast.*

★ Hotel Pumilio
$$$$ | **HOTEL** | **FAMILY** | A peaceful retreat just five minutes outside bustling Jacó, this all-suites hotel is surrounded by lush rain forest and has tastefully decorated

A beautiful heron perched near the beach at Jacó

rooms with fully equipped kitchens and patios overlooking the pool, mountains, and gardens. **Pros:** quiet location; beautiful and clean rooms; excellent staff. **Cons:** restaurant serves breakfast only; very firm beds; far from beach. $ *Rooms from: $273 ✉ Jacó ✈ From Herradura's stoplight 2 km (1 mile) on Rte. 34 south, 1 km (½ mile) to left ☎ 2643–5678, 800/410–8018 in U.S. ⊕ www.hotelpumil-io.com* ⌁ *16 rooms* ⅼⓄⅼ *Free Breakfast.*

Jacó Laguna Resort

$$$$ | HOTEL | On the quiet southern end of Jacó beach, this property is clean and comfortable and just far enough from town to offer a peaceful night of sleep. **Pros:** in low season, guests are generously upgraded; great tiki bar; ideal location. **Cons:** weak Wi-Fi signal in some rooms; mattresses lack support; hallway noise. $ *Rooms from: $271 ✉ Corner of C. Madrigal and Avda. Pastor Díaz, Jacó ☎ 2643–3362, 215/942–5135 in U.S. ⊕ www.jacolagunaresort.com* ⌁ *30 rooms* ⅼⓄⅼ *No Meals.*

Nightlife

Whereas other beach towns may have a bar or two, Jacó has an avenue full of them, with enough variety for many different tastes. After-dinner spots range from restaurants perfect for a quiet drink to loud bars with pool tables and dance clubs. You can even try your luck at one of the town's casinos.

BARS

Orange Pub

BARS | This is a good choice for a cocktail, after-dinner drinks, or a late-night meal. It has a big bar in back, pool tables, and DJs and dancing on weekends. ✉ *Avda. Pastor Díaz, north of Il Gale-one mall, across from C. Bohio, Jacó* ☎ *8888–8022.*

CASINOS

Croc's Casino

CASINO | Only in Jacó would you find a mini Las Vegas, with a casino of slot machines, table games, and free cocktails for gamblers. There's always a game on the big screen and country music playing poolside. For those who've had one too many rounds, you can stay the night at the massive Croc's resort, which is comfortable but devoid of Costa Rican character. ⊠ *Jacó* ✛ *Take 2nd entrance into Jacó at Maxi Pali store. Follow "T," turn right, casino is 1 km (½ mile) down on left, oceanfront* ☎ *800/809–5506 in U.S. or Canada, 4001–5398* ⊕ *www. crocscasinoresort.com.*

LIVE MUSIC
★ PuddleFish Brewery
LIVE MUSIC | This colorful bistro has live music several days of the week and handcrafted brews made in-house. ⊠ *South end of Playa Jacó at the entrance of Calle Madrigal, Jacó* ✛ *100 meters (328 feet) southwest of the Delta gas station* ☎ *4703–6301* ⊕ *www.puddlefishbrewery. com.*

Shopping

Souvenir shops with mostly the same mass-produced merchandise are crowded one after the other along the main street in the center of town. Most of the goods, like wooden crafts and seed jewelry, are run-of-the-mill souvenir fare, but a few shops have more unusual items. If you plan on buying any surf-related products, this is your place, as even surf wax is hard to come by once you leave Jacó. Jacó Walk, a shopping area with retail stores, restaurants, entertainment venues, cultural exhibits, and business offices all in one open space, is worth a visit.

CRAFTS
Cocobolo
CRAFTS | Named for the tropical hardwood of the cocobolo tree, this large shop is jam-packed with wooden handicrafts hanging from the ceiling, walls, and shelves. It's much of what you find in other stores, but with more tasteful items and a richer variety. In addition to wood carvings, they sell clothing, hammocks, jewelry, and locally made crafts. ⊠ *Avda.*

Pastor Díaz, Jacó ✛ *300 meters (984 feet) north of Banco Nacional, next to Jass Surf Shop* ☎ *2643–3486.*

FOOD AND CANDY
Fruity Monkey Poop / Costa Rica Coffee Experience
FOOD | For locally grown coffee and reasonably priced artisan crafts, this place offers the best shopping in Jacó. They serve marvelous iced coffees, natural iced teas, and fresh-roasted coffee. Be sure to try a sample of their chocolate, pineapple licorice, and "Fruity Monkey Poop" (actually just candied nuts). ⊠ *Avda. Pastor Díaz, across from Banco Nacional and Mas X Menos market, Jacó* ☎ *2643–6197* ⊕ *www.facebook.com/ FruityMonkeyPoopCR.*

SPORTING GOODS
Cartón
SPORTING GOODS | Cartón sells new and used boards and shapes for some of Costa Rica's top surfers. It's not only the shape, but also the artwork that makes Cartón's boards so extraordinary. Their two-hour surf lessons are held just past the surf shop at Madrigal Beach. They also offer surf tours. ⊠ *C. Madrigal, near gas station, Jacó* ☎ *2643–3762 7210–9799.*

Jass Surf Shop
SPORTING GOODS | As Jacó's first surf shop, this well-stocked store has a good variety of surf gear at decent prices. They sell new and used surfboards and stand-up paddleboards, and will buy back your board at the end of your trip for half the purchase price. Two-hour surf lessons cost $50. ⊠ *Avda. Pastor Díaz, next to La Perla, 200 meters (656 feet) north of Banco Nacional, Jacó* ☎ *2643–3850.*

Activities

ATV TOURS
Because ATV tours have only been popular in Costa Rica for about a decade, the vehicles are in relatively good condition. But they're not exactly the most

eco-friendly way to see the area's rain forest and wildlife, and rollovers always pose a risk. Some operators will ask you to put up a credit card voucher of roughly $1,000.

CANOPY TOURS
★ Rainforest Adventures
LOCAL SPORTS | A modified ski lift offers easy access to the tropical transitional forest, with eight-seat gondolas that float through the treetops within a 222-acre private nature reserve. The company has guided tours that explain aspects of the local ecology, sustainability programs, as well as a variety of eco-adventures. There is also a butterfly garden, and a "Trano-py" tour that combines the tram with a 10-cable zipline tour. A top attraction is a 164-foot waterfall climbing tour that includes ziplines, forest trekking, and a free fall. The International Ecotourism Society named Rainforest Adventures one of the most sustainable theme parks in the world. It is also considered to be one of the safest due to their double cables, chest harnesses, platform railings, certified guides, braking system, and high-tech equipment inspected annually. ⊠ *3 km (2 miles) west of Jacó, Jacó* ☎ *2224–5961* ⊕ *www.rainforestadventure.com* ⊡ *From $79.*

HORSEBACK RIDING
Discovery Horseback Tours
HORSEBACK RIDING | During these 2½-hour trail rides on healthy horses, you'll spend some time in the rain forest and also stop at a small waterfall where you can take a dip. The jungle spa will get you dirty at some mud baths, and another tour takes you on a sunset ride on the beach. For experienced riders only, the Bird's Eye View is a 2½-hour challenging ride through rivers and rain forest. Tours start at 8:30 and 2:00 weekdays, and only at 8:30 on Saturday. ⊠ *Jacó* ☎ *8838–7550* ⊕ *www.horseridecostarica.com* ⊡ *From $90 (cash only).*

KAYAKING AND CANOEING
Kayak Jacó
CANOEING & ROWING | **FAMILY** | Looking for waters calmer than those at Jacó Beach? Kayak Jacó takes you to secluded beaches for sea-kayaking tours and Hawaiian-style outrigger canoe trips that are appropriate for everyone in the family, from children to grandparents. The half-day tours include snorkeling (conditions permitting) at secluded beaches. A 2½-hour night tour (available December–mid-April) starts at sunset and ends with s'mores and a bonfire on the beach. You can also charter a private sailboat. ⊠ *Playa Agujas, Jacó* ☎ *2643–1233* ⊕ *www.kayakjaco.com* ⊡ *From $70. Transportation to/from your hotel $25.*

SURFING
Jacó has several beach breaks, all of which are best around high tide. Surfboard-toting tourists abound in Jacó, but you don't need to be an expert to enjoy the surf, as waves are often small enough for beginners, especially around low tide. Abundant surf shops rent boards and give lessons, usually closer to the south end of the beach where most surf schools set up camp. Prices range from $50 to $60 for two hours and usually include a board and transportation. If you plan to spend more than a week surfing, it might be cheaper to buy a used board and sell it back at the standard half price before you leave. Otherwise, you'll be paying airline transportation fees around $150 one way, and most likely your board will arrive damaged despite your bubble-wrapping efforts. For rental, Jacó has plenty of surf shops with solid quivers, with cheaper boards starting at $10 an hour. If you don't have much experience, don't go out when the waves are really big—Jacó sometimes gets very powerful swells, which result in dangerous rip currents. During the rainy season, waves are more consistent than in the dry months, when Jacó sometimes lacks surf.

Tortuga Surf School

SURFING | Private surf lessons with Tortuga include board rental, water, fruit, and ISA-certified instructors (International Surfing Association). They also offer 7-, 14-, or 22-day Surf and Stay camps that combine lodging, lessons, and local excursions. ✉ *Hotel Perico Azul, C. Santana and Avda. Pastor Díaz, Jacó* ☎ *8847–6289* ⊕ *www.tortugasurfcamp. com* ✉ *From $65.*

SWIMMING

The big waves and dangerous rip currents that make surfing so popular here can make swimming dangerous. Lifeguards are on duty only at specific spots and only sporadically. If the ocean is rough, stay on the beach—dozens of swimmers have drowned here over the years.

When the ocean is calm, especially around low tide, you can swim just about anywhere along Playa Jacó. The sea is always calmer near the beach's northern and southern ends, but the ocean bottom is littered with rocks there, as it is in front of the small rivers that flow into the sea near the middle of this beach.

TOUR OPERATORS

You don't have to physically step into any tour office, because everyone from a reception desk attendant to a boutique salesperson can book you a local adventure. Almost every tour can pick you up at your hotel's doorstep.

■ **TIP→ Keep in mind that part of your price tag includes the salesperson's commission, so if you hear higher or lower prices from two different people, it's likely a reflection of a shift in the commission. You can try negotiating a better deal directly from the outfitter.**

Adventure Tours

ADVENTURE TOURS | Although this company is best known for having the safest ATV tours with the longest routes, we recommend their eco-friendly adventures like canopy tours, white-water rafting,

Riptides

Riptides (or rip currents), common in Jacó and Manuel Antonio's Playa Espadilla, are dangerous and have led to many deaths over the years. If you get caught in one, don't panic and don't try to swim against it as paddling to shore will simply expend your energy. Riptides are generally less than 100 feet wide, so simply swim parallel to shore until you feel the power dissipate. Once you are out of the current, swim back to the beach. The best policy is not to go in deeper than your waist when the waves loom large, and never swim alone.

kayaking, and canyoning. For nature lovers, they have monkey tours and croc tours. ✉ *Avda. Pastor Díaz, in center of Playa Jacó, behind Subway, Jacó* ☎ *2643–5720, 800/761–7250 in North America* ⊕ *www.adventuretourscostarica.com* ✉ *From $59.*

Playa Hermosa

5 km (3 miles) south of Jacó, 113 km (70 miles) southwest of San José.

On the other side of the rocky ridge that forms the southern edge of Playa Jacó is Playa Hermosa, a swath of dark-gray sand and driftwood stretching southeast as far as the eye can see, with consistent waves for surfers. For nonsurfers, outdoor options include horseback and canopy tours in the nearby forested hills, but all of these can be done from other beaches. As for the town itself, there's really not much, which is part of the attraction for travelers who want to escape Jacó's crowds and concrete towers. Most of the restaurants, bars, and hotels have cropped up one after the other on a thin stretch separating the highway and the beach. From June to December, olive ridley turtles nest on the beach at night, especially when there's not much moonlight.

■ TIP→ Note: there is a second Playa Hermosa on the Guanacaste Pacific coast.

GETTING HERE AND AROUND

If you have a car, take the coastal highway 5 km (3 miles) past Jacó. You'll see the cluster of businesses on the right. If you don't have your own transportation, take a taxi from Jacó or a local bus toward Quepos.

Not that Playa Hermosa

"*¡Ojo!*" as they say. Watch out: Costa Rica has two Playa Hermosas. Don't confuse this one with the larger, more developed beach of the same name on the Guanacaste Pacific coast. Each has its fans, but the Central Pacific's Playa Hermosa is better known to Costa Ricans and to surfers.

Beaches

Playa Hermosa

BEACH | Despite its name, "Beautiful Beach" is hardly spectacular. The southern half of the wide beach lacks palm trees or other shade-providing greenery; its sand is scorching hot in the afternoon; and frequent rip currents make it unsafe to swim when there are waves. But surfers find beauty in its consistent, hollow surf breaks. Beginner surfers should stick to Jacó since waves here are powerful and punchy, and will close out on big days. The beach's northern end is popular because it often has waves when other spots are flat, and the ocean is cleaner than at Jacó, except after heavy rains when there is floating debris. There is also plenty of forest covering the hills, and scarlet macaws sometimes gather in the Indian almond trees near the end of the beach. Amenities are all at the Backyard Bar. **Amenities:** food and drink; showers; toilets. **Best for:** sunset; surfing. ✉ *Playa Hermosa.*

Hotels

The Backyard Hotel

$$ | **HOTEL** | Surfers are the main clientele in these beachfront rooms with high ceilings, clay-tile floors, and sliding-glass doors that open onto semiprivate balconies and terraces, most of which have good views of Playa Hermosa. **Pros:** steps from the surf; gated parking; friendly staff. **Cons:** no breakfast; thin sheets and towels; back rooms get road noise. [$] *Rooms from: $140* ✉ *Costanera, southern end of town, Playa Hermosa* ☎ *2643–7011* 🌐 *www.backyardhotel.com* 🛏 *8 rooms* 🍴 *No Meals.*

Surf Inn

$$ | **B&B/INN** | Right in front of Hermosa's beach break, a mural of tall palms and peeling waves marks the entrance to this well-priced inn, which offers small apartments and studios. **Pros:** almost half price in low season; surfers' paradise; kitchens in rooms. **Cons:** studios are dark; two-night minimum stay on weekends and holidays; full payment due at booking, which is nonrefundable. [$] *Rooms from: $120* ✉ *Costanera, Playa Hermosa* ✣ *Next to Backyard Hotel, 200 meters (656 feet) south of soccer field* ☎ *8899–1520, 2643–7184* 🌐 *www.surfinnhermosa.com* 🛏 *6 units* 🍴 *No Meals.*

Activities

You can arrange activities throughout the Central Pacific from Playa Hermosa. Most tour operators and outfitters include transportation in their prices.

For more options, see Activities in Jacó, above, or consult your hotel's reception.

SURFING

Most people who bed down at Playa Hermosa are here for the same reason—the waves that break just a shell's toss away. There are a half dozen breaks scattered along the beach's northern end, and the surf is always best around high tide. Hermosa's conditions change rapidly, depending on the tides, wind, and swell activity. Because it is a beach break, though, the waves here often close out, especially when the surf is more than 8 feet. If you don't have much experience, don't go out when the waves are really big—Hermosa sometimes gets very powerful swells, which result in dangerous rip currents. If you're a beginner, don't go out at all. Surf instructors in Hermosa take their students to Jacó, an easier place to learn the sport. If you need to rent a board, some hotels have their own quiver and will allow you to rent by the hour ($10).

Nika Surfboards

SURFING | For all your surfing needs, Nika has ding repair, surf lessons, and boards for rent or sale. ✉ *Costanera, 4 km (2½ miles) south of Hermosa on road to Esterillos, Playa Hermosa* ☎ *2643–2871* ⊕ *www.nikasurfboards.com* 📧 *2-hr lessons $50.*

Esterillos Este

20 km (12 miles) southeast of Playa Hermosa, 3 km (2 miles) northwest of Playa Bejuco.

Just 20 minutes southeast of Jacó, Playa Esterillos is divided into three sections; Este (East), Central, and Oeste (West). While Esterillos Oeste and Central are inhabited by locals, the undeveloped area of Esterillos Este is where you'll find several boutique hotels capitalizing on the seclusion and beachfront location. Head-high waves break year-round, making it one of the most consistent surf spots in Costa Rica. At low tide, the dark stretch of sand is unbelievably wide, inviting beachcombers for a leisurely stroll. Almond trees and swaying palms frame the shoreline, and you can walk for miles without seeing another soul. If you want to get away from it all, the isolation and "best-kept secret" feel make Esterillos Este the perfect escape.

GETTING HERE AND AROUND

From Playa Hermosa, head 20 km (12 miles) south on the coastal highway (Costanera). Pass Esterillos Oeste and Esterillos Central before turning right onto the dirt road labeled Esterillos Este. Continue ½ km (¼ mile) to the beach road and follow the signs in either direction to your hotel.

ESSENTIALS

The nearest medical facilities are at the hospital in Parrita, 15 minutes south on the coastal highway. There is a shopping center outside of Esterillos Este past Playa Bejuco: a grocery store, gym, and several shops and services including an ATM are available. Supplies can also be purchased at the Mini Super in Playa Bejuco or at the Super Sol in Esterillos Oeste. Other services can be found north in Jacó or south in Parrita.

Beaches

Playa Esterillos

BEACH | Serious surfers from Jacó and Playa Hermosa head to Playa Esterillos to ditch the crowds when waves are pumping. This isolated beach break dishes up hollow barrels, and gets more swell than neighboring surf spots. It works best at high tide with a south or southwest swell direction, but beginners will want to stay clear of the pounding waves. Lessons ($60) and board rental ($20) can be organized through Encantada Ocean Cottages, but if you're a novice surfer, it's best to stick to the inside whitewash with supervision. At low tide, this dark beach looks like a chocolate field, perfect for beachcombing or an afternoon stroll. You can

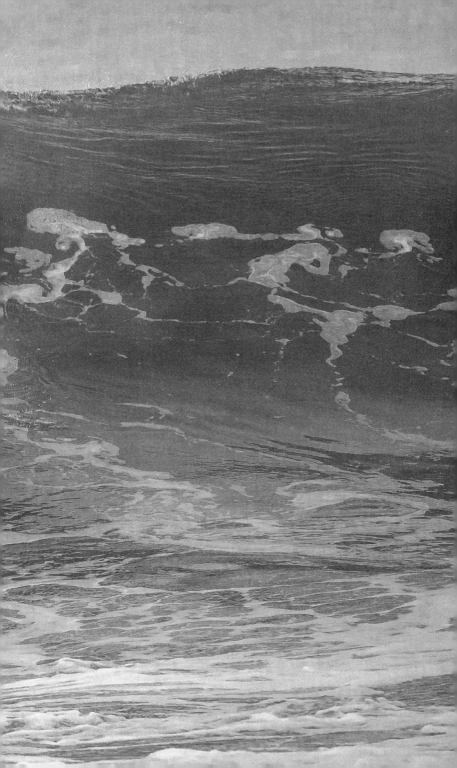

walk for miles without seeing another set of prints in the sand. Other than a couple sodas in Esterillos Oeste, there are no beach amenities, and those within local hotels are exclusively for guests. Just offshore in Esterillos Oeste is a mermaid statue that you can walk to at low tide. If you drive here, don't leave any valuables in the car. **Amenities:** parking (roadside; no fee). **Best for:** solitude; surfing. ✉ *Playa Esterillos, Costanera Sur, Esterillos Este* ✣ *20 mins south of Playa Jacó.*

Hotels

Alma Del Pacifico Beach Hotel & Spa
$$$$ | **HOTEL** | Combining Costa Rica's vibrant architecture with modern design, this tranquil property reminiscent of tropical-deco decor, offers spacious rooms and colorful beach bungalows with indoor-outdoor rain showers and private gardens. **Pros:** gorgeous and tranquil property; spacious rooms; creative and colorful design. **Cons:** hard mattresses; simple breakfast; wild beach, far from town. [$] *Rooms from: $283* ✉ *3 km (2 miles) north of Playa Bejuco, next to Encantada Cottages, Esterillos Este* ☎ *2778–7070* 🌐 *www.almadelpacificohotel.com* 🛏 *20 rooms* 🍴 *Free Breakfast.*

★ **Encantada Ocean Cottages**
$$ | **HOTEL** | **FAMILY** | Framing a blue-tiled pool are freestanding cottages with thoughtful and creative touches like luxurious bedding atop artsy bed frames (made from repurposed pallets), colorful throws, polished cement floors, and lofts with twin beds. **Pros:** peaceful location with 24-hour security; surf lessons and board rental available along with daily yoga classes; comfy beds. **Cons:** often full; low water pressure; smaller breakfast. [$] *Rooms from: $150* ✉ *Next to Alma Del Pacifico Beach Hotel, Esterillos Este* ☎ *4702–5847 in Costa Rica, 310/807–3434 in the U.S., 506/6038–2574 WhatsApp* 🌐 *www.encantadacostarica.com* 🛏 *7 units* 🍴 *Free Breakfast.*

Activities

HORSEBACK RIDING

The Riding Adventure
HORSEBACK RIDING | Beach riding is the specialty here. Trips set out from a cattle ranch 20 minutes south of Jacó and include a stop at a waterfall for swimming or trail walking. Tours take place twice daily and include a stop at the Pelican restaurant for lunch. Transportation from your hotel can be arranged for $10, or you can start at the meeting point for beach tours next to Monterey Del Mar Hotel in Esterillos Este. ✉ *Monterey Del Mar Hotel, Esterillos Este* ☎ *8834–8687, 6080–0501* 🌐 *www.theridingadventure.com* 🎟 *From $65.*

Quepos

23 km (14 miles) south of Parrita, 174 km (108 miles) southwest of San José.

This hot and dusty town is the gateway to Manuel Antonio, and also serves as the area's hub for banks, supermarkets, and other services. Because nearby Manuel Antonio is so much more attractive, there is little reason to stay here, but many people stop for dinner, for a night on the town, or to go sportfishing. Quepos's name stems from the indigenous tribe that inhabited the area until the Spanish conquest wiped them out. For centuries the town of Quepos barely existed, until the 1930s, when the United Fruit Company built a banana port and populated the area with workers from other parts of Central America. The town thrived for nearly two decades, until Panama disease decimated the banana plantations in the late 1940s. The fruit company then switched to less lucrative African oil palms, and the area declined. Only since the 1980s have tourism revenues lifted the town out of its slump, a renaissance owed to the beauty of the nearby beaches and nature reserves.

Forests around Quepos were destroyed nearly a century ago, but the massive Talamanca Mountain Range, some 10 km (6 miles) to the east, holds one of the largest expanses of wilderness in Central America.

GETTING HERE AND AROUND

The drive from San José to Quepos is less than three hours. Follow the directions for Jacó and continue south another 40 minutes. Buses from San José's Tracopa bus station (Avenida 5, Calles 14–16) drop you off in downtown Quepos. SANSA runs multiple flights per day, 20 minutes one way, between San José and Quepos (XQP), as well as direct flights between Quepos and Palmar Sur in the Southern Pacific and La Fortuna in the Northern Lowlands.

RENTAL CARS Alamo. ⊠ *Downtown, next to Pali supermarket, Quepos* ☎ *2242–7733, 2777–3344, 800/462–5266 in U.S.*

TAXIS Taxi services. ☎ *2777–3080, 2777–1207.*

ESSENTIALS

BANKS/ATMS BAC San José. ⊠ *Avda. Central, Quepos* ☎ *2295–9797.* **Banco Nacional.** ⊠ *Calle 2, Quepos* ☎ *2777–1157.*

MEDICAL ASSISTANCE Centro Medico Quepos. ⊠ *Rancho Grande de Quepos, Quepos* ☎ *2777–1727.* **Farmacia La Económica.** ⊠ *Main Rd., Quepos* ⊹ *In front of market at La Galeria Comercial* ☎ *2777–2130, 2777–3213.*

POST OFFICE Correos. ⊠ *Avda. Central, next to soccer field, Quepos* ☎ *2777–1471.*

TOURIST INFORMATION Instituto Costarricense de Turismo. ⊠ *Quepos* ⊹ *25 meters (82 feet) east of docks* ☎ *2299–5800, 2777–4221 in Quepos, 866/267–8274 in North America* ⊕ *www.ict.go.cr.*

Sights

Rainforest Spices / Villa Vanilla

FARM/RANCH | Thirty minutes north of Quepos, this spice plantation produces vanilla, cinnamon, cocoa, pepper, allspice, turmeric, and a variety of exotic fruits, essential oils, and medicinal plants. Half-day tours include a visit to the harvesting warehouse, a walk through the fields, and a tasting of Ceylon cinnamon and chocolate gourmet treats prepared by the in-house pastry chef. If you get hooked on the vanilla-bean cheesecake, the cardamom ice cream, or the cinnamon tea, you can stock up on organic spices at the shop on your way out. Tastings and transportation from the Quepos–Manuel Antonio area are included in the tour price. Be sure to bring bug spray. ⊠ *16 km (10 miles) east of Quepos, Quepos* ⊹ *Take paved road toward hospital and airport, at gas station intersection, continue east. After 6 km (4 miles), pass through Naranjito and continue 1 km (½ mile) to "Y" intersection. Stay left, continue 5 km (3 miles) to Villa Vanilla on left* ☎ *2779–1155, 8839–2721* ⊕ *www.rainforestspices.com* ☑ *$45.*

Rainmaker Conservation Project

NATURE PRESERVE | This private nature reserve is spread over Fila Chota, a lower ridge of the Talamanca Range 22 km (13 miles) northeast of Quepos, and protects more than 1,500 acres of lush and precipitous forest, with river-walk or canopy-bridge routes to follow in the lower section. The reserve is home to many of Costa Rica's endangered species, and you may spot birds here that you won't find in Manuel Antonio. You are likely to see scarlet macaws and toucans, due to a repopulation of the species in the Quepos Biological Corridor. Their long-time resident sloth "Charlie Rainmaker" helps educate guests about rain-forest conservation. The reserve encompasses five ecozones and represents 75% of the species found in Costa Rica. It isn't as good a place to see animals as the national park, but Rainmaker's forest is different—lusher and more precipitous—and the view from its bridges is impressive. Guided tours are available from Manuel Antonio, or you can stop and take a self-guided tour on your way to or from Quepos. The park also offers an early-morning bird-watching tour and a night reptiles-and-amphibians hike. The restaurant serves lunch ($8), and there's an on-site microbrewery that utilizes Rainmaker's mountain waters. It's best to visit Rainmaker in the morning, since—true to its name—it often pours in the afternoon. ✉ *Quepos* ⊕ *22 km (13 miles) northeast of Quepos* ☎ *8588–2586, 540/349–9848 in U.S., 8960–3836 park cell* 🌐 *rainmakercostarica.com* 🎟 *From $20 (cash only).*

🍴 Restaurants

Runaway Grill

$$$ | **SEAFOOD** | This favorite with sportfishermen ("You hook 'em, we cook 'em") is the town's best place for seafood, serving everything from shrimp scampi to fresh tuna with mushrooms to fried snapper and orange chicken. Their location, overlooking the marina, offers the best view in town. **Known for:** spicy crab dip; kids' menu; fresh tuna and ceviche. [$] *Average main: $20* ✉ *Marina Pez Vela, Quepos* ☎ *2774–9095* 🌐 *www.runaway-grill.com.*

🏃 Activities

There's a tour operator or travel agency on every block in Quepos that can sell you any of about a dozen tours, but some outfitters give discounts if you book directly through them. The dry season is the best time to explore the area's rain forests. If you're here during the rains, do tours first thing in the morning.

CANOPY TOURS

★ Canopy Safari

ZIP LINING | **FAMILY** | There are many zipline tours in the area that take you flying through the treetops, but Canopy Safari has earned a reputation for long and fast-paced rides. The company's privately owned forest is about a 30-minute car ride from Quepos, and the tour includes gliding down 11 ziplines, a Tarzan swing, two rappel lines, and a visit to the on-site butterfly garden and serpentarium. Tours take place at 8 and 11 and include either breakfast or lunch. They also offer rafting tours. ✉ *Office downtown, next to Poder Judicial, Quepos* ☎ *2777–0100, 888/765–8475 in North America* 🌐 *www.canopysafari.com* 🎟 *Tour $85.*

FISHING

Quepos is one of the best points of departure for deep-sea fishing in southwestern Costa Rica. The best months for hooking a marlin are from October to February and in May and June, whereas sailfish are abundant from November to May and are caught year-round. From May to October you're more likely to catch yellowfin tuna, roosterfish, mahimahi, and snapper. Sailfish and marlin are always catch-and-release.

KAYAKING AND RAFTING

Iguana Tours

KAYAKING | Guides show off the area's natural beauty on white-water rafting trips on the Naranjo (Class III–IV) and Savegre (Class II–III) rivers and kayak adventures at sea or in a mangrove estuary. They also offer bird-watching, horseback riding, catamaran trips, and canopy tours. ✉ *Downtown Quepos, across from soccer field, Quepos* ☎ *2777–2052* 🌐 *www.iguanatours.com* 🎟 *From $65.*

Quepos, the gateway to Manual Antonio, is the area's hub with banks, supermarkets, and other services.

Manuel Antonio

3 km (2 miles) south of Quepos, 179 km (111 miles) southwest of San José.

You need merely reach the top of the forested ridge on which many of Manuel Antonio's hotels are perched to understand why it is one of Costa Rica's most popular destinations. That sweeping view of beaches, jungle, and shimmering Pacific dotted with rocky islets confirms its reputation. Unlike the tropical forests in other parts of the country, Manuel Antonio's humid tropical forest remains green year-round. The town itself is spread out across a hilly and curving 5-km (3-mile) road that originates in Quepos and deadends at the entrance to Manuel Antonio National Park. Along this main road, near the top of the hill, or on Punta Quepos are the area's most luxurious hotels and fine-dining restaurants, surrounded by rain forest with amazing views of the beaches and offshore islands. The only problem with staying in one of those hotels is that you'll need to drive or take public transportation to and from the main beach and national park, about 10 minutes away. More hotel and restaurant options are available at the bottom of the hill, within walking distance of the beach, but they lack the sweeping view.

GETTING HERE AND AROUND

Manuel Antonio is a 15-minute drive over the hill from Quepos and 25 minutes from the Quepos airport. Between SANSA and Skyway, a flight from San José and Quepos (XQP) will be easy to find. Flying time is 20 minutes. There are also direct flights between Quepos and La Fortuna and Quepos and Liberia. Buses depart from San José's Tracopa bus station (Avenida 5, Calles 14–16) for Manuel Antonio four times a day, at 6 am, noon, and 6 and 7:30 pm, traveling the opposite direction at 6 and 9:30 am, noon, and 5 pm. They pick up and drop off passengers in front of hotels on the main Quepos–Manuel Antonio road. Shuttle service Interbus offers hotel-to-hotel service to and from San José, Jacó,

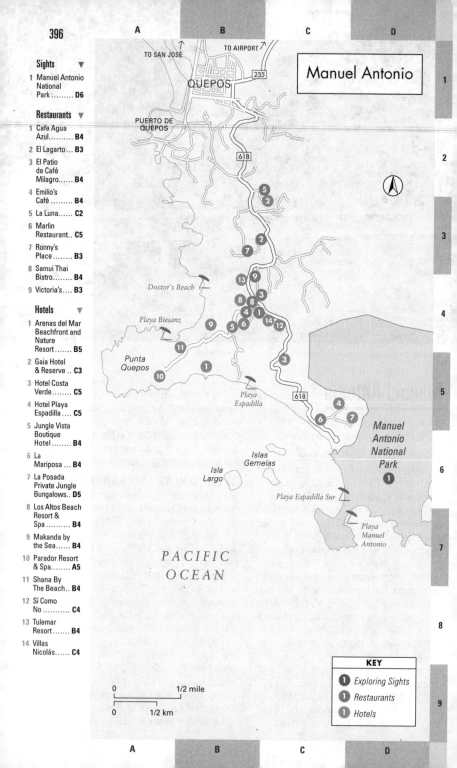

Manuel Antonio

TO SAN JOSÉ
TO AIRPORT
QUEPOS
235
PUERTO DE
QUEPOS
618

Doctor's Beach

Playa Biesanz

Punta
Quepos

Playa
Espadilla

618

Islas
Gemelas

Isla
Largo

Playa Espadilla Sur

Manuel
Antonio
National
Park

Playa
Manuel
Antonio

PACIFIC
OCEAN

0   1/2 mile
0   1/2 km

KEY

1 Exploring Sights
1 Restaurants
1 Hotels

Monteverde, Arenal, and major North Pacific beaches. The trip from San José takes about 2½ hours by car or 3½ hours by bus. A local public bus makes the 20-minute trip from Quepos to Manuel Antonio every half hour from 7 to 7, then hourly until 10 pm.

RENTAL CARS Economy. ⊠ *Next to Banco Promérica, across from Salsipuedes, Manuel Antonio* ☎ *2777–5353.*

TAXIS Taxi Services. ☎ *2777–1207.*

ESSENTIALS

BANK/ATM Banco Promérica. ⊠ *Main road, at top of hill, between Economy Rent a Car and Cafe Milagro, Manuel Antonio* ☎ *2505–7000.*

 Sights

★ **Manuel Antonio National Park**
(*Parque Nacional Manuel Antonio*)
NATIONAL PARK | FAMILY | Costa Rica's smallest park packs in an assortment of natural attractions, from wildlife sheltered by rain forest to rocky coves teeming with marine life. Meandering trails framed by guácimo colorado, mangrove, and silk-cotton trees serve as refuge to sloths, iguanas, agoutis, coatis, raccoons, monkeys, and birds. This is one of the country's best places to see squirrel monkeys and white-faced capuchin monkeys. The great diversity of wildlife is easily spotted from the well-maintained trails, and because the animals are so used to humans, you're likely to see them up close, especially near groups of tourists eating lunch at the beach. Security guards now inspect bags at the park entrance as new restrictions allow visitors to bring only fruit, sandwiches, and nonalcoholic beverages. The mass amounts of junk food stolen and consumed by wildlife has led to serious health problems for the animals. As tempting as it may be, do not feed the wildlife.

Just beyond the entrance, the park's main trail leads to Playa Manuel Antonio, with white sand and submerged volcanic rock great for snorkeling. A second trail winds through the rain forest and spills onto Playa Espadilla Sur, the park's longest beach, which is often less crowded due to rough waters. Farther east, Playa Escondido (Hidden Beach) is rocky and secluded, but not open to the public due to safety precautions; however, you can view it from afar.

Despite its size, Manuel Antonio is Costa Rica's most-visited national park before Poás Volcano. A few tips to make the most of a visit:

Park entrance tickets are sold exclusively at Coopealianza offices in Quepos and Manuel Antonio, one of which is located 50 meters (164 feet) before the park entrance. Tickets are valid for one year from date of purchase, for a single visit. Hire a private guide with ICT certification issued by the Costa Rica Tourism Board.

Arrive as early as possible—between 7 and 8 am is the best time to see animals (and it's cooler, too). Keep in mind the park closes at 3 pm.

Beware of manzanillo trees (indicated by warning signs)—their leaves, bark, and applelike fruit secrete a gooey substance that irritates the skin.

⚠ **It's common for noncertified guides to approach tourists and offer their services. Even if you ask to see identification, they might show only a Costa Rican ID or a driver's license. Make sure that you hire only a guide that has a badge reading "ICT" with a valid expiration date. Noncertified guides often charge as much as ICT-approved guides, but tours last only an hour to 90 minutes (as opposed to three hours), and you won't see a fraction of the wildlife you might with an experienced guide.**

For more information, see the highlighted listing in this chapter. ⊠ *Manuel Antonio* ☎ *2777–5185* ✉ *$18* ⊙ *Closed Tues.*

Beaches

When the surf is up, riptides are a dangerous problem on Playa Espadilla, Manuel Antonio's main beach, which runs parallel to the road near the park's entrance.

■ **TIP→ Never leave your valuables unattended while you're swimming.**

Playa Biesanz

BEACH | For a less turbulent swim and smaller crowds than at other Manuel Antonio beaches, head to this quiet beach within a sheltered cove. There are a few tide pools near a cluster of rocks and, during low tide, you can see fragments of turtle traps dating back to AD 900, when the area was inhabited by the indigenous Quepoa people. You can rent snorkeling gear for $10 and kayaks for $30. Prepare to pay $1–$2 to the unofficial parking attendant who monitors cars. Bring your own food, drinks, and bug spray since there are no amenities and a few mosquitoes on the jungle trail. You're likely to see monkeys and butterflies on the trail connecting the road to the sand. **Amenities:** none. **Best for:** snorkeling; solitude. ✉ *Near Hotel Parador, Manuel Antonio.*

Playa Espadilla

BEACH | As the road approaches Manuel Antonio National Park, it skirts the lovely, forest-lined beach of Playa Espadilla, which stretches for more than 2 km (1 mile) north from the rocky crag that marks the park's border to the base of the ridge that holds most of the hotels. One of the most popular beaches in Costa Rica, it fills up with sunbathers, surfers, volleyball players, strand strollers, and sandcastle architects on dry-season weekends and holidays. For most of the year, it is surprisingly quiet, especially at the northern end below Arenas del Mar. Even on the busiest days it is long enough to provide an escape from the crowd, which tends to gather around the restaurants and lounge chairs near

In the Thick of It

There's more rain forest on private land than in Manuel Antonio National Park, which means it's not unusual to see many of the animals the park is famous for from the balcony of your hotel room or from your breakfast table. It also means that local landowners play an important role in conserving the area's flora and fauna.

its southern end. Though many people often swim and surf here, beware of rough seas and deadly rip currents. There are usually lifeguards on duty closest to the park. If you plan on surfing on the north end, beware of the rocks lurking just below the break closest to the cliffs. You can access this isolated section of Playa Espadilla by way of a 1-km (½-mile) dirt road near Arenas del Mar. There's free parking on the sand, accessible by four-wheel-drive vehicles only. **Amenities:** food and drink. **Best for:** surfing; walking. ✉ *Manuel Antonio.*

Playa Manuel Antonio

BEACH | The town's safest swimming area is sheltered Playa Manuel Antonio, the second beach in the national park. Its white sand makes it attractive for lounging around, and the warm, clean water is good for snorkeling. There are plenty of palm trees where you can find shade on this wide stretch of sand, and just outside the park are vendors selling fresh coconut water and lychees. Keep watch over your food as raccoons and monkeys are known to steal lunches while people are swimming. Huge mounds of lava rock shelter this cove on both sides of the rugged coastline. Several shacks just outside the park rent beach chairs for about $15 a day. Beaches inside the national park do not have lifeguards or food vendors, unlike those near the

You can hike to white-sand beaches in Manuel Antonio National Park—just one of the reasons it is so popular.

entrance. **Amenities:** parking; showers; toilets. **Best for:** snorkeling; swimming; walking. ✉ *6 km (4 miles) south of Quepos; near park entrance, Manuel Antonio.*

🍴 Restaurants

Cafe Agua Azul

$$$ | **SEAFOOD** | Follow your nose to this simple second-floor room offering breathtaking views by day and a deliciously inventive selection of seafood by night. The lunch menu is strong on salads, burgers, and sandwiches, but the dinner options include some of the best entrées in town, like seared tuna over a tequila-and-lime cucumber salad and calamari sautéed with capers and olives. **Known for:** seafood pasta with a Parmesan cream tomato sauce; nightly seafood specials; blackened fish sandwich. [$] *Average main: $20* ✉ *Main road, above Villas del Parque office, 2nd fl., Manuel Antonio* ☎ *2777–5280* ⏲ *Closed Oct.*

El Lagarto

$$$$ | **STEAKHOUSE** | Meat lovers can get their fix at this local grill, where sizzling cuts are seared on a wood-fire grill and served on chopping blocks. The bar serves powerful margaritas and daiquiris, but it's the grass-fed beef from neighboring La Fortuna that you'll want to try. **Known for:** grass-fed beef served with baked potato; grilled seafood; killer sunset views. [$] *Average main: $30* ✉ *Manuel Antonio* ✥ *200 meters (656 feet) north of the soccer field* ☎ *2777–6932* 🌐 *www.ellagartobbq.com* ⏲ *No lunch.*

El Patio de Café Milagro

$$$ | **CAFÉ** | This cozy café is the only place in town that serves its own fresh-roasted coffee, with an eclectic menu serving inventive dishes like chilled avocado soup, mango chayote salad, roasted pork with sautéed papaya, and dorado with Caribbean salsa. Top sellers include jerk chicken, fish tacos, and the fish of the day with passion fruit sauce. **Known for:** live music (usually acoustic) every night 7–10; kombucha and craft beer on tap;

fresh roasted coffee. $ *Average main: $17* ⊠ *Main road to park, across from Los Altos, Manuel Antonio* ☎ *2777–2272* ⊕ *elpatiodecafemilagro.com.*

★ Emilio's Café

$$ | MEDITERRANEAN | Just inside the doors of this popular café you'll find sweeping views, organic cuisine, and a chic vibe that sets the stage for all kinds of good eats (and drinks). Breakfast offerings include eggs Benedict, waffles, or delectable French toast, while sesame-crusted tuna, falafel pita, or one of the vegetable sandwiches served with homemade pesto or salsa picante are available for lunch or dinner. **Known for:** a Mediterranean spin on classics like ceviche and poke; excellent coffee; a wide range of delectable homemade desserts. $ *Average main: $12* ⊠ *Manuel Antonio* ⊹ *40 meters (131 feet) before Hotel Mariposa* ☎ *8655–5965, 2777–6807* ⊘ *Closed Tues.*

★ La Luna

$$$$ | INTERNATIONAL | It's hard to know what's more impressive—the view or the cuisine at this restaurant without walls, where the sun melts into the Pacific and La Luna (the moon) takes center stage. Innovative starters range from Gorgonzola-and-tomato tarts to honey-garlic calamari. **Known for:** ginger-and-panko-crusted tuna; happy hour with tapas and cocktails; fine-dining tasting menu with wine pairing. $ *Average main: $30* ⊠ *Gaia Hotel, Km 2.7 Carretera Quepos, Manuel Antonio* ☎ *2777–9797* ⊕ *www.gaiahr.com.*

Marlin Restaurant

$$$ | COSTA RICAN | The outdoor tables are pretty much always full, owing to a location on Manuel Antonio's busiest corner, across the street from the beach near the national park entrance. This is a convenient place to grab breakfast after an early-morning hike—maybe banana pancakes or a *típico*, with eggs and *gallo pinto* (black beans and rice). **Known for:** fresh fish; margaritas with a beach view; casado (typical Costa Rican food). $ *Average main: $17* ⊠ *Main road, south of hill, on corner across from bus stop and beach, Manuel Antonio* ☎ *2777–1134.*

Ronny's Place

$$$ | COSTA RICAN | Just behind the original location is a new and improved venue where a spectacular sunset view comes with friendly, attentive service and a tempting menu that includes such typical tico dishes as *sopa negra* (black-bean soup), ceviche, shrimp and fish on a skewer, and filet mignon wrapped with bacon and topped with a mushroom sauce. Up a long dirt road, this is the best place in town to soak in the ocean views—especially when accompanied by a glass of their famous white-wine-and-vodka sangria. **Known for:** seafood platters with whole red snapper; coconut crusted jumbo shrimp; piña coladas served in pineapples. $ *Average main: $20* ⊠ *Manuel Antonio* ⊹ *1 km (½ mile) west of main road, down dirt road across from Amigos del Río* ☎ *2777–5120* ⊕ *www.ronnysplace.com* ⊘ *Closed Sept. 15–30.*

Samui Thai Bistro

$$$ | THAI | FAMILY | The chefs at this popular corner restaurant have mastered Thai cuisine with a Costa Rican twist, starting with the ginger fish, cashew chicken, lobster pad Thai, and green curry that will have you planning your next vacation to Thailand. Daily specials are the way to go, based on the freshest catch of the day and creative sides like mango salad or fried rice served in a pineapple bowl. **Known for:** ginger fish; authentic Thai dishes; curry puffs. $ *Average main: $18* ⊠ *Manuel Antonio* ⊹ *On corner of main street, Los Altos Plaza* ☎ *2101–7058* ⊕ *www.facebook.com/samuicr.*

Victoria's

$$$ | ITALIAN | This Italian eatery is the perfect place to stop for brick oven pizza or homemade pastas. Thin and crispy top picks include New York style with pepperoni, sausage, and ham, or pesto-chicken pizza with toasted

The Pacific coast is backed by mangrove, rain, transitional, and tropical dry forests.

walnuts and caramelized onions. **Known for:** live music Saturday; banana flambé; homemade meatballs. $ *Average main: $24* ⊠ *Diagonally across from Tulemar, Manuel Antonio* ☎ *2777–5143* ⊕ *www. victoriasgourmet.com* ⊗ *No lunch.*

Hotels

Arenas del Mar Beachfront and Nature Resort

$$$$ | **RESORT** | On hillsides sloping down to two pristine, almost-deserted beaches, chic and elegant rooms are decorated with gorgeous natural fabrics and local art and have huge private terraces with comfortable outdoor seating. **Pros:** best of both worlds: luxury and eco-consciousness; free shuttle, minibar, and laundry service; wonderful bird-watching and wildlife viewing; beach with surf lessons and lifeguard. **Cons:** humidity can leave bathrooms somewhat musty; pricey; very steep paths and stairs. $ *Rooms from: $550* ⊠ *El Parador road at far west end of Playa Espadilla, Manuel Antonio* ☎ *2104–0589, 888/240–0280 in U.S.*

⊕ *www.arenasdelmar.com* ⇄ *37 rooms* ⊙ *Free Breakfast.*

Gaia Hotel & Reserve

$$$$ | **HOTEL** | **FAMILY** | On 13 acres of private reserve, this boutique hotel is contemporary and very chic, with rooms rendered in slate, hardwood, and rattan with Italian fittings. **Pros:** outstanding service; free shuttle to beach and national park; best spa in Manuel Antonio. **Cons:** rooftop pools are shallow and impractical; 3 km (2 miles) from the beach; children over 13 only. $ *Rooms from: $460* ⊠ *Km 2.7 Carretera Quepos, near Plaza Yara, Manuel Antonio* ☎ *2777–9797, 800/226–2515 in U.S.* ⊕ *www.gaiahr.com* ⇄ *21 units* ⊙ *Free Breakfast.*

Hotel Costa Verde

$$$ | **RESORT** | **FAMILY** | Their motto, "still more monkeys than people" is not an understatement, as you're likely to see howler and white-faced monkeys on the forest trails surrounding these varied accommodations (including three converted from airplanes). **Pros:** great ocean views; wildlife; daily yoga. **Cons:** 1½ km (1

mile) from the beach; service inconsistent; most efficiencies suffer road noise. $ *Rooms from: $160* ✉ *Road to national park, on south side of hill, on left, Manuel Antonio* ☎ *2777–0584, 866/854–7958 in North America* ⊕ *www.costaverde.com* ⤴ *75 rooms* ⍾ *Free Breakfast.*

Hotel Playa Espadilla

$$$ | HOTEL | FAMILY | Simple but spacious mint-green and cream rooms are a short walk from the beach and are surrounded by green lawns bordered on two sides by the tall trees of Manuel Antonio National Park. **Pros:** surrounded by forest; close to beach and national park; guests can use amenities at sister property Cabinas Espadilla. **Cons:** showers often lack hot water; basic rooms; service inconsistent. $ *Rooms from: $194* ✉ *150 m on side road from Marlin Restaurant, 1st left, 300 m before park entrance, Manuel Antonio* ☎ *2777–0903* ⊕ *www.espadilla.com* ⤴ *16 rooms* ⍾ *Free Breakfast.*

Jungle Vista Boutique Hotel

$$$ | HOTEL | FAMILY | The name says it all at this new property with artfully crafted studios and apartments tucked on the lush hillside of Manuel Antonio. **Pros:** lovely pool; access to sister property; central location. **Cons:** some street noise; jungle attracts bugs; steep hill. $ *Rooms from: $250* ✉ *Manuel Antonio* ✛ *100 meters (328 feet) west of Hotel Mariposa* ☎ *2777–0818, 888/760–7546 in U.S.* ⊕ *www.junglevistahotel.com* ⤴ *22 rooms* ⍾ *Free Breakfast.*

La Mariposa

$$$ | RESORT | The best view in town—a sweeping panorama of verdant hills, the aquamarine ocean, and offshore islands—is the claim to fame for this array of spacious rooms tucked between the jungle and gardens ablaze with colorful flowers. **Pros:** gorgeous views; free shuttle to the beach; infinity pool. **Cons:** some ocean-view balconies lack privacy; sections of hotel slightly dated; 2 km (1 mile) from beach. $ *Rooms from: $234* ✉ *West of main road, right after Barba*

Roja, across from Mango Moon Hotel, Manuel Antonio* ☎ *2777–0355, 800/572–6440 in U.S.* ⊕ *www.lamariposa.com* ⤴ *70 rooms* ⍾ *Free Breakfast.*

La Posada Private Jungle Bungalows

$$ | RESORT | This cluster of distinctive A-frame bungalows, nestled on the edge of the national park and also just a short walk from the beach, is as close as you'll get to sleeping in the park. **Pros:** good value; near beach and park; friendly staff. **Cons:** small pool; rooms slightly dated; chaotic outside the hotel during park hours. $ *Rooms from: $140* ✉ *Manuel Antonio* ✛ *250 meters (820 feet) up side road from Marlin Restaurant, at park entrance* ☎ *2777–1446* ⊕ *www.laposada-jungle.com* ⤴ *12 units* ⍾ *Free Breakfast.*

★ Los Altos Beach Resort & Spa

$$$$ | RESORT | FAMILY | These three- and four-bedroom Balinese-inspired luxury condo suites boast 2,500 square feet of living space with industrial kitchens, slate floors, granite counters, rich hardwoods, and rattan furnishings. **Pros:** great views; free cooking classes and water aerobics; ideal for families; enormous rooms. **Cons:** $150 charge per room over two guests; only high-rise in Manuel Antonio (a bit of an eyesore); higher-level suites cost more. $ *Rooms from: $450* ✉ *Km 4 on road to Manuel Antonio National Park, across from Café Milagro, Manuel Antonio* ☎ *2777–8888, 888/803–1332 in U.S.* ⊕ *losaltosresort.com* ⤴ *28 condos* ⍾ *Free Breakfast.*

Makanda by the Sea

$$$$ | RESORT | These bright, spacious white-and-cream villas are among the area's most tasteful (and expensive) accommodations, and the hypnotic views of the jungle-framed Pacific Ocean make this secluded rain-forest retreat worth every penny. **Pros:** tranquil; yoga on Wednesday and Friday; ocean views. **Cons:** spotty Wi-Fi; slippery steps; no children under 16; 10-minute hike to the beach. $ *Rooms from: $500* ✉ *1 km (½ mile) west of La Mariposa, Manuel*

Antonio ☎ 2777–0442, 888/625–2632 in North America 🌐 www.makanda.com 🛏 31 units 🍴 Free Breakfast.

Parador Resort & Spa

$$$$ | RESORT | Terra-cotta floors, steamer trunks, marble statues, bronzed knights, and elaborate antiques create a high-end Spanish colonial style at this beachfront resort perched on the end of a secluded peninsula. **Pros:** outstanding service; tranquil location; free shuttle to national park. **Cons:** 15-minute drive to Manuel Antonio National Park; pool closes at 7 pm; pricey food. [$] *Rooms from: $283 ✉ End of peninsula at Biesanz Beach, Manuel Antonio ☎ 2777–1414 🌐 www.hotelparador.com 🛏 122 rooms 🍴 Free Breakfast.*

Shana By The Beach

$$$ | RESORT | With some of the best service in Manuel Antonio and updated rooms, Shana By the Beach is a lovely option with jungle- or ocean-view balconies in every room. **Pros:** attentive service; daily food and drink specials; sleek design. **Cons:** weak Wi-Fi signal in some rooms; steep driveway; not oceanfront. [$] *Rooms from: $225 ✉ Manuel Antonio ⊕ Road to Quepos, 300 meters (984 feet) downhill from La Mansión Inn ☎ 2777–7373 🌐 www.shanahotel.com 🛏 74 rooms 🍴 Free Breakfast.*

Sí Como No

$$$$ | RESORT | FAMILY | This sustainable resort sits atop one of the most idyllic hillsides in Manuel Antonio. **Pros:** neighboring wildlife refuge; nice views; good restaurants. **Cons:** standard rooms overpriced; a few suites too close to road; 3 km (2 miles) from beach. [$] *Rooms from: $279 ✉ Road to park, just after Villas Nicolás, right-hand side, Manuel Antonio ☎ 2777–0777, 888/742–6667 in North America 🌐 www.sicomono.com 🛏 54 units 🍴 Free Breakfast.*

★ **Tulemar Resort**

$$$$ | HOTEL | Tucked inside the peaceful 33-acre gated Tulemar Gardens, circular glass villas perched on jungle hillsides are connected by paved trails that meander past four swimming pools and spill onto the beach. **Pros:** accommodating staff; exceptional design; within private gated reserve surrounded by wildlife. **Cons:** not wheelchair accessible; condo-hotel means some services are lacking; some units don't have ocean views. [$] *Rooms from: $295 ✉ Tulemar Gardens, next to Los Altos Beach Resort, Manuel Antonio ☎ 2777–0580, 800/518–0831 in North America 🌐 www.tulemarresort.com 🛏 35 units 🍴 No Meals.*

Villas Nicolás

$$$ | HOTEL | On a hillside about 3 km (2 miles) from the beach, these terraced, privately owned Mediterranean-style villas have impressive views and offer one and two bedrooms, kitchens, and (in most) large balconies with hammocks. **Pros:** good location; most rooms have great views; grounds are well maintained. **Cons:** a bit of hike to the beach; no TVs; fee to use beach towels; some units need updating. [$] *Rooms from: $160 ✉ Road to park, across from Hotel Byblos, Manuel Antonio ☎ 2777–0481 🌐 www.villasnicolas.com 🛏 21 rooms 🍴 Free Breakfast.*

🍸 Nightlife

BARS

Barba Roja

BARS | As one of Manuel Antonio's first restaurants, this is still one of the best places to go for sunset cocktail hour, live music, and local beers on tap. *✉ Main road, 100 meters (328 feet) before Cafe Milagro, Manuel Antonio ☎ 2777–0331 🌐 www.barbarojarestaurant.com.*

MUSIC CLUBS
Victoria's

LIVE MUSIC | This upscale Italian restaurant is also a popular nightspot, with great wine and a romantic atmosphere. ✉ *Main road, diagonally across from Tulemar, Manuel Antonio* ☎ *2777–5143* ⊕ *www. victoriasgourmet.com.*

Shopping

There's no shortage of shopping in this town. The beach near the entrance to the park is lined with a sea of vendors who sell T-shirts, hats, and colorful beach wraps. More-authentic handicrafts are sold at night by artisans positioned along the sidewalk in central Manuel Antonio.

Regalame

ART GALLERIES | This appealing art gallery is a showplace for paintings, drawings, pottery, woodwork, and jewelry by area artists. ✉ *Next to Sí Como No Hotel, Manuel Antonio* ☎ *2777–0777.*

Activities

CANOPY TOURS
El Santuario Canopy Adventure Tour

ZIP LINING | Just 20 minutes from Manuel Antonio National Park, this canopy tour boasts the longest single zipline in Central America, extending nearly 1½ km (1 mile) over the treetops. Tours include 14 platforms, 3 towers, 6 bridges, 3 nature walks, and 1 double-belay rappel. The company has double-anchored ziplines with built-in braking systems. Transportation and lunch are included in the tour fee. ✉ *Manuel Antonio* ☎ *2777–6908, 877/914–0002 in U.S.* ⊕ *www.elsantuariocanopyadventure.com* ✍ *Tour $80.*

Tití Canopy Tour

ZIP LINING | You'll find a relatively slow-paced zipline tour here—a rarity in Costa Rica—on 10 cables through a forest reserve that is contiguous with the national park. On the last platform there are dual lines, so you can race. Lunch is included. Guides go above and beyond to make you feel comfortable and safe and will help you spot animals. ✉ *Costanera Hwy., Manuel Antonio* ✛ *150 meters (492 feet) south of Quepos Hospital* ☎ *2777–3130* ⊕ *www.titicanopytour.com* ✍ *$75.*

HIKING

Highly visited Manuel Antonio National Park is the obvious place to go, but you can also gain a rich appreciation of the local forests' greenery and wildlife in private reserves like Greentique Wildlife Refuge and Rainmaker.

◼ **TIP → Bring binoculars!**

HORSEBACK RIDING
Brisas del Nara

HORSEBACK RIDING | This outfitter takes riders of all ages and levels through the protected Cerro Nara mountain zone, 8 km (5 miles) from Manuel Antonio, and ends with a swim in a natural pool at the foot of a 300-foot waterfall. Full-day tours include three hours on horseback, along with breakfast and lunch; the ride on the half-day tour lasts two hours. For those who want a little less trot in their tour, they have a safari-truck option that visits many of the same attractions. ✉ *Manuel Antonio* ☎ *2779–1235, 8718–2085* ⊕ *www.horsebacktour.com* ✍ *From $65.*

KAYAKING
Iguana Tours

KAYAKING | Half-day sea-kayaking trips from Quepos to snorkel at Playa Biesanz in Manuel Antonio National Park require some experience when the seas are high. On a mellower paddle through the mangrove estuary of Isla Damas you might see monkeys, sloths, and various birds. If you'd like to kick back and relax, try the catamaran. White-water rafting tours are also available. Lunch is included. ✉ *Downtown Quepos, across from Catholic church, Quepos* ☎ *2777–2052, 506/8706–9584 WhatsApp* ⊕ *www.iguanatours.com* ✍ *From $65.*

SNORKELING AND DIVING
The islands that dot the sea in front of Manuel Antonio are surrounded by volcanic rock reefs with small coral formations. They attract schools of snapper, jacks, barracudas, rays, sea turtles, moray eels, and other marine life.

Oceans Unlimited
SCUBA DIVING | This PADI five-star career development center offers all-day diving excursions to Caño Island, local dives, and PADI-certification courses; rental equipment is included. A half-day, two-tank dive for certified divers at Manuel Antonio is $109. Note that tours leave from Quepos. ✉ *Marina Pez Vela, Quepos* ☎ *2519–9544* ⊕ *www.scubadiving-costarica.com* 🍽 *From $109; Caño Island day trip $175.*

SURFING
Manuel Antonio Surf School (*MASS*)
SURFING | Beginner surfers are in good hands with this reputable surf school that guarantees every student will get up on a wave by the end of the session. They teach the mechanics of surfing, wave theory, and offer lessons for all levels at several breaks in Manuel Antonio, Isla Damas, and Dominical. Three-hour group lesson fees include transportation, gear, snacks, and certified instruction. Half-day tours to Damas Island include lunch. If just one lesson isn't enough, they have a surf retreat five minutes outside Dominical. Solo surfers traveling without boards can rent from their solid quiver. ✉ *C. Principal, across from Pajaro Azul, Manuel Antonio* ☎ *2777–4842* ⊕ *www.manuelantoniosurfschool.com* 🍽 *Lessons from $70, tours from $100, rentals from $10* 🍽 *Cash only.*

TOUR OPERATORS
Manuel Antonio's list of outdoor activities is almost endless. Tours generally range from $40 to $100 per person and can be booked through your hotel's reception desk or directly through the outfitter. During the rainy season, some outdoor options might lose their appeal, but clouds usually let loose in the afternoon, so take advantage of sunny mornings. Most nature-themed activities go on rain or shine.

Jade Tours
PRIVATE GUIDES | The certified and knowledgeable guides at Jade Tours will turn your park trek through the national park into an entertaining biology class, as they point out camouflaged wildlife in the treetops. Try the mangrove night tour for a spooky learning adventure. Their team has more than a decade of experience and will help you snap all those picture-perfect images of Costa Rica's flora and fauna through their high-powered scope. Included in the rate are transportation, park entrance, and eco-friendly snacks. ✉ *Manuel Antonio* ☎ *2777–0932, 8632–8760* ⊕ *www.costaricajadetours.com* 🍽 *$55.*

★ Johan Chaves Nature and Birding Tours
PRIVATE GUIDES | Raised in Manuel Antonio, Johan Chaves provides three-hour guided tours of the national park that start bright and early at 7:30. Johan's true passion for wildlife and nature make him one of the most sought-after guides in the region, so reserve (by email) well in advance. In addition to being an expert birder, he is extremely knowledgeable about animal behavior and Costa Rica's history. He has a talent for keeping children intrigued on the trail and for spotting wildlife around every turn. Bring water, sunscreen, walking shoes, bug spray, a camera, and swimsuit if you plan to linger at the beach following the tour. The fee includes park entrance and transportation to and from your hotel. ✉ *Manuel Antonio* ☎ *2779–1189, 8850–4419 mobile* ⊕ *manuelantoniobirdwatching.com* 🍽 *$46 cash only.*

WHITE-WATER RAFTING

The three white-water rivers in this area have limited seasons, when the rains from August to October raise them to their perfect peak. The **Naranjo River** offers a short but exciting run, with Class III–V rapids calling for some experience (April–December only). The **Parrita River** provides a relatively mellow (Class II–III) white-water route, but it's only navigable in two-person inflatable duckies. The **Savegre River** has two navigable stretches: a Class II–III lower section that's a mellow trip perfect for neophytes, and a more rambunctious upper section of Class III–IV rapids. It flows past patches of rain forest that are usually navigable year-round, and it's also good for fly-fishing.

Amigos del Río (*ADR*)

WHITE-WATER RAFTING | Catering to all levels of adrenaline junkies, Amigos del Río has six-hour rafting trips on the Savegre River (Class III rapids), four-hour trips on the Naranjo River (Class III–IV), and five-hour trips on the El Chorro section of the Naranjo River (Class IV–V). Included in the rate are breakfast, lunch, transportation, equipment, and bilingual guides. Tours depart at 7 and 11:30 am daily. The Naranjo River tour runs May to December, El Chorro runs from January to April, and Savegre trip is available year-round. ✉ *2 km (1 mile) on main road to Manuel Antonio National Park, 100 m past Hotel Gaia, Manuel Antonio* ☎ *2777–0082, 877/393–8332 in North America* ⊕ *www.amigosdelrio.net* 🌐 *From $125.*

H2O Adventures

WHITE-WATER RAFTING | The Manuel Antonio franchise for Ríos Tropicales, the biggest rafting outfitter in the country, runs kayaking excursions and rafting trips on the Naranjo River, departing daily at 8 and 1 from Quepos. For something less turbulent, they have a rafting trip down the Savegre River at 8 and 1 suitable for ages 5 to 70. Transportation and lunch are included. ✉ *250 meters (820 feet) east from Catholic church, Quepos* ☎ *2777–4092, 506/8959–8989 WhatsApp, 888/532–3298 in U.S.* ⊕ *www.h2ocr.com* 🌐 *From $124.*

Chapter 10

THE OSA PENINSULA AND THE SOUTH PACIFIC

Updated by
Marlise Kast-Myers

⦿ Sights ★★★★★ 🍴 Restaurants ★★☆☆☆ 🛏 Hotels ★★★★☆ 🛍 Shopping ★☆☆☆☆ 🍸 Nightlife ★☆☆☆☆

WELCOME TO THE OSA PENINSULA AND THE SOUTH PACIFIC

TOP REASONS TO GO

★ **Bird-watching:** Spot beauties such as the scarlet macaw and resplendent quetzal.

★ **Enormous Corcovado National Park:** The last refuge of endangered jaguars and tapirs.

★ **Kayaking:** Head to the Golfo Dulce or along the jungly channels of the Sierpe or Colorado River.

★ **Mountain hikes:** Hiking paths here range from easy daytime treks around luxurious lodges to Costa Rica's toughest: 12,532-foot Cerro Chirripó.

★ **Wild places to stay:** Relax in the country's top ecolodges, rustic thatch-roof beach bungalows, and cozy mountain cabins.

1 Zona de Los Santos. Beautiful, mountainous coffee region.

2 San Gerardo de Dota. Top nature destination with great hiking trails.

3 San Isidro de El General. Bustling market town and the gateway to Chirripó National Park.

4 San Gerardo de Rivas. Wild, scenic place for bird-watching, hiking, and Chirripó National Park.

5 San Vito. Agricultural market town with Italian flair.

6 Dominical. A lively surfer haven next to lush forest.

7 Ballena Marine National Park. 10 km (6 miles) of pristine beaches and a chance to watch dolphins and migrating whales.

8 Golfito. The eastern Golfo Dulce draws anglers and kayakers.

9 Playa Zancudo. Slow-paced beach town with good sportfishing.

10 Playa Pavones. Surfing town with bird-watching nearby.

11 Puerto Jiménez. Frontierlike town and gateway to Corcovado National Park.

Ballena National Marine Park

12 Corcovado National Park. 1,153 square km (445 square miles) of rain forest straight out of a David Attenborough nature documentary.

13 Cabo Matapalo. Rain forest meets the sea at the southern tip of the Osa Peninsula.

14 Carate. Remote, black volcanic-sand beach that feels like the end of the road.

15 Drake Bay. Adventure-filled destination great for hiking, snorkeling, and boating.

CHIRRIPÓ NATIONAL PARK

Chirripó National Park

Chirripó National Park is all about hiking. The ascent up Mt. Chirripó, the highest mountain in Costa Rica, is the most popular, challenging, and exclusive hike in the country.

From the trailhead to the peak, you gain more than 8,000 feet of elevation, climbing through shaded highland forest, then out into the wide-open, windswept wilds of the *páramo*, scrubby moorland similar to the high Andes. It's a 48-km (30-mile) round-trip, and you need at least three days to climb to the base, explore the summits, and descend. The chilly stone Hostel Casa Terbi is the only available accommodation, with small rooms of four bunks each, shared bathrooms, and a no-frills kitchen for use. Trails from the hostel lead to the top of Chirripó and the nearby peak of Terbi, as well as half a dozen other peaks and glacier lakes. A scenic hiking route starts from the small pueblo of San Jerónimo, 40 km (25 miles) southwest of San Gerardo. It's a shorter trail, at 14½ km (9½ miles) each way, with spectacular views.

BEST TIME TO GO

Between sometimes freezing temperatures and more than 150 inches of rain a year, timing is of the essence here. The best months are in the dry season (January–May). The park is open all year, but during much of October, and all of November and December, the trails are often too wet and slippery to hike safely.

FUN FACT

A climb up Chirripó is a rite of passage for many young Costa Ricans, who celebrate their graduation from high school or college with a group expedition.

BEST WAYS TO EXPLORE

HIKING

There's no getting around it: the only way to explore this park is on foot. And the only way is up. It's a tough climb to Mt. Chirripó's base camp—6 to 10 hours from the official park entrance, depending on your physical condition—so most hikers head out of San Gerardo de Rivas before the first light of day. You can hire porters to lug your gear up and down for you, so at least you can travel relatively light.

People who live in Costa Rica train seriously for this hike, so be sure you are in good enough shape to make the climb. Smart hikers also factor in a couple of days in the San Gerardo de Rivas area to acclimate to the high altitude before setting out. The hike down is no picnic, either: your knees and ankles will be stretched to their limits. But it's an adventure every step of the way—and the bragging rights are worth it.

MOUNTAIN HIGHS

The base-camp hostel at Los Crestones is at 11,152 feet above sea level, so you still have some hiking ahead of you if you want to summit the surrounding peaks. Take your pick: Chirripó at 12,532 feet; Ventisqueros at 12,467 feet; Cerro Terbi at 12,336; and, for the fainter of heart, Mt. Uran at 11,811 feet.

BIRD-WATCHING

Although your eyes will mostly be on the scenery, there are some highland species of birds that thrive in this chilly mountain air. Watch for the volcano junco, a sparrowlike bird with a pink beak and a yellow eye ring. Only two hummingbirds venture up this high—the fiery-throated hummingbird, which lives up to its name; and the volcano hummingbird, which is the country's smallest bird.

Planning to hike in Chirripó? Prepare for high altitudes.

TOP REASONS TO GO

YOU DID IT!

The sheer sense of accomplishment at completing this tough hike is the number one reason to take on this challenge. You need to be in very good shape.

OCEAN VIEWS

On rare, perfectly clear days, the top of Chirripó is one of the few places in the country where you can see both the Pacific and Atlantic oceans.

TOP OF THE WORLD

The exhilaration of sitting on top of the world, with only sky, mountain peaks, and heath as far as the eye can see, motivates most visitors to withstand the physical challenges and the spartan conditions in the hostel.

UNIQUE ENVIRONMENT

A climb up Chirripó gives visitors a unique chance to experience extreme changes in habitat, from pastureland through rain forest and oak forest to bleak, scrubby páramo (a high-elevation ecosystem).

BALLENA MARINE NATIONAL PARK

A whale breaches in Ballena Marine National Park.

Great snorkeling, whale-watching, and beachcombing draw visitors and locals to Ballena Marine National Park, which protects four relatively tranquil beaches as well as a mangrove estuary, a remnant coral reef, and a vast swath of ocean.

Playa Uvita, fronting the small town of Bahía Ballena, is the longest, widest, and most visited beach, and the embarkation point for snorkeling, fishing, and whale-watching tours. Restaurants and *cabinas* line the nearby main street of the town. Playa Colonia, the most easily accessible beach, has safe swimming and a view of rocky islands. Playa Ballena, south of Playa Colonia, is a lovely strand backed by lush vegetation. Finally, tiny Playa Piñuela is the prettiest of the park beaches, in a deep cove that serves as the local port. It's also the narrowest beach, with a pebbled slope down to the sand. Along with the tropical fish you'll see while snorkeling, you may be lucky enough to see humpback whales and dolphins.

(For more information, see the review in this chapter.)

BEST TIME TO GO

December to April is the best time for guaranteed sunny beach weather, as well as for sightings of humpback whales with their young. The whales also roam these waters in late July through late October. Bottlenose dolphins abound in March and April.

FUN FACT

Playa Uvita features a tombolo, a long swath of sand connecting a former island to the coast. At low tide, the exposed brown sandbar resembles a whale's tail.

BEST WAYS TO EXPLORE

BEACHCOMBING

The park's beaches are ideal to explore on foot, especially Playa Uvita, which has the longest and widest stretch of sand. Visitors and locals flock here in the late afternoon to catch spectacular sunsets. Don't forget your camera! At low tide, you can walk out onto the Whale's Tail sandbar. During the day, you'll see moving shells everywhere—hermit crabs of every size are constantly scuttling around. Although it all looks idyllic—and it mostly is—don't leave valuables unattended on the beach.

CAMPING

If you brought a tent, pitch it here. Camping on the beach is allowed at Playas Ballena, Colonia, and Piñuela. You can't beat the price, as camping is included in the park admission. Every beach has *sanitarios* (basic toilets) and cold-water showers. But bring your own drinking water. Costa Ricans are avid (and often noisy) campers, so try to avoid busy weekends and school holidays.

IN AND ON THE WATER

Swimming here is relatively safe, but check with the park ranger or your hotel about the best swimming spots. Watch for the *banda amarilla* (yellow ribbon) signs that indicate dangerous currents. Whale- and dolphin-watching excursions are also a fun option—bottlenose dolphins are most often spotted, but humpback whales, especially mothers with babes, are the stars of the show. If you want to be the captain of your boat, sea kayaks are a popular way to explore the park's mangroves and river estuaries. Playa Ventanas, just south of the park's official border, has tidal rock caves you can kayak through.

Playa Uvita's wide beach is uncrowded.

TOP REASONS TO GO

ALONE TIME

If solitude is what you're after, the park's beaches are relatively uncrowded, except on weekends and school holidays when locals come to camp and relax. Neither Playa Colonia nor Playa Piñuela see a lot of traffic, so you can have them virtually to yourself almost anytime. Just don't hang out after dark.

BEACHES

Miles of wide, sandy beach backed by palm trees and distant green mountain ridges make this one of the most scenic and accessible coastlines in the country. Playa Uvita and Playa Ballena, with their warm, swimmable waters and soft sand, attract the most beachgoers.

WHALES AND DOLPHINS

Catching sight of a mother humpback whale with her young swimming alongside is a thrill you won't soon forget. And watching dolphins cavorting around your boat is the best entertainment on water.

CORCOVADO NATIONAL PARK

Corcovado National Park

For those who crave untamed wilderness, Corcovado National Park is the experience of a lifetime. Covering one-third of the Osa Peninsula, the park is blanketed primarily by rain forest and holds Central America's largest remaining tract of lowland Pacific rain forest.

The remoteness of Corcovado and the difficult access to its interior make it one of the country's most pristine parks—barely disturbed by human presence—where massive, vine-tangled primary-forest trees tower over the trails, and birds and wildlife abound. Your chances of spotting endangered species are better here than anywhere else in the country, although it still takes a combination of luck and determination. The rarest and most sought-after sightings are the jaguar and Baird's tapir. Corcovado also has the largest population of scarlet macaws in the country. Bordering the park are some of Costa Rica's most luxurious eco-friendly jungle lodges and retreats.

(For more information, see the review in this chapter.)

BEST TIME TO GO

Dry season (January–May) is the best time to visit, but it's also the most popular. With only a limited number of camping spots available, it's crucial to reserve well in advance if you want to stay overnight in the park. New rules require that you are accompanied by a certified guide. June through August will be wetter, but may also be a little cooler. The long-distance trails are virtually impassable from September to December, when most visitors arrive in boats.

BEST WAYS TO EXPLORE

BIRD-WATCHING AND WILDLIFE

The holy grail of wildlife spotting here is a jaguar or a Baird's tapir. You may be one of the lucky few to see one of these rare, elusive animals. In the meantime, you can content yourself with coatis, peccaries, and agoutis on the ground and, in the trees, some endemic species of birds you will see only in this part of the country: Baird's trogon, riverside wren, and black-cheeked ant-tanager, to name a few.

GETTING HERE AND AROUND

The easiest way to visit the park is on a guided day trip by boat to the San Pedrillo station, organized by a lodge or tour company in Drake Bay, Sierpe, or Uvita. The well-heeled can fly in on an expensive charter plane to the Sirena airfield. But no matter how you arrive, the only way to explore is on foot. There are no roads, only hiking trails. If you have a backpack, strong legs, a certified guide, and a reservation for a tent site you can enter the park on foot at three staffed ranger stations and spend up to five days deep in the wilds.

HIKING

There are two main hiking routes to Corcovado. When you're planning your itinerary, keep in mind that the hike between any two ranger stations takes at least a day. The hike from La Leona to Sirena is about 16 km (10 miles) and requires crossing a wide river mouth and a stretch of beach best negotiated at low tide. Some people plan this hike before dawn to avoid the blistering sun. The 25-km (15½-mile) route from Los Patos to Sirena is the coolest trail, through forest all the way.

71 reptile species live in the park, including the eyelash viper.

TOP REASONS TO GO

FLORA AND FAUNA

The sheer diversity of flora and fauna and the chance to see wildlife completely in the wild are the main draws here. The number of cataloged species, to date, includes 500 trees, 150 orchids, 375 birds, 124 mammals, 123 butterflies, 71 reptiles, 46 amphibians, and more than 8,000 insects.

OFF THE BEATEN TRACK

Day visitors get to taste the thrill of being completely off the beaten track, in an untamed natural world. But for campers at La Sirena and San Pedrillo stations, the chance to spend days roaming miles of trails without hearing a single man-made sound is a rare treat.

TEST YOUR LIMITS

The physical challenges of hiking in high humidity and living basically, along with the psychological challenge of being completely out of touch with "the real world," can be rewarding.

Visitors go south to heed the call of the wild. The jewels in the South Pacific crown are the idyllic Golfo Dulce and the wild Osa Peninsula, brimming with wildlife and natural adventures. There is no place like it, especially when you travel off the grid, far from the sounds of modern civilization. With miles of undulating Pacific coastline, there is rarely a crowded beach. Up in the highlands, the hiking and bird-watching are unsurpassed.

The South Pacific encompasses everything south of San José, down to the border with Panama, and all the territory west of the Talamanca Mountains, sloping down to the Pacific coast. Adventures abound in this rugged region. On land, hiking, bird-watching, horseback riding, and wildlife viewing are the main activities, along with some thrilling tree-climbing, ziplining, and waterfall-rappelling opportunities. On the water, there's surfing, snorkeling, diving, fishing, sea kayaking, and whale- and dolphin-watching, as well as swimming and beachcombing.

What makes many of these activities special is that, given the wildness of the locations, the focus is more on nature than on entertainment. No matter what you're doing, you'll come across interesting flora and fauna and natural phenomena. Another key to what sets this area apart is the large number of trained naturalist guides. Most ecolodges have resident guides who know not only where to find the birds and wildlife, but also how to interpret the hidden workings of the natural world around you.

The hiking in the south is simply spectacular, so don't leave home without your hiking boots. The most challenging hike in the country is Chirripó Mountain, a 6- to 10-hour haul up to the national-park hostel, a base camp for exploring surrounding peaks. Dramatic but less challenging hikes include the well-maintained, wide trails in the cool high-altitude forests of the Savegre Valley; the dramatic Coastal Path south of Drake; and forest trails to waterfalls and swimming holes in the Golfo Dulce, Osa Peninsula, and around Dominical.

MAJOR REGIONS
The most remote part of Costa Rica, the South Pacific encompasses the southern half of Puntarenas Province and La Amistad International Biosphere. The region

descends from mountainous forests just an hour south of San José to the humid Golfo Dulce and the richly forested Osa Peninsula, six to eight hours from the capital by car.

Famous for spectacular mountain vistas, high-altitude coffee farms, cloud-forest ecolodges, and challenging mountain hikes, the **Central Highlands** of Cerro de la Muerte are less than an hour south of San José, climbing up the Pan-American Highway.

The **Valle de El General** (the General's Valley) area encompasses vast expanses of highland wilderness on the upper slopes of the Talamanca mountains and the high-altitude páramo of Chirripó National Park, as well as prosperous agricultural communities amid vast, sunbaked fields of pineapple and sugarcane. It is bounded to the north and west by the central highlands of the massive Cordillera de Talamanca and to the south by La Amistad International Park.

On the other side of a mountain ridge, just a scenic hour-long drive west of San Isidro de El General, you reach the sunny southern Pacific coast, with its miles of beaches for surfing, strolling, kayaking, and snorkeling. In addition to surfer haven **Dominical, Ballena Marine National Park** alone encompasses almost 10 km (6 miles) of protected beaches. Scattered along the coast are small communities with increasing numbers of international residents and interesting restaurants and lodging options.

One of only three tropical fjords in the world, the **Golfo Dulce** has 600-foot-deep waters in the center of a usually placid gulf where you can watch dolphins swim and humpback whales feed. At Chacarita, 33 km (20 miles) south of Palmar Sur, the southern coast assumes a split personality. Heading west, you reach the Osa Peninsula and, eventually, the Pacific Ocean and the wildest region of Costa Rica. Continuing due south brings you to the

Golfo Dulce, which means "Sweet Gulf," reflecting the usually tranquil waters. This gulf creates two shorelines: an eastern shore that is accessible only by boat above Golfito, and a western shore, which is the eastern side of the Osa Peninsula. South of Golfito the coast fronts the Pacific Ocean once again (rather than the calm gulf), with wilder beaches that beckon surfers and nature lovers.

You'll find the country's most breathtaking scenery and most abundant wildlife on the **Osa Peninsula,** a third of which is protected by Corcovado National Park. And complementing the peninsula's lush forests and pristine beaches is the surrounding sea, with great fishing, snorkeling, diving, and some surfing. There are two sides to the Osa: the gentler Golfo Dulce side, much of it accessible by car, albeit along rough roads; and the much wilder and dramatic Pacific side, which is accessible only by boat, by plane, or by hiking a sublimely beautiful coastal trail.

Planning

When to Go

PEAK SEASON: JANUARY TO APRIL

The dry season has the most reliably sunny weather. But be aware that the climate swings wildly in the south, from bracing mountain air to steamy coastal humidity. In the mountains it's normally around 24°C (75°F) during the day and 10°C (50°F) at night. Temperatures can fall close to freezing on the upper slopes of Cerro de la Muerte and elsewhere, so be sure to pack warm layers. Temperatures in coastal areas are usually 24°C–32°C (76°F–90°F), but it's the humidity that does you in.

OFF-SEASON: SEPTEMBER TO DECEMBER

The rainy season can be very wet indeed, especially September through November. The wet season is longest in the Osa Peninsula, where showers usually last through January. Roads sometimes flood and many lodges close in the rainiest months (October and November). Elsewhere during the long rainy season, mornings tend to be brilliant and sunny, with refreshing rain starting in mid-afternoon. Many lodges offer discounted "green season" rates. Often, there is a two- or three-week period of dry weather with brilliant sunshine in late June into July, a mini-summer called *el veranillo*.

SHOULDER SEASON: EARLY DECEMBER AND APRIL TO MAY

Early December, when the landscape is lush and green after months of rain and crowds of tourists have yet to arrive, can be delightful in most of the Southern Zone. April into May is another good time to visit, when crowds have thinned out and the rains are just starting to freshen up the landscape.

Planning Your Time

You need at least a week to truly experience any part of the Osa Peninsula. Even if you fly, ground transportation to your lodge may be painfully slow, so plan two days for travel alone. It's best to choose one base and take day trips from there. In three weeks, you can experience the entire region, including mountains, beaches, and the Osa Peninsula.

If you are driving south, keep in mind that Cerro de la Muerte is often covered with fog in the afternoon, so plan to cross the mountains in the morning. This mountain road has been much improved, but it's safer—not to mention more scenic—to drive it in dry, clear weather. More and more visitors take the coastal highway these days, but they miss out on the dramatic mountain vistas.

Don't try to cover too much ground on a set schedule. It is simply impossible to overestimate how long it takes to drive a certain route or make transportation connections in this part of the country, especially during rainy season, when flooding and landslides can close roads and bad weather can delay flights. But remember, getting there is part of the adventure.

Getting Here and Around

AIR

Costa Rica's domestic airline, SANSA, has direct flights from San José to Puerto Jiménez, Drake Bay, and Golfito. Their small planes hold 14 to 19 passengers.

BUS

Bus fares from San José average about $10, depending on distance and number of stops. The best way to get around the region's roads is by bus—let someone else do the driving. Bus fares are cheap, and you'll meet the locals. But the going is generally slow, departures are often very early in the morning, and schedules change so frequently that you'll want to confirm the day before you travel.

Based in Dominical, Monkey Ride has large, air-conditioned shuttle-van services in each direction between San José and the Dominical/Uvita/Ojochal area starting at $60 per person.

BUS CONTACT Monkey Ride. ⊠ *Main St., Pueblo del Río, Dominical* ☎ *2787–0454* ⊕ *www.monkeyridecr.com.*

CAR

Driving in the southern reaches of the South Pacific can be rough, especially in rainy season. If you decide to drive, make sure your vehicle has 4WD, high clearance, and a spare tire. Give yourself lots of daylight time to get to where you're going (the sun sets around 5:30). You can also fly to Golfito or the Osa Peninsula and rent a 4WD vehicle. The Southern Zone was the very last part of Costa Rica to be settled, and the first road from San José to San Isidro wasn't begun until the 1950s.

Health and Safety

You are more likely to suffer from dehydration than any other health issue. Carry plenty of water wherever you go, wear a hat, and use sturdy hiking boots and long pants when hiking trails where biting insects may strike or the occasional snake might be sleeping in the sun. Do not leave any valuables in your car or your room—always put them in the safe provided by your hotel or lodge.

Money Matters

ATMs are sprouting up everywhere in the Southern Zone. The places you won't find a bank are remote communities, for example the beaches south of Golfito on the mainland, or in Drake Bay and lodges south of Puerto Jiménez.

Restaurants

Count on finding lots of fresh fish and tropical fruits on the menu, whether at a roadside *soda* (casual eatery) serving *comida típica* (typical food) or a sophisticated restaurant in Dominical or Ojochal. Up in the mountains, don't miss out on eating fresh, farmed trout. The food at most remote ecolodges is excellent.

Hotels

Expect reasonable comfort in unbelievably wild settings. Most accommodations are in small hotels, lodges, and cabins run by hands-on owners, many of them foreigners who fell in love with the country during a vacation here and stayed. Generally speaking, the farther south and more remote the lodge, the more expensive it is. Bad roads (causing supply problems) and lack of electricity and communications make hotel-keeping costly, especially in the Osa Peninsula and Golfo Dulce, where a fresh egg can cost up to a dollar. When comparing per-person prices, take into account that most of these places include meals, transport, guides, and unique locations.

The country's premier ecolodges are almost all in the Southern Zone, ranging from simple tents to sophisticated lodges. But keep in mind that if you yearn to be close to nature, you have to be prepared for encounters of the natural kind in your shower or bedroom. Keep a flashlight handy for nighttime trips to the bathroom and always wear shoes.

HOTEL AND RESTAURANT PRICES

Restaurant prices are the average cost of a main course at dinner or, if dinner is not served, at lunch. Hotel prices are the lowest cost of a standard double room in high season. Restaurant and hotel reviews have been shortened. For full information, visit Fodors.com.

What it Costs in U.S. Dollars			
$	$$	$$$	$$$$
RESTAURANTS			
under $10	$10–$15	$16–$25	over $25
HOTELS			
under $75	$75–$150	$151–$250	over $250

Tours

Costa Rica Expeditions

ECOTOURISM | The most experienced ecotourist outfit in Costa Rica specializes in customizing countrywide nature tours led by expert, bilingual, local naturalist guides. ☎ 2521–6099 ⊕ www.costaricaexpeditions.com ✉ From $250 per person, per day.

Horizontes Nature Tours

ECOTOURISM | This expert ecotourist company arranges small-group and custom tours with naturalist guides and ornithologists, including nature-photography tours. They can also offer guided day trips to Corcovado National Park, cultural tours in Puerto Jiménez, or volunteer opportunities with a sea turtle rescue organization. ☎ 2222–2022, 888/786–8748 toll-free in U.S. ⊕ www.horizontes.com ✉ From $1,500.

Traveling with Kids

The Southern Zone is like Outward Bound for families, where kids and parents can face challenges (such as no TVs or video games!) and have fun together. Plunge the family into real-life adventures with added educational value. You might inspire a future herpetologist or marine biologist among your progeny.

Go horseback riding to waterfalls and swimming holes. Steal into the night with infrared flashlights to scout out frogs and other fascinating, nocturnal creepy-crawlies. Paddle a kayak in a calm gulf where dolphins play. Rappel down a waterfall, climb inside a hollow tree, or zipline through the canopy.

The more remote areas of the south are ideal for kids ages seven and up. Babies and all their paraphernalia are hard to handle here, and toddlers are tough to keep off the ground where biting insects and snakes live.

Visitor Information

There aren't many official tourist offices in the south. The Dominical Information Center is a great source for everything from bus schedules to maps to tour arrangements. There is also a hard-to-find, official government tourist office in Río Claro, en route to Golfito. Always ask for recommendations from your hosts.

Lodge and hotel owners know their turf and they want happy guests, so they are unlikely to steer you astray.

Zona de Los Santos

Santa María de Dota is 65 km (40 miles) south of San José.

Empalme, at Km 51 of the Pan-American Highway, marks the turnoff for Santa María de Dota, the first of the picturesque coffee-growing towns, named after saints, that dot this mountainous area known as the Zona de Los Santos (Zone of the Saints). The route itself is about 24 km (15 miles) long.

GETTING HERE AND AROUND

From San José, drive southeast on the paved Pan-American Highway, heading toward Cartago, then follow the signs south for San Isidro de El General. The two-lane road climbs steeply, and there are almost no safe places to pass heavy trucks and slow vehicles, but the views are worth it. Make an early start, because the road is often enveloped in mist and rain in the afternoon. It typically takes about 90 minutes to reach Km 51, where you turn right at Empalme to reach Santa María de Dota, 14 km (8½ miles) along a wide, curving, paved road.

Sights

Ruta de Los Santos (*Route of the Saints*)
SCENIC DRIVE | The scenic road that winds through the high-altitude valleys from Empalme to San Pablo de León is appropriately called the Ruta de Los Santos—the towns it passes are named after saints. It's nicely paved to facilitate shipping the coffee produced in the region. On the 30-minute drive from Empalme to San Pablo de León Cortés, you travel through misty valleys ringed by precipitous mountain slopes terraced with lush, green coffee plants. The 24-km (15-mile) route also captures the

essence of a fast-disappearing traditional tico way of life built around agriculture. Stately churches anchor bustling towns full of prosperous, neat houses with pretty gardens and a few vintage 1970s Toyota Land Cruiser trucks parked in the driveways.

Restaurants

Café de Los Santos
$ | CAFÉ | This pretty café, within sight of the town's majestic church in San Marcos de Tarrazú, showcases the area's high-altitude arabica Tarrazú coffee, the "celestial drink" for which this zone is famous. **Known for:** homemade sweet and savory pastries; vintage photos of oxcarts and coffee harvests; 30 specialty coffee drinks. ⓢ *Average main: $5* ✉ *San Marcos de Tarrazú* ⊹ *6 km (4 miles) west of Santa María de Dota; 200 meters (656 feet) east of church* ☎ *2546–7881* ☉ *Closed Sun.*

Mutute Café Boutique Tarrazú
$ | COSTA RICAN | A giant, colorful *chorreador,* the traditional wooden stand for making coffee with a socklike filter, marks the spot for this tiny but sophisticated café, a showplace for the award-winning, high-altitude coffee from the nearby Tarrazú coffee region. Watch baristas expertly concoct flavorful espresso and cappuccino, complete with artistic swirls in the milk foam. **Known for:** handsome packages of coffee to buy; easy parking; homemade fig cake. ⓢ *Average main: $5* ✉ *Empalme, Km 51, Pan-American Hwy.* ☎ *2571–2323.*

Hotels

Toucanet Lodge
$$ | B&B/INN | FAMILY | For serenity and mountain greenery, you can't beat this lodge in a secluded valley with panoramic views and the opportunity to see hummingbirds and some of the 200-plus highland species on the lodge's list, including the resplendent quetzal.

Pros: fresh mountain air; seclusion and tranquility; excellent birding trails. **Cons:** bumpy dirt-road access; some steps to climb to cabins; simple furnishings. ⓢ *Rooms from: $84* ✉ *Hwy. 315, 7 km (4½ miles) east of Santa María de Dota, Copey* ⊹ *To get here from Pan-American Hwy., turn at sign for Copey and follow scenic dirt road 8 km (5 miles)* ☎ *2541–3045* ⊕ *www.toucanetlodge.com* ⇥ *8 rooms* ☉| *Free Breakfast.*

Shopping

Coopedota Santa Maria
FOOD | The best place to buy local coffee is where 800 farmers bring their raw coffee beans to be roasted and packed into jute bags at the first carbon-neutral coffee producer in the world. You can buy three dozen different coffee beverages and export-quality coffee at the café shop for about $10 per pound (about half the price you'll pay at the airport). Choose between light or dark roast and *en grano* (whole bean) or *molido* (ground). A variety of tours are offered (from $35), covering everything from processing to tasting to the cooperative's innovative recycling. Check out the website for details of tours or email to make reservations. ✉ *C. Ctl., Santa María de Dota* ☎ *2541–2827 for coffee tour, 2541–0102 café* ⊕ *www.coopedota.com.*

San Gerardo de Dota

89 km (55 miles) southeast of San José, 52 km (32 miles) south of Santa María de Dota.

Cloud forests, invigorating mountain air, well-maintained hiking trails, and excellent bird-watching make San Gerardo de Dota one of Costa Rica's premier nature destinations. The tiny hamlet is in the narrow Savegre River valley, 9 km (5½ miles) down a twisting, partially paved track that descends abruptly to the west from the Pan-American Highway. The peaceful surroundings look more like the Rocky Mountains than Central America, but hike down the waterfall trail and the vegetation quickly turns tropical again. Beyond hiking and bird-watching, activities include horseback riding and ziplining.

GETTING HERE AND AROUND

The drive from San José takes about three hours, and from Santa María de Dota about an hour. At Km 80 on the Pan-American Highway, turn down the dirt road signed "San Gerardo de Dota." It's a harrowing, twisting road with signs warning drivers to gear down and go slow. Some newly paved sections help ease the steepest curves. Tourist vans often stop along the road when the guides spot birds; grab your binoculars and discreetly join them!

🍴 Restaurants

Kahawa

$ | **COSTA RICAN** | Perched on the boulder-strewn bank of the rushing Savegre River, this handsome blond-wood-and-stone rancho specializes in serving up fresh trout in myriad ways at riverside tables, perfect for bird-watching. If you're not a fan of fish, try the *kuku tamu*, a chicken breast sandwich with *chiverre* (black seed squash) preserve, red onion, fresh cheese, mustard, and arugula. **Known for:** trout fillet with coconut sauce; homemade desserts; fried trout tacos. [$] *Average main: $9* ✉ *San Gerardo de Dota, San Gerardo* ✣ *From Pan-American Hwy. at Km 80, about 8 km (5 miles) down steep road to San Gerardo de Dota* ☎ *2740–1081* 🌐 *kahawa.co* 🕒 *No dinner.*

🛏 Hotels

★ **Dantica Lodge and Gallery**

$$$ | **B&B/INN** | High style at high altitude, this avant-garde lodge clinging to the side of a mountain has unbeatable valley views, great bird-watching, luxury accommodations, a sophisticated restaurant, and the top ecological sustainability rating. **Pros:** superior rooms have whirlpool bathtubs; top-notch Latin American craft gallery; excellent restaurant. **Cons:** some casitas close to road; high altitude; steep, narrow trails to forest casitas. [$] *Rooms from: $159* ✉ *Road to San Gerardo de Dota, 4 km (2 miles) west of Pan-American Hwy., San Gerardo* ☎ *2740–1067* 🌐 *www.dantica.com* 🛏 *12 rooms* 🍴 *Free Breakfast.*

Paraíso Quetzal Lodge

$$ | **B&B/INN** | A paradise for resplendent quetzals, this rustic but comfortable lodge is amid cloud-enshrouded mountains and valleys with 16 km (10 miles) of hiking and birding trails through ancient oak forests dripping with moss and epiphytes. **Pros:** cozy, heated cabins with modern bathrooms; nature photographer's outdoor studio; excellent espresso. **Cons:** steep paths to some cabins; very cold nights; very simple food. [$] *Rooms from: $83* ✉ *Km 70, Pan-American Hwy., Cerro de la Muerte* ☎ *2200–0241, 8810–0234* 🌐 *www.paraisoquetzal.com* 🛏 *14 rooms* 🍴 *No Meals.*

★ **Savegre Hotel, Natural Reserve & Spa**

$$$ | **B&B/INN** | Famous for miles of bird-watching trails and expert guides, this lodge has comfortable, spacious rooms with two double beds and modern bathrooms, some with bathtubs, set in colorful, bird-attracting gardens. **Pros:** room heaters and fireplaces; weekday rates from $85; pleasant riverside spa. **Cons:** different menus for all-inclusive guests; many tour groups; steep trails and high altitude may tax some visitors. [$] *Rooms from: $165* ✉ *C. San Gerardo, Km 80, Pan-American Hwy., San Gerardo* ✣ *Take very steep road for 9 km (5½ miles) to hotel entrance, a bridge over Río Savegre* ☎ *2740–1028* 🌐 *www.savegre.com* 🛏 *50 rooms* 🍴 *Free Breakfast.*

A male white-throated mountain-gem hummingbird flying next to a bromelia.

Trogón Lodge
$$$ | B&B/INN | FAMILY | Set in a riotous garden filled with fuchsias, hydrangeas, and hummingbirds, Trogón Lodge is more picturesque hideaway than hiking-heavy destination. **Pros:** picturesque garden and river setting; convivial public areas; small but excellent gift shop. **Cons:** shared verandas; can be noisy with families; steep, short trails that end at road. [$] *Rooms from: $154* ✉ *San Gerardo de Dota, San Gerardo* ✛ *At Km 80 on Pan-American Hwy., follow very steep, partially paved road down 7½ km (4½ miles)* ☎ *2740–1051 lodge, 2293–8181 for reservations only* ⊕ *www.trogonlodge.com* ⇱ *25 rooms* ❂❘ *Free Breakfast.*

 Activities

BIRD-WATCHING
Although you can see many birds from your cabin porch and viewing platform, most bird-watching requires hiking, some of it along steep paths made extra challenging by the high altitude (from 7,000 to 10,000 feet above sea level). Come fit and armed with binoculars and layers of warm clothing. The early mornings are brisk up here, but you'll warm up quickly with the sun and the exertion of walking.

★ Savegre Hotel, Natural Reserve & Spa
BIRD WATCHING | With the best bird guides in the area, including veteran birder Marino Chacon ($120 for a half day), this hotel organizes the best highland birding and hiking tours in the oak forests and surrounding mountains. For nature photographers, the Batsú Garden ($25) is an outdoor studio with battery-charging facilities for cameras and computers, perched on a hillside garden overlooking a bird-friendly orchard. ✉ *Savegre Hotel, Natural Reserve & Spa, Km 80, Pan-American Hwy., San Gerardo* ☎ *2740–1028* ⊕ *www.savegre.com.*

Tropical Feathers
BIRD WATCHING | Guided by Noel and Carlos Ureña, expert birders with 20 years of experience, Tropical Feathers offers multiday bird-watching packages and arranges customized tours, including wildlife-photography tours, in the San

Isidro de El General and Dominical area, as well as the entire country. Half-day birding tours start at $100 for two people; $150 including transportation. Check the website for excellent photos and bird lore. ☎ 2771–9686 ⊕ www.costaricabirdingtours.com.

HIKING

Some of the best hiking in the country is in this valley.

Savegre Hotel, Natural Reserve & Spa

HIKING & WALKING | This world-renowned bird-watching hotel runs a daylong, guided, natural-history hike that starts with a drive up to the páramo (high-altitude ecosystem) of Cerro de la Muerte. The trail descends through oak forest into the valley. Miles of prime bird-watching and hiking trails wind through the private forest reserve. Night temperatures on the slopes of Cerro de la Muerte can approach freezing. Pack accordingly for cold mornings. ⊠ Savegre Hotel, Natural Reserve & Spa, C. San Gerardo, San Gerardo ☎ 2740–1028 ⊕ www.savegre.com ☎ $150 per person, including transportation.

San Isidro de El General

54 km (34 miles) south of San Gerardo de Dota.

Although San Isidro de El General has no major attractions, the bustling market town is a good place to have lunch, get cash at one of the many ATMs, or fill your tank—the main highway into town is lined with service stations, some operating 24 hours. Advice to map readers: there are other San Isidros in Costa Rica, but this is the only San Isidro de El General. Just to confuse matters more, this town also goes by the name Peréz Zeledón. The town is the jumping-off point for hiking the scenic highlands around San Gerardo de Rivas, and climbing the country's highest peak, Mt. Chirripó. There's also excellent bird-watching

in nearby nature reserves, including the original homestead, now a museum, of famed ornithologist Alexander Skutch.

GETTING HERE AND AROUND

The Pan-American Highway takes you straight into San Isidro de El General. It's 129 km (80 miles) south of San José and about 1½ hours' drive south of the San Gerardo de Dota highway exit. Truck traffic can be heavy and painfully slow. For folks in a hurry, there's a daily 35-minute SANSA flight from San José to the San Isidro airstrip, leaving San José at 7:55 am and returning at 8:40 am. Buses to Dominical leave from the San Isidro de El General bus terminal, southeast of the cathedral, near the Pan-American Highway. Buses bound for San Gerardo de Rivas, the starting point of the trail into Chirripó National Park, depart from San Isidro de El General at 5:30 am from the central park and at 2 pm from a stop at the central market.

ESSENTIALS

BANKS/ATMS ATH Coopealianza. ⊠ South side of central park beside Hotel Chirripó, San Isidro ☎ 4800–2000. **Banco Nacional.** ⊠ North side of central park, San Isidro ☎ 2212–2000.

HOSPITAL Hospital Escalante Pradilla. ⊠ Off main street, east of municipal stadium, San Isidro ☎ 2785–0700.

PHARMACY Farmacia Santa Marta. ⊠ Northwest of central park, across from cultural center, San Isidro ☎ 8937–6628.

POST OFFICE Correo. ⊠ From southeast corner of central park, 1 block south, San Isidro.

Sights

Centro Biológico Las Quebradas

(Las Quebradas Biological Center)
NATURE PRESERVE | **FAMILY** | In a lush valley 7 km (4½ miles) northeast of San Isidro de El General, this community-managed nature reserve protects 1,853 acres of dense forest in which elegant tree ferns

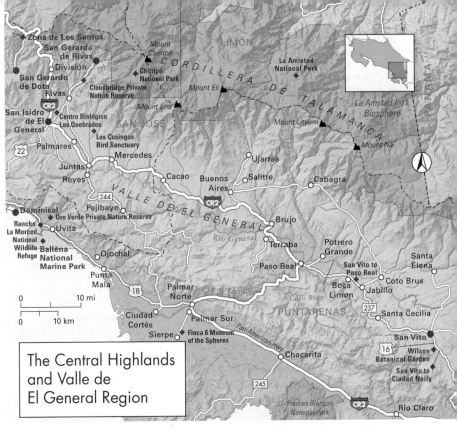

The Central Highlands and Valle de El General Region

grow in the shadows of massive trees, and colorful tanagers and euphonias flit about the foliage. Five kilometers (3 miles) of trails wind uphill through the forest and along the Río Quebradas, which supplies water to San Isidro de El General and surrounding communities. There's also an easily accessible sensory garden, with plants to smell and taste, and a butterfly garden. To get here from the Pan-American Highway, head 7 km (4½ miles) northeast at the sign for Las Quebradas. The reserve is 2 km (1 mile) north of town on an unpaved road. ⊠ Off Pan-American Hwy., 7 km (4½ miles) northeast of San Isidro de El General, Quebradas ☎ 2771–4131 ⊕ www.fudebi-ol.com ☑ $4 ☖ Must have a reservation to visit weekends.

Los Cusingos Bird Sanctuary

HISTORIC HOME | This property contains birding trails and the house of the late Dr. Alexander Skutch, the region's preeminent ornithologist and coauthor of *A Guide to the Birds of Costa Rica*, the birders' ultimate companion. His 190-acre estate, an island of forest amid a sea of new farms and housing developments, is now run by the nonprofit Centro Científico Tropical (Tropical Science Center), which has improved 2 km (1 mile) of trails and maintains the simple house where Dr. Skutch lived—without electricity—from 1941 until his death in 2004, just a week shy of his 100th birthday. Room by room, the moldy books, piles of journals, vintage typewriter, and humble bedrooms and kitchen speak to Skutch's lifelong philosophy of simplicity. Among the 200 or so bird species that still visit the property are *cusingos* or fiery-billed araçaris—colorful, small members of the toucan family, for which the property is named—and mixed tanager flocks. The sanctuary is a half-hour's drive southeast of San Isidro de El General in the town of Quizarrá. Just show up, or call ahead if you want a guided tour. ✉ *15 km (10 miles) southeast of San Isidro de El General, Quizarrá* ⊕ *South on Pan-American Hwy., cross bridge over Río General and watch for small, blue Riserva Biológica sign on left, take that turn, through town of Peñas Blancas, past cemetery and watch for sign on right for Quizzará and Los Cusingos* ☎ *2738–2070* 🌐 *www.cct.or.cr* 🎫 *$17.*

Restaurants

El Trapiche de Nayo

$ | **COSTA RICAN** | **FAMILY** | The panoramic valley view is worth a stop at this rustic roadside restaurant that serves the kind of food Ticos eat at *turnos* (village fund-raising festivals), including *gallos,* thick tortillas cooked on a wood stove, which you stuff with cooked hearts of palm, root vegetables, or chicken in salsa. Some Saturdays, raw sugarcane is pressed in an antique mill and boiled in huge iron cauldrons. **Known for:** decent restrooms; homemade molasses-flavored fudge; mondongo (tripe soup). [$] *Average main: $9* ✉ *Pan-American Hwy., 6 km (4 miles) north of San Isidro de El General, San Isidro* ☎ *2771–7267, 8361–3652.*

Kafe de la Casa

$ | **COSTA RICAN** | As hip as it gets in downtown San Isidro, this café serves excellent cappuccino and homemade muffins or an all-day breakfast in a funky, retro-rustic atmosphere combining 1950s diner and tico country. There's also a full menu of meat and chicken dishes. **Known for:** healthy yogurt smoothies; cultural happenings; monster plate of bocas (snacks) to share. [$] *Average main: $9* ✉ *C. 4, Avda. 3, behind MUSOC bus station, San Isidro* ☎ *2770–4816* ⏲ *Closed Sun.*

Hotels

Hacienda Alta Gracia

$$$$ | **RESORT** | Aimed at very well-heeled equestrians, this breathtakingly luxurious resort high above the lush valley of the General River has a stable of 48 beautiful horses to groom and ride, capacious casitas, a sybaritic spa, two swimming pools, and sophisticated dining. **Pros:** high-tech TVs and computers in casitas; designer bathrooms; private airstrip. **Cons:** more suited to couples and teens than young children; need to be tech-savvy to operate all the in-room devices; long walks to casitas or wait for electric cart ferry. [$] *Rooms from: $629* ✉ *Santa Teresa de Cajón de Perez Zeledón, San Isidro* ⊕ *20 km (13 miles) south of San Isidro de El General on Pan-American Hwy., then left onto Cajón road about 10 km (6 miles)* ☎ *2105–3000 hotel, 855/812–2212 toll-free* 🌐 *aubergeresorts.com/altagracia* 🛏 *50 rooms* 🍴 *Free Breakfast.*

Hotel Los Crestones

$ | **HOTEL** | Flowering hedges make this pleasant and affordable motel feel homey, even though it's near the sometimes-noisy stadium (the quietest rooms are Nos. 18 to 27). **Pros:** affordable prices; close to downtown; gated property, secure parking, and easy wheelchair access. **Cons:** some rooms lack A/C; breakfast not included; noisy rooms at the front. [$] *Rooms from: $65* ✉ *Road to Dominical, southwest side of stadium, San Isidro* ☎ *2770–1200* 🌐 *www.hotel-loscrestones.com* 🛏 *27 rooms* 🍴 *No Meals.*

Activities

HIKING

The major tourist draw is climbing Mt. Chirripó (the highest peak is about 12,532 feet) in Chirripó National Park. There is a limit of 52 hikers in the park on any one day. The park closes the last two weeks of May, and the last weekend in February.

All lodging, food, and porter arrangements are now made by a local cooperative, **Consorcio Aguas Eternas** (⊕ *www. chirripo.org* ☎ *2742–5200*).

A system is in place to make reservations easier and hiking safer, with tour packages that include lodging before the hike, porters, guides, and accommodation in the park hut.

See Hotel de Montaña El Pelícano for details.

Alternatively, opt for a different hike in the surrounding area.

San Gerardo de Rivas

20 km (12½ miles) northeast of San Isidro.

Chirripó National Park is the main reason to venture to San Gerardo de Rivas, but if you aren't up for the physically challenging adventure of hiking up Chirripó it's still a wildly scenic place, reminiscent of the Himalayas, to spend a day or two. Spread over steep terrain at the end of the narrow valley of the boulder-strewn Río Chirripó, San Gerardo de Rivas has cool mountain air, excellent bird-watching, invigorating hiking trails, and ethereal views.

GETTING HERE AND AROUND

The good news is that most of the winding road from San Isidro de El General to San Gerardo de Rivas is paved. There are a few gravel patches and some steep, narrow stretches, however, so 4WD is recommended. Buses run twice a day from San Isidro.

Sights

Chirripó National Park

(*Parque Nacional Chirripó*)

TRAIL | The main attraction of this national park is Mt. Chirripó, the highest mountain in Costa Rica and a mecca for both hikers and serious summiteers. It's a 48-km (30-mile) round-trip hike, with an elevation gain of 6,890 feet to reach the hostel, and another 1,000 feet to reach the summit. You need to be very fit and acclimatize before setting out. The round-trip usually takes three days: one day to climb to the hostel, one day to explore the surrounding summits, and one day to descend.

With the number of hikers limited to 52 per day on the San Gerardo route, and only 15 hikers per week from the San Jerónimo trail, it's becoming an ever more exclusive experience to hike here. Lodging at the summit hut is set at $35 per night. Though the hostel is slightly more comfortable than it used to be, keep in mind that it is still fairly basic, with bunk beds and no hot water for showers. It's chilly at the top, so be sure to pack lots of layers. The maximum stay at the hostel is three days, two nights. Lodging and food service in the simple restaurant are arranged by Consorcio Aguas Eternas, which also can provide all the gear you need, from pillows, towels, and sleeping bags to porters to haul them. Depending on which of the various meal packages and local lodging before and after the hike you choose, prices for a hike start at about $250 per person. Porter fees are set at about $4 per kilo, and charged each way. The easiest way to arrange a hike is through one of the hotels that belong to the consortium, such as Hotel de Montaña El Pelícano, which can arrange all the details, from park reservation to lodging, food, and gear. ⊠ *Consorcio Aguas Eternas, Main street, south side of soccer field, San Gerardo* ☎ *2742–5200* ✉ *infochirriposervicios@gmail.com* 🖬 *$18 per day park fee; $35 per day for lodging in park, plus food* 🕙 *Closed 2 wks in Nov.*

Cloudbridge Private Nature Reserve

NATURE PRESERVE | **FAMILY** | This private nature reserve staffed by volunteers and a senior biologist has an easy trail to a waterfall, plus almost 12 km (8 miles) of river and ridge trails, including one trail that utilizes 4 km (2½ miles) of the Chirripó National Park trail. It's a pleasant alternative for hikers who aren't up to the challenge of Chirripó or haven't reserved a spot far in advance. You can take a guided 3½-hour tour past two waterfalls and learn about the flora and fauna of the cloud forest for $35. There's also an art gallery featuring nature paintings by artist Linda Moskalyk, and accommodations in four fully equipped houses (starting at $70, two-night minimum). Volunteers often occupy the simple rental cabins, so check the website for availability. There's no admission fee to hike in the reserve, but donations are requested. ✉ *2½ km (1½ miles) northeast of San Gerardo de Rivas, San Gerardo* ☎ *8856–5519* ⊕ *www.cloudbridge.org* 🍽 *By donation.*

 Restaurants

El Descanso

$$ | **CONTEMPORARY** | The kind of extraordinary restaurant you hope to stumble on in the most unlikely place, this intimate five-table wood-and-bamboo dining room is presided over by chef Esteban Acuña, whose family owns the attached small hotel. Drawing on his California training, Acuña gives local ingredients contemporary twists, flavored with herbs from the adjoining garden. **Known for:** creamy soups, cold and hot; chocolate volcano flourless cake; mushroom-and-herb-stuffed whole trout. $ *Average main: $12* ✉ *Hotel El Descanso, Hwy. 242, 5 mins north of Canáan, San Isidro* ☎ *2256–0304.*

Hotels

Hotel de Montaña El Pelícano

$ | **B&B/INN** | On a precipitous ridge, this modest wooden lodge is an affordable and comfortable launching pad for a hike up Chirripó, or a pleasant spot to relax and breathe in fresh mountain air and scenery and watch birds. **Pros:** official Chirripó hike operator; one-of-a-kind folk art museum; two pools, one designated for kids. **Cons:** very steep drive to hotel; friendly but slow service; smallish rooms in main lodge. $ *Rooms from: $72* ✉ *Main road, south of Chirripó National Park office, San Gerardo* ✛ *500 meters (1,640 feet) north of Canaan High School* ☎ *2742–5050* ⊕ *hotelpelicano.com* 🛏 *13 rooms* 🍽 *Free Breakfast.*

Río Chirripó Retreat

$$$ | **B&B/INN** | **FAMILY** | In one of the most beautiful mountain settings imaginable, this yoga-centric riverside lodge, reminiscent of a Himalayan temple, is pure pleasure, from the lush flower gardens to the sophisticated room design to the open-air yoga studio within sound of the rushing river. **Pros:** enchanting riverside setting; excellent breakfasts loaded with fresh fruits; room balconies with river views. **Cons:** yoga groups may dominate; smallish double rooms; no sit-down lunch. $ *Rooms from: $178* ✉ *San Gerardo de Rivas* ☎ *2742–5109* ⊕ *www.riochirripo. com* 🛏 *10 rooms* 🍽 *Free Breakfast.*

Activities

Costa Rica Trekking Adventures

HIKING & WALKING | Selva Mar runs tours around San Gerardo de Rivas, and will coordinate and guide a trip to Chirripó. For a four-day, three-night climb including basic lodging and all meals, it's $440 for one person or a hefty discount for two or more. ✉ *San Gerardo* ☎ *2771–4582* ⊕ *chirripo.com.*

San Vito

110 km (68 miles) southeast of San Isidro, 61 km (38 miles) northeast of Golfito.

Except for the tropical greenery, the rolling hills around the bustling hilltop town of San Vito could be mistaken for a Tuscan landscape. The town actually owes its 1952 founding to 200 Italian families who converted forest into coffee, fruit,

Gesneriaceae flowers

and cattle farms. A remnant of the Italian flavor lingers on in the statue dedicated to the *pioneros* standing proudly in the middle of town. San Vito today is a bustling agricultural market town, the center of the Coto Brus coffee region. Many coffee pickers are from the Guaymí indigenous group, who live in a large reserve nearby and also over the border in Panama. They're easy to recognize by the women's colorfully embroidered, long cotton dresses.

GETTING HERE AND AROUND

If you're driving south from San Isidro, your best route is along the wide, smooth Pan-American Highway via Buenos Aires to Paso Real, about 70 km (43 miles). Then take the scenic high road to San Vito, 40 km (25 miles) farther along. This road is paved and it's the most direct and prettiest route. Another route, which many buses take, is via Ciudad Neily, about 35 km (22 miles) northeast of Golfito, and then 24 km (15 miles) of winding steep road up to San Vito, at

almost 3,280 feet above sea level. There are direct buses from San José four times a day, and buses from San Isidro twice a day.

ESSENTIALS

Most of the banks in town have cash machines that accept foreign cards.

BANKS/ATMS ATH Coopealianza. ✉ *Center of town, 200 meters (656 feet) east of Catholic church and north of hospital, San Vito* ☎ *2773–3763.* **Banco Nacional.** ✉ *Across from south side of central park, San Vito* ☎ *2212–2000.*

HOSPITAL Hospital San Vito. ✉ *South of town, on road to Wilson Botanical Garden, San Vito* ☎ *2773–1100.*

PHARMACY Farmacia Assisi. ✉ *Center of town, main street, San Vito* ☎ *2773–5580.*

POST OFFICE Correo. ✉ *Far north end of town, beside police station, San Vito* ☎ *2773–3130.*

Sights

★ Wilson Botanical Garden

GARDEN | A must-see for gardeners and bird-watchers, the world-renowned Wilson Botanical Garden is enchanting even for those who are neither. Paths through the extensive grounds are lined with exotic plants and shaded by avenues of palm trees and 50-foot-high bamboo stalks. In 1961, U.S. landscapers Robert and Catherine Wilson bought 30 acres of coffee plantation and started planting tropical species, including palms, orchids, bromeliads, and heliconias. Today the property extends over 635 acres, and the gardens hold around 2,000 native and more than 3,000 exotic species. The palm collection—more than 700 species—is the second largest in the world. Fantastically shaped and colored bromeliads, which usually live in the tops of trees, have been brought down to the ground in impressive mass plantings, providing one of many photo opportunities. Guided walks are conducted at 7:30 am and 1:30 pm.

The garden was transferred to the Organization for Tropical Studies in 1973, and in 1983 it became part of Amistad Biosphere Reserve. Under the name Las Cruces Biological Station, Wilson functions mainly as a research and educational center, so there is a constant supply of expert botanists and biologists to take visitors on natural-history tours in the garden and the adjoining forest trails. Birders can hike to the new canopy tower in the forest, funded by the local San Vito Birding Club, to get up to eye level with birds in the treetops. Twice a month, members of the San Vito Bird Club lead free birding tours of the garden, complete with binoculars and field guides to share. Check 🌐 *www.sanvitobirdclub.org* for the bird-walk schedule. If you spend a night at the garden lodge, you have the garden all to yourself in the late afternoon and early morning, when wildlife is most active. Guests also have access to the Río Java trail, where monkeys abound. ✉ *Road to Ciudad Neily, 6 km (4 miles) south of San Vito, San Vito* ☎ *2773–4004* 🌐 *www.tropicalstudies.org* 🎫 *Guided tour from $34 per person.*

Restaurants

Pizzería Liliana

$$ | **ITALIAN** | **FAMILY** | At the classiest restaurant in town you can treat yourself to authentic pizza made from all-natural ingredients, or dig into the macaroni *sanviteña* style: with white sauce, ham, and mushrooms. The classics are here as well, and they're all homemade—lasagna, cannelloni, and ravioli—as well as hearty chicken and meat dishes. **Known for:** kids menu; one of the few places open late; generous portions. [$] *Average main: $11* ✉ *San Vito* ✥ *500 meters (1,640 feet) west of central square, up short hill* ☎ *2773–3080.*

Hotels

Cascata del Bosco Hotel

$$ | **B&B/INN** | Just 200 meters (656 feet) from the entrance to Wilson Botanical Garden, this collection of four totally private, round bungalows, set amid gardens and forest teeming with birds, is designed for nature lovers. **Pros:** close to Wilson Botanical Garden; attractive cabins; affordable and consistent rates. **Cons:** not a lot of parking; bar can be noisy on weekends; no phones in rooms. [$] *Rooms from: $75* ✉ *Las Cruces* ✥ *200 meters (656 feet) from entrance to Wilson Botanical Garden* ☎ *2773–3208* 🌐 *www.cascatadelbosco.com* 🛏 *4 rooms* 🍴 *Free Breakfast.*

★ Wilson Botanical Garden

$$$ | **B&B/INN** | The best features of the dozen comfortable rooms here, in three modern buildings built of glass, steel, and wood, are the private balconies cantilevered over a forested ravine, perfect for bird-watching. **Pros:** 24-hour access to botanical garden and nature trails;

En Route

San Vito to Ciudad Neily. The 33-km (21-mile), recently paved road from San Vito to Ciudad Neily is twisting and spectacular, with views over the Coto Colorado plain to the Golfo Dulce and Osa Peninsula beyond. You can stop halfway at **Mirador La Torre** to enjoy excellent fruit*naturales* (fruit juice) and the view from their counter stools. Watch out for some tricky curves where there are no guardrails. ✉ *San Vito.*

San Vito to Paso Real. The paved, scenic road from San Vito to Paso Real travels along a high ridge with sweeping valley views on either side. Halfway between Boca Limón and Las Vueltas, stop to enjoy a *refresco* and the views at open-air **Restaurante La Carreta.** As the road descends, the wide valley of El General River opens up before you, planted with miles of spiky pineapples and tall sugarcane. Few passing opportunities require a lot of patience, especially in the valley if you find yourself caught in a slow-moving convoy of trucks hauling pineapple and sugarcane. ✉ *San Vito.*

excellent birding and wildlife viewing; chance to meet researchers. **Cons:** modest rooms; possible noise from adjoining terraces; family-style meals served on a strict schedule. [$] *Rooms from: $188* ✉ *Las Cruces Biological Station, Road to Ciudad Neily, 6 km (4 miles) south of San Vito, San Vito* ☎ *2524–0607 Organization for Tropical Studies office in San José, 2773–4004 Wilson Botanical Garden reception* 🌐 *tropicalstudies.org/portfolio/las-cruces-research-station* 🛏 *12 rooms* 🍴 *All-Inclusive.*

Dominical

34 km (21 miles) southwest of San Isidro, 40 km (25 miles) south of Quepos.

Sleepy fishing village–turned–surfer town, Dominical has undergone a lively makeover, with a paved beach road, new restaurants and shops, and a farmers' market on Friday morning. As more and more luxury villas pop up all over the hillsides above the beaches, you're likely to find the private-jet set rubbing elbows with the bohemian hippie crowd. It's still a major surfing destination, attracting surfers of all ages, with a lively restaurant and nightlife scene. Favorite local hangouts come and go, so don't hesitate to try something new.

Dominical's real magic lies beyond the town, in the surrounding terrestrial and marine wonders: the rain forest grows right up to the beach in some places, and the ocean offers world-class surfing.

Much of the lush forest that covers the steep hillsides above the beaches is protected within private nature reserves. Several of these reserves, such as Hacienda Barú, protect significant tracts of the rain forest.

GETTING HERE AND AROUND

The paved road west over the mountains and down to Dominical is scenic at its best and fog-shrouded at its worst. There are lots of curves and a few dicey landslide areas, so take your time and enjoy the scenery along the hour-long drive from San Isidro de El General. From Quepos, the paved Costanera Highway makes for an easy half-hour drive to Dominical, although you do have to contend with huge transport trucks barreling along. Buses from San Isidro de El General leave six times a day, three times a day from Quepos. If you want to avoid driving altogether, Monkey Ride has air-conditioned vans with room for six to eight passengers that make trips to and from San José (starting at $49). There's an ATM in the Pueblo del Río center; if you need a full-service bank, the nearest is in Uvita.

RENTAL CARS Solid Car Rental. ✉ *Hwy. 34, Uvita, Dominical* ✛ *Across the street from the Sandias de Colonia grocery store* ☎ *2442–6000 San José office, 800/390–7065 in the U.S., 8898–5415 cell in Uvita* ⊕ *www.solidcarrental.com.*

TOURS

Costa Rica Dive and Surf

ADVENTURE TOURS | This outfit offers inshore dives in Ballena Marine National Park ($99) or around Caño Island ($175), as well as Caño Island snorkeling tours including lunch ($130), plus surf lessons ($50 for a two-hour lesson, max three persons). Boats and dive equipment are in a new facility in Uvita. ✉ *Main street, Dominical* ✛ *20 meters (65 feet) south of church* ☎ *2743–8679* ⊕ *www.costaricadiveandsurf.com.*

Dominical Adventures

ADVENTURE TOURS | As well as surfing lessons, this operator organizes Class II and III white-water rafting trips on the Guabo or Savegre River ($100), and more challenging Class III and IV rafting on the Coto Brus River ($125). Sea and mangrove kayak tours are available for $65. Gentler tube floats down the Barú River are $60 per person. Check the website for a daily surf report. A private learn-to-surf lesson is $70. ✉ *Main street, across from Pueblo del Río, Dominical* ☎ *8897–9540* ⊕ *www.dominicaladventures.com.*

Pineapple Kayak Tours

ADVENTURE TOURS | Catering to kayakers and paddleboarders of all ages and skill levels, this outfit takes you paddling through mangroves, past Playa Ballena's Whale's tail, and in the Ventanas caves. Tours start at $60 per person. ✉ *Main street, Dominical* ✛ *Next to police station* ☎ *8873–3283* ⊕ *www.pineapplekayaktours.com.*

VISITOR INFORMATION

Along with providing free bus schedules and town maps, Dominical Information is a reliable, all-in-one information center that arranges adventure tours on, over, and under the water, along with horse tours, ziplines, and rappelling down waterfalls. You can take an ATV tour to a hidden waterfall.

CONTACTS Dominical Information. ✉ *Pueblo del Río, Main street, Dominical* ☎ *2787–0454, 323/285–8832 in the U.S.* ⊕ *www.dominicalinformation.com.*

 # Sights

★ Hacienda Barú

WILDLIFE REFUGE | FAMILY | This leading eco-tourism and conservation wildlife refuge offers spectacular bird-watching tours and excellent naturalist-led hikes (starting at $36), a thrilling Flight of the Toucan canopy tour ($52), a chance to spend the night in the jungle ($158), or self-guided walks along forest and mangrove trails ($15). The refuge also manages a turtle-protection project and nature-education program in the local school. You can stay in basic cabins or in poolside rooms—or just come for the day. ✉ *Costanera Hwy., 3 km (2 miles) north of Dominical, Dominical* ☎ *2787–0003* ⊕ *www.haciendabaru.com* ✉ *From $15.*

★ Nauyaca Waterfalls

WATERFALL | FAMILY | This massive double cascade, the longer one tumbling down 150 feet, is one of the most spectacular sights in Costa Rica. The falls (aka Barú River Falls) are on private property, so the only ways to reach them are on horseback, hiking, or riding in an open truck. Arrive before 1 pm as access to the waterfalls closes at 2 pm. ✉ *Hwy. to San Isidro de El General, 10 km (7 miles) northeast of Dominical, Dominical* ✛ *On the road to Platanillo* ☎ *2787–0541, 6280–1790* ⊕ *nauyacawaterfallscostarica.com* ✉ *$10 to hike.*

Nauyaca waterfalls is a three-tier waterfall and well worth the visit.

Parque Reptilandia

WILDLIFE REFUGE | FAMILY | With more than 300 specimens, this impressive collection includes snakes, lizards, frogs, turtles, and other reptilian creatures, housed in visitor-friendly terrariums and large enclosures. Stars of the exhibit are a Komodo dragon, Gila monsters, and a 150-pound African spur-thighed tortoise that likes to be petted. Kids love the maternity ward showcasing newborn snakes. More mature snakes live under a retractable roof that lets in sun and rain. Although snakes are generally more active in sunlight, this is still a great rainy-day activity. Guided night tours can also be arranged to watch nocturnal animals. If you're not squeamish, snake-feeding day is Friday, spread out from 10 am to 3 pm. ⊠ *Road to San Isidro, 11 km (7 miles) east of Dominical, Dominical* ☎ *8308–8855* ⊕ *www.crreptiles.com* ⊠ *$12.*

Poza Azul

WATERFALL | FAMILY | Hidden in a forest above Dominicalito Beach, this waterfall is considerably smaller than Nauyaca Waterfalls, but it has a lovely swimming hole at its base. The pool is often populated by local kids when school is out and by surfers late in the afternoon. Pay strict attention to the posted sign that warns not to leave anything of value in your parked car. Avoid holiday times and weekends, when there are often large crowds. The best time to visit is during rainy season between the months of June and December. ⊠ *Dominical* ⊹ *Off the main hwy., turn left past the Dominicalito soccer field and through a stream; follow the road straight uphill for about 300 meters (984 feet) to where the road widens. (If the stream is too high to cross, go back to the highway and drive south to the next left turn, where there's a bus stop, and go through a small village, over the new bridge, then turn right up the mountain for 300 meters [984 feet]).*

Beaches

Playa Dominical

BEACH | Long and flat, Playa Dominical is good for beachcombing among all the flotsam and jetsam that the surf washes up onto the brown sand. There's shade and parking under palm trees along the new brick-paved road that parallels the beach. The water is relatively clean and local businesses make sure things look tidy. Photo opportunities abound here, with buff surfers riding the waves and vendors' clotheslines of colorful sarongs flapping in the sea breeze. Tortilla Flats restaurant is practically on the beach. Huge waves and dangerous rip currents make it primarily a surfing beach. In high season, flags mark off a relatively safe area for swimming, under the watchful gaze of a professional lifeguard. **Amenities:** food and drink; lifeguards; parking (no fee). **Best for:** surfing; walking. ✉ *Dominical.*

Playa Dominicalito

BEACH | This wide beach is usually calmer and more suited to boogie boarding and beginner surfers. There are hidden rocks near the shore, so the best time to swim is at low tide. This is one of the best walking beaches, with lots of shade under tall palms and beach almond trees early in the morning. The sun sets behind a huge rocky outcropping topped with tiny palm trees, an ideal shot for photographers. There is an unofficial campground running parallel to the beach, which is popular with locals, especially during Easter, Christmas, and school holidays. **Amenities:** parking (no fee). **Best for:** solitude; sunset; walking. ✉ *Dominical* ✥ *About 1 km (½ mile) south of Playa Dominical.*

Restaurants

Cafe Mono Congo

$ | VEGETARIAN | Pull up a counter stool or sit at a table on the popular riverside terrace at this friendly café with creative vegetarian and gluten-free dishes, organic juices, local and imported craft beers on tap, kombuchas, and herbal teas. Desserts are not only gluten-free, they are addictive: the chocolate papaya pie combines dark chocolate with papaya to make a rich mousse filling for a date, almond, and coconut crust. **Known for:** pineapple barbecue veggie burger; excellent organic coffee; quinoa bowl. [$] *Average main: $8* ✉ *Pueblo del Río, Main St., Dominical* ☎ *8485–5523, 6312–8766 WhatsApp, for ordering* 🌐 *cafemonocongo.com.*

Dominical Sushi

$$ | JAPANESE | With a view over the Barú estuary, this open-air Japanese restaurant serves local seafood in all the usual rolls and sashimi, with some tropical twists, plus imported Sapporo beer, sake, or green tea. Dark bamboo furniture, Japanese lanterns, and colored globes set the modern, minimalist scene, while smooth, jazzy music sets a cool mood. **Known for:** ahi poke salad with raw tuna; cool jazz soundtrack; tico shrimp roll with mango. [$] *Average main: $12* ✉ *Pueblo del Río, Main street, Dominical* ☎ *7018–9935* 🌐 *www.dominicalsushi.com.*

El Pescado Loco

$ | SEAFOOD | Beer-battered onion rings, fresh hand-cut fries, and fried pickles have taken Dominical by storm at this laid-back alfresco kiosk in the Pueblo del Río complex on the riverfront. The fish tacos are outstanding—crispy beer-battered fish fillets accompanied by guacamole, red cabbage, and a spicy sauce are folded into a thin soft tortilla. **Known for:** beer-battered mushroom tacos; gluten-free tortillas; outstanding fish tacos. [$] *Average main: $8* ✉ *Pueblo del Río,*

Main street, Dominical ☎ 717/877-9259 in U.S. ⊕ elpescadoloco.business.site ⊟ No credit cards ⊗ Closed Sun.

★ La Parcela

$$$ | **COSTA RICAN** | Picture a dream location: a high headland jutting out into the sea with vistas up and down the coast, and throw in a breeze-swept terrace, polished service, a boat-shape bar, and some fine seaside cuisine, and you are at La Parcela. The turquoise and white decor is reminiscent of Greece, the sunsets are spectacular, and shrimp and lobster dishes are pricey but excellent. **Known for:** grilled tuna with pasta; tres leches and vegan avocado pie; beer-battered fish tacos. $ Average main: $17 ⊠ 4 km (2½ miles) south of Dominical, off Costanera Hwy., Dominical ☎ 2787–0016 ⊕ www.laparcelacr.com.

Phat Noodle

$$ | **INDONESIAN** | Spice up your day with skewers of Indonesian satays and generous bowls of peanutty pad Thai and red or green curry at this hip open-air caravansary under a high corrugated-metal green roof. The kitchen, in a gaily painted converted bus, turns out portions large enough to share. **Known for:** veggie spring rolls; happy hour specials from 2–6 daily; coconut ceviche. $ Average main: $14 ⊠ Main street, across the street from Pueblo del Río, Dominical ☎ 2787–0017 ⊕ www.phatnoodlecostarica.com.

Ricar2 Restaurant

$$ | **ECLECTIC** | **FAMILY** | This alfresco restaurant tucked beside a bona fide Boeing 727 (minus the engine) delivers generous portions of upscale pastas, succulent meats, and tasty fish and seafood, including Peruvian-style ceviches. During the day kids can frolic in the swimming pool and adults can order spicy tropical chicken wings. **Known for:** spicy chicken wings; live-music evenings; red snapper in a mushroom cream sauce. $ Average main: $14 ⊠ Dominical ✛ 1½ km (1 mile) northeast of Dominical, on road from San Isidro de El General ☎ 506/2787–0172.

Tortilla Flats

$$ | **SOUTHWESTERN** | This perennially popular and casual surfer hangout is right across from Dominical Beach, which you can spy through a fringe of palm trees. Favorite menu items are the fresh-baked baguette sandwiches stuffed with interesting combinations and the excellent margaritas and flavored daiquiris, usually downed at the huge U-shape bar. **Known for:** great location across from the beach; live bands some evenings; falafel wrap. $ Average main: $13 ⊠ Across from Dominical Beach, Dominical ☎ 8841–1616.

Hotels

Lodgings in the lowlands of Dominical and the area a little to the north are closer to the beach, but tend to be hot and muggy and not as comfortable as the more luxurious, private, and breezy places up in the hills above Dominicalito, to the south.

Coconut Grove Oceanfront Cottages

$$ | **HOUSE** | **FAMILY** | Directly on the beach, this well-maintained cluster of equipped cabins and beach houses is ideal for travelers who want to fend for themselves, turn off the air-conditioning at night, and fall asleep to the sound of the ocean. **Pros:** best location in town (right on beach); close enough to feel cool ocean breezes; fully equipped kitchens, A/C, satellite TV, and Wi-Fi. **Cons:** guests must love animals; very steep driveway; 20-year-old property could use an update. $ Rooms from: $95 ⊠ Dominicalito Beach, Km 147, Costanera Hwy., 3 km (2 miles) south of Dominical, Dominical ☎ 2787–0130 ⊕ www.coconutgrovecr. com ⊟ No credit cards ⇆ 5 rooms ⎮◎⎮ No Meals.

Cuna del Angel Hotel and Spa

$$$ | **B&B/INN** | With an excellent restaurant, a lush garden, a pretty infinity pool, and exceptional service, this elegant hotel is a heavenly spot for those who like to indulge themselves. **Pros:** delightful decor; excellent restaurant also serves gluten-free dishes; friendly, professional service in hotel. **Cons:** water pressure is sometimes low; steep steps to Jungle Rooms and restaurant; remote location means you need a car to reach the beach. $ *Rooms from: $226 ⊠ Costanera Hwy., Puertocito, 9 km (5 miles) south of Dominical, Dominical ☎ 2787–4343 ⊕ www.cunadelangel.com ⤳ 22 rooms* ❍| *Free Breakfast.*

Hacienda Barú National Wildlife Refuge and Ecolodge

$$ | **B&B/INN** | **FAMILY** | This wildly family-friendly, comfortable ecolodge makes a great base for exploring vast tracts of surrounding forest (both primary and secondary), plus there are mangroves, a beach with nesting turtles, and 366 bird species. **Pros:** prime wildlife viewing; excellent guides; great value. **Cons:** no A/C (but rooms are well ventilated with ceiling and wall fans); pool is in full sun (wear sunscreen!); older cabins are not fancy. $ *Rooms from: $131 ⊠ Off Costanera Hwy., 3 km (2 miles) north Dominical, Dominical ☎ 2787–0003 ⊕ www.haciendabaru.com ⤳ 12 rooms* ❍| *Free Breakfast.*

Suites Charter Boutique

$$$ | **HOTEL** | Even if you've had your fill of flights to Costa Rica, this boutique hotel housed inside a refurbished airplane is one experience you'll be bragging about for years. **Pros:** unique design; good value; spacious rain shower. **Cons:** on busy road; no meals; tiny airplane windows mean no natural light. $ *Rooms from: $160 ⊠ Dominical ✛ 2 km (1 mile) northwest of Dominical, on road from San Isidro de El General ☎ 2787–0172 ⤳ 1 room* ❍| *No Meals.*

Villas Alturas

$$$ | **B&B/INN** | One of the best lodging deals on this coast, these seven, no-frills villas are in a sublime, lofty setting, with a large swimming pool and a huge terrace overlooking a million-dollar view of the Pacific. **Pros:** excellent value; good poolside restaurant; wildlife refuge on-site. **Cons:** long way down to beach and activities; sparsely furnished villas; long, steep drive requiring 4WD. $ *Rooms from: $220 ⊠ Off Costanera Hwy., Dominical ✛ 7 km (4½ miles) south of Dominical, 800 meters (2,624 feet) up steep hill ☎ 2200–5440 ⊕ www.villasalturas.com ⤳ 7 rooms* ❍| *Free Breakfast.*

Villas Río Mar

$$ | **HOTEL** | **FAMILY** | This three-star affordable resort hotel, with two pools, minigolf, and tennis courts is upriver from Dominical beach on exquisitely landscaped grounds filled with orchids, bougainvillea, and hibiscus. **Pros:** huge pool; lovely grounds; excellent restaurant. **Cons:** 15-minute walk to the main beach; rate does not include tax; children can be noisy in pool. $ *Rooms from: $85 ⊠ Off main hwy. into town, 1 km (½ mile) west of Dominical, Dominical ☎ 2787–0052 ⊕ www.villasriomar.com ⤳ 63 rooms* ❍| *Free Breakfast.*

Nightlife

During the high season, Dominical hops at night, and when the surfers have fled to find bigger waves, there are enough locals around to keep some fun events afloat.

Fuego Brew Co.

BARS | With an on-site, full-scale brewery below and a rancho restaurant above, this hip brewpub with live music many nights has become the liveliest nightspot in town. Belly up to the long bar, relax in a quieter lounge area, or take a table overlooking the garden and the Barú River estuary. Above-average bar food and pizza accompany the many beers on tap; you can order a flight of four ales to taste, then order your favorite. It's open till 10:30. *⊠ Off main street, next door to yoga center, Dominical ☎ 7059–9753 ⊕ www.fuegobrew.com.*

Shopping

Mama Toucan's Natural & Organic Foods

FOOD | Colorful and comfortably air-conditioned, this whole-foods store is a treat to browse in. Along with the fresh organic vegetables, there is a wide selection of gluten-free foods, including bagels and breads, and a deli with ready-to-eat vegan and gluten-free snacks and sandwiches. The ice cream, sorbet, and gelato made with coconut milk are delicious whether you are a vegan or an omnivore. The shop also carries hard-to-find, imported specialty foods, spices, and excellent local chocolates. It's open from 7 to 8 daily. ⊠ *Pueblo del Río, Main St., Dominical* ☎ *8872–5445* ⊕ *www.mamatoucans.com.*

 Activities

FISHING

Angling options range from expensive sportfishing charters to a trip in a small boat to catch red snapper and snook for supper. The five most common fish species here, in the order in which you are likely to catch them, are sailfish, dorado, yellowfin tuna, wahoo, and marlin.

HORSEBACK RIDING

Don Lulo

HORSEBACK RIDING | FAMILY | Horseback-riding tours to Nauyaca Waterfalls depart Monday to Saturday at 9 am from Don Lulo's stables. The tour ($85) includes lunch at the family homestead near the falls. You can swim in the cool pool beneath the falls, so bring a bathing suit and sunscreen. There is a river to cross, but otherwise the 12-km (7½-mile) ride is easy. You can also ride in an open truck ($32) or hike in on your own ($10). Be sure to reserve a day in advance. In rainy season, raincoats are provided. ⊠ *Road to San Isidro, 10 km (6 miles) northeast of Dominical, Dominical* ☎ *2787–0541, 2787–0542* ⊕ *www.nauyacawaterfallscostarica.com.*

SURFING

The surfing is great in Dominical, thanks to the runoff from the Barú River mouth, which constantly changes the ocean bottom and creates well-shaped waves big enough to keep intermediate and advanced surfers challenged. The best surfing is near the river mouth, and the best time is two hours before or after high tide, to avoid the notorious riptides.

Dominical Adventures

ADVENTURE TOURS | One-on-one, two-hour surfing lessons are $60; group lessons are $50 per person. All lessons include local transportation, surfboard, rash guard, fruit, and soft drinks. Board rental starts at $15 per day for a longboard. ⊠ *Main street, across from mercadito, Dominical* ☎ *2787–0431, 8897–9542* ⊕ *www.dominicaladventures.com.*

Dominical Surf School

SURFING | Owned and operated by Costa Rican surf champion Debbie Zec, this surf school holds lessons at several local breaks and can take surfers to nearby Playa Dominical between Quepos and Uvita. Their standard ratio is two students per instructor, and they offer two-hour courses from beginner to advanced. Rates include equipment and drinking water. ⊠ *Dominical* ☎ *8853–4860* ⊕ *www.dominicalsurfschool.com* 🛏 *From $60.*

Ballena National Marine Park

20 km (12 miles) southeast of Dominical.

Named for the whales (*ballenas,* in Spanish) that seasonally migrate here, this park protects marine life in miles of ocean, as well as 10 km (6 miles) of coastline, incorporating four separate beaches, each with its own character. Opportunities abound for fishing, whale- and dolphin-watching tours, kayaking, camping, beachcombing, and swimming. Sunsets here are unbeatable.

GETTING HERE AND AROUND

The park area includes the communities of Uvita, Bahía Ballena, and Ojochal, all easily accessible off the Costanera, a wide, paved highway now officially called Carretera Nacional Pacifica Fernández. As soon as you get off the highway, however, the roads are often bumpy and dusty. Alternatively, take a taxi or bus from Dominical. Eight buses leave Dominical, starting at 4:45 am until 5:30 pm daily, and there are longer-haul buses that pass along the Costanera and can drop you off in Uvita. Each of the park's four sectors, open 7 to 6, has a small ranger station where you pay your $7 admission.

ESSENTIALS

HOSPITAL Dome Plaza Medical Services. ⊠ Dome Plaza, Uvita ✛ 50 meters (164 feet) south of bridge ☎ 2743–8595 doctor, 2743–8418 dentist, 2743–8558 pharmacy.

VISITOR INFORMATION

The Uvita Information Center (closed Sunday and lunch, noon–2) is a one-stop shop for tours, hotel bookings, transportation and shuttle services, mail services, and general tourist information that connects easily with some of the smaller, harder-to-reach ecotourism projects in the Costa Ballena. The center shares office space with a rental-car agency, so look for the big Toyota sign.

CONTACTS Uvita Information Center. ⊠ On Costanera Hwy., across from BM Supermarket, Uvita ✛ Adjacent to the Flor de la Sabana Restaurant ☎ 2743–8072 ⊕ www.uvita.info.

 Sights

★ **Ballena Marine National Park**
(Parque Nacional Marino Ballena)
BEACH | FAMILY | Named for the whales who use this area as a nursery, the park has four separate Blue Flag beaches stretching for about 10 km (6 miles) and encompasses a mangrove estuary, a remnant coral reef, and more than 12,350 acres of ocean, home to tropical fish, dolphins, and humpback whales. Playa Uvita is the most popular sector of the park, with the longest stretch of beach and shallow waters calm enough for kids. Restaurants line the road to the Playa Uvita park entrance, but there are no food concessions within the park. Access to each of the four beaches—from north to south, Uvita, Colonia, Ballena, and Piñuela—is off the Costanera Highway. Although the official park offices are open 7 am to 6 pm, visitors can stay on longer, especially to view sunsets or camp. ⊠ Entrance at Playa Uvita, about 20 km (12 miles) south of Dominical, Uvita ☎ 8705–1629 ⊠ $7.

Finca 6 Museum of the Spheres
RUINS | About an hour from Uvita, you can learn about the mystery of Costa Rica's pre-Columbian spheres—massive, perfectly round stones uncovered in the 1930s—in this archaeological museum, built on a recently designated UNESCO World Heritage site near Sierpe, the port for boats to Drake Bay. Dating from 800 to 1500 AD, these carefully arranged spheres of varying sizes cover acres of land, popping up miles from the source of the rock used to carve them. Anthropologists speculate they may have served as agricultural calendars or as ceremonial sites similar to Stonehenge. All of the theories are outlined, in English and Spanish, along with displays of period pottery, sculpture, and other artifacts in a light and airy new museum, a branch of San José's National Museum. Much of the museum is outdoors, to view archaeological sites and see the spheres in situ. The sun is hot, so come early and bring along a hat and a water bottle. Squirrel monkeys and birds inhabit the wooded areas along the trails, so it's a good idea to carry binoculars and cameras, too. If you are on your way to the Osa Peninsula, by car or boat, don't miss this opportunity to encounter a surviving vestige of indigenous culture. ⊠ 8 km (5 miles) west of turnoff from Costanera

to Palmar Sur, on road to Sierpe; look for Finca 6 sign on left, just before small bridge ✚ *45 km (28 miles) south of Uvita, on Costanera Hwy., to turnoff for Palmar Sur, then follow signs to airport and Sierpe* ☎ *2211–5847* ⊕ *www.museocostarica.go.cr* ✉ *$7* ⊘ *Closed Mon.*

Oro Verde Private Nature Reserve
NATURE PRESERVE | You'll find excellent bird-watching and hiking in this nature preserve, uphill from the Costanera. Family-run, the property has well-groomed trails through a majestic, primary forest reserve. Early-morning, three-hour birding tours start at 6 ($40 per person, two person minimum) and end with a hearty home-cooked breakfast. In the afternoon, you can set out for a three-hour birding walk. For a totally different perspective on wildlife, join the naturalist-guided night tour, from 6 to 9 pm. The best way to book is through the Uvita Information Center. ✉ *Km 159, Costanera Hwy., 3 km (2 miles) uphill from Rancho La Merced, Uvita* ☎ *2743–8889, 8843–8833.*

Rancho La Merced National Wildlife Refuge
FARM/RANCH | **FAMILY** | Ride the range on a 1,250-acre property combining forest and pasture ($55) or gallop along the beach at sunset on horseback ($60). Riding tours also include a guide and helmets, and kid-size saddles are available. All tours begin at the pleasant reception center, where you can freshen up in clean, modern restrooms. For $8 you can explore the 10 km (6 miles) of hiking trails on your own with a trail map that includes a wildlife picture guide. ✉ *Km 159, Costanera Hwy., north of Uvita, Uvita* ☎ *2743–8032, 8861–5147* ⊕ *www.rancholamerced.com* ✉ *From $50.*

Uvita Market
MARKET | From 9 am to 2 pm on Saturday, the place to be is this combination farmers' market and weekly gathering place for locals. About 20 vendors show up to sell organic produce, chocolate, homemade cheeses and hot sauces, fresh fish, baked goods, jams, and frozen gourmet dinners and soups to take home. You can also feast on ready-to-eat breakfast burritos, tamales, cakes, cookies, and the freshest, best doughnuts in the country, made right on the spot. Artists sell painted masks, colorful textiles, and beautiful wildlife photographs. Every third Saturday there's a garage-sale table, too. This is a great place to meet English-speaking locals as they meet and greet. Some weeks, there's live music by local bands. You'll find the market just off the Costanera Highway, across from the Banco de Costa Rica and down a short side road. Just look for all the parked cars. ✉ *Off Costanera Hwy., across from Banco de Costa Rica, Uvita.*

Uvita Waterfall
(*Catarata Uvita y Jardin de Mariposas*) **WATERFALL** | It doesn't get much better than waterfalls, butterflies, and waterslides all in one. There's a short hike to reach the reward of several cascades that drop into freshwater swimming holes. As you jump—or slide—from the platform, monkeys often swing overhead from tree to tree, making this a surreal jungle experience. Secure pathways with metal railings guide the way. There are restrooms (with showers), a snack bar, and a butterfly garden with blue morphos fluttering about. Bring water shoes if you have them, as rocks can be slippery. To have the place to yourself, come early or arrive later in the day. ✉ *Calle Bejuco, Uvita* ✚ *Near Hostel Waterfall Lodge* ☎ *8915–4345* ✉ *$4.*

Beaches

Playa Ballena
BEACH | This lovely strand is backed by lush vegetation and is fairly easy to get to from the main highway, along a short, bumpy dirt road. There's free parking close to the beach. **Amenities:** showers; toilets. **Best for:** swimming; walking. ✉ *Ballena Marine National Park, 4 km (2½ miles) south of Playa Colonia access road, off Costanera Hwy., Ojochal* ✉ *$7.*

Playa Colonia

BEACH | This beach is safe for swimming and has a view of rocky islands, which you can visit by kayak. The access road is a well-graded dirt road. There is a sandy break for surfing, with gentle waves for beginners. In high season, vendors sell cold drinks and souvenirs at the beach entrance. It's the only beach where cars can park practically on the beach. **Amenities:** food and drink; showers; toilets. **Best for:** swimming. ✉ *Ballena Marine National Park, 2 km (1¼ miles) south of Playa Uvita along Costanera Hwy., Ballena Marine National Park* 🎟 *$7.*

Playa Piñuela

BEACH | Nestled in a deep cove with views of small islands, tiny Playa Piñuela is the prettiest, and many times the most private, of the Ballena Marine National Park beaches. It's not always the best beach for swimming at high tide, however, since the shore is strewn with large stones and the waves can be a little rough. At low tide, the smooth, sandy beach emerges. The access road is very bumpy but also short. **Amenities:** showers; toilets. **Best for:** walking. ✉ *Ballena Marine National Park, 3 km (2 miles) south of Playa Colonia, off Costanera Hwy., Ojochal* ✣ *Turn off Costanera just past Km 172 marker* 🎟 *$7.*

★ **Playa Uvita**

BEACH | At the northern end of Ballena Marine National Park, wide, palm-fringed Playa Uvita stretches out along a tombolo (a long swath of sand) connecting a former island to the coast. At low tide, you can walk out to the famous "whale tail," where you'll get magnificent views of the hills and jungles of Uvita (and maybe spot a macaw). This is the most popular beach, especially on weekends, with shallow waters for swimming. On weekdays you may have it almost to yourself. It's also the launching spot for boat tours and the favorite vantage point for spectacular sunsets. There is no parking at the beach, but there are private parking lots along the road leading to the park entrance, charging $4 a day. **Amenities:** food and drink; showers; toilets. **Best for:** sunset; swimming; walking. ✉ *Ballena Marine National Park, Uvita* 🎟 *$7.*

Playa Ventanas

BEACH | This scenic beach has interesting tidal caves, popular for sea kayaking. Coconut palms edge the beach, which is sometimes pebbly, with quite a dramatic surf, especially at high tide when the waves break against huge offshore rock formations. The ocean views are rivaled by the vistas of green, forested mountains rising up behind the beach. You can camp here and use very basic toilets and cold-water showers. There's a new access road to the beach and a guarded parking area ($3 for the day). But it is advisable to not leave anything of value in your car. **Amenities:** parking (fee); showers; toilets. **Best for:** walking. ✉ *Ballena Marine National Park, 1½ km (1 mile) south of Playa Piñuela, off Costanera Hwy., Ojochal.*

🍴 Restaurants

The Bamboo Room

$$ | **MODERN CANADIAN** | Bamboo decks the walls at this hilltop restaurant with a spectacular view of land and sea, but it's the upscale menu that grabs one's attention due to its innovative takes on fish, shrimp, chicken, and out-of-the-ordinary bar food. Crunchy, panko-crispy shrimp make appearances in salads and on their own, and the beer-battered sea bass keeps customers on repeat. **Known for:** butternut squash gnocchi; occasional live music; salad with panko-crisp shrimp. [$] *Average main: $13* ✉ *Alma Hotel, C. Perezoso, Ojochal* ☎ *8380–5353* 🕒 *Closed Tues.–Thurs.*

★ **Citrus Gastro Bar**

$$$ | **ECLECTIC** | Tangy, tart, and refreshing, this ultrasophisticated restaurant lives up to its name, both in its daring decor and inventive fusion menu spanning the globe from the Far East, across the Mediterranean to chef Marcella Marciano's culinary homeland, France. The menu careens from classic French escargots and *moules marinières* to Japanese wasabi-spiced shrimp, to Indian chicken curry. **Known for:** choco-choco flourless cake; chic and romantic setting; seafood platter in lemon-garlic sauce. $ *Average main: $20* ⊠ *Plaza Tangara main road in Ojochal, Ojochal* ☎ *2786–5175, 8304–1717* ⊕ *www.citrusrestaurante. com* ☾ *Closed Sun.*

★ Exotica Restaurant

$$$ | FRENCH | Fabulous French cuisine with tropical accents served on an intimate alfresco patio in the tiny French-Canadian enclave of Ojochal keeps this romantic restaurant at the top of locals' list of go-to special-occasion restaurants. Raked sand, red lanterns, and "curtains" of fairy lights set the tone for a menu that includes an intriguing Tahitian fish carpaccio bathed in a creamy banana and coconut marinade, a hearty serving of fish or shrimp in a banana-curry sauce, or a spicy Vietnamese chicken soup. **Known for:** spicy Vietnamese chicken soup; reasonably priced international wine list; chili-spiced flourless chocolate cake. $ *Average main: $20* ⊠ *Main road into Ojochal, off Costanera Hwy., Ojochal* ☎ *2786–5050* ☾ *Closed Sun.; Sept.–Oct.; and Mon. May–Aug. No lunch.*

Tilapias El Pavón

$$ | COSTA RICAN | FAMILY | To enjoy an authentically tico day in the country, follow a winding river road about 20 minutes up to this family-run tilapia fish farm in the tiny hamlet of Vergel, where you catch your own tilapia on the way. The cooks at the open-air wooden restaurant overlooking the scenic fishponds will fry up your fish in 10 minutes, presenting it whole or filleted, with rice, salad, yuca, and excellent *patacones* (fried, mashed plantains), plus a pitcher of refreshing fruit naturale, a feast for less than $11. You can work up

an appetite on a short hike to a spectacular, nearby waterfall with a swimming hole (bring your swimsuit and binoculars for bird-watching), then catch your own tilapia. **Known for:** crisp fried plantain patacones; fishponds set in gardens; fried, breaded, or grilled fresh tilapia. $ *Average main: $10* ⊠ *3 km (2 miles) south of Ojochal, then just before bridge in Punta Mala, follow dirt road 4 km (2½ miles) uphill to tiny hamlet of Vergel, Punta Mala* ☎ *2200–4721* ▭ *No credit cards.*

☕ Coffee and Quick Bites

Pancito Café

$ | FRENCH | Besides crusty baguettes, buttery croissants, and divine pastries to go, this French bakery near the entrance to Ojochal serves hearty breakfast omelets and light lunches of fish soup, sandwiches, quiches, crepes, salads, and mussels with French fries. Customers perch on high stools at tables and counters in this casual thatch-roof café, many with their laptops open, taking advantage of the free Wi-Fi. **Known for:** salade niçoise; pork rillettes; moules frites (mussels with French fries). $ *Average main: $8* ⊠ *Plaza de Los Delfines, off Costanera Hwy. at entrance to Ojochal, Ojochal* ☎ *506/2786–5774, 8729–4115* ▭ *No credit cards* ☾ *No dinner.*

Sibu Coffee & Chocolate

$ | CAFÉ | It's not always easy to find a great cup of coffee around Uvita, but the espresso here, brewed using organic coffee beans from the high-altitude Dota region, is excellent and ready by 7 am. Pair it with a homemade pastry for a heavenly morning. **Known for:** chocolate-and-almond cake; freshly roasted coffee beans to buy; best macchiato in the area. $ *Average main: $9* ⊠ *Uvita* ✛ *Across from BM supermercado in center of Uvita* ☎ *2743–8674.*

🛏 Hotels

Cristal Ballena Boutique Hotel & Spa
$$$ | **B&B/INN** | **FAMILY** | High on a hillside with spectacular ocean views framed by giant traveler's palm trees, this Austrian-owned hotel is a luxurious base for exploring the area. **Pros:** wonderful swimming pool for serious swimmers and loungers; great ocean, mountain, and sky views; luxurious rooms. **Cons:** stairs to manage between rooms and restaurant; steep walk down to beach; a little away from the center of town. $ *Rooms from: $248* ⊠ *Costanera Hwy., 7 km (4 miles) south of Uvita, Uvita* ☎ *2786–5354, 8390–6863* ⊕ *www.cristal-ballena.com* 🛏 *19 rooms* ⊺⊚⊺ *Free Breakfast.*

El Castillo
$$$$ | **B&B/INN** | With one of the most spectacular ocean views on the Costa Ballena, this modern "castle" is a luxury boutique hotel with nine ultrachic guest quarters with private terraces. **Pros:** million-dollar view; luxury accommodation; scenic pool with room to swim laps. **Cons:** no children under 16; overpriced restaurant; some noise from trucks on nearby Costanera. $ *Rooms from: $300* ⊠ *C. Perezoso, off Costanera Hwy., Ojochal* ✛ *500 meters (1,640 feet) south of Ojochal* ☎ *2786–5543 hotel, 214/329–9866 in U.S.* ⊕ *www.elcastillocr.com* 🛏 *9 rooms* ⊺⊚⊺ *Free Breakfast.*

★ Kurá
$$$$ | **B&B/INN** | Stunning contemporary design, high-tech comforts, and a lofty location overlooking the Pacific combine to set a whole new standard of luxury at this adults-only property. **Pros:** the ultimate in contemporary design and comfort; excellent restaurant; no children under 16. **Cons:** a long, steep drive down to the beach; isolation, for good or bad; some rooms don't have blackout curtains. $ *Rooms from: $850* ⊠ *1 km (½ mile) above Uvita, to parking lot; hotel transport up to Kurá, Bahía Ballena* ☎ *8521–3407, 800/728–0466 toll-free*

U.S. ⊕ *www.kuracostarica.com* ⊙ *Closed Oct.* 🛏 *8 rooms* ⊺⊚⊺ *Free Breakfast.*

La Cusinga Eco-Lodge
$$$ | **B&B/INN** | **FAMILY** | Along with one of the best sunset views along the coast, this comfortable ecolodge on a high cliff bordering Ballena Marine National Park has spacious, airy cabins and a forest trail to a pristine beach. **Pros:** magnificent views; forest and beach access; pleasant restaurant. **Cons:** two rooms lack ocean views; remote; steep path between cabins and lodge. $ *Rooms from: $219* ⊠ *Bahía Ballena* ✛ *Between Km 166 and 167 on Costanera Hwy., south of Dominical* ☎ *2770–2549 reservation office, 8318–8598 lodge* ⊕ *www.lacusingalodge.com* 🛏 *18 rooms* ⊺⊚⊺ *Free Breakfast.*

Rancho Pacifico
$$$$ | **B&B/INN** | Nestled into the mountainside overlooking the Pacific, these private, chic, one-, two-, and three-bedroom villas and suites are the ultimate getaway. **Pros:** private and romantic 18-plus adults-only atmosphere; jungle setting and gorgeous views; great restaurant. **Cons:** isolated; some rooms don't have A/C (but not really necessary at these elevations); steep roads require 4WD to get here. $ *Rooms from: $495* ⊠ *1 Rancho Pacifico Rd., Uvita* ☎ *8715–7397* ⊕ *ranchopacifico.com* 🛏 *7 units* ⊺⊚⊺ *Free Breakfast.*

Rio Tico Safari Lodge
$$ | **B&B/INN** | **FAMILY** | You may feel as though you're on a luxury safari when you step inside one of these spacious South African tents perched on sturdy wooden platforms cantilevered over a rushing mountain river. **Pros:** gorgeous natural setting; luxury tents; homemade bread and granola for breakfast. **Cons:** no A/C; no dinner restaurant; steps to climb up and down from main lodge to tents. $ *Rooms from: $81* ⊠ *3 km (2 miles) south of Ojochal on Costanera, turn off just before bridge in Punta Mala near Km 179, 4 km (2½ miles) up winding dirt road to Vergel de Punta Mala, Punta Mala*

☎ 8996–7935, 4000–0680 ⊕ www.rioti-co.com ↪ 12 rooms ⊮I Free Breakfast.

★ Vista Celestial

$$$$ | **HOTEL** | These modern 1,000-square-foot villas, on the rain-forested peak over-looking Costa Ballena and the "whale tail," feel lavish and luxurious; each has indoor and outdoor showers and large soaking tub, private terraces with infinity plunge pool, posh beds, and heavenly views. **Pros:** stunning views in a wild setting; spacious cabinas with all the amenities; beautiful common area with lounge, pool, and Jacuzzi. **Cons:** pricey; there are some steps from the restaurant to villas (but they will give you a ride); trekking up the mountain can be tough—you need 4WD. $ Rooms from: $485 ⊠ Uvita ✛ 2 km (1 mile) northeast of the Catarata de Uvita ☎ 8523–0627 ⊕ www.vistacelestial.com ↪ 5 villas ⊮I Free Breakfast.

Yaba Chigui Lodge

$$ | **B&B/INN** | You'll be charmed by this boutique ecolodge at jungle's edge, a modern representation of indigenous dwellings. **Pros:** Costa Rican hospitality; delicious breakfasts; eco-conscious. **Cons:** not on beach; only four cabinas; thin walls. $ Rooms from: $120 ⊠ Ojochal ✛ 1½ km (1 mile) after C. Papagayo ☎ 2786–5120 ⊕ yabachigui.com ↪ 4 cabinas ⊮I Free Breakfast.

Nightlife

The Bamboo Room

CABARET | Ojochal has a whole new lease on nightlife with live music at sunset, Friday, Saturday, and Monday at the Bamboo Room in the Alma Hotel. You could see owner-musician John on the piano, or Ken Nickell, a songwriter, singer, and storyteller. ⊠ Alma Hotel, C. Perezoso, Ojochal ☎ 8380–5353 ⊕ almacr.com/the-bamboo-room.

Mosaic Wine Bar

WINE BARS | One of the coolest bars in Uvita was appropriately birthed out of conversation and cocktails among friends. That 2017 discussion of "what if" popped the cork on a jungle wine bar that brings sushi, charcuterie, and over 40 bottles from around the globe to your table. Not sure what to order? Just ask Casey, the owner and certified sommelier to find the perfect blend for your palate. If you fall in love with a particular glass, you can buy a bottle from their wine shop. ⊠ Uvita ✛ 300 meters (984 feet) past the BCR towards the Uvita Waterfall ☎ 2215–0068.

Activities

DIVING AND SNORKELING

The best spot for snorkeling in the park is at the north end of Playa Ballena, near the whale's tail.

Bahía Aventuras

BOAT TOURS | Bilingual guides lead half-day tours in covered boats that combine whale- and dolphin-watching with snorkeling for $90. Whale season begins at the end of December and runs until end of February, and July to October. A boat tour of the Terraba Sierpe Mangrove costs $85. If you want to try your luck, you can fish from a 23-foot boat designed and built locally; a half day for up to four people costs $790, and a full day for a group of up to eight people around Caño Island costs $1,250. There is a pleasant waiting room at the tour office, with clean, accessible bathrooms and parking. ⊠ Bahía Ballena ☎ 2743–8362, 8846–6576 ⊕ www.bahiaaventuras.com.

Dolphin Tours of Bahía Ballena

FISHING | This tried-and-true tour company takes a minimum of two people on four-hour boat tours that combine dolphin- and whale-watching with snorkeling, a visit to ocean caverns, and a rocky island bird sanctuary for $85 per person. All-day fishing trips for snook and red snapper cost $1,200 for up to four anglers. ☎ 2743–8013, 8825–4031 ⊕ www.dolphintourcostarica.com.

ZIPLINING
Osa Canopy Tour
ZIP LINING | Ziplines are a dime a dozen in Costa Rica, but this one gets rave reviews. With 11 platforms and more than 3 km (2 miles) of cable, you will certainly get your money's worth. For the really adventurous, there are also two rappelling stations (one 30 feet high, the other 90 feet) and a Tarzan swing. Count on flying through the forest, 100 feet high at times, for two to three hours, all for $75 per person. The maximum weight for a zipliner is 230 pounds. Call ahead to reserve three days in advance. ⊠ *Ticket office at Km 196, Costanera Hwy., south of Uvita, Bahía Ballena* ☎ *2788–7555, 8884–1237* ⊕ *www.osacanopytour.com.*

Golfito

130 km (81 miles) south of Uvita, 339 km (212 miles) southeast of San José.

Overlooking a small gulf (hence its name) and hemmed in by a steep bank of forest, Golfito has a scenic location. Lodges supply kayaks for paddling the gulf's warm, salty, and crystal clear waters. When the sun sets behind the rolling silhouette of the Osa Peninsula, you can sometimes spot phosphorescent fish jumping. Fishing, both commercial and for sport, is the main activity here, with lively marinas providing slips to visiting yachts and charter fishing boats.

Golfito was once a thriving banana port—United Fruit arrived in 1938—with elegant housing and lush landscaping for its plantation managers. After United Fruit pulled out in 1985, Golfito slipped into a state of poverty and neglect. The town itself consists of a pleasant, lushly landscaped older residential section and a long strip of scruffy commercial buildings. Visiting U.S. Coast Guard ships dock here, and small cruise ships moor in the harbor. The Costa Rica Coast Guard Academy is also here.

GETTING HERE AND AROUND
From San José the trip used to take eight hours, along paved roads crossing over often-foggy mountains. But with the new toll road from San José, connecting to the paved Costanera Highway, travel time has been cut to five hours. Your best bet, especially if you are visiting a lodge on the gulf, is to fly to Golfito, which takes only about an hour. Direct buses from San José leave twice daily, at 7 am and 3:30 pm, following the longer mountain route; the 6:30 am bus from San José uses the faster Costanera route.

Taxis and boats take you wherever you need to go in and around Golfito. You can hire taxi boats at the city dock in Golfito (about $90 round-trip, often negotiable, to go to area lodges or across the Golfo Dulce to Puerto Jiménez). The only way to reach the remote Golfo Dulce lodges above Golfito is by boat. Early morning is the best time, when the water in the gulf is at its calmest. Most lodges include the boat transport in their rates.

A long-planned marina is now in place, with slips and a fuel dock, as well as a bait and tackle shop and upscale restaurant, with hopes for a hotel and more shops in the future.

For tour, lodging, and general tourist information, check out ⊕ *www.golfito-costarica.com*, a website managed by longtime Golfito residents.

TAXI Taxi service. ⊠ *Taxi stand beside gas station in center of town, near municipal dock, Golfito* ☎ *2775–2020.*

ESSENTIALS
BANKS/ATMS ATH Coopealianza. ⊠ *North end of town, across from hospital, Golfito* ☎ *2775–0025.* **Banco Nacional.** ⊠ *South of hospital on main road through Golfito, Golfito* ☎ *2212–2000.*

HOSPITAL Hospital de Golfito Manuel Mora Valverde. ⊠ *400 meters (1,312 feet) north of the Catholic church, near Deposito, Golfito* ☎ *2775–7800.*

The view of Golfo Dulce from the road to Puerto Jiménez

PHARMACY Farmacia Golfito. ✉ *Main street, across from city park, Golfito* ☎ *2775–2442.*

POST OFFICE Correo. ✉ *Off main road, south of central park, Golfito.*

 Sights

American Zone
NEIGHBORHOOD | The northwestern end of town is the so-called American Zone, full of handsome wooden houses where the expatriate managers of United Fruit lived amid flowering trees imported from all over the world. Many of these vintage houses, built of durable Honduran hardwoods, are now being spruced up. Eccentric garden features, such as a restored railway car, make the neighborhood worth a stroll. If you're on foot, there's also excellent birding in and around the gardens. ✉ *Golfito* ✛ *Northwestern end of town.*

Piedras Blancas National Park (*Parque Nacional Piedras Blancas*)
NATIONAL PARK | There is some good birding in the dense forest here, which is also an important wildlife corridor connecting to Corcovado National Park. Follow the main road northwest through the American Zone and past the airstrip and a housing project. The place where a dirt road heads into the rain forest is great for bird-watching. There are marked trails from the entrance near the marina, but the park is best explored with a guide; the best birding is along the road. ✉ *Adjacent to Golfito National Wildlife Refuge, Golfito* 🜄 *$11 (cash only)* ⊘ *Closed Sun.*

 Restaurants

Banana Bay
$$ | AMERICAN | For consistently good American-style food, you can't beat this marina restaurant with a view of expensive yachts and sportfishing boats. Locals complain that the prices are high, but portions are hefty and include generous

salads, sizzling hamburgers, and a delicious grilled dorado sandwich with a mountain of fries. **Known for:** grilled fish sandwich; free Wi-Fi; BLT and burgers with a pile of hot fries. $ *Average main: $13* ✉ *Main street, south of town dock, Golfito* ☎ *2775–0383.*

Restaurante Mar y Luna

$$ | **SEAFOOD** | This pleasant terrace restaurant jutting out over the water has the best harbor view in Golfito, along with jaunty nautical decor and the coolest breezes in town. The seafood-heavy lineup includes grilled whole fish served in a variety of ways, including Caribbean style with coconut milk and a side of patacones (fried, mashed plantain). **Known for:** seafood soup with coconut milk; harbor view; fish tacos. $ *Average main: $15* ✉ *South end of main street, north of Hotel Las Gaviotas, Golfito* ☎ *2775–0192* ⊕ *www.hotelmaryluna.com.*

Hotels

The atmosphere of the in-town hotels differs dramatically from that of the lodges in the delightfully remote east coast of the Golfo Dulce. The latter is a world of jungle and blue water, birds and fish, and desert-island beaches, with lodges accessible only by boat from either Golfito or Puerto Jiménez.

Casa Roland Marina Resort

$$ | **HOTEL** | Everything at this luxury resort—designed like an art deco ocean liner incongruously dry-docked in Golfito's American Zone—is first-class, and guests stroll among gleaming hardwoods, polished brass, and stained glass. **Pros:** style and luxury; excellent service; resort facilities for bargain price. **Cons:** often deserted and too quiet with few guests; A/C is sometimes too cold; dark hallways and low ceilings on lower floor. $ *Rooms from: $120* ✉ *American Zone, Golfito* ☎ *2775–3405* ⊕ *www.casarolandgolfito. com* ⮌ *53 rooms* ⦿| *Free Breakfast.*

Esquinas Rainforest Lodge

$$$$ | **B&B/INN** | **FAMILY** | This well-managed ecolodge in a 35-acre nature preserve bordering Piedras Blancas National Park is run by Austrians who have successfully instilled some sense of Teutonic order in the jungle. **Pros:** top-notch trails and wildlife-viewing opportunities in unique natural setting; excellent meals; saltwater pool. **Cons:** some trails are challenging, and you need to be steady on your feet; lodge is geared to nature lovers who aren't looking for luxury; no A/C and it can get hot here. $ *Rooms from: $310* ✉ *Near village of La Gamba, 5 km (3 miles) west of Villa Briceño turnoff, Golfito* ☎ *2741–8001* ⊕ *www.esquinaslodge. com* ⮌ *18 rooms* ⦿| *All-Inclusive.*

★ Playa Cativo Lodge

$$$$ | **B&B/INN** | Planted between the tranquil Golfo Dulce and tropical forest, this luxury ecolodge brilliantly fuses high design, luxe comfort, and gastronomic flights of fancy in two restaurants with an eco-consciousness dictated by its castaway location accessible only by boat. **Pros:** castaway seclusion; high-style bathrooms with vintage tiles; two innovative restaurants. **Cons:** not as much privacy in main lodge; only one room has A/C; stairs to upper suites, but views are worth it. $ *Rooms from: $570* ✉ *Playa Cativo, Golfito* ☎ *506/2775–6262* ⊕ *www.playacativo.com* ⮌ *18 rooms* ⦿| *All-Inclusive.*

★ Playa Nicuesa Rainforest Lodge

$$$$ | **RESORT** | Hands down, this is the best ecolodge on the gulf, combining comfortable, upscale accommodations and great food with an emphasis on adventure on both land and sea. **Pros:** everything you need to have an active vacation; excellent food and service; rate includes boat transport. **Cons:** some insects outside the mosquito netting at night; pebbly beach; no A/C. $ *Rooms from: $510* ✉ *Golfo Dulce, accessible only by boat from Golfito or Puerto Jiménez, Golfito* ☎ *2258–8250 in San*

José, 2222–0704 in San José, 866/504–8116 in U.S. toll-free ⊕ www.nicuesal-odge.com ⊗ Closed Oct.–Nov. 15 ⤵ 10 rooms ❘◎❘ All-Inclusive.

Nightlife

Happy hour is popular in Golfito. The bar at Banana Bay Marina is hopping every day from 5 to 7, when locals come to watch the sunset. The lively bar at Samoa del Sur has a mix of Ticos and foreigners, mostly of the hard-drinking fishermen type. On Friday night there's karaoke and dance music at the huge, high-tech disco-bar by the pool at the Casa Roland Marine Resort.

Fish Hook Marina & Lodge
BARS | The curved, polished-wood bar at this marina is cooled by breezes off Golfito Bay. It's a pleasant place to meet locals, tell fish tales, and sit and watch the sunset over the bay. Drink specials, including $2 beers and $6 cocktails, are offered all day long. ⊠ *Main street, south of Banana Bay, Golfito* ☎ *2775–1624* ⊕ *www.fishhookcr.com.*

Activities

FISHING
The open ocean holds plenty of sailfish, marlin, and roosterfish during the dry months, as well as mahimahi, tuna, and wahoo during the rainy season; there's excellent bottom fishing any time of year. Captains are in constant radio contact with one another and tend to share fish finds.

Banana Bay Marina
FISHING | This marina houses a fleet of four charter fishing boats, fitted with tournament-quality tackle and skippered by English-speaking, world-record-holding captains. A day's fishing averages $1,100 for up to three people. Food and beverage included. ⊠ *Golfito* ☎ *2775–0255, 2775–0003* ⊕ *www.bananabaymarina-golfito.com.*

Playa Zancudo

51 km (32 miles) south of Golfito.

Life here is laid-back and casual, centering on walking the beach, fishing, kayaking, paddleboarding, swimming, and hanging out at the local bars and restaurants. Zancudo has a good surf break at the south end of the beach, but it pales in comparison with Playa Pavones a little to the south. Swimming is especially good two hours before or after high tide, especially at the calmer north end of the beach. The water is always warm.

If you get tired of playing in the surf and sand, you can arrange a boat trip to the nearby mangrove estuary to see birds and crocodiles. Zancudo is also home to one of the area's best sportfishing operations, headquartered at the Zancudo Lodge.

GETTING HERE AND AROUND
The road from Golfito is fully paved for the first 11 km (7 miles), but after the turnoff at El Rodeo, you'll encounter some rough patches. A bridge has finally replaced the ancient cable ferry, making the trip a little shorter, but count on 1½ hours to get here. Instead of driving, you can hire a boat at the municipal dock in Golfito for the 25-minute ride ($80 for two) or take a cheaper *collectivo* (communal) boat that leaves from Golfito's Samoa del Sur Hotel twice a week; check the schedule at the hotel because it varies throughout the year. A taxi ride from Golfito to Zancudo costs about $85, so the boat is a bargain.

Getting around Playa Zancudo doesn't take much, since there's really only one long, dusty road parallel to the beach. You can rent a bike at Cabinas Sol y Mar, Coloso del Mar, or Tres Amigos Supermercado for about $10 per day.

WATER TAXI Cabinas Los Cocos. ⊠ *Beach road, Zancudo* ☎ *2776–0012.*

Beaches

Playa Zancudo

BEACH | For laid-back beaching involving hammocks strung between palms and nothing more demanding than watching the sunset, you can't beat Playa Zancudo, with its miles of wide, flat beach and romantic views of the Osa Peninsula across the Golfo Dulce. The water is amazingly warm for swimming and except for local holiday times, this beach is pretty much deserted. It isn't picture-perfect: the 10 km (6 miles) of dark, volcanic sand is sometimes strewn with flotsam and jetsam. But there's a constant breeze — often too windy — and a thick cushion of palm and almond trees between the beach and the dirt road running parallel. Away from the beach breezes, be prepared for biting *zancudos* (no-see-ums). **Amenities:** food and drink. **Best for:** sunset; swimming; walking. ✉ *Zancudo.*

Restaurants

Coloso del Mar Restaurant

$ | **SEAFOOD** | Fabulous fish burritos, steak with tropical sauce, and a savory fillet of sea bass with a smoky jalapeño cream sauce are a few of the delights at this screened-in-porch restaurant in a bright-yellow clapboard cottage on the beach. Chicken or fish curry is popular with the locals. **Known for:** banana pancakes; service with a smile; fish cakes and creamy mashed potatoes. [$] *Average main: $9* ✉ *Main road, Zancudo* ✣ *200 meters (656 feet) north of Soda Tranquilo* ☎ *2776–0050* 🌐 *www.colosodelmar.com* ⏲ *No lunch.*

Restaurant Sol y Mar

$ | **ECLECTIC** | On a porch with a palm-fringed beach view, this thatch-roof restaurant is open year-round and has an eclectic menu ranging from spicy quesadillas and burritos to pizza and fresh fish. There's a touch of Thai here, too; one of the most popular dishes is mahimahi in a coconut-curry sauce. **Known for:** homemade desserts; huge breakfasts; deep fried chicken. [$] *Average main: $9* ✉ *Cabinas Sol y Mar, Main road, south of Cabinas Los Cocos, Zancudo* ☎ *2776–0014.*

Hotels

Cabinas Los Cocos

$$ | **HOUSE** | This secluded cluster of self-catering cabins right on the beach, under palm trees swaying in the breeze, is designed for parties of two to four people who want to kick back and enjoy the beach. **Pros:** like having your own beach house on an idyllic beach; friendly host helps you get the most out of your stay; Wi-Fi in cabins. **Cons:** no phone in cabins; no TV; no A/C, but there are ceiling fans and ocean breezes. [$] *Rooms from: $96* ✉ *Beach road, north of Cabinas Sol y Mar, Zancudo* ☎ *2776–0012* 🌐 *www.loscocos.com* 🛏 *4 rooms* 🍴 *No Meals.*

Cabinas Sol y Mar

$ | **B&B/INN** | Just as the name implies, Cabinas Sol y Mar have plenty of sun and sea, as well as a beach fringed by coconut palms and apricot-color wooden cabinas with porches where you can take in the spectacular views of the Osa Peninsula year-round. **Pros:** beach location; bargain price; lively restaurant and bar. **Cons:** bare-bones furniture; no-frills bathrooms; no A/C or TV. [$] *Rooms from: $65* ✉ *Main road, south of Cabinas Los Cocos, Zancudo* ☎ *2776–0014* 🌐 *www.zancudo.com* 🛏 *6 rooms* 🍴 *No Meals.*

★ The Zancudo Lodge

$$$$ | **ALL-INCLUSIVE** | The carefully groomed grounds of this top-notch, luxury beachfront resort are a riot of tropical foliage and flowers, shaded by massive mango trees. **Pros:** laundry service included; excellent fishing boats and captains; there's A/C, which is rare in these parts. **Cons:** minimum three-night stay; not child friendly (no kids under 18); pricey for the area. [$] *Rooms from:*

$385 ✉ *Main road, northern end of town, Zancudo* ☎ *2776–0008, 800/854–8791 in U.S. toll-free* ⊕ *www.zancudolodge.com* ☯ *Closed June–Oct.* ⇨ *15 rooms* ⍐ *Free Breakfast.*

 Activities

FISHING

If you've got your own gear, you can do some good shore fishing from the beach or the mouth of the mangrove estuary, or hire a local boat to take you out into the gulf. The main edible catches are yellow-fin tuna, snapper, and snook; catch-and-release fish include marlin, roosterfish, and swordfish.

The Zancudo Lodge

FISHING | This luxury lodge runs the biggest charter operation in the area, with 16 boats ranging in length from 28 to 36 feet, including two TwinVee catamarans and two state-of-the-art Contender 32STs. During high season, fishing packages are $1,100 per day for up to four anglers. ✉ *Main road, north end of town, Zancudo* ☎ *2776–0008* ⊕ *www. zancudolodge.com.*

KAYAKING

The kayaking is great at the beach and along the nearby Río Coto Colorado, lined with mangroves. You can also test your balance on a paddleboard over ocean waves or on the river.

Cabinas Los Cocos

KAYAKING | The popular tour ($70 per person, minimum three passengers) takes you for a 1½-hour motorboat ride up the Coto Colorado River, then a magical two-hour kayak tour along a jungly mangrove channel and a relaxing paddle, moving downstream with the current, back to the river mouth. Captain Susan can identify the birds you'll see along the way. The lodge also rents user-friendly sit-on-top kayaks with backrests for $5 per hour, and paddleboards (with instruction) at $20 for two hours. ✉ *Beach road, north of Cabinas Sol y Mar, Zancudo* ☎ *8829–5007.*

Playa Pavones

53 km (33 miles) south of Golfito.

Surfing is the main draw here, especially from April to September when the waves are most reliable. But the dramatic scenery, looking across the Golfo Dulce to the Osa Peninsula, along with a very laid-back vibe, make it a popular destination year-round. The area is not heavily developed but there are some excellent restaurants in town, and nearby Tiskita Jungle Lodge is a birder's paradise.

GETTING HERE AND AROUND

There's no avoiding the bumpy road from Golfito to Conte, where the road forks north to Zancudo and south to Pavones. But the dirt road to Pavones is usually well graded. A public bus leaves from Golfito twice a day, and the trip takes about two hours. A taxi from the airstrip in Golfito costs upward of $80.

TAXIS 4X4 Taxi Service. ✉ *Golfito* ☎ *8533–2614.*

 Beaches

Playa Pavones

BEACH | Driving along remote Playa Pavones, one of the most scenic beaches in Costa Rica, you catch glimpses through the palms of brilliant blue water, white surf crashing against black rocks, and the soft silhouette of the Osa Peninsula. This area at the southern edge of the mouth of Golfo Dulce attracts serious surfers, as one of the world's longest left-hand waves in the world. The pristine black-sand beaches and virgin rain forest lure beach goers watching the show. The coast is very rocky, so it's important to ask locals before surfing or swimming. One of the best places to swim is in the Río Claro, under the bridge or at the river mouth (dry season only). The town of Pavones itself is a helter-skelter collection of guesthouses and sodas a few blocks from the beach. **Amenities:** food and drink. **Best for:** surfing; swimming; walking. ✉ *Pavones.*

🍴 Restaurants

Café de la Suerte

$ | **VEGETARIAN** | Fortunately for food lovers, the "Good Luck Café" serves truly astonishing vegetarian food, along with intriguing exotic juices and thick fruit smoothies. The homemade yogurt is a revelation: light, almost fluffy, and full of flavor, served over a cornucopia of fruits, sprinkled with the café's own granola, and mixed into refreshing fruit-flavored lassis. **Known for:** creamy quiches; vegetarian lasagna; delectable brownies. [$] *Average main: $8* ✉ *Main street, next to soccer field, Pavones* ☎ *2776–2388, 8381–4347* 💳 *No credit cards* 🕒 *Closed Oct., Nov., and Sun. Aug.–Mar. No dinner most nights.*

La Bruschetta (*La Piña*)

$$ | **ITALIAN** | **FAMILY** | This kitschy Italian spot within earshot of the surf serves savory bruschetta and 16 varieties of the town's most authentic pizza: crispy, with a thin crust, Neapolitan-style. The four-seasons pizza is a triumph, with thin, spicy pepperoni, flavorful ham, olives, eggplant, peppers, onion, and zucchini. **Known for:** filet mignon; funky, fun atmosphere; knockout gnocchi. [$] *Average main: $15* ✉ *Main road between Pavones and Punto Banco, north of La Ponderosa Beach and Jungle Resort, Pavones* ✥ *Look for the "La Piña" sign* ☎ *2776–2174.*

🛏 Hotels

★ La Ponderosa Beach and Jungle Resort

$$ | **B&B/INN** | The world-famous Playa Pavones surf break is a 10-minute walk from La Ponderosa, the area's only beach resort and several cuts above the usual surfer hangout, with accommodations verging on luxurious. **Pros:** great value with all-inclusive option; close to beach and town; magnificent garden and forest trails. **Cons:** mosquitoes love the garden when there's no breeze; often full; tends to attract a younger crowd. [$] *Rooms from: $115* ✉ *Road between Pavones and Punta Banco, on beach, Pavones* ☎ *2776–2076* 🌐 *www.laponderosapavones.com* 🛏 *8 rooms* 🍽 *All-Inclusive.*

★ Tiskita Jungle Lodge

$$$$ | **ALL-INCLUSIVE** | This last-outpost ecolodge, near the border with Panama, is a draw for bird-watchers as well as nature lovers, yoga enthusiasts, and adventurers who want to really get away from it all in relative comfort and at an affordable, all-inclusive price. **Pros:** unrivaled wildlife viewing and birding; splendid natural isolation; friendly, knowledgeable owners. **Cons:** no A/C; not a lot of privacy in joined double and triple cabins, which share verandas; some steep walks to cabins in forest. [$] *Rooms from: $285* ✉ *On road between Pavones and Punta Banco, 6 km (4 miles) south of Playa Pavones, Pavones* ☎ *2296–8125* 🌐 *www.tiskita.com* 🕒 *Closed May–Nov. except to groups of 8 or more* 🛏 *17 rooms* 🍽 *All-Inclusive* ☞ *All-inclusive package includes all meals, 2 guided tours.*

🏃 Activities

SURFING

Pavones is famous for one of the longest left-hand waves in the world, thanks to the mouth of the Río Claro. The most consistent waves are from April to September, and that's when the surfing crowd heads down here from the Central Pacific beaches. But even at the crest of its surfing season, Pavones is tranquility central compared with the surfing hot spots farther north.

Sea Kings Surf Shop

SURFING | You can buy top-of-the-line surfboards and other gear here, along with heavy-duty sunscreen, board wax, and the latest in surfer wear. You can also rent surfboards for $15 per day. ✉ *Main street, near Café de la Suerte, Pavones* ☎ *2776–2015* 🌐 *www.facebook.com/SeaKingsSurfShop.*

Puerto Jiménez

130 km (86 miles) west of Golfito, 364 km (226 miles) from San José.

You might not guess it from the rickety bicycles and ancient pickup trucks parked on the main street, but Puerto Jiménez is the largest town on the Osa Peninsula and the main gateway to the rest of the peninsula and to Corcovado National Park. This one-iguana town has a certain frontier charm, with an interesting, funky edge provided by ecolodge owners and backpacking nature lovers. A bayside promenade has added a touch of civility, with benches where you can sit and admire the gulf views. At night, elegant street lamps light your way to the restaurants along the waterfront.

This is the last civilized outpost on the peninsula. Heading south, you fall off the grid. Cell service is spotty, so make your phone calls, send your email, get cash, and stock up on supplies here. Be prepared for the humidity and mosquitoes—Puerto Jiménez has plenty of both.

If you need a refreshing dip, head southeast of the airport to Playa Platanares, where there is a long stretch of beach with swimmable, warm water. At low tide, you can also walk out onto a narrow, pebbly beach beside the town dock.

The main reason to come to Puerto Jiménez is to spend a night before or after visiting Corcovado National Park, because the town has the best access to the park's two main trailheads and an airstrip with flights from San José. It's also the base for the *colectivo* to Carate.

GETTING HERE AND AROUND

Because the drive is long, most visitors fly to Puerto Jiménez from San José. Driving from Golfito is a little easier these days thanks to the paved road all the way from Rincón to Puerto Jiménez; even the formerly potholed road between Chacarita and Rincón has been paved. A

faster option from Golfito is the motorboat launches, which make the trip in 45 minutes for only $6, leaving Golfito at 7:30, 10, 11:30, 1, and 3:15. Going in the opposite direction, the fast launches to Golfito leave Puerto Jiménez at 6, 8:45, 11:30, 2, and 4:15. The schedule changes frequently, so check before you head to the dock. Be sure to arrive 15 minutes early, because the boats often depart as soon as they are full. You can also hire a private taxi at the city dock in Golfito for about $100, which can drop you off in Puerto Jiménez or at your lodging.

A colectivo taxi—actually an open truck with bench seats—leaves Puerto Jiménez daily at 6 am and 1:30 pm for Cabo Matapalo and Carate. At $9 it's the cheapest way to travel, but the trip is along a bumpy road and is not recommended in rainy season (May through December). It leaves from a stop 200 meters (656 feet) west of the Super 96.

Once you arrive in Puerto Jiménez, you can get around on foot or bicycle.

RENTAL CARS Alamo. ☒ *Airport St., Puerto Jiménez* ☎ *2735–5175* ⊕ *alamocostarica.com.*

ESSENTIALS

BANK/ATM Banco Nacional. ☒ *Main street, 1 block north of Corcovado BM Supermarket, Puerto Jiménez* ☎ *2735–5020.*

POST OFFICE Correo. ☒ *Main street, west side of soccer field, Puerto Jiménez* ☎ *2735–5045.*

VISITOR INFORMATION

The National Parks Service office has information about hiking trails in Corcovado National Park and maps in an office for visitors, at the entrance to the complex, on the right-hand side. This is the only office where you can buy your entrance ticket ($15 per day, two-day minimum) to Corcovado National Park. You cannot buy tickets at the ranger stations, even if you have a reservation. The office is open

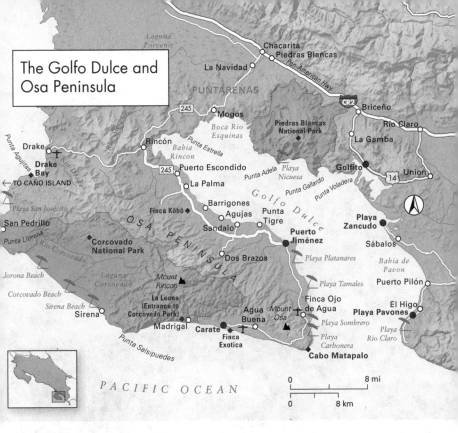

The Golfo Dulce and
Osa Peninsula

weekdays 8 to 4. For information (ask for the English version) on visiting the park, send an email request (pncorcovado@gmail.com) for an online brochure.

CONTACTS National Parks Service Headquarters. ✉ *Road running north, parallel to airstrip, Puerto Jiménez* ☎ *2735–5036.*

🍽 Restaurants

Marisquería Corcovado

$$ | SEAFOOD | If you want to enjoy a little local atmosphere, join the anglers, families, and backpackers at this tiny restaurant that has spilled over into a large waterfront garden. You can spend $9 for a plate of grilled fish or $36 on lobster. **Known for:** lobster when available; gulf view and breezes; grilled fresh fish. $ *Average main: $14* ✉ *On waterfront, east of city dock, Puerto Jiménez* ☎ *2735–5659.*

★ Pearl of the Osa

$$ | ECLECTIC | Head to this casually chic, open-air beachfront restaurant for the most upscale and memorable dining, with a dazzling, postcard-perfect beach view and the most sophisticated menu in the Puerto Jiménez area. Standouts on the tantalizing menu include a four-soup sampler: black bean with egg, avocado, and cilantro; warm carrot ginger with red-pepper coulis; and a cold, spicy gazpacho as well as a green version. **Known for:** coffee ice cream; vegetarian choices; fish tacos and shrimp salad. $ *Average main: $15* ✉ *Iguana Lodge grounds, Playa Platanares, 5 km (3 miles) south of airstrip, Puerto Jiménez* ☎ *8848–0752* ⊕ *www.iguanalodge.com.*

PizzaMail.lt

$ | ITALIAN | This cheerful, family-run café comes with an authentic pedigree: the Colovattis are from Trieste, and the pizza is simply the best in the area. The crust is toasty crisp on the outside and chewy inside, topped with high-quality fixings and sauce made fresh every day. **Known for:** authentic Italian pastas; cheerful atmosphere; fabulous pizza and calzones. $ *Average main: $9* ⊠ *Main street, across from soccer field, Puerto Jiménez* ☎ *2735–5483* ⊗ *Closed Tues. and Sept.–Nov. No lunch.*

Restaurante Carolina

$ | COSTA RICAN | This simple alfresco restaurant in the heart of Puerto Jiménez is the most likely spot to meet locals and run into just about every visitor in town, making it a good place to pick up information. It serves decent comida típica, salads, pasta, reliably fresh seafood, and excellent fruit smoothies. **Known for:** good meeting place; comida típica; fruit shakes. $ *Average main: $8* ⊠ *Main street, near police station, Puerto Jiménez* ☎ *2735–5185.*

 ## Hotels

Playa Platanares is only about 6 km (4 miles) outside Puerto Jiménez, but lodgings there have a different feeling from those in town because they are on a lovely and quiet beach. Bosque del Río Tigre is also outside town, but inland, in a forested area beside a river, on the northeastern edge of Corcovado Park.

★ Bosque del Río Tigre Lodge

$$$$ | B&B/INN | You can't get any closer to nature than this off-the-grid lodge, famous for its excellent birding and hiking trails, wedged between forest and the banks of the Río Tigre. **Pros:** a birder's paradise; great hiking trails; fabulous food. **Cons:** limited electricity; must love living very close to nature; shared bathroom and outdoor showers. $ *Rooms from: $344* ⊠ *Riverside, in Dos Brazos de Río Tigre, 12 km (7½ miles) northwest of Puerto Jiménez, Dos Brazos del Tigre* ✛ *Turn off main hwy. at sign for Dos Brazos and follow dirt road to village and beyond, to river* ☎ *8768–8383 WhatsApp, 8705–3729 text messages only* ⊕ *www.bosquedelriotigre.com* ⊗ *Closed May, Sept., and Oct.* ⇥ *5 rooms* ⦿❨ *All-Inclusive.*

★ Danta Corcovado Lodge

$$ | B&B/INN | FAMILY | Follow the giant tapir-footprint signs to this extraordinary, rustic lodge, reminiscent of an Adirondacks camp but with oversize, whimsical wood furniture, all within hiking distance of the western edge of Corcovado National Park. **Pros:** proximity to Corcovado National Park; comfortable rusticity; unique design. **Cons:** close encounters of the insect kind in cabins; restaurant a little pricey; no A/C. $ *Rooms from: $120* ⊠ *Road from La Palma to Guadalupe, 3 km (2 miles) northwest of La Palma, La Palma* ☎ *2735–1111* ⊕ *www.dantalodge.com* ⇥ *9 rooms* ⦿❨ *Free Breakfast.*

★ Iguana Lodge

$$$$ | B&B/INN | If a long stretch of deserted beach is your idea of heaven, check out this idyllic lodge with two-story cabins set in an exquisite botanical garden. **Pros:** tranquil tropical setting; complimentary kayaks and paddleboards; breakfast included in casita rooms. **Cons:** club rooms are small and can be noisy; be prepared to get friendly with an insect or two; casitas are pricey. $ *Rooms from: $285* ⊠ *Playa Platanares, 5 km (3 miles) south of airport, Puerto Jiménez* ☎ *8848–0752* ⊕ *www.iguanalodge.com* ⇥ *11 rooms* ⦿❨ *Free Breakfast.*

Nightlife

Pearl of the Osa

GATHERING PLACES | Tuesday night there's a barbecue with tiki torches, a bonfire, and tables right on the beach. Come at 5:30 to watch the sunset; it's a good idea to reserve ahead. ⊠ *Playa Platanares, next to Iguana Lodge, Puerto Jiménez* ☎ *8848–0752.*

⚡ Activities

TOUR OPERATOR
Osa Tropical
OTHER TOURS | Isabel Esquivel runs the best general tour operation on the peninsula. Whatever travel question you ask the locals, they will usually reply "Ask Isabel," whether it's help with arranging flights, ground transportation, hotel rooms, rental houses, guided tours, or car rentals. ⊠ *Main street, across from Banco Nacional, Puerto Jiménez* ☎ *2735–5722, 2735–5062* ⊕ *www. osa-tropical.com.*

BIRD-WATCHING
The birding around the Osa Peninsula is world renowned, with more than 400 species. Regional species include Baird's trogon, yellow-billed cotinga, whistling wren, black-cheeked ant-tanager, the glorious turquoise cotinga, and, of course, the brilliant, impossible-to-miss scarlet macaws, which make frequent visits to the almond trees around town and all along the coast.

★ Bosque del Río Tigre Lodge
BIRD WATCHING | The area's best English-speaking birding guides are at Bosque del Río Tigre Lodge, just west of Puerto Jiménez, in prime birding habitat, with river, forest, and open areas. A three-hour morning bird walk starts at 5:30 am; it does not include transportation to lodge, but it does include coffee and banana bread beforehand and a hearty breakfast afterward. ⊠ *12 km (7½ miles) northwest of Puerto Jiménez, at end of dirt road and across shallow river, Dos Brazos del Tigre* ☎ *8705–3729* ⊕ *www.bosquedelriotigre.com* ✉ *$63 per person for three-hour bird walk.*

Rincón
BIRD WATCHING | One of the best spots on the peninsula to spot a rare and highly endangered yellow-billed cotinga is along the north side of the bridge over the river at Rincón. Scan the forested hills above the road. Turquoise cotingas are also spotted here. Make sure to get there before 7 am for the best birding. ⊠ *Main road, 40 km (25 miles) north of Puerto Jiménez, Rincón.*

BOATING
Cabinas Jiménez Adventure Boat Tour
SNORKELING | If you just want to get out onto the water, Captain John offers four-hour tours on a covered boat. You can explore the gulf, look for dolphins, do some snorkeling, or try plane boarding. Snacks, fruit, and soft drinks are included ($75 per person, minimum six people). The boat sails at 7:30 am. ⊠ *Cabinas Jiménez, on waterfront, Puerto Jiménez* ☎ *2735–5090* ⊕ *www.cabinasjimenez. com.*

FISHING
Puerto Jiménez is a major fishing destination, with plenty of billfish, tuna, snapper, and snook, almost all year, with the exception of June and July, when things slow down. The best offshore fishing is between December and April. Charter captains follow the fish up and down the Pacific coast, so ask at your hotel for their recommendation of the best fishing boats currently in town.

Tropic Fins Adventures
FISHING | Head out onto the Golfo Dulce or the open ocean on a sportfishing adventure aboard a custom-built 28-foot Ocean Runner, equipped with all the latest fishing equipment, a full cooler, plenty of snacks, and a healthy lunch. Captain Cory Craig, a transplanted Canadian, has been fishing these waters for more than a decade. The boat comfortably accommodates four anglers. Half-day excursions are $750; full-day trips, which can last up to nine hours, depending on how the fish are biting, are $1,100. Package tours include flight from San José, plus lodging, meals, and fishing. ⊠ *Playa Platanares, Puerto Jiménez* ☎ *8834–6079* ⊕ *www.tropicfins.com.*

Beach views at Drake Bay on the Osa Peninsula

HIKING

★ Osa Aventura

HIKING & WALKING | Many hiking guides have come on the scene since Corcovado made guides compulsory. But this long-standing company has been specializing in multiday hiking adventures into the park for more than 20 years. Hikers stay in way-off-the-beaten-track rustic lodges en route to Corcovado National Park. Osa Aventura employs bilingual biologists to lead hikes and conduct scientific research projects in which visitors can sometimes participate. ✉ *Puerto Jiménez* ☎ *2735–5670, 8372–6135* ⊕ *www. osaaventura.com* ✉ *$552 for guided hike with two nights in the park, all meals and equipment, for two hikers.*

Osa Wild

HIKING & WALKING | The focus here is on sustainable tourism, including horseback-riding treks, nighttime insect tours, kayak tours, visits to local farms, and low-impact, low-cost biologist-guided tours into Corcovado National Park. A three-day, two-night hike into the park for two averages $408 per person and includes transportation, guide, entrance fees, accommodation in tents, and all the necessary camping gear. Reserve at least a month ahead. You can rent bikes here for $10 per day. ✉ *Main street, north of Banco Nacional, across from gas station, Puerto Jiménez* ☎ *2735–5848, 8716–5775* ⊕ *www.osawildtravel.com.*

Tigre Sector

HIKING & WALKING | If you have a sturdy vehicle, it's just a 30-minute drive west to the village of Dos Brazos and the Tigre Sector of Corcovado Park. This is the newest official park entrance, with a brand-new ranger station and a community tourist center offering guided day hikes, horseback rides, and bird-watching. Few hikers come to this pristine part of the park because it's more difficult to access, which means you'll likely have it to yourself. But you must be accompanied by a certified guide, available in Dos Brazos. ✉ *Dos Brazos de Río Tigre, off main hwy. between Rincón and Puerto*

Jiménez, Puerto Jiménez ☎ *8691–4545*
⊕ *www.corcovadoeltigre.com.*

KAYAKING
Puerto Jiménez is a good base for
sea-kayaking trips on the calm Golfo
Dulce and for exploring the nearby mangrove rivers and estuaries.

Aventuras Golfo Dulce
KAYAKING | Alberto Robleto has amassed
an impressive fleet of kayaks with
excellent safety equipment for snorkeling, dolphin-watching, and bird-watching
tours. The most popular tours are the
three-hour mangrove tour and the sunset
kayaking tour on the gulf, when dolphins
are often jumping (each tour $52). There's
also a kayaking tour to witness the
bioluminescence phenomenon, offered
eight days before and after a new moon.
✉ *Road to Playa Platanares, southeast
of airport, Puerto Jiménez* ☎ *2735–5195*
⊕ *www.aventurastropicales.com.*

Corcovado National Park

The crown jewel of the country's national
park system, Corcovado is the ultimate
in off-the-grid adventure. The only way
to see it is on foot, with a certified
naturalist guide to interpret the incredible
biodiversity that has made this park the
most rewarding and challenging natural
experience in the country.

GETTING HERE AND AROUND
The easiest way to visit remote Corcovado
National Park is by boat from Drake Bay
or on foot from Carate. A 20-minute boat
trip from Drake Bay gets you to the San
Pedrillo entrance. The boat trip from Drake
Bay to Sirena takes 45 minutes to one
hour. From Carate airfield, where the road
and therefore taxis from Puerto Jiménez
stop, it's about a 45-minute walk along
the beach to La Leona park entrance. You
also can access the park for guided day
tours from Corcovado el Tigre (⊕ *www.
corcovadoeltigre.com*) or from the Los
Patos entrance near La Palma.

You can hire a private taxi in Puerto
Jiménez ($90) to take you to Carate, pay
$15 per person for a shared taxi or, the
cheapest option, hop on the colectivo
pickup truck for $9. Since all visitors must
be accompanied by a guide, transportation to the park is usually included in the
cost of an overnight package tour.

 Sights

★ Corcovado National Park
(*Parque Nacional Corcovado*)
NATIONAL PARK | This is the last and larg-
est outpost of virgin lowland rain forest
in Central America, and it's teeming
with wildlife. Visitors who tread softly
along the park's trails may glimpse
howler, spider, and squirrel monkeys,
coatimundis, peccaries (wild pigs),
poison dart frogs, scarlet macaws, and,
very rarely, jaguars and tapirs.

Most first-time visitors to Corcovado
come on a daylong boat tour from Drake
Bay or hike in from Carate, Los Patos,
or Dos Brazos del Río Tigre. But to get
to the most pristine, wildlife-rich areas,
you need to walk, and that means a
minimum of three days: one day to walk
in, one day to walk out, and at least one
day inside the park. Park policy requires
every visitor to be accompanied by a
certified naturalist guide. Whichever
guide or tour company you hire can make
the park reservation and pay the park
entrance fees for you in Puerto Jiménez.
All accommodation and food within the
park are now provided by a local community consortium called ADI Corcovado
(*reservaciones@adicorcovado.org*).

The daily limit on the number of overnight visitors at the Sirena station is 70,
bunking down in platform tents with all
meals and bedding provided. No outside
food is allowed. There's also camping ($4)
at the San Pedrillo sector, but without
meals or bedding. Ranger stations are
officially open from 7 am to 4 pm daily,
but you can walk in almost any time with

a certified guide, as long as you have reserved and paid in advance. For safety reasons, there is no longer any night walking permitted into or out of the park. For more information, see the highlighted listing in this chapter. ⊠ *Corcovado National Park, Carate* ⊕ *www.sinac.go.cr* ✆ *$15 per day.*

Hotels

Meals and lodging at Sirena station are now organized by ADI Corcovado, a community organization that has greatly improved everything from platform tents to meals to bathrooms. All reservations have to be arranged and paid for in advance by emailing *reservaciones@ adicorcovado.org.*

Camping is your only option inside the national park. You must reserve camping and prepared meals well in advance since there's room for only 70 campers at La Sirena. Excellent meals served in the Sirena station cost $20 for breakfast, $25 for lunch or dinner (children half price). Meal times are 6–8 am for breakfast, noon–1 for lunch, and 6–7 for dinner. Accommodation is in bunkbeds on a covered platform, with bedding included, $30 per night. You cannot prepare any food in the park, but you can bring in trail mix and snacks. There's a shop at Sirena where you can buy snacks and bottled water. Camping at San Pedrillo, with your own gear and no meals, is $4 per night. The maximum stay in the park is four nights and five days. Guides are mandatory; therefore, the guide making all the arrangements is usually included in a guided package tour.

🏃 Activities

If your reason for coming to the Osa Peninsula is Corcovado National Park, choose a lodge that has resident naturalist guides. On the Drake Bay and gulf sides of the park, all the lodges arrange guided trips into Corcovado, most with their own guides. Tour operators in Puerto Jiménez and Drake Bay also run guided trips in the park.

HIKING

Corcovado has 13 ecosystems within its boundaries, ranging from mangroves and swamps to lowland rain forest. The park also has more forest giants (trees that stand 165 to 264 feet high) than anywhere in Central America.

There are two main hiking routes to Corcovado. One begins near La Palma, at Los Patos entrance. The other is a beach trail—an easy, if hot, 3½-km (2¼-mile), 45-minute shore walk from Carate to La Leona entrance, followed by a 16-km (10-mile) walk to La Sirena. You can hike from Drake Bay to San Pedrillo; it's 14 km (8½ miles) and you need to pay attention to tides and some rocky sections. You can also take a boat to the San Pedrillo station and hike the trails there, as well as camp. There are two other, less-traveled official entrances to the park with ranger stations: Los Planes, inland from Drake Bay, and a new entrance at El Tigre, west of Puerto Jiménez.

Hiking is always tough in the tropical heat, but the forest route from Los Patos is cooler than the beach hike to La Leona. Although it is possible to hike La Leona at high tide, it's more difficult because you have to walk on a slope rather than the flat part of the beach. The hike between any two stations takes all day.

The hike from La Leona to Sirena requires crossing one big river mouth and a stretch of beach that can be crossed only at low tide. Some guides do it very early in the morning, just before sunrise, to avoid the blistering heat along the beach.

The hike from Los Patos to Sirena is shady all the way; it's 25 km (about 14 miles) and takes about eight hours. Bring plenty of water along. The Sirena ranger station and El Tigre sector have great trails that can easily fill a couple of days.

Swimming on the beach near Sirena is not advised because of rip currents and bull sharks. Also steer clear of the brackish Río Sirena, home to crocs, bull sharks, and snakes. The only advisable swimming area is the Río Claro.

Cabo Matapalo

21 km (14 miles) south of Puerto Jiménez.

The southern tip of the Osa Peninsula, where virgin rain forest meets the sea at a rocky point, retains the kind of natural beauty that people travel halfway across the world to experience. From its ridges you can look out on the blue Golfo Dulce and the Pacific Ocean, sometimes spotting whales in the distance. The forest is tall and dense, with the highest and most diverse tree species in the country, usually draped with thick lianas.

The name Matapalo refers to the strangler fig, which germinates in the branches of other trees and extends its roots downward, eventually smothering the supporting tree by blocking the sunlight. Flocks of brilliant scarlet macaws and troops of monkeys are the other draws here.

GETTING HERE AND AROUND

If you drive one hour south from Puerto Jiménez, be prepared for a bumpy ride and a couple of river crossings. During the height of rainy season, in October and November, cars are sometimes washed out along rivers to the ocean. Most hotels arrange transportation in 4WD taxis or their own trucks. The cheapest—and the roughest—way to travel is by colectivo ($10), which leaves Puerto Jiménez at 6 am and 1 pm. Buses do not serve Cabo Matapalo.

 Restaurants

Martina's Bar & Restaurant
$$ | CONTEMPORARY | Formerly known as Bar Buena Esperanza, as the road sign still says, this is the coolest, liveliest—and only!—upscale bar-restaurant on the road from Puerto Jiménez to Carate. It would still be the best even if there were others, thanks to a short but scrumptious menu featuring contemporary versions of local fish, pork, chicken, and salads. **Known for:** panko-encrusted mahimahi with tropical fruit salsa; gnocchi with fresh vegetable sauce, Parmesan, and arugula salad; grilled sesame tuna with Thai coleslaw. $ *Average main: $15* ⊠ *On road to Carate, just before Río Carbonera crossing, in Matapalo, Cabo Matapalo* ☎ *8360–9979* ⊘ *Closed last week of Aug.*

🛏 Hotels

★ Bosque del Cabo
$$$$ | RESORT | Atop a cliff at the tip of Cabo Matapalo, this lodge has unparalleled views of the Golfo Dulce merging with the endless blue of the Pacific, as well as 750 acres of primary forest, home to plenty of monkeys and peccaries, as well as the occasional puma and ocelot. **Pros:** luxurious bungalows; fabulous trails and guides; congenial atmosphere among guests at cocktail hour and dinner. **Cons:** limited electricity supply; rates do not include $40 round-trip transfer fee per person; steep trail to beach and back. $ *Rooms from: $580* ⊠ *Road to Carate, 22 km (14 miles) south of Puerto Jiménez, Cabo Matapalo* ☎ *2735–5206, 4070–2025 at lodge* ⊕ *www.bosquedelcabo.com* ⇄ *18 units* ❍ *All-Inclusive.*

★ El Remanso Rainforest Wildlife Lodge
$$$$ | B&B/INN | This tranquil, sophisticated retreat in a forest brimming with birds and wildlife, 400 feet above a mostly deserted beach studded with tide pools, has luxurious two- to five-person cabinas with screened windows, king-size beds,

The view from the deck of the Toucan cabina at Bosque del Cabo

contemporary bathrooms with spacious showers, and private decks with forest and ocean views. **Pros:** gorgeous natural setting; jungle views; easy access to beach. **Cons:** no hair dryers; steep drive down to lodge; no A/C. $ *Rooms from: $550* ⊠ *Main road to Carate, Cabo Matapalo* ✛ *22 km (14 miles) south of Puerto Jiménez* ☎ *2735–5569 office, 8814–5775* ⊕ *www.elremanso.com* ⇨ *16 rooms* ⊙ *All-Inclusive.*

★ Lapa Ríos

$$$$ | ALL-INCLUSIVE | Set in a vast, private nature reserve, with a breathtaking view from the lodge's high jungle ridge, this is the first and most spectacular ecolodge in Costa Rica, garlanded with numerous awards for its mix of sustainability, conservation, service, and comfort. **Pros:** excellent, professional service; price includes tours and transportation and all à la carte meals; retains local flavor with friendly, well-trained staff. **Cons:** steep trail to get to beach (unless you take the shuttle service); minimum three-night stay in high season; many steps to climb to most cabins. $ *Rooms from: $1,148* ⊠ *Road to Carate, 20 km (12 miles) south of Puerto Jiménez, Cabo Matapalo* ☎ *2735–5130* ⊕ *www.laparios.com* ⇨ *17 rooms* ⊙ *All-Inclusive.*

Activities

TOUR OPERATOR

★ Everyday Adventures

ADVENTURE TOURS | Andy Pruter, an engaging, experienced outfitter, might call his company Everyday Adventures, but his trips are anything but. He will take you on guided adrenaline-pumping activities: rappelling down waterfalls ($100), climbing up a 70-foot strangler fig vine ($75), and hiking the rain forest ($60). Or you can go all out with a combination rappelling-and-climbing tour for $140. ⊠ *Cabo Matapalo* ☎ *8353–8619* ⊕ *www.psychotours.com.*

SURFING

On the eastern side of Cabo Matapalo, on Pan Dulce beach, waves break over a platform that creates a perfect, very forgiving right, drawing surfers from far and wide, especially beginners.

Pollo Surf School

SURFING | Local surf expert Oldemar (aka Pollo) Fernandez offers daily lessons at Pan Dulce Beach at his Pollo Surf School. Soft-top boards and rash guards make learning a little less painful. Expect to pay $60 per person for a two-hour group lesson, or $120 for a private lesson. Pollo also offers 1½-hour stand-up paddle-board tours, starting at the beach ($55, minimum age 14). ✉ *Cabo Matapalo* ☎ *8366–6559, 8363–1481* 🌐 *www.pollo-surfschool.com.*

Carate

60 km (37 miles) west of Puerto Jiménez.

Carate is literally the end of the road. The volcanic black-sand beach stretches for more than 3 km (2 miles), with dramatically high surf that's perfect for boogie boarding and body surfing. Swimming is best and safest around low tides. The main entertainment at the beach is watching the noisy but magnificent scarlet macaws feasting on nuts in the beach almond trees that edge the shore. Though remote, lodges now have Wi-Fi and some mobile phone coverage.

GETTING HERE AND AROUND

The road from Matapalo to Carate covers 40 suspension-testing km (25 miles); there is a bridge over the Agua Buena River and the road is periodically graded and relatively smooth—but that can all change to a sea of mud with one drenching wet season. You're better off taking the colectivo from Puerto Jiménez *(see Getting Here and Around in Puerto Jiménez, above)*.

Or give yourself a break and fly via charter plane to Carate's small airport, which has been upgraded recently; arrange flights through your lodge. From here it's 3 km (2 miles), roughly a 40-minute walk along the beach to La Leona ranger station entrance to Corcovado National Park. In rainy season (May to December) it is sometimes impossible to cross the raging Río Carate that separates the landing strip from the beach path to the park, and you may end up stranded on either side. Parking at the store in Carate is $5 per day.

Hotels

★ Finca Exotica

$$$ | **ALL-INCLUSIVE** | A garden paradise that lives up to its name, this combination organic farm and sophisticated ecolodge is an otherworldly experience, meant to be slowly and thoughtfully absorbed over a three-night minimum stay. **Pros:** discounts with cash payments; exotically delicious food; charming hosts. **Cons:** must enjoy being in a totally natural setting; communal dining; no A/C or hot water. [$] *Rooms from: $220* ✉ *Main road, east of Carate airstrip, Carate* ☎ *4070–0054, 8359–8408 WhatsApp* 🌐 *www.fincaexotica.com* 🕒 *Closed Sept. 15–Nov. 15* 🛏 *14 rooms* 🍴 *All-Inclusive.*

Lookout Inn Lodge

$$$ | **B&B/INN** | **FAMILY** | This lively barefoot inn—shoes come off at the bottom step, and steps here are plentiful—is set on a precipitous hillside with a spectacular panorama that includes a colorful garden and scarlet macaws foraging in the almond trees that line the beach. **Pros:** proximity to beach and access on foot to Corcovado Park; excellent food; party atmosphere. **Cons:** some mosquitoes; no A/C or power outlets in rooms; very steep climb to lodge and down to beach. [$] *Rooms from: $200* ✉ *Main road to Carate, east of Carate landing strip, Carate* ☎ *2735–5431* 🌐 *www.lookout-inn.com* 🛏 *11 rooms* 🍴 *Free Breakfast.*

Boat trips are a must to explore the wild Osa Peninsula.

★ Luna Lodge

$$$$ | B&B/INN | Perched on a sublime mountaintop overlooking rain forest and ocean, this is the quintessential yoga retreat, though it's universally enjoyed for its remoteness and proximity to wildlife. **Pros:** scenic setting for peace, yoga, and therapeutic massages; quiet paradise with no children under five; excellent birding. **Cons:** beach is quite a hike; large yoga groups come for retreats; extremely steep road up to lodge. $ *Rooms from: $450* ⊠ *2 km (1 mile) up a steep, partially paved road from Carate, Carate* ☎ *4070–0010, 888/760–0760* ⊕ *www.lunalodge. com* ⊅ *18 rooms* ⍜ *All-Inclusive.*

🏃 Activities

Activities here revolve around Corcovado National Park and its environs. Hiking, horseback riding, canopy tours, and other adventures must be organized through your hotel.

Drake Bay

18 km (11 miles) north of Corcovado, 40 km (25 miles) southwest of Palmar Sur, 310 km (193 miles) south of San José.

This is castaway country, a real tropical adventure, with plenty of hiking and some rough but thrilling boat rides to get here. The rugged coast that stretches south from the mouth of the Río Sierpe to Corcovado probably doesn't look much different from what it did in Sir Francis Drake's day (1540–96), when, as legend has it, the British explorer anchored here. Small, picture-perfect beaches with surf crashing against dark volcanic rocks are backed by steaming, thick jungle. Nature lodges scattered along the coast are hemmed in by the rain forest, which is home to troops of monkeys, sloths, scarlet macaws, and hundreds of other bird species.

The cheapest accommodations in the area can be found in the town of Drake, which is spread out around the bay. A trio of upscale nature lodges—Drake Bay

Wilderness Resort, Aguila de Osa Inn, and La Paloma Lodge—are clumped near the Río Agujitas on the bay's southern end. They all offer comprehensive packages, including trips to Corcovado and Caño Island. Lodges farther south, such as Copa del Arbol, Punta Marenco Lodge, and Casa Corcovado, run excursions from even wilder settings.

GETTING HERE AND AROUND

The fastest way to get to Drake Bay is to fly directly to the airstrip. You can also fly to Palmar Sur and take a taxi to Sierpe and then go on a thrilling, if bumpy, boat ride to Drake Bay. From the airport, it's a 25-minute taxi ride to Sierpe. You can pay $20 per person for a seat in a communal boat. These small, open boats leave at low tide, usually 11 to 11:30 am for the one-hour trip to Drake. You need to be at the dock at least an hour early to ensure a seat. There is also boat service from Drake Bay to Sierpe, from the beach, between 7 and 7:30 am, and around 2:30 in the afternoon. Many lodges arrange boat transportation from Drake Bay or Sierpe, and captains will often stop along the way to view wildlife in the river mangroves.

From Rincón you can drive to Drake on a 30-km (19-mile) sometimes-graded dirt road. The drive from Rincon is much easier now as all major streams and rivers have bridges, so you can pass by car year-round. A 4x4 is still recommended or at least a 4x2 with high clearance as there are still some steep climbs with rocks.

Getting here by bus is not easy. Buses leave Puerto Jiménez for La Palma about every two hours from 6 am to 8 pm, connecting in La Palma with buses to Drake Bay at 11:30 am and 4 pm daily, except Sunday. Buses leave Drake at 4:30 am and 1 pm heading for La Palma, to connect with buses in Rincón de Osa to either Puerto Jiménez or San José. These bus schedules often change, so be sure to check with a local source. The drive from San José to Drake is a scenic, but exhausting, seven hours long.

Hotels

★ Casa Corcovado Jungle Lodge

$$$$ | B&B/INN | FAMILY | This hilltop jungle lodge has it all: exquisite bungalows in the closest location to Corcovado National Park, extensive gardens, two swimming pools, a beach, excellent tours, naturalist guides, and first-class service. **Pros:** unrivaled location adjoining national park; excellent tours, service, and facilities; reasonably priced. **Cons:** no A/C; steep road to beach; an adventure to get here: be prepared for a thrilling, wet landing. $ *Rooms from: $915* ✉ *Northern border of Corcovado, Drake* ☎ *2256–3181, 888/896–6097 in U.S. toll-free, 2206–4611 lodge* ⊕ *www.casacorcovado.com* ☉ *Closed Sept.–mid-Nov.* ⌨ *14 rooms* ⦿ *All-Inclusive.*

★ Copa de Arbol Beach & Rainforest Resort

$$$$ | RESORT | Copa de Arbol is ultraluxurious, ultracool (comes with air-conditioning), ultra-expensive, and is idyllically situated between crashing ocean surf and dense jungle, right on the coastal path walking trail that connects Drake Bay to Corcovado. **Pros:** comfort, hotel-like luxury in the jungle; idyllic location; spacious rooms. **Cons:** boat transportation and tours not included; lots of steps to negotiate; accessible only by boat (with a wet landing) or on foot. $ *Rooms from: $660* ✉ *Along coastal path, one beach north of Playa Caletas, Drake* ☎ *831/246–4265 in U.S, 8935–1212* ⊕ *www.copadearbol.com* ⌨ *10 rooms* ⦿ *All-Inclusive.*

Drake Bay Wilderness Resort

$$$$ | B&B/INN | FAMILY | Perfect for multigenerational families, this beautifully maintained resort is the best deal in Drake Bay and has the most kid-friendly grounds, with lots of flat, open space for romping, plus a refreshing saltwater swimming pool and rocky tidal pools to explore. **Pros:** great location; excellent food; free perks (laundry service, snacks at sunset, and kayaks to borrow). **Cons:** no A/C in open-air dining room; minimum

three-day stay; not much privacy in the cabins with open screen windows. [$] *Rooms from: $600* ✉ *Southern end of bay, at mouth of Río Agujitas, Drake* ☎ *2775–1716* 🌐 *www.drakebay.com* 🛏 *20 rooms* 🍴 *All-Inclusive.*

Jinetes de Osa
$$ | **B&B/INN** | This small bay-side hotel overlooking the beach and almost hidden behind flowering hedges is the most comfortable and reasonably priced place to stay in the village of Drake. **Pros:** convenient location; affordable rates; adventuresome, active clientele. **Cons:** access is on foot, since the tide washes right up to the lodge steps; many steps up to hillside rooms; standard rooms are smallish with no A/C. [$] *Rooms from: $130* ✉ *West side of bay, Drake* ☎ *8996–6161* 🌐 *www.completelycostarica.com* 🛏 *15 rooms* 🍴 *Free Breakfast.*

★ La Paloma Lodge
$$$$ | **B&B/INN** | Sweeping ocean views, impeccably appointed accommodations, and lots of tropical-foliage privacy make this lodge the area's most romantic option. **Pros:** ocean views and easy access to beach; great service; interesting guests from all over the world. **Cons:** small pool; three-night minimum stay; steep, long climbs to some ranchos. [$] *Rooms from: $766* ✉ *On Drake Bay, near Drake Bay Wilderness Resort, Drake* ☎ *2239–0954 office in San José, 2775–1684 lodge* 🌐 *www.lapalomalodge.com* ⏲ *Closed Sept. and Oct.* 🛏 *11 rooms* 🍴 *All-Inclusive.*

Activities

TOUR OPERATORS

Jinetes de Osa
DIVING & SNORKELING | Experienced guides run popular diving ($140 for a two-tank dive), snorkeling ($90), and dolphin-watching ($120) tours. ✉ *West side of bay, Drake* ☎ *8996–6161* 🌐 *www.completelycostarica.com.*

★ The Night Tour
WILDLIFE-WATCHING | **FAMILY** | When you're on the Osa Peninsula, the wildest nightlife is outdoors. Join entomologist Tracie Stice (also known as the Bug Lady) and herpetologist Gianfranco Gomez on their night tour of insects, bats, reptiles, and anything else creeping or crawling around at night. Tracie is a wealth of bug lore, with riveting insect stories from around the world. Top-of-the-line Petzl headlamps help you see in the dark. Tours are $50 per person. Book ahead because these nightly tours, at 7:30 pm, are popular. ✉ *Drake* ☎ *8701–7356* 🌐 *www.thenighttour.com.*

Reel Escape
FISHING | With its ideal location close to the offshore fish-filled Furuno banks and river mouths along the coast, this charter operation has great fishing options aboard a 35-foot CABO sportfishing boat equipped with twin 450 CAT engines. There's a full-size galley, bathroom, and shower on board, and top-of-the-line fishing gear. Bilingual Capt. Willy Atencio has fished internationally, but he has come home to his native Drake Bay. He and his mates will transport you to the boat, take you where the fish are, then clean and fillet your catch. Half-day, inshore trips accommodate up to four fishers, are aboard a 26-foot panga with a 250-horse-powered Yamaha outboard motor, and cost $475. A full-day offshore (lunch included) expedition aboard the CABO runs $1,600 for up to five fishers. ✉ *Drake Bay* ☎ *8824–3036, 855/372–5322 toll-free in U.S.* 🌐 *www.fishdrakebay.com.*

Chapter 11

TORTUGUERO AND THE CARIBBEAN COAST

Updated by
Marlise Kast-Myers

11

Sights	⦿ Restaurants	⌂ Hotels	⊖ Shopping	♆ Nightlife
★★★☆☆	★★★★☆	★★★★☆	★★★☆☆	★★☆☆☆

WELCOME TO TORTUGUERO AND THE CARIBBEAN COAST

TOP REASONS TO GO

★ **Dolphin-watching:** Bottlenose, tucuxi, and Atlantic spotted dolphins ply the southern Caribbean coast.

★ **Food and flavors:** Leave *gallo pinto* (rice and beans) behind in favor of mouthwatering *rondón* (meat or fish stew) or *caribeño* (Caribbean) rice and beans, stewed in coconut milk.

★ **Music:** Mix reggae and calypso with your salsa. Rhythms waft in from the far-off Caribbean islands, and homegrown musicians are making names for themselves, too.

★ **Sportfishing:** World-class tarpon and snook attract serious anglers to the shores off Tortuguero National Park.

★ **Turtles:** People from around the world flock to the northern Caribbean for the annual nesting of four sea turtle species.

1 The Sarapiquí Loop. The Sarapiquí Loop circles Braulio Carrillo National Park, rare for its easy-to-access primary rain forest.

2 Puerto Viejo de Sarapiquí. A prime spot for wildlife viewing, the lesser-known Puerto Viejo is home to nature-themed activities.

3 Tortuguero. The roadless northern Caribbean coast encompasses the coastal jungles and canals leading to and through Tortuguero National Park.

4 Cahuita. A sloth sanctuary, national park, and several beaches are big draws here.

5 Puerto Viejo de Talamanca. A hot spot for backpackers, this colorful town is home to wildlife refuges.

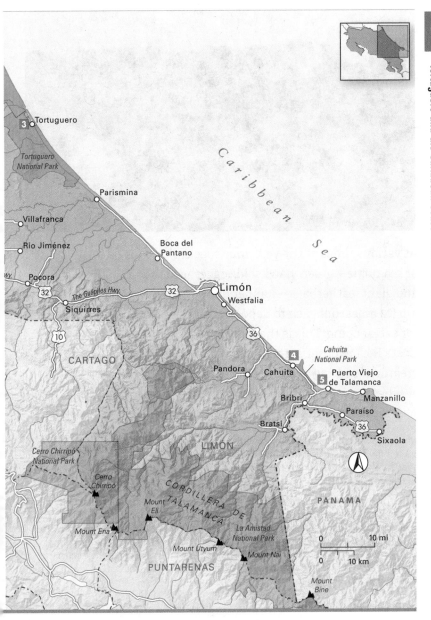

TORTUGUERO NATIONAL PARK

Tortuguero National Park

At various times of the year, four species of sea turtle—green, hawksbill, loggerhead, and giant leatherback—lumber up the 35 km (22 miles) of beach to deposit their eggs for safekeeping. This is the best place in Costa Rica to observe these magnificent creatures' nesting and hatching rituals.

In 1975 the Costa Rican government established Tortuguero National Park to protect the sea turtle population, which had been decimated after centuries of being hunted for its eggs and shells. Still, despite preservation efforts, fewer than 1% of the hatchlings will make it to adulthood.

Turtles may be the top draw here, but keep your eyes peeled for other species: tapirs, jaguars, anteaters, ocelots, howler monkeys, capuchin monkeys, three-toed sloths, collared and white-lipped peccaries, coatis, and blue morpho butterflies also populate the park. You can wander the beach when the turtles aren't nesting, but riptides make swimming dangerous, and shark rumors persist.

BEST TIME TO GO

The green turtle's July-through-October nesting season is the most popular time to visit. It rains here (a lot!) year-round, so expect to get wet no matter when you go. February through April is a tad drier.

FUN FACT

One of nature's mysteries is how turtles find their way back to the same beach where they hatched. It's thought that the sand leaves a biological imprint on the turtle hatchlings during their scurry to the sea.

BEST WAY TO EXPLORE

BIRD-WATCHING AND WILDLIFE

This is a birder's dream destination. Some of the rarer species you'll find here include the snowy cotinga, palm warbler, and yellow-tailed oriole. Waterbirds and herons abound. On a recent foray, members of the Birding Club of Costa Rica were treated to a close-up view of a wide-eyed rufescent tiger-heron chick sitting in his nest, squawking impatiently for food. You'll also see iguanas, caimans, and sloths. Bird-watching and wildlife spotting sometimes collide: while watching two beautiful agami herons feeding on a muddy bank, birders were shaken up by the sudden splash of a crocodile attacking the herons. Happily, the herons were quicker off the mark than the birders were!

BOAT RIDES

It's not quite *The African Queen,* but a boat ride along the narrow vine-draped canals here is close. Once you're off the main canal, the specially designed, narrow tour boats glide relatively quietly (using mandated electric motors) and slowly, which makes for better wildlife spotting and fewer waves that erode the lagoon banks. Another alternative is to rent a kayak and go at your own speed along the canals.

TOURS

Most visitors opt for a fully escorted tour with one of the big lodges, because you're looked after from the moment you're picked up at your San José hotel until you're dropped off a day or two or seven later. All include a couple of standard tours of the park in their package prices. It's entirely possible to stay at a smaller in-town place and make à la carte arrangements yourself.

Turtle hatchlings make their way to the sea.

TOP REASONS TO GO

LUXURY IN THE JUNGLE

Don't let tales of Tortuguero's isolation dissuade you from making a trip. No question: the place is remote. But the lodges up here package everything (overnight lodging, meals, tours, and, best of all, guided round-trip transportation) into one price, in true "leave the driving to them" fashion. You won't lift a finger.

PLANE OR BOAT ONLY

Whoever coined the old adage "Getting there is half the fun" might have had Tortuguero in mind. Plane and boat are the only ways to get to this no-road sector of Costa Rica. If you have the time, the fully escorted boat trips to and from the jungle give you a real Indiana Jones experience.

TURTLES

Tortuguero takes its name from the Spanish word for turtle (*tortuga*), and here you'll get the chance to observe the nesting and hatching of four species of sea turtle.

CAHUITA NATIONAL PARK

Cahuita National Park

In a land known for its dark-sand beaches, the coral-based white sand of Cahuita National Park (Parque Nacional Cahuita) is a real standout.

The only Costa Rican park jointly administered by the National Parks Service and a community, it starts at the southern edge of the village of Cahuita and runs pristine mile after pristine mile southward. Whereas most of the country's protected areas tender only land-based activities, this park entices you offshore as well.

Roughly parallel to the coastline, a 7-km (4-mile) trail passes through the forest to Cahuita Point. A hike of a few hours along the trail—always easiest in the dry season—lets you spot howler and white-faced capuchin monkeys, coatimundis, armadillos, and raccoons. The coastline is encircled by a 2½-square-km (1-square-mile) coral reef. The park was first created to protect this reef. You'll find superb snorkeling off Cahuita Point, but sadly, the coral reef is slowly being killed by sediment, intensified by deforestation and the erosive effects of the 1991 earthquake that hit the coast.

BEST TIME TO GO

As elsewhere on this coast, you can expect rain here no matter the time of year. February through April and September and October are drier months, and offer the best visibility for snorkeling; they are the least desirable months if you're here to surf, however.

FUN FACT

Here is Costa Rica's only national park with two-tiered entry fees. You'll pay $5 if you enter in the village of Cahuita. The entrance at Puerto Vargas, several kilometers south of town, charges $10.

BEST WAY TO EXPLORE

BEACHING IT

The waves here are fabulous for bodysurfing along the section of beach at the Puerto Vargas entrance. This wide swath of shoreline is also great for strolling, jogging, or just basking in the Caribbean sun, but be careful of riptides along this stretch of coast. The safest swimming is in front of the camping area.

CYCLING

Cycling makes a pleasant way to see the park in the dry season. Seemingly everybody in Cahuita and Puerto Viejo de Talamanca rents bicycles. (The southern entrance to the park is close enough to Puerto Viejo that it could be your starting point, too.) The park trail gets muddy at times, and you run into logs, river estuaries, and other obstacles.

HIKING

A serious 7-km (4-mile) hiking trail runs from the park entrance at Kelly Creek all the way to Puerto Vargas. Take a bus or catch a ride to Puerto Vargas and hike back around the point in the course of a day. Remember to bring plenty of water, food, and sunscreen.

SNORKELING

Tour operators in Cahuita will bring you to a selection of prime snorkeling spots offshore. If you want to swim out on your own, the best snorkeling spot is off Punta Vargas at the south end of the park. Along with the chance to see some of the 500 or so species of tropical fish that live here, you'll see some amazing coral formations, including impressive elk horn, majestic blue stag horn, and eerie yellow brain corals. When the water is clear and warm, the snorkeling is great. But that warm water also appeals to jellyfish—if you start to feel a tingling sensation on your arms or legs, head for shore.

Look up to spot wildlife on a hike in Cahuita National Park.

11

Tortuguero and the Caribbean Coast   CAHUITA NATIONAL PARK

TOP REASONS TO GO

EASY ACCESS

With one of its two entrances sitting in "downtown" Cahuita, access to the park is a snap. But ease of access does not mean the place is overrun with visitors. Fortunately, this is no Manuel Antonio.

LOTS OF LODGING

Closeness to Cahuita and Puerto Viejo de Talamanca and their spectrum of lodging options means you'll have no trouble finding a place to stay that fits your budget. You can even camp in the park if you're up for roughing it.

CORAL REEF

Costa Rica's largest living coral reef just offshore means the snorkeling is phenomenal here. Watch for blue parrotfish and angelfish as they weave their way among equally colorful species of coral, sponges, and seaweeds. Visit during the Caribbean coast's two mini dry seasons for the best visibility.

The tourist brochures tout the country's Caribbean coast as "the other Costa Rica." Everything about this part of Costa Rica seems different: different culture, different history, different climate, and different activities. (Expect different prices, too. Your travel dollar goes further here than elsewhere in the country.) This region was long ago discovered by European adventure seekers—you're quite likely to hear Dutch, German, and Italian spoken by the visitors here—but is lesser known in North American circles.

The ethnic mix differs markedly here, as it does all along the Caribbean coast of Central America. The region was first settled by the British, and then, throughout the 19th century, by the descendants of Afro-Caribbean slaves who came to work on the banana plantations and construct the Atlantic railroad. That makes the Caribbean coast the best place in the country to find English speakers, although the language is disappearing as Spanish takes over.

It is rainier here than in other parts of Costa Rica, and the rain is distributed pretty evenly year-round without a distinct dry season—though October (when the rest of Costa Rica is getting deluged with rain) is the driest month. The region will never draw the typical fun-in-the-sun crowd that frequents the drier Pacific coast, but it does offer a year-round forested lushness and just as many activities at a more reasonable price.

MAJOR REGIONS

The Sarapiquí Loop circles Braulio Carrillo National Park, rare for its easy-to-access primary rain forest.

The **Southern Caribbean coast** stretches south from port-of-call Limón to Panama. Towns along the coast have an Afro-Caribbean vibe that echoes Jamaica—and some of them are more backpackerish than others. Beaches are fringed with forest, and waters are rough. Surfers make the trip for Salsa Brava.

Planning

When to Go

HIGH SEASON: FEBRUARY TO APRIL

Climate is the Caribbean's bugaboo and will forever prevent it from becoming the same high-powered tourist destination that the northern Pacific coast is. (Frankly, we consider that to be a blessing.) The Caribbean lacks a true dry season, though February to April could be called a "drier" season, with many sunny days and intermittent showers. Yet, despite weather patterns that differ from the rest of Costa Rica, places here charge high-season rates from December to April, just as they do elsewhere in the country. Prices skew a bit lower in the Caribbean, though, than elsewhere in Costa Rica.

LOW SEASON: MAY TO AUGUST AND DECEMBER THROUGH JANUARY

The heaviest rains (and periodic road closures) come in December and January, high season elsewhere in Costa Rica. During the rainiest months visitors are fewer. May through August sees rain, too, although not quite as much. The popularity of this part of the country among European travelers means that July and August become mini high seasons here, often with a slight increase in lodging prices. Tortuguero sets its own seasons, with higher prices the norm during the prime turtle-watching months of July through September.

SHOULDER SEASON: SEPTEMBER TO NOVEMBER

Want in on a little secret? When the rest of Costa Rica settles into the soggiest time of year, the sun comes out and the weather begins to dry up in this part of the country. The Caribbean coast makes the perfect refuge from the insufferably wet months of September and October elsewhere.

Planning Your Time

Attractions near Braulio Carrillo National Park lend themselves to day trips from San José. Tour operators also have whirlwind daylong Tortuguero trips from the capital. We recommend you avoid these—the area really deserves two or, ideally, three days. Choose a single Caribbean destination and stay put if you have just a few days; Cahuita and Puerto Viejo de Talamanca are ideal for that purpose. If you have a week, you can tackle the north and south coasts.

Getting Here and Around

AIR

SANSA flies daily from San José to the small airport in Limón (LIO) and the airstrip in Tortuguero (TTQ).

CONTACTS SANSA. ☎ 2290–4100, 877/767–2672 in North America ⊕ www. flysansa.com.

BUS AND SHUTTLE

Grupo Caribeños buses, some snazzy double-deckers, connect San José's Gran Terminal del Caribe with hourly service to Guápiles, Siquirres, and Limón. Autotransportes MEPE, which has a lock on bus service to the south Caribbean coast, has a reputation for being lackadaisical but is really quite dependable. Its San José buses depart from the capital's Terminal Atlántico Norte. MEPE drivers and ticket sellers are accustomed to dealing with foreigners; even if their English is limited, they'll figure out what you want. MEPE occasionally runs extra buses to Cahuita and Puerto Viejo de Talamanca during the high season. Bus fares to this region are reasonable. From San José, expect to pay $4 to Guápiles, $7 to Limón, $11 to Cahuita, $12 to Puerto Viejo de Talamanca, and $16 to Sixaola on the Panamanian border.

If you prefer a more private form of travel, consider taking a shuttle. Comfortable air-conditioned vans of the nationwide company Interbus or the Caribbean-based Caribe Shuttle depart from San José hotels daily for Cahuita and Puerto Viejo de Talamanca. Reserve tickets ($59 one way) at least a day in advance.

BUS CONTACTS Autotransportes MEPE. ✉ C. 9, Avda. 12, San José ☎ 2758–0618 ⊕ www.mepecr.com. **Caribe Shuttle.** ☎ 2750–0626, 800/274–6191 in North America ⊕ www.caribeshuttle.com. **Grupo Caribeños.** ✉ C. Ctl., Avda. 13, Barrio Tournón ☎ 2222–0610 ⊕ www.facebook.com/grupocaribenos. **Interbus.** ☎ 4100–0888 ⊕ www.interbusonline.com.

CAR

With the exception of Tortuguero, this region is one of the country's most accessible. The southern coast is a three- to four-hour drive from San José, over mostly decent roads (by Costa Rican standards), and public transportation is frequent and reliable. Gas stations are plentiful between Guápiles and Limón, but their numbers dwindle to two on the southern coast between Limón and Puerto Viejo de Talamanca. The northern Caribbean coast is another story: the total absence of roads means you have to arrive by plane or boat. Most travelers go with a tour booked through one of the large Tortuguero lodges.

If you're driving here, remember that fog often covers the mountains in Braulio Carrillo National Park, north of San José, by early afternoon. Cross this area in the morning if you can. Always exercise utmost caution on the portion of highway that twists and turns through the park: You'll share the highway with large trucks. Check road conditions before you set out; occasional landslide closures through Braulio Carrillo necessitate leaving San José from the southeast, passing through Cartago, Paraíso, and Turrialba, then rejoining the Caribbean Highway at Siquirres, a detour that adds a tiring extra 90 to 120 minutes onto your trip.

See The Central Valley, Chapter 5.

Health and Safety

All the standard tropical precautions apply when traveling in the Caribbean region. This is a very warm part of the country, so carry water, wear a hat, and use plenty of sunscreen. The undertow is dangerous along virtually the entire coast, making swimming risky. Wear mosquito repellent in low-lying coastal areas, where a few cases of dengue and chikungunya have been reported. Costa Ricans, most of whom have never been here, will caution you on safety in this region. Crime here is no worse than anywhere else in the country.

Money Matters

ATMs are becoming more common in this part of the country, although we recommend, if possible, stocking up on cash in San José. You'll find cash machines in Puerto Viejo de Sarapiquí, Guápiles, Guácimo, Siquirres, and several in Limón. Puerto Viejo de Talamanca has two; Cahuita has one. ATMs in smaller towns may run out of cash on weekends. Remember: many smaller places—there are a lot of those here in the Caribbean—do not accept credit cards.

Restaurants

The many open-air dining spots out here provide you with that ultimate tropical dining experience, with Puerto Viejo de Talamanca offering one of Costa Rica's most varied dining scenes. Think seafood, chicken, coconut, and fruits in the Caribbean. Restaurateurs take advantage of the bounty of the land and sea in this part of the country.

Hotels

The glitzy high-rise resorts of the Pacific coast are nowhere to be found in the Caribbean. The norm here is small, independent lodgings, usually family owned and operated. Fewer visitors in this region mean plenty of decent lodging at affordable prices most of the year. But tourism *is* growing, so it's risky to show up without reservations. Despite weather patterns that differ from the rest of the country, most Caribbean lodgings charge high-season rates from Christmas through Easter, just like elsewhere in Costa Rica. Many also impose another mini high season in July and August, prime vacation months for the region's predominantly European tourist clientele. Surprisingly few places here have air-conditioning, but sea breezes and ceiling fans usually provide sufficient ventilation. Smaller places frequently don't take credit cards; those that do may give discounts if you pay with cash.

HOTEL AND RESTAURANT PRICES

Restaurant prices are the average cost of a main course at dinner or, if dinner is not served, at lunch. Hotel prices are the lowest cost of a standard double room in high season. Restaurant and hotel reviews have been shortened. For full information, visit Fodors.com.

What it Costs in U.S. Dollars			
$	$$	$$$	$$$$
RESTAURANTS			
under $10	$10–$15	$16–$25	over $25
HOTELS			
under $75	$75–$150	$151–$250	over $250

Package Tours

One of Costa Rica's most remote regions is also one of its prime tourist destinations. No roads lead to Tortuguero on the northeast coast, so plane or boat are your only options. If you don't want to bother with logistics, consider booking a package tour with one of the lodges. It will include all transport from San José and back, overnights, meals, and guided tours. Prices look high at first, but considering all you get, they are quite reasonable. Other types of regional tours are also available: **Horizontes** (☎ *2222–2022*) tours include naturalist guides and transport by 4WD vehicle.

The Sarapiquí Loop

The area immediately north of the San José metro area doesn't leap to mind when discussing ecotourism in Costa Rica, but it should. The Sarapiquí River gave its name to this region at the foot of the Cordillera Central mountain range. To the west is the rain forest of Braulio Carrillo National Park, and to the east are Tortuguero National Park and Barra del Colorado National Wildlife Refuge. These splendid national parks share the region with thousands of acres of farmland, including palm, banana, and pineapple plantations, as well as cattle ranching. Cheap land and rich soil brought a wave of Ticos to this area a half century ago. Until the construction of Highway 126 in 1957, which connects the area to San José, this was one of the most isolated parts of Costa Rica, with no tourism. Government homesteading projects brought many residents, who cleared massive swaths of the rain forest for cattle grazing and agriculture. Now, old-growth lowland rain forest, montane cloud forest, and wetlands exist only within the borders of the national parks and several adjoining private reserves. A growing selection of nature lodges have set up shop here, and you can enjoy their offerings 60 to 90 minutes after you leave the capital. (Just try getting to the Osa Peninsula on the southern Pacific coast in that same time.)

Sights

★ Rainforest Adventures

OTHER ATTRACTION | Just beyond the northeastern boundary of Braulio Carrillo National Park, about 15 km (9 miles) before the Caribbean-slope town of Guápiles, a 1,200-acre reserve houses a privately owned and operated engineering marvel: a series of gondolas strung together in a modified ski-lift pulley system. Each of the 24 gondolas holds six people plus a bilingual biologist-guide equipped with a walkie-talkie to request brief stops for snapping pictures. The ride covers 2½ km (1½ miles) in 80 minutes. The price includes a biologist-guided walk through the area for ground-level orientation before or after the tram ride. Several add-ons are possible, too, with frog and butterfly exhibits, a medicinal-plant garden, and a zipline canopy tour on-site, as well as a half-day birding tour. There is also on-site lodging. You can arrange a personal pickup in San José for a fee, or there are public buses (on the Guápiles line) every half hour from the Gran Terminal del Caribe in San José. Drivers know the tram as the *teleférico*. Many San José tour operators offer a day tour that combines the tram with another half-day option; combos with the Britt Coffee Tour, near Heredia, are especially popular. These folks operate a similar facility near the Central Pacific town of Jacó as well as in Panama and the Caribbean islands of Jamaica, Saint Lucia, and St. Maarten. ✉ *Hwy. 32, 10 km (6 miles) northeast of Braulio Carrillo National Park, Braulio Carrillo National Park* ☎ *2224–5961 in San José* ⊕ *www.rainforestadventure.com* ☞ *Tram $68, multi-activity packages $103.*

Puerto Viejo de Sarapiquí

80 km (48 miles) north of San José.

One of Costa Rica's lesser-known eco-destinations has been developing a growing selection of nature-themed activities in recent years. In the 19th century, Puerto Viejo de Sarapiquí was a thriving river port and the only link with the coastal lands straight east. Fortunes nose-dived with the construction of a full-fledged port in the town of Moín near Limón, and today Puerto Viejo has a slightly run-down air. The activities of the Nicaraguan Contras made this a danger zone in the 1980s, but now that the political situation has improved, boats once again ply the old route up the Sarapiquí River to the San Juan River on the Nicaraguan border, from where you can travel downstream to Barra del Colorado or Tortuguero. (The relationship between Costa Rica and Nicaragua could be called "icy," but that need not concern you as a visitor.) A few tour companies have Sarapiquí River tours with up to Class III rapids in the section between Chilamate and La Virgen, with plenty of wildlife to see. If you prefer to leave the driving to them, many of the lodges operate boat tours on the tamer sections of the river. Don't confuse Puerto Viejo de Sarapiquí with Puerto Viejo de Talamanca on the south Caribbean coast. Locals refer to both as simply "Puerto Viejo." We use the complete names of both towns to avoid any mix-up.

GETTING HERE AND AROUND

The Braulio Carrillo Highway runs from Calle 3 in San José and passes the Zurquí and Quebrada González sectors of Braulio Carrillo National Park. It branches at Santa Clara, north of the park, with the paved Highway 4 continuing north to Puerto Viejo de Sarapiquí. Alternatively, an older winding road connects San José with Puerto Viejo de Sarapiquí, passing through Heredia and Vara Blanca. The

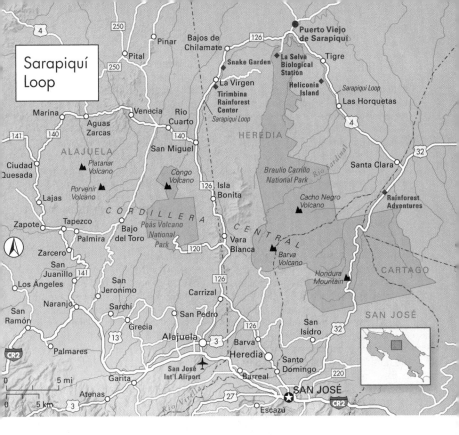

Sarapiquí Loop

former route is easier, with less traffic; the latter route is more scenic but narrow, and if you are at all prone to motion sickness, the newer road is a safer bet. Heavy rains sometimes cause landslides that block the newer highway near the Zurquí Tunnel inside the park, in which case you have to go via Vara Blanca. Check conditions before you set out. Get an early start; fog begins to settle in on both routes by the middle of the afternoon.

■ **TIP→** There are gas stations on the Braulio Carrillo Highway at the turnoff to Puerto Viejo de Sarapiquí, as well as just outside town. Fill the tank when you get the chance.

Grupo Caribeños buses travel several times daily via both routes—more frequently via the newer route, though—and leave from San José's Gran Terminal del Caribe.

ESSENTIALS

BANK/ATM Banco Nacional. ⊠ *Across from post office, Puerto Viejo de Sarapiquí* ☎ *2212–2000* ⊕ *www.bncr.fi.cr.*

MEDICAL CLINIC Red Cross. (*Cruz Roja*) ⊠ *West end of town, Puerto Viejo de Sarapiquí* ☎ *2766–6254.*

PHARMACY Farmacia Alfa. ⊠ *50 meters (164 feet) northeast of Parque Central, next to MExpress, Puerto Viejo de Sarapiquí* ☎ *2766–6348.*

POST OFFICE Correos. ⊠ *Across from Banco Nacional, Puerto Viejo de Sarapiquí* ⊕ *correos.go.cr.*

Sights

Heliconia Island

GARDEN | Some 70 species of the heliconia, a relative of the banana, are among the collections that populate 5 acres of botanical gardens on this island in the Sarapiquí River. Expect to see ample bird and butterfly life, too. ⊠ *La Chaves, 8 km (5 miles) south of Puerto Viejo de Sarapiquí, Puerto Viejo de Sarapiquí* ☏ *8331–9929* ⊕ *www.heliconiaisland. com* ⌑ *From $12.*

★ La Selva Biological Station

NATURE SIGHT | FAMILY | At the confluence of the Puerto Viejo and Sarapiquí rivers, La Selva packs about 700 bird species, 700 tree species, and 500 butterfly species into just 15 square km (6 square miles). Sightings might include the spider monkey, poison dart frog, agouti, collared peccary, and dozens of other rare creatures. Extensive, well-marked trails and swing bridges, many of which are wheelchair accessible, connect habitats as varied as tropical wet forest, swamps, creeks, rivers, secondary regenerating forest, and pasture. The site is a project of the Organization for Tropical Studies (OTS), a research consortium of 63 U.S., Australian, South African, and Latin American universities, and is the oldest of three biological stations OTS operates in Costa Rica. (OTS also operates one research station in South Africa.) To see the place, take an informative three-hour morning or afternoon nature walk with one of La Selva's bilingual guides, who are among the country's best. Walks start every day at 8 am and 1:30 pm. For a completely different view of the forest, set off on a guided two-hour walk at 5:45 am or the night tour at 7 pm. If you get at least seven people together, you can enroll in the daylong Bird-Watching 101 course, which can be arranged anytime for $80 per person; if you have at least six, you can tag along with one of the resident research scientists for a half day. Young children won't feel left out either,

with a very basic nature-identification course geared to them. Even with all the offerings, La Selva can custom-design excursions to suit your own special interests, too. Advance reservations are required for the dawn and night walks and any of the courses. ✥ *Drive 6 km (4 miles) south from Puerto Viejo de Sarapiquí, and look for signs on west side of road. La Selva is a $12 taxi ride from Puerto Viejo de Sarapiquí* ☏ *2766–6565, 2524–0607 in San José, 919/684–5774 in North America* ⊕ *www.tropicalstudies. org* ⌑ *From $40.*

Snake Garden

OTHER ATTRACTION | FAMILY | One of a growing number of Costa Rica's serpentaria, the Snake Garden shows off some 60 species of reptiles, including all the poisonous snakes (and most of the nonpoisonous ones) found in Costa Rica, as well as pythons, anacondas, and rattlesnakes from elsewhere in North and South America. You can handle a few specimens upon request and under supervision. ⊠ *Centro Neotrópico Sarapiquís, La Virgen de Sarapiquí, Puerto Viejo de Sarapiquí* ☏ *2761–1004* ⊕ *www. sarapiquis.com* ⌑ *$33.*

Tirimbina Rainforest Center

NATURE PRESERVE | This working biological research station, 17 km (11 miles) southwest of Puerto Viejo, encompasses 750 acres of primary forest and 8 km (5 miles) of trails, some of them traversing hanging bridges at canopy level. Tours introduce you to bats, frogs, and other common but often misunderstood creatures, and show off the beauty of the forest. Reservations are recommended for all activities, and required for the bat, frog, birding, and night tours. ⊠ *La Virgen de Sarapiquí, Puerto Viejo de Sarapiquí* ☏ *4020–2900* ⊕ *www.tirimbina.org* ⌑ *From $29.*

Hotels

Hotel Gavilán

$$ | **HOTEL** | In 2020, a Spanish couple purchased this little paradise where beautiful gardens run down to the river; they added a pool, free tai chi classes, and a menu blending Spanish and Costa Rican dishes. **Pros:** lovely gardens; many activities; great for birders. **Cons:** not all rooms have A/C; Wi-Fi in common areas only; need a car to stay here; rustic rooms. [$] *Rooms from: $80* ✉ *700 meters (2,296 feet) north of Comando Atlántico (naval command), Puerto Viejo de Sarapiquí* ☎ *8343–9480* 🌐 *www.gavilanlodge.com* 🛏 *20 rooms* 🍴 *Free Breakfast.*

Sarapiquís Rainforest Lodge

$$ | **HOTEL** | **FAMILY** | Within the Centro Neotrópico Sarapiquís, an environmental educational center and garden, you can stay the night inside indigenous-inspired circular *palenque* (huts) with palm-thatch roofs. **Pros:** large rooms; private terraces; buffet-style restaurant. **Cons:** sometimes difficult to find space; A/C is extra; some rooms need updating. [$] *Rooms from: $119* ✉ *Centro Neotrópico Sarapiquís, La Virgen de Sarapiquí, 17 km (11 miles) southwest of Puerto Viejo, Puerto Viejo de Sarapiquí* ☎ *2761–1004* 🌐 *www.sarapiquis.com* 🛏 *40 rooms* 🍴 *Free Breakfast.*

★ **Selva Verde Lodge**

$$$ | **HOTEL** | Built on stilts over the Sarapiquí River on the edge of a 2-square-km (1-square-mile) private tropical rain forest reserve, the lodge caters primarily to those seeking natural-history tours. **Pros:** ecology-minded staff; many activities; great for birders. **Cons:** sometimes difficult to find space in high season; steep walk to reach a few bungalows; popular with tour groups. [$] *Rooms from: $166* ✉ *Chilamate, Puerto Viejo de Sarapiquí* ✣ *7 km (4 miles) west of Puerto Viejo de Sarapiquí* ☎ *2761–1800, 833/344–5835 in North America* 🌐 *www.selvaverde.com* 🛏 *70 units* 🍴 *Free Breakfast.*

Tirimbina Rainforest Lodge

$$ | **B&B/INN** | A variety of comfy lodge accommodations put you close to this research complex's many fun nature-themed activities. **Pros:** access to the reserve without a guide; terrific rates for what's offered; rooms have A/C, a rarity in this region. **Cons:** can be difficult to find space; caters to groups, so not a place to go if you crave privacy; standard rooms are a bit spartan. [$] *Rooms from: $89* ✉ *La Virgen de Sarapiquí, Puerto Viejo de Sarapiquí* ✣ *17 km (11 miles) southwest of Puerto Viejo* ☎ *4020–2900* 🌐 *www.tirimbina.org* 🛏 *25 rooms* 🍴 *Free Breakfast.*

Activities

RAFTING

The Virgen del Socorro area is one of the most popular put-in points for white-water rafters, and offers both Class II and III rapids. The upper Sarapiquí River gets wilder and woolier with Class IV rapids to navigate. Trips leaving from the Chilamate put-in are more tranquil, with mostly Class I rapids. The put-in point depends on the weather and season. Several operators lead tours on the Sarapiquí River.

TOUR OPERATORS

Hotel Gavilán Río Sarapiquí

WILDLIFE-WATCHING | The hotel runs wildlife-watching and birding tours from its site on the river near Puerto Viejo de Sarapiquí. ✉ *700 meters (2,297 feet) north of Comando Atlántico (naval command), Puerto Viejo de Sarapiquí* ☎ *8343–9480* 🌐 *www.gavilanlodge.com* 🎟 *From $49.*

Tortuguero

30 minutes by air and 4 hours by road and boat northeast of San José.

Some compare these dense layers of green set off by brilliantly colored flowers—a vision doubled by the jungle's reflection in mirror-smooth canals—to the Amazon. That's stretching it, but there's

Steep hills and heavy rainfall make this country a mecca for white-water sports.

still an "Indiana Jones" mystique to the journey up here, especially when you get off the main canals and into the narrower lagoons. The region remains one of those Costa Rican anomalies: roadless and remote, it's nevertheless one of the country's most visited places. The tourism seasons here are defined not by the rains or lack thereof (with 200 inches of rain annually, Tortuguero is wet most of the year) but by the months of prime turtle hatching.

The stretch of beach between the Colorado and Matina rivers was first mentioned as a nesting ground for sea turtles in a 1592 Dutch chronicle. Nearly a century earlier, Christopher Columbus compared traversing the north Caribbean coast and its swimming turtles to navigating through rocks. Because the area is so isolated—there's no road here to this day—the turtles nested undisturbed for centuries. By the mid-1900s, however, the harvesting of eggs and poaching of turtles had reached such a level that these creatures faced extinction. In 1963

an executive decree regulated the hunting of turtles and the gathering of eggs, and in 1970 the government established Tortuguero National Park; modern Tortuguero bases its economy on tourism. When the 2020 COVID-19 pandemic hit Tortuguero, the lack of tourism revenue hampered its ability to fund turtle-conservation efforts. Without that added vigilance that the community is famous for, egg poaching increased once again. Tourism dollars continue to help restore the equilibrium.

A system of canals running parallel to the shoreline provides safer access to the region than the dangerous journey up the seacoast. You can continue up the canals (natural and man-made) that begin in Moín, near Limón, and run all the way to Tortuguero. Or you can embark at various points north of Guápiles and Siquirres, as do public transportation and most of the package tours. (The lodges' minivans bring you from San José to the put-in point, where you continue your journey by boat.)

Just north of the national park of the same name, the hamlet of Tortuguero is a pleasant little place with 600 inhabitants, four churches, two bars, a handful of souvenir shops, and a small selection of inexpensive lodgings, mostly occupied by backpackers. And one more plus: there are no motor vehicles here, a refreshing change from the traffic woes that plague the rest of Costa Rica. You can also take a stroll on the 32-km (20-mile) beach, but avoid swimming here because of strong riptides and large numbers of bull sharks and barracuda.

GETTING HERE AND AROUND

It's easier than you'd think to get to remote Tortuguero. Flying is the quickest (and most expensive) option. SANSA flies daily to and from San José.

If you're staying at one of the lodges, its boat will meet you at the airstrip.

The big lodges all have packages that include transportation from and back to San José, along with lodging, meals, and tours. Guide-staffed minivans pick you up at your San José–area hotel and drive you to their own put-in site, usually somewhere north of Siquirres, where you board a covered boat for the final leg on the canals to Tortuguero. The trip entails sightseeing and animal viewing. The trip back to San José stops only for a lunch break. This is the classic "leave the driving to them" way to get to Tortuguero.

A boat from the port of Moín, near Limón, is the traditional budget method of getting to Tortuguero if you are already on the Caribbean coast. Arrive at the docks before 10 am and you should be able to find someone to take you there. The going price is $40 per person each way, and travel time is about three hours.

If you arrive in Moín in your own vehicle, JAPDEVA, Costa Rica's Atlantic port authority, operates a secure, guarded parking facility for your car while you are in Tortuguero.

It's entirely possible to make the trip independently via public transportation from San José, and it's a good option if you are staying in the village rather than at a lodge. A direct bus departs from San José's Gran Terminal del Caribe to Cariari, north of Guápiles, at 9 am. At Cariari, disembark and walk five blocks to the local terminal, where you can board an 11:30 am bus for the small crossroads of La Pavona. From here, boats leave at 1 pm to take you to Tortuguero, arriving around 3 pm. La Pavona has secure parking facilities. The charge is $10 per night. The Cariari–La Pavona–Tortuguero bus-boat service is provided by COOPETRACA for $10 one way. Cariari has only spartan accommodation; La Pavona has none.

BUS AND BOAT CONTACTS COOPETRACA. ☎ *2767–7137.*

Water taxis provide transportation from multiple points in the village to the lodges. Expect to pay about $5 to $10 per trip.

ESSENTIALS

This unstaffed kiosk with free brochures offers information on the town's history, the park, turtles, and other wildlife.

VISITOR INFORMATION Kiosk. ☒ *Town center, Tortuguero.*

Sights

Sea Turtle Conservancy

WILDLIFE REFUGE | Florida's Sea Turtle Conservancy runs a visitor center and a museum with excellent animal photos, a video narrating local and natural history, and detailed discussions of the latest ecological goings-on and what you can do to help; there's a souvenir shop next door. For the committed ecotourist, the John H. Phipps Biological Field Station, which is affiliated with the conservancy and has been operating in Tortuguero since 1959, has camping areas and dorm-style quarters with a communal kitchen. If you want to get involved in the

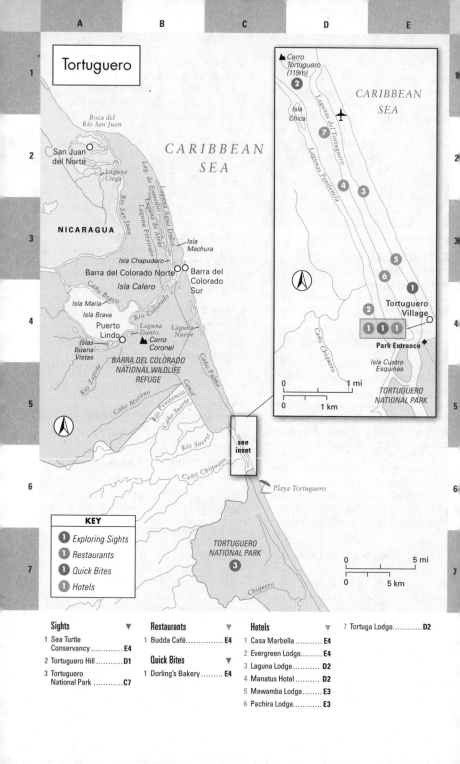

Tortuguero

CARIBBEAN SEA

CARIBBEAN SEA

Boca del
Río San Juan

San Juan
del Norte

Laguna
Ciega

NICARAGUA

Isla
Machura

Isla Chapudero

Barra del Colorado Norte

Barra del
Colorado
Sur

Isla Calero

Isla Maria

Isla Brava

Puerto
Lindo

Laguna
Danto

Laguna
Nueve

Islas
Buena
Vistas

Cerro
Coronel

**BARRA DEL COLORADO
NATIONAL WILDLIFE
REFUGE**

Río Zapote

Caño Bravo

Río Colorado

Caño Palma

Canal

Caño Moreno

Río Penitencia

Caño Suerte

Río Suerte

see
inset

Caño Chiquero

Playa Tortuguero

**TORTUGUERO
NATIONAL PARK**

Chiquero

Inset:

Cerro
Tortuguero
(119m)

Isla
Chica

Lagunas del Tortuguero

Lagunas Penitencia

Tortuguero
Village

Park Entrance

Isla Cuatro
Esquinas

**TORTUGUERO
NATIONAL PARK**

| 0 | | 1 mi |
| 0 | | 1 km |

KEY

- **1** *Exploring Sights*
- **1** *Restaurants*
- **1** *Quick Bites*
- **1** *Hotels*

| 0 | | 5 mi |
| 0 | | 5 km |

life of the turtles, help researchers track turtle migration (current research, using satellite technology, has tracked turtles as far as the Florida Keys), or help catalog the population of neotropical migrant birds, arrange a stay in advance through the center's offices in Florida. ⊠ *Tortuguero* ⊹ *From beach at north end of village, walk north along path and watch for sign* ☎ *2709–8091, 352/373–6441 in North America* ⊕ *www.conserveturtles. org* ✉ *$2.*

Tortuguero Hill (*Cerro del Tortuguero*)
MOUNTAIN | For a hike with a view, climb the steps nearly 400 feet to the top of Cerro del Tortuguero. This inactive volcano marks the highest point in the region, and rewards hikers with panoramic views of the Tortuguero canals and rain forest. If you book this experience as an organized tour through your lodge, expect to pay around $40. Otherwise, the 2.1 km (1.3 mile) hike will set you back a small $3 access fee, plus the cost of your boat taxi. Check the boat schedule to plan your return trip accordingly. ⊠ *Cerro Tortuguero of Sector Barra del Colorado Wildlife Refuge, Tortuguero* ⊹ *15-min boat ride from Tortuguero town* ✉ *$3.*

★ **Tortuguero National Park** (*Parque Nacional Tortuguero*)
NATIONAL PARK | **FAMILY** | There is no better place in Costa Rica to observe sea turtles nesting, hatching, and scurrying to the ocean. The July–October nesting season for the green turtle is Tortuguero's most popular time to visit. Toss in the hawksbill, loggerhead, and leatherback—the three other species of sea turtle that nest here, although to a lesser extent—and you expand the season from February through October. Hatching takes place September to December. You can undertake night tours only with an authorized guide, who will be the only person in your party with a light, and that will be a light with a red covering. Photography, flash or otherwise, is strictly prohibited. The sight of a mother turtle furiously digging

Did You Know?

Some people still believe turtle eggs to be an aphrodisiacal delicacy, and some bars around Costa Rica (illegally) serve them as snacks. It's a big part of the human contribution to the turtles' disappearance.

in the sand to bury her eggs is amazing, even from several yards away, and the spectacle of a wave of hatchlings scurrying out to sea is simply magnificent. This outstanding natural resource is also home to 138 mammal species including manatees, monkeys, and jaguars.

For more information see the highlighted listing in this chapter. ⊠ *South of Tortuguero village, Tortuguero* ☎ *2709–8086 Tortuguero National Park, 1192 national parks hotline in Costa Rica* ⊕ *www.sinac. go.cr* ✉ *$17.*

🏖 Beaches

Playa Tortuguero
BEACH | The crashing waves and misty air (it rains a lot in Tortuguero) give you the unsettling feeling that you're standing at the edge of the world. Swimming and surfing are simply not possible here—sharks are present along this stretch of coast, for one thing—but by night, depending on the season, this beach comes alive with the age-old ritual of Tortuguero's four species of sea turtles laying and burying their eggs. They then hatch and the baby turtles scurry out to sea, a spectacle that's viewable only in the company of a licensed guide. Sunbathing? People-watching? Who needs those when this is the real show? **Amenities: none. Best for:** solitude; sunrise; walking. ⊠ *North of Tortuguero village, Tortuguero.*

🍴 Restaurants

If you stay at one of the big lodges up here, an all inclusive package is available if you want your meals included, both in Tortuguero and on your way to and from. Usually *not* included in package prices are alcoholic beverages, soda, and bottled water. Ask to be sure.

If you're staying in town, you have simple, but satisfying, restaurant options including cafés and *sodas* (mom-and-pop restaurants serving traditional Costa Rican cuisine).

Budda Café
$ | **ITALIAN** | Pizza, crepes, pastas, and fresh fish are on the menu at this small, canal-side café in the center of town. Wood lattice over the windows, a thatch roof, and, not surprisingly, a small Buddha statue make up the furnishings. **Known for:** friendly service; cool canal-side setting; good cocktail selection. [$] *Average main: $8* ✉ *Next to police station, Tortuguero* ☎ *2709–8084* 🌐 *www.buddacafe.com.*

☕ Coffee and Quick Bites

Dorling's Bakery
$ | **CAFÉ** | What this small bakery misses in ambience and decor, it makes up for in quality baked goods to go. This is a great place to stop for breads made with banana, carrot, and *natilla* (sour cream), or for something more substantial, grab pizza, pasta, or sandwiches before a day of sightseeing. **Known for:** canal views; variety of breads; hearty, fortifying breakfasts. [$] *Average main: $5* ✉ *Tortuguero* ✣ *25 meters (82 feet) north of Catholic church* ☎ *8816–2020, 2767–0444* ⏲ *No dinner.*

🛏 Hotels

The big lodges here offer one- or two-night excursion packages. Given the choreography it takes to get up here, opt for a more leisurely two-night stay if you can. Rates look expensive at first glance, but prices usually include everything from guides, tours, meals, and snacks to minivan and boat transportation, and in some cases air travel from and back to San José. The $17 entrance fee to Tortuguero National Park may or may not be included in the package price; ask to make sure. If you calculate what you get, the price is actually quite reasonable, and the tours are undeniably great fun. Some lodges do not have phones, although all have radio contact with the outside world. All reservations must be made with their offices in San José. Be sure to travel light; you get a baggage allowance of 25 pounds, strictly enforced. There's simply no space in the boats for you to bring more. Since you're likely returning to San José at the completion of your Tortuguero tour, your hotel in the capital *might* allow you to store your bigger bags there. Ask ahead of time.

★ Casa Marbella
$ | **B&B/INN** | This B&B, the best of the in-town lodgings, is a real find, with complimentary use of kayaks, rain boots, kitchen facilities, Wi-Fi, and a full breakfast to boot. **Pros:** knowledgeable, enthusiastic owner; immaculate rooms; walking distance to all village attractions. **Cons:** no access to lodge-package amenities; can be difficult to find availability; some pedestrian street noise. [$] *Rooms from: $65* ✉ *Across from Catholic church, Tortuguero* ☎ *2709–8011* 🌐 *casamarbella.tripod.com* 🛏 *14 rooms* 🍴 *Free Breakfast.*

★ Evergreen Lodge
$$$$ | **RESORT** | The Evergreen offers an entirely different (and intimate) concept in Tortuguero lodging: whereas other lodges have cabins arranged around a clearing, at Evergreen they are built on stilts and penetrate deep into the forest. **Pros:** seclusion from other lodges; no minimum night stay required, like at most lodges; informative tours with knowledgeable guides. **Cons:** farther from town than other lodges; quietest of area

accommodation, so not a place if you look for action; rustic rooms. $ *Rooms from: $500* ⊠ *2 km (1 mile) from Tortuguero village on Canal Penitencia, Tortuguero* ☎ *2709–8213, 2222–6840 in San José* ⊕ *www.evergreentortuguero. com* ⊅ *66 cabins* ❍❘ *All-Inclusive.*

Laguna Lodge

$$$$ | RESORT | Laguna is the largest of the Tortuguero lodges, with a mix of concrete and wood buildings spread out over 12 acres of grounds on a thin sliver of land between the ocean and the first canal inland, and it hums with activity. **Pros:** family pool; unique architecture; open-air restaurant that extends over the canal. **Cons:** not for those who crave solitude; some rooms on the basic side; large numbers of guests. $ *Rooms from: $534* ⊠ *Between ocean and first canal inland, Tortuguero* ☎ *2709–8082, 2253–1100 in San José* ⊕ *www.lagunatortuguero.com* ⊅ *106 rooms* ❍❘ *All-Inclusive.*

Manatus Hotel

$$$$ | RESORT | Amenities such as air-conditioning, satellite television, fitness centers, and spa treatments are typically not found in Tortuguero, but one of the area's most luxurious hotels has them all. **Pros:** intimate surroundings; numerous creature comforts not ordinarily found here; friendly staff with knowledgeable guides. **Cons:** food is unimpressive; quiet seclusion, so not a place to go if you seek action; fills up quickly in high season. $ *Rooms from: $540* ⊠ *Across river, about 1 km (½ mile) north of village, Tortuguero* ☎ *2709–8197, 2239–7364 in San José* ⊕ *www.manatuscostarica.com* ⊅ *12 rooms* ❍❘ *All-Inclusive.*

Mawamba Lodge

$$$$ | RESORT | Nestled between the river and the ocean, Mawamba is the perfect place to kick back and relax, and it is also the only jungle lodge within walking distance (about 10 minutes) of town. **Pros:** many activities; walking distance to village; includes meals, guided tours, and transportation. **Cons:** no A/C; trip

to beaches and sunset dinner cruise aren't included in the price; rustic rooms. $ *Rooms from: $508* ⊠ *½ km (¼ mile) north of Tortuguero on ocean side of canal, Tortuguero* ☎ *2709–8181, 2293–8181 in San José* ⊕ *www.mawamba.com* ⊅ *54 cabinas* ❍❘ *All-Inclusive.*

Pachira Lodge

$$$$ | RESORT | This is the prettiest of Tortuguero's lodges, but not the costliest—the owners here market competitively and keep prices reasonable. **Pros:** many activities; hotel has private walking trails; beautiful surroundings. **Cons:** no a/c in rooms; not for those who crave solitude; large numbers of guests. $ *Rooms from: $490* ⊠ *Across river from Sea Turtle Conservancy, Tortuguero* ☎ *2709–8172, 2257–2242 in San José, 800/644–7438 in North America* ⊕ *www.pachiralodge.com* ⊅ *94 rooms* ❍❘ *All-Inclusive.*

★ Tortuga Lodge

$$$$ | RESORT | Lush lawns, orchids, and tropical trees surround this thatch riverside lodge, renowned for its nature packages and top-notch, personalized service. **Pros:** many activities; seclusion from other lodges; top-notch guides and service. **Cons:** this is farther from the park than most lodges in the area; two-night minimum stay; noise from two daily flights. $ *Rooms from: $592* ⊠ *Across river from airstrip, 2 km (1 mile) from village, Tortuguero* ☎ *2709–8034, 2521–6099 in San José, 800/672–8704* ⊕ *www.tortugalodge.com* ⊅ *28 rooms* ❍❘ *All-Inclusive.*

🏃 Activities

FISHING

You have your choice of mackerel, tarpon, snook, and snapper if you fish in the ocean; snook and calba if you fish in the canals. If you opt for the latter, the National Parks Service levies a $30 license fee (you are fishing in the confines of Tortuguero National Park), good for one month. Operators include the fee in your tour price.

The magnificent emerald basilisk is just one of the creatures found in Tortuguero National Park.

Eddie Brown

FISHING | With 40 years of experience, longtime area fishing expert Eddie Brown and his brother Roberto offer half-day fishing packages for $275; daylong excursions are $500. ✉ *Tortuguero* ☎ *8834–2221* ⊕ *www.captaineddiebrown.com.*

Tortuguero Sport Fishing

FISHING | Known as "Primo" to everyone in town, Elvin Gutiérrez takes two passengers out on the ocean for two hours or more, at $80 per hour, or for a full nine-hour day ($550). Prices include boat, guide, and refreshments. ✉ *Tortuguero* ☎ *2709–8115* ⊕ *www.tortuguerosport-fishing.com.*

TOURS

Tortuguero is one of those "everybody's a guide" places. Quality varies, but most guides are quite knowledgeable. If you stay at one of the lodges, guided tours are usually included in your package price (check when you book). If you hire a private guide, $20 to $25 per person per hour is the going rate, depending on the excursion, with most lasting three hours.

Casa Cecropia (*Cacao Tour*)

CULTURAL TOURS | When in Costa Rica, dive into chocolate with a history lesson where you can taste the cacao fruit, smell the roasted beans, and transform them into artisanal chocolate. Two-hour tours require reservations and are available in Spanish, English, and French. ✉ *Tortuguero village, next to entrance to Tortuguero National Park, Tortuguero* ☎ *2709–8196* ⊕ *www.casacecropia.com* 💵 *$25* ⏱ *Tours at 10:30 am and 4 pm; reservation required.*

Riverboat Francesca

GUIDED TOURS | Local indigenous Miskito guide Sven Watson is legendary for his bird- and animal-spotting skills. The family's riverboat, *Francesca*, can take you up the canals for two-day, one-night excursions to Tortuguero for $235 to $250 per person, depending on the lodge used. As with all Tortuguero excursions, Watson offers a more leisurely three-day, two-night trip as well. If you're interested only in seeing the canals, a four-hour tour ($85) includes lunch. Trips begin at the

Caribbean port of Moín, 5 km (3 miles) northwest of Limón. ☎ *2226–0986 in San José, 810/433–1410 in North America* ⊕ *www.tortuguerocanals.com.*

Sea Turtle Conservancy

OTHER TOURS | Call or stop by the visitor center at the Sea Turtle Conservancy to get a recommendation for good local guides. (Someone is not always there, though.) ✉ *Tortuguero* ☎ *2709–8091, 352/373–6441 in North America* ⊕ *www. conserveturtles.org.*

Victor Barrantes

ADVENTURE TOURS | Local guide and area expert Victor Barrantes conducts hiking and boating tours around the area, including treks to Tortuguero Hill, as well as turtle tours July–October. ✉ *Tortuguero* ☎ *8928–1169* ⊕ *tortugueroinfo.tripod. com* ✉ *From $30.*

TURTLE-WATCHING

If you want to watch the *deshove* (egg laying), contact your hotel or the parks office to hire a certified local guide, required on turtle-watching excursions. Note that you won't be allowed to use a camera—flash or nonflash—on the beach, and only your guide is permitted to use a flashlight (and that must be covered with red plastic), because lights can deter the turtles from nesting. Wear dark clothing if you can, and avoid loud talking. Smoking is prohibited on the tours.

■ **TIP→ A few unscrupulous locals will offer to take you on a turtle-watching tour outside the allowed February–November season, disturbing sensitive nesting sites in the process. If it's not the season, don't go on a turtle excursion. As the signs around town admonish: "Don't become another predator."**

Cahuita

44 km (26 miles) southeast of Limón.

Dusty Cahuita (pronounced *cah-WEE-tah*), its main street flanked by wood-en-slat cabins, is a backpackers' vacation town—a hippie hangout where you can be immersed in Afro-Caribbean culture. Tucked in among the backpackers' digs are a few surprisingly nice get-away-from-it-all lodgings, and restaurants with some tasty cuisine at decent prices. After years of negative crime-related publicity, Cahuita has beefed up security and has made a well-deserved come-back on the tourist circuit. No question that nearby Puerto Viejo de Talamanca has overtaken Cahuita and become the hottest spot on the southern Caribbe-an coast. But as Puerto Viejo grows exponentially, Cahuita's appeal is that it remains small and manageable. It's well worth a look.

GETTING HERE AND AROUND

Autotransportes MEPE buses travel from San José's Terminal Atlántico Norte seven times a day—plan on four hours for the trip—and approximately hourly through-out the day from Limón and Puerto Viejo de Talamanca. The bus terminal here sits at the entrance to Cahuita, about four blocks from the town center. You can give yourself a wider selection of times than the six daily San José–Cahu-ita services: hourly Grupo Caribeños buses connect San José with Limón, and hourly MEPE buses connect Limón with Cahuita. The MEPE and Caribeños terminals are one block apart in Limón. Walking could be an option if you're not laden with bags and if it's still light out. Unlike MEPE vehicles, Caribeños buses are air-conditioned.

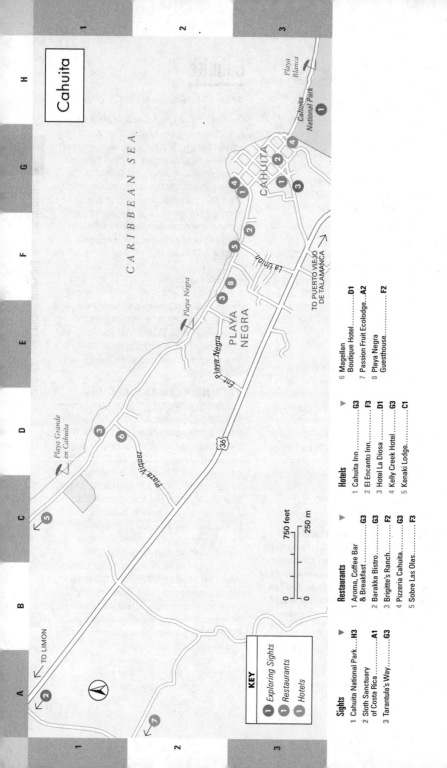

Cahuita

CARIBBEAN SEA

Playa Grande en Cahuita

Playa Negra

PLAYA NEGRA

Playa Blanca

Cahuita National Park

CAHUITA

La Union

TO PUERTO VIEJO DE TALAMANCA

Plaza Vizquez

Ent. Playa Negra

TO LIMON

36

KEY

1 Exploring Sights
1 Restaurants
1 Hotels

0   750 feet
0   250 m

Sights

1 Cahuita National Park....**H3**
2 Sloth Sanctuary
 of Costa Rica **A1**
3 Tarantula's Way......**G3**

Restaurants ▶

1 Aroma, Coffee Bar
 & Breakfast.............**G3**
2 Barakka Bistro.............**G3**
3 Brigitte's Ranch...........**F2**
4 Pizzeria Cahuita..........**G3**
5 Sobre Las Olas............**F3**

Hotels ▶

1 Cahuita Inn................**G3**
2 El Encanto Inn............**F3**
3 Hotel La Diosa **D1**
4 Kelly Creek Hotel.........**G3**
5 Kenaki Lodge.............**C1**

6 Magellan
 Boutique Hotel.........**D1**
7 Passion Fruit Ecolodge...**A2**
8 Playa Negra
 Guesthouse.............**F2**

Car travel is straightforward: watch for signs in Limón and head 45 minutes south on the coastal highway. Road conditions fluctuate with the severity of the previous year's rains and with the speed at which highway crews patch the potholes (the road's blacktop surface makes it a never-ending battle).

If driving from Limon, you'll pass several banana farms that account for 80% of Costa Rica's plantations.

Cahuita has three entrances from the highway: the first takes you to the far north end of the Playa Negra road, near the Magellan Inn; the second, to the middle section of Playa Negra, near the Atlántida Lodge; and the third, to the tiny downtown.

The proximity of the Panamanian border means added police vigilance on the coastal highway. No matter what your mode of travel, expect a passport inspection and cursory vehicle search at a police checkpoint just north of Cahuita. If you're on public transportation, you may be required to disembark from the bus while it's searched.

NAVIGATING CAHUITA

Cahuita's tiny center is quite walkable, if dusty in the dry season and muddy in the wet season once you get off the few paved streets. It's about a 30-minute walk to the end of the Playa Negra road to Hotel La Diosa. Always take a taxi to or from Playa Negra and Playa Grande after dark. Cahuita has a couple of officially licensed red taxis, but most transportation is provided informally by private individuals. To be on the safe side, have your hotel or restaurant call a driver for you.

Bicycles are a popular means of utilitarian transportation in Cahuita. Seemingly everyone rents basic touring bikes for $20 per day, but quality varies widely— and note that no one rents helmets.

Recycle!

Unfortunately, it's difficult to recycle in most places in Costa Rica, but Cahuita and Puerto Viejo de Talamanca have made it a breeze. Separate and deposit your aluminum cans and glass and plastic beverage bottles in the *Recicaribe* barrels you'll see in either community.

ESSENTIALS

BANK/ATM Banco de Costa Rica. ⊠ *Bus terminal at entrance to town, Cahuita* ☎ *2211–1111.*

PHARMACY Farmacia Quiribrí. ⊠ *Bus terminal, Cahuita* ☎ *2755–0505.*

POST OFFICE Correos. ⊠ *Bus terminal, Cahuita* ⊕ *correos.go.cr.*

Sights

Cahuita National Park

(*Parque Nacional Cahuita*)

NATIONAL PARK | With rain forest extending right to the edge of a curving, utterly undeveloped 3-km (2-mile) white sand beach, this popular national park is the stuff of picture postcards. The park was created to protect the 2½-square-km (1-square-mile) coral reef that encircles the coast and offers excellent snorkeling off Cahuita Point. Trails into the rain forest reveal a wealth of wildlife. February through April and September and October are slightly drier months, and offer the best visibility for snorkeling. A nice touch to the infrastructure here is the "plastic walk," a boardwalk path made of recycled plastic. Visitors in wheelchairs can be wheeled down to the surf in the park's own chairs. The location means you'll find a great selection of in-town dining and lodging options within a few blocks of the park's northern entrance, making this one of

Kayaking is a popular activity in Tortuguero.

the country's easiest protected areas to visit. Choose from two park entrances: one is in downtown Cahuita; the other is at Puerto Vargas, just off the main road, 5 km (3 miles) south of town. If you don't have a car, you can get here easily via bike or taxi. ⊠ *Southern end of Cahuita, Cahuita* ☎ *2755–0461 Cahuita entrance, 2755–0302 Puerto Vargas entrance, 1192 national parks hotline in Costa Rica* 🖃 *Donation at Cahuita entrance; $5 at Puerto Vargas entrance.*

★ Sloth Sanctuary of Costa Rica

NATURE PRESERVE | FAMILY | This full-fledged nature center a few miles northwest of Cahuita is well worth a stop. Many of the sloths that live on the premises are here because of illness or injury and are not on display to the public, but Buttercup, the very first of their charges, holds court in the nature-focused gift shop. She has been joined by Leno, a Bradypus male— that's one of the two sloth species found in Costa Rica—who can be found in the aquarium. A visit is a good way to learn about these little-known animals. Your admission contributes to further care and research by the good-hearted folks who operate the facility. Reservations are required for a special insider's tour ($150) that takes you behind the scenes into the sloth clinic and nursery. ⊠ *Cahuita* ✛ *9 km (5 miles) northwest of Cahuita; follow signs on Río Estrella delta* ☎ *6450–0312 WhatsApp* ⊕ *www.slothsanctuary.com* 🖃 *From $28* ⊗ *Closed Mon.* ☞ *Tours on the hr 8–2.*

Tarantula's Way

OTHER ATTRACTION | If you want a primer on things that creep and crawl in the night, here's the tour for you. An expert guide takes you on a two-hour walk through a jungle setting, and you'll spot ants, frogs, lizards, snakes, and, of course, tarantulas. Advance reservations are required. Group size is limited to six. No tours are given on rainy nights. ⊠ *Cahuita* ✛ *300 meters (984 feet) west of bus station at entrance to town* ☎ *8720–3253* 🖃 *$40.*

Beaches

Playa Blanca (*White Beach*)
BEACH | Costa Rica's Caribbean coast has no true white-sand beaches, but Cahuita's in-town beach is as close as it gets (*blanca* means "white" in Spanish). Right at the town entrance to the national park, you're a few steps from local eateries. The park's jungle comes right up to the beach's edge, creating one of those postcard-perfect views. The undertow can be strong here; swimmers are more likely to venture out near the center of the beach. Use caution in any case. **Amenities:** food and drink. **Best for:** sunrise; walking. ✉ *Town center, Cahuita.*

Playa Grande
BEACH | Beyond the Atlántida Lodge, Playa Negra's black sand lightens to a dark brown. Whether this constitutes a separate beach or not is open for debate, but the lodgings out here distinguish their stretch of sand as "Playa Grande." You're much farther from town here; the beach feels even more isolated. Do be careful—as with all beaches on this coast, the undertow makes swimming risky. Restaurant Bananas has food and drinks just 100 meters (328 feet) south of Playa Grande. Camping is permitted on the beach for a small fee. **Amenities:** none. **Best for:** sunrise; walking. ✉ *Cahuita* ☎ *8558–5285 camping.*

Playa Negra (*Black Beach*)
BEACH | Cahuita's Playa Negra—it's not the same as the beach of the same name in Puerto Viejo de Talamanca—fronts a narrow road heading north out of the town center. Depending on the stretch of sand, it puts you a few steps from eateries. Your fellow beachgoers will likely be surfers. Remember: the waves that make for good surfing conditions cause problems for swimming. Most stretches of black-sand Playa Negra feel isolated. If there aren't visitors around, don't linger. **Amenities:** food and drink. **Best for:** sunrise; surfing; walking. ✉ *Cahuita.*

Restaurants

Aroma, Coffee Bar & Breakfast
$$ | **VEGETARIAN** | Fortify yourself for a day of sightseeing with a vegan breakfast, perhaps banana pancakes or crepes, at this semi-open-air spot. For lunch, dig into a variety of vegan burgers and salads (mango is a favorite) with fruit cheesecakes for dessert. **Known for:** cheery owners; extensive vegan menu, a rarity in Costa Rica; great selection of smoothies. [$] *Average main: $13* ✉ *Cahuita* ✣ *50 meters (164 feet) northeast of bus station* ☎ *8808–6445* ⏲ *Closed Thurs. No dinner.*

★ **Barakka Bistro**
$$$ | **ITALIAN** | An expat Italian-French couple have fused the cuisines of their respective countries into Cahuita's most stylish and cozy dining spot. Combine a ricotta cannelloni with a croque madame in bechamel sauce, or steak tartare with a variety of bruschettas. **Known for:** macadamia pesto; attentive service; innovative blending of two cuisines. [$] *Average main: $17* ✉ *Cahuita* ✣ *50 meters (164 feet) southeast of Coco's Bar* ☎ *6079–5602* 🌐 *www.facebook.com/barakkabistrocahuita* ⏲ *Closed Mon. and Tues.*

Brigitte's Ranch
$ | **CAFÉ** | Fuel up for the day's activities at this informal, open-air café on the Playa Negra road. A hearty breakfast—served until 11 am—of banana pancakes and fruit with honey or pineapple jam does the trick. **Known for:** American-style omelets; tasty gallo pinto; hearty, fortifying breakfasts. [$] *Average main: $7* ✉ *Playa Negra road, 1½ km (1 mile) from town, Cahuita* ☎ *2755–0053* 🌐 *www.brigittecahuita.com* ⏲ *No lunch or dinner.*

Pizzeria Cahuita
$$ | **PIZZA** | Pastas and meat entrées are on the menu, but the real draw here is the 30 varieties of thin-crust pizza whipped up and served with style by a gregarious Italian family from Ravenna. The Cuatro Quesos (four cheeses) with mozzarella, Gorgonzola, Parmesan, and

Respecting Costa Rica's Animals

Yes, sloths are adorable. But if you came to Costa Rica with dreams of holding one, think again: the experience of hugging, petting, or offering food to an animal to manipulate it for photos is unlawful (not to mention, they actually hate to be touched by an unfamiliar person). Such irresponsible actions put you at risk—these are still wild animals, after all—and harm the animal's health and viability as they mend for potential rehabilitation into the wild.

If you're visiting one of the country's many animal-rescue centers, remember that every responsible center will turn down any visitor request to hold or pet the animals. Even the workers treating the animals try to limit

tactile contact as much as possible. A few unethical sites allow visitors to touch the animals and snap pics. Do not participate.

In response to the disturbing trend of the "animal selfie" in which visitors try to hold animals or entice them with food into that "perfect" photo op, Costa Rica has even started the hashtag #StopAnimalSelfies on social media to bring a halt to this practice and encourage you to share respectful photos without holding the animals, at a safe distance. Your social-media post will be just as endearing with only the animal in the photo, and you'll know that you helped to keep them safe and healthy.

---

fontina is the most popular. **Known for:** friendly service; takeout; handmade ravioli. $ *Average main: $15* ⊠ *Cahuita* ✛ *50 meters (164 feet) east of police station* ☎ *2755–0179* ⊗ *Closed Thurs.*

Sobre Las Olas
$$ | SEAFOOD | The name means "over the waves," and this is one of the few dining spots in Cahuita perched this close to the shore. Red snapper is the house specialty, but other seafood and pasta dishes are on the menu, too, along with affordable sandwiches and lighter fare. **Known for:** fresh sushi; terrific ocean views; good wine selection. $ *Average main: $14* ⊠ *Playa Negra road, just north of El Encanto, Cahuita* ☎ *6074–7573* ⊗ *Closed Wed.*

 Hotels

★ Cahuita Inn
$$$ | HOTEL | Grab a hammock and sway away your cares at this beachfront property that is spotless, modern, comfortable, and possibly the best deal in

Cahuita. **Pros:** gracious hosts; authentic Italian restaurant; sleek rooms. **Cons:** often booked; tiny pool; not centrally located. $ *Rooms from: $160* ⊠ *Cahuita* ✛ *50 meters (164 feet) east of the Cahuita's Police station* ☎ *2755–0179* ⊕ *www.cahuitainn.com* ⇶ *5 rooms* ⫶◯⫶ *Free Breakfast.*

★ El Encanto Inn
$$ | B&B/INN | Cahuita doesn't get more serene than these lodgings spread out in a garden with an extensive bromeliad collection. **Pros:** friendly owners; good value for what's offered; central location without being right in the heart of things. **Cons:** friendly dogs on-site, so not a place to go if you dislike canines; some reports of patchy Wi-Fi; not for young travelers looking for a scene. $ *Rooms from: $98* ⊠ *Cahuita* ✛ *200 meters (656 feet) west of police station on Playa Negra road* ☎ *2755–0113* ⊕ *www.elencantocahuita.com* ⇶ *11 units* ⫶◯⫶ *Free Breakfast.*

Hotel La Diosa

$$ | **HOTEL** | Brightly painted stone or wood cabins—most have air-conditioning, a rarity here—are scattered around the grounds at this place on the far north end of Playa Grande. **Pros:** snorkeling tours to Playa Blanca; A/C available; friendly service. **Cons:** breakfast not included; car required to get around; far from sights. [$] *Rooms from: $95* ✉ *2 km (1 mile) north of town at end of Playa Negra road, Cahuita* ☎ *2755–0055, 800/854–7761 in North America* 🌐 *www.hotelladiosa.net* 🛏 *10 cabins* 🍴 *No Meals.*

Kelly Creek Hotel

$ | **B&B/INN** | This wonderful budget option in a handsome wooden hotel sits on the creek bank across a short pedestrian bridge from the Cahuita National Park entrance. **Pros:** good value; gracious owner; closest property to the national park. **Cons:** breakfast not included; two-night minimum stay; dark rooms. [$] *Rooms from: $70* ✉ *Next to park entrance, Cahuita* ☎ *8459–6480, 2755–0007* 🛏 *4 rooms* 🍴 *No Meals.*

Kenaki Lodge

$$ | **B&B/INN** | The rooms and bungalows at this serene lodge have dark hardwood floors and vaulted ceilings and are decorated with bright tropical colors. **Pros:** quiet seclusion; good value for what's offered; ample parking (a rarity here). **Cons:** group events may create commotion in dining area; bungalows usually booked for a year or more at a time; far from town and sights. [$] *Rooms from: $104* ✉ *Playa Grande, Cahuita* ✣ *Far north end of Playa Negra road* ☎ *2755–0485* 🌐 *www.kenakilodge.com* 🛏 *6 units.*

Magellan Boutique Hotel

$$ | **B&B/INN** | One of Cahuita's most elegant lodgings, this group of bungalows is graced with tile-floor terraces facing a pool and gardens growing on an ancient coral reef. **Pros:** every room has a private terrace; creature comforts include cable TV and Netflix; A/C in all rooms. **Cons:** staff can be too businesslike; breakfast not included; far from sights. [$] *Rooms from: $101* ✉ *2 km (1 mile) north of town at end of Playa Negra road, Cahuita* ☎ *2755–0035* 🌐 *www.magellanboutique-hotel.com* 🛏 *7 units* 🍴 *No Meals.*

Passion Fruit Ecolodge

$$ | **HOTEL** | Five houses, each named for a tropical fruit, congregate on lush, secluded gardens on the highway outside of Cahuita. **Pros:** bright, cheery houses; friendly service; pool (a rarity in these parts). **Cons:** a car is needed to stay here; breakfast costs extra; far from the beach. [$] *Rooms from: $105* ✉ *5 km (3 miles) north of town on highway, Cahuita* ☎ *8939–9823* 🌐 *passionfruitecolodge.com* 🛏 *5 houses* 🍴 *No Meals.*

★ **Playa Negra Guesthouse**

$$ | **HOTEL** | This gracious, Québécois-owned lodging set in lush, hibiscus-strewn gardens has become a Cahuita favorite. **Pros:** stylish surroundings; attentive owners; terrific rates for what's offered. **Cons:** a car is needed to get around; not all units have A/C; friendly dogs on-site, so not a place to stay if canines aren't your thing. [$] *Rooms from: $105* ✉ *Playa Negro road, Cahuita* ✣ *50 meters (164 feet) north of soccer field* ☎ *8556–2870* 🌐 *www.playanegra.cr* 🛏 *3 units* 🍴 *No Meals.*

🍸 Nightlife

Aside from the local bars, Cahuita's nightlife centers on restaurants, all pleasant places to linger over dinner for the evening.

Chao's Paradise

BARS | If you're out this way, Chao's makes for a pleasant open-air space for a beer and some seafood and fries. After dark, get here and back by taxi. ✉ *Playa Negra road, Cahuita* ✣ *50 meters (164 feet) north of soccer field* ☎ *8950–2546.*

Wildlife-watching in Cahuita National Park

Cocorico

CAFÉS | Italian eatery Cocorico shows movies many evenings at 7:30. ✉ *Main road, Cahuita* ☎ *2755–0409.*

Reggae Bar

BARS | As befits the name of the place, reggae music is on tap here a few evenings of the week. You're bound to hear "No Woman, No Cry" and all the other anthems. After dark, take a taxi to and from here. ✉ *Playa Negra road, Cahuita* ✛ *50 meters (164 feet) north of soccer field* ☎ *2755–0209* ⊕ *www.facebook.com/reggaebar.cahuita.*

Shopping

Farmers' Market

MARKET | Small by U.S. standards, this farmers' market has a handful of vendors selling fresh produce and meats in the community center building. Open Sunday 6 am to noon. ✉ *Salon Communal, Main St., Cahuita* ✛ *2 blocks north of Central Parquecito.*

Activities

Cahuita is small enough that its tour operators don't focus simply on the town and nearby national park, but instead line up excursions around the region, even as far away as the Tortuguero canals to the north and Bocas del Toro, Panama, to the south.

★ The Biologist from Cahuita

GUIDED TOURS | Dutch biologist and longtime resident David Geurds imparts his knowledge in a terrific selection of half-day and evening hiking tours in the area. ✉ *Cahuita* ☎ *8997–4714* ⊕ *banani-to-tours.jimdofree.com.*

Brigitte's Ranch

HORSEBACK RIDING | Here you can rent good bikes for $15 per day, as well as take part in half- or full-day horseback-riding excursions from $70. Chocolate tours can be arranged for $25, and jungle night tours for $35. ✉ *Playa Negra road, 1½ km (1 mile) from town, Cahuita* ☎ *2755–0053* ⊕ *www.brigittecahuita.com* ✉ *From $25.*

Willie's Tours

ADVENTURE TOURS | The town's largest tour operator can set you up with a variety of adventures, including rafting, kayaking, hiking the national park, and visiting indigenous reserves for a glimpse into traditional life. Willie's also offers tours that take you farther afield, north to Tortuguero and south to Bocas del Toro, Panama. ⊠ Main St., Cahuita ✛ 100 meters (328 feet) north of Coco's Bar ☎ 2755–1024 ⊕ www.williestourscostarica.com ✉ From $35.

Puerto Viejo de Talamanca

16 km (10 miles) south of Cahuita.

This muddy, colorful little town is one of the hottest spots on the international budget-travel circuit, and swarms with backpackers, surfers, and New Agers. For better or for worse, though, Puerto Viejo de Talamanca has outgrown its surfer roots and you'll find plenty of more "grown-up" offerings on the road heading southeast and northwest out of town.

At the last count, some 50 nationalities were represented in this tiny community, and most are united in concern for the environment and orderly development of tourism—few want to see the place become just another Costa Rican resort community. Some locals bemoan the loss of their town's innocence, as drugs and other evils have surfaced, but this is still a fun town to visit, with a great variety of hotels, cabinas, and restaurants in every price range. Unlike some other parts of Costa Rica, no one has been priced out of the market here.

Locals shorten the name to just "Puerto Viejo" (British settlers called the area "Old Harbour") but we use the complete name to avoid confusion with the other Puerto Viejo covered in this chapter: Puerto Viejo de Sarapiquí in northern

Costa Rica. (Note that you may also see this Caribbean town referred to as "Puerto Viejo de Limón.") You have access to the beach right in town, and the Salsa Brava, famed in surfers' circles for its pounding waves, is here off the coast, too. The best strands of Caribbean sand are outside the village: Playa Cocles, Playa Chiquita (technically a series of beaches), and Punta Uva, all dark-sand beaches, line the road heading southeast from town. Playa Negra—not to be confused with the Playa Negra near Cahuita—is a black-sand beach northwest of town. Punta Uva, with fewer hotels and the farthest from the village, sees fewer crowds and more tranquility. Playa Negra shares that distinction, too—for now—but developers have eyed the beach as the next area for expansion.

GETTING HERE AND AROUND

The turnoff to Puerto Viejo de Talamanca is 10 km (6 miles) down the coastal highway south of Cahuita. (The highway then continues southeast to Bribri and Sixaola at the Panamanian border). The village lies another 5 km (3 miles) beyond the turnoff. The paved road passes through town and continues to Playas Cocles and Chiquita and Punta Uva all the way to the village of Manzanillo. "Periodically potholed" describes the condition of the road from the highway into town and as far as Playa Cocles. The newer paved sections beyond Cocles haven't disintegrated (yet). Autotransportes MEPE buses travel from San José's Terminal Atlántico Norte seven times a day—plan on 4½ hours for the trip—and approximately hourly throughout the day from Limón and Cahuita. The town has no actual bus terminal. If you arrive on public transportation, you disembark at a bus shelter strewn with a few beer bottles on the street fronting the beach. (It makes an awful first impression, but this is an enjoyable town, so keep your disappointment in check.) The MEPE ticket office is about a half block away. All buses from San José go into Puerto

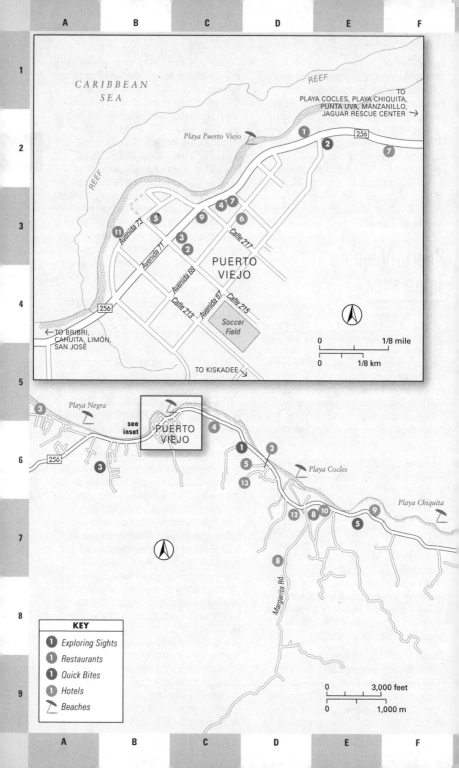

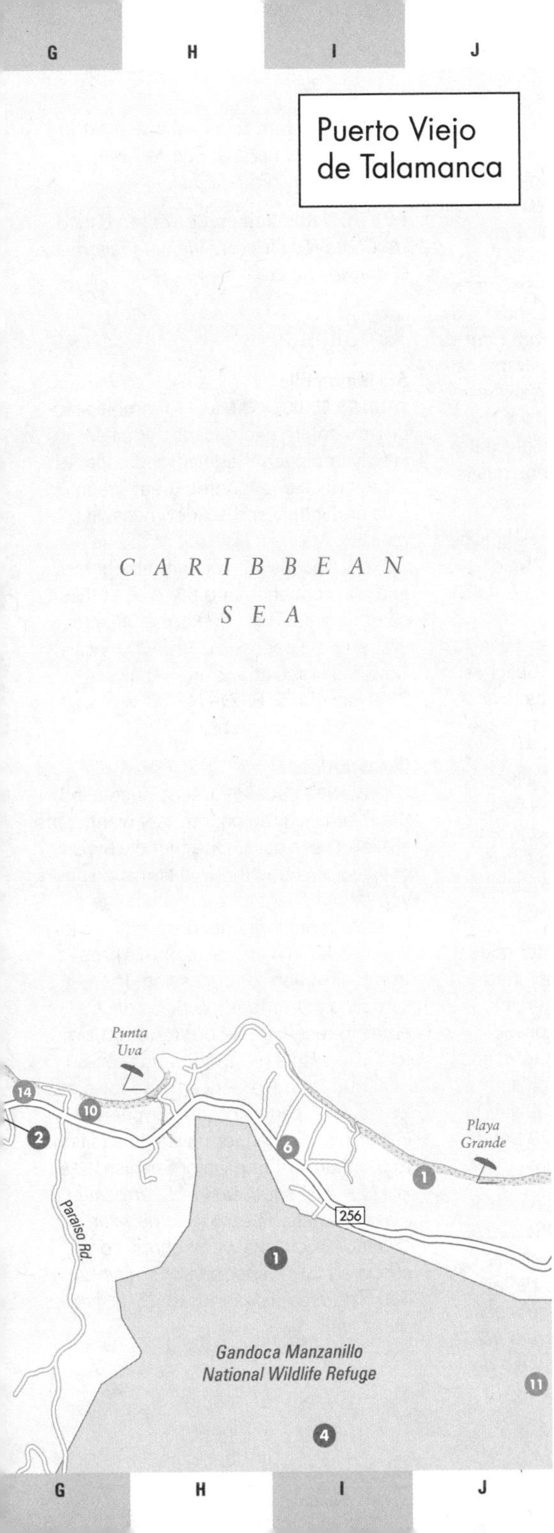

G
H
I
J
Puerto Viejo de Talamanca
CARIBBEAN SEA
Punta Uva
Playa Grande
Paraiso Rd.
256
Gandoca Manzanillo National Wildlife Refuge

Sights

1 Ara Manzanillo I8
2 Chocorart G7
3 Finca la Isla Botanical Garden A6
4 Gandoca-Manzanillo National Wildlife Refuge I9
5 Jaguar Rescue Center E7

Restaurants

1 Amimodo D2
2 Bread & Choclate C3
3 Café Viejo C3
4 Chile Rojo C3
5 Como en Mi Casa ArtCafe B3
6 El Refugio Grill I7
7 Koki Beach C3
8 La Pecora Nera E7
9 Restaurant Tamara C3
10 Selvin's G7
11 Stashus con Fusion B3

Quick Bites

1 Caribeans D6
2 De Gustibus Bakery E2

Hotels

1 Almonds & Corals J8
2 Azania Bungalows D6
3 Banana Azul A5
4 Blue Conga Hotel C6
5 Cariblue Beach & Jungle Resort D6
6 Casa Verde Lodge C3
7 Escape Caribeño F2
8 Geckoes Lodge D7
9 Hotel Aguas Claras E7
10 Le Caméléon E7
11 Nature Observatorio J9
12 Physis Caribbean B&B D7
13 Terrazas del Caribe D6
14 Tree House Lodge G7

Viejo de Talamanca; most, though not all, Limón-originating buses do as well, but a couple drop you off on the highway. Check if you board in Limón. You can give yourself a wider selection of times than the six daily San José–Puerto Viejo services. Hourly Grupo Caribeños buses connect San José with Limón, and hourly MEPE buses connect Limón with Puerto Viejo. The MEPE and Caribeños terminals are one block apart in Limón. Walking could be an option if you're not weighed down with bags and if it's still light out. Unlike MEPE vehicles, Caribeños buses are air-conditioned.

Local buses ply the 15-km (9-mile) paved road between Puerto Viejo and Manzanillo every two hours during the day. Unless your schedule meshes exactly with theirs, you're better off biking or taking a taxi to and from the far-flung beaches along the way. Most taxi service is unofficial here. To be on the safe side, have your hotel or restaurant call one for you. Taxis charge roughly $5 to Playa Negra, $7 to Playa Cocles, $10 to Playa Chiquita, $12 to Punta Uva, and $17 to Manzanillo. Indian-made "tuktuks" provide some Puerto Viejo taxi service. Picture a covered three-wheel auto rickshaw.

You can manage the town center quite easily on foot, though it is dusty in the dry season and muddy when it rains. The main street is, thankfully, paved. Everyone gets around by bike here, and seemingly everyone has one for rent (invariably without a helmet). Quality varies widely; expect to pay $20 per day for a good bike.

ESSENTIALS
BANKS/ATMS Banco de Costa Rica. ⊠ *50 meters (164 feet) south of bridge at entrance to town, Puerto Viejo de Talamanca* ☎ *2750–0707* ⊕ *www.bancobcr. com.* **Banco Nacional.** ⊠ *25 meters (82 feet) south of Correos, Puerto Viejo de Talamanca* ⊕ *www.bncr.fi.cr.*

PHARMACY Farmacia Caribe. ⊠ *Next to Banco de Costa Rica, Puerto Viejo de Talamanca* ☎ *2750–0698.*

POST OFFICE Correos. ⊠ *Next to Banco de Costa Rica, Puerto Viejo de Talamanca* ⊕ *correos.go.cr.*

Sights

Ara Manzanillo
WILDLIFE REFUGE | FAMILY | An ambitious project begun two decades ago has slowly improved the survival prospects for the once-endangered great green (*Ara ambiguus*) and scarlet macaws (*Ara macao*). A daily 3 pm tour of the field station here acquaints you with the breeding and reintroduction into the wild of these colorful birds. Throughout the 98-acre property are approximately 100 macaws. Advance reservations are required. ⊠ *Manzanillo* ☎ *8971–1436* ⊕ *www. aramanzanillo.org* 🎫 *$20.*

Chocorart
FARM/RANCH | FAMILY | Cacao once ruled the Talamanca region, but few plantations are left these days. One friendly Swiss couple continues the tradition and shows you the workings of their chocolate plantation on their chocolate tour. Follow the little-known life cycle of this crop from cultivation to processing. There's sampling at the tour's conclusion. Call or email to reserve a 2-hour tour, and aim to come with a group to avoid the $80 minimum tour fee. Since these folks are Swiss, they can tailor the commentary in German, French, or Italian, in addition to the standard English or Spanish. ⊠ *6 km (4 miles) southeast of Puerto Viejo at Playa Chiquita, Puerto Viejo de Talamanca* ☎ *8866–7493* ⊕ *www.facebook.com/ chocorart* 🎫 *$25 per person; minimum of $80* ⊙ *Closed weekends* ☞ *By appointment only.*

Finca la Isla Botanical Garden
(*Jardín Botánico Finca la Isla*)
GARDEN | At the Finca la Isla Botanical Garden, you can explore a working tropical-fruit, spice, and ornamental-plant farm. Sloths abound, and you might see a few poison dart frogs. A guided tour (three-person minimum, must be reserved in advance) lasts two hours and includes admission and a glass of the farm's homemade fruit juice. Tours can be arranged in advance on days outside the Friday through Monday opening hours. You get the fruit juice if you wander around on your own, too (a $1 tour book is available in English, Spanish, French, Dutch, and German). Watch the demonstration showing how cacao beans are turned into chocolate, and sample some of the product at the end of the tour. ✉ *½ km (¼ mile) west of Puerto Viejo at Playa Negra, Puerto Viejo de Talamanca* ☎ *8886–8530* ⊕ *www.costaricaorganicsfarm.com* ✉ *From $6* ⊘ *Closed Tues.–Thurs.*

Gandoca-Manzanillo National Wildlife Refuge (*Refugio Nacional de Vida Silvestre Gandoca-Manzanillo*)
WILDLIFE REFUGE | The refuge stretches along the southeastern coast from southeast of Puerto Viejo de Talamanca to the town of Manzanillo and on to the Panamanian border. Its limits are not clearly defined. Because of weak laws governing the conservation of refuges and the rising value of coastal land in this area, Gandoca-Manzanillo is less pristine than Cahuita National Park and continues to be developed. (Development thins out the farther you get from Puerto Viejo and the closer you get to the village of Manzanillo.) However, the refuge still has plenty of rain forest, *orey* (a dark tropical wood) and *jolillo* (a species of palm) swamps, 10 km (6 miles) of beach where four species of turtle lay their eggs, and almost 3 square km (1 square mile) of *cativo* (a tropical hardwood) forest and coral reef. You'll most likely spot monkeys, sloths, and perhaps even snakes. The Gandoca estuary is a nursery for tarpon and a wallowing spot for crocodiles and caimans. ✉ *15 km (9 miles) southeast of Puerto Viejo de Talamanca, Gandoca-Manzanillo National Wildlife Refuge* ☎ *2750–0398 for ATEC, 1192 national parks hotline in Costa Rica* ✉ *Free* ⊘ *Closes daily at 3 pm.*

★ **Jaguar Rescue Center**
(*Centro de Rescate Jaguar*)
WILDLIFE REFUGE | **FAMILY** | Many regard a visit to the Jaguar Rescue Center as the highlight of their trip to Puerto Viejo de Talamanca. The name is a bit misleading since there are actually no jaguars at the rescue. The original rescued animal here was an orphaned, injured jaguar cub that ultimately did not survive. His memory lives on in the facility's name. Primarily howler monkeys, sloths, birds, caimans, and lots of snakes make up the charges of the capable staff here. The goal, of course, is to return the animals to the wild, but those that are too frail are assured a permanent home here. Your admission fee for the 90-minute tour at 9:30 or 11:30 am (English or Spanish) helps fund the rescue work. (Tours in French, German, or Dutch can be arranged with advance notice.) Touching the animals is not permitted, for your safety as well as theirs. ✉ *3 km (2 miles) southeast of Puerto Viejo, between Playa Cocles and Playa Chiquita, Puerto Viejo de Talamanca* ☎ *2750–0710* ⊕ *www.jaguarrescue.foundation* ✉ *From $22* ⊘ *Closed Sun.*

 Beaches

Playa Chiquita
BEACH | Nothing against Puerto Viejo, but the farther you get from town, the quieter things get—to put it bluntly, the "riff-raff" factor lessens out here. The downside is that you'll find fewer visitors congregating on dark-sand Chiquita, and isolated stretches of beach can spell trouble. Stay only if you see a lot of other people around. The undertow is strong

out here. Swim at your own risk, preferably in company, and don't venture out too far. **Amenities:** none. **Best for:** sunrise; surfing; walking. ✉ *6 km (4 miles) southeast of Puerto Viejo de Talamanca, Puerto Viejo de Talamanca.*

Playa Cocles

BEACH | The sand gets a bit lighter and the crowd slightly more upscale—it is still Puerto Viejo, though—a couple of kilometers outside of town. Fewer vendors will pester you here than in the town itself, and it'll be mostly you and other travelers. (If there's nobody around, don't linger. There's always safety in numbers.) As with all Puerto Viejo area beaches, the undertow can be strong on Cocles. Never venture out too far. **Amenities:** food and drink. **Best for:** partiers; sunrise; surfing; walking. ✉ *Puerto Viejo de Talamanca ✛ 2 km (1 mile) southeast of Puerto Viejo de Talamanca.*

Playa Negra (Black Beach)

BEACH | Not to be confused with Cahuita's beach of the same name, Puerto Viejo's black-sand Playa Negra lies close to town but is relatively undeveloped. That situation is expected to change in coming years, but for now you'll likely have this stretch of sand north of town to yourself. While this sounds idyllic, remember that there's always safety in numbers on beaches in this area. Be careful about going into the water; the undertow can be strong. **Amenities:** none. **Best for:** sunrise; surfing; walking. ✉ *1 km (½ mile) north of Puerto Viejo de Talamanca, Puerto Viejo de Talamanca.*

Playa Puerto Viejo

BEACH | The clutter of the unnamed in-town beach epitomizes Puerto Viejo. Locals gather here. The strong undertow makes swimming risky along this stretch, but surfers delight in the consistently good waves. The upside is that you're just a few steps from the in-town restaurants. **Amenities:** food and drink. **Best for:** partiers; sunrise; surfing; walking. ✉ *In town, Puerto Viejo de Talamanca.*

Punta Uva

BEACH | The area's most beautiful beach—with dark sand like all area strands—lies a long way from Puerto Viejo and offers splendid isolation from the commotion of town. *Uva* means "grape" in Spanish, and the beach gets its name from the sea-grape trees found out here. A few nearby restaurants can take care of your culinary needs. As always here, there's the undertow to contend with. Be careful and never venture too far out into the water. **Amenities:** food and drink. **Best for:** sunrise; surfing; walking. ✉ *9 km (5½ miles) south of Puerto Viejo de Talamanca, Puerto Viejo de Talamanca.*

Restaurants

Amimodo

$$$ | **ITALIAN** | The name translates to "my way," and the exuberant Italian owners really do it their way, combining the cuisine of their native northern Italy with Caribbean flavors. Antipasto might be classic bruschetta or *jamón de atún* (tuna ham) with avocado dressing, and ravioli might be stuffed with tropical shrimp, pineapple, and curry, with avocado sauce on the side. **Known for:** tropical veranda setting; exuberant service; ever-changing creative menu. $ *Average main: $20* ✉ *In front of Salsa Brava, Puerto Viejo de Talamanca* ☎ *2750–0257.*

Bread & Chocolate

$$ | **CAFÉ** | The takeaway line for brownies—made with their own processed cocoa—forms at the gate before this place opens at 6:30 am. Stick around, though, for a hearty breakfast of cinnamon-oatmeal pancakes, French toast, or creamy scrambled eggs, washed down with a cup of French-press coffee. **Known for:** fresh-baked goods; homemade sauces; jerk chicken. $ *Average main: $10* ✉ *Puerto Viejo de Talamanca ✛ 50 meters (164 feet) south of post office* ☎ *2750–0723* ⊕ *www.breadandchocolatecr.com* ⊘ *Closed Mon. No dinner.*

Café Viejo

$$$ | **ITALIAN** | This is the hot place to see and be seen on Puerto Viejo's main drag. The owners learned to cook at the knee of their Italian grandmother back in Rimini, and have concocted a menu, several pages long, of pizzas and handmade pastas. **Known for:** impressive pizza variety; place to view Puerto Viejo's passing parade; traditional Italian cooking. $ *Average main: $18* ✉ *Avda. 71, corner of C. 215, Puerto Viejo de Talamanca* ☎ *2750–0817* ⊕ *www.cafeviejo. com* ⊗ *Closed Tues. No lunch.*

Chile Rojo

$$ | **THAI** | Not a thing about the name or furnishings reflects its Thai and Middle Eastern offerings, but this restaurant does a brisk business. Choose from Thai grilled tuna, falafel, hummus, samosas, or sushi. **Known for:** lamb curry; friendly, leisurely service; vegetarian dishes and fresh sushi. $ *Average main: $12* ✉ *Main St. oceanfront, Puerto Viejo de Talamanca* ☎ *2750–0421.*

Como en Mi Casa ArtCafe

$ | **VEGETARIAN** | Everything is made on-site at this small second-floor café. Start off the day with an order of vegan pancakes and fruit smoothie, or ease into lunch with veggie burritos and a tomato, oregano, and olive oil bruschetta. **Known for:** friendly service; many gluten-free offerings; fresh homemade bread. $ *Average main: $9* ✉ *100 meters (328 feet) east of bus stop, Puerto Viejo de Talamanca* ☎ *8674–2853* ⊕ *www.facebook. com/vegeterianglutenfreefood* ⊗ *Closed Tues. No dinner.*

★ **El Refugio Grill**

$$$ | **ARGENTINE** | This tiny rancho-style restaurant in the middle of a forest clearing is one of Costa Rica's top Argentine restaurants. The menu varies throughout the year and might consist of beef in chimichurri sauce, spinach crepes, curried shrimp, mussels in white wine, or grilled tuna. **Known for:** hearty Argentine menu; homemade guacamole and chips;

intimate and secluded forest setting. $ *Average main: $20* ✉ *Punta Uva, Puerto Viejo de Talamanca* ☎ *2759–9007* ⊗ *Closed Wed.*

Koki Beach

$$$ | **ECLECTIC** | This slightly elevated terrace restaurant with colorful furniture (and colorful characters) is a great place to watch Puerto Viejo's parade of evening passersby and the ocean waves lapping on the beach across the street. The mostly surf-and-turf menu means lots of shrimp and sea bass and lots of beef and chicken, all served on or off skewers according to your preference. **Known for:** good drink selection; place to see and be seen; live music. $ *Average main: $18* ✉ *Oceanfront, on main street, Avda. 71 and C. 219, Puerto Viejo de Talamanca* ☎ *2750–0902* ⊕ *kokibeach.blogspot.com* ⊗ *Closed Mon. No lunch.*

★ **La Pecora Nera**

$$$$ | **ITALIAN** | For nearly 30 years, the owner of this Italian restaurant has gone to great lengths to assure ingredients are authentic, including importing olive oil and wine from Italy. You'll be surprised at all the additional light Tuscan entrées, appetizers, and desserts the chef-owner has concocted that day. **Known for:** exuberant owner; leisurely dining experience; innovative Italian menu. $ *Average main: $30* ✉ *3 km (2 miles) southeast of town at Playa Cocles, Puerto Viejo de Talamanca* ☎ *2750–0490* ⊕ *www.lapeco-raneracr.com* ⊗ *Closed Mon. No lunch.*

Restaurant Tamara

$$ | **CARIBBEAN** | Puerto Viejo's first restaurant still dishes up tasty, authentic Caribbean food, like fresh fish or chicken in Caribbean sauce. They're known for their rondón (coconut stew), tamara shrimp, and fresh ceviche. **Known for:** solid Caribbean menu; reggae music; great people-watching. $ *Average main: $11* ✉ *219 A St., at Avda. 67, Puerto Viejo de Talamanca* ⊹ *200 meters (656 feet) east of Super Diamante* ☎ *2750–0148.*

Selvin's (*Blanca & Selvin's*)
$$ | **CARIBBEAN** | Blanca, the owner of this longtime standby at Punta Uva, cooks up a menu of rondón, rice and beans, lobster, shrimp, and chicken with sweet mole sauce. The cool breezes of the seaside setting could not be more pleasant. **Known for:** friendly service; irregular hours; hearty Caribbean cooking. [$] *Average main: $13* ✉ *Puerto Viejo de Talamanca* ✣ *7 km (4½ miles) southeast of town at Punta Uva* ☎ *2750–0664* 🌐 *www.selvinpuntauva.com* 🕓 *Closed Mon.–Thurs.*

★ **Stashus con Fusion**
$$ | **ECLECTIC** | This restaurant epitomizes Puerto Viejo: lively, organic, popular, but confident enough not to seek trendiness. Ordering is by sauces: Thai peanut, Indonesian-Caribbean curry, Mexican chipotle, Jamaican jerk-style, or Malaysian-guayaba curry, which is served on vegetables, chicken, shrimp, or fish (marlin or tuna). **Known for:** mix-and-match menu; organic offerings; live music. [$] *Average main: $13* ✉ *Beach Front Rd., between entrance of town and bus stop, Puerto Viejo de Talamanca* ☎ *8385–6887* 🌐 *www.stashusconfusion.com* 🕓 *Closed Wed. No lunch.*

Coffee and Quick Bites

Caribeans
$ | **CAFÉ** | At first glance, this small café could use a spelling lesson, but since Caribeans deals in coffee and chocolate, the play on words is apt. Treat yourself to a latte, mocha, or coconut cappuccino, all made from organic, fair-trade coffee from the Turrialba region in the far-eastern Central Valley, and roasted here. **Known for:** locally roasted beans; coconut cappuccino; organic, fair-trade coffee. [$] *Average main: $9* ✉ *2 km (1 mile) southeast of town at Playa Cocles, Puerto Viejo de Talamanca* ☎ *2750–0504* 🌐 *www.caribeanscr.com* 🕓 *Closed Sun.*

De Gustibus Bakery
$ | **BAKERY** | Follow your nose to this bakery where breads, cakes, and pastries lure customers from the point of "just a bite" to breakfast-on-repeat—it's hard to resist the chocolate-filled cream puffs, cinnamon rolls, French toast, and pancakes. Swing by later in the day for a vegan burger or burrito. **Known for:** exceptional breakfasts; chocolate pastries; French toast. [$] *Average main: $8* ✉ *Carretera Principal, Puerto Viejo de Talamanca* ✣ *50 meters (164 feet) south of Restaurante Amimodo* ☎ *2756–8397* 🌐 *www.facebook.com/degustibusbakery.*

Hotels

Almonds & Corals (*Almendros y Corales*)
$$ | **RESORT** | Hidden in a beachfront jungle within the Gandoca-Manzanillo Wildlife Refuge, Almonds & Corals features scattered bungalows raised on stilts and linked by boardwalks lighted by kerosene lamps. **Pros:** rustic comfort; close to beach and Manzanillo Reserve; cool jungle surroundings. **Cons:** need a car to stay here; could use a bit of upkeep; no A/C. [$] *Rooms from: $130* ✉ *Near end of road to Manzanillo, Gandoca-Manzanillo National Wildlife Refuge* ☎ *2759–9056, 2271–3000 in San José* 🌐 *www.almondsandcorals.com* 🛏 *24 bungalows* 🍴 *Free Breakfast.*

Azania Bungalows
$$ | **B&B/INN** | Eleven thatch-roof A-frame bungalows are spread around Azania's ample gardens, and each sleeps four. **Pros:** good value; good Argentine restaurant; rustic elegance. **Cons:** bungalows are dark inside; mosquito netting provided is necessary; difficult to make reservations. [$] *Rooms from: $105* ✉ *1½ km (1 mile) southeast of town at Playa Cocles, Puerto Viejo de Talamanca* ☎ *2750–0540* 🌐 *www.azania-costarica.com* 🛏 *11 bungalows* 🍴 *Free Breakfast.*

Punta Uva Beach has a strong undertow.

Banana Azul

$$ | **RESORT** | When Canadian owner, Colin Brownlee bought a grazing pasture on the beach, little did he know that 12 years later, it would become one of the most popular boutique hotels on the Caribbean, complete with its own supermarket, tour company, beauty salon, and villas. **Pros:** friendly management and staff; seclusion (set away from hubbub of town); beachfront massages available. **Cons:** best to have a car to stay here; can be difficult to find space; no kids under 16 allowed, so not an option for families. [$] *Rooms from: $135* ✉ *Puerto Viejo de Talamanca* ✥ *1½ km (1 mile) north of Puerto Viejo at end of Playa Negra* ☎ *2750–2035, 305/846–8220* 🌐 *www.bananaazul.com* 🛏 *25 rooms* 🍴 *Free Breakfast.*

★ Cariblue Beach & Jungle Resort

$$$ | **HOTEL** | The youthful Italian owners came here to surf years ago, stayed on, and built a lodging that combines refinement with that hip Puerto Viejo vibe in exactly the right proportions. **Pros:** daily free activities including yoga; live music on weekends; A/C. **Cons:** can be difficult to make reservations; can be difficult to find a parking space; ideal to have a car to stay here. [$] *Rooms from: $200* ✉ *2 km (1 mile) southeast of town at Playa Cocles, Puerto Viejo de Talamanca* ☎ *2750–0035, 305/749–5269 in North America* 🌐 *www.cariblue.com* 🛏 *43 rooms* 🍴 *Free Breakfast.*

Casa Verde Lodge

$ | **HOTEL** | If you've graduated from your backpacker days and are a bit more flush with cash but still want to be near the action, this old standby on a quiet street a couple of blocks from the center of town is ideal. **Pros:** good value; immaculately kept up; nicest in-town lodging. **Cons:** businesslike staff; two of the rooms don't have private baths; difficult to find vacancies. [$] *Rooms from: $55* ✉ *Puerto Viejo de Talamanca* ✥ *200 meters (656 feet) south and 200 meters (656 feet) east of bus stop* ☎ *2750–0015* 🌐 *www.facebook.com/CasaVerdeLodge* 🛏 *19 units* 🍴 *No Meals.*

Escape Caribeño

$$ | **B&B/INN** | The wonderfully friendly Italian owners—who treat you like family—are what make this place, with immaculate hardwood bungalows lining a pleasant garden amply populated with hummingbirds, just outside town. **Pros:** central location without being right in town; gregarious owners; friendly staff. **Cons:** spartan in some places; some rooms get noise from the road; some rooms are small. [$] *Rooms from: $110* ✉ *Puerto Viejo de Talamanca* ✥ *150 meters (492 feet) after Veterinaria Arroyo Solano* ☎ *2750–0103* 🌐 *www.escapecaribeno.com* 🛏 *14 bungalows* 🍴 *Free Breakfast.*

★ **Geckoes Lodge**

$$$ | **B&B/INN** | Impeccable service gives this place an edge among the area's handful of set-back-in-the-woods lodgings, and the Wi-Fi, private plunge pool, and barbecue that come with each house are unexpected touches in a setting such as this. **Pros:** wonderful, personalized service; lush, sumptuous surroundings; private plunge pools. **Cons:** only three accommodations; best to have a car to stay here; can be difficult to find. [$] *Rooms from: $240* ✉ *Margarita Road in Cocles, 3 km (2 miles) southeast of town and 1 km (½ mile) inland at Playa Cocles, Puerto Viejo de Talamanca* ☎ *2750–0908* 🌐 *www.geckoeslodge.com* 🛏 *2 houses* 🍴 *No Meals.*

★ **Hotel Aguas Claras**

$$$$ | **HOTEL** | Luxury has arrived to Puerto Viejo with this five-star boutique hotel that has carefully curated an unparalleled property with a Caribbean vibe splashed with design, art, and comfort. **Pros:** beachfront; optional full-board meal plan; classy modern-bohemian style. **Cons:** no children under eight, so not ideal for families; slow service; often booked solid. [$] *Rooms from: $290* ✉ *Punta Cocles, Puerto Viejo de Talamanca* ✥ *500 meters (1,640 feet) south of Villas Caribe* ☎ *4040–0418, 2750–0131* 🌐 *www.hotelaguasclaras.com* 🛏 *26 rooms* 🍴 *Free Breakfast.*

Le Caméléon

$$$$ | **HOTEL** | This boutique hotel fronting Playa Cocles is decidedly un–Puerto Viejo in its luxury, but if you're in the mood for a splurge here on the coast, this is the spot. **Pros:** stylish luxury; attentive staff; many amenities. **Cons:** expensive; beach club across a busy road; slow service. [$] *Rooms from: $299* ✉ *Playa Cocles, Puerto Viejo de Talamanca* ✥ *200 meters (656 feet) east of soccer field* ☎ *2750–3096* 🌐 *www.lecameleonhotel.com* 🛏 *58 rooms* 🍴 *Free Breakfast.*

Nature Observatorio

$$$$ | **B&B/INN** | If you're looking for some "Guess where we stayed!" bragging rights following your return from Costa Rica, this lodging option 82 feet high in a tree provides them. **Pros:** definitely has the "wow" factor; the ultimate in seclusion; platform can sleep up to six people. **Cons:** cannot come and go as you please; hoisting yourself to the platform requires physical strength; not for those with fear of heights. [$] *Rooms from: $460* ✉ *South of Manzanillo village, Gandoca-Manzanillo National Wildlife Refuge* ☎ *8628–2663, 647/344–5843 in North America* 🌐 *www.natureobservatorio.com* 🛏 *1 platform* 🍴 *All-Inclusive.*

★ **Physis Caribbean B&B**

$$ | **B&B/INN** | If you want to experience the area's well-known vibe but have outgrown Puerto Viejo's backpacker digs, this lodging—meaning "nature" in Latin—is the ticket. **Pros:** hip, knowledgeable owners; impeccable service; immaculate rooms. **Cons:** one room is on the small side; may be a little too hip for some visitors; no children under 10, so not ideal for families. [$] *Rooms from: $96* ✉ *Miss Winny Town Rd., Puerto Viejo de Talamanca* ✥ *1½ km (1 mile) southeast of town at Playa Cocles* ☎ *2750–0941* 🌐 *www.physiscaribbean.net* 🛏 *4 rooms* 🍴 *Free Breakfast.*

Terrazas del Caribe

$$ | **HOTEL** | The consolation prize for not being beachfront is a fully equipped apartment with a kitchen and terrace

Crossing into Panama via Sixaola

Costa Rica's sleepy border post at Sixaola fronts Guabito, Panama's equally quiet border crossing, 44 km (26 miles) south of the turnoff to Puerto Viejo de Talamanca. Both are merely collections of banana-plantation stilt houses and a few stores and bars; neither has any lodging or dining options, but this is a much more low-key crossing into Panama than the busy border post at Paso Canoas on the Pan-American Highway near the Pacific coast. If you've come this far, you're likely headed to **Bocas del Toro**, the real attraction in northwestern Panama. This archipelago of 68 islands continues the Afro-Caribbean and indigenous themes seen on Costa Rica's Atlantic coast, and has opportunities for diving, snorkeling, swimming, and wildlife viewing. The larger islands are home to a growing selection of hotels and restaurants—everything from funky to fabulous. Boats at Almirante, Panama, on the mainland 36 km (22 miles) from the border, transport you to the islands.

If you decide to stay overnight in "Bocas," you'll likely base yourself on Isla Colón, the main island. You'll find the best dining and lodging selections here in Bocas Town, (Picture Puerto Viejo de Talamanca, but with paved streets and not quite so much clutter.) More secluded accommodation has sprung up in recent years on some of the outer islands, and there's something undeniably cool about bopping from island to island in one of the motorized launches that serve as the archipelago's taxi system.

Tips:

- Locals appear to cross the border at will in both directions. You may not do so. Go through official passport formalities.
- Costa Rican rental vehicles may not exit the country.
- Panama is one hour later than Costa Rica. Set your watch ahead.
- Panama uses the U.S. dollar as its currency, but calls it the balboa. No one will accept or exchange your Costa Rican colones.

surrounding a swimming pool with a Jacuzzi and waterfall. **Pros:** secure parking; great pool bar; clean and spacious rooms. **Cons:** not beachfront; breakfast not included; rooms lack character. [$] *Rooms from: $119* ✉ *Puerto Viejo de Talamanca* ✣ *400 meters (1,312 feet) southwest of Azania St, near Cocles beach* ☎ *2750–0949* 🌐 *www.terrazas-delcaribe.com* 🛏 *24 units* 🍴 *No Meals.*

Tree House Lodge

$$$ | HOTEL | This lodging complex among forested ground contains six large, stylish houses, all at ground level, one of which is built around a tree (that's the Tree House). **Pros:** attention to style in furnishings; all houses have kitchens, and most have A/C and Jacuzzis; unique architecture. **Cons:** easiest to stay here if you have a car; a bit on the pricey side; far from sights. [$] *Rooms from: $200* ✉ *Punta Uva, Puerto Viejo de Talamanca* ☎ *2750–0706* 🌐 *www.costaricatree-house.com* 🛏 *6 units* 🍴 *No Meals.*

🍸 Nightlife

The distinction between dining spot and nightspot blurs as the evening progresses, as many restaurants become pleasant places to linger after dinner. You'll also find bars with live music on certain nights. The town's main drag is packed with pedestrians, bicycles, and a few cars most evenings, the block between Café Viejo and Hot Rocks getting the most action. Wander around; something is bound to entice you. Be aware that some of the strictly local hangouts get pretty rough around the edges at night.

■ TIP➜ **When out after dark, ask a staff member at the restaurant, bar, or club to call you a taxi when you're ready to call it an evening.**

BARS

Hot Rocks
BARS | A wonderful breeze wafts through this huge, semi-open-air U-shape bar just off the beach. Nights are dedicated variously to bingo, karaoke, live music, and open-mic performances. ⊠ *Avda. 71 and C. 217, Puerto Viejo de Talamanca* ☎ *2100–4507.*

PV Bar de Vino (*Puerto Viejo Wine Bar*)
WINE BARS | The bar's pretty, semi-open-air setting with lots of greenery makes a nice place to sip wine and nosh on tapas (Spanish-style appetizers). ⊠ *Puerto Viejo de Talamanca ✛ 3 km (2 miles) southeast of Puerto Viejo between Playa Cocles and Playa Chiquita* ☎ *8584–3234.*

Tasty Waves Cantina
BARS | Tuesday is $2 taco night at the lively, sometimes rowdy, Tasty Waves Cantina. There's live music on Friday and karaoke on Saturday. Movies get under way at 7:30 pm on Monday and occasionally other nights of the week as well. ⊠ *Playa Cocles, 1 km (½ mile) southeast of town, Puerto Viejo de Talamanca* ☎ *2750–0507* ⊕ *www.facebook.com/TastyWavesCantina.*

◖ Shopping

Vendors set up stands at night on the beach road heading out of town toward Playa Cocles, cheap jewelry being the prime fare. But the town counts a couple of honest-to-goodness souvenir shops, too.

Feria Agrícola y Artesanel
(*Agricultural and Craft Fair*)
MARKET | Puerto Viejo's Saturday-morning farmers' market is a good place to stock up on fresh fruits and veggies for that weekend beach picnic. It takes place in a building just south of the bus stop. ⊠ *Puerto Viejo de Talamanca ✛ 50 meters (164 feet) south of bus stop* ☎ *2750–0883.*

Tienda del Mar
MIXED CLOTHING | Really two stores in one, Tienda del Mar sprawls around a street corner in the center of town and specializes in bright, colorful batik clothing of all sizes, as well as more run-of-the-mill T-shirts, sandals, wood carvings, ceramics, and postcards. ⊠ *Avda. 71, next to Restaurant Tamara, Puerto Viejo de Talamanca* ☎ *2750–0762.*

Wanderlust
SOUVENIRS | This shop near the bus stop offers a good selection of locally made crafts and colorful clothing. They carry national brands of swimwear, as well as Lycra made from recycled plastics. ⊠ *Puerto Viejo de Talamanca ✛ 50 meters (164 feet) southeast of bus stop* ☎ *8755–7217.*

Activities

RAFTING

Exploradores Outdoors

WHITE-WATER RAFTING | Rafting excursions lie about two hours away, but one San José–based outfitter has an office here. Exploradores Outdoors is highly regarded and has one- and two-day excursions on the Pacuare River, with a pickup point here or in San José and the option to start in one place and be dropped off at the other. The outfitter also offers sea-kayaking excursions off the coast of the Gandoca-Manzanillo Wildlife Refuge. ✉ *Puerto Viejo de Talamanca* ⊕ *200 meters (656 feet) south of Salsa Brava* ☎ *2750–2020, 2222–6262 in San José, 646/205–0828 in North America* ⊕ *www.exploradoresoutdoors.com* 🖾 *From $59.*

SURFING

Surfing is the name of the game in Puerto Viejo, for everyone from newbies to Kelly Slaters. The best conditions are late December through March, but there's action all year. Longtime surfers compare the south Caribbean with Hawaii, but without the "who do you think you are?" attitude. There are a number of breaks here, most famously **Salsa Brava,** which translates to "wild sauce." It breaks fairly far offshore and requires maneuvering past some tricky currents and a shallow reef. Hollow and primarily right-breaking, Salsa Brava is one gnarly wave when it gets big. If it gets *too* big, or not big enough, check out the breaks at Punta Uva, Punta Cocles, or Playa Chiquita. Boogie boarders and bodysurfers can also dig the beach-break waves at various points along this tantalizingly beautiful coast.

Rocking J's

SURFING | If you've always wanted to try surfing, consider the friendly 90-minute surf school ($40) offered through Rocking Js hostel. They'll start you out with a small wave near the bus stop. A two-hour private lesson will run you $60. You can also rent equipment here. ✉ *Rockin' J's hostel, at Salsa Brava Beach, Puerto Viejo de Talamanca* ☎ *2750–0665* ⊕ *www.rockingjs.com.*

TOUR OPERATORS

As in Cahuita, tour operators and outfitters here can set up tours and activities anywhere on the south Caribbean coast.

Terraventuras

SPECIAL-INTEREST TOURS | This well-established operator can lead you around Puerto Viejo de Talamanca and Cahuita, or take you on excursions to Tortuguero, the Gandoca-Manzanillo Wildlife Refuge, and Bocas del Toro in Panama. Take your pick from cooking classes, horseback riding, snorkeling adventures, jungle tours, and more. It also rents good-quality surfboards, bicycles, boogie boards, and snorkeling gear. ✉ *Puerto Viejo de Talamanca* ⊕ *100 meters (328 feet) south of bus stop* ☎ *2750–0750* ⊕ *www.terraventuras.com* 🖾 *From $60.*

Caution

The conditions that make the Caribbean so popular among surfers spell danger for swimmers. A few drownings occur each year. Strong riptides can pull you out to sea, even in waist-deep water, before you realize what's happening. Never swim alone in these parts—good advice anywhere.

Index

514

Photo Credits

Front Cover: D. Hurst / Alamy Stock Photo [Description: Closeup of a three-toed sloth, Costa Rica]. **Back cover, from left to right:** Tito Slack/Shutterstock, Ondrej Prosicky/Shutterstock, Dudarev Mikhail/Shutterstock **Spine:** William Berry/Shutterstock **Interior, from left to right:** 2018 SL-Photography/Shutterstock (1) MlennyPhotography/iStockphoto (2) Kobby Dagan/Shutterstock (5) **Chapter 1: Experience Costa Rica:** LOUIS-MICHEL DESERT/Shutterstock (6-7) Simon Dannhauer / Shutterstock (8) Petrsalinger/Dreamstime (9) Simon Hack/Dreamstime (9) Tzooka/Dreamstime (10) Bryce Jackson / Shutterstock (10) Dartamonov / Shutterstock (10) Tricia Daniel / Shutterstock (10) Damsea / Shutterstock (11) SL-Photography / Shutterstock (11) LMspencer / Shutterstock (12) Kevin Wells Photography / Shutterstock (12) Wollertz/Dreamstime (12) BGSmith / Shutterstock (12) Oliverjw | Dreamstime.com (13) Bogdan Lazar/Dreamstime (13) Simon Dannhauer / Shutterstock (14) Julian_Trejos (14) Lindsay Fendt / Alamy Stock Photo (15) Simon Dannhauer/shutterstock (18) Aleivac63/Dreamstime (18) Pablo Hidalgo/Dreamstime (18) Simon Dannhauer/istock (18) AutumnSkyPhotography/istock (19) Courtesy_Playa Nicuesa Rainforest Lodge, Golfito (20) Courtesy_Harmony Hotel (20) Courtesy_Dantica Cloud Forest Lodge (20) Courtesy_Lapa Rios Lodge (21) Courtesy_Arenal Observatory Lodge, Arenal (21) ALLEKO/istock (22) Jarib/istock (23) **Chapter 3: Biodiversity:** Worldswildlifewonders/Shutterstock (77) Costa Rica Tourist Board (ICT) (79) urosr / Shutterstock (82-83) Worldswildlifewonders/Shutterstock (84) danmike (84) Courtesy of Costa Rica Tourism (85) Wollertz 2017\Charles Wollertz\iStockphoto (86) Anky10\Dreamstime (86) Ibenk_88/Shutterstock (86) Alexey Stiop\iStockphoto (86) Martin Mecnarowski/Shutterstock (87) EML / Shutterstock (87) Junior Braz/Shutterstock (87) Nacho Such/Shutterstock (87) Tanguy de Saint-Cyr/Shutterstock (88-89) Underworld/Shutterstock (90) Worldswildlifewonders/Shutterstock (90) Dudarev Mikhail/Shutterstock (91) Olaf Oczko/Shutterstock (92) 2010 s74/Shutterstock (92) Jbphotography\t\Dreamstime (92) Carlos Avila Soto/Shutterstock (92) Mirco1\Dreamstime (93) Chrismrabe\Dreamstime (93) Ondrej Prosicky/Shutterstock (93) Nature's Charm/Shutterstock (93) Simon Dannhauer/Shutterstock (94-95) Mr. James Kelley/Shutterstock (96) Gianfranco Vivi/Shutterstock (96) Ronald Reyes (97) JoséAndrés 22 CR\iStockphoto (98) Bob Pool/Shutterstock (98) Whiskybottle\Dreamstime (98) Natali22206/Shutterstock (98) worldswildlifewonders / Shutterstock (99) Vaclav Sebek/Shutterstock (99) Martin Pelanek/Shutterstock (99) Petr Salinger/Shutterstock (99) SL-Photography/Shutterstock (100-101) Dieniti\Dreamstime (102) Nature's Charm/Shutterstock (102) John Fader\iStockphoto (103) Raymond Pauly\iStockphoto (104) Phortun/Shutterstock (104) E.P. Mallory/Flickr (104) Jarib\iStockphoto (104) Kjwells86\Dreamstime (105) Clm138/Dreamstime.com (105) Ondrej Prosicky/Shutterstock (105) Kjorgen\Dreamstime (105) Henkbogaard\Dreamstime (106-107) Jeroen Mikkers/Shutterstock (108) Lacomino FRiMAGES/Shutterstock (108) Thornton Cohen (109) KanchanaRH/Shutterstock (110) Ondrej Prosicky/Shutterstock (110) Saini Goutam/Shutterstock (110) Vladislav T. Jirousek/Shutterstock (110) Juan Aceituno/Shutterstock (111) Jeroen Mikkers/Shutterstock (111) Nature's Charm/Shutterstock (111) Seadam\Dreamstime (111) Zeljkokcanmore\Dreamstime (112-113) SimonDannhauer\Dreamstime (114) Alberto Carrera\iStockphoto (114) Juan Amighetti/Costa Rica Tourist Board (ICT) (115) Stephen Orsillo/Shutterstock (116) Jarib/Shutterstock (116) Edda Dupree_iStockphoto (116) Lindasj22/Shutterstock (116) Joost van Uffelen/Shutterstock (117) Nature's Charm/Shutterstock (117) Nikky de Graaf/Shutterstock (117) Petr Simon/Shutterstock (117) Nobito/Shutterstock (118) **Chapter 4: San José:** Mbrand85/Shutterstock (119) Lindy Drew (122) Lindy Drew (123) JeanFrancoisSchmitz/Flickr (132) Dchulov/Dreamstime (136) Lupita Rojas Solis/Shutterstock (138) Mihai-Bogdan Lazar/Shutterstock (144) Tossy (156) **Chapter 5: The Central Valley:** jvcostarica (159) Marco Diaz Segura/Shutterstock (162) United Nations Development Programme/Flickr (163) Thorsten Spoerlein/Shutterstock (163) Jason Kremkau (164) GerryP/Shutterstock (165) Michal Sarauer/Shutterstock (165) Michal Sarauer/Shutterstock (166) Dmitry Chulov/Shutterstock (167) Galyna Andrushko/Shutterstock (167) Lindy Drew (174) Luis Alvarado Alvarado/Shutterstock (183) Suriyo tataisong/Shutterstock (187) SALMONNEGRO-STOCK/Shutterstock (189) Mario Wong Pastor/Shutterstock (189) North Wind Picture Archives / Alamy (190) Rob Crandall/Shutterstock (190) Steve Bly / Alamy (190) Gianfranco Vivi/Shutterstock (191) Kobby Dagan/Shutterstock (191) Kenneth Hong/Flickr [CC BY-ND 2.0] (192) Angela Hampton Picture Library / Alamy (192) Noiz Stocker/Shutterstock (192) Jordi Cami / Alamy (192) J1 / Alamy (193) photolibrary.com (193) Arco Images GmbH / Alamy (193) Marvin Dembinsky Photo Associates / Alamy (193) Kobby Dagan/Shutterstock (198) Lindy Drew (201) Dancarod/Shutterstock (202) Neil McAllister/Alamy (205) Pafnuti/Shutterstock (208) **Chapter 6: Arenal, Monteverde, and the Northern Lowlands:** Msoberma (211) Colin D. Young / Shutterstock (214) racegirl (215) vogelmutter (215) Felzum/Dreamstime.com (216) RussiseeO/Shutterstock (217) Henk Bogaard/Shutterstock (217) Sportster (222) Dmitriyrnd\Dreamstime (230) tiffnco (232) Thornton Cohen / Alamy (235) Rainforest Adventures Costa Rica (236) tiffnco (238) Justine Evans / Alamy (239) Kevin Schafer / Alamy (239) THEPALMER (239) Bobhilscher\Dreamstime (242) Mirco1\Dreamstime (244) Dieniti\Dreamstime (254) **Chapter 7: Guanacaste:** Nickolay Stanev/Shutterstock (257) Nicousnake\Dreamstime (260) Xenia_Photography/Shutterstock (261) Steven Rojas/Shutterstock (261) Andy119/Shutterstock (262) Alfredohr2000\Dreamstime (263) Alexey Stiop\iStockphoto (263) Miroslav Denes/Shutterstock (277) SL-Photography/Shutterstock (284-265) Antonio Jorge Nunes/Shutterstock (286) mboja (287) chinamom (287) Juan Amighetti/Costa Rica Tourist Board (ICT) (288) Sam Chadwick/Shutterstock (288) imagebroker / Alamy (288) Stefan Neumann/Shutterstock (293) Pufferfishy\Dreamstime (301) Marisa A Petherbridge/Shutterstock (306) Mihai-Bogdan Lazar/Shutterstock (316-317) underworld/Shutterstock (318) Angela N Perryman/Shutterstock (318) Jorge A. Russell/Shutterstock (319) Larry Satterberg/Shutterstock (322) **Chapter 8: The Nicoya Peninsula:** Jeffry Gonzalez/Shutterstock (329) Gianfranco Vivi/Shutterstock (332) Salparadis/Shutterstock (333) Tanya Keisha\Ursula1964\Dreamstime (333) Underworld/Shutterstock (346) RChoi\iStockphoto (350) Jorge A. Russell/Shutterstock (357) Fotos593/Shutterstock (359) Juhku/Shutterstock (365) **Chapter 9: Manuel Antonio and the Central Pacific Coast:** Thorsten Spoerlein/Shutterstock (367) Stefan Neumann/Shutterstock (370) Headout Agencja Reklamowa/Shutterstock (371) Simon Dannhauer/Shutterstock (371) Jorge A. Russell/shutterstock (380) Leethal33 (384) Jorge A. Russell/shutterstock (390) Jorge A. Russell/Shutterstock (391) Mabelin Santos/Shutterstock (395) Romiana Lee/Shutterstock (399) Daniel Karfik/Shutterstock (401) **Chapter 10: The Osa Peninsula and the South Pacific:** Marco Diaz Segura/

Photo Credits

Shutterstock (407) Saintdags/Shutterstock (410) Raul Cole/Shutterstock (411) Saintdags/Shutterstock (411) Claude Huot / Shutterstock (412) Simon Dannhauer/Shutterstock (413) Jason Kremkau (413) Ondrej Prosicky/Shutterstock (414) Wirestock Creators/Shutterstock (415) Margus Vilbas Photography/Shutterstock (415) Henk Bogaard/Shutterstock (423) JYJ pictures/Shutterstock (429) Mikolaj Ostaszewski\iStockphoto (433) Eisenlohr\iStockphoto (442) Reimar/Shutterstock (446) Seadam\Dreamstime (454) Seadam\Dreamstime (455) Rainer Lesniewski/Shutterstock (458) Monica Richards (462) PAUL ATKINSON/Shutterstock (464) **Chapter 11: Tortuguero and the Caribbean Coast:** Francesco Ricca Iacomino\iStockphoto (467) Lisastrachan\Dreamstime (470) Carlos Miguel Forero\iStockphoto (471) Dchulov\Dreamstime (471) Simon Dannhauer/Shutterstock (472) McKerrell Photography/Shutterstock (473) Dam@seaphotoart.com\iStockphoto (473) Errol Barrantes/Costa Rica Tourist Board (ICT) (482) Tossy (488) Marco Lissoni/Shutterstock (492) Rodrigo Montenegro/Costa Rica Tourist Board (ICT) (496) Simon Dannhauer/Shutterstock (505) **About Our Writers:** All photos are courtesy of the writers.

*Every effort has been made to trace the copyright holders, and we apologize in advance for any accidental errors. We would be happy to apply the corrections in the following edition of this publication.

Notes

Notes

Notes

Notes

Notes

Notes

Notes

Notes

Fodor's ESSENTIAL COSTA RICA

Publisher: Stephen Horowitz, *General Manager*

Editorial: Douglas Stallings, *Editorial Director;* Jill Fergus, Amanda Sadlowski, *Senior Editors;* Kayla Becker, Brian Eschrich, Alexis Kelly, *Editors;* Angelique Kennedy-Chavannes, *Assistant Editor*

Design: Tina Malaney, *Director of Design and Production;* Jessica Gonzalez, *Graphic Designer;* Erin Caceres, *Graphic Design Associate*

Production: Jennifer DePrima, *Editorial Production Manager;* Elyse Rozelle, *Senior Production Editor;* Monica White, *Production Editor*

Maps: Rebecca Baer, *Senior Map Editor;* David Lindroth, Mark Stroud (Moon Street Cartography), *Cartographers*

Photography: Viviane Teles, *Senior Photo Editor;* Namrata Aggarwal, Neha Gupta, Payal Gupta, Ashok Kumar, *Photo Editors;* Eddie Aldrete, *Photo Production Intern;* Kadeem McPherson, *Photo Production Associate Intern*

Business and Operations: Chuck Hoover, *Chief Marketing Officer;* Robert Ames, *Group General Manager;* Devin Duckworth, *Director of Print Publishing*

Public Relations and Marketing: Joe Ewaskiw, *Senior Director of Communications and Public Relations*

Fodors.com: Jeremy Tarr, *Editorial Director;* Rachael Levitt, *Managing Editor*

Technology: Jon Atkinson, *Director of Technology;* Rudresh Teotia, *Lead Developer*

Writers: Marlise Kast-Myers, Jeffrey Van Fleet, Rachel White

Editor: Alexis Kelly

Production Editor: Elyse Rozelle

4th edition

ISBN 978-1-64097-539-2

ISSN 2578-3068

SPECIAL SALES
This book is available at special discounts for bulk purchases for sales promotions or premiums. For more information, e-mail SpecialMarkets@fodors.com.

PRINTED IN CANADA

10 9 8 7 6 5 4 3 2 1

About Our Writers

Journalist and author **Marlise Kast-Myers** has traveled to more than 80 countries and has lived in Switzerland, Dominican Republic, Spain, and Costa Rica. Before settling in Southern California, she completed a surfing and snowboarding expedition across the world. Following the release of her memoir, *Tabloid Prodigy*, Marlise co-authored over 40 *Fodor's Travel Guides* including books on Cancún, San Diego, Panama, Puerto Rico, Peru, Los Cabos, Corsica, Riviera Maya, Sardinia, Vietnam, and Costa Rica. She served as a photojournalist for *Surf Guide to Costa Rica* and authored *Day and Overnight Hikes on the Pacific Crest Trail*. Based in San Diego County, she lives at the historic Betty Crocker Estate where she and her husband, Benjamin, operate an antiques business, Brick n Barn. Her website is ⊕ *www.marlisekast.com*. She updated The Nicoya Peninsula; Manuel Antonio and the Central Pacific Coast; The Osa Peninsula and the South Pacific; and Tortuguero and the Caribbean Coast chapters for this guide.

Freelance writer **Jeffrey Van Fleet** has spent the better part of the last two decades enjoying Costa Rica's long rainy season and Wisconsin's cold winters. (Most people would do it the other way around.) At this point, he has covered almost every country south of the Rio Grande for various Fodor's guidebooks. He updated the San José and Central Valley chapters and Travel Smart, Experience Costa Rica, and Biodiversity sections for this edition.

Rachel White is a wanderer and writer chasing the sun from Michigan to Costa Rica. In between, she ushers her four children to as many other countries as she can. She is a contributor *Fodor's Belize: With a Side Trip to Guatemala, Michigan Home and Lifestyle*, ⊕ *www.mother.ly*, and is working on a children's picture book. For this edition, Rachel updated the Arenal and Guanacaste chapters. Follow her escapades on Instagram @rachel_cherry_white_writes.

PENGUIN CANADA

THE SERPENT'S TALE

ARIANA FRANKLIN, a former journalist, is a biographer and author of the novels *City of Shadows*, *Mistress of the Art of Death*, and *Grave Goods*. She is married with two daughters and lives in England.

The
Serpent's Tale

ARIANA FRANKLIN

The
Serpent's Tale

PENGUIN
CANADA

PENGUIN CANADA

Published by the Penguin Group

Penguin Group (Canada), 90 Eglinton Avenue East, Suite 700,
Toronto, Ontario, Canada M4P 2Y3 (a division of Pearson Canada Inc.)

Penguin Group (USA) Inc., 375 Hudson Street, New York, New York 10014, U.S.A.
Penguin Books Ltd, 80 Strand, London WC2R 0RL, England
Penguin Ireland, 25 St Stephen's Green, Dublin 2, Ireland
(a division of Penguin Books Ltd)
Penguin Group (Australia), 250 Camberwell Road, Camberwell, Victoria 3124, Australia
(a division of Pearson Australia Group Pty Ltd)
Penguin Books India Pvt Ltd, 11 Community Centre, Panchsheel Park,
New Delhi – 110 017, India
Penguin Group (NZ), 67 Apollo Drive, Rosedale, North Shore 0745,
Auckland, New Zealand (a division of Pearson New Zealand Ltd)
Penguin Books (South Africa) (Pty) Ltd, 24 Sturdee Avenue, Rosebank,
Johannesburg 2196, South Africa

Penguin Books Ltd, Registered Offices: 80 Strand, London WC2R 0RL, England

Published in Penguin Canada paperback by Penguin Group (Canada),
a division of Pearson Canada Inc., 2008
Published in this edition, 2009

1 2 3 4 5 6 7 8 9 10 (OPM)

Copyright © 2008 by Ariana Franklin

Manufactured in the U.S.A.

Library and Archives Canada Cataloguing in Publication data available
upon request to the publisher.

ISBN: 978-0-14-305285-2

American Library of Congress Cataloging in Publication data available.

Visit the Penguin Group (Canada) website at **www.penguin.ca**

Special and corporate bulk purchase rates available; please see
www.penguin.ca/corporatesales or call 1-800-810-3104, ext. 477 or 474

To Dr. Mary Lynch, M.D., FRCP, FRCPI,
consultant cardiologist.

My literally heartfelt thanks.

PROLOGUE

The two men's voices carried down the tunnels with reverberations that made them indistinguishable but, even so, gave the impression of a business meeting. Which it was. In a way.

An assassin was receiving orders from his client, who was, the assassin thought, making it unnecessarily difficult for himself, as such clients did.

It was always the same; they wanted to conceal their identities, and turned up so masked or muffled you could hardly hear their instructions. They didn't want to be seen with you, which led to assignations on blasted heaths or places like this stinking cellar. They were nervous about handing over the down payment in case you stabbed them and then ran off with it.

If they only realized it, a respectable assassin like himself *had* to be trustworthy; his career depended on it. It had taken time, but Sicarius (the Latin pseudonym he'd chosen for himself) was becoming known for excellence. Whether it was translated from the Latin as "assassin" or "dagger," it stood for the neat removal of one's political opponent, wife, creditor, without suspicion being provable against oneself.

Satisfied clients recommended him to others who were afflicted, though they pretended to make a joke of it: "You could use the fellow they call Sicarius," they'd say. "He's supposed to solve troubles like yours."

And when pressed for information: "I don't know, of course, but rumor has it he's to be contacted at the Bear in Southwark." Or Fillola's in Rome. Or La Boule in Paris. Or at whatever inn in whichever area one was plying for trade that season.

This month, Oxford. In a cellar connected by a long tunnel to the undercroft of an inn. He'd been led to it by a masked and hooded servant—oh, really, *so* unnecessary—and pointed toward a rich red-velvet curtain strung across one corner, hiding the client behind it and contrasting vividly with the mold on the walls and the slime underfoot. Damn it, one's boots would be *ruined.*

"The ... assignment will not be difficult for you?" the curtain asked. The voice behind it had given very specific instructions.

"The circumstances are unusual, my lord," the assassin said. He always called them "my lord." It pleased them. "I don't usually like to leave evidence, but if that is what you require ..."

"I do, but I meant spiritually," the curtain said. "Does your conscience not worry you? Don't you fear for your soul's damnation?"

So they'd reached that point, had they, the moment when clients distanced their morality from his, he being the low-born dirty bastard who wielded the knife and they merely the rich bastards who ordered it.

He could have said, "It's a living and a good one, damned or not, and better than starving to death." He could have said, "I don't have a conscience, I have standards, which I keep to." He could even have said, "What about *your* soul's damnation?"

But they paid for their rag of superiority, so he desisted. Instead, he said cheerily, "High or low, my lord. Popes, peasants, kings, varlets, ladies, children, I dispose of them all—and for the same price: seventy-five marks down and a hundred when the job's done." Keeping to the same tariff was part of his success.

"Children?" The curtain was shocked.

Oh, dear, dear. *Of course* children. Children inherited. Children were obstacles to the step-father, aunt, brother, cousin who would come into the estate once the little moppet was out of the way. And more difficult to dispose of than you'd think …

He merely said, "Perhaps you would go over the instructions again, my lord."

Keep the client talking. Find out who he was, in case he tried to avoid the final payment. Killing those who reneged on the agreement meant tracking them down, inflicting a death that was both painfully inventive and, he hoped, a warning to future clients.

The voice behind the curtain repeated what it had already said. To be done on such and such a day, in such and such a place, by these means the death to occur in such and such a manner, this to be left, that to be taken away.

They always want precision, the assassin thought wearily. Do it this way, do it that. As if killing is a science rather than an art.

Nevertheless, in this instance, the client had planned the murder with extraordinary detail and had intimate knowledge of his victim's comings and goings; it would be as well to comply ...

So Sicarius listened carefully, not to the instructions—he'd memorized them the first time—but to the timbre of the client's voice, noting phrases he could recognize again, waiting for a cough, a stutter that might later identify the speaker in a crowd.

While he listened, he looked around him. There was nothing to be learned from the servant who stood in the shadows, carefully shrouded in an unexceptional cloak and with his shaking hand—oh, bless him—on the hilt of a sword stuck into a belt, as if he wouldn't be dead twenty times over before he could draw it. A pitiful safeguard, but probably the only creature the client trusted.

The location of the cellar, now ... it told the assassin something, if only that the client had shown cunning in choosing it. There were three exits, one of them the long tunnel, down which he'd been guided from the inn. The other two might lead anywhere, to the castle, perhaps, or—he sniffed—to the river. The only certainty was that it was somewhere in the bowels of Oxford. And bowels, as the assassin had reason to know, having laid bare quite a few, were extensive and tortuous.

Built during the Stephen and Matilda war, of course. The assassin reflected uneasily on the tunneling that had, literally, undermined England during the thirteen years of that unfortunate and bloody fracas. The strategic jewel that was Oxford, guarding the country's main routes south to north and east to west, where they crossed the Thames, had suffered badly. Besieged and re-besieged, people had dug like moles both to get in and to get out. One of these days, he thought—and God give it wasn't today—the bloody place would collapse into the wormholes they'd made of its foundations.

Oxford, he thought. A town held mainly for King Stephen and, therefore, the wrong side. Twenty years on, and its losers still heaved with resentment against Matilda's son, Henry Plantagenet, the ultimate winner and king.

The assassin had gained a deal of information while in the area—it always paid to know who was upside with whom, and why—and he thought it possible that the client was one of those still embittered by the war and that the assignment was, therefore, political.

In which case it could be dangerous. Greed, lust, revenge: Their motives were all one to him, but political clients were usually of such high degree that they had a tendency to hide their involvement by hiring yet another murderer to kill the first, *i.e., him*. It was always wearisome and only led to more bloodletting, though never his.

Aha. The unseen client had shifted, and for a second, no more, the tip of a boot had shown beneath the curtain hem. A boot of fine doeskin, like one's own, and *new*, possibly recently made in Oxford—again, like one's own.

A round of the local boot makers was called for.

"We are agreed, then?" the curtain asked.

"We are agreed, my lord."

"Seventy-five marks, you say?"

"In gold, if you please, my lord," the assassin said, still cheerful. "And similarly with the hundred when the job's done."

"Very well," the client said, and told his servant to hand over the purse containing the fee.

And in doing so made a mistake which neither he nor the servant noticed but which the assassin found informative. "Give Master Sicarius the purse, my son," the client said.

In fact, the clink of gold from the purse as it passed was hardly less satisfactory than that the assassin now knew his client's occupation.

And was surprised.

ONE

The woman on the bed had lost the capacity to scream. Apart from the drumming of her feet and the thump of her fists against the sheets, her gyrations were silent, as if she were miming agony.

The three nuns, too, kneeling at either side, might have been aping intercession; their mouths moved soundlessly, because any noise, even the sibilance of a whispered prayer, set off another convulsion in the patient. They had their eyes closed so as not to see her suffering. Only the woman standing at the end of the bed watched it, showing no expression.

On the walls, Adam and Eve skipped in innocent tapestried health among the flora and fauna of the Garden while the Serpent, in a tree, and God, on a cloud, looked on with amiability. It was a circular room, its beauty now mocking the ghastliness of its owner: the fair hair that had turned black and straggled with sweat, the corded veins in the once-white neck, lips stretched in the terrible grin.

What could be done had been done. Candles and burning incense holders heated a room where the lattices and shutters had been stuffed closed so as not to rattle.

Mother Edyve had stripped Godstow, her convent, of its reliquaries in order to send the saints' aid to this stricken woman. Too old to come herself, she had told Sister Havis, Godstow's prioress, what to do. Accordingly, the tibia of Saint Scholastica had been tied to the flailing arm, droplets from the phial containing Saint Mary's milk poured on the poor head, and a splinter of the True Cross placed into the woman's hand, though it had been jerked across the room during a spasm.

Carefully, so as not to make a noise, Sister Havis got up and left the room. The woman who had been standing at the end of the bed followed her. "Where you going?"

"To fetch Father Pol. I sent for him; he's waiting in the kitchen."

"No."

Like the stern but well-born Christian she was, Havis showed patience to the afflicted, though this particular female always made her flesh creep. She said, "It is time, Dakers. She must receive the viaticum."

"I'll kill you. She ain't going to die. I'll kill the priest if he comes upstairs."

It was spoken without force or apparent emotion, but the prioress believed it of this woman; every servant in the place had already run away for fear of what she might do if their mistress died.

"Dakers, Dakers," she said—always name the mad when speaking to them so as to remind them of themselves—"we cannot deny the rite of holy unction's comfort to a soul about to begin its

journey. Look ..." She caught hold of the housekeeper's arm and turned her so that both women
faced into the room where their muttered voices
had caused the body on the bed to arch again. Only
its heels and the top of its head rested on the bed,
forming a tortured bridge.

"No human frame can withstand such torment,"
Sister Havis said. "She is dying." With that, she
began to go down the stairs.

Footsteps followed her, causing her to hold fast
to the banister in case she received a push in the
back. She kept on, but it was a relief to gain the
ground and go into white-cold fresh air as she
crossed to the kitchen that had been modeled on
that of Fontevrault, with its chimneys, and stood
like a giant pepper pot some yards away from the
tower.

The flames in one of the fireplaces were the only
light and sent leaps of red reflection on the drying
sheets that hung from hooks normally reserved for
herbs and flitches of bacon.

Father Pol, a mousy little man, and mousier than
ever tonight, crouched on a stool, cradling a fat
black cat as if he needed its comfort in this place.

His eyes met the nun's and then rolled in inquiry
toward the figure of the housekeeper.

"We are ready for you now, Father," the prioress
told him.

The priest nodded in relief. He stood up,
carefully placed the cat on the stool, gave it a last
pat, picked up the chrismatory at his feet, and
scuttled out. Sister Havis waited a moment to see

if the housekeeper would come with them, saw that she would not, and followed Father Pol.

Left alone, Dakers stared into the fire.

The blessing by the bishop who had been called to her mistress two days ago had done nothing. Neither had all the convent's trumpery. The Christian god had failed.

Very well.

She began to move briskly. Items were taken from the cupboard in the tiny room that was her domain next to the kitchen. When she came back, she was muttering. She put a leather-bound book with a lock on the chopping block. On it was placed a crystal that, in the firelight, sent little green lights from its facets wobbling around the room.

One by one, she lit seven candles and dripped the wax of each onto the block to make a stand. They formed a circle round the book and crystal, giving light as steady as the ones upstairs, though emitting a less pleasant smell than beeswax.

The cauldron hanging from a jack over the fire was full and boiling, and had been kept so as to provide water for the washing of the sickroom sheets. So many sheets.

The woman bent over it to make sure that the surface of the water bubbled. She looked around for the cauldron's lid, a large, neatly holed circle of wood with an iron handle arched over its center, found it, and leaned it carefully on the floor at her feet. From the various fire irons by the side of the hearth, dogs, spits, etc., she picked out a long poker and laid that, too, on the floor by the lid.

"Igzy-bidzy," she was muttering, "sishnu shishnu, adony-manooey, eelam-peelam ..." The ignorant might have thought the repetition to be that of a child's skipping rhyme; others would have recognized the deliberately garbled, many-faithed versions of the holy names of God.

Dodging the sheets, Dame Dakers crossed to where Father Pol had been sitting and picked up the cat, cradling and petting it as he had done. It was a good cat, a famous ratter, the only one she allowed in the place.

Taking it to the hearth, she gave it a last stroke with one hand and reached for the cauldron lid with the other.

Still chanting, she dropped the cat into the boiling water, swiftly popping the lid in place over it and forcing it down. The poker was slid through the handle so that it overlapped the edges.

For a second the lid rattled against the poker and a steaming shriek whistled through the lid's holes. Dame Dakers knelt on the hearth's edge, commending the sacrifice to her master.

If God had failed, it was time to petition the Devil.

Eighty-odd miles to the east as the crow flew, Vesuvia Adelia Rachel Ortese Aguilar was delivering a baby for the first time—or trying to deliver it.

"Push, Ma," said the fetus's eldest sister helpfully from the sidelines.

"Don't you be telling her that," Adelia said in East Anglian. "Her can't push til the time comes." At this stage, the poor woman had little control over the matter.

And neither do I, she thought in desperation. *I don't know what to do.*

It was going badly; labor had been protracted to the point where the mother, an uncomplaining fenwoman, was becoming exhausted.

Outside, on the grass, watched by Adelia's dog, Mansur was singing nursery rhymes from his homeland to amuse the other children—all of whom had been delivered easily with the aid of a neighbor and a bread knife—and it was a measure of Adelia's desperation that at this moment she relished neither his voice nor the strangeness of hearing a castrato's angelic soprano wafting minor-key Arabic over an English fenland. She could only wonder at the endurance of the suffering woman on the bed, who managed to gasp, "Tha's pretty."

The woman's husband remained uncharmed. He was hiding himself and his concern for his wife in the hut's undercroft with his cow. His voice came up the wooden flight of stairs to the stage—part hayloft, part living quarters—where the women battled. "Her never had this to-do when Goody Baines delivered 'em."

Good for Goody Baines, Adelia thought. But those babies had come without trouble, and there had been too many of them. Later, she would have to point out that Mistress Reed had given birth to nine in twelve years; another would probably kill her, even if this one did not.

However, now was not the moment. It was necessary to keep up confidence, especially that of the laboring mother, so she called brightly, "You be thankful you got me now, bor, so you just keep that old water bilin'."

Me, she thought, *an anatomist, and a foreigner to boot. My speciality is corpses. You have a right to be worried. If you were aware of how little experience I have with any parturition other than my own, you'd be frantic.*

The unknown Goody Baines might have known what to do; so might Gyltha, Adelia's companion and nursemaid to her child, but both women were independently paying a visit to Cambridge Fair and would not be back for a day or two, their departure having coincided with the onset of Mistress Reed's labor. Only Adelia in this isolated part of fenland was known to have medical knowledge and had, therefore, been called to the emergency.

And if the woman in the bed had broken her bones or contracted any form of disease, Adelia could indeed have helped her, for Adelia was a doctor—not just wise in the use of herbs and the pragmatism handed down from woman to woman through generations, and not, like so many men parading as physicians, a charlatan who bamboozled his patients with disgusting medicines for high prices. No, Adelia was a graduate of the great and liberal, forward-thinking, internationally admired School of Medicine in Salerno, which defied the Church by enrolling women into its studies if they were clever enough.

Finding Adelia's brain on a par with, even excelling, that of the cleverest male student, her professors had given her a masculine education, which, later, she had completed by joining her Jewish foster father in his department of autopsy.

A unique education, then, but of no use to her now, because in its wisdom—and it *was* wisdom—Salerno's School of Medicine had seen that midwifery was better left to midwives. Adelia could have cured Mistress Reed's baby, she could have performed a postmortem on it were it dead and revealed what it died of—but she couldn't birth it.

She handed over a basin of water and cloth to the woman's daughter, crossed the room, and picked up her own baby from its wicker basket, sat down on a hay bale, undid her laces, and began to feed it.

She had a theory about breast-feeding, as she had for practically everything: It should be accompanied by calm, happy thoughts. Usually, when she nursed the child, she sat in the doorway of her own little reed-thatched house at Waterbeach and allowed her eyes and mind to wander over the Cam fenland. At first its flat greenness had fared badly against the remembered Mediterranean panorama of her birth, with its jagged drama set against a turquoise sea. But flatness, too, has its beauty, and gradually she had come to appreciate the immense skies over infinite shades of willow and alder that the natives called carr, and the richness of fish and wildlife teeming in the hidden rivers.

"Mountains?" Gyltha had said once. "Don't hold with mountains. They buggers do get in the way."

Besides, this was now the homeland of the child in her arms, and therefore infinitely beloved.

But today, Adelia dared not indulge either her eyes or her mind for her baby's sake. There was another child to be saved, and be damned if she was going to let it die through her own ignorance. Or the mother, either.

Silently apologizing to the little thing in her arms, Adelia set herself to envisaging the corpses she'd dissected of mothers who'd died with their fetuses yet undelivered.

Such pitiable cadavers, yet when they were laid out on the marble table of the great autopsy hall in Salerno, she'd withheld compassion from them, as she'd learned to do with all the dead in order to serve them better. Emotion had no place in the art of dissection, only clear, trained, investigative reasoning.

Now, here, in a whiskery little hut on the edge of the civilized world, she did it again, blanking from her mind the suffering of the woman on the bed and replacing it with a map of interior organs, positions, pressures, displacements. "*Hmm.*"

Hardly aware she was doing it, Adelia withdrew her baby from her left, now empty, breast and transferred it to the other, still calculating stresses on brain and navel cord, why and when suffocation occurred, blood loss, putrefaction ... "*Hmm.*"

"Here, missis. Summat's coming." The daughter was guiding her mother's hands toward the bridle that had been tied to the bed head.

Adelia laid her child back in its basket, covered herself up, and went to the bottom of the bed.

Something was indeed emerging from the mother's body, but it wasn't a baby's head, it was a baby's backside.

Goddamn. A breech birth. She'd suspected it but, by the time she'd been brought in, engagement in the uterus had taken place and it was too late to insert her hand and revolve the fetus, even if she'd had the knowledge and daring.

"Ain't you going to tug it out?" the daughter asked.

"Not yet." She'd seen the irreparable damage caused by pulling at this stage. Instead, she addressed the mother. "*Now* you push. Whether you want to or not, *push*."

Mistress Reed nodded, put part of the bridle in her mouth, clamped her teeth on it, and began pushing. Adelia gestured to the girl to help her drag the mother's body farther down the bed so that her buttocks hung over the edge and gravity could play its part.

"Hold her legs straight. By the ankles, behind me, *behind* me, that's right. Well done, mistress. Keep pushing." She herself was on her knees, a good position for delivering—and praying.

Help us, Lord.

Even so, she waited until a navel appeared with its attached cord. She touched the cord gently—a strong pulse. *Good, good.*

Now for it.

Moving quickly but with care, she entered her

hand into the mother's cavity and released one leg, then the other, flexing the tiny knees.

"Push. *Push*, will you."

Oh, beautiful, sliding out by themselves *without having to be pulled* were two arms and a torso up to the nape of the neck. Supporting the body with one hand, Adelia laid the other on the little back and felt the tremor of a pulse.

Crucial now. Only minutes before suffocation set in. *God, whichever god you are, be with us now*.

He wasn't. Mistress Reed had lost strength, and the baby's head was still inside.

"Pass over that pack, *that* pack." In seconds, Adelia had extracted her dissection knife, always kept clean.

"Now." She placed the daughter's hand on Mistress Reed's pubic region. "Press." Still supporting the little torso, she made a cut in the mother's perineum. There was a slither and, because the knife was still in her fingers, she had to catch the baby in the crook of her elbows.

The daughter was shouting, "That's out, Dadda."

Master Reed appeared at the head of the ladder in a smell of cow dung. "Gor dang, what is it?"

Stupid with relief, Adelia said, "It's a baby." Ugly, bloodied, soapy, froglike, with its feet tending toward its head as they had in the womb, but undamaged, breathing, and, when tapped on its back, objecting to life in general and its emergence into it in particular—to Adelia, as beautiful a sight and sound as the world was capable of producing.

"That's as may be, but what *is* it?"

"Oh." Adelia put down the knife and turned the miracle over. It was male, quite definitely male. She gathered herself. "I believe the scrotum swelling to be caused by bruising and will subside."

"He's a'going to be popular if it don't, ain't he?" Master Reed said.

The cord was severed, Mistress Reed was stitched and made decent for visitors, and the baby was wrapped in a fleece and put into his mother's arms.

"Here, missis, you got a name as we can call him after?" her husband wanted to know.

"Vesuvia Adelia Rachel Ortese Aguilar," Adelia said apologetically.

There was silence.

"What about him?" Master Reed pointed at the tall figure of Mansur, who had come up with the siblings to view the miracle.

"Mansur bin Fayîi bin Nasab Al-Masaari Khayoun of Al Amarah."

More silence.

Mansur, whose alliance with Gyltha was enabling him to understand English even if it gave him little chance to speak it, said in Arabic, "The prior comes, I saw his boat. Let them call the boy Geoffrey."

"Prior Geoffrey's here?" Adelia was down the ladder in a trice and running to the tiny wooden platform that served as a quay—all homes in the fenland had access to one of its innumerable rivers, its children learning to maneuver a coracle as soon as they could walk.

Clambering out of his barge with the help of a liveried oarsman was one of Adelia's favorite people. "How are you here?" she said, hugging him. "*Why* are you here? How is Ulf?"

"A handful, but a clever handful. He thrives." Gyltha's grandson, and, so it was said, the prior's as well, had been set to serious study at the priory school and would not be allowed to leave it until the spring sowing.

"I am so pleased to see you."

"And I you. They told me at Waterbeach where you were gone. It appears that the mountain must come to Mohammed."

"It's still too mountainous," Adelia said, standing back to look at him. The prior of Saint Augustine's great canonry in Cambridge had been her first patient and, subsequently, her first friend in England; she worried about him. "You have not been keeping to my diet."

"*Dum vivimus, vivamus*," he said. "Let us live while we live. I subscribe to the Epicureans."

"Do you know the mortality rate among Epicureans?"

They spoke in fast and classical Latin because it was natural to them, though it caused the men in the prior's barge to wonder why their lord was concealing from them what he was saying to a woman and, even more wondrous, how a woman could understand it.

"Oh, but you are well come," Adelia said, "just in time to baptize my first delivery. It will comfort his parents, though he is a healthy, glorious child."

Adelia did not subscribe to the theory of Christian infant baptism, just as she didn't subscribe to any of what she regarded as barbarous tenets held by the world's three major faiths. A god who would not allow that baby upstairs into the Kingdom of Heaven if it died before being sprinkled with certain words and water was not a god she wanted anything to do with.

But his parents regarded the ceremony as vital, if only to ensure the boy a Christian burial should the worst happen. Master Reed had been about to send for the shabby, peripatetic priest who served the area.

The Reed family watched in silence as bejewelled fingers wetted their son's forehead and a voice as velvety-rich as its owner's vestments welcomed him into the faith, promising him life eternal and pronouncing him "Geoffrey in the name of the Father, and of the Son, and of the Holy Ghost, amen."

"Fen people never say thank you," Adelia apologized, as, carrying her baby, she joined the prior in his barge, the dog called Ward scrambling in with her, leaving Mansur to follow in their rowing boat. "But they never forget, either. They were grateful but amazed. You were too much for them, as if archangel Gabriel had come down in a shaft of gold."

"*Non angeli, sed angli*, I fear," Prior Geoffrey said, and such was his fondness for Adelia that he, who had lived in Cambridgeshire for thirty years, remained complacent at being instructed in the ways of the fens by this woman from southern Italy.

Look at her, he thought, *dressed like a scarecrow, accompanied by a dog that will necessitate fumigation of the bench it sits on, the finest mind of her generation hugging her bastard for joy at having delivered a brat into a hovel.*

Not for the first time, he wondered about her parentage, of which she was as ignorant as he. Brought up by a Salernitan couple, a Jew and his Christian wife, who'd found her abandoned among the stones of Vesuvius, her hair was the dark blond sometimes seen on Greeks or Florentines. Not that anybody could see it at the moment, hidden in that unspeakable cap.

She is still the oddity she was when we first met on the road to Cambridge, Prior Geoffrey thought. *I returning from the pilgrimage to Canterbury, she in a cart, accompanied by an Arab and a Jew. I put her down as their trull, not recognizing the virginity of a scholar. Yet when I began to bawl in pain— Lord, how I bawled, and Lord, what pain it was—despite all my company of Christians, only she played the Samaritan. In saving my life that day she reduced me, me, to stammering adolescence by manipulating my most intimate parts as if they were mere tripes to be cooked. And still I find her beautiful.*

She had been obeying a summons even then, brought from her work with the dead of Salerno to be part of a team in disguise led by the investigating Jew, Simon of Naples, to find out who was killing Cambridge's children—a matter that seriously bothered the King of England because it was leading to riot and, therefore, a depletion of his taxes.

This being England and not freethinking Salerno, it had been necessary for Mansur, Adelia's servant, to set up as the doctor, with Adelia herself pretending to be his assistant during their investigation. Poor, good Simon—even though a Jew, the prior remembered him in his prayers—had been murdered in his search for the killer, and Adelia herself had nearly lost her life, but the case had been resolved, justice imposed, and the king's taxes restored to his treasury.

In fact, so useful had been Adelia's forensic skill in the matter that King Henry had refused to let her return to Italy in case he should need her again. A miserly and greedy ingratitude typical of kings, Prior Geoffrey thought, even while he rejoiced that it had made the woman his neighbor.

How much does she resent this exile? It wasn't as if she'd been rewarded. The king had done nothing—well, he'd been abroad—when Cambridge's doctors, jealous of a successful interloper, had driven her and Mansur out of town and into the wilderness of the fens.

Sick and suffering men and women had followed them, and still did, not caring if treatment was at the hands of foreign unbelievers but only that it made them well.

Lord, I fear for her. Her enemies will damn her for it. Use her illegitimate child as proof that she is immoral, take her before the Archdeaconal Court to condemn her as a sinner. And what can I do?

Prior Geoffrey groaned at his own guilt. *What friend have I been to her? Or to her Arab? Or Gyltha?*

Until he had himself teetered on the edge of death and been dragged back by Adelia, he had followed the Church's teaching on science that only the soul mattered, not the body. Physical pain? It is God's purpose, put up with it. Investigation? Dissection? Experiments? *Sic vos ardebitis in Gehenna*. So will ye burn in hell.

But Adelia's ethos was Salerno's, where Arab, Jewish, and even Christian minds refused to set barriers on their search for knowledge. She had lectured him: "How can it be God's purpose to watch a man drowning when to stretch out one's hand would save him? *You* were drowning in your own urine. Was I to fold my arms rather than relieve the bladder? No, I knew how to do it and I did it. And I knew because I had studied the offending gland in men who'd died from it."

An oddly prim little thing she'd been then, unsophisticated, curiously nunlike except for her almost savage honesty, her intelligence, and her hatred of superstition. She had at least gained something from her time in England, he thought— more womanliness, a softening, and, of course, the baby—the result of a love affair as passionate and as unsuitable as that of Héloïse and Abelard.

Prior Geoffrey sighed and waited for her to ask why, busy and important man that he was, he had sailed forth to look for her.

The advent of winter had stripped the fens of leaves, allowing the sun unusual access to the river so that its water reflected back exactly the wild shapes of naked willow and alder along the banks. Adelia, voluble with relief and triumph, pointed out the names of the birds flying up from under the barge's prow to the stolid baby on her lap, repeating their names in English, Latin, and French, and appealing to Mansur across the water when she forgot the Arabic.

How old is my godchild now? the prior wondered, amused. *Eight months? Nine?* "Somewhat early to be a polyglot," he said.

"You can't start too soon."

She looked up at last. "Where are we going? I presume you did not come so far on the chance of baptizing a baby."

"A privilege, *medica*," Prior Geoffrey said. "I was taken back to a blessed stable in Bethlehem. But no, I did not come for that. This messenger"—he beckoned forward a figure that had been standing, cloaked and transfixed, at the barge prow—"arrived for you at the priory with a summons, and since he would have had difficulty finding you in these waters, I volunteered to bring him."

Anyway, he'd known he must be at hand when the summons was delivered; she wouldn't want to obey it.

"Dang bugger," Adelia said in pure East Anglian—like Mansur's, her English vocabulary was being enlarged by Gyltha. "*What?*"

The messenger was a skinny young fellow, and Adelia's glare almost teetered him backward. Also, he was looking, openmouthed, to the prior for confirmation. "This is the lady Adelia, my lord?" It was, after all, a name that suggested nobility; he'd expected dignity—beauty, even—the sweep of a skirt on marble, not this dowdy thing with a dog and a baby.

Prior Geoffrey smiled. "The lady Adelia, indeed."

Oh, well. The young man bowed, flinging back a cloak to show the arms embroidered on his tabard, two harts rampant and a golden saltire. "From my most reverend master, the lord Bishop of Saint Albans."

A scroll was extended.

Adelia didn't take it. The animation had leeched out of her. "What does *he* want?" It was said with a frigidity the messenger was unused to. He looked helplessly at the prior.

Prior Geoffrey intervened; he had received a similar scroll. Still using Latin, he said, "It appears that our lord bishop needs your expertise, Adelia. He's summoned you to Cambridge—something about an attempted murder in Oxfordshire. I gather it is a matter heavy with political implications."

The messenger went on proffering his scroll; Adelia went on not taking it. She appealed to her friend. "I'm not going, Geoffrey. I don't want to go."

"I know, my dear, but it is why I have come. I'm afraid you must."

"I don't want to see him. I'm happy here. Gyltha, Mansur, Ulf, and this one ..." She dandled the child at him. "I like the fens, I like the people. Don't make me go."

The plea lacerated him, but he hardened his heart. "My dear, I have no choice. Our lord bishop sends to say that it is a matter of the king's business. The *king's*. Therefore, you have no choice, either. You are the king's secret weapon."

TWO

Cambridge hadn't expected to see its bishop again so soon. Eighteen months ago, after his appointment to the see of Saint Albans, the town had turned out for him with all the pomp due a man whose word ranked only a little below that of God, the Pope, and the Archbishop of Canterbury.

With equal pomp, it had seen him off on an inaugural circuit of his diocese that, because it was huge, like all England's sees, would take him more than two years to complete.

Yet here he was, before his time, without the lumbering baggage train that had accompanied him when he left, and with gallopers coming only a few hours ahead to warn of his arrival.

Still, Cambridge turned out for him. In strength. Some people fell on their knees or held up their children to receive the great man's blessing; others ran at his stirrup, babbling their grievances for him to mend. Most just enjoyed the spectacle.

A popular man, Bishop Rowley Picot. One of Cambridge's own. Been on Crusade. A king's appointee to the bishopric, too, not the Pope's. Which was good, King Henry II being nearer and more immediately powerful than the Vatican.

Not one of your dry-as-a-stick bishops, either: known to have a taste for hunting, grub, and his drink, with an eye for the ladies, so they said, but given all that up since God tapped him on the shoulder. And hadn't he brought to justice the child murderers who'd terrorized the town a while back?

Mansur and Adelia, followed disconsolately by the bishop's messenger, had insisted on scouring Cambridge's fair for Gyltha, and now, having found her, Mansur was holding her up so that she could peer over the heads of the crowd to watch the bishop go by. "Dressed like a Christmas beef, bless him," Gyltha reported down to Adelia. "Ain't you going to let little un look?"

"No," Adelia said, pressing her child more closely to her.

"Got a crosier and ever'thing," Gyltha persisted. "Not sure that hat suits un, though."

In her mind's eye, Adelia saw a portly, portentous, mitered figure representing, as most bishops did, the hypocrisy and suffocation of a church that opposed not only herself but every advance necessary for the mental and physical health of mankind.

There was a touch on her shoulder. "If you would follow me, mistress. His lordship is to grant you an audience in his house, but first he must receive the sheriff and celebrate Mass."

"*Grant us a audience*," Gyltha mimicked as Mansur lowered her to the ground. "That's rich, that is."

"*Um.*" The bishop's messenger—his name had turned out to be Jacques—was still off-balance; Saracens and fishwives were not the sort of people he was in service to deal with. Somewhat desperately, he said, "Mistress, I believe my lord expects his interview to be with you only."

"This lady and gentleman come with me," Adelia told him, "or I don't go."

Being in Cambridge again was distressing her. The worst moments of her life, and the best, had passed in this town; the place was haunted by spirits whose bones rested in peace while others still shrieked to a god that hadn't heard them.

"The dog, too," she added, and saw the poor messenger's eyes roll. She didn't care; it had been a concession to come at all. When she'd stopped off at her house on the way in order to pack suitable winter clothing for them all, she had gone so far as to wash her hair and change into her best dress, shabby though it now was. Further than that, she would not go.

The episcopal residence—the bishop had one in every major town in the diocese—was in Saint Mary's parish, a building now abuzz with servants preparing it for unexpected habitation.

Followed by the dog, Ward, the three were shown into a large upstairs chamber where dust sheets were now being whisked off heavy, ornate furniture. An open door at its far end revealed the gilt and plaster of a bedroom where footmen were hanging brocade drapes from the tester of a magnificent bed.

One of them saw Mansur looking in and crossed the room to shut the door in his face. Ward lifted his leg and piddled against the door's carved arch.

"Tha's a good dog," Gyltha said.

Adelia hefted the rush basket holding her sleeping baby onto a brassbound chest, fetched a stool, undid her bodice laces, and began the feed. *What a remarkable child*, she thought, gazing down at it, accustomed to the quiet of the fens yet showing no fear, only interest, amid the hubbub that had been Cambridge today.

"*Well*," Gyltha said to her. The two women hadn't had a moment until now in which to talk privately.

"Exactly."

"What's his lordship want with you, then?"

Adelia shrugged. "To look into an attempted murder in Oxfordshire, so Prior Geoffrey said."

"Didn't think you'd come for that."

"I wouldn't have, but it's on the king's orders, apparently."

"Oh, bugger," Gyltha said.

"Indeed." Henry Plantagenet's was the ultimate command; you could squirm under it, but you disobeyed it at your peril.

There were times when Adelia resented Henry II bitterly for marooning her on the island of Britain so that, having discovered her talents at reading the secrets of the dead, he could use them again. There were other times when she didn't.

Letters had originally passed between the English king and his royal kinsman, William of Sicily, requesting help for the problem in Cambridge that only Salerno's investigative tradition could provide. It had been a shock to everybody that Salerno obliged by sending a mistress of the art of death rather than a master, but things had turned out well—for Henry II, at least. So much so that other letters had passed between him and King William requesting—and granting—that Adelia stay where she was awhile longer.

It had been done without her request or permission, an act of naked piracy, typical of the man. "I'm not an object," she'd shouted at him. "You can't borrow me, I'm a human being."

"And I'm a king," Henry told her. "If I say you stay, you stay."

Damn him, he hadn't even *paid* her for all she'd done, for the danger, for the loss of beloved friends—to the end of her days, she would mourn for Simon of Naples, that wise and gentle man whose companionship had been like a second father's. And her dog, a much lesser loss but, nevertheless, a grief.

On the other hand, to weight the scale, she had retained her dear Mansur, gained an affection for England and its people, been awarded the friendship of Prior Geoffrey, Gyltha and her grandson, *and*, best of all, acquired her baby.

Also, although the Plantagenet was a crafty, hot-tempered, parsimonious swine, he was still a great king, a very great king, and not just because he ruled an empire of countries stretching from the borders of Scotland to the Pyrenees. The quarrel between him and his Archbishop of Canterbury, Thomas à Becket, would damn him forever, ending as it had in the archbishop's murder. But Henry'd had the right of it, in Adelia's opinion, and it had been disastrous for the world that the Jew-hating, self-aggrandizing, backward-looking Becket's refusal to allow any reform of the equally backward-looking English Church had driven his king into uttering the dreadful cry *"Who will rid me of this turbulent priest?"* For immediately it had been taken up by some of his knights with their own reasons for wanting Becket dead. They'd slipped away across the Channel to Canterbury and committed a deed that had resulted in making a martyred saint out of a brave but stupid and blinkered man while, at the same time, giving the Church every excuse to scourge a king who'd wanted to curb its power and allow greater justice to his people with laws more fair, more humane than any in the world.

Yes, they called Henry Plantagenet a fiend, and there were times when Adelia thought he probably was, but she also knew that his ferocious blue eyes saw further into the future than any other man's. He'd succeeded to the throne of an England blasted and impoverished by civil war and given it a secure prosperity that was the envy of other lands.

It was said his wife and his sons resented and had plotted against him and, again, Adelia could see why—he was so far ahead of everybody else, so quick, that their relationship with him could provide no more than metaphorically clinging to his stirrup as he rode.

Yet when the Church would have put Adelia on trial during her search for the murderer of Cambridge's children, it was this busy king who'd found time to step in and exonerate her.

Well, so he should, she thought. *Wasn't I saving him trouble and money? I'm not his subject, I am a Sicilian; he has no right to coerce me into his service.*

Which would have been an unquestionably reasonable sentiment if, sometimes, Adelia didn't feel that to be in the service of Henry II of England was a privilege.

Nevertheless, she damned his eyes for him and, for the sake of her child's digestion, tried to clear him from her mind. Trouble was, the vast room around her reflected a Church that made her angrier than Henry ever could. Here was nothing that was not rigidly and opulently religious—the bishop's massive chair, a cushioned, gold-inlaid prie-dieu where his lordship could kneel in comfort to the Christ, who'd died in poverty, air stuffy with incense. Urging herself to despise it, Adelia contrasted it with Prior Geoffrey's room at the priory, which was all the holier for its reminders of the profane—fishing rods in a corner, the smell of good food, an exquisite little bronze Aphrodite brought back from Rome, the framed letter from a pupil he was proud of.

She finished feeding. Gyltha took the child from her to burp it, an occupation both women vied for—there was no more satisfying sound than that tiny belch. Because the newly lit brazier had not yet begun to warm the room, Gyltha added another blanket to the basket before she put it in the shadows to let the baby sleep. Then she went to stand by the brazier and looked around with complacence. "Murder, eh? Old team and old days back again."

"*Attempted* murder," Adelia reminded her. "And no, they aren't."

"Do make a change to go travelin', though," Gyltha said. "Better'n a winter iced into they bloody fens."

"You love winter in the fens. So do I." Adelia had learned to skate.

"Don't mean as I can't enjoy somewheres else." Old as she was, Gyltha had an adventurous spirit. She gave a rub to her backside and nodded toward the basket. "What's his lordship going say to our little treasure, then?"

"I can only hope," Adelia said, "that he won't ask whose it is."

Gyltha blinked. "Ooh, that's nasty. He's not a'goin' to do that, 'course he not a'goin' to do that. What's set your maggots bitin'?"

"I don't want us to be here, Gyltha. Bishops, kings, they've got no right to ask anything of me. I won't do it."

"You got any choice, girl?"

There was a step on the landing outside. Adelia gritted her teeth, but it was a small priest who came in. He carried the holder of a lit candle in one hand and a slate book in the other, raising the light high and making a slow arc with it, peering at each face with shortsighted eyes.

"I am Father Paton, his lordship's secretary," he said. "And you are ... yes, yes." To make sure, he put his book on a table, opened it, and held the candle near. "An Arab male and two females, yes." He looked up. "You will be provided with transport, service, and provisions to Oxford and back, a winter cloak each, firing, plus a rate of a shilling a day each until such time as his lordship is satisfied the work be done. You will have no expectation beyond that."

He peered at his slate once more. "Ah, yes, his lordship has been informed of a baby and expressed his willingness to give it his blessing." He waited for appreciation. Getting none, he said, "It can be conveyed to him. Is it here?"

Gyltha moved to stand between him and the basket.

The priest didn't see his danger; instead, he looked once more at his slate and, unused to dealing with women, addressed Mansur. "It says here you are some sort of doctor?"

Again, there was no reply. Apart from the priest, the room was very still.

"These are your instructions. To discover the culprit whom, three days ago"—he checked the date—"yes, it was the celebration of Saint Leocadia ... three days ago, made an attempt on the life of the woman Rosamund Clifford of Wormhold Tower near Oxford. You will require the help of the nuns of Godstow in this endeavor." He tapped the slate with a bony finger. "It must be pointed out that, should the aforesaid nuns offer you free accommodation at the convent, your payment shall be reduced accordingly."

He peered at them, then returned to the main thrust. "Any information is to be sent to his lordship immediately as it is gained—a messenger to be provided for the purpose—and you will tell no one else of your findings, which must be unearthed with discretion."

He scanned his book for more detail, found none, and clapped it shut. "Horses and a conveyance will be at the door within an hour, and food is being prepared in the meantime. To be provided without charge." His nose twitched at his generosity.

Was that all? No, one more thing. "I imagine the baby will prove a hindrance to the investigation; therefore, I have commissioned a nurse to look after it in your absence." He seemed proud to have thought of it. "I am informed the going rate is a penny a day, which will be deducted ... Ow, *ow*, put me down."

Dangling by the back of his surplice from Mansur's hand, he had the appearance of a surprised kitten.

He's very young, Adelia thought, *although he will look the same at forty. I would be sorry for him if he didn't frighten me so much; he'd have taken my baby away without a thought.*

Gyltha was informing the struggling kitten. "You see, lad," she said, bending to put her face close, "we come to see Bishop Rowley."

"No, no, that is impossible. His lordship departs for Normandy tomorrow and has much to do before then." Somehow, horizontally, the little priest achieved dignity. "I attend to his affairs ..."

But the door had opened and a procession was entering in a blaze of candles, bearing at its center a figure from an illuminated manuscript, majestic in purple and gold.

Gyltha's right, Adelia thought immediately, *the miter doesn't suit him*. Then she took in the set of jowls, the dulled eyes, so changed from the man she remembered.

No, we're wrong: It does.

His lordship assessed the situation. "Put him down, Mansur," he said in Arabic.

Mansur opened his hand.

Both pages carrying his lordship's train leaned out sideways to peer at the ragbag of people who had floored Father Paton. A white-haired functionary began hammering on the tiles with his wand of office.

Only the bishop appeared unmoved. "All right, steward," he said. "Good evening, Mistress Adelia. Good evening, Gyltha, you look well."

"So do you, bor."

"How's Ulf?"

"At school. Prior says as he's doing grand."

The steward blinked; this was lèse-majesté. He watched his bishop turn to the Arab. "Dr. Mansur, *as-salaam alaykum*."

"*Wa alaykum as-salaam.*"

This was worse. "My lord ..."

"Supper will be served up here as quickly as may be, steward. We are short of time."

We, thought Adelia. The episcopal "we."

"Your vestments, my lord ... Shall I fetch your dresser?"

"Paton will divest me." The bishop sniffed, searching for the source of a smell. He found it and added, "Also, bring a bone for the dog."

"Yes, my lord." Pitiably, the steward wafted the other servants from the room.

The bishop processed to the bedroom, the secretary following and explaining what he had done, what they had done. "I cannot understand the antagonism, my lord, I merely made arrangements based on the information supplied to me from Oxford."

Bishop Rowley's voice: "Which seem to have become somewhat garbled on the journey."

"Yet I obeyed them as best I could, to the letter, my lord ... I cannot understand ..." Outpourings of a man misjudged came to them through the open door as, at the same time, Father Paton divested his master of cope, dalmatic, rochet, pallium, gloves, and miter, layer after layer of embroidered trappings that had employed many needlewomen for many years, all lifted off and folded with infinite care. It took time.

"Rosamund Clifford?" Mansur asked Gyltha.

"You know her, you heathen. Fair Rosamund as they sing about—the king's pet fancy. Lots of songs about Fair Rosamund."

That Rosamund. Adelia remembered hearing the ha'penny minstrels on market days, and their songs—some romantic, most of them bawdy.

If he's dragged me here to involve me in the circumstances of a loose woman ...

Then she reminded herself that she, too, must now be numbered among the world's loose women.

"So she've near been murdered, has she?" Gyltha said, happily. "Per'aps Queen Eleanor done it. Tried to get her out of the way, like. Green jealous of Rosamund, Eleanor is."

"The songs say that as well, do they?" Adelia asked.

"That they do." Gyltha considered. "No, now I think on't, can't be the queen as done it; last I heard, the king had her in prison."

The mighty and their activities were another country, in another country. By the time reports of what they were up to reached the fens, they had achieved the romance and remoteness of myth, nothing to do with real people, and less than nothing compared to a river flooding or cows dead from the murrain or, in Adelia's case, the birth of a baby.

Once, it had been different. During the war of Stephen and Matilda, news of their comings and goings was vital, so you could know in advance— and hopefully escape—whichever king's, queen's, or baron's army was likely to come trampling your crops. Since much of the trampling had taken place in the fens, Gyltha had then been as aware of politics as any.

But out of that terrible time had emerged a Plantagenet ruler like a king from a fairy tale, establishing peace, law, and prosperity in England. If there *were* wars, they took place abroad, blessed be the Mother of God.

The wife Henry brought with him to the throne had also stepped out of a fairy tale—a highly colored one. Here was no shy virgin princess; Eleanor was the greatest heiress in Europe, a radiant personality who'd ruled her Duchy of Aquitaine in her own right before wedding the meek and pious King Louis of France—a man who'd bored her so much that the marriage had ended in divorce. At which point nineteen-year-old Henry Plantagenet had stepped forward to woo the beautiful thirty-year-old Eleanor and marry her, thus taking over her vast estates and making himself ruler of a greater area of France than that belonging to its resentful King Louis.

The stories about Eleanor were legion and scandalous: She'd accompanied Louis on crusade with a bare-breasted company of Amazons; she'd slept with her uncle Raymond, Prince of Antioch; she'd done this, done that ...

But if her new English subjects expected to be entertained by more naughty exploits, they were disappointed. For the next decade or so, Eleanor faded quietly into the background, doing her queenly and wifely duty by providing Henry with five sons and three daughters.

As was expected of a healthy king, Henry had other children by other women—what ruler did not?—but Eleanor seemed to take them in her stride, even having young Geoffrey, one of her husband's bastards by a prostitute, brought up with the legitimate children in the royal court.

A happy marriage, then, as marriages went.

Until ...

What had caused the rift in the lute? The advent of Rosamund, young, lovely, the highest-born of Henry's women? His affair with her became legendary, a matter for song; he adored her, called her *Rosa Mundi*, Rose of all the World, had tucked her away in a tower near his hunting lodge at Woodstock and enclosed it in a labyrinth so that nobody else should find the way through ...

Poor Eleanor was in her fifties now, unable to bear any more children. Had menopausal jealousy caused her rage? Because rage there must certainly have been for her to goad her eldest son, Young Henry, into rebellion against his father. Queens had died for much less. In fact, it was a wonder her husband hadn't executed her instead of condemning her to a not uncomfortable imprisonment.

Well, delightful as it was to speculate on these things, they were all a long way away. Whatever sins had led to Queen Eleanor's imprisonment, they had been committed in Aquitaine, or Anjou, or the Vexin, one of those foreign places over which the Plantagenet royal family also ruled. Most English people weren't sure in what manner the queen had offended; certainly Gyltha was not. She didn't care much. Neither did Adelia.

There was a sudden shout from the bedroom. "It's *here*? She's brought it *here*?" Now down to his tunic, a man who looked younger and thinner but still very large stood in the doorway, staring around him. He loped to the basket on the table. "My God," he said, "my God."

You dare, Adelia thought, *you* dare *ask whose it is*.

But the bishop was staring downward with the awe of Pharaoh's daughter glimpsing baby Moses in the reeds. "Is this him? My God, he looks just like me."

"She," Gyltha said. "*She* looks just like you."

How typical of church gossips, Adelia thought viciously, that they would be quick to tell him she'd had his baby without mentioning its sex.

"A daughter." Rowley scooped up the child and held her high. The baby blinked from sleep and then crowed with him. "Any fool can have a son," he said. "It takes a man to conceive a daughter."

That's *why I loved him*.

"Who's her daddy's little moppet, then," he was saying, "who's got eyes like cornflowers, so she has—yes, she has—just like her daddy's. And teeny-weeny toes. *Yumm, yumm, yumm*. Does she like that? Yes, she does."

Adelia was helplessly aware of Father Paton regarding the scene. She wanted to tell Rowley he was giving himself away; this delight was not episcopal. But presumably a secretary was privy to all his master's secrets—and it was too late now, anyway.

The bishop looked up. "Is she going to be bald? Or will this fuzz on her head grow? What's her name?"

"Allie," Gyltha said.

"*Ali?*"

"Almeisan." Adelia spoke for the first time, reluctantly. "Mansur named her. Almeisan is a star."

"An Arab name."

"Why not?" She was ready to attack. "Arabs taught the world astronomy. It's a beautiful name, it means the shining one."

"I'm not saying it isn't beautiful. It's just that I would have called her Ariadne."

"Well, you weren't there," Adelia said nastily.

Ariadne had been his private name for her. The two of them had met on the same road, and at the same time that she'd encountered Prior Geoffrey. Although they hadn't known it then, they were also on the same errand; Rowley Picot was ostensibly one of King Henry's tax collectors but privately had been clandestinely ordered by his royal master to find the beast that was killing Cambridgeshire's children and thereby damaging the royal revenue. Willy-nilly, the two of them had found themselves following clues together. Like Ariadne, she had led him to the beast's lair. Like Theseus, he had rescued her from it.

And then, like Theseus, abandoned her.

She knew she was being unfair; he'd asked—begged—her to marry him, but by this time he'd earned the king's approbation and was earmarked for an advancement that needed a wife devoted to him, their children, his estates—a conventional English chatelaine, not a woman who neither would nor could give up her duty to the living and dead.

What she couldn't forgive him for was doing what she'd told him to do: leave her, go away, forget, take up the king's offer of a rich bishopric.

God torment him, he might have *written*.

"Well," she said, "you've seen her, and now we are leaving."

"Are we?" This was Gyltha. "In't we going to stay for supper?"

"No." She had been looking for insult from the first and had found it. "If someone has attempted to harm this Rosamund Clifford, I am sorry for it, but it is nothing to do with me."

She crossed the room to take the baby from him. It brought them close so that she could smell the incense from the Mass he'd celebrated clinging to him, infecting their child with it. His eyes weren't Rowley's anymore, they were those of a bishop, very tired—he'd traveled hard from Oxford—and very grave.

"Not even if it means civil war?" he said.

The pork was sent back so that the smell of it should not offend Dr. Mansur's nose and dietary law, but there were lampreys and pike in aspic, four different kinds of duck, veal in blanc-mange, a crisp, golden polonaise of bread, a sufficiency for twenty, and—whether it displeased Mohammedan nostrils or not—enough wine for twenty more, served in beautiful cameo-cut glass bowls.

Once it had all been placed on the board, the servants were sent from the room. Father Paton was allowed to remain. From the straw under the table came the crunch of a dog with a bone.

"He *had* to imprison her," Rowley said of his king and Queen Eleanor. "She was encouraging the Young King to rebel against his father."

"Never understood that," Gyltha said, chewing a leg of duck. "Not why Henry had his boy crowned king along of him, I mean. Old King and Young King ruling at the same time. Bound to cause trouble."

"Henry'd just been very ill," Rowley told her. "He wanted to make sure of a peaceful succession if he died—he didn't want a recurrence of another Stephen and Matilda war."

Gyltha shuddered. "Nor we don't, neither."

It was a strange dinner. Bishop Rowley was being forced to put his case to a Cambridgeshire housekeeper and an Arab because the woman he needed to solve it would not look at him. Adelia sat silent and unresponsive, eating very little.

He's a different creature, there's nothing of the man I knew. Damn him, how was it so easy for him to stop loving me?

The secretary, disregarded by everybody, ate like a man with hollow legs, though his eyes were always on his master, as if watching for further unepiscopal behavior.

The bishop explained the circumstances that had brought him hurrying from Oxford, part of his diocese, and tomorrow would take him to Normandy to search out the king and tell him, before anybody else did, that Rosamund Clifford, most beloved of all the royal mistresses, had been fed poisonous mushrooms.

"Mushrooms?" Gyltha asked. "Could've been mischance, then. Tricky things, mushrooms, you got to be careful."

"It was deliberate," the bishop said. "Believe me, Gyltha, this was not an accident. She became very ill. It was why they called me to Wormhold, to her sickbed; they didn't think she'd recover. Thanks to the mercy of Christ, she did, but the king will wish to know the identity of the poisoner, and I want, I *have*, to assure him that his favorite investigator is looking into the matter ..." He remembered to bow to Mansur, who bowed back. "Along with his assistant." A bow to Adelia.

She was relieved that he was maintaining the fiction in front of Father Paton that it was Mansur who possessed the necessary skills for such an investigation—not her. He had betrayed himself to a charge of immorality by saying that Allie was his, but he was protecting her from the much more serious charge of witchcraft.

Gyltha, enjoying her role as interrogator, said, "Can't've been the queen sent her them mushrooms, can it? Her being in chains and all?"

"I wish she *had* been in bloody chains." Rowley was Rowley again for a moment, furious and making his secretary blink. "The blasted woman escaped. Two weeks ago."

"Deary dear," Gyltha said.

"Deary dear indeed, and was last seen heading for England, which, in everybody's opinion bar mine, would give her time to poison a dozen of Henry's whores."

He leaned across the table to Adelia, sweeping a space between them, spilling his wine bowl and hers. "*You* know him, you know his temper. *You've* seen him out of control. He loves Rosamund, truly loves her. Suppose he shouts for Eleanor's death like he shouted for Becket's? He won't mean it, but there's always some bastard with a reason to respond who'll say he's doing it on the king's orders, like they did with Becket. And if their mother's executed, *all* the boys will rise up against their father like a tide of shit."

He sat back in his chair. "Civil war? It'll be here, everywhere. Stephen and Matilda will be nothing to it."

Mansur put his hand protectively on Gyltha's shoulder. The silence was turbulent, as if from noiseless battle and dumbed shrieks of the dying. The ghost of a murdered archbishop rose up from the stones of Canterbury and stalked the room.

Father Paton was staring from face to face, puzzled that his bishop should be addressing the doctor's assistant with such vehemence, and not the doctor.

"Did she do it?" Adelia asked at last.

"No." Rowley wiped some grease off his sleeve with a napkin, and replenished his bowl.

"Are you sure?"

"Not Eleanor. I know her."

Does he? Undoubtedly, there was tender regard between queen and bishop; when Eleanor and Henry's firstborn son had died at the age of three, Eleanor had wanted the child's sword taken to Jerusalem so that, in death, little William might be regarded as a holy crusader. It was Rowley who'd made the terrible journey and lain the tiny sword on the high altar—so *of course* Eleanor looked on Rowley kindly.

But like everything else in royal matters, it was King Henry who'd arranged it, Henry who'd given Rowley his orders, Henry who'd received the intelligence of what was going on in the Holy Land that

Rowley'd brought back with him. Oh, yes, Rowley Picot had been more the king's agent than the queen's sword carrier.

But still claiming special knowledge of Eleanor's character, the bishop added, "Face-to-face, she'd tear Rosamund's throat out ... but not poison. It's not her style."

Adelia nodded. She said in Arabic, "I still don't see what you want of me. I am a doctor to the dead ..."

"You have a logical mind," the bishop said, also in Arabic. "You see things others don't. Who saved the Jews from the accusation of child murder last year? Who found the true killer?"

"I had assistance." That good little man Simon of Naples, the *real* investigator who had come with her from Salerno for the purpose and had died for it.

Mansur, unusual for him, struck in, indicating Adelia. "She must not be put in such danger again. The will of Allah and only the will of Allah saved her from the pit last time."

Adelia smiled fondly at him. Let him attribute it to Allah if he liked. Actually, she had survived the child killer's lair only because a dog had led Rowley to it in time. What neither he, nor God, nor Allah had saved her from were memories of a nightmare that still reenacted themselves in her daily life as sharply as if they were happening all over again— often, this time, to young Allie.

"Of course she won't be in danger again," the bishop told Mansur with energy. "This case is completely different. There's been no murder here, only a clumsy attempt at one. Whoever tried to do it is long gone. But don't you see?" Another bowl tipped as he thumped the board. "*Don't you see? Everybody* will believe Eleanor to be the poisoner; she hates Rosamund *and* she was possibly in the neighborhood. Wasn't that Gyltha's immediate conclusion? Won't it be the world's?" He took his eyes away from Mansur and to the woman opposite him. "In the name of God, Adelia, *help me.*"

With a jerk of her chin toward the door, Gyltha nudged Mansur, who nodded, rose, and took an unwilling Father Paton by the scruff of his neck.

The two who remained seated at the table didn't notice their going. The bishop's gaze was on Adelia; hers on her clasped hands.

Stop resenting him, she was thinking. *It wasn't abandonment; mine was the refusal to marry, only mine the insistence we shouldn't meet again. It is illogical to blame him for keeping to the agreement.*

Damn him, though, there should have been something all these months—at least an acknowledgment of the baby.

"How are you and God getting along?" she asked.

"I serve Him, I hope." She heard amusement in his voice.

"Good works?"

"When I can."

She thought, *And we both know, don't we, that you would sacrifice God and His works, me and your daughter, all of us, if doing so would serve Henry Plantagenet.*

He said quietly, "I apologize for this, Adelia. I

would not have broken our agreement not to meet again for anything less."

She said, "If Eleanor *is* proved guilty, I won't lie. I shall say so."

"Ya-*hah*." Now *that* was Rowley, the energy, the shout that shivered the wine in its jug—here, for an instant, was her joyous lover back again.

"Couldn't resist, could you? Are you taking the baby with you? Yes, of course, you'll still be breast-feeding—damned odd to think of you as lactating stock."

He was up and had opened the door, calling for Paton. "There's a basket of mushrooms in my pack. Find it and bring it here." He turned to Adelia, grinning. "Thought you'd want to see some evidence."

"You devil," she said.

"Maybe, but this devil will save its king and its country or die trying."

"Or kill me in the process." *Stop it*, she thought, *stop sounding like a wronged woman; it was your decision.*

He shrugged. "You'll be safe enough, nobody's out to poison *you*. You'll have Gyltha and Mansur— God help anyone who touches you while they're around—and I'm sending servants along. I presume that canine eyesore goes, too?"

"Yes," she said. "His name's Ward."

"One more of the prior's finds to keep you safe? I remember Safeguard."

Another creature that had died saving her life. The room was full of memories that hurt—and with the dangerous value of being shared.

"Paton is *my* watchdog," he said conversationally. "He guards my virtue like a bloody chastity belt. Incidentally, wait until you see Fair Rosamund's labyrinth—biggest in Christendom. Mind you, wait til you see Fair Rosamund herself, she's not what you'd expect. In fact—"

She interrupted. "Is it at risk?"

"The labyrinth?"

"Your virtue."

All at once, he was being kind. "Oddly enough, it isn't. I thought when you turned me down ... but God was kind and tempered the wind to the shorn lamb."

"And when Henry needed a compliant bishop." *Stop it, stop it.*

"And the world needed a doctor, not another wife," he said, still kind. "I see that now; I have prayed to see it; marriage would have wasted you."

Yes, yes. If she had agreed to marriage, he'd have refused the bishopric the king had urged on him for political expediency, but for her, there had been the higher priority of her calling. She'd have had to abandon it—he'd demanded a wife, not a doctor, especially not a doctor to the dead.

In the end, she thought, *neither of us would bestow the ultimate, sacrificial gift on the other.*

He got up and went to the baby, making the sign of the cross on her forehead with his thumb. "Bless you, my daughter." He turned back. "Bless you, too, mistress," he said. "God keep you both safe, and may the peace of Jesus Christ prevail over the Horsemen of the Apocalypse." He sighed. "For I can hear the sound of their hooves."

Father Paton came in carrying a basket and gave it to his lordship, who then gestured for him to leave.

Adelia was still staring at Rowley. Among all this room's superfluity of wealth, the turmoil she'd experienced in it as shades of the past came and went, one thing that should belong to it—its very purpose—had been missing; she had just caught its scent, clear and cold: sanctity, the last attribute she'd expected to find in him. Her lover had become a man of God.

He took the chair beside her to give her details of the attempt on Rosamund's life, putting the basket in front of her so that she could examine its contents. In the old days, he couldn't have sat beside her without touching her; now it was like sitting next to a hermit.

Rosamund loved stewed mushrooms, he told her; it was well known. A lazy servant, out gathering them for her mistress, had been handed some by an old, unidentified woman, a crone, and had taken them back without bothering to pick more.

"Rosamund didn't eat them all, some had been kept for later, and while I was with her I took the remainder to bring with me. I thought you might be able to identify the area they came from or something—you know about mushrooms, don't you?"

Yes, she knew about mushrooms. Obediently, Adelia began turning them over with her knife while he talked.

It was a fine collection, though withering now: boletes that the English called Slippery Jack, winter oysters, cauliflower, blewits, hedgehogs. All very tasty but extraordinarily, *most* extraordinarily, varied; some of these species grew exclusively on chalk, some under pine trees, others in fields, others in broadleaf woodland.

Deliberately or not, whoever gathered these had spread the net wide and avoided picking a basketful that could be said to come from a specific location.

"As I say, it was quite deliberate," the bishop was saying. "The crone, whoever she was, made a point of it—they were for the Lady Rosamund, nobody else. Whoever that crone was, she hasn't been seen since. Disappeared. Slipped in a couple of malignant ones, do you see, hoping they'd poison the poor woman, and it's only through the mercy of God ..."

"She's dead, Rowley," Adelia said.

"What?"

"If these fungi duplicate what Rosamund ate, she's dead."

"No, I told you, she recovered. Much better when I left her."

"I know." Adelia was suddenly so sorry for him; if she could have changed what she was going to say, she would have. "But it's what happens, I'm afraid." She speared the killer with her knife and lifted it. "It's a feature of this one that those who eat it apparently get better for a while."

Innocuous-looking, white-gilled, its cap now aged into an ordinary brown but still retaining a not unpleasant smell. "It's called the Death Cap. It grows everywhere; I've seen it in Italy, Sicily,

France, here in England; I've seen its effect, I've worked on the corpses who ate it—too many of them. It is always, *always* fatal."

"No," he said. "It can't be."

"I'm sorry, I'm so *sorry*, but if she ate one of these, even a tiny bite ..." He had to know. "Sickness and diarrhea at first, abdominal pain, and then a day or two when she'd seem to be recovering. But all the while the poison was attacking her liver and kidneys. There's absolutely no cure. Rowley, I'm afraid she's gone."

THREE

No question now of the bishop crossing from England to Normandy in order to calm a turbulent king. The king's beloved was dead, and the king would be coming to England himself, riding the air like a demon to ravage and burn—maybe, in his rage, to kill his own wife if he could find her.

So, at dawn, the bishop rode, too, another demon loose on the world, to be ahead of the king, to find the queen and get her away, to be on the spot, to locate the real culprit, to be able to say: "My lord, hold your hand; *this* is Rosamund's killer."

To avoid Armageddon.

With the bishop went those for his purpose, a pitiful few compared to his lordship's usual train: two men-at-arms, a groom, a secretary, a messenger, a carriage, horses, and remounts. Also an Arab doctor, a dog, two women, and a baby— and to hell if they couldn't keep up.

They kept up. Just. Their carriage, Father Paton's "conveyance," was splendidly carved, enclosed against the weather by purple waxed cloth with matching cushions among the straw inside, but it was not intended for speed. After three hours of it, Gyltha said that if she stayed in the bugger much longer she'd lose her teeth from rattling, and the poor baby its brains.

So they transferred to horses, young Allie being placed and padded into a pannier like a grub in a cocoon; Ward, the dog, was stuffed less gently into the other. The change was made quickly to stay up with the bishop, who wouldn't wait for them.

Jacques the messenger was sent ahead to prepare the bishop's palace at Saint Albans for their brief stay overnight and, then, next day, to the Barleycorn at Aylesbury for another.

It was cold, becoming colder the farther west they went, as if Henry Plantagenet's icy breath were on their neck and getting closer.

They didn't reach the Barleycorn, because that was the day it began to snow, and they left the roads for the Icknield Way escarpment, where avenues of trees and the chalk under their horses' hooves made the going easier and therefore faster.

There were no inns on these high tracks, and the bishop refused to waste time by descending to find one. "We'll make camp," he said.

When, eventually, he allowed them to dismount, Adelia's muscles protested as she struggled to get off her horse. She looked with anxiety toward Gyltha, who was struggling off hers. "Are you surviving?" Tough as leather the fenwoman might be, but she was still a grandmother and entitled to better treatment than this.

"I got sores where I wou'n't like to say."

"So have I." And stinging as if from acid.

The only one looking worse than they did was

Father Paton, whose large breakfast at Saint Albans had been jolting out of him, amidst groans, for most of the way. "Shouldn't have gobbled it," Gyltha told him.

Baby Allie, on the other hand, had taken no harm from the journey; indeed, snuggled in her pannier, she appeared to have enjoyed it, despite her hurried feeds when Bishop Rowley had permitted a stop to change horses.

Carrying her with them, the two women retired to the cart and ministered to their wounds with salves from Adelia's medicine chest. "The which I ain't letting Father Fustilugs have any," Gyltha said vengefully of Father Paton. She'd taken against him.

"What about Mansur? He's not used to this, either."

"Great lummox ..." Gyltha liked to hide her delight in and love for the Arab. "He'd not say a word if his arse was on fire."

Which was true; Mansur cultivated stoicism to the point of impassivity. His sale as a little boy to Byzantine monks who'd preserved the beauty of his treble singing voice by castration had taught him the futility of complaining. In all the years since he'd found sanctuary with Adelia's foster parents and become her bodyguard and friend, she'd never heard him utter a querulous sentence. Not that he uttered many words in strange company anyway; the English found him and his Arab dress outlandish enough without the addition of a child's squeaky speaking voice issuing from a man six feet tall with the face of an eagle.

Oswald and Aelwyn, the men-at-arms, and Walt, the groom, were uneasy in their dealings with him, apparently crediting him with occult powers. It was Adelia they treated like dirt—though never if Rowley was looking. At first she'd put their discourtesies down to the rigors of the journey, but gradually they became too marked to be disregarded. Unless the bishop or Mansur was nearby, she was never assisted onto a horse nor down, and the occasions when she went off into the trees to answer a call of nature were accompanied by low, offensive whistles. Once or twice she heard Ward yelp as if he'd been kicked.

Nor had she and Gyltha been provided with sidesaddles. Rowley had ordered them, but somehow, in the haste, they'd been forgotten, leaving the women perforce to ride astride, an unseemly posture for a lady though, actually, one that Adelia preferred because she considered sidesaddles injurious to the spine.

Nevertheless, the omission had been uncivil and, she thought, intended.

To church servants like these, she was a harlot, of course; either the bishop's trull or the Saracen's, perhaps both. For them it was bad enough to be chasing across country in bad weather to attend the funeral of a king's mistress without dragging another whore along with them.

"What's she with us for?"

"God knows. Clever with her brains, so they say."

"Clever with her quim more like. Is that his lordship's bastard?"

"Could be anybody's."

The exchange had been made where she could overhear it.

Damn it, this would harm him. Rowley had been appointed by Henry II against the wishes of the Church, which had wanted its own man to fill the post of Saint Albans and still hoped for a reason to dismiss the king's candidate. Knowledge that he'd fathered an illegitimate child would give his enemies their chance.

Damn the Church, Adelia thought. Our affair was over before he became a bishop. Damn it for imposing impossible celibacy on its people. Damn it for hypocrisy—Christendom was littered with priests wallowing in varieties of sin. How many of *them* were condemned?

And damn it for its hatred of women—an abuse of half the world's inhabitants, so that those who refused to be penned into its sheepfold were condemned as harlots and heretics and witches.

Damn you, she thought of the bishop's men, *are you so innocent? Are all your children born in wedlock? Which of you jumped over the broomstick with a woman rather than legally marry her?*

And damn you, Bishop Rowley, for placing me in this situation.

Then, because she was feeding Allie, she damned them all again for making her angry enough to damn them.

Father Paton escaped her curses; unlovable as he was, he at least treated her like he treated everybody else—as a sexless and unfortunate expense.

The messenger, Jacques, a gauche, large-eared, somewhat overeager young man, seemed more kindly inclined to her than the others, but the bishop kept him on the gallop with taking messages and preparing the way ahead, so she saw little of him.

With imperceptible difference, the Icknield Way became the Ridgeway. The cold was gaining an intensity that leeched strength out of humans and horses, but they were at least approaching the Thames and the Abbey of Godstow, which stood on one of its islands.

Jacques rejoined the company, appearing from the trees ahead like a mounted white bear. He shook himself free of snow as he bowed to Rowley. "Abbess Mother Edyve sends greetings to your lordship and her joy to accommodate you and your party whenever you will. Also, I was to say that she expects the body of the Lady Rosamund to be brought to the convent by river today."

Rowley said heavily, "So she is dead."

"I trust so, my lord, for the nuns intend to bury her."

His bishop glared at him. "Go back there. Tell them we should arrive tonight and that I am bringing a Saracen doctor to examine Lady Rosamund's corpse and determine how she died." He turned to Adelia and said in Latin, "You'll want to see the body, won't you?"

"I suppose so." Though what it could tell her, she wasn't sure.

The messenger stopped long enough to stuff

bread, cheese, and a flask of ale into his saddlebag before remounting.

"Shouldn't you rest first?" Adelia asked him.

"Don't mind for me, mistress. I sleep in the saddle."

She wished *she* could. To stay in it at all took strength. Father Paton's provision of cloaks had been of the cheapest wool and, wearing them, she, Gyltha, and Mansur would have frozen to death on horseback if it hadn't been for the rough mantles of beaver fur they had brought with them. The fenland was full of beaver, and these were gifts from a grateful trapper Adelia had nursed through pneumonia.

That afternoon the travelers descended from the hills to the village of Thame and the road leading to Oxford. It was getting dark, still snowing, but the bishop said, "Not far now. We'll press on with lanterns."

It was terrible going; the horses had to be rugged even though they were kept moving. Soon they had to be fitted with headbands that fringed their eyes, usually a device to keep off flies, so they would not be blinded by the thick flakes that swirled and stuck to the lashes.

It was impossible to see beyond a yard. If the road hadn't run between hedges, they would have lost their way, lanterns or no lanterns, and ended in a field or river. When the hedges disappeared at a crossroads, Rowley had to call a halt until they found the right track again, which meant the men had to search for it, all the time calling to each other in case any one of them blundered away—an error that, in this cold, would cost him his life.

For the baby's sake as well as their own, the women were forced to reenter the carriage and stay there. Father Paton had already done so, complaining that if he stayed in the cold he would lose the use of his secretarial writing hand.

They hooked one of the lanterns to the arch over their heads and began heaping straw to make a bed, tucking Allie between them to benefit from the heat of their bodies. The cold lanced in like needles through the eyelets where the canopy was tied to its struts, so icy that it nullified the smell of the straw and even of the dog at their feet.

They were going at walking pace—Mansur was leading the horses—but deep pits in the track concealed by snow caused the carriage to fall and tip with bone-jarring suddenness so that rest was impossible. In any case, anxiety for what the others were suffering outside precluded sleep.

Gyltha said admiringly of Rowley, "He ain't a'going to stop, is he?"

"No." This was a man who'd pursued a murderer across the deserts of Outremer. An English blizzard wasn't going to defeat him. Adelia said, "Have no concern for him: He's showing none for ..." There was a lurch of the carriage, and she grabbed at a strut with her right hand and her baby with her left to stop them being thrown from one side to the other. The lantern swung through an arc of one hundred eighty degrees, and Gyltha lunged upward to snuff out its candle in case it set fire to the canopy.

"... us," Adelia finished.

In the darkness and at an angle, they could hear Father Paton praying for deliverance while, outside, screeching Arabic curses rained on horses that refused to pull. One or another was effective; after another grinding jerk, the carriage went on.

"You see," came Gyltha's voice, as if resuming a conversation, "Rowley, he remembers the war betwixt Matilda and Stephen. He's a youngster compared to me, but he was born into it, and his parents, they'd have lived through it, like I did. King Stephen, he died natural in his bed. And Queen Matilda, she's still going strong. But the war betwixt them ... weren't so for us commoners. We died over and over. It was like ... like we was all tossed in the air and stayed there with nothing to hold to. The law went, ever'thing went. My pa, he was dragged off his fields one day to build a castle for Hugh Bigod. Never came back. Took three years a'fore we heard he was crushed flat when a stone fell. We near starved without un."

Adelia heard the deep intake of breath, heavier than a sigh. Simple sentences, she thought, but what weight they carried.

Gyltha said, "We lost our Em an' all. Older than me she was, about eleven. Some mercenaries came through and Ma ran with my brothers and me to hide in the fen, but they caught Em. She was screaming when they galloped off with her, I can hear her now. Never did find out what happened, but she was another as didn't come back."

It was a lecture. Adelia had heard Gyltha talk

about the thirteen-year war before, but only in general terms, never like this; as witness to its chaos, the old woman was calling up specters that still gave her pain. Feudalism might be harsh for those at its bottom end, but it was at least a protection. Adelia, who had been brought up both protected and privileged, was being told what happened when order crumbled and civilization went with it.

"Nor it weren't no good praying to God. He weren't listening."

Men gave way to basest instincts, Gyltha said. Village lads, decent enough if controlled, saw those controls disappear and themselves became thieves and rapists. "Henry Plantagenet, now, he may be all sorts, but with him a'coming king it stopped, d'you see. It stopped; the ground was put back under us. The crops grew like they had, the sun come up of a morning and set of nights, like it should."

"I see," Adelia said.

"But you can't *know*, not really," Gyltha told her. "Rowley do. His ma and pa, they was commoners, and they lived through it like I did. He'll move mountains so's it don't happen again. He's seeing to it so's my Ulf, bless him, can go to school with a full belly as nobody'll slit open. Bit of traveling? Few snowflakes? What's that?"

"I've only been thinking of myself, haven't I?" Adelia said.

"And the baby," Gyltha said, reaching over to pat her. "And a fair bit of his lordship, I reckon. Me, I'll follow where he goes and happy to help."

She had raised their venture to a plane that left Adelia ashamed and exposed to her own resentment. Even now, she couldn't give credence to the reasoning that caused them to be doing what they were doing, but if the bishop, who did, was right and they could prevent civil war by it, then she, too, must be happy to give of her best.

And I am, she thought, grimacing. *Ulf is safe at school; Gyltha and Mansur and my child are with me. I am happy that Bishop Rowley is happy in a god who has taken away his lusts. Where else should I be?*

She shut her eyes and gave herself up to patient endurance.

Another great lurch woke her. They'd stopped. The canvas was lifted, letting in a draft of wicked cold and showing a face blue and bearded by ice. She recognized it as the messenger's; they had caught up with him. "Are we there?"

"Nearly, mistress." Jacques sounded excited. "His lordship asks, will you come out and look at this?"

It had stopped snowing. A moon shone from a sky full of stars onto a landscape almost as beautiful. The bishop and the rest of his entourage stood with Mansur in a group at the beginning of a narrow, humped stone bridge, its parapets perfectly outlined in snow. Loud water hidden by the drop on the left suggested a weir or millrace. To the right was the gleam of a smooth river. Trees stood like white sentinels.

As Adelia came up, Rowley pointed behind her. She looked back and saw some humped cottages. "That's the village of Wolvercote," he said. He turned her so that she was now facing across the bridge to where the stars were blanked out by a complexity of roofs. "Godstow Abbey." There was a suggestion of light coming from somewhere among its buildings, though any windows on this side were dark.

But it was what was in the middle of the bridge that she must look at. The first thing she saw was a saddled horse, not moving, head and reins drooping downward, one leg bent up. The groom, Walt, stood at its head, patting its neck. His voice came shrill and querulous through the stillness. "Who'da done this? He's a good un, this un, who'da done it?" He was more concerned for the horse than for the dead man sprawled facedown in the snow beside it.

"Robbery and murder on the King's Highway," Rowley said quietly, his breath wreathing like smoke. "Plain coincidence and nothing to do with our purpose, but I suppose you'd better look, bodies being your business. Just be quick about it, that's all."

He'd kept everyone else back like she'd taught him; only the groom's footprints and his own showed going to the bridge in the snow, and only his returned. "I had to make sure the fellow was dead," he said. "Take Mansur with you for the look of it." He raised his voice. "The lord Mansur can read traces left on the ground. He speaks little English, so Mistress Adelia will interpret for him."

Adelia stayed where she was for a moment, Mansur beside her. "What time is it, do you know?" she asked in Arabic.

"Listen."

She unbound her head from its muffler. From the other side of the bridge, solitary, faraway, but clear over the rush of noisy water, came a sweet female voice raised in a monotone. It paused and was answered by the disciplined response of other voices.

She was hearing a chime of the liturgical clock, an antiphon. The nuns of Godstow had roused from their beds and were chanting Vigils.

It was four o'clock in the morning, near enough.

Mansur said, "Was not the galloper here earlier? He may have seen something."

"When were you here, Jacques? The doctor wants to know."

"In daylight, mistress. That poor soul wasn't lying there then." The young man was aggrieved and upset. "I delivered his lordship's message to the holy sisters and rode straight back across the bridge to rejoin you all. I was back with you before the moon came up, wasn't I, my lord?"

Rowley nodded.

"When did it stop snowing?" From what she could see of the body, there were only a few flakes on it.

"Three hours back."

"Stay here."

Mansur took up a lantern, and they went forward together to kneel by the body. "Allah, be good to him," Mansur said.

As her foster father had taught her, Adelia took a moment to pray to the spirit of the dead man who was now her client. "Permit your flesh and bone to tell me what your voice cannot."

He lay facedown, too neatly for someone who'd fallen off a horse, legs straight, arms splayed above the head, cloak and tunic down over his hams. His cap, like his clothes, was of good but slightly worn wool, and it lay a few inches away, the brave cock-pheasant feather in it broken.

She nodded to Mansur. Gently, he raised the wavy brown hair from the neck to touch the skin. He shook his head. He'd attended on enough corpses with Adelia to know it would be impossible to estimate the time of death; the body was frozen—had begun to freeze the moment life left it, would stay frozen long enough to delay the natural processes.

"*Hmm.*"

Expertly, acting together, they turned the corpse over. Two half-shut brown eyes regarded the sky with disinterest, and Mansur had to force the frozen lids down over them.

He was young: twenty, twenty-one, perhaps less. The heavy arrow in his chest came from a crossbow and had gone deep, probably being driven farther in by the fall that had broken its flights. Mansur held the lantern so that Adelia could examine the wound; there was blood around it but only a few smears on the snow occupying the space that the body had vacated when it was turned.

She guided Mansur's hand so that the lantern illuminated the corpse's neck. "*Hmmm.*"

A scabbard with a sword still in it was attached to a belt with a tarnished buckle engraved with a crest. The same crest had been embroidered on a gaping, empty purse.

"Come along, Doctor. You can do all this when we take him to the nunnery." Rowley's voice.

"Be quiet," Adelia told him in Arabic. He'd hurried her all the way from Cambridge; now he could damn well wait. There was something wrong here; perhaps it was why Rowley had called for her to investigate it, some part of his mind noticing the anomalies even while part was intent on another murder altogether.

There was an anguished plea from Walt, the groom. "This here poor bugger's in pain, my lord. Naught to be done. 'S time he was finished."

"Doctor?"

"*Wait*, will you?" Irritably, she got up and went over to where the horse and the groom stood, regarding the ground as she went. "What's the matter with it?"

"Hamstrung. Some godless swine cut his tendon." Walt pointed to a slash across the horse's leg just above the hock. "See? That's deliberate, that is."

The snow here was bloodied black and showed that the animal had thrashed around before managing to rise on its three uninjured legs.

"Can it be mended?" All she knew about horses was which end you faced.

"*He's hamstrung.*" Answering stupid questions from a woman no better than she should be added to Walt's anger.

Adelia returned to Mansur. "The animal has to be dispatched."

"Not here," he said. "The carcass will block the bridge." And bridges were vital; not to repair them, or to render them unusable, was a hostile act causing such hardship to the local economy that the law came down heavily on those who committed it.

"What in *hell* are you two about?" Rowley had come up.

"There's something wrong here," Adelia told him.

"Yes, somebody robbed and killed this poor devil. I can see that. Let's load him up and get on."

"No, it's more than that."

"*What* is?"

"Give me time," she shouted at him, and then, realizing, "the doctor needs time."

The bishop blew out his cheeks. "Why did I bring her, Lord? Answer me that. Very well, let's at least see to his horse."

Adelia insisted on going first, slowly leading the way past Walt and the crippled animal and down the other side of the bridge, Mansur beside her holding the lantern so that light fell on the ground at each step.

Everything that was not white was black; boot marks, hoofprints, too jumbled to be distinguished from one another. There'd been a lot of activity where the bridge rejoined the road near the great gatehouse of the convent. A lot of blood.

Mansur pointed.

"Oh, well done, my dear," she said. Under the

shadow of heavy oak branches lolling over the convent wall, clear prints led to others—writing a story for those who could read it. "*Hmm.* Interesting."

Behind her, the bishop and groom soothed the jerkily limping horse as they led it, discussing where it should be put down. Would the nuns want the carcass? Good eating on a horse. But butchery and skinning would be arduous in this weather; better to cut its throat among the trees where the convent wall bent into a forest. "They can get it later if they want it."

"Doubt there'll be much left by then, my lord." It wasn't only humans that appreciated the eating on a horse.

Walt relieved the animal of its tack. There was a roll attached to the saddle protected by oilcloth. "Oo-op now, my beauty, oo-op." Murmuring gentle equine things, he led it toward the trees.

"Could we hide the body there as well?" Adelia wanted to know.

"If we do, there will be not much left of that, either," Mansur said.

Rowley joined them. "Will you hurry *up*, you two. We'll all be bloody icicles in a minute."

Adelia, who had shivered from cold all the way from Cambridge, was no longer aware of it. "We don't want the body discovered, my lord."

The bishop tried for patience. "It *is* discovered, mistress. We discovered it."

"We don't want the killer to find it."

Rowley cleared his throat. "You mean, let's not

tell him? He knows, Adelia. He shot a bolt into the lad's chest. He's not coming back to make sure."

"Yes, he is. You'd have seen it yourself if you hadn't been in such a rush." She nudged Mansur. "Look as if you're instructing."

With Rowley between them, Mansur speaking of their findings in Arabic, and Adelia, on the other side, appearing to translate, they told him the story of a killing as the marks in the snow had told it to them.

"We can't be sure of the time. *After* it stopped snowing is all we can guess. Anyway, late enough this night for nobody to be about. They waited for him here, near the gates."

"They?"

"Two men." Rowley was pulled into the shadow of the oak. Footprints were just visible in the snow. "See? One wears hobnails, the other's boots have bars across the soles, maybe clogs bound with strips. They arrived here on horseback and took their horses into those trees, where Walt has gone. They came back on foot and stood here. They ate as they waited." Adelia retrieved a crumb of something from the ground, and then another. "Cheese." She held them to the bishop's nose.

He recoiled. "As you say, mistress."

Vigils over, the convent was silent again. From deeper in among the trees of the forest came Walt's prayer, "And the Lord have mercy on thy poor soul, if thee have one."

A long scream like a whistle, a heavy crash. Silence.

Walt emerged, simultaneously wiping his dagger on his cloak with one hand and his eyes with the other. "Goddamn, I hates a'doing that."

The bishop patted him on the shoulder and sent him to join the others on the far side of the bridge. To Adelia and Mansur, he said, "They knew he was coming, then?"

"Yes. They were waiting for him." Even the most desperate robber didn't loiter in the hope of a passerby in the early hours of a freezing night.

They must have thought themselves lucky that the blizzard had passed, she thought, not knowing they were imprinting their guilt in the resultant snow for Vesuvia Adelia Rachel Ortese Aguilar, *medica* of the renowned School of Medicine in Salerno, expert on death and the causes of death, to happen along and decipher it.

For which they were going to be sorry.

It had been a cold wait; they'd stamped their feet to keep warm. In her mind, Adelia waited with them, nibbling phantom cheese. Perhaps they had listened to the sound of Compline being sung before the nuns retired to bed for the three hours until Vigils. Apart from that it would have been quiet except for an owl or two, perhaps, and the shriek of a vixen.

Here he comes, the rider. Up the road that leads from the river to the convent, his horse's hooves muffled by the earlier snow but still audible in the silence.

He's nearing the gates, slowing—does he mean to go in? But Villain Number One has stepped out in front of him, the crossbow cocked and straining. Does the rider see him? Shout out? Recognize the man? Probably not; the shadows are dark here. Anyway, the bolt has been loosed and is already deep in his chest.

The horse rears, sending its rider backward and tumbling, breaking the bolt's flights as he falls. Villain Number Two snatches at the reins, leads the terrified horse to the trees, and tethers it there.

"He's on the ground and dying—a crossbow quarrel is nearly always fatal wherever it hits," Adelia said, "but they made sure. One or other of them—whoever he was has big hands—throttled him as he lay on the ground."

"God have mercy," the bishop said.

"Yes, but here's the interesting thing," Adelia told him, as if everything else had been commonplace. "*Now* they drag him to the center of the bridge. See? The toes of his boots make runnels in the snow. They throw his cap down beside him—dear *Lord*, they're stupid. Did they think a man fallen from his mount looks so tidy? Legs together? Skirts down? You saw that, didn't you? And then, *then*, they fetch his horse to the bridge and slice its leg."

"They do not take him into the trees," Mansur pointed out. "Nor the horse. Neither would have been found if they'd done that, not until the spring, and by then, no one could see what had happened to them. But no, they drag him to where the first person across the bridge in the morning will see him and raise the hue and cry."

· "Not giving the killers as much time to get away as they might have." The bishop was reflective. "I see. That's ... eccentric."

"*This* is what's eccentric," Adelia said. They'd come up to the body again. At the bottom of the bridge where the others were gathered, somebody had made a makeshift brazier and lit a fire. Faces, ghastly in the reflection of the flames, turned hopefully in their direction. "You goin' to be much longer?" Gyltha shouted. "Little un's due a feed, and we'm dyin' of frostbite."

Adelia ignored her. She still didn't feel the cold. "Two men," she said, "and they are poor, judging from their footwear. Two men kill our rider. Granted, they take the money from his purse, but they leave the purse, a good one that has his family crest on it. They leave his boots, his cloak, the silver buckle, his fine horse. What thief does that?"

"Perhaps they were disturbed," Rowley said.

"Who disturbs them? Not us. They are long gone before we come up. They had time to strip this poor soul of everything he ... had. They do not. Why, Rowley?"

The bishop thought it through. "They want him found."

Adelia nodded. "It is vital to them."

"They want him to be identified."

Adelia's exhaled breath was a stream of satisfaction. "Exactly. It must be known who he is and that he is dead."

"I see." Rowley considered. "Hence the suggestion that we hide his body. I don't like it, though."

"But that will bring them back, Rowley," Adelia said, and for the first time she touched him, a tug on his sleeve. "They've taken pains to have this poor young man's death declared to the world. They'll come back to find out why it isn't. We can be waiting for them."

Mansur nodded. "Some fiend intends to profit by this killing, Allah ruin him."

Adelia jiggled the bishop's sleeve again. "But not if the boy seems merely to have gone away, just disappeared."

Rowley was doubtful. "There'll be someone at home, worrying for him."

"If so, they'll want his murderers found."

"He ought to be buried with decency."

"Not yet."

Pulling his arm from her grasp, the bishop went away from her. Adelia watched him go to the parapet of the bridge and lean over it, looking at the roaring water that showed white in the moonlight.

He hates it when I do this, she thought. He was prepared to love the woman but not the doctor. Yet it was the doctor he invited along, and he must bear the consequences. I have a duty to that dead boy, and I will not abandon it.

Now she was cold.

"Very well." He turned round. "You may be fortunate in that Godstow possesses an icehouse. Famous for it."

While the body was being wrapped in its cloak and its possessions collected, Adelia went to the fire to feed her baby.

The Bishop of Saint Albans gathered his men

around him to tell them what Dr. Mansur had discovered from reading the signs in the snow.

"With the mercy of God, we may hope to catch these killers. Until then, not one of you—I say again, *nobody*—is to mention what we have seen this night. We shall keep this body reverently, but secretly, hidden in order to find out who comes back for it—and may God have mercy on their souls, for we shall not."

It was well done. Rowley had fought in Outremer on Crusade and found that men responded better for knowing what their commander was about than those merely given reasonless commands.

He drew an assenting growl from the circle about him, the messenger's particularly fervent— he and the others spent much of their lives on the road, and they saw the rider on the bridge as any one of themselves fallen to the predators infesting the highways. As Good Samaritans, they had been too late to save the traveler's life, but they could at least bring his killers to justice.

Only Father Paton's frown suggested that he was assessing how much the corpse was going to cost the ecclesiastical purse.

Baring their heads, the men took the body up and put it in the cart. With everybody walking beside it, leading their horses, they crossed the bridge to Godstow nunnery.

FOUR

$\mathcal{G}$odstow Abbey with its surrounding grounds and fields was actually a large island formed by curves of the Thames's upper reaches and tributaries. Although the porter who unbarred its gates to the travelers was a man, as were the groom and ostler who saw to their horses, it was an island ruled by women.

If asked, its twenty-four nuns and their female pensioners would have insisted that it was the Lord God who had called them to abandon the world, but their air of contentment suggested that the Lord's wish had coincided exactly with their own. Some were widows with money who'd heard God's call at their husband's graveside and hurried to answer it at Godstow before they could be married off again. Some were maidens who, glimpsing the husbands selected for them, had been overwhelmed by a sudden vocation for chastity and had taken their dowries with them into the convent instead. Here they could administer a sizable, growing fiefdom efficiently and with a liberal hand—and they could do it without male interference.

The only men over them were Saint Benedict, to whose rule they were subject and who was dead these six hundred and fifty years; the Pope, who was a long way away; the Archbishop of Canterbury, often ditto; and an investigative archdeacon who, because they kept their books and their behavior in scrupulous order, could make no complaint of them.

Oh, and the Bishop of Saint Albans.

So rich was Godstow that it possessed *two* churches. One, tucked away against the abbey's western wall, was small and acted as the nuns' private chapel. The other, much larger, stood on the east, near the road, and had been built to provide a place of worship for the people of the surrounding villages.

In effect, the abbey was a village in itself, in which the holy sisters had their own precincts, and it was to these that the travelers were taken by the porter. A maid carrying a yoke squeaked at the sight of them and then curtsied, spilling some milk from the buckets. The porter's lantern shone on passageways and courtyards, the sudden, sculptured pillars of a cloister where the shutters of the porter's windows opened to show white-coiffed heads like pale poppies whispering, "Bishop, the bishop," along the row.

Rowley Picot, so big, so full of energy and intent, so loudly male, was a cockerel erupting into a placid coop of hens that had been managing happily without him.

They were met by the prioress, still pinning her veil in place, and begged to wait in the chapter house where the abbess would attend them. In the meantime, please to take refreshment. Had the ladies any requirements? And the baby, such a fine little fellow, what might be done for him?

The beauty of the chapter house relied on the sweep of unadorned wooden crucks and arches. Candles lit a tiled floor strewn with fresh rushes and were reflected back in the sheen of a long table and chairs. Besides the scent of apple logs in the brazier, there was a smell of sanctity and beeswax— and now, thanks to Ward, the stink of unsavory dog.

Rowley strode the room, irritated by the wait, but, for the first time since the journey began, Adelia fed young Allie in the tranquillity the baby deserved. Its connection with Rosamund Clifford had made her afraid that the abbey would be disorderly, the nuns lax and no better than they should be. She still had bad memories of Saint Radegund's in Cambridge, the only other religious English sisterhood she'd encountered until now—a troubled place where, eventually, a participant in child killing had been unmasked.

Here at Godstow the atmosphere spoke of safety, tidiness, discipline, everything in its place.

She began to doze, lulled by the soporific mutterings of Father Paton as he chalked the reckonings onto his slate book. "To cheese and ale on the journey ... to provender for the horses ..."

A nudge from Gyltha got her to her feet. A small, very old nun, leaning on an ivory-topped walking stick, had come in. Rowley extended his hand; the nun bent creakily over it to kiss the episcopal ring on his finger. Everybody bowed.

The abbess sat herself at the head of the board, took trouble to lean her stick against her chair, clasped her hands, and listened.

Much of Godstow's felicity, Adelia realized within minutes, was due to this tiny woman. Mother Edyve had the disinterested calm of elderly people who had seen everything and were now watching it come around for the second time. This young bishop—a stripling compared to her—could not discompose her, though he arrived with a Saracen, two women, a baby, and an unprepossessing dog among his train, telling her that he had found a murdered man outside her gates.

Even the fact that the bishop wished to conceal the corpse in her icehouse was met calmly. "Thus you hope to find the killer?" she asked.

"Killer*sss*, Abbess," the bishop hissed impatiently. Once again, he went over the evidence found by Dr. Mansur and his assistant.

Adelia thought that Mother Edyve had probably grasped it the first time; she was merely giving herself time to consider. The wrinkly lidded eyes embedded into a face like creased calfskin closed as she listened, her veined hands reflected in the high polish of the table.

Rowley ended with, "We are assured that there are people who wish the young man's death and name to be broadcast; when there is only silence, they may return to find out why."

"A trap, then." It was said without emphasis.

"A trap is necessary to see justice done," Rowley persisted, "and only you to know about it, Abbess."

He is asking a great deal of her, Adelia thought. To conceal a body unmourned and unburied is surely against the law and certainly unChristian.

On the other hand, according to what Rowley had told her, this old woman had kept both her convent and her nuns inviolate during thirteen years of civil war, much of it waged in this very area, a feat suggesting that the rules of men, and even God's, must have been tinkered with somewhere along the line.

Mother Edyve opened her eyes. "I can tell you this, my lord: The bridge is ours. It is our convent's duty to maintain its structure and its peace and, by extension therefore, to catch those who commit murder on it."

"You agree, then?" Rowley was taken aback; he'd expected resistance.

"However," the abbess said, still distantly, as if he hadn't spoken, "you will need the assistance of my daughter prioress." Sliding it along her belt from under her scapular, Mother Edyve produced the largest chatelaine Adelia had ever seen; it was a wonder it didn't weigh her to the floor. Among the massive keys attached to it was a small bell. She rang it.

The prioress who had first greeted them came in. "Yes, Mother?"

Now that she could compare them, Adelia saw that Sister Havis had the same flat face and the same calfskin, though slightly less crinkled, complexion as the abbess. "Daughter prioress," then, was not a pious euphemism; Edyve had brought her child with her to Godstow when she took the veil.

"Our lord bishop has with him a consignment for our icehouse, Sister Havis. It will be stored there secretly during Lauds." A key was detached from the great iron ring and handed over. "There shall be no mention of it to any soul until further notice."

"Yes, Mother." Sister Havis bowed to her bishop, then to her mother, and left. No surprise. No questions. Godstow's icehouse, Adelia decided, must have stored more than sides of beef in its time. Treasure? Escapers? Situated as it was between the town of Wallingford, which had held out for Queen Matilda, and Oxford Castle, where King Stephen's flag had flown, there might well have been a need to hide both.

Allie was wriggling, and Gyltha, who was holding her, looked interrogatively at Adelia and then at the floor.

Adelia nodded, clean enough. Allie was put down to crawl, an exercise she was refusing to perform, preferring to hitch herself along on her backside. Wearily, the dog Ward disposed himself so that his ears could be pulled.

Rowley wasn't even thanking the abbess for her cooperation; he had moved on to a matter more important to him. "And now, madam, what of Rosamund Clifford?"

"Yes, the Lady Rosamund." It was spoken as distantly as ever, but Mother Edyve's hands tightened slightly. "They are saying it was the queen poisoned her."

"I was afraid they would."

"And *I* am afraid it may precipitate war."

There was a silence. Abbess and bishop were in accord now, as if they shared a foul secret. Once again, trampling horsemen milled around the memories of those who had known civil war, emitting to Adelia a turbulence so strong that she wanted to pick up her baby. Instead, she kept an eye on her in case the child made for the brazier.

"Has her corpse arrived?" Rowley asked abruptly.

"No."

"I thought it had been arranged; it was to be carried here for burial." He was accusatory, the abbess's fault. *Whereas*, thought Adelia, *any other bishop would have commended a convent that refused to inter a notorious woman in its ground.*

Mother Edyve looked down the side of her chair. Allie was trying to pull herself up by one of its legs. Adelia rose to go and remove her but the abbess held her back with an admonishing finger, then, without a change of expression, took the little bell from her chatelaine and passed it down.

You know babies, Adelia thought, comforted.

"Our foundation is indebted to the Lady Rosamund for many past kindnesses." Mother Edyve's voice tweeted like a distant bird. "We owe her body burial and all the services for her soul. It was arranged, yet her housekeeper, Dakers, refuses to release the corpse to us."

"Why not?"

"I cannot say, but without her consent, it is difficult to amend the situation."

"In the name of God, *why* not?"

Something, and it might have been a gleam of amusement, disturbed the immobility of the abbess's face for half a second. From the floor by her chair came a tinkling as Allie investigated her new toy. "I believe you visited Wormhold Tower during the lady's illness, my lord?"

"You know I did. Your prioress ... Sister Havis fetched me from Oxford to do so."

"And both of you were led through the labyrinth surrounding the tower?"

"Some crackbrained female met us at the entrance to it, yes." Rowley's fingers tapped on the table; he hadn't sat down since entering the room.

"Dame Dakers." Again, the suggestion of amusement like the merest breath on a pond. "I understand she will admit nobody since her mistress died. She adored her. My lord, I fear without she guides you through the labyrinth, there is no way of gaining the tower."

"I'll gain it. By God, I'll gain it. No body shall remain unburied whilst I am bishop here ..." He stopped, and then he laughed; he'd brought one through the gates with him.

It is his saving grace, Adelia thought as she melted and smiled with him, to see the incongruity of things. She watched him apologize to the abbess for his manner and thank her for her amiability—until she saw that the nun's pale old eyes had turned and were watching *her* watching *him*.

The abbess returned to the subject. "Dame Dakers's attachment to her mistress was"—the adjective was carefully considered—"formidable. The unfortunate servant responsible for bringing in the fatal mushrooms has fled from the tower in fear of her life and has sought sanctuary with us."

"She's here? Good. I want to question her." He corrected himself. "With your *permission*, madam, I should like to question her."

The abbess inclined her head.

"And if I may trespass on your kindness a little more," Rowley went on, "I would leave some of my party here while Dr. Mansur and his assistant accompany me to Wormhold Tower and see what may be done. As I say, the good doctor here has investigative abilities that can enable us ..."

Not yet. Not today. For God's sake, Rowley, we've traveled hard.

Adelia coughed and caught Gyltha's eye. Gyltha nudged Mansur, who stood next to her. Mansur looked round at them both, then spoke in English and for the first time. "Your doctor advise rest first." He added, "My lord."

"Rest be damned," Rowley said, but he looked toward Adelia, who must go with him when he went, or why was she here?

She shook her head. *We need rest, Rowley. You need it.*

The abbess's eyes had followed the exchange and, if it had told her nothing else, though it probably had, she'd learned enough to know the matter was settled. "When you have disposed of the unfortunate gentleman's body, Sister Havis will see to your accommodation," she said.

I t was still very dark and very cold. The nuns were chanting Lauds in their chapel, and everybody else with a duty to do was performing it within the complex of buildings, out of sight of the main gates, where a covered carriage containing a dead man had been left just inside them.

Walt and the men-at-arms were guarding it. They stood, stamping and slapping their arms to keep warm, stolidly ignoring the inquisition of the convent porter, who was leaning out of a bottom window in the gatehouse. Sister Havis told him sharply to withdraw his head, close the shutters, and mind his own business. "Keep thy silence, Fitchet."

"Don't I?" Fitchet was aggrieved. "Don't I always keep it?" The shutters slammed.

"He does," Sister Havis said. "Mostly." Holding the lantern high, she stalked ahead of them through the snow.

Walt led the horses after her, the bishop, Oswald, and Aelwyn marching beside him, with Adelia and Mansur above them on the cart's driving seat.

Rowley, aware now that he had tired her, would have left Adelia in the room that had been prepared for her and Gyltha and the baby in the guesthouse, but this dead young man was her responsibility. However good the reason, his body was being treated disgracefully at her behest; she must accord it what respect she could.

They were following the wall that ringed the convent's extensive buildings and gardens to where it ran into the woods in which, on the other side, lay the dead man's dead horse.

The rush of water that they'd heard from on the bridge became loud; they were close to the river, either the Thames itself or a fast stream running into it that gushed up even colder air. The noise became tremendous.

Mansur pointed; he and Adelia were seated high enough on the cart to see over the wall and, when trees allowed, across the water itself. There was their bridge and, on its far side, a water mill.

The Arab was saying something—she couldn't hear him—perhaps that the mill had been in darkness when they'd stood on the bridge so that they hadn't noticed it. Now light came through tiny windows set in its tower, and its great wheel was being turned by the race.

They'd pulled up. Sister Havis had stopped at a large stone hut built flush with the wall on this side and was unlocking its door.

The nun's lantern showed the inside of the hut to be empty apart from a ladder and a few tools. The floor was slabbed with stone, but most of its space was taken up by a great curve of iron set with handles, like the lid of an immense pot.

Sister Havis stood back. "It will need two to lift it." She had the same emotionless voice as her mother.

Aelwyn and Oswald exerted themselves to raise the lid, displaying the blackness of a hole and releasing a chill that was palpable even in the air of the hut, and with it a smell of straw and frozen meat.

The bishop had taken the lantern from the prioress and was down on his knees by the side of the hole. "Who built this?"

"We do not know, my lord. We discovered it and maintain it. Mother Abbess believes it was here long before our foundation."

"The Romans, I wonder?" Rowley was intrigued. The ladder was carried over and put in place so that he could descend. His voice came up with an echo, still asking questions, Sister Havis answering them with detachment.

Yes, its position so far from the convent butchery was inconvenient, but presumably its builders had placed it here to be close to a part of the river that was embanked so that the chamber would suffer no erosion while yet benefiting from the cooling proximity of running water.

Yes, the convent still pickled and salted most of its animals after the Michaelmas slaughter, since even Godstow could not provide feed for them all during the winter, but freezing some carcasses enabled its people to have occasional fresh meat into the spring, or later.

Yes, of course, the mill pond over the way needed a very cold winter to turn to ice, but all winters were cold these days and the last freeze had been exceptional, providing them with sufficient frozen blocks to last until summer. Yes, his lordship would see a drain that took away any melted water.

"Marvelous."

Adelia coughed with intent. Rowley's head appeared. "What?"

"The obsequies, my lord."

"Oh, of course."

The body was lain on the slabs.

Rigor mortis had passed off, Adelia was interested to see, but that would be from the comparative warmth provided by the wrapping of straw and the shelter of the cart; down in that freezing hole, it would return.

The sure, strong voice of the Bishop of Saint Albans filled the hut. "*Domine, Iesu Christe, Rex gloriae* ... Free the souls of all faithful departed from infernal punishment and the deep pit ... nor let them fall into darkness, but may the sign-bearer Saint Michael lead them into the holy light which you promised ..."

Adelia silently added her own requiem prayer: *And may those who love you forgive me for what we do.*

She went down the pit ahead of the body, joining Oswald and the bishop. A dreadful place, like the inside of an enormous brick egg insulated throughout by thick, netted straw over which more netting held the ice blocks. On their hooks, butchered sides of beef, lamb, venison, and pig, whitened by frost, hung so close together that she could not pass through without brushing her shoulders against them.

She found a space and straightened, to have her cap caught in the talons of game birds hanging from their own gallows.

Teeth chattering—and not just from the cold— she and the others guided the feet of the dead man as Aelwyn and Walt lowered him.

Together they laid him down under the birds, positioning him so that if there were drips, they would not fall on his face.

"I'm sorry. I'm so sorry." When the others had climbed out of the hole, she stayed by the dead man for a moment to make him a promise. "Whether we catch your killers or not, I will not leave you here for long."

It was almost too long for her; she was so cold she couldn't manage the ladder and Mansur had to hoist her out.

The abbess gave up her house to Rowley, saying it was a relief to do so; its steep steps to the front door had become difficult for her. In that he was her superior in God, she could do no less, although it gave him access to the inner courtyard with its cloister, chapel, refectory, and nuns' dormitory, which were otherwise barred to men overnight. Having taken a look at Father Paton and deciding that he wasn't a sexual threat, either, she put the secretary in with his master.

Jacques, Walt, Oswald, and Aelwyn were accommodated in the male servants' quarters.

Mansur was given a pleasant room in the men's guesthouse. Gyltha, Adelia, the baby, and the dog were accommodated just as pleasantly in the females' wing next to the church. Angled outside steps led up to each guest's private door, which, since they were on the top floor, gave the two women a view westward over the track to Oxford and the abbey's fields where they sloped down to the Thames.

"Duck down," said Gyltha, examining a large

bed. "An' no fleas." She investigated further. "And some saint's put hot bricks to warm it."

Adelia wanted nothing so much as to lie down on it and sleep, and, for a while, all three of them did just that.

They were awakened by bells, one of them tolling as if in their ear and setting the water ewer shivering in its basin on the room's table.

Ready to flee, Adelia picked up Allie where she lay between her and Gyltha. "Is it a fire?"

Gyltha listened. The massive strokes were coming from the church tower nearby, and with them came the chime of other bells, tinnier and much farther away. "It's Sunday," she said.

"Oh, to *hell*. It's not, is it?"

However, courtesy and Adelia's consciousness of their indebtedness to the abbess demanded that they attend the morning worship to which Godstow was summoning its people.

And more than just its own people. The church in the outer courtyard was open to everybody, lay and religious—though not, of course, to infidels and the smellier dogs, thus leaving Mansur and Ward still in their beds—and today everybody within walking range was struggling through snow to get to it. The village of Wolvercote came across the bridge en masse, since its own church had been allowed to fall into ruin by the lord of the manor.

The attraction was the bishop, of course; he was as miraculous as an angel descended. A view of his cope and miter alone was worth the tithes everybody had to pay; he might be able to cure the little un's cough; for sure he could bless the winter sowing. Several poorly looking milch cows and one limping donkey were already tied up by the water trough outside, awaiting his attention.

The clergy entered by their own separate doorway to take their seats in the glorious stalls of the choir under the church's equally glorious fan-vaulted roof.

By virtue of his tonsure, Father Paton sat next to the nuns' chaplain, a little dormouse of a man, opposite the rows of nuns that included among their black ranks two young women in white veils who had a tendency to giggle; they found Father Paton funny.

Most bishops used their homilies to wag a finger at sin in general, often in Norman French, their mother tongue, or in Latin on the principle that the less the congregation understood, the more in awe it would be.

Rowley's was different, and in an English his flock could understand. "There's some buggers are saying poor Lady Rosamund has died at the Queen Eleanor's hand, which it is a wickedness and a lie, and you'll oblige our Lord by giving it no credit."

He left the pulpit to stride up and down the church, lecturing, hectoring. He was here to discover what or who had caused Rosamund's death, he said, "For I do know she was dearly loved in these parts. Maybe 'twas an accident, maybe 'twasn't, but if it weren't, both king and queen'll see to it the villain be punished according to law. In the meantime, 'tis beholden on us all to keep our counsel and the precious peace of our Lord Jesus Christ."

Then he kneeled down on the stones and straw to pray, and everyone in church kneeled with him.

They love him, Adelia thought. *As quickly as that, they love him. Is it showmanship? No, it isn't. He's beyond that now. Beyond me, too.*

When they rose, however, one man—the miller from across the bridge, judging from the spectral whiteness with which flour had ingrained his skin—raised a question. "Master, they say as how the queen be upsides with the king. Ain't going to be no trouble twixt 'em, is there?"

He was backed by a murmur of anxiety. The civil war in which a king had fought a queen was only a generation in the past; nobody here wanted to see another.

Rowley turned on him. "Which is your missus?"

"This un." The man jerked a thumb at the comfortable lady standing beside him.

"And a good choice you made there, Master Miller, as all can see. But tell me you ain't been upsides with her along the years some'eres, or her ain't been upsides with you, but you diddun start a war over it. Reckon as royalty ain't no different."

Amid laughter, he returned to his throne.

One of the white-veiled girls sang the responsory in honor of the bishop's presence and sang it so exquisitely that Adelia, usually deaf to music, waited impatiently through the congregation's answers until she sang again.

So it was nice to find the same young woman waiting for her in the great courtyard outside after the clergy had filed out. "May I come and see the baby? I love babies."

"Of course. I must congratulate you on your voice; it is a joy to hear."

"Thank you. I am Emma Bloat."

"Adelia Aguilar."

They fell into step, or, rather, Adelia stepped and Emma bounced. She was fifteen years old and in a state of exaltation over something. Adelia hoped it was not the bishop. "Are you an oblate?"

"Oh, no. Little Priscilla is the one taking the veil. I am to be married."

"Good."

"It *is*, isn't it? Earthly love ..." Emma twirled in sheer joie de vivre. "God must reckon it as high as heavenly love, mustn't he, despite what Sister Mold says, or why does He make us feel like this?" She thumped the region of her heart.

"'It is better to marry than to burn,'" quoted Adelia.

"Huh. What I say is, how did Saint Paul know? He didn't do either."

She was a refreshing child and she did love babies, or she certainly loved Allie, with whom she was prepared to play peep-bo longer than Adelia had believed possible without the brain giving way.

It seemed that the girl must have privilege of some kind, since she was not called back to join the sisters' afternoon routine. *Wealth or rank?* Adelia wondered. *Or both?*

She showed no more curiosity about this influx of strangers to the convent than if they had been toys provided for her amusement, though she demanded that they be curious about her. "Ask me about my husband-to-be, ask me, ask me."

He was beautiful, apparently, *oh* so beautiful, gallant, wild with love for her, a writer of romantic poems that rivaled any Paris might have sent to Helen.

Gyltha raised her eyebrows to Adelia, who raised her own. This was happiness indeed, and unusual to be found in an arranged marriage. For arranged it was; Emma's father, she told them, was a wine merchant in Oxford and was supplying the convent with the best Rhenish to pay for having her educated as befitted a nobleman's wife. It was he who had procured the match.

At this point, Emma, who was standing by the window, laughed so much that she had to hold on to the mullion.

"Your intended's a lord, then?" Gyltha asked, grinning.

The laughter went, and the girl turned to look out of the window as if its view could tell her something, and Adelia saw that when the exuberance of youth went, beauty would take its place.

"The lord of my heart," Emma said.

It was difficult for the travelers to forgather in order to discuss and plan. Lenient as Godstow was, it could not tolerate the step of a Saracen into its inner courtyard. For the bishop to visit the women's quarters was equally out of place. There was only the church, and even there a nun was always present at the main altar, interceding with God for the souls of such departed as had paid for the privilege. However, it had a side chapel devoted to Mary, deserted at night yet lit by candles— another gift from the dead that they might be remembered to the Holy Mother—and the abbess had given her permission for its use as a meeting place, as long as they were quiet about it.

The day's large congregation had left no warmth behind. Blazing candles on the shrine sent out light and heat only a few feet, leaving the ogival space around them in icy shadow. Entering by a side door, Adelia saw a large figure kneeling before the altar, his cowled head bowed and the fingers of his hands interlaced so tightly that they resembled bare bone.

Rowley got up as the women entered. He looked tired. "You're late."

"I had to feed the baby," Adelia told him.

From the main body of the church came the drone of a nun reading the commemorations from the convent register. She was being literal about it. *"Lord, in Thy mercy, bless and recognize the soul of Thomas of Sandford, who did provide an orchard in Saint Giles's, Oxford, to this convent and departed this life the day after Martinmas in the year of our Lord 1143. Sweet Jesus, in Thy Mercy, look kindly on the soul of Maud Halegod, who did give three silver marks ..."*

"Did Rosamund's servant tell you anything?" Adelia whispered.

"*Her?*" The bishop didn't bother to lower his voice. "The female's rattle-headed; I'd have got more out of the bloody donkeys I've had to bless all bloody afternoon. She kept bleating, I swear, like a sheep."

"You probably frightened her." In full regalia, he'd have been overwhelming.

"Of course I didn't frighten her. I was charming. The woman's witless, I tell you. You see if you can get some sense out of her."

"I shall."

Gyltha had found some hassocks piled in a cupboard and was distributing them in a circle, where the candlelight fell on them, each one displaying the blazon of a noble family that didn't want to dirty its knees when it came to church.

"Hassocks are sensible," Adelia said, putting one under the sleeping Allie's basket in order to keep it off the stones. Ward settled himself on another. "Why don't the rich endow hassocks for the poor? They'd be remembered longer."

"The rich don't want us comfortable," Gyltha said. "Ain't good for us. Give us ideas above our station. Where's that old Arab?"

"The messenger's fetching him."

He came, having to stoop through the side door, wrapped in a cloak, Jacques behind him.

"Good," Rowley said. "You can go, Jacques."

"*Ummm.*" The young man shifted in complaint.

Adelia took pity on him. Messengers had an unenviable and lonely job, spending their time crisscrossing the country with a horse as their only companion. Their masters were hard on them: letters to be delivered quickly, replies brought back even quicker; excuses, such as bad weather, falls, difficult country, or getting lost, discounted in favor of the suspicion that the servant had been wasting his time and his employer's money in some tavern.

Rowley, she thought, was being particularly hard on this one; there was no reason why the young man should not be included in their discussions. She suspected that Jacques's sin lay in the fact that, though he wore the sober Saint Albans livery, he compensated for his lack of height by wearing raised boots and a high plume in his hat, which led to the suspicion that he was following the trend introduced by Queen Eleanor and her court for males as well as women to subscribe to fashion—an idea welcomed by the young generation but condemned as effete by men, like Rowley, like Walt and Oswald, whose choice of clothing material had always been either leather or chain mail.

Walt had been heard to describe the messenger, not inaccurately, as looking like "a stalk of celery wi' roots attached," and Rowley had grumbled to Adelia that he feared his messenger was "greenery-yellery" and "not good, plain old Norman English," both epithets he reserved for men he regarded as effeminate. "I shall have to send him away. The boy even wears scent. I can't have my missives delivered by a popinjay."

This, thought Adelia, *from a man whose ceremonial robes dazzled the eye and took half an hour to put on.*

She decided to intercede. "Are we taking Master Jacques with us to Rosamund's tower tomorrow?"

"Of course we are." Rowley was still irritable. "I may need to send messages."

"Then he'll know as much as we know, my lord. He already does."

"Oh, very well."

From the altar beyond the screen that separated them, the ceaseless muttering of prayer for the dead went on as, with different nuns taking up the task, it would go on all night.

"... of your mercy, the soul of Thomas Hookeday, hayward of this parish, for the sixpence he did endow ..."

Rowley produced the saddle roll that had belonged to the dead man on the bridge. "Hasn't been time to look through it yet." He unbuckled the straps and put it on the floor to unroll it. With Jacques standing behind them, the four sat round and considered its contents.

Which were few. A leather bottle of ale. Half a cheese and a loaf neatly wrapped in cloth. A hunting horn—odd equipment for a man traveling without companions or dogs. A spare cloak with fur trimming, surprisingly small for what had been a tall man—again, carefully folded.

Wherever the youngster had been heading, he was banking on finding food and lodging there; the bread and cheese wouldn't have sustained him very far.

And there was a letter. It appeared to have been pushed just under the flap between the buckles of the leather straps that secured the roll.

Rowley picked it up and smoothed it out.

"'To Talbot of Kidlington,'" he read. "'That the Lord and His angels bless you on this Day that enters you into Man's estate and keep you from the Path of Sin and all unrighteousness is the dearest hope of your affct cousin, Wlm Warin, gentleman-at-law, who hereby sends: two silver marks as an earnest of your inheritance, the rest to be Claimed when we do meet. Written this day of Our Lord, the sixteenth before the Kalends of January, at my place of business next Saint Michael at the North Gate of Oxford.'"

He looked up. "Well, there we are, then. Now we know our body's name."

Adelia nodded slowly. "*Hmm*."

"What's wrong with *that*? The boy's got a name, a twenty-first birthday, and an affectionate cousin with an address. Plenty for you to work on. What he hasn't got is two silver marks. I imagine the thieves took those."

Adelia noted the "you"; this was to be her business, not the bishop's. "Don't you think it odd," she asked, "if the family arms on his purse were not to tell us who he was, here is a letter that does. It gives us almost too much information. What affectionate writer calls his cousin Talbot of Kidlington rather than just Talbot?"

Rowley shrugged. "A perfectly standard superscription."

Adelia took the letter from him. "And it's on vellum. Expensive for such a brief, personal note. Why didn't Master Warin use rag paper?"

"All lawyers use vellum or parchment. They think paper is *infra dignitatem*."

But Adelia mused on. "And it's crumpled, just shoved between the buckles. Look, it's torn on one of them. Nobody treats vellum like that—it can always be scraped down to use again."

"Perhaps the lad was in a rush when he received it, stuffed it away quickly. Or he was angry because he was expecting more than two marks? Or he doesn't give an owl's hoot for vellum. Which"—the bishop was losing his patience—"at this moment, I don't, either. What is your point, mistress?"

Adelia considered for a moment.

Whether the body in the icehouse was that of Talbot of Kidlington or not, when alive it had belonged to a neat man; his clothing had told her that. So did the care he'd expended on wrapping the contents of his saddle roll. People with such tidy habits—and Adelia was one of their number—did not carelessly thrust a document on vellum into an aperture with the flat of the hand, as this had been.

"I don't think he even saw this letter," she said. "I think the men who killed him put it there."

"For the Lord's sake," Rowley hissed at her, "this is overelaboration. Adelia, highway villains do not endow their victim with correspondence. What are you saying? It's a forgery to put us off the track? Talbot of Kidlington isn't Talbot of Kidlington? The belt and the purse belong to someone else entirely?"

"I don't know." But something about the letter was wrong.

Arrangements were made for the next day's excursion. Adelia would accompany bishop, messenger, groom, and one of the men-at-arms on a ride upriver, using the towpath to Rosamund's tower while Mansur and the other man-at-arms would travel by water, bringing a barge on which to carry back the corpse.

While discussion went on, Adelia took the opportunity to examine the blazons on all the hassocks. None of them matched the device on the young man's purse or belt.

Rowley was talking to Gyltha. "You must stay here, mistress. We can't take the baby with us."

Adelia looked up. "I'm not leaving her behind."

He said, "You'll have to, it won't be a family outing." He took Mansur by the arm. "Come along, my friend, let's see what the convent has in the way of boats." They went out, the messenger with them.

"*I'm not leaving her,*" Adelia shouted after him, causing a momentary pause in the recital of souls from beyond the screen. She turned to Gyltha. "How *dare* he. I won't."

Gyltha pressed on Adelia's shoulders to force her down onto a hassock, then sat beside her. "He's right."

"He's not. Suppose we get cut off by snow, by anything? She needs to be fed."

"Then I'll see as she is." Gyltha took Adelia's hand and bounced it gently. "It's time, girl," she said. "Time she was weaned proper. You're a'drying up; you know it, the little un knows it."

Adelia was hearing the truth; Gyltha never told

her anything else. In fact, the weaning process had been going on for some weeks as her breast milk diminished, both women chewing food to a pap and supplementing it with cow's milk to spoon into Allie's eager mouth.

If breast-feeding, which the childless Adelia had considered would be an oozing embarrassment, had proved to be one of life's natural pleasures, it had also been the excuse to have her child always with her. For motherhood, while another joy, had burdened her with a tearing and unexpected anxiety, as if her senses had been transferred into the body of her daughter, and, by a lesser extension, into that of all children. Adelia, who'd once considered anyone below the age of reason to be alien and had treated them as such, was now open to their grief, their slightest pain, any unhappiness.

Allie suffered few of these emotions; she was a sturdy baby, and gradually Adelia had become aware that the agony was for herself, for the two-day-old creature that had been abandoned by an unknown parent on a rocky slope in Italy's Campania nearly thirty years before. During her growing up it had not mattered; an incident, even amusing in that the couple who'd discovered her had commemorated an event all three had considered fortunate by giving her Vesuvia as one of her names. Childless, loving, clever, eccentric, Signor and Signora Aguilar, both doctors trained in the liberal tradition of Salerno's great School of Medicine, he a Jew, she a Catholic Christian, had found in Adelia not only a beloved daughter but a brain that superseded even their intelligence, and had educated it accordingly. No, abandonment hadn't mattered. It had, in fact, turned out to be the greatest gift that the real, unknown, desperate, sorrowing, or uncaring mother could have bestowed on her child.

Until that child had given birth to a baby of her own.

Then it came. Fear like a typhoon that wouldn't stop blowing, not just fear that Allie would die but fear that she herself would die and leave the child without the mercy that had been bestowed on her. Better they both die together.

Oh, God, if the poisoner was not content merely with Rosamund's death ... or if the killers from the bridge were waiting en route ... or if she should leave her child in a Godstow suddenly overwhelmed by fire ...

This was obsession, and Adelia had just enough sense to know that, if it persisted, it would damage both herself and Allie.

"It's time," Gyltha said again, and since Gyltha, most reliable of women, said it was, then it was.

But she resented the ease with which Rowley demanded a separation that would cause her grief and, however unfounded, fear as well. "It's not up to him to tell me to leave her behind. I hate leaving her, I hate it."

Gyltha shrugged. "His child, too."

"You wouldn't think so."

The messenger's voice came from the door. "My apologies, mistress, but his lordship asks that you will interview Bertha."

"Bertha?"

"Lady Rosamund's servant, mistress. The mushrooming one."

"Oh, yes."

Apart from the unremitting prayers for the dead in the church and the canonical hours, the convent had shut down, leaving it in a total, moonless black. The compass of light from Jacques's lantern lit only the bottom of walls and a few feet of pathway lined by snow as he led the two women to their quarters. There Adelia kissed her baby good night and left Gyltha to put her to bed.

She and the messenger went on alone, leaving the outer courtyard for open ground. A faint smell suggested that somewhere nearby were vegetable gardens, rotted now by the frost.

"Where are you taking me?" Her voice went querulous into the blackness.

"The cowshed, I'm afraid, mistress." Jacques was apologetic. "The girl's hidden herself there. The abbess put her to the kitchens, but the cooks refused to work with her, seeing it was her hand that fed the poison to the lady Rosamund. The nuns have tried talking to her but they say it's difficult to get sense from the poor soul, and she dreads the arrival of the lady's housekeeper."

The messenger chatted on, eager to prove himself worthy of inclusion into his bishop's strange, investigative inner circle.

"About the blazon on the poor young man's purse, mistress. It might profit you to consult Sister Lancelyne. She keeps the convent's cartulary and register, and has a record of the device of every family who's made a gift at some time or another."

He'd been making good use of his time. It was a messenger's attribute to persuade himself into the good books of the servants of households he visited. It got him better food and drink before he had to set off again.

Walls closed in again. Adelia's boots splashed through the slush of what, in daytime, must be much-used lanes. Her nose registered that they were passing a bakehouse, now a kitchen, a laundry, all silent and invisible in the darkness.

More open land. More slush, but here and there footprints in a bank of snow where someone had stepped off the path.

Menace.

It came at her, unseen, unaccountable, but so strong that she hunched and stood still under its attack as if she were back in the alleys of Salerno and had seen the shadow of a man with a knife.

The messenger stopped with her. "What is it, mistress?"

"I don't know. Nothing." There were footprints in the snow, valid, explicable footprints no doubt, but for her, remembering those on the bridge, they pointed to death.

She forced herself to trudge on.

The acrid stink of hot iron and a remnant of warmth on the air told her they were passing a smithy, its fire banked down for the night. Now a stable and the smell of horse manure that, as they walked on, became bovine—they had reached the cowshed.

Jacques heaved open one of the double doors to reveal a wide, bespattered aisle between partitioned stalls, most of which were empty. Few beasts anywhere survived the Michaelmas cull—there was never enough fodder to see herds through the winter—but farther up the aisle, the lantern shone on the crusted backsides and tails of the cows that had been left alive to provide winter milk.

"Where is she?"

"They said she was here. Bertha," Jacques called. "*Bertha.*"

From somewhere in the dark at the far end of the shed came a squeak and rustle of straw as if an extra-large mouse were making for its hole.

Jacques lit their way up the aisle and shone the lantern into the last of the stalls before hanging it from the hook of an overhead beam. "She's there, I think, mistress." He stood back so Adelia could see inside it.

There was a big pile of straw against the stall's back wall. Adelia addressed it. "Bertha? I mean you no harm. Please talk to me."

She had to say it several times before there was a heave and a face was framed in the straw. At first, with the lantern sending downward light on it, Adelia thought it was a pig's, then saw that it belonged to a girl with a nose so retroussé as to present only nostrils, giving it the appearance of a snout. Small, almost lashless eyes fixed on Adelia's face. The wide mouth moved and produced sound high up the scale. "Non me faux," it sounded like. "Non me faux, non me faux."

Adelia turned back to Jacques. "Is she French?"

"Not as far as I know, mistress. I think she's saying it was not her fault."

The bleat changed. "Donagemme."

"'Don't let her get me,'" Jacques translated.

"Dame Dakers?" Adelia asked.

Bertha hunched in terror. "Turmeinamouse."

"'She'll turn me into a mouse,'" Jacques said helpfully.

The irresistible thought came, shamefully, that in the case of this child, the dame's powers to turn her into an animal would not be stretched very far.

"Antrappi." Bertha was becoming less frightened and more confidential, poking forward now to show a thin upper neck and body under head and hair colored the same as the straw that framed them. Her gaze became fixed on Adelia's neck.

"'And catch I in a trap,'" Jacques said.

Adelia was getting the hang of Bertha's speech. Also, she had become angry, as she always did at the suggestion of magic, appalled that this girl should be terrorized by black superstition. "Sit up," she said.

The porcine little eyes blinked and Bertha sat up instantly, spilling straw. She was used to being bullied.

"Now," Adelia said, more quietly, "nobody blames you for what happened, but you *must* tell me how it came about."

Bertha leaned forward and poked at Adelia's necklet. "What be that purty thing?"

"It's a cross. Haven't you seen one before?"

"Lady Ros do have similar, purtier nor that. What be for? Magic?" This was awful. Had nobody taught the girl Christianity?

Adelia said, "As soon as I can, I shall buy you one of your own and explain it to you. Now, though, you must explain things to *me*. Will you do that?"

Bertha nodded, her eyes still on the silver cross.

So it began. It took infinite labor on Adelia's part and wearisome, evasive repetition on Bertha's, pursuing the theme that it wasn't her fault, before any relevant information could be teased from her. The girl was so ignorant, so credulous, that Adelia's opinion of Rosamund became very low—no servant should be so deprived of education. *Fair Rosamund*, she thought. Not much fairness in the neglect of this sad little thing.

It was difficult to estimate her age; Bertha herself didn't know it. Between sixteen and twenty, Adelia guessed, half-starved and as unaware of how the world wagged as any mole in its run.

Jacques, unnoticed, had slid a milking stool against her hocks, allowing her to sit so that she and Bertha were on a level. He remained standing directly behind her in shadow, saying not a word.

Ever since she'd heard of Rosamund's death, Adelia had believed that what she would eventually uncover was the tale of a sad accident.

It wasn't. As Bertha gained confidence and Adelia understanding, the story that emerged showed that Bertha had been the accomplice, albeit unwittingly, to deliberate murder.

On the fatal day, she said, she'd gone into the

forest surrounding Wormhold Tower to gather kindling, not mushrooms, pulling a sledge behind her to pile it with such dead branches as could be reached with a crook.

Lowest of all Rosamund's servants, it had already been a bad morning for her. Dame Dakers had walloped her for dropping a pot and told her that Lady Rosamund was sick of her and intended to send her away, which, Bertha being without family to turn to, would have meant having to tramp the countryside begging for food.

"Her's a dragon," Bertha whispered, looking round and up in case Dame Dakers had flown in, flapping her wings, to perch on one of the cowshed's beams. "Us calls her Dragon Dakers."

Miserably, Bertha had gathered so much fuel—afraid of Dragon Dakers's wrath if she didn't—that, having tied the bundled wood to the sledge, she found it impossible to pull, at which point she had sat down on the ground and bawled her distress to the trees.

"And then *her* come up."

"Who came?"

"*Her* did. Old woman."

"Had you ever seen her before?"

"'*Course* not." Bertha regarded the question as an insult. "Her didn't come from our parts. Second cook to Queen Eleanor, she was. The *queen*. Traveled everywhere with un."

"That's what she told you? She worked for Queen Eleanor?"

"Her did."

"What did this old woman look like?"

"Like a old woman."

Adelia took a breath and tried again. "How old? Describe her. Well-dressed? In rags? What sort of face? What sort of voice?"

But Bertha, lacking both observation and vocabulary, was unable to answer these questions. "Her was ugly, but her was kind," she said. It was the only description she could give, kindness being so rare in Bertha's life that it was remarkable.

"In what way was she kind?"

"Her gave I them mushrooms, didn't her? Magic, they was. Said they'd make Lady Ros look on I with"—Bertha's unfortunate nose had wrinkled in an effort to recall the word used—"favor."

"She said your mistress would be pleased with you?"

"Her did."

It took time, but eventually something of the conversation that had taken place in the forest between Bertha and the old woman was reconstructed.

"*That's what I do for my lady, Queen Eleanor,*" the old woman had said. "*I do give her a feast of these here mushrooms, and her do look on me with favor.*"

Bertha had inquired eagerly whether they also worked on less-exalted mistresses.

"*Oh, yes, even better.*"

"*Like, if your mistress were going to send you off, she wouldn't?*"

"*Send you off? Promote you more like.*"

Then the old woman had added, "*Tell you what I'll*

do, Bertha, my duckling, I like your face, so I'll let you have my mushrooms to cook for your lady. Fond of mushrooms, is she?"

"Dotes on 'em."

"There you are, then. You cook her these and be rewarded. Only you must do it right away now."

Amazed, Adelia wondered for a moment if this was a fairy tale that Bertha had concocted in order to conceal her own guilt. Then she abandoned the thought; nobody had ever bothered to tell Bertha fairy tales in which mysterious old women offered girls their heart's desire—or any fairy tales at all. Bertha was incapable of concoction, anyway.

So that day in the forest, now eager and full of strength, Bertha had tied the basket of mushrooms to the wood on her sledge and dragged both back to Wormhold Tower.

Which was almost deserted. *That*, Adelia thought, *was significant*. Dame Dakers had left for the day to go to a hiring fair in Oxford in order to find a new cook—cooks, it seemed, never endured her strictures for long and were constantly leaving. The other staff, free of the housekeeper's eye, had taken themselves off, leaving Fair Rosamund virtually alone.

So, in an empty kitchen, Bertha had set to work. The amount of fungi had been enough for two meals, and Bertha had divided them, thinking to leave some for tomorrow. She'd put half into a skillet with butter, a pinch of salt, a touch of wild garlic, and a sprinkling of parsley, warmed them over a flame until the juices ran, and then taken the dish up to the solar where Rosamund sat at her table, writing a letter.

"Her could write, you know," Bertha said in wonder.

"And she ate the mushrooms?"

"Gobbled 'em." The girl nodded. "Greedy like."

The magic had worked. Lady Rosamund, most unusually, had smiled on Bertha, thanked her, said she was a good girl.

Later, the convulsions had begun ...

Even now, Adelia discovered, Bertha did not suspect the crone in the forest of treachery. "Accident," she said. "Weren't the old un's fault. A wicked mushroom did get into that basket by mistake."

There was no point in arguing, but there had been no mistake. In the selection Bertha had saved and Rowley had shown Adelia, the Death Cap was as numerous as any other species—and carefully mixed in among them.

Bertha, however, refused to believe ill of someone who'd been nice to her. "Weren't her fault, weren't mine. Accident."

Adelia sat back on her stool to consider. Such an undoubted murder, only Bertha could believe it an accident, only Bertha could think that royal servants roamed the forest bestowing gifts of enchanted mushrooms on anyone they met. There had been meticulous planning. The old woman, whoever she was, had spun a web to catch the particular fly that was Bertha on the particular day when Rosamund's dragon, Dakers, had been absent from her mistress's side.

Which argued that the old woman had been

privy to the movements of Rosamund's household, or instructed by someone who was.

Rowley's right, Adelia thought, *someone wanted Rosamund dead and the queen implicated.* If Eleanor *had* ordered it done, she'd hardly have chosen an old woman who'd mention her name. No, it hadn't been Eleanor. Whoever had done it had hated the queen even more than Rosamund. Or maybe merely wanted to enrage her husband against her and thereby plunge England into conflict. Which they might.

The shed had become quiet. Bertha's mumbles that it wasn't her fault had faded away, leaving only the sound of cows' chewing and the slither of hay as they pulled more from their mangers.

"For God's sake," Adelia asked Bertha desperately, "didn't you notice *anything* about the old woman?"

Bertha thought, shaking her head. Then she seemed puzzled. "Smelled purty," she said.

"She smelled pretty? In what way pretty?"

"Purty." The girl was crawling forward now, her nose questing like a shrew's. "Like you."

"She smelled like me?"

Bertha nodded.

Soap. Good scented soap, Adelia's one luxury, used only two hours ago in the allover wash to cleanse her from her travels. Bars of it, made with lye, olive oil, and essence of flowers, were sent to her once a year by her foster mother from Rome—Adelia had complained in one of her letters of the soap in England, where the process was based on beef tallow, making its users smell as if they were ready for the oven.

"Did she smell like flowers?" she asked. "Roses? Lavender? Chamomile?" And she knew it was useless. Even if Bertha was conversant with these plants, she would know them only by local names unfamiliar to Adelia.

It had been a gain, though. No ordinary old woman gathering mushrooms in a forest would smell of perfumed soap, even supposing she used soap at all.

Rising to her feet, Adelia said, "If you smell her scent again on anybody else, will you tell me?"

Bertha nodded. Her eyes were fixed on the cross at Adelia's throat, as if, ignorant of its meaning, it still spoke to her of hope.

And what hope has she, poor thing?

Sighing, Adelia unfastened the chain from her neck and slid it with its cross into Bertha's dirty little hand, closing her fingers over it. "Keep this until I can buy you one of your own," she said.

It cost her to do it, not because of the cross's symbolism—Adelia had been exposed to too many religions to put all her faith in a single one—but because it had been given to her by Margaret, her old nurse, a true Christian, who had died on the journey to England.

But I have known love. I have my child, an occupation, friends.

Bertha, who had none of these things, clasped the cross and, bleating with pleasure, dived back into the straw with it.

As they walked back through the night, Jacques said, "Do you believe that little piggy can sniff out your truffle for you, mistress?"

"It's a long shot," Adelia admitted, "but Bertha's nose is probably the best detector we have. If she should smell the old woman's scent again, it will be on someone who buys foreign soap and can tell us who their supplier is, who, in turn, could provide us with a list of customers."

"Clever." The messenger's voice was admiring.

After a while, he said, "Do you think the queen *was* involved?"

"Somebody wants us to think so."

FIVE

*O*n the rise above a gentle valley, a dog and four riders from Godstow reined in and considered the building and appurtenances crowning the opposite hill.

After some silence, Adelia said, unwisely, "How on earth do tradesmen penetrate it?"

"Gift of flowers and a nice smile used to do it in my day," the bishop said.

She heard a snort from the two men on either side of her.

"I mean the labyrinth," she said.

Rowley winked. "So do I."

More snorts.

Oh, dear, sexual innuendo. Not that she could blame them. From here, the view of Wormhold Tower and what surrounded it looked, well, *rude*. A very high, thin tower capped by a close-fitting cupola—it even had a tiny walkway around its tip to accentuate the penile resemblance—rose from the ring of a labyrinth that men apparently saw as female pubic hair. It presented an outline that might have been scrawled on the top of its hill by a naughty, adolescent giant. A graffito against the skyline.

The bishop had led them here at a canter, afraid the weather might stop them, but now that the tower was in sight, anxiety had left him relieved and, obviously, with time to enjoy ribaldry.

Actually, it had been an easy journey northward, using the river towpath that ran from Godstow to within a half-mile of the tower. So easy, in fact, that Adelia had been invigorated by it and lost her own fear that the weather would hamper her return to her child.

Such bargemen as they'd encountered had warned them that more snow was on the way, but there was no sign of it. It was a cloudless day, and although the sun hadn't melted the previous night's fall, it had been impossible not to rejoice in a countryside like white washing spread out to dry against a laundered blue sky.

Farther south, on the river they'd just left, Mansur, the bishop's two men-at-arms, and a couple of Godstow's men were bringing up a barge on which to take the body of Rosamund back to the convent—once Bishop Rowley had retrieved it.

First, though, the labyrinth that surrounded the dead woman's stronghold had to be got through—a prospect that was stimulating the old Adam in Adelia's companions.

"I told you," Rowley said, addressing Adelia but winking at Walt. "Didn't I say it was the biggest chastity belt in Christendom?"

He was trying to provoke her. *Ignore it.* "I hadn't thought it would be quite so large," she said, and then sighed at herself. Another double entendre to make the men snigger.

Well, she hadn't. The labyrinth at Saint Giorgio's in Salerno was considered by the town to be a wonder, supposed to represent in length and complexity the soul's journey through life. But this thing opposite her now was a colossus. It encircled the tower, forming a ring so thick that it took up a wide section of this side of the hill and disappeared behind it. Its outer wall was nine or ten feet high, while, at this distance, its interior seemed to be filled entirely by white wool.

The prioress of Godstow had warned her about it before she set out. "Blackthorn," Sister Havis had told her with disgust. "Can you credit it? Walls of granite with blackthorn planted against them."

What Adelia was looking at was stone and hedge, twisting and turning in frozen undulation.

Not a belt, Adelia thought. *A snake. A huge, constricting serpent.*

Walt said, "Reckon as that's a bugger for its hedgers," nearly causing Rowley to fall off his horse. Jacques was smiling broadly, happy at seeing his bishop unbend.

Sister Havis had said what Adelia could expect. The original labyrinth, she'd said, had been built round his keep by a mad Saxon necromancer and enlarged by his equally mad dispossessor, a Norman, one of the Conqueror's knights, in order to stop his enemies from getting in and his women from getting out.

The Norman's descendants had been dispossessed in their turn by Henry Plantagenet, who'd found it a convenient place in which to install his mistress, abutting, as it did, the forest of Woodstock, where he kept a hunting lodge.

"Architectural vulgarity," Sister Havis had called it, angrily. "An object of male lewdness. Local people are in awe of it, even while they jeer at it. Poor Lady Rosamund. I fear the king found it amusing to put her there."

"He would." Adelia knew Henry Plantagenet's sense of humor.

And Rowley's.

"Of course I can penetrate it," the bishop was saying now, in answer to a question from Jacques. "I've done it. A wiggle to the right, another to the left, and everybody's happy."

Listening to the laughter, Adelia began to be sorry for Rosamund. Had the woman minded living in a place that invited, almost *demanded*, salacious comment from every man who saw it?

Poor lady. Even dead, she was being shown little respect.

With snow resting on the walls and branches of the surrounding labyrinth, the tower looked to be rising from a mass of white fuzz. Adelia was irresistibly reminded of a patient, an elderly male whom her foster father was attending and on whose body he was instructing Adelia how to repair a hernia in the groin. Suddenly, much to his abashed surprise, the patient had sustained an erection.

That's what's scrawled against the sky, she thought, *an old man's last gasp*.

She turned on Rowley. "How. Do. We. Get. In,"

she said, clearly, "and try to remember there's a dead woman in there."

He jerked a thumb. "We ring the bell."

Transfixed by the tower, she hadn't noticed it, though it stood only a few yards away on the hillside, next to a horse trough.

Like everything else belonging to Wormhold, it was extraordinary, an eight-foot-high wooden trapezoid set into the ground, from which hung a bell as massive as any in a cathedral's chimes.

"Go on, Jacques," the bishop said. "Ding-dong."

The messenger dismounted, walked up to the bell, and swung the rope hanging from its clapper.

Adelia clung to her mare as it skittered, and Walt snatched the reins of Jacques's to prevent it from bolting. Birds erupted from the trees, a rookery fell to circling and cawing as the bell's great baritone tolled across the valley. Even Ward, most unresponsive of mongrels, looked up and gave a bark.

The reverberations hung in the air and then settled into a silence.

Rowley swore. "Again," he said. "Where's Dakers? Is she deaf?"

"Must be," Jacques said. "That would waken the dead." He realized what he'd said. "Beg pardon, my lord."

For a second time the great bell tolled, seeming to shake the earth. Again, nothing happened.

"Thought I saw someone," Walt said, squinting against the sun.

So did Adelia—a black smudge on the tower's walkway. But it had disappeared now.

"She'd answer to a bishop, should've worn my episcopal robes," Rowley said. He was in hunting clothes. "Well, there's nothing for it. We can find our own way through—I remember it perfectly."

He set his horse down the hill to the valley, cloak flying. Less precipitately, the others followed.

The entrance in the labyrinth's wall when they reached it sent the men off again. Instead of an arch, two stone ellipses met at top and bottom, forming a ten-foot cleft resembling the female vulva, the inference being emphasized by the stone-carved surround in the shape of snakes coiling into various fruits and out again.

It was difficult to get the horses to enter, though the cleft was big enough; they had to be blindfolded to step through, showing, in Adelia's opinion, more decency than the remarks made by the men tugging at their reins.

Being inside wasn't nice. The way ahead of them was fairly wide, but blackthorn covered it, shutting out the sun to enfold them in the dim, gray light of a tunnel and the smell of dead leaves.

The roof was too low to allow them to remount. They would have to walk the horses through.

"Come on." Rowley was hurrying, leading his horse at a trot.

After a few bends, they could no longer hear birdsong. Then the way divided and they were presented with two tunnels, each as wide as the one by which they'd come, one going left, the other right.

"This way," said the bishop. "We turn northeast toward the tower. Just keep a sense of direction."

The first doubt entered Adelia's mind. They shouldn't have had to choose. "My lord, I'm not sure this is ..."

But he'd gone ahead.

Well, he'd been here before. Perhaps he did remember. Adelia followed more slowly, her dog pattering after her, Jacques behind him. She heard Walt bringing up the rear, grumbling. "Wormhold. Good name for this snaky bugger."

*Wyrm*hold. *Of course. Wyrm.* In marketplaces, the professional storytellers—that the English still called skalds—frightened their audience with tales of the great snake/dragon that squirmed its way through Saxon legends just as the mimicking tunnels coiled through this labyrinth.

Wistfully, Adelia remembered that Gyltha's Ulf loved those stories and played at being the Saxon warrior—what was his name?—who'd killed one such monster.

I miss Ulf. I miss Allie. I don't want to be in the Wyrm's lair.

Ulf had described it to her with relish. *"Horrible it was, deep in the earth and stunk with the blood of dead men."*

Well, they were spared that stench at least. But there was the smell of earth, and a sense of being underground, pressed in with no way out. *Which is what the Daedalus who concocted this swine intended*, she thought. It explained the blackthorn; without it, they could have climbed a wall, seen where they were heading, and breathed fresh air, but blackthorn had spines that, like the Wyrm, tore flesh to shreds.

It didn't frighten her—she knew how to get out—but she noticed that the men with her weren't laughing now.

The next bend turned south and opened into three more tunnels. Still unhesitating, Rowley took the alley to the right.

After the next bend, the way divided again. Adelia heard Rowley swear. She craned her neck to look past his horse for the cause.

It was a dead end. Rowley had his sword out and was stabbing it into a hedge that blocked the way. The scrape of metal on stone showed that there was a wall behind the foliage. "Goddamn the bastard. We'll have to back out." He raised his voice. "Back out, Walt."

The tunnel wasn't wide enough to turn the horses without scratching them on head and hindquarters, not only injuring them but also making them panic.

Adelia's mare didn't want to back out. It didn't want to go on, either. Sensibly, it wanted to stand still.

Rowley had to squeeze past his own horse to take hers by the bridle in both hands and push until he persuaded the animal to retreat back to the cul-de-sac's entrance, where they could re-form their line.

"I *told* you we should keep going northeast," he said to Adelia, as if she had chosen the route.

"Where *is* northeast?"

But, irritated, he'd set off again, and she had to try and drag her reluctant mare into a trot to keep him in sight.

Another tunnel. Another. They might have been wrapped in gray wool that was thickening around them. She'd lost all sense of direction now. So, she suspected, had Rowley.

In the next tunnel, she lost Rowley. She was at a division and couldn't see which branch he'd taken. She looked back at Jacques. "Where's he gone?" And, to the dog, "Where is he, Ward? Where's he gone?"

The messenger's face was grayish, and not just from the light straining through the roof; it looked older. "Are we going to get out, mistress?"

She said soothingly, "Of course we shall." She knew how he felt. The thorned roof rounded them in captivity. They were moles without the mole's means of rising to the surface.

Rowley's voice came, muffled. "Where in hell *are* you?" It was impossible to locate him; the tunnels absorbed and diverted sound.

"Where are *you*?"

"In the name of God, stay *still*, I'm coming back."

They kept shouting in order to guide him. He shouted in his turn, mostly oaths. He was swearing in the Arabic he'd learned on crusade—his choice language when he cursed. Sometimes his voice was so near it made them jump; then it would fade and become hollow, raving against labyrinths in general and this one in particular. Against Dame Dakers and her bloody serpent. Against Eve with *her* bloody serpent. Even, appallingly, after blackthorn tore his cloak, against Rosamund and her bloody mushrooms.

Ward cocked his ears this way and that, as if enjoying the tirade, which, his mistress thought, he probably was, being another male.

It's women to be blamed, always women. He wouldn't curse the man who built this horror, or the king who imprisoned Rosamund in the middle of it.

Then she thought, *They're frightened. Well, Walt may not be, but Rowley is. And Jacques definitely is.*

At last a tall shape loomed out of the shadow ahead, leading a horse and coming toward her. It yelled, "What are you standing there for, woman? Get back. We should have taken the last turning."

Again, it was her fault. Again, the mare wouldn't move until the bishop took its bridle and pushed.

So that he shouldn't be embarrassed in front of the other two men, Adelia lowered her voice. "Rowley, this isn't a labyrinth."

He didn't lower his. "No, it isn't. We're in the entrails of Grendel's bloody mother, that's what, goddamn her."

It came to her. *Beowulf.* That was the name. Beowulf, Ulf's favorite among all legendary Saxon warriors, killer of the Wyrm, slayer of the half-human monster Grendel and of Grendel's awful avenging mother.

"*Waste bitch, boundary walker,*" Ulf had said of Grendel's mother, meaning she prowled the edge between earth and hell in woman's shape.

Adelia began to get cross. Why was it women who were to blame for everything—*everything*, from the Fall of Man to these blasted hedges?

"We are not in a labyrinth, my lord," she said clearly.

"Where are we, then?"

"It's a maze."

"Same difference." Puffing at the horse: "Get *back*, you great cow."

"No, it isn't. A labyrinth has only one path and you merely have to follow it. It's a symbol of life or, rather, of life and death. Labyrinths twist and turn, but they have a beginning and an end, through darkness into light."

Softening, and hoping that he would, too, she added, "Like Ariadne's. Rather beautiful, really."

"I don't want mythology, mistress, beautiful or not, I want to get to that sodding tower. What's a maze when it's at home?"

"It's a trick. A trick to confuse. To *amaze*."

"And I suppose Mistress Clever-boots knows how to get us out?"

"I do, actually." God's rib, he was sneering at her, sneering. She'd a mind to stay where she was and let him sweat.

"Then in the name of Christ, *do* it."

"Stop bellowing at me," she yelled at him. "You're bellowing."

She saw his teeth grit in the pretense of a placatory smile; he always had good teeth. Still did. Between them, he said, "The Bishop of Saint Albans presents his compliments to Mistress Adelia and please to escort him out of this hag's hole, for the love of God. How will you do it?"

"My business." Be damned if she'd tell him.

Women were defenseless enough without revealing their secrets. "I'll have to take the lead."

They were forced to back the horses to one of the junctions where there was just enough room to turn each animal round without damage, though not enough to allow one to pass another, so Adelia ended up leading Walt's mount, Walt leading the messenger's behind her, Jacques behind him with hers, Rowley bringing up the rear with his own.

The maneuver was achieved with resentment. Even Jacques, her ally, said, "How are *you* going to get us out, then, mistress?"

"I just can." She paused. "Though it may take some time."

She stumped along in front, holding Walt's mount's reins in her right hand. In the other was her riding crop, which she trailed with apparent casualness so that it brushed against the hedge on her left.

As she went, she chuntered to herself. *Lord, how disregarded I am in this damned country. How disregarded all women are.*

She was back to the reasoning that had made her refuse to marry Rowley. At the time, he'd been expecting the king to offer him a barony, not a bishopric, thus allowing him a wife. Mad for him though she was, acceptance would have meant slipping her wrists into metaphorical golden fetters and watching him lock them on. As his wife, she could never have been herself, a *medica* of Salerno.

Adelia possessed none of the requisite feminine arts: She couldn't dance well, didn't play the lute, had never touched an embroidery frame—her sewing restricted to cobbling back together those cadavers she had dissected. In Salerno, she had been allowed to pursue skills that suited her, but in England there had been no room for them; the Church condemned any woman who did not toe its line—for her own safety, she had been forced to practice as a doctor in secret, letting a man take the credit.

As Baron Rowley's wife she would have been feted, complimented, bowed to, just as long as she denied her true being. And how long could she have done that? *I am who I am.*

Ironically, the lower down the social scale women were, the greater freedom they had; the wives of laborers and craftsmen could work alongside their men—even, sometimes, when they were widowed, take over their husband's trade. Until she'd become Adelia's friend and Allie's nurse, Gyltha had conducted a thriving business in eels and had called no man her master.

Adelia trudged on. *Hag's hole. Grendel's mother's entrails.* Why was this dreadful place feminine to the men lost in it? Because it was tunneled? Womblike? *Is this woman's magic? The great womb?*

Is that why the Church hates me, hates all women? Because we are the source of all true power? Of life?

She supposed that by leading them out of it, she was only confirming that a woman knew its secrets and they did not.

Great God, she thought, *it isn't a question of hatred. It's fear. They are frightened of us.*

And Adelia laughed quietly, sending a suggestion of sound reverberating backward along the tunnel, as if a small pebble was skipping on water, making each man start when it passed him.

"What in hell was that?"

Walt called back stolidly, "Reckon someone's laughing at us, master."

"Dear God."

Still grinning, Adelia glanced over her shoulder to find Walt looking at her. His gaze was amused, friendlier than it had been. It was directed at her riding crop, still dragging along the left-hand hedge. He winked.

He knows, she thought. She winked back.

Heartened by this new ally, she nevertheless quickened her pace because, when she'd turned, she'd had to squint to make out Walt's expression. His face was indistinct, as if seen through haze.

They were losing the light.

Surely it was still only afternoon outside, but the low winter sun was leaving this side of the labyrinth, whichever side it was, in shadow. She didn't want to imagine what it would be like in blackness.

It was frightful enough anyway. Following the left-hand hedge wherever it went took them into blind alleys time and again so that they became weary with the travail of reversing increasingly restless horses. Each time, she could hear Rowley stamping. "Does the woman know what in hell she's doing?"

She began to doubt it herself. There was one tormenting question: *Are the hedges continuous?* If there was a gap, if one part of this maze was separated from the rest, then they could wander until it suffocated them.

As the tunnels darkened, the shadows conglomerated into a disembodied face ahead of her, malignant, grinning, mouthing impossible things. *You won't get out. I've closed the clefts. You are sewn in. You won't see your baby again.*

The thought made her hands sweat so that the riding crop slipped out of her grasp and, in clutching for it, she bumped into the hedge and set off a small avalanche of frozen snow onto her head and face.

It refreshed her common sense. *Stop it, there's no such thing as magic.* She shut her eyes to the gargoyle and her ears to Rowley's curses—the nudge had set off a shower all along the line—and pressed on.

Walt said, as if passing the time of day, bless him, "'Tis marvelous to me how they do keep this thorn in trim. Two cuts a year, I reckon. Needs a powerful number of men to do that, mistress. Takes a king to pay them sort of wages."

She supposed it *was* marvelous in its way, and he was right, the maze would require a small army to look after it. "Not only cut it but sweep it," she said. For there were no clippings on the paths. "I wouldn't want my dog to get a thorn in his paw."

Walt considered the animal pattering along behind Adelia, with which he had now been confined at close quarters for some time. "Special breed, is he? Never come across his like afore." Nor, his sniff said, would he rush to do so again.

She shrugged. "I've got used to it. They're bred for the stink. Prior Geoffrey of Cambridge gave me this one's predecessor when I came to England so that I could be traced if I got lost. And then gave me another when the first one ... died."

Killed and mutilated when she'd tracked down the murderer of Cambridge children to a lair a thousand times more awful than this one. But the scent he'd left to be followed had saved her then, and both the prior and Rowley had ever since insisted that she be accompanied by just such another.

She and Walt continued to chat, their voices absorbing into the network of shrubbery enfolding them. Walt had stopped despising her; it appeared that he was on good terms with women. He had daughters, he told her, and a capable wife who managed their smallholding for him while he was away. "The which I be away a lot, now Bishop Rowley's come. Chose me out of all the cathedral grooms to travel with un, so he did."

"A good choice, too," Adelia told him, and meant it now.

"Reckon 'twas. Others ain't so partial to his lordship. Don't like as he's friend to King Henry, them being for poor Saint Thomas as was massacry-ed at Canterbury."

"I see," she said. She'd known it. Rowley, having been appointed by the king against their wishes, was facing hostility from the officers and servants of his own diocese.

Whether the blame heaped on Henry Plantagenet for the murder of Thomas à Becket on the steps of his own cathedral was justified, she had never been sure, even though, in his temper, the king had called for it while in another country. Had Henry, as he'd screamed for the archbishop's death, been aware that some of his knights, with their own reasons for wanting Becket dead, would gallop off to see it done?

Perhaps. Perhaps not.

But if it hadn't been for King Henry's intervention, the followers of Saint Thomas would have condemned her to the whipping post—and nearly had.

She was on Henry's side. The martyred archbishop had seen no difference between the entities of Church and of God. Both were infallible. The laws of both must be obeyed without question and without alteration as they always had been. Henry, for all his faults the more human man, had wanted changes that would benefit not the Church but his people. Becket had obstructed him at every turn, and was still obstructing him from the grave.

"Me and Oswald and Master Paton and young Jacques, we was all new to our jobs, see," Walt was saying. "We didn't have no grumble with Bishop Rowley, not like the old guard, as was cross with him for being a king's man. Master Paton and Jacques, they joined selfsame day as he was installed."

So with the great divide between king and martyr running through the diocese of Saint Albans, its new bishop had chosen servants as fresh to their roles as he was to his.

Good for you, Rowley. Judging by Walt and Jacques, you've done well.

The messenger, however, was proving less imperturbable than the groom. "Should we shout for help, my lord?" Adelia heard him ask Rowley.

For once, his bishop was gentle with him. "Not long now, my son. We're nearly out."

He couldn't know it, but, in fact, they were. Adelia had just seen proof that they were, though she was afraid the bishop would receive little satisfaction from it.

Walt grunted. He'd seen what she'd seen—ahead in the tunnel was a pile of rounded balls of manure.

"That un dropped that as we was coming in," Walt said quietly, nodding toward the horse Adelia was leading; it had been his own, the last in line when they entered the maze. The four of them would soon be out—but exactly where they had started.

"It was always an even chance." Adelia sighed. "Bugger."

The two men behind hadn't heard the exchange, nor, by the time the hooves of the front two horses had flattened them in passing, did just another lot of equine droppings have any significance for them.

Another bend in the tunnel. Light. An opening.

Dreading the outburst that must follow, Adelia and her horse stepped through the cleft leading out of the Wyrm's maze to be met by clean, scentless cold air and a setting sun illuminating the view of a great bell hanging from a trapezoid set in a hill they had descended more than two hours before.

One by one, the others emerged. There was silence.

"I'm sorry, I'm sorry," Adelia shouted into it. She faced Rowley. "Don't you see, if a maze is continuous, if there aren't any breaks, and *if* all the hedges are connected to each other and you follow one of them and stick rigidly to it wherever it goes, you'll traverse it eventually, you *must*, it's inevitable, only ..." Her voice diminished into a misery. "I chose the left-hand hedge. It was the wrong one."

More silence. In the dying light, crows flapped joyously over the elm tops, their calls mocking the earthbound idiots below.

"Forgive me," the Bishop of Saint Albans said politely. "Do I understand that if we'd followed the right-hand hedge, we could have eventually reached the destination we wanted in the first bloody place?"

"Yes."

"The right-hand hedge?" the bishop persisted.

"Well ... obviously, to go back it would be on the left-hand again ... *Are* you taking us back in?"

"Yes," the bishop said.

Lord, Lord, he's taking us back in. We'll be here all night. I wonder if Allie's all right.

They rang the great bell again, in case the figure they'd seen on the tower's walkway had relented, but, by the time they'd watered the horses at the trough, it was obvious that he or she had not.

Nobody spoke as loins were girded and a lantern lit. It was going to be very dark in there.

Rowley swept his cap off his head and knelt. "Be with us, Lord, for the sake of Thy dear Son."

Thus, the four reentered the maze. Knowing that it had an end made their minds easier, though the cost of constantly twisting and turning and backing out of the blind alleys was higher now that they were tiring.

"How'd you learn of mazes, mistress?" Walt wanted to know.

"My foster father. He's traveled extensively in the East, where he saw some, though not as big."

"Proper old Wyrm, this, i'n it? Reckon there's a way through as we'm not seeing."

Adelia agreed with him. To be girded to this extent from the outside world would be an intolerable inconvenience; there had to be a straighter route. She suspected that some of the blind ends that appeared to be stone and hedge walls were not lined by masonry at all; they were gates with blackthorn trained over them that could open and shut on a direct path.

No good to her and the others, though. Investigating each one to see if it were movable would take too long and would result only in having to make further choices of tunnels that ended in fixtures.

They were condemned to the long way through.

They made it in silence. Even Walt stopped talking.

Nighttime brought the maze to life. The long-dead trickster who had designed it still tried to frighten them, but they knew him now. Nevertheless, the place had its own means of instilling dread; lantern light lit a thick tube of laced branches as if the men and the woman in it were struggling through an interminable gray stocking infested by creatures that, unseen, rustled out their dry existence in its web.

By the time they emerged, it was too dark to see whether the cleft they stepped through was ornamented like the entrance. They'd lost interest, anyway; amusement had left them.

The tunnels had to some extent protected them from the bitter air that assailed them now. Apart from an owl that, disturbed by their coming, took off from a wall with a slow clap of wings, there was no sound from the tower that faced them across the bailey. It was more massive than it had appeared from a distance, rising sheer and high toward a sky where stars twinkled icily down on it like scattered diamonds.

Jacques produced another lantern and fresh candles from his saddlebag and led them toward a blacker shape in the shadows at the tower's base that indicated the steps to a door.

Nobody had crossed the bailey since the snow fell; nothing human, anyway—there were animal and bird prints aplenty. But the place was an obstacle course. Snowy bumps proved to be abandoned goods: a broken chair, pieces of cloth, a barrel with its staves crushed on one side, battered pans, a ladle. The snow covered a scene of chaos.

Walt, stumbling, revealed a bucket with a dead hen inside. The corpse of a dog, frozen in the act of snarling, lay at the end of its chain.

Rowley gave the bucket a kick that dislodged the hen's carcass. "The disloyal, thieving *bastards*."

Was that what this was?

It had been said that when William the Norman died, his servants immediately stripped their king's body and ran off with such of his possessions as they could carry, leaving his knights to find the great and terrible Conqueror's corpse naked on the floor of an empty palace room.

Had Rosamund's servants done the same the moment their mistress was dead? Rowley called it disloyalty, but Adelia remembered what she'd thought of Rosamund's neglect of Bertha; loyalty could come only of exchange and mutual regard.

The door to the tower, when the four reached it, was of thick, black oak at the top of a flight of wickedly glistening steps. There was no knocker. They hammered on it but neither dead nor living answered them. The sound echoed as if into an empty cave.

Keeping together—nobody suggested separating—they filed around the tower's base, through arched entrances to courtyards, to where another door proved as immovable as the first. It was, at least, on ground level.

"We'll ram the swine."

First, though, the horses had to be cared for. A path led to a deserted stable yard containing a well that responded with the sound of a splash when Walt dropped a stone down it, allaying his fear that its depths would prove frozen. The stalls had straw in them, if somewhat dirty, and their mangers had been replenished with oats not long before their former occupants had been stolen.

"Reckon as it'll do for now," Walt said grudgingly.

The others left him chipping ice from the well's windlass.

The pillagers had been arbitrary and hurried. An otherwise deserted byre held a cow that had resisted theft by being in the act of delivering its calf. Both were dead, the calf still in its birth sac.

Dodging under a washing line on which hung sheets as stiff as metal, they explored the kitchen buildings. The scullery had been stripped of its sink, the kitchen of everything except a massive table too heavy to lift.

Trying the barn, they found indentations in its earth floor to show where a plow and harrow had once stood. And ...

"What's this, my lord?"

Jacques was holding up his lantern to a large contraption in a corner by a woodpile.

It was metal. A flanged footplate formed the base of two upright struts attached to it by heavy springs. Both sets of struts ended in a row of triangular iron teeth, shaped to fit into the corresponding row of the other's.

The men paused.

Walt rejoined them, to stare. "Seen 'em as'll take your leg," he said slowly. "Never like this un, though."

"Neither have I," Rowley told him. "God be merciful, somebody's actually oiled it."

"What is it?" Adelia asked.

Without answering, Rowley went up to the contraption and grasped one set of its teeth. Walt took the other and, between them, they pulled the two sets of struts' rows apart until each lay flat on the ground opposite the other, teeth gaping upward. "All right, Walt. Careful now." Rowley bent and, keeping his body well away, extended an arm to fumble underneath the mechanism. "Works by a trigger," he said. Walt nodded.

"What *is* it?" Adelia asked again.

Rowley stood and picked up a log from the woodpile. He gestured for Adelia to keep her dog away. "Imagine it lying in long grass. Or under snow."

Almost flat, as the thing was now, it would be undetectable.

It's a mantrap. Oh, God help us.

She bent and grasped Ward's collar.

Rowley chucked the log onto the contraption's metal plate.

The thing leaped upward like a snapping shark. The teeth met. The clang seemed to come later.

After a moment, Walt said, "Get you round the whatsis, that would, begging your pardon, mistress. No point in gettin' you out, either."

"The lady didn't care for poachers, it seems," the bishop said. "Damned if I go wandering her woods." He dusted his hands. "Come on, now. This won't beat the Bulgars, as my old granddad used to say. We need a ram."

Adelia stayed where she was, staring at the mantrap. At two and a half feet high, the teeth would engage around the average man's groin, spiking him through. As Walt had said, releasing the victim would make no difference to an agonizing and prolonged death.

The thing was still vibrating, as if it were licking its chops.

The bishop had to come back for her.

"Somebody made it," she said. "Somebody oiled it. For use."

"I know. Come along, now."

"This is an awful place, Rowley."

"I know."

Jacques found a sawing horse in one of the outhouses. Holding it sideways by its legs and running with it, he and Walt managed to break down the tower's back door at the third attempt.

It was nearly as cold inside as out. And more silent.

They were in a round hall that, because of the tower's greater base, was larger than any room they were likely to find upstairs. Not a place for valued visitors to wait; it was more a guardroom. A couple of beautiful watchman's chairs, too heavy to be looted, were its saving grace. For the rest, hard benches and empty weapon racks made up the furniture. Cressets had been torn from the walls, a chandelier from its chain.

Some tapers clipped into their holders were strewn among the rushes of the floor. Lighting them from the lantern, Rowley, Adelia, and Walt took one each and began the ascent of the bare staircase running upward around the wall.

They found the tower to be one circular room placed on another, like a tube of apothecary's pills wrapped in stiff paper and set upright, the door to each reached by a curving flight and a tiny landing. The second they came to was as utilitarian as the first, its empty racks, some dropped strands of polishing horsetail, and the smell of beeswax suggesting an overlarge cleaning cupboard.

Above that, the maids' room: four wooden beds and little else. All the beds were stripped of palliasse and covering.

Each room was deserted. Each was marginally less uncomfortable than the one below. A sewing room—looted, for the most part, but the bench tables set under each arrow slit to catch the light carried torn strips of material and an errant pincushion. A plaster dummy had been smashed to the floor, and shards of it were seemingly kicked onto the landing.

"They hated her," said Adelia, peering in through the arched doorway.

"Who?"

"The servants."

"Hated who?" The bishop was beginning to puff.

"Rosamund," Adelia told him. "Or Dame Dakers."

"With these stairs? I don't blame 'em."

She grinned at his laboring back. "You've been eating too many episcopal dinners."

"As you say, mistress." He was unoffended. It was a rebuff; in the old days, he'd have been indignant.

I must remember, she thought. *We are no longer intimate; we keep our distance.*

The fourth room—or was it the fifth?—had not

been looted, though it was starker than any. A truckle bed, its gray, knitted bedspread rigidly tucked in. A deal table on which stood ewer and basin. A stool. A plain chest with a few bits of women's clothing, equally plain and neatly folded.

"Dakers's room," Adelia said. She was beginning to get the feel of the housekeeper, and was daunted by it.

"Nobody's here. Leave it."

But Adelia was interested. Here, the looters had desisted. Here, she was sure, Dragon Dakers had stood on the stairs, as frightening as Bertha described her, and stopped them from going farther.

Rosamund's escutcheon was carved into the eastern section of the west wall above Dakers's bed; it had been painted and gilded so that it dominated the gray room. Raising her candle to look at it, Adelia heard an intake of breath from Rowley in the doorway that wasn't due to exertion.

"God's teeth," he said, "that's madness."

A carved outer shield showed three leopards and the fleur-de-lis, which every man and woman in England now recognized as the arms of their Angevin Plantagenet king. Inside it was a smaller shield, checkered, with one quarter containing a serpent, the other a rose.

Even Adelia's scanty knowledge of heraldry was enough to know that she was looking at the escutcheon of a man and his wife.

The bishop, staring, joined her. "*Henry*. In the name of God, Henry, what were you *doing* to allow this? It's madness."

A motto had been carved into the wall beneath the escutcheon. Like most armorial mottos, it was a pun. *Rosa Mundi*.

Rose of all the world.

"Oh, dear," Adelia said.

"Jesus have mercy," Rowley breathed. "If the queen saw this ..."

Together, motto and escutcheon made the taunt of all taunts: *He prefers me to you. I am his wife in all but name, the true queen of his heart.*

The bishop's mind was leaping ahead. "Damnation. Whether Eleanor's seen it or not is irrelevant. It's enough for others to assume that she knows of it and had Rosamund killed because of it. It's a reason to kill. It's flaunting usurpation."

"It's a bit of stone with patterns on it put up by a silly woman," Adelia protested. "Does it matter so much?"

Apparently, it did—and would. Pride mattered to a queen. Her enemies knew it; so did the enemies of the king.

"*I'll* kill the bitch if she isn't dead already," said the man of God. "I'll burn the place down, and her in it. This is an invitation to war."

She was puzzled. "You've been here before, I'd expect you to have seen it already."

He shook his head. "We met in the garden; she was taking the air. We gave thanks to God for her recovery, and then Dakers led me back through the Wyrm. Where *is* Dakers?"

He pushed past Jacques and Walt, who stood blinking in the doorway, and attacked the stairs, shouting for the housekeeper. Doors slammed open as he looked into the next room, dismissed it, and raced upward to the next.

They hurried after him, the tower resounding with the crash of boots and the click of a dog's paws on stone.

Now they were climbing past Rosamund's apartments. Dakers, if it *was* Dakers, had been able to preserve them in all their glory. Adelia, trying to keep up, was vouchsafed glimpses of spring and autumn come together. Persian carpets, Venetian goblets, damask divans, gold-rich icons and triptychs, arras, statuary: the spoils of an empire laid at the feet of an emperor's mistress.

Here were glazed windows, not the arrow slits of the rooms below. They were shuttered, but the taper's light as Adelia passed reflected an image of itself in lattices of beautiful and expensive glass.

And through the open doors came perfume, subtle but strong enough to delight a nose deadened by cold and the foul pelt of a dog.

Adelia sniffed. Roses. He even captured roses for her.

Above her, another door was flung against its jamb. A sharp exclamation from the bishop.

"What is it, what is it?" She reached him on the last landing; there were no more stairs. Rowley was standing facing the open door, but the lit candle in his hand was down by his side, dripping wax onto the floor.

"What *is* it?"

"You were wrong," Rowley said.

The cold up here was extraordinary.

"Was I?"

"She's alive. Rosamund. Alive after all."

The relief would have been immeasurable if it hadn't been that he was so strange and there was no light in the room he was facing.

Also, he was making no effort to enter.

"She's sitting there," he said, and made the sign of the cross.

Adelia went in, the dog following her.

No perfume here, the cold obliterated scent. Each window—at least eight of them encircled the room—was open, its glazed lattice and accompanying shutter pushed outward to allow in air icy enough to kill. Adelia felt her face shrivel from it.

Ward went ahead. She could hear him sniffing round the room, giving no sign that he encountered anybody. She went in a little farther.

The glow of the taper fell on a bed against the northerly wall. Exquisite white lace swept from a gilded rondel in the ceiling to part over pillows and fall at either side of a gold-tasseled coverlet. It was a high and magnificent bed, with a tiny ivory set of steps placed so that its owner might be assisted to reach it.

Nobody was in it.

Its owner was sitting at a writing table opposite, facing a window, a pen in her hand.

Adelia, her taper now vibrating a little, saw the glancing facets of a jeweled crown and ash-blond hair curling from it down the writer's back.

Go nearer. You have to. It can't harm you. It can't.

She willed herself forward. As she passed the bed, she stepped on a fold of its lace lying on the floor, and the ice in it crunched under her boot.

"Lady Rosamund?" It seemed polite to say it, even knowing what she knew.

She took off her glove to touch the figure's unexpectedly large shoulder and felt the chill of stone in what had once been flesh. She saw a white, white hand, its wrist braceleted with skin, like a baby's. Thumb and forefinger were supporting a goose quill as if it had only seconds ago drawn the signature on the document on which they rested.

Sighing, Adelia bent to look into the face. Open, blue eyes were slightly cast downward so that they appeared to be rereading what the hand had just written.

But Fair Rosamund was very dead.

And very fat.

SIX

"*D*akers," Adelia said. "Dakers did this."

Only Dame Dakers could be refusing to let her dead mistress go to her grave.

Rowley was recovering. "We'll never get her in the coffin like that. For the love of God, *do* something. I'm not rowing back to Godstow with her sitting up and looking at me."

"Show some respect, blast you." Banging the last window closed, Adelia turned on him. "You won't be rowing, and she won't be sitting."

Both were compensating in their own way for the impact of a scene that had unmanned him and unnerved her.

Jacques was staring from the doorway, but Walt, having peered in, had retired downstairs in a hurry. Ward, unperturbed, was scratching himself.

Used to dead bodies as she was, Adelia had never feared one—until now. Consequently, she'd become angry. It was the corpse's *employment* ... Rosamund hadn't died in that position—if it were the mushrooms that had killed her, the end would have been too violent. No, Dakers had dragged the still-warm carcass onto the Roman chair, arranged it, and then either waited for rigor mortis to set in or, if rigor had already passed, held it in place until the cold coming through the open windows had fixed head, trunk, and limbs as they were now, frozen in the attitude of writing.

Adelia knew this as surely as if she'd seen it happen, but the impression that the dead woman had got up, walked to her table, sat down, and picked up a pen could not be shaken off.

Rowley's peevishness merely disguised the revulsion that had thrown him off balance, and Adelia, who felt the same, responded to it with irritation. "You didn't tell me she was fat."

"Is it relevant?"

No, it wasn't, of course it wasn't, but it was a sort of aftershock. The image Adelia had gained of Fair Rosamund by repute, from meeting Bertha, from tramping through the dreadful maze, from seeing the even more dreadful mantrap, had been of a beautiful woman with the indifference to human suffering of an Olympian goddess: physically lovely, pampered, aloof, cold as a reptile—but slim. Definitely slim.

Instead, the face she'd bent down to peer into had looked back at her with the innocent chubbiness integral to the obese.

It altered things. She wasn't sure why, but it did.

"How long has she been dead?" Rowley demanded.

"What?" Adelia's mind had wandered into inconsequential questioning of the corpse. *Why, with your weight, did you live at the top of this tower? How did you get down the stairs to meet Rowley in the garden? How did you get back up?*

"I *said*, how long has she been dead?"

"Oh." It was time to collect her wits and do the job she'd been brought here to do. "Impossible to be exact."

"Was it the mushrooms?"

"How can I tell? Probably yes."

"Can you flatten her?"

God's rib, he was a crude man. "She'll flatten herself," Adelia said, shortly, "just get some heat into this damned room." Then she asked, "Why did Dakers want her to be seen *writing*, do you suppose?"

But the bishop was on the landing, shouting to Walt to bring braziers, kindling, firewood, candles, pushing Jacques into descending and helping the groom, then going down himself on another search for the housekeeper, taking energy with him and leaving the chamber to the quiet of the dead.

Adelia's thoughts rested wistfully on the man whose calm assistance and reassurance had always been her rock during difficult investigations—for never was one likely to be more difficult than this. Mansur, however, was on the barge bringing Rosamund's coffin upriver and, even supposing he had arrived at the landing place that served Wormhold Tower a quarter of a mile away, he, Oswald, and the men with them had been told to stay there until the messenger fetched them.

Which could not be tonight. Nobody was going to face the maze of the Wyrm again tonight.

She had only one light; Rowley had taken his taper with him. She put hers on the writing table as near to the corpse's hand as possible without burning it—a minuscule start to the thawing out of the body that not only would take time but would be messy.

Adelia brought to mind the pigs on which she had studied decomposition at the farm in the hills above Salerno, kept for the purpose by Gordinus, her teacher of the process of mortification. From the various carcasses, her memory went to those frozen in the icehouse he'd had built deep into rock. She calculated weights, times; she envisaged needles of ice crystals solidifying muscle and tissue ... and the resultant juices as they melted.

Poor Rosamund. She would be exposed to the outrages of corruption when everything in her chamber spoke of a being who'd loved elegance.

Poor Dakers, who had, undoubtedly, loved her mistress to the point of madness.

Who had also put a crown on her mistress's head. A real crown, not a fashionable circlet, not a chaplet, not a coronal, but an ancient thing of thick gold with four prongs that rose in the shape of fleur-de-lis from a jeweled brim—the crown of a royal consort. This, Dakers was saying, is a queen.

Yet the same hand had brushed the lovely hair so that it hung untrammeled over the corpse's shoulders and down its back in the style of a virgin.

Oh, get to it, Adelia told herself. She was not here to be fascinated by the unplumbable depths of human obsession but to find out why someone had found it good that this woman should die and, thereby, who that someone was.

She wished there was some noise from down-stairs to ameliorate the deathly quiet of this room. Perhaps it was too high up for sound to reach it.

Adelia turned her attention to the writing table, an eerie business with the shuttered glass on the other side of it acting on it like the silvering of a looking glass, so that she and the corpse were reflected darkly.

A pretty table, highly polished. Near the dead woman's left hand, as if her fingers could dip into it easily, was a bowl of candied plums.

The bowl was a black-and-red pot figured with athletes like the one her foster father had found in Greece, so ancient and precious that he allowed no one to touch it but himself. Rosamund kept sweet-meats in hers.

A glass inkwell encased in gold filigree. A smart leather holder for quills, and a little ivory-and-steel knife to sharpen them. Two pages of the best vellum, both closely written, lying side by side, one under the right hand. A sand shaker, also glass, in gold filigree matching the inkwell, its sand nearly used up. A tiny burner for melting the wax that lay by it in two red sticks, one shorter than the other.

Adelia looked for a seal and found none, but there was a great gold ring on one of the dead fingers. She picked up the taper and held it close to the ring. Its round face was a matrix that when pressed into softened wax would embed the two letters RR.

Rosamund Regina?

Hmm.

It had mattered to Dakers that Rosamund be recognized as literate—no mean accomplishment in England, even among high-born women. Why else had she been petrified like this? Obviously, she *had* been literate. The table's implements showed heavy use; Rosamund had written a lot.

Was Dakers merely proud that you could write? *Or is there some other significance that I'm not seeing?*

Adelia turned her attention to the two pieces of vellum. She picked up the one directly in front of the corpse—and found it indecipherable in this light; Rosamund's literacy had not extended to good calligraphy— here was a cramped scrawl.

She wondered where Rowley was with more candles, blast him. It was taking the bishop a long time to return. For just a second, Adelia registered the fact, then found that by extending the parchment above her head with one hand, putting the taper dangerously close underneath it with the other, and squinting, it was just possible to make out a superscription. What she held was a letter.

"To the Lady Eleanor, Duchess of Aquitaine and supposed Queen of England, greetings from the true and very Queen of this country, Rosamund the Fair."

Adelia's jaw dropped. So, very nearly, did the letter. This wasn't lèse-majesté, it was outright, combative treason. It was a challenge.

It was *stupid*.

"Were you insane?" The whisper was absorbed by the room's silence.

Rosamund was sending a challenge to Eleanor's authority, and must have known it was one the queen would have to respond to or be forever humiliated.

"You were taking a risk," Adelia whispered. Wormhold Tower might be difficult to seize, but it wasn't impregnable; it couldn't withstand the sort of force that an infuriated queen would send against it.

The deadness of the corpse whispered back, *Ah, but instead did the queen send an old woman with poisoned mushrooms?*

None of the above, Adelia thought to herself, because Eleanor didn't receive the letter. Most likely, Rosamund had never intended to send it; isolated in this awful tower, she'd merely amused herself by scribbling fantasies of queenship onto vellum.

What else had she written?

Adelia replaced the letter on the table and picked up its companion document. In the dimness, she made out another superscription. Another letter, then. Again, it had to be held up so that the taper shone upward onto it. This one was easier to read.

"To the Lady Eleanor, Duchess of Aquitaine and supposed Queen of England, greetings from the true and very Queen of this country, Rosamund the Fair."

The wording was exactly the same. And it was more decipherable only because somebody else had written it. This hand was very different from Rosamund's scrawl; it was the legible, sloping calligraphy of a scholar.

Rosamund had copied her letter from this one.

Ward gave a low growl, but Adelia, caught up in the mystery, paid him no attention.

It's here. I am on the brink of it.

Waving the parchment gently, she thought it out, then saw in the mirror of the window that she was, in fact, tapping Rosamund's head with it.

And stopped, she and the corpse each as rigid as the other. Ward had tried to warn her that someone else had entered the tower room; she'd paid no notice.

Three faces were reflected in the glass, two of them surmounted by crowns. "I am delighted to make your acquaintance, my dear," one of them said—and it wasn't talking to Adelia.

Who, for a moment, stood where she was, staring straight ahead, trying to subdue shivering superstition, gathering all her common sense against belief in the wizardry of conjurement.

Then she turned and bowed. There was no mistaking a real queen.

Eleanor took no notice of her. She walked to one side of the table, bringing with her a scent that subsumed Rosamund's roses in something heavier and more Eastern. Two white, long-fingered hands were placed on the wood as she bent forward to look into the face of the dead woman. "Tut, tut. You *have* let yourself go." A beringed forefinger nudged the Greek pot. "Do I suspect too many sweeties and not enough sallets?"

Her voice belled charmingly across the chamber. "Did you know that poor Rosamund was fat, Lord Montignard? Why was I not told?"

"Cows usually are, lady." A man's voice, coming from a shape lounging in the doorway and holding a lantern. There was an indistinct, taller figure in mail standing behind him.

"So rude," said Eleanor, apologetically, to the body in the chair. "Men are unfair, are they not? And you must have had so many compensating qualities ... generosity with your favors, things like that."

The cruelty was not only verbal but also accentuated by the two women's physical disparity. Against the tall sweep of the queen's shape, that showed slender even in the fur wrapping it round, Rosamund appeared lumpen, her tumbling hair ridiculous for a mature woman. Compared to the delicate spikes on the white-gold crown Eleanor wore, Rosamund's was an overweight piece of grandiloquence.

The queen had come to the document. "My dear, another of your letters to me? And God froze you to ice in the middle of penning it?"

Adelia opened her mouth and then shut it; she and the men in the doorway were merely sounding boards in the game that Eleanor of Aquitaine was playing with a dead woman.

"I am sorry I was not here at the time," the queen was saying. "I had but landed from France when I received word of your illness, and there were other matters I had to see to rather than be at your deathbed." She appeared to sigh. "Always business before pleasure."

She picked up the letter and held it at arm's length, unable to read it in the light but not needing to. "Is this like the others? *Greetings to the supposed queen from the true one?* Somewhat repetitious, don't you think? Not worth keeping, yes?"

She crumpled the parchment and tossed it onto the floor, grinding it out on the stones with the twist of an excellent boot.

Slowly, slowly, Adelia bent slightly sideways and down. She slipped the document she'd been holding into the top of her right boot and felt her dog lick her hand as she did it. He was keeping close.

Facing the mirroring window, she looked to see if the man in the doorway had noticed the movement. He hadn't. His attention was on Eleanor; Eleanor's on Rosamund's corpse.

The queen was cupping her ear as if listening to a reply. "You don't mind? So generous, but they say you were always generous with your favors. Oh, and forgive me, this bauble is mine." Eleanor had lifted the crown off the dead woman's head. "It was made for the wives of the counts of Anjou two centuries ago, and *how dare he give it to a stinking great whore like you ...*"

Control had gone. With a scream, the queen sent the crown spinning away toward the window opposite them both as if she meant to smash the glass with it. Ward barked.

What saved Eleanor's life was that the crown hit the window with the padded underside of its brim. If the glass had shattered, Adelia—dazedly watching the mirroring window shake as the missile bounced off it—would not have seen the reflection of Death slithering toward them. Nor the knife in its hand.

She didn't have time to turn round. It was coming for Eleanor. Instinctively, Adelia flung herself sideways, and her left hand contacted Death's shoulder.

In trying to deflect the knife, she misjudged and had her right palm sliced open by it. But her shove changed the momentum of the attacker, who went tumbling to the floor.

The scene petrified: Rosamund sitting unconcernedly in her chair; Eleanor, just as still, facing the window in which the attack had been reflected; Adelia standing and looking down at the figure lying sprawled facedown at her feet. It was hissing.

The dog approached it, sniffing, and then backed away.

So for a second. Then Lord Montignard was exclaiming over the queen while the mailed man had his boot on the attacker's back and a sword raised in his two hands, looking at Eleanor for permission to strike.

"No." Adelia thought she'd shrieked it, but shock diminished the word so that it sounded quietly reasonable.

The man paid her no attention. Expressionless, he went on looking at the queen, who had a hand to her head. She seemed to collapse, but it was to kneel. The white hands were steepled, the crowned head bowed, and Eleanor of Aquitaine prayed. "Almighty God," she said, "accept the thanks of this unworthy queen for stretching out Your hand and reducing this, my enemy, to a block of ice. Even in death she did send her creature against me, but You turned the blade so that, innocent and wronged as I am, I live on to serve You, my Lord and Redeemer."

When Montignard helped her to her feet, she was amazingly calm. "I saw it," she said to Adelia. "I saw God choose you as his instrument to save me. Are you the housekeeper? They say this strumpet had a housekeeper."

"No. My name is Adelia. I am Adelia Aguilar. I assume that is the housekeeper. Her name is Dakers." Pointing to the figure on the floor, her hand dripped blood over it.

Queen Eleanor paid it no attention. "What do you do here, then, girl? How long have you lived here?"

"I don't. I'm a stranger to this place. We arrived an hour or so ago." A lifetime. "I've never been here before. I had only just come up the stairs and discovered ... this."

"Was this creature with you?" Eleanor dabbled her fingers in the direction of her still-supine attacker.

"No. I hadn't seen her, not until now. She must have hidden herself when she heard us come up the stairs."

Montignard came close to wave the tip of a dagger in her face. "You wretch, it is your queen you talk to. Show respect or I slit your nose." He was a willowy young man, very curly, very brave now.

"My lady," Adelia added dully.

"Stop it, Monty," the queen snapped, and turned to the man in mail. "Is the place secured, Schwyz?"

"Secure?" Still without expression, Schwyz managed to convey his opinion that the tower was about as secure as a slice of carrot. "We took four men in the barge and three downstairs." He didn't address the queen by her title, either, but Adelia noticed that Montignard didn't threaten to slit Schwyz's nose for it; the man stood square on thick legs, more like a foot soldier than a knight, and nobody was in any doubt that if Eleanor had given the nod, he'd have skewered the housekeeper like a flapping fish. And Montignard, for that matter.

A *mercenary*, Adelia decided.

"Did these three men downstairs bring you with them?" the queen asked.

"Yes." Dear Lord, she was tired. "My lady," she added.

"Why?"

"Because the Bishop of Saint Albans asked me to accompany him." Rowley could answer the questions; he was good at that.

"Rowley?" The queen's voice had altered. "*Rowley's* here?" She turned to Schwyz. "Why was I not told?"

"Four men in the boat and three downstairs," Schwyz repeated stolidly. His accent was London with a trace of something more foreign. "If a bishop is among them, I don't know it." He didn't care, either. "We stay the night here?"

"Until the Young King and the Abbot of Eynsham arrive."

Schwyz shrugged.

Eleanor cocked her head at Adelia. "And why has his lordship of Saint Albans brought one of his women to Wormhold Tower?"

"I can't say." At that moment, she didn't have the energy to recount the train of events, and certainly not to make them comprehensible. She was too tired, too shocked, too struck down by horrors even to refute the imputation of being "one of his women," though not to wonder how many he was known to have.

"We shall ask him," Eleanor said brightly. She looked down at the writhing shape on the floor. "Raise her."

The courtier Montignard pushed forward and made a fuss of kicking the would-be assassin's knife across the floor. Hauling her upright from under Schwyz's boot, he maintained her with one arm round the chest and put the point of his dagger to her neck with the other.

It *was* Death, a better facsimile than any in the marketplace mystery plays. The hood of a black cloak had wrinkled back to disclose the prominent cheekbones and teeth of a skull with pale skin so tight that the only indication, in this bad light, to show that the face had any at all was a large and sprouting mole on the upper lip. The eyes were set deep; they might have been holes. All it lacked was the scythe.

It was still hissing sporadically, the words mixed with spittle. "... dare to touch the true queen, you dissembler ... my Master, my most northerly Lord ... burn your soul ... cast you ... utmost obscenity."

Eleanor leaned forward, cupping her ear again, then stood back. "Demons? *Belial?*" She turned to her audience. "The woman threatens me with Belial. My dear, I married him."

"Only let me strangle her, lady. Let me cauterize this pus," Montignard said. A pearl of blood appeared from where the tip of the dagger pierced the woman's skin.

"Leave her alone." Adelia managed a shout now. "She's mad, and she's half dead already, leave her alone." Instinctively, she'd put her fingers round the woman's wrist, feeling a hideously slow pulse among bones almost as cold as Rosamund's. Dear God, how long had she been hiding in this ice chamber?

"She needs warmth," Adelia said to Eleanor. "We must warm her."

The queen looked at Adelia's dripping hand held out to her in appeal, then at the housekeeper. She shrugged. "We are informed the creature needs warming, Monty. I imagine that does not entail putting it into the fire. Take it downstairs, Schwyz, and see to it. Gently, now. We shall question it later."

Scowling, the courtier handed his captive over to Schwyz, who took her to the door, gave an order to one of his men, saw her taken away, and came back. "Madam, we should leave. I cannot defend this place."

"Not yet, Master Schwyz. Go about your duties."

Schwyz stumped off, not a happy man.

The queen smiled at Adelia. "You see? You ask

for the woman's life, I give it. Noblesse oblige. Such a gracious monarch am I."

She was impressive; Adelia gave her that. The prickling weakness of shock that threatened to collapse Adelia's legs left this woman seemingly untouched, as if attempted assassination was the everyday round of royalty. Perhaps it was.

Montignard hesitated. He nodded toward Adelia. "Leave you alone with this wench, lady? I shall not. Does she wish you harm? I do not know."

"My lord." Eleanor had a metaphorical whip in her boot. "Whoever she may be, she saved my life. Which"—the whip cracked—"*you* were too slow to do. Now go attend to that eyesore. Also, we could profit from some warmth ourselves. See to it. And bring me the Bishop of Saint Albans."

Self-preservation helped Adelia to mumble, "And some brandy. Send up brandy." She'd just properly seen the wound in her hand; it went deep and, goddamn all assassins, she needed her right hand.

The queen nodded her permission. She showed no sign of leaving the chamber and descending to another. While Adelia considered that perverse, not to say unhallowed, considering the poor body occupying it, she was grateful to be spared the stairs. Sidling out of the royal sight, she sank down onto the floor by the side of the bed and stayed there.

People came and went, things were done, the bed stripped and its covers and mattress sent downstairs to be burned—the queen was insistent about that.

A beautiful young woman, presumably one of Eleanor's attendants, came in, fluttered at the sight of Rosamund, fainted prettily, and had to be taken out again. Maids, manservants—how many had she brought with her?—carried in braziers, candles enough to light the Vatican, incense and oil burners, lamps, flambeaux. Adelia, who'd thought she'd never be warm again, began to think kindly and soporifically of the cold. She closed her eyes ...

"... in hell are you doing here? If he's coming, he'll come straight for this tower." It was Rowley's voice, very loud, very angry.

Adelia woke up. She was still on the floor by the bed. The chamber was hotter; there were more people in it. Rosamund's body, ignored, sat at its table, though some merciful soul had covered the head and shoulders with a cloak.

"You dare address my glorious lady like that? She goes where she pleases." This was Montignard.

"I'm talking to the queen, you bastard. Keep your snout out of ... *it*." He jerked the last word— somebody had punched him.

Peering under the bed, Adelia saw the bottom half of the queen and all of Rowley kneeling in front of her. His hands were tied. Mailed legs—she recognized one pair as Schwyz's—stood behind him and, to the side, Montignard's fine leather boots, one of them raised for another kick.

"Leave him, my lord," Eleanor said icily. "This is

the language I have come to expect from the Bishop of Saint Albans."

"It's called truth, lady," Rowley said. "When did you ever hear anything else from me?"

"Is it? Then the question is not what *I* do here, but what *you* do."

It'll come in a minute, Adelia thought. The appalling coincidence of this forgathering must seem sinister to a queen who'd just been attacked.

Cautiously, she began undoing the strings of the purse hanging from her belt and feeling for the small roll of velvet containing the surgical instruments she always carried when traveling.

"I told you. I came on your behalf." Rowley jerked his head in the direction of the writing table. "My lady, rumor is already blaming you for Rosamund's death ..."

"*Me?* Almighty God killed her."

"He had help. Let me find out whose—it's why I came, to find out ..."

"In the dark? This night of nights?" Montignard interrupting again. "You come and at the same time a demon rushes out of the wall to stab the queen?"

Here it was. Adelia's hand found the tiny, lethally sharp knife in the roll and loosened it so that its handle protruded. What to do with it she wasn't sure, but if they hurt him ...

"*What?* What demon?" Rowley asked.

Eleanor nodded. "The housekeeper, Dampers. Did you hire her to kill me, Saint Albans?"

"*Elean-oor.*" It was the protesting growl of one old friend to another; everybody else in the chamber was diminished by the claim of a hundred shared memories. It made the queen go back in her tracks.

"Well, well," she said, more gently, "I suppose you must be absolved, since it was your leman who pushed aside the blade."

Adelia's hand relaxed.

"My leman?"

"I forgot you have so many. The one with the foreign name and no manners."

"Ah," the bishop said. "*That* leman. Where is she?"

Using her one good hand, Adelia pulled herself up by the bed frame and stood where everybody could see her. She felt afraid and rather foolish.

Awkwardly, Rowley looked round. He had blood on his mouth.

Their eyes met.

"I rejoice that she served such a mighty purpose, madam," the Bishop of Saint Albans said slowly. He looked back at the queen. "Keep her if you will, she's of no use to me—as you say, she has no manners."

Eleanor shook her head at Adelia. "See how easily he discards you? All men are knaves, king or bishop."

Adelia began to panic. *He's abandoning me to her. He can't. There's Allie. I must get back to Godstow.*

Rowley was answering another question. "Yes, I have. Twice. The first time I came was when she was taken ill—Wormhold is part of my diocese; it was my duty. And tonight when I heard of her death. That's not the point ..." Being bound and on his knees wasn't going to stop the bishop from lecturing the queen. "In the name of God, Eleanor, why didn't you make for Aquitaine? It's madness for you to be here. Get away. I beg you."

"*'That's not the point'*?" Eleanor had heard only what was important to her. Her cloak swished across the floor as she retrieved Rosamund's letter from it. "This is the point. This, *this*. I have received ten such." She smoothed the letter out and held it out. "You and the whore were in league with Henry to set her up as queen."

There was a moment's quiet as Rowley read.

"God strike me, I knew nothing of it," he said— and Adelia thought that even Eleanor must hear that he was appalled. "Nor does the king, I swear. The woman was insane."

"*Evil.* She was *evil.* She shall burn in this world as in the next—her and all that is hers. The brush- wood is being put in place, ready for the flame. A fitting end for a harlot. No Christian burial for her."

"Jesus." Adelia saw Rowley blanch and then gather himself. Suddenly, the tone of his voice changed to one that was wrenchingly familiar; it had got her into his bed. "Eleanor," he said gently, "you are the greatest of queens, you brought beauty and courtesy and music and refinement to a realm of savages, you civilized us."

"Did I?" Very soft, all at once girlish.

"You know you did. Who taught us chivalry toward women? Who in hell taught me to say please?" He followed up the advantage of her laugh. "Do not, I beg you, commit an act of vandalism that will resound against you. No need to burn this tower; let it stand in its filth. Retire to Aquitaine, just for a while, give me time to find out who actually killed Rosamund so that I can treat with the king. For the sake of Christ crucified, lady, until then *don't antagonize him*."

It was the wrong note.

"Antagonize him?" Eleanor said sweetly. "He had me imprisoned at Chinon, Bishop. Nor did I hear your voice amongst those raised against it."

She signaled to the men behind Rowley, and they began dragging him out.

As they reached the doorway, she said clearly, "You are Henry Plantagenet's man, Saint Albans. Always were, always will be."

"And yours, lady," he shouted back, "And God's."

They heard him swearing at his captors bumping him down the stairs. The sound became fainter. There was a silence like the dust-settling quiet that comes after a building has crashed to the ground.

Schwyz had stayed behind. "The *schweinhund* is right that we should leave, lady."

The queen ignored him; she was circling, agitated, muttering to herself. Shrugging resignation, Schwyz went away.

"He'd never hurt you, lady," Adelia said. "Don't hurt him."

"Don't love him," the queen snapped back.

I don't, I won't. *Just don't hurt him*.

"Let me take out his eyes, my queen." Montignard was breathing hard. "He would assassinate you with that demon."

"Of course he wouldn't," Eleanor said—and

Adelia let out a breath of relief. "Rowley told the truth. That woman, Dampers ... I had inquiries made, and it is well known she was mad for her mistress, *ugh*. Even now, she would kill me ten times over."

"Really?" Montignard was intrigued. "They were Sapphos?"

The queen continued to circle. "Am I a killer of whores, Monty? What can they accuse me of next?"

The courtier bent and picked up the hem of her cloak to kiss it. "You are the blessed Angel of Peace come to Bethlehem again."

It made her smile. "Well, well, we can do nothing more until the Young King and the abbot arrive." From downstairs came the sound of furniture being overturned and the slamming of shutters. "What is Schwyz *doing* down there?"

"He puts archers at each window ready to defend. He is afraid the king will come."

The queen shook her head indulgently, as if at overenthusiastic children. "Even Henry can't travel fast in this weather. God kept the snow off for me, now he sends it to impede the king. Well then, I shall stay here in this chamber until my son comes." She looked toward Adelia. "You too, yes?"

"Madam, with your permission I shall join the—"

"No, no. God has sent you to me as a talisman." Eleanor smiled quite beautifully. "You will stay here with me and"—she walked over to the body and snatched off its covering cloak—"together we shall watch Fair Rosamund rot."

So they did.

What Adelia remembered of that night afterward were the hour-long silences when she and the queen were alone—apart from Montignard, who fell asleep—and during which Eleanor of Aquitaine sat, untiring, her back straight as a plumb line, eyes directed at the body of the woman her husband had loved.

She also remembered, though with disbelief, that at one point a young courtier with a lute came in and strolled about the chamber, singing winsomely in the langue d'oc, and that, after receiving no response from his queen and even less from the corpse, he wandered out again.

And the heat. Adelia remembered the heat of the braziers and a hundred candle flames. At one point, she begged for relief. "May we not open a window for a minute, madam?" It was like being in a pottery kiln.

"No."

So Adelia, the lucky charm, privileged by her status as God-sent savior to royalty, sat in its presence, crouching on the floor with her cloak under her while the queen, still in her furs, sat and watched a corpse.

Eleanor's eyes left it only when they brought the brandy, and Adelia, instead of drinking the spirit, tipped it over the cut in her hand and took a needle and silk thread from the traveling pack of instruments in her pocket.

"Who taught you to cleanse with brandy?" Eleanor wanted to know. "I use twice-distilled Bordeaux myself ... Oh, here, I shall do it."

Tutting at Adelia's attempt to stitch the wound together with her left hand, she took the needle and thread and did it instead, putting in seven ligatures where Adelia herself would have used only five, thus making a neater, if more painful, job of it. "We who went on Crusade had to learn to treat the wounded, there were so many," she said briskly.

Most of them caused by the ineptitude of the King of France, its leader, according to Rowley, after his own, much later, time in the Holy Land.

Not that the Church had condemned Louis for it, preferring instead to dwell on the scandal Eleanor, then his queen, had caused by insisting on going with him and taking with her a train of similarly adventurous females.

"Born to trouble as the sparks fly upwards, that lady," Rowley had said of her, not without admiration. "Her and her Amazons. And an affair with Uncle Raymond of Toulouse when she arrived in Antioch. What a woman."

Something of that daring remained; her very presence here showed as much, but time, thought Adelia, had twisted it into desperation.

"Is that ... *urgh*." Adelia wished to be brave, but the queen was plying the needle with more skill than gentleness. "Was that where you learned ... how to thread a maze? In the ... *oofff* ... East?" For there was no sign that Eleanor had spent as much time blundering around Wormhold's hedges as she and the others had.

"My lady," insisted the queen.

"My lady."

"It was, yes. The Saracen is skilled in such devices, as in so much else. I have no doubt your bishop also learned the trick of it from the East. Rowley went there on my orders ... a long time ago." Her voice had softened. "He took the sword of my dead little son to Jerusalem and laid it on Christ's own altar."

Adelia was comforted; the bond between Eleanor and Rowley made by that vicarious crusade went deep. It might be stretched to its limit in present circumstances, but it still held. The queen had taken him prisoner; she wouldn't allow him to be killed.

She's a mother, Adelia thought. *She'll let me go back to my baby.* There would be an opportunity to ask for that when she and the queen were better acquainted. In the meantime, she still had to learn all she could about Rosamund's murder. *Eleanor hadn't ordered it. Who had?*

Taper light had been kinder to the queen than the blazing illumination around them now. Elegance was there and always would be, so was the lovely, pale skin that went with auburn hair, now hidden, but wrinkles were puckering at her mouth and the tight, gauze wimple around her face did not quite hide the beginning of sagging flesh under the chin. Slender, yes, fine bones, yes. Yet there was another sag above the point where a jeweled belt encircled her hips.

No wonder, either. Two daughters by her first husband, Louis of France, and, since their divorce, eight more children from her marriage to Henry Plantagenet, five of them sons.

Ten babies. Adelia thought of what carrying Allie had done to her own waistline. *She's a marvel to look as she does.*

There wouldn't be any more, though; even if king and queen had not been estranged, Eleanor must now be, what, fifty years old?

And Henry probably not yet forty.

"There," the queen said, and bit through the needle end of the silk now holding Adelia's palm together. Producing an effusion of lace that served her as a handkerchief, she bound it efficiently round Adelia's hand and tied it with a last, painful tug.

"I am grateful, my lady," Adelia said in earnest.

But Eleanor had returned to her watch, her eyes on the corpse.

Why? Adelia wondered. *Why this profane vigil? It's beneath you.*

The woman had escaped from a castle in the Loire Valley, had traveled through her husband's hostile territory gathering followers and soldiers as she went, had crossed the Channel and slipped into southern England. All this to get to an isolated tower in Oxfordshire. And in winter. True, most of the journey had obviously been made before the roads became as impassable as they now were—to arrive at the tower, she must have been camped not far away. Nevertheless, it was a titanic journey that had tired out everybody but Eleanor herself. *For what? To gloat over her rival?*

But, Adelia thought, *the enemy is vanquished, petrified into a winter version of Sodom and Gomorrah's block of salt.*

An assassination has been thwarted by me and an Eleanor-preserving God. Rosamund turns out to have been fat. All this is sufficient, surely, to satisfy any lust for revenge.

But not the queen's, obviously; she must sit here and enjoy the vanquished one's decomposition. *Why?*

It wasn't because she'd envied the younger mistress the ability to still bear children. Rosamund hadn't had any.

Nor was it as if Rosamund had been the only royal paramour. Henry swived more women than most men had hot dinners. "Literally, a father to his people," Rowley had said of him once, with pride.

It was what kings did, almost an obligation, a duty—in Henry's case, a pleasure—to his realm's fertility.

To make the damn crops grow, Adelia thought sourly.

Yet Eleanor's own ducal ancestors themselves had encouraged the growth of acres of Aquitanian crops in their time; she'd been brought up not to expect marital fidelity. Indeed, when she'd had it, wedded to the praying, monkish King Louis, she'd been so bored she'd petitioned for divorce.

And hadn't she obliged Henry by taking one of his bastards into her household and rearing him? Young Geoffrey, born of a London prostitute, was proving devoted and useful to his father; Rowley had a greater regard for him than for any of the king's four remaining legitimate sons.

Rosamund, only Rosamund, had inspired a hatred that raised the heat of this awful room, as if Eleanor's body was pumping it across the chamber so that the flesh of the woman opposite would putrefy quicker.

Was it that Rosamund had lasted longer than the others, that the king had shown her more favor, a deeper love?

No, Adelia said to herself. *It was the letters.* Menopausal as Eleanor was, she'd believed their message: Another woman was being groomed to take her place; in both love and status, she was being overthrown.

If it *had* been Eleanor who'd poisoned Rosamund, it was tit for tat. In her own way, Rosamund had poisoned Eleanor.

Yet Rowley had been right: This queen hadn't murdered anybody.

There was no proof of it, of course. Nothing that would absolve her. The killing had been plotted at long range; people would say she had ordered it while she was still in France. There was nothing to scotch the rumor—apart from Eleanor's own word.

But it wasn't her style. Rowley had said so, and Adelia now agreed with him. If Eleanor had engineered it, she would have wanted to be present when it happened. This curiously naïve, horrible overseeing of her rival's disintegration was to compensate her for not having been there to enjoy the last throes.

But damn it, I don't have to witness it with you. All at once, Adelia was overwhelmed by the obscenity of the situation. She was tired, and her hand stung like fire; she wanted her child. Allie would be missing her.

She stood up. "Lady, it is not healthy for you to be here. Let us go downstairs."

The queen looked past her.

"Then I will," Adelia said.

She walked to the door, skirting Montignard, who was snoring on the floor. Two spears clashed as they crossed, blocking the doorway in front of her; the first man-at-arms had been reinforced by another.

"Let me by," she said.

"You want to piss, use a pot," one of the men said, grinning.

Adelia returned to Eleanor. "I am not your subject, lady. My king is William of Sicily."

The queen's eyes remained on Rosamund.

Adelia gritted her teeth, fighting desperation. *This is not the way. If I'm to see Allie again, I must be calm, make this woman trust me.*

After a while, followed by her dog, Adelia began circling the chamber, not looking for a way out—there was none—but using this trapped time to find out where Dakers had hidden herself.

It couldn't have been under the bed or Ward would have sniffed her out; he didn't have the finest nose in the world, it being somewhat overwhelmed by his own scent, but he wouldn't have missed that.

Apart from the bed, the room contained a prie-dieu, smaller than the one in the bishop's room at Saint Albans but as richly carved. Three enormous chests were stuffed with clothes.

A small table held a tray that had been brought in for the queen's supper: a chicken, veal pie, a cheese, a loaf—somewhat mildewed—dried figs, a jug of ale, and a stoppered bottle of wine. Eleanor hadn't touched it. Adelia, who'd last eaten at the nunnery, sliced heavily into the chicken and gave some to Ward. She drank the ale to satisfy her thirst and took a glass of wine with her to sip as she explored.

An aumbry contained pretty bottles and phials with labels: *Rose oyl. Swete violet. Rasberrie vinigar for to whiten teeth. Oyle of walnut to smooth the hands.* Nearly all were similarly cosmetic, though Adelia noted that Rosamund had suffered from breathing problems—*I'm not surprised, with your weight*—and had taken elecampane for it.

The bed took up more of the center of the room than was necessary by standing a foot or so out from the wall. Behind it was a tapestry depicting the Garden of Eden—obviously a favorite subject, because there was another, a better one, on the same theme on the easterly wall between two of the windows.

Going closer, so that she stood between the bed and the hanging, Adelia felt a blessed coolness.

The tapestry was old and heavy; the considerable draft emerging from underneath it did not cause it to shift. Where in the one on the other wall Adam and Eve sported in joyful movement, here cruder needlework stood them opposite each other amid unlikely trees, as frozen as poor Rosamund herself. The only depiction of liveliness was in the coiling green toils of the serpent—and even that was moth-eaten.

Adelia went closer; the chill increased.

There was a small gap in the canvas where the snake's eye should have been—and it wasn't the moth that had caused it. It had been deliberately made; there was buttonhole stitching round its edges.

A spy hole.

She had to exert some strength to push the hanging aside. Icy air came rushing out at her, and a stale smell. What she saw was a tiny room, corbeled into the tower's wall. Rosamund hadn't had to use chamber pots; hers was the luxury of a garderobe. Set into a curved bench of polished wood was a bottom-shaped, velvet-lined hole over a drop to the ground some hundred feet below. Soap in the shape of a rose lay in a holder next to a little golden ewer. A bowl within hand's reach contained substantial wipes of lamb's wool.

Good for Rosamund. Adelia approved of garderobes, as long as the pit beneath them was dug out regularly; they saved maidservants having to go up and down stairs carrying, and often slopping, noisome containers.

She was not so enamored of the mural painted on the plastered walls; its eroticism being more suited to a bordello than to a privy, but perhaps Rosamund had enjoyed looking at it while she sat there, and undoubtedly Henry Plantagenet would have. Although, come to think of it, had even he been aware of the existence of the garderobe and its spy hole?

Adelia moved behind the tapestry so that she could apply her eye to the hole—and found that she could see right down the bed to the writing desk and the window beyond.

Here, then, was where Dakers had concealed herself and—unpleasant thought—had watched her, Adelia, at her investigations. What patience and what stamina to endure the cold; only fury inspired at seeing Eleanor snatch the crown off her mistress's head had impelled her out of it.

But the careful stitching around the peephole indicated that tonight wasn't the only time somebody had employed their time looking through it.

It would have been invited guests who'd ventured up to this floor—it was an English custom for the higher classes to entertain in their bedrooms. If Dakers had spied on them, she would have to have taken up position in the garderobe— with Rosamund's permission and knowledge.

To watch the guests? The king? The bed and its activities?

Speculation opened an avenue that Adelia did not want to explore, still less the relationship between mistress and housekeeper.

To hell with the queen's permission; she needed to breathe clean air. She slid herself out from under the hanging. Eleanor appeared not to have noticed. Adelia went to the nearest window, lifted the lattices' catch, pulled it inward, and pushed the shutters open. Kicking a footstool into position, she stood on it and leaned out.

The bitter night sky crackled with stars. Peering downward to the ground, she saw scattered watch fires with armed men moving around them.

Oh, God, if they're putting brushwood around the tower's base ... if a breeze comes up and blows a spark from one of the fires ...

She and Eleanor were at the top of a chimney.

That was enough fresh air. Shivering, not merely from the cold, Adelia closed the shutters. In doing so, she put too much weight on one side of the footstool and returned to the floor in a noisy scramble.

Glancing at the queen, expecting a rebuke, she wondered if Eleanor was in a trance; the queen's eyes had not shifted from Rosamund. From his position on the floor, Montignard kicked out, muttered, and then continued to snore.

Adelia bent down to replace the footstool and saw that its marquetry top had come adrift, revealing that it was, in fact, the lid of a box on legs. There were documents inside. She scooped them out and returned to her former place on the floor at the other side of the bed to read them.

Letters again, half a dozen or more, all of them addressed to Eleanor, all purporting to have been written by Rosamund, yet in the same hand as the one Adelia had put into her boot.

Each had the same jeering superscription and, in this light, she was able to read what followed; it was not always the same in every letter, but the inherent message was repeated over and over.

"Today did my lord king sport with me and tell me of his adoration ..." "My lord king has this moment left my bed ..." "He speaks of his divorce from you with longing ..." "... the Pope will look kindly on divorce on the grounds of your treachery to my

lord king in that you do inflame his sons against him." "... the arrangements for my coronation at Winchester and Rouen." "... my lord king will announce to the English who is their true queen."

Poison in ink, drip, drip.

And the writer had penned them for Rosa-mund to duplicate in her own hand. He or she— more likely he—had even attached notes for her instruction.

"Be more legible, for the queen did scoff at your lettering and call you ignoramus."

"Write quickly that this may reach the queen on her anniversary as she does set much store by that date and will be the more affected."

"Hurry, for my messenger must come to Chinon, where the queen is kept, before the king moves her elsewhere."

And most telling of all: "We win, lady. You shall be queen before summer comes again."

At no point did the instructor name himself. But, thought Adelia, he was someone who'd been near enough to Eleanor to know that she had ridiculed Rosamund's writing.

And a fool. If his hope was to engineer a divorce between Henry and Eleanor and set Rosamund up as queen, he was lacking the most fundamental political sense. Henry would never divorce Eleanor. For one thing, even if wifely treason was grounds for divorce—and Adelia didn't think it was—Henry had caused too much offense to the Church over the death of Becket and had suffered for it; he dare not offend again. For another, he had a regard for the order of things. Even more important to him was the fact that by losing Eleanor, he would lose her great Duchy of Aquitaine, and Henry, though a beast, was a beast that never gave up land.

In any case, the easygoing English might wink at their king's mistress, but not a mistress imposed on them as queen; it would be an insult.

I know that, and I'm a foreigner.

And yet these letters had been good enough to inspire a stupid, ambitious woman to copy and send them, good enough to inflame a queen into escaping and urging war by her sons against their father.

Rowley could be right; the person who had written these things had done so to create war.

There was a loud sniff from the other side of the room. Eleanor spoke in triumph. "She is going. She has begun to stink."

That was quicker than expected. Surprised, Adelia looked up to where Rosamund was still stiffly inclined over her work.

She looked round further and saw that, in search of comfort, Ward had settled himself on the trailing end of the queen's ermine cloak. "I'm afraid that's merely my dog," she said.

"*Merely?* Get him off. What does he do here?"

One of the men-at-arms who'd been nodding in the doorway roused himself and came in to deposit Ward on the landing outside, then, at a nod from his queen, returned to his post.

Eleanor shifted; she'd become restive. "Saint Eulalie grant me patience. How long will this take?" The vigil was becoming tiresome.

Adelia nearly said, "A while yet," and then didn't. Until she knew more about the situation, she had better stay in the role of a woman whom the queen accepted as a somewhat soiled part of Rowley's baggage train but who'd nevertheless been chosen by God to save the royal life and was being kept close to the royal side as a reward.

But you should know more about me, Adelia thought, irritated. *I am dying with curiosity; so should you be. You should know more about everything: how Rosamund died, why she wrote the letters, who dictated them ... you should have had the room searched and found these exemplars before I did. It's not enough to be a queen; you should ask questions. Your husband does.*

Henry Plantagenet was a ferret and an employer of ferrets. He'd nosed out Adelia's profession in a second and penned her up in England, like one of the rarer animals in his menagerie, until he found a use for her. He knew exactly how things stood between her and his bishop; he'd known when their baby was born—and its sex, which was more than the child's father had known. A few days afterward, to prove that he knew, a royal messenger in plain clothes had delivered a gloriously lacy christening gown to Adelia's fenland door with a note: "Call her what you will, she shall always be Rowley-Powley to me."

Compared to the king, Eleanor walked within a circle of vision encompassing only her personal welfare and the certainty that God was most closely concerned with it. The questions she'd asked in this chamber had related solely to herself.

Adelia wondered whether she should enlighten her. Rowley and the queen must have corresponded in the past; she would know his writing. Showing her these documents would at least prove that he hadn't written them for Rosamund to copy. She might even recognize the penmanship and know who had.

Wait, though. There were two crimes here.

If Mansur or her foster father had been watching Adelia at that moment, they would have seen her adopt what they called her "dissecting face," the mouth tightened into a line, eyes furious with concentration, as they always were when her knife followed the link of muscle to sinew, pursued a vein, probed, and cut effect in order to find cause.

What made her a brilliant anatomist, Dr. Gershom had once told her, was instinct. She'd been offended. "Logic and training, Father." He'd smiled. "Man provided logic and training, maybe, but the Lord gave you instinct, and you should bless him for it."

Two crimes.

One, Rosamund had copied inflammatory letters. Two, Rosamund had been murdered.

Discovering whom it was who had urged Rosamund to write her letters was one thing. Discovering her murderer was another. And both solutions were contradictory, as far as Eleanor of Aquitaine and the Bishop of Saint Albans were concerned.

For the queen, the letter writer would be the villain and must be eliminated. Eleanor didn't give a damn who'd killed Rosamund—would, if she learned who it was, probably reward him.

But for Rowley, the murderer was endangering the peace of the kingdom and must be eliminated. And his claim was the greater, because murder was the more terrible crime.

It would be better, at this stage, to give Rowley open ground for *his* investigation rather than complicating it by allowing the queen to pursue *hers*.

Hmm.

Adelia gathered up the documents on her lap, put them back in the footstool box, and replaced its lid. She would do nothing about them until she could consult Rowley.

Eleanor continued to fidget. "Has this benighted tower no place of easement?"

Adelia ushered her toward the garderobe.

"Light." The queen held out her hand for a candle, and Adelia put one into it—reluctantly. She would see the naughty paintings.

If Adelia could have been any sorrier for the woman, it was then. When you came down to it, Eleanor was consumed by sexual jealousy as raging as that of any fishwife catching her husband in flagrante, and was being stabbed by reminders of it at every turn.

Adelia tensed herself for a storm, but when the queen emerged from under the hanging she looked tired and old, and was silent.

"You should rest, madam," Adelia said, concerned. "Let us go down ..."

There was noise from the stairs, and the two guards in the doorway uncrossed their spears and stood at attention.

A great hill of a man entered, sparkling with energy and frost and dwarfing Schwyz, who followed him in. He was enormous; kneeling to kiss the queen's hand only put his head on a level with hers.

"If I'd been here, my dear, 'twouldn't have happened," he said, still kneeling. He pressed Eleanor's hand to his neck with both of his, closing his eyes and rocking with the comfort of it.

"I know." She smiled fondly at him. "My dear, dear abbot. You'd have put your big body in the way of the knife, wouldn't you?"

"And gone rejoicing to Paradise." He sighed and stood up, looking down at her. "You going to burn 'em both?"

The queen shook her head. "I have been persuaded that Dampers is mad. We will not execute the insane."

"Who? Oh, Dakers. She's mad, sure enough, I told you she was. Let the flame have her, I say. And her bloody mistress with her. Where is the whore?"

He strode across the room to the table and poked the corpse's shoulder. "Like they said, cold as a witch's tit. Bit of fire'd warm them both up, get 'em ready for hell." He turned to wag his finger at Eleanor. "I'm a simple Gloucestershire man, as you know, and, Sweet Mary save me, a sinner, too, but I love my God, and I love my queen with all my soul, and I'm for putting their enemies to the torch." He spat on Rosamund's hair. "That's the Abbot of Eynsham's opinion of *you*, madam."

The visitor had caused Montignard to stand up. He was busily and jealously—and uselessly—trying to gain the queen's attention by urging her to eat. Eynsham, a man built more for tossing bales of hay than for shepherding monastic sheep, dominated the room, taking the breath out of it with the power of his body and voice, filling it with West Country earthiness and accent.

Bucolic he might have been, but everything he wore was of expensive and exquisite clerical taste, though the pectoral cross that had swung from his neck as he bent to the queen was overdone—a chunk of dull gold that could have battered a door in.

He'd taken years off Eleanor; she was loving it. Apart from the egregious Montignard, her courtiers had been too weary from traveling to make much fuss over her escape from death.

Or my part in it, Adelia thought, suddenly sour. Her hand was hurting.

"Bad news, though, my glory," the abbot said.

Eleanor's face changed. "It's Young Henry. Where is he?"

"Oh, he's right enough. But the chase was snappin' at our heels all the way from Chinon, so the Young King, well, he decides to make for Paris 'stead of yere."

Suddenly blind, the queen fumbled for the arm of her chair and sank into it.

"Now, now, it's not as bad as that," the abbot said,

his voice deep, "but you know your lad, he never did take to England—said the wine was piss."

"What are we to do? What are we to do?" Eleanor's eyes were wide and pleading. "The cause is lost. Almighty God, what are we to do now?"

"There, there." The abbot knelt beside her, taking her hands in his. "Nothing's lost. And Schwyz here, we've been speaking together, and he reckons it's all to the good. Don't ee, Schwyz?"

At his urging, Schwyz nodded.

"See? And Schwyz do know what he's about. Not much to look at, I grant, but a fine tactician. For here's the good news." Eleanor's hands were lifted and hammered against her knees. "You hear me, my glory? Listen to me. Hear what our commander Jesus have done for us—He've brought the King of France onto our side. Joined un to Young Henry, yes he has."

Eleanor's head came up. "*He has?* Oh, at last. God be praised."

"King Louis as ever is. He'll bring his army into the field to fight alongside the son against the father."

"God be praised," Eleanor said again. "*Now* we have an army."

The abbot nodded his great head as if watching a child open a present. "A saintly king. Weedy husband he was to you, I'll grant, but we ain't marrying him, and God'll look kindly on his valor now." He hammered Eleanor's knees again. "D'you see, woman? Young Henry and Louis'll raise their banner in France, we'll raise ours here in England,

and together we'll squeeze Old Henry into submission. Light will prevail against Dark. Twixt us, we'll net the old eagle and bring un down."

He was forcing life into Eleanor; her color had come back. "Yes," she said, "yes. A pronged attack. But have we the men? Here in England, I mean? Schwyz has so few with him."

"Wolvercote, my beauty. Lord Wolvercote's camped at Oxford awaiting us with a force a thousand strong."

"Wolvercote," repeated Eleanor. "Yes, of course." Despondency began to leave her as she climbed the ladder of hope the abbot held for her.

"Of *course* of course. A thousand men. And with you at their head, another ten thousand to join us. All them as the Plantagenet has trampled and beggared, they'll come flocking from the Midlands. Then we march, and oh what joy in Heaven."

"Got to get to fuck Oxford first," Schwyz said, "and quick, for fuck's sake. It's going to snow, and we'll be stuck in this fuck tower like fuck Aunt Sallies. At Woodstock, I told the stupid bitch it couldn't be defended. Let's go straight to Oxford, I said. I can defend you there. But *she* knew better." His voice rose from basso to falsetto. *"Oh, no, Schwyz, the roads are too bad for pursuit, Henry can't follow us here."* The tone reverted. "Henry fuck can, I know the bastard."

In a way, it was the strangest moment of the night. Eleanor's expression, something between doubt and exaltation, didn't change. Still kneeling by her side, the abbot did not turn round.

Didn't they hear him?

Did I?

For Adelia had been taken back to the lower Alps of the Graubünden, to which, every year, she and her foster parents had made the long but beautiful journey in order to avoid the heat of a Salerno summer. There, in a villa lent to them by the Bishop of Chur, a grateful patient of Dr. Gershom's, little Adelia had gone picking herbs and wildflowers with the goatherd's flaxen-haired children, listening to their chat and that of the adults—all of them unaware that little Adelia could absorb languages like blotting paper.

A strange language it had been, a guttural mixture of Latin and the dialect of the Germanic tribes from which those alpine people were descended.

She'd just heard it again.

Schwyz had spoken in Romansh.

Without looking round, the abbot was giving the queen a loose translation. "Schwyz is saying as how, with your favor on our sleeve, this is a war we'll win. When he do speak from his heart, he reverts to his own patter, but old Schwyz is your man to his soul."

"I know he is." Eleanor smiled at Schwyz. Schwyz nodded back.

"Only he can smell snow, he says, and wants to be at Oxford. An' I'll be happier in my bowels to have Wolvercote's men around us. Can ee manage the journey, sweeting? Not too tired? Then let you go down to the kitchens with Monty and get some hot grub inside ee. It'll be a cold going."

"My dear, dear abbot," Eleanor said fondly, rising, "how we needed your presence. You help us to remember God's plain goodness; you bring with you the scent of fields and all natural things. You bring us courage."

"I hope I do, my dear. I hope I do." As the queen and Montignard disappeared down the stairs, he turned and looked at Adelia, who knew, without knowing how she knew, that he had been aware of her all along. "Who's this, then?"

Schwyz said, "Some drab of Saint Albans's. He brought her with him. She was in the room when the madwoman attacked Nelly and managed to trip her up. Nelly thinks she saved her life." He shrugged. "Maybe she did."

"Did she now?" Two strides brought the abbot close to Adelia. A surprisingly well-manicured hand went under her chin to tip her head back. "A queen owes you her life, does she, girl?"

Adelia kept her face blank, as blank as the abbot's, staring into it.

"Lucky, then, aren't you?" he said.

He took his hand away and turned to leave. "Come on, my lad, let us get this *festa stultorum* on its way."

"What about her?" Schywz jerked a thumb toward the writing table.

"Leave her to burn."

"And *her*?" The thumb indicated Adelia.

The abbot's shrug suggested that Adelia could leave or burn as she pleased.

She was left alone in the room. Ward, seeing his

chance, came back in and directed his nose at the tray with its unfinished veal pie.

Adelia was listening to Rowley's voice in her mind. *"Civil war ... Stephen and Matilda will be nothing to it ... the Horsemen of the Apocalypse ... I can hear the sound of their hooves."*

They've come, Rowley. They're here. I've just seen three of them.

From the writing table came a soft sound as Rosamund's melting body slithered forward onto it.

SEVEN

By going against the advice of its commander and dragging her small force with her to Wormhold Tower, Eleanor had delayed its objective—which was to join up with the greater rebel army awaiting her at Oxford.

Now, with the weather worsening, Schwyz was frantic to get the queen to the meeting place— armies tended to disperse when kept idle too long, especially in the cold—and there was only one sure route that would take her there quickly: the river. The Thames ran more or less directly north to south through the seven or so miles of countryside that lay between Wormhold and Oxford.

Since the queen and her servants had ridden from their last encampment, accompanied by Schwyz and his men on foot, boats must be found. And had been. A few. Of a sort. Enough to transport the most important members of the royal party and a contingent of Schwyz's men but not all of either. The lesser servants and most of the soldiers were going to have to journey to Oxford via the towpath—a considerably slower and more difficult journey than by boat. Also, to do so, they

were going to have to use the horses and mules that
the royal party had brought with them.

All this Adelia gathered as she emerged into the
tower's bottom room, where shouted commands
and explanations were compounding chaos.

A soldier was pouring oil onto a great pile of
broken furniture while servants, rushing around,
screamed at him to wait before applying the flame
as they removed chests, packing cases, and boxes
that had been carried into the guardroom only
hours before. Eleanor traveled heavy.

Schwyz was yelling at them to leave everything;
neither those who were to be accommodated in the
few boats nor those who would make the trek
overland to Oxford could be allowed to carry
baggage with them.

Either they didn't hear him or he was ignored. He
was being maddened further by Eleanor's insistence
that she could not proceed without this servant or
that and, even when agreement was reached, by the
favored ones' refusal to stand still and be counted.
Part of the trouble seemed to be that the
Aquitanians doubted the honesty of their military
allies; Eleanor's personal maid shrieked that the
royal wardrobe could not be entrusted to "sales
mercenaries," and a man declaring himself to be the
sergeant cook was refusing to leave a single pan
behind for the soldiers to steal. So outside the tower,
soldiers struggled with frozen harnesses to ready the
horses and mules, and the queen's Aquitanians
argued and ran back and forth to fetch more
baggage, none of which could be accommodated.

There and then Adelia decided that whatever else happened, she herself would make for the towpath if she could—and quickly. Among this amount of disorganization, nobody would see her go and, with luck and the Lord's good grace, she could walk to the nunnery.

First, though, she had to find Rowley, Jacques, and Walt.

She stood on the stairs looking for them in the confusion before her; they weren't there, they must have been taken outside. What she did see, though, was a black shape that kept to the shadow of the walls as it made its way toward the stairs, jumping awkwardly like a frog because its feet were hobbled. The rope that had been put round its neck flapped as it came.

Adelia drew back into the dark of the staircase, and as the creature hopped up the first rise, caught it by its arm. "No," she said.

The housekeeper's hands and feet had been tied tightly enough to restrain a normal woman, but whoever had done it hadn't reckoned with the abnormal: Dakers had hopped from wherever her guards had left her in order to try and join her mistress at the top of the tower.

And still would if she could. As Adelia grabbed her, Dakers threw her thin body to shake her off. Unseen by anyone else, the two women struggled.

"You'll *burn*," hissed Adelia. "For God's sake, do you want to burn with her?"

"*Yes-s-s.*"

"I won't let you."

The housekeeper was the weaker of the two. Giving up, she turned to face Adelia. She had been roughly treated; her nose was bleeding, and one of her eyes was closed and puffy. "Let me go, let me go. I'll be with her. I *got* to be with her."

How insane. How sad. A soldier was readying the tower's destruction; servants were oblivious to all but their own concerns. Nobody cared if the queen's would-be assassin died in the flames, might even prefer it if she did.

They can't do that. She's mad. One of the reasons Adelia loved England was that if Dakers were brought to trial for her attempt on the queen's life, no court in the country, seeing what she was, would sentence her to death. Eleanor herself had held to it. Restrain the woman with imprisonment, yes, but the reasonable, ancient dictum of *"furiosus furore solum punitur"* (the madness of the insane is punishment enough) meant that anyone who'd once possessed reason but by disease, grief, or other accident had lost the use of his or her understanding must be excused the guilt of his or her crime.

It was a ruling that agreed with everything Adelia believed in, and she wasn't going to see it bypassed, even if Dakers herself was a willing accessory and preferred to die, burning, alongside Rosamund's body. Life was sacred; nobody knew that better than a doctor who dealt with its absence.

The woman was pulling away from her again. Adelia tightened her grip, feeling a physical revulsion; she, who was never nauseated by corpses, was repelled by this living body she had to clutch so closely to her, by its thinness—it was like hugging a bundle of sticks—by its passion for death.

"Don't you want to avenge her?" She said it because it was all she could think of to keep the woman still, but, after a minute, a measure of sanity came into the eyes glaring into hers.

The mouth stopped hissing. "Who did it?"

"I don't know yet. I'll tell you this much, it wasn't the queen."

Another hiss. Dakers didn't believe her. "She paid so's it could be done."

"No." Adelia added, "It wasn't Bertha, either."

"I know that." Contemptuously.

There was a sudden, curious intimacy. Adelia felt herself sucked into whatever understanding the woman possessed, saw her own worth as an ally calculated, dismissed—and then retrieved. She was, after all, the *only* ally.

"I find things out. It's what I do," Adelia said, slackening her grip a little. Suppressing distaste, she added, "Come along with me and we'll find things out together."

Once more she was weighed, found wanting, weighed again, and adjudged as possibly useful.

Dakers nodded.

Adelia fumbled in her pocket for her knife and cut the rope round the housekeeper's ankles and took the noose from round the neck over her head. She paused, unsure whether to free her hands as well. "You promise?"

The only good eye squinted at her. "You'll find out?"

"I'll try. It's why the Bishop of Saint Albans brought me here." Not very reassuring, she thought, considering that the Bishop of Saint Albans was leaving the place as a prisoner and Armageddon was about to break out.

Dakers held out her skinny wrists.

Schwyz had left the guardroom in order to gain control of the situation in the bailey outside. Some of the servants had gone with him; the few that remained were still gathering their goods and didn't notice the two women sidling out.

There was equal confusion in the bailey. Adelia covered Dakers's head with the hood of her cloak and then put up her own so that they would be just two more anonymous figures in the scurry.

A rising wind added to the noise as it whirled little showers of snowflakes that were slow to melt. Moonlight came and went like a guttering candle.

Disregarded, still clutching Dakers, Adelia moved through the chaos with Ward at her heels, looking for Rowley. She glimpsed him on the far side of the bailey, and it was a relief to see that Jacques and Walt were with him, all three roped together. Nearby, the Abbot of Eynsham was arguing over them with Schwyz, his voice dominating the noise made by the wind and bustle. "... I don't care, you tyrant, I need to know what they know. They come with us." Schwyz's retort was whirled away, but Eynsham had won. The three prisoners were prodded toward the crowd at the gateway, where Eleanor was getting up on a horse.

Damn, damn *it*. She *must* talk to Rowley before they were separated. Whether she could do it unnoticed ... and with a failed assassin in tow ... yet she dared not let go of Dakers's hand.

And Dakers was laughing, or, at least, a low cackle was emerging from the hood round her face. "What is it?" Adelia asked, and found that in taking her eyes off Rowley and the others she had lost sight of them. "Oh, be *quiet*."

Agonized with indecision, she towed the woman toward the archway that led to the outer bailey and the entrance to the maze. The wind blew the servants' cloaks open and closed as they milled about so that the golden lion of Aquitaine on their tabards flickered in the light of the torches. Soldiers, tidy in their padded jackets, tried to impose order, snatching unnecessary and weighty items away from clutching arms and restraining their owners from snatching them back. Only Eleanor was calm, controlling her horse with one hand and shielding her eyes with the other in order to watch what was being done, looking for something.

She saw Ward, like a small, black sheep against the snow, and pointed the animal out to Schwyz with a gloved finger as she gave an order. Schwyz looked round and pointed in his turn. "That one, Cross," he shouted at one of his men. "Bring her. That one with the dog."

Adelia found herself seized and hoisted onto a mule. She struggled, refusing to let go of Dakers's hand.

The man called Cross took the line of least resistance; he lifted Dakers as well so that she clung on to Adelia's back. "And bloody stay there," he yelled at them. With one hand on the mule's bridle and his body pinning Adelia's leg, he took his charges through the archway and into the outer bailey, holding back until the rest of the cavalcade joined them.

Eleanor rode to the front, Eynsham just behind her. The open gates of the maze yawned like a black hole before them.

"Go straight through, Queen of my heart," the abbot called to her joyfully. "Straight as my old daddy's plow."

"Straight?" the queen shouted back.

He spread his arms. "Didn't you order I to learn the whore's mysteries? Diddun I do it for ee?"

"There's a direct way through?" Eleanor was laughing. "Abbot, my abbot. '*And the crooked shall be made straight ...*'"

"'*... and the rough places plain,*'" he finished for her. "That old Isaiah, he knew a thing or two. I am but his servant, and yours. Go, my queen, and the Lord's path shall lead you through the whore's thicket."

Preceded by some of her men, one holding a lantern, Eleanor entered the maze, still laughing. The cavalcade followed her.

Behind them, Schwyz gave another order and a lit torch arched through the air onto the piled tinder in the guardroom ...

The abbot was right; the way through the maze had been made straight. Alleys were direct passageways into the next. Blocking hedges revealed themselves as disguised, now open, doors.

Mystery had gone. The wind took away the maze's silence; the hedges around them bent and shivered like ordinary storm-tossed avenues. Some insidious essence had been withdrawn; Adelia couldn't be sorry. What she found extraordinary was that if the strange abbot who declared himself a devotee of the queen could be believed, Rosamund herself had shown him the secret of the way through.

"You know that man?" she asked over her shoulder. Flinching, she felt Dakers's thin chest heave up and down against her back as the housekeeper began cackling again.

"Ain't he the clever one." It wasn't so much a reply as Dakers's commentary to herself. "Thinks he's bested our wyrm, so he do, but that's still got its fangs." Perhaps it was part of her madness, Adelia thought, that there was no animosity in her voice toward a man who, self-confessed, had visited Rosamund in her tower in order to betray her to the queen.

They were through the maze within minutes. Swearing horribly at the mule, Cross urged it into a trot so that Adelia and Dakers were cruelly bumped up and down on its saddleless spine as it charged the hill.

The wind strengthened and drove snow before it in sporadic horizontal bursts that shut out the moon before letting it ride the sky again. As they crested the hill it slammed, shrieking, into their faces.

Adelia looked back and saw Rowley, Jacques, and Walt being prodded out of the maze by the spears of the men behind them.

There was a howl of triumph from Dakers; her head was turned to the tower—a black, erect, and unperturbed outline against the moon.

"That's right, that's right," Dakers screamed, "our lord Satan did hear me, my darling. I'll be back for ee, my dear. Wait for me."

The tower wasn't burning. It should have been a furnace by now, but despite broken furniture, oil, a draft, and a torch, the bonfire hadn't caught. Something, some *thing*, had put out the fire.

Its door faced the wind, Adelia told herself. The wind carried snow and extinguished the flames.

But what couldn't be extinguished was the image of Rosamund, diabolically preserved, waiting in that cold upper chamber for her servant to return to her ...

It was a sad little flotilla at the river: rowing boats, punts, an old wherry, all found moored along the banks and commandeered by Schwyz's soldiers. The only vessel of any substance was the barge that Mansur and Oswald and the Godstow men had brought upriver to collect Rosamund's body. Adelia looked for Mansur and, when she didn't see him, became frightened that the soldiers had killed him. These were crude men; they reminded her of the followers of Crusade armies passing through Salerno who'd been prepared to slaughter anybody with an appearance different from their own. There *was* a tall figure standing in the barge's prow, but the man was cloaked and hooded like everybody else and the snow hindered identification. It could be Mansur, it could be a soldier.

She tried reassuring herself with the fact that Schwyz and his men were mercenaries and more interested in utility than the slaughter of Saracens; they would surely see the need to keep alive every skilled boatman they had to take them to Oxford.

The chaos that had reigned in Wormhold's bailey was now redoubled as Eleanor's people fought to accompany their queen on the Godstow barge—the only one with a cabin. If there was someone managing the embarkation, he was overwhelmed.

The mercenary Cross, in charge of Adelia and Dakers, waited too long for orders; by the time he realized there weren't going to be any, the barge was dangerously overladen with the queen's servants and baggage. He and the two women were waved away from it.

Cursing, he hauled them both along to the next vessel in line and almost threw them into its stern. Ward made a leap and joined them.

It was a rowing boat. An *open* rowing boat tied by a hawser onto the stern of the Godstow barge. Adelia shrieked at the soldier, "You can't put us here. We'll freeze." Exposed to the lacerating wind in this thing, they'd be dead long before they reached Oxford, two corpses as rigid as Rosamund's.

The boat shuddered as three more people were forced into it by another guard, who clambered in after them. A voice deeper than Adelia's and more used to carrying overrode the wind: "In the name of God, man, do you want to kill us? Get us under cover. Ask the queen, that lady there saved her life." The Bishop of Saint Albans had joined her, and her protest. Still roped to Jacques and Walt and at a spear's end, he nevertheless carried authority.

"I'm getting it, aren't I?" Cross shouted back. "Shut your squalling. Sit there. In front of the women."

Once everybody was settled to his satisfaction, he produced a large bundle that turned out to be an old sail and called to his companion, addressing him as Giorgio, to help him spread it.

Whatever their manners, he and his companion were efficient. The wind tried to whip the canvas away from them, but Dakers and Adelia were made to sit on one end of it before it was looped back and up, bringing it forward so that it covered them as well as the three prisoners and, finally, the two soldiers themselves, who took their seat in the prow. Their efforts had been self-preservation; they were coming, too. With deliberate significance, Giorgio placed a stabbing sword across his knees.

The sail was dirty and smelly, and rested heavily on the top of everybody's head, not quite wide enough for its purpose, so that covering themselves fully against the slanting wind on one side left a gap on the other. Ice formed over it immediately, rendering it stiff but also making a protective layer. It was shelter of a sort.

The river was being whipped into a fury that slopped wavelets of icy water over the gunwales. Adelia heaved Ward onto her lap, covered him with her cloak, and put her feet up against Rowley's back to keep them out of the wet—he was on the thwart immediately in front of her on the starboard side where the gap was. Jacques sat between him and Walt.

"Are you all right?" She had to shout against the shriek of the wind.

"Are you?" he asked.

"Splendid."

The messenger was also trying to be brave. Adelia heard him say, "Boat trip—makes a nice change."

"It'll come out of your wages," the bishop told him. Walt grunted.

There was no time for more. The two soldiers were yelling at them to bail "before this bloody scow goes under," and were handing out receptacles with which to do it. The three prisoners were given proper bailers while two jugs were passed to the women. "And put your bloody backs to it."

Adelia began bailing—if the boat sank beneath them, they'd be dead before they could scramble to the bank. As fast as she could, she chucked icy water out into the river. The river chucked it back.

Seen through the gap in the sail, the scudding snow was vaguely illuminated by the lamp on the stern of the barge ahead and the prow of whatever vessel was behind them, providing just enough light for Adelia to recognize the pitifully inadequate jug with which she was bailing. It was of silver and had lately stood on the tray on which a servant had brought food and drink to Eleanor in Rosamund's chamber. The Aquitanians had been right; the mercenaries—the two in this boat, at any rate—were thieves.

Adelia experienced a sudden fury that centered on the stolen jug but had more to do with being cold, tired, wet, in extreme discomfort, and frightened for her life. She turned on Dakers, who was doing nothing. "Bail, blast you."

The woman remained motionless, her head lolling. *Probably dead*, Adelia thought.

Anger had afflicted Rowley as well. He was shouting at his captor to free their hands so he and Jacques and Walt could bail faster—they were being slowed by having to scoop the water up and out in awkward unison.

He was again told to shut his squalling, but after a minute Adelia felt the boat rock even more heavily and then heard the three men in front of her swearing. She gathered from their abuse that they'd been cut free of one another but the separate pieces of rope that bound each pair of wrists were still in place.

Still, the three could now bail quicker—and did. Adelia transferred her fury to Dakers for dying after all she, Adelia Aguilar, had done for her. "Sheer ingratitude," she snapped, and grabbed the woman's wrist. For the second time that night, she felt a weak pulse.

Leaning forward so that she nearly squashed the

dog on her lap, she jerked Dakers's feet out of the bilge and, to warm them, pushed one between the bodies of Rowley and Jacques and the other between Jacques and Walt.

"How long are we going to sit here?" she screamed over their heads at the soldiers. "God's rib, when are we going to *move*?"

But the wind screamed louder than she could; the men didn't hear her. Rowley, though, nodded his head in the direction of the gap.

She peered out at the whirling curtain of snow. They were moving, had been moving for some time, and had reached a bend in the river where a high bank of trees must have been sheltering them a little.

Whether the barge in front, to which they were attached, was being poled by men or pulled by a horse, she didn't know—a dreadful task for either. It was probably being poled; they seemed to be going faster than walking pace. The wind at their backs and the flow of the river was helping them along, sometimes too much—the prow of their boat bumped into the stern of the barge, and the soldiers were having to take turns to struggle out from under the sail cover to fend off with an oar.

How far Oxford was she didn't know, either, but at this rate of progress, Godstow could only be an hour or so away—and there, somehow, she must get ashore.

With this determined, Adelia felt calmer, a doctor again—and one with an ailing patient on her hands. Part of her extreme irritation had been because she was hungry. It came to her that Dakers was probably even hungrier than she was, faint from it—there'd been no sign of food in the Wormhold kitchen when they'd investigated it.

Adelia, though she might condemn the thieving mercenaries, hadn't come empty-handed out of Rosamund's chamber, either; there'd been food left on the queen's tray, and hard times had taught her the value of foraging.

Well, Rosamund wasn't going to eat it.

She delved into her pocket and brought out a lumpy napkin, unfolded it, broke off a large piece from the remains of Eleanor's veal pie, and waved it under Dakers's nose. The smell of it acted as a restorative; it was snatched from her fingers.

Making sure the soldiers couldn't see her—she could barely see them in the darkness under the sail—she leaned forward again and slid the cheese she'd also filched between Jacques and Rowley until she felt the roped hand of one of them investigate it, grasp it, and squeeze her own hand in acknowledgment. There came a pause in the three men's bailing, during which, she guessed, the cheese was being secretly portioned, causing the soldiers to shout at them again.

The remains of the veal pie she divided between herself and Ward.

After that there was little to be done but endure and bail. Every so often, the sail drooped so heavily between them that one of the men had to punch it from underneath in order to rid it of the snow weighting it.

The level of water slopping below her raised legs refused to go down, however much she threw over the side; each breath she expelled wetted the cloak muffling her mouth, freezing immediately so that her lips became raw. The sailcloth scraped against her head as she bent and came up again. But if she stopped, the cold would congeal the blood in her veins. Keep on bailing, stay alive, live to see Allie again.

Rowley's elbow jerked into her knees. She went on bailing, lean, dip, toss, lean, dip, toss; she'd been doing it forever, would continue forever. Rowley had to nudge her again before she realized she could stop. There was no water coming in.

The wind had lessened. They were in a muffled silence, and light of a sort—was it day?—came through the window of the sail's gap, beyond which snow was falling so thickly it confused the eye into giving the impression that the boat was progressing through air filled with swansdown.

The cold also coming in through the gap had numbed her right side and shoulder. She leaned forward and pressed against Rowley's back to preserve some warmth for the two of them, pulling Dakers with her so that the housekeeper's body was against Jacques's.

Rowley turned his head slightly, and she felt his breath on her forehead. "Well?"

Adelia shifted higher to peer over his shoulder. Despite the fall in the wind, the swollen river was running faster than ever and putting the rowing boat in danger of crashing into the barge or veering against a bank.

One of the soldiers—she thought it was Cross, the younger of the two—was fending off, having abandoned the shelter of the sail so that it drooped over his companion, who was hunched over the prow thwart, exhausted or asleep, or both.

There was no movement, either, from Walt or Jacques. Dakers was still slumped against Jacques's back.

Adelia nosed Rowley's hood away from his ear and put her lips against it: "They're going to raise Eleanor's standard at Oxford. They think the Midlands will rise up and join her rebellion."

"How many men? At Oxford, how many men?"

"A thousand, I think."

"Did I see Eynsham back there?"

"Yes. Who is he?"

"Bastard. Clever. Got the ear of the Pope. Don't trust him."

"Schwyz?" she asked.

"Bastard mercenary. First-class soldier."

"Somebody called Wolvercote is in charge of the army at Oxford."

"A bastard."

That disposed of the main players, then. She rested her face against his cheek in momentary contentment.

"Got your knife?" he asked.

"Yes."

"Cut this bloody rope." He jiggled his bound hands.

She took another look at the soldier crouching by the prow; his eyes were closed.

"Come on." Rowley's mouth barely moved. "I'll be getting off in a minute." They might have been journeying luxuriously together and he'd remembered a prior destination to hers.

"No." She put her arms round him.

"Don't," he said. "I've *got* to find Henry. Warn him."

"No." In this blizzard, nobody would find anybody. He'd die. The fen people told tales about this sort of snowstorm, of unwary cottagers, having ventured out in it to lock up their poultry or bring in the cow, unable to find their way back through a freezing, whirling thickness that took away sight and sense of direction so that they ended up stiff and dead only yards from their own front doors. "No," she said again.

"Cut this bloody rope."

The soldier in the prow stirred and muttered, "What you doing?"

They waited until he settled again.

"Do you want me to go with my hands tied?" Rowley breathed.

Christ *God*, how she loathed him. And loathed Henry Plantagenet. The king, always the king if it costs my life, yours, our child's, all happiness.

She delved into her pocket, gripped the knife, and seriously considered sticking it into his leg. He couldn't then go wandering about in a circle and end up as a mound of ice in some field.

"I hate you," she told him. Tears were freezing on her eyelashes.

"I know. Cut the bloody rope."

Holding the knife, she slid her right arm farther around him, all the time watching the man in the prow, wondering why she didn't alert him so that Rowley would be restrained ...

She couldn't. She didn't know what fate Eleanor intended for her prisoner or, even if it was a benign one, what Eynsham or Schwyz might do.

Her fingers found his hands and walked their way to the rope round his wrists. She began cutting, carefully—the knife was so sharp that a wrong move could open one of his veins.

One strand severed, another. As she worked, she hissed bile. "Your leman, am I? No use to you, am I? I hope you freeze in hell—and Henry with you."

The last strand went, and she felt him flex his hands to get their circulation back.

He turned his head so that he could kiss her. His chin scraped her cheek.

"No use at all," he said, "except to make the sun come up."

And he was gone.

Jacques took charge. Adelia heard him put a sob into his voice, telling the furious Cross that the collision with the bank had caused the bishop to fall overboard.

She heard the mercenary's reply: "He's dead meat, then."

Jacques burst into a loud wail but smoothly took Ward off Adelia's lap, shifted her so that she sat between him and Walt with the sleeping Dakers resting on her back, and returned the dog to its place under her cloak.

She was barely aware of the change. *Except to make the sun come up.*

I'll make the sun come up if I see him again. I'll kill him. Dear Lord, keep him safe.

The snow stopped, and the heavy clouds that carried it rolled away westward. The sun came out and Cross rolled back the sail, thinking there was warmth to be had.

Adelia took no notice of that, either, until Walt nudged her. "What's up with he, mistress?"

She raised her head. The two mercenaries were sitting on the prow thwart opposite. The one called Cross was trying to rouse his companion. "Come on, Giorgio, upsy-daisy. Weren't your fault we lost the bloody bishop. Come on, now."

"He's dead," Adelia told him. The man's boots were fixed in the solidified bilge water. Just another frozen corpse to add to the night's list.

"Can't be. *Can't* be. I kept him in the warm, well, warm as I could." Cross's bad-tempered face was agonized.

Lord, this death is important to this man. It should be important to me.

For the look of the thing, Adelia stretched so that her hand rested against the dead man's neck where a pulse should be. He was rigid. She shook her head. He'd been considerably older than his friend.

Jacques and Walt genuflected. She took the living soldier's hand in one of hers. "I'm sorry,

Master Cross." She spoke the end words: "May God have mercy on his soul."

"He was bloody sitting here, keeping warm, I thought."

"I know. You did your best for him."

"Why ain't you lot dead, then?" Anger was returning. "You was sitting same as him."

Useless to say that they had been bailing and therefore moving, just as Cross himself, who, even though exposed to the wind, had been active in preventing collision. And poor Giorgio had been alone, with no human warmth next to him.

"I'm sorry," she said again. "He was old, the cold was too much for him."

Cross said, "Taught me soldiering, he did. We been through three campaigns together. Sicilian, he was."

"So am I."

"Oh."

"Don't move him," she said sharply.

Cross was trying to gather the body up so as to lay it along the thwart. Like Rosamund's, its rigor would persist until it encountered heat—there was none in this sun—and the sight of it on its back with knees and hands curved like a dog's was not one its friend would want to see.

Walt said, "By Gor, ain't that Godstow by there?"

Allie.

She realized that she was surrounded by a glittering, diamond-hard landscape that she had to shade her eyes to look at. Trees had been upended, their roots like ghastly, desperate, twiggy fingers frozen in the act of appeal. For the rest, the countryside appeared flattened by the monstrous weight of snow fallen on it so that what had been dips in the ground were merely smooth shallows among the rises they interspersed. Straight threads of smoke rising against a cornflower-blue sky showed that the lumps scattered on the rise above the bank were half-buried houses.

There was a small, humped bridge in the distance, white as marble; she and Rowley had stood on it one night in another century. Beyond that—she had to squeeze her eyes nearly shut to see—many threads of smoke and, where the bridge ended, a wood and the suggestion of gates.

She was opposite the village of Wolvercote. Over there, though she couldn't see it, stood the nunnery of Godstow. Where Allie was.

Adelia stood, slipped, and rocked the boat in her scramble to get up again. "Put us ashore," she told Cross, but he didn't seem to hear her. Walt and Jacques pulled her down.

The galloper said, "No good, mistress, even supposing ..."

"Look at the bank, mistress," Walt told her.

She looked at it—a small cliff where flat pasture should have been. Farther in, what appeared to be enormous frozen bushes were, in fact, the spread branches of mature oak trees standing in drifts that must be—Adelia estimated—fifteen feet or more deep.

"We'd never get through," Jacques was saying.

She pleaded, begged, while knowing it was true;

perhaps when the inhabitants disinterred themselves, they would dig tunnels through the snow to
reach the river, but until then, or until it thawed,
she was separated from the convent as if by a
mountain barrier. She would have to sit in this boat
and be swept away past Allie, only God knowing
how or when, or *if*, she could get back to her.

They'd passed the village now. They were nearly
at the bridge that crossed the tributary serving the
mill. The Thames was widening into the great sweep
that would take it around the convent's meadows.

And something was happening to it ...

The barge had slowed. Its sides were too high to
see what was occurring on its deck, but there was
activity and a lot of swearing.

"What's the matter?"

Walt picked up one of the bailers, dipped it over
the side, brought it back, and stirred his finger in it.
"Look at this."

They looked. The cupped water was gray and
granulated, as if somebody had poured salt into it.
"What is it?"

"It's ice," Walt said softly. "It's bloody ice." He
looked around. "Must be shallower here. It's ice,
that's what it is. The river's freezing up."

Adelia stared at it, then up at Walt, then back to
the river. She sat down suddenly and gave thanks
for a miracle as wonderful as any in the Bible; liquid
was turning solid, one element changing into
another. They would have to stop. They could walk
ashore and, many as they were, they could dig their
way through to the convent.

She looked back to count the boats behind them.

There were no boats. As far as the eye could see, the river was empty, graying along this stretch but gaining a blueness as it twisted away into a dazzling, silent distance.

Blinking, she searched for a sight of the contingent that should have been accompanying them along the towpath.

But there was no towpath—of course there wasn't. Instead, where it had been, was a wavy, continuous bank of frozen snow, taller than two men in some places, with its side edge formed by wind and water as neatly as if some titanic pastry cook with a knife had sheared off the ragged bits of icing round the top of a cake.

For a second, because her mind was directed only at reaching her daughter, Adelia thought, *It doesn't matter, there are enough of us to dig a path ...*

And then, "Dear Lord, where are they?" she said. "All those people?"

The sun went on shining beautifully, unfairly, pitilessly, on an empty river where, perhaps, in its upper reaches men and women sat in their boats as unmoving as Giorgio sat in this one, where, perhaps, corpses rolled in sparkling water.

And what of the riders? Where were they, God help them? Where was Rowley?

The answering silence was terrible because it was the only answer. It trapped the oaths and grunts of effort from the barge as if in a bell jar, so that they echoed back in an otherwise soundless air.

The men on board it labored on, plunging poles

through the shallow, thickening water until they found purchase on the river bottom and could push the barge another yard, another ...

After a while, the bell jar filled with sounds like the cracks of whips—they were encountering surface sheet ice and having to break through it.

They inched past the point of the river where it divided and a stream turned off toward the mill and the bridge. There was no noise from the millrace, where a fall of water hung in shining stillness.

And, oh, God Almighty save our souls, in all this wonder, somebody had used the bridge as a gibbet; two glistening, distorted figures hung from it by the neck—Adelia, looking up, glimpsed two dead faces looking quizzically sideways and down at her, saw two pairs of pointing feet, as if their owners had been frozen in a neat little dancing jump.

Nobody else seemed to notice, or care. Walt and Jacques were using the oars to pole the rowing boat along so that it didn't drag on the barge. Dakers sat next to her now, her hood over her face; somebody had placed the sail around the two of them to keep them warm.

They inched past the bridge and into an even wider bend where the Thames ran along a Godstow meadow—which, astonishingly, still was a meadow. Some freak of the wind had scoured it of snow so that a great expanse of frosted grass and earth provided the only color in a white world.

And here the barge stopped because the ice had become too thick to proceed farther. It didn't matter, *it didn't matter*—there was a scar leading down the rise from the convent to the shore and, at the bottom of it, convent men with shovels were shouting and waving, and everybody in the two boats was shouting and waving back as if it were they who were marooned and had glimpsed a rescuing sail coming toward them ...

Only then did Adelia realize that she had been sustained through the night on borrowed energy and it was now being debited out of her body so quickly that she was close to the languor that comes with death. It had been a very near thing.

They had to disembark onto ice and cross it to reach land. Ward's paws slipped and he went down, sliding, until he could scrabble resentfully up again. An arm went round Adelia's waist to help her along and she looked up into the face of Mansur. "Allah is merciful," he said.

"Somebody is," she said. "I was so frightened for you. Mansur, we've lost Rowley."

Half-carried, she stumbled across the ice beside him and then across the flattened grass of the meadow.

Among the small crowd ahead, she glimpsed Eleanor's upright figure before it disappeared into the tunnel that led up to the convent gates, a steep, thin pathway with walls twice head height on either side. It had been dug to take Rosamund's coffin; instead, it received a litter made out of oars and wrapped around with sailcloth, under which rested the contorted body of a mercenary soldier.

A beautiful tunnel, though. At its top stood an

elderly woman, her studied impassivity displaying her relief. "You took your time."

As Adelia fell, babbling, into her arms, Gyltha said, "A'course she's well. Fat and fit as a flea. Think as I can't look after her? Gor dang, girl, you only left her yesterday."

EIGHT

*I*f her heart sank at the prospect of feeding and housing the forty or so exhausted, bedraggled, frostbitten men, women, and dogs shambling through her gates, Mother Edyve gave no sign of it, though it must have sunk further when she saw that they included the Queen of England and the Abbot of Eynsham, neither of them friends to Godstow, to say nothing of a troop of mercenary soldiers.

It didn't occur to her that she was welcoming a force of occupation.

She ordered hot possets for her guests. She surrendered her house to Queen Eleanor and her maids, lodged the abbot and Montignard in the men's guesthouse with their and the queen's male servants, and quartered Schwyz on the gatekeeper. She put the queen's dogs and hawks in her own kennels and mews, distributing the other mercenaries as widely as she could, billeting one on the smith, another in the bakery, and the rest among individual—and aged—retainers and pensioners in the houses that formed a small village within the convent walls.

"So's they'm split up and not one of 'em where there's girls," Gyltha said approvingly. "She's a wily one, that Ma Edyve."

It was Gyltha who had carried the report of the
events at Wormhold to the abbess. Adelia was too
tired and, anyway, hadn't been able to face telling
her of Rowley's death.

"She don't believe it," Gyltha said on her return.
"No more don't I. Now, then, let's be seeing to you
two."

Mansur hated fuss and kept declaring that he was
well, but he had been exposed to the open cold while
poling the barge as Adelia, Jacques, and Walt had
not, and she and Gyltha were worried about him.

"Look what you done to your hands, you great
gawk," Gyltha said. Her disquiet always took the
form of anger. Mansur's palms were bleeding where
his mittens, and then his skin, had worn through
against the wood of the pole.

Adelia was concerned more for his fingers, which
were white and shiny where they emerged from the
wrecked mittens. "Frostbite."

"They cause me no pain," Mansur said stolidly.

"They will in a minute," Adelia promised.

Gyltha ran to Mansur's lodging to get him a dry
gown and cloak, and brought back with her a bucket
of hot water from the kitchen and would have
plunged her lover's hands into it, but Adelia
stopped her. "Wait til it cools a little."

She also prevented Gyltha from hooking the
brazier nearer to him. The condition of frostbite had
interested her foster father after he'd seen the effects
of it during their holidays in the Alps—he had actually
braved a winter there to study it—and his conclusion
had been that the warming must be gradual.

Young Allie, always deprived of burning herself on the brazier—it was kept within a guard—turned her attention to trying to pull the bucket over her head. Adelia would have enjoyed watching the resulting tussle between Gyltha and that remarkable child if her own toes hadn't ached agonizingly with the return of blood to frozen muscle and bone.

She estimated the worth of dosing herself and Mansur with willow-bark decoction for the pain and then rejected it; each of them was a stoic, and the fact that her toes and his fingers were turning red without blistering indicated that the affliction was mild—better to keep the drug for those in whom it might be worse.

She crawled onto the bed to suffer in comfort. Ward leaped on after her, and she had neither the energy nor will to turn him off. The dog had shared his body heat with her on the boat—what were a few fleas if she shared hers with him?

"What did you do with Dakers?" she asked.

"Oh, her." Gyltha had not taken to the walking skeleton that Adelia had dragged, unaware that she *was* dragging it, through the convent gates, but had seen, *because* Adelia was dragging it, that there was a necessity to keep it alive. "I give her to Sister Havis, and she give her to Sister Jennet in the infirmary. She's all right, ugly thing."

"Well done." Adelia closed her eyes.

"Don't you want to know who's turned up here since you been away?"

"No."

When she woke up, it was afternoon. Mansur had gone back to the men's guesthouse to rest. Gyltha was sitting beside the bed, knitting—a skill she'd picked up from one of her Scandinavian customers during her eel-selling days.

Adelia's eyes rested on the chubby little figure of Allie as it hitched itself around the floor on its bottom, chasing the dog and grimacing to show the one tiny tooth that had manifested itself in her lower gum since her mother had last seen her. "I swear I'll never leave you again," she told her.

Gyltha snorted. "I keep telling you, 'twas only thirty hours."

But Adelia knew the separation had been longer than that. "It was nearly permanent," she'd said, and added painfully, "For Rowley, it has been."

Gyltha wouldn't countenance it. "He'll be back, large as life and twice as natural. Take more than a bit of old snow to finish off that lad." To Gyltha, the Right Reverend Lord Bishop of Saint Albans would always be "that lad."

"He can stay away for me," Adelia said. She clung on to her grievance against him like a raft to keep her from being subsumed in grief. "He didn't care, Gyltha, not for his life, not Allie's, not mine."

"Except to make the sun come up."

"A'course he didn't, he's out to stop a war as'll take more lives than yours. God's work that is, and the Lord'll watch over un according."

Adelia clung to that, too, but she had been deeply frightened. "I don't care, if it's God's work, let Him do it. We are leaving. As soon as the snow clears, we're all slipping away back to the fens."

"Oh, ar?" Gyltha said.

"It's not '*oh, ar*.' I mean it." In the fens, her life had been acceptable, regulated, useful. She'd been ripped away from it, subjected to, and then abandoned in, physical and mental turmoil by the man *at whose request* she had become embroiled in it in the first place. Almost worse than anything, he had revived in her an emotion that she'd thought to be dead, that was better dead.

"Except to make the sun come up."

Damn him, don't think of it.

Gaining anger, she said, "It's all high politics, anyway. That's what Rosamund's killing was, as far as I can see—an assassination to do with queens and kings and political advantage. It's outside my scope. Was it the mushrooms? Yes, it probably was. Do I know who sent them? No, I don't, and there's an end to it. I'm a doctor, I won't be drawn into their wars. God's rib, Gyltha, Eleanor abducted me, *abducted* me—I nearly ended up joining her damned army."

"Shouldn't have saved her life, then, should you?"

"What was I to do? Dakers was coming at her with a knife."

"You sure you don't want to know who else's turned up?"

"No. I only want to know whether anybody's likely to stop us going."

But it appeared that in the physical collapse affecting all the travelers, even Eleanor, on their arrival at the convent, nobody had spared a thought for the woman who had saved the queen's life—or, for that matter, the woman who had nearly taken it. The priority had been a place to get warm and to sleep.

Perhaps, Adelia thought, the queen had forgotten Dakers and herself altogether and, when the roads were open again, would proceed to Oxford without attending to either. By which time Adelia would be beyond reach, taking Gyltha, Mansur, and Allie with her and leaving Dame Dakers to her own hideous devices—she no longer cared what they were.

Gyltha went to fetch their supper from the kitchen.

Adelia leaned down from the bed, picked up her daughter, pressing her nose against the warm satin of the child's cheek, and propped her up against her own knees so that they faced each other.

"We're going home, aren't we, mistress? Yes, we are. We won't get involved in their old wars, will we? No, we won't. We'll go far off, we'll go back to Salerno, we don't care what that nasty old King Henry says, do we? We'll find the money from somewhere. It's no good making faces ..." For Allie was extending her lower lip and showing her new tooth in an expression reminiscent of the camel in Salerno's menagerie. "You'll like Salerno, it's warm. We'll take Mansur and Gyltha and Ulf, yes, we will. You miss Ulf, don't you? So do I."

On an investigation like this—*had* she been going to proceed with it—Gyltha's grandson would have been her eyes and ears, able to go about unremarked as only an eleven-year-old urchin could, his plain, very plain, features giving the lie to his extreme intelligence.

Nevertheless, Adelia thanked her God that Ulf, at least, was out of harm's way. She found herself wondering, though, what the boy would have said about the situation ...

Allie started wriggling, wanting to continue with her persecution of Ward, so Adelia set her down absently, listening to a harsh little voice in her head that asked questions like an insistent crow.

Two murders, ain't there? Rosamund's and the fella on the bridge? You think they're connected?

"I don't know. It doesn't matter," she answered out loud.

It was goin' to depend on who turned up, weren't it? Somebody was, to see why there hadn't been no fuss about the dead un on the bridge? Whoever done it wanted him dead, din't they? An' wanted a hullabaloo about it, din't they?

"Such was my assumption. But there hasn't been time, the snow would have delayed them."

Somebody's come.

"I don't care. I'm going home, I'm frightened."

Leavin' the poor bugger in the icehouse, is that it? Very godly, I'm sure.

"Oh, shut up."

Adelia liked order; in a sense, it was what her profession was about—and you could say this for the dead, they didn't make unexpected moves or threaten you with a knife. To be out of control and at the whim of others, especially the malignantly inclined, as she had been at Wormhold and on the river, had discomposed her very being.

The convent enfolded her; the long, low, plain room spoke soothingly of proportion. It was dark outside now, and the glow of the brazier gave a shadow to each of the beams in the ceiling, making a pleasingly uniform pattern of dark and not-so-dark stripes against white plaster. Even muffled by the wool that Gyltha had stuffed in the cracks of the shutters to keep out the cold, the distant sound of the nuns singing Vespers was a reassurance of a thousand years of disciplined routine.

And all of it an illusion, because a corpse lay in its icehouse and, seven miles away, a dead woman sat at a writing table, both of them waiting ... for what?

Resolution.

Adelia pleaded with them: *I can't give it to you, I'm frightened, I want to go home.*

But jagged, almost forgotten images kept nudging at her mind: snowy footprints on a bridge, a letter crumpled in a saddlebag, other letters, copied letters, Bertha's piglike nose snuffling at a scent ...

Gyltha returned carrying a large pot of mutton and vegetables in broth, some spoons, a loaf tucked under one arm, and a leather bottle of ale under the other. She poured some of the broth into Allie's bowl and began mashing it to a pulp, putting the pieces of meat into her mouth and chewing them with her big, strong teeth until they, too, were pulp, then returning them to the bowl. "Turnip and barley," she said. "I'll say this much for the sisters, they do a fair supper. And good, warm milk from the cow with little un's porridge this morning."

Reluctantly, because to mention one of the convent's problems was somehow to solidify it, Adelia asked, "Is Bertha still in the cowshed?"

"Won't come out, poor soul. That old Dakers still want to scrag her?"

"I don't think so, no."

Feeding Allie, who was making spirited attempts to feed herself, took concentration that allowed no thought for anything else.

When they'd wiped food off her hair as well as off their own, the child was put down to sleep and the two women ate their supper in silence, their feet stretched out to the brazier, passing the ale bottle back and forth between them.

Warm, the pain beginning to lessen, Adelia thought that such security as there was in her world rested at this moment in the gaunt old woman on the stool opposite hers. A day didn't go by without a reminder of the gratitude she owed to Prior Geoffrey for their introduction, nor a strike of fear that Gyltha might leave her, nor, for that matter, puzzlement at why she stayed.

Adelia said, "Do you mind being here, Gyltha?"

"Ain't got no choice, girl. We'm snowed up. Been snowing again, if you'd notice. Path down to the river's gone and blocked itself again."

"I mean, galloping across country to get here, away from home, murder ... everything. You never complain."

Gyltha picked a strand of mutton from her teeth, considered it, and popped it back into her mouth. "Somewhere to see, I suppose," she said.

Perhaps that was it. Women generally had to stay where they were put, which in Gyltha's case had been Cambridgeshire fenland, a place that Adelia found endlessly exotic but that was undoubtedly very flat. Why should not Gyltha's heart drum to adventure in foreign places like any crusader's? Or long to see God's peace retained in her country as much as Rowley did? Or require, despite the risk, to see God's justice done on those who killed?

Adelia shook her head at her. "What would I do without you?"

Gyltha poured the remnants of the broth from Adelia's bowl into hers and put it down on the floor for Ward. "For a start, you wouldn't have no time to find out who done in that poor lad, nor who it was done for Rosamund," she said.

"Oh," Adelia said, sighing. "Very well, tell me."

"Tell ee what?" But Gyltha was smirking a satisfied smirk.

"You know very well. Who's arrived? Who's been asking questions about the boy in the icehouse? Somebody wanted him found and, sure as taxes, that somebody is going to question why he hasn't been. Who is it?"

It was more than one. As if blown ahead of the snow that had now encased them, four people had arrived at Godstow during Adelia's absence.

"Master and Mistress Bloat of Abingdon, they're

ma and pa to that young Emma as you took to. Come to see her married."

"What are they like?"

"Big." Gyltha spread her arms as if to encompass tree trunks. "Big bellies, big words, big voices—he has, anyhow, bellows like a bull as how he ships more wine from foreign parts than anybody else, sells more'n anybody else—for a nicer price than anybody else, I wouldn't be surprised. Hog on a high horse, he is."

By which Adelia gathered that Master Bloat reveled in a position he'd not been born to. "And his wife?"

In answer, Gyltha arranged her mouth into a ferocious simper, picked up the ale bottle, and ostentatiously prinked her little finger as she pretended to drink from it. She hadn't taken to the Bloats.

"Unlikely murderers, though," Adelia said. "Who else?"

"Their son-in-law-as-will-be."

Another person with a valid reason for coming to Godstow. "*Aaaah.*" So the beautiful, gallant writer of poetry had come to take his bride. How nice for that wild, charming girl, how nice that love would lighten the winter darkness for a while at least. "How did he get here?"

Gyltha shrugged. "Arrived from Oxford afore the blizzard set in, like the others. Seems he's lord of the manor over the bridge, though he don't spend much time there. Run-down old ruin, Polly says it is." Gyltha had made friends in the kitchen.

"His pa as took Stephen's side in the war had a castle further upriver during the war, the which King Henry made un pull it down."

"Is he as handsome as Emma thinks he is?"

But Adelia saw that here was another that hadn't been taken to—this time, in depth. "Handsome is as handsome does," Gyltha said. "Older'n I expected, and a proper lord, too, from his way of ordering people about. Been married before, but her died. The Bloats is lickin' his boots for the favor of him making their girl a noblewoman." Gyltha leaned forward slightly. "And him kindly accepting two hundred marks in gold as comes with her for a dowry."

"Two hundred marks?" An immense sum.

"So Polly says. In gold." Gyltha nodded. "Ain't short of a shilling or two, our Master Bloat."

"He can't be. Still, if he's prepared to purchase his daughter's happiness ..." She paused. "*Is* she happy?"

Gyltha shrugged. "Ain't seen her. She's kept to the cloisters. I'da thought she'd come rushing to see this Lord Wolvercote ..."

"*Wolvercote?*"

"That's his lordship's name. Suits him, an' all; he do look proper wolfish."

"Gyltha ... Wolvercote, that's the man ... he's the one who's raised an army for the queen. He's supposed to be at Oxford, waiting for Eleanor to join him."

"Well, he ain't, he's here."

"*Is* he now? But ..." Adelia was determined to follow the gleam of romance where it led. "He's not a likely murderer, either. It speaks well for him if he's prepared to delay a war because he can't wait to marry young Emma."

"He's delayin' it," Gyltha pointed out, "for young Emma plus two hundred marks. *In* gold." She leaned forward, pointing with her knitting needle. "You know the first thing he do when he got back to the village? Finds a couple of rogues robbin' his manor and hangs 'em quicker'n buttered lightning."

"The two on the bridge? I wondered about them."

"Sister Havis ain't happy. She made a right to-do about it, according to Polly. See, it's the abbey's bridge, and the sisters don't like it being decorated with corpses. 'You take 'em down now,' she told his lordship. But he says as it's *his* bridge, so he won't. And he ain't."

"Oh, dear." So much for romance. "Well, who's the fourth arrival?"

"Lawyer. Name of Warin. Now he *has* been asking questions. Very worried about his young cousin, seemingly, as was last seen riding upriver."

"Warin, Warin. He wrote the letter the boy carried." It was as if an ice barrier was melting and allowing everything to flood back into her memory. *Your affct cousin, Wlm Warin, gentleman-at-law, who hereby sends: two silvr marks as an earnest of your inheritance, the rest to be Claimed when we do meet.*

Letters, always letters. A letter in the dead man's saddlebag. A letter on Rosamund's table. Did they connect the two murders? Not necessarily. People wrote letters when they could write at all. On the other hand ...

"When did Master Warin arrive seeking his cousin?"

"Late last night, afore the blizzard. And he's a weeper. Crying fit to bust for worry as his cousin might've got caught in the snow, or been waylaid for his purse. Wanted to cross the bridge and ask at the village, but the snow started blowing, so he couldn't."

Adelia worked it out. "He was quick off the mark to know the boy was missing, then. Talbot of Kidlington—it must be him in the icehouse—was only killed the night before."

"Is that a clue?" The gleam in Gyltha's eye was predatory.

"I don't know. Probably not. Oh, dear *God*, what now?"

The church bell across the way had begun to toll, shivering the ewer in its bowl, sending vibrations through the bed. Allie's mouth opened to yell, and Adelia scrambled to get to her and cover her ears. "What is it? What is it?" This was no call to worship.

Gyltha had her ear to the shutters, trying to listen to shouts in the alley below. "Everybody to the church."

"Is it fire?"

"Dunno. Summoning bell, more like." Gyltha ran to the line of pegs where their cloaks hung. Adelia began wrapping Allie in her furs.

Outside, groups of people hurried from both ends of the alley and joined the congestion in the noisy church porch, where those pausing to let others go in chattered in alarm, asking one another questions and receiving no answers. They took noise in with them ... and quieted.

Though it was crowded, the church was silent and mostly dark, all light concentrated on the chancel, where men sat in the choir stalls, *men*, some of them in mail. The bishop's throne had been placed in front of the altar for Queen Eleanor to sit in; she wore her crown, but the enormous chair dwarfed her.

Beside her stood a knight, helmeted, his cloak flung back to show the scarlet-and-black blazon of a wolf's head on the chest of his tabard. A gauntleted hand rested on his sword's hilt. He was so still he might have been a painted sculpture, but his was the figure that drew the eye.

The trickle of sound that came in with newcomers dried up. Godstow's entire population was here now, all those who could walk, at least. Adelia, fearing that the child in her arms might be crushed, looked round for space and was helped up onto a tomb by people already standing on it. Gyltha and Ward joined her.

The bell stopped tolling; it had been mere background to what was developing and only became noticeable now by its cessation.

The knight nodded, and a liveried man behind the choir stalls turned and opened the vestry door, which was the entrance used by the religious.

Mother Edyve came in, leaning on her cane, followed by the nuns of Godstow. She paused as she reached the chancel and regarded the men who occupied the places reserved for her and the sisters. The Abbot of Eynsham sat there, so did Schwyz, Montignard, others. None of them moved.

There was a hiss of appalled breath from the congregation, but Mother Edyve merely cocked her head and limped past them, a finger raised to beckon at her flock as she went down the steps to stand with the congregation.

Adelia peered round the nave, looking for Mansur. She couldn't see him; instead, she found herself looking at mailed men with drawn swords standing at intervals along the walls, as if the ancient stones had sprung rivets of steel and iron.

Warders.

She turned back. The knight in the chancel had begun speaking.

"You all know me. I am the Lord of Wolvercote, and from this moment I claim this precinct of Godstow in the name of our Lord Savior and my gracious liege lady, Queen Eleanor of England, to be held against the queen's enemies until such time as her cause prevails throughout this land."

It was a surprisingly high, weak voice from such a tall man, but in that silence it didn't need strength.

There was a murmur of disbelief. Behind Adelia, somebody said, "What do he mean?"

Somebody else muttered, "Gor bugger, is he tellin' us we're at war?"

There was a shout from the nave: "What enemies is that, then? We ain't got no enemies, we're all snowed up." It sounded to Adelia like the voice of the miller who had questioned Bishop Rowley. There was a general, nervous snigger.

Immediately, two of the men-at-arms against the southern wall barged forward, hitting people aside with the flat of their swords until they reached the interrupter. Seizing his arms, they pulled him through the crowd to the main doors.

It *was* the miller. Adelia got a glimpse of a round face, its mouth open in shock. The men dragging him wore the wolf's head blazon. A boy ran after them. "Pa. Leave my pa alone." She couldn't see what happened after that, but the doors slammed shut and silence descended again.

"There will be no disobedience," said the high voice. "This abbey is now under military rule, and you people are subject to martial law. A curfew will be imposed ..."

Adelia struggled with disbelief. The most shocking thing about what was happening was its stupidity. Wolvercote was alienating the very people he needed as friends while the snow lasted. *Needlessly.* As the miller said, there was no enemy. The last she'd heard, the nearest military force was at nearby Oxford—and that was Wolvercote's own.

Oh, God, a stupid man—the most dangerous animal of them all.

In the choir stalls, Montignard was smiling at the queen. Most of the others were watching the crowd in the nave, but the Abbot of Eynsham was examining his fingernails while the scowl on

Schwyz's face was that of a man forced to watch a monkey wearing his clothes.

He wouldn't have done this, Adelia thought. *He's a professional. I wouldn't have done it, and I don't know anything about warfare.*

"... the holy women will keep to their cloister, rationing will be introduced while the snow lasts, and one meal a day shall be eaten communally—gentles in the refectory, villeins in the barn. Apart from church services, there shall be no other gatherings. Any group of more than five people is forbidden."

"That's done for his bloody meals, then," Gyltha breathed.

Adelia grinned. Here was stupidity in extremis; the kitchen staff alone numbered twenty; if they couldn't congregate, there would be no cooking.

Whatever that man is up to, she thought, *this is not the way to do it.*

Then she thought, *But he doesn't know any other. This is a man for whom frightened people are obedient people.*

And we are frightened. She could feel it, collective memory like a chill lancing through body heat in the church. An old helplessness. The Horsemen were with them, introduced into their peace by a stupid, stupid swine.

For what?

Adelia looked to where Schwyz and Abbot Eynsham sat, radiating discomposure. If this is the queen's war, they are all on the same side. Is Wolvercote establishing himself over his allies before he can be challenged? Grabbing authority *now*? Not the Abbot of Eynsham, not Schwyz, nor any other to win the glory, if glory was to be won. Wolvercote had arrived to find the queen of England at hand and must establish himself as her savior before anyone else could. If she succeeded under his generalship, Wolvercote might even be the true regent of England.

I'm watching a man throw dice.

He'd come to the end of his orders. He was turning, kneeling to Eleanor, his sword proffered, hilt first, for her to touch. "Always your servant, lady. To you and God in majesty, I swear my fealty."

And Eleanor was touching the hilt. Standing up. Skirting him to get to the chancel steps. Raising her small fist. Looking beautiful.

"I, Eleanor, Queen of England, Duchess of Aquitaine, do swear that you are my people and that I shall love and serve you as I love and serve my gracious Lord, Jesus Christ."

If she expected applause, she didn't get any. But she smiled; she was sure of her charm. "My good and faithful vassal, Lord Wolvercote, is a man of war, yet he is also a man of love, as shall be witnessed by his marriage to one of your own within a day or two, a celebration to which everyone here shall be invited."

That didn't get any applause, either, but from somewhere deep within the congregation, some-body farted. Loudly.

The men-at-arms turned their heads this way and that, looking for the culprit, but, though a shiver swept through the crowd, every face remained stolid.

How I love the English, Adelia thought.

The Abbot of Eynsham was on his feet, retrieving the situation by administering a blessing. At the "go in peace," the doors opened and they were allowed to file out between a phalanx of armed men who directed them to go home without talking.

Back in their room, Gyltha tore off her cloak. "Are they all gone daft, or is it me?"

"They have." She put Allie onto the bed; the child had been bored by the proceedings and had fallen asleep.

"What's to be gained by it?"

"Infighting," Adelia said. "He's making sure he's queen's champion before she can get another. Did you see Schwyz's face? Oh, poor Emma."

"'Queen's champion'?" scoffed Gyltha. "If Godstow wasn't for Henry Plantagenet before, it bloody is now—that's what the queen's champion's gone and done."

There was a knock on the door.

It was the mercenary, Cross, truculent as ever. He addressed Gyltha but pointed his chin at Adelia. "She's got to come along of me."

"And who are you? Here, you're one of them." Angrily, Gyltha pushed the man out onto the steps. "She ain't going anywhere with you, you pirate, and you can tell that bloody Wolvercote I told you so."

The mercenary staggered under the assault as he held it off. "I ain't Wolvercote's, I'm Schwyz's." He appealed to Adelia. "Tell her."

Gyltha kept pushing. "You're a bastard Fleming, whoever you be. Get away."

"Sister Jennet sent me." It was another appeal to Adelia; Sister Jennet was Godstow's infirmarian. "The doctor wants you for summat. Urgent."

Gyltha ceased her assault. "What doctor?"

"The darky. Thought he was a bargee, but turns out he's a doctor."

"A patient," Adelia said, relieved. Here was something she could deal with. She bent down to kiss Allie and went to get her bag. "Who is it? What's the trouble?"

Cross said, "It's Poyns, ain't it?" as if she should know. "His arm's bad."

"In what way bad?"

"Gone sort of green."

"*Hmmm.*" Adelia added her bundle of knives to the bag's equipment.

Even as they left, accompanied by Ward, Gyltha was giving the mercenary little shoves. "An' you bring her back as good as she goes, you scavengin' bugger, or it's me you'll answer to. And what about your bloody curfew?"

"Ain't my curfew," Cross shouted back. "'S Wolvercote's."

It was in operation already. Ward gave a grunt in reply to the bark of a fox somewhere out in the fields, but apart from that, the abbey was quiet. As they skirted the church and turned up by the barn, a sentry stepped out of the doorway of the little round pepper pot of a building that served as the convent's lockup.

The flambeau above the doorway shone on his helmet. He had a pike in his hand. "Who goes there?"

"Infirmary, mate," Cross told him. "This here's a nurse. Pal of mine's poorly."

"Give the password."

"What bloody password? I'm a queen's soldier, same as you."

"In the name of Lord Wolvercote, give us the password, see, or I'll run you through."

"Listen here, friend ..." Avoiding the pike, Cross shambled up to the sentry, apparently to explain, and hit him on the jaw.

He was a short man, Cross, but the taller sentry went down as if poleaxed.

Cross didn't even look at him. He gestured to Adelia. "Come *on*, will you?"

Before obeying, she stooped to make sure the sentry was breathing. He was, and beginning to groan.

Oh, well, it had been a password of sorts.

"I'm coming."

Sister Jennet was imperiling her immortal soul by bringing in on one of her cases a man she thought to be a heathen doctor. Nor was she doing it any good, either, by acquiescing to the presence of his "assistant," a woman whose relationship with the bishop had caused speculation among the sisterhood.

Yet that same bishop during his visit had spoken of the skill and scope of Arab medicine in general and of this practitioner in particular, and if she was religious, Sister Jennet was also a doctor manqué; it was against every instinct of her nature to watch one of her patients die from a condition about which she could do nothing but a Saracen could.

The tug and counter-tug of the battle within her was apparent in the anger with which she greeted Adelia. "You took your time, mistress. And leave this dog outside. It's bad enough that I have to countenance mercenaries in the ward." The infirmaress glared at Cross, who cowered.

Adelia had seen infirmaries where Ward's presence would have improved the smell. But not here. She looked around her; the long ward was as clean as any she'd encountered. Fresh straw on its boards, the scent of burning herbs from the braziers, white sheets, every patient's head cropped close against lice, and the ordered bustle of the attendant nuns suggesting that here was efficient care for the sick.

She shut Ward outside. "Perhaps you would tell me what I can do."

Sister Jennet was taken aback; Adelia's manner and plainness of dress were unexpected in a bishop's moll. Somewhat mollified, the infirmaress explained what she required of Dr. Mansur. "... but we are both imprisoned in the damned Tower of Babel."

"I see," Adelia said. "You can't understand him." Mansur probably understood quite well but could not move without her.

"Nor he me. It is why I sent for you. You speak his tongue, I understand." She paused. "Is he as

skilled as Bishop Rowley declared him to be?" At
the mention of the name, her eyes flickered to
Adelia's face and away.

"You will not be disappointed," Adelia promised
her.

"Well, anything is better than the village barber.
Don't stand there. Come along." She glared again
at the mercenary. "You, too, I suppose."

The patient was at the far end of the ward.
They'd put woven screens of withies round the
bed, but the smell coming from beyond confirmed
the reason for Sister Jennet's need of unChristian
help.

He was a young man, his terror at his surroundings enhanced by the tall, white-robed, dark-faced
figure looming over him. "It don't hurt," he kept
saying. "It don't hurt."

Mansur spoke in Arabic. "Where have you
been?"

Adelia replied in the same tongue. "Summoned
to church. We're under military rule."

"Who are we fighting?"

"God knows. Snowmen. What have we got
here?"

Mansur leaned forward and gently lifted a
covering of lint from the boy's left arm.

"No time to waste, I think."

There wasn't. The mangled lower arm was black
and discharging stinking, yellow pus.

"How did it happen?" Adelia demanded in
English—and added, as she so often had to, "The
doctor wants to know."

Cross spoke up. "Caught it under a cartwheel on the march to the tower, clumsy young bugger. Put some ointment on it, can't you?"

"Can you leave him his elbow?" Mansur asked.

"No." The telltale signs of necrosis were already racing upward beyond the joint.

"We'll be lucky if we can save his life."

"Why did the little woman not do it herself earlier?"

"She can't. She's not allowed to shed blood."

The Church's proscription against surgery was absolute. Sister Jennet could not disobey it.

Mansur's hawklike nose wrinkled. "They would leave him to die?"

"They were going to send for the Wolvercote barber." The horror of it overcame her. "A *barber*, dear God."

"A barber who sheds blood? He need not shave me, Imshallah."

Even had he been called in, the barber would have had to do his work in the kitchen to avoid offending God's nose with bloodshed in the area of the sacred cloister. Now, so would Adelia. This added tussle of medicine versus her religion caused such turbulence in Sister Jennet that she made arrangements for the operation in a rap of furious orders, and watched Mansur carry her patient out of the ward as if she hated them both. "And you," she shouted at the despised Cross, "you crawl back to your kennel. They don't want you."

"We do," Adelia told her. "He ... er, he knows the password."

However, the procession of doctor, patient, doctor's assistant, her dog, mercenary, and two nuns bearing clean linen and palliasse went unchallenged as it emerged via the door from the infirmary chapel and turned left toward the kitchen.

Adelia let the others go in first and caught Cross by the front of his jerkin before he could enter. She was going to need him; the patient would be less frightened if Cross, his friend, were present. She didn't like Cross much—well, he didn't like her—but she thought she could trust him to keep silent. "Listen to me, that boy's arm has to come off, and I ..."

"What you mean 'come off'?"

She kept it simple. "There's poison spreading up your friend's arm. If it gets to his heart, he will die."

"Ain't the darky going to say magic words over it or summat?"

"No, he's going to amputate, cut it off. Or rather, I am going to do it for him but ..."

"Can't. You're a woman."

Adelia shook him; there wasn't time for this. "Have you seen the state of the doctor's hands? They're in bandages. You will hear him talk and see me work but ..."

"He's going to tell you what to do, is that it?" Cross was slightly reassured. "Here, though, what's my lad going to do without his bloody arm?"

"What's he going to do without his bloody life?" Adelia shook the man again. "The point is ... you must swear never to tell anybody, *anybody*, what you see tonight. Do you understand?"

Cross's unlovely, troubled face cleared. "*Is* magic, ain't it? The darky's going to do sorcery, that's why the nuns ain't allowed to see."

"Who's your patron saint?"

"Saint Acacias, a'course. He always done well by me."

"Swear on him that you will not tell."

Cross swore.

The kitchen was deserted for the night. The nuns prepared its enormous chopping block with the palliasse and clean sheets for the patient to lie on, then bowed and left.

Young Poyns's eyes were goggling in his head and his breathing was fast; he was feverish and very frightened. "It don't hurt. It don't hurt at all."

Adelia smiled at him. "No, it wouldn't. And it won't, you're going to go to sleep." She got the opium bottle and a clean cloth out of her bag. Mansur was already lowering her net of knives into the bubbling pot of water hanging from a jack over the fire; hot steel cut better than cold.

The light in the kitchen, however, was insufficient. "You," she said to Cross. "Two candles. One in each hand. Hold them where I tell you, but don't let them drip."

Cross was watching Mansur raise the knives from the pot and take them out of the net with his bandaged hands. "You sure he knows what he's doing?"

"*Candles*," Adelia hissed at him. "Help or get out."

He helped; at least, he held the candles, but as she put the opium-soaked cloth over the patient's face, he tried to intervene. "You're smotherin' him, you bitch." Mansur held him back.

She had a few seconds; the boy must not breathe the opium too long. "This arm has to come off. You know that really, don't you? He may die anyway, but he can't live if I don't operate right away."

"*He's* telling you what to do, though?" Cross had begun to be overawed by Mansur, who, with his strength, his robe, and kaffiyeh, was impressive. "He's a sorcerer, ain't he? That's why he talks funny."

"You'll have to appear to be instructing me," Adelia said in Arabic.

Mansur began gabbling in Arabic.

She had to work fast, thanking God that opium grew plentifully in the Cambridgeshire fens and she had brought a good supply but measuring its benignity against its danger.

The world shrank to a tabletop.

Since he had to keep talking, Mansur chose as his theme *Kit b'Alf Layla wa-Layla*, also known as *The Book of a Thousand Nights*. So an Oxfordshire convent kitchen rang with the high-pitched voice of a castrato recounting in Arabic the stories that the Persian Scheherazade had concocted for her sultan husband three hundred years earlier in order to delay her execution. He'd told them to Adelia as a child and she had loved them. Now she heard them no more than she heard the pop and crackle of the fire.

Had Rowley, saved from the cold waters, entered the kitchen, Adelia wouldn't have looked up, nor recognized him if she had. The mention of her child's name would have brought the response "Who?" There was only the patient—not even him, really, just his arm. Fold back the flaps of skin.

"*Suturae.*"

Mansur slapped a threaded needle into her outstretched hand and began mopping blood.

Arteries, veins.

Saw the bone or cleave it? How the patient might manage his life with only a shoulder stump was not her concern; her thinking could only advance at the speed of the operation.

A heavy object thumped into the kitchen waste pail.

More stitches. Ointment, lint, bandage.

At last she wiped her forearm across her forehead. Slowly, her vision expanded to take in the beams and pots and a roaring fire.

Somebody was bothering her. "What's he say? Will he be all right?"

"I don't know."

"That was wunnerrful, though, weren't it?" Cross was shaking Mansur warmly by the hand. "Tell him he's a marvel."

"You're a marvel," Adelia said in Arabic.

"I know."

"How are your hands, my dear?" she asked. "Can you carry him back to the infirmary?"

"I can."

"Then wrap him up warm and be quick before the soporific wears off. Careful of his shoulder. Tell Sister Jennet he's likely to vomit when he comes round. I'll be along in a minute."

"He'll live now, won't he? Going to be all right, the lad, ain't he?"

She turned on the botherer. She was always bad-tempered at this point; it had been a race and, like a runner, she needed time to recover and—Cross, was it?—wasn't giving her any.

"The doctor doesn't *know*," she said—to hell with the bedside manner; it wasn't as if this man had been nice to her on the boat. "Your friend has youth on his side, but his injury was poisoned for too long and"—she leaned in to the attack—"*should have been treated before this*. Now go away and leave me alone."

She watched him slouch off after the laden Mansur, then sat herself by the fire, making lists in her head. There was plenty of willow bark, thanks be; the patient would need it for the pain. If he lived.

The stink of decomposition coming from the kitchen pail was a worry to her; after all, this was the kitchen that served their food. A rat appeared from behind a cupboard, its whiskers twitching in the direction of the pail. Adelia reached for the woodpile and threw a log at it.

What to do with severed limbs? In Salerno, she'd had other people to dispose of them. She'd always suspected they mixed them with the pigs' swill; it was one of the reasons she had been wary of eating pork.

Wrapping herself in her cloak and carrying the bucket, she went out into the alley to find some place of disposal. It was shockingly cold after the kitchen's heat, and very dark.

Farther down the alley someone began screaming. Went on screaming.

"I can't," Adelia said out loud. "I just can't." But she began blundering toward the sound, hoping somebody else would get there first and deal with whatever it was.

A lantern came bobbing out of the darkness with the sound of running. "Who's that?" It was the messenger, Jacques. "Oh, it's you, mistress."

"Yes. What is that?"

"I don't know."

They trotted toward it, being joined as they went by other lanterns that gave glimpses of alarmed faces and slippered feet.

Past the laundry, past the smithy, past the stables—all of it déjà vu, and horrible because Adelia now knew where the screams were coming from.

The cowshed doors were open, with people clustering around outside them, some trying to comfort a hysterical milkmaid, though most were transfixed and gaping, holding their lanterns high so that light shone on the dangling figure of Bertha.

A strap round her neck hung her from a hook in a beam. Her bare toes pointed downward toward a milking stool where it lay on its side among the straw.

The nuns lamented over the dead girl. What, they asked, could have possessed her to commit suicide, that so very grievous sin? Had she not known that God was the owner of her life and, consequently, that she had committed an unlawful act against God's own dominion, forbidden by Scripture and Church?

No, Adelia thought angrily, *Bertha hadn't known that; nobody would have taught her*.

Guilt, the sisters said. Hers was the hand that had given poisoned mushrooms to Rosamund; remorse had overcome her.

But they were good and charitable women, and though Bertha would have to be interred in uncon-secrated ground outside their convent walls, they took the body to their own chapel to keep a vigil over it in the meantime. They chanted prayers for the dead as they went. The crowd from the cowshed followed them.

Bertha had never had so much attention. Death in such a small community, after all, was always an event; felo-de-se was unheard of and worthy of much attention.

As she followed the procession through the dark alleys, Adelia stayed angry, thinking how wrong it was that a creature who had been denied so much in her short life must now be denied even a Christian burial.

Jacques, walking beside her, shook his head. "Terrible thing this is, mistress. To hang herself, poor soul. Felt herself responsible for Lady Rosamund's death, I reckon."

"She didn't, though, Jacques. You were there. '*Not my fault, not my fault*.' She said it over and over." It was one thing Bertha had been clear about.

"Well, then, she was mortal afraid of Dame Dakers. Couldn't face her, I reckon."

Yes, she had been afraid of Dakers. That would be the verdict. Either Bertha had suffered intolerable remorse for the death of her mistress or she had been so terrified of what Dakers would do to her that she had preferred to take her own life.

"It's wrong," Adelia said.

"A sin," Jacques agreed. "God have mercy on her soul all the same."

But it was wrong, everything was *wrong*. The scene of Bertha hanging from the hook had been wrong.

They were approaching the chapel. Such laypeople as had been accompanying the body stopped. This was the nuns' territory; they must stay outside. Even if she could have gone on, Adelia couldn't bear it anymore, not Jacques and his gloomy chatter, not the accompanying, expostulating men and women, not the nuns' chanting. "Where's the guesthouse from here?"

Jacques showed her the way back. "A good night's sleep, mistress. That's what you need."

"Yes." But it wasn't fatigue, though she was very tired, it was the wrongness of everything. It hammered at her mind like something wanting to come in.

The messenger lighted her up the steps and then went off, muttering and shaking his head.

Gyltha had heard the screaming even from their room and had called out the window to find its cause. "Bad business," she said. "They're saying sorrow made her do it, poor mite."

"Or perhaps she was frightened that Dame Dakers would turn her into a mouse and give her to the cat, yes, I know."

Gyltha looked up from her knitting, alerted. "Oh, ar? What's this?"

"It's wrong." Adelia fondled Ward's ears, then pushed the dog away.

Gyltha's eyes narrowed, but she said nothing more on the subject. "How's the Fleming?"

"I don't think he'll survive." Adelia wandered to their communal bed and soothed back her sleeping daughter's hair.

"Serve un right." Gyltha didn't hold with mercenaries, whose extensive use during the Stephen and Matilda war had made them universally loathed. Whether they came from Flanders or not—and most of them did—the name "Fleming" had become a euphemism for rape, pillage, and cruelty. "One thing about the king," she said, "he got rid of all they bastards, and now Eleanor's bringing 'em back."

"*Hmmm.*"

Gyltha raised her eyebrows. She'd prepared a hot posset—the room smelled deliciously of hot milk and rum. She handed a beaker to Adelia. "You know what time it is?" She pointed to the hour marks on the candle by the bed. "Time you was in bed. Nearly morning. They'll be singing Matins soon."

"It's all wrong, Gyltha."

Gyltha sighed; she knew the signs. "It'll keep til morning."

"No, it won't." Adelia roused herself and refastened her cloak. "A measure, I need a measure. Have we any string?"

There was cord that they used to bind their traveling packs. "And I want that back," Gyltha said. "Good cord that is. Where you going?"

"I left the medicine bag in the kitchen. I'd better go and get it."

"You stay there," Gyltha told her sharply. "You ain't going nowhere without that old Arab goes, too."

But Adelia had gone, taking the cord and a lantern with her. Not to the kitchen. She made her way to the nuns' chapel. It was dawn.

They had laid Bertha's body on a catafalque in the little nave. The sheet they'd covered it with dragged all the vague light from the high windows to its own oblong whiteness, condemning the rest of the space to a misty dust.

Adelia strode up the nave, the shushing of her feet in the rushes disturbing the quiet so that the nun on her knees at the foot of the catafalque turned to see who it was.

Adelia paid her no attention. She put the lantern on the floor while she turned back the sheet.

Bertha's face had a bluish tint; the tip of her tongue was just visible where it stuck out of the side of her mouth. This, with her tiny nose, gave her a look of impudence, like some fairy child.

The nun—she was one Adelia didn't know—hissed her concern as Adelia picked up the lantern and, with the other hand, pulled back Bertha's lids to expose the eyes.

There were flecks of blood in their whites. Only to be expected.

Getting onto her knees, Adelia held the lantern as close as she could to the neck. There were lines from the edges of the strap that the girl had hung by, but there were other marks—gouges that traveled down the throat.

And running horizontally around the skin of the neck beneath the strap bruises was a line of tiny circular indentations.

The nun was on her feet, trying to flap Adelia away from the body. "What are you doing? You are disturbing the dead."

Adelia ignored her, didn't even hear her. She recovered Bertha's face with the sheet and turned it back at the other end, lifting the girl's skirts to expose the lower body.

The nun ran from the chapel.

The vagina showed no sign of tearing or, as far as it was possible to see, any trace of semen.

Adelia replaced the sheet.

Damn. There *was* a way of knowing. Her old tutor, Gordinus, had shown her by opening the necks of prisoners who'd been hanged and comparing their hyoid bones with bones of those who'd been garroted—a form of execution peculiar to a district of Pavia, which had inherited it from the Romans. *"See, my dear? The bone is rarely broken in garroting, whereas it is, almost invariably, in hanging. Thus, if we are suspicious in a case of strangulation, we may distinguish whether it was self-inflicted or the result of an attack by another. Also, in the case of hanged suicides, there is seldom bleeding into the neck muscles, whereas if we find it in a corpse supposed to have hanged itself, we have cause to be suspicious that we are looking at a case of murder."*

A dissection ... if she could just do a dissection ... Oh, well, she'd have to rely on measurements ...

"And what is this?" The deep voice rang through the chapel, dispelling its quiet, seeming to disturb the dust motes and bring in a sharper light.

The nun was gabbling. "Do you see her, my lord? This woman ..."

"I see her." He turned on Adelia, who had run the cord from the top of Bertha's head to her bare toes. "Are you mad? Why do you dishonor the dead, mistress? Even one such as this?"

"*Hmmm.*" Having made a knot in it, Adelia wound the cord around her hand and began vaguely wandering toward the door.

Splendid in breadth and height and color, the abbot blocked her way. "I *asked*, mistress, why you interfere with the poor soul lying there?" The West Country accent had gone, replaced by schooled vowels.

Adelia moved past him. *The strap*, she thought, *perhaps it's still in the cowshed. And my chain.*

The abbot watched her go and then, with a sweep of his arms, sent the nun back to her vigil.

Outside, despite a suicide, the presence of a queen, occupation by her mercenaries, and the terrible cold, the wheel of the abbey's day was being sent spinning. Slipping on dirty, nobbling ice, Godstow's people hurried past her to reawaken damped-down fires and start their work.

Jacques caught up with Adelia as she passed the stables. "I waited, mistress. What's to be done with this?" He was carrying a bucket and swung it in front of her so that she had to stop. It contained an arm; Adelia stared at it for a moment before remembering that, in what seemed like another epoch, she had performed an amputation.

"I don't know. Bury it somewhere, I suppose." She pressed on.

"Bury it," Jacques said, looking after her. "And the ground like bloody iron."

The cowshed in daylight. Warm, despite the open doors. Sun shining onto its bespattered floor, quiet except for a rhythmic swish from one of the stalls, where a young woman was milking. The stool she sat on was the one that had been kicked over underneath Bertha's hanging body.

Her name, she said, was Peg, and it was she who, entering the shed early to begin the morning's milking, had discovered Bertha. The sight had sent her into screams, and she'd had to run back home for a drop of her mother's soothing cordial before she could face returning to the scene and start work.

"'Tis why I'm so late today. These poor beasts've been lowing for me to come and relieve 'em but 'twas the shock, d'ye see. Opened the doors and there she was. Never get over it, I won't. This old shed, 'twill never be the same again, not to me it won't."

Adelia knew how she felt; the comforting smell of animal flatulence and straw, the innocent homeliness of the place had been invaded. An ancient beam from which a body had hung was now a gibbet. She wouldn't get over it, either. Bertha had died here, and of all the deaths, Bertha's cried out the loudest.

"Can I help ye, mistress?" Peg wanted to know, carrying on milking.

"I'm looking for a necklet, a cross and chain. I gave it to Bertha. She isn't wearing it now, and I'd like to put it in her grave with her."

Peg's cap went askew as she shook her head without it losing contact with the cow's ribs. "Never seen un."

In her mind's eye, Adelia resurrected the scene of an hour or so ago. A man—she thought it was Fitchet the gatekeeper—had run forward, righted the stool that lay below Bertha's feet, stood on it, and lifted the body so that the strap it hung by came free of the beam's hook.

What, then? That's right, that's right, other men had helped him lay the body down. Somebody had undone the strap and tossed it away. The people clustering around, hopelessly trying to revive the dead girl, had hindered Adelia from seeing whether her cross and chain was on Bertha's neck. If it had been, the strap had covered it and pressed it tightly against the girl's skin as she hanged, forcing its links into her flesh and causing those indentations.

But if she *hadn't* been wearing it ...

Adelia began looking around.

In a cobwebby corner, she found the strap. It was a belt, an old one. A worn rivet showed where the owner had been wont to fasten it, but at the far end of the leather, another rivet had been badly contorted where it had been slipped over the hook on the beam and taken the weight of Bertha's body.

"Where did she get a belt from, I wonder?" Adelia asked herself out loud, putting it over her shoulder.

"Dunno, she never had no belt," Peg said.

That's right. She hadn't. Adelia walked slowly to the far end of the cowshed, kicking up wisps of hay as she went to see if they hid anything.

Behind her came the swish of milk as it went into the pail and Peg's reflective voice: "Poor thing, I can't think what come to her. 'Course, she were a bit of a looby, but even so ..."

"Did she say anything to you?"

"Said a lot, always muttering away up the other end there, enough to give you goose bumps, but I paid her no mind."

Adelia reached the stall that Bertha had occupied. It was dark here. She balanced the lantern on top of a partition and went down on her knees to start sifting the straw, feeling through it to the hard-packed earth underneath.

She heard Peg address her cow, "You're done then, madam," and the friendly slap on its rump as the milkmaid left it to go on to the next, and the sound of footfalls as some new person entered the shed, and Peg's voice again: "And a good morning to you, Master Jacques."

"Good morning to *you*, Mistress Peg."

There was flirtation in both voices that brought a lightness to the day. Jacques, Adelia thought, despite his sticking-out ears and breathy over-eagerness, had made a conquest.

He came hurrying up the aisle and paused to watch Adelia as she scrabbled. "I buried it, mistress."

"What? Oh, good."

"Can I help whatever it is you're doing, mistress?" He was becoming used to her eccentricities.

"No."

Because she'd found it. Her fingers had encountered the harsh thread of metal, little and broken—the cross was held by the fastening, but farther along, the links had snapped.

God help us all. This, then, was where it had happened. In this dark stall, Bertha had torn at her own neck in an attempt to dislodge the necklet with which strong hands were strangling her.

Oh, the poor child.

Adelia again saw Bertha crawling toward her, sniffing, telling her what the old woman in the forest, who had given her the mushrooms for Rosamund, had smelled like.

"Purty. Like you."

The memory was unbearable. The short, sad little life ending in violence ... *Why? Who?*

"Mistress?" Jacques was becoming troubled by her stillness.

Adelia picked herself up. Gripping the necklet, she walked with the messenger down to where Peg was pouring her full pail of foaming milk into a bigger bucket, her backside giving a provocative wiggle at Jacques's approach.

The milking stool. She knew now that Bertha had been murdered, but there was just one more proof ...

As Peg went to collect the stool to take it to the next cow, Adelia was ahead of her. "May I have this for a moment?"

Peg and Jacques stared as she took the stool and placed it directly under the hook in the beam. She unwound the length of cord from her hand and pushed it toward Jacques. "Measure me."

"Measure you, mistress?"

"*Yes.*" She was becoming irritable. "From my crown to my feet."

Shrugging, he held one end of the cord to the top of Adelia's head and let it drop. He stooped and pinched the place where it touched the ground. "There. You're not very tall, mistress."

She tried to smile at him—his own lack of height bothered him; without his raised boots, he wouldn't be much higher than she was. Looking at the cord where he held it, she saw that it extended a little way from the knot she had made when she'd measured the corpse on the catafalque. She was nearly two inches taller than Bertha had been.

Now to see.

Peg said, "She got excited yesterday, round about evening milkin', now I come to think on it."

"Who did? Bertha?"

"Said she'd got summat to tell the lady with the cross and went rushin' out. That's what she'd call a nun, I suppose, on account of she didn't know better."

No, Adelia thought, *it was me. I was the lady with the cross.* "Where did she go?"

"Can't have been far," Peg said, "for she were soon back and takin' on like she'd seen the devil stinkin' of sulphur. Summat about acres."

"Dakers?" Jacques asked.

"Could've been."

"Must've seen Dame Dakers," Jacques said. "She was mortal afraid of that woman."

Adelia asked, "She didn't say what it was she wanted to tell the nun?"

"Kept mutterin' something about wasn't her, 'twas him."

Adelia steadied herself against a stall's stanchion, grasping it hard. "Could it have been: '*It wasn't a her, it was a him*'?"

"Could've been."

"*Hmmm.*" She wanted to think about it, but the cows farther up the line were lowing with discomfort, and Peg was becoming restive at the annexation of her milking stool.

Adelia slipped the belt into its buckle and put it round her neck, pulling it close. Stepping up on the stool, she tried extending the free piece of the belt to the hook, managing only to make the end of the leather touch it, leaving a gap between hook and rivet. She stood on tiptoe; rivet and hook still didn't meet—and she was taller than Bertha had been.

"It's too short," she said. "The belt's too short."

That was what had bothered her. The sight of the dangling body had been too shocking to take in at the time, but her mind had registered it—*Bertha's feet could not have reached the stool to kick it away.*

She began choking, struggling to get the buckle undone before unseen arms could lift her up and attach the belt to the hook; she couldn't breathe.

Jacques's hands fumbled at her neck and she fought them, as Bertha had fought those of her killer. "All right, mistress," he said. "Steady. Steady now." When he'd got the belt off, he held her arm and stroked her back as if soothing a frightened cat. "Steady now. Steady."

Peg was watching them as if at the capering insane. Jacques nodded at her, indicating the stool, and with relief she took it up and went back to her cows.

Adelia stood where she was, listening as Peg's capable, cold-chapped hands squeezed and relaxed on the cow's teats, sending milk into the pail with the regularity of a soft drumbeat.

"It wasn't a her, it was a him."

Jacques's eyes questioned her; he, at least, had understood what she'd been about.

"Well," Adelia said, "at least now Bertha can be buried in consecrated ground."

"Not suicide?"

"No. She was murdered."

She saw again how his young face could age.

"Dakers," he said.

NINE

*T*he nuns thought the same.

"Let me understand you," Mother Edyve said. "You are saying that Dame Dakers hanged that poor child?"

They were in the chapter house; the abbess was in conclave with her senior nuns.

They had not welcomed Adelia. After all, they had serious matters to mull over: Their abbey had been as good as invaded; dangerous mercenaries occupied it; there were bodies hanging from their bridge; if the snow continued, they would soon run out of supplies. They did not want to listen to the outlandish, unsettling report of a murder—*murder?*—in their midst.

However, Adelia had done one thing right: She had brought Mansur along. Gyltha had persuaded her. "They won't pay you no mind," she'd said, "but they might attend to that old Arab." And after a few hours' sleep, Adelia had decided she was right. Mansur had been recommended to the nuns by their bishop, he looked impressive, he stood high in the estimation of their infirmaress; above all, he was a man, and as such, even though a foreigner, he carried more weight than she did.

It had been difficult to get a hearing until the chapter meeting was over, but Adelia had refused to wait. "This is the king's business," she'd said. For so it was; murder, wherever it occurred, came under royal jurisdiction. The lord Mansur, she told them, was skilled in uncovering crimes, had originally been called to England by Henry II's warrant to look into the deaths of some Cambridgeshire children—well, so he had, in a way—and the killer had been found.

Apologizing for Mansur's insufficiency in their language, she had pretended to interpret for him. She'd begged them to examine for themselves the marks on Bertha's neck, had shown them the evidence by which she proved murder ... and heard her voice scrabbling at them as uselessly as Bertha's fingers had scrabbled at the necklet strangling her.

She answered Mother Edyve, "The lord Mansur is not accusing Dame Dakers. He is saying that *somebody* hanged Bertha. She did not hang herself."

It was too gruesome for them. Here, in their familiar, wooden-crucked English chapter house, stood a towering figure in outlandish clothing—a heathen, king's warrant or not—telling them what they did not want to hear through the medium of a woman with a dubious reputation.

They didn't have investigative minds. It seemed as if none of them, not even their canny old abbess, possessed the ferocious curiosity that drove Adelia herself, nor any curiosity at all. All questions had been answered for them by the resurrection of Jesus Christ and the rule instituted by Saint Benedict.

Nor were they too concerned with earthly justice. The murderer, if a murderer there was, would be sentenced more terribly when he faced the Great Judge, to whom all sins were known, than by any human court.

The belt, the broken chain, and the measuring cord lay snaked on the table before them, but they kept their eyes away.

Well, yes, they said, but was the lack of distance between Bertha's feet and the milking stool significant? Surely that poor misguided girl could have somehow climbed onto one of the cowshed stalls with the belt round her neck and jumped? Who knew what strength was given to the desperate? Certainly, Bertha had been in fear of what Dame Dakers might do to her, but did not that in itself argue felo-de-se?

Rowley, if only you were here ...

"It was murder," Adelia insisted. "Lord Mansur has proved it was murder."

Mother Edyve considered the matter. "I would not have credited Dakers with the strength."

Adelia despaired. It was like being on a toasting fork—whichever side was presented, it was flipped over so that the other faced the fire. If Bertha had been murdered, then Dakers, revenging Rosamund's death, had been the murderer—who else could it have been? If Dakers wasn't the murderer, then Bertha had not been murdered.

"Perhaps one of the Flemings did it, Wolvercote's or Schwyz's," Sister Bullard, the cellaress, said. "They are lustful, violent men, especially in liquor. Which reminds me, Mother, we must set a guard on the cellars. They are already stealing our wine."

That opened a floodgate of complaint: "Mother, how are we to feed them all?"

"Mother, the mercenaries ... I fear for our young women."

"And our people—look how they beat the poor miller."

"The courtiers are worse, Mother. The lewd songs they sing ..."

Adelia was sorry for them. On top of their worries, here were two strange persons, who had arrived at Godstow in company with a murdered body from the bridge, now suggesting that another killer was at large within the abbey's very walls.

The sisters did not—indeed, *could* not—blame them for either death, but Adelia knew from some sideways looks from under the nuns' veils that she and Mansur had acquired the taint of carrion.

"Even if what Lord Mansur says is true, Mother," said Sister Gregoria, the almoner, "what can be done about it? We are snowed up; we cannot send for the sheriff's coroner until the thaw."

"And while the snow lasts, King Henry cannot rescue us," Sister Bullard pointed out. "Until he can, our abbey, our very existence, is in peril."

That was what mattered to them. Their abbey had survived one conflict between warring monarchs; it might not survive another. If the queen should oust the king, she would necessarily reward the blackguard Wolvercote, who had secured her victory—and Lord Wolvercote had long desired Godstow and its lands. The nuns could envisage a future in which they begged for their bread in the streets.

"Allow Lord Mansur to continue his inquiries," Adelia pleaded. "At least do not bury Bertha in unconsecrated ground until all the facts are known."

Mother Edyve nodded. "Please tell Lord Mansur we are grateful for his interest," she said in her fluting, emotionless voice. "You may leave us to question Dame Dakers. After that, we shall pray for guidance in the matter."

It was a dismissal. Mansur and Adelia had to bow and leave.

Discussion broke out behind them almost before they'd reached the door—but it was not about Bertha. "Yes, but where *is* the king? How may he come to our aid if he doesn't even know we are in need of it? We cannot trust that Bishop Rowley reached him—I fear for his death."

As the two went out of the chapter house door, Mansur said, "The women are frightened. They will not help us search for the killer."

"I haven't even persuaded them there *is* a killer," Adelia said.

They were skirting the infirmary when, behind them, a voice called Adelia's name. It was the prioress. She came up, puffing. "A word, if I may, mistress." Adelia nodded, bowed a farewell to Mansur, and turned back.

For a while, the two women went in silence.

Sister Havis, Adelia realized, had not spoken a word during the discussion in the chapter house. She was aware, too, that the nun did not like her. To walk with her was like accompanying the apotheosis of the cold that gripped the abbey, a figure denuded of warmth, as frozen as the icicles spiking the edge of every roof.

Outside the nuns' chapel, the prioress stopped. She kept her face averted from Adelia, and her voice was hard. "I cannot approve of you," she said. "I did not approve of Rosamund. The tolerance that Mother Abbess extends to sins of the flesh is not mine."

"If that's all you have to say ..." Adelia said, walking away.

Sister Havis strode after her. "It is not, but it has to be spoken." She withdrew a mittened hand from under her scapular and held it out to bar Adelia's progress. In it were the broken necklet, the measuring cord, and the belt. She said, "I intend to use these objects as you have done, in investigation. I shall go to the cowshed. Whatever your weaknesses, mistress, I recognize an analytical soul."

Adelia stopped.

The prioress kept her thin face turned away. "I travel," she said. "Mine is the work to administer our lands around the country, in consequence of which I see more of the dung heap of humanity than do my sisters. I see it in its iniquity and error, its disregard for the flames of hell which await it."

Adelia was still. This was not just a lecture on sin; Sister Havis had something to tell her.

"Yet," the prioress went on, "there is greater evil. I was present at Rosamund Clifford's bedside; I witnessed her terrible end. For all that she was adulterous, the woman should not have died as she did."

Adelia went on waiting.

"Our bishop had visited her a day or two before; he questioned her servants and went away again. Rosamund was still well then, but he believed from what he'd been told that there had been a deliberate attempt to poison her, which, as you and I know, subsequently succeeded." Suddenly, the prioress's head turned and she was glaring into Adelia's eyes. "Is that what he told you?"

"Yes," Adelia said. "It was why he brought us here. He knew the blame would fall on the queen. He wanted to uncover the real killer and avert a war."

"He set great store by you, then, mistress." It was a sneer.

"*Yes, he did,*" Adelia hissed back at her. Her feet were numb with standing, and her grief for Rowley was undoing her. "Tell me whatever you want to tell me, or let me go. In God's name, are we discussing Rosamund, Bertha, or the bishop?"

The prioress blinked; she had not expected anger.

"Bertha," she said, with something like conciliation. "We are discussing Bertha. It may interest you to know, mistress, that I took charge of Dame Dakers yesterday. The female is deranged, and I did not want her roaming the abbey. Just before

Vespers I locked her in the warming room for the night."

Adelia's head went up. "What time is evening milking?"

"*After* Vespers."

They had begun walking in step. "Bertha was still alive then," Adelia said. "The milkmaid saw her."

"Yes, I have talked to Peg."

"I *knew* it wasn't Dakers."

The prioress nodded. "Not unless the wretched female can walk through a thick and bolted door. Which, I may say, most of my sisters are prepared to believe that she can."

"You may say, you may say." Adelia stopped, furious. "Why didn't you say all this in chapter?"

The prioress faced her. "You were making yourself busy proving to us that Bertha was murdered. I happened to know Dakers could not have killed her. The question then arose, who did? And why? It was not a wolf I wanted to loose amongst sisters who are troubled and frightened enough already."

Ah. At last, Adelia thought, *a logical mind. Hostile, cold as winter to me, but brave.* Here, beside her, was a woman prepared to follow terrible events to their terrible conclusion.

She said, "Bertha had some knowledge about the person who gave her the mushrooms in the forest. She didn't know she had it. It came to her yesterday, and I think, I *think*, that she left the cowshed to come and tell me. Something, or perhaps it was someone, stopped her, and she went back again. To be strangled and then hanged."

"Not a random killing?"

"I don't believe so. Nor was there any sexual interference, as far as I can tell. It wasn't robbery, either; the chain was not stolen."

Unconsciously, they had begun pacing up and down together outside the chapel. Adelia said, "What she told Peg was that it wasn't a her, it was a him."

"Meaning the person in the forest?"

"I think so. I think, I *think*, Bertha remembered something, something about the old woman who gave her the mushrooms for Rosamund. I think it came to her that it wasn't an old woman at all—her description always sounded ... I don't know, odd."

"Old women peddling poisoned mushrooms aren't odd?"

Adelia smiled. "Overdone, then. Playacting. I think that's what Bertha wanted to tell me. *Not a her but a him.*"

"A man? Dressed as a woman?"

"I think so."

The prioress crossed herself. "The inference being that Bertha could have told us who it was that killed Rosamund ..."

"Yes."

"... but was strangled before she could tell us ... *by that same person.*"

"I think so."

"I was afraid of it. The Devil stalks secretly amongst us."

"In human form, yes."

"'I shall not fear,'" quoted Sister Havis. "'I shall not fear for the arrow that flieth by day, for the matter that walketh in darkness, nor for the Devil that is in the noonday.'" She looked at Adelia. "Yet I do."

"So do I." Oddly, though, not as much as she had; there was a tiny comfort in having passed on what she knew to authority, and here, though personally hostile, was almost the only authority the convent could offer.

After a while, Sister Havis said, "We have had to take the body from the bridge out of the icehouse. A man came asking for him, a cousin, he said—a Master Warin, a lawyer from Oxford. We laid out the body in the church for its vigil and so that he might identify it. Apparently, it is that of a young man called Talbot of Kidlington. Is he another of this devil's victims?"

"I don't know." She realized she had been saying "I" all this time. "I shall consult with the Lord Mansur. He will investigate."

The slightest flicker of amusement crossed the prioress's face; she knew who the investigator was. "Pray do," she said.

From the cloister ahead of them came the sound of laughter and singing. It had, Adelia realized, been going on for some time. Music, happiness, still existed, then.

Automatically, the prioress began walking toward it. Adelia went with her.

A couple of the younger nuns were screaming joyously in the garth as they dodged snowballs being pelted at them by a scarlet-clad youth. Another young man was strumming a viol and singing, his head upraised to an upper window of the abbess's house, at which Eleanor stood laughing at the antics.

This, in the sanctum. Where no layman should set foot. Probably never had until now.

From Eleanor's window came a trail of perfume, elusive as a mirage, shimmering with sensuality, a siren scent beckoning toward palm-fringed islands, a smell so lovely that Adelia's nose, even while it analyzed—bergamot, sandalwood, roses—sought longingly after its luxury before the icy air took it away from her.

Oh, Lord, I am so tired of death and cold.

Sister Havis stood beside her, rigid with disapproval, saying nothing. But in a minute the players saw her. The scene froze instantly; the troubadour's song stopped in his throat, snow dropped harmlessly from the hand of his companion, and the young nuns assumed attitudes of outraged piety and continued their walk as if they had never broken stride. The snowballer swept his hat from his head and held it to his chest in parodied remorse.

Eleanor waved from her window. "Sorry," she called, and closed the shutters.

So I am not the only taint, Adelia thought, amused. The queen and her people were bringing the rich colors of worldliness into the convent's black-and-white domain; the presence of Eleanor, which had undermined an entire Crusade, threatened

Godstow's foundations as even Wolvercote and his mercenaries did not.

Then the amusement went. *Did she bring a killer with her?*

Adelia was too tired to do much for the rest of the morning except look after Allie while Gyltha went off to meet friends in the kitchen. It was where she picked up a good deal of information and gossip.

On her return, she said, "They're busy cooking for young Emma's wedding now that Old Wolfie's turned up. Poor soul, I wouldn't fancy marryin' that viper. They're wondering if she's having second thoughts—she's keeping to the cloister and ain't spoke a word to him, so they say."

"It's bad luck to see your bridegroom before the wedding," Adelia said vaguely.

"I wouldn't want to see *him* after," Gyltha said. "Oh, and later on the sisters is going to see about them hangin' off the bridge. Abbess says it's time they was buried." She took off her cloak. "Should be interestin'. Old Wolfie, he'll be the sort as likes corpses decoratin' the place." There was a gleam in her eye. "Maybe as there'll be a battle atwixt 'em. Oh, Lord, where you going *now*?"

"The infirmary." Adelia had remembered her patient.

Sister Jennet greeted her warmly. "Perhaps you can convey my gratitude to the Lord Mansur. Such a neat, clean stump, and the patient is progressing well." She looked wistful. "How I should have liked to witness the operation."

It was the instinct of a doctor, and Adelia thought of the women lost to her own profession, as this one was, and thanked her god for the privilege that had been Salerno.

She was escorted down the ward. All the patients were men—"women mainly treat themselves"—most of them suffering from congestion of the lungs caused, the infirmaress said, by living on low-lying ground subject to unhealthy vapors from the river.

Three were elderly, from Wolvercote. "These are malnourished," the infirmaress said of them, not bothering to lower her voice. "Lord Wolvercote neglects his villagers shamefully; they haven't so much as a church to pray in, not since it fell down. It is God's grace to them that we are nearby."

She passed on to another bed where a nun was applying warm water to a patient's ear. "Frostnip," she said.

With a pang of guilt, Adelia recognized Oswald, Rowley's man-at-arms. She'd forgotten him, yet he had been one of those, along with Mansur, poling the barge that the convent had sent to Wormhold.

Walt was sitting at his bedside. He knuckled his forehead as Adelia came up.

"I'm sorry," she told Oswald. "Is it bad?"

It looked bad. Dark blisters had formed on the outer curve of the ear so that the man appeared to have a fungus attached to his head. He glowered at her.

"Shoulda kept his hood pulled down," Walt said cheerfully. "We did, didn't we, mistress?" The mutual suffering on the boat had become a bond.

Adelia smiled at him. "We were fortunate."

"We're keeping an eye on the ear," Sister Jennet said, equally cheerful. "As I tell him, it will either stay on or fall off. Come along."

There were still screens round young Poyns's bed—not so much, Sister Jennet explained, to provide privacy for him as to prevent his evil mercenary ways from infecting the rest of the ward.

"Though I must say he has not uttered a single oath since he's been here, which is unusual in a Fleming." She pulled the screen aside, still talking. "I can't say the same for his friend." She shook a finger at Cross, who, like Walt, was visiting.

"We ain't bloody Flemings," Cross said wearily.

Adelia was not allowed to look at the wound. Dr. Mansur, apparently, had already done so and declared himself satisfied.

The stump was well bandaged and—Adelia sniffed it—had no smell of corruption. Mansur, having attended so many operations with her, would have been able to tell if there was any sign of mortification.

Poyns himself was pale but without fever and taking food. For a moment, Adelia allowed herself to glory in him, orgulous as a peacock at her achievement, even while she marveled at the hardihood of the human frame.

She inquired after Dame Dakers; here was

another she had neglected, and for whom she felt a responsibility.

"We keep her in the warming room," Sister Jennet said, as of an exhibit. "Once she was recovered, I couldn't let her stay here—she frightened my patients."

I n a monastery, the warming room would have been the scriptorium where such monks as had the skill spent their days copying manuscripts while carefully guarded braziers saved their poor fingers from cramping with cold.

Here were only Sister Lancelyne and Father Paton—he came as a surprise; Adelia had forgotten the existence of Rowley's secretary. Both were writing, though not books.

Thin winter sun shone on their bent heads and on the documents with large seals attached to them by ribbon covering the table at which they sat.

Adelia introduced herself. Father Paton screwed up his eyes and then nodded; he'd forgotten her also.

Sister Lancelyne was delighted to make her acquaintance. She was the sort of person to whom gossip was without interest unless it was literary. Nor did she seem to know that Rowley was lost. "Of course, you came with the bishop's party, did you not? Please extend to his lordship my gratitude for Father Paton; *what* I would do without this gentleman ... I had vowed to arrange our cartulary and register in some sort of order, a task that proved beyond me until his lordship sent this Hercules into my Augean stables."

Father Paton as Hercules was something to savor; so was Sister Lancelyne herself, an old, small, gnomelike woman with the bright, jewellike eyes of a toad; so was the room, shelved from floor to ceiling, each shelf stacked with rolls of deeds and charters showing their untidy, sealed ends.

"Alphabetical order, you see," chanted Sister Lancelyne. "That is what we have to achieve, and a calendar showing which tithe is due to us on what day, what rent ... but I see you are looking at our book."

It was the *only* book, a slim volume bound in calfskin; it had a small shelf to itself that had been lined with velvet like a jewel box. "We have a Testament, of course," Sister Lancelyne said, apologizing for the lack of library, "and a breviary, both are in the chapel, but ... oh, dear." For Adelia had advanced on the book. As she took its spine between finger and thumb to remove it, there was a gasp of relief from the nun. "I see you care for books; so many drag at its top with a forefinger and break ..."

"Boethius," Adelia said with pleasure. "'*O happy race of men if love that rules the stars may also rule your hearts.*'"

"'*To acquire divinity, become gods,*'" exulted Sister Lancelyne. "'*Omnis igitur beatus deus ... by participation.*' They imprisoned him for it."

"And killed him. I know, but as my foster father says, if he hadn't been in prison, he would never have written *The Consolation of Philosophy*."

"We only have the *Fides and Ratio*," said Sister Lancelyne. "I long for ... no, mea culpa, I *covet* the rest as King David lusted on Bathsheba. They have an entire *Consolation* in the library at Eynsham, and I ventured to beg the abbot if I might borrow it to copy, but he wrote back to say it was too precious to send. He does not credit women with scholarship and, of course, you can't blame him."

Adelia was not a scholar herself—too much of her reading had largely and necessarily been expended on medical treatises—but she possessed a high regard for those who were; the talk of her foster father and her tutor, Gordinus, had opened a door to the literature of the mind so that she'd glimpsed a shining path to the stars, which, she promised herself, she would investigate one day. In the meantime, it was nice to discover it here among shelves and the smell of vellum and this little old woman's unextinguished desire for knowledge.

Carefully, she replaced the book. "I was hoping to find Dame Dakers with you."

"Another great help," Sister Lancelyne said happily, pointing to a hooded figure squatting on the floor, half-hidden by the shelves.

They'd given Rosamund's housekeeper a knife with which to sharpen their quills. Goose feathers lay beside her, and she held one in her hand, the shreds of its calamus scattered on her lap. A harmless occupation, and one she must have engaged in a hundred times for Rosamund, yet Adelia was irresistibly reminded of something being dismembered.

She went to squat beside the woman. The two scribes had gone back to their work. "Do you remember me, mistress?"

"I remember you." Dakers went on shaving the quill end, making quick movements with the knife.

She had been fed and rested; she looked less bleached, but no amount of well-being was ever going to plump the skin over Dakers's skeleton, nor was it going to distract her hatred. The eyes bent on her work still glowed with it. "Found my darling's killer yet?" she asked.

"Not yet. Did you hear of Bertha's death?"

Dakers's mouth stretched, showing her teeth. She had—and happily. "I summoned my master to punish her, and he's a'done it."

"What master?"

Dakers turned her head so that Adelia stared full into her face; it was like looking into a charnel pit. "There is only The One."

Cross was waiting for her outside, and loped truculently alongside as she walked. "Here," he said, "what they goin' to do with Giorgio?"

"Who? Oh, Giorgio. Well, I suppose the sisters will bury him." The corpses were piling up at Godstow.

"Where, though? I want him planted proper. He was a Christian, was Giorgio."

And a mercenary, thought Adelia, which might, in Godstow's eyes, put him in the same category as others who'd relinquished their right to a

Christian grave. She said, "Have you asked the nuns?"

"Can't talk to 'em." Cross found the holy sisters intimidating. "*You* ask 'em."

"Why should I?" The sheer gracelessness of this little man ...

"You're a Sicilian, ain't you? Like Giorgio. You said you was, so you got to see him planted proper, with a priest and the blessing of ... what was that saint had her tits cut off?"

"I suppose you mean Saint Agnes," Adelia said coldly.

"Yeah, her." Cross's unlovely features creased into a salacious grin. "They still carry her tits around on festival days?"

"I'm afraid so." She had always considered it an unfortunate custom, but the particularly horrible martyrdom of poor Saint Agnes was still commemorated in Palermo by a procession bearing the replicas of two severed breasts on a tray, like little nippled cakes.

"He thought a lot of Saint Agnes, Giorgio did. So you tell 'em."

Adelia opened her mouth to tell *him* something, then saw the mercenary's eyes and stopped. The man agonized for his dead friend, as he had agonized for the injured Poyns; there was a soul here, however ungainly.

"I'll try," she said.

"See you do."

In the large open area beyond the grain barn, one of Wolvercote's liveried men was walking up and down outside the pepper pot lockup, though what he might be guarding Adelia couldn't imagine.

Farther along, the convent smith was pounding at the ice on the pond to crack a hole through which some aggrieved-looking ducks might have access to water. Children—presumably his—were skimming around the edges of the pond with bone skates strapped to their boots.

Wistfully, Adelia paused to watch. The joy of skating had come to her late—not until she'd spent a winter in the fens, where iced rivers made causeways and playgrounds. Ulf had taught her. Fen people were wonderful skaters.

To skim away from here, free, letting the dead bury the dead. But even if it were possible, she could not leave while the person was at liberty who had hung Bertha up on a hook like a side of meat ...

"You skate?" Cross asked, watching her.

"I do, but we have no skates," she said.

As they approached the church, a dozen or so nuns, led by their prioress, came marching out of its doors like a line of disciplined, determined jackdaws.

They were heading for the convent gates and the bridge beyond, one of them pushing a two-wheeled cart. A sizable number of Godstow's lay residents scurried behind them expectantly. Adelia saw Walt and Jacques among the followers and joined them; Cross went with her. As they passed the guesthouse, Gyltha came down its steps with Mansur, Allie cocooned in her arms. "Don't want to miss this," she said.

At the gates, Sister Havis's voice came clear. "Open up, Fitchet, and bring me a knife."

Outside, a path had been dug through the snow on the bridge to facilitate traffic between village and convent. Why, since it led to nowhere else, Lord Wolvercote had thought it necessary to put a sentry on it was anybody's guess. But he had—and one who, facing a gaggle of black-clad, veiled women, each with a cross hanging on her chest, still found it necessary to ask, "Who goes there?"

Sister Havis advanced on him, as had Cross upon his fellow the night before. Adelia almost expected her to knock him out; she looked capable of it. Instead, the prioress pushed aside the leveled pike with the back of her hand and marched on.

"I wouldn't arse about, friend," Fitchet advised the sentry, almost sympathetically. "Not when they're on God's business."

When she'd glimpsed the bodies from the boat, Adelia had been too cold, too scared, too occupied to consider the manner in which they'd been hanged—only the image of their dangling feet had stayed in her memory.

Now she saw it. The two men, their arms tied, had been stood on the bridge while one end of a rope was attached round each neck and the other to one of the bridge's stanchions. Then they'd been thrown over the balustrade.

Bridges were communication between man and man, too sacred to be used as gallows. Adelia wished that Gyltha hadn't brought Allie; this was not going to be a scene she wanted her daughter to watch. On the other hand, her child was looking around in a concentration of pleasure; the surrounding scenery was a change, a lovely change, from the alleys of the convent where she was taken for her daily outings in fresh air. The bridge formed part of a white tableau, its reflection in the sheeted river below was absolute, and the waterfall on its mill side had frozen in sculptured pillars.

The mill wheel beyond was motionless and glistened with icicles as if from a thousand stalactites. It was an obscenity for distorted death to decorate it. "Don't let her see the bodies," she told Gyltha.

"Get her used to it," Gyltha said. "Her'll see plenty of hangings as she grows. My pa took me to my first when I were three year old. Enjoyed it, too, I did."

"I don't want her to enjoy it."

Getting the bodies up wasn't going to be easy; they were weighted by accumulated ice, and the rope holding them was stretched so tightly over the balustrade that it had frozen to it.

Walt joined Adelia. "Prioress says we ain't to help; they got to do it theyselves, seemingly."

Sister Havis considered for a moment and then gave her orders. While one used Fitchet's knife to scrape the ice from the ropes, the tallest of the nuns, the cellaress, leaned over, stretching her arm to grasp the hair of one of the hanging men. She lifted, giving the rope some slack.

A seagull that had been pecking at the man's eyes flew off, yelping, into the clear sky. Allie watched it go.

"Haul, my sisters." The prioress's voice rang after it. "Haul for the mercy of Mary."

A row of black backsides bent over the balustrade. They hauled, their breath streaming upward like smoke.

"What in hell are you women doing?"

Lord Wolvercote was on the bridge, to be no more regarded by the sisters than the seagull. He stepped forward, hand on his sword. Fitchet and Walt and some other men rolled up their sleeves. Wolvercote looked round. His sentry's helpless shrug told him he would get no help against God's female battalion. He was outnumbered. He shouted instead, "Leave them. This is *my* land, *my* half of the bridge, and villains shall hang from it as and when I *see fit*."

"It's our bridge, my lord, as you well know." This was Fitchet, loud but weary with the repetition of an old argument. "And Mother Abbess don't want it decorated with no corpses."

One body was up now, too stiff to bend, so the sisters were having to lift it vertically over the balustrade, its cocked head angled inquiringly toward the man who had sentenced it to death.

The nuns laid him on the cart, then returned to the balustrade to raise his fellow.

The dispute had brought the miller's family to their windows, and faces lined the sills to watch the puffs of air issuing like dragons' breath from the two arguing men.

"They were *rogues*, you dolt. Thieves. In possession of stolen property, and I made an example of them, as I have a right to do by infangthief. Leave them *alone*."

He was tall, dark-complexioned, age about thirty or so, and would have been handsome if his thin face hadn't settled into lines of contempt that at the moment were emphasized by fury. Emma had talked joyously of her future husband's poetry, but Adelia saw no poetry here. Only stupidity. He had made an example of the two thieves; they'd been hanging here for two days, and the river's lack of traffic meant that anybody who was going to see them had already done it. A more sensible man would have bowed to the inevitable, given his blessing, and walked away.

Wolvercote can't, Adelia thought. He sees the sisters as undermining his authority, and it frightens him; he must be cock of the heap or he is nothing.

Infangthief. She searched her memory—one of the English customary laws; Rowley had once mentioned it, told her, "*Infangthief? Well, it's a sort of legal franchise that certain lords of the manor hold by ancient right to pass the death penalty on thieves caught on their property. The king hates it. He says it means the buggers can hang anybody they've a mind to.*"

"*Why doesn't he get rid of it, then?*"

But ancient rights, apparently, were not to be discarded without resentment, even rebellion, by those who held them. "*He will—in time.*"

The second corpse had been retrieved, and sacking was laid over both. The nuns were beginning to push their loaded cart back across the bridge, their feet slipping on the ice.

"See, my duck," Gyltha said to Allie. "That were fun, weren't it?"

Sister Havis stopped as they passed Wolvercote, and her voice was colder than the dead men. "What were their names?"

"Names? What do you want their names for?"

"For their graves."

"They didn't have names, for God's sake. They'd have gone on to take the chalice off your own damned altar if I hadn't stopped them. They were *thieves*, woman."

"So were the two crucified with Our Lord; I don't remember Him withholding mercy from them." The prioress turned and followed her sisters.

He couldn't leave it. He called after her, "You're an interfering old bitch, Havis. No wonder you never got a man."

She didn't look back.

"They're going to bury them," Adelia said. "Oh, dear."

Jacques, nearby, grinned at her. "It's a fairly usual custom with the dead," he said.

"Yes, but I didn't look at their boots. And you," she said to Gyltha. "Take that child home." She hurried after the nuns and delayed the cart by standing in front of it. "Would you mind? Just a minute?"

She knelt down in the snow so that her eyes were on a level with the legs of the corpses and raised the sacking.

She was transferred to the bridge when she had first seen it, at nighttime, when the awful burden it carried and the footprints in its snow had told her the sequence of murder as clearly as if the two killers had confessed to it.

She heard her own voice speaking to Rowley: "*See? One wears hobnails, the other's boots have bars across the soles, maybe clogs bound with strips. They arrived here on horseback and took their horses into those trees ... They ate as they waited ...*"

Facing her was a pair of stout hobnailed boots. The other corpse had lost the footwear from its right foot, but the clog on its left had been retained by the tight bands of leather passing under the sole and cross-gartered around the lower leg.

Carefully, she replaced the sacking and stood up. "Thank you."

Nonplussed, the nuns with the cart continued on their way. Sister Havis's eyes met Adelia's for a moment. "Were they the ones?"

"Yes."

Walt overheard. "Here, is these the buggers as done for that poor horse?"

Adelia smiled at him. "And the traveler. Yes, I think so." She turned and found that Wolvercote had approached to see what she'd been up to. The crowd of abbey people waited to hear the exchange.

"Do you know where they came from?" she asked him.

"What do you care where they came from? I found them robbing my house; they had a silver cup, *my* silver cup, and that's all I needed to know." He turned to the porter. "Who is this female? What's she doing here?"

"Came with the bishop," Fitchet told him shortly.

Walt piped up, proprietorially: "She's with the darky doctor. She can tell things, she can. Looks at things and knows what happened."

It was badly phrased. Adelia hunched as she waited for the inevitable.

Wolvercote looked at her. "A witch, then," he said.

The word dropped into the air like ink into pristine water, discoloring it, webbing it with black, spiky traces before graying it forever.

Just as the allusion to Havis as a frustrated virgin would be a label that stuck to her, so the surrounding people hearing the name "witch" applied to Adelia would always remember it. The word that had stoned and set fire to women. There was no appeal against it. It tinged the faces of the men and women listening. Even Jacques's and Walt's showed a new doubt.

She castigated herself. *Lord, what a fool; why didn't I wait?* She could have found some other opportunity to look at the men's boots before they were buried. But no, she'd had to make sure immediately. Thoughtless, *thoughtless*.

"Damn it," she said. "*Damn*." She looked back. Lord Wolvercote had gone, but everybody else was looking in her direction; she could hear the murmurs. The damage had been done.

Breathily, Jacques came loping up to her. "I don't think you're a witch, mistress. Just stay in your room, eh? Out of sight, out of mind. Like Saint Matthew says: '*Sufficient unto the day is the evil thereof.*'"

But the day was not gone yet. As they passed through the gates of the convent, a fat man, wild-eyed, emerged out of the church door farther along. He gestured at Jacques. "You," he shouted, "fetch the infirmaress."

The messenger went running. The fat man turned and rushed back into the church.

Adelia teetered outside. "*Sufficient unto the day ...*" *There's been enough evil, and you've brought some of it on yourself. Whatever this is, it is not for you.*

But the sounds coming from inside the building were of distress.

She went in.

The sunshine was managing poorly within the large church, where, by day, candles were unlit. Glacial shafts of sun were lancing into the dark interior from the high, narrow windows above the clerestory, splashing a pillar here and there and cutting across the nave in thin stripes that avoided the middle, where the distress was centered.

Until her eyes adjusted to the contrast, Adelia couldn't make out what was happening. Slowly, it took shape. There was a catafalque, and two burly figures, a male and a female, were trying to drag something off it.

The something—she could see it now—was young Emma, very still, but her hands were gripping the far side of the catafalque so that her body could not be shifted away from the body that lay beneath her.

"Leave un, girl. Come on up now. 'Tis shameful, this. Gor dang it, what be it with her?" The fat man's voice.

The woman's was kinder but no less disturbed. "Yere, yere, don't take on like this, my duck, you'm upsetting your pa. What's this dead un to you? Come on up now."

The fat man looked around in desperation and caught sight of Adelia standing in the doorway, illuminated by the sun behind her. "Here, you, come and give us a hand. Reckon our girl's fainted."

Adelia moved closer. Emma hadn't fainted; her eyes were wide and stared at nothing. She had thrown herself so that she lay arched over the corpse under her. The knuckles of her gripping hands were like tiny white pebbles against the black wood of the catafalque beneath it.

Going closer still, Adelia peered down.

The nuns had put coins over the eyes, but the face was the face of the dead young man on the bridge, whom she and Rowley had lowered into the icehouse. This was Master Talbot of Kidlington. Only minutes before, she had been examining the boots of his murderers.

She became aware that the fat man was blustering—though not at her. "Fine convent this is, leaving dead people round the place. It's right upset our girl, and I don't wonder. Is this what we pay our tithes for?"

The infirmaress had come into the church, Jacques with her. Exclamation and exhortation created a hubbub that had an echo, Sister Jennet's crisp pipe—"Now, now, child, this will not do"— interspersed with the bellows of the father, who was becoming outraged and looking for someone to blame, while the mother's anxiety made a softer counterpoint to them both.

Adelia touched Emma's clawed hand, gently. The girl raised her head, but what she saw with those tormented eyes Adelia couldn't tell. "Do you see what they've done? To him, to *him*?"

The father and Sister Jennet were standing away now, openly quarreling. The mother had stopped attending to her daughter in order to join in.

"Control yourself, Master Bloat. Where else should we have lain a body but in a church?" Sister Jennet did not add that as far as Godstow and bodies were concerned, they were running out of space.

"Not where a man can fall over it; that's not what we pay our tithes for."

"That's right, Father, that's right ..." This was Mistress Bloat. "We was just being shown round, wasn't us? Our girl was showing us round."

Emma's eyes still stared into Adelia's as if into the Pit. "Do you see, oh, God, do you see?"

"I see," Adelia told her.

And she did, wondering how she could have been so blind not to see it before. So *that* was why Talbot of Kidlington had been murdered.

TEN

*W*here were you going to elope to?"

"Wales."

The girl sat on a stool in the corner of Adelia and Gyltha's room. She'd torn the veil off her head, and long, white-blond hair swayed over her face as she rocked back and forth. Allie, upset by the manifestations of such grief, had begun to bawl and was being jiggled quiet again in her mother's arms. Ward, also showing an unexpected commiseration, lay with his head on Emma's boots.

She'd fought to be there, literally. When at last they'd been able to prise her away from the body, she'd stretched her arms toward Adelia, saying, "I'll go with her, *her*. She understands, *she knows*."

"Dang sight more'n I do," Master Bloat had said, and Adelia had rather sympathized with him—until, that is, he'd tried to drag his daughter off, putting a hand over her mouth so that her noise would attract no more attention than it had.

Emma had been his match, twisting and shrieking to beat him off. At last Sister Jennet had advised compliance. "Let her go with this lady for now. She has some medical knowledge and may be able to calm her."

They could do nothing else, but from the looks Master and Mistress Bloat gave her as she helped their daughter toward the guesthouse, Adelia was aware that she'd added two more to her growing list of enemies.

She managed to persuade the girl to drink an infusion of lady's slipper, and it calmed her enough that she could answer questions, though Gyltha, who was gently rubbing the back of Emma's neck with rose oil, frowned at Adelia every time she asked one. A silent argument was going on between them.

Leave the poor soul alone, for pity's sake.

I can't.

She's breaking her heart.

It'll mend. Talbot's won't.

Gyltha might sorrow for the stricken one, but Adelia's duty as she saw it was to Talbot of Kidlington, who had loved Emma Bloat and had ridden to the convent through snow to take her away and marry her, an elopement so financially disastrous to a third party—Adelia's thoughts rested on the Lord of Wolvercote—that it had ordered his killing.

Master Hobnails and Master Clogs hadn't been waiting on an isolated bridge on a snowy night for any old traveler to come along; common scoundrels though they undoubtedly were, they weren't brainless. They knew, because somebody had told them, that at a certain hour a certain man would ride up to the convent gates ... Kill him.

They *had* killed him, and then they'd fled over the bridge to the village—to be killed themselves.

By the very man who'd employed them in the first place?

Oh, yes, Wolvercote fitted that particular bill nicely.

Though perhaps not entirely. Adelia still puzzled over the lengths someone had gone to in order to make sure that the corpse was identified as Talbot's. She supposed, if it *was* Wolvercote, he'd wanted Emma to know of her lover's death as soon as possible, and that her hand—and her fortune—was now his again.

Yes, but presumably, when Talbot didn't turn up, that way would have been made open. Why did the corpse have to be put under her nose, as it were, right away? And why in circumstances that pointed the accusing finger so directly at Wolvercote himself?

Do you see what they've done?

Who were the "they" that Emma thought had done it?

Adelia put Allie on the floor, gave her the teething ring that Mansur had carved for the child out of bone, and sat herself by Emma, smoothing back the long hair and mouthing "I have to" over her head at Gyltha.

The girl was almost apathetic with shock. "Let me stay here with you." She said it over and over. "I don't want to see them, any of them. I can't. You've loved a man, you had his child. You understand. They don't."

"'Course you can stay," Gyltha told her.

"My love is dead."

So is mine, Adelia thought. The girl's grief was her own. She forced it away. There'd been murder done, and death was her business. "You were going to Wales?" she asked. "In *winter*?"

"We'd had to wait, you see. Until he was twenty-one. To get his inheritance." The sentences came in pieces with an abstracted dullness.

To Talbot of Kidlington, That the Lord and His angels bless you on this Day that Enters you into Man's estate.

And on that day Talbot of Kidlington had set out to carry off Emma Bloat with, if Adelia remembered aright, the two silver marks that had been enclosed in Master Warin's letter.

"His inheritance was two silver marks?" Then she recalled that Emma didn't know about the marks because she didn't know about the letter.

The girl barely noticed the interjection. "The land in Wales. His mother left it to him, Felin Fach ..." She said the name softly, as if it had been spoken often, a sweet thing held out to her in her lover's voice. "'*Felin Fach*,' he used to say. '*The vale of the Aêron, where salmon leap up to meet the rod and the very earth yields gold.*'"

"Gold?" Adelia looked a question at Gyltha. *Is there gold in Wales?*

Gyltha shrugged.

"He was going to take possession as soon as he gained his majority. It was part of his inheritance, you see. We were going there. Father Gwilym was waiting to marry us. '*Funny little man, not a word of English ...*'" She was quoting again, almost smiling. "'*Yet in Welsh he can tie as tight a marriage knot as any priest in the Vatican.*'"

This was dreadful; Gyltha was wiping her eyes. Adelia, too, was sorry, so sorry. To watch suffering like this was to be in pain oneself, but she had to have answers.

"Emma, who knew you were going to elope?"

"Nobody." Now she did actually smile. "'*No cloak, or they'll guess. I'll have one for you. Fitchet will open the gate ...*'"

"Fitchet?"

"Well, of course Fitchet knew about us; Talbot paid him."

Apparently, the gatekeeper counted as nobody in Emma's reckoning.

The girl's face withered. "But he didn't come. I waited in the gatehouse ... I waited ... I thought ... I thought ... oh, Sweet Jesus, show mercy to me, I *blamed* him ..." She began clawing the air. "Why did they kill him? Couldn't they just take his purse? Why kill him?"

Adelia met Gyltha's eyes again. That was all right, then; Emma put her lover's killing down to robbers—as, at this stage, it was probably better that she should. There was no point in inflaming her against Wolvercote until there was proof of his culpability. Indeed, he might be innocent. If he hadn't known of the elopement ... But Fitchet had known.

"So it was a secret, was it?"

"Little Priscilla knew, she guessed." Again, that entrancement at being taken back to the past; the subterfuge had been thrilling. "And Fitchet, he smuggled our letters in and out. And Master Warin, of course, because he had to write the letter to Felin

Fach so that Talbot could take seisin of it, but they were all sworn not to tell." Suddenly, she gripped Adelia's arm. "Fitchet. He wouldn't have told the robbers, would he? He *couldn't*."

Adelia gave a reassurance she didn't feel; the number of nobodies who'd known about the elopement was accumulating. "No, no. I'm sure not. Who is Master Warin?"

"Were they waiting for him?" She had her nails into Adelia's skin. "Did they know he was carrying money? *Did they know?*"

Gyltha intervened. "A'course they didn't." She pulled Emma's hand off Adelia's arm and enfolded it in her own. "Just scum, they was. Roads ain't safe for anybody."

Emma looked wide-eyed at Adelia. "Did he suffer?"

Here, at least, was firm ground. "No. It was a bolt to the chest. He'd have been thinking of you, and then ... nothing."

"Yes." The girl sank back. "Yes."

"Who is Master Warin?" Adelia asked again.

"But how can I go on without him?"

We do, Adelia thought. *We have to*.

Allie had hitched herself over to replace Ward by pushing him off and settling her bottom on Emma's boots. She put a pudgy hand on the girl's knee. Emma stared down at her. "Children," she said. "We were going to have lots of children." The desolation was so palpable that for the other two women the firelit room became a leafless winter plain stretching into eternity.

She's young, Adelia thought. *Spring will come to her again one day perhaps, but never with the same freshness.* "Who is Master Warin?"

Gyltha tutted at her; the girl had begun to shake. *Stop it now.*

I can't. "Emma, who is Master Warin?"

"Talbot's cousin. They were very attached to each other." The poor lips stretched again. "'*My wait-and-see Warin. A careful man, Emma, but never did a ward have such a careful guardian.*'"

"He was Talbot's guardian? He handled his business affairs?"

"Oh, don't worry him with them now. He will be so ... I must see him. No, I can't ... I can't face his grief ... I can't face anything."

Emma's eyelids were half down with the fatigue of agony.

Gyltha wrapped a blanket round her, led her to the bed, sat her down, and lifted her legs so that she fell back on it. "Go to sleep now." She returned to Adelia. "And you come wi' me."

They went to the other side of the room to whisper.

"You reckon Wolvercote done in that girl's fella?"

"Possibly, though I'm beginning to think the cousin-cum-guardian had a lot to lose when Talbot came into his estates. If he's been handling Talbot's affairs ... It's starting to look like a conspiracy."

"No, it ain't. It was robbery pure and simple, and the boy got killed in the course of it."

"He didn't. The robbers *knew.*"

"No, they bloody didn't."

"Why?" She'd never seen Gyltha like this.

"A'cause that poor girl's going to have to marry Old Wolfie now whether she likes it or don't, and better if she don't think it was him as done for her sweetheart."

"Of course she won't have to ..." Adelia squinted at the older woman. "*Will* she?"

Gyltha nodded. "More'n like. Them Bloats is set on it. He's set on it. That's why her wanted to elope, so's they couldn't force her."

"They can't force her. Oh, Gyltha, they *can't*."

"You watch 'em. She's a high-up, and it happens to high-ups." Gyltha looked toward Heaven and gave thanks that she was common. "Nobody didn't want me for my money. Never bloody had any."

It did happen. Because it hadn't happened to Adelia, she hadn't thought of it. Her foster parents, that liberal couple, had allowed her to pursue her profession, but around her in Salerno, young, well-born female acquaintances had been married off to their father's choice though they cried against it, part of a parental plan for the family's advancement. It was that or continual beating. Or the streets. Or a convent.

"She could choose to become a nun, I suppose."

"She's their only child," Gyltha said. "Master Bloat don't want a nun, he wants a lady in the family—better for business." She sighed. "My auntie was cook to the De Pringhams and their poor little Alys was married off screamin' to Baron Coton, bald old bugger that he was."

"You have to say yes. The Church says it's not legal otherwise."

"*Hunh.* I never heard as little Alys said yes."

"But Wolvercote's a bully and an idiot. You know he is."

"So?"

Adelia stared into Emma's future. "She could appeal to the queen. Eleanor knows what it is to have an unhappy marriage; she managed to get a divorce from Louis."

"Oh, yes," Gyltha said, raising her eyes. "The queen's sure to go against the fella as is fighting her battle for her. Sure to." She patted Adelia's shoulder. "It won't be so bad for young Em, really ..."

"Not bad?"

"She'll have babies, that's what she wants, ain't it? Anyways, I don't reckon she'll have to put up with un for long. Not when King Henry gets hold of un. Wolvercote's a traitor, and Henry'll have his tripes." Gyltha inclined her head to consider the case. "Might not be bad at all, really."

"I thought you were sorry for her."

"I am, but I'm facing what she's facing. Bit o' luck she'll be widowed afore the year's out, then she'll have his baby and his lands ... Yes, I reckon it might turn out roses."

"*Gyltha.*" Adelia drew back from a practicality unsuspected even of this practical woman. "That's foul."

"That's business," Gyltha said. "That's what high-ups' marriage is, ain't it?"

Jacques was kept busy that day, bringing messages to the women in the guesthouse. The first was from the prioress: "To Mistress Adelia, greetings from Sister Havis, and to say that the girl Bertha will be interred in the nuns' own graveyard."

"Christian burial. Thought you'd be pleased," Gyltha said, watching Adelia's reaction. "What you wanted, ain't it?"

"It is. I'm glad." The prioress had ended her investigation and managed to persuade the abbess that Bertha had not died by her own hand.

But Jacques hadn't finished. He said dutifully, "And I was to warn you, mistress, you're to remember the Devil walks the abbey."

There lay the sting. The nuns' agreement that a killer was loose in Godstow made his presence more real and added to its darkness.

Later still that morning, the messenger turned up again. "To Mistress Adelia, greetings from Mother Edyve, and will she return Mistress Emma to the cloister? To keep the peace, she says."

"Whose peace?" Gyltha demanded. "I suppose them Bloats is complaining."

"So is the Lord Wolvercote," said Jacques. He grimaced, wrinkling his eyes and showing his teeth as one reluctant to deliver more bad news. "He's saying ... well, he's saying ..."

"What?"

The messenger blew out his breath. "It's being said as how Mistress Adelia has put a spell on Mistress Emma and is turning her against her lawful husband-to-be."

Gyltha stepped in. "You can tell that godless arse-headed bastard from me ..."

A hand on her shoulder stopped her. Emma was already wrapping herself in her cloak. "There's been trouble enough," she said.

And was gone down the steps before any of them could move.

Inside the abbey, the various factions trapped within its walls fractured like frozen glass. A darkness fell over Godstow that had nothing to do with the dimming winter light.

In protest against its occupation, the nuns disappeared into their own quadrangles, taking their meals from the infirmary kitchen, their exercise in the cloister.

The presence of two bands of mercenaries began to cause trouble. Schwyz's were the more experienced, a cohesive group that had fought in wars all over Europe and considered Wolvercote's men mere country ruffians hired for the rebellion—as, indeed, many of them were.

But the Wolvercoters had smarter livery, better arms, and a leader who was in charge—anyway, there were more of them; they bowed to nobody.

Schwyz's men set up a still in the forge and got drunk; Wolvercote's raided the convent cellar and got drunk. Afterward, inevitably, they fought one another.

The nights became dreadful. Godstow's people and guests cowered in their rooms, listening to the fighting in the alleys, dreading a crashed-in door and the entry of liquored mercenaries with robbery or rape on their minds.

In an effort to protect their property and women, they formed a militia of their own. Mansur, Walt, Oswald, and Jacques, like dutiful men, joined it in patrolling—but the result was that, more often than not, the nightly brawls became tripartite affairs.

An attempt by the chaplain, Father Egbert, to minister to the flock the nuns had deserted ended when, during Sunday-evening communion, Schwyz shouted at Wolvercote, "Are you going to discipline your men, or do I do it for you?" and a fight broke out between their adherents that spread even to the Lady Chapel, smashing lamps, a lectern, and several heads. One of Wolvercote's men lost an eye.

It was as if the world had frozen and would not turn, allowing no other weather to reach a beleaguered Oxfordshire than a bright sun by day and stars that filled the sky at night, neither bringing any relief from the cold.

Every morning, Adelia pushed open the shutters briefly to allow air into their room and searched the view for ... what? Henry Plantagenet and his army? Rowley?

But Rowley was dead.

There had been more snow. It was impossible to distinguish river from land. There was no human life out there, hardly any animal life.

Crisscross patterns like stitching showed that

birds, frantic with thirst, had hopped around in the early dawn to fill their beaks with snow, but where were they? Sheltering in the trees that stood like iron sentinels across the river, perhaps. Could they withstand this assault? Where were the deer? Did fish swim beneath that ice?

Watching a solitary crow flap its way across the blue sky, Adelia wondered whether it saw a dead, pristine world in which Godstow was the only circle of life. As she stared at it, the crow folded its wings and fell to earth, a small, untidy black casualty in the whiteness.

If the nights weren't bad enough, Godstow's days became morbid with the *hit-hit* of picks hacking out graves in the frozen earth while the church bell tolled and tolled for the dead as if it had lost the capacity to ring for anything else.

Adelia was keeping to the guesthouse as much as possible; the looks from people she encountered if she went out and their tendency to cross themselves and make the sign of the evil eye as they passed her were intimidating. But there were some funerals she had to attend.

Talbot of Kidlington's, for one. The nuns reappeared for that. A little man at the front of the congregation, who Adelia supposed was the cousin, Master Warin, wept all through it, but Adelia, skulking at the back, saw only Emma, white and dry-eyed, in the choir, her hand clasped tightly in little Sister Priscilla's.

A funeral for Bertha. This was held at night and in the privacy of the abbess's chapel, attended by the convent chapter, the milkmaid, Jacques, and Adelia, who'd folded Bertha's hands around a broken chain and a silver cross before the plain, pine coffin was interred in the nuns' own graveyard.

A funeral for Giorgio, the Sicilian. No nuns this time, but most of the Schwyz mercenaries were there, and Schwyz himself. Mansur, Walt, and Jacques came, as they had to Talbot's. So did Adelia. She'd begged a reluctant Sister Havis for Giorgio to be treated as a Christian, arguing that they knew no harm of him apart from his profession. Due to her, the Sicilian was lowered into a cold Christian grave with the blessing of Saint Agnes.

There was no word of thanks from his friend Cross. He left the graveyard after the interment without speaking, though later three pairs of beautifully fashioned bone skates complete with straps were left outside Adelia's door.

A funeral for two Wolvercote villagers who'd succumbed to pneumonia. Sister Jennet and her nurses attended, though Lord Wolvercote did not.

A funeral for the two hanged men. Nobody except the officiating priest was present, though those bodies, too, each went into a churchyard grave.

His duty done, Father Egbert closed the church and, like the nuns, retired to an inner sanctum. He would not, he said, hold regular services when any mercenary was likely to be in the congregation; the advent of Christ's birth was not to be despoiled by a load of feuding heathens who wouldn't recognize the Dove of Peace if it shat on their heads. Which he hoped it would.

It was a sentence on the whole community. No *Christmas?*

A shriek went up, loudest of all from the Bloats; they'd come to see their girl married at the Yule feast. And their girl, thanks to malefic influence from a woman no better than she should be, was now saying she didn't want to marry at all. This wasn't what they paid their tithes for.

One voice, however, was raised above theirs. With more effect. Sister Bullard, the cellaress, was, materially, the most important person in the abbey and the one who'd become the most sorely tried. Even with the convent's new militia trying to protect it, her great barn of a cellar suffered nightly raids on its ale tuns, wine vats, and foodstuff.

Worried that the entire convent would soon be unable to feed itself, she turned to the only earthly authority left to her—the Queen of England.

Eleanor had been staying to her own apartments, paying little attention to anything except the effort to keep herself amused. Finding the rest of the abbey tedious, she had ignored its troubles. However, marooned as she was on the island of Godstow for the duration of the snow, she had to listen to Sister Bullard telling her that she faced discord and starvation.

The queen woke up.

Lord Wolvercote and Master Schwyz were summoned to her rooms in the abbess's house, where it was pointed out to them that only under her banner could they attract allies—and she had no intention of leading rabble, which, at the moment, was what they and their men were becoming.

Rules were laid down. Church services would resume—to be attended only by the sober. Wolvercote's men must cross the bridge each night to sleep at their lord's manor in the village, leaving only six of their number behind to join Schwyz's men in enforcing the curfew.

No more raids on the cellar by either side—any mercenary doing so, or found fighting, was to be publicly flogged.

Of the two culprits, Lord Wolvercote should have come out of the meeting better; Schwyz, after all, was being paid for his services, whereas Wolvercote was rendering his for free. But the Abbot of Eynsham was also present, and, as well as being a friend to Schwyz, he had the cleverer and more persuasive tongue.

It was noted by those who saw Lord Wolvercote emerge from the queen's presence that he was snarling. "A'cause he don't get young Emma, neither," Gyltha reported. "Not yet, at any rate."

"Are you sure?"

"Certain sure," Gyltha said. "The girl's been pleading with Mother Edyve, and she's asked for Eleanor's protection. The which the queen says old Wolfie ought to wait."

Again, this had come from the convent kitchen, where Gyltha's friend Polly had helped the royal servants carry refreshment to the meeting between the queen and the mercenary leaders. Polly had learned many things, one of them being that the queen had complied with Mother Edyve's request for Emma's marriage to Wolvercote to be delayed indefinitely, "until the young woman has recovered from the affliction to her spirits that now attends them."

Polly reported that "his Wolfie lordship weren't best pleased."

Adelia, relieved, didn't think the Bloats would be, either. But by now, everybody knew what the affliction was that attended Emma's spirits and, according to Gyltha, there was general sympathy for her, much of which sprang from the equally general dislike for Wolvercote.

There was more good news from the kitchen. With order restored, Eleanor had, apparently, announced that the church was to be reopened, services resumed, and, when it came, Christ's Mass to be celebrated with a feast.

"Proper old English one, too," Gyltha said, a pagan gleam in her eye. "Caroling, feastin', mummers, Yule log, and all the trimmin's. They're killin' the geese and hangin' them this very minute."

It was typical of Eleanor, Adelia thought, that having saved the convent's store of food and drink, she now imperiled it. Feasting the entire community would be an enormous and expensive undertaking. On the other hand, the queen's orders had been necessary and perceptive; they might well defuse a situation that was becoming intolerable.

And if a feast could introduce gaiety into Godstow, by God, it needed it.

With the resurgence of Eleanor's energy came an invitation. "To Mistress Adelia, a summons from her gracious lady, Queen Eleanor." Jacques brought it.

"You running errands for royalty now?" Gyltha asked at the door. The messenger had found brighter clothes from somewhere, curled hair hid his ears, and his perfume reached Adelia, who was across the room.

He'd also found a new dignity. "Mistress, I am so favored. And now I must go to the Lord Mansur. He, too, is summoned."

Gyltha watched him go. "Aping they courtiers," she said with disapproval. "Our Rowley'll kick his arse for him when he comes back."

"Rowley's not coming back," Adelia said.

When Mansur strode into the royal chamber, one of the courtiers muttered audibly, "And now we entertain heathens." And as Adelia followed behind with Ward ambling at her heels, "Oh, Lord, *look* at that cap. And the *dog*, my dear."

Eleanor, however, was all kindness. She came sweeping forward, offering her hand to be kissed. "My Lord Mansur, how pleased we are to see you." To Adelia: "My dear child, we have been remiss. We have been kept busy with matters of state, of course, but even so I fear we have neglected one with whom I fought against the devil's spawn."

The long upper room had been the abbess's, but now it was definitely Eleanor's. For surely Mother Edyve had not scented it with the richness of the heathen East nor filled it with artifacts so colorful—shawls, cushions, a gloriously autumnal triptych—that they eliminated the naïve, biblical pastels on her walls. Mother Edyve had never knelt at a prie-dieu made from gold, nor would her bedposts have roared with carved lions, nor had gossamer, floating like cobwebs, descended from the bed's tester over her pillow, nor male courtiers like adoring statuary, nor a beautiful minstrel to fill the abbatial air with a love song.

Yet, Adelia thought, still astonished by the bed—how had they got the thing on the boat?—the effect was not sexual. Sensual certainly, but this was not the room of a houri, it was merely ... Eleanor.

It had certainly drawn Jacques into its spell. Lounging in a corner, he bowed to her, beaming and waggling his fingers. So here he was, and—to judge from the joy exuding from him, his even higher boots, and a new style of hair that hid his wide ears—in Aquitanian fashion paradise.

The queen was plying Mansur with dried dates and almond-paste sweetmeats. "We who have been to Outremer know better than to offer you wine, my lord, but"—a click of elegant royal fingers toward a page—"our cook magicks a tolerable sherbet."

Mansur kept his face stolidly blank.

"Oh, dear," Eleanor said. "Does the doctor not understand me?"

"I fear not, lady," Adelia said. "I translate for him." Mansur was fairly fluent in Norman French, which was being spoken here, but the pretense that he was restricted to Arabic had served the two of them well, and probably would again; it was surprising what he learned when among those who believed him not to understand. And if Bertha's killer was somewhere among this company ...

What could be wanted of him? He was being treated with honor for someone whose race the queen had gone on Crusade to defeat.

Ah, Eleanor was asking her to pass on praise to Mansur for his medical skill in saving the life of "one of dear Schwyz's mercenaries"; Sister Jennet had sung *so* highly of him.

That was it, then. A good physician was always worth having. Christian disdain for Arab and Jew did not extend to their doctors, whose cures among their own people—partly brought about, Adelia believed, by their religions' strict dietary laws—gave them a high reputation.

So she herself was here merely as an interpreter.

But no, apparently she was a witness to Eleanor's courage; history was being changed.

Propelling her around by a hand on her shoulder, the queen told the story of what had happened in the upper room of Wormhold Tower, where, in the presence of a rotting corpse, a sword-wielding demon had appeared.

Eleanor, it seemed, had held up a calm hand to

it. "Thou art a Plantagenet fiend, for that race is descended from demons. In the name of Our Savior, go back to thy master."

And lo, the fiend had dropped its sword and slunk back whence it had come.

What did I do? Adelia wondered.

"... and this little person here, my own Mistress Athalia, then picked up the sword the fiend had dropped, though it was still very hot and stank of sulphur, and threw it out of the casement."

Glad I could help. Adelia speculated on whether the queen believed her own nonsense and decided she didn't. Perhaps Dakers's attack had shocked and embarrassed her so that she must now present it to her advantage. Or perhaps she was playing games. She was bored; all these people were bored.

Having *ooh*ed and *aah*ed throughout the recital, the courtiers applauded—except Montignard, who, with a dirty look at Adelia, burst out with, "But it was I who ministered to you afterwards, lady, did I not?" though the list of the things he had done was overlaid by a slow hand clap from the Abbot of Eynsham leaning against one of the bedposts.

Eleanor turned on him, sharp. "Our neglect is actually yours, my lord. We charged you to look after our brave Mistress Amelia, did we not?"

The abbot surveyed Adelia from the tips of her snow-rimed boots to the unattractive cap with its earflaps on her head and down again until his eyes met hers. "Lady, I thought I had," he said.

The queen was still talking. Shocked, Adelia didn't hear her. The man wished her harm, had tried to procure it. At the same time, she felt his regard, like that of a swordsman saluting another. In a way she had not yet fathomed, she, Vesuvia Adelia Rachel Ortese Aguilar, known only in this place as the Bishop of Saint Albans's fancy and a useful picker up of demonic swords, mattered to Lord Abbot of Eynsham. He'd just told her so.

The queen's hands were spread out in a question, and she was smiling. The courtiers were laughing. One of them said, "The poor thing's overwhelmed."

Adelia blinked. "I beg your pardon, lady."

"I *said*, dear, that you must join us here; we cannot have our little helpmeet living in whatever hole the abbey provides. You shall move in with my waiting women, I am sure they have room, and you shall take part in our sport. You must be so bored out there."

You *are*, Adelia thought again. Eleanor probably *did* secretly feel she had a debt for having her life saved, but even more, she needed a new pet to play with. Ennui was everywhere, in the screech of female bickering coming from the next room where the waiting women waited, in the pettish laughter directed at herself, the sense that they had run out of butts for their wit and required another.

This, after all, was a company and queen that left one castle once it had begun to stink and moved on to the next, hunting, entertaining, and being entertained, kept clean and fed by an army of cooks, fullers, laundresses, and servants, many of whom had been left behind on the trail to war that Eleanor had taken, and even more subsequently lost to the snow. Without these resources, they festered.

One of the courtiers was ostentatiously holding his nose over Ward, though the young man's own person, let alone his linen, was hardly more delectable.

Move in with them all? Lord, help me. She wasn't going to accept an invitation to step into an overcrowded hell, even when extended by a queen.

On the other hand, if one of these was Bertha's killer, how better to sniff him out than by asking questions and, hopefully, receiving answers? *Move in with them?* No, but if, by day, she could have access to the royal chambers ...

Adelia bowed. "Lady, you are all goodness. As long as my baby would not disturb your nights ..."

"A child?" The queen was intrigued. "Why didn't they tell me? A little boy?"

"A girl," Adelia told her. "She is teething and therefore wakeful ..."

There was a light scream from Montignard. "*Teething?*"

"A synonym for screaming, so I do understand," Eynsham said.

"Our two lords do not like babies," Eleanor confided to Adelia.

"I do, sweet lady." This was the abbot again. "So I do. Lightly broiled with parsley, I find them right toothsome."

Adelia pressed on. "Also, I must assist my master, Dr. Mansur here, when he is called to the infirmary at night as he so often is. I keep his potions."

"A synonym for stinks and rattling pots," the abbot said.

Montignard was clasping his hands beseechingly. "Lady, you'll not have a wink of rest. If that bell tolling the hours and the sisters singing them were not enough, we'll have the screech of babies and Lord knows what devilry ... you'll be exhausted."

Bless him, Adelia thought.

Eleanor smiled. "Such a hedonist you are, my swain." She reflected, "I *do* need my sleep, yet I am reluctant not to reward the girl."

"Oh, let her come and go," Eynsham said wearily, "though *not* in them clothes."

"Of course, of *course*. We shall dress her."

It was a new thing, it would pass the time.

It was also Adelia's passport—though she had to pay for it. She was carried through to the women's room, its door not quite closed, so that male heads poking round it added a chorus of comment to the humiliation of being stripped to her chemise while swathes of material were held against her skin and capless head to be pronounced too this, too that, not *mauve*, my dear, not with that complexion—so corpselike. Where *had* she found such fine white linen for her chemise? Was she Saxon that she was so fair? No, no, Saxons had blue eyes, probably a Wend.

She wasn't even asked whether she wanted a new gown. She didn't; she dressed to disappear. Adelia was an observer. The only impact she ever wished to make was on her patients, and then not as a woman. Well ... she'd wished to make an impact on

Rowley, but she'd done that without any clothes on at all ...

The poor seamstresses among the queen's ladies weren't consulted, either, though the necessary needlework to transform whatever material was decided on into a bliaut for her—very tight at the top, very full in the skirt, sleeves narrow to the elbow, then widening almost to the ground—would be onerous, especially as Eleanor was demanding that it should have filigree embroidery at the neck and armholes, and be finished for the Christmas feast.

Adelia wondered at seamstresses being taken to war and at anyone who required a military transport to contain presses full of dazzlingly colored brocades, silks, linens, and samite.

In the end, Eleanor decided on velvet of a dark, dark blue that had, as she said, "the bloom of the Aquitanian grape."

When the queen did something, she did it whole-heartedly: a flimsy veil—she herself demonstrated how it should be attached to the barbette—a thin, gold circlet, a tapestried belt, embroidered slippers, a cope and hood of wool fine enough to draw through a ring, all these things were Adelia's.

"Only your due, my dear," Eleanor said, patting her head. "It was a very nasty demon." She turned to Eynsham. "We're safe from it now, aren't we, Abbot? You said you'd disposed of it, did you not?"

Dakers. What had they done to Dakers?

"Couldn't have it wandering around loose to attack my heart's lady again, could I?" The abbot was jovial. "I found un hiding among the convent books and, doubting it could read, would have hanged it there and then. But there was an outcry from the good sisters so, *pendent opera interrupta*, I had it put in the convent lockup instead. We'll take it with us when we go and hang it then"—he winked—"if it ain't frozen to death in the meantime."

There was appreciative laughter in which Eleanor joined, though she protested, "No, no, my lord, the female is possessed, we cannot execute the insane."

"Possessed by the evil of her mistress. Better dead, lady, better dead. Like Rosamund."

It was a long night. Nobody could retire until the queen gave her permission, and Eleanor was inexhaustible. There were games, board games, fox and geese, Alquerque, dice. Everybody was required to sing, even Adelia, who had no voice to speak of and was laughed at for it.

When it was Mansur's turn, Eleanor was enraptured and curious. "Beautiful, beautiful. Is that not a castrato?"

Adelia, sitting on a stool at the queen's feet, admitted it was.

"How interesting. I have heard them in Outremer but never in England. They can pleasure a woman, I believe, but must remain childless. Is that true?"

"I don't know, lady." It was, but Adelia wasn't prepared to discuss it in this company.

The room became hot. More games, more singing.

Adelia began to nod, jerked awake each time by a draft from the door as people came and went.

Jacques was gone—no, there he was, bringing more food from the kitchen. Montignard was gone, and Mansur, no, they had come back from wherever they'd been. The abbot was gone, reappearing with string to satisfy Eleanor's sudden desire to play cat's cradle. There he was again, this time with Mansur, a table between them, their heads bent over a chess-board. A courtier entered, clutching snow to cool the wine ... another young man, the one who'd thrown snowballs at the nuns, was singing to a lute ...

Adelia forced herself to her feet. Crossing to the chess table, she surveyed the board. "You're losing," she said in Arabic.

Mansur didn't look up. "He is the better player, Allah curse him."

"Say something more."

He grunted. "What do you want me to say? I am tired of these people. When do we go?"

Adelia addressed Eynsham. "My lord Mansur instructs me to ask you, my lord, what you can tell him about the death of the woman, Rosamund Clifford."

The abbot raised his head to look at her and, again, there was that piercing connection. "Does he? Does he indeed? And why should my lord Mansur want to inquire of it?"

"He is a doctor; he has an interest in poison."

Eleanor had heard Rosamund's name. She called across the room, "What is that? What are you saying?"

Immediately, the abbot was another man, bucolic, convivial. "The good doctor do want to know about bitch Rosamund's death. Wasn't I with you when we heard of it, my sweeting? Didn't they tell us as we was landing, having crossed from Normandy? Didn't I fall to my knees and give thanks to the Great Revenger of all sin?"

Eleanor held out her hands to him. "You did, Abbot, you did."

"But you knew Rosamund before that," Adelia said. "You said so when we were at Wormhold."

"Did I know Rosamund? Oh, I knew her. Could I allow vileness unchecked in my own county? My old daddy would have been ashamed. How many days did I spend in that Jezebel's lair, a Daniel exhorting her to fornicate no more?" He was playing to the queen, but his eyes never left Adelia's.

More songs, more games, until even Eleanor was tired. "To bed, good people. Go to bed."

As he escorted Adelia home, Mansur was broody, chafed by his defeat at chess, of which he was himself a skilled exponent. "He is a fine player, that priest. I do not like him."

"He had a hand in Rosamund's death," Adelia said, "I know it; he was taunting me with it."

"He was not there."

True, Eynsham had been across the Channel when Rosamund died. But there was *something* ...

"Who was the fat one with the pox?" Mansur asked. "He took me outside to show me. He wants a salve."

"Montignard? Montignard has the pox? Serve him right." Adelia was irritable with fatigue. It was nearly dawn. A Matins antiphon from the direction of the chapel accompanied them as they trudged.

Mansur raised the lantern to light her up the guesthouse steps. "Has the woman left the door unbarred for you?"

"I expect so."

"She should not. It is not safe."

"Then I'll have to wake her, won't I?" Adelia said, going up. "And her name's Gyltha. Why don't you ever say it?" *Damn it*, she thought, *they're as good as married.*

She stumbled over something large that rested on the top step, nearly sending it over the edge and down to the alley. "Oh, dear God. Mansur. *Mansur.*"

Together, they carried the cradle into the room; the child in it was still asleep and wrapped in her blankets. She seemed to have taken no harm from being left in the cold.

The candle had gone out. Gyltha sat unmoving in the chair on which she had been waiting for Adelia to come back. For an appalling moment, Adelia thought she'd been murdered—the woman's hand was dangling over the place where the cradle always lay.

A snore reassured her.

The three of them sat in a huddled group around the cradle, watching Allie sleep, as if afraid she would evaporate.

"Someone come in here and stole her? Put her on the step?" Gyltha couldn't get over it.

"Yes," Adelia told her. One inch farther on the step, just one inch ... In her mind she kept seeing the cradle turn in midair as it fell into the alley some twenty feet below.

"Someone come in here? And I never heard un? Put her out on the step?"

"Yes, *yes*."

"Where's the sense in it?"

"I don't know." But she did.

Mansur voiced it: "He is warning you."

"I know."

"You ask too many questions."

"I know."

"What questions?" Gyltha, in her panic, wasn't keeping up. "*Who* don't want you asking questions?"

"I don't know." If she had, she would have groveled to him, squirmed at his feet in supplication. *You've won. You're cleverer than I am. Go free, I won't interfere. But leave me Allie.*

ELEVEN

The instinct was to hide with Allie in the metaphorical long grass, like a hare and leveret in their form.

When the queen sent Jacques to inquire for her, Adelia sent back that she was ill and could not come.

The killer conversed with her in her head.

How submissive are you now?

Submissive, my lord. Totally submissive. I shall do nothing to displease you, just don't hurt Allie.

She knew him now, not who he was but what he was. Even as he'd plucked Allie's cradle from under the sleeping Gyltha's hand and put it on the steps, he'd revealed himself.

Such a simple expedient to reduce his opponent to impotence. If she didn't fear him so much, she could admire it—the audacity, the economy, the *imagination* of it.

And it had told her for which killings he had been responsible.

There had been two lots of murder, she knew that now, neither one having anything to do with the other; only the fact that she'd witnessed the corpses of both within a short time had given them a seeming relationship.

Talbot of Kidlington's death was the most straightforward, because it had been for the oldest of reasons: gain.

Wolvercote had good reason to kill the boy; the elopement with Emma would have deprived him of a valuable bride.

Or the inheritance Talbot had gained on his twenty-first birthday would have deprived his guardian of an income, for Master Warin could have been defrauding the boy—it wasn't unknown for an heir to come into his estates only to find that they'd gone.

Or, and this was a possibility Emma herself had raised while not believing it, Fitchet had alerted two friends to the fact that a young man would be arriving at the convent by night with money in his purse. After all, the gatekeeper had been acting as go-between for the two lovers—presumably for a fee—which indicated he was corruptible.

Or—the least likely—the Bloats had discovered their daughter's plan and had hired killers to prevent it.

Such was Talbot's murder.

Yet not one on the list of his likely killers fitted the character of the man who'd crept into the guest-house and put Allie's cradle on the steps outside. The smell of him was different, it had none of the direct brutality with which Talbot had been eliminated.

No, this man was ... what? Sophisticated? Professional? *I do not kill unless I must. I have given you a warning. I trust you will heed it.*

He was the murderer of Rosamund and Bertha.

There was more snow. The sides of the track that had been dug down to the Thames fell in under it.

It was left to Gyltha to fetch their meals from the kitchen, to empty their chamber pots in the latrine, and to gather firing from the woodpile.

"Ain't we ever a'going to take that poor baby for some air?" she wanted to know.

"No."

I am outside, watching. How submissive are you?

Totally submissive, my lord. Don't hurt my child.

"Nobody can't snatch her, not with that old Arab along of us."

"No."

"We stay here, then, with the door barred?"

"Yes."

But of course, they couldn't ...

The first alarm came at night. Somewhere a handbell was ringing and people were shouting.

Gyltha leaned out of the window to the alley. "They're yellin' fire," she said. "I can smell smoke. Oh, dear Lord, preserve us."

Bundling Allie into her furs, they dressed themselves, snatching up what belongings they could before carrying her down the steps.

Fire, that greatest of threats, had brought out everybody on this side of the abbey. Fitchet came running from the gates carrying two buckets; men were emerging out of the guesthouse: Mansur, Master Warin.

"Where is it? Where is it?"

The ringing and hubbub was coming from the direction of the pond.

"Barn?"

"Lockup, sounds like."

"Oh, God," Adelia said. "*Dakers*." She handed Allie to Gyltha and began running.

Between the pond and the lockup, Peg was swinging a bell as if she were thwacking an unruly cow with it. She'd seen the flames on her way to the milking. "Up there." She pointed with the bell toward the narrow slit that allowed air into the little beehive building of stone that was the convent lockup.

Volunteers, already forming a line, shouted to hasten the smith as he hammered an iron spar into the pond to gain water for their pails.

Mansur came up beside Adelia. "I smell no fire."

"Neither do I." There was a slight smitch in the air, nothing more, and no flames apparent in the lockup's slit.

"Well, there damn was," Peg said.

The door to the lockup opened and a bad-tempered sentry came out. "Oh, get on home," he shouted. "No need for this rumpus. Straw caught fire, is all. I stamped it out." It was Cross. He locked the door behind him and gestured at the crowd with his spear. "Go on. Get off with you."

Relieved, grumbling, people began to disperse.

Adelia stayed where she was.

"What is it?" Mansur asked.

"I don't know."

Cross leveled his spear at her as she came up to him from the shadows. "Get back there, nothing to see. Go home ... oh, it's you, is it?"

"Is she all right?"

"Old Mother Midnight? She's all right. Hollered a bit, but she's dandy in there now, bloody sight dandier than it is out here. Warm. Gets her meals regular. What about the poor buggers got to guard her, that's what I say."

"What started the fire?"

Cross looked shifty. "Reckon as she kicked the brazier over."

"I want to see her."

"That you don't. Captain Schwyz told me: 'No bugger talks to her. No bugger to go near 'cept to bring her meals. And keep the bloody door locked.'"

"And who told Schwyz? The abbot?"

Cross shrugged.

"I want to see her," Adelia said again.

Mansur reached out and took the spear from the mercenary's hand with the ease of pulling up a weed.

Blowing out his cheeks, Cross unlatched an enormous key from his belt and put it in the lock. "Just a peep, mind. Captain's bound to be here in a minute; he'll have heard the rumpus. Bloody peasants, bloody rumpus."

It *was* only a peep. Mansur had to lift Adelia up so that she could see over the mercenary's shoulder as he blocked the door to stop them from going in.

What light there was inside came from burning logs in a brazier. Except for an ashy patch on one side, a deep ring of straw circled the curve of the stone walls. Something moved in it.

Adelia was reminded of Bertha. For a moment, a pair of eyes in the straw reflected the glow from the brazier and then disappeared.

Boots could be heard crunching the ice as their owner came toward them. Cross tore his spear away from Mansur. "Captain's coming. Get away, for God's sake."

They got away.

"Yes?" Mansur asked as they walked.

"Somebody tried to burn her to death," Adelia said. "The slit's up on the back wall, on the opposite side from the entrance. I think somebody tossed a lighted rag through it. If Cross was guarding the door, he wouldn't have seen who it was. But he knows it happened."

"The Fleming said the brazier tipped over."

"No. It's bolted to the floor. There was no sign that a brand fell out of it. Somebody wanted to kill her, and it wasn't Cross."

"She is a sad, mad *bint*. Perhaps she tried to burn herself."

"No." It was a natural progression. Rosamund, Bertha, Dakers. All three had known—in Dakers's case, still did—something they should not.

If it hadn't been for Cross's quick reaction in putting the fire out, the last of them would have been silenced.

Early the next morning, armed mercenaries broke into the chapel where the nuns were at prayer and carried off Emma Bloat.

Adelia, sleeping in, heard of it when Gyltha came scurrying back from the kitchen where she'd been to fetch their breakfast. "Poor thing, poor thing. Terrible to-do 'twas. Prioress tried to stop 'em and they knocked her down. In her own chapel. *Knocked her down.*"

Adelia was already dressing. "Where did they take Emma?"

"Village. Wolvercote it was, and his bloody Flemings. Carried her to his manor. Screaming, so they said, poor thing, poor thing."

"Can't they get her back?"

"The nuns is gone after her, but what can they do?"

By the time Adelia reached the gates, the rescue party of nuns was returning across the bridge, empty-handed.

"Can nothing be done?" Adelia asked as they went by.

Sister Havis was white-faced and had a cut below her eye. "We were turned back at spearpoint. One of his men laughed at us. He said it was legal because they had a priest." She shook her head. "What sort of priest I don't know."

Adelia went to the queen.

Eleanor had just been acquainted with the news herself and was raging at her courtiers. "Do I command savages? The girl was under my protection. Did I or did I not tell Wolvercote to give her time?"

"You did, lady."

"She must be fetched back. Tell Schwyz—where is Schwyz?—tell him to gather his men ..." She looked around. Nobody had moved. "*Well?*"

"Lady, I fear the ... *um* ... damage is done." This was the Abbot of Eynsham. "It appears that Wolvercote keeps a hedge priest in the village. The words were said."

"Not by the girl, I'll warrant, not under those circumstances. Were her parents present?"

"Apparently not."

"Then it is abduction." Eleanor's voice was shrill with the desperation of a ruler losing control of the ruled. "Are my orders to be ignored in such a fashion? Are we living in the caves of brute beasts?"

Apart from Adelia's, the queen's was the only anger in the room. Others, the men, anyway, were disturbed, displeased, but also faintly, very faintly, amused. A woman, as long as it wasn't their own, carried off and bedded was broad comedy.

There was an embryonic wink in the abbot's eye as he said, "I fear our lord Wolvercote has taken the Roman attitude towards our poor Sabine."

There was nothing to be done. Words had been said by a priest; Emma Bloat was married. Like it or not, she had been deflowered and—as it was in every male mind—probably enjoyed it.

Helpless, Adelia left the room, unable to bear its company.

In the cloister walk, one of Eleanor's young men, lost to everything about him, was blocking the way as he walked up and down, strumming a viol and trying out a new song.

Adelia gave him a push that sent him staggering. The door of the abbey chapel at the end of the cloister beckoned to her, and she marched in, only knowing, on finding it blessedly empty, that she was wild for a solace that—and she knew this, too— could not be granted.

She went to her knees in the nave.

Dear Mother of God, protect and comfort her.

The icy, incense-laden air held only the reply: *She is cattle as you are cattle. Put up with it.*

Adelia pummeled the stones and made her accusation out loud. "Rosamund dead, Bertha dead. Emma raped. Why do You allow it?"

The reply came: "There will be medicine for our complaint eventually, my child. You of all people, with your mastery of healing, should know that."

The voice was a real one, dry and seemingly without human propulsion, as if it rustled out of the mouth on its own wings to flutter down from the tiny choir to the nave.

Mother Edyve was so small, she was almost hidden in the stall in which she sat, her hands folded on her walking stick, her chin on her hands.

Adelia got up. She said, "I have intruded, Mother. I'll go."

The voice alighted on her as she made for the door. "Emma was nine years old when she came to Godstow, bringing joy to us all."

Adelia turned back. "No joy now, not for her, not for you," she said.

Unexpectedly, Mother Edyve asked, "How is Queen Eleanor taking the news?"

"With fury." Because she was sour with a fury of her own, Adelia said, "Angry because Wolvercote has flaunted her, I suppose."

"Yes." Mother Edyve rubbed her chin against her folded hands. "You are unjust, I think."

"To Eleanor? What can she do except rant? What can any of us do? Your joyful child's enslaved for life to a pig, and even the Queen of England is helpless."

"I have been listening to the songs they sing to her, to the queen," Mother Edyve said. "The viol and the young men's voices—I have been sitting here and thinking about them."

Adelia raised her eyebrows.

"What is it they sing of?" Mother Edyve asked. "*Cortez amors?*"

"Courtly love. A Provençal phrase. Provençal fawning and sentimental rubbish."

"Courtly love, yes. A serenade to the unattainable lady. It is most interesting—earthly love as ennoblement. We could say, could we not, that what those young men yearn for is a reflected essence of the Holy Mary."

Silly old soul, thought Adelia, savagely. "What those young men yearn for, Abbess, is not holiness. This song will end in a high-flown description of the secret arcade. It's their name for the vagina."

"Sex, of course," said the abbess, amazingly, "but with a gentler longing than I have ever heard ascribed to it. Oh, yes, basically, they are singing to more than they know; they sing to God the Mother."

"God the *Mother*?"

"God is both our father and our mother. How could it be otherwise? To create two sexes yet favor only one would be lopsided parentage, though Father Egbert chides me for saying so."

No wonder Father Egbert chided; it was a wonder he didn't excommunicate. God masculine and feminine?

Adelia, who considered herself a modern thinker, was confounded by a perception of an Almighty who, in every religion she knew of, had created weak and sinful woman for man's pleasure, human ovens in which to bake his seed. A devout Jew thanked God daily that he had not been born female. Yet this little nun was plucking the beard from God's chin and providing Him not only with the breasts but also with the mind of a female.

It was a philosophy of most profound rebellion. But now that Adelia came to consider her, Mother Edyve was a rebel, or she would not have been prepared to flout the Church by giving space in her graveyard to the body of a king's whore. Only independence of mind could at the same time be extending charitable thought to a queen who had brought nothing but turbulence into the abbey with her.

"Yes," the birdlike voice went on, "we grieve for the lopsidedness of the world as the Almighty Feminine must grieve for it. Yet God's time is not our time, we are told; an age is but a blink of an eye to one who is Alpha and Omega."

"Ye-es." Frowning, Adelia moved nearer and sat sideways on the chancel steps, hugging her knees, staring at the still figure in the stall.

"I have been thinking that in Eleanor we are witnessing a blink," it said.

"Eh?"

"Yes, for the first time to my knowledge, we have a queen who has raised her voice for the dignity of women."

"*Eh?*"

"Listen," the abbess said.

The trouvère in the cloister had finished composing his song. Now he was singing it, the lovely tenor of his voice flowing into the gray chapel like honey. "*Las! einssi ay de ma mort exemplaire, mais la doleur qu'il me convendra traire, douce seroit, se un tel espoir avoie ...*"

If the singer was dying of love, he'd chosen to set his pain to a melody as pretty as springtime. Despite herself, Adelia smiled; the combination ought to win him his lady, all right.

"*... Dame, et se ja mes cuers riens entreprent, don mes corps ait honneur n'avancement, De vous venracom loneins que vos soie ...*"

So if his heart ever undertook anything that would bring him honor, it would come from the beloved, however far away she was.

The music that attended Eleanor wherever she went had, to Adelia's indiscriminatory ear, been another of her affectations, the incipient background of a woman with every frailty ascribed to the feminine nature: vain, jealous, flighty, one who, in order to assert herself, had chosen to go to war to challenge a man greater than she was.

Yet the abbess was attending to it as if to holy script.

Attending to it with her, Adelia reconsidered. She'd dismissed the elaborate, sighing poetry of the male courtiers, their interest in dress, their perfumed curls, because she judged them by the standard of rough masculinity set by a rough male world. *Was* regard for gentleness and beauty decadent? *Rowley*, she thought, with a tearing rush of fondness, *would say that it was*—he loathed femininity in men; he equated his messenger's liking for scent with the worst excesses of the Emperor Caligula.

Eleanor's version, though, could hardly be decadence, because it was new. Adelia sat up. *By God, it was new.* The abbess was right; deliberately or not, the queen was carrying into the uncultured farmyard of her domains an image of women demanding respect, people to be considered and cherished for their personal value rather than as marketable goods. It demanded that men *deserve* women.

For a moment back there in the queen's apartment, Eleanor had held Wolvercote up to her courtiers, not as a powerful male gaining what was his but as a brute beast dragging its prey into the forest to be gnawed.

"I suppose you're right," she said, almost reluctantly.

"... *vous que j'aim très loyaument ... Ne sans amours, emprendre nel saroie.*"

"But it's a pretense, it's artificial," Adelia protested. "Love, honor, respect. When are they ever extended to everyday women? I doubt if that boy actually practices what he's singing. It's ... it's a pleasant hypocrisy."

"Oh, I have a high regard for hypocrisy," the little nun said. "It pays lip service to an ideal which must, therefore, exist. It recognizes that there is a Good. In its own way, it is a token of civilization. You don't find hypocrisy among the beasts of the field. Nor in Lord Wolvercote."

"What good does the Good do if it is not adhered to?"

"That is what I have been wondering," Mother Edyve said calmly. "And I have come to the conclusion that perhaps the early Christians wondered it, too, and perhaps that Eleanor, in her fashion, has made a start by setting a brick in a foundation on which, with God's help, our daughters' daughters can begin to build a new and better Jerusalem."

"Not in time for Emma," Adelia said.

"No."

Perhaps, Adelia thought drearily, *it was only a very old woman who could look hopefully on a single brick laid in a wasteland.*

They sat a while longer, listening. The singer had changed his tune and his theme. "*I would hold thee naked in my arms at eve, that we might be in ecstasy, my head against thy breast ...*"

"That, too, is love of a sort, nevertheless," Mother Edyve said, "and perhaps all one to our Great Parent, who made our bodies as they are."

Adelia smiled at her, thinking of being in bed with Rowley. "I have been convinced that it is."

"So have I, which speaks well for the men we have loved." There was a reflective sigh. "But don't tell Father Egbert."

The abbess got up with difficulty and tested her legs.

Warmed, Adelia went to help her settle her cloak. "Mother," she said on impulse, "I am afraid for Dame Dakers's safety."

A heavily veined little hand flapped her away; Mother Edyve had become impatient to go. "You are a busy soul, child, and I am grateful for it, but you may leave Dakers's safety to me."

As she hobbled out, she said something else, but the words were indistinct, something like, "After all, I have the keys to the lockup."

By the end of that day, Adelia had changed. Perhaps it was anger at Emma Bloat's rape. Perhaps it was anger at the attempt on Dakers's life. Perhaps it was the courage inspired by Mother Edyve.

Whatever it was, she knew she couldn't cower in the guesthouse anymore while murderers and abductors went unchecked.

In essence, the killer of Rosamund and Bertha had made a contract with her: *Leave me alone and your child is safe.*

A shameful contract. Nevertheless, she would have abided by it, taking it as a given that he would not kill again.

But he'd tossed a burning rag through an aperture as if the living woman inside was rubbish.

I can't allow that, she told him.

She was afraid, very afraid indeed; her baby would have to be protected as no child ever had been, but she, Adelia, could not live, *her daughter* could not live, at the cost of other people's deaths.

"Where you going?" Gyltha called after her.

"I'm going to ask questions."

She found Jacques in the cloister, being taught how to play the viol by one of the troubadours. The courtiers were colonizing the place. *And the nuns,* she thought, *are now too intimidated by everything that has happened to stop them.*

She dragged the unwilling messenger away toward the almonry and sat him and herself down on a mounting block.

"Yes, mistress?"

"I want you to help me find out who ordered the killing of Talbot of Kidlington."

He was set aback. "I don't know as I'm up to that, mistress."

She ignored him and recounted the list of those she suspected: "Wolvercote, Master Warin, the gatekeeper, and the Bloats." She went into detail.

He rubbed his chin; it was closely shaved now, like all the young men's at Eleanor's court.

"I can tell you one thing, if it helps," he said. "Lawyer Warin made a to-do when he was intro-duced to my lord Wolvercote in church. '*So honored to make your acquaintance, my lord. We have not met, but I have long wished to know ...'* He made a point of it—I was there and heard him. If he mentioned that they had not encountered each other before, he must have said it three or four times."

"How did Wolvercote greet Master Warin?"

"Like he treats everybody, as if he'd been squirted out of a backside." He grimaced, afraid of having offended her. "Sorry, mistress."

"But you believe Warin was insisting they hadn't met before when, really, they had?"

Jacques thought about it. "Yes, I do."

Adelia was shivering. Ward had crept under her skirts and was pressing against her knees for warmth. A gargoyle on the gutter of the abbess's house opposite gaped at her, its chin bearded with icicles.

I am watching you.

She said, "Emma thought kindly of Master Warin, which means that Talbot did, too, which also means the boy trusted him ..."

"And confided his intention to elope?" The messenger was becoming interested.

"I know he did," she said. "Emma told me so. The boy told Warin he was choosing his birthday as the day for the elopement so that he could take possession of his inheritance ..."

"Which, unbeknownst, Master Warin had squandered ..." This was exciting.

Adelia nodded. "Which, indeed, Master Warin may have squandered, thereby necessitating his young cousin's removal ... "

"... and it dawns on Master Warin that he has an ally in Lord Wolvercote. Old Wolfie will be deprived of a bride and a fortune if the elopement goes ahead."

"Yes. So he approaches Lord Wolvercote and suggests Talbot should die."

They sat back to think it through.

"Why was it so urgent that Talbot's body be identified right away?" Adelia wondered.

"That's easy, mistress. Lawyer Warin may be pressed for money—he looks a man who likes to live well. If he's Talbot's heir, it would take too long to prove to a coroner that the estate of the anonymous corpse was his. That takes a long time. Courts are slow. His creditors would come in before he inherited."

"And it would suit Wolvercote for Emma to realize that her lover was dead. Yes, it's all of a piece," she said. "It was Wolvercote who provided the killers. Warin probably didn't know any."

"And got rid of them once they'd done the deed. It could be so, mistress."

Talking it over had hardened the case for Adelia, turning theory to reality. Two men had conspired to blot out a young life. Wickedness was discussed in lawyers' offices as business, considered in manor houses over a flagon of wine; men were instructed in it. Normality, goodness were commodities to be traded for greed. Innocence was helpless against it. *She* was helpless against it. It gibbered at her from the rooftops.

"How to prove it, though?" Jacques asked.

"Plotters distrust one another," she said. "I think it can be done, but I shall need you to help me."

She let him go then, and hurried back to the guesthouse, unable to shake off her fear for Allie.

"Right as a shilling," Gyltha said. "Look at her."

But Adelia knew that Gyltha, too, was afraid, because she'd told Mansur to move in with them, day and night.

"Anyone as doesn't like it can go and ... well, you know what," she said. "So you do what you got to do. Mansur's on guard."

But so was the killer ...

N ow she had to go and see Father Paton. This time she did it carefully, waiting until night, watching for watchers, slipping from shadow to shadow until she was protected by the narrow walk that led to the warming room stairs.

Sister Lancelyne was at Vespers, and the little priest was alone, poring over the cartulary by candlelight, none too pleased to be interrupted.

Adelia told him everything, *everything*, beginning with finding Talbot's body on the bridge—the little priest might have missed it while he'd been keeping warm in the cart—proceeding to the happenings at Wormhold, to the return to Godstow and the death of Bertha, her suspicions of who did what, the threat to Allie, the threat to Dame Dakers.

He didn't want to hear it. He kept shifting and glancing longingly at the documents open in front of him. This was a tale reeking of the cardinal sins, and Father Paton preferred humanity in the abstract. "Are you certain?" he kept asking. "Surely not. How dare you reckon such things?"

Adelia persisted, skewering him with logic like a pin through a butterfly. She didn't like him much; he didn't like her at all, but he was separated from the battle in which she was engaged, and his mind was like one of his own ledgers; she needed it as a register.

"You must keep it all very, very secret," she told him. "Mention it to nobody except the king." This bloodless little man had to be the repository of her knowledge so that, in the event of her death, he could pass it on to Henry Plantagenet. "When the king comes, he will know what to do."

"But I do not."

"Yes, you do." And she told him what it was that he must look for.

"This is impudence." He was shocked. "In any case, I doubt that, even if it is extant, it will prove your case."

Adelia doubted it, too, but it was all she had in her armory. She attempted an encouragement that she didn't feel. "The king *will* come," she said, "and he *will* prevail in the end." That was her only certainty. Eleanor might be extraordinary, but she had pitted herself against one who straddled his kingdom like a colossus; she could not win.

There Father Paton agreed with her. "Yes, yes," he said, "a queen is only a woman, unable to fight any cause successfully, let alone her own. All she may expect is God's punishment for rebelling against her rightful lord."

He turned on Adelia. "You, too, mistress, are a mere woman, sinful, impertinent, and right or wrong, you should not be questioning your betters."

She held her temper and instead dangled a carrot. "When the king *does* come," she said, "he'll want to know who murdered Rosamund. There will be advancement for the man that can tell him who it was."

She watched the priest's mouth purse as he entered possible promotion to an abbacy, even a bishopric, into a mental balance sheet against the risk and lèse-majesté of what he was being asked to do.

"I suppose I shall be serving God, who is all truth," he said slowly.

"You will," she said, and left him to get on with it.

And then it was Christmas.

The church was so packed with bodies for Angel Mass that it was actually hot, and the smell of humanity threatened to overwhelm the fresh, bitter scent of holly and ivy garlands.

Adelia almost sweltered in her beaver cloak. She kept it on because, underneath, she was wearing the bliaut that Eleanor's seamstresses had finished just in time and knew that she looked so nice in it, with all the other trimmings the queen had given her, that she felt she would attract attention.

"You show yourself," Gyltha had protested. "You don't look half bad." Which, from her, was praise.

But the instinct to keep out of the killer's eye was still strong. Perhaps she would take off her cloak at the coming feast; perhaps she wouldn't.

The choir stalls, once more reserved for the nuns, provided a black-and-white edging to the embroidered, bedecked altar with its blaze of candles and the robes of the abbot and two priests as they moved through the litany like glowing chess pieces.

The magic was infallible.

The queue for Communion included murderous men, hostile factions, every gamut of human weakness and sorrow, yet, as it moved quietly forward, it was gripped by the same awe. At the rail, the miller knelt beside one of the men who had belabored him. Adelia received the host from the Abbot of Eynsham, whose hands rested for a second in blessing on the head of Baby Allie. The cup passed from a Wolvercote mercenary to one of Schwyz's before each lumbered back to his place, chewing and exalted.

There was common and growing breathlessness as Mary labored in her stable a few yards away. The running footfalls of the shepherds came nearer and nearer. Angels chanted above the starlit, snow-stacked church roof.

When the abbot, raising his arms, announced a deep-throated "The Child is born," his exhortation to go in peace was lost in a great shout of congratulation, several of the women yelling advice on breast-feeding to the invisible but present Mary and prompting her to "make sure and wrap that baby up warm now."

Bethlehem was here. It was now.

As Adelia filed into the great barn, Jacques pushed through the crowd to touch her shoulder. "The queen's greeting, mistress, and she will be disappointed if you are not wearing the gifts she gave you."

Reluctantly, Adelia took off her cloak with its hood, revealing the bliaut and the barbette, and felt naked. Walt, who was beside her, looked at her and stared. "Wondered who this stranger was," he said. She supposed that, too, was a compliment. And indeed, she received a lot of surprised looks—most of them friendly. For this was another gift Eleanor had, unconsciously, given her; by showing her favor, the queen had cleansed her of the taint of witch-craft.

Though Eleanor and her court had made plans for its entertainments, the feast in the barn was expropriated by the English.

Expropriated? It was run away with.

Charming Aquitanian carols were drowned in roaring wassails as the flaming Yule log, dragged in on the end of a harness by an ox, was set on a hearth in the middle of the great square formed by the tables in the barn. A minstrel in the gallery— actually, the hayloft—tried singing to the diners, but since, it turned out, all the convent's people and most of the village had been invited and were making too much noise to hear him, he gave up and descended to eat with the rest.

It was a Viking meal. Meat and more meat. The icehouse had yielded its best. Eleanor's cook had, literally, battled for his art in the kitchen, but his winter sallats and frumenty, his pretty painted pastry castles and delicate flower-water jellies had been so overwhelmed and dripped on by lard and blood-gravy that he'd been taken poorly and now sat staring into space as his apprentice popped comforting little squares of roast pork into his mouth.

There were no courses, either. The convent servants had coped for too long with Godstow's overflowing and demanding guests, and the advent of Christmas had worked them even harder. They'd spent the last few days in the scorching heat of cooking fires and in decorating the barn until it resembled a glade in a forest; they weren't bloody going to miss the feast for which they'd sweated by running back and forth to the kitchens. Everything they'd cooked—savory, sweet, sauced, plain, breads and pudding—was dumped on the tables in one glorious heap while they clambered onto the benches nearest the barn doors to enjoy it.

This was a good thing; there was so much carving to be done at once, so much handing of dishes up and down the tables, so many shouts back and forth for "some of that stuffing for my lady," "a slice off the gander, if you please," "pass up the turnip mash, there" that a camaraderie of gustation grew between high and low, though it did not extend to the dogs waiting under the tables for scraps and squabbling when one fell their way.

Ward kept close to Adelia's knees, where he was fed royally—his mistress was a small eater and, in order not to offend Mansur, who was sitting beside her and kept heaping her platter, she secretly slipped hunks of meat to her dog.

Eleanor, Adelia saw, was taking it all well. With good humor, the queen had put on the monstrous crown of ivy and bay leaves presented to her by the smith's wife, thereby ruining her own simple headdress and adding to the growing paganism of the night by her sudden resemblance to an earth goddess.

Apart from the royal cook, the only person to take no part in the jollity was Emma, a glacial, unmoving figure sitting next to her husband, who ignored her. Adelia tried to catch her eye, and then didn't; the girl looked at nothing.

How were Master and Mistress Bloat going to deal with the situation? Adelia wondered. Were they condemning the abduction of their daughter?

No, they'd decided to overlook it. They'd placed themselves on the inner side of one of the tables opposite the abductor, though Wolvercote was rebuffing most of their attempts to engage him in conversation.

Master Bloat even tried to stand up and make a toast to the happy couple, but the volume of noise increased alarmingly as he did so, and Emma, coming to life for the first time, regarded her father with a look so bitter that the man's words withered in his mouth and he sat down again.

With Mansur on her left and Allie tied firmly in a sling to her hip—there was to be no more abduction of daughters—Adelia turned her attention to the man on her right. She had taken pains to get a seat next to him.

Master Warin had kept to himself until now, and the fact that he had to ask her, politely, who she was and did not react unfavorably when she told him her name showed that he had been isolated from convent gossip.

He had a nervous habit of licking his lips and had none of the smooth superiority of most lawyers, an unremarkable person who'd softened but did not try to hide a strong Gloucestershire accent. Adelia got the impression that gaining legal qualification had been hard for him, both financially and intellectually, and that he confined himself to *consilio et auxilio*, advising on wills, assarts, boundary disputes, contracts of service, all the minutiae of everyday law, though important enough to those involved with them.

When she commiserated with him on the death of his young cousin, he wet his lips again and real tears came into his shortsighted eyes: The murder had bereft him of family, he told her, since he had no wife as yet. "How I envy you this bonny little girl, mistress. I would dearly like children."

Adelia had built a case against the lawyer. She had to keep reminding herself that *somebody* had passed on the information that led to killers waiting on the bridge for Talbot of Kidlington, and none was more likely than this little man, who said of Talbot, "We were closer than cousins. He was my younger brother after his parents died. I looked after him in everything."

But while it was modest, his clothing was of a quality not to be expected of a family lawyer, and the large seal ring on his finger was entirely of gold; Master Warin did himself well. Also, his taste did not run to mead and ale; his grabs at the wine jug as it was passed round were frequent.

Adelia applied the spur. "Your cousin didn't confide to you his intention to run away with Mistress Bloat, then?" she asked.

"Of course not." Master Warin's voice became sharp. "A lunatic idea. I would have dissuaded him from it. Lord Wolvercote is an important man. I would not have him shamed by one of my family."

He was lying. Emma had said he'd been part of the elopement conspiracy.

"Did you know him, then? Wolvercote?"

"I did not." Master Warin's tongue wriggled around his lips. "We met in church the other night for the first time."

Lying again. This was her man.

"I'd only wondered if you knew what your cousin was planning, because people are saying that you came here hot on his heels ..."

"Who says that?"

"You arrived at the abbey so soon after ..."

"That is a calumny. I was worried for my cousin traveling in the snow. Who are these slanderers?

Who are *you*? I don't need to sit here ..." His tongue flickering like a snake's, Master Warin grabbed his wine cup and moved away to find a seat farther down the table.

Mansur turned his head to watch the lawyer's agitated progress. "Did he kill the boy?" he asked in Arabic.

"In a way. He told Wolvercote so that Wolvercote could kill him."

"As guilty, then."

"As if he shot the bolt himself, yes. He could have said he knew about the elopement and turned up at the abbey in order to stop it, thus explaining why he was so prompt on the scene. But he wouldn't say that—I gave him the opportunity—because people would think he was in Wolvercote's pocket, and he insists they never met. Actually, it wouldn't condemn him if he said they had, but they conspired together to kill the boy, you see, and it's warping his judgment. Guilt is making him distance himself from Wolvercote when he doesn't need to."

"He betrayed his own kin, Allah spit on him. Can we prove it?"

"We'll try." Adelia took Allie out of the sling and rubbed her cheek against her daughter's downy head. How much more depressing was the banal ordinariness of a murderer like little Lawyer Warin than the brutality of a Wolvercote.

There was a sudden push, and she was shoved to one side by Cross taking the place that Warin had left and bringing with him the chill of outside.

"Move up there." The mercenary began reaching for dishes like a starving man.

"What have you been up to?" she asked.

"What you think I been up to? Marching up and down outside that bloody lockup. And a waste of bloody time that was. She's gone."

"Who's gone?"

"The demon. Abbot hisself told me she was a demon. Who'd you think?"

"Dakers? Dakers has gone?" She was on her feet, startling Allie, who'd been sucking the marrow of a beef bone. "Oh, dear God, they've taken her."

Cross looked up at her, gravy dripping from his mouth. "What you on about? Nobody ain't taken her. She's vanished. That's what demons do, they vanish."

Adelia sat down. "Tell me."

How it had been done, or even when, Cross couldn't tell her, because he didn't know; nobody knew. It hadn't been discovered until a short while ago when, on instructions from the cellaress, a kitchen servant had brought a tray of Christmas food for its prisoner and Cross had used his key to open the lockup's door.

"'S on a ring, the key is, see," he said. "Each guard passes it on to the next one as takes over. Oswald passed it to me when I went on duty, an' Walt'd passed it to him when *he* went on duty, and they both swears they never opened that bloody door, an' I know I didn't, not til I unlocked it just now ..."

There was a pause while he scooped beef into his mouth.

"*And*?" Adelia asked, impatient.

"An' so I fits the key in the lock, turns it, opens the door, and the boy goes in with the basket, and there she was ... gone. Place as bare as a baby's arse."

"Somebody must have let her out." Adelia was still worried.

"No, they bloody ain't," Cross said. "I tell you, nobody din't open the bloody door til then. She's vanished. 'S what demons do. Turned herself into a puff a smoke and out through one of the slits, that's what she done."

He'd called for Schwyz to come to the lockup, he said, nodding toward the empty space on the upper table where the mercenary leader had been sitting. Sister Havis, too, had been summoned.

"But, like I told 'em, you won't find her a'cause she's vanished, gone back to hell where she come from. What else you expect from a demon? Here he comes, look, shittin' hisself six ways from Sunday."

A scowling Schwyz had entered the barn and was striding up to the table where the Abbot of Eynsham sat next to the queen. All the diners were too busy carousing and eating to pay him any attention, except those to whom he had to deliver the news. Adelia saw that Eleanor merely raised her eyebrows, but the abbot immediately got to his feet; he seemed to be shouting, though the noise in the barn was too great for Adelia to hear him.

"He's wanting the abbey searched," Cross said, interpreting. "No bloody chance of that, though. Nobody ain't leaving Yule food to go huntin' a demon in the dark. I ain't, I know that."

So much was obvious. The abbot was talking urgently to Lord Wolvercote, who was shrugging him off like a man who didn't care. Now he was appealing to the abbess, whose response, while more courteous, showed a similar refusal to be of help.

As she spread her hands to indicate the uselessness of interrupting the diners, Mother Edyve's eyes rested for a moment without expression on Adelia's across the room.

After all, I have the keys to the lockup.

"What you laughing at?" Cross asked.

"At a man hoist with his own petard."

However the abbess had managed the escape, whichever of Dakers's guards had been commanded to turn a blind eye, the Abbot of Eynsham could neither accuse nor punish. He was the one who, in locking her up, had demonized Rosamund's housekeeper; he could not now complain if, as Cross said, she had done what demons did.

Still grinning, Adelia leaned forward to tell Gyltha, who was on the Arab's other side, what had happened.

"Good luck to the old gargoyle." Gyltha took another swig from her beaker; she'd been imbibing with energy for some time.

Mansur said in Arabic, "Convent men have been digging a path through the snow down to the river. The abbess ordered it. I overheard the man Fitchet say it was so that the queen could go skating on the ice. Now I think that they have been making an escapeway for Rosamund's woman."

"They've let her leave? In this weather?" It wasn't funny anymore. "I thought they'd hide her somewhere in the abbey."

Mansur shook his head. "It is too crowded, she would be found. She will survive if Allah wills it. It is not far to Oxford."

"She won't go to Oxford."

There was only one place Dame Dakers would be making for.

For the rest of the meal and as the tables were put aside to clear the barn for dancing, Adelia thought of the river and the woman who would be following its course northward. Would the ice hold her? Could she survive the cold? Had the abbot, who would know where she was heading, sent men and dogs after her?

Mansur, looking at her, said, "Allah protects the insane. He will decide whether the woman lives or dies."

But it was because Dakers was insane and friendless and knew too much that Adelia's shoulders were bowed by responsibility for her.

Allah, God, whoever You are, look out for her.

However, in seeing to young Allie, who, having fed and slept and now woken up again, needing to be wiped top and bottom and to have her clouts changed, and demanding entertainment, Adelia was forced to dwell on what was immediate.

There was entertainment in plenty. The troubadours had gathered in the hayloft and were now playing with a force and rhythm that couldn't be denied; the queen and her court danced to the music with toe-pointing, hand-arching elegance at one end of the barn while, at the other, the English jounced in swinging, noisy rings.

A convent pensioner was juggling apples with a dexterity that belied his years, and the smith, against the advice of his wife, was swallowing a sword.

Activity and grunts from under the hayloft eventually produced a wild assortment of figures that proceeded to put on an impromptu and scatological version of Noah's flood so exuberantly that the dancers paused to become its audience.

Adelia, sitting on the ground with a crowing, pointing Allie against her knees, found herself enjoying it. It was doubtful if Noah would have recognized the species capering up this invisible gangplank into an invisible ark. The only real animal, the convent donkey, outperformed the rest of the cast by dropping a pungent criticism of their performance on the foot of a unicorn, played by Fitchet, making Gyltha laugh so hard that Mansur had to drag her away until she recovered.

For all their sophistication, Eleanor's party couldn't resist the applause accorded to such vulgarism. They joined in, dropping refinement and showing themselves to be clowns manqués as they appeared in startling wigs and skirts, faces painted with flour and madder.

What was it about some men that they must ape women, Adelia thought, even as she booed an irascible Mrs. Noah, played with brio by Montignard, belaboring Noah for being drunk.

Was that Jacques under the warts, straw hair, and extended bosom of Japhet's wife? Surely that wasn't the Abbot of Eynsham black-faced and whirling so fast on his toes that his petticoat flared in a blur?

Allie, still clutching her marrow bone, had fallen asleep again. It was time to go to bed before the manic hilarity of the night descended into brawling, as it almost inevitably would. Already Schwyz's men and Wolvercote's had separated into drunken coteries and were focusing blearily on one another in a way suggesting that the spirit of Christmas was on its last legs.

Wolvercote himself had already gone, taking Emma with him. The queen was thanking the abbess before departing, and Mother Edyve was signaling to her nuns. Master Warin had disappeared. The smith, clutching his throat, was being led away by his wife.

Adelia looked around for Gyltha and Mansur. Oh, dear, her beloved Arab—possibly the only sober person in the barn apart from herself—had been inveigled into doing his sword dance for the delight of some convent servants, and Gyltha was gyrating round him like an inebriated stoat. Not a drinker usually, Gyltha, but she could never resist alcohol when it was free.

Yawning, Adelia picked up Allie and took her to the corner in which they'd left the cradle, put the child in it, took away the marrow bone, gave it to Ward, covered up her daughter, and raised the cradle's little leather hood, then settled down beside it to wait.

And fell asleep to dream a frenetic, rowdy dream that turned hideous when a bear picked her up and, clutching her to its pelt, began dragging her away into the forest. She heard growling as Ward attacked the bear and then a yelp as it kicked him away.

Struggling, almost smothered, her legs trailing, Adelia woke up fully. She was being pulled into the darkest corner under the hayloft in the arms of the Abbot of Eynsham. He slammed her so hard against the outer wall that bits of lathe and plaster showered them both, pushing his great body against her.

He was very, very drunk and whispering. "You're his spy, you bitch. The bishop. I know you ... pretending to be prim with me, you whore, I know ... what you got up to. How's he do it? Up the arse? In your mouth?"

Brandy fumes enveloped her as his blackened face came down onto hers.

She jerked her head away and brought up her knee as sharply as she could, but the ridiculous skirt he was wearing gave him protection and, though he grunted, his weight stayed on her.

The whispering went on and on. "... think you're so clever ... see it in your eyes, but you're a stinking strumpet. A spy. I'm better than Saint Albans ... I'm *better* ..." His hand had found her breast and was squeezing it. "Look at me, I can do it ... Love me, you bitch, love *me* ..." He was licking her face.

Outside the suffocating cubicle she was trapped in, somebody was intervening, trying to pull the heaving, hissing awfulness off her. "Leave her, Rob, she's not worth it." It was Schwyz's voice.

"Yes, she is. She looks at me like I'm shit ... like she knows."

There was the sound of a loud smack, then air and space. Relieved of weight, Adelia slid down the wall, gasping.

The abbot lay on the ground, onto which Mansur had flattened him. He was weeping. Beside him, Schwyz was on his knees, giving comfort like a mother. "Just a whore, Robert, you don't want that."

Mansur stood over them both, sucking his knuckles but impassive as ever. He turned and held out his hand to Adelia. She took it and got to her feet.

Together, they walked back to the cradle. Before they reached it, Adelia paused, wiping her face, smoothing her clothes. Even then, she couldn't look down at her child. How impure they made you feel.

Behind her, Schwyz's soothing went on, but the wail of the abbot rose high above it. "Why Saint Albans? *Why not me?*"

With Mansur carrying the cradle, they collected a staggering, singing Gyltha and walked back to the guesthouse through the welcome cold of the night.

Adelia was too deep in shock to be angry, though she knew she would be; after all, she had more regard for herself than women who, miserably, expected assault as the price for being women. But even while her body was shaking, her mind was trying to fathom the reason for what had happened. "I don't understand," she said, wailing. "I thought he was a different sort of enemy."

"Allah punish him, but he would not have hurt you, I think," Mansur said.

"What are you talking about? He *did* hurt me. He tried to rape me."

"He is incapable, I think," Mansur said. His own condition had made a judge of such things; he found the sexuality of so-called normal men interesting. Though castrated, unable to have children, he himself could still have sex with a woman, and there was lofty pity in his voice for one who could not.

"He seemed capable enough to me." Sobbing, Adelia stopped and scooped up snow to rub over her face. "Why are you so tolerant?"

"He wants, but he cannot have. I think so. He is a talker, not a doer."

Was that it? Inadequacy? Among all the filth, there had been a despairing appeal for love, sex, *something*.

Rowley had said of him, "*Bastard. Clever. Got the ear of the Pope.*"

And with all the cleverness, this friend of popes must, when drunk, plead for a despised woman's regard like a child for somebody else's toy.

Because *she* despised *him*?

And I do, she thought. If there was vulnerability, it made the abbot the more loathsome to her. Adelia preferred her enemies straightforwardly and wholeheartedly without humanity.

"I hate him," she said—and *now* she was angry. "Mansur, I'm going to bring that man down."

The Arab bent his head. "Let us pray that Allah wills it."

"He'd better."

Fury was cleansing to the mind. Nevertheless, as Mansur persuaded Gyltha to stop kissing him and go to sleep, Adelia washed herself all over in a bowl of icy water from the ewer. And felt better.

"I'll bring him down," she said again, "somehow."

For a minute, which was all that could be borne of the cold, she opened one of the shutters to look out on the geometric shadows that the pitches of the abbey's roofs were throwing onto the stretch of snow beyond its walls.

A blacker runnel scarred the moonlit whiteness where a new track had been dug to the river. They were linked now, the abbey and the Thames. For the first time, there was an escape route from this seething, overfilled cauldron of humanity where paragons and monsters fought the ultimate, yet never-ending, battle in suffocating collision.

At least one soul had taken it. Somewhere in that metallic wilderness, Dakers was risking her life not, Adelia knew, in order to disappear from her captors but to reach the thing she loved, though it was dead.

TWELVE

*W*hen, early next morning, Adelia opened the shutters on Saint Stephen's Day, it was to find that something had happened to the view from the guesthouse. Yes, of course, a new path was leading down to the bank—they'd cut rough steps in it—but it was more than that; the sense of isolation was gone, and expectation had taken its place.

It was difficult to see why; dawn was blessing the deserted countryside with its usual ephemeral touch of apricot. The snow was as solid as it had been and contained no human footprints as far as the eye stretched.

Yet the white forest across the river was, somehow, less rigid ...

"They're here."

Mansur joined her at the window. "I see nothing."

"I thought I saw something in those trees."

They stood looking. Adelia's excitement trickled away; the expectation was in her, not in the view.

"Wolves, most like," said Gyltha, who was skulking at the rear of the room, avoiding the light. "I heard them last night, horrid close they was."

"Was that when you were vomiting into the chamber pot?" Adelia asked interestedly.

Gyltha ignored her. "Right up to the walls, they were. I reckon they found young Talbot's horse as was left in the woods."

Adelia hadn't heard them—it had been bears that prowled her sleep. But Gyltha was probably right; it would be wolves among the trees—less frightening than those inside the walls.

Yet the leap of hope that Rowley was alive and had brought the king and his men to them had been so volcanic that she couldn't relinquish it altogether. "There *could* be an army hiding out there," she said. "It wouldn't attack without knowing the strength of the force inside the abbey—the sisters might get hurt. He'd wait, Henry would wait."

"What for?" Mansur asked.

"Yes, what for?" Gyltha was being determinedly talkative to show that she wasn't suffering. "He wouldn't need an army to take this place—me and little Allie could storm it by ourselves. And how'd the king get here? No, old Wolf knows he's safe til the snow melts. He ain't even posted lookouts."

"He has now," Mansur said.

Adelia leaned out. Gyltha joined her. Immediately below, a man in Wolvercote scarlet and black was patrolling the walkway running along the hopelessly inadequate castellations of the convent wall, his morning shadow falling rhythmically on the merlons as he passed and disappearing at each crenel. He had a pike in one hand and a rattle in the other.

"What's he guarding us from?" Gyltha asked. "Magpies? There ain't no army out there. Nobody don't fight in winter."

"Henry does," Adelia said. She was hearing Rowley's voice, vibrating from the near-incredulous pleasure with which he'd spoken of his king's exploits, recounting the tale of the young Plantagenet when, fighting for his mother's right to the throne of England against his uncle Stephen, he'd crossed the Channel with a small army in a bitter Christmas gale, catching his enemies hibernating—and beating them.

Until now, Wolvercote had been relying on an English winter to keep his enemy as powerless to move as he was. But whether it was because the umbilical path through the snow now connected the convent to the outside world, or whether there was something in the air today, Saint Stephen's Day, he had set a guard ...

"He's afraid." Adelia's own voice vibrated. "He thinks Henry's coming. And he could, Mansur, the king *could*—his men could skate upriver and get here." She had another thought: "I suppose Wolvercote could even skate his men down to Oxford and join the other rebels. Why hasn't he?"

"The man Schwyz thought of it. He is the better tactician," Mansur said. "He asked Fitchet if it could be done. But further down, the Thames is deeper and has more tributaries, its ice does not hold and cannot be risked. Nobody can go or come that way." Mansur spread his hands in apology to

Adelia for disappointing her. "Local knowledge. No one moves until the snow melts."

"And close them bloody shutters," Gyltha said. "You want this baby to freeze?" Suddenly gentle, she added, "Nobody in the outside world don't know we're here, my duck."

"The woman is right," Mansur said.

They've lost hope, she thought. *They've given Rowley up for dead at last.* Godstow festered like an unsuspected bubo in the world's white flesh, waiting to spread its poison. Only the birds overhead could know that it flew the pennant of a rebel queen—and birds weren't likely to tell anybody.

But today, against all evidence, hope told Adelia that there was something beyond these shutters. At least there were steps leading to the river, and the river, however treacherous, led to the outside world. It was sunny, and there was an indefinable feeling in the air.

She'd been afraid too long, besieged too long, threatened too long, shut in dark rooms during daylight like a hostage—they all had.

Hearing talk and laughter, she gave the shutters a push that threw them back against the wall and leaned out again.

Farther along, the convent gates were opening and a crowd of chattering men and women were assembling outside them. In their center was a slim, elegant figure dressed in furs with a sheen that glowed in the sun.

"The queen's going skating," Adelia said. She turned round. "And so are we. All of us. Allie, too."

Everybody did. It was, after all, Saint Stephen's Day, which, by tradition, belonged to the servants, whom, since they could not go home to their villages, had to enjoy it in situ. Tonight it would be their privilege to have their own private feast on last night's leftovers.

Almost every worker in the abbey tumbled out onto the ice, some without skates but all carrying the traditional clay box that they rattled invitingly under the noses of the guests.

Having made her contribution, Adelia turned to delighting her daughter by attaching her belt to the cradle and skimming the child in it over the ice as she skated. Others on skates similarly obliged those who had none, so that the wide sweep of the Thames became a whirl of sledges and trays, of puffed jokes and pink cheeks, through which a smiling queen sailed, swanlike, with her courtiers gaggling after her.

The nuns joined them after Lauds, the younger ones shrieking happily and vying with Sister Havis, who, while making it seem stately, outraced them all.

A brazier was placed on the ice near the bank and a chair carried to it so that Mother Edyve could sit by its warmth in company with the walking wounded that Sister Jennet had brought from the infirmary. Ward, whose attempts to scrabble along behind Adelia kept ending with his legs splaying into a quadrant, gave up the battle and settled down to sulk on the piece of carpet under the abbess's chair.

Adelia saw her patient and skated over to him, dragging the cradle behind her. "Are you progressing well?"

Poyns's young face was abeam. "Right nicely, mistress, I thank ee. And the abbess is giving me a job, assistant gatekeeper to Master Fitchet. Don't need two arms in gatekeepin'."

Adelia smiled back at him. *What* a nice abbey this was.

"And thank Master Man ... Manum ... thank the doctor for me; God and the saints bless him."

"I will."

Tables appeared bearing some remnants of the Christmas feast.

Sitting on somebody's homemade sledge on the far bank where Ward joined them, Adelia and Gyltha masticated Allie's dinner for her and ate their own, ignoring the child's persistent "Bor, bor," asking to be taken onto the ice again.

"She means 'more,'" Adelia said proudly. "That's her first word."

"Them's her first orders," Gyltha said. "Who's a little tyrant, then?" She abandoned her lamb chop to Ward, picked up the belt, and skated off with the cradle, throwing up a spray of ice behind her.

Adelia and her dog sat on. From here she had a panorama of the convent walls. There were now two of Wolvercote's men patrolling, both of them keeping their eyes on the trees behind her. A figure stood at one of the windows in the men's guesthouse—she thought it was Master Warin.

No sign of the abbot, thanks be to God; he'd

become dreadful to her, as, with her rejection, she must have become dreadful to him—and would be punished for it.

The bridge had been closed; she could tell that because some Wolvercote villagers were crowding the far side of it, wistfully watching the merrymakers on ice. Others were digging their own path down to the river.

Behind her, in the forest that she'd hoped would be hiding Henry Plantagenet and his army, she could hear the shouts of the younger convent men as, careless of wolves, they scoured the undergrowth in the hunt for a wren, their noise indicating that they were not encountering anything larger.

She looked back to see their figures running through the trees, faces blackened with soot, as tradition demanded they should be. Why it was necessary to catch a wren at all on Saint Stephen's Day she did not understand; she could never fathom English customs. Pagan, most of them.

She returned to watching the scene on the ice.

Wolvercote was talking to Eleanor at the food table. Where was Emma?

Adelia wondered what it was that had stirred the man into setting a watch now, when he had neglected any precaution for so long. Perhaps he'd sensed the same alertness in the air that so invigorated herself—or had just glimpsed another opportunity to assert his control. Either way, he was a fool as well as a brute; what point was there in guarding the abbey and, apparently, readying it in case of siege when nearly all its occupants were capering outside its walls, any one of whom could carry news of his presence in it to his enemy?

She was glad of it—the liberation. If it hadn't meant leaving her nearest and dearest behind, she'd have been tempted to skate off and find Henry for herself.

But Schwyz had just come out of the abbey gates and was viewing the indisciplined joyousness below him like a man who could organize things better. And, damn him, he was *going* to organize them better. Descending the steps, approaching Wolvercote, berating ...

Within minutes he'd stationed his mercenaries at each end of the river's bend. Nobody would get away now. He was actually scolding Eleanor, pointing her toward the convent gate ... She was shaking her head, having too much fun, skating away from him.

They'd have to go in soon; the sun was getting low, withdrawing brightness and such warmth as it had bestowed. At last, Eleanor's clear diction was heard thanking Mother Edyve for the entertainment. "So refreshing ..." People were beginning to climb the steps of the track.

"Mistress," said a crisp voice behind Adelia. It was Father Paton.

Rowley's little secretary looked incongruous on skates, but he balanced on them neatly, his mittened, inky hands crossed on his chest as if protecting himself from the unworthy. "I have it," he said.

She stared at him. "You ... *found* it? I can't believe ...

it was such a long shot." She had to pull herself together. "And is it the same?"

"Yes," he said, "I regret to say that the similarity with the one you gave me is undeniable."

"It would stand up in a court of law?"

"Yes. There are peculiarities common to each that even the illiterate would recognize. I have it here, I have them both ..." He began unbuckling the large scrip hanging from his belt.

Adelia stopped him. "No, no, I don't want them. You keep them, and my affidavit. Keep them very safe until the time comes ... and in the name of Jesus, tell nobody you have them."

Father Paton pursed his lips. "I have written my own account of this affair, explaining to whomsoever it may concern that I have done what I have done because I believe it to be the will of my master, the late Bishop of Saint Albans ..."

There was a swirl of ice as the bishop's messenger encircled them and came to a sliding stop.

Jacques's face was ruddy with exercise; he looked almost handsome, though his bishop would not have approved of the elaborate, hand-twirling, very Aquitanian bow he gave Adelia. "It's done, mistress. With good fortune, they're meeting in the church at Vespers. You and this gentleman should take your positions early."

"What nonsense is this?" Father Paton disapproved of Jacques only slightly less than he did of Adelia.

"Jacques has been delivering two invitations that I've written, Father," she told him. "We are going to eavesdrop; we are going to prove who contrived the death of Talbot of Kidlington."

"I will have nothing to do with all your supposed killings. You expect me to eavesdrop? Preposterous. I refuse."

"What supposed killings?" Jacques asked, puzzled.

"We shall *be* there," Adelia told the priest. She cut off his protests. "Yes, you shall. We need an independent witness. God in Heaven, Father, a young man was put to death."

A rough figure with an even rougher voice had come up to them. "Get inside, you lot, and quick about it." Cross had his arms held wide to scoop the three of them toward the steps.

Glad to go, Father Paton skated off.

"*Can* he help us with Bertha's death?" Jacques asked.

"I'm not telling you again," Cross said. "The chief says inside, so get bloody inside."

Jacques obeyed. Adelia lingered.

"Come on, now, missis. 'S getting chilly." The mercenary took her arm, not unkindly. "See, you're shaking."

"I don't want to go in," she said. The convent walls would imprison her and the killer together again; she was being dragged back into a cage that held a monster with blood on its fangs.

"You ain't staying here all night." As he pulled her over the ice, Cross shouted over his shoulder at the wren hunters in the trees, "Time to go in, lads."

When they reached the steps, he had to haul Adelia up them like an executioner assisting a prisoner to the gallows.

Behind them, a crowd of men emerged from the trees of the far bank, shouting in triumph over a small cage twisted from withies in which fluttered a frightened wren. They were hooded, covered in snow, their black faces rendering them unrecognizable.

And if, whooping and capering with the rest, there was one more figure going in through the convent gates than had left them, nobody noticed it.

The convent carpenter had laid boards across the end rafters of the church's Saint Mary side chapel in order to facilitate the removal and replacement of struts that showed signs of rotting, creating a temporary and partial little loft in which the two people now hiding in it could listen but not see. Adelia and Father Paton were, quite literally, eavesdroppers.

It had taken considerable urging to get the priest to accompany her into the rafters. He'd protested at the subterfuge, the risk, the indignity.

Adelia hadn't liked it, either. This wasn't her way of doing things, it was arbitrary, unscientific. Worse, the fear she felt at being once more in the abbey sapped her energy, leaving her with a deadening feeling of futility.

But coming in through the chapel's door, a draft had wavered the candles burning on the Virgin's altar, one of them lit by Emma for Talbot of Kidlington, and so she had bullied, shamed, and cajoled. "We have a duty to the dead, Father." It was the bedrock of her faith, as fundamental to her as the Athanasian Creed to Western liturgy, and perhaps the priest had recognized its virtue, for he had stopped arguing and climbed the ladder Jacques set for them.

Now Vespers had chimed, the faint chanting from the cloisters had stopped. The church was empty—ever since the mercenaries had proved troublesome, the nuns had transferred the vigil for their dead to their own chapel.

Somewhere a dog barked. Fitchet's mongrel, probably—a bristled terror at whose every approach Ward, not renowned for his courage, lay down and rolled over.

They were too far back in the loft to see anything below. Only a glow from the altar candles in the church proper reached them so that they could, at least, make out the wagon roof above them. It gave Adelia the impression that she and the priest were lying on the thwarts of an upended boat. Uncomfortably.

Fierce little beads that were the eyes of the bats hanging from the lathes overhead glared down at her.

A scamper nearby caused Father Paton to squeak. "I abhor rats."

"Be quiet," she told him.

"This is foolishness."

Perhaps it was, but they couldn't alter it now—

Jacques had taken the ladder away, replacing it in the bell tower next door from whence it had come, perching himself in the shadows at the tower's top.

A latch clicked. The unoiled hinges of the chapel's side door protested with a screech. Somebody hissed at the noise. The door closed. Silence.

Warin. It would be the lawyer; Wolvercote wouldn't creep as this one crept.

Adelia felt a curious despair. It was one thing to theorize about a man's guilt, another to have it confirmed. Somewhere below her stood a creature who'd betrayed the only relative he had, a boy in his care, a boy who'd trusted him and had been sent to his death.

A rasp of hinges again, this time accompanied by the stamp of boots. There was a vibration of energy.

"Did you send me this?" Wolvercote's voice. Furious. If Master Warin protested, the listeners did not hear him because Wolvercote continued without pause. "Yes you did, you whoreson, you puling pot of pus, you stinking spittle, you'll not tax me for more, you crapulous bit of crud ..."

The tirade, its wonderful alliteration unsuspected from such a source, was accompanied by slaps, presumably across Master Warin's face, that resounded against the walls like whip cracks—each one making Father Paton jump so that Adelia, lying beside him in the rafters, flinched in unison.

The lawyer was keeping his head, though it had to be buzzing. "Look, look, my lord. In the name of Christ, *look*." The onslaught stopped.

He's showing *his* letter.

Apart from giving the time and place of the suggested meeting, the message she'd written to each man had been short: *We are discovered.*

There was a long pause while Wolvercote—not a reading man—deciphered the note sent to Warin. The lawyer said quietly, "It's a trap. Somebody's here."

There were hurried, soft footfalls as Warin searched, the opening of cupboards—a thump of hassocks falling to the floor as they were dislodged. "Somebody's *here.*"

"*Who's* here? *What* trap?" Wolvercote was staying where he was, shouting after Warin as the little man went into the body of the church to search that, too. "Didn't you send me this?"

"What's up there?" Master Warin had come back. "We should look up there."

He looked upward. The impression that the man's eyes could see through the boards tensed Adelia's muscles. Father Paton didn't move.

"Nobody's up there. How could anybody get up there? What trap?"

"My lord, somebody knows." Master Warin had calmed himself a little. "My lord, you shouldn't have hanged the knaves. It looked badly. I'd promised them money to leave the country."

So you *supplied the killers.*

"Of course I hanged the dogs." Wolvercote was still shouting. "Who knew if they would keep their mouths shut. God curse you, Warin, if this is a ploy for more payment ..."

"It is not, my lord, though Sweet Mary knows it was a great service I rendered you ..."

"Yes." Wolvercote's tone had become quieter, more considering. "I am beginning to wonder why."

"I told you, my lord. I would not have you wronged by one of my own family; when I heard what the boy intended ..."

"And no benefit to you? Then why in hell did you come here? What brought you galloping to the abbey to see if he was dead?"

They were moving off into the nave of the church, their voices trailing into unintelligible exchanges of animosity and complaint.

After a long time, they came back, only footsteps giving an indication of their return. The door scraped open. Boots stamped through it as loudly as they had come.

Father Paton shifted, but Adelia clamped his arm. *Wait*. They won't want to be seen together. Wolvercote has left first.

Silence again. A quiet little man, the lawyer.

Now he was going. She waited until she heard the fall of the latch, then wriggled forward to peer over the boards.

The chapel was empty.

"Respectable men, a baron of the realm, ogres, ogres." Father Paton's horror was tinged with excitement. "The sheriff shall be told, I must write it down, yes, write it down. I am witness to conspiracy and murder. The sheriff will need a full affidavit. I am an important deponent, yes, I would not have believed ... a baron of the realm."

He could hardly wait for Jacques to bring the ladder. Even as he descended it, he was questioning the messenger on what had been said in the church.

For a moment, Adelia lay where she was, immobile. It didn't matter what else had been said; two murderers condemned themselves out of their own mouths, as careless of the life they had conspired to take as of a piece of grass.

Oh, Emma.

She thought of the bolt buried in the young man's chest, stopping that most wonderful organ, the heart, from beating, the indifference of the bowman who'd loosed it into the infinite complexity of vein and muscle, as indifferent as the cousin who had ordered it to be loosed, as the lord who'd paid him to do it.

Emma, Emma.

Father Paton scuttled back to the warming room—he wanted to write out his deposition right away.

There was a bright, cold moon, no necessity for a lantern. As Jacques escorted her home, he told her what he'd managed to hear in the church. Mostly it had been repetition of the exchanges in the chapel. "By the time they left," he said, "they were deciding it was a trick played on them. Lord Wolvercote did, anyway, he suspects his mercenaries. Lawyer Warin was still atremble, I'll wager he leaves the country if he can."

They said good-bye at the foot of the guesthouse steps.

Unbelievably tired, Adelia dragged herself up, taking the last rise gingerly as she always did, now with the memory of an event that hadn't happened but in which, constantly, she watched a cradle tumble over the edge.

She stopped. The door was slightly open, and it was dark inside. Even if her little household had gone to sleep, a taper was always left burning for her—and the door was never left open.

She was reassured by Ward coming to greet her, the energetic wag of his tail releasing more odor than usual. She went in.

The door was shut behind her. An arm encircled her chest, a hand clamped itself across her mouth. "Quietly now," somebody whispered. "Guess who."

She didn't need to guess. Frantically, she wriggled around in the imprisoning arms until she faced the man, the only man.

"You *bastard*," she said.

"True, to an extent," he said, picking her up. He chucked her onto the nearest bed and planted himself on top of her. "Ma and Pa married eventually, I remember exactly, I was there."

There wasn't time to laugh—though, with his mouth clamped onto hers, she did.

Not dead—deliciously living, the smell of him so right, he was rightness, *everything* was right now that he was here. He moved her to the very soul and very, *very* much to her innards, which turned liquid at his touch. She'd been parched for too long.

Their bodies pumping like huge wings took them higher and higher on a flight into cataclysmic air and then folded into the long, pulsing drop to a truckle bed in a dark, cold room.

When the earth stopped rocking and settled, she wriggled from underneath him and sat up.

"I knew you were nearby," she said. "Somehow, I knew."

He grunted.

She was energized, as if he had been a marvelous infusion bringing her body back to life.

She wondered if there would be another baby, and the thought made her happy.

Her lover had relapsed into postcoital inertia. She jabbed a finger into his back. "Where's Allie? Where are Gyltha and Mansur?"

"I sent them to the kitchens, the servants are having a revel." He sighed. "I shouldn't have done that."

So that she could look at him, she got up and stumbled for the table, felt around, pinched some tinder out of its box, struck a flint, and lit a taper at its flame.

He was thin, oh, bless him, but beautiful. In trousers —now down around his hocks—like a peasant, his face smeared with what looked like tree bark.

"A wren hunter," she said, delighted. "You came in with the wren hunters. Has Henry come?"

"Had to get in somehow. Thank God it's Saint Stephen's Day, or I'd have had to climb the bloody wall."

"How did you know we'd be at Godstow?"

"With the river freezing? Where else would you be?"

He wasn't responding properly. "We could be dead," she pointed out. "We nearly were."

He sat up. "I was in the trees," he said, "watched you skating. Very graceful, a little shaky on the turns, perhaps ... By the saints, that's a bonny baby, isn't she?"

Our baby, Adelia thought. *She's our bonny baby.*

She punched his shoulder, not altogether playfully. "Damn you, Rowley. I suffered, I thought you were dead."

"I knew that bit of the Thames," he said, "that's why I got off, belongs to Henry, part of Woodstock forest; there's a river keeper close by—I'd baptized his child for him. I made for his cottage, wasn't easy but I got there." He sat up suddenly. "Now then ... what's to do here?"

"Rowley, I *suffered.*"

"No need. The keeper took me to Oxford—we used snowshoes. Bloody place was teeming with rebels, every bastard that had fought for Stephen and suffered for it was in arms and flying Eleanor's standard or Young Henry's. We had to bypass the town and make for Wallingford instead. Always a royal stronghold, Wallingford. The FitzCounts held it for the empress during the war. I knew the king'd go there first." He wiped his forehead with the back of his hand. "Jesus save me, but it was hard going."

"Serves you right," she said. "Did you find the king? Is he here?"

"More that he found me, really. I was laid up at Wallingford with a rheum in the chest, I damn near died. What I needed was a doctor."

"I'm sorry I couldn't attend," she said tartly.

"Yes, well, at least I could keep an eye on the river from there. And sure enough, he came, and a fleet of boats with him." Rowley shook his head in wonder. "He was in Touraine, putting down Young Henry's rebellion, when he heard about Rosamund. God punish that boy, now he's joined with Louis of France against his own father. *Louis*, I ask you." Rowley's fists went to the sides of his head in disbelief. "We all knew he was an idiot, but who'd have dreamed the treacherous little whelp would go to his father's greatest enemy for aid?"

He leaned forward. "And Eleanor had urged him to do it. Do you know that? Our spies told us. Urged their son against his father."

"I don't care," she told him. "I don't care what they do. What is happening *now*?"

But she couldn't shift him. He was still with Henry Plantagenet, who had captured two Touranian castles from the Young King's supporters before making tracks for England with a small army in the heaviest winter in years.

"How he did it I don't know. But here he comes, up the Thames, trailing boats full of men behind him. Did I tell you he was *rowing*? The barge crew weren't going fast enough for the bugger, and there he was, pulling at an oar like a pirate and swearing the sky black."

"Where is he now?"

"On his way." There was a pause. "He wants to see you."

"Does he?"

"Sent me to fetch you. Wants to know if it was Eleanor that did for Rosamund. I said you'd be able to tell him yea or nay."

"Great God," she said. "Is that why you've come?"

"I'd have come anyway. I was worried about leaving you ... but I should've known you were safe enough." He cocked his head, sucking his teeth as if in admiration at her capacity for survival. "God kept you in His hand. I asked Him to."

"'*Safe enough*'?" It was a screech. "You left me to die in an open boat." He had to hush her. She went on more quietly. "'Safe enough'? We've been cooped up with killers, your daughter, all of us. There's been murder done here, betrayal ... weeks, *weeks* I've been afraid ... for Allie, for all of us ... weeks." She scrubbed the tears off her cheeks with her fists.

"Ten days, it was," he said gently. "I left you ten days ago." He was on his feet, pulling up his trousers, adjusting his shirt. "Get dressed and we'll go."

"Go where?"

"To Henry. I said he wants to see you."

"Without Allie? Without Gyltha and Mansur?"

"We can hardly take them with us; I've found a path through the snow, but it'll be rough traveling, even on horses, and I only brought two."

"No."

"Yes." It was a sigh. "I was afraid of this. I told the king. 'She won't come without the child,' I said." He made it sound like a whim.

She'd had enough. "Will you tell me? *Where is Henry?*"

"Oxford, at least that's where he was heading."

"Why isn't he here?"

"Look," he said reasonably, "Godstow's a side issue. The important thing is Oxford. Henry's sending young Geoffrey Fitzroy up here with a small force, it shouldn't need more—Mansur says Wolvercote and Schwyz have few men. Henry's not arriving in person ..." She saw the flash of a grin. "I don't think our good king trusts himself to meet Eleanor face-to-face; he might run her through. Anyway, it's somewhat embarrassing to arrest one's own wife."

"When? When will this Geoffrey come?"

"Tomorrow. That's if I can get back to guide him and tell him the placements here—make sure he doesn't kill the wrong people."

He will do it, she thought. *He will track back through this dreadful countryside, disgruntled because I won't leave our daughter behind but assured that she and I will be safe enough. He is all maleness and bravery, like his damn king, and we understand each other not at all.*

Well, she thought, *he is what he is, and I love him.*

But a chill was growing; there was new strangeness; she'd thought it was the old Rowley back—and for a while, gloriously, it had been, but there was constraint. He talked with the remembered insouciance yet didn't look at her. He'd put out a hand to wipe the tears from her face, then withdrawn it.

She said, because she was impelled to, "Do you love me?"

"Too much, God help me," he said. "Too much for my soul. I shouldn't have done it."

"Done what?"

"Almighty God forgive me. I promised, I swore an oath that if He kept you safe, I would abstain from you, I would not lead you to sin again. It was touching you that did it. I want you too much. Feeling you was ... too much."

"What am I? Something to be given up for Lent?"

"In a way." His voice had become measured, a bishop's. "My dear, every Sunday I have to preach against fornication in one church or another, hearing my own exhortation mingling with God's whisper, 'You are a hypocrite, you lust for her, you are damned and she is damned.'"

"Much to be said for hypocrisy," she said dully. She began dragging on her clothes.

"You must see. I can't have you punished for my sin. I left you to God. I made a bargain with Him. 'While she is safe, Lord, I am Your servant in all things.' I swore the oath in the king's presence, to seal it." He sighed. "And now look what I've gone and done."

She said, "I don't care if it is sin."

"I do," he said heavily. "I'd have married you, but no, you would keep your independence. So Henry had his bishop. But a bishop, don't you see? A keeper of other people's souls. His own, yours ..."

Now he looked at her. "Adelia, it matters. I thought it would not, but it does. Beyond the panoply and the choirs—you wouldn't believe the singing that goes on—there is a still, small voice ... nagging. Say you understand."

She didn't. In a world of hatred and killing, she did not understand a God who regarded love as a sin. Nor a man who obeyed that deity.

He was raising his hand as if about to make the sign of the cross over her. She hit it. "Don't you dare," she said. "Don't you dare bless me."

"All right." He began struggling into his clothes. "Listen to me, though. When Geoffrey attacks, *before* he attacks, you're to go to the cloister—he'll keep the fighting away from there. Take Allie and the others. I've told Walt to make sure you get there ...'She's important to the king,' I said."

She didn't listen. She'd never been able to compete with Henry Plantagenet; for sure she wouldn't be able to outrival God. It was winter, after all. To an extent, for her now, it always would be.

Like a fishhook in the mind, something dragged her attention away from despair. She said, "You told Walt?"

"Mansur fetched him here while I was waiting ... Where have you been, by the way?"

"You told Walt," she said.

"And Oswald—they didn't know where Jacques was, nor Paton, but I told them to spread the word, I want all my men ready—they'll need to get to the gates and open them to Geoffrey ..."

"Dear Christ," she said.

Ward was snarling softly.

She almost tripped as she made for the door so that she slammed against it. She slid the bolt across, then put her ear to the wood and listened. They wouldn't have long, only the grace of God had allowed the two of them this long. "How were you going to get out?"

"Cross the gatekeeper's palm with silver. What is it?"

"*Shssh.*"

The sound of boots running through the slush of the alley. "They're coming for you. Oh, God. Oh, God."

"Window," he said. He crossed the floor and jerked the shutters open so that moonlight lit the chamber.

Window, yes.

They dragged blankets off the bed and knotted them together. As they slung them out of the window, the assault on the door began. "Open. Open up." Ward hurled himself at it, barking.

Rowley tied the blanket rope round the mullion and heaved back on it to test it. "After you, mistress."

She was always to remember the polite quirk of his hand as at an invitation to dance. "I can't," she said. "They won't hurt me. It's you."

He glanced down and then back at her. "I *have* to go. I've got to guide them in."

"I know." The door was being assaulted; it wasn't a strong door, it would give any minute. "Do it, then," she hissed.

He grinned, took a falchion from his belt, and gave it to her. "See you tomorrow."

As he reached the parapet, she tried to undo the knot around the mullion and then, because it was too tight, began sawing at it with the blade, glancing out every other second. She saw him make for the nearest crenel and jump, cloak flying. It was deep snow, a soft enough landing for him. But could he get to the steps?

He had. As, behind her, the door splintered and a dreadful yelp came out of Ward's throat, she saw her man skidding across the ice like a boy.

She was thrown to one side. Schwyz roared, "There he is. Opposite bank. Loso. Johannes."

Two men leaped for the door. Another took Schwyz's place at the window, frantically winding a crossbow, his foot in its stirrup. He aimed, loosed. "*Ach, scheiss.*" He looked at Schwyz. "*Nein.*"

Adelia closed her eyes, then opened them. There was another step on the outside landing.

A giant figure bowed its head to get through the door and looked calmly around. "Perhaps it would be better if we relieved Mistress Adelia of her dagger."

She wouldn't have used it on a human being in any case. She handed it over, hilt first, to the Abbot of Eynsham, who had written the letters for Rosamund to copy and send to the queen, and then had her killed.

He thanked her, and she went down on her knees to attend to Ward, where he had crawled under one of the beds. As she felt the kicked and broken rib, he looked at her with self-pitying eyes. She patted him. "You'll live," she said. "Good dog. Stay here."

Politely, the abbot held her cloak for her while she put it on, then her hands were tied behind her back and a gag put in her mouth.

They took her to the gatekeeper's lodge.

There was nobody else about; the abbey had gone to bed. Even if she'd been able to shout for help, nobody at this end of the convent would have heard her—or come to her rescue if they had. Master and Mistress Bloat were not on her side. Lawyer Warin most definitely was not. There was no sign of Wolvercote's men, but they wouldn't have helped her, either.

The great gates were open, but all activity was centered in the lodge chamber that led off the porch, where Schwyz's men hurried to and fro.

They pushed Adelia inside. Fitchet was dead on the floor, his throat cut. Father Paton lay alongside him, coughing out some of his teeth.

She slid to kneel beside the priest. Beneath the bruises, his face showed indignation. "Kep' hi'n me," he said. "Too le'ers." He tried harder. "Took the lett-ers."

Men were fastening hoods and cloaks, collecting weapons into bundles, emptying Fitchet's food cupboard, and rounding up some frightened hens into a crate.

"Did our worthy gatekeeper possess such a thing as wine?" The abbot asked. "No? Tut, tut, how I *loathe* ale." He sat on a stool, watching the bustle, fingering the huge cross on his chest.

The two mercenaries who had chased after Rowley came in, panting. "He had horses."

"*Siech.* That ends it, then. We go." Schwyz took hold of the pinion round Adelia's hands and jerked her to her feet with an upward pull that nearly displaced her shoulders. He dragged her over to the abbot. "We don't need her, let me kill the whore."

"Schwyz, my dear, good Schwyz." Eynsham shook

his great head. "It seems to have escaped your notice that at this moment, Mistress Adelia is the most valuable object in the convent, the king's desire for her company being such that he sends a bishop to collect her—whether for her sexual prowess or such information as she may possess is yet to be determined. She is our trump card, my dear, the Atalantean golden apple that we may have to throw behind us to delay pursuit ..." He reflected. "We might even appease the king by handing her back to him, should he catch up with us ... yes ... that is a possibility."

Schwyz had no time for this. "Do we take her or not?"

"We do."

"And the priest?"

"Well, there I fear we must be less forgiving. Master Paton's possession of the letters is unfortunate. He has evidence I would not wish king or queen to hear, even supposing he could voice it, which—"

"Christ's eyes, do I *finish* him?"

"You do."

"*Nnnnnn.*" Adelia threw herself forward. Schwyz pulled her back.

"I know, I know." The abbot nodded. "These things are upsetting, but I have no wish to lose the queen's esteem, and I fear Father Paton could disabuse her of it. Did you provide him with my text on which dear Rosamund based her letters? Of course you did. What an enterprising little soul you are."

He was talking. He'd condemned the priest to death and he was talking, amused.

"Since I stand in high regard with our blessed Eleanor, it would be—what is the word?—*inconvenient* if she knew I was the goad that pricked her into further rebellion. In view of my desertion, she might tell Henry. As it is, she will be informed of a murderous intruder to the abbey, d'ye see, and that we, the good Schwyz and myself, are in brave pursuit to stop him before he reaches the king's lines. In fact, of course, we are leaving the lady to her inevitable fate; the snow has proved too much for us, the amiable Lord Wolvercote too little ... As Master Schwyz says of that gentleman in his rough way—he couldn't fight a sack of shit."

Schwyz had let go of her and was walking toward Father Paton.

Adelia closed her eyes. *God, I beg you.*

A whimper from Father Paton, a hot smell. A hush, as if even this company was awed by the passage of a soul to its maker.

Then somebody said something, somebody else laughed. Men began carrying bundles and crates out to the porch and down to the river.

The abbot's finger went under Adelia's chin and tilted her head.

"You interest me, madam, you always have. How does a foreign slut like yourself command the attention not only of a bishop but a king? And you, forgive me, without an apparent grace to bless yourself with."

Keeping her eyes closed, she jerked away from him, but he grasped her face and angled it back and forth. "Do you satisfy them both? At the same time? Are you a mistress of threesomes? Do you excel at *lit à trois*? Cock below and behind? Arsehole and *pudendum muliebre*? What my father in his elegant way used to call a bum-and-belly?"

There would be a lot of this before the end, she thought.

She looked straight into his eyes.

Great God, he's a virgin.

How she knew it in that extremity ... but she knew it.

The face above hers diminished into an agonized, pleading vulnerability—*Don't know me, don't know me*—before it resumed the trompe l'oeil that was the Abbot of Eynsham.

Schwyz had been shouting at them both; now he came and hauled Adelia upright. "She better be no trouble," he said. "We got enough to carry."

"I am *sure* she won't be." The abbot smiled on Adelia. "We could send to the kitchen for the baby if you prefer and take it with us, though whether it would survive the journey ..."

She shook her head.

Eynsham, still smiling, gestured toward the door. "After you, mistress."

She went through it and down the ice steps like a lamb.

THIRTEEN

The moon had edged a little toward the west, so that two more cloaked mercenaries cast long, sharp, stunted shadows on the ice as they loaded a large sledge with the packages the others were bringing down. One of them picked up Adelia and slung her on top of the bundles, hurting her arms as she landed on them. Somebody else slung a tarpaulin over her, and she had to toss her head round until a fold fell back and she could see.

Go south, she thought. *Make them go south, Henry's there. Lord, make them go south.*

The abbot, Schwyz, and some of the other men were clustered around her, balancing against the sides of the sledge as they put on skates, intent, not talking.

They have to go south—they don't know the king's attacking Oxford.

Oh, but of course they did. They knew everything—Rowley had inadvertently told them.

Lord, send them south.

The abbot made experimental pirouettes on the ice, admiring his shadow in the steel mirror of the river. "Yes, yes," he said. "One never forgets."

He paid no attention to Adelia—she was luggage now. He nodded at Schwyz, who nodded at his men.

Two mercenaries picked up trails of harness leading from the sledge and heaved themselves into the straps. Somebody else mounted the sledge's running board behind Adelia and grasped the guiding struts.

The abbot looked up at the convent walls lowering above him. "Queen Eleanor, sweet broken reed, farewell. *Veni, vidi, vadi,*" then raised his eyes to the star-sprinkled sky. "Well, well, on to better things. Let us go."

"And quiet about it," Schwyz said.

The sledge hissed as it moved.

They headed north.

Adelia retched into her gag. Nothing to stop him from killing her now.

For a while, she was so afraid that she could hardly see. He was going to kill her. *Had* to kill her.

Appalling sadness overtook her. Images of Allie missing her, growing up without her, small, needy. *I'll die loving you. Know it, little one, I never stopped loving you.*

Then the guilt. *My fault, darling; a better mother would have passed it by, let them all slaughter one another—no matter, as long as you and I weren't wrenched apart. My fault, my grievous fault.*

On and on, grief and fear, fear and grief, as the untidy, white-edged banks slid by and the sledge whispered and grated and the men pulling it grunted with effort, their breath puffing wisps of smoke into the moonlight, taking her further and further into hell.

Discomfort forced itself on her attention—the

bundle beneath her had spears in it. Also, the gag tasted abominable and her arms and wrists hurt.

Suddenly irritable, she shifted, sat up, and began to take notice.

Two mercenaries were pulling the sledge. Another was behind. Four skated on either side, Schwyz and the abbot ahead. Nine in all. None of them her friend Cross—she hadn't been able to make out the faces of the two mercenaries packing the sledge, but both were thinner than Cross.

No help, then. Wherever they were headed, Schwyz was taking only his most trusted soldiers; he'd abandoned the others.

Where are we going? The Midlands? There was still smoldering discontent against Henry Plantagenet in the Midlands.

Adelia shifted and began investigating the sacking with her wrists, tracing the spears in it along the shafts to their blades. *There.*

She pressed down and felt a point prick into her right palm. She began trying to rub the rope against the side of the blade but kept missing it and encountering the spear point instead so that it went uselessly into the rope's fibers and out again, an exercise that might eventually unpick them if she had a week or two to spare ...

It was something to do, though, to fight off the inertia of despair. Of course Eynsham would have her killed. Her use to him as a bargaining counter would last only until he could be sure Henry wasn't pursuing him—and the chance of that receded with every mile they went north. Most of all, he would kill her because she'd seen the worm wriggling in that brilliant, many-faceted, empty carapace, and he had seen her see it.

Her arms were becoming tired ...

Tears still wet on her face, Adelia dozed.

It was heavy going for the men pulling the sledge, and even for those merely skating. Afraid of pursuit, they hadn't lit torches, and though the moon was bright, the ice gave a deceptive, smooth sheen to branches and other detritus that had been frozen into it so that the mercenaries fell frequently or had to make detours round obstructions— occasionally heaving the sledge over them.

In her sleep, Adelia was vaguely aware of being rolled around during the portages and of muffled swearing, aware, too, that men were taking rests on the sledge, crawling under the tarpaulin with her to get their strength back before giving up their place to the next. There was nothing sexual in it—they were too exhausted—and she refused to wake up. Sleep was oblivion ...

Another passenger came aboard, exhaling with the relief at being off the ice. Fingers fumbled at the back of her head and undid the gag. "No need for this now, mistress. Nor this." Gently, somebody pushed her forward and a knife sawed at the rope round her wrists. "There. More comfy?"

There was a waft of sweet, familiar scent. Licking her mouth, Adelia flexed her shoulders and hands. They hurt. They were still traveling, and it was still very cold, but the stars had dulled a little; the moon shone through a light veil of mist.

"You didn't need to kill Bertha," she said.

There was a pause.

"I rather think I did," Jacques said reasonably. "Her nose would have betrayed me sooner or later. I'm afraid the poor soul literally sniffed me out."

Yes. Yes, she had.

Bertha crawling forward in the cowshed, snuffling, using the keenest sense she had to try and describe the old woman in the forest who'd given her the mushrooms for Rosamund.

"Smelled purty ... like you."

It wasn't me, Bertha. It was the man standing behind me. "A him. Not a her."

The girl had been sniffing the messenger's scent—the perfume that was a feature of him even when he dressed up as an old woman picking mushrooms.

"Do you mind?" he asked now. It was solicitous, hoping she wasn't upset. "She wasn't much of a loss, really, was she?"

Adelia kept her eyes on the two mercenaries dragging the sledge.

Jacques tucked the tarpaulin round her and sat sideways to peer into her face, reasonable, explaining, no longer the wide-eyed young man with big ears, much older, at ease. She supposed that's what he was, a shape-changer; he could be what he wanted when circumstances demanded.

He'd taken Allie in her cradle and put her on the step.

"Ordinarily, you see, there is no need for what I call auxiliary action, as there was in Bertha's case," he said. "Usually, one fulfills one's contract and moves on. All very tidy. But this particular employment has been complicated—interesting, I don't deny, but complicated." He sighed. "Snowed up in a convent, not only with one's employer but, as it turns out, a *witness* is not an experience one wants repeated."

A killer. *The* killer.

"Yes, I see," Adelia said.

After all, she'd lived with revulsion ever since she'd become aware that he'd poisoned Rosamund. To use him in the necessary business of getting Wolvercote and Warin to convict themselves in the church had been an exercise in terror, but she'd been unable to think of any other stratagem to placate him. By then she'd sniffed the mind that permeated the abbey with a greater menace than Wolvercote because it was free of limitation, a happy mind. Kill this one, spare that, remain guiltless.

It had been necessary to amuse it, like a wriggling mouse enthralling the cat. To gain time, she'd let it watch her play at solving the one murder of which it was innocent. To keep the cat's teeth out of the neck of a mouse that asked questions.

She asked, "Did Eynsham order you to kill her?"

"Bertha? Lord, no." He was indignant. "I do have initiative, you know. Mind you"—an elbow nudged Adelia's ribs—"he'll have to pay for her. She'll go on his account."

"His account," she said, nodding.

"Indeed. I am not the abbot's vassal, mistress. I really must make that clear; I am independent; I travel Christendom providing a service—not everybody approves of it, I know, but it is nevertheless a service."

"An assassin."

He considered. "I suppose so. I prefer to think of it as a profession like any other. Let's face it, Doctor, your own business is termed witchcraft by those who don't understand it, but we are both professionals pursuing a trade that neither of us can lay public claim to. We both deal in life and death." But she'd touched his pride. "How did I give myself away? I did try to warn you against too much curiosity."

His visits to Bertha, his constant proximity, the indefinable sense of menace that lurked in the cowshed when he was there. The scent that Bertha had recognized. A freedom to roam the abbey, unnoticed, that no one else possessed. In the end, he was the only one it could have been.

"The Christmas feast," she said.

She'd known for sure then. In the capering, warty old woman of Noah's ark, she'd recognized a grotesque of the crone that Bertha had seen in the forest.

"Ah," he said. "I really should avoid dressing up, shouldn't I? I have a weakness for it, I'm afraid."

She asked, "When did Eynsham hire you to kill Rosamund?"

"Oh, ages ago," he said. "I'd only recently come to England to pick up commissions. Well, I'll tell you when it was; I'd just become the bishop's messenger—in my line of work, it's always useful to have a reason to travel the countryside. Incidentally, mistress, I hope I gave the bishop good service ..."

He was in earnest. "I like to think I'm an excellent servant, no matter what the work."

Yes, excellent. When Rowley had crept into the abbey and alerted his men, it hadn't occurred to him that his messenger should not be informed of the coming attack along with the rest—not the irritating, willing Jacques, one of his own people.

"In fact, I shall miss working for Saint Albans," he was saying now, "but as soon as Walt told me the king was coming, I had to inform Eynsham. I couldn't let Master Abbot be taken, could I? He owes me money."

"Is that how it goes?" she asked. "The word is spread? Assassin for hire?"

"Virtually, yes. I haven't lacked employment so far. The contractor never likes to reveal himself, of course, but do you know how I found out this one was our abbot?"

The joy of it raised his voice, launching an owl off its tree and making Schwyz, up ahead, turn and swear at him. "Do you know how I recognized him? Guess."

She shook her head.

"His boots. Master Abbot wears exceptionally fine boots, as I do. Oh, yes, and he addressed his servant as 'my son,' and I said to myself, *By the saints, here is a churchman, a rich churchman.* All I had to do was ask around Oxford's best bootmakers. The problem, you see, is to get the other half of the fee, isn't it?" He was sharing their occupational troubles. "So much as down payment, so much when the job's done. They never like to pay the second installment, don't you find that?"

She didn't say anything.

"Well, I do. Getting the other half of the fee is why I've had to attach myself to my lord Eynsham like fish glue. Actually, in this instance, it isn't his fault; circumstances have been against him: the retreat from Wormhold, the snow ... but apparently we're calling in at his abbey on the way north—that's where he keeps the gold, in his abbey."

"He'll kill you," she said. It was an observation to keep him talking; she didn't mind one way or the other. "He'll get Schwyz to cut your throat."

"*Aren't* they an interesting couple? *Doesn't* Schwyz adore him? They met in the Alps, apparently. I have wondered whether they were ... well, *you* know ... but I think not, don't you? I'd welcome your medical opinion ..."

One of the mercenaries in harness was slowing down, wheeling his arm for the messenger to take his place.

The voice in Adelia's ear became a confidential whisper, changing from a gossip's to an assassin's. "Don't worry for me, mistress. Our abbot has too many enemies that need to be silenced *in* silence. Schwyz leaves a butcher's trail behind. I don't. No, no, my services will always be in demand. Worry for yourself."

He threw back the tarpaulin in order to get off the sledge.

"Will it be you who kills me, Jacques?" she asked.

"I do hope not, mistress," he said politely. "That would be a shame."

And he was gone, refusing to take his place in the harness. "My good fellow, I am not an ox."

Not human, either, she thought, a *lusus naturae*, a tool, no more culpable for what it did than an artifact, as blameless as a weapon stuck on a wall and admired by the owner for its beautiful functionality.

The lingering trail of his perfume was obliterated by a smell of sweat and damp dirt from the next man who crawled under the tarpaulin to fall asleep and snore.

The abbot had taken position on the step behind her, but instead of helping to propel the sledge along, he became a passenger, his weight slowing the men pulling it to a stumping crawl that threatened their balance. They were complaining. At an order from Schwyz, they removed their skates and, to give them better purchase, continued in their boots.

Which, Adelia saw, were splashing. The sledge had begun to send up spray as it traveled. There were no stars now, and the vague moon had an even more vague penumbra. Schwyz had lit a torch and was holding it high as he skated.

It was thawing.

From over her head came a fruity boom: "I don't wish to complain, my dear Schwyz, but any more of this and we'll be marching on the river bottom. How much further?"

"Not far now."

Not far to where? Having been asleep and not knowing for how long, she couldn't estimate how far they'd come. The banks were still their featureless, untidy conglomeration of reed and snow.

It was even colder now; the chill of increasing damp had something to do with it, but so had fear.

Eynsham would be reassured by their unpursued
and uninterrupted passage up the river. Once he
was in safe territory, he could rid himself of the
burden he'd carried to it.

"Up ahead," Schwyz called.

There was nothing up ahead except a dim
twinkle in the eastern sky like a lone star bright
enough to penetrate the mist that hid the others. A
castle showing only one light? A turret?

Now they were approaching a landing stage,
white edged and familiar.

Then she knew.

Rosamund had been waiting for her.

Adelia had remembered Wormhold as a place
of jagged, shocking flashes of color where men
and women walked and talked in madness.

Now, through the dawn mist, the tower returned
to what it was—a mausoleum. Architectural innuendo
had gone. And the maze, for those who dragged the
sledge through slush into it, was merely a straight and
dreary tunnel of gray bushes leading to a monument
like a giant's tombstone against a drearier sky.

The door above its steps stood open, sagging
now. The unlit bonfire remained untouched in the
hall where a mound of broken furniture, like the
walls, shone with gathering damp in Schwyz's
torchlight.

As they went in, a scuttle from escaping rats
accentuated the hall's silence, as did the abbot's
attempt to raise the housekeeper. "Dakers. Where

are you, little dear? 'Tis your old friend come to call. Robert of Eynsham."

He turned to Schwyz as the echo faded. "She doesn't know it was me as had her locked up, does she?"

Schwyz shook his head. "We fooled her, Rob."

"Good, then I'm still her ally. Where *is* the old crow? We need our dinner. *Dakers.*"

Schwyz said, "We can't stay long, Rob. That bastard'll be after us."

"My dear, stop attributing the powers of Darkness to him, we've outmaneuvered the bugger." He grimaced. "I suppose I'd better go up and search for my letters. If our Fair Rosamund kept one, she might have kept others. I *told* the fat bitch to burn them, but did she? Women are *so* unreliable." He pointed at the bonfire. "Get that alight when the time comes. Some food first, I think, a nap, and then, when our amiable king arrives, we'll be long gone, leaving a nice warm fire to greet him. *Dakers.*"

He must know where she is, Adelia thought. The only life here is in the top room with the dead.

"Up you go, then." Schwyz turned away to give orders to his men, and then turned back. "What do you want done with the trollop?"

"*This* trollop?" The abbot looked down at Adelia. "We'll hang on to her until the last minute, I think, just in case. She can come up and help me look for the letters."

"Why? She'll be better down here." Schwyz was jealous.

The abbot was patient with him. "Because I

didn't see any letters lying around when we were here last, but little Mistress Big Eyes had one, hadn't you, my dear? If she found one, she can find the others. Bind her hands, if you like, but in front this time and not too tight; she's looking wan."

Adelia's hands were pinioned again—not gently, either.

"Up, up." The abbot pointed her toward the stairs. "Up, up, up." To the mercenary, he said, "Tell the men to put their minds to my dinner. And Schwyz ..." The tone had changed.

"What?"

"Set a damn good watch on that river."

He's frightened, Adelia thought suddenly. *He, too, credits Henry with supernatural powers. Oh, dear God, let him be right.*

Going up the tiny, wedge-shaped, slippery, winding steps without the balancing use of hands was not easy, but Adelia did better than the abbot, who was grunting with effort before they reached the second landing. That was the stage where the tower cut them off from the noise at its base, imposing a silence in which the echo of their footsteps troubled the ears as if they disobeyed an ordinance from the dead. *Go back. This is a tomb.*

Light that was hardly light at all came, sluggish, through the arrow slits onto the same broken mess that had littered the landings when she'd climbed up here with Rowley. Nobody had swept it away, nobody ever would.

Up and up, past Rosamund's apartments, empty of their carpets and gold ornaments now, looted by mercenaries, maybe even the Aquitanians, while Eleanor had kept her vigil over a corpse. Much good it had done them; loot and looters had gone to the bottom of the Thames.

They were getting close to the top now.

I don't want to go in there. Why doesn't it stop? It's impossible I should die here. Why doesn't somebody stop this?

The last landing, the door a crack open but with its ornate key in the lock.

Adelia stood back. "I'm not going in."

Gripping her shoulder, the abbot pushed her in front of him. "Dakers, my dame. Here's the Abbot of Eynsham, your old friend, come to pay his respects to your mistress."

A smell like a blast of wind teetered him on the threshold.

The room was furnished as Adelia had last seen it. No looting here—there hadn't been time.

Rosamund no longer sat at the writing table, but something lay on the bed with the frail curtains framing it and a cloak covering its upper half.

There was no sign of Dakers, but, if she had wanted to preserve her mistress still, she had made the mistake of closing the windows and lighting funerary candles.

"Dear God." With a handkerchief to his nose, the abbot hurried around the room, blowing out candles and opening the windows. "Dear God, the whore *stinks*. Dear God."

Moist, gray air refreshed the chamber slightly.

Eynsham came back to the bed, his eyes fascinated.

"Leave her," Adelia advised him.

He whipped the cloak off the body and let it fall to the floor. "*Aach.*"

Her lovely hair fanned out from the decomposing face onto a pillow, with another pillow propping her crown near the top of her head. The crossed hands on her breast were mercifully hidden by a prayer book. Feet bulged wetly out of the tiny gold slippers that peeped from under the graceful, carefully arranged folds of a gown as blue as a spring sky. Patches of ooze were staining its silk.

"My, my," said the abbot softly. "*Sic transit Rosa Mundi.* So the rose of all the world rots like any other ... Rosamund the Foul ..."

"*Don't you dare,*" Adelia shouted at him. If she'd had her hands free, she'd have hit him. "Don't you *dare* mock her. You brought her to this, and, by God, this is what you'll come to—your soul with it."

"*Oof.*" He stepped back like a child faced by a furious parent. "Well, it's a horror ... admit it's a horror."

"I don't care. You treat her with respect."

For a moment he was wrong-footed by his own lapse in taste. Tentatively, standing well back from the bed, his hand traced a blessing in the air toward it. "*Requiescat in pace.*" After a moment, he said, "What *is* that white stuff growing out of her face?"

"Grave wax," Adelia told him. Actually, it was very interesting; she'd not seen it on a human flesh before, only on that of a sow at the death farm.

For a moment she was a mistress in the art of death again, aware only of the phenomenon in front of her, vaguely irritated that lack of time and means were preventing her from examining it.

It's because she was fat, she thought. The sow in Salerno had been fat, and Gordinus had kept it in an airtight tin chest away from flies. *"You see, my child? Bereft of insects, this white grease—I call it* corpus adipatus—*will accrete on plumper areas, cheeks, breasts, buttocks, et cetera, and hold back putrefaction, yes, actually delay it. Though whether it causes the delay or the delay causes it is yet to be determined."*

Bless him, Gordinus had called it a marvel, which it was, and damn it that she was seeing it manifest on a human corpse only now.

It was especially interesting that the room's new warmth was, to judge from what was seeping through Rosamund's gown, bringing on putrefaction at the selfsame time. That couldn't be caused by flies—could it?—there were none at this time of year ... blast it, if her hands were free, she could find out what was breeding under the material ...

"Oh, what?" she asked crossly. The abbot was pulling at her.

"Where does she keep the letters?"

"What letters?" This opportunity to advance knowledge might never come again. If it wasn't flies ...

He swung her round to face him. "Let me explain the position to you, my dear. In all this I have only been pursuing my Christian duty to bring down a king who had the good Saint Thomas murdered on the steps of his own cathedral. I intended a civil war that our gracious queen would win. Since that outcome now seems unlikely, I need to retrieve my position because, if Henry finds my letters, Henry will send them to the Pope. And will the Holy Father sanction what I have done to punish the wicked? Will he say, 'Well done, thou good and faithful Robert of Eynsham, you have advanced our great cause'? He will not. He must pretend outrage, because a worthless whore was poisoned in the process. He will wash his Pilate's hands. Will there be oak leaves? Reward? Ah, no."

He stopped savoring the sound of his own voice. "Find those letters for me, mistress, or when Henry comes he will discover in the ashes of his bordello the bones of not just one of his harlots but two." He was diverted by a happy thought. "Together, in each other's arms, perhaps. Yes, perhaps ..."

He mustn't see that she was afraid; he *mustn't* see that she was afraid. "In that case, the letters will be burned, too," she said.

"Not if the bitch kept them in a metal box. Where are they? You had one, mistress, and were quick enough to show it around. *Where did she keep the letters?*"

"On the table, I took it from the table."

"If she kept one, she kept more." He shouted for the housekeeper again. "*Dakers*. She'll know. Where is the hellhag?"

And then Adelia knew where Dakers was.

All the visits he'd made to this room, and he'd never known he was observed from a garderobe with a spy hole. He didn't know now.

Eynsham was examining the table, sweeping its writing implements aside, sending the ancient bowl in which Rosamund had kept sweetmeats onto the floor, where it broke. He bent to look under the table. There was a grunt of satisfaction. He came up holding a crumpled piece of vellum. "Is this all there was?"

"How could I know?" It was the letter Rosamund had been writing to the queen, that Eleanor in her fury had thrown to the floor. Adelia had given the abbot's template to poor Father Paton and, if she died for it, she wasn't going to tell this man that there were others hidden in a box stool only inches from his right boot.

Let him doubt, let there be a worm of worry for as long as he lives.

Great God, he's reading it.

The abbot had lumbered to the open window and was holding the parchment to the light. "Such an appalling hand the trollop had," he said. "Still, it's amazing she could write at all."

And let Dakers doubt *him*. No wonder the housekeeper had laughed as they were taken to the boats that night; she'd seen Eynsham, who had always been Rosamund's friend and, therefore, would be a friend to her.

If she was listening now, if she could be got to switch sides ...

Adelia raised her voice. "Why did you make Rosamund write letters to Eleanor?"

The abbot lowered the parchment, partly exasperated, partly amused. "Listen to the creature. Why does she ask a question when her brain cannot possibly encompass the answer? What use to tell you? How can you even approach in understanding the exigencies that we, God's agents, are put to in order to keep His world on its course, the descent we must make into the scum, the instruments we must use—harlots like that one on the bed, cutthroats, all the sweepings of the cesspit, to achieve a sacred aim."

He was telling her anyway. A wordy man. A man needing the reassurance of his own voice and, even more, the sanctification of what he had done.

And still hopeful. It surprised her. That he was having to abandon his great game as a lost cause and desert his championship of Eleanor was stimulating him, as if certain he could retrieve the situation with charm, tactics, a murder here or there, using the false urbanity, his common-man-with-learning, all the air in the balloon that had bounced him into the halls of popes and royalty ...

A mountebank, really, Adelia thought.

Also a virgin. Mansur had seen it, told her, but Mansur, with the superiority of a man who could hold an erection, had discounted the agony of supposed failure turned to malevolence. Another churchman might bless a condition that ensured his chastity, but not this one; he wanted, lusted after, that most natural and commonplace gift that he was denied.

Perhaps he was making the world pay for it, meddling with brilliance in high politics, pushing men and women round his chessboard, discarding this one, moving that one, compensating himself for the appalling curiosity that kept him outside their Garden of Eden as he jumped up and down in an effort to see inside it.

"To stimulate war, my dear," he was saying. "Can you understand that? Of course you can't—you are the clay from which you were made and the clay to which you will return. A war to cleanse the land of a barbarous and unclean king. To avenge poor Becket. To return England to God's writ."

"Rosamund's letters would do all that?" she asked.

He looked up. "Yes, as a matter of fact. A wronged and vengeful woman, and believe me, nobody is more vengeful than our gracious Eleanor, will escape any bonds, climb any mountains, cross all oceans to wreak havoc on the wrongdoer. And thus she did."

"Then why did you have Rosamund poisoned?"

"Who says I did?" Very sharp.

"Your assassin."

"The merry Jacques has been chattering, has he? I must set Schwyz onto that young man."

"People will think the queen did it."

"The king does, as was intended," he said vaguely. "Barbarians, my dear, are easily manipulated." He turned back to the letter and continued to read. "Excellent, oh excellent," he said. "I'd forgotten ... To the '*supposed Queen of England ... from the true and very Queen of this country, Rosamund the Fair.*' What I had to endure to persuade that tedious wench to this ... Robert, Robert, such a subtle fellow you are ... "

A draft twitched at Adelia's cloak. The hanging behind Rosamund's bed had lifted. As air came up the corbel of the hidden garderobe and into the room, it brought a different, a commoner stench to counter that of the poor corpse on the bed. It was cut off as the hanging dropped back.

Adelia walked across to the window. The abbot was still holding the letter to the light, reading it. She took up a position where, if he looked up, he would see her and not the figure creeping down the side of the bed. It had no knife in its hand, but it was still death—this time, its own.

Dakers was dying; Adelia had seen that yellowish skin and receded eyes too often not to know what they meant. The fact that the woman was walking at all was a miracle, but she was. And silently.

Help me, Adelia willed her. *Do something*. Without moving, she used her eyes in appeal. *Help me.*

But Dakers didn't look at her, nor at the abbot. All her energy was bent on reaching the staircase.

Adelia watched the woman slip between the partially open door and its frame without touching either and disappear. She felt a tearing resentment. *You could have hit him with something.*

The abbot had sat himself in Rosamund's chair as he read, still muttering bits of the letter out loud. "'... *and I did please the king in bed as you never did, so he told me* ...' I'll wager you did, girl. Sucking and licking, I'll wager you did. '... *he did moan with delight* ...' I'll wager he did, you filthy trollop ..."

He's exciting himself with his own words.

As Adelia thought it, he glanced up—into her eyes. His face gorged. "What are you looking at?"

"Nothing," she told him. "I am looking at you and seeing nothing."

Schwyz was calling from the stairs, but his voice was drowned in Eynsham's scream: "You judge *me*? *You*, a whore ... judge *me*?"

He got up, a gigantic wave rising, and engulfed her. He clutched her to his chest and carried her so that her feet trailed between his knees. Blinded, she thought he was going to drop her out of the window, but he turned her round, holding her high by the scruff of the neck and her belt. For a second, she glimpsed the bed, heard the grunt as she was thrown down onto what lay on it.

As Adelia's body landed on the corpse, its belly expelled its gases with a whistle.

The abbot was screaming. "Kiss her. Kiss, kiss, kiss ... suck, lick, you bitches." He pushed her face into Rosamund's. He was twisting Adelia's head like a piece of fruit, pressing it down into the grease. "Sniff, suck, lick ..."

She was suffocating in decomposing flesh.

"Rob. Rob."

The pressure on her head lessened slightly, and she managed to turn her smeared face sideways and breathe.

"Rob. *Rob*. There's a horse in the stable."

It stopped. It had stopped.

"No rider," Schwyz said. "Can't find a rider, but there's somebody here."

"What sort of horse?"

"Destrier. A good one."

"Is it his? He can't be here. Jesus save us, is he *here*?"

The slam of the door cut off their voices.

Adelia rolled off the bed and groped her way across the floor to one of the windows, her tied hands searching outside the sill for its remnant of snow. She found some and shoved it into her mouth. Another window, more snow into the mouth, scrubbing her teeth with it, spitting. More, for the face, nostrils, eyes, hair.

She went from window to window. There wasn't enough snow in the world, not enough clean, numbing ice …

Drenched, shaking, she slumped into Rosamund's chair, and with her pinioned hands still scrubbing at her neck, she laid her head on the table and gave herself up to heaving, gasping sobs. Uninhibited, like a baby, she wept for herself, for Rosamund, Eleanor, Emma, Allie, all women everywhere and what was done to them.

"What are you bawling for?" a male voice said, aggrieved. "You think that's bad? Try spending time cooped up in a shithole with Dakers for company."

A knife ripped the rope away from round her hands. A handkerchief was pushed against her cheek. It smelled of horse liniment. It smelled beautiful.

With infinite care, she turned her head so that her cheek rested on the handkerchief and she could squint at him.

"Have you been in there all the time?" she asked.

"All the time," the king told her.

Still with her head on the table, she watched him walk over to the bed, pick up his cloak, and replace it carefully over the corpse. He went to the door to try its latch. It didn't move. He bent down to peer through the keyhole.

"Locked," he said, as if it was a comfort.

The ruler of an empire that stretched from the border of Scotland to the Pyrenees was in worn hunting leathers—she'd never seen him in anything else; few people did. He walked with the rolling bandiness of a man who spent more time in the saddle than out of it. Not tall, not handsome, nothing to distinguish him except an energy that drew the eye. When Henry Plantagenet was in the room, nobody looked anywhere else.

Deeper lines ran from his nose to the corners of his mouth than when she'd last seen him, there was a new dullness in his eyes, and his red hair was dimmer; something had gone out of him and not been replaced.

Relief brought a manic tendency to giggle. Adelia began rubbing her wrists. "Where are your men, my lord?"

"Ah, well there ..." Grimacing, he came back from the door and edged round the table to peer cautiously out. "They're on their way, only a few, mind, but picked men, fine men. I had a look at the situation in Oxford and left young Geoffrey to take it before he moves on to Godstow."

"But ... did Rowley find you? You know the queen is at Godstow?"

"That's why Geoffrey'll take it next," he said irritably. "He won't have any trouble in either place. The rebels, God rot 'em, I'll eat them alive, were practically running up the white flag at Oxford already, so ..."

"My daughter's at Godstow," she said. "My people ..."

"I know, Rowley told me. Geoffrey knows, I told *him*. Stop wittering. I've seen snowmen with more defensive acumen than Wolvercote. Leave it to young Geoffrey."

She supposed she'd have to.

He glanced round. "How is little Rowley-Powley, anyway? Got a tooth yet? Showing a flair for medicine?"

"She's well." He could always melt her. But it would be nice to get out of here. "These picked men of yours ..." she said. This was Rowley all over again. Why didn't they ever bring massed troops?

"They're on their way," he said, "but I fear I outstripped them." He turned back to the window. "They'd told me she still wasn't buried, you see. My lads are bringing a coffin with them. Buggers couldn't keep up."

They wouldn't have; he must have ridden like a fiend, melting the snow in front of him, to say good-bye, to mend the indecency inflicted on his woman.

"Hadn't long arrived before you turned up," he said. "Heard you coming up the stairs, so Dakers and I beat a retreat. First rule when one's outnum-bered—learn the enemy's strength."

And learn that Rosamund, in her stupidity and ambition, had betrayed him. Like his wife, like his eldest son.

Adelia felt an awful pity. "The letters, my lord ... I'm so sorry."

"Don't mention it." He wasn't being polite; she

mustn't refer to it again. Since he'd covered the corpse, he hadn't looked at it.

"So here we are," he said. Still cautious, he leaned out. "They're not keeping much of a watch, I must say. There's only a couple of men patrolling the courtyard—what in hell are the rest doing?"

"They're going to fire the tower," she told him, "and us in it."

"If they're using the wood in the hall, they'll have a job. Wouldn't light pussy." He leaned farther out of the window and sniffed. "They're in the kitchen, that's where they are ... something's cooking. Hell's bollocks, the incompetent bastards are taking the time to eat." He loathed inefficiency, even in his enemies.

"I don't blame them." She was hungry, she was *ravenous*. A magic king had skewed this death chamber into something bearable. Without sympathy, without concession to her as a woman, by treating her as a comrade, he had restored her. "Have you got any food on you?"

He struck his forehead with the heel of his hand. "Well, there, and I left the festive meats behind. No, I haven't. At least, I don't think so ..." He had a pocket inside his jacket and he emptied its contents onto the table with one hand, his eyes still on the courtyard.

There was string, a bradawl, some withered acorns, needle and twine in a surprisingly feminine sewing case, a slate book and chalk, and a small square of cheese, all of them covered in oats for his horse.

Adelia picked out the cheese and wiped it. It was like chewing resin.

Now that she was more composed, events were connecting to one another. This king, this violent king, this man who, intentionally or not, had set on the knights that stirred Archbishop Becket's brains onto the floor of his cathedral, had sat quietly behind a hanging and listened, without sound, without moving, to treachery of extreme magnitude. And he'd been armed.

"Why didn't you come out and kill him?" she asked, not because she wished he had but because she truly wanted to know how he'd restrained himself from it.

"Who? Eynsham? Friend to the Pope? Legate *maleficus*? Thank you, he'll die, but not at my hand. I've learned my lesson."

He'd given Canterbury to Becket out of trust, because he loved him—and from that day his reforms had been opposed at every turn. The murder of the Jew-hating, venomous, now-sainted archbishop had set all Christendom against him. He'd done penance for it everywhere, allowing the monks of Canterbury to whip him in public, only just preventing his country from being placed under the Pope's interdict banning marriage, baptism, burial of the dead ...

Yes, he could control his anger now. Eleanor, Young Henry, even Eynsham, were safe from execution.

Adelia thought how strange it was that, locked in a chamber with a man as helpless as herself, at the top of a tower that any minute could be a burning chimney, she should be at ease.

He wasn't, though; he was hammering the mullion. "Where are they, in God's name? Jesus, if I can get here fast, why can't they?"

Because you outstripped them, Adelia thought. *In your impatience, you outstrip everybody, your wife, your son, Becket, and expect them to love you. They are people of our time and you are not; you see beyond the boundaries they set; you see me for what I am and use me for your advantage; you see Jews, women, even heretics, as human beings and use them for your advantage; you envisage justice, toleration, unattainable things. Of course nobody keeps up with you.*

Oddly enough, the one mind she could equate with his was Mother Edyve's. The world believed that what was now was permanent, God had willed it, there could be no alteration without offending Him.

Only a very old woman and this turbulent man had the sacrilegious impudence to question the status quo and believe that things could and should be changed for the betterment of all people.

"Come on, then," he said, "we've got time. Tell me. You're my investigator—what did you find out?"

"You don't pay me for being your investigator." She might as well point this out while she had the advantage.

"Don't I? I thought I did. Take it up with the Exchequer. Get on, get on." His stubby fingers drummed on the windowsill. "Tell me."

So she told him, from the beginning.

He wasn't interested in the death of Talbot of

Kidlington. "Silly bugger. I suppose it was the cousin, was it? Never trust the man who handles your money ... Wolvercote? Vicious, that family. All rebels. My mother hanged the father from Godstow Bridge, and I'll do the same for the son. Go on, go on, get to the bits that *matter*."

He meant Rosamund's death, but it all mattered to Adelia, and she wasn't going to let him off any of it. She'd been clever, she'd been brave, it had cost too many lives; he was going to know everything. After all, he was getting it free.

She plowed on, occasionally nibbling at the cheese. Drops from melting icicles splashed on the sill. The king watched the courtyard. The body of the woman who'd begun it all lay on her bed and rotted.

He interrupted. "Who's that ... *Saints' bollocks, he's stealing my horse*. I'll rip him, I'll mince his tripes, I'll ..."

Adelia got up to see who was stealing the king's destrier.

A thickening mist hid the hill and gave an indistinct quality to the courtyard below, but the figure urging the horse into a gallop toward the maze entrance was recognizable, though he was bending low over its neck.

Adelia gave a yelp. "Not him, not him. He mustn't get away. Stop him, for God's sake, *stop him*."

But there was nobody to stop him; some of Schwyz's men had heard the hooves and were running toward the maze, uselessly.

"Who was it?" the king asked.

"The assassin," she told him. "Dear God, he mustn't get away. I want him punished." For Rosamund, for Bertha ...

Something had happened to frighten him if Jacques was deserting Eynsham and the second installment of his precious payment.

Then she was pulling at the king's sleeve. "It's your men," she said. "He must have heard them. They're here. Shout to them. Tell them to go after him. Will they catch him?"

"They'd better," he said. "That's a bloody good horse."

But if Henry's men *had* arrived and the assassin had heard them and decided to cut his losses, there was no sign of them in the courtyard and no sound.

Together, Adelia and the king watched the pursuers return, shrugging, to disappear toward the kitchen.

"Are you *certain* your men are on their way?" she asked.

"We won't see them til they're ready. They'll be coming through the rear of the maze."

"There's another entrance?"

The king smirked. "Imitate the mole, never leave yourself only one exit. Get on with it, tell me the rest."

Jacques's escape anguished her. She thought of the little unmarked grave in the nuns' cemetery ...

The king's fingers were tapping again, so she took up her tale where she'd left off.

There was another interruption. "Hello, where's Dakers going?"

Adelia was beside him in an instant. The mist had begun to play tricks, ebbing and flowing in swirls that deceived the eye into seeing unmelted mounds of snow as crouching men and animals, but it didn't hide the thin black figure of Rosamund's housekeeper crawling toward the maze.

"What's that she's dragging?"

"God knows," the king said. "A sawing horse?"

It was something large and angular, too much for the human bundle of bones that collapsed after each pull but which managed to steady itself to pull again.

"She's mad, of course," the king said. "Always was."

It was agonizing to watch such effort, but watch they did, having to keep refocusing their eyes as Dakers inched her burden along like an ant through the shifting grayness.

Leave it, whatever it is, Adelia begged her. *They haven't seen you. Go and die at your own choosing.*

Another blink and there was only fog.

"So ..." the king said. "You'd taken one of Eynsham's templates from this chamber to Godstow and given it to the priest ... Go on."

"His handwriting is distinctive, you see," she told him. "I've never seen another like it, very curly—beautiful, really—he uses classically square capitals but fills them in with whirls and his minuscule ..."

Henry sighed, and Adelia hurried on. "Anyway, Sister Lancelyne, she's Godstow's librarian, once wrote to Eynsham asking if she might borrow the abbot's copy of Boethius's *Consolation* in order to copy it, and he'd written back, refusing ..."

She saw again the learned little old nun among her empty shelves. "If ever we get out of here, I'd like Sister Lancelyne to have it."

"A whole *Philosophy*? Eynsham has a Boethius?" The Plantagenet eyes gleamed; he was greedy for books and totally untrustworthy when it came to other people's.

"*I should like,*" Adelia said clearly, "Sister Lancelyne to have it."

"Oh, very well. She'd better look after it. Get on, get on."

"And while we're about it"—there had to be some profit out of this—"if Emma Bloat should be widowed ..."

"She will be," the king promised. "Oh, yes, she will be."

"She's not to be forced into marriage again."

With her own fortune and Wolvercote's lands, Emma would be a prize. She would also, as the widow of one of his barons, be in the king's gift, a valuable tradable object in the royal marketplace.

"Is this a horse fair?" the king asked. "Are you haggling? With *me*?"

"Negotiating. Regard it as my fee."

"You'll ruin me," he said. "Very well. Can we proceed? I need evidence of Eynsham's calumny to show the Pope, and I doubt he'll regard curly handwriting as proof."

"Father Paton thought it was." Adelia winced. "Poor Father Paton."

"Anyway ..." Henry was looking around the table. "The bastard seems to have taken his template with him."

"There are others. What we can't prove is that he employed an assassin to kill ... who did kill."

"I shouldn't worry about that," the king said. "He'll probably tell us."

I've condemned a man to torture, she thought. Suddenly, she was tired and didn't want to say any more. If Schwyz managed to put a flame to the bonfire in the hall, there was no point to it, anyway.

She abridged what was left. "Then Rowley arrived. He told Walt, that's his groom, to look after me when the attack came. Walt, not knowing, told the assassin, who told Eynsham—who is very afraid of you and decided to run and take me with him." It sounded like the house that Jack built. That's all," she said, closing her eyes, "more or less."

Drips from the icicles were increasing, pattering like rain onto the windowsills of a silent room.

"Vesuvia Adelia Rachel Ortese Aguilar," the king said, musing.

It was an accolade. She opened her eyes, tried to smile at him, and closed them again.

"He's a good lad, young Geoffrey," Henry said. "Very loving. God bless him. I got him on a prostitute, Ykenai—strange name, the saints only know what race her parents were, because she doesn't. Big woman, comfortable. I still see her occasionally when I'm in London."

Adelia was awake now. He was telling her something, a tit for tat, payment for her trouble. This was about Rosamund without mentioning her name.

"I set her up in a pie shop, Ykenai, and very successful it's been, except it's making her bigger than ever. We talk about pies, there's a lot to making pies."

Big women, comfortable, bouncy mattresses, as Rosamund had been. Women who talked about little things, who didn't test him. Women as different from Eleanor as chalk to cheese—and maybe he'd loved both.

Wife and mistress both treacherous. Whether Rosamund had been ambitious herself or had been stirred into it by a devious abbot, the result was the same; she had nearly sparked a war. The only female refuge this man, this *emperor*, had left lived in a London pie shop where at least one loyal son had been born to him.

Henry's voice came from the window, nastily. "While he was with you, did the Bishop of Saint Albans tell you of his oath?" He wanted to hurt someone else who'd been betrayed.

"Yes," she said.

"He swore it in front of me, you know. Hand on the Bible, '*I swear by the Lord God and all the saints of Heaven that if You will guard her and keep her safe, I shall withhold myself from her.*'"

"I know," she said.

"Hah."

For the first time in days, she could hear the chatter of birds, as if small, frozen hearts were being thawed back to life.

Henry reached over and took the remnant of cheese out of her fingers, squashed it, and scattered the crumbs along the windowsill.

A robin flew down immediately to peck, its wings almost touching his hand before flying off again.

"I'll bring spring back to England," its king said. "They won't beat me, by Christ, they won't."

They have beaten you, Adelia thought. *Your men aren't coming. Everybody betrays you.*

Henry's head had gone up. "Hear that?"

"No."

"I did. They're here." His sword rasped from its scabbard. "Let's go down and fight the bastards."

They weren't *here*. It was birds he'd heard. The two of them would stay here forever and decompose alongside Rosamund.

She dragged herself to the window.

Alarmed men were emerging from the kitchen, turning this way and that, confused by the fog, running back to fetch weapons. She heard Schwyz's shout: "Round the other side. It came from the rear."

The Abbot of Eynsham was taking undecided steps toward the entrance to the maze, then away from it.

"*Yes*," Adelia said.

Henry's dagger that had cut her hands free was on the table. She took it up with a ferocious joy. She wanted to fight somebody.

But she couldn't. For one thing ... "My lord, we're locked in."

He was standing on tiptoe, feeling around the top of the coronal that held the curtains of Rosamund's bed. His hand came away with a key in it. He waved it at her. "Never get into a hole without a second exit."

Then they were out of the door and pattering down the stairs, Henry leading.

Two landings down, they met one of Schwyz's men running up, sword drawn. Whether he was trying to find somewhere to hide or had come for her, Adelia never knew. His eyes widened as he saw the king.

"Wrong way," Henry told him, and stuck him through the mouth. The man fell. The king ran him through again, raising him on the swordpoint as if on a skewer, and flicked him off so that he was thrown round the next bend. Kept flicking him, a heavy man, round the next and the next, though he was long dead by the time they reached the hall.

The air outside was discordant with shouts and the clash of metal. The fog had thickened; it was difficult to make out who was fighting whom.

The king disappeared, and Adelia heard a gleeful howl of "*Dieu et Plantagenet*" as he found an enemy.

It was like being in the middle of battling unseen ghosts. With the dagger ready, she began walking cautiously forward to where she'd last seen Eynsham. One killer had escaped; she'd be damned if another thwarted justice. This one would if he could; not a courageous man, the abbot; he killed only through others.

Two heavy figures appeared on her left, their swords sparking as they fought. She jumped out of their way and they vanished again.

If I call him, he will come, she thought. She was still a bargaining counter; he'd want to use her as a shield. She had a knife, she could threaten him into standing still. "Abbot." Her voice was high and thin. "Abbot."

Something answered her in a voice even higher. In astonishment. In a crescendo of agony that rose into a falsetto beyond what was human. In shrieks that pulsed through the mist and overrode all noise of battle and silenced it. It overrode everything.

It was coming from the direction of the maze. Adelia began running toward it, sliding in the slush, falling, picking herself up, and blundering on. Whatever it was had to be helped; hearing it was unendurable.

Somebody splashed past her. She didn't see who it was.

A wall of bushes loomed up. Frantically, she used her hands to follow it round toward the maze entrance, toward the screaming. It was diminishing now; there were words in it. Prayer? Pleading?

She found the entrance and plunged inside.

Curiously, it was easier to see in here, merely gloomy, as if the tunnels were bewilderment enough and had regimented the mist into their own coils. The hedged doors were open, still giving straight passage.

He'd gone a long way in, almost to the exit that led to the hill. The sound was softening into mumbles, like somebody discontented. As Adelia came up, it stopped altogether.

The last paroxysm had sent the abbot arching backward over the mantrap so that his stomach curved outward. His mouth was stretched open; he looked as if he'd died roaring with laughter.

She edged round to the front. Schwyz was scrabbling at the mess where the machine's fangs had bitten into Eynsham's groin. "It's all right, Rob," he was saying. "It's all right." He looked up at Adelia. "Help me."

There was no point. He was dead. It would take two men to force the mantrap open. Only hate like the fires of hell had given Dakers the strength to lever the struts apart so that their jaws lay flat in the dirt, waiting to snap up the man who'd had Rosamund poisoned.

The housekeeper had sat herself a couple of feet away so that she could watch him die. And had died with him, smiling.

There was a lot of clearing up to do.

They brought the wounded down to Adelia on the landing stage, because she didn't want to return to the tower. There weren't many, and none were badly injured, most needing only a few stitches, which she managed with the contents of the king's sewing case.

All were Plantagenet men; Henry hadn't taken any prisoners.

She didn't ask what had happened to Schwyz; she didn't care much. Probably, he hadn't, either.

One of the barges that came upriver from Godstow contained Rosamund's much-traveled coffin. The Bishop of Saint Albans was aboard another. He'd been with Young Geoffrey at the storming of the abbey and looked tired enough to fall down. He kept his distance on seeing Adelia, though he thanked his God for her deliverance. Godstow had been liberated without loss on the Plantagenet side. Wolvercote, now in chains, was the only one who'd put up any resistance.

"Allie's safe and well," Rowley said. "So are Gyltha and Mansur. They were cheering us on from the guesthouse window."

There was nothing else she needed to know. Yes, one thing. "Lawyer Warin," she said. "Did you find him?"

"Little sniveling fellow? He was trying to escape via the back wall, so we put him in irons."

"Good."

The thaw was proceeding quickly. Untidy plates of ice floating downriver and bumping into the landing stage became smaller and smaller. She watched them; each one carried its own little cloud of thicker fog through the mist.

It was still very cold.

"Come up to the tower," Rowley said. "Get warm."

"No."

He put his cloak around her, still without touching her. "Eleanor got away," he said. "They're hunting the woods for her."

Adelia nodded. It didn't matter one way or the other.

He shifted. "I'd better go to him. He'll need me to bless the dead."

"Yes," she said.

He walked away, heading for the tower and his king.

Another coffin was carried to the landing stage, assembled from pieces of the bonfire. Dakers would be accompanying her mistress to the grave.

The rest of the dead were left piled in the court-yard until the ground should be soft enough to dig a common grave.

Henry came, urging on the loading, shouting to the oarsmen that if they didn't row their hearts out, he'd have their bollocks; he was in a hurry to get to Godstow and then on to Oxford. He ushered Adelia aboard. The Bishop of Saint Albans, he told her, was staying behind to see to the burials.

The fog was too thick to allow a last glimpse of Wormhold Tower, even if Adelia had looked back, which she didn't.

The Plantagenet wouldn't go inside the cabin, being too concerned with piloting the rowers away from shoals, occasionally jotting notes on his slate book and studying the weather. "There'll be a breeze soon," he said.

He didn't let Adelia go inside, either; he said she needed air and sat her down on a thwart in the stern. After a while, he joined her. "Better now?"

"I'm going back to Salerno," she told him.

He sighed. "We've had this conversation before."

They had, after the last time he'd used her to investigate deaths. "I am not your subject, Henry, I'm Sicily's."

"Yes, but this is England, and I say who comes and goes."

She was silent, and he began wheedling. "I need you. And you wouldn't like Salerno now, not after England; it's too hot, you'd dry up like a prune."

She compressed her lips and turned her head away. *Damn him, don't laugh.*

"Eh?" he said. "Wouldn't you? Eh?"

She had to ask. "Did you know Dakers would set the mantrap for Eynsham?"

He was astonished, hurt. If he hadn't been trying to woo her, he'd have been angry. "How could I see what in hell the woman was dragging? It was too damn foggy."

She'd never know. For the rest of her life, she'd be questioned by the image of the two of them, him and Dakers, sitting together in the garderobe, planning. "*He'll die, but not by my hand,*" he had said. He'd been so certain.

"Nasty things, mantraps," he said. "Never use 'em." And paused. "Except for deer poachers." And paused. "Who deserve 'em." He paused again. "And then only ones that take the leg."

She'd never know.

"I am returning to Salerno," she said, very clear.

"It'd break Rowley's heart, oath or not."

It would probably break hers, but she was going anyway.

"You'll stay." The nearest oarsmen turned round at the shout. "I've had enough of rebellion."

He was the king. The route to Salerno passed through vast tracts of land where nobody traveled without his permission.

"It's his oath, isn't it?" he said, wheedling again. "I wouldn't have made it myself, but then, I'm not bound to chastity, thank the saints. We'll have to see what we can do about that—I yield to nobody in my admiration for God, but He's no good in bed."

I t was a quick journey; the thaw was putting the Thames into full spate, carrying the barge at speed. Henry spent the rest of the time making notes in his slate book. Adelia sat and stared into nothingness, which was all there was to see.

But the king was right, a light breeze had come up by the time they approached Godstow, and from some way off, the bridge became just visible. It appeared to be busy; the middle span was empty, but at each end people were milling around a single still figure.

As the barge passed the village, the activity among the group on this side of the bridge became clearer.

It was a hanging party. Taller than anybody else, Wolvercote stood in the middle of it with a noose around his neck while a man attached the other end of the rope to a stanchion. Beside him, the much smaller figure of Father Egbert muttered in prayer.

A young woman was watching the scene from the abbey end. The crowd of people behind her was keeping back, but one of them—Adelia recognized the matronly shape of Mistress Bloat—tugged at her daughter's hand as if she were pleading. Emma paid no attention. Her eyes never left the scene on the other side of the bridge.

Seeing the barge, a young man leaned over the bridge's parapet. His voice came clear and jolly.

"Greetings, my lord, and my thanks to God for keeping you safe." He grinned. "I knew He would."

The oarsmen reversed their rowing stroke so that the boat could keep its position against the flow of the water and allow the exchange between king and son. Above them, Wolvercote kept his gaze on the sky. The sun was beginning to come out. A heron rose out of the rushes and flapped its gawky way farther downriver.

Henry put aside his slate book. "Well done, Geoffrey. Is everything secured?"

"All secure, my lord. And, my lord, the pursuers I put after the queen have sent word. She is caught and being brought back."

Henry nodded. Pointing up at Wolvercote, he said, "Has he made confession for his sins?"

"For everything except his treachery to you, my lord. He refuses to be absolved for rebellion."

"I wouldn't absolve the swine anyway," Henry said to Adelia. "Even the Lord'll have to think twice." He called back, "Tip him over, then, Geoffrey, and God have mercy on his soul." He gestured to his oarsmen to row on.

As the boat passed by, two of the men lifted Wolvercote up and steadied him so that he stood balanced on the parapet.

Father Egbert raised his voice to begin the absolution: "*Dominus noster Jesus Christus ...*"

Adelia turned away. She was near enough now to see Emma's face; it was completely expressionless.

"... *Deinde, ego te absolvo a peccatis tuis in nominee Patris, et Filii, et Spiritus Sancti. Amen.*"

There was a thump of suddenly tightened rope. Jeers and cheering went up from both ends of the bridge.

Adelia couldn't watch, but she knew when Wolvercote had stopped struggling because it wasn't until then that Emma turned and walked away.

A crowd of soldiers, nuns, and serving people, nearly everybody in the abbey had gathered on the meadow below the convent to cheer King Henry in.

For Adelia there were only three, a tall Arab, an elderly woman, and a child whose small hand was being flapped up and down in welcome.

She bowed her head in gratitude at the sight of them.

After all, I have no need for any but these.

Allie seemed to have learned another word, because Gyltha was trying to make her say it, first encouraging the baby and then pointing toward Adelia, who couldn't hear it through the cheering.

There was a shout from the opposite bank that cut through the noise. "My lord, my lord. We have recovered the queen, my lord."

At an order from Henry, the barge veered across the river toward a group of horsemen arriving through the trees. A man with the insignia of a captain of the Plantagenet guard was dismounting, while one of his soldiers helped the queen down from his horse where she'd been riding pillion.

A gate in the barge's taffrail was opened and a gangplank laid across the gap between it and the bank. The captain, a worried-looking man, came aboard.

"How did she get across the river?" Henry asked.

"There was an old wherry further down, my lord. We think Lord Montignard poled her across ... my lord, he tried to delay her capture, he fought like a wolf, my lord ... he ..."

"They killed him," the queen called from the bank. She was brushing the soldier's restraining hand off her arm like a speck of dust.

The king went forward to help her aboard. "Eleanor."

"Henry."

"I like the disguise, you look well in it."

She was dressed like a boy, and she did look well in it, though as a disguise it would have fooled nobody; her figure was slim enough, but the muddy, short cloak and boots, the angle of the cap she'd stuffed her hair into, were worn with too much style.

The cheering from the abbey had stopped; there was an open-mouthed silence as if people on the far bank were watching a meeting between warring Olympians and waiting for the thunderbolts.

There weren't any. Adelia, crouched in the stern, watched two people who had known each other too well and been too long together to surprise now; they had conceived eight children and seen one of them die, ruled great countries together, made laws together, put down rebellions together, quarreled, laughed, and loved together, and if, now, all that had ended in a metaphorical attempt to disembowel each other, it was still in their eyes and hung in the air between them.

As if, even now, she couldn't bear to look anything but feminine for him, Eleanor took off her cap and sent it spinning into the river. It was a mistake; the boy's costume became grotesque as the long, graying hair of a fifty-year-old woman fell over its shoulders.

Gently, mercifully, her husband took off his cloak and put it around her. "There, my dear."

"Well, Henry," she said, "where's it to be this time? Back to Anjou and Chinon?"

The king shook his head. "I was thinking more of Sarum."

She tutted. "Oh, not Sarum, Henry, it's in England."

"I know, my love, but the trouble with Chinon was that you insisted on escaping from it."

"But Sarum," she persisted. "So dull."

"Well, well, if you're a good girl, I'll let you out for Easter and Christmas." He gestured to the rowers to take up their oars. "For now, though, we're making for Oxford. Some rebels there are waiting for me to hang them."

An enraptured Adelia woke up in panic. There was a river between her and her child. "My lord, my lord, let me off first."

He'd forgotten her. "Oh, very *well*." And to the rowers, "Make for the other bank."

Against fast running water, the procedure was lengthy, and the king tutted irritably all through it. By the time the barge was settled at a disembarking point on the requisite bank, it had gone long past the abbey, and Adelia was handed ashore on a deserted stretch of meadow into mud that she sank in up to the tops of her boots.

The king liked that. He leaned over the taffrail, humor restored. "You'll have to squelch back," he said.

"Yes, my lord. Thank you, my lord."

The barge took off, its dipping and rising oars sending glittering droplets back onto the surface of the water.

Suddenly, the king was running along the barge's length to the stern so that he could tell her one more thing. "About the bishop's oath," he called, "don't worry about it. '... *if You will guard her and keep her safe* ...' Very nicely phrased."

She called back, "Was it?"

"Yes." The rapidly increasing distance between them was forcing him to shout. "Adelia, you're my investigator into the dead, like it or not ..."

All she could see now was the Plantagenet three-leopard pennant fluttering as the barge rounded a wooded bend, but the king's voice carried cheerfully over its trees: "You're *never* going to be safe."

AUTHOR'S NOTE

Fair Rosamund Clifford holds a bigger place in legend than she does in historical records, which make only brief references to her, and I hope her shade does not haunt me for my fictional portrayal.

The English Register of Godstow Nunnery, edited by Andrew Clarke and published by the Early English Text Society, shows that the abbey was both highly regarded and efficiently administered at this time. It was also broad-minded enough to bury the body of Henry II's mistress, Rosamund Clifford, in front of the altar, where the tomb became a popular shrine. However, the great bishop, Hugh of Lincoln, though he had been a friend of Henry's, was shocked to find it there when he visited the convent in 1191, two years after the king's death, and ordered it to be disinterred and reburied somewhere less sacred in the convent grounds.

Most of the rebellion of Henry II's family took place on the continent but, since the nice thing for a novel writer is the gap in medieval records, I have dared to interpose one such rising in England, where we do know at least that some of his discontented barons were quick to join in Young Henry and Eleanor's fight.

Eleanor of Aquitaine survived the death of Henry and the imprisonment he imposed on her. In fact, she survived all her sons as well, except King John. In her seventies, she crossed the Pyrenees to arrange the marriage of a granddaughter, and suffered an abduction and, later, a siege. She died at the age of eighty-two and was laid to rest beside her husband and Richard the First, their son, in the Abbey of Fontevrault, where their effigies are still to be seen in its beautiful church.

I make no apology for the way in which my characters go by water between Godstow and various places. The Thames around the island on which the remains of the convent stand is navigable to a fair way farther up even now, and there is every likelihood that its tributaries have changed their courses over the years, and those of the Cherwell, now disappeared, provided better going than the lesser roads. As Professor W. G. Hoskins, the father of landscape archaeology, says in his *Fieldwork to Local History* (Faber and Faber), "In medieval and later times a large proportion of inland trade went by river, far more than has ever been generally realised." Also, there are references to the Thames freezing during the very cold winters of the twelfth century.

Incidentally, beavers were common in English rivers during the twelfth century. It was later, in the 1700s, that they were hunted to extinction for their fur.

And, unlikely as it seems, opium *was* grown in the East Anglian fens, not only in the twelfth but in succeeding centuries—it is thought that the Romans brought the poppy to England, as they brought so much else. The tincture fen people called "Godfrey's Cordial"—a mixture of opium and treacle—was still in use in the twentieth century.

One by one, all of Henry's sons turned against him, and he died at Chinon in 1189, probably from bowel cancer, knowing that his youngest and most loved, John, had joined the rebellion of the elder brother, Richard.

I have given the manor of Wolvercote a fictitious lord for the purposes of this story; the real owner of the manor at this time was a Roger D'Ivri, and I have no evidence that D'Ivri was involved in any rebellion against Henry II, though it is interesting that, whether he wanted to or not, he later gave the manor to the king, who gave it to Godstow Abbey.

The reference to paper as a writing material in chapter four may offend the general view that paper did not reach Europe, certainly northern Europe, until the fourteenth century. Granted, it wasn't used much in the twelfth century—scribes and monkish writers were snobbish about it and preferred vellum—but it was around, though probably of poor quality. Viz the interesting article posted on the Internet: "Medieval Ink" by David Carvalho.

The trick of getting out of a multicursal maze I owe to that lovely writer on landscape, Geoffrey Ashe, and his *Labyrinth and Mazes*, published by Wessex Books.

The real Abbot of Eynsham, whoever he was, must be absolved of the wickedness that I attribute to his fictional counterpart. As far as I know, he lived a blameless life and had high regard for women—though, in that case, he would have been a rare specimen among medieval churchmen.

The idea of God as both father and mother was famously encapsulated in the writings of the feminine mystic Julian of Norwich in the fourteenth century, but the concept was deep in much Christian thinking long before that, and so the conversation between the Abbess of Godstow and Adelia in chapter eleven of this book is not necessarily anachronistic.

In the Middle Ages, the title of doctor was bestowed on followers of philosophy, not physicians, but I have applied it in the modern sense here to simplify meaning for readers and myself.

ACKNOWLEDGMENTS

As always, my gratitude to my agent, Helen Heller, for her wise judgment of plot and pace. And to Rachel Kahan, my editor at Penguin Group (USA), for the same. Also to the London Library, which contains everything an inquiring author needs to know, and to its staff.

And last but never least, to my husband, Barry, and the family for their patience—especially my daughter Emma, who shoulders secretarial burdens so well and leaves me free to write.

Thank you.

Following is an excerpt of
the next vibrant and exciting mystery from

ARIANA FRANKLIN ...

Grave Goods

Coming soon from Penguin Group (Canada)

And God was angry with His people of Somerset so that, in the year of Our Lord 1154, on the day after the feast of Saint Stephen, He caused an earthquake that it might punish them for their sins ...

Thus wrote Brother Caradoc in Saint Michael's chapel on top of Glastonbury Tor, to which he'd scrambled, gasping and sobbing, so as to escape the devastation that God with His earthquake had wrought on everything below. For two days he and his fellow monks had been up there, not daring to descend because they could still hear aftershocks making their abbey tremble and looked down, appalled, at more giant waves submerging the little island villages in the Avalon marshes.

Two days, and Caradoc was still wet and had a pain in his poor old chest. When the earthquake struck and his fellow monks had scampered from the shivering abbey, making for the tor that was always their refuge in times of danger, he'd run with them, hearing Saint Dunstan, strictest of saints though dead these 166 years, telling him to rescue the *Book of Glastonbury* first. *Caradoc, Caradoc, do your duty though the sky falls.*

But it was bits of masonry that had been falling, and Caradoc had not dared to run into the abbey library and fetch the great jewel-studded book—it would have been too heavy for him to carry up the hill anyway.

The slate book that was always attached to the rope girdle round his waist had been weighty enough, almost too much for an old man laboring up a five-hundred-foot, steeply conical hill. His nephew, Rhys, had helped him, pushing, dragging, shouting at him to go faster, but it had been a terrible climb, terrible.

Now, in the cold, dry and unshaken shelter of the chapel that Joseph of Arimathea had built when he'd brought the cruets containing Christ's sacred blood and sweat from the Holy Land, Brother Caradoc did his duty as the abbey's annalist. In feeble taper light and apologetically using Saint Michael's altar as a table, he chalked this latest event in Glastonbury's history onto slate pages so that, later, he could transcribe them onto the vellum of the Great Book.

> And the Lord's voice was heard in the screams of people and the squealing of animals as the ground undulated and opened beneath them, in the fall of great trees, in the toppling of candles and the roar of resultant flames as houses burned.

The pain in his chest increased, and the shade of Saint Dunstan went on nagging him. *The Book must be saved, Caradoc. The history of all our saints cannot be lost.*

"I haven't got to the wave yet, my lord. At least let there be some record of it." He went on writing.

Loudest of all, Our Lord spoke in the noise of an approaching wave that raised itself higher than a cathedral in the bay and ran up the tidal rivers of the Somerset Levels, sweeping away bridges as it came and drowning all in its path. Through His mercy, it only reached the lower levels of our abbey so that it still stands, but ...

The Book, Caradoc. Tell that idle nephew of yours to fetch it.

Brother Caradoc looked to his fellow monks, immobile and huddled for warmth on the choir floor, some of them snoring. "He sleeps, my lord."

When doesn't he? St. Dunstan asked with some justice. *Either sleeping or singing unsuitable songs, that boy. He'll never make a monk. Kick him awake.*

Gently, Brother Caradoc prodded a pair of skinny young ankles with his foot. "Rhys, Rhys. Wake up, bach."

He was a good boy in his way: Rhys the novitiate, a lovely tenor, but St. Dunstan was right: The lad cared more for singing profane songs than psalms, and the other monks constantly berated him for it, keeping him busy to cure his idleness. Tired out now, he merely grunted and slept on.

Well, let him rest. Caradoc began writing again. He hadn't yet recorded the fissure in the graveyard. Yes, he must put that in. For, as he'd run from the quaking buildings, he had seen a deep hole opening up in the abbey's burial ground between the two pyramids that had stood in it as long as time had gone. He wrote:

> *As if the end of the world had come and the Almighty had sounded the Last Trump so that the dead might rise from their graves.*

The Book! St. Dunstan shouted. *Caradoc, would you leave the record of our days to looters?*

No, he couldn't do that. So Brother Caradoc put down his chalk and, though his shivers were becoming uncontrollable and the pain across his chest an iron bar, he made for the door of the chapel and began stumbling down the winding terrace of the tor. He knew now that the Last Trump had sounded for him and that, even if he couldn't save the Book, he must die trying, or, at least, take his last breath in the beloved abbey that had been his home these last thirty years.

A lot of precious breath it cost him as he wavered downward, falling over hummocks, his gasps sending sheep galloping, but gravity was on his side and it propelled him down to the gate, which swung open at his touch, under the chevroned Norman arch, and into the grounds. He staggered onward as far as the vegetable garden, where he collapsed amongst Brother Peter's lettuces, unable to go farther.

Now he could peer down the incline toward the towering church. There had been damage; the old bell tower had collapsed, and gaps showed where some corners were sheared away. The waters that encircled the grounds had not reached so far, therefore the Great Book and all the relics of the saints would still be untouched. Beyond them, though, the village outside the walls was still and smokeless, its pasture littered with dirty white lumps that were the corpses of sheep.

Caradoc experienced anguish for the drowned people and animals, for the ruined hayricks, cornfields—it would be a hard summer for the survivors, and an even harder winter.

Yet holy Glastonbury still stood. Beautiful it was, crystalline under the bright new moon reflected in its skirt of floodwater, an island of glass. *The* Island of Glass.

Sucking in breath that couldn't fill his lungs, he turned his eyes to the graveyard awaiting him.

A flicker of movement caught his eye. Three cowled figures were pulling on ropes that dragged something up the slope from the abbey's great gate. Too far away for him to hear any sound they made, they seemed like ghosts. And perhaps, Caradoc thought, that is what they are. For what human could be abroad and busy in this devastation when even the owls and nightingales were silent?

He couldn't make out what it was they were hauling. It had the shape of a great log or a canoe. Then, as the figures came to the fissure in the ground that the earthquake had opened, he saw what it was: a coffin.

They were lowering it into the fissure. Now they were kneeling, and from the throat of one of them came a great shriek. "Arthur, Arthur. May God have mercy on your soul and mine."

There was a moan from the dying monk. "Is King Arthur dead then?"

For Caradoc, though a Glastonbury monk these thirty years, had believed that King Arthur was merely resting, waiting until he was called to rise and fight the Devil's hordes once more. And he rested here.

Avalon was Glastonbury, Glastonbury was Avalon, the Isle of Glass indeed, and Arthur slept somewhere amongst these hills with their hidden caves and crystal springs, Arthur the Brave, Arthur of the Welsh, who'd resisted the seaborne invaders and kept the flame of Christianity flickering in Britain during its Dark Ages.

It had been Caradoc's joy that he could serve God in the place where Arthur had been brought to be mended from his wounds after the last great battle.

Was he dead then? Was great Arthur dead?

The earth trembled again, lightly, like a dog settling itself to sleep. Caradoc heard other voices, this time calling his name. An arm went under his head and he looked up into the frightened eyes of his nephew.

"Look, bach," Caradoc said, trying to point. "They are burying King Arthur. Three of his lords in hooded cloaks, see."

"Lie still now, Uncle," Rhys said and shouted up the hill to the other, searching monks, "I've found him. Here, he's by here."

"There, boy," Caradoc said. "Between the pyramids, in the fissure. I saw them lower his coffin, I heard them mourning him."

"A vision, was it?" Rhys asked, peering toward the graveyard and seeing nothing.

"A vision, clear as clear," Caradoc said. "There's sad it is that Arthur is dead."

"Whisht now, Uncle," Rhys said. "There's help on the way." To calm and comfort the old man, he began singing, not a hymn, but a song that Welsh mothers sang to their children—a song of Arthur Pendragon.

> *"... when the land rang with minstrels' song*
> *the sharpening of weapons,*
> *the splash of oars coming into harbor,*
> *a ripple of water in the sea-cave ..."*

Caradoc's eyes closed and he smiled. "Good, good," he whispered. "At least I shall lie where King Arthur lies. There's company."

When the other monks came upon him, they found Rhys still singing as he cradled a dead man.

They buried Brother Caradoc the next morning. If there had ever been a fissure in the graveyard, the earthquake's last tremor had filled it in, for there was no sign of it.

Nor did Rhys ap Gruffid tell anybody of what his uncle said he had seen. Rhys, who was not suited to be a monk and knew that he never would be, was a Welshman through and through and it would not do for these English to know that Arthur was dead.

So, for twenty-four years the two pyramids guarded the place where an old monk had seen Arthur buried and nobody knew the importance of what lay between them.

Until ...

March A.D. 1176, a wind was hurtling down a ravine in Wales, blowing the haulms of reeds and the flare of torches in the same, streaming angle as the hair on the severed heads that topped the line of poles leading up to the Plantagenet tents. It sent grass, leaves, and branches nodding in vehement agreement.

With a spike through each of their Welsh brains, the heads couldn't nod, though they revolved slightly so that their blank eyes shifted as if dividing their attention between the bottom of the ravine, where English soldiers were digging burial pits, and a limping mailed figure who was dragging a woman up the steep slope toward the tents.

As she was pulled level with the poles, the woman broke into a wail of Welsh lamentation, peering at each head and calling out what, presumably, were their names.

The mailed man paused, puffing—she was a big lady to haul. "Look," he said, "they were killed in battle. *Battle*. Understand? My lads got a bit carried away with their bodies, that's all. The king doesn't behead prisoners, at least not often—he's a good king. *Good.*"

But the woman was ignorant of English, no matter how loudly it was emphasized. *"Duw, Duw,"* she cried, lifting her arms to the sky. The man had to get behind her and push before she'd go farther.

The opening of the bigger tent was lit from inside, outlining the also mailed figure of Henry II, who stood at its entrance shouting at a line of bound men being made to kneel in front of him— while a man-at-arms undid the king's hauberk at the back and carefully peeled it off.

"There was no *point* to this, you stupid bastards. No *point.*" To the interpreter at his side, the king said, "Tell 'em that. Tell them I've made peace with Lord Deheubarth or however the bugger pronounces it. They won't have to pay any more taxes with me as their king than they pay him already." He paused. "Well, not much more." He pressed a cloth against his left arm to stop the bleeding. "Now look what they've done. Tell them I've had to mount an expensive campaign to put down their bloody rebellion, I've lost good men, *they've* lost good men, I won't be able to use my shield arm for bloody days, and they'll be taxed for it until their brains squeak—that's if they've got any and if I don't gouge them out. Tell 'em that. Tell them Arthur is *dead.*"

At the sound of the name, the kneeling prisoners raised their heads as one man and a shout of "Bywyd hir Arthur" rippled along the line.

"'Arthur live forever,'" translated the interpreter, helpfully.

Henry Plantagenet exhaled with violence. "I know what it means." He extended his wounded arm. "The bastard who did this was shouting it. They all shout it. Tell them Arthur is dead. I'm as proud of him as the next man but he lived about seven hundred years ago and ... There you are, Bishop. And who in hell is *this*?"

The lady from the hill had arrived in the tent with her companion.

Rowley, Bishop of Saint Albans, lifted off his helmet, then the coif beneath, and rubbed his nose where the nasal had chafed it. "I believe she's from the village down the valley, my lord. She was wandering among the dead—looking for her son, I think."

"It seems she's found him," Henry said. The woman had cried out and thrown herself at one of the prisoners, toppling him over in her joy. "Yes, that's his mother all right ..." For now the woman had taken to slapping the prisoner around his head with some force. "You usually like 'em slimmer and younger."

Rowley ignored the slur. "My lord, one of our men down there, he speaks a bit of Welsh, he seems to think she's got something valid to tell us and wants to ransom her son to get at it."

"What in hell can she possibly ... oh, all *right*. Fulk, take the others away, all except that one and the lady. And send up that pill-pissing butcher who calls himself a doctor."

Fulk signaled to two of his men, who began kicking the prisoners to their feet. "Do you want me to hang them, my lord?"

"No, Fulk, I don't," Henry told him, wearily. "I want to enlist them. I want them to teach my bloody archers a thing or two, and they can't do that with their necks stretched."

As the prisoners were taken away, the king turned to Rowley and gestured to an unusually long bow propped in a corner. "How do they do it? I tried and I could hardly bend that damn thing, but those wizened little bastards pull it back as easily as a pump handle."

"It's a skill we've got to learn, no doubt about that," Rowley said. He set about taking off his chausses.

"And the penetration ... one flight just missed me and hit a tree. I pulled it out later. Nine inches in, it was. I swear, nine inches into solid oak. If it hadn't been for the wind ..."

"That's what saved me. The wind swerved mine and took off most of its force." The bishop looked morosely at the calf of his leg. "Still went in, though, and, *damnation*, it's taken a couple of links in with it."

"That'll need cauterizing, then," the king said, cheering up. "And now, Owain, my man, what are those two yammering about?"

The interpreter, an elderly border Welshman with the gift of making himself near invisible, had been attending to the conversation of mother and son in the tent entrance, most of it pursued by the woman. "Interesting, my lord. Urging him to tell you about Arthur, so she is. Something about Glastonbury and a vision ..."

"Arthur?" The king, who had collapsed onto a stool, sat up.

"What I can make of it, my lord, the son's not a soldier by rights, he was with the holy men at Glastonbury a time ago and she wants him to tell you something that happened, a vision, a burial, I can't make it out at all ..."

"Glastonbury? He can speak English?"

"So it would seem, my lord, but he's reluctant ..."

Henry turned to a crouching page. "Fetch a block. And fetch Fulk back. Tell him to bring an axe."

Apart from the sobbing pleas of the mother to her son, the tent fell quiet. Every now and then the wind from outside sent the burning logs of the brazier into a flare so that the shadows of the men who sat round it sharpened and then faded again.

The entry of the doctor and his assistant added the smell of drying blood—their hands and aprons were covered in it—to that of bruised grass, sweat, and steel.

"How's De Boeuf?" the king asked.

"I have hopes for him, my lord. Thirty stitches but, yes, I have hopes."

"And Sir Gerard?"

The doctor shook his head. "I'm afraid not, my lord."

"Shit," the king said. When the doctor took his arm to examine it, he jerked it away. "Attend to my lord bishop first. His leg'll need cauterizing."

"So will that arm, my lord. The cut's gone deep." The doctor picked up the brazier's poker and stuck it into the glowing ash.

Accompanied by the page, who was weighed down with an axe, Fulk came in, cradling three feet of tree trunk like a baby. He set it down, relieved the page of the axe, and, at a nod from his king, dragged the prisoner to the block, shook him so that he folded to his knees in front of it, and showed him the axe. The blade gleamed in the firelight.

"Take the woman out," Henry said. "No, first get this fellow's name."

"Rhys," the interpreter said.

"Now then, Rhys ..." He had to wait until the page, with some difficulty, hauled the screaming Welshwoman out of the tent. "Tell me about Arthur."

The prisoner's eyes kept blinking in terror. He was a tall, lanky man, probably in his thirties, with unfortunate teeth and straggling fair hair. His voice, however, was captivating and, isolated from his comrades, with the yells of his mother audible outside the tent, and the axe's blade practically touching his nose, he used it to answer questions.

No, no, he hadn't fought with the rebels, not actually fought, they'd taken him along to put their prowess to song. Very content he was, personally, with King Henry Plantagenet to reign, and there was a fine name for a eulogy that he'd be happy to provide anytime.

Yes, yes, he'd spent a year as an oblate in

England, in Glastonbury. His uncle Caradoc ap Gruffid had been a monk there, see, but he, Rhys ap Gruffid ap Owein ap Gwilym ...

Fulk hit him.

... had decided his vocation lay in the bardic world and he'd wandered away back to Wales to learn the harp. A fine bard he'd become as it turned out, oh yes, his "Marwnat Pwyll"—well, "Death Song for Pwyll" it was in English—was considered the finest composition since Taliesin had ...

Fulk hit him again.

"Oh, well then, the vision. It was of Arthur in his coffin being buried and lamented. My uncle Caradoc saw it. Just after the earthquake it was, see, and terrible that was, the ground heaving like a ship ..."

Slapping him was useless; the man wasn't being obstructive, he was physically incapable of keeping to the point. It was a matter of waiting it out.

Eventually, wearily, the king said, "So your uncle saw a vision of Arthur's burial. In the monks' grave-yard at Glastonbury, between the two pyramids."

"Yes, yes, very old those pyramids, very exotic ..."

"Take him away, Fulk. Better keep him separate from the rest. They're not going to be happy with him." Henry turned to his bishop. "What's your opinion, Rowley?"

The Bishop of Saint Albans's attention was being dominated by the tweezers that were picking shreds of chainmail from his leg.

He tried to consider the matter. "There are true visions, I don't say there aren't, but a dying old man ..."

"Worth telling Glastonbury about it, though?" While his friend havered, the king said, "I need Arthur dead, my son. If there's something down in that fissure, I want it dug up and shown to every bloody Celt from·here to Brittany. No more revolts because a warrior from the Dark Ages is going to lead them to freedom. I want Arthur's bones and I want them on display."

"If they're there, Henry. *If* they're there, they'd require some sort of verification."

The poker-end in the brazier had become a molten white and the doctor was lifting it out.

Henry II showed his vicious little teeth in a grin as he held out his arm; he was going to get some reward from the situation. "And you know who can provide that verification—*saints' bollocks.*" The smell of scorched flesh pervaded the tent.

"Not her, my lord," the bishop pleaded, watching the poker approach his leg. "She's— *goddamn*—she's ... *oof* ... earned the right to be left in peace. So have I."

"She's my investigator of the dead, Rowley. That's what I pay her for."

"You don't pay her, my lord."

"Are you sure?" The king puzzled over it, then said, "If she gives me a dead Arthur, my son, she can name her price."